Land Transfer and Finance

ASPEN PUBLISHERS

Land Transfer and Finance

Cases and Materials

Fifth Edition

Curtis J. Berger
Late Lawrence A. Wien Professor of Real Estate Law
Columbia University School of Law

Quintin Johnstone
Justus S. Hotchkiss Professor of Law, Emeritus
Yale Law School

Marshall Tracht
Professor of Law
Hofstra University School of Law

Wolters Kluwer
Law & Business

AUSTIN   BOSTON   CHICAGO   NEW YORK   THE NETHERLANDS

Aspen Publishers
Attn: Permissions Department
76 Ninth Avenue, 7th Floor
New York, NY 10011-5201

To contact Customer Care, e-mail customer.care@
aspenpublishers.com, call 1-800-234-1660, fax 1-800-901-9075, or
mail correspondence to:

Aspen Publishers
Attn: Order Department
PO Box 990
Frederick, MD 21705

Printed in the United States of America.

1 2 3 4 5 6 7 8 9 0

ISBN 978-0-7355-6275-2

Library of Congress Cataloging-in-Publication Data

Berger, Curtis J.
    Land transfer and finance: cases and materials/Curtis J. Berger,
Quintin Johnstone, Marshall Tracht. — 5th ed.
        p. cm.
    Includes index.
    ISBN 978-0-7355-6275-2
    1. Vendors and purchasers — United States — Cases. I. Johnstone,
Quintin. II. Tracht, Marshall E. III. Title.

KF665.A4A93 2007
346.7304'37 — dc22

                                                    2007007085

About Wolters Kluwer Law & Business

Wolters Kluwer Law & Business is a leading provider of research information and workflow solutions in key specialty areas. The strengths of the individual brands of Aspen Publishers, CCH, Kluwer Law International and Loislaw are aligned within Wolters Kluwer Law & Business to provide comprehensive, in-depth solutions and expert-authored content for the legal, professional and education markets.

CCH was founded in 1913 and has served more than four generations of business professionals and their clients. The CCH products in the Wolters Kluwer Law & Business group are highly regarded electronic and print resources for legal, securities, antitrust and trade regulation, government contracting, banking, pension, payroll, employment and labor, and healthcare reimbursement and compliance professionals.

Aspen Publishers is a leading information provider for attorneys, business professionals and law students. Written by preeminent authorities, Aspen products offer analytical and practical information in a range of specialty practice areas from securities law and intellectual property to mergers and acquisitions and pension/benefits. Aspen's trusted legal education resources provide professors and students with high-quality, up-to-date and effective resources for successful instruction and study in all areas of the law.

Kluwer Law International supplies the global business community with comprehensive English-language international legal information. Legal practitioners, corporate counsel and business executives around the world rely on the Kluwer Law International journals, loose-leafs, books and electronic products for authoritative information in many areas of international legal practice.

Loislaw is a premier provider of digitized legal content to small law firm practitioners of various specializations. Loislaw provides attorneys with the ability to quickly and efficiently find the necessary legal information they need, when and where they need it, by facilitating access to primary law as well as state-specific law, records, forms and treatises.

Wolters Kluwer Law & Business, a unit of Wolters Kluwer, is headquartered in New York and Riverwoods, Illinois. Wolters Kluwer is a leading multinational publisher and information services company.

Summary of Contents

Contents

Chapter Two

Basic Financing Considerations of the Real Estate Transaction

Chapter Three

Chapter Four

Contents of Sale

Chapter 5

Title Protection   471

Chapter 6

Preface

The scope and organization of this book reflect our belief that virtually every real estate transaction draws upon the lawyer's knowledge of relevant contract, financing, taxation, and titles doctrine and upon his or her familiarity with the institutional context of the real estate market. Thus, the book is both doctrinal and institutional — sometimes heavily one, sometimes heavily the other. The sections on finance and title insurance, for example, stress the descriptive, whereas the section on the "contract of sale" reinforces the doctrinal and analytical skills students have been gaining since the first day of law school. We have tried for a balance to suit our own tastes and, we hope, those of other instructors.

We have written this book for a nationwide market, fully cognizant, however, that land law has many local variations. We expect that a teacher may want to key into the text statutes, forms, and even court decision to illustrate the practice of the community where the students are most likely to work. At the same time, we believe that real estate transactions, like commerce in goods, are undergoing a strong nationalizing influence, and we hope that the book reflects this trend.

As with many casebooks, we are certain that more than one way will be found in which to organize and teach the materials inside. For example, those teaching a two-unit course may decide to assign only chapters two, four and five. Those offering an advanced course in land transaction problems may concentrate on chapters six and seven. Other teachers of a basic land transaction course no doubt will find coverage of all seven chapters appropriate, with perhaps selective omission consistent with the teacher's priorities.

May 2007

Acknowledgments

American Bar Association Section of Taxation, Committee on Financial Transactions, Subcommittee on Asset Securitization, Legislative Proposal to Expand the REMIC Provisions of the Code to Include Nonmortgage Assets, 46 Tax L.R. 299 (1991). Reprinted by permission.

American Bar Association, Special Committee on Residential Real Estate Transactions, Residential Real Estate Transactions: The Lawyer's Proper Role, 14 Real Prop. Prob. and Tr. J. 585-590 (Fall 1979). Reprinted by permission of the Section of Real Property, Probate and Trust Law. Copyright © 1979 by the American Bar Association, Chicago, Illinois.

Arnold, Real Estate Transactions — Structure and Analysis with Forms. Reprinted by permission.

Barnett, Marketable Title Acts — Panacea or Pandemonium, 53 Cornell L. Rev. 45, 92-94 (1967). Copyright © 1967 by Cornell University and Fred B. Rothman and Company.

Basye, Trends and Progress — The Marketable Title Acts, 47 Iowa L. Rev. 261-267 (1962). Copyright © 1962 by the University of Iowa (Iowa Law Review). Reprinted by permission.

Berger, Condominium: Shelter on a Statutory Foundation, 63 Colum. L. Rev. 987 (1963). Copyright © 1963 by the Directors of the Columbia Law Review Association. Reprinted by permission.

Berger, Land Ownership and Use 226-227 (3d ed. 1982). Reprinted by permission.

Berman, "Once a Mortgage, Always a Mortgage" — The Use (and Misuse) of Mezzanine Loans and Preferred Equity Investments, Stan. J. L. Bus. & Fin. 76 (2005). Reprinted by permission.

Bixby, The Vendor–Vendee Problem: How Do We Slice the Insurance Pie?, 19 The Forum 112-114, 127-128 (1983), a publication of the American Bar Association. Reprinted by permission.

Black, Loan Workout Strategies, 4 Prob. & Prop. 39 (March/April 1990). Reprinted by permission.

CALIFORNIA ASSOCIATION OF REALTORS®, California Residential Purchase Agreement and Joint Escrow Instructions. Reprinted by permission.

CALIFORNIA ASSOCIATION OF REALTORS®, Exclusive Authorization and Right to Sell (Multiple Listing). Reprinted by permission.

Christie, Antitrust Update, 62 Title News No. 7, at 21 (1983). Reprinted by permission.

Comment, Enhancing the Marketability of Land: The Suit to Quiet Title, 68
     Yale L.J. 1245, 1265, 1277, 1283 (1959). Reprinted by permission of the
     Yale Law Journal Company and Fred B. Rothman and Company.
Cribbett and Johnson, Principles of the Law of Property 210-212 (3d ed.
     1989). Copyright © 1989 by Foundation Press. Reprinted by
     permission.
Cross, The Record "Chain of Title Hypocrisy," 57 Colum. L. Rev. 787-796
     (1957). Copyright © 1957 by the Directors of the Columbia Law Review
     Association. All rights reserved. Reprinted by permission.
Currier, Finding the Broker's Place in the Typical Residential Real Estate
     Transaction, 33 U. Fla. L. Rev. 655-681 (1981). Copyright © 1981 by the
     University of Florida Law Review. Reprinted by permission of the
     University of Florida Law Review.
Del Cotto, Sale and Leaseback: A Hollow Sound When Tapped?, 37 Tax L.
     Rev. 1, 3-9 (1981). Reprinted by permission.
Fidelity National Title Insurance Company, Loan and Owner's Policies of
     Title Insurance. Reprinted by permission.
FTC and Shopping Center — Dos and Don'ts for Major Tenants, 3 Real Est.
     L. Rep. No. 11 (April 1974). Copyright © 1975 by Warren, Gorham and
     Lamont, 210 South Street, Boston, MA 02111. All rights reserved.
     Reprinted by permission.
Goldstein & Weber, The Art of Negotiating, 37 N.Y.L. Sch. L. Rev. 326
     (1992). Reprinted by permission.
Halper, Planning and Construction Clauses in a Subordinated Ground
     Lease, 17 Real Estate L.J. 48 (1988). Reprinted by permission.
Hawkins, Comments of Barry Hawkins, 24 Quinnipiac Law Review 597
     (2006). Reprinted by permission.
Homburger, Real Estate Sale-Leasebacks 1-2, 2-4 (1992). Reprinted by
     permission.
Hyatt, Condominium and Home Owner Associations: Formation and De-
     velopment, 24 Emory L.J. 977, 980-983 (1975). Reprinted by
     permission.
Johnstone, Land Transfers: Process and Processors, 22 Val. L. Rev. 493, 520-
     521, 544-545 (1988). Reprinted by permission.
Johnstone, Private Mortgage Insurance, 39 Wake Forest L. Rev. 783, 784-
     787, 792-794, 802-803, 827-828, 830-831, 836 (2004). Reprinted by
     permission.
Konikoff, CFO's Guide to Real Estate Appraisals, 534 PLI/Real 843, 850-859
     (2006). Reprinted by permission.
Lefcoe, Yield Maintenance and Defeasance: Two Distinct Paths to Commer-
     cial Mortgage Prepayment, 28 Real Est. L.J. 202 (2000). Reprinted by
     permission.
Levin and Roberts, Future Forms of Financing — Lending Devices
     Addressed to Inflation and Tight Money, reprinted in American Bar
     Association, Real Property, Probate and Trust Law Section, Financing

Real Estate During the Inflationary '80s, at 31 (1981). Reprinted by permission of the American Bar Association from Financing Real Estate Transactions During the Inflationary '80s, a publication of the Section of Real Property, Probate and Trust Law. For more information about the publication contact the American Bar Association.

Lifton, Practical Real Estate in the '80s: Legal, Tax and Business Strategies 390-398, 497-499 (2d ed. 1983). Reprinted by permission of Law and Business, Inc.

Lifton, Real Estate in Trouble: Lender's Remedies Need an Overhaul, 31 Bus. Law. 1927, 1931-1945 (1976). Copyright © 1976 by the American Bar Association and its Section of Corporation, Banking and Business Law.

Malloy, The Secondary Mortgage Market — A Catalyst for Change in Real Estate Transactions, 39 Sw. L.J. 991, 1001-1018 (1986). Reprinted by permission.

The Mortgage and Real Estate Executive's Report 5-7 (June 16, 1985). Copyright © 1985 by Warren, Gorham and Lamont. All rights reserved. Reprinted by permission.

Note, Iowa's Prohibition of Title Insurance — Leadership or Folly?, 33 Drake L. Rev. 683, 695-701 (1983-1984). Reprinted by permission.

Note, Reforming the Vendor's Remedies for Breach of Installment Land Contracts, 47 S. Cal. L. Rev. 191, 205-206 (1973). Reprinted by permission of the Southern California Law Review.

Note, The Tract and Grantor–Grantee Indices, 47 Iowa L. Rev. 481-485 (1962). Copyright © 1962 by the University of Iowa (Iowa Law Review). Reprinted by permission.

Patton, Evolution of Legislation on Proof of Title to Land, 30 Wash. L. Rev. 224, 228-235 (1955). Reprinted by permission of the Washington Law Review and the Fred B. Rothman Company.

Prather, Foreclosure of the Security Interest, 1957 Ill. L.F. 420-427. Copyright © 1957 by the Board of Trustees of the University of Illinois. Reprinted by permission.

Restatement Third, Property (Mortgages), secs. 2.1, 2.3 and 3.2, copyright 1997 by the American Law Institute. Reprinted by permission. All rights reserved.

Roberts, Disclosure Duties in Real Estate Sales and Attempts to Reallocate Risks, 34 Conn. L. Rev. 1 (2001). Reprinted by permission.

Salin, Usury, reprinted in 15 Encyclopedia of the Social Sciences 193-197 (1934). Copyright © 1934, 1962 by MacMillan Publishing Company. Reprinted by permission of MacMillan Publishing Company from Encyclopedia of the Social Sciences.

Schill, The Impact of Capital Markets on Real Estate Law and Practice, 32 J. Marshall L. Rev. 269 (1999). Reprinted by permission.

Seneker, II, How to Document Securitized Commercial Real Estate Loans, ALI-ABA 2006. Reprinted by permission.

Smith and Lubbell, Real Estate Financing: Protecting the Lender with Title
Insurance, 5 Real Est. Rev. No. 1, at 14 (Winter 1985). Copyright ©
1985 by Warren, Gorham and Lamont. All rights reserved. Reprinted
by permission.

Stark, Foreclosing on the American Dream, An Evaluation of State and
Federal Foreclosure Laws, 51 Okla. L.R. 229, 229-231, 235-236, 247-
250 (1998). Reprinted by permission.

Sterk, Minority Protection in Residential Private Governments, 77 B.U.L.
Rev. 273, 288-307, 320-329 (1997). Reprinted by permission.

Thomas, The Mortgaging of Long Term Leases, 39 Dicta 363, 379-382
(1962). Reprinted by permission of the Denver Bar Association.

Whalen, Commercial Ground Leases, 2d ed. 1-2, 8-10, 17-19 (Prac. L. Inst.
2002). Reprinted by permission.

York, The Ground Lease and the Leasehold Mortgage, 99 Banking L.J. 709-
721 (1982). Reprinted by permission.

Yuhas and Fellows, Sale-Leasebacks Revisited: The Old and the New Federal
Law, 31 Real Est. L.J. 9 (2002). Reprinted by permission.

Zerwick, Creation and Maintenance of a Title Plant, 34 Natl. Capitol Area
Realtor No. 1, at 11 (1966). Reprinted by permission from the January
1966 issue of Realtor Magazine.

Land Transfer and Finance

CHAPTER ONE

The Professional and the Land Transaction: Brokers and Lawyers

A. THE ROLE OF THE BROKER

Real estate brokers and the salespersons who work for them comprise one of the largest white collar service occupations in the United States.[1] They usually are the first service professionals to become involved in real estate sales transactions. Their business is facilitating the sale of land by bringing buyers and sellers together, thereby helping to create a market in land. Owners wishing to sell commonly list their properties with one or more brokers, and prospective buyers approach brokers for information about properties that may meet their needs. Brokers usually show listed properties to prospective buyers, explain sales terms and procedures, and often act as intermediaries in negotiating contract and deed provisions. Among other services commonly performed by real estate brokers are counseling and advising buyers and sellers; preparing transaction legal documents, such as contracts of sale and deeds; and administering the closing of real estate transactions.[2] Real estate brokers also often act as intermediaries in the leasing of land. Probably a majority of real estate sales in the United States are made with the assistance of brokers. A much smaller percentage of leases are made with real estate broker help.

Most brokered sales of real estate are of individual dwelling units; but brokers are used for selling all other kinds of land parcels, including commercial, industrial, and agricultural properties. Commercial and industrial brokers frequently serve a much larger geographic area than do residential brokers; and commercial and industrial brokers generally have a wider range of knowledge about real estate markets, potential land uses, contract of sale terms, and financing possibilities than do their counterparts specializing in single-family dwelling units. Contracts

---

1. On real estate brokerage and laws pertaining to real estate brokers, see Burke, Law of Real Estate Brokers (2d ed. 1992, cum. supp. 2006); Rohan et al, Real Estate Brokerage Law and Practice (1985 & annual supps.).

2. A recent survey of a sizable sample in many states of real estate brokers specializing in commercial real estate disclosed that in working time spent, in order of priority of time put in, brokers' activities were as follows: (1) negotiating sales and purchases, (2) negotiating leases, (3) analysis and counseling, (4) prospecting for clients, (5) contract preparation, (6) locating development sites, (7) managing own assets, (8) property management, (9) financing, and (10) construction and development. In income derived from activities, the priorities were somewhat different and were as follows: (1) negotiating sales and purchases, (2) negotiating leases, (3) managing own assets, (4) prospecting for clients, (5) locating development sites, (6) analysis and counseling, (7) property management, (8) contract preparation, (9) financing, and (10) exchanging. Epley, Characteristics of the U.S. Commercial Real Estate Agent, 32 Real Estate Rev. 38 (Winter 2004). No doubt many real estate brokers specializing in residential real estate, including sale of single-family residences, engage in the same activities as those listed above for commercial brokers.

by brokers with parties to real estate transactions usually are in writing. When sellers are contracting with brokers, the brokerage contract, commonly referred to as a listing agreement, is usually entered into when the property is listed with the broker for sale. Almost always, brokers are paid on commissions, 6 percent of the sales price commonly being the agreed to compensation. Ordinarily, if the broker does not help effectuate a sale, no commission or other compensation is earned. In sale transactions, real estate brokers generally are considered the legal agents of sellers, not buyers; and commissions, when earned, are owed only by sellers. However, brokers commonly provide advice and assistance to buyers as well as sellers, a dual service role raising troublesome conflict of interest problems.

Sales of real estate, especially sales of single-family homes, are greatly facilitated in most local communities by multiple listing services. A multiple listing service is often referred to as an MLS. An MLS is an organization of brokers in a locality that provides centralized pooling of sales listings made with individual broker members of the service. All broker members of the MLS may seek to sell any of the pooled properties. If a sale of a pooled property is made by a broker other than the original listing broker, the brokerage commission is shared with the original listing broker. An MLS facilitates sales by expanding the number of brokers attempting to sell properties listed for sale.

NOTE

There are three common types of seller listing arrangements with brokers: open, exclusive, and exclusive right to sell. Under an open listing, the seller is obligated to pay a commission only to the broker who is the procuring cause of sale. If the property is listed with more than one broker, only the broker who is the procuring cause of sale is entitled to a commission, and no broker receives a commission if the owner sells the property on his own without any broker locating the buyer or facilitating the sale transaction. Under an exclusive listing, the seller contracts with a particular broker to be the exclusive agent to sell the property. If another broker is the procuring cause, the broker with the exclusive agency must be paid a commission, as well as the broker who is the procuring cause. However, the seller owes no commission if he or she sells the property without the aid of a broker. The exclusive right to sell listing differs from an exclusive listing in that, under the former, the broker is entitled to a commission even if the seller makes the sale without the aid of a broker. Sales made through a multiple listing service often involve exclusive or exclusive right to sell listings with the listing broker. Other members of the service may be selling brokers and as such are agents of the listing broker. The listing broker and the seller broker making the sale then share in the commission on agreed terms. All types of listing agreements ordinarily have an express termination date.

Brokers and the salespersons who work for them are separately licensed by the state in which they work,[3] examinations and other requirements for brokers' licenses being more stringent than those for salespersons. Most states impose some educational requirements concerning the work of salespersons and brokers

___

3. As a means of deterring real estate brokerage activities by unlicensed brokers, a statute in Hawaii has an unusually severe sanction for those retaining an unlicensed broker. The statute, Hawaii Rev. Stat. § 454-458, includes the following: "Any contract entered into by any person with any unlicensed mortgage broker or solicitor shall be void and unenforceable." In Beneficial Hawaii, Inc. v. Kida, 30

before a person may take the licensing examination, 60 classroom hours being a common requirement. Licensing examination pass rates vary considerably from state to state, with the pass rate being below 50 percent in some states.[4] There are approximately 616,000 licensed real estate brokers in the United States, 16 percent of them inactive, and approximately 1,477,000 licensed real estate salespersons in the United States, 16 percent of them inactive.

Most real estate brokerage offices serve only a limited geographic area: a town, section of a big city, or a suburban community. Most real estate brokerage firms have only one office, but multiple-office firms have become more common, some of them operating nationwide. Franchising has spread rapidly in recent years, such as companies like Coldwell Banker and Century 21. Under franchise arrangements, local offices are independently owned, but affiliation with a national or regional franchise operation gives referral and advertising advantages to the local offices. Real estate brokerage has become more competitive. Contributing to this has been more discount brokers offering more limited services for a lower commission when sales occur. Also, Internet listings by sellers have increased the volume of sales made without use of a broker.

The real estate brokers' trade association structure is strong and influential at the local, state, and national levels, and membership in most organizations is open to both brokers and salespersons. The national association is the National Association of Realtors (NAR). There are state associations, affiliated with the NAR, in every state, and 1,442 NAR-affiliated local boards scattered nationwide. Membership in the national organization requires membership, as well, in a state affiliate. There are 1,322,000 NAR members.[5] Only broker members of the NAR may use the licensed term "realtor," while salesperson members are referred to as "realtor-associates." Many of the local boards operate multiple listing services, and many also approve widely used printed forms of deeds, leases, contracts of sale, listing agreements, and other common real estate transaction legal documents. The NAR has promulgated a Code of Ethics and Standards of Practice to which members are expected to adhere; and it has set up a number of member subgroups, including the Society of Industrial Realtors and the American Institute of Real Estate Appraisers. The real estate brokers' trade associations are powerful lobbying bodies at national, state, and local levels.

Mortgage brokers are also important in real estate, especially in larger transactions. This type of broker, for a fee, brings together mortgage lenders and borrowers, with real estate as the loan security. Borrowers making use of mortgage broker services often are having difficulty finding a lender on acceptable terms, and the lenders often are seeking the relatively high returns that frequently are possible in real estate mortgage loans. Mortgage broker fees commonly are 1 to 3 percent of the loan and are ordinarily paid by the borrower. Some mortgage brokers also are real estate brokers. In some states, mortgage brokers are licensed, but generally these intermediaries are subject to less government regulation than are real estate brokers or lawyers.

P.2d 895 (Haw. 2001), the Supreme Court of Hawaii relied on this statute in holding void and unenforceable a mortgage and a promissory note securing the mortgage.

4. On state by state educational requirements for real estate brokers and salespersons, see Olazabal & Sacasas, Real Estate Agent as "Superbroker," Defining and Bridging the Gap Between Residential Realtors' Abilities and Liabilities in the New Millenium, 30 Real Estate L.J. 173, 223-230 (2001).

5. The above numbers of licensed real estate brokers and salespersons, inactive percentages, and the numbers of affiliated local boards and NAR members are as of 2006 and were obtained from the NAR.

The business of real estate brokerage is very competitive, the competition coming both from brokerage firms competing with one another and from other business firms — including some banks, some business consulting firms, and some law firms — competing with real estate brokerage firms. Competition as well is coming from an increasing volume of Internet listings by sellers that has eliminated the use of brokers in many sales transactions.[6]

Controversy has long existed between lawyers and real estate brokers over brokerage activities in providing such law-related services to parties to real estate transactions as preparing legal documents — including contracts of sale, deeds and leases, administering the closing of real estate transactions, and providing legal advice. Lawyers have asserted that such services by brokers are illegal and are prohibited by unauthorized practice laws. However, there is considerable legal authority that, with certain qualifications and exceptions, permits real estate brokers to provide some legal services to parties engaged in real estate transactions. But there is extensive variation among the states permitting the brokers to perform legal services as to just what services and what qualifications and exceptions apply. The frequently commented on Opinion 26 case sets forth one such position, a position favorable to brokers provided that certain notice precautions are followed. Another aspect of unauthorized practice law applicable to real estate brokers is that in many states the applicable law is ambiguous and uncertain. Moreover, as the trend is toward broadening somewhat the legal services role of real estate brokers, older case law extensively restricting that role often is of questionable validity today. Even where the law prohibiting real estate brokers from providing legal services is relatively clear, enforcement in many states is lax and violations by brokers are prevalent, especially in residential real estate transactions.

Currier, Finding the Broker's Place in the Typical Residential Real Estate Transaction

33 U. Fla. L. Rev. 655-681 (1981)

The real estate broker's place in the residential real estate conveyancing process is not well understood. The law most often casts the broker as the seller's legal agent. This does not always accord with the expectations of home sellers and buyers about the broker's function; indeed, brokers themselves frequently take a broader view of their role than the law of agency implies. A broker who disregards the law's proscriptions, however, and seeks to fulfill the parties' expectations risks sanction if a disappointed seller or buyer later complains. Should fear of penalty lead the broker to keep his conduct within the boundaries of agency law, the parties to a transaction, particularly the buyer, may be denied the aid and counsel they need and expect from the broker.

Disparity between the legal model imposed on brokers and the expectations of the parties creates a dilemma for brokers and prompts consumer uncertainty about the broker's role. The law governing the real estate broker's place in a residential

---

6. On Internet listing competition, see Rohan et al, Real Estate Brokerage Law and Practice, Ch. 10 (1985 and annual supps.). For competition generally in real estate residential brokerage and recommendations for making that industry even more competitive, see symposium, 35 Real Estate L.J. 11 (2006).

real estate transaction and the expectations of sellers and buyers about the broker's role need reconciliation. . . .

A Perspective on the Role of the Real Estate Broker

Most persons initiate residential real estate transactions by contacting a real estate broker.[2] The broker generally knows the local housing market, is experienced in the conveyancing process, and can present a house to many potential buyers. Sellers may consequently seek local brokers in an effort to obtain the timely sale of their property at the maximum price, on favorable terms. Brokers may thus be able to help sellers achieve their objectives in the real estate market and guard the seller from having to exert great personal effort. . . .

Potential buyers may also be concerned about purchasing a home because of the high transactional costs associated with real estate transactions. Inspecting a house for defects is often financially impossible,[7] and the conveyancing process is becoming increasingly complex. In addition, individuals participate in this market relatively infrequently during their lifetimes[9] despite the mobility of the population and the high volume of real estate transactions. The unfamiliarity of the process thus contributes to the anxiety many potential home buyers feel when entering the real estate market. . . .

The broker and buyer spend a considerable amount of time together during the often lengthy home search period. Inevitably, as several houses are visited, comparisons will be made regarding floor plans, neighborhood character, and the like. The shared experience of buyer and broker makes the broker the logical buyer's advisor

2. "Broker" is used in this article as a generic term to describe both the real estate broker and the real estate salesperson. All 50 states require licensing as a condition to lawfully acting as either a real estate broker or real estate salesperson. P. Goldstein, Real Estate Transactions 29 (1980). Real estate brokering consists of a person acting for another for compensation in the negotiation or attempted negotiation of the sale, purchase, exchange or rental of any interest in real property. See, e.g., Fla. Stat. § 475.01(3) (1981). Although qualifications for licensing vary, typically the broker's license is more difficult to obtain than a salesperson's license. For example, in Florida a person must complete a 51-hour course and pass an examination to be licensed as a real estate salesperson. Id. § 475.17(2). To qualify for a broker's license, a person must have twelve months' experience as a licensed salesperson in the office of a registered broker, take an additional 48-hour course, and pass another examination. Id. Salespersons can perform most brokerage services, but they must be employed by, and act under the supervision of, a licensed broker. Id. § 475.01(4). Nothing prohibits a person licensed as a broker from acting as a salesperson for another broker or for a business association acting as a broker. In a large real estate brokerage firm many persons may be licensed as brokers although the business may be registered only in the names of the partners or a few of the active members. It is difficult to generalize about what brokerage activities cannot be performed by salespersons. . . .

Realtors are brokers who belong to the National Association of Realtors, which is the largest brokers' trade group. It has been active through local boards of realtors in operating multiple listing services and other aspects of the real estate business. . . .

7. This has been recognized at least with respect to new homes: "An experienced builder who has erected and sold many houses is in a far better position to determine the structural condition of a house than most buyers. Even if a buyer is sufficiently knowledgeable to evaluate a home's condition, he rarely has access to make any inspection of the underlying structural work, as distinguished from the merely cosmetic features." Duncan v. Schuster-Graham Homes, Inc., 194 Colo. 441, 444, 578 P.2d 637, 638–39 (1978).

9. Mobility among owners of homes is significantly less than among renters. Despite a high rate of mobility within the general population and the fact that about 64 percent of all housing units are owner-occupied, U.S. Dept. of Commerce, Bureau of the Census, 1979 Statistical Abstract of the United States 782 (hereinafter cited as Statistical Abstract), a family is not likely to make more than a few home purchases during its existence. Id. at 122; Speare, Home Ownership, Life Cycle State and Residential Mobility, 7 Demography 449 (1970).

as alternative courses are weighed and sifted. The broker's advice is influential because of his expertise.

Current conveyancing practices involve the broker with the buyer beyond the search-and-locate stage. A buyer may reasonably continue to rely on the broker's assistance as the offer is formulated and the final contract negotiated. The broker aids the buyer in preparing the offer that forms the basis of the land sale contract between seller and buyer. Although the buyer can reject the broker's aid and consult an attorney, time pressure may militate against this. The buyer may also feel the broker is the best person to advise him.

Both sellers and buyers contact brokers to help them achieve their differing goals in a real estate transaction. Sellers' objectives are straightforward and not as dependent on the development of a personal relationship with the broker for their success. Buyers' special needs, on the other hand, create a reliance on brokers during the natural progression of the broker-buyer relationship. A broker, however, experiences difficulty in performing the tasks expressly or impliedly entrusted to him by the lawyer while remaining within the legal rules currently governing his conduct.

REAL ESTATE BROKERS AND THE LAW OF AGENCY

In practice both home buyers and home sellers have legitimate claims to the broker's loyalty. An analysis of agency law, however, reveals that the legal system affords more favorable treatment and greater protection to the broker-seller relationship than to that of the broker-buyer. This greater protection is derived from the legal effect of the listing agreement between the seller and broker, in which the seller promises to pay a commission to the broker thus making the broker his agent. Regardless of both the amount of time the broker and buyer spend together and the personal relationship that may develop between them, the broker is seldom considered the buyer's agent.

In the majority of cases, a written, exclusive right-to-sell agreement establishes the agency relationship between seller and broker. Under this contract, the seller promises to pay an agreed commission to the broker if the house sells during the listing period. The commission must be paid whether the sale results from the efforts of the listing broker, another broker, or the seller. Other forms of listing property with a broker are possible, but brokers promote the exclusive right to sell the model, arguing that it assures the broker's best attention and effect to sell the property. In theory, sellers *must* count on the listing broker's efforts under an exclusive right to sell agreement to avoid potential liability for more than one commission. In practice, however, the listing broker will agree to cooperate with another broker and share the commission unless the listing broker has another offer in hand; part of a certain commission is better than the chance of a whole commission.

Cooperation among brokers is so sensible that it has become formalized in the multiple listing services (MLS) that permeate real estate markets across the country. The MLS concept is simple — brokers agree to pool listings and split commissions. Multiple listing services mitigate the harshness of exclusive right-to-sell listing agreements. A seller's property is included in the inventory of all MLS members by listing it with one, and the brokers' advance agreement to cooperate effectively eliminates the potential double commission problem.

Buyers as well as sellers benefit from MLS operations. One MLS member can show a house listed by any other member without having to arrange that member's cooperation in advance. Given the substantial market share of many multiple listing services, the "one-stop shopping" method appears to be a very efficient way to canvass available housing opportunities. Another consequence of the MLS arrangement, however, is not so advantageous to buyers. The agreement to pool listings and share commissions creates ties among member brokers that make each a subagent of every other member broker.

Once the broker becomes the seller's agent,[29] the law imposes certain duties on the broker. Because of the agency relationship's fiduciary character, the broker is subject to the duties of loyalty, honesty and full disclosure to his principal. These duties bind the agent because of the nature of an agency arrangement and do not depend on the listing agreement's terms. Basic principles of agency law require the broker to disclose information to the seller that would help him in the bargaining process. The broker must further refrain from disclosing information to the buyer that would harm the seller, unless failure to make the revelation amounts to fraud or misrepresentation.

The standard agency model works well for most purposes in the conveyancing process. It regulates the broker's behavior vis-à-vis the seller. For example, the broker cannot secretly profit by buying property he has agreed to sell at a bargain price and then reselling it at a profit. Self-dealing is not prohibited, but the broker must disclose his intentions to deal personally in the property and not take advantage of his superior knowledge to gain from the trust the seller has reposed in him.

Although a broker may advise a seller of his opinions concerning offers received, the law clearly states that all such decisions are the seller's. Offers must be communicated to the seller regardless of the broker's evaluation of whether they should be accepted, rejected, or countered. A high standard of care applies to the broker's conduct regarding the accuracy and sufficiency of the advice. Failing to meet it, the broker risks possible disciplinary proceedings and sanctions.[36]

In contrast to the seller's legal relationship with the broker, the home buyer's position is a perilous one. Reposing confidence and trust in the broker, the buyer is potentially exposed to manipulation and exploitation. Brokers can successfully meet a buyer's complaints about alleged mistreatment with a defense based upon the law of agency. Of course, actions in fraud and misrepresentation afford some

29. Agency is a consensual relationship between two persons wherein one of them, the principal, empowers the other, the agent, to act and the agent assumes to so act. Restatement (Second) of Agency § 1 (1958); Defosses v. Notis, 333 A.2d 83 (Me. 1975). Generally, the broker is a special agent, as opposed to a general one. A special agent represents the principal in a discrete number of transactions without involving a continuity of service. Restatement (Second) of Agency § 3 (1958). Ingalls v. Rice, 511 S.W.2d 78, 80 (Tex. Civ. App. 1974); Stenson v. Thrush, 36 Wash. 2d 726, 728, 219 P.2d 977, 978 (1950). The authority of the broker is confined to selling a described piece of real property for a given price. In practice the broker does not sell the property but solicits offers and aids in negotiating a sale on terms acceptable to the seller.

36. A broker may be denied his commission for not performing in a satisfactory manner the duties owed to the seller-principal. See, e.g., Security Aluminum Window Mfg. Corp. v. Lehman Assocs., Inc., 108 N.J. Super. 137, 260 A.2d 248 (Super. Ct. App. Div. 1970) (compensatory and punitive damages assessed against broker who led principal to believe that an offer of only $25,000 had been made when in fact a $50,000 offer had been received). The broker's license may be suspended or revoked for violation of a duty imposed on the broker by law or contract, without regard to whether the victim of the misconduct sustained loss or damage. Fla. Stat. § 475.25(1)(1981). Additionally, members of the National Association of Realtors can be penalized by their local board for violating that group's Code of Ethics. Sanctions range from a reprimand to expulsion from the local chapter.

protection to the buyer. The buyer may alternatively assert an express agency relationship exists between himself and the broker or that mistreatment by a broker, while not amounting to fraud or misrepresentation, breaches duties owed to him even though he is not the broker's principal.

Establishing a formal agency relationship with a real estate broker, however, will be difficult for the buyer. The seller's contractual arrangement with the broker, because of its formality and an assumption that it arose first, may preempt any relationship buyer claims with the broker. The mere fact that the listing agreement is in writing, however, should not elevate the broker-seller relationship to a superior position;[39] rather, the listing agreement should be considered only one of many material facts necessary to determine who the broker's principal was in a particular transaction.

The person whose relationship with the broker began first could assert a stronger claim to the agent's loyalty. There is an unarticulated presumption that the broker-seller relationship is the initial one. Buyers thus bear the burden of overcoming this presumption; however, the presumption itself is questionable. The home buyer and the broker may be working together prior to the time the seller's house is listed. In tight real estate markets, a land sale contract may be entered within hours or days of listing. It is unlikely that these sudden sales result from the home buyer just happening into a broker's office moments after the listing has been obtained.

A buyer's claim that the broker is his agent is weakened because the seller pays the broker's compensation. Although one can act as an agent gratuitously, most brokers sell real estate to earn a living. Work done in the normal transaction is expected to lead to a commission. It seems reasonable, therefore, to expect the broker to give his allegiance to the party who is paying him. While the listing agreement legally obligates the seller to pay the commission, the home buyer may be paying all or part of the commission indirectly. Sellers often increase the price if they employ a broker so that the sale's net proceeds equal what might have been obtained by selling privately. The buyer thus effectively pays the commission, despite the fact that liability for the commission rests on the seller. In practice, the broker collects his commission at closing from money provided by the buyer. If a transaction does not close, the buyer may pay some compensation to the broker as an element of the seller's damages in an action on the purchase and sale agreement.[45] If the superiority of the broker-seller relationship is based on the broker's compensation flowing from the seller, it is therefore undermined to the extent that the commission is buried in the sales price.

Although custom dictates that the seller pays the commission, the mere fact that the seller agrees to make this payment is not sufficient to create an agency relationship between seller and broker. Sometimes facts and circumstances demonstrate

39. The listing agreement does not come under the Statute of Frauds because it provides for the broker's services in connection with the sale of land, not for the actual transfer of any interest in property. E.g., Jefcoat v. Singer Hous. Co., 619 F.2d 539, 543 (5th Cir. 1980). Some states nonetheless insist that brokerage contracts be in writing. E.g., Idaho Code § 9-508 (1979).

45. Seller can recover incidental damages flowing from the buyer's breach of the land sale contract, including any commissions for which the seller becomes liable. See Uniform Land Transaction Act 2-507(a). Land sale contracts typically let the seller keep as liquidated damages any deposit the buyer has made in lieu of, or as part of, an action for damages against a breaching buyer. A Maryland court recently held that the seller must elect between forfeiture of the deposit or an action for damages. Blood v. Gibbons, 288 Md. 268, 418 A.2d 213 (Md. 1980). If the seller keeps the deposit and does not seek damages, the broker usually accepts one-half the deposit (up to the amount of the commission) as compensation for services.

the broker was really acting for the buyer in the transaction. When such a case arises, the seller's agreement does nothing more than determine how the broker is to be compensated for his efforts.

Nothing theoretically prohibits a buyer from hiring a broker, agreeing to pay a fee for services, and thus creating a principal-agent relationship. In practice, however, this seldom occurs. The organization and operation of the residential brokerage business discourages such arrangements. Home buyers understand that brokers will receive compensation from sellers, and they know that brokers will work with them without additional charge. Formal contracts are not solicited by buyers and brokers do not insist on them. The broker ends up a seller's agent in law, and an extension of the seller in the transaction. Despite the hours spent together and closeness of their relationship, buyer and broker become, at least in theory, adversaries in the negotiation process.

One argument remains for a buyer who feels mistreated by a broker who is the seller's agent and whose conduct does not amount to fraud. A buyer can assert the breach of certain duties brokers owe even to non-principal parties in a real estate transaction. The foundation of these duties is somewhat obscure. One source is the National Association of Realtors' Code of Ethics. Under it member brokers must deal honestly and in good faith with all non-principals, including buyers. Another source is the notion that the broker's license is a privilege conferred by the state in exchange for which the broker must act in the public interest. Dealing honestly and fairly with all members of the public is part of the broker's duty of furthering the public interest.

The idea that the broker must deal straightforwardly with the public adds dimension to the simple picture that emerges from strict application of agency law to the relationships among the parties in residential real estate transactions. That the brokers' professional organization has a code of conduct recognizing the needs of buyers implies that brokers believe they serve both parties to a real estate transaction and that agency law inaccurately reflects their dual role in the market place. . . .

Given the reasonable expectations both sellers and buyers harbor concerning the broker's loyalty, alternative ways of handling the legal relationships among the parties must be evaluated. Legal theory must be brought closer to the operation of the residential real estate market. Perhaps the tangled web of conflicting rights and duties could be clarified by only slight changes in the law. The viability of any alteration must be assessed in the context of the present structure of the real estate market. An examination of the advantages and problems with a number of possible reforms is necessary.

DUAL AGENCY

Recognizing a principal-agent relationship between broker and buyer along with the broker's traditional duties to the seller would provide legal support for the buyer's expectations regarding the broker's role as an advisor and give the broker a solid foundation upon which to engage in counseling activity. The duality of fiduciary responsibilities to parties who are often adversaries, however, conflicts with the agent's duty to serve the principal's interests above all others. The inherent shortcomings of dual agency considerably undercut its usefulness in coping with the problems considered here. . . .

Before the broker can act as dual agent, the knowledge and consent of both principals must be obtained. Achieving such consent in the current market structure might be difficult. . . .

Another approach, related to dual agency, would permit a broker to represent the buyer's interests if another broker listed the house. Throughout this article the assumption has been that only one broker works on a sale, dealing with both buyer and seller. In the context of multiple listing services, however, the most suitable homes are likely to have been listed by someone other than the broker working with the buyer. In such a situation, a natural division of labor may result, serving the legitimate needs of each party—the listing broker can act as seller's agent, and the broker, who has established a relationship with the buyer and who shows him the house (the selling broker) can act as the buyer's agent. The parties may be comfortable with this arrangement, but it does not square with the legal framework which applies to the typical transaction. Legally, the selling broker is the seller's agent because of the multiple listing agreement signed by member brokers, which provides for splitting the commission between the brokers who participate in a conveyance. Courts have not been reluctant to hold the selling broker responsible to the seller, even though the two have no express agreement. To work for the buyer under the current legal framework, therefore the selling broker would have to become a dual agent. . . .

DISCLOSURE

The confusion about the broker's role in the conveyancing process can be viewed as a consumer protection problem. Attention has been focused recently on the frequent abuses consumers suffer in the property conveyancing process. These abuses relate primarily to expenses for obtaining financing and transferring title. Mandatory disclosure has become a significant consumer protection method. The seller or creditor must disclose pertinent information, including statements about the consumer's legal rights and the concomitant duties of the retailers, lenders, and others with whom they deal. . . .

The principle of disclosure could nevertheless be applied to the real estate brokerage industry. Brokers could be required by law or regulation to inform buyers of the agency relationship the broker has directly with some sellers, through listing agreements, and indirectly with others, through multiple listing arrangements. The broker would have to explain that he may not volunteer more information than the owner of the home would have to disclose nor give advice about the appropriate price or subjective qualities of the houses inspected. If a dual agency approach is adopted, statements could be formulated for presentation to both parties at the outset of the broker's dealings with each of them.

Disclosure would reveal to buyers the constraints agency law places on the broker's actions and disabuse them of the belief that the broker is working for them. In the absence of a viable comprehensive solution to the problems considered here, disclosure in some form would aid buyers. Brokers and those who regulate them should give serious attention to the best form of disclosure and the best time for it. Disclosure, however, cannot solve the more fundamental problem of providing counsel to buyers. Disclosure helps but it is no cure for the lack of advice and guidance buyers expect.

MIDDLEMAN

A broker may act as a middleman in a real estate[103] conveyance. This characterization emphasizes the broker's independent objective to earn a commission in the transaction. As a middleman, the broker is limited to bringing the parties together and may not take an active part in the negotiations for either party. The middleman posture limits the broker to doing less than either party expects. Such a constrained role makes the usual commission the broker receives seem exorbitant. Casting the broker as a middleman may cure the conflict of interest problems, but it is overkill, eliminating the substance of the broker's participation in the conveyancing process.

BUYER'S AGENT

If buyers require the services and counsel of agents with expertise in real estate, a direct and obvious way to meet the demand is for some brokers to work exclusively for buyers. Nothing in the law of agency or real estate brokerage bars such an activity. Indeed, many cases holding brokers responsible to buyers involve agents employed to find property for buyers rather than to sell for owners.

Because buyer's agents would be a new development in residential real estate transactions, changes in the manner of conducting business would be required. A major difficulty would be determining the compensation of the buyer's agent. To make this agent's duties of loyalty and disclosure clear, his compensation ought to come solely from the buyer-principal.

If buyers have to pay the same price for a house plus a fee to secure the loyalty of the broker, they might avoid entering into such agency agreements, despite the benefits such an arrangement might offer. Obviously, buyer reception of the idea depends on the fee. In the multiple broker situation the selling broker usually gets the larger share of the commission. For this new concept to work, therefore, more than an incidental amount will need to be paid by the buyer because the broker must forego the customary selling broker's percentage of the commission.

A buyer may pay less for a house if he employs an agent to negotiate directly with the seller and the listing broker, however. A commonly held assumption is that the commission is buried in the sale price and, practically speaking, paid by the purchaser when a broker is involved in a transaction. Some buyers explore "for sale by owner" listings expecting to pay less for a house.[106] If the selling broker's share of the commission were not subtracted from the proceeds the seller received at closing because the purchaser paid for these services directly, the seller should

103. A broker may claim middleman status to avoid the charge that he acted as agent for both parties without their consent to a dual agency. Harry M. Fine Realty Co. v. Stiers, 326 S.W.2d 392, 398 (Mo. App. 1959). Because dual agencies can be created, the broker need not reduce his participation to that of middleman. Mallory v. Watt, 100 Idaho 119, 122, 594 P.2d 629, 632 (1979). An excellent conception of the middleman's role is provided by an early North Dakota case: "A broker is simply a middleman . . . when he has no duty to perform but to bring the parties together, leaving them to negotiate and to come to an agreement themselves without any aid from him. If he takes . . . any part in the negotiations, however, he cannot be regarded as a mere middleman, no matter how slight a part it may be." Jensen v. Bowen, 37 N.D. 352, 358, 164 N.W.4, 5 (1917).

106. There is an apparent lack of empirical verification of whether buyers save all or part of the commission by purchasing directly from the seller without the aid of a broker. Brokers hint that the commission is buried in the price. The National Association of Realtors gives as a reason for owners to list their homes that: "[I]n a Sale by Owner, the Realtor's commission is always deducted by the buyer and the seller is left to do all the work for nothing." National Association of Realtors, Sales Handbook 71 (1975).

accept a lower price for his house. The price of the house would, therefore, be lower by an amount approaching or equal to the fee paid by the buyer to employ the broker at the outset of the search process. Costs, therefore, should not inhibit the introduction of a buyer's agent into the conveyancing process.

Another question to consider is whether enough brokers would undertake such an activity to make it viable. If a broker could somehow be a buyer's agent for some clients and continue to list property, the industry might not resist this change. Even if buyers' agents were prohibited from listing property the concept might still work. So many people hold real estate sales and brokerage licenses that one could expect a significant number to become buyers' agents to capture revenues such activity would generate. Certainly, many details and questions would have to be carefully thought out before the implementing of such a radical change in the way residential real estate sales are presently transacted. Given a problem as pervasive as this one, however, imagination and experimentation are necessary.

CONCLUSION

Home buying and selling are important events in the personal lives of most Americans. Counsel and aid ought to be available for those who want it. Although most real estate brokers understand the significance of their responsibilities and treat both buyer and seller with consideration, the law defining the broker's role in the conveyancing process is vague and inconsistent with the understanding of the parties involved. For the sake of brokers, sellers, and buyers, brokers' duties should be clarified. If possible, the duties should be defined in a way that meets the reasonable expectations of the parties.

NOTES

1. In commercial real estate transactions it is commonplace for there to be brokers representing only buyers. But in residential sales this type of broker relationship is unusual, although it may be becoming more frequent. See Ferguson and Plattner, The Growing Importance of Buyers' Brokers, 21 Real Estate Review no. 4, at 83 (1992).

2. Dual agency, in which the broker legally is agent of both buyer and seller, is permitted in some states in some circumstances. An advantage of this form of broker representation is that the brokerage commission paid by each party generally is less than if the broker were representing but one of them. Broker dual agency, however, poses a serious conflict of interest problem to the broker: how to deal with the diverse interests of the parties being represented by the broker so as to avoid illegally favoring one of the parties over the other one. Connecticut by statute permits dual agency. See Conn. Gen. Stat. Ann. § 20-325g (1999). The Connecticut statute relies largely on buyer and seller signing a written informed consent form and disclosure requirements on the broker as protection of the parties when brokers are dual agents. It is questionable whether these requirements provide sufficient protection from the risk of brokers unduly favoring one side over the other.

3. Another form of brokerage contract, one aimed at limiting brokers' legal risks, is the nonagent contract, also known by other names, including transaction broker contract. This form of brokerage control is expressly permitted by the law of some states. Nonagent brokerage limits broker liability by permitting brokers to enter into brokerage contracts in which the broker's services to be provided are sufficiently limited that the broker is not legally an agent and hence not subject to most of the fiduciary obligations that an agent owes the principal. For statutes permitting nonagent brokerage contracts, see Colo. Rev. Stat. Ann. § 12-61-807 (2003) and Minn. Stat. Ann. § 82-197, subd. 4 (IV) (1999). For discussion of nonagent brokerage contracts, see Pancak et al, Real Estate Agency Reform: Meeting the Needs of Buyers, Sellers, and Brokers, 25 Real Est. L.J. 345, 355-358 (1997); Wilson, Nonagent Brokerage: Real Estate Agents Missing in Action, 52 Okla. L. Rev. 85 (1999).

Federal Trade Commission, The Residential Real Estate Brokerage Industry

F.T.C. Staff Rep. 7, 16, 17, 63, 110-112, 145-146 (1983)

Listing brokers perform a number of tasks designed to facilitate the sale of a home. Commonly, one of the most important of these is listing the home with the local "multiple listing service" (or "MLS"). This service, generally owned and operated by a local association of brokers, is an information sharing or exchange mechanism, the use of which is reserved to its broker members. It is a means of informing the members, who are potentially "cooperating brokers," of the seller's desire to sell. The listing broker will describe the property, the asking price, any unusual features, outstanding mortgages, and so forth in the "MLS listing" and also indicate his or her willingness to "split" the commission with any cooperating broker who finds a suitable buyer, indicating the percent of the commission which will be given as a split (typically, this may amount to half of the total commission due on sale of the property).

Buyers often work with brokers to find suitable homes to buy. While a broker commonly will inform a prospective buyer of the broker's own listings first, he or she will then turn to the local MLS to find additional listings which may meet the buyer's needs. If the buyer makes a selection, the buyer makes an "offer" to purchase the home. This offer typically will be at a price below that originally asked by the seller. A process of negotiation often follows with "counter-offers" relating to price and other terms (who will pay for a termite inspection, for example) changing hands through the intermediation of the broker. . . .

Most MLSs allow only exclusive right-to-sell listing contracts to be processed using their facilities. Only 18 percent of the MLSs which responded to an FTC survey of such institutions reported accepting exclusive agency listings [broker receives a commission if another broker sells the property during the listing period but not if the seller does], and only 11 percent would accept open listings. Most brokers presumably prefer exclusive right-to-sell listings [broker receives a commission if the property is sold during the listing period regardless of who sells it]. Such listings have two obvious effects. They prevent the seller from selling the property without paying the broker a commission when the broker has spent serious time and effort in trying to dispose of it. And they also prevent a seller from putting pressure on a dilatory broker during the listing period by threatening to find a buyer and sell the house him or herself. . . .

The growth of the MLSs during the last 60 years has been the most important development in the modern brokerage industry. The historical reasons for and effects of multiple listing give important insights into today's industry. Today, 92 percent of sellers using brokers have their homes listed on an MLS. A number of industry commentators have concluded that the MLS is essential for a broker to compete and effectively market homes in most areas.

All MLSs impose conditions of membership. These rules and regulations may have a substantial impact on the nature and degree of competition in the industry. Of the MLSs we surveyed for this Report, 94 percent were affiliated with a local Board of Realtors. Membership in the Board usually is required to obtain access to a Realtor MLS. However, even where Realtor membership is not a condition, 89 percent of the brokers who participate in the MLSs were, on average, Realtors. Realtor membership, in turn, means accepting a number of conditions, including compliance with the NAR's Code of Ethics and payment of its membership dues (which include dues for membership in all three levels of the NAR structure — local, state, and national). . . .

The concept of multiple listing was based upon the need to devise an efficient method for marketing exclusive listings. With an exclusive listing only one broker had direct rights and incentives to sell the house. By the 1920's, however, sellers had become aware of the advantages of obtaining exposure through many brokers. For this reason exclusive listings had become nearly impossible for brokers to obtain. The open listing was the general rule.

From the broker's point of view, open listings were associated with a number of problems. These problems related to competition among listing brokers, competition with sellers, and duplication of effort by brokers. . . .

The MLSs and exclusive listing agreements, when used together, reduced the problems presented by unfettered competition. With an exclusive listing, only one broker could claim the commission. Other brokers could not work directly with the seller. Cooperation of other brokers with the exclusive listing broker (someone with whom they could anticipate dealing cooperatively on many different future sales and therefore with whom they could establish an ongoing professional relationship) was the basis of the new marketing system. "They have replaced the old spirit of competition for one of cooperation, and it has brought peace where there was strife, and harmony where discord reigned." [H. Nightengale, California Real Estate at 12 (April 1924).] . . .

Open listings were also associated with competition with the seller. Substantial numbers of sellers at that time were making direct sales to buyers even after listing their homes with a broker who spent time and effort to sell it. The MLSs and the exclusive-right listing agreement helped to stop this. The MLSs would accept only exclusive-right listings, and the exclusive-right listings most brokers came to insist upon in most transactions guaranteed the broker a commission even if the seller procured the buyer. . . .

Open listings sometimes might be given to as many as 20 brokers. Many of these brokers might spend time trying to sell the property only to find that they could not deliver the property to a prospective buyer. Either the property had been sold, withdrawn from the market, or the price had gone up. Listings were considered the broker's inventory, the stock on his shelves. Open listings, however, were analogized to perishable goods. A broker had no certainty that they would remain viable, saleable listings.

This waste of time and the inability to deliver properties even if purchasers were found are problems which brokers still associate with open listings. The exclusive contracts required by most MLSs eliminated these perceived problems by binding the seller to a specific listing period and a specific price. Further, with an exclusive, the listing broker receives some protection from other brokers and from the seller. Even if another, cooperating broker or the owner sells the listing, the initial, listing broker will receive a substantial portion of the commission. . . .

Note, Sub-Agency in Residential Real Estate Brokerage: A Proposal to End the Struggle with Reality

61 S. Cal. L. Rev. 401 (1988)

The residential real estate brokerage industry is in a state of confusion. Brokers do not know who they represent. Consumers do not know who represents them. The cause of much of this confusion is the doctrine of "sub-agency," by which two brokers in a real estate transaction *both* represent the seller.

The typical home sale involves two real estate brokers, the "listing broker" and the "cooperating broker." The listing broker contracts with the seller to arrange the sale of the property. This contract takes the form of a "listing agreement," and creates an express agency relationship between the listing broker and the seller. As a result of this relationship, the listing broker owes duties of care and of "utmost good faith and loyalty" to the seller. The most widely used standard form listing agreement authorizes the listing broker to place the listing on the Multiple Listing Service (MLS) in the area, and to appoint sub-agents to assist the broker in marketing the property. The MLS is a system whereby listings are pooled and distributed to all brokers who subscribe to the service. These brokers can bring buyers to the listed property and receive a share of the commission paid by the seller. . . .

The strongest argument for eliminating sub-agency is that it does not reflect reality. Buyers reasonably believe that cooperating brokers represent them. Moreover, *sellers* overwhelmingly believe that cooperating brokers are buyers' agents. This belief is shared by the cooperating brokers themselves. Words like "cooperation" and "sub-agency" are used throughout the industry, but *not* in the context of owing fiduciary duties to sellers or working on their behalf. Rather, the terms are euphemisms for fee-splitting. Becoming a sub-agent merely allows the broker access to the property and the possibility of collecting a share of the fee if the sale is consummated. Assuming brokers act according to their beliefs and expectations, one must conclude that cooperating brokers actually negotiate on behalf of their buyers. This conclusion is supported by empirical evidence. . . .

The uniform beliefs and expectations of consumers and brokers undermines reliance on the "custom of the industry" as a justification of sub-agency. The most that can be said is that only "cooperation" and fee-splitting are industry customs. Neither consumers nor brokers expect a cooperating broker to owe a duty of loyalty to the seller or to work for anyone but the buyer. Sellers do not expect cooperating brokers to negotiate the highest possible price, nor do they expect to be held responsible for the wrongful acts of the cooperating broker. Moreover, all parties to the transaction will be surprised upon learning that a cooperating broker acts as a dual agent. . . .

The optimal solution to the sub-agency problem should accomplish the following:

    (a) impose duties and liabilities only where the parties reasonably expect them;

    (b) provide a standard of conduct to which brokers can conform *before* problems arise in the transaction;

    (c) encourage balanced representation and protection of both buyer and seller;

    (d) avoid the conflict of interest caused by dual agency;

    (e) maintain the benefits of the MLS as an information exchange while at the same time maximizing competition throughout the real estate brokerage industry; and

    (f) incorporate practical workability and political feasibility.

The current system of sub-agency utterly fails to satisfy the first four criteria, and has serious problems with the last two. Neither consumers nor brokers expect or consent to have cooperating brokers work on behalf of sellers, and there are problems of potential dual agency and vague fiduciary duties. While the MLS is maintained, competition in the brokerage industry is not what it should be.

Outright elimination of sub-agency avoids the dual agency problem (except in the case of in-house sales), conforms to the reasonable expectations of the parties, and encourages balanced representation of both parties in the transaction. Such an elimination also provides a clear standard of conduct for the cooperating broker. However, arguments have been made doubting the continued viability of the MLS without subagency. Moreover, in light of vehement opposition from the NAR, the elimination of sub-agency may not be politically feasible.

The literature contains three other solutions to the sub-agency problem short of outright elimination. The first two — making the cooperating broker an agent of *both* buyer and seller or increasing common law fiduciary duties to the buyer — are actually problematic symptoms of sub-agency rather than its cure. The third — disclosure of the brokers' agency relationships — may be a step in the right direction, but is insufficient to rectify the sub-agency problem. . . .

A limited concept of sub-agency would retain the doctrine's positive aspects while avoiding most of the negative ramifications. Under limited sub-agency, the cooperating broker is a "sub-agent" of the listing broker. However, the scope of the sub-agency does not include owing a duty of loyalty to the seller. The cooperating broker's duty to the listing broker and seller would be limited to:

(a) facilitating the bargaining process by participating in an exchange of information regarding the seller's property and the buyer's offer; and

(b) serving as a conduit for the disclosure of non-confidential material facts regarding the seller's property. In performing this limited agency, the cooperating broker can show the seller's property to the buyer and relay information given by the seller or listing broker (either directly or through MLS information) to the buyer.

The cooperating broker will, however, be the primary agent of the buyer. Thus, the broker will owe a duty to obtain the lowest price and the best possible terms for the buyer, and to refrain from disclosing confidential information to the listing broker or seller. The cooperating broker will be free to give advice to the buyer on the amount of the initial offer, and discuss intangible factors which may affect the buyer's decision but do not reach the level of material fact. Since the cooperating broker will owe no duty of loyalty to the seller, a conflict of interest will not exist.

Limited sub-agency offers tremendous advantages. The expectations of all parties to the transaction are consistent with the legal duties imposed upon them. Neither the seller nor the listing broker would be held accountable for the independent misdeeds of the cooperating broker, although they would remain liable for their own misrepresentations or concealment. Buyers would receive representation and negotiation on their behalf without accompanying dual agency problems. Moreover, artificial rescission based on undisclosed dual agency would be eliminated.

Cooperating brokers could conform their conduct to the law without extensive knowledge of legal technicalities, simply by representing the buyer and keeping the market open for sellers. The cooperating broker would not be accountable to the seller for advising the buyer on the proper "low ball" offer, or for failing to point out legal intricacies regarding the transaction. The cooperating broker would be accountable to the seller only for the misrepresentation or concealment of material facts regarding the buyer, which could affect the seller's decision to enter into the transaction on the terms ultimately agreed upon. By producing a ready, willing, and able buyer, the cooperating broker can quality for the fee-split, and even enforce the right to a fee as a "procuring cause" of the sale.

Limited sub-agency also maintains the MLS as a valuable marketing mechanism. The need for qualified professionals to participate in the dissemination and analysis of listing information, along with the desire to maintain a system of cooperation among brokers in order to maximize exposure of and access to available homes, should justify restricting the use of the MLS to licensed real estate brokers. For the same reason, limit sub-agency is politically feasible, and, in fact, is a pleasing compromise between ardent single agency advocates and vehement sub-agency disciples.

Single agency is encouraged, since buyer brokers will no longer have to worry about formally rejecting sub-agency to avoid the dual agency problem. Limited sub-agency will be more efficacious and less costly, since it conforms to the parties' current actions and beliefs. The need for extensive disclosure and education programs is reduced, as is litigation caused by unknown duties.

Thus, the proper legal solution to the question of sub-agency is to create a presumption that the cooperating broker in the typical residential real estate transaction is the primary agent of the buyer, with duties of care, good faith, and loyalty. The cooperating broker should be seen as the sub-agent of the listing broker, and thus an agent of the seller, only for the purpose of providing the best possible market exposure for the seller's property (not including directing buyers to it) and of maximizing the exchange of information.

The current system of sub-agency creates undue confusion among brokers and consumers. It is time courts and legislatures took action to end the struggle with reality and conform the law to the reasonable expectations and actual conduct of the parties in residential real estate transactions.

Because the two brokers are said to have "cooperated" in the sale, this second broker has been dubbed the "cooperating broker." The cooperating broker may also be called the "selling broker" or "selling agent" on the theory that he or she is authorized through the MLS to "sell" the property. Despite the confusing name, most buyers rely on the advice of the cooperating broker, the majority believing that cooperating brokers represent them. Commentators have uniformly characterized this belief as reasonable in light of the cooperating broker's close relationship with the buyer. Moreover, many cooperating brokers see themselves as buyers' agents.

Despite the belief of the parties, a majority of jurisdictions hold that in a typical MLS transaction the cooperating broker is a sub-agent of the listing broker, and as such an agent of the seller. This notion of subagency is so counter-intuitive in light of actual experience that commentators often precede a statement of the rule with a "legalese" disclaimer, stating that the cooperating broker is "*legally* the subagent of the seller." The notion of sub-agency causes not only rhetorical confusion (by calling what many believe to be the buyer's broker the "selling agent"), but also practical confusion with respect to the cooperating broker's duty of loyalty. . . .

In a majority of jurisdictions, the cooperating broker in a typical residential real estate transaction is deemed the sub-agent of the listing broker. In the standard form multiple listing agreement, the seller authorizes the listing broker to refer the listing to the MLS, and to appoint sub-agents to assist the broker in procuring a buyer. The cooperating broker accepts the listing broker's offer of sub-agency by commencing negotiation on behalf of the buyer to purchase the property.

As a sub-agent, the cooperating broker owes the same fiduciary duties of good faith and loyalty to the seller as does the listing broker. In addition, the seller is responsible to the buyer for the misdeeds of the cooperating broker. The listing broker is also responsible for the acts of the cooperating broker. . . .

A minority of courts hold that the cooperating broker in a typical MLS transaction is the agent of the buyer and not of the seller. These courts look beyond the MLS fee-split to the facts of the particular transaction, taking a cynical view of the implications of the MLS.[82] The fact that the transaction goes through the MLS is

---

82. Facts emphasized in finding the cooperating broker an agent of the buyer and not of the seller include:

   1. the cooperating broker working to locate suitable property for the buyer before the seller comes into the picture; . . .

insufficient to establish an agency relationship between the cooperating broker and the seller. Moreover, receipt of a portion of the fee paid by the seller does not establish such a relationship. Courts are motivated to undertake this factual analysis because they view the MLS not as a device for the creation of agency relationships, but simply as a clearinghouse for information which brokers can use to set up deals inexpensively and effectively.

In re Opinion No. 26 of the Committee on the Unauthorized Practice of Law

654 A.2d. 1344 (N.J. 1995)

PER CURIAM.

We again confront another long-simmering dispute between realtors and attorneys concerning the unauthorized practice of law. *See New Jersey State Bar Ass'n v. New Jersey Ass'n of Realtor Bds.*, 93 N.J. 470, 461 A.2d 1112 (1983). Title companies are also involved. Our resolution of the dispute turns on the identification of the public interest. Since our decision today permits sellers and buyers in real estate transactions involving the sale of a home to proceed without counsel, we find it necessary to state the Court's view of the matter at the outset. The Court strongly believes that both parties should retain counsel for their own protection and that the savings in lawyers fees are not worth the risks involved in proceeding without counsel. All that we decide is that the public interest does not require that the parties be deprived of the right to choose to proceed without a lawyer.

The question before us is whether brokers and title company officers, who guide, control and handle all aspects of residential real estate transactions where neither seller nor buyer is represented by counsel, are engaged in the unauthorized practice of law. That many aspects of such transactions constitute the practice of law we have no doubt, including some of the activities of these brokers and title officers. Our power to prohibit those activities is clear. We have concluded, however, that the public interest does not require such a prohibition. Sellers and buyers, to the extent they are informed of the true interests of the broker and title officer, sometimes in conflict with their own interests, and of the risks of not having their own attorney, should be allowed to proceed without counsel. The South Jersey practice, for it is in that part of the state where sellers and buyers are most often unrepresented by counsel in residential real estate transactions, may continue subject to the conditions set forth in this opinion. By virtue of this decision, those participating in such transactions shall not be deemed guilty of the unauthorized practice of law so long as those conditions are met. Our decision in all respects applies not only to South Jersey, but to the entire state.

Under our Constitution, this Court's power over the practice of law is complete. *N.J. Const.* art. 6, §2, 13. We are given the power to permit the practice of law and to

---

2. the cooperating broker's lack of contact with the seller; . . .
3. the seller's lack of control over the cooperating broker's action. . . .

prohibit its unauthorized practice. We have exercised that latter power in numerous cases. . . .

The question of what constitutes the unauthorized practice of law involves more than an academic analysis of the function of lawyers, more than a determination of what they are uniquely qualified to do. It also involves a determination of whether non-lawyers should be allowed, in the public interest, to engage in activities that may constitute the practice of law. As noted later, the conclusion in these cases that parties need not retain counsel to perform limited activities that constitute the practice of law and that others may perform them does not imply that the public interest is thereby advanced, but rather that the public interest does not require that those parties be deprived of their right to proceed without counsel. We reach that conclusion today given the unusual history and experience of the South Jersey practice as developed in the record before us.

We determine the ultimate touchstone — the public interest — through the balancing of the factors involved in the case, namely, the risks and benefits to the public of allowing or disallowing such activities. In other words, like all of our powers, this power over the practice of law must be exercised in the public interest; more specifically, it is not a power given to us in order to protect lawyers, but in order to protect the public, in this instance by preserving its right to proceed without counsel. . . .

I

PROCEEDINGS BELOW

Opinion No. 26 of the Committee on the Unauthorized Practice of Law, 130 *N.J.L.J.* 882 (March 16, 1992), was issued in response to an inquiry, one of many, from the New Jersey State Bar Association. The inquiry sought a determination of whether the South Jersey practice constituted the unauthorized practice of law. That practice, described in detail later, concerns the sale of a home generally financed by a purchase money mortgage. The essence of the South Jersey practice is that from the beginning of the transaction to the end, neither seller nor buyer is represented by counsel. Every aspect of the transaction is handled by others, every document drafted by others, including the contract of sale, affidavit of title, bond and mortgage. The Committee on the Unauthorized Practice of Law (the Committee), relying largely on our decisions in *New Jersey State Bar Association v. New Jersey Association of Realtor Boards*, 93 *N.J.* 470, 461 A.2d 1112 (1983); *Cape May County Bar Association v. Ludlam*, 45 *N.J.* 121, 211 A.2d 780 (1965); *New Jersey State Bar Association v. Northern New Jersey Mortgage Associates*, 32 *N.J.* 430, 161 A.2d 257 (1960), and its own prior determination in Opinion No. 11 of the Committee on the Unauthorized Practice of Law, 95 *N.J.L.J.* 1345 (December 28, 1972), ruled that the ordering of a title search by the broker, the preparation of conveyancing and other documents by title officers, their clearing of title questions, and indeed the activities of both broker and title officers at the closing itself, where neither buyer nor seller was represented by counsel, that all of these activities constituted the unauthorized practice of law. The decision was interpreted widely as prohibiting the South Jersey practice, in effect prohibiting a seller and buyer from proceeding with the sale of a home without counsel. . . .

Specifically, we rule as follows: a real estate broker may order a title search and abstract; an attorney retained by a title company or a real estate broker may not prepare conveyance documents for a real estate transaction except at the specific written request of the party on whose behalf the document is to be prepared; a title company may not participate in the clearing of certain legal objections to title, see *infra* at 359, 654 A.2d at 1362; and the practice of conducting closings or settlements without the presence of attorneys shall not constitute the unauthorized practice of law. We hold further, however, that unless the broker conforms to the conditions set forth later in this opinion, all participants at the closing who have reason to believe those conditions have not been complied with will be engaged in the unauthorized practice of law, and any attorney with similar knowledge so participating in such a transaction will have committed unethical conduct.

II

THE SOUTH JERSEY PRACTICE

Although the variations are numerous, the South Jersey practice complained of typically involves residential real estate closings in which neither buyer nor seller is represented by counsel, and contrasts most sharply with the North Jersey practice if one assumes both parties are represented there. Obviously, that is not always the case: the record shows that about sixty percent of the buyers and about sixty-five percent of the sellers in South Jersey are not represented by counsel. In North Jersey, only one half of one percent of buyers, and fourteen percent of sellers, proceed without counsel.

In North Jersey, when both seller and buyer are represented by counsel, they sign nothing, agree to nothing, expend nothing, without the advice of competent counsel. If, initially without counsel, they sign a contract of sale prepared by the broker, they ordinarily then retain counsel who can revoke that contract in accordance with the three-day attorney review clause. They are protected, and they pay for that protection. The seller in North Jersey spends on average $750 in attorney fees, and the buyer in North Jersey spends on average $1,000. The buyer in South Jersey who chooses to proceed without representation spends nothing. The South Jersey seller whose attorney does no more than prepare the deed and affidavit of title, usually without even consulting with the seller, spends about $90. South Jersey buyers and sellers who are represented throughout the process, including closing, pay an average of $650 and $350, respectively.[2] Savings obviously do not determine the outcome of this case; they are but one factor in the mix of competing considerations.

The typical South Jersey transaction starts with the seller engaging a broker who is ordinarily a member of the multiple listing system. The first broker to find an apparently willing buyer gets in touch with the seller and ultimately negotiates a sale price agreeable to both. The potential buyer requires financing arrangements which are often made by the broker. Before the execution of any sales contract the broker puts the buyer in touch with a mortgage company to determine if the buyer qualifies for the needed loan.

---

2. It is suggested that although the parties under the South Jersey practice save the cost of counsel, the savings may be offset to some extent because they nonetheless pay others for services attorneys in North Jersey customarily provide.

At this preliminary stage, no legal obligations of any kind are likely to have been created, except for those that arise from the brokerage relationship itself.

Assuming the preliminary understanding between the seller and buyer remains in effect, the broker will present the seller with the standard form of contract used in that area (usually a New Jersey Association of Realtors Standard Form of Real Estate Contract). That form includes, pursuant to our opinion in *New Jersey State Bar Association v. New Jersey Association of Realtor Boards*, 93 N.J. 470, 461 A.2d 1112 (1983), notice that the attorney for either party can cancel the contract within three business days. If the seller signs the contract, and does not within three days retain counsel, the seller will have become legally bound to perform numerous obligations without the benefit of any legal advice whatsoever, some of which may turn out to be onerous, some costly, some requiring unanticipated expense, and some beyond the power of the seller to perform, with the potential of substantial liability for such nonperformance. Many sellers will not understand just what those obligations are, and just what the risks are. Not only has the seller not retained a lawyer, the only person qualified to explain those risks. Worse yet, the only one the seller has had any contact with in the matter is the broker, whose commission depends entirely on consummation of the transaction, and whose interest is primarily — in some cases it is fair to say exclusively — to get the contract signed and the deal closed.

After the seller signs the contract, the broker delivers it to the buyer for execution. The buyer may not know if the description of the property is precisely that assumed to be the subject of the purchase. The buyer may have no idea if the title described in the contract is that with which he would be satisfied, no sound understanding of what the numerous obligations on the part of the seller mean, and no fair comprehension of whether all of the possible and practical concerns of a buyer have been addressed by the contract. No lawyer is present to advise or inform the buyer; indeed, there is no one who has the buyer's interest at heart, only the broker, whose interests are generally in conflict with the buyer's. . . .

For both seller and buyer, it is that contract that substantially determines all of their rights and duties. Neither one of them can be regarded as adequately informed of the import of what they signed or indeed of its importance. At that point the broker, who represents only the seller and clearly has an interest in conflict with that of the buyer (the broker's interest is in consummation of the sale, the buyer's in making certain that the sale does not close unless the buyer is fully protected) performs a series of acts on behalf of the *buyer*, and is the only person available as a practical matter to explain their significance to the buyer. The broker orders a binder for title insurance, or a title commitment to make sure that the *buyer* is going to get good title. The buyer has no idea, and hopefully never will have, whether the broker ordered the right kind of title search, a fairly esoteric question that only an experienced attorney can determine.

The broker also orders numerous inspection and other reports, all primarily of interest to the buyer, to make certain that not only is the title good, but that there are no other problems affecting the premises, the house and their use. . . .

The seller in the meantime is happy to hear from no one, for it suggests there are no problems. Eventually, the seller is told that a deed will be arriving drafted by an attorney selected by the broker, the instrument that our decisions clearly require may be drafted only by the seller's attorney. *Cape May County Bar Ass'n v. Ludlam*, 45 N.J. 121, 211 A.2d 780 (1965). Of course, the purpose of that ruling was to assure competent counsel in the drafting of such a uniquely legal document, but "competent" always meant counsel who understood the entire transaction. In South Jersey, the attorney selected by the broker, while theoretically representing the seller, may be primarily interested in the broker, the source of the attorney's "client" and the likely source of future "clients," and consequently primarily interested in completing the sale. That attorney is likely to prepare a deed satisfactory to the title company — in fact that attorney often does not even contact the seller. He or she may have no idea of anything in the contract of sale other than the description of the land and the fact that a certain kind of deed is required. No advice on the substance of the transaction comes from such an attorney even though the seller may get the impression that, since an attorney drafted the deed, the seller's interests are somehow being protected. In fact, the only protection those interests ever received, other than those that happened to appear in the form contract, is in the numbers inserted in that contract, the total purchase price, the down payment, and the closing date, for those are probably the only terms of that contract fully understood by the seller.

The buyer's position is even worse when the closing occurs. The seller will at least know that he or she got paid. Legal training is not required for that fact, even though there is no practical assurance that the seller will not thereafter be sued. The buyer, on the other hand, wants something that is largely incomprehensible to almost all buyers, good and marketable title, one that will not result in problems in the future. What the buyer gets before closing is a "title binder," a piece of paper that may suggest something about the quality of the seller's title, but that is very much in need of explanation for any substantial understanding of its meaning. The title company is required to mail to the unrepresented buyer notice of any exceptions or conditions associated with the title insurance policy. *N.J.S.A.* 17:46B–9. This notice, which must be sent five days prior to the closing, must also notify the buyer of the right to review the title commitment with an attorney. *Ibid.* If the buyer chooses not to retain an attorney, there is no one to give the buyer that understanding other than the broker and the title agent. The broker's knowledge will often be inadequate, and the conflicting interest apparent. The title company similarly has a conflicting interest, for it too is interested in completion of the transaction, the *sine qua non* of its title premium. But the title company is also interested in good title, for it is guaranteeing that to the mortgage company, as well as to the buyer. "Good title," however, may be one on which the title company and the mortgagee are willing to take a risk, but one on which a buyer might or should not be willing to, if the buyer knew what the risk was. . . .

The day for closing arrives and everyone meets, usually at the offices of the title company. Seller and buyer are there, each without an attorney; the broker is there, and the title officer is there, representing both the title company and the mortgagee. The funds are there. And the critical legal documents are also on hand: the mortgage and the note, usually prepared by the mortgagee; the deed, along with the affidavit of title, prepared by the attorney selected by the broker or by the title company; the settlement statement, usually prepared by the title company, indicating how much is owed, what deductions should be made for taxes and other costs and what credits are due; and the final marked-up title binder, which evidences the obligation of the title company to issue a title policy to the buyer, and which at that point is probably practically meaningless to the buyer. All are executed and delivered, along with other documents, and the funds are delivered or held in escrow until the title company arranges to pay off prior mortgages and liens.

It would take a volume to describe each and every risk to which the seller and buyer have exposed themselves without adequate knowledge. But it takes a very short sentence to describe what apparently occurs: the deal closes, satisfactory to buyer and seller in practically all cases, satisfactory both at the closing and thereafter.

III

THE UNAUTHORIZED PRACTICE OF LAW

As noted above, this transaction in its entirety, the sale of real estate, especially real estate with a home on it, is one that cannot be handled competently except by those trained in the law. The most important parts of it, without which it could not be accomplished, are quintessentially the practice of law. The contract of sale, the obligations of the contract, the ordering of a title search, the analysis of the search, the significance of the title search, the quality of title, the risks that surround both the contract and the title, the extent of those risks, the probability of damage, the obligation to close or not to close, the closing itself, the settlement, the documents there exchanged, each and every one of these, to be properly understood must be explained by an attorney. And the documents themselves to be properly drafted, must be drafted by an attorney. Mixed in with these activities are many others that clearly do not require an attorney's knowledge, such as the ordering of inspection and other reports, and the price negotiation. But after that, even though arguably much can be accomplished by others, practically all else, to be done with full understanding, requires the advice of counsel. . . .

In this case, the record clearly shows that the South Jersey practice has been conducted without any demonstrable harm to sellers or buyers, that it apparently saves money, and that those who participate in it do so of their own free will presumably with some knowledge of the risk; as Judge Miller found, the record fails to demonstrate that brokers are discouraging the parties from retaining counsel, or that the conflict of interest that pervades the practice has caused material damage to the sellers and buyers who participate in it. Given that record, and subject to the conditions mentioned hereafter, we find that the public interest will not be compromised by allowing the practice to continue. We note again that our prior decisions and those of the Committee on this issue did not have the benefit of such a record and were premised on the irrefutable finding that the activities of the non-lawyers in the South Jersey practice constituted the practice of law. That they do, but with the benefit of the record before us it is equally clear that the practice does not disserve the public interest.

Of decisive weight in our determination is the value we place on the right of parties to a transaction to decide whether or not they will retain counsel. We should not force them to do so absent persuasive reasons. Given the importance in our decision of the assumption that the parties have chosen not to retain counsel, and without coercion have made that decision, we have attached a condition to the conclusion that the South Jersey practice does not constitute the unauthorized practice of law. The condition is designed to assure that the decision is an informed one. If that condition is not met, the brokers (and title officers, if aware of the fact) are engaged in the unauthorized practice of law, and attorneys with knowledge of that fact who participate are guilty of ethical misconduct. . . .

We do not here adopt a "consumerism" that invariably requires that services be made available at the lowest price no matter how great the risk. The record suggests that despite their conflict of interest, brokers' ethical standards have resulted in some diminishment of those risks. Unlike prior cases, there is no finding here, for instance, that brokers are discouraging retention of counsel, no suggestion that title companies are paying rebates to referring brokers. Today's public, furthermore, not only has the benefit of the attorney-review clause, but is presumably better educated about the need for counsel, the function of attorneys, and the legal aspects of the sale of the home. The public continues, in South Jersey, to choose not to be represented. We assume that the public has simply concluded that the perceived advantages are worth those risks.

We do not adopt a rule, however, that so long as informed consent from the parties is obtained, any conduct that might otherwise constitute the unauthorized practice of law is permitted. Most of the practices restricted to attorneys can be performed, and may be performed, only by them regardless of the informed consent of the parties and regardless of the lower cost of using non-attorneys. All we decide is that in *this* case, concerning *this* practice, the record demonstrates that the public interest will not be compromised by allowing what would otherwise be the unauthorized practice of law if the parties are adequately informed of the conflicting interests of brokers and title officers and of the risks involved in proceeding without counsel.

We emphasize the nature of the public interest standard applied in this case. It is the same as in the cases allowing brokers to prepare real estate sales contracts and certified public accountants to prepare inheritance tax returns. No suggestion was made or implied in those cases that the public was better served if they used brokers and certified public accountants rather than lawyers for the services involved. On the contrary, the conditions imposed by this Court in both — requiring that the parties be informed in advance of their right to retain counsel — reflect our judgment that the parties would be well advised to obtain counsel. We decided only that the protection that lawyers provide and parties need — the basic rationale for prohibiting the unauthorized practice of law — was sufficiently addressed in those cases by assuring that the parties knowingly rejected it; we decided only that the public interest in those cases did not require depriving parties of their right to proceed without counsel, did not require the protection of counsel against their will. . . .

Our required disclosure notice goes beyond that of other cases, reflecting our determination to assure that the parties who decide not to retain lawyers know the conflicting interests of others and know that there are risks of proceeding without one.

There is a point at which an institution attempting to provide protection to a public that seems clearly, over a long period, not to want it, and perhaps not to need it — there is a point when that institution must wonder whether it is providing protection or imposing its will. It must wonder whether it is helping or hurting the public.[5] We have reached that point in this case. Although we have strong

5. We note that in Arizona, after its Supreme Court prohibited brokers from preparing real estate sales contracts, the people approved a constitutional amendment that provided that licensed real estate brokers "shall have the right to draft or fill out and complete" real estate documents, including deeds, mortgages, and contracts of sale. *Ariz. Const.* art. XXVI, § 1.

doubts, the evidence against our doubt requires that we allow this practice to continue with some form of added protection, recognizing, however, that like the attorney-review clause, the added protection may not be effective. . . .

Our decision, while allowing continuation of the South Jersey practice, imposes new conditions on that practice and serious consequences for non-compliance. In order that brokers and others may adjust their practices to comply with those conditions, our decision will not become effective until sixty days from the date of this opinion and will apply to all real estate contracts subject to this opinion that are thereafter executed and to the transactions based on those contracts.

The decision of the Committee, Opinion No. 26, is affirmed in part, and reversed in part, and judgment entered declaring the rights of the participants in New Jersey residential real estate transactions in accordance with this opinion.

For affirmance in part, reversal in part — Chief Justice WILENTZ and Justices HANDLER, POLLOCK, O'HERN, GARIBALDI, and STEIN — 6.

Opposed — None.

APPENDIX A
NOTICE

TO BUYER AND SELLER:
YOU MUST READ THIS NOTICE BEFORE SIGNING THE CONTRACT

The Supreme Court of New Jersey requires real estate brokers to give you the following information before you sign this contract. It requires us to tell you that you must read all of it before you sign. Here is the information for both buyer and seller:

1. I am a real estate broker. I represent the seller. I do not represent the buyer. The title company does not represent either the seller or the buyer. Furthermore, both the seller and the buyer should know that it is in my financial interest that the house be sold and that the closing be completed. My fee is paid only if that happens. The title company has the same interest, for its insurance premium is paid only if that happens.

2. I am not allowed, and I am not qualified, to give either the seller or the buyer any legal advice. Neither the title company nor any of its officers are allowed to give either the seller or buyer any legal advice. Neither of you will get any legal advice at any point in this transaction unless you have your own lawyer. If you do not hire a lawyer, no one will represent you in legal matters either now, or at the closing. I will not represent you and the title company and its officers will not represent you in those matters.

3. The contract attached to this notice is the most important part of the sale. It determines your rights, your liabilities, and your risks. It becomes final when you sign it — unless it is cancelled by your lawyer within three days — and when it does become final you cannot change it, nor can any attorney you may hire thereafter change it in any way whatsoever.

4. The buyer especially should know that if he or she has no lawyer, no one will be able to advise him or her what to do if problems arise in connection with the purchase of this property. Those problems may be about

various matters, including the seller's title to the property. They may affect the value of the property. If either the broker or title company sees that there are problems and that because of them you need your own lawyer, they should tell you. However, it is possible that they may not recognize the problems or that it may be too late for a lawyer to help. Also, they are not *your* lawyers, and they may not see the problem from your point of view.

5. Whether you, seller or buyer, retain a lawyer is up to you. It is your decision. The purpose of this notice is to make sure you have some understanding of the transaction, the risks, who represents whom, and what their interests are, when you make that decision. The rules and regulations concerning brokers and title companies prohibit each of them from suggesting that you are better off without a lawyer. If anyone makes that suggestion to you, you should carefully consider whose interest they are serving. The decision whether to hire a lawyer to represent your interests is yours and yours alone.

NOTES AND QUESTIONS

1. Do you believe that most parties to New Jersey residential home sales, before signing a sales contract, will carefully read and comprehend the notice required by the New Jersey court?

2. Opinion 26 is an example of the law in one state as to what legal services may be provided by real estate brokers to parties to real estate transactions. Examples from other states appear below, although obviously what is authorized by some of these opinions is so limited that brokers are almost entirely excluded from legally providing legal services to parties engaged in real estate transactions. Examples are these: Conway-Bogue Realty Ins. Co. v. Denver Bar Assn., 312 P.2d 998 (Colo. 1957), real estate brokers may prepare legal documents in connection with sale, leasing, or lending transactions in which they are acting as brokers provided that no separate charge is made for the legal document preparation services; Pope County Bar Assn. v. Suggs, 624 S.W.2d 828 (Ark. 1981), real estate brokers may prepare for parties to real estate transactions a wide range of standardized real estate transfer legal documents; State v. Indiana Real Estate Assn., Inc., 191 N.E.2d 711 (Ind. 1963), real estate brokers may fill in the forms of most standardized legal instruments in real estate transactions, other than deeds, if the form legal instruments were prepared by attorneys, but the brokers may not give legal advice to the parties or make a separate charge for their instrument preparation services; Chicago Bar Assn. v. Quinlan & Tyson, Inc., 214 N.E.2d 77 (Ill. 1966), real estate brokers may fill in the usual form of preliminary real estate contract or offer to purchase as these services are incidental to legitimate real estate brokerage services; Duncan & Hill Realty v. Dept. of State, 405 N.Y.S.2d 339 (N.Y. App. Div. 1978), a real estate broker may prepare simple real estate contracts of sale, but the court narrowly construes the term "simple legal contract" and also prohibits real estate brokers from giving legal advice to the parties to real estate transactions. An added test as to what constitutes unauthorized practice of law by a nonlawyer that has been applied to accountants and could be applied to real estate brokers is the difficult or doubtful legal question test. If the legal services require determination of difficult or doubtful questions

of law, a nonlawyer may not provide those services to others. See Agran v. Shapiro, 273 P.2d 619 (Cal. App. 1954). On unauthorized practice by real estate brokers, see generally Burke, Law of Real Estate Brokers § 13.1 (2d ed. 1992, cum. supp. 2006); Rohan et al, Real Estate Brokerage Law and Practice, ch. 7 (1985 & ann. supps.); Goudey, Too Many Hands in the Cookie Jar: The Unauthorized Practice of Law by Real Estate Brokers, 75 Or. L. Rev. 889 (1996); Palomar, The War Between Attorneys and Lay Conveyancers — Empirical Evidence Says "Cease Fire," 31 Conn. L. Rev. 423 (1999).

3. In Arizona, by constitutional provision, real estate brokers may "draft or fill out and complete, without charge, any and all instruments incident thereto, including, but not limited to, preliminary purchase agreements and earnest money receipts, deeds, mortgages, leases, assignments, releases, contracts for sale of realty, and bills of sale." Ariz. Const. art. 26, § 1. This constitutional provision was adopted in 1962 by popular referendum following an Arizona Supreme Court opinion highly restrictive as to what documents title companies and brokers could prepare. State Bar of Arizona v. Arizona Land Title & Trust Co., 90 Ariz. 76, 366 P.2d 1 (1961), on rehearing, 91 Ariz. 293, 371 P.2d 1020 (1962). The Arizona Association of Realtors campaigned vigorously for the constitutional amendment. On the Arizona constitutional provision and the case that preceded it, see Romero, Theories of Real Estate Broker Liability: Arizona's Emerging Malpractice Doctrine, 20 Ariz. L. Rev. 767, 785–786 (1978).

4. The Supreme Court of Washington, on grounds of separation of powers, held as unconstitutional a statute that authorized escrow agents to prepare contracts of sale, deeds, mortgages, and other documents in relation to escrow transactions. Bennion, Van Camp, Hagen & Ruhl v. Kassler Escrow, Inc., 96 Wash. 2d 443, 635 P.2d 730 (1981). The court subsequently adopted a court rule proposed by the state bar, Washington Admission to Practice Rule 12, permitting certain lay persons to qualify as closing officers under court regulation and control. Closing officers are authorized to prepare and complete certain form documents, including deeds and contracts of sale. The court rule apparently avoided the possibility of a constitutional amendment permitting preparation of real estate transfer instruments by lay persons.

5. Why, in your opinion, is enforcement of laws as to unauthorized practice of law by real estate brokers so lax in much of the United States?

6. Another important unauthorized practice problem involves out-of-state lawyers. To what extent can out-of-state lawyers represent parties in states where the lawyers are not licensed to practice? And to what extent can such lawyers represent parties in a real estate transaction when the land is located in a state where the lawyers are not licensed to practice? ABA Model Rules 5.5 and 8.5, which have been adopted in a number of states, in some of these states with some modifications, permit such multijurisdictional practice with certain restrictions.

7. In all states there is an exemption from unauthorized practice for nonlawyers who provide legal services for themselves, pro se representation. This exemption applies to individuals as well as to corporations and other organizations that rely on nonlawyer employees for their pro se services, including such services as those concerning real estate transactions. However, the usual requirement is that when a corporation or other organization appears before a court in a representative capacity, as distinct from a witness capacity, the only employees of the organization who may appear before the court in a representative capacity, as distinct from a

witness capacity, are lawyer employees admitted in the state or otherwise legally authorized to make such appearances. On pro se representation see Wolfram, Modern Legal Ethics 803–806 (1986); Restatement of the Law Third, The Law Governing Lawyers 37–38 (2000).

8. Are unauthorized practice laws really needed to protect parties to real estate transactions? Are not tort and contract laws, together with the adverse market reputation consequences of a broker or out-of-state lawyer engaging in conduct harmful to parties to real estate transactions, sufficient to deter adequately such wrongful conduct? Moreover, are not all unauthorized practice laws merely means for further strengthening the legal monopoly of lawyers over legal services in the jurisdiction where the lawyers are admitted to practice, and is not that monopoly of questionable merit? What is your opinion on these questions and what legal solution to the problem of unauthorized practice by real estate brokers do you believe is preferable and why?

9. Although lawyers commonly are authorized to act as real estate brokers, conflict of interest and other professional ethics problems can arise when they do. On these problems, see Mortland, Attorneys as Real Estate Brokers: Ethical Considerations, 25 Real. Prop., Prob. & Tr. J. 755 (1991).

B. BROKERS' DUTIES TO BUYERS, SELLERS, AND OTHER PARTIES TO REAL ESTATE TRANSACTIONS

Sellers' brokers frequently develop close relationships with prospective buyers when the brokers are attempting to sell properties. But if a selling broker unduly favors a prospective buyer to the disadvantage of the seller this may constitute sanctionable breach of duty to the broker's principal, the seller. Also, if in the course of the broker's attempting to find a satisfactory buyer the broker unduly favors the interests of a prospective buyer or the interests of the broker over those of the broker's principal, this too is a violation of the broker's duties to the principal and can result in sanctions being imposed on the broker. The next case is an example of a seller's broker being held to have engaged in such improper conduct.

Not only do real estate brokers have duties to their principals, usually a seller, but they also have duties to those on the other side, usually a buyer. Brokers' duties to their principals are largely determined by the brokerage contract and the law of agency. Their duties to other parties to real estate transactions are largely determined by tort law and by statutes and case law particularly applicable to brokers. An influencing factor of importance to brokerage law in many residential real estate transactions is the unfamiliarity of many parties to these transactions with the law governing the transactions and the frequent mistaken perception by residential real estate buyers that the seller's broker is their broker. Some states have sought to provide added protection to buyers and sellers of residential properties by imposing obligations on the broker to disclose to buyer and seller information as to whom the broker is representing. Also, some states require that sellers' brokers of residential properties inspect the property being offered for sale and notify prospective buyers of what the inspection has disclosed as to the value and desirability of the property.

Daubman v. CBS Real Estate Co.

580 N.W.2d 552 (Neb. 1998)

I. STATEMENT OF CASE

Claiming that defendant-appellant CBS Real Estate Co. and its agent, defendant-appellant Arlene Engelbert, breached their fiduciary duties, plaintiffs-appellees, Allen E. Daubman and his wife, Renee A. Daubman, sought the return of the real estate sales commission they paid. Following a bench trial, the district court entered judgment in favor of the Daubmans. CBS and Engelbert appealed to the Nebraska Court of Appeals, claiming that the district court had erred in (1) finding that they breached their fiduciary duties, (2) failing to find that the Daubmans ratified and otherwise acquiesced in their actions, (3) finding that the Daubmans sustained damages, and (4) awarding prejudgment interest. Concluding that the evidence failed to support the district court's judgment, the Court of Appeals vacated the judgment and remanded the cause with directions to dismiss. See *Daubman v. CBS Real Estate Co.*, 6 Neb.App. 390, 573 N.W.2d 802 (1998). The Daubmans thereupon successfully petitioned for further review, claiming, in summary, that the Court of Appeals erroneously set aside the district court's factual findings. For the reasons hereinafter set forth, we reverse, and remand with direction.

II. SCOPE OF REVIEW

This action is one for assumpsit for money had and received, an action which may be brought where a party has received money which in equity and good conscience should be repaid to another. *Kramer v. Kramer*, 252 Neb. 526, 567 N.W.2d 100 (1997); *Wrede v. Exchange Bank of Gibbon*, 247 Neb. 907, 531 N.W.2d 523 (1995). In such a circumstance, the law implies a promise on the part of the person who received the money to reimburse the payor in order to prevent unjust enrichment. *Kramer, supra; Wrede, supra.* The action, although falling under the common-law class of assumpsit, is really in the nature of a bill in equity and lies wherever the party should by equity and natural principles of justice refund the money. *Boman v. Olson*, 158 Neb. 636, 64 N.W.2d 310 (1954). Although founded on equitable principles, an action in assumpsit for money had and received is an action at law. *Kramer, supra; Wrede, supra.*

The judgment and factual findings of the trial court in an action at law tried to the court without a jury have the effect of a verdict and will not be set aside unless clearly wrong. *In re Estate of Wagner*, 253 Neb. 498, 571 N.W.2d 76 (1997). In reviewing an action at law, an appellate court reviews the evidence in the light most favorable to the prevailing party. *Id.* However, regarding questions of law, an appellate court is obligated to reach a conclusion independent of determinations reached by the lower courts. *State v. Hill*, 254 Neb. 460, 577 N.W.2d 259 (1998).

III. FACTS

As the Daubmans were considering building a new home, they wished to explore the amount for which they could sell their current home. To that end, they contacted Engelbert, a real estate saleswoman working through CBS. Engelbert met with the Daubmans, and the Daubmans asked her to prepare a competitive market analysis on the property to determine its market value. Engelbert prepared the analysis and forwarded the results to the Daubmans.

Engelbert informed the Daubmans that she was working with Thomas and Brenda Pedersen, who were looking for a residence similar in features and price to the Daubman property. According to Allen Daubman, Engelbert also stated that the Pedersens "had been pre-approved for credit in an amount more than necessary to purchase [the] home." Engelbert also stated, according to Allen Daubman, that the Pedersens had sufficient financial ability to purchase the home and that financing would not be a problem; that the Pedersens were preapproved with a particular lender for a $180,000 loan. Engelbert contradicted Allen Daubman, testifying that she did not state that the Pedersens had been preapproved for a particular amount of credit. Rather, Engelbert claims that she told the Daubmans not that the Pedersens were preapproved but that they were "qualified buyers, that [she] had been working with them, that . . . they had a savings plan, they had been paying off their debts, and they had the cash to close." Engelbert admitted telling the Daubmans that the Pedersens were capable of buying the home.

Engelbert offered to show the property to the Pedersens if the Daubmans signed a "one-party listing agreement" with CBS granting it an exclusive right to sell the property to the Pedersens only. The next day, the Daubmans signed the one-party listing agreement. Pursuant to this agreement, the Daubmans agreed to give CBS the sole and exclusive right to sell the property for $139,950 "cash or as terms agreed" to the Pedersens only, and to pay CBS a cash commission of 7 percent of the gross sales price. At the time the agreement was signed, the Daubmans notified Engelbert that they might be interested in leasing back the property or moving into an apartment, since they were contemplating building a new home, which would not be completed before the sale of their current property closed.

Engelbert showed the property to the Pedersens that same day, and later that day the Pedersens requested that Engelbert prepare an offer. Engelbert prepared an offer, which provided that the Pedersens would purchase the property for $132,000 and rent the property back to the Daubmans for a period of time. That evening, Engelbert presented the offer to the Daubmans.

Allen Daubman testified that upon receiving the offer, he told Engelbert that he was not interested, that he was very disappointed, and that he no longer wished to pursue the matter with the Pedersens. He further explained to Engelbert that he was concerned about the Pedersens' ability to obtain financing, based on the fact that their offer provided for a 95-percent loan. According to Allen Daubman, Engelbert was insistent on working something out and stated that the Pedersens' credit was "squeaky-clean." Engelbert denies using the term "squeaky-clean."

The Daubmans' plan to build a new home would require several financial obligations, including renting an apartment. Thus, if the Pedersens could not obtain a loan, the Daubmans could face the situation of not having their house sold but having to pay rent on an apartment and payments on a construction loan. To offset their risk, the Daubmans suggested to Engelbert that the Pedersens make a $5,000 nonrefundable earnest deposit. According to Allen Daubman, Engelbert recommended very strongly against such a proposal, saying that it was unnecessary, and reiterated that the Pedersens were financially strong, asserting that "they had been saving money in anticipation of buying a house; that they had cleaned up their bills; and that financing, again, should not be any problem whatsoever."

The following day, Allen Daubman prepared and faxed a counteroffer to CBS, specifying a purchase price of $139,900; an earnest deposit of $2,000; approval of financing in 30 days; closing within 30 days; and possession to be given the Pedersens at closing, all contingent upon the Pedersens being able to obtain financing of 95 percent of the purchase price at 8.5 percent for 30 years. The counteroffer would also allow the Daubmans to continue listing and showing the property for purposes of obtaining backup offers in the event the Pedersens were unable to obtain financing.

The next day, the Pedersens requested that CBS prepare another offer. The new offer provided that they would purchase the property for $139,900 with an earnest deposit of $2,000, conditional on their obtaining a conventional loan secured by a mortgage or deed of trust on the property in the sum of $132,900. The offer further provided that the Pedersens were to apply for financing within 5 business days of its acceptance and that if financing was not approved within 30 days of acceptance of the offer, the offer would be null and void, and the earnest deposit would be returned to the Pedersens. The offer further provided that if processing of the Pedersens' loan application was not completed within 30 days, the time limit would be automatically extended until the lending agency either approved or rejected the application. The transaction was to be closed on July 29, 1992, by an escrow agent and possession given to the Pedersens on July 30. The Daubmans accepted the offer on June 12, 1992, on the condition that the possession date be subject to the availability of a mover acceptable to them. The Pedersens accepted this condition.

The Pedersens met with Residential Mortgage Services on June 15, 1992, to apply for a loan, with Engelbert in attendance. At the appointment, Engelbert did not learn of any information that would jeopardize the Pedersens' loan application, and after the appointment, she communicated the information she learned to Allen Daubman. On June 25, the Daubmans entered into an agreement for the construction of a new home. On July 9, Residential Mortgage Services notified Engelbert that it probably would not be able to make a loan to the Pedersens and recommended that the loan application be moved to another lender.

After learning of the probable denial by Residential Mortgage Services, Engelbert contacted Capital Financial Services to determine whether it could approve a loan to the Pedersens on the terms contained in their purchase agreement. On July 10, 1992, Capital Financial Services informed Engelbert that it could probably make the loan and asked her to have the loan file transferred to it. On the same day, the loan file was moved from Residential Mortgage Services to Capital Financial Services, and the Pedersens made an appointment to meet with a Capital Financial Services representative on July 13. Engelbert testified that she personally gave the loan file to the representative.

After moving the loan file, Engelbert informed the Daubmans on July 10, 1992, of the transfer, that the chances for loan approval were good, and that she would know more on July 13. According to Allen Daubman, Engelbert told him on July 10 that she assisted the Pedersens in making a separate second loan application with a different lender on July 9. The Daubmans had not authorized CBS or Engelbert to seek alternative financing on behalf of the Pedersens in the event the first financial institution turned them down. Allen Daubman asked Engelbert why she moved the Pedersens over to a second lender without first calling him, and stated that the purchase agreement was now null and void because the Pedersens had not made the second loan application within the 5-day period. Engelbert told Allen Daubman that he was wrong and that

> as long as any loan application is pending, not just the first one, but any loan application is pending, when the 30-day time period under the purchase agreement hits, that I had no choice but to wait until whatever loan application was pending is either approved or rejected by that particular lender.

Allen Daubman was concerned that if he insisted the purchase agreement was void, he could face possible legal actions by the Pedersens and CBS. Engelbert testified that she now realized that Allen Daubman's interpretation of the purchase agreement was correct and that the rejection from Residential Mortgage Services rendered the purchase agreement null and void.

The Pedersens applied for a loan to Capital Financial Services on July 13, 1992. Also on that day, Allen Daubman requested that Engelbert ask the Pedersens if they would delay the closing and possession until the end of August. The Pedersens rejected this request. Allen Daubman then asked Engelbert to contact the Pedersens and ask them if they would agree to make the $2,000 deposit nonrefundable so that the Daubmans could sign a 6-month apartment lease at the Washington Heights apartment complex. The Pedersens rejected this request as well.

Engelbert and Allen Daubman met with a representative of Capital Financial Services on July 16, 1992, to discuss the Pedersens' loan prospects. On July 17, Allen Daubman faxed a letter to Engelbert informing her that in order to perform according to the purchase agreement and vacate the property at the end of July, the Daubmans needed to sign a 6-month apartment lease. However, because the Pedersens' loan had not yet been approved, the Daubmans were unwilling to sign the apartment lease. Thus, Allen Daubman suggested that the parties enter into an amendment whereby the Pedersens would make the $2,000 deposit nonrefundable and the Pedersens would be given an additional 2 weeks to obtain loan approval. According to Allen Daubman, before even discussing the proposal with the Pedersens, Engelbert told him that the proposed amendment would not be acceptable to the Pedersens. Engelbert denies that she prematurely told Allen Daubman that the Pedersens would deny the amendment. On July 18, the Pedersens rejected the amendment.

The Daubmans had located an apartment in the Washington Heights apartment complex, and the complex operator was willing to lease to them on a 6-month basis. The operator told the Daubmans that they eventually needed to sign the lease, but was not pressing them to do so. The Daubmans were trying to delay the signing as long as possible. When the Pedersens told Engelbert that they would not agree to the Daubmans' amendment, Brenda Pedersen also informed Engelbert that she had called the complex operator to check on the availability of apartments there. After speaking with the Pedersens, Engelbert called the complex operator to find out whether any apartments were available for lease, notwithstanding that the Daubmans had not authorized her to do so. According to Engelbert, "because Mrs. Pedersen had called, [the operator] was starting to put two and two together and asked me if it was about the Daubmans. And I said yes." Engelbert then called the Daubmans on July 18, 1992, and informed them of the Pedersens' rejection of the amendment. Shortly after talking to Engelbert about the proposed amendment, the complex operator called the Daubmans and insisted that they sign the lease no later than the evening of July 27.

Shortly after the "apartment incident," Allen Daubman contacted a senior vice president of CBS, indicated that he no longer wished to work with Engelbert, and requested that another salesperson handle the matter. According to Allen Daubman, he also told the vice president during this conversation that he did not think it was appropriate that CBS receive a commission. The vice president denied that Daubman indicated at this time that he did not want to pay a commission.

Engelbert learned on July 21, 1992, from the vice president that Allen Daubman did not want her calling him. Engelbert called Capital Financial Services on July 20, 21, 22, and 23 and visited their office on July 24 to find out the status of the Pedersens' loan. She learned that Capital Financial Services had received mortgage approval that day and would be receiving formal loan approval on July 27. Engelbert prepared and faxed a letter to Allen Daubman that afternoon explaining this. On July 27, Engelbert learned that the Pedersens received formal loan approval and called Allen Daubman the same day to communicate this news to him.

On July 27, 1992, the Daubmans entered into a 6-month apartment lease. On July 30, Allen Daubman informed CBS that he did not want the escrow agent to pay CBS a commission and sent a letter to the escrow agent demanding that no moneys be withheld by it and paid to CBS for its services. The escrow agent informed Allen Daubman that it could not close the sale unless either the Daubmans agreed to allow it to deduct the commission or CBS agreed to forfeit its commission. Neither the Daubmans nor CBS would so agree. CBS' vice president told Allen Daubman that the commission had to be paid out of the closing, despite the fact that neither the listing agreement nor the purchase agreement so provided.

An employee of the escrow agent testified that in the event of a commission dispute, either the parties have to resolve the problem or the real estate agent has to give authorization to close without withholding the commission. According to this witness, "I can't go on what a seller is telling me until I get authorization from the [real estate] company to not charge a commission or whatever."

On July 31, 1992, Allen Daubman faxed an agreement to the CBS vice president informing him that the Daubmans would allow the sale to be closed and the commission to be paid out of the proceeds of the sale of the house if CBS agreed that such payment would be without prejudice to any claim the Daubmans might have over whether the commission was payable under the circumstances. The vice president agreed, and Allen Daubman then instructed the escrow agent to close the sale.

CBS received a commission of $9,793 on August 3, 1992, and the parties stipulated that the Daubmans had suffered no damages, special or general. Finding that Engelbert and, through her, CBS had breached the fiduciary duties they owed the Daubmans, the district court awarded the Daubmans the amount of the commission, together with prejudgment interest from and after July 31, 1992, and costs.

IV. ANALYSIS

We begin our analysis by focusing on the issues raised by the Daubmans' petition for further review. In considering whether the evidence supports the district court's finding that Engelbert and CBS breached their fiduciary duties to the Daubmans and whether such breach justifies a forfeiture of their commission, we recall that generally, an agent is required to act solely for the benefit of the principal in all matters connected with the agency and adhere faithfully to the instructions of the principal. *Fletcher v. Mathew,* 233 Neb. 853, 448 N.W.2d 576 (1989); *Walker Land & Cattle Co. v. Daub,* 223 Neb. 343, 389 N.W.2d 560 (1986); *Allied Securities, Inc. v. Clocker,* 185 Neb. 524, 176 N.W.2d 914 (1970). An agent and principal are in a fiduciary relationship such that the agent has an obligation to refrain from doing any harmful act to the principal. *Fletcher, supra; Grone v. Lincoln Mut. Life Ins. Co.,* 230 Neb. 144, 430 N.W.2d 507 (1988).

More specifically, a real estate agent owes the principal a fiduciary duty to use reasonable care, skill, and diligence in performing her or his obligations and to act honestly and in good faith. *Barta v. Kindschuh,* 246 Neb. 208, 518 N.W.2d 98 (1994). The rule requiring an agent to act with utmost good faith toward the principal places the agent under a legal obligation to make a full, fair, and prompt disclosure to the principal of all facts within the agent's knowledge which are or may be material to the matter in connection with which the agent is employed, which might affect the principal's rights and interests or influence the principal's action in relation to the subject matter of the employment, or which in any way pertain to the discharge of the agency which the agent has undertaken. *Brezina v. Hill,* 202 Neb. 773, 277 N.W.2d 224 (1979). In a number of instances, we have held that a real estate agent's breach of duty prevented the collection of a commission. E.g., *Elson v. Pool,* 235 Neb. 469, 455 N.W.2d 783 (1990) (agent forged principal's signature); *Firmature v. Brannon,* 223 Neb. 123, 388 N.W.2d 119 (1986) (agent denigrated property); *Brezina, supra* (to protect buyer, agent signed and filed purchase agreement in violation of selling principal's wishes); *Vogt v. Town & Country Realty of Lincoln, Inc.,* 194 Neb. 308, 231 N.W.2d 496 (1975) (agent had undisclosed interest in purchase); *Allied Securities, Inc., supra* (agent had undisclosed interest in purchase); *Schepers v. Lautenschlager,* 173 Neb. 107, 112 N.W.2d 767 (1962) (agent had undisclosed interest in purchase and failed to inform principal of prospective purchaser willing to pay more than sale price); *Pearlman v. Snitzer,* 112 Neb. 135, 198 N.W. 879 (1924) (agent failed to declare he already had buyer at price above which agent was to recover commission); *Campbell v. Baxter,* 41 Neb. 729, 60 N.W. 90 (1894) (agent received commission from both buyer and seller); *Jansen v. Williams,* 36 Neb. 869, 55 N.W. 279 (1893) (agent interfered with principal's right of direct sale).

The district court based its legal conclusion that Engelbert placed her interests and those of the Pedersens above those of the Daubmans upon the following specific findings of fact:

> [E]very effort was made by . . . Engelbert to consummate sale of the premises with the Pedersens only. When the Pedersens' financial condition was shown to be precarious . . . Engelbert took several steps to keep the transaction alive for the Pedersens, and, more to the point, even when events became detrimental to the [Daubmans]. As the series of events became more convoluted and the [Daubmans] made arrangements to enter into a six-month lease of an apartment during construction of their new home . . . Engelbert on her own initiative contacted their lessor to ascertain for herself whether the Daubmans could continue to lease the property if there was a delay in the closing of the sale of [the] Daubmans' home. This "end run" is the most glaring example of extent to which . . . Engelbert put her own interests and the interests of the Pedersens ahead of the [Daubmans']. More damaging was the fact that closing of the sale of the Daubman home was contingent upon payment of Engelbert's and CBS' commission.

Since the listing agreement restricted Engelbert to selling only to the Pedersens, the fact that that was her sole effort could not have constituted a breach of her duty to the Daubmans. Moreover, while Engelbert and CBS refused to voluntarily forfeit their commission, it was the escrow agent that refused to close the transaction unless either the commission was voluntarily forfeited by Engelbert and CBS or the Daubmans allowed it to be paid. Thus, neither does this occurrence support the district court's legal conclusion.

However, Engelbert's effort with regard to the Pedersens' loan applications is another matter. Because it was not until July 13, 1992, that the Pedersens met with Capital Financial Services and because Engelbert took the position that the Daubmans had no choice but to wait and see whether Capital Financial Services approved or rejected the Pedersens' loan application, the Daubmans faced a considerable time problem. The purchase agreement provided that the Pedersens would take possession on July 30. Thus, the Daubmans would need to rent an apartment in order to vacate by that date. Residential Mortgage Services took 24 days on the Pedersens' loan application, and there was no way of telling exactly how long Capital Financial Services would take to either approve or reject the Pedersens' application. Moreover, as part of her effort to complete the sale no matter what the effect on the Daubmans, Engelbert, without the Daubmans' knowledge, contacted the operator of the apartment complex to check on the availability of apartments and confirmed to the operator that her inquiry concerned the Daubmans, with the result that the Daubmans were pressured into executing a lease by July 27. Although Engelbert was authorized to sell only to the Pedersens, she should not have continued to push the sale when the situation began to look detrimental to the interests of the Daubmans.

In addition, it must be remembered that although Engelbert claimed she stated only that the Pedersens were prequalified, Allen Daubman testified that Engelbert erroneously told them that the Pedersens had been preapproved with a particular lender for a $180,000 loan, enough to buy their home. While the district court made no specific finding with regard to this issue, the rule that in a bench trial, the trial court's entry of judgment in favor of a party warrants the conclusion that the trial court found in that party's favor on all issuable facts requires that we conclude the district court resolved this issue in favor of the Daubmans. See, *Peterson v. Kellner*, 245 Neb. 515, 513 N.W.2d 517 (1994); *Burgess v. Curly Olney's, Inc.*, 198 Neb. 153, 251 N.W.2d 888 (1977). (This rule is not made inapplicable merely because in addition to a general finding, the trial court also mentioned certain matters specifically. *Burgess, supra.*)

The district court's factual findings with regard to Engelbert's treatment of the Pedersens' loan applications, her contact with the apartment complex operator, and her representation as to the preapproval of the Pedersens for a loan support the district court's legal conclusion that Engelbert and, through her, CBS put their interests in completing the sale, and thereby collecting the commission, and the interests of the Pedersens in acquiring the property ahead of the Daubmans' interests in selling the property in a manner and under a time schedule which least inconvenienced them. All of Engelbert's actions taken together support the district court's legal conclusion that she and, through her, CBS materially breached the duties they, as agents, owed their principals, the Daubmans. . . .

V. JUDGMENT

For the foregoing reasons, we reverse the judgment of the Court of Appeals and remand the cause thereto with the direction that it affirm the judgment of the district court, modified in accordance with this opinion.

REVERSED AND REMANDED WITH DIRECTION.

NOTES

1. The *Daubman* case is an example of the protracted bargaining and negotiation that can occur when real estate parcels, including residential parcels, have been offered for sale. It also is an example of the risks that real estate brokers can incur in being overly zealous in trying to make a sale.

2. In TPL Associates v. Helmsley-Spear, Inc., 536 N.Y.S.2d 754 (1989), the defendant, Helmsley-Spear, Inc., a brokerage firm, was the broker for the seller of commercial property. The facts as alleged are that six of defendant's brokers owned substantial interests in the purchaser, one of them a 22.5 percent interest. It is further alleged that defendant informed the plaintiff, prior to the contract of sale for the property being signed, that none of defendant's brokers had more than a nominal interest in the purchaser. After the closing, when plaintiff discovered that brokers working for defendant held much more than a nominal interest in the purchaser, plaintiff refused to pay the final brokerage commission installment of $43,000 and brought this action to recover the $43,000 brokerage commission installment that it earlier had paid. The trial court dismissed the complaint for failure to state a valid cause of action and the plaintiff appealed. The appellate court reversed and in its opinion stated the following:

> [The trial court] erred in treating the relationship between the parties as one at arms' length, rather than as a fiduciary relationship between principal and agent. An agent is charged with a duty of loyalty and may not have interests in the subject transaction which are adverse to those of his principal. Where a conflict of interest exists, nothing less than full and complete disclosure is required of the agent. . . .
>
> A breach by the agent of this duty of loyalty is a fraud for which the agent is answerable in damages, and any compensation paid to him may be forfeited. In accord is Darby v. Furman Co., 513 S.E.2d 848 (S.C. 1999), in which the brokerage firm's agent who represented the seller in making a sale was a partner in the buyer, so the seller was entitled to return of the brokerage commission of $28,500. However, the brokerage firm would have been entitled to the commission if the seller had received proper advance written notice of the agent's interest in the buyer.

Haldiman v. Gosnell Development Corp.

155 Ariz. 585, 748 P.2d 1209 (Ct. App. 1988)

GREER, Judge. The primary issue presented in this appeal is whether a real estate agent who is an employee of the seller owes a duty of full and frank disclosure to the buyer in a real estate transaction. . . .

Since this is an appeal from a summary judgment, we view the facts most favorably to the appellant. The appellant, Meredith Haldiman, entered into a contract on August 5, 1982, to purchase a townhome, which was to be constructed by appellee Gosnell Development Corporation (Gosnell). The purchase contract, entitled an "Agreement to Purchase" (purchase agreement), was prepared by appellee Gael Boden, an employee of Gosnell and a licensed real estate salesman. Haldiman was not represented by her own real estate agent, nor did she obtain outside legal advice.

Boden prepared the purchase agreement on a Gosnell form, by typing in the blanks, including the purchaser's name, the development, the home site, the plan, options and price. The total purchase agreement consisted of two pages. It provided, inter alia:

> 5. If Purchaser fails to comply in timely fashion with all terms and conditions of this Agreement or otherwise should fail to complete the Purchase, GDC [Gosnell Development Corporation] may elect to (a) terminate this Agreement by delivery of written notice to Purchaser and may retain any monies received and/or collect monies due, including but not limited to earnest monies and amounts due for options incorporated into the Residence, as liquidated and agreed damages, or (b) seek specific performance, and/or (c) pursue any other right or remedy provided by law. . . .
>
> 8. This Agreement and any subsequent executed agreements constitute the Agreement between the parties hereto and neither shall be bound by any understanding, negotiation, discussion, agreement, promise or representation expressed or implied, which is not set forth herein or in subsequent agreements executed by both parties. . . .
>
> 12. Purchaser acknowledges having read and understood each of foregoing terms and conditions. *Purchaser should not execute this Agreement if any of the provisions are unclear or objectionable to Purchaser.*

Pursuant to the agreement, Haldiman paid a $2,000 earnest money deposit.

Boden subsequently prepared an additional agreement, an "Option/Change Order Agreement" (option agreement) which was executed on August 27, 1982. This second agreement set forth the options that Haldiman chose for her new home and their prices. Pursuant to that agreement, she paid a deposit of $1,300 for the options.

Boden signed both agreements as a "marketing representative" of Gosnell. Haldiman was provided copies of the two agreements. Boden apparently made no explanation of the terms of the purchase agreement at the time of execution. He did not, for example, explain that pursuant to its terms, Haldiman's deposit would not be refunded if she was unable to close escrow because she did not qualify for financing or was unable to sell her former home. Neither did he suggest that the purchase agreement be conditioned upon Haldiman's ability to obtain reasonable financing or to sell her existing home.

Close of escrow was set for January, 1983, when it was anticipated that construction of the unit would be completed. Gosnell was ready and able to close escrow at that time, but Haldiman was unable to secure financing because she had not yet sold her former home. Gosnell extended her a four and one-half month grace period within which to sell her home. By May, 1983, she still had not sold her home and was unable to close escrow. On May 6, 1983, Gosnell notified Haldiman by letter that it was terminating the purchase agreement because of Haldiman's failure to comply with the terms and conditions of the agreement and close escrow in a timely fashion. She was given a final deadline of May 16, 1983. Haldiman failed to close escrow, and pursuant to the purchase agreement, Gosnell terminated the agreement and retained both the $2,000 earnest money deposit and $1,300 option deposit Haldiman had paid.

Haldiman filed a complaint against Gosnell and Gael Boden alleging that Gosnell wrongfully retained the total of $3,300 she had deposited with Gosnell (Count I) and that Gael Boden represented her in the transaction and had breached his duty to give her full and frank advice and to treat her fairly (Count II). Count II was resolved in favor of Gosnell and Boden upon their motion for summary judgment, and Count I was resolved by arbitration in Gosnell's favor. On appeal, Haldiman claims that the trial court improperly granted the defendants' motion for summary judgment and that the court should have held, as a matter of law, that Boden owed Haldiman a duty of full and frank disclosure. . . .

WAS A DUTY OWED?

Real estate salesmen and brokers owe a duty of good faith and loyalty to their principal. Vivian Arnold Realty Co. v. McCormick, 19 Ariz. App. 289, 293, 506 P.2d 1074 (1973). They must exercise reasonable due care and diligence to effect a sale to the principal's best advantage. Id.; Haymes v. Rogers, 70 Ariz. 257, 219 P.2d 339 (1950). They must also disclose to their clients information they possess pertaining to the transaction involved. Jennings v. Lee, 105 Ariz. 167, 461, P.2d 161 (1969).

In Morley v. J. Pagel Realty & Insurance, 27 Ariz. App. 62, 550 P.2d 1104 (1976), Division Two of this court extended this duty one step further. The question before the court was the extent of a real estate broker's duty to his client and specifically, whether the broker should have advised his clients, the sellers, to require security for the buyer's performance. The court stated:

> In the case at bench, appellants [the sellers] seek to hold appellees [the real estate broker] liable for failing to inform them that the Haydens' offer contemplated no security and that a mortgage should be required. Although this information might be beyond the average person, it is common knowledge in the real estate business. We think that as part of appellees' duty to effect a sale for appellants on the best terms possible and to disclose to them all the information they possess that pertained to the prospective transaction, appellees were bound to inform appellants that they should require security for the Haydens' performance.

Id. at 65, 550 P.2d at 1107. The court specifically stated, however, that its holding was a narrow one and should not be extended beyond the facts before it. Id. at 65-66, 550 P.2d at 1107-08. The court then stated:

> It [the holding] is reinforced by art. 26, §1 of the Arizona Constitution. Having achieved, by virtue of this provision, the right to prepare any and all instruments incidental to the sale of real property, including promissory notes, *real estate brokers and salesmen also bear the responsibility and duty of explaining to the persons involved the implications of these documents.*

Id. at 66, 550 P.2d at 1108 (emphasis added). Haldiman argues that this last phrase suggests that the court was opening the door to an increased duty of salesmen *to persons other than their principal or client.* She urges this court to adopt a broad interpretation of *Morley*. For the reasons stated below, however, we decline to do so.

We first point out that the *Morley* court specifically stated that its holding was narrow and should not be extended beyond the facts before it. From this very clear statement, we can only conclude that the court meant just that. Its subsequent statement is dicta at best, and therefore not controlling as precedent. Town of Chino Valley v. City of Prescott, 131 Ariz. 78, 638 P.2d 1324 (1981), *appeal dismissed,* 457 U.S. 1101, 102 S. Ct. 2897, 73 L. Ed. 2d 1310, *rehearing denied,* 459 U.S. 899, 103 S. Ct. 199, 74 L. Ed. 2d 160 (1982).

The Arizona Supreme Court, when subsequently presented with a similar question to that in *Morley,* refused to impose a duty of disclosure on a real estate agent who was not working for the seller. Buffington v. Haas, 124 Ariz. 36, 601 P.2d 1320 (1979). That court concluded:

> there was not an agency relationship between appellant Haas [the real estate salesman] and appellee Buffington. Haas had no obligation to inform the appellee that under the contract she did not retain a security interest in her property. Morley v. J. Pagel Realty & Ins., 27 Ariz. App. 62, 550 P.2d 1104 (1976). *He also had no obligation to inform her as to the contents of the escrow instructions.* . . .

Haldiman nevertheless suggests that this court should impose a duty on real estate agents to explain the implication of real estate documents even in the absence of an agency relationship. She suggests that this duty would be in the public's best interest, and that the court could ensure that *all* parties to a real estate transaction were informed, thereby reducing litigation involving mistake, misrepresentation and misunderstanding in real estate transactions. Although certainly a laudable goal, this court cannot simply create a legal duty because it might reduce litigation in the future. Haldiman does not expressly argue that Boden was her agent, although she does state in her affidavit that Boden represented her in connection with the real estate transaction and gave her real estate advice. As a matter of law, however, Boden could not have been Haldiman's agent.

Part of Boden's job was to write purchase contracts for potential Gosnell home purchasers, which is exactly what he did for Haldiman. This brief relationship now forms the basis of Haldiman's claim that he represented her and gave her real estate advice in the transaction. Haldiman's belief that Boden represented her, or was in essence her agent, does not, however, make him her agent. See, e.g., Warren v. Mangels Realty, 23 Ariz. App. 318, 321, 533 P.2d 78, 81 (1975) ("Warren's mental characterization of Mangels as his 'agent' could not by some magical process convert Mangels into one"). The facts are clear, despite Haldiman's belief and claim, that Boden was an employee of Gosnell and represented Gosnell only. An agent may not, in the absence of the principal's consent, act on behalf of an adverse party. Valley Natl. Bank v. Milmoe, 74 Ariz. 290, 296, 248 P.2d 740, 744 (1952). Haldiman has not presented any evidence, or even alleged, that Gosnell gave Boden per mission to represent Haldiman in the transaction. Boden, on the other hand, claims he worked exclusively for Gosnell and at no time represented or worked for Haldiman. Accordingly, Boden only represented Gosnell and could not have been Haldiman's agent.

Haldiman also argues that Boden is liable because he was negligent for failing to adhere to the standards of his profession, citing Darner Motor Sales, Inc. v. Universal Underwriters Insur. Co., 140 Ariz. 383, 682 P.2d 388 (1984). *Darner,* however, involved an insurance agent who failed to explain the implications of an insurance policy *to his client.* The *Darner* court phrased the issue precisely: "What duty does a licensed insurance agent *owe to a client or customer?*" 140 Ariz. at 397, 682 P.2d at 402 (emphasis added). Other cases, both prior to and subsequent to *Darner* have similarly involved professionals who failed to adhere to the standards of their profession when dealing with their clients. In Rossell v. Volkswagen of America, 147 Ariz. 160, 166, 709 P.2d 517, 523 (1985), the Arizona Supreme Court summarized these cases and the nature of the duty they imposed:

> Volkswagen argues that case law already recognizes that in negligent design cases a manufacturer is not liable absent a showing that he failed to conform to the standard of care in design followed by other manufacturers. We do not agree. Darner Motor Sales, Inc., v. Universal Underwriters Insurance Co., 140 Ariz. 383, 682 P.2d 388 (1984); Boyce v. Brown, 51 Ariz. 416, 77 P.2d 455 (1938); and Riedisser v. Nelson, 111 Ariz. 542, 534 P.2d 1052 (1975), are, for instance, cases involving *professionals (insurance broker and physicians) sued by their clients or patients.* National Housing Industries, Inc., v. E. L. Jones Development Co., 118 Ariz. 374, 576 P.2d 1374 (App. 1978), involves the liability of a professional engineer to the assignee of its client, a developer. . . . *They do involve, instead, the liability of professionals who generally work in close relationship with their clients or patients.* (Emphasis added).

In light of the foregoing, Boden did not have a broker/client relationship with Haldiman, and thus did not breach a duty to uphold real estate professional standards. Cf. *Darner,* supra. Haldiman has no cause of action for Boden's failure to suggest that the purchase contract be conditioned upon financing and selling her home, or his failure to explain that she could not recover her deposits if she failed to close escrow for any reason. . . . We affirm the judgment of the trial court as to the substantive issues, and we remand for a redetermination of attorneys' fees incurred below. . . .

NOTE

Buyers seeking to purchase homes often are uninformed as to their legal relationship with the brokers they are dealing with. Brokers are usually so solicitous of the buyers' preferences and interests that buyers commonly believe that the brokers are representing them, a belief held by the prospective buyer in the *Haldiman* case. The likelihood of confusion is even greater when properties are listed with a multiple listing service and the buyer is dealing with the selling broker rather than the listing broker. Functionally, at least, it appears very much as though the selling broker is representing the buyer. Some states have sought to avoid buyer and seller misunderstanding as to broker legal representation in home sale transactions by requiring that brokers make written disclosures to buyers and sellers as to the nature of the broker relationship. For example, New York has a real estate broker disclosure law requiring broker disclosure to prospective buyers and sellers by appropriate prescribed written form. The statutory forms set forth in simple language the nature of the agency and the duties of the broker, and require a signed acknowledgment by the prospective buyer or seller that the party signing has received the disclosure notice and understands it. The law applies only to residential real estate transactions. N.Y. Real Prop. Law Ann. § 443 (McKinney Supp. 1992).

Haymes v. Rogers

70 Ariz. 257, 219 P.2d 339 (1950)

DE CONCINI, Justice. Kelley Rogers, hereinafter called appellee, brought an action against L. F. Haymes, hereinafter referred to as appellant, seeking to recover a real estate commission in the sum of $425. The case was tried before a jury which returned a verdict in favor of appellee. The said appellant owned a piece of realty which he had listed for sale with the appellee, real estate broker, for the sum of $9,500. The listing card which appellant signed provided that the commission to be paid appellee for selling the property was to be five (5%) percent of the total selling price. Tom Kolouch was employed by the said appellee as a real estate salesman, and is hereafter referred to as "salesman."

On February 4, 1948, the said salesman contacted Mr. and Mrs. Louis Pour, prospective clients. He showed them various parcels of real estate, made an appointment with them for the following day in order to show them appellant's property. The salesman then drew a diagram of the said property in order to enable the Pours to locate and identify it the next day for their appointment. The Pours, however, proceeded to go to appellant's property that very day and encountering the appellant, negotiated directly with him and purchased the property for the price of $8,500. The transcript of evidence (testimony) reveals that the appellant knew the Pours had been sent to him through the efforts of appellee's salesman but he did not know it until they verbally agreed on a sale and appellant had accepted a $50 deposit. Upon learning that fact he told the Pours that he would take care of the salesman.

Appellant makes several assignments of error and propositions of law. However, we need only to consider whether the trial court was in error by refusing to grant a motion for an instructed verdict in favor of the defendant.

One of the propositions of law relied upon by the appellant is as follows: "The law requires that a real estate broker employed to sell land must act in entire good faith and in the interest of his employer, and if he induces the prospective buyer to believe that the property can be bought for less, he thereby fails to discharge that duty and forfeits all his rights to claim commission and compensation for his work."

There is no doubt that the above proposition of law is correct. . . .

The facts here are clear and undisputed. The salesman informed the purchasers that he had an offer at $8,250 for the property from another purchaser which he was about to submit to appellant. He further told them he thought appellant would not take $8,250 but would probably sell for a price between $8,250 and $9,500 and that they in all probability could get it for $8,500. The agent was entirely without justification in informing the purchasers that the property might be bought for $8,500, since that placed the purchasers at a distinct advantage in bargaining with the principal as to the purchase price of the realty. As a general rule an agent knows through his contacts with his principal, how anxious he is to sell and whether or not the principal will accept less than the listed price. To inform a third person of that fact is a clear breach of duty and loyalty owed by the fiduciary to his principal. Such misconduct and breach of duty results in the agent's losing his right to compensation for services to which he would otherwise be entitled. 2 Am. Jur. 235, Agency, section 299, Restatement of Agency, section 469. . . .

This determination makes a consideration of the other grounds for appeal unnecessary. Under the circumstances the court should have directed a verdict for the defendant, appellant.

Judgment reversed.

La Prade, C.J., and Stanford and Phelps, JJ., concur.

UDALL, Justice (dissenting). I dissent for the reason that as I construe the record in the instant case the facts do not disclose such bad faith or gross misconduct on the part of the broker as to disentitle him to compensation.

There is no disagreement between us as to the high standard which the law prescribes must be maintained in dealings between an agent and his principal. . . . The difficulty comes in applying the law to the facts of this case.

The great majority of the reported cases denying a brokerage fee involves instances where (1) the agent acts adversely for the purpose of securing a secret profit for himself or otherwise advancing his own welfare at the expense of that of his employer; (2) an agent disclosing the necessitous circumstances of his principal; (3) the agent is guilty of fraud or dishonesty in the transaction of his agency; (4) his conduct is disobedient or constitutes a willful and deliberate breach of his contract of service; or (5) where he withholds information from his principal which it is his duty to disclose. . . . I submit, however, that the facts before us do not place the conduct of this broker within any of the prohibitions above enumerated and I have been unable to find a single case where the courts have denied compensation under a factual situation comparable to that presented by this record. . . .

An analysis of the testimony before us, when taken as it must be in the light most favorable to a sustaining of the judgment, shows but four questionable matters. First, the agent advised his principal, before the Pours came onto the scene, that in his opinion the listed sales price of $9500 was excessive. This statement was made after repeated efforts to sell to others at the list price had failed. I can see nothing improper in this. Second, the agent advised Pour (the ultimate purchaser whom he had procured) that his principal, the owner, then had on his desk for acceptance or rejection an offer of $8250 which offer, in his opinion, the seller would not accept. There may have been some impropriety in this disclosure of his principal's business but I cannot read into this slip such gross misconduct as to warrant denying him compensation. Third, complaint is made that the broker failed to exert his best efforts to effect a sale to the Pours at the list price of $9500. In my opinion there is no merit to this contention because it is clear that the broker did advise the prospective purchasers that the owner's asking price was $9500 and it further appears that appellant perfected the sale with the Pours the evening of the first day they were contacted and before the broker's salesman had an opportunity to keep an appointment for the following day at 1:00 P.M., when he was to show them the property in question. It is unthinkable to believe that any purchaser would buy property without first seeing it. The majority evidently do not base the reversal upon any of these derelictions so finally we consider what is urged as the broker's most serious breach of duty to act in good faith and for the interest of the appellant, to wit, his unauthorized statement that the owner might accept less than the list price. To keep the record straight I quote from the cross-examination of salesman Tom Kolouch:

> "*Q.* And you also told them at that time that you were pretty sure if they would offer $8500 for the property that they would get it?
> *A.* I told them they might try $8500. I didn't tell them for sure they would get it because I wasn't setting a price on the other man's property.
> *Q.* And you told them if they would offer $8500 that they might get the property?
> *A.* They might have, yes.
> *Q.* And there wasn't anything said at that time about their offering $9500 for the property?
> *A.* I told them the price was $9500 on our list."

And the following is Mr. Pour's version of the matter:

> "*Q.* He told you to go out there and offer $8500 for the property?
> *A.* No, he told me it was listed for more, but he didn't think this offer would go through, and if I met somewhere in between I might get it."

In effect, as I view it, all the appellee intended by his statements to the Pours was to hold their interest in the property until he could show it to them and the parties could be brought together. I understand it to be the law that the ultimate duty of the broker toward his principal is to procure a purchaser ready, willing and able to purchase upon terms agreed upon by the owner and the purchaser. How then can it be said that the effort of the broker in the instant case in attempting to interest a purchaser and bring the purchaser and owner together by stating that the property might possibly be purchased for less than the quoted price (something which every prospective purchaser would be justified in assuming and which is a hope in the mind of every buyer) amounted to a breach of his duty to act for his principal's best interest? Will not the court's opinion be construed as holding that if a broker states to a purchaser or even indicates in any manner that property might be acquired for less than the listed price his right to a commission is thereby forfeited? If such be the declared law of this state it will certainly give a wide avenue of escape to unscrupulous realty owners from paying what is justly owed to agents who have been the immediate and efficient cause of the sale of their property. . . .

I would affirm the judgment as entered by the learned trial court.

On Rehearing: 70 Ariz. 408, 222 P.2d 789 (1950)

De Concini, Justice. In our former opinion . . . we held that as a matter of law there was bad faith shown on the broker's part which precluded him from recovery of his commission. In the light of the motion for rehearing and a reexamination of the evidence and instructions we are constrained to change our view. . . .

The defendant below requested an instruction on bad faith which the trial court refused to give. . . .

The evidence in this case presents a close question as to good or bad faith on the part of the broker. The trial court should have submitted that issue to the jury to decide. . . .

In this case the appellant sold the property to a purchaser whom he knew was sent to him by the appellee's salesman. Therefore, in the absence of bad faith the broker is entitled to his commission when he is the procuring cause of sale. . . .

Judgement is reversed and the case remanded for a new trial with directions to submit the question of bad faith on the part of the appellee to the jury. Judgment reversed.

La Prade, C.J. and Udall, Stanford and Phelps, JJ., concurring.

NOTES

1. In Moore and Co. v. T-A-L-L, Inc., 792 P.2d 794 (Colo. 1990), a broker was held to have forfeited its commission of over $70,000 by breaching its fiduciary duties to the seller. The forfeiture was ordered even though there was no finding that the seller sustained a monetary loss as a result of the breach of fiduciary duties. The duties breached consisted of disclosing confidential information to the buyer, negotiating with the buyer on terms not disclosed to the seller, and failing to offer advice and assistance to the seller on possible alternative offering terms.

2. A broker owes a duty to prospective buyers to submit their bids to the seller. In Stevens v. Jayhawk Realty Co., 236 Kan. 90, 689 P.2d 786 (1984), plaintiff's willingness to offer a price higher than that of the successful bidder was never communicated by the broker to the seller; as a result, plaintiff asserted that he lost money by failing to acquire a parcel of land on which he could turn a profit. Plaintiff sued the broker, the trial court awarded plaintiff damages of $37,000, but the judgment was reversed on appeal because the broker's alleged misconduct caused no loss to plaintiff since seller was aware of plaintiff's willingness to pay a higher price but despite this chose to sell to a lower bidder.

3. As to broker's duties to seller, aside from the usual fiduciary obligation of honesty and forthrightness, broker has to reach some level of competence. Causing the principal to miss a good deal or enter a bad one may cost the broker the commission. In Schoenberg v. Benner, 251 Cal. App. 2d 154, 59 Cal. Rptr. 359 (1967), broker recommended that seller sell to an impecunious buyer. Buyer had given broker a false statement of the value of his assets. Broker could easily have tried to confirm buyer's statement but failed to do so. Seller conveyed outright to this buyer; seller received from buyer $20,000 cash (of which $7,500 went to broker) and buyer's promise to pay an additional $117,500, a promise not secured by a mortgage on the transferred land. Buyer then mortgaged the unencumbered land to a bona fide purchaser bank and absented himself with the proceeds. Seller was awarded a $125,000 judgment against the broker. On broker's action over against buyer, the court held that the buyer's misbehavior fell short of legal fraud on the broker. Also, failure of broker to provide seller with adequate information on prospective buyer's financial condition can prevent broker from being entitled to a commission even

though broker produced an ostensibly able and willing buyer on the seller's terms. Gatlinburg Real Estate Co. v. Booth, 651 S.W.2d 203 (Tenn. 1983).

4. Listing agreements typically have a limited duration, and Statutes of Frauds typically require that listing agreements include in writing their duration. As an added inducement to the duration being in writing, a California statute, Cal. Bus. & Prof. Cod. § 10176(f) (West Supp. 2006), provides that a licensed broker is subject to disciplinary action for the practice of claiming a commission under an exclusive listing that does not contain "a definite, specified date of final and complete termination."

5. Some states have funds from which those damaged by wrongful acts of real estate brokers may recover at least some of their losses. Illinois's statute provides:

Ill. Comp. Stat. 454/20-85 (Smith-Hurd Supp. 2006)

Recovery from Real Estate Recovery Fund

§ 20-85. Recovery from Real Estate Recovery Fund. OBRE [Office of Banks and Real Estate] shall maintain a Real Estate Recovery Fund from which any person aggrieved by an act, representation, transaction, or conduct of a licensee or unlicensed employee of a licensee that is in violation of this Act or the rules promulgated pursuant thereto, constitutes embezzlement of money or property, or results in money or property being unlawfully obtained from any person by false pretenses, artifice, trickery, or forgery or by reason of any fraud, misrepresentation, discrimination, or deceit by or on the part of any such licensee or the unlicensed employee of a licensee and that results in a loss of actual cash money, as opposed to losses in market value, may recover. The aggrieved person may recover, by order of the circuit court of the county where the violation occurred, an amount of not more than $10,000 from the Fund for damages sustained by the act, representation, transaction, or conduct, together with costs of suit and attorney's fees incurred in connection therewith of not to exceed 15% of the amount of the recovery ordered paid from the Fund. However, no licensed broker or salesperson may recover from the Fund unless the court finds that the person suffered a loss resulting from intentional misconduct. The court order shall not include interest on the judgment. The maximum liability against the Fund arising out of any one act shall be as provided in this Section, and the judgment order shall spread the award equitably among all co-owners or otherwise aggrieved persons, if any. The maximum liability against the Fund arising out of the activities of any one licensee or one unlicensed employee of a licensee, since January 1, 1974, shall be $50,000. Nothing in this Section shall be construed to authorize recovery from the Fund unless the loss of the aggrieved person results from an act or omission of a licensed broker, salesperson, or unlicensed employee who was at the time of the act or omission acting in such capacity or was apparently acting in such capacity and unless the aggrieved person has obtained a valid judgment as provided in Section 20–90 of this Act. No person aggrieved by an act, representation, or transaction that is in violation of the Illinois Real Estate Time-Share Act or the Land Sales Registration Act of 1989 may recover from the Fund.

Many states have similar funds, called client security funds, for lawyers' defalcations. Most such lawyer funds are administered by a bar association and financed by assessments on all lawyers in the state. See Turney & Holtaway, Client Protection Funds — Lawyers Put Their Money Where Their Mouths Are, The Prof'l. Lawyer 18 (Feb. 1998); Comment, Attorney Misappropriation of Clients' Funds: A Study in Professional Responsibility, 10 U. Mich. J.L. Ref. 415, 423-432 (1977).

Easton v. Strassburger

152 Cal. App. 3d 90, 199 Cal. Rptr. 383 (1984)

KLINE, Presiding Justice. Valley of California, Inc., doing business as Valley Realty (appellant), appeals from a judgment for negligence entered in favor of Leticia M. Easton (respondent). Appellant was one of six defendants in the action, which was brought by respondent for fraud (including negligent misrepresentation) and negligence in the sale of residential property.

FACTS

In the case below, all defendants were found liable to respondent for negligence. However, because Valley Realty alone has appealed, we limit our review of the record only to those facts which affect the liability of that party.

Viewing the evidence in the light most favorable to respondent, as we must, the record discloses the following facts: The property which is the subject of this appeal is a one-acre parcel of land located in the City of Diablo. The property is improved with a 3,000 square foot home, a swimming pool, and a large guest house. Respondent purchased the property for $170,000 from the Strassburgers in May of 1976 and escrow closed in July of that year. Appellant was the listing broker in the transaction.

Shortly after respondent purchased the property, there was massive earth movement on the parcel. Subsequent slides destroyed a portion of the driveway in 1977 or 1978. Expert testimony indicated that the slides occurred because a portion of the property was fill that had not been properly engineered and compacted. The slides caused the foundation of the house to settle which in turn caused cracks in the walls and warped doorways. After the 1976 slide, damage to the property was so severe that although experts appraised the value of the property at $170,000 in an undamaged condition, the value of the damaged property was estimated to be as low as $20,000. Estimates of the cost to repair the damage caused by the slides and avoid recurrence ranged as high as $213,000.

Appellant was represented in the sale of the property by its agents Simkin and Mourning. It is uncontested that these agents conducted several inspections of the property prior to sale. There is also evidence they were aware of certain "red flags" which should have indicated to them that there were soil problems. Despite this, the agents did not request that the soil stability of the property be tested and did not inform respondent that there were potential soil problems.

During the time that the property was owned by the Strassburgers there was a minor slide in 1973 involving about 10 to 12 feet of the filled slope and a major slide in 1975 in which the fill dropped about eight to 10 feet in a circular shape 50 to 60 feet across. However, the Strassburgers did not tell Simkin or Mourning anything about the slides or the corrective action they had taken.

Respondent purchased the property without being aware of the soil problems or the past history of slides.

In December of 1976 respondent filed suit against appellant, the Strassburgers, and three other named defendants.[1] As against appellant, respondent alleged

---

1. These three defendants—San Ramon Builders, George Sauer and H.M. Bull—were sued for negligent construction only.

causes of action for fraudulent concealment, intentional misrepresentation, and negligent misrepresentation.

Appellant filed a cross-complaint against the Strassburgers seeking full indemnity, or, in the alternative, partial indemnity.

The action was tried before a jury. As to appellant, the judge instructed the jury only as to negligent misrepresentation and simple negligence, since the actions for fraudulent concealment and intentional misrepresentation had been voluntarily dismissed. The jury returned a special verdict finding that all named defendants had been negligent, and assessed damages of $197,000. Negligence was apportioned among the parties under the principals of comparative negligence in the following percentages: Appellant — 5%; Strassburgers — 65%; George Sauer and San Ramon Builders — 15%; H.M. Bull — 10%. The jury also found a non-party (a cooperating broker) five percent responsible.

Appellant contends that the judgment must be reversed or modified for the following reasons: 1) The trial judge incorrectly instructed the jury on a real estate broker's duty to investigate and disclose defects in property; 2) no expert testimony was produced on two key issues in the case: the standard of care applicable to appellant, and appellant's failure to meet this standard of care; 3) the evidence presented at trial was insufficient to establish that appellant was negligent; 4) the jury based its award on the wrong measure of damages; and 5) appellant was improperly denied indemnity against the Strassburgers.

For reasons we shall explain, we find that none of appellant's arguments require reversal of the judgment against it. We agree, however, that appellant was improperly denied indemnification.

DISCUSSION

I

Appellant's primary contention is that the trial judge committed error by giving the jury an instruction specifying a real estate broker's duty to investigate and disclose defects in property he lists for sale.

In analyzing the validity of this contention, it must be kept in mind that the judgment against appellant was for *simple negligence* only. To establish liability for such negligence, respondent was not required to show that appellant had actual knowledge of the soils problems (as would have been required to prove intentional misrepresentation or fraudulent concealment) or that a misrepresentation had been made as to the soils condition of the property (as is required to establish negligent misrepresentation). (Carroll v. Gava (1979) 98 Cal. App. 3d 892, 895, 159 Cal. Rptr. 778; Huber, Hunt & Nichols, Inc. v. Moore (1977) 67 Cal. App. 3d 278, 304, 136 Cal. Rptr. 603.) We are concerned here only with the elements of a simple negligence action; that is, whether appellant owed a legal duty to respondent to use due care, whether this legal duty was breached, and finally whether the breach was a proximate cause of appellant's injury. (United States Liab. Ins. Co. v. Haidinger-Hayes, Inc. (1970) 1 Cal. 3d 586, 594, 83 Cal. Rptr. 418, 463 P.2d 770; 4 Witkin, Summary of Cal. Law (8th Ed. 1974) Torts, § 488, p.2749.)

Whether a defendant owes a duty of due care to a particular plaintiff is a question of law. (Peter W. v. San Francisco Unified Sch. Dist. (1976) 60 Cal. App. 3d 814, 822, 131 Cal. Rptr. 854; 4 Witkin, supra, Summary of Cal. Law, Torts, § 493, p.2756).

Appellant does not contend that it was under no duty to exercise due care to prevent injury to respondent.[2] Rather, appellant objects to the manner in which this duty was characterized by the trial court. More particularly, appellant challenges the following instruction: "A real estate broker is a licensed person or entity who holds himself out to the public as having particular skills and knowledge in the real estate field. He is under a duty to disclose facts materially affecting the value or desirability of the property that are known to him or which through reasonable diligence should be known to him." *broker's duty*

Appellant argues that this instruction elevates a broker's duty beyond the level established by the case law, contending that a broker is only obliged to disclose known facts and has no duty to disclose facts which "should" be known to him "through reasonable diligence." In effect, appellant maintains that a broker has no legal duty to carry out a reasonable investigation of property he undertakes to sell in order to discover defects for the benefit of the buyer. Appellant further argues that since this instruction indicated to the jury that a broker is under such a duty as a matter of law, the giving of the instruction constitutes reversible error.

It is not disputed that current law requires a broker to disclose to a buyer material defects known to the broker but unknown to and unobservable by the buyer. (Cooper v. Jevne (1976) 56 Cal. App. 3d 860, 866, 128 Cal. Rptr. 724; Lingsch v. Savage (1963) 213 Cal. App. 2d 729, 733, 29 Cal. Rptr. 201; see also regulations of the Department of Real Estate set forth in Cal. Admin. Code, tit. 10, § 2785, subd. (a)(3).) The *Cooper* case contains the most complete judicial articulation of the rule: "It is the law of this state that where a real estate broker or agent, representing the seller, knows facts materially affecting the value or the desirability of property offered for sale and these facts are known or accessible only to him and his principal, and the broker or agent also knows that these facts are not known to or within the reach of the diligent attention and observation of the buyer, the broker or agent is under a duty to disclose these facts to the buyer. (Lingsch v. Savage [1963] 213 Cal. App. 2d [729, 29 Cal. Rptr. 201] . . .)." (56 Cal. App. 3d at 866, 128 Cal. Rptr. 724.) If a broker fails to disclose material facts that are known to him he is liable for the intentional tort of "fraudulent concealment" or "negative fraud." (Warner Const. Corp. v. City of Los Angeles (1970) 2 Cal. 3d 285, 293-294, 85 Cal. Rptr. 444, 466 P. 2d 996; Cooper v. Jevne, supra, 56 Cal. App. 3d at 866, 128 Cal. Rptr. 724; Lingsch v. Savage, supra, 213 Cal. App. 2d at 735-736, 29 Cal. Rptr. 201.) As noted, however, appellant's liability was here grounded on negligence rather than fraud. The issue, then, is whether a broker is negligent if he fails to disclose defects which he should have discovered through reasonable diligence. Stated another way, we must determine whether the broker's duty of due care in a residential real estate transaction includes a duty to conduct a reasonably competent and diligent inspection of property he has listed for sale in order to discover defects for the benefit of the buyer.

Admittedly, no appellate decision has explicitly declared that a broker is under a duty to disclose material facts which he should have known. We conclude, however, that such a duty is implicit in the rule articulated in *Cooper* and *Lingsch,* which speaks

---

2. Despite the absence of privity of contract, a real estate agent is clearly under a duty to exercise reasonable care to protect those persons whom the agent is attempting to induce into entering a real estate transaction for the purpose of earning a commission. (Merrill v. Buck (1962) 58 Cal. 2d 552, 561-562, 25 Cal. Rptr. 456, 375 P.2d 305; see also, Earp v. Nobmann (1981) 122 Cal. App. 3d 270, 290, 175 Cal. Rptr. 767.)

not only to facts known by the broker, but also and independently to facts that are *accessible* only to him and his principal.[3] *Cooper,* supra, 56 Cal. App. 3d at p.866, 128 Cal. Rptr. 724; *Lingsch,* supra, 213 Cal. App. 2d at p.735, 29 Cal. Rptr. 201, italics added.)

The primary purposes of the *Cooper-Lingsch* rule are to protect the buyer from the unethical broker and seller and to insure that the buyer is provided sufficient accurate information to make an informed decision whether to purchase. These purposes would be seriously undermined if the rule were not seen to include a duty to disclose reasonably discoverable defects. If a broker were required to disclose only known defects, but not also those that are reasonably discoverable, he would be shielded by his ignorance of that which he holds himself out to know. The rule thus narrowly construed would have results inimical to the policy upon which it is based. Such a construction would not only reward the unskilled broker for his own incompetence, but might provide the unscrupulous broker the unilateral ability to protect himself at the expense of the inexperienced and unwary who rely upon him. In any case, if given legal force, the theory that a seller's broker cannot be held accountable for what he does not know but could discover without great difficulty would inevitably produce a disincentive for a seller's broker to make a diligent inspection. Such a disincentive would be most unfortunate, since in residential sales transactions the seller's broker is most frequently the best situated to obtain and provide the most reliable information on the property and is ordinarily counted on to do so.

As one commentator has observed: "Real estate brokers are often in a very commanding position with respect to both sellers and buyers of residential property. The real estate broker's relationship to the buyer is such that the buyer usually expects the broker to protect his interests. This trust and confidence derives from the potential value of the broker's service; houses are infrequently purchased and require a trained eye to determine value and fitness. In addition, financing is often complex. Unlike other commodities, houses are rarely purchased new and there are virtually no remedies for deficiencies in fitness. In some respects the broker-buyer relationship is akin to the attorney-client relationship; the buyer, like the client, relies heavily on another's acquired skill and knowledge, first because of the complexity of the transaction and second because of his own dearth of experience." (Comment, A Reexamination of the Real Estate Broker-Buyer-Seller Relationship (1972) 18 Wayne L. Rev. 1343.) Thus, as stated by Judge Cardozo, as he then was, in a different but still relevant context: "The real estate broker is brought by his calling into a relation of trust and confidence. Constant are the opportunities by concealment and collusion to extract illicit gains. We know from our judicial records that the opportunities have not been lost. . . . He is accredited by his calling in the minds of the inexperienced or the ignorant with a knowledge greater than their own." (Roman v. Lobe (1926) 243 N.Y. 51, 54-55 [152 N.E. 461, 462; 50 A.L.R. 1329, 1332] quoted in Richards Realty Co. v. Real Estate Comr. (1956) 144 Cal. App. 2d 357, 362, 300 P.2d 893; see also Jacobson, Broker's Liability for Sale of Defective Homes (1977) 52 L.A. Bar Journal 346, 347, 353 and Note, Real Estate Brokers' Duties to Prospective Purchasers (1976) Brigham Young L. Rev. 513, 514-515.)

---

3. For reasons we describe presently, where the cause of action is for negligence rather than fraud the undisclosed material facts need not be either actually known by the broker or accessible *only* to him or his principal. (See text, infra, at pp. 390–391.)

Definition of the broker's duty to disclose as necessarily including the responsibility to conduct a reasonable investigation thus seems to us warranted by the pertinent realities. Not only do many buyers in fact *justifiably* believe the seller's broker is also protecting their interest in securing and acting upon accurate information[4] and rely upon him, but the injury occasioned by such reliance, if it be misplaced, may well be substantial. However, the broad definition of the duty we adopt is supported not simply by the magnitude of the benefit thus conferred on buyers but also by the relative ease with which the burden can be sustained by brokers. It seems relevant to us, in this regard, that the duty to disclose *that which should be known* is a formally acknowledged professional obligation that it appears many brokers customarily impose upon themselves as an ethical matter. Thus, The Code of Ethics of the National Association of Realtors[5] includes, inter alia, the provision that a broker must not only avoid . . . concealment of pertinent facts," but "has an affirmative obligation to discover adverse factors that a reasonably competent and diligent investigation would disclose."[6] (National Assoc. of Realtors,

4. See Sinclair, The Duty of the Broker to Purchasers and Prospective Purchasers of Real Property in Illinois (1981) 69 Ill. Bar. J. 260, 263-264, wherein the author states: "In the typical residential real estate transaction, however, the buyer, in particular, may be intentionally or inadvertently led under such circumstances to believe the broker will represent his interest even where he is aware the broker has a listing agreement with the seller. Since the broker's commission is generally paid as a percentage of the sales price, the broker's interest is more closely identified with that of the seller than of the buyer. Where the buyer is unappreciative of the potentially divided loyalty of the broker, he may be lulled into relying on the broker to his significant detriment. Misplaced reliance by the buyer can extend beyond the issue of price to questions regarding quality of title, condition of the premises, and proration of closing costs, property taxes, recording fees, and other expenses."

5. Pursuant to Evidence Code section 452, subdivision (h), we may take judicial notice of relevant criteria promulgated by a private professional association. (See Matchett v. Superior Court (1974) 40 Cal. App. 3d 623, 627, 115 Cal. Rptr. 317; and People v. Moran (1974) 39 Cal. App. 3d 398, 406, fn. 6, 114 Cal. Rptr. 413.) We do so here for the limited purpose of showing that, with respect to situations similar to that here presented (see infra, fn. 6), a significant number of real estate brokers have formally acknowledged the professional responsibility to conduct a reasonable investigation of listed property for the benefit of a buyer with whom the broker is not in privity of contract. We note that, since the Code was adverted to in respondent's brief, appellant has been afforded an opportunity to meet such information in its reply brief and at oral argument (Evid. Code, § 459, subd. (d)) even though such an opportunity is not required where, as here, the matter of which judicial notice is taken is not "of substantial consequence to the determination of the action." (Id.)

6. In fact, one of the examples provided by the Association to explain the operation of Article 9 is analogous to the facts of this case: "Shortly after REALTOR A negotiated the sale of a home to Buyer B a complaint came to the Board charging REALTOR A with failure to disclose a substantial fact concerning the property. The charge was that the house was not connected to the city sanitary sewage system, but had a septic tank, whereas the buyer claimed he had every reason to believe the house was connected with the sewer line. [¶] In a statement to the Board's Grievance Committee, Buyer B agreed that the subject was not discussed during his various conversations with REALTOR A about the house. However, he pointed out that his own independent inquiries had revealed that the street on which the house was located was 'sewered' and he had naturally assumed the house was connected. He had since determined that every other house on the street for several blocks in both directions was connected. He stated that REALTOR A, in not having disclosed the exceptional situation, had failed to disclose a pertinent fact. [¶] REALTOR A's defense in a hearing before the Board's Professional Standards Committee was (1) that he did not know that this particular house was not connected with the sewer; (2) that in advertising the house he had not represented it as being connected; (3) that at no time, as Buyer B conceded, had he orally stated that the house was connected; that the fact under discussion was not a 'pertinent fact' within the meaning of the Code of Ethics. [¶] The Committee determined that the absence of sewer connection in an area where other houses were connected was a substantial and pertinent fact in the transaction; that the absence of any mention to this fact in advertising or oral representation made it no less pertinent; that ascertaining the failure of previous owners to connect with the available sewer line was within REALTOR A's obligation under Article 9 of the Code; that he was, therefore, in violation of Article 9." (National Association of Realtors, supra, Interpretations of the Code of Ethics, at p.74).

It may be observed that the defect in this example — the lack of a conventional sewage connection — would not in the circumstances described likely be as apparent to a broker as the defect at issue in the case at bar.

Interpretations of the Code of Ethics (7th ed. 1978) art. 9.) This implicit duty of all real estate agents, regardless whether they are members of the aforementioned Association and bound by its Code of Ethics,[7] is reflected in the law. Thus, for example, in Brady v. Carman (1960) 179 Cal. App. 2d 63, 3 Cal. Rptr. 612, the court noted that "[t]he defendant . . . is a real estate agent, and as such is supposed to possess ordinary professional knowledge concerning the . . . natural characteristics of the property he is selling. . . , it should have been apparent that the [buyers] were ignorant concerning the nature of an easement and how it could limit their use of the property. . . . [*The broker*] *was obliged as a professional man to obtain information* about the easement *and make a full disclosure* of the burdens it imposed on the land." (Id., at pp. 68-69, 3 Cal. Rptr. 612, italics added.) It is true that Brady v. Carman was an action based on fraud, not, as in the present case, negligence; but we do not conceive that the existence of the professional duty to obtain information described in that case may be allowed to vary with the cause of action.

In sum, we hold that the duty of a real estate broker, representing the seller, to disclose facts, as that fundamental duty is articulated in *Cooper* and *Lingsch*, includes the affirmative duty to conduct a reasonably competent and diligent inspection of the residential[8] property listed for sale and to disclose to prospective purchasers all facts materially affecting the value or desirability of the property that such an investigation would reveal.

With respect to the application of this holding, it is vitally important to keep in mind that in *Cooper* and *Lingsch* the basis of liability was fraud, not negligence. The fundamental duty to disclose set forth in those and other real estate fraud cases has application only where it is alleged that the broker either had actual knowledge of the material facts in issue or that such facts were "accessible *only* to him and his principal" (*Cooper,* supra, 56 Cal. App. 3d at p.866, 128 Cal. Rptr. 724; *Lingsch,* supra, 213 Cal. App. 2d at p. 735, 29 Cal. Rptr. 201, italics added), so that the broker may constructively be deemed to have had actual knowledge. The implicit duty to investigate is not considered in those cases simply because it is superfluous to the issue of fraud. However, in cases where, as here, the cause of action is for negligence, not fraud, it need not be alleged or proved that the broker had actual knowledge of the material facts in issue nor that such facts were accessible *only* to him or his principal and that he therefore had constructive knowledge thereof.

The real estate fraud cases also require that the undisclosed material facts be such as "are not known to or within the reach of the diligent attention and observation of the buyer." (*Cooper,* supra, 56 Cal. App. 3d p.866, 128 Cal. Rptr. 724; *Lingsch,* supra, 213 Cal. App. 2d at p. 735, 29 Cal. Rptr. 201.) We decline to place a similar limitation on the duty to investigate here articulated. Such a limitation might, first of all, diminish the broker's incentive to conduct the

7. It appears that appellant's agents, Simkin and Mourning, who were both members of the Contra Costa County Board of Realtors, were members of the Association and subject to the Code, since only brokers who are members of the Association are entitled to use the copyrighted name "Realtor."

8. We express no opinion here whether a broker's obligation to conduct an inspection for defects for the benefit of the buyer applies to the sale of commercial real estate. Unlike the residential home buyer who is often unrepresented by a broker, or is effectively unrepresented because of the problems of dual agency (see generally, 1 Miller & Starr, Current Law of California Real Estate (1983 Supp.) § 4.18, pp. 25-29; Comment, Dual Agency in Residential Real Estate Brokerage: Conflict of Interest and Interests in Conflict (1982) 12 Golden Gate L.Rev. 379), a purchaser of commercial real estate is likely to be more experienced and sophisticated in his dealings in real estate and is usually represented by an agent who represents only the buyer's interests. (Comment, supra, 12 Golden Gate L.Rev. at 383.)

reasonably competent and diligent inspection which the law seeks to encourage. Furthermore, general principles of comparative negligence provide adequate protection to a broker who neglects to explicitly disclose *manifest* defects. (See generally, Li v. Yellow Cab Co. (1975) 13 Cal. 3d 804, 119 Cal. Rptr. 858, 532 P.2d 1226.) The duty of the seller's broker to diligently investigate and disclose reasonably discoverable defects to the buyer does not relieve the latter of the duty to exercise reasonable care to protect himself. Cases will undoubtedly arise in which the defect in the property is so clearly apparent that as a matter of law a broker would not be negligent for failure to expressly disclose it, as he could reasonably expect that the buyer's own inspection of the premises would reveal the flaw. In such a case the buyer's negligence *alone* would be the proximate cause of any injury he suffered.

Accordingly, we find that the instruction at issue in this case was legally correct, for, as the trial judge stated to the jury, a seller's broker in a residential real estate transaction *is* "under a duty to disclose facts materially affecting the value or desirability of the property . . . which through reasonable diligence should be known to him."

Appellant also argues that the instruction was improper because the sentence therein just quoted was immediately preceded by the definition of a broker as a "licensed person or entity who holds himself out to the public as having particular skills and knowledge in the real estate field." Appellant maintains that the proximity of these two sentences led the jury to believe that the duty to disclose is imposed by the license. We disagree. The proximity of the two sentences does not of itself suggest that the duty described in the second sentence arises *because* of the licensing law. There is no connecting language which logically identifies the license referred to in the first sentence as the source of the duty described in the second. The instruction merely sets forth two accurate and independent statements. In any event, since we have held that the duty was correctly defined, a misapprehension by the jury as to its source, if there were any misapprehension, would not have been prejudicial.

The challenged instruction was not erroneous in any respect.

II

Appellant next contends that the judgment must be reversed because the verdict was not supported by substantial evidence. Again, we cannot agree. . . .

Real estate agents hold themselves out to the public as professionals, and, as such, are required to make reasonable use of their superior knowledge, skills and experience within the area of their expertise. (4 Witkin, supra, Summary of Cal. Law, §518, p.2783). Because such agents are expected to make use of their superior knowledge and skills, which is the reason they are engaged, and because the agents in this case were or should have been alert to the signs of soils problems earlier described, the jury was well within the bounds of reason when it concluded that a reasonably diligent and competent inspection of the property would have included something more than a casual visual inspection and a general inquiry of the owners.

The judgment for negligence against appellant was amply supported by the evidence.

NOTES AND QUESTIONS

1. Shortly after the *Easton* case was decided, the California legislature passed this statute apparently intended to codify the *Easton* position on broker obligations to disclose physical defects to buyers:

§ 2079. Real estate brokers; inspections and disclosures
It is the duty of a real estate broker . . . to a prospective purchaser of residential real property comprising one to four dwelling units, including a manufactured home as defined in Section 18007 of the Health and Safety Code, to conduct a reasonably competent and diligent visual inspection of the property offered for sale and to disclose to that prospective purchaser all facts materially affecting the value or desirability of the property that such an investigation would reveal, if that broker has a written contract with the seller to find or obtain a buyer or is a broker who acts in cooperation with such a broker to find and obtain a buyer.

§ 2079.2. Real estate brokers; standard of care
The standard of care owed by a broker under this article is the degree of care that a reasonably prudent real estate licensee would exercise and is measured by the degree of knowledge through education, experience, and examination, required to obtain a license under Division 4 (commencing with Section 10000) of the Business and Professions Code.

§ 2079.3. Scope of inspection
The inspection to be performed pursuant to this article does not include or involve an inspection of areas that are reasonably and normally inaccessible to such an inspection, nor an affirmative inspection of areas off the site of the subject property or public records or permits concerning the title or use of the property, and, if the property comprises a unit in a planned development as defined in Section 11003 of the Business and Professions Code, a condominium as defined in Section 783, or a stock cooperative as defined in Section 11003.2 of the Business and Professions Code, does not include an inspection of more than the unit offered for sale, if the seller or the broker complies with the provisions of Section 1368. [underlined words added by 1994 amendment]

§ 2079.4. Breach of duty; limitation of actions
In no event shall the time for commencement of legal action for breach of duty imposed by this article exceed two years from the date of possession, which means the date of recordation, the date of close of escrow, or the date of occupancy, whichever occurs first.

§ 2079.5. Buyers or prospective buyers; duty of reasonable care
Nothing in this article relieves a buyer or prospective buyer of the duty to exercise reasonable care to protect himself or herself, including those facts which are known to or within the diligent attention and observation of the buyer or prospective buyer.

§ 2079.7. Environmental hazards; duty to disclose
(a) If a consumer information booklet described in Section 10084.1 of the Business and Professions Code is delivered to a transferee in connection with the transfer of real property, . . . a seller or broker is not required to provide additional information concerning, and the information shall be deemed to be adequate to inform the transferee regarding, common environmental hazards, as described in the booklet, that can affect real property.

(b) Notwithstanding subdivision (a), nothing in this section either increases or decreases the duties, if any, of sellers or brokers, . . . or alters the duty of a seller or broker to disclose the existence of known environmental hazards on or affecting the real property.

California Civil Code Ann. (West Supp. 2006.)

Given the *Easton* opinion, why do you believe the California legislature passed the above statute? Should not the *Easton* opinion suffice on the broker negligence issue? The California statute applies only to one to four dwelling-unit properties. Should it not also apply to all properties, commercial and industrial included?

2. Most jurisdictions have shown little inclination to go as far as California in imposing broker liability for failure to search for and disclose to prospective buyers hidden but discoverable defects in properties being offered for sale. A federal appeals court, for instance, has refused to find that the sweeping *Easton* tort law innovation is the law of Maryland even though a Maryland statute authorizes suspension of a real estate broker's license for "failure to disclose . . . to any person with whom such licensee is dealing, any material fact . . . relating to the property with which such licensee is dealing, which such licensee knew or should have known." Herbert v. Saffell, 877 F.2d 267, 274 (4th Cir. 1989). For arguments supporting adoption by more states of the *Easton* search and disclose obligation, especially as to environmental pollution hazards, see Comment, A Toxic Nightmare on Elm Street: Negligence and the Real Estate Broker's Duty in Selling Previously Contaminated Residential Property, 15 B.C. Envtl. Aff. L. Rev. 547 (1988).

3. Similar disclosure obligations of sellers' brokers to buyers also have been held to apply to buyers' brokers obligations to sellers. See, e.g., Lombardo v. Albi, 14 P.3d 288 (Ariz. 2000), in which the buyer's broker failed to inform the sellers prior to closing that the buyers probably could not perform by the closing date due to inadequate financial resources and the buyer's broker was aware of the buyer's financial situation. This failure to disclose resulted in delays costly to the sellers and resulting in loss to the sellers for which the buyer's broker is liable.

4. Brokers can also be tortiously liable to buyers for fraud or misrepresentation by making material false statements to buyers about properties offered for sale. Examples are false statements as to rental income, freedom from termites, annual property taxes, or outstanding liens. If the false statement is merely an opinion, no liability follows; but the line between statements of fact and opinion often is unclear. Brokers are in the business of bringing about sales and may be tempted in dealing with buyers to overstate what is attractive and understate what is unattractive about listed properties. This approach can be risky to the brokers involved. Brokers may protect themselves from such liability by express statements to buyers, preferably in writing, that the brokers are not warranting the condition of the premises and recommending that buyers have the premises inspected by an expert property inspector. On broker liability and protective steps that may be taken, see Hagglund and Weimer, Caveat Realtor: The Broker's Liability for Negligent and Innocent Misrepresentations, 20 Real Est. L.J. 149 (1991).

C. BUYER'S AND SELLER'S DUTIES TO BROKER

An obvious duty of buyers and sellers when they employ brokers is to comply with terms of the brokerage contract, including payment of the brokerage commission when earned. The type of listing provided for in the brokerage contract can be determinative of the brokerage payment obligations of the buyer or seller who has retained the broker. For example, was the listing agreement open, exclusive, or exclusive right to sell? It is also possible under some brokerage contracts that the broker can be entitled to a commission even though no sale occurred. As the next two cases show this can result from such seller conduct as seller withdrawal of the property from sale or inaccurate information about the property provided by the seller in the listing with the broker. Every brokerage contract imposes legal obligations not only on the broker but also on the person who has retained the broker, the broker's clients.

Contract law, however, is not the only possible basis of liability of buyers and sellers to their brokers. Some conduct by buyers or sellers may be tortious and entitle the broker to damages, possibly even punitive or exemplary damages. The article by Professor Black cited later in this section briefly considers the noncontractual remedies that may be available to brokers from their clients.

Blank v. Borden

524 P.2d 127 (Cal. 1974)

SULLIVAN, Justice. In the instant case we confront the question whether the familiar withdrawal-from-sale provision in an exclusive-right-to-sell contract between an owner of real property and a real estate broker exacts an unlawful penalty within the meaning of sections 1670 and 1671 of the Civil Code. We conclude that it does not. . . .

On April 26, 1970, defendant Erica Borden and plaintiff Ben Blank, a real estate broker, entered into a written agreement for the purpose of securing a purchaser for defendant's weekend home in Palm Springs. The agreement, a printed form contract drafted by the California Real Estate Association, was entitled "Exclusive Authorization and Right to Sell" and by its terms granted Blank the exclusive and irrevocable right to sell the property for the seven-month period extending from the date of the agreement to November 25, 1970. It further provided that if the property were sold during the said period the agent would receive 6 percent of the selling price, and that "if said property is *withdrawn from sale,* transferred, conveyed, leased without the consent of Agent, or made unmarketable by [the owner's] voluntary act during the term hereof or any extension thereof," the agent would receive 6 percent of the "price for the property" stated elsewhere in the agreement. (Italics added.) Relevant portions of the agreement are set forth [below].

EXCLUSIVE AUTHORIZATION AND RIGHT TO SELL
California Real Estate Association
Standard Form

1. RIGHT TO SELL. I hereby employ and grant Ben Blank Company, here-in-after called "Agent," the exclusive and irrevocable right to sell or exchange [the described real property]. . . .

2. TERM. Agent's right to sell shall commence on April 26, 1970 and expire at midnight on November 25, 1970.

3. TERMS OF SALE. (a) The price for the property shall be the sum of $85,000.00. . . .

4. COMPENSATION TO AGENT. I hereby agree to compensate Agent as follows: (a) Six % of the selling price if the property is sold during the term hereof, or any extension thereof, by Agent, on the terms herein set forth or any other price and terms I may accept, or through any other person, or by me, or six % of the price shown in 3(a), if said property is withdrawn from sale, transferred, conveyed, leased without the consent of Agent, or made unmarketable by my voluntary act during the term hereof or any extension thereof. . . .

5. If action be instituted on this agreement to collect compensation or commissions, I agree to pay such sum as the Court may fix as reasonable attorney's fees. . . .

Dated April 26, 1970,   Palm Springs,
                                                                                California
x [signature]
_____

Erica Borden, Owner

12. In consideration of the execution of the foregoing, the undersigned Agent agrees to be diligent in endeavoring to obtain a purchaser.

                                                                                California

BEN BLANK COMPANY
_____

Agent

By [signature]
_____

Ben Blank

The findings of the trial court describe subsequent events in the following terms:

"5. Plaintiff at once began a diligent effort to obtain a purchaser for said property, including but not limited to the expenditures of monies for advertisements in the newspaper, but on or about June 26, 1970, while said exclusive sales contract was still in effect and while plaintiff was making a diligent effort to obtain a purchaser, defendant, without reason or justification, orally notified plaintiff that the property was no longer for sale and that he had no further right to make efforts to sell same or collect a commission, all in direct violation of said exclusive sales contract."

Determining that the foregoing constituted a withdrawal from sale within the terms of the agreement,[2] the trial court concluded that plaintiff Blank was entitled to compensation according to the agreement's provisions. Accordingly it rendered judgment in favor of plaintiff Blank in the amount of $5,100 (6 percent of $85,000) plus interest. Defendant has appealed.

At the outset we quickly dispose of two contentions relating to the substantiality of the evidence in support of the findings of the trial court which we have quoted above.

First, it is contended that there was no support for the finding that plaintiff was making a diligent effort to find a purchaser for the property when it was withdrawn

_____

2. Apparently the property had not been returned to the market or sold by the time of trial. Defendant testified that she and her husband were at that time using the house as their principal residence.

from the market; this, it is urged, resulted in a failure of consideration. . . . There is evidence in the record that plaintiff contacted several parties — members of the country club on whose golf course the property fronted as well as other persons — with respect to the property, and that he ran newspaper advertisements concerning the property during the two months which preceded defendant's withdrawal of the property. The fact that plaintiff had produced no *offers* prior to the withdrawal of the property from the market of course does not in itself compel a finding that he was not making diligent efforts to find a purchaser.

Second, it is contended that the finding concerning defendant's withdrawal of the property from the market lacks substantial support. Again, however, our examination of the record discloses ample evidence to support the finding. The withdrawal occurred in the course of an argument which took place at the property between plaintiff and defendant's then fiance, Dr. Archer Michael.[3] Defendant was also present at the time. When Dr. Michael, after making statements which might reasonably be construed as threats of physical violence, told plaintiff to take his sign off the property and leave because his services were no longer wanted, plaintiff asked defendant whether she concurred. She replied that she did, and plaintiff departed. It was only after receiving a letter from plaintiff's attorney demanding payment pursuant to the contract that she attempted to soften her position and requested that plaintiff continue his efforts to sell the property. It was wholly within the province of the trial court, as finder of fact, to determine that the withdrawal was complete and unequivocal when made and that defendant's subsequent efforts through counsel to recant were ineffective and irrelevant.

We are thus brought to the single significant issue in this case, namely, the extent of recovery to which plaintiff is entitled under the contract.

It has long been the law of this state that any right to compensation asserted by a real estate broker must be found within the four corners of his employment contract. . . . By the same token, however, "[t]he parties to a broker's contract for the sale of real property are at liberty to make the compensation depend upon any lawful conditions they see fit to place therein. [Citations.]" (Leonard v. Fallas (1959) 51 Cal. 2d 649, 652, 335 P.2d 665, 668.) In short it is the *contract* which governs the agent's compensation, and that contract is strictly enforced according to its lawful terms.

It is equally well settled in this state that a withdrawal-from-sale clause in an exclusive-right-to-sell contract is lawful and enforceable, a claim for compensation under such a clause being not a claim for damages for breach of that contract but a claim of indebtedness under its specific terms. . . .

Defendant contends, however, albeit somewhat obliquely, that such clauses should be denied enforcement as an unlawful penalty[4] under the terms of Civil Code sections 1670 and 1671. The same argument was urged upon the court in Baumgartner v. Meek, 126 Cal. App. 2d 505, 272 P.2d 552, and was rejected in the following language: "We think this contention cannot be sustained in view of the contrary holdings in the cases referred to [i.e., Kimmell v. Skelly, supra, 130 Cal. 555, 62 P. 1067; Walter v. Libby (1945) 72 Cal. App. 2d 138, 164 P.2d 21; Fleming v. Dolfin (1931) 214 Cal. 269, 4 P.2d 776; Mills v. Hunter (1951) 103 Cal. App. 2d 352,

3. Subsequent to the events here in question but prior to judgment Dr. Michael and defendant were married.
4. "The term 'penalty' has traditionally been utilized to designate, inter alia, a charge which is deemed to be void because it cannot qualify as proper liquidated damages. . . ."

229 P.2d 456]. The distinction between an action for breach of the promise by the owner not to revoke or deal through others or sell himself during the stipulated term, wherein damages are sought for such breach, and a contractual provision whereby, in consideration of the services of the broker to be and being rendered, the owner directly promises that if he sells through others or by himself or revokes he will pay a sum certain, is made clear in the cited cases, particularly in the quotations we have taken from the opinion in Kimmell v. Skelly. The action is for money owed, an action in debt, and the only breach involved is the failure to pay the promised sum." (126 Cal. App. 2d at p. 512, 272, P.2d at p. 556.)

We agree with the *Baumgartner* court that the withdrawal-from-sale clause in an exclusive-right-to-sell contract does not constitute a void penalty provision. . . .

. . . Its terms in no sense contemplate a "default" or "breach" of an obligation by the owner upon whose occurrence payment is to be made.[5] On the contrary, the clause in question presents the owner with a true option or alternative: if, during the term of an exclusive-right-to-sell contract, the owner changes his mind and decides that he does not wish to sell the subject property after all, he retains the power to terminate the agent's otherwise exclusive right through the payment of a sum certain set forth in the contract.

We do not see in this arrangement the invidious qualities characteristic of a penalty or forfeiture. As indicated above, what distinguishes the instant case from other situations in which a form of alternative performance is used to mask what is in reality a penalty or forfeiture is the element of rational choice. . . .

In the instant case . . . the contract clearly reserves to the owner the power to make a realistic and rational choice in the future with respect to the subject matter of the contract. Rather than allowing the broker to proceed with his efforts to sell the property, the owner, in the event that at any time during the term of the contract he changes his mind and decides not to sell after all, may withdraw the property from the market upon payment of a sum certain. In these circumstances the contract is truly one which contemplates alternative performance, not one in which the formal alternative conceals a penalty for failure to perform the main promise.[7]

Further considerations support our determination that the contractual provision here at issue should be enforced according to its terms. First, it is important to

5. Although the trial court's findings of fact and conclusions of law speak in terms of "breach" of the exclusive-right-to-sell contract, the judgment must be sustained if correct. "No rule of decision is better or more firmly established by authority, nor one resting upon a sounder basis of reason and propriety, than that a ruling or decision, itself correct in law, will not be disturbed on appeal merely because given for a wrong reason. . . ."

7. The distinction we make here is discussed by McCormick in the following terms: "[I]n . . . an alternative contract the promise to pay may be a penalty, and void as such. If a contract provides that A will either convey land then worth about $10,000 within six months at a price of $10,000 or will pay $250, it is quite clear that a reasonable man might look forward to either choice as a reasonable possibility and there is no reason for hesitating to enforce the promise to pay if the land is not conveyed. If, on the other hand, A's promise provides that he shall either pay $100 on January 1st or $200 on demand thereafter, a different situation is presented. No reasonable man would, when the contract was made, consider that there was any rational choice involved (conceding the ability to pay either sum) in determining which course to pursue. If he can do so, he will pay the lesser sum, and the agreement necessarily is founded on this assumption, and the only purpose and effect of the formal alternative is to hold over him the larger liability as a threat to induce prompt payment of the lesser sum. Consequently, while an alternative promise to pay money when it presents a conceivable choice is valid, yet, if a contract is made by which a party engages himself either to do a certain act or to pay some amount which at the time of the contract no one would have considered an eligible alternative, the alternative promise to pay is unenforceable at a penalty." (McCormick, Damages, § 154, pp. 617-618.) (Fns. omitted.)

recognize that we are not here concerned with a situation wherein the party who seeks to enforce the clause enjoyed a vastly superior bargaining position at the time the contract was entered into. On the contrary, the contract before us was one which was freely negotiated by parties dealing at arm's length.[8] While contracts having characteristics of adhesion must be carefully scrutinized in order to insure that provisions therein which speak in terms of alternative performance but in fact exact a penalty are not enforced, . . . we believe that in circumstances such as those before us interference with party autonomy is less justified. . . .

Moreover, it must be emphasized that the basic contract before us shares with other purely "commission" contracts the quality of being essentially result-oriented. Regardless of the amount of effort expended by the broker under such a contract, he is entitled to no compensation at all unless a sale occurs. By the same token, when a sale *is* effected, the compensation received is a percentage of the sale price — and this is paid regardless of the amount of effort which has been expended by the broker. If in this context we view the owner's exercise of a withdrawal-from-sale clause as an anticipatory "breach" of the main contract, the "damage" sustained by the broker would not be measured in the amount of effort expended by him prior to the "breach" but rather would be measured in terms of the value of the lost *opportunity* to effect a sale and thereby receive compensation. . . . The determination of this value would clearly degenerate into an examination of fictional probabilities — e.g., whether the broker, if allowed to continue his efforts for the full term of the contract, would have been successful in locating a buyer and effecting a sale. This consideration further strengthens our conviction that in these circumstances the contract of the parties, entered into in a context of negotiation and at arm's length, should govern their rights and duties. . . .

For the foregoing reasons we hold that the withdrawal-from-sale clause in an exclusive-right-to-sell real estate contract, long a part of real estate marketing practice in this state and long held to be valid and enforceable according to its terms, does not exact an unlawful penalty in violation of sections 1670-1671 of the Civil Code. The judgment below, which enforced the clause before us upon a showing that the explicitly stated conditions for its enforcement were present, was fully supported by the evidence and correct in all respects.

The judgment is affirmed.

Wright, C.J., and McComb, Mosk and Clark, JJ., concur.

BURKE, Justice (dissenting). I dissent. The majority never reach the question whether the "commission-on-withdrawal" clause in the instant case was an invalid penalty clause or an enforceable liquidated damages clause. (See Civ. Code, §§ 1670, 1671.) Instead, the majority neatly sidestep this issue by labelling the brokerage contract as one contemplating an "alternative performance" by the owner in the event he exercises his "true option" to withdraw the property from sale. To the contrary, the issue in this case cannot be avoided by the facile use of labels — otherwise any illegal penalty could be disguised as a "true option by the promisor to pay a substantial sum for the privilege of breaking his contract. When we examine the essential nature of the exclusive brokerage contract, it becomes patently obvious that defendant *promised* to afford plaintiff broker the exclusive and irrevocable right to sell the property during a specified period, that defendant

8. The owner of real property has a considerable range of choice as to the type of arrangement he wishes to enter into with the broker he selects to effect the sale. (See, I Miller & Starr, Current Law of Cal. Real Estate, pp. 212-219.)

breached that promise by withdrawing the property from sale, that the contract itself specifies the *damages* for the breach, and that accordingly we must determine whether or not the damage provision was a penalty or liquidated damages provision. . . .

Nowhere in the contract is any mention made of any "option" given to defendant to withdraw the property from sale. Instead, the language of the contract makes it apparent that a withdrawal of the property without the broker's consent would constitute a breach of the owner's promise to grant an irrevocable right to sell the property during the specified period.[1] Indeed, it seems wholly naive to assume, as the majority do, that a property owner would have bargained for the "option" of withdrawing the property from sale, given the consequences of exercising that option, namely, the payment of the *full* commission which would have been payable to the broker had he sold the property for the original $85,000 asking price.

The majority suggest that defendant was given a "realistic and rational choice" under the contract to withdraw the property from sale, and that the contract was "freely negotiated" at "arm's length." Yet as the majority acknowledge in the first sentence of their opinion, the "commission-on-withdrawal" provision is a "familiar" one; in fact, the provision probably is contained in every exclusive brokerage contract in this state.[2] In other words, no "true option" or "rational choice" is involved in this case — owners seeking to sell their property under an exclusive contract have no practical alternative but to agree to the "commission-on-withdrawal" provision. . . .

The specified damages could, of course, approximate actual damages in a situation in which the broker had negotiated a sale of the property at the original asking price, for in that situation the broker's actual loss would be the commission he otherwise would have earned. But the "commission-upon-withdrawal" clause purports . . . to require payment of the full commission whether or not a sale had been arranged. In that regard, the clause seemingly could not represent a reasonable effort to estimate the fair *average* compensation as required in *Garrett*. Moreover, as indicated in prior cases, ordinary valuation of a broker's services is not so impracticable or extremely difficult as to justify use of a specified damages provision. . . .

NOTES AND QUESTIONS

1. What risks affecting brokers do withdrawal clauses in exclusive right to sell brokerage contracts seek to guard against?

2. How should brokers be compensated if property is listed with a multiple listing service under an exclusive right to sell agreement that includes a no withdrawal clause, the listing broker and several selling brokers make substantial but varying

1. The trial court found that plaintiff had made diligent efforts to sell the property and that defendant without justification withdrew the property from sale, "in direct *violation* of said exclusive sales contract." (Italics added.) Accordingly, the trial court awarded plaintiff as his "commission" the sum of $5,100, representing six percent of the proposed sales price of $85,000, "as provided for in said contract in the event of a *breach* of said exclusive sales contract. . . . As a result of the foregoing, plaintiff has been damaged in the sum of $5,100.00. . . ." (Italics added.)

2. "*The standard forms* of exclusive right to sell listings in *common use provide* . . . that the seller's withdrawal of the property from the market entitles the broker to his full commission immediately, regardless of whether he has procured a buyer before the time of the removal." (Italics added: California Real Estate Transactions [C.E.B.], § 5.18, p. 137.) As the majority herein point out, "The agreement [was] a printed form contract drafted by the California Real Estate Association. . . ." (p. 32.)

efforts to sell the property, but before any sale contract is entered into the seller withdraws the listing?

3. The principal obligation of buyers and sellers to their broker is the contractual obligation to pay the broker a commission when earned. But other legal concepts may also be relevant in some situations. Among these concepts are fraud, the duty not to unreasonably interfere with an agent's work, tortious interference with a contractual relationship, and tortious conspiracy to deprive the broker of a commission. For a discussion of these concepts, with supporting case law authority, see Black, Client Liability to Real Estate Brokers: From Contract to Punitive Damages, 25 Real Estate L.J. 78 (1996).

Dworak v. Michals

320 N.W.2d. 485 (Neb. 1982)

BUCKLEY, District Judge. This is an action brought by plaintiff, Douglas J. Dworak, a licensed real estate broker, against defendants, F. R. Michals, Sr., and Nebraska Real Estate Corporation, for the sum of $5,376, the same representing the amount of commission plaintiff claimed he was entitled to for having produced ready, willing, and able buyers to purchase an apartment complex owned by Michals and listed for sale with defendant Nebraska Real Estate Corporation, of which he was president.

The action was tried to the court, which determined the plaintiff was not entitled to a commission but was entitled to $250, which was one-half of the earnest money deposit, and entered judgment for that amount against both defendants. From this judgment plaintiff appeals.

The material facts are not disputed. The listing contract between Michals and Nebraska Real Estate Corporation was executed on April 6, 1977. It provided for a 6 percent commission in the event a purchaser was found "who is ready, willing and able to purchase the property before the expiration of this listing." It was a Multiple Listing Service contract, which meant that the listing was promulgated to all member realtors of the Multiple Listing Service in the Lincoln, Nebraska, area. This was accomplished by distribution of a Multiple Listing "sheet" or "ticket" which contained a photograph of the building and information concerning the property, which included an "income estimate" and "expense estimate." The income estimate specified 12 five-room apartments at $215 per month rent and 10 garages renting for $15 monthly.

Plaintiff, at that time a self-employed realtor and a member of the Lincoln Multiple Listing Service, received the listing on April 12, 1977. He contacted Michael Johanns and A. J. Swanson, whom he knew were interested in buying an apartment building for investment purposes. He gave them a copy of the listing sheet and took them through the property. Johanns and Swanson used the income and expense information on the listing sheet to calculate the cash flow, i.e., whether or not the rental income would be sufficient to cover all expenses, including the projected mortgage payment. They relied on the information on the listing sheet in making their cash flow calculations, which they determined would meet their requirements.

They then submitted an offer to purchase the property for $256,000 on April 14, 1977, which offer was accepted by Michals on the same day. The offer was accompanied by a $500 deposit, which was held by defendant Nebraska Real Estate Corporation.

While the buyers were in the process of securing a mortgage loan, the appraiser for the mortgage lender called Johanns on May 3 and told him that while he was at the property many tenants expressed extreme concern over the increase in rents planned for June 1, and that many of them threatened to move. Johanns relayed this to Swanson. Since both buyers were totally unaware of any planned increase in rents, Swanson immediately called Michals, who admitted that at about the same time the property was listed for sale the tenants were sent notices of an increase in rent, averaging about $15 per unit, effective June 1. He also admitted that the rents as shown on the listing sheet were not the rents currently in effect but in fact were the rents to be charged on June 1. When Swanson demanded that some form of action be taken over the situation, Michals immediately agreed to release the buyers from the purchase contract, which they elected to do, and the release was executed on the following day, with the $500 deposit returned to the buyers. The plaintiff Dworak first learned of the release later and, after his demand for a commission was refused, brought this suit.

The parties agree that if plaintiff is entitled to a commission it would be in the sum of $5,376, which is 2.1 percent of the sales price and his share as a nonlisting broker of the total commission due. Plaintiff contends he is entitled to the commission because he produced buyers who were ready, willing, and able to purchase the property when the contract to purchase was signed, notwithstanding that the sale was never closed. Defendants contend that plaintiff's commission would not be earned until the sale is consummated, unless the failure to consummate is the fault of the seller. They then contend that in fact the sale did not close because the buyers became unwilling and backed out of the agreement.

As to the applicable law, the defendants are correct. In the case of Cornett v. Nathan, 196 Neb. 277, 242 N.W.2d 855 (1976), we analyzed the law in this area. First, we noted that "[t]his court has consistently held that a broker has not earned his commission unless he produces a buyer who is ready, able, and willing to buy on terms satisfactory to the seller." Id. at 279, 242 N.W.2d at 857. In Wisnieski v. Coufal, 188 Neb. 200, 204, 195 N.W.2d 750, 753 (1972), we said: "A broker earns his commission and becomes entitled thereto when he produces a purchaser who is ready, able, and willing to purchase at a price and upon terms specified by the principal or satisfactory to him." In Huston Co. v. Mooney, 190 Neb. 242, 245, 207 N.W.2d 525, 527 (1973), this court said: "Ordinarily a real estate broker, who for a commission undertakes to sell land on certain terms and within a specified period, is not entitled to compensation for his services unless he produces a purchaser within the time limited who is ready, able, and willing to buy upon the terms prescribed."

In *Cornett*, however, the buyer was financially unable to consummate the sale. It is not clear whether this condition existed when he signed the agreement to purchase. We recognized that the intent of the parties in the usual listing agreement is that the seller expects to pay a commission only if the sale is completed, because, in most cases, the only source capable of paying the commission is the proceeds from the sale of the property. We further recognized that the reason for the payment of substantial commission fees is the requirement placed upon the real estate broker that he produce not just a person who will sign an agreement to purchase on hopes and expectation, but one who is ready, willing, and able to pay.

We then went on in *Cornett* to disapprove any notion that the commission is earned as soon as the seller accepts an offer to purchase, noting that to do this would place an unreasonable and unrealistic burden on the seller to determine the buyer's readiness, willingness, and ability to complete the purchase at the time the offer to purchase is made. Rather, we placed this burden and the risk involved on the broker, since this would be his most important function in earning his commission.

We then concluded in *Cornett* that where the buyer is financially unable to close the sale, the broker has not earned his commission. In support of this conclusion, we cited the following language from Ellsworth Dobbs, Inc. v. Johnson, 50 N.J. 528, 551, 236 A.2d 843, 855 (1967): "When a broker is engaged by an owner of property to find a purchaser for it, the broker earns his commission when (a) he produces a purchaser ready, willing and able to buy on the terms fixed by the owner, (b) the purchaser enters into a binding contract with the owner to do so, and (c) the purchaser completes the transaction by closing the title in accordance with the provisions of the contract." This three-part test, as generally stated, would apply to the unwilling as well as the financially unable buyer. Since the rationale previously stated for requiring consummation of the sale for the broker to earn the commission would be just as applicable to the buyer who becomes unwilling as it would to the buyer who becomes unable, we adopt the three-part test set out in *Ellsworth Dobbs* as the general rule to determine when a real estate broker earns his commission.

The adoption of this rule, however, does not alter the obligation of the seller to pay a commission if the sale is not completed due to the fault or refusal of the seller. We have always held that, in such event, the broker has a right to the commission called for. See, Jones v. Stevens, 36 Neb. 849, 55 N.W. 251 (1893); Howell v. North, 93 Neb. 505, 140 N.W. 779 (1913); Lincoln Realty Co. v. Garden City Land & Immigration Co., 94 Neb. 346, 143 N.W. 230 (1913); Wisnieski v. Coufal, supra. This is also recognized in Ellsworth Dobbs, Inc. v. Johnson, supra, where the court, after setting out the three-part test, went on to say: "If the contract is not consummated because of lack of financial ability of the buyer to perform or because of any other default of his . . . there is no right to commission against the seller. On the other hand, if the failure of completion of the contract results from a wrongful act or interference of the seller, the broker's claim is valid and must be paid. In short, *in the absence of default by the seller,* the broker's right to commission against the seller comes into existence only when his buyer performs in accordance with the contract of sale." (Emphasis supplied.) Id. at 551, 236 A.2d at 855.

This case, then, turns on the question of whether the buyers Johanns and Swanson had a legal right to refuse to go further with the sale. If not, they become unwilling buyers and plaintiff is not entitled to a commission. If they did, the failure to close the sale is attributable to Michals and plaintiff has earned his commission.

The trial court found that the buyers backed out of a valid purchase contract. We feel the evidence is insufficient to support that finding. The decision of Johanns and Swanson not to complete the sale was based on the representation of the rents on the listing sheet and their discovery that those rents were not the current rents but new rent increases effective almost immediately after they would become the new landlord. They faced the risk of tenants leaving, with resultant vacant units and an insufficient cash flow, the very thing they relied on in their purchase offer.

It would also lock them in from June 1 as to future rent adjustments. And, as Johanns put it, "there was a general pervasive fear of whether I could trust this seller."

The buyers could have defended an action by Michals for specific performance on the ground of misrepresentation. The facts support the essential elements, namely, a representation as a statement of fact, untrue when made, known to be untrue by the maker, with the intention that it be acted upon, and acted upon with resulting detriment. Moser v. Jeffrey, 194 Neb. 132, 231 N.W.2d 106 (1975); Buhrman v. International Harvester Co., 181 Neb. 633, 150 N.W.2d 220 (1967).

Defendants argue that the buyers were not entitled to rely on the rents shown on the listing sheet because the listing contract states: "MULTI-DWELLING LISTING. This information, although believed to be accurate, is not guaranteed." This statement does not appear on the listing sheet given to the buyers and containing the information the buyers relied on. There is no evidence that "this information" includes the statements on the listing sheet, but even if it did, neither plaintiff nor the buyers ever saw the listing contract between the defendants or otherwise were aware of it.

Defendants produced a Lincoln real estate broker who gave an expert opinion that it would be proper to list rents on the listing ticket in April that would not be effective until June, even though no notation such as "effective June 1" was made on the ticket. The expert further testified that the information is not adequate to form the basis of a purchase. But even if the listing sheet was acceptable by real estate standards, or more information is needed by the buyer, this does not alter the fact that the representations as to rents currently in effect were made and, considering the obvious purpose of the information on the sheet is to give a prospective buyer more knowledge about the property, including its investment potential, that the seller knows and intends that this information is likely to be disseminated to the prospective buyer.

It is, of course, the rule that the finding of the trial court in a jury-waived law action will not be disturbed on appeal unless clearly wrong. Henkle & Joyce Hardware Co. v. Maco, Inc., 195 Neb. 565, 239 N.W.2d 772 (1976). Here, there is no evidence in conflict which is relevant to the determination of the right of the buyers to refuse to consummate the sale. It becomes a matter of law and we find that the buyers did have a lawful right to decide not to complete the purchase and that, therefore, the failure to complete the contract to sell is attributable to the conduct of Michals, which therefore entitles the plaintiff to his commission.

Plaintiff's entitlement to the commission is from the seller Michals, but not from defendant Nebraska Real Estate Corporation. The Multiple Listing Service contract obligates the parties to pay 2.1 percent of the sales price, or 35 percent of the 6 percent total commission, to a member broker, such as plaintiff, who procures the buyer. The plaintiff, then, is a third-party beneficiary of the listing contract. The beneficiaries of a contract may recover thereon, though not named as parties, when it appears by express stipulation, or by reasonable intendment, that the rights and interests of such beneficiaries were contemplated and being provided for therein. Fowler v. Doran, 123 Neb. 37, 241 N.W. 759 (1932). Since defendant Nebraska Real Estate Corporation did not receive the commission, the plaintiff's right to recover the commission due him is against defendant Michals.

The judgment of the District Court is reversed and the cause remanded with directions to enter judgment for the plaintiff against defendant Michals in the sum of $5,376 plus interest from May 15, 1977, that being the date of the scheduled closing of the sale, and to dismiss the action as to defendant Nebraska Real Estate Corporation.

Reversed and remanded with directions.

NOTES AND QUESTIONS

1. It is often declared to be the prevailing American position that absent a contract between broker and seller expressly to the contrary, the broker who produces a buyer ready, able, and willing to buy on the seller's terms is entitled to a commission. Movement away from this position is apparent, with a growing number of courts approving the three-part test set forth in the New Jersey case of Ellsworth Dobbs, Inc. v. Johnson and discussed in Dworak v. Michals. The *Dobbs* test is protective of the seller and places added risks on the broker, including no commission if the buyer changes his or her mind after expressing willingness to buy on the seller's terms.

Which is preferable: the prevailing American position or the *Dobbs* test? Should most residential sellers' lack of familiarity with brokers' practices and laws governing brokerage agreements and real estate transactions be a significant consideration in determining which of the above is preferable?

2. In a jurisdiction in which the broker is entitled to a commission by procuring a purchaser ready, willing, and able to purchase but without a closing having occurred, it has frequently been held that if the purchaser is financially unable to purchase, the broker has not procured an "able" purchaser and is not entitled to a commission. What this means is that to assure that brokers will have earned their commissions they should make advance credit checks of their prospective buyers. But should such credit check burdens be placed on brokers or should the buyers' financial capability of performing be a risk placed on sellers? On the "able" purchaser problem in real estate broker commission cases see Burke, Law of Real Estate Brokers, § 3.2.2 (1992 & Ann. Supps.).

3. The seller, as principal, owes an obligation of good faith to the broker, and whether or not there is an extension agreement, the seller may not terminate the brokerage contract or wait out its termination for the purpose of avoiding payment of the broker's commission and after termination sell to a buyer introduced by the broker. Moshovitis v. The Bank Companies, 694 A.2d 64 (D.C. 1997); Snyder v. Schram, 547 P.2d 102 (Or. 1976). See also Werner v. Katal Country Club, 650 N.Y.S.2d 866 (1996), in which the court said: " . . . a broker is entitled to recover a commission where the owner terminates his or her activities in bad faith and as a mere device to escape the payment of the commission."

4. Death of an owner who has listed property for sale with a broker ordinarily terminates the agreement, irrespective of any stated termination date in the agreement between owner and broker. This is consistent with the common agency rule that the agency relationship terminates at the death of the principal. However, the agency relationship may be extended beyond the death of the listing owner by expressly so providing, as by a clause stating: "Above contract binding on heirs and assigns." Wilbur Smith and Associates v. National Bank of South Carolina, 274 S.C. 296, 263 S.E.2d 643 (1980).

D. THE ROLE OF THE LAWYER

Real estate transactions, including representation of buyers and sellers, historically have been a major source of lawyers' work and continue so today. However, due to enhanced competition from nonlawyers, in many communities nonlawyers have largely displaced lawyers in providing legal services for the sale, rental, or mortgaging of single-family residential real estate. Much of this competition has come from other service occupations, particularly real estate brokers, but lawyers have also been displaced by an increase in parties to single-family residential transactions acting pro se and providing such services for themselves. The previously considered *Opinion 26* case and the notes following that case consider the unauthorized practice limitations on nonlawyers providing legal services in real estate transactions. In many states such limitations have become less restrictive over time. It also should be emphasized here that in many states enforcement of these unauthorized practice limitations has been very lax and violations by nonlawyers are common.

In commercial real estate transactions lawyer competition from nonlawyers has been much less extensive than in single-family residential transactions. This competitive disparity, the reasons for it, and the likely future for lawyers in residential and commercial real estate transactions are considered hereafter by Barry Hawkins, a highly respected Connecticut lawyer, whose practice is concentrated in commercial real estate transactions.

The excerpt from the ABA Special Committee report that follows describes the steps needed to consummate a routine home purchase and sale financed by a mortgage. Similar procedures are commonly involved in transfers of nonresidential properties, although added steps frequently may be taken in connection with sales of some kinds of nonresidential land parcels. The ABA report is a position paper on the need for lawyers in residential real estate transactions, as viewed by the practicing bar, and is a response to criticism of the amount of lawyers' fees as an item in overall land sale costs. Although published some years ago, the procedures described in the ABA report are still commonly followed in most residential and nonresidential real estate transactions in the United States.

American Bar Association, Special Committee on Residential Real Estate Transactions, Residential Real Estate Transactions: The Lawyer's Proper Role

14 Real Prop. Prob. and Tr. J. 581, 585–590 (1979)

THE BROKERAGE CONTRACT

Initially a seller will enter into a brokerage contract with a real estate agent. In many jurisdictions this contract is not required to be in writing with all of the usual dangers of unwritten contracts. A special peril faced by sellers who have not had the advantage of legal counsel is that they may employ more than one broker and, in the absence of a clear understanding concerning the conditions under which the brokerage fee is earned, the seller may become liable to pay more than one fee.

In practice, a high percentage of brokerage contracts are in writing. A common assumption is that the contract is simple and standardized. In fact, a properly drawn contract will anticipate a number of legal problems of some complexity, such as the right of the seller to negotiate on the seller's own behalf, the effect of multiple listings, the disposition of earnest money if the buyer defaults, the rights of the broker if the seller is unable to proffer a marketable title, the duration of any exclusive listing and, as already brought out, the point at which the brokerage fee is earned. Most of the terms are negotiable and, in theory, a new contract should be drawn each time a broker is employed.

Standardized forms, where carefully drawn, have certain advantages. There are no objections to form contracts per se, as used by either brokers or other participants in the land transfer transaction. The objections to form contracts are that they may be inappropriate to the particular transaction, badly drawn initially or incorrectly filled in.

Any seller signing such a contract should have it approved by the seller's lawyer before signing. The seller should have the lawyer explain its meaning and be on hand to see that it is properly executed. (It is presumed that if the seller consults a lawyer, the lawyer will advise against entering into any oral agreement.) In other words, the seller needs the traditional legal services embraced in the expression "advice, representation and drafting." The broker needs similar services at one time or another and receives them from the broker's own lawyer as needed. In routine transactions the broker is sufficiently familiar with the details to be able to handle the matter without resort to professional assistance.

The Preliminary Negotiations

When the broker has found a potential buyer, negotiations between the buyer and the seller will begin, with the broker acting in the role of intermediary. In some cases the seller will leave to the broker all the work of negotiation and will merely ratify the agreement reached with the buyer.

It is generally thought that neither the buyer nor the seller needs a lawyer in the course of the negotiations. In theory this assumption is correct because neither party is bound until a written sales contract is signed. In fact, a great deal of trouble can be avoided if both the buyer and the seller consult their own lawyers during the course of the negotiations. If they are to make a proper bargain, they must know what to bargain about.

Aside from the question of price, which seems paramount in the minds of both parties, they should consider such problems as the mode of paying the purchase price and the tax consequences resulting therefrom, the status of various articles as fixtures or personal property, the time set for occupancy and the effect of loss by casualty pending the closing.

They can make whatever agreement they want, but they should anticipate all important questions and be certain a complete understanding has been reached. Failure to do so in the preliminary negotiations may mean, at the time for signing a contract, that they will have to start negotiations all over again. Worse, they may enter into a contract highly disadvantageous to one or the other, so uncertain as to require litigation to determine its meaning, or so ambiguous as to be void for indefiniteness.

The Commitment for Financing

Before entering into a sales contract, it would be desirable for the buyer to obtain as much of a commitment as possible for necessary financing.

Many lenders, however, refuse to make the necessary inspections, appraisals and credit investigations to make such a commitment until the buyer can exhibit a signed purchase and sale agreement, and many buyers are reluctant to risk losing the property to a higher offer by deferring the execution of the purchase and sale agreement. All of this leads to the common practice of including in the agreement a "subject to financing" clause which should be examined by the lawyers for the parties before the contract is signed.

Finding a willing lender is not part of a lawyer's professional duties. In practice a lawyer, being a person of affairs, may be able to render this service. Legal expertise is exercised when the lawyer advises the buyer about problems the buyer should anticipate in coming to terms with the lender. By way of illustration, the buyer will seldom have any understanding of the potential effect of an acceleration clause. The buyer should know what the legal and practical consequences of such a clause will be. The buyer should also obtain an estimate of the closing costs that will have to be paid and should obtain legal advice as to all items found in the estimate.

The commitment contract between the lender and buyer will normally be prepared by the lender's lawyer. Before it is accepted, the buyer's lawyer should ascertain that it properly anticipates all important contingencies, comports with the oral agreement previously reached and binds the lender.

Normally the lender has much greater financial expertise than the buyer. This advantage may not have been of as much importance formerly as it is today, because the financing of homes has in many instances become extremely complex. For this reason, when dealing with the lender the buyer is in need of legal assistance.

THE CONTRACT OF SALE

Once an informal agreement has been reached, the buyer and the seller will enter into a formal contract of sale. The importance of this document cannot be overemphasized. Once it is signed, the rights and obligations of the parties are fixed. Each transaction is unique and, in theory, a contract should be specially drafted for each.

The interested parties are the broker, the buyer and the seller. The contract should contain an appropriate provision with regard to the broker's commission. The buyer and the seller want assurance that the writing reflects their understanding. If they have not received legal advice during the preliminary negotiations, they will need to know what questions should have been anticipated and whether firm and advantageous provisions are found in the document. When the instrument is executed, their lawyers should be present to assure that the proper formalities are observed to make it binding. Here again the parties need legal services in the form of drafting, advice, and representation.

This need is not avoided by the use of forms. Even if the form is properly drawn, the printed portion may not adequately express the particular agreement made between the parties, or the words used in filling in blanks may distort its effectiveness. As a matter of practice standardized forms are widely used, and it is recognized that this practice likely will continue. It is recommended that local bar associations draft standard forms of sales agreements, and that joint seminars with real estate brokers and others regarding residential real estate transactions be held regularly. Whenever forms are used, any insertion should be carefully checked by the buyer's and seller's lawyers, and the appropriateness of the form for the particular transaction should be determined by the buyer's and seller's lawyers. The buyer and the seller are often unaware of what the contract means, what they should anticipate, and what steps are needed to make the instrument binding. They should be advised by their own legal counsel.

Prior to the time the contract is signed, the buyer and the seller should have detailed advice about many legal aspects of the transaction. For example, they may not be aware of the need to anticipate the question of who bears the loss or damage to, or destruction of, buildings on the premises between the time the contract is signed and the time of closing. They also may be unaware of the existence of such problems as whether the contract so changes the interest of the seller as to affect insurance policies; whether either the buyer or seller, or both, should execute new wills; whether federal and state gift and death tax matters are involved; whether joint tenancies or tenancies by the entireties will be affected; and the like.

DETERMINING THE STATUS OF THE TITLE

After the contract of sale is executed, the state of the seller's title must be determined to the satisfaction of both the buyer and the lender. This is generally the most important legal work connected with the transaction. The initial examination will be made by the lawyer for the buyer, the seller, the lender, or the title insurer, relying upon the official land title records or an abstract thereof, or a title plant maintained by a title insurance company. Where a lawyer's certificate is relied upon, either the lender or the buyer, or both, may desire additional protection in the form of a title insurance policy.

Whoever makes the title examination, the buyer's lawyer should inform the buyer of the limitations, if any, which impair the title. The buyer should also receive formal protection by a written opinion from the lawyer, an owner's title insurance policy, or both. If the buyer applies for title insurance, the buyer's lawyer should negotiate the provisions to be included or excluded from the policy. The lawyer should also make clear to the buyer what the policy means. In particular, the exceptions to coverage contained in the policy should be explained.

The use of standardized exceptions is common to title insurance. They are complex and restrictive and are frequently not understood by the layman.

Each title insurance policy is unique in that it may contain exceptions peculiar to that individual title. The buyer must first be made aware of the existence of these exceptions and must then be made to understand them. If the exception is to a $10,000 mortgage and the buyer sees the provision, the buyer will probably not mistake its meaning. But if the exception is to "all of the conditions and restrictions found in deed of X to Y, recorded in the office of the clerk of the court of Z County, in Deed Book 309 at page 873," the buyer will not, in the first place, realize that the exception is important, or, if the buyer does, will not understand its meaning without assistance from the lawyer.

THE SURVEY

Survey problems arise in many transactions, and the lawyers for all parties should inform their clients of such problems. At some time prior to the approval of title the buyer, the lender, or the title insurance company may demand a survey. The primary purpose of the survey will be to find whether the legal description of the land conforms to the lines laid down on the ground. An additional purpose may be to determine whether structures on the premises violate restrictive covenants or zoning ordinances or constitute an encroachment. When the survey has been completed, the parties should have their lawyers advise them about any legal implications of the surveyor's findings and the scope and extent of the surveyor's certification.

CURATIVE ACTION

In some cases curative action is needed to make titles marketable. Any such curative action should be carried out by a lawyer for the seller, the buyer, or the lender. If the curative action is carried out by the lawyer for the seller, it should be checked for sufficiency by the lawyers for the buyer and lender; if by the lawyer for the buyer, by the lawyer for the lender; and if by the lawyer for the lender, by the lawyer for the buyer.

* * * *

DRAFTING INSTRUMENTS

Before closing, a lawyer should draft the deed, mortgage and the bond or note secured by the mortgage. As a matter of convenience these papers are commonly drafted by the mortgagee's attorney, although the representative of either of the other parties is equally qualified. Whoever does the work, the product should be examined by lawyers for each of the other two parties and the title insurance company, and they should be advised whether the instruments are effective and create the interests intended.

The drafting of these instruments is sometimes considered merely routine work. This is not true. For example, the description of the parties must be so phrased as to prevent confusion, and the description of the land must be complete and accurate. The importance of the form of warranties is often overlooked. By way of illustration, if the title is encumbered by equitable covenants or utility easements, either or both may be acceptable to the buyer and lender, but they should be excepted from the warranty.

How title is to be taken should have been provided in the initial contract between the buyer and the seller, and the buyer should be advised as to the tax and other effects of the manner in which title is taken.

Of equal importance are other special agreements reached earlier in the transaction. The controlling law may provide that the deed supersedes prior understandings so that if they are not embraced in the deed they are nullified. Each deed must therefore be examined to determine whether it carries out what has been agreed upon.

* * * *

OBTAINING TITLE INSURANCE

Where a title insurance policy for the buyer is based on the certificate of a lawyer not employed by a title insurance company, the lawyer may make an application for the initial binder and, after closing, send in a final certificate and procure a policy. This is work for which the lawyer normally, and properly, should be paid by the client to the extent the lawyer is not paid for these services as the agent of the title company.

The lawyer should not accept compensation from a title insurance company solely for referring business to that company. This is, of course, clearly improper and contrary to the recorded position of the American Bar Association. The Real Estate Settlement Procedures Act specifically prohibits the acceptance of any "kickbacks" from the title insurance company.

CLOSING

A closing statement is generally prepared prior to final closing. The statement may take various forms and is designed to indicate the allocation of debits and credits to the various parties. In some cases it is prepared by a layman, in others by a lawyer. The buyer's and seller's lawyers should make certain their clients understand the nature and amount of all closing costs. The American Bar Association supported the adoption of legislation requiring a uniform closing statement in all government-related mortgage transactions. In addition it is recommended that local bar associations draft uniform closing statement forms for use in all other real estate transactions. Even a standard closing form in itself is not sufficient, unless the parties are assured by their own lawyers of the appropriateness of each item.

Unless there is an escrow closing, a further check of title should be made immediately prior to closing. If this check is not made, it is possible that the parties will be unaware that the title has been impaired between the time of the original examination and the closing date. This further check will generally be carried out by the lawyer, abstracter or title insurance company certifying or insuring title.

The closing is the proceeding at which the parties exchange executed instruments, make required payments, and conclude the formal aspects of the transaction. At this point the buyer, the seller, and the lender should be represented by their own lawyers. They require advice and may need representation if a disagreement arises. They should be assured that the legal documents they exchange create the interests intended, that they receive the protection to which they are entitled and that correct payments have been made to those entitled to receive them.

As a part of the closing, arrangements must be made for insurance, taxes, and other incidents of ownership. Instruments must be recorded and a final check of title made. Disbursements must be made and documents distributed to the parties entitled to receive them. Title insurance policies, where called for, must be procured. If a lawyer handles the closing, the lawyer will attend to all or virtually all of these details.

Symposium on the Future of the Legal Profession, Comments of Barry Hawkins[*] on the Future of the Legal Profession in Connecticut

24 Quinnipiac L. Rev. 597 (2006)

There are two separate segments of real estate law practice: residential and commercial. Many lawyers, whose practices concentrate on real estate, practice in only one of these two segments. Residential real estate law practice is increasingly commodity driven, with transactions that are repetitive in nature, using standardized procedures

* Barry Hawkins is a partner in the Stamford, Connecticut, office of a major Connecticut law firm.

and standardized documents. In this type of practice, competition from nonlawyers is intense, with lenders, title companies, and brokers performing much or all of the legal work in a large percentage of residential real estate transactions. The result of this competition is that lawyers have largely disappeared from representing clients in residential real estate transactions in some Connecticut communities, and they are likely to largely disappear from this segment of the practice throughout the state in the future. The only way lawyers can retain this work is by developing high volume operations, with most of the work being done by paralegals. Lawyers, of course, will retain some work related to residential real estate in representing plaintiffs or defendants in claims against nonlawyers for the nonlawyers' alleged negligence or other misconduct when performing legal services in some residential real estate transactions.

My practice is concentrated in commercial real estate, the segment far less vulnerable to competition from nonlawyers than the residential segment. One reason for this lesser vulnerability is that commercial real estate transactions commonly are quite complex, frequently involving a number of different fields of law. This complexity helps in making commercial real estate attractive to lawyers and discouraging to nonlawyers. Among anticipated changes in the Connecticut commercial real estate market that will enhance the volume of lawyer work in this field is the increase in redevelopment of existing built-up urban areas, with many new or extensively remodeled commercial structures replacing structures that were there before. Although residential real estate law practice will no doubt dwindle still further, commercial real estate law practice seems destined to expand.

QUESTIONS

What Hawkins describes as occurring in Connecticut also is occurring in most other states. In your opinion, what can law firms and the organized bar do to enable law firms to retake their lost share of the legal services market for residential real estate transactions? One option obviously is exerting pressure for stricter unauthorized practice laws that will more extensively and unequivocally exclude brokers and other nonlawyer firms from providing legal services in residential real estate conveyancing or mortgaging transactions. Another option is to try to achieve more rigorous enforcement of existing unauthorized practice laws that prohibit nonlawyers from providing legal services in real estate conveyancing or mortgaging transactions. Still another option is for law firms to more aggressively compete with nonlawyers for legal services work in the residential land transactions market by increased efficiency, enhanced volume of such work per law firm, much lower fee charges to clients, and much more extensive advertising and other marketing efforts. But are any of these options realistic and what prospects are there that relevant sectors of the legal profession will aggressively attempt any of them or be successful in recapturing a large share of the residential land transactions legal services market if they do so? What is your opinion?

THE NEGOTIATION ROLE OF LAWYERS

Negotiation is an important skill in most all types of law practice, most particularly in practices specializing in real estate transactions. Many lawyers are poor negotiators and many law students show early signs of becoming poor negotiators. Some students, for example, are overly aggressive, some are too meek, and many are frequently ill-prepared on the facts and the law on matters under consideration. Every law student should give thought to how he or she intends to deal with this important aspect of law practice and should consciously seek to develop an effective emotional, tactical, and intellectual approach to this aspect of lawyers' work, an approach also suited to the particular student's personality. The Goldstein and Weber article could prove helpful in this endeavor. The article is based on the practical experience of the authors, highly successful lawyers in New York City. The authors' observations obviously are applicable not only to negotiation of real estate transactions but to negotiation of other kinds of transactions as well.

Charles A. Goldstein & Sarah L. Weber, The Art of Negotiating

37 N.Y.L. Sch. L. Rev. 326 (1992)

I. Introduction

Negotiating is an art. A negotiation is a planned effort to achieve something almost as elusive as beauty—mutual agreement. In a commercial context, the skilled negotiator envisions the deal as painters contemplate the images of their paintings. The final outcome of each artistic endeavor is the result of applied creativity. A painter employs brushes and paints on canvas. The negotiator's tools are speech, prose, humor, and body language, resulting in mechanically applied text on paper.

An element common to all types of art is the intellect—an ability to understand the medium and creatively to shape the form. Early in their careers, painters learn certain basic concepts relating to color, shapes, and sizes, as well as how to apply such concepts imaginatively to their work. They begin with primary colors; they learn to blend them; and they determine which combinations work best for them. Similarly, negotiators develop basic skills. They learn to refine them, and they determine how to employ them to make a deal. Note that people possess such skills at various levels and that we are speaking of art, not science. Each negotiation—like each work of art—takes on a different character. Just as each artist is influenced and inspired by events, places, people, and cultures, so is each negotiator. In this article, we identify the negotiator's basic skills, suggest how to develop them, and illustrate their application.

II. Skills of a Negotiator

A. Understand Your Client

In the United States, attorneys, as agents of their clients, generally play an important role in the negotiation of business deals. For an attorney to negotiate a deal effectively for or with a client, the attorney must understand the client's goals, requirements, and business. The attorney should comprehend the client's priorities, including the elements which the client is willing to concede and those that the client considers vital.

Your role as the attorney negotiating on behalf of your client will be easier if you have knowledgeable clients who clearly know what they want to achieve. Part of your task is to help your clients articulate, enumerate, and prioritize their objectives. In doing this, you help them and, at the same time, you prepare yourself. In the course of assisting your clients, you help them on at least five fronts: (1) you attempt to provide them with information; (2) you analyze the "legal context" of the transaction; (3) you give them the benefit of your experience in dealing with the issues at hand; (4) you help them explore their options; and (5) as devil's advocate, you challenge their assumptions and positions. It is not your business to make decisions for your client; the client, not the lawyer, "calls the shots." Your client sees the transaction in a unique light — through the client's knowledge of the facts, business sense, experience, sense of acceptable risk, and relationship with the other side. Only the client can decide whether the risks are worthwhile and acceptable. If well advised, the client will decide what is important to both sides and which points are "dealbreakers."

B.   KNOW THE LAW AND YOUR CLIENT'S FACTS

Your knowledge will have a direct impact on your negotiating abilities. Here, as elsewhere, knowledge is power. Your knowledge of statutes and of the common law is indispensable and is one of the most important contributions you will make to the negotiating process. Although it is useful to be able to write clearly, it is essential to know how your words will be interpreted by a court should a dispute arise. Your knowledge of both the law's substantive terms and the interpretation courts have given those terms directly influences your ability to draft a contract. For example, very often it is not necessary to negotiate or to draft matters clearly covered by applicable law. In New York, landlords need not "beat to death" their insistence on absolute discretion in granting or in withholding consent to assignment by their commercial tenants of a leasehold interest. It is enough to say that their consent is required. Here, the law is clear, and resources would be squandered if too much effort was expended to negotiate or to draft this point. Is a landlord, however, required to mitigate a tenant's damages if the latter defaults on the lease? Here, the law is not clear. In such a context, it is worth everyone's resources to delineate the parties' respective rights and obligations carefully. In the course of your practice, you will learn what must be said and what is better left unsaid.

Your knowledge of the *facts* of a deal is equally essential. You must know the context within which the law will apply, the way that issues will arise, and, indeed, which issues are likely to arise. Your client is not interested in academic dissertations. For example, an attorney representing a purchaser of a building should be so familiar with the building itself — through having examined it, studied inspection reports, met with management personnel, etc. — that the attorney can anticipate matters requiring representations, answers, and particular agreements.

In addition, your knowledge of your client's business goes hand-in-hand with your understanding of the facts. An attorney representing a purchaser of a building must understand what the client finds interesting and what the client expects to achieve. The attorney must know how the client intends to finance the purchase, what the client intends to do with the property, and how the client intends to make a profit. Your knowledge of your client's business will allow you to shape a deal to meet the client's needs. For example, if the purchaser plans to syndicate the deal, the transaction should have a structure, and the contract should contain certain conditions that facilitate syndication. This purchaser's attorney should also understand income-tax law, securities law, partnership law, and generally keep in mind the practical reality of the situation.

C. Reputation

Your reputation will play a role in your ability to negotiate effectively. You will become known in the legal and business communities by the way you handle a deal and by your knowledge or lack of it. You must expect to deal with some of the same people with whom you have negotiated previously or with people who have heard about you. A reputation as a strong negotiator can give you increased power before you come to the table. And once you have established a good reputation, it is important to preserve that reputation lest you dissipate one of your key assets. On the other hand, you should never underestimate your opponent, whatever his or her reputation may be. Preconceived notions about your opponent based on the opinions of others can prove very dangerous. They may lead you to fail to perceive opportunities when you can gain significant advantages in the deal, or — worse — to assume inappropriately aggressive stances, thus killing the deal.

D. Rapport

Rapport plays a role in all negotiations. Going into a negotiation, your goal should be to establish meaningful communication in an atmosphere in which people are willing to resolve differences. It is often wise to make people comfortable in discussing the issues. The nature of your relationship with your opponent will not necessarily be friendly, but it should be marked by trust and confidence. You want the other side to feel that it makes sense to pursue the deal and to work *with* you rather than *against* you.

The personality of each negotiator affects the rapport among the negotiating parties. Depending on the setting of the negotiation, the type of deal, your bargaining power, and your opponent, you may want to emphasize certain characteristics and to play down others. For example, a lender's attorney with a "stiff" attitude will not kill a mortgage deal if the borrower can only get financing from that lender. On the other hand, a borrower's attorney who seems evasive, untrustworthy, or too aggressive may find the deal evaporate in his or her hands. In addition, you may want to shift some of the burden of negotiating to your associate, depending on the circumstances and on the type of transaction. If your opponent appears inexperienced or insecure, it may be a good idea to designate someone from your side whose credentials are less obvious to negotiate with the opponent to alleviate the opponent's defensiveness. Remember, the object is not to put on a brilliant performance, but to be effective.

To some degree, all attorneys are "actors." Most attorneys have diverse experiences and have represented landlords as well as tenants, lenders as well as borrowers, and sellers as well as purchasers. As a result, they know how to argue both sides of each question. While the ability to articulate your thoughts and to persuade the other side is essential, it is perhaps more important to be able to understand your opponent's objectives and requirements. This enables you to plan your overall negotiating strategy. In addition, you should expect that at times there will be misunderstandings and difficult discussions. Charm and a sense of humor — in addition to perspective, a sense of priorities and of balance, and a thorough knowledge of the law — will help you overcome any rough spots.

One of the most important attributes a negotiator should have is the ability to bargain and to strategically compromise different points in a manner that promotes the negotiation. As discussed earlier, the more information you have, the better your ability will be to compromise strategically. Although to some extent this seems to be an innate talent, it can certainly be developed and refined through years of observing others and of experiencing your own negotiations.

E. ATTITUDE

A good reputation, experience, prestige, presumed power, knowledge, or your client's importance may cause you to "bully" or intimidate the attorney on the other side. Although many attorneys use this tactic, a common defect of this approach is that it may cause the other side to be defensive and distrustful. This approach may have an even more negative effect if the other side refuses to consider the deal because they have to negotiate with what they believe is an unreasonable attorney. In such a situation, if you are a "bully," then even if your client loves you, chances are that the client will still want to proceed with the deal and will hire a different attorney. Obviously, this is a result you will want to avoid.

To be a successful dealmaker, you should inspire people to trust you and rely upon what you say. The development of a relationship of trust requires that the documents that follow any phase of the negotiation accurately reflect the agreements that the parties have made. It is inexcusable if, for example, after months of negotiating, attorneys prepare "final" documents for execution that change, or covertly add to, the provisions that the parties have already agreed upon. If the documents must go beyond the agreement as it stands, an explanation is necessary. Otherwise, a time will come when no one will want to negotiate with you (much less have you represent them), except those you would rather not represent.

Taking advantage of mistakes made by your opponent is also a bad idea. For business people, it is often an acceptable way to get ahead. For example, your client, who is buying a building, is unlikely to tell the seller that the leasing market is better than the seller thought and that the purchase price is on the low side. Attorneys, however, are in a different position. As agents, they should not take advantage of their opponents' mistakes because they will never build the relationship of trust and confidence necessary to effect a deal. Generally, however, an attorney does not have an obligation to educate the other attorney as to the law, or to point out perceived errors of judgment. If, however, you know that the attorney said something he or she could not have meant, or failed to draft something of importance to him or her through mere inadvertence, you will do your client harm by not bringing the error to the other side's attention.

III. APPLICATION OF SKILLS

Now that we have described some of the attributes of a successful negotiator, let's go to the table and see how they are applied.

WHO WILL NEGOTIATE FOR YOUR CLIENT AND WHEN

Prior to commencing a negotiation, your client should decide who, between the two of you, will do the actual negotiating. The client may decide that he or she wants to negotiate certain points, usually only the basic business terms, in a separate meeting with the business people on the other side, and that the attorneys should negotiate all of the other points. On the other hand, the client may decide to negotiate all of the points of the deal side by side with you. The latter approach proves to be very effective after you have represented your client in several deals and have developed a style that complements the client's own. The client may also choose to take the "good guy/bad guy" approach, allowing one party to play an understanding and agreeable role and allowing the other party to play a tough and inflexible role. Sometimes this approach may be taken inadvertently because of your client's or your own personality. You should note that your opponents may take offense to this approach, rendering the "bad guy" ineffective; then again, they may not.

RHYTHM AND LENGTH

Each negotiation has a particular rhythm. It is in your favor if you can bang the drum and set the beat by which issues are raised. In most cases, it is best to start the negotiation slowly in terms of raising difficult issues, to prove to the other side that you are a reasonable person. Meaningful discussion in the initial meetings will often lead to a smooth long-term negotiation. Sometimes, however, this approach is utilized for different motives. For example, if you have never dealt with your opponent, you may choose to reserve discussion on problematic, albeit important, issues and initially raise points that can be resolved easily to build a positive relationship with your opponent. This same approach may also be taken if you have previously dealt with the other side and you know how difficult they are. If you are dealing with obstinate people and you raise the problematic issues first, the other side may leave the negotiation at your first meeting or fight you on every point. In either case, you may never have the opportunity to establish a sturdy foundation from which to continue the negotiations. . . .

    The rhythm and length of a negotiation are interconnected factors. The fear always exists that a lengthy negotiation may result in a breakdown of communication between the parties. Delays resulting from redrafting documents or in setting up meetings may have the inadvertent effect of killing a deal because the parties have too much time to think, to worry, or to find another deal. In addition, the longer it takes to close the deal, the greater the risk that unanticipated negative events will intervene. Many deals that were negotiated for months, and even years, fell apart in one day following the October 1987 market crash. An ability to proceed with due diligence, to respond rapidly, to create a sense of direction and a promise of fast agreement allows you to corner the other side and to close the doors of escape. Of course, deliberate delay when the other side is anxious is also a strategy. Delaying a negotiation can be used to your advantage if you are waiting for certain events to occur or for certain factors to reveal themselves (for example, a change in interest rates). But, in such a case, be sure you know who wants the deal the most. . . .

WHICH SIDE WILL LEAD, AND WHEN

Determining which side will lead a negotiation and set its framework may affect the control of the deal. Taking control of a negotiation may seem like a good idea because it enables you to define the issues, thus shifting the onus onto the other side to come up with counterproposals. In certain situations, however, it may actually be better for you to let the other side lead, particularly if you are ignorant of its overall position. If you hear your opponent's position first, for example, it may reveal that the other side is willing to give you more than you had anticipated. In any case, it will give you a position from which to continue the negotiations. By using this approach you may also avoid the situation in which you lead with a point that your opponent will not or is not yet ready to concede — thus risking an early killing of the deal.

Leverage is a part of all negotiations. Usually one side will have more bargaining chips than the other and will seek to take advantage of that fact. For example, if you are acting as a lender providing financing for the development of an office building when such financing is scarce, you will use that leverage to structure the deal to your advantage. Leverage also influences the rhythm of a negotiation. In the landlord–tenant scenario, if the market has an abundance of leasable space, the landlord may choose to offer the tenant a "pre-negotiated" lease. Here, the landlord is telling the tenant that it has recognized the latter's points and has accommodated the tenant on such points to the extent acceptable to the landlord. The effect of this approach is to focus the negotiations on more important issues, as well as to make the landlord appear amenable to a deal. In a market with little space, however, a landlord may choose to capitalize on the situation by offering the tenant a "take-it-or-leave-it" lease and fighting them on every point, including more-or-less inconsequential ones.

DRAFTING

Taking control of a negotiation by controlling the drafting of documents is usually advantageous. Here again, you are building a framework within which the other side must work. One advantage of drafting a document is that you will discover the issues that have not been "thought through" at the negotiating table. The result of such a process is that you can formulate positions on these aspects and put them on the table in a form you prefer. Indeed, your client may reexamine whether the client wants to do the deal at all unless certain issues can be resolved in the client's favor. Another advantage of control over the drafting is the power it gives you to influence the pace at which the deal proceeds.

On the other hand, in certain circumstances it may advance the progress of the negotiation if you allow the other side to present you with what should be a mutually acceptable document, unless you anticipate that the other side will be obstinate with respect to all or most of the issues. One of the disadvantages of drafting a document is that the language of the document is often construed against its drafter. Also, as we mentioned earlier, in certain cases you may want to find out your opponent's initial position by having the opponent draft the document.

The circumstances of a transaction frequently dictate the appropriate party to draft a document. The seller of a building, for example, possesses information relating to the building and is therefore the appropriate party to prepare the contract of sale. In addition, depending on the side of the deal that you are on, it may or may not be pivotal to control the drafting of the document. A property seller will want control over the drafting of the contract because the typical purchaser will insist on many representations and covenants concerning the property, whereas usually the purchaser's only important obligation will be to pay the purchase price.

In certain situations, the other side will attempt to wrest control of the drafting by giving you a document that they have prepared, instead of commenting on the document you have prepared. For example, in a leasing scenario the landlord's attorneys usually draft the lease. A franchise tenant that has a strong bargaining position and a legitimate need to have all of its leases on a common form for financing and operational purposes, however, is likely to prepare its own lease.

When to Postpone Deal Points and When Not To

At the negotiating table, it is best not to defer resolution of points, unless the other side has reserved decision on the same issues. Otherwise, the negotiations may go on forever. Ideally, issues raised in later negotiations should be issues that require revisitation because of agreed-upon changes in the deal, new issues that have arisen or that have taken on new importance as a result of the development of the deal, or issues that were inadvertently overlooked because they were not thought out completely. Then again, sometimes a client wants the attorney to handle the first meeting alone and to negotiate a difficult point in order to glean insight from the discussion and then reserve decision on the point. This permits the client either to negotiate beyond what the attorney negotiated or to show that the client is a true statesperson and can give up points that the attorney did not or could not.

Some people use this technique of renegotiating points to take what we call a "second bite of the apple." At the start of a negotiation, you may decide to save certain issues for discussion at later meetings for the reasons we discussed earlier. The danger inherent in the use of such a tactic is that if your opponent determines that you saved a crucial issue in bad faith, it may kill the deal, resulting in a waste of time and of money. When your opponent takes a second bite of the apple, you are likely to be annoyed; remember that when you try it. . . .

"Winning"

Who "wins" a negotiation is a question of objectives. The winner of a negotiation is the one who achieves what he or she wants from it. A truly successful negotiation is one in which all the parties are satisfied that they have achieved their important objectives. Thus, everyone can "win."

It is important to note, however, that "winning" requires you to set priorities. As in life, people do not get everything they want out of a negotiation, but you can get the combination of things that are truly important to you in the order you desire. If a deal fails, the person who had more to lose is the "loser," and if a deal succeeds, the person who needed it most is the "winner," because that person could least afford to have it fail. Although you should take pains to understand the objectives of your opponent, whether or not your opponent has achieved, or failed to achieve, *his* or *her* objectives is immaterial if you have achieved *yours*.[21] A truly successful

---

21. Winning a negotiation is not a contest of egos. The winner of a negotiation is not measured by how much one bullied the other side or proved one's intellect. For example, if you think a building is worth $1,000,000 and you negotiate to buy it for that amount, you should be satisfied, although your opponent may think the building is worth less. After all, this is the way that transactions occur—because

negotiation is one in which all the parties feel satisfied that they have achieved their important objectives.

IV. CONCLUSION

The true test of whether you, as an attorney, are a successful negotiator is whether you have the ability to effect transactions. If you are good, you will be able to effect a high percentage of your transactions. If you are *really* good, you will effect transactions that others thought could not have been done. The ability to resolve differences among the parties creatively and in a manner that advances your client's goals is the ultimate measure of your negotiating abilities.

There is no sure-fire formula to follow to be a successful negotiator. It is a combination of different factors, including luck. We have attempted to explain to you some of the skills that you, as an attorney, may want to develop. The more you read, observe, and experience, the more astute a negotiator you will become.

E. LAWYERS' DUTIES TO BUYERS, SELLERS, AND OTHER PARTIES TO REAL ESTATE TRANSACTIONS

Lawyers are subject to extensive legal restrictions and obligations in their practices, including their duties to buyers and sellers or other parties in real estate transactions. Many of these restrictions and obligations are imposed by detailed court rules on professional responsibility. In most every state the courts have adopted, with some modifications, the American Bar Association's Model Rules of Professional Conduct as the principal set of court rules governing lawyers' professional conduct.[7] The modifications from the most recent version of the ABA Model Rules of Professional Conduct differ somewhat from state to state. Of particular importance in real estate transactions are the professional conduct rules on conflict of interest and protection of client confidences, notably ABA Model Rules 1.6 through 1.13. These rules are relevant to many aspects of lawyers' real estate practice. As an example of the interpretive difficulties and underlying policy differences that can be encountered in applying these or comparable disciplinary rules, we will concentrate on one very troublesome issue: Can a lawyer concurrently represent multiple diverse interests, such as those of both buyer and seller, in a real estate transaction? The next case, In the Matter of Dolan, involves such multiple interests. Of special importance in this case was a court rule, Disciplinary Rule 5-105, a rule that was later largely replaced by ABA Model Rule 1.7. ABA Model Rule 1.7 provides as follows:

Rule 1.7 Conflict of Interest: Current Clients

(a) Except as provided in paragraph (b), a lawyer shall not represent a client if the representation involves a concurrent conflict of interest. A concurrent conflict of interest exists if:

---

one side thinks it is doing better than the other. A buyer of a building believes that if the buyer owned the building, he or she would not sell it for the price at which it was purchased; and the seller of a building may believe that if the buyer is willing to pay the price for the building, it is worthwhile for the seller to sell it.

7. 2007 American Bar Association, Model Rules of Professional Conduct.

(1) the representation of one client will be directly adverse to another client; or

(2) there is a significant risk that the representation of one or more clients will be materially limited by the lawyer's responsibilities to another client, a former client or a third person or by a personal interest of the lawyer.

(b) Notwithstanding the existence of a concurrent conflict of interest under paragraph (a), a lawyer may represent a client if:

(1) the lawyer reasonably believes that the lawyer will be able to provide competent and diligent representation to each affected client;

(2) the representation is not prohibited by law;

(3) the representation does not involve the assertion of a claim by one client against another client represented by the lawyer in the same litigation or other proceeding before a tribunal; and

(4) each affected client gives informed consent, confirmed in writing.

New Jersey has adopted Rule 1.7 with these recent changes to Rule 1.7(b):

(b) Notwithstanding the existence of a concurrent conflict of interest under paragraph (a), a lawyer may represent a client if:

(1) each affected client gives informed consent, confirmed in writing, after full disclosure and consultation, provided, however, that a public entity cannot consent to any such representation. When the lawyer represents multiple clients in a single matter, the consultation shall include an explanation of the common representation and the advantages and risks involved;

(2) the lawyer reasonably believes that the lawyer will be able to provide competent and diligent representation to each affected client;

(3) the representation is not prohibited by law; and

(4) the representation does not involve the assertion of a claim by one client against another client represented by the lawyer in the same litigation or proceeding before a tribunal.

In the Matter of Dolan

76 N.J. 1, 384 A.2d 1076 (N.J. 1978)

PER CURIAM. A complaint was filed with the Middlesex County Ethics Committee charging respondent with conflicts of interest in connection with certain real estate transactions. After receipt of the Committee's report the Court directed the Central Ethics Unit to file a petition for an Order to Show Cause, which issued in due course. That petition asserts that respondent's conduct constituted violations of DR 5-105, DR 8-101, and DR 9-101, dealing respectively with conflicts, abuse of public position, and the appearance of impropriety.

I

The public position which respondent held during the times pertinent hereto was that of municipal attorney for the Borough of Carteret, to which he was appointed at the beginning of 1971. For some time prior to the events in question the Borough had implemented a policy of urban renewal pursuant to Federal Housing Authority (FHA) procedures. By ordinance it created the Carteret Redevelopment Agency

(Agency), consisting of six members, five of whom were appointed by the municipal governing body. The Agency's function was to solicit proposals from developers for utilization of certain tracts for low and moderate income multi-family dwelling units. Gulya Brothers, Inc., a developer, submitted a proposal for a townhouse project on one of the tracts, which the Agency accepted. Thereafter, on April 5, 1971, Gulya Bros. Redevelopment Corp. (Gulya) was established for the purpose of purchasing the land from the Agency and developing it, and marketing the town-houses which it erected thereon.

Upon acceptance of Gulya's proposal the Agency was required to obtain the necessary approvals from the municipal planning board, board of adjustment and governing body. Additionally, it was obliged to convey to the developer marketable title to the tracts involved. In due course the Agency, which was represented by its own counsel, successfully processed applications before the appropriate municipal bodies, and on November 15, 1971, the Borough gave final approval to the project.

Thereafter Gulya's attorney sought financing for the project on behalf of the developer but was unsuccessful. To aid in this endeavor the developer's attorney sought out the respondent, who had "handled matters for him in the past," was "familiar with mortgage financing," and had done "some extensive real estate work." In May or June of 1972 respondent, at the instance of Gulya's attorney, discussed the project with the principals of Gulya and at that point took over the representation of the developer, with the full consent of previous counsel. Prior to this respondent had not represented Gulya in any capacity whatsoever. Specifically, he had not appeared on the developer's behalf before the Agency; neither had he represented either the planning board or board of adjustment at the time of the Agency's applications to those bodies or at any other time. Respondent was, however, attorney for the Borough when the Council acted favorably on the board of adjustment's recommendation to grant the Agency's application for the necessary variances for this project.

Respondent's efforts on Gulya's behalf produced the required financing through a New Jersey mortgage company. The financing consisted of both the construction mortgage and permanent mortgages available to the buyers of the townhouses. Respondent's representation of the developer continued throughout the initial construction stage of the project, during which time he was, as has been indicated, attorney for the municipality in which the development was located, albeit that representation of the municipality was not in any wise in connection with any business of or application on behalf of the developer.

Respondent also represented the mortgage company in sales involving perma-nent mortgages used in the purchase of townhouses from Gulya. In those same transactions he came to act as well on behalf of purchasers-mortgagors of the housing units at their closings of mortgage loan and title, under the following circumstances. In order to market the townhouses the developer engaged a real estate agent, whose function it was to attract buyers and assist those buyers in obtaining FHA approvals. It was the agent who led the buyers through whatever preliminary steps were required leading to execution of the contracts, and it was the agent who secured execution of those contracts. Respondent did not enter the picture until after the contracts had been signed by the buyer. The contract forms utilized by the agent, pursuant to these procedures, contained the following clauses:[1]

---

1. These clauses have not been directly attacked in these proceedings and we do not pass on their propriety.

> Purchaser shall be responsible for paying the closing attorneys for the mortgage (sic) their legal fee for examination of title and recording of deed and mortgage and shall also be responsible for and shall pay for survey, mortgage title insurance, hazard insurance premium, escrow funds for taxes and insurance, appraisal and inspection fees and a one percent processing fee except as may be otherwise provided herein. . . .
>
> If purchaser uses seller's attorney, the seller will pay the legal fee for title examination, recording of deed and mortgage, survey, mortgage title insurance, appraisal and inspection fees.

By virtue of the arrangement last referred to either respondent or an associate in his office attended closings not only for the seller in sixteen instances, but also for the purchasers-mortgagors in at least fourteen of those closings.[2] At these closings purchasers were notified for the first time of the potential conflicts of interest arising out of respondent's multiple representations. They were presented with and executed two separate waiver and consent forms, one acknowledging and approving respondent's representation of purchaser and seller and the other acknowledging and approving his representation of mortgagor, mortgagee, and seller.

As may be seen, then, there are two separate areas of potential conflict of interest called to our attention by the Committee report and the Central Ethics Unit's presentment.[3] The first centers about respondent's representation of the builder-developer while at the same time serving as attorney for the Borough of Carteret. The second focuses on his representation at the closing of the seller, the purchasers-mortgagors and the mortgagee under circumstances casting doubt on the informed nature of the consents given by the buyers to this multiple representation.

II

We address first the asserted conflict presented by respondent's representation of the developer while concurrently acting as borough attorney. Respondent points out that at no time did his representation of Gulya involve any dealings or transactions with the Borough. All applications to municipal boards necessary to permit the Agency to convey clear title to the developer had been completed before respondent's representation of the developer commenced. Throughout the course of negotiations with the Agency involving Borough-related matters, Gulya was represented by its own attorney who eventually called on respondent for assistance when financing loomed as an obstacle.

With all of this, however, the fact remains that respondent's conduct was directly contrary to the mandate of this Court in In re A. and B., 44 N.J. 331, 209 A.2d 101 (1965). There it was noted that while in some situations it may be proper (within the

---

2. In a letter answer to the complaint, marked in evidence at the Committee's hearing, respondent indicated that "one or two of the people did bring their own attorney to the closing."

3. A third area emerges, although it was not touched upon in the complaint, testimony, report or presentment. It is the arrangement under which respondent represented both Gulya and the mortgage company with respect to the construction mortgage — again at a time when he was municipal attorney. Much of the thrust of his opinion can be directed with equal force to that relationship even though it has not been presented to us directly.

proscription of DR 5-105) for an attorney to engage in dual representation, nevertheless

> the subject of land development is one in which the likelihood of transactions with a municipality and the room for public misunderstanding are so great that a member of the bar should not represent a developer operating in a municipality in which the member of the bar is the municipal attorney or the holder of any other municipal office of apparent influence. We all know from practical experience that the very nature of the work of the developer involves a probability of some municipal action, such as zoning applications, land subdivisions, building permits, compliance with the building code, etc.
>
> It is accordingly our view that *such dual representation is forbidden even though the attorney does not advise either the municipality or the private client with respect to matters concerning them. The fact of such dual representation itself is contrary to the public interest.* [44 N.J. at 334–35, 209 A.2d at 103 (emphasis added).]

While in a sense this rule may be deemed somewhat harsh, particularly in a situation where, as here, the representation of both municipality and developer was at no time in connection with a transaction involving both clients, we are strongly of the view that the public interest demands strict adherence to the letter of In re A. and B., supra. A municipal attorney's public obligations are such that he must take particular pains to avoid the shadow of suspicion which inevitably is cast when he begins to entangle himself in a representative capacity in the legal affairs of a developer operating within the municipality. If the municipal attorney is not a full-fledged member of the "municipal family," he is least in such a close and confidential relationship with it as to warrant his not representing those who may benefit (or, as here, have already benefitted) from successful applications by others (here, the Agency) to the planning board and zoning board of adjustment.

In this case the affirmative action of those municipal boards, while made at the Agency's behest, inured to the benefit of Gulya. Those applications were, in a very real sense, in Gulya's interest, were made at a time when respondent represented the Borough, and were then followed by respondent's representation of Gulya in connection with the same development project. This representation ignored the clear admonition of In re A. and B., supra, and hence merits our disciplinary action.

III

We turn our attention to the conflict presented by respondent's multiple representation of seller, purchaser-mortgagor, and mortgagee.[4] At the outset we recognize the emphasis that our disciplinary rules place on the desirability of completely

---

4. In an analogous context, the not uncommon practice by some lending institutions of requiring real estate mortgagors to be represented by the lender's attorney has not gone unnoticed by the Legislature. N.J.S.A. 46:10A-6 prohibits such a practice in a mortgage loan transaction where the mortgagee is a consumer. Senate Bill 35, an amendment to this statute which has passed the Senate and is now before the Assembly Banking and Insurance Committee, expands the scope of the statute to prohibit such a practice in all mortgage loan transactions, regardless of whether the mortgagee is a consumer or a commercial party.

independent counsel. Specifically, DR 5-105 prohibits multiple representation except under certain severely circumscribed circumstances.[5] See In re A. and B., supra, 44 N.J. at 335, 209 A.2d 101 (Schettino, J., concurring). The sense of our rules is that an attorney owes complete and undivided loyalty to the client who has retained him. The attorney should be able to advise the client in such a way as to protect the client's interests, utilizing his professional training, ability and judgment to the utmost. Consequently, if any conflicting interest could arise which would stand in the way of that kind of unstinting zeal, then the client must be so informed and the attorney may continue his limited representation only with the client's informed consent.

In a real estate transaction, the positions of vendor and purchaser are inherently susceptible to conflict. In re Kamp, 40 N.J. 588, 595, 194 A.2d 236 (1963). This is likewise the case with a borrower-lender relationship. Id. at 596, 194 A.2d 236. The requirements of an attorney involved in such multiple representations of purchaser, vendor and mortgagee are set out in Justice Proctor's opinion in In re Kamp, supra, where he said:

> Full disclosure requires the attorney not only to inform the prospective client of the attorney's relationship to the seller, but also to explain in detail the pitfalls that may arise in the course of the transaction which would make it desirable that the buyer have independent counsel. The full significance of the representation of conflicting interests should be disclosed to the client so that he may make an intelligent decision before giving his consent. If the attorney cannot properly represent the buyer in all aspects of the transaction because of his relationship to the seller, full disclosure requires that he inform the buyer of the limited scope of his intended representation of the buyer's interest and point out the advantages of the buyer's retaining independent counsel. A similar situation may occur, for example, when the buyer of real estate utilizes the services of the attorney who represents a party financing the transaction. To the extent that both parties seek a marketable title, there would appear to be no conflict between their interest. Nevertheless, a possible conflict may arise concerning the terms of the financing, and therefore at the time of the retainer the attorney should make clear to the buyer the potential area of conflict. In addition, if the buyer's interests are protected only to the extent that they coincide with those of the party financing the transaction, the attorney should explain the limited scope of this protection so that the buyer may act intelligently with full knowledge of the facts. [40 N.J. at 595–96, 194 A.2d 240.]

See also N.J. Advisory Committee on Professional Ethics, Opinion 51, 87 N.J.L.J. 705 (1964).

5. DR 5-105. Refusing to Accept or Continue Employment if the Interests of Another Client May Impair the Independent Professional Judgment of the Lawyer

(A) A lawyer shall decline proffered employment if the exercise of his independent professional judgment in behalf of a client will be or is likely to be adversely affected by the acceptance of the proffered employment, except to the extent permitted under DR 5-105(C).

(B) A lawyer shall not continue multiple employment if the exercise of his independent professional judgment in behalf of a client will be or is likely to be adversely affected by his representation of another client, except to the extent permitted under DR 5-105(C).

(C) In situations covered by DR 5-105(A) and (B), except as prohibited by rule, opinion, directive or statute, a lawyer may represent multiple clients if he believes that he can adequately represent the interests of each and if each consents to the representation after full disclosure of the facts and of the possible effect of such representation on the exercise of his independent professional judgment on behalf of each.

(D) If a lawyer is required to decline employment or to withdraw from employment under DR 5-105, no partner or associate of his or his firm may accept or continue such employment.

In the application of these principles to the matter before us we are mindful of the circumstances surrounding this type of transaction, namely, the purchase of low and moderate income dwellings with federally guaranteed financing, which serve to distinguish it from the conventional transfer of real estate. There is less flexibility in the terms. Federal auspices in this context brings with it a certain rigidity which leaves little room for negotiation of price and such other commonly negotiable features as limits and rates on borrowed money. The prescribed forms for bond and mortgage contain fixed terms from which variance is rarely, if ever, permitted. Nevertheless, the severely strictured nature of the relationship between mortgagor and mortgagee in no wise serves to diminish the essential obligation of full and timely disclosure. The opportunity for conflict to arise — for instance, in terms of a condition of title acceptable to one party but not the other — while perhaps remote is by no means non-existent. More apparent is the possibility that as between buyer and developer-seller there may ripen some disagreement respecting the physical condition of the premises. Without presuming to suggest an exhaustive list of potential areas of conflict, we draw attention to these as the kinds of matters of which consenting purchasers-mortgagors should be made aware before they consent to the attorney representing another party to the transaction.

Here the consent forms executed by purchasers at the eleventh hour amounted to little more than a perfunctory effort formally to comply with *Kamp's* admonition. After the respondent was retained, he had an "immediate" duty to explain to the client the nature of his relationship with the seller and inform the client of the significance of any consent that the client may have given to dual representation. In re Kamp, supra, 40 N.J. at 596, 194 A.2d 236; see In re Lanza, 65 N.J. 347, 350–51, 322 A.2d 445 (1974).

The problems that can arise from the failure to heed that instructive warning are graphically demonstrated in the matter before us. The record reveals that a purchaser objected to signing one of the consent forms after the conflict of interest situation had been explained to him (because he believed it might place him in the position of approving a conflict which was "illegal"), but ultimately he executed the form as the result of persuasion from his wife and a desire to avoid the serious disruption of his moving plans resulting from any adjourned or cancelled closing. Although we agree with the Committee's conclusion that the consent form was signed voluntarily in the literal sense that neither respondent nor the seller exerted any overt pressure on the client, nevertheless we are left with the impression, as was the Committee, that execution of the form was due more to the exigencies of the situation than to an unfettered will. And this need not and should not have been. The circumstances surrounding the execution of the consent form in this instance and in every other instance where the forms were executed in like fashion should not have been permitted to arise. The record before us reveals that respondent's office dealt with the purchasers "for several weeks before . . . the closing." Somewhere in that interval the time should have been taken and the opportunity created to explain to the purchasers the potential conflicts — the "pitfalls" — so as to allow for execution of the consent forms after due deliberation.

While the practicalities of this type of purchase may generate joint representation of low or middle income purchasers-mortgagors and their sellers and mortgagees by a single attorney, those practicalities in no sense justify any relaxation of the requirement of full, complete and timely explanation of the pitfalls and implications of such representation and the potential for conflict. Indeed, given the increased likelihood that this class of clients may be without the resources to obtain separate representation, the need for meticulous observance of the requirement of full disclosure and informed consent is underscored.

IV

While tenable arguments have been made in favor of a complete bar to any dual representation of buyer and seller in a real estate transaction, see e.g., In re Lanza, supra, 65 N.J. at 353, 322 A.2d 445 (Pashman, J., concurring); In re Rockoff, 66 N.J. 394, 397, 331 A.2d 609 (1975) (Pashman, J., concurring), on balance we decline to adopt an inflexible per se rule. Confining ourselves to the type of situation before us (assuredly there are others, entirely unrelated to financial pressures), the stark economic realities are such that were an unyielding requirement of individual representation to be declared, many prospective purchasers in marginal financial circumstances would be left without representation. That being so, the legal profession must be frank to recognize any element of economic compulsion attendant upon a client's consent to dual representation in a real estate purchase to be circumspect in avoiding any penalization or victimization of those who, by force of these economic facts of life, give such consent.

This opinion should serve as notice that henceforth where dual representation is sought to be justified on the basis of the parties' consents, this Court will not tolerate consents which are less than knowing, intelligent and voluntary. Consents must be obtained in such a way as to insure that the client has had adequate time — manifestly not provided in the matter under consideration — to reflect upon the choice, and must not be forced upon the client by the exigencies of the closing. This applies with equal force to the dual representation of mortgagor and mortgagee.

In view of respondent's impeccable record, including a history of significant public service and contributions to the legal profession, we conclude that appropriate discipline is exercised by the imposition of this public reprimand.

Pashman, J., concurring in the reprimand.[*]

For reprimand: Chief Justice Hughes, Justices Mountain, Sullivan, Pashman and Clifford and Judge Conford — 6.

Opposed: None.

PASHMAN, J., concurring and dissenting. While I applaud the Court's tightening of the rules governing multiple representation in real estate transactions by further narrowing its permissible circumstantial basis, I am afraid that its effort to provide an additional safeguard for consumers of legal services simply does not go far enough. The prophylactic rule announced herein will do little to enhance the likelihood that the quality of representation provided in such circumstances will duplicate that which would be provided by counsel with undivided loyalty. Similarly, the Court's admonition that attorneys must avoid "any penalization or victimization" of clients who, as a result of economic constraints, consent to dual representation will be far from effective to prevent the various abuses endemic in such situations.

On two previous occasions I have sought to enumerate the compelling reasons supporting adoption of a per se rule forbidding dual representation in certain

---

[*] Only as to § 11 of the majority opinion.

situations where an irreconcilable conflict of loyalty so inheres in the circumstances that adequate protection of the interests of each of the multiple clients is precluded. In re Lanza, 65 N.J. 347, 353, 322 A.2d 445 (1974) (Pashman, J., concurring); In re Rockoff, 66 N.J. 394, 397, 331 A.2d 609 (1975) (Pashman, J., concurring). I write now to reiterate my adherence to those principles and to note my continuing concern with the Court's present posture in this troublesome area of professional ethics. The result herein continues the Court's acceptance of dual representation in circumstances where, notwithstanding full disclosure and knowing consent by the derivative client,[1] the intrinsic degree of divided allegiance is so intolerable that the proscribed adverse effect on the exercise of the attorney's independent professional judgment on behalf of that client must ipso facto be conclusively presumed.[2] See D.R. 5-105(B). In so doing, the Court relies on the fiction that a lay client can effectively consent to dual representation and perpetuates the cruel myth that adequate representation can be provided in such cases by an attorney who supposedly can simultaneously protect the inevitably adverse interest of his two masters. The reality, of course, is that it is well-nigh impossible for the derivative client to be so well attuned to the numerous legal nuances of the transaction that his consent can be said to have been truly informed.[3] The propriety of according dispositive effect to consent so obtained is further undermined when it is frankly acknowledged that the consent is induced by the derivative client's reliance on a promise by the attorney which cannot be fulfilled — the promise of adequate representation of each of his two clients.

Surely the Court is not so naive as to the economic realities of such transactions as its utopian stance would indicate. Any conflicting interests which are potentially disruptive of the ultimate goal — the expeditious consummation of the sales transaction — must inevitably be resolved in favor of the primary client and for that same reason will probably not even be brought to the attention of the derivative client. This problem is even more aggravated in circumstances such as those of the instant case where the

---

1. The derivative client is the client whose representation by the attorney derives from his participation in a transaction with the party who is the primary client of the attorney. The derivative client is the client to whom disclosure is made and from whom consent to the dual representation is sought.

2. See New Jersey Supreme Court Advisory Committee on Professional Ethics, Opinion 212, 94 N.J.L.J. 553 (1971) (improper for attorney to continue to represent either party to real estate transaction after controversy has arisen between them).

3. The most frequent topics of controversy at closing are:

A) Difficulties with the quality of title deliverable by the seller.
B) Disputes over alleged structural defects.
C) Warranties.
D) Unfinished work.
E) Leaks.
F) Cellar problems.
G) Construction of roads and sidewalks in the development on schedule.
H) Drainage problems.
I) Problems as to utilities.
J) Defective masonry foundations.
K) Mortgage and tax escrows — amount and interest.
L) Escrows of a part of seller's money to assure compliance with above problems, including schedule for release of funds.
M) Appropriate remedies for compliance with any agreements concerning the above.

There are, of course, innumerable variations of such problems within the above general areas. These are in addition to the many subjects as to which intolerable conflicts of interest result if the attorney provides dual representation at the contract negotiation stage as well as at the closing of title.

primary client of the attorney is a developer with whom the attorney has a potentially long-term and profitable relationship. Consequently, the attorney has a substantial economic stake in maintaining the continued goodwill of this primary client. As our Advisory Committee on Professional Ethics has observed, in such situations.

> . . . the attorney, either consciously or unconsciously, will be influenced by a desire to maintain his economically profitable relationship with the seller. The developer has more homes to sell, hence more profitable professional employment for the attorney. The desire to maintain his relationship will make it difficult in any given case for the attorney to devote himself to the interests of a buyer with the same degree of vigor and undivided loyalty which would be the case were such desire not present. This motivation may very probably cause the attorney's representation of the buyer to be less searching, less demanding and in general less effective than would be the case were the attorney not reluctant to risk the loss of what for him has become a profitable monopoly.
>
> A second point, interrelated with the first, stems from the fact that the attorney acquires a very extensive intimate knowledge of the developer and of the tract in question as the result of the work he carries out for the owner. If the developer will not be able or willing to construct roads as rapidly as is represented, if a subcontractor is not doing his work well, if drainage problems exist and have not been solved, if there is a question as to when and how all utilities will be introduced, if, as an example only, the masonry foundations of various homes have proven defective, the attorney in each case will perforce possess this knowledge. These are only a few of the possibilities. Anyone who has had direct contact with projects of this sort will be able to add other examples from his own experience. Undertaking a dual representation, the attorney will find himself in an impossibly equivocal position. As representing the seller, he must use all reasonable and proper means to see that the proposed sale of his client's property is consummated; as representing the buyer, he has an obligation to reveal any information which would be of genuine interest or help to the buyer in determining whether to make the purchase and in protecting his rights after the contract has been signed. It is apparent that this twofold obligation cannot be met in circumstances where the attorney's knowledge embraces any fact, known to him as the result of his relationship with the seller, which, if known to the buyer, might influence him to reject the purchase or to insist upon terms or conditions less favorable to the seller.
>
> As mentioned above, there is a very definite interrelationship between these two factors the existence of which we have sought to emphasize. In general they will not be present in the ordinary isolated transaction where an attorney represents both buyer and seller. On the other hand they would seem to be endemic in the kind of situation we are considering. Accordingly, it seems clear that unless in any given case these factors for some reason fail to exist or unless their influence can be minimized to the point of complete insignificance, they constitute an *insurmountable impediment* to the kind of dual representation here being considered. [New Jersey Supreme Court Advisory Committee on Professional Ethics, Opinion 51, 87 N.J.L.J. 705 (1964); (emphasis added).]

Even assuming that dual representation in an "ordinary isolated" real estate transaction should not be per se impermissible, the practice is wholly unsupportable where the attorney involved is the representative of a developer. The attorney's economic disincentive to be vigilant in safeguarding the buyer's interests in such a case is too strong, and a per se prohibition is absolutely imperative. Dual representation in these circumstances forces the derivative client to play with a stacked deck. I cannot countenance the Court's continued tolerance of such farcical and often duplicitous behavior by some members of the legal profession. The injustice of this is heightened by the fact that it occurs in what for most consumers is the transaction of greatest personal and financial moment in their lifetime in which their need for adequate representation is acute.

I am similarly distressed by this Court's continuing condonation of the concept of "limited" dual representation, first sanctioned in In re Kamp, 40 N.J. 588, 595–596, 194 A.2d 236 (1963). By securing the derivative client's consent to such a limitation on his duty, the attorney, in addition to his plenary representation of the primary client, "represents" the derivative client also as to some matters involved in the closing of title but not as to others. In practical terms what this arrangement means is that at the settlement table, moments after having purportedly acted on behalf of the derivative client's interest, the attorney will turn on his "former" client and act solely as the advocate for the primary client as to the matters reserved from dual representation. One can readily imagine the bewilderment of the derivative client as he sees the attorney transformed from ally to enemy in a matter of seconds. He didn't bargain for that result when he gave his "consent" to the limits of the dual representation he would receive. Agreeing to allow an attorney not to press certain matters on your behalf is not equatable with agreeing to have him press those very matters against you. This incongruous situation would be ludicrous were it not so tragic. Yet the Court sees fit to perpetuate such an arrangement; which in reality is nothing less than a travesty of the attorney-client relationship and mocks the very concept of the professionalism of lawyers. The impropriety of permitting an attorney to act as both the advocate and adversary of a client in a single transaction is too obvious even for statement.

The Court fails to make its position more palatable by noting that meaningful independent representation for the purchasers in the instant transactions would have been unlikely in any event because of the "rigidities" occasioned by the fact that the housing program involved was under "federal auspices." I am not persuaded that inadequate representation should be acceptable because on some occasions adequate representation might not bear any significant fruit.

Moreover, the Court's assumption that adoption of a per se prohibition of dual representation in a real estate transaction would somehow prevent persons of modest means from being represented at all is unwarranted. The more likely result of a per se rule will be to alert such persons to the gravity of the contemplated transaction and consequently impel them to secure their own counsel. In this regard it is not inappropriate for us to notice the greater access by consumers to information concerning the cost of legal services as a result of fee advertising in this post-*Bates*[4] era. Considering the more than adequate number of attorneys in this state, it is very likely that representation in such relatively uncomplicated matters as residential real estate settlements at moderate fees will be readily available. Furthermore, the cost of obtaining independent counsel is normally only an incremental addition to the cost of the entire transaction and is a cost that most purchasers would willingly bear if they were aware of its potentially significant benefit. The assumption that such persons will totally forego legal representation rather than spending a relatively insignificant additional amount for an attorney is dubious at best. Naturally, many purchasers will leap at the opportunity to avoid a purportedly unnecessary extra expense when they are misled into believing that the

4. Bates v. Arizona State Bar Association, 433 U.S. 350, 97 S. Ct. 2691, 53 L. Ed. 2d 810 (1977).

seller's attorney can and will give them equally effective representation for free or at a lesser cost than if they obtained their own representation.[5] However, it does not necessarily follow that prohibition of dual representation will deprive most purchasers of the services of an attorney.

Were these purchasers not induced to believe that the quality of the derivative representation they would receive from the seller's attorney is the equivalent of any representation they could receive from their own counsel, it is reasonable to assume that they would have obtained independent representation. In short, the Court allows dual representation to be a self-justifying practice by accepting the theory that its sine qua non role in the provision of housing to persons of limited means is proven by the fact that so many persons consent to it. I am unable to concur in that assessment. The incidence of exploitation of unsophisticated purchasers as a result of the conflicting loyalties of an attorney with "two clients" counsels against our making such tenuous assumptions.

It is virtually impossible for an attorney to contend for that which duty to another client requires him to oppose. This impossible fact pattern prevents the fulfillment of that undivided loyalty owed by a lawyer to his client. We must decisionally or by Canons of Ethics discourage an attorney from taking any chances where such a highly charged potential for conflict exists. Misconduct may be found despite disclosure and consent.

Absent any explicit demarcation of the line beyond which attorneys tread at their peril in this murky area of ethical behavior, I believe it is inappropriate for the Court to broaden the concept of the type of consent required to avoid a finding of impropriety and then to apply it in an ex post facto manner to the conduct of the particular respondent before us. Is it fair to premise a finding of misconduct on a practice whose ethically violative nature has only this day been explicitly defined? I think not, and for that reason dissent from the disciplinary action taken against Mr. Dolan for conduct only technically improper under the present state of the law and which would in all likelihood not have occurred if this Court had provided attorneys with the needed guidance in the first place. By starkly dramatizing the plethora of pitfalls which await attorneys who are fool-hardy enough to chance a misstep in this precipitous area of professional ethics, this case underscores the critical need for a per se prohibition of dual representation which will deter attorneys at the threshold of that hazardous journey.

While I concur in the reprimand of the respondent for the conduct described in Section II of the Court's opinion, I hasten to add that my comments herein on the issue of multiple representation are not addressed to Mr. Dolan's particular conduct. It is an unfortunate fact of life that respondent is not alone in treading at the razor's edge of ethical behavior. However, as he was in technical compliance with the disciplinary rules as presently formulated, there

---

5. In this regard it is noteworthy that in the instant case the developer's standardized agreement of sale contained the following specially inserted provision:

If purchaser uses seller's attorney, the seller will pay the legal fee for title examination, recording of deed and mortgage, survey, mortgage title insurance, appraisal and inspection fees.

The substantial saving for the purchasers resulting from their utilization of the seller's attorney makes this offer quite persuasive, and vitiates the voluntariness of its acceptance. The Court fails to comment on the ethical implications of this clause although a functionally indistinct practice was condemned in In re Kamp, 40 N.J. 588, 598, 194 A.2d 236 (1963).

is no valid basis for imposing any sanction for the multiple representation disclosed in this record.

NOTES AND QUESTIONS

1. States that currently have not adopted the Model Rules of Professional Conduct are New York, Ohio, and California. New York and Ohio have rules based on an earlier version of the ABA Model Rules, the ABA Model Code of Professional Responsibility, but with extensive variations. California has never adopted either the ABA Model Rules or Model Code, but in many respects its rules are similar to the ABA Model Rules or Model Code.

Most federal courts also have rules on professional conduct for lawyers who appear before them, with substantial variation among federal districts on what rules are applicable. Some districts adopt the professional conduct rules of the state where the court sits; some adopt the professional conduct rules of the state where the court sits but with specified exceptions; some treat the state rules merely as guides, not binding authority; and some have no rules but leave determinations of ethical conduct standards for lawyers up to the discretion of each judge. On federal court authority to set standards of lawyer conduct, see Zacharias & Green, Federal Court Authority to Regulate Lawyers: A Practice in Search of a Theory, 56 Vand. L. Rev. 1303 (2003).

2. Conflict of interest is a common professional responsibility problem facing lawyers. It can arise in all kinds of law practices and in all kinds of law offices. Potential conflict may require a lawyer not to accept proffered representation, and if an actual conflict arises a lawyer may be disqualified from continuing to represent one or more clients. Under some circumstances, consent of affected parties, with adequate disclosure as to the nature of the conflict, may justify the lawyer in acting in a conflict of interest situation.

In real estate transactions, lawyers often are asked to represent concurrently parties with differing interests, such as a buyer and seller or mortgagor and mortgagee. Almost invariably this poses a conflict of interest issue. Although there is some ambiguity and uncertainty in the Rules of Professional Conduct on conflict of interest and in the case law interpreting those Rules, the restrictions imposed by the Rules and case law are clear enough to constitute warning signals of when lawyers *may* be in conflict of interest violation if they decide to engage in certain conduct.

3. The Connecticut Supreme Court in Westport Banks v. Corcoran, Malin & Aresco, 605 A.2d 862 (1992), had this to say about conflict of interest when a lawyer represents both lender and borrower in making a title search and issuing a title opinion needed in a real estate loan transaction:

Rule 1.7 of the Rules of Professional Conduct sets forth the general rule on conflicts of interest in an attorney-client relationship. Rule 1.7(a) states in pertinent part that a "lawyer shall not represent a client if the representation of that client will be directly adverse to another client, *unless* . . . [t]he lawyer reasonably believes the representation will not adversely affect the relationship with the other client . . . and . . . [e]ach client consents after consultation. . . .

In Connecticut, banks often rely on the skill and judgment of a single loan closing attorney to conduct a title search and issue a title opinion. See, e.g., T. Witherspoon,

E. Sostman & P. Culver, Basic Real Estate Law in Connecticut (1988) p. 44. Many loan transactions occur every day, without incident, in which a single attorney searches the title and issues a title opinion. Indeed, when an attorney conducts a title search on behalf of a lender and a borrower, both the lender and borrower have similar interests in obtaining an accurate title opinion letter. The lender seeks an accurate opinion letter so that its loan may be adequately secured. The borrower also seeks an accurate opinion letter so that it may procure the loan from the lender and learn of any encumbrances that would affect title to the property. The two parties seek the same result, namely, that no encumbrance on the property will interfere with the granting of the loan. This supports the view that an attorney could reasonably view his relationship with the lender and borrower as nonadversarial. Moreover, the Connecticut Bar Association has "sanctioned the practice of a single attorney representing multiple parties, including a mortgage lender and borrower, in a real estate transaction where there is no actual conflict of interest and where there has been full disclosure and consent of the parties with respect to representation by the single attorney. Informal Opinion 1-74 (1974); See CBA Formal Opinion No. 30 (1978) for a discussion of the issues involved." Connecticut Bar Association Committee on Professional Ethics, Informal Opinion 83-25 (1983).

The defendants argue, as the trial court reasoned, that there is a potential for a conflict of interest. "A possible conflict[, however,] does not itself preclude the representation. The critical questions are the likelihood that a conflict will eventuate and, if it does, whether it will materially interfere with the lawyer's independent professional judgment in considering alternatives or foreclose courses of action that reasonably should be pursued on behalf of the client. Consideration should be given to whether the client wishes to accommodate the other interest involved." Rules of Professional Conduct, Rule 1.7, comment. As we stated earlier, in the initial stages of a loan transaction, the lender and borrower have similar interests in securing an accurate title opinion letter. If an unforeseen conflict arises after representation has been undertaken, an attorney should withdraw from the representation of the client. Id.; see also Rules of Professional Conduct, Rule 1.16. That does not mean, however, as the defendants' argument suggests, that the potential for such a conflict must preclude an attorney from representing a borrower and lender simultaneously.

4. In Baldasarre v. Butler, 625 A.2d 458 (N.J. 1993), a case concerning dual representation by a lawyer of both buyer and seller in a real estate transaction, the New Jersey Supreme Court in its opinion stated the following:

This case graphically demonstrates the conflicts that arise when an attorney, even with both clients' consent, undertakes the representation of the buyer and the seller in a complex commercial real estate transaction. The disastrous consequences of Butler's dual representation convinces us that a new bright-line rule prohibiting dual representation is necessary in commercial real estate transactions where large sums of money are at stake, where contracts contain complex contingencies, or where options are numerous. The potential for conflict in that type of complex real estate transaction is too great to permit even consensual dual representation of buyer and seller. Therefore, we hold that an attorney may not represent both the buyer and the seller in a complex commercial real estate transaction even if both give their informed consent.

5. In every real estate sale or mortgage closing are not the interests of the parties so inherently conflicting that no lawyer should ever be permitted to represent buyer

and seller, or borrower and lender, in the same closing transaction? Why is such an absolute prohibition on dual representation not imposed by the Rules of Professional Conduct or the court?

6. Lawyers are subject to very extensive conflict of interest legal restraints, far more than are real estate brokers. Why the disparity, and can and should this disparity be changed by substantially increasing conflict of interest legal restraints on real estate brokers?

7. Conflict of interest restrictions on lawyers are based in part on preventing possible confidential information disclosure by the lawyers. In a recent case, Continental Resources v. Schmalenberger, 656 N.W.2d 730 (N.D. 2003), the Supreme Court of North Dakota disqualified a law firm from representing plaintiffs in a controversy over oil and gas leases. The court concluded that a lawyer in the firm being disqualified previously had done title work for the defendant as to title to the leases, that this work was substantially related to the matter being litigated, and that while performing the title work the lawyer could have obtained confidential information from the defendant, hence the disqualification. The court's opinion in part includes the following:

> "Loyalty is an essential element in the lawyer's relationship to a client." Comment, N.D.R. Prof. Conduct 1.7. "The duty of confidentiality continues after the client-lawyer relationship has terminated." Comment, N.D.R. Prof. Conduct 1.6. "An integral purpose of the rule of confidentiality is to encourage clients to fully and freely disclose to their attorneys all facts pertinent to their cause with absolute assurance that such information will not be used to their disadvantage." Damron v. Herzog, 67 F.3d 211, 215 (9th Cir. 1995). "'Clients must feel free to share confidences with their lawyers. This will not occur if we permit lawyers to be today's confidants and tomorrow's adversaries.'" Clinard v. Blackwood, 46 S.W.3d 177, 188 (Tenn. 2001) (quoting Penn Mut. Life Ins. Co. v. Cleveland Mall Assocs., 841 F.Supp. 815, 818 (E.D. Tenn. 1993)). As the court said in Analytica, Inc. v. NPD Research, Inc., 708 F.2d 1263, 1266-67 (7th Cir. 1983) (citations omitted):
>
> > For rather obvious reasons a lawyer is prohibited from using confidential information that he has obtained from a client against that client on behalf of another one. But this prohibition has not seemed enough by itself to make clients feel secure about reposing confidences in lawyers, so a further prohibition has evolved: a lawyer may not represent an adversary of his former client if the subject matter of the two representations is "substantially related," which means: if the lawyer could have obtained confidential information in the first representation that would have been relevant in the second. It is irrelevant whether he actually obtained such information and used it against his former client, or whether—if the lawyer is a firm rather than an individual practitioner—different people in the firm handled the two matters and scrupulously avoided discussing them.
>
> Confidentiality is promoted through N.D.R. Prof. Conduct 1.9, which provides:
>
> A lawyer who has formerly represented a client in a matter shall not thereafter:
>
> > (a) Represent another person in the same matter in which that person's interests are materially adverse to the interests of the former client; or
> > (b) Represent another person in a substantially related matter in which that person's interests are materially adverse to the interests of the former client unless the former client consents after consultation; or

> (c) Use information relating to the representation to the disadvantage
> of the former client in the same or a substantially related matter except as
> Rule 1.6 would require or permit with respect to a client.

Thus, a lawyer may not represent another client in the same matter in which that client's interests are materially adverse to the interest of the former client, or, without a former client's consent, represent another client in a substantially related matter in which that client's interests are materially adverse to the interests of the former client.

Among other professional responsibility rules particularly relevant to lawyers representing clients in real estate transactions are these ABA Model Rules of Professional Conduct adopted as court rules by most states: Rule 1.5 on fees, Rules 7.1 through 7.3 on advertising and other forms of marketing by lawyers, and Rule 5.5 on multijurisdictional practice. A substantial minority of states have not adopted the most recent ABA version of Model Rule 5.5 and the law in those states more extensively restricts multijurisdictional practice by lawyers than does the latest ABA version of Rule 5.5.

8. In many states lawyers may provide brokerage services to their clients without being licensed as real estate brokers. But there is authority prohibiting a lawyer from claiming or accepting a brokerage commission from a client for the sale of real estate if the lawyer also is providing legal services to that client in the same sale transaction. See, for example, In re Roth, 577 A.2d 490 (N.J. 1990), in which the court held that a lawyer claiming or accepting a brokerage commission under such circumstances would violate the conflict of interest restrictions imposed by Rule 1.7(c) of the New Jersey Rules of Professional Conduct.

CHAPTER TWO

Basic Financing Considerations of the Real Estate Transaction

At the heart of most real estate transactions lies the fact that a buyer seeks financing on terms as favorable as prevailing conditions and the buyer's own circumstances permit. Tax, business, and investment-yield factors generally make it unwise to acquire the property "free and clear"—a choice that most buyers do not even have. From the young marrieds who are buying their first home to the hard-bitten professionals who are enlarging their empire, the questions (though hardly the answers) are the same: What are the sources of real estate loans? On what basis are loans available? If financing alternatives exist, how does one choose between them? In the pages that follow, we will examine in turn the mortgage market, major mortgage lending institutions, mortgage insurers, common mortgage provisions, and basic security transactions, including remedies of secured creditors when borrowers default. The chapter closes with consideration of prejudicial treatment of some home buyers and what has and should be done about it.

The mortgage market is unusually complex in organization and operation and is under constant pressure to change. Currently, it is in a period of particularly acute change. The lawyer specializing in real estate transactions should be knowledgeable about how the mortgage market functions, about the contributions and expectations of the major participant groups in that market, and about how and why the market is changing. The law of real estate finance cannot be understood without a broad-based understanding of the mortgage market.

A. THE MORTGAGE MARKET

Generally, the term "mortgage market" refers to the market in which loans are made to finance the acquisition, construction, or improvement of real property, the real property being security for the moneys loaned.[1] The total of real estate mortgage debt outstanding in the United States is tremendous and has increased rapidly in recent years. In 2004 real estate mortgage debt outstanding in this country was $10.5 trillion, up from $3.8 trillion in 1990.[2] The largest percentage of this debt was in

---

1. Mortgage proceeds sometimes are applied to uses unrelated to real property. Tuition payments are a common example. Mortgages may also be written as collateral security for the guaranty of the debts of another person, or for obtaining proceeds for use on property other than the mortgaged property.

2. U.S. Dept. of Commerce, Statistical Abstract of the United States: 2006, Table 1180.

one-to-four unit residential properties, which in 2004 totaled $8.1 trillion. The remainder in 2004 was allocated as follows: commercial properties, $1.7 trillion; multifamily residential properties, $.6 trillion; and farm properties, $.2 trillion.[3] The dollar volume of mortgage debt outstanding can be expected to increase in the future as the economy expands, the population increases, and the value of the dollar declines due to inflationary forces. The mortgage market is cyclical as to availability of funds. At times loan money is tight, at times relatively easy to obtain. The current state of the economy locally and nationally, the financial condition of institutional lenders of mortgage funds, the degree of competition among lenders, and the current level of interest rates are among factors that influence whether mortgage moneys are relatively difficult or easy to obtain. Obviously, too, the more credit-worthy the borrower and the more economically favorable the mortgage terms to the lender, the more likely mortgage loan applications will be approved by the lender.

The tremendous influx of new funds needed by the real estate mortgage market has been aided greatly in recent years from an expanding national and even international secondary market in mortgage-backed securities. A high percentage of all new mortgages now move into a secondary market that issues securities on selected pools of such mortgages. These securities have a much broader market than would the individual mortgages sold unsecuritized.

Originators of mortgage loans should be distinguished from those who later purchase this form of debt. Originators make the decisions as to whether or not to loan, they negotiate loan terms, commonly prepare the loan documents, and advance loan funds on the security of land interests. Many originators continue to hold at least some of the loans they originate until the loans are paid off or otherwise terminated; but, increasingly, originators are selling their loans in the secondary market.

Not only does the availability of mortgage money tend to be cyclical, easier to obtain at some times than others, but borrowers' delinquencies on mortgage debt obligations and lender foreclosures of mortgages also tend to be cyclical.[4] Predictably, both delinquencies and foreclosures are higher in economic recession periods.

A separate aspect of the mortgage market is mortgage servicing. Mortgage servicing is the collection from mortgagors of principal and interest payments, remittance of proceeds to the lenders, making certain that insurance and taxes on the mortgaged property have been paid, and taking corrective action when borrowers are delinquent in their payments. Accurate records also must be kept on all these transactions. Servicing is a continuing procedure, for most all

---

3. Id.

4. Illustrative of the cyclical character of mortgage delinquencies and foreclosures is the data during the past quarter-century or so. From 1990 to 2004 the percentage of one-to-four unit residential mortgage loans being serviced that were delinquent at the end of the year, as disclosed by a survey regularly conducted by the Mortgage Bankers Association of America, varied from a high of 5.1 percent in 2001 and 2002 to a low of 4.2 percent in 1995. U.S. Dept. of Commerce, Statistical Abstract of the United States: 2006, Table 1181. As was to be expected, subprime mortgage loans had much higher delinquency rates than those for the averages of all mortgage loans. The subprime delinquency rate varied from a high of 14.3 in 2002 to a low of 10.4 in 2004. Id. The survey also disclosed annual variations in rates of one-to-four unit residential mortgage loan foreclosures. The percentage of all such loans in the study that were in the process of foreclosure at the end of the year varied from a low of 0.9% in 1990 and 1995 to a high of 1.5% in 2001 and 2002. Id. For subprime loans the comparable foreclosure rate varied from a high of 9.4 percent in 2000 and 2001, to a low of 4.0 percent in 2004. Id.

mortgages are amortized, with required regular installments of interest and principal, often on a monthly basis. Many lenders do their own servicing, but there is a trend for the servicing function to be split off and to be handled by specialist servicers who do not own the loans they service. Payment for servicing is a small percentage of the outstanding loan balance, typically one-quarter to one-half of one percent per year. There are substantial economies of scale to mortgage servicing, and it can be very profitable if a sufficient volume of mortgages is being serviced. Some of the large servicers at any one time have servicing responsibility for tens of thousands of mortgages. Modern servicing operations are heavily computerized.

The mortgage market, like the stock market, in effect is not one market but many. The market for one-family homes differs from that for high-rise apartments, and separate markets exist for each major form of real estate improvement: one- to four-family residence; multiple dwelling; commercial (stores and office buildings); industrial. There are also separate markets for new structures and old; for well-maintained structures and run-down ones; for luxury housing and low-rent; for urban real estate and rural; for improved real estate and raw land; for segregated neighborhoods and interracial; for construction loans and "permanent" financing; for private ownership and public, and so on. Some of these markets cast a weak shadow, but in time one learns how and where to find them.

The mortgage market is also organized into primary and secondary markets. The term "secondary" causes some confusion, since it is used in two dissimilar ways. In one of its senses, secondary market refers to activity in junior liens (for example, the second mortgage), as distinguished from the market in first mortgages. But secondary also refers to a sequence of events whereby a mortgage (be it senior or junior) changes ownership, often by prearrangement even before the mortgage is placed; an originating or primary lender sells (assigns) the mortgage to a secondary lender. Of tremendous importance to the growth in this latter form of secondary market has been mortgage securitization in which mortgages are purchased by a securitizing entity that then issues and sells securities backed by these mortgages.[5] The largest mortgage

5. The following briefly describes the securitization process:

The mechanics of a typical mortgage securities market transaction are simple: a lender originates mortgages, pools them together (or sells them to another entity, often called a "conduit," which forms a pool from mortgages originated by several primary lenders), and transfers the pool to a trustee. The trustee issues certificates representing either an equity or a debt participation in the pool. The certificates are then sold by the pooling entity or conduit (each of which is also called the "warehouser") to investors. The warehouser may continue to service the mortgage loans comprising the pool or may contract with a loan servicing entity for the performance of this duty. The investors thus receive the benefits of investing in home loan mortgages without incurring the costs in efficiency associated with individual investors originating and servicing the loans, and without being forced to concentrate their risk in one loan or make a very large investment in order to diversify. The loan originator obtains the advantage of liquidity for its mortgage portfolio with the consequent ready availability of more capital to put back into the housing sector. The servicer charges as its fee a portion of the spread between the interest rate on the underlying mortgages and the coupon rate on the securities issued off the pool. The housing market (and, ultimately, the home buyer) benefits from the increased availability of mortgage money.
Comment, The Secondary Mortgage Market and State Regulation of Real Estate Financing, 36 Emory L.J. 971, 981 (1987).

On mortgage securitization see also Frankel, Securitization: Structural Finance, Financial Asset Pools, and Asset-Backed Securities (1991 & Supp. 1998) (considers various forms of securitization, including securitization of mortgages); Fiedler & Devoe, The Explosion of Commercial Property Securitization, Real Est. Rev., Winter 1995, at 5; Pittman, Economic and Regulatory Developments Affecting Mortgage Related Securities, 64 Notre Dame L. Rev. 497 (1989).

securitizers are two federal government sponsored and regulated private companies, the Federal National Mortgage Association (Fannie Mae) and the Federal Home Loan Mortgage Corporation (Freddie Mac). A substantial volume of mortgages also are purchased and securitized by private companies that do not receive federal sponsorship benefits, such as those benefits granted Fannie Mae and Freddie Mac.

Malloy, The Secondary Mortgage Market — A Catalyst for Change in Real Estate Transactions

39 Sw. L.J. 991, 1013-1018 (1986)

III. IMPLICATION FOR CHANGE FOSTERED BY THE SECONDARY MORTGAGE MARKET

The implications of the secondary mortgage market manifest themselves in two broad and interrelated ways. First, the market has changed the manner in which parties interact within the context of a real estate transaction. Second, the market has altered the traditional view of the proper role of state and federal government in administering and developing the law of real property.

Dramatic growth in secondary mortgage market activity has significantly influenced the way in which homebuyers/borrowers, lenders, developers, and investors interact. The increasing access to interregional, national, and international capital markets has changed the very nature and structure of traditional housing and real estate market operations. For instance, the flow of funds through the secondary mortgage market to primary mortgage lenders affects housing affordability. Most homebuyers apply for loans at local banks and savings institutions. These institutions, especially in high growth areas like the sunbelt, depend to a great extent on the availability of interregional, national, or international funds to supply their capital requirements. Purely local concerns of the parties to the transactions must, therefore, give way to the intrusion of national standards of uniformity and investment acceptability. Thus, if homebuyers expect a continuing supply of affordable homefinancing, they must also accept the conditions of access to nonlocal capital markets that will make new sources of investment capital available for local real estate development. Because the secondary market can attract and direct these new sources of capital and should thereby reduce financing costs for homebuyers, homebuyers have an interest in maintaining a strong secondary market.

An active secondary mortgage market also benefits local mortgage lenders by providing them with the opportunity to originate and service many more loans than

---

Indicative of the importance of securitization is the following data: of the $10.5 trillion in mortgage debt outstanding at the end of 2004, the largest holders of this debt were federal government agency and federal government sponsored agency pools (a form of securitization), $3.5 trillion; commercial banks, $2.6 trillion; asset-backed securities issuers, $1.5 trillion; and savings institutions, inlcuding thrifts, $1.1 trillion. U.S. Dept. of Commerce, Statistical Abstract of the United States: 2006, Table 1180.

Most mortgages that have been securitized are on residential properties. But since the early 1980s a substantial market in commercial real estate mortgage securities has developed, aided by the willingness of national credit-rating agencies to rate these financings. See Shenker and Coletta, Asset Securitization: Evolution, Current Issues and New Frontiers, 69 Tex. L. Rev. 1369, 1399-1403 (1991). Also see Lee, The Commercial Mortgage-Backed Securities Frontier, 5 Rl. Est. Fin. J., no. 5, at 80 (1989); and Tomlinson & Carroll, The Awakening of the Commercial Secondary Market, 50 Mortgage Banking 67 (Nov. 1989).

would be possible if they merely held all of their loans in portfolio until maturity. The market increases the local mortgage lenders' liquidity and thereby enhances long-term profitability by giving them greater access to the capital markets and better protection against interest rate changes. The market also provides indirectly a source of substantial income through loan origination and servicing fees.

Both the reduction in home financing costs and the increased ability to provide loans to a given local market constitute positive economic benefits for real estate development. These positive economic benefits for the homebuyer/borrower and lender, however, are not without their costs. A local mortgage lender that aggressively taps nonlocal markets for primary mortgage funds may shift from using and managing local funds for local investments to mass retailing of loans, local and otherwise, for sale in the secondary mortgage market. In this manner the local mortgage lender may redefine its self-image and restructure its operations to facilitate the directing of local individual needs into prepackaged arrangements that are acceptable for resale rather than tailoring services to meet local and individual needs. As a result, the borrower and lender relationship changes and becomes less personal.

Investor requirements of the secondary mortgage market also affect the projects of real estate developers. Consequently, developers should seek to modify their projects to ensure that project construction standards and legal documentation will be acceptable to the major secondary market entities. If the developer ensures that the secondary market will accept the primary mortgage loans secured by the developed property, then more primary mortgage lenders will be willing to extend mortgage financing to the project based on the greater liquidity of such mortgages. Even if the developer plans to offer its own purchase money mortgage financing to individual property buyers, it should consider the requirements of the secondary mortgage market investor. If the underlying purchase money mortgages satisfy investor expectations by resembling other standard mortgages, then the developer retains the potential to issue builder bonds. In this manner access to the capital markets can be used to finance continued real estate development.

Through the secondary mortgage market, the homebuyer/borrower, lender, developer, and investor interact. Even though the secondary market investor does not directly participate in the underlying transaction, the importance of the secondary market process to the continued financing of real estate development makes the investor an indirect participant. The indirect participation of unrelated investors has significantly changed the point of reference for interaction in real estate transactions. Increasingly, direct parties must refer to the objectives and business standards of unknown investors as benchmarks for the conduct of what superficially appears to be a local real estate transaction.

In addition to changing the manner in which parties to a real estate transaction interact, the secondary mortgage market has affected the perceived roles of state and federal government in administering and developing real property law. The financing of real estate development increasingly appears to require access to interregional, national, and international capital markets. The ability of state government alone to administer and develop appropriate law is thus diminishing. The nonlocal capital markets require a degree of uniformity in both documentation and underlying real property law so that investors can easily access alternative investments without detailed investigation of particular lenders and particular state law. Likewise, the ability of secondary mortgage market entities to issue securities based on mortgages requires a substantial degree of national uniformity in order to make the underlying pooling arrangements manageable.

With the success and variety of the various mortgage-related securities currently available, pressure to facilitate the further development of the secondary mortgage market has increased. The success of the market in bringing new sources of capital to real estate development has bestowed upon the market a reputation as the "goose that lays the golden eggs." Indeed, real estate transactions appear to be capable of attracting a substantial portion of the billions of dollars available for capital investment if the appropriate legal changes are made to facilitate a competitive market for the origination, issuance, and resale of mortgage-related securities.

The success of the secondary mortgage market has demonstrated that real estate transactions are matters of national, not purely state and local, concern. The success and viability of a national housing policy and of a national policy to revive our financially troubled lending institutions depends, at least in part, on a healthy secondary mortgage market that by its very nature is national in scope. Consequently, for the law to facilitate a competitive market in mortgage-related securities authority must exist at the national level to coordinate, administer, and develop appropriate regulations and legal doctrines.

NOTE

1. For other discussions of secondary mortgage markets see Downs, The Revolution in Real Estate Finance, chs. 12 and 13 (1985); Lore, Mortgage-Backed Securities: Developments and Trends in the Secondary Mortgage Market (1985); Biller, The Significance of Income Taxation for Securitized Mortgages and the Secondary Mortgage Market, 9 Am. J. Tax Policy 283 (1991); Fernandez, Globalization of Mortgage-Backed Securities, 1987 Colum. Bus. L. Rev. 357; Fiedler & Devoe, The Explosion of Commercial Property Securitization, 24 Real Est. Rev. 5 (Winter 1995); Hu, Secondary Market, The American Model, 51 Mortgage Banking 14 (April 1991). On secondary financing see 2 Madison et al., The Law of Real Estate Financing §§ 8.1-8.24 (2006).

B. MAJOR MORTGAGE LENDING INSTITUTIONS

1. Commercial Banks

Real estate mortgage lending is an important although not predominate activity of most commercial banks. These banks are major holders and originators of long-term real estate mortgage debt on residential, commercial, and farm properties, and also are the largest funders of secured loans for real estate construction projects. Through management of pension funds, they also invest moneys in real estate mortgages. Further, they provide lines of credit to mortgage companies for originating and holding mortgages until assigned to permanent lenders, often referred to as loan warehousing. Generally, commercial banks prefer shorter-term loans because of the greater liquidity of these loans, and they find lending on construction projects particularly attractive because the loans are short-term and provide high yields. In addition to their real estate mortgage loans, commercial banks have always been heavily involved in short-term loans to businesses for such purposes as acquiring inventories, expanding output, or other short-term operational needs. Many of these loans are for large sums of money. Consumer loans for household hard goods and other consumer needs are another facet of commercial bank lending. Most commercial banks also maintain trust departments that manage the assets of inter vivos and testamentary trusts. Many, as well, invest extensively in government debt securities. Because of the diversity of their activities, commercial banks have been referred to as financial department stores. They acquire their funds from a variety of sources, including demand and time deposits from individuals and businesses.

The overall importance of commercial banks as mortgage lending institutions has been declining as a result of increased competition from other lending institutions, including mortgage securitizers, and increased resort of commercial borrowers to the commercial paper market.[6] Competitive forces also are reflected in the vast expansion in the size and number of outlets of the larger banks through mergers and acquisitions, with a few banks having outlets in all sections of the country and expanding their operations overseas.

2. Savings Institutions

Savings institutions long have been of great importance in originating and funding real estate mortgage loans, especially home loans on single-family dwellings. They include savings and loan associations (S&Ls) and savings banks often referred to as thrifts.[7] Of these two types of lenders, S&Ls collectively are much more significant, as their volume of mortgage originations and mortgage debt held is far greater than that of the savings banks. There also are many more S&Ls than savings banks; and the S&Ls are located in all sections of the United States, whereas savings banks are mostly located in New England and the Middle Atlantic states.

S&Ls and savings banks are referred to as thrifts because they historically have encouraged ordinary people to save and do so by depositing their savings with the thrifts that then lend these funds to ordinary people, primarily for home acquisition or home improvement. This still is their principal mode of operation. S&Ls began in the pre-Civil War period as savings institutions that lent only to their members and only to finance home purchases. Some S&Ls still are organized as mutual institutions in which their depositors are members, share in gross income as interest or dividends on deposits, and elect the governing board. Other savings and loans are structured as stock associations, owned and operated much as other business corporations. Some savings banks are mutual institutions, owned and operated for the benefit of their depositors.

The savings institutions' overall significance as mortgage lending institutions has declined in recent years. Some have become insolvent and closed down, some have been turned into commercial banks. Highly speculative lending in the 1980s, especially by S&Ls in some parts of the country, led to a number of irretrievable defaults and insolvencies.[8] The federal government, largely as a result of its insurance of savings deposits up to $100,000 per deposit account, was forced to fund most depositor losses, at a cost of many billions of dollars to the federal government. One development that has reduced the risks encountered by many savings institutions is that they now act mostly as originators of mortgage loans, selling the loans in the secondary market shortly after origination, rather than holding them until maturity.

---

6. On more recent changes in commercial banking, see Macey and Miller, America's Banking System: The Origins and Future of the Current Crisis, 69 Wash. U.L.Q. 769 (1991).

7. Credit unions also are often classified as thrifts.

8. On the S&L crisis, see an excellent symposium, Financial Institutions and Regulations, The S&L Crisis: Death and Transfiguration, 59 Fordham L. Rev. S1-S459 (1991). See also a symposium, Savings & Loan Crisis: Lessons and a Look Ahead, 2 Stanford L. & Policy Rev., no. 1, 4-158 (1990); and Tucker, Meire, and Rubenstein, The RTC: A Practical Guide to the Receivership/Conservatorship Process and the Resolution of Failed Thrifts, 25 U. Rich. L. Rev. 1 (1990).

3. Mortgage Companies

Also known as mortgage banks, these institutions are major originators of mortgages, mostly on residential properties, for large institutional lenders. Before World War II, mortgage companies were virtually unknown but are now key intermediaries, especially in the financing of home sales, including newly built residential properties. A high percentage of their originations are of mortgages backed by FHA or VA. The major customers of mortgage companies are life insurance companies, but most types of mortgage lenders acquire mortgages from mortgage companies to some extent. During the short interval of time between mortgage origination and disposal, mortgage banks usually finance their mortgage acquisitions with commercial bank credit lines. Mortgage banks ordinarily make a modest net return from originations but it is mortgage servicing that makes them profitable. When mortgages are disposed of by mortgage companies, they commonly retain the servicing. Most mortgage banks are small local businesses, but a few are sizable multistate operations.

It also is relevant here to make reference to mortgage brokers that although not lenders are also frequently highly important to the origination of many mortgage loans. Mortgage brokers assist borrowers, mostly home buyers, in finding mortgage loans on terms acceptable to the borrowers. Most all local communities have one or more mortgage brokerage companies and these companies generally are small, low-cost operations serving borrowers in the locality where they are based. Some mortgage banks are mixed function operations, acting as lenders in some transactions, brokers in others.

4. Mortgage Securitizers

Most real estate mortgages are sold by the originators to others. Some of these mortgage purchasers hold the mortgages as investors, but many securitize the mortgages and then sell the securities. By far the largest purchasers and securitizers of one- to four-unit residential properties are two federal government sponsored companies, the Federal National Mortgage Association (Fannie Mae) and the Federal Home Loan Mortgage Corporation (Freddie Mac). Many commercial mortgages also are securitized, mostly by private, non-federally sponsored companies. Fannie Mae and Freddie Mac and their operations are considered more fully just below. Their mortgage operations are massive. The mortgage debt outstanding on one- to four-unit residences in the United States held by Fannie Mae or Freddie Mac or securitized in securities issued by one of the two companies is about $3 trillion.

Johnstone, Private Mortgage Insurance

39 Wake Forest L. Rev. 783, 827-828 & 830-831 (2004)

Fannie Mae [Federal National Mortgage Association] and Freddie Mac [Federal Home Loan Mortgage Association] are federally chartered, private corporations. The stock of each is listed on the New York Stock Exchange and held by many thousands of stockholders. The original Fannie Mae was first authorized by Congress in 1934 and chartered as a corporation wholly owned by the federal government in 1938. In 1968, the original Fannie Mae was partitioned into two separate but distinct corporations, one retaining the original Fannie Mae name of Federal

National Mortgage Association, and the other to be known as the Government National Mortgage Association ("Ginnie Mae"). The new Fannie Mae is not only a private company but also a GSE.[208] Ginnie Mae is a federal government corporate entity, fully federally owned, and a unit within the Department of Housing and Urban Development. Ginnie Mae was created to take over some of the higher risk mortgage programs of the original Fannie Mae that were considered to be in need of more extensive federal financial backing. Freddie Mac was created in 1970, but since its inception has been a private company and classified as a GSE.

Fannie Mae and Freddie Mac long have had much the same objectives, have performed much the same functions, and have been subject to the same or very similar legal regulations. Their principal objectives are apparent from federal statutes and regulations and can be briefly summarized as these: increasing home ownership by residents; increasing the flow of capital to housing; increasing the liquidity of mortgage loans on housing; promoting access to credit for housing in all geographic areas, including underserved areas; and stabilizing mortgage credit over time. The principal functions of both Fannie Mae and Freddie Mac are the purchase and the securitization of home mortgages, both conventional mortgages and those insured by the FHA or guaranteed by the VA. When mortgages are securitized by Fannie Mae or Freddie Mac, the mortgages are pooled, and shares in the pool are sold to investors. Fannie Mae and Freddie Mac guarantee timely payment of interest and principal on the mortgage-backed securities they issue. So far as is practicable, and whether or not the mortgages are later securitized, the mortgages purchased by either company must meet the quality, type, and class standards generally imposed by private institutional mortgage investors. High risk conventional mortgages on 1- to 4-unit dwelling units, those with LTVs over 80% at time of purchase, may not be purchased by either company unless the credit quality of the mortgage at the time of purchase has been enhanced in one of three ways: a qualified insurer has insured or guaranteed the mortgage; the seller has retained a participation in the mortgage of not less than 10%; or the seller has agreed to repurchase or replace the mortgage on demand of the company in the event of default. Of major importance to PMI companies is that the usual lender preference for loans they will make is for the first option, and a PMI company is the usual qualified insurer selected. This has greatly increased the insurance volume of PMI companies. . . .

Of tremendous importance to the financial viability and competitive effectiveness of Fannie Mae and Freddie Mac are the financial benefits, in essence subsidies, the federal government makes available to the two companies.[224] Among these subsidies, mandated by statute, are exemptions of Fannie Mae and Freddie Mac

---

208. GSEs have been defined as follows:

In general, GSEs are financial institutions established and chartered by the federal government, as privately owned entities, to facilitate the flow of funds to selected credit markets, such as residential mortgages and agriculture. In addition to Fannie Mae, Freddie Mac, and the Federal Home Loan Banks, the Farm Credit System and Farmer Mac [Farmer's Home Administration] are GSEs.

U.S. CONGRESSIONAL BUDGET OFFICE [CBO], FEDERAL SUBSIDIES AND THE HOUSING GSEs 1, n.2 (2001). Another Congressional Budget Office report states that: "The major defining characteristic of a GSE, however, is that the federal government is perceived to back the obligations of the sponsored enterprise with an implicit guarantee." CBO MAY 1996 REPORT at ix.

224. For the various federal subsidies of Fannie Mae and Freddie Mac, see CBO MAY 1996 REPORT, *supra* note 19, at 9-11; CBO MAY 2001 REPORT, *supra* note 20, at 13-14. These studies are among the series of studies on the effects of the privatization of Fannie Mae and Freddie Mac that are required by statute, 12 U.S.C. § 4602 (2000).

from state and local government taxes[225] and from costly Securities and Exchange Commission requirements and fees.[226] There also are subsidies that provide each company with substantial additional financial support. This additional financial support includes authorizing the U.S. Treasury to lend up to $2.25 billion to each company and legally qualifying each company's debt as being eligible for use as collateral for public deposits, for unlimited investment by federally chartered banks and thrifts, and for purchase by the Federal Reserve.[227] The special legal status granted to Fannie Mae and Freddie Mac by the federal government has enhanced the companies' profitability and increased the credit standing, market acceptance, and the liquidity of the mortgage-backed securities that the companies guarantee. This preferred treatment by the federal government has also led the financial markets to perceive that the federal government is implicitly guaranteeing the companies' securities, adding still further to the companies' financial strength and profitability. A 2001 study by the Congressional Budget Office estimated that the federal subsidies to the two companies in 2000 totaled $10.7 billion, with about $1 billion of this from tax and regulatory exemptions and the remainder from subsidies reducing the companies' borrowing costs and reducing the cost to the companies of guaranteeing the mortgage-backed securities they issue. These annual subsidies undoubtedly have remained very substantial in the years since 2000.

5. Other Mortgage Lenders

There are a variety of other private real estate mortgage lenders. Most of these lenders' mortgage loan holdings are held as long-term investments. One such type of investor is the life insurance company. In a sense, the primary business of the life insurance companies is investing, with insurance policy premiums financing their investment operations and their profits largely attributable to successful investing. Over the last quarter-century life insurance companies in the United States consistently have held a total of about a quarter of a trillion dollars in real estate mortgages.[9] Pension funds, analogous to life insurance companies in the massive amounts of money they allocate to investments, also have large mortgage holdings. Real estate investment trusts (REITs) are still another type of mortgage lender. Some are equity REITs, that own real estate, and their income comes largely from rentals. But others are mortgage REITs, whose holdings are mortgage investments. One attraction of REITs as forms of investment is their favorable income tax treatment.[10] Individuals, too, hold a significant number of real estate mortgages. Many of these individuals are sellers who have taken back purchase money mortgages. Some are family members who have loaned money to other family members, often at below-market rates. And the second mortgage market, with its typical high interest, has

---

225. 12 U.S.C. § 1723a(c) (excepting real property taxes from the exemption).

226. *Id.* § 1719(e) (applicable to Fannie Mae); *id.* § 1455(g) (applicable to Freddie Mac).

227. *Id.* § 1719(c) (applicable to Fannie Mae); *id.* § 1455(c) (2000) (applicable to Freddie Mac).

9. U.S. Dept. of Commerce, Statistical Abstract of the United States: 2006, Table 1211.

Although the total dollar value of life insurance company investments in mortgages has been relatively constant, as a percentage of their total assets, there has been a substantial decline in their mortgage holdings, given the consistent increase in the dollar value of their total assets. For example, in 1990 life insurance company total mortgage holdings were 19 percent of their total assets but only 7 percent in 2003. Id.

10. On REITs, see Garrigan & Parsons (eds.), Real Estate Investment Trusts (1995); Madison et al., The Law of Real Estate Financing § 3:26 (2005); McCall, REITs and Securities Laws: A Quick Guide to the Basics, 13 Prob. & Prop. 17 (Mar/Apr 1999); Witner, REITs: The Revolution in Real Estate Financing, 22 Real Est. L.J. 248 (1994).

long attracted individuals looking for high-yield investments. But overall, both in numbers of mortgages held and their total dollar volume, it is institutional lenders, not individual lenders, that dominate the real estate mortgage market.

Life insurance companies, with assets of 1.3 trillion dollars, are major investment entities. In a sense, their primary business is investing, with insurance policy premiums financing their investment operations and their profits largely attributable to successful investing. About 65 percent of their assets are investments in government and corporate securities, but about 20 percent are in mortgage loans. Most of their mortgage loans are on nonresidential properties, and they often loan large amounts on individual properties. Some of these large-scale mortgage financings are highly innovative and complex transactions, carefully crafted by among the best real estate lawyers in the nation. As life insurance companies may make equity investments in real estate, some of their financing transactions also include joint ventures and sale-leasebacks. Some companies are organized as stock companies, others as mutuals.

C. MORTGAGE INSURERS

Insurance of real estate mortgages is limited mostly to insurance of mortgages on one- to four-unit residential properties. Accurate current data is lacking but apparently about one-third of all outstanding mortgages on one- to four-unit residential properties are now covered by mortgage insurance. Nearly all of this insurance is written either by one of the private mortgage insurance companies (PMIs) or by one of two federal government agencies, the Federal Housing Administration (FHA) or the Veterans' Administration (VA). In recent years the total dollar amount of mortgage insurance originations by PMIs has been appreciably greater than the combined dollar amount of mortgage insurance originations by FHA and VA. The article excerpt appearing below considers mortgage insurance and mortgage insurers in some detail and although concerned principally with private mortgage insurance, it does consider as well FHA and VA mortgage insurance.

Johnstone, Private Mortgage Insurance

39 Wake Forest L. Rev. 783, 784-787, 792-794, 802-803, 836 (2004)

A large percentage of 1- to 4-unit home mortgages are covered by PMI. The market for PMI has long been heavily influenced by the market involvement of both federal agencies and private agencies subsidized by the federal government. Two of these federal agencies, the FHA and the VA, insure mortgage loans and are major competitors of PMI companies in the mortgage insurance market.[4] VA coverage

---

4. Another federal agency, the Department of Agriculture's Rural Housing Service ("RHS"), also insures mortgage loans. Loans are insured by RHS for a variety of rural area needs, such as housing for domestic farm labor and low-income families. . . . In terms of either the number of loans insured or the total dollar amount of all loans insured, the RHS's mortgage insurance program is miniscule compared to that of either the FHA or the VA. . . .

A few states also have mortgage insurance programs, relatively modest in gross volume of coverage compared to that of the PMI companies or the FHA or the VA, in which the state or a state agency insures homes or nonresidential projects serving community needs that otherwise would have difficulty finding adequate financing. . . .

often is referred to as a guaranty rather than insurance, but in essence it is insurance, and in this Article will generally be referred to as mortgage insurance. The FHA share of the home loan mortgage insurance market is much larger than that of the VA, as the VA only insures home mortgage loans of military veterans and, under some circumstances, their spouses. The secondary market for FHA and VA loans is aided considerably by another federal agency, the Government National Mortgage Association ("Ginnie Mae"), a unit within the Department of Housing and Urban Development. Ginnie Mae guarantees the timely payment of principal and interest on securities issued by private institutions backed by pools of federally insured mortgage loans, including loans insured by the FHA and the VA. Most FHA- and VA-insured loans are securitized and most of these securities are guaranteed by Ginnie Mae.[7] Ginnie Mae charges a variety of fees for its services, including guaranty fees and commitment fees. Ginnie Mae has consistently operated at a profit and has never had to exercise its right to borrow funds from the U.S. Treasury in financing its operations.

In the competition among PMI companies and the FHA and the VA, each side has certain advantages over the other in attracting customers for their home mortgage insurance coverage. Among the advantages of FHA and VA coverage over PMI coverage are that underwriting standards for FHA and VA coverage are less strict than those for PMI companies, an attraction particularly to lower-income home buyers. The FHA also has a competitive advantage in that it insures the full amount of the mortgage loan loss, whereas PMI typically insures only the top 20 to 30% of any such loss and the VA only insures 50% or less. And some borrowers and some lenders apparently feel more protected if their loans are insured by the federal government than if they have private insurer protection, another competitive advantage of the FHA and the VA over PMI coverage. Advantages of PMI over FHA or VA coverage in attracting mortgage insurer customers include lower cost than FHA coverage; availability for large loans over the maximums that the FHA will insure; availability for a far greater number of loans than the VA can insure, given the VA's restriction to insuring loans only of qualifying veterans or their spouses; and lender preference for the more efficient settlement procedures of PMI companies than those of the FHA or the VA. If competition between PMI and FHA-VA mortgages is measured in terms of the number of new insured mortgage originations, in the past several years the PMI companies annually have had more new insured mortgage originations than the FHA and the VA combined. In 2002, PMI companies had 2.3 million such originations, compared to less than two-thirds that many for FHA-VA combined. . . .

Primary PMI is the form of mortgage insurance that provides mortgage default protection, at specified coverage percentages, for individual mortgage loans, and includes a separate insurer commitment for each loan. The insureds are lenders, mostly institutional lenders, such as savings and loan companies, commercial banks, and mortgage banks. But mortgagors, the borrowers, are usually responsible for payment of PMI policy premiums. . . .

PMI policies do not cover all of the insured's loss — only a contractually agreed percentage of it. The percentage is generally between the top 20% and the top 30% of the insured's loss claim if loan default and resulting loss to the insured occur.

---

7. In fiscal year 2003, 92.6% of the combined total of loans insured by the FHA and the VA were guaranteed by Ginnie Mae. . . . Ginnie Mae, 2003 Annual Report (2004).

The loss covered by mortgage insurance, known as the claim amount, is calculated pursuant to the insurance agreement and includes a percentage of unpaid loan principal, past due interest, and certain expenses. Occasionally the coverage percentage exceeds the top 30%, with the top 40 percentage about as high as coverage ever goes, except for bulk insurance coverage, which often is 45 to 50% or more. The percentage depends on the perceived risk: the greater the risk, the higher the percentage. The limited percentage of PMI insurance coverage in effect creates a form of co-insurance, as the risk is shared by the insurer and the lender and results in the lender more carefully evaluating loan applications. A lower percentage also may result in a lower insurance premium, as the insurer's exposure then is less than if the percentage were higher. Primary PMI generally has a high risk of borrower default and claim payment on the insured loan. The LTV at the time the insurance was written is an important indication of the extent of the loan risk; the higher the ratio, usually, the higher the risk of default. Most all mortgage loans insured by primary PMI policies have LTV at or above 80%, with many exceeding 90% and some exceeding 97%. Some companies in recent years also have been insuring a substantial number of mortgages at 103% LTV. This subprime segment of the market has been growing and results in a larger share of the PMI market being high risk. . . .

Pool mortgage insurance insures groups of individual mortgages. It generally provides 100% coverage for any default losses on mortgages in the pool but is subject to an aggregate loss limit on all mortgage loans in the pool. The pooling often occurs for the purpose of issuing securities on the assembled mortgages. Securitizing mortgages has emerged as an important development in the securities field. Hundreds of mortgages are often included in a pool. The liability of the pool insurer typically is limited to between 5 and 25% of the original principal balance of mortgages in the pool. Mortgage loans in the pool may or may not have primary mortgage insurance. . . .

At the close of 2002, the total PMI net pool risk-in-force in the United States was $12.3 billion, up from $7.2 billion in 1999. In recent years, pool risk-in-force, net of reinsurance, has been about 5% of all mortgage insurance risk-in-force, the remaining 95% being non-pooled primary mortgage insurance risk-in-force. . . .

V. CONCLUSIONS

[Mortgage insurance] is an important form of risk sharing that makes lenders more willing to provide mortgage loans for home buyers, especially those home buyers with very limited cash resources. It also makes higher risk home mortgage loans more salable in the secondary mortgage market and thereby contributes considerably to the volume of securitized mortgages, a large and growing sector of the securities market. The net effect of [mortgage insurance] is that it helps substantially in increasing the percentage of occupant home ownership, particularly for families with lower or moderate incomes. . . .

D. MORTGAGE PROVISIONS

Some years ago Professor Charles Haar coined the phrase "credit trio" to describe the usual provisions of a mortgage. The trio consists of down payment, length of mortgage, and rate of interest. By manipulating these terms, Congress, through its FHA and VA programs; and state officials, through their control over mortgage lenders, can make housing finance cheaper or more expensive, and home buying easier or more difficult. Since the 1930s, the juggling of mortgage terms has been a key feature of the nation's housing programs. In other areas as well, especially in the realm of the high-voltage operators, the shaping of the credit terms in a deal negotiation may ultimately determine whether the deal can be made. One talent that marks the real estate "pro" is the knack for working out the debt arrangements to make an otherwise dubious transaction feasible and even inviting.

We will discuss each member of Professor Haar's trio, and then consider some other provisions commonly included in real estate mortgages.

1. Down Payment and the Loan-to-Value Ratio

Suppose that a buyer can make a $12,000 down payment on a $80,000 house. To complete the purchase, he or she will need a $68,000 mortgage loan. In describing the mortgage, we use the term *loan-to-value ratio*, which states the percentage relationship between the size of the loan (mortgage debt) and the real estate's appraised value;[11] in our example, the loan-to-value ratio would be 85 percent. In making a mortgage loan, regulated lenders must comply with any maximum loan-to-value ratio that federal and state laws have fixed for each group of lenders. Often the loan-to-value ceiling will also depend upon the class or age of property given as security. It is self-evident that as the loan-to-value ceiling rises, the buyer's cash down payment requirements drop, provided, of course, that lenders are willing to make maximum loans. During tight-money eras, lenders — as a matter of internal policy — may refuse to make loans at, or even near, the ceiling percentage.

Until the mid-1930s, official loan-to-value ceilings were set far below present levels. Typically, the pre-Depression home mortgage was not supposed to exceed 50 to 60 percent of appraised value. Such limits, strictly obeyed, would have weakened the housing boom of the 1920s, since, despite good times, few families had the $5000 or $10,000 in liquid assets needed for a cash down payment. To get around the conservative limit, lenders often stretched their appraisals to the point of incredulity; and if, despite the inflated ratio, a homebuyer remained shy of cash, easy access to second, third, and even fourth mortgages from the seller or from private lenders made it quite simple to acquire real estate with little of one's own money in the transaction.

When incomes and real estate values tumbled during the 1930s, overextended borrowers and lenders suffered alike. Mortgage delinquency reached all-time highs as more than one million American families lost their homes through foreclosure between 1930 and 1935. The real estate market became so depressed that in all of

---

11. "The exact legislative definition can be quite important. The wording in different statutes — 'appraised value,' 'estimated value,' 'reasonable normal value,' 'estimated replacement cost,' 'actual cost,' 'necessary current cost,' 'reasonable value' — affects the size of the resulting down payment considerably. Accounting terms often conceal significant social policy decisions. [The] substitution of the words 'replacement value' for 'market value' may substantially reduce the amount of equity capital which the builder has to provide." Haar, Federal Credit and Private Housing 60 (1960).

1933 only 120,000 residential starts occurred, fewer than one-tenth the number eight years before.

Only heart massage seemed likely to quicken the economy, and the National Housing Act of 1934 proved a useful and enduring stimulant. It introduced the federally insured mortgage, a guarantee to lenders that the government, not they, would bear any loss resulting from a defaulted loan. Yet a willing lender is only one party to a real estate transaction; a borrower able to raise the down payment and handle the long-term debt is a vital second. To escape the Depression, something more than old forms was needed, and Congress responded by lifting the loan-to-value ceiling for the FHA-insured mortgage well above any level once believed safe. For example, the purchaser of a $15,000 house could obtain a $13,500 FHA-insured mortgage, reducing his down payment requirement to $1500. Had the house been conventionally financed, the buyer would have needed at least $6000.

Fairly high loan-to-value ceilings have remained a key feature of government-backed mortgages, with the ratio at times even reaching 100 percent.[12] And as their confidence in the economy returned after World War II, lenders specializing in conventional loans wanted also to deal with low down-payment borrowers. Entreaties to state legislatures and to Congress brought an easing of loan-to-value limits on noninsured loans, in some cases almost to the level of FHA and VA mortgages. To illustrate: California now lets its state-chartered savings and loan associations make a 100 percent loan on some properties. Cal. Fin. Code § 7509 (West 1999). With the advent of private mortgage insurers, conventional lenders can now shift the risk of default on high loan-to-value mortgages.

Other factors that cushion the lender's risk when making seemingly dangerous loans are exacting credit standards, a steady full employment economy, and a housing demand that exceeds the available supply. Time also works in the lender's favor, even though, as we shall see, the rate of mortgage reduction usually begins quite modestly. The pressures of inflation and scarcity tend to force up real estate values, adding to the owner's equity wholly apart from mortgage reduction. Moreover, inflation also allows the debtor to repay fixed dollars of debt service with dollars of shrinking value, thereby making default itself less likely.

An introduction to leverage. The professional investor knows emphatically the value of *leverage,* a congenial exercise in applied arithmetic that allows one to catapult his yield by reducing his down payment. To explain how leverage works, let us start with an investor who buys a $10 million apartment house that throws off $1,500,000 after expenses. On an all cash purchase, he will earn a 15 percent cash yield on his investment. Suppose instead that he borrows to make the purchase: first $5,000,000, then $9,000,000. If the mortgages bear 12 percent interest, and if the annual debt service (that is, the combined amount of interest and principal reduction) is designed to pay off the mortgages in 25 years, the cash flow and cash yield appear below:

---

12. During the peak building years of 1950 and 1955, no-down-payment VA loans accounted for 44 and 40 percent, respectively, of all new one- to four-family home sales. Haar, Federal Credit and Private Housing 58 n.4 (1960).

Congress, in 1961, initiated the § 221(d)(3) program, which was intended to stimulate non-profit groups (such as hospitals, churches, labor unions, colleges) to produce housing for "moderate" income tenants. An essential feature of this program was the 100 percent mortgage.

(a) $5,000,000 mortgage, $5,000,000 cash
     down payment

Cash flow before debt service	$1,500,000
Less debt service	$ 633,000
Cash flow after debt service	$ 867,000
Cash yield on $5,000,000 down payment	17.34%

(b) $9,000,000 mortgage, $1,000,000 cash
     down payment

Cash flow before debt service	$1,500,000
Less debt service	$1,139,400
Cash flow after debt service	$ 360,600
Cash yield on $1,000,000 down payment	36.06%

If we were to continue to project cash yield based on ever-shrinking down payments, the investment return would approach infinity. And by placing elsewhere the cash that mortgaging replaces, the investor can expand and diversify his holdings.

It is useful to understand how leverage can bring a geometric increase in investment return. Note that it depends upon the investor turning a profit on the borrowed funds; this, in turn, depends upon a favorable spread between the "points" (points equal percentage) of debt service and the "free and clear" rate of return on the investment. To illustrate this principle with the $5,000,000 mortgage:

(1)	Free and clear return (at 15%) on $5,000,000 of borrowed funds	$750,000
(2)	Debt service (at 12.66 points) on $5,000,000 mortgage	$633,000
(3)	Profit on the borrowed funds (1 minus 2)	$117,000
(4)	Profit on the equity or down payment funds	$750,000
(5)	Overall cash flow (3 plus 4)	$867,000

Thus our investor has enhanced his rate of return by adding the $117,000 profit on the borrowed moneys to the regular 15 percent yield that his down payment generates. By increasing the spread between free and clear return and debt service costs, or by increasing the ratio of borrowed to equity capital, the investor will improve his leverage advantage. To test your understanding, repeat this calculation for a $9,000,000 mortgage.

It follows, inevitably, that leverage will produce negative results if the assumptions above are reversed and the mortgage debt service costs exceed the free and clear rate of investment return. Suppose, in our example, that the free and clear return on an all-cash investment is only $1,300,000 (13 percent) and that the investor can only obtain a 15-year mortgage on any moneys that he borrows. If we assume the same 12 percent interest rate, the annual debt service for each $1,000,000 of mortgage comes to $144,600 (14.46 points). We now have an unfavorable spread between the "points" of debt service and the "free and clear" rate of investment return. The impact on cash yield, assuming a $5,000,000 mortgage, appears below:

$5,000,000 mortgage, $5,000,000 cash
   down payment
Cash flow before debt service $1,300,000
Less debt service $ 723,000

Cash flow after debt service $ 577,000
Cash yield on $5,000,000 down payment   11.54%

And, as the borrowed funds increase, the disadvantage grows geometrically. You might work out the figures for a $6,000,000 mortgage, a $7,000,000 mortgage, etc.

With medicine, one dose may be restorative, five doses fatal. So, too, with leverage. If it is too great, it may ruin. The investor (and the lender) gamble that operating income will be enough to carry the debt. In the first example, where $5,000,000 was borrowed, $867,000 was left after debt service; when $9,000,000 was borrowed, only $360,600 remained. These amounts, $867,000 and $360,600, are the margin of solvency. If the margin disappears (rentals down, expenses up), the investor faces the uninviting options of finding cash elsewhere or defaulting on his loan, unless he is able to refinance the debt so as to reduce or postpone the debt service requirements. Needless to say, the slimmer the margin of solvency, the shakier the investment. History records more than one real estate empire that was leveraged into oblivion.

2. *Length of Mortgage*

trio?

(The due date of a loan, i.e., its length or maturity, is the second of the credit quartet. Prior to the New Deal, real estate loans were seldom written for longer than 10 to 15 years.[13] But with the advent of the FHA-insured mortgage, and its policy of easier down payment requirements, the practice of relatively short-term loans had to be reexamined. All else equal, an $80,000 loan bears twice the debt service of a $40,000 loan. Higher loan-to-value ratios may bring more buyers into the market, but higher debt service payments will drive them away again. To hold down the level of debt service, Congress enabled the FHA to insure 25-year mortgages, for that time (1934) a revolutionary idea. Table 2-1 shows that extending the mortgage's length can help offset the debt service increase of a higher loan-to-value ratio. The figures cover a 12 percent mortgage and real estate valued at $80,000.

As the table shows, the debt service on a $64,000, 25-year mortgage costs little more than that on a $40,000, 10-year mortgage. Even a $72,000 mortgage, extended for 40 years, results in debt service less than one-third higher than that of the much smaller, short-term loan.

---

13. In 1925, the average contract length for home mortgages issued by life insurance companies and savings and loan associations, respectively, was 6.0 years and 10.9 years. Haar, Federal Credit and Private Housing 58 n.3 (1960).

TABLE 2-1
Monthly Debt Service Related to Length of Mortgage
and Loan-to-Value Ratio
(*in dollars*)

	10 Years	25 Years	40 Years
Loan-to-Value Ratio			
50 Percent ($40,000)	573.88	421.29	403.40
80 Percent ($64,000)	918.21	674.06	645.44
90 Percent ($72,000)	1,032.99	758.32	726.12

The combination, then, of higher loan-to-value ratios and longer maturities became the key to FHA's effort to energize the housing market. Both credit changes were needed to reflect the savings and the incomes of potential buyers. Congress has since further liberalized the maturities on government-backed loans, with 40-year terms now authorized for some programs and 30- and 35-year terms available for most others. Conventional loans have also become much longer.

A stretched-out loan is not all to the buyer's advantage. The longer he repays the loan, the more slowly his equity builds and the larger will be his total interest charges. A 12 percent, $40,000, 10-year mortgage, costs $28,880 in interest; the interest on a 25-year mortgage would come to $86,400! Some might boggle at this sum. Given, however, the migratory habits of American households, 25-year mortgages rarely go to term. Most mortgages are paid off long before maturity, often when the property is sold to a refinancing buyer. Moreover, the differences are less startling when present value discounting is applied to the absolute amounts. And the deductibility of home mortgage interest payments for taxpayers itemizing their expenses further shrinks the "actual" outlays.

a. "Due-on" Clauses

If the mortgagor "sells, conveys, alienates . . . said property or any part thereof, or any interest therein . . . in any manner or way, whether voluntarily or involuntarily . . . mortgagee shall have the right at its option, to declare said note . . . secured hereby . . . immediately due and payable without notice."

This "due-on" clause, a standard provision in mortgages and deeds of trust, became the hurricane eye of a decade-long controversy, which Congress finally quelled in 1982. At issue was whether courts would (or could) enforce such clauses, where the mortgagee's security was unthreatened by a transfer of title, and where the mortgagee hoped simply to gain from a fortuitous event a higher interest yield. In short: the transferee would be credit-worthy, but the lender would not approve a mortgage takeover at the original, lower interest rate.

The California courts led the assault on such clauses. The courts of at least three other states (Arizona, Arkansas, and Michigan) also restricted enforceability of such clauses, as also did at least five state legislatures (Colorado, Iowa, New Mexico, Utah, and Virginia).

Believing that restrictions on the lender's ability to accelerate a loan upon transfer of the security would adversely affect lenders due to the loss of cash flow, net income, and access to secondary mortgage markets, the Federal Home Loan Bank Board (FHLBB), in 1976, issued a regulation that curbed state power over "due-on" provisions with respect to loans held by federally chartered thrift institutions. The United States Supreme Court, in Fidelity Fed. Sav. & Loan Assn. v. de la Cuesta, 458 U.S. 141, 102S. Ct. 3014 (1982), upheld the regulation, ruling that Congress had delegated to the FHLBB the power to preempt state law as to such institutions under its regime.

Persuaded that even broader relief was necessary, Congress passed the Garn-St. Germain Depository Institutions Act of 1982, Pub. L. 97320, 96 Stat. 1469. This measure, and the regulations thereunder, cover essentially all lenders, individual and institutional, and all properties, residential and commercial. There remain, however, some key exceptions to the Act's coverage. One of these postponed the Act's preemption for a three year "window period," ending October 15, 1985, for many loans in states that restricted enforcement of due-on-sale clauses before passage of the Act. In accord with the Act, a few states have extended the October 15, 1985, date for some loans, in some instances permanently.[14] In addition, the Act does not cover certain specified transfers, some of them involuntary or other transfers involving transferees likely to have difficulty raising cash to pay off the underlying obligation if the due-on clause was to be enforced. The exemption section of the Act, 12 U.S.C.A. § 1701j-3(d) (2001) provides:

> With respect to a real property loan secured by a lien on residential real property containing less than five dwelling units, including a lien on the stock allocated to a dwelling unit in a cooperative housing corporation, or on a residential manufactured home, a lender may not exercise its option pursuant to a due-on-sale clause upon —
>
> (1) the creation of a lien or other encumbrance subordinate to the lender's security instrument which does not relate to a transfer of rights of occupancy in the property;
>
> (2) the creation of a purchase money security interest for household appliances;
>
> (3) a transfer by devise, descent, or operation of law on the death of a joint tenant or tenant by the entirety;
>
> (4) the granting of a leasehold interest of three years or less not containing an option to purchase;
>
> (5) a transfer to a relative resulting from the death of a borrower;
>
> (6) a transfer where the spouse or children of the borrower become an owner of the property;
>
> (7) a transfer resulting from a decree of a dissolution of marriage, legal separation agreement, or from an incidental property settlement agreement, by which the spouse of the borrower becomes an owner of the property;
>
> (8) a transfer into an inter vivos trust in which the borrower is and remains a beneficiary and which does not relate to a transfer of rights of occupancy in the property; or
>
> (9) any other transfer or disposition described in regulations prescribed by the Federal Home Loan Bank Board.

Good to Know

14. On window period exemptions, see 1 Nelson and Whitman, Real Estate Finance Law 404-408 (4th ed. 2002). Michigan, New Mexico, and Utah have permanently extended the exemptions. Arizona and Minnesota extended them for short periods that have now expired. Id. at 408.

NOTES AND QUESTIONS

1. In explaining its support for the 1982 legislation, Congress stated that restrictions on the enforceability of "due-on" clauses had led to inflated home prices, higher mortgage origination fees, higher interest rates on newly issued mortgages, the advantaging of existing home owners to the disadvantage of home buyers, and the encouragement of riskier lending practices. A "Due-on-Sale Task Force" assembled by the FHLBB concluded that the imposition of due-on-sale restrictions nationwide would create, within two years, annual losses exceeding $1.0 billion for federal and state savings and loan associations. Barad and Layden, Due-on-Sale Law as Preempted by the Garn-St. Germain Act, 12 Real Est. L.J. 138, 140 (1983).

2. What arguments are there justifying each of the specified exemptions set forth above in § 1701j-3(d) of the Garn-St. Germaine Act?

b.   Mortgage Prepayment

As the next case makes clear, the right to prepay is not automatic. Unless the parties have agreed otherwise, the lender may stand on the original bargain and insist that payments continue, as provided for, until maturity. But it is common for mortgages expressly to include the right to prepay. However, it is also common for real estate loan instruments to permit prepayment only if a premium is paid by the mortgagor for the privilege of prepaying. The usual reason that mortgagors desire to prepay is that interest rates have declined and the mortgagors wish to refinance at the current lower rates.

Peter Fuller Enterprises v. Manchester Savings Bank

152 A.2d 179 (NH 1959)

Bill in equity, in which plaintiffs seek, among other relief, reformation of certain mortgage notes and a determination of their right to pay off these notes which are secured by real and personal property mortgages.

There are two notes executed by plaintiff Peter Fuller Enterprises, Inc., and endorsed by Peter Fuller, the other plaintiff, payable to Manchester Savings Bank in the principal amounts of $200,000 and $50,000 and another payable to Amoskeag Industries, Inc. in the principal amount of $220,000. All three notes provide for quarterly payments of interest and principal payments in specified amounts payable monthly beginning April 28, 1958 to April 28, 1963 "whereupon the entire unpaid balance shall become due and payable; sixty (60) days default in payment of any interest or principal payment to make the entire balance due and payable."

[On February 13, 1959, plaintiffs tendered to the respective payees the interest due to date and the unpaid principal of each note which was refused. They claimed the tender was improperly refused and made no more payments. They further claimed that by their failure to make the payments due February 28, March 28, and April 28, 1959, the maturity of the notes had been automatically accelerated.]

Before a hearing on the merits, plaintiffs filed a motion the amended prayer of which was "that the said mortgages on the real estate and chattels of Peter Fuller Enterprises, Inc. held by defendants be now discharged upon the mortgagors furnishing such securities in substitution for said mortgages as the Court shall find justice requires."

At a hearing on said motion counsel for plaintiffs stated and offered to provide that they "may lose a sale that will be at least one hundred and fifty thousand dollars more advantageous to them than any other sale they have been offered" and "that a failure to discharge these mortgages, particularly the chattel mortgages, would subject the debtor to irreparable harm and damage and a very serious financial loss."

The Court (Griffith, J.) found for the purposes of the motion "that it would appear you [plaintiffs] might suffer substantial by the failure to discharge the mortgage at this time and that equity would seem to indicate that you were entitled to a discharge of the mortgage upon some basis that would completely secure the defendants as far as a monetary performance of their contract was concerned."

Thereupon the following issues were reserved and transferred to this court without ruling:

"1) Whether or not the Trial Court has authority at this stage of the proceeding and after its findings as disclosed in the record which findings were excepted to by the petitioners, to order a discharge of the mortgages described in the petition upon the condition that the petitioners substitute therefore a sum of cash, to be deposited in New Hampshire banks, equal to the unpaid principal and interest to April 1963, plus a sum sufficient to offset any loss in credits against the state tax levied on savings banks' assets, or by the furnishing of any other security which the Court might order to secure the petitionees.

"2) Whether or not the Trial Court has authority after

"a) a hearing on the merits, and

"b) a ruling that notes and mortgages described in the petition are valid instruments as written and not mature until 1963, and

"c) a finding that the petitioners might suffer substantial financial loss by reason of their failure to obtain discharges of the mortgages described in the petition

to order a discharge of the mortgages upon the condition that the petitioners substitute therefore a sum of cash, to be deposited in New Hampshire banks, equal to the unpaid principal and interests to April 1963, plus a sum sufficient to offset any loss in credits against the state tax levied on savings banks' assets, or by the furnishing of any other security which the Court might order to secure the petitioners, or by requiring said cash or other security to be paid on said notes according to their terms."

LAMPRON, Justice. . . . Every negotiable instrument is payable at the time fixed therein. RSA 337:85. The mortgages the dominant feature of which is security for the performance of the primary obligations evidenced by the notes become void upon payment according to terms or by legal tender thereof. RSA 479:6; Blaisdell v. Coe, 83 N.H. 167, 168, 139 A. 758, 65 A.LR. 626. A mortgagor, however, in the absence of a provision so providing has no right to pay in advance of maturity. Buffum v. Buffum, 11 N.H. 451, 456; Trahant v. Perry, 253 Mass. 486, 149 N.E. 149; I Glenn Mortgages, s. 50, p. 319; 59 C.J.S. Mortgages § 447, p. 695. Plaintiffs argue that by their failure to make the payments due as indicated above, the maturity of the notes has been automatically accelerated by their provision that "sixty (60) days default in any interest or principal payment to make the entire unpaid balance due and payable."

It is stated in an annotation in 159 A.L.R. beginning at page 1077 that a majority of jurisdictions hold that such a clause is not self-operative but leaves an option to the creditor whether or not to take advantage of it and that without some action on his part the full amount will not become immediately due merely on the happening of a default. See cases cited pp. 1084, 1085. The rationale of these decisions is that the provision is primarily for the benefit of the creditor who should be free to decide whether such protection is necessary under the circumstances of the default and the obligor should not be entitled to take advantage of his own wrong and cause an automatic change of maturity. P. 1088.

[margin note: Other jurisdictions go both ways]

Other jurisdictions hold that under such a clause the entire principal of the note and mortgage becomes automatically due without the necessity of a declaration of the right or an election on the part of anyone. See cases cited. Id., pp. 1079, 1080. The basis of these holdings is that the provision exists for the benefit of both parties and courts have no right to make a new contract different from the expressed words of the parties. Id., p. 1082.

[margin note: NH]

We have no decision in New Hampshire on this point but we are of the opinion that the better view is that such a clause should be interpreted not as self-operating but as conferring an option on the holder to accelerate the maturity and so hold for the following reasons. In many instances mortgage loans are made by lenders as an investment and the period for which they run can affect the rate of interest and other terms thereof. If an acceleration clause such as the one in this case were held to be automatic, the borrower by his own default could convert a mortgage from a five-year mortgage to a sixty-day mortgage. Keene Five Cent Sav. Bank v. Reid, 10 Cir., 123 F. 221, 224; Kleiman v. Kolker, 189 Md. 647, 57 A.2d 297. Furthermore even though in the instant case such an interpretation is considered a hardship, in most cases if the clause were self-operating, the holder could not exercise leniency in overlooking failures to make payments when due, thus the whole loan would be brought down on the head of the debtor at once. Chafee, Acceleration Provisions in Time Paper, 32 Harv. L. Rev. 765-769. . . .

The Trial Court has found for the purposes of the motion to discharge the mortgages in advance of a hearing on the merits that plaintiffs might suffer substantial loss by their failure to obtain these discharges at this time. . . .

The plaintiffs argue in support of the Trial Court's authority that since the mortgage is merely security for the debt the Court should have authority to substitute other security for it, provided it is equivalent in value, for if the creditors' rights to payment of the debt are fully protected they may not complain.

Defendants take the position that the Trial Court has no authority to interfere with the private contractual rights voluntarily entered into by the parties. They argue that any alteration of the security arrangement by the Trial Court is a substitution of the court's judgment for that of the mortgagees as to the adequacy of the security.

"In the nature of things obligations arising from contractual relations cannot justly and reasonably be displaced by other obligations. . . . There is no law or judicial power by which considerations of equity may reform contracts which are free from legal attack on grounds of fraud and mistake." Lemire v. Haley, 91 N.H. 357, 361, 362, 19 A.2d 436, 440. The hardship which will result to the plaintiffs in this case is not one "the possibility of which was not evident at the time the agreement was executed." Bourn v. Duff, 96 N.H. 194, 198, 72 A.2d 501, 504. Hardship resulting from what may prove to be an improvident bargain fairly and voluntarily assumed by contract does not entitle a party to be relieved of its undertaking in equity. 96 N.H. 198, 199, 72 A.2d 501. Cf. Caron Inc. v. Manchester Federal Savings & Loan Association, 90 N.H. 560, 10 A.2d 668. The answer to transferred issue No. 1 is "no." . . .

It is not the duty of this court nor do we deem it good practice to advise the parties in advance of hearing as to their rights under all possible facts which might be proved. White Mountain Freezer Co. v. Murphy, 78 N.H. 398, 403, 101 A. 357. No decision holding that a court will order a discharge of a mortgage the condition of which has not been performed so as to enable the mortgagor to make a profit on an advantageous sale has been presented to us. Nor has any statutory law in our state granting such authority to the Trial Court been brought to our attention. Cf. RSA 511:48-50, 53. Williams v. Mathewson, 73 N.H. 242, 60 A. 687; Perry v. Champlain Oil Company, 99 N.H. 451, 114 A.2d 885; Lefebvre v. Waldstein, 101 N.H. 451, 146 A.2d 270. Our answer to issue No. 2 is "no."

The bill in equity for reformation not having been heard on the merits the order is remanded.

All concurred.

NOTES AND QUESTIONS

1. Facts appearing in a letter from Donald R. Bryant, Esq., attorney for petitioners, help to illuminate the lawsuit. The disputed loans had financed the purchase of a local textile business. Amoskeag Industries, Inc., which was one of the creditors, was an organization of Manchester citizens interested in retaining the city's major industry. Unluckily, the textile business turned out to be precarious and, by October 1959, only six months after signing the secured notes, the petitioners had decided to sell out if they could find a buyer. When efforts to sell the entire business collapsed, the petitioners obtained an offer for just the machinery from J. P. Stevens Company, which intended to move it to a Southern mill. The Stevens offer was $150,000 higher than any other offer that the petitioners received, but it could not be accepted unless the notes were paid and the mortgage on the machinery discharged. The payee's clear interest was in obstructing the sale of the machinery to an out-of-state organization. The case was settled, after the New Hampshire Supreme Court decision and before trial, by the payment of a 3 percent penalty ($12,925).

Textile manufacturing at one time was a major industry in New England and, as typified by the facts in the Peter Fuller case, many textile manufacturers and even some of their equipment moved from New England to towns in the U.S. Southeast. Recently these Southeast towns have faced a similar loss as much of the textile industry has become based overseas, especially in some Asian countries.

2. Lenders will usually grant at least a limited, conditional privilege of prepayment, if the borrower bargains for such a privilege when seeking the loan commitment. But to exercise the privilege, the borrower must often pay a substantial premium, the so-called prepayment penalty. A sample prepayment clause appears below:

> The further privilege is reserved commencing with the first regular quarterly installment due date in the fourth loan year . . . and on any regular quarterly installment

due date thereafter of making payments in multiples of Five Thousand ($5,000) Dollars on the principal in excess of . . . [Five Hundred Thousand Dollars in any one loan year — the approximate regular annual principal payment] provided . . . that any such payment in excess of the said Five Hundred Thousand Dollars ($500,000) in any one loan year shall be subject to a prepayment charge of three percent (3%) on such excess during the fourth loan year and declining one-quarter (¼%) each loan year thereafter. . . . Cf. Westminister Investing Corp. v. Equitable Assurance Society of the United States, 443 F.2d 653 (D.C. Cir. 1970).

3. A standard attack on clauses imposing a prepayment penalty has been that the penalty is a usurious exaction. The standard judicial response has been that the sum exacted is not interest, but an agreed upon payment for exercising a privilege. Secured Real Estate Loan Prepayment and the Prepayment Penalty, 51 Calif. L. Rev. 923 (1963), collects the cases and argues that perhaps particular prepayment penalties can be struck down as forfeitures disproportionate to the harm caused to mortgages from prepayment. What *is* the lender's loss if the borrower seeks prepayment at a time when interest rates are generally higher than when the mortgage was first placed? On the other hand, suppose that interest rates have fallen below where the prepayment penalty will fully compensate the lender for its reinvestment losses? Would it be fairer — to lender and borrower alike — for the parties to hinge the prepayment charge, if any, to the differential in interest rates; that is, the greater the drop in interest rates, the greater the prepayment charge? Might this system result in the borrower collecting a premium from the lender for prepayments made when interest rates have risen?

4. In some states, mortgage prepayment penalties in certain circumstances are prohibited by statute. An extreme example is this Pennsylvania statute, Pa. Stats. Ann., tit. 41, § 405 (West 1999).

> Residential mortgage obligations contracted for on or after the effective date of this act [Jan. 30, 1974] may be prepaid without any penalty or other charge for such prepayment at any time before the end of the period of the loan.

On the validity of mortgage provisions prohibiting prepayment, see Annot., Validity and Construction of Provision of Mortgage or Other Real Estate Financing Contract Prohibiting for a Fixed Period of Time, 81 A.L.R. 4th 423 (1990).

5. On the evolution of mortgage prepayment law, see Alexander, Mortgage Prepayment: The Trial of Common Sense, 72 Cornell L. Rev. 288 (1987). Alexander stresses that a dominant theme in the history of mortgage prepayment law has been tension between equitable principles of property law and rigid application of contract law. Rigorous application of contract formalism, that prohibited prepayment without consent of the creditor, emerged during the early nineteenth century, with twentieth century courts and legislatures often reversing this approach by easing the harshness of its application.

Creditors' interests in mortgages, Alexander concludes, have become largely commercial investments, with a majority of mortgages becoming commercial paper securitized in the secondary mortgage market. Alexander believes that residential mortgage debtors should have similar flexibility to mortgagees in marketing their debt obligations to third persons. He suggests that this flexibility be encouraged by a rule that if a creditor refuses prepayment, the debtor has a nonwaivable right to have the mortgage released from the property upon adequate substitute security being provided. Substitute security could be a guarantee from a highly rated credit institution that payment would be made of the underlying debt, and the credit institution might even assume the debt. The original mortgagor, of course, would normally pay the credit institution for guaranteeing or assuming the debt. The suggested security substitution proposal would not prevent prepayment penalties from being included in mortgage debt agreements. However, Alexander argues, the prospect of debts being transferred without prepayment becoming necessary would tend to reduce prepayment benefits to lenders and hold down amounts charged for the privilege of prepaying. Alexander is of the opinion that residential homeowner mortgagors are particularly deserving of more favorable treatment in relation to prepayment of their mortgage debt obligations.

3. Rate of Interest

a. Introduction

The third member of the trio, the rate of interest, gets the greatest attention — and deservedly — from lenders, borrowers, consumer advocates, lawmakers, and builders. Because interest payments are the largest item of housing expense for many homeowners and landlords, interest rate levels have much to do with the ability of consumers to afford decent shelter and with the willingness of both homebuyers and suppliers to engage in new shelter investment. A family earning $35,000 yearly would exhaust its entire housing budget on interest costs alone if its shelter (whether owned or rented) were financed by a $70,000, 14 percent mortgage — not a fanciful illustration, since in many areas even modest dwellings cost over $75,000 and 14 percent mortgage interest rates were prevalent in the recent past and no doubt will be reached again in the future.

Interest rate levels also are major influences on the market for all kinds of nonresidential real estate and affect the prices at which such properties may be sold, the viability of many development projects, and even the prospects of some owners in financial difficulties of acquiring financing that will enable them to retain title to their properties.

b. Adjustable Rate Mortgages

Adjustable rate mortgages (ARMs) have become a common form of real estate financing in the United States, especially for home purchases.[15] Also known as variable rate mortgages (VRMs), these types of real estate mortgage loans began to appear in the 1970s, and by 1990 it is estimated that about one-quarter of one- to four-family residential mortgage debt was ARM debt. The major feature of an ARM

---

15. On adjustable rate mortgages, see Nelson and Whitman, Real Estate Finance Law § 11.4 (4th ed. 2002); Powell on Real Property § 37.16 (2005); Badger, Adjusting to the Perils of ARMs, 51 Mortgage Banking 53 (Aug. 1991); Hoff, Arm Servicing, An Exotic Species, 51 Mortgage Banking 35 (June 1991); Garrigan & Mueller, Pricing Adjustable Rate Mortgage Loans, 21 Real Estate Rev., no. 2, p. 64 (1991).

is that, by its terms, the interest rate fluctuates in response to the rate of inflation as measured by some statistical index. The applicable index is specified in the loan document, and a variety of indexes are used, usually some national or regional cost of money that is readily available but that the particular lender cannot control. Examples are the weekly average yield on United States Treasury securities, adjusted to a constant maturity of one year; the Federal Reserve discount rate; and one of the widely adhered to prime rates. As a safeguard to borrowers, there generally is a cap on how much ARM interest rates may fluctuate in any adjustment interval, for example in any one year, or how much the adjustment rate may fluctuate over the life of the loan. Five percent is a common cap on interest rate movement during the life of the loan.

When mortgage financing is being arranged, borrowers often have the option of fixed rate or adjustable rate mortgage terms. In recent years, an appeal to borrowers of adjustable rate over fixed rate financing has been that the former, at the time the loan is made, often has been substantially lower than the latter. The adjustable rate frequently has been two percentage points or more lower than the fixed rate. Borrowers are most likely to be attracted to ARMs when interest rates generally are high and the expectation is that they will be declining in the near future.

Competition among lenders has resulted in different kinds of ARMs being offered. In addition to different indexes and caps, other variations include the convertible ARM, giving the borrower the option of converting to a fixed rate loan after a specified period of time; the negative amortization ARM, that enables the borrower to add interest increases onto the principal due, thereby stabilizing the amount of installment payments; and the fixed payment ARM, in which installment payments are constant as a result of abnormally high principal payments that cushion any interest rate increases.

A major advantage of ARMs is that they help relieve the financial squeeze on thrift institutions from lending long and borrowing short. In rising interest periods, if thrifts hold ARMs, the expanding return from ARMs interest helps the thrifts pay for expanding costs, including rising costs of money to the thrifts in retaining or expanding short-term and demand deposits. ARMs also are somewhat helpful in reducing cyclical fluctuations in the real estate market by encouraging real estate sales in high-interest periods. Many buyers who are deterred by high fixed-rate mortgages are willing to buy with ARM financing, knowing that their costs will decline with the decline in inflation.

There are, however, some disadvantages to ARMs. They are costlier to service than fixed-rate mortgages because of the interest adjustments that must be made. Evidence also has recently been surfacing of widespread servicing errors in the amount and timing of ARM interest adjustments, errors generally unfavorable to borrowers. Further, the uncertainties as to the amount of ARM interest payments and complexities in regulation of ARMs reduce the attraction of these mortgages to the secondary market.

ARMs are subject to extensive legal regulation, designed in large part to protect borrowers from lender overreaching and to enhance borrower understanding of this financing form. Much of the ARM regulation is by federal agencies, including the Federal Reserve Board, the Comptroller of the Currency, the Federal Home Loan Bank Board, and the Department of Housing and Urban Development. Regulations cover such matters as permissible caps, required disclosure to consumers of rate adjustments and rate adjustment procedures, and conditions that must be met for federal agencies to purchase or insure ARMs. Some states, by statute, also regulate ARM terms, including permissible interest rate fluctuations.[16]

How the adjustable rate mortgage works: Suppose that R borrows $50,000 on an ARM, which calls for an initial interest rate of 12.0 percent, a 25-year maturity, and annual debt service (based on monthly payments) of $6,320. Five years later, interest rates have risen to 13.0 percent and an ARM adjustment is required. What is the ARM adjustment? Under present theory, it might take one of three forms:

(1) *Maturity remains constant; debt service rises to reflect increased interest rate.* At the end of five years, R will have reduced his mortgage balance from $50,000 to $47,825. The interest rate having risen to 13.0 percent, the debt service must be adjusted upward so as to pay off the unpaid balance, at the higher rate, in the remaining 20 years. The revised annual debt service installment: $6,724. The annual debt service increase: $404.

(2) *Debt service remains constant; maturity extended.* This formula would seek to avoid entirely the risk of default that might follow higher debt service payments. In order to maintain the level of debt service, while adjusting for higher interest rates, the mortgage term must be extended. After five years, when R's mortgage balance is $47,825, the annual debt service of $6,320 — adjusted for a 13.0 percent interest rate — will require another 32 years in which to amortize that balance. Thus, the ARM maturity must be extended twelve years.

(3) *Combination of debt service increase and maturity extension.* This formula would seek to reduce the risk of default that might follow higher debt service payments while avoiding extreme extensions of the mortgage term. The parties might agree, for example, that any maturity extension would not exceed a fixed duration — viz., 25 years; and that the borrower would pay higher debt service to complete the adjustment. In the illustration above, R would be obliged after five years to pay an

---

16. For example, Pa. Stat. Ann. ch. 41, § 301(e) (Purdon 1999), which, for residential mortgages, provides in part: . . . variable interest rate mortgages may be written provided no increase in interest provided for in any provision for a variable interest rate contained in a security document, or evidence of debt issued in connection therewith shall be lawful unless such provision is set forth in such security document, or in any evidence of debt issued in connection therewith, or both, and such document or documents contain the following provisions:

(1) That the index for determining increase or decrease in interest rate shall be the lawful rate of interest . . .

(2) A requirement that when an increase in the interest rate is required by a movement in a particular direction of the prescribed standard an identical decrease is required in the interest rate by a movement in the opposite direction of the prescribed standard.

(3) The rate of interest shall change not more often than once during any semiannual period and at least six months shall elapse between any two such changes.

(4) The change in the interest rate shall be one-fourth of one per cent in any semiannual period, and shall not result in a rate more or less than two and five-tenths percentage points greater or less than the rate for the first loan payment due after the closing of the loan.

(5) The rate of interest shall not change during the first annual period of the loan.

(6) Subject to the provisions of paragraphs (3), (4) and (5), an increase or decrease in the interest rate shall be effected when the index moves in such percentage that the difference between the present index rate and present mortgage rate varies not less than one-fourth of a percentage point from the difference between the index and mortgage rates at the date of the first contracted loan repayment.

(7) The contracted periodic payment may at the option of the borrower be increased or decreased in dollar amount equal to any periodic increase or decrease in interest requirement, or the contracted periodic payment may at the option of the borrower be retained constant provided the maturity of the mortgage is not extended beyond forty years from the date of said mortgage or five years beyond the original maturity date for which said mortgage was written, whichever is the shorter.

adjusted annual debt service of $6,475, to reflect an extended maturity from 20 to 25 years. The annual debt service increase: $155.

One key variable is the index to which interest rates are geared. For the borrower's protection, the index used should not be one that the lender can manipulate. Thus, an index based on changes in the dividend rate on deposits would clearly be unsuitable. Short-term rates, e.g., the rate on prime commercial paper, change too frequently and swing too widely to be a useful index. The Consumer Price Index measures *current* inflation whereas interest rates reflect *anticipated* inflation; thus, the CPI does not seem entirely suitable, either.

c.   Limitations on the Lender's Return: Usury

Usury is a less pervasive problem in real estate finance than it has been in the past. The main reasons for this are that an increasing number of financing transactions have been exempted from usury laws and many states also have raised permissible interest ceilings substantially. However, usury can still be a problem to lenders and borrowers, and in many states usury law is a maze of exemptions and interest ceilings, not always consistent or rational. In real estate transactions, usury can be a particularly troublesome consideration in very risky deals in which lenders want a high return for taking on high risks. Especially vulnerable to usurious charges are desperation borrowers who are in serious financial straits and willing to pay abnormally high rates to obtain money to meet emergency demands.

(1)   Usury Laws — Historical Antecedents

Salin, Usury

15 Encyclopedia of the Social Sciences 193-197 (Seligman ed. 1934)

In the course of its history the concept of usury has covered a variety of meanings. Originally it referred to all returns derived from the lending of capital and carried no moral opprobrium. With the growing condemnation of the financial abuses of the moneylenders the term came to be confined to credit transactions carrying excessive charges and thus acquired a distinct ethical connotation. In the Middle Ages all direct payments for loans were deemed usurious and condemned as sinful. In modern times the term was again narrowed down and now it refers <u>only to excessive loan charges, while the payment of moderate rates is covered by the more</u> <u>neutral term interest.</u> . . .

The ethical nature of the concept of usury renders it impossible to formulate permanent and definite criteria of what constitutes a usurious transaction. As long as freedom of contract remains the corner stone of economic organization, it is not the economist but the legislator who must decide at what point a voluntary economy transaction constitutes an abuse of economic freedom and thus an act of usury. [I]n certain periods the moral views of the legislative bodies were identical with those of the majority of the people, while at other times there was a wide divergence in this respect, so that usages which were officially outlawed were nevertheless sanctioned in economic life. Thus while concepts such as price, wage, interest, are economic categories transcending time, usury is a historical category understood only in the light of the moral and legal norms prevailing in a particular period.

. . . The earliest prohibition of usury is to be found in the Mosaic code (Leviticus xxv:36 and Deuteronomy xxiii:20). The restriction, however, applied only to Jews; the taking of interest from aliens was permitted. In Athens the legislation of Solon intended to ease the financial burden of the agricultural population, limited the rate of interest. In Rome the Twelve Tables established a minimum of 10 percent. Subsequently Justinian reduced the legal rate considerably, to 6 percent for general loans, 8 percent for manufacturers and merchants, 4 percent for persons in high positions and 12 percent for the foenus nauticum [a loan advanced to finance maritime trade]. The more drastic restrictions of the Justinian code were inspired by the growing influence of the teachings of the ancient philosophers and of the young Christian church.

The ancient Attic philosophers [Plato and Aristotle] realized the social dangers inherent in a system which encourages the pursuit of gain for gain's sake, and by condemning moneylending they hoped to strike at the very roots of profit economy. The ban on gains derived from moneylending was also influenced by the naturalistic conception of money and interest. . . . Money, Aristotle held, is an inorganic object used as a medium of exchange and therefore cannot breed new coins. He who demands payment for the lending of money causes money to beget money and thus acts contrary to the laws of nature.

The antichrematistic tone of the ancient philosophers was in perfect accord with the teachings of the rising church. While the attitude of the church was based primarily on the Scriptural command Mutuum date nihil inde sperantes (Lend, hoping for nothing again, St. Luke vi:35), the theologians drew freely upon the anti-usury arguments of the philosophers. In the Roman church Ambrose of Milan formulated the principle which dominated ecclesiastic teaching for almost a thousand years: everything which accrues to the capital constitutes usury. While couched primarily in moral terms, this rigorous prohibition derived its social justification from the fact that under conditions of a primitive economy most loans were contracted by the needy for purposes of consumption and the borrower usually found himself in a worse position at the end than at the beginning of the loan period. Moreover because of the absence of business opportunities in the early Middle Ages, when the usury doctrine of the church took shape, the holder of funds did not forego any loss of profit by parting temporarily with his capital. The absolute prohibition of usury was further justified in terms of contemporary economic theory; it was argued that a loan transaction involving the transfer of ownership of the sum of money to the borrower really constituted a sale in which in accordance with the medieval principle of equivalence of exchange the lender, that is, the seller of money, might expect in return only the exact equivalent of the amount originally advanced. The fact that a period of time intervened between the offering and the return of the sum was dismissed with the argument that time is divine and can therefore command no price. Unlike the situation in ancient Greece and Rome, it was no longer necessary to determine at which rate a charge for money loan became usurious and punishable; all charges above the principal were held usurious. Usury was no mere transgression of the law but a mortal sin punishable by excommunication. This rigid measure originally applied only to the clergy but was subsequently extended to all lay Christians.

While the church consistently prohibited the charging of a price for loans throughout the Middle Ages, a person in need of money who was willing to shoulder the cost was never deprived completely of the possibility of borrowing money. Aside from the various devices designed to evade the anti-usury laws, as, for instance, the practice of sale and resale whereby the prospective lender fictitiously sold to the borrower a commodity on credit at a high price and simultaneously repurchased it for cash at a lower price, the difference constituting an interest charge for an actual loan, the medieval borrower could turn to the Jewish moneylenders and pawnbrokers, who did not come under the jurisdiction of the church and were tolerated in their moneylending operations. Later Christian traders, notably the Lombards and the Caorsini, engaged to an increasing extent in the banking business; and although they were generally condemned as usurers, they came in time to enjoy the privileges of the princes and even of the church. Under the impact of economic necessity the church authorities themselves began to reinterpret the all comprehensive concept of usury in favor of a more liberal policy toward financial transactions. Thus while it denied to the creditor the right to charge a price for his loans, the church permitted the collection of a fine in case the debtor did not return the principal at the time specified in the loan agreement. There developed the practice of inserting a penal clause (poena conventionalis) into the loan agreements whereby a nominal, brief, gratuitous loan period was set; after its expiration the debtor automatically was liable for the payment of the fine in addition to the repayment of the principal. But even in the absence of a penal clause the creditor was allowed, by invoking the principle damnum emergens, to recover for any damages he might have suffered as a result of the loan. It was but one step further to the application of the principle of lucrum cessans, whereby the lender had a right to indemnity if he could prove that he had to forego a potential profit as a result of the loan; this proof was rendered easier with the growth of investment opportunities, and later it was waived for merchants and manufacturers. . . .

Under the impact of capitalistic development the original conceptions of the church fathers receded into the background. By the eighteenth century the status of moneylending came to resemble that prevailing in ancient Rome; the question was no longer whether it was permissible to charge a price for capital but at what rate the charge became excessive and therefore usurious. Most states attempted to fix maximum rates of interest. But soon even such restrictions drew the attack of the advocates of the newly emerging doctrine of freedom of enterprise. . . . Of greatest significance was the demand for complete freedom put forward by Jeremy Bentham in his famous Defense of Usury (London 1787). In the name of personal liberty Bentham demanded the same degree of freedom for money trade as that prevailing in commodity trade. Taking as his point of departure the familiar argument that every rational person knows best how to defend his interests and that there is therefore no reason for government interference, he maintained that the state which aims to aid the poor by restricting the interest rate excludes them at the same time from the sources of credit. Similarly impressive was the common contention that a restriction of the rate of interest necessarily results in a shortage of capital and consequently in an increase in the cost of credit. . . .

The advances of economic liberalism wiped the anti-usury laws from the statute books of most countries. England removed its ban on usury in 1854, Holland in 1857, Belgium in 1865 and Prussia and the North German Federation in 1867. In the United States the overwhelming majority of the states still retain their anti-usury laws, but these have little effect on the actual movement of interest rates. The sweeping repeal of the anti-usury laws did, however, produce in most countries a flood of credit abuses, sufficient to warrant the prompt reintroduction of protective measures. In the latter part of the nineteenth century Germany, Austria and other countries and England in 1900 found it necessary to enact measures covering all cases in which the moneylender took undue advantage of the inexperience or carelessness of the borrower, particularly when the latter was led to accept excessive financial changes through fraud or misrepresentation on the part of the former. In some countries and in various states of the United States the whole field of small loans, most of which are in the nature of consumption loans, was placed under the special protection of the law to prevent financial exploitation of the small and as a rule economically weak borrower. . . .

NOTE

For a brief summary of various other rationales supporting anti-usury laws, including arguments by Adam Smith and John Maynard Keynes, see Benfield, Money, Mortgages, and Migraine — The Usury Headache, 19 Case W. Res. L. Rev. 819, 831-833 (1968). For a comprehensive survey of contemporary usury law in the United States, see Madison et al., The Law of Real Estate Financing §§ 5:21-5:25 (2005).

(2)   Selected Usury Issues

(a)   When Is a Transaction "Usurious"?

Moran v. Kenai Towing and Salvage, Inc.

523 P.2d 1237 (Alaska 1974)

CONNOR, Justice. This appeal presents a dispute over the disposition of the proceeds from an insurance policy following a fire loss.

In 1968 Kenai Towing and Salvage, Inc., was the owner of certain improved real property in the vicinity of Kenai, Alaska. On the property was a building which had been erected by Kenai Towing & Salvage, Inc., at its own expense. The company was in financial difficulty. It approached Jack Moran for a loan. The parties agreed that as security for the loan Kenai would convey title to the real property to Moran, and Moran would then lease the property to Kenai with an option to purchase. This arrangement would enable Kenai to reobtain the property when the lease obligations had been fulfilled. The initial loan occurred in September of 1968. Including closing costs, it was in the amount of $11,586.38. Kenai executed a warranty deed conveying title to Moran. Moran executed a lease with an option to purchase in favor of Kenai; the monthly payments were to be $300, with each payment fully credited to the purchase price. The lease was dated September 4, 1968; the warranty deed was dated September 20, 1968.

Thereafter more money was sought by Kenai, and Moran lent an additional $7,515.88. The parties terminated the earlier lease with option and entered into a new lease with a purchase option dated October 24, 1968. This "lease with option" bound Kenai unconditionally to pay $500 a month for five years, commencing November 1, 1968. It also bound Moran unconditionally to convey title to Kenai upon receipt of the last lease payment. By August 11, 1969, the total paid under both leases was $5,100.

On July 13, 1969, a fire totally destroyed the building located on the real property.

Under the October 24, 1968, lease Kenai was to maintain fire insurance on the building at its own expense, in an amount of at least $60,000. The precise language of this clause in the lease was: "During the term of this lease, lessees shall, at their own expense, maintain fire insurance covering the interest of the lessor in the demised premises in an amount not less than Sixty Thousand Dollars ($60,000.00)." Kenai was unable to pay for the insurance. It was agreed that Moran would do so, and that Kenai would reimburse Moran therefore. The total annual premiums for the first year were $2,029.

The parties had intended the sale with lease-back transaction to be a method of securing repayment of the $19,767.26 lent by Moran to Kenai. Moran himself believed the property to be worth between $75,000 and $100,000. He had evinced no interest in buying the property as a permanent owner, and no negotiations had taken place between the parties as to an absolute sale of the property.

After the fire a dispute arose between the parties over the disposition of the insurance proceeds. Moran claimed entitlement to the entire amount of the insurance proceeds. Kenai took the position that Moran was entitled to the proceeds in an amount not exceeding the amount loaned, plus fire insurance premiums paid, less a reduction because of usury.

Kenai brought a declaratory judgment action against Moran. The fire insurers paid $52,500 into the registry of the court as the agreed amount of insurance payable on the loss. The case was tried by the court, and ultimately a judgment was entered which provided that from the fire insurance proceeds Moran should be paid $19,767.26, with interest at 8 percent plus the insurance premiums paid by him, less payments received, and that Kenai should be paid the balance of the proceeds, $33,471.67. Kenai was also awarded costs and an attorney's fee.

Moran appeals from the judgment, claiming various errors committed by the superior court. Kenai cross-appeals, claiming that the court erred in failing to find that the loan from Moran was usurious. . . .

We must first observe that the "lease with purchase option" in this case is really a device to secure repayment of a debt. It is no different functionally than a mortgage or contract for the sale of land. Hervey v. Rhode Island Locomotive Works, 93 U.S. 664, 23 L. Ed. 1003 (1877); McKeeman v. Commercial Credit Equipment Corp., 320 F. Supp. 938 (D. Neb. 1970); American Can Co. v. White, 130 Ark. 381, 197 S.W. 695 (Ark. 1917). . . .

The loan in this case was in the amount of $19,767.26. It was to be repaid in monthly installments of $500, beginning November 1, 1968, and continuing for five years. The amount to be paid by Kenai to Moran was, therefore, $30,000, over a five year period. Even if one were to assume no reduction of principal until the end of five years, the rate of interest is more than 10 percent. A simple interest rate, with a constant reduction of principal, would be considerably greater.

The maximum interest rate which could be charged lawfully on this type of loan in 1968 was 8 percent. On its face this loan was usurious.

In Metcalf v. Bartrand, 491 P.2d 747, 750 (Alaska 1971), we adopted the rule of Wilcox v. Moore, 354 Mich. 499, 93 N.W.2d 288 (1958). The court in *Wilcox* stated that in determining whether a transaction is usurious, a court must look to the real *test* nature of the transaction, in order to avoid "the betrayal of justice by the cloak of words, the contrivances of form, or the paper tigers of the craft." Id. at n.1,291. Intent to violate the usury law will be presumed when the loan agreement unequivocally calls for an impermissible rate of return on the indebtedness. Metcalf v. Bartrand, supra, 491 P.2d at 750-751.

That the transaction here was cast in terms of a "lease with option to purchase" does not save it from the application of the usury statute. Lease-purchase contracts or contracts for the sale of land are often used as devices to disguise usurious loans. When this is the case, courts unhesitatingly pierce through the transaction to determine whether, in substance, a usurious loan was negotiated. Metcalf v. Bartrand, supra at 750-751; McKeeman v. Commercial Credit Equipment Corp., 320 F. Supp. 938 (D. Neb. 1970); Burr v. Capital Reserve Corp., 71 Cal. 2d 983, 80 Cal. Rptr. 345, 458 P.2d 185 (1969).

We hold, therefore, that the superior court's finding was clearly erroneous. Under the applicable statutory provision, usury results in a forfeiture of the entire interest on the debt. It follows that the judgment in this case must be modified. The superior court allowed Moran $2,102.60 as interest on the loans, computed at 8 percent. This amount must instead be deducted from the sum that Moran will receive under the judgment, and Kenai's share of the recovery should be increased accordingly.

We affirm the judgment, as modified. We remand for the entry of a modified judgment.

Affirmed in part, reversed in part.

NOTES AND QUESTIONS

1. The incidence of usurious transactions is higher when major money market interest rates are high, but even when these market interest rates are low, very high-risk borrowers often are vulnerable to being charged usurious interest rates.

2. The successful usury defense requires that three elements be shown: (1) the transaction was in fact a "loan or forbearance"; (2) the debtor was in fact *required* to pay excessive "interest"; and (3) the lender had "wrongful intent," which most courts view as anything more than innocent mistake.

"Loan" transactions are usually quite straightforward. The borrower simply issues his note or bond to evidence the obligation. Rarely does the note reveal an interest rate that blatantly violates the usury limit except where the lender may wrongly believe that one of the usury exceptions applies, page 166 infra. The *Moran* case typifies the *disguised* loan where the parties, at the "lender's" instance, dress up the transaction to conceal its real nature. Some other disguises are described in Benfield, Money, Mortgages, and Migraine — The Usury Headache, 19 Case W. Res. L. Rev. 819, 866-873 (1968). These include "selling" part of the borrower's business to the lender for a nominal price, or "selling" real estate or other property to the lender at one price (the moneys needed) and agreeing unconditionally to repurchase the asset at a second, higher price, where the difference exceeds the allowable interest rates for the interval between sale and purchase.

"Forbearance" occurs when, at the loan's maturity, the lender agrees not to press collection of the debt until some later date. If the lender exacts a charge for agreeing to forbear, it will be treated as loan interest.

3. The borrower may bear many expenses in connection with a loan, but only expenses that are "interest" or interest-like are subject to the usury defense. Loan expenses include charges for credit reports, appraisals, title examinations, title insurance, mortgage preparation, surveys, inspections, tax and insurance escrows, recording, bank attorneys, loan "origination," and mortgage brokers.

Points charged by lenders when loans are originated commonly are held to be interest for usury purposes. A case so holding is Abramowitz v. Barnett Bank, 394 So. 2d 1033 (Fla. Dist. Ct. App. 1981), in which it is stated at 1035 (citations omitted): "A lender will not be allowed to impose any miscellaneous fees or service charges on the front end of a loan when that sum, added to the interest charged, exceeds the maximum rate of interest. Application of such fees to pay the general overhead of a lender . . . are not sufficient to alter the characterizations of these charges as interest. It is also well established that a borrower can be charged the actual reasonable expenses of making a particular loan. However bogus charges for services not actually rendered will not be allowed to cloak the extraction of illegal interest." In the *Abramowitz* case, the bank charged one point (one percent) to originate a $400,000 loan, the $4,000 fee deducted from the loan proceeds paid the borrower. A bank officer admitted that part of the $4,000 went to pay the bank's normal overhead expenses, such as salaries and utilities. The loan was held usurious.

Adjustable rate mortgage interest also is generally considered interest for usury purposes unless exempted by statute. See Annot., Usury in Connection With Loan Calling for Variable Interest Rate, 18 A.L.R. 4th 1068 (1982). But prepayment premiums or penalties almost always have not been considered interest in determining whether a transaction is usurious. Arguments in support of this position include that the payment is for loss to the mortgagee of a favorable loan and that in many cases making a prepayment is optional with the mortgagor and hence is a charge for exercising a privilege and not interest. See Annot., Construction and Effect as to Interest Due of Real Estate Mortgage Clause Authorizing Mortgagor to Prepay Principal Debt, 86 A.L.R. 3d 599 (1978).

A safeguard measure, if there is concern that a particular transaction may be usurious, is to include a cap provision in the loan document stating that interest charged shall not exceed the maximum permitted by applicable usury laws.

4. In their concern with inflation, lenders have sought an even sturdier hedge against the declining dollar than record-breaking interest rates. Lenders frequently insist upon a profit-sharing set-up, which may take one of several forms. Consider as to each arrangement its vulnerability to the claim of usury:

a. Lender's participation in income as contingent interest: The borrower agrees to pay to the lender a specified percentage of his income from the mortgaged property as well as the fixed interest on the loan. The percentage base is variously defined (e.g., gross income, gross receipts, net income, etc.). Cf. Jameson v. Warren, 91 Cal. App. 590, 267 P. 372 (1928); Brown v. Cardoza, 67 Cal. App. 2d 187, 153 P.2d 767 (1944) (usury can result where fixed rate at or near the ceiling and the contingent fee places return substantially above the ceiling); contra Lyons v. National Savings Bank, 113 N.Y.S.2d 695 (Sup. Ct. 1952).

b. Lender's participation in proceeds of refinancing or resale: The borrower agrees that if he sells the property or refinances the mortgage above the existing balance, the lender will receive a percentage of the sales price or excess mortgage proceeds. Cf. Thomassen v. Carr, 250 Cal. App. 2d 341, 58 Cal. Rptr. 297 (1967) (usury did not result where lender received 30 percent of the developers' sales profit "in lieu of" interest).

c. Lender's participation by receipt of ownership interest: The lender receives an *ownership* share in the venture for which he pays little or nothing. Compare Mission Hill Development Corp. v. Western Small Business Investment Co., 260 Cal. App. 2d 923, 67 Cal. Rptr. 505 (1968) (parties intended to evade usury laws) with Bokser v. Lewis, 383 Pa. 507, 119 A.2d 67 (1956) (no intent found).

5. *How to compute the interest rate:* Ordinarily, the computation of the basic interest rate involves a routine calculation. Where the lender collects "extras," however, the calculation becomes more difficult and may involve vital policy choices. To take a simple illustration: The lender charges at the outset a $500 "origination fee" on a $10,000, two-year loan bearing 6 percent interest: Is the first year's yield 11 percent (and possibly usurious)? Looking at this and similar transactions, the court would probably prorate the fee, treating it as interest earned over the entire loan period; this would result in an average yield of 8.5 percent yearly. French v. Mortgage Guaranty Co., 16 Cal. 2d 26, 104 P.2d 655 (1940); Home Savings and Loan Assn. v. Bates, 76 N.M. 660, 417 P.2d 798 (1968). The result would be unchanged even if the borrower prepaid the loan after one year. Why is that? Cf. French v. Mortgage Guaranty Co., supra; B. F. Saul Co. v. West End Park North, Inc., 250 Md. 707, 246 A.2d 591 (1968).

Where the interest charge is partly tied to a profit-sharing arrangement, should courts vary their usual practice of viewing the entire loan period? To illustrate the problem: On a $100,000, 10-year loan, the borrower agrees to pay annually 5 percent interest and 10 percent of his net profits; under this sharing arrangement, the bank receives $6,000 ($5,000 + $1,000) in year one, and $13,000 ($5,000 + $8,000) in year two. The borrower then claims usury. If the court treats the profit-sharing arrangement as an interest equivalent, how should the interest rate be measured: year two alone; the average for years one and two; no measurement until the 10-year loan period ends?

6. One means of avoiding local usury restrictions, with some case law support, is for the parties to contract that the law of another designated state, with more lenient usury laws, shall determine the validity of interest rates. This approach was upheld in Continental Mortgage Investors v. Sailboat Key, Inc., 395 So. 2d 507 (1981), in which the opinion of the Florida Supreme Court states at 507-508: "The question presented is whether the courts of this state will recognize a choice of law provision designating foreign law in an interstate loan contract which calls for interest prohibited as usury under Florida law but supportable under the chosen foreign law [Massachusetts]. We conclude that in an interstate commercial loan transaction with which several states have contacts and in which usury is implicated, Florida courts will recognize a choice of law provision provided by the parties so long as the jurisdiction chosen in the contract has a normal relationship with the transaction. Under the circumstances of this case, we hold that Continental Mortgage Investors, a real estate investment trust organized under the laws of Massachusetts with its only office in Massachusetts where it carries on its business, has a sufficient nexus with Massachusetts to support a choice of law provision in favor of that state's law." In the *Continental* case, the land involved and the borrower were located in Florida.

(b) Exempt Transactions

The usury statute itself, fraught as it is with exceptions, belies the imputation of a strong public policy.

Continental Mortgage Investors v. Sailboat Key, Inc.,
395 So. 2d 507, 509 (Fla. 1981)

The realm of usury is fraught not only with exception, but also with paradox. The very word "usurious" strongly connotes an unclean act and, indeed, where usury occurs, the penalties often are stringent and sometimes even criminal. Yet usury law exemptions cover many more loan situations than do the ceilings. Major exemptions include the consumer loan, which may carry rates as high as 3 percent monthly when made by licensed regulated lenders; the credit sale of goods; loans by credit unions and pawnbrokers; and some installment or industrial loan transactions that control most consumer and business borrowing outside the area of real estate finance. Exemptions also apply to many loans secured by real estate, of which the corporate borrower exemption is particularly important.

Feller v. Architects Display Buildings, Inc.

54 N.J. Super. 205, 148 A.2d 634 (App. Div. 1959)

SCHETTINO, J.A.D. Appeal was taken by the defendants Architects Display Buildings, Inc., a corporation of New Jersey (hereafter referred to as "Architects") and Charles S. Cohan, individually, from a Superior Court, Chancery Division, summary judgment foreclosing two mortgages, one in the amount of $250,000 and the other $50,000. . . .

The trial court pointed out in its oral findings and opinion on April 25, 1958 that:

"The defendant corporation has filed a defense by amended pleadings which seeks to set up in the main three legal defenses: (1) usury; (2) that the transaction was a violation of the Banking Act, and, (3) that there is a violation to the Real Estate Broker's Act."

In support of its amended answer and counterclaim, defendant Architects submitted three affidavits, as follows: (a) affidavit of its president, Charles S. Cohan, dated February 28, 1958; (b) affidavit of Charles S. Cohan, dated March 28, 1958, and (c) affidavit of Samuel D. Lewin, attorney and title searcher, dated March 28, 1958. No other proof was submitted or offered by Architects.

The facts are as follows: Architects had been constructing a building on premises located on Route 22, Mountainside, New Jersey, and had completed about 70% of the work. In order to complete it, it sought mortgage loans from a man named Sturm. He offered to lend to Architects $250,000 in consideration for advance interest of $11,460 and a "service charge" of $28,540 which would leave a net of $211,000. Architects accepted the offer by a letter dated January 30, 1957 confirming the terms of the agreement. Pursuant to the terms, Architects on February 4, 1957 mortgaged its premises to Sturm for the sum of $250,000, due December 30, 1957. The mortgage secured Architects' promissory note of $250,000 to the order of Sturm. The mortgage provided that "In the event that said note and this mortgage are not paid on the due date the Mortgagor shall pay a service charge at the rate of 1/23 of 1% per day from the date of default to the date of actual payment."

The mortgage also provided that "The within mortgage is given to secure advances to be made for the construction of a building on the mortgaged premises and to secure other charges, all in accordance with the terms of a commitment signed by the mortgagee and approved and accepted by the mortgagor; said commitment is dated January 30, 1957." The note incorporated all the terms of the mortgage. Payment of this note was personally guaranteed by Architects' president, Charles S. Cohan. Mr. Cohan, although not a lawyer, had studied for the bar.

On the same day all of Architects' stockholders, consisting of Charles S. Cohan, Florence B. Cohan, his wife, and Ethel Cohan, his sister, executed their consent to the execution of the mortgage and note and also executed a subordination of indebtedness to the loan of $250,000. By letter dated February 4, 1957 Architects also agreed that Sturm could assign to plaintiffs the original loan letter agreement dated January 30, 1957, the note, the mortgage and the assignment of a certain lease affecting the premises. On February 4, 1957 Sturm transferred to plaintiffs the mortgage and note. Architects admitted the receipt of the $210,000 in accordance with the loan agreement and admitted that no part of the $250,000, the interest or charges has been paid.

On April 24, 1957 Architects borrowed an additional $50,000 from plaintiffs. This loan was secured by a mortgage containing provisions to the effect that it was given to secure a series of 11 promissory notes. The mortgage provided that "In the event that any of the notes secured by this mortgage are not paid on the due date said note in default shall bear interest at the rate of 1/23 of 1% per day from the due date to the date of actual payment. . . . Architects admitted receipt of $41,000 of this stated loan of $50,000 pursuant to the terms of the agreement. The series of 11 notes was endorsed by Charles S. Cohan, individually. The first ten of said notes were each in the sum of $2,000, due and payable on the first day of each month starting with July 1, 1957 and ending on April 1, 1958, inclusive, and the eleventh note was in the sum of $30,000 due April 24, 1958. The notes due July 1, 1957 through November 1, 1957, inclusive were paid by Architects. The note due December 1, 1957 was not paid and remained unpaid for more than 15 days. Each note provided that "in the event of the non-payment of any one of said series and such default continues for a period of 15 days, then at the option of the holder of any of the said notes, all or any part of the remaining unpaid notes shall forthwith become due and payable." By reason of the default in the payment of the December 1, 1957 note plaintiffs exercised the right to claim the principal unpaid balance of $40,000 represented by the notes due December 1, 1957 through April 1, 1958, inclusive, and April 24, 1958, were immediately due and payable. Architects admits that the sum of $40,000 has not been paid and that no interest or charges thereon have been paid.

acceleration clause

As we view the record, we agree with the trial court that the case was a proper one for summary judgment. . . . N.J.S.A. 31:1-6 provides:

"Corporation not to make defense of usury.

"No corporation shall plead or set up the defense of usury to any action brought against it to recover damages or enforce a remedy on any obligation executed by said corporation."

Our Supreme Court has stated in In re Greenberg, 21 N.J.213, 220, 121 A.2d 520 (1956), and Gelber v. Kugel's Tavern, 10 N.J. 191, 196, 89 A.2d 654 (1952), that if the corporate form is used to cloak a loan which in fact is intended to be a loan to an individual, the alter ego of the corporation, then this statutory provision will not bar the plea of usury. In *Gelber* the Supreme Court stated that if the corporation to which the loan was ostensibly made was specifically incorporated at the request of the lenders' agent and subsequent to the application for the loan, the defense of usury would apply. The court stated (10 N.J. at page 196, 89 A.2d at page 656):

". . . It is generally recognized . . . that an individual may recover usurious payments on loans made in fact to the individual though in form disguised as loans to a corporation and evidenced by obligations executed by it to hide the fact that the lender has exacted an illegal rate of interest from the real borrower."

The Supreme Court pointed out that on the evidence the jury should have been permitted to determine the reason for the incorporation and if the jury found it was created as a cloak to evade the usury law, then the corporate shell would not benefit the lender.

But in the case before us the undisputed history of Architects does not help defendants at all. Architects was incorporated on May 24, 1956. On May 29, 1956 it acquired title to the premises involved herein. In July 1956 it began to build and by January 30, 1957, according to Mr. Cohan's depositions, "The building was enclosed, with the exception of window-walls. . . . Oh, I would say about seventy percent" of the construction was completed. We hold that the loans were made to an existing corporation.

Architects through its president contends that the obligations were entered into by Mr. Cohan and Architects as co-makers and therefore the defense of usury should apply as one of the borrowers was an individual who could have the benefit of the defense of usury. Mr. Cohan's depositions dissipate this contention. Mr. Cohan was a guarantor of the corporate obligation and not a co-maker. Mr. Justice Brennan in *Gelber* stated (10 N.J. at page 196, 89 A.2d at page 656):

". . . If, however, the loans are actually made to the corporation direct, usury is not a defense even to the endorsers of the corporate obligations issued for the loans, [citations]."

We hold that the defense of usury is not applicable.

A corollary point is raised with reference to the charge of 1/23 of 1% interest per day after default as being a penalty. As to the first loan, i.e., $250,000, the due date was December 30, 1957. For the period of time from the date of the loan, February 4, 1957 to December 30, 1957, plaintiffs received $11,460 advance interest payments plus the service charge of $28,540 which plaintiffs concede amounts to interest as well by deducting the amount from the face amount of the loan. By the terms of the loan no default could take place until after December 30, 1957. It is the general rule in the case of a corporate borrower that it is not illegal to provide for a higher rate of interest than the legal rate after maturity, but if such rate is unconscionably high it will be unenforceable because it amounts to a penalty. 3 Williston on Contracts, § 781, p. 2196; 5 ibid., § 1416, p. 3945; 6 ibid., § 1969, p. 4803; cf. Restatement, Contracts, § 536; cf. Ramsey v. Morrison, 39 N.J.L. 591 (Sup. Ct. 1877); cf. In re Tastyeast, Inc., 126 F.2d 879 (3rd Cir., 1942), certiorari denied Modern Factors Co. v. Tastyeast, Inc., 316 U.S. 696, 62 S. Ct. 1291, 86 L. Ed. 1766 (1942). Here the rate before maturity amounted to about 19% and the rate after maturity is 15.87%. The latter being less it is not unconscionable and so is enforceable.

However, as to the interest payments after default on the $50,000 loan, a different factual situation exists. There, advance interest in the amount of $8,500 was retained by plaintiffs for the period from April 24, 1957 to April 24, 1958. Default took place on December 1, 1957. Plaintiffs urged and the trial court agreed that interest at the default rate of 1/23 of 1% per day ran from December 1, 1957 which was within the period for which interest had been paid. On the basis of $8500, the interest rate on the $50,000 loan is computed to be 17%. Were we to allow an additional 1/23 of 1% per day the defendant would be paying 17% plus 15.87%, totalling 32.87%, on the unpaid $40,000 balance from the accelerated maturity date. This is clearly unconscionable and unenforceable as a penalty. Error was therefore committed in allowing any additional interest on the unpaid balance of that loan for the period from December 1, 1957 through April 24, 1958. The trial court was correct in allowing the 1/23 of 1% rate after the maturity date of April 24, 1958 to the date of judgment, May 9, 1958 and legal rate thereafter. . . .

Modified and remanded for action not inconsistent with this opinion and with costs.

NOTES AND QUESTIONS

1. The corporate borrower exemption has spread to a majority of states. New York was first, in 1850, after a bank had outraged the financial community by successfully pleading the usury law to avoid repayment of a loan that had saved it from permanent insolvency. Dry Dock Bank v. American Life Insurance & Trust Co., 3 N.Y. 344 (1850). In several other states, rate limits for corporate borrowers are above those for noncorporate borrowers. What is the present justification for treating corporations less protectively?

2. In New York, the exemption does not apply to a corporation whose principal asset is a one- or two-family dwelling, when the corporation is organized or the controlling interest acquired within six months prior to the obtaining of a loan secured by the asset. N.Y. Gen. Oblig. Law §5-521 (McKinney 2001). See also Ky. Rev. Stat. Ann. § 360.025(2) (2002). Why this exemption within an exemption?

3. In Washington, a corporate borrower engaged in a trade or business may raise the usury defense only when a natural person is also liable on the loan. Wash. Rev. Code Ann. § 19.52.030 (Supp. 1991). In short, the immunity of the individual inures to the corporation. This reverses the situation in the main case where the disability of the corporation attaches to the individual. What are the arguments for and against each rationale?

4. An individual borrows at a usurious rate and gives a mortgage to secure the debt. He then transfers the real estate to a corporation, which takes title subject to the mortgage. May the corporation interpose the usury defense in a mortgage foreclosure action? Cf. Kahn v. Sohmer, 12 A.D.2d 659, 212 N.Y.S.2d 85 (1961).

5. In a number of states, some seller-financed transactions are exempt from the usury laws. Among cases so holding is Mandelino v. Fribourg, 23 N.Y.2d 145, 242 N.E.2d 823 (1968), in which the Court of Appeals held that the purchase money mortgage in that case was not a "loan" within the meaning of the usury statute, as the statute applies to a loan or forbearance not to a sale. In another New York case, this statement is made: "There is no usury in the normal purchase money mortgage transaction where a seller demands a higher price because the consideration is not all in cash. However, a lender of money may not utilize the form of a purchase money mortgage to cloak a usurious loan." Butts v. Samuels, 5 A.D. 1008, 174 N.Y. S.2d 325, 326 (1958).

6. In some states, loans for large sums of money are exempt from usury laws. For example, two and one-half million dollars in New York, N.Y. Gen. Oblig. Law § 5-501-6b (McKinney 2001); and over a half-million dollars in Florida, unless rate constitutes criminal usury, Fla. Stat. Ann. § 687.03 (West 2003).

7. On the unconscienability concept as applied to high interest rate situations see Bender, Rate Regulation at the Crossroads of Usury and Unconscienability, 31 Hous. L. Rev. 721 (1994).

(c)   The Penalties for Usury

Szerdahelyi v. Harris

67 N.Y.2d 42, 490 N.E.2d 517 (1986)

OPINION OF THE COURT

SIMONS, Judge.

The issue is whether a lender, by tendering a return of excess interest paid by a borrower on a usurious loan, may establish a right to recover the loan principal plus legal interest. Section 5-511 of the General Obligations Law provides otherwise but defendants claim that the 1965 amendment to section 5-519 of the General Obligations Law, not previously interpreted by this court, permits them to relieve themselves of the illegality and revive the void contract. We hold that it does not.

The question arises from these facts. Plaintiff and Patrick Laurent were tenants in an apartment building that was converted to cooperative ownership. Plaintiff elected to purchase their apartment but she was unable to secure a conventional mortgage without Laurent, who was then out of the country. Accordingly, she consulted Martin Harris who was attorney for Laurent and his brother. Harris tried to secure a mortgage but when he was unable to do so, he approached some of his clients in an effort to arrange a short-term loan for plaintiff that could be superseded by a mortgage upon Laurent's return. Defendant Mensch was one of those Harris approached. She agreed to make the loan by liquidating all or part of her interest in a Dreyfus account that paid a return of approximately 18% per year, provided that the loan was fully secured and that the return was sufficient to compensate her for any loss arising from the liquidation of her account. Harris claimed that to ensure this he contacted the Banking Department and was told that a return of 21% was permissible. In fact, the maximum allowable interest rate at the time, as fixed by Banking Law § 14-a, was 16%.

On November 17, 1981, plaintiff purchased the cooperative apartment. The purchase was financed by her check for $14,161.33 and a check for $25,000 drawn on the Mensch account with Dreyfus Liquid Assets, Inc. payable to the order of attorney Harris, as her agent, and indorsed by him. Harris delivered the checks to the cooperative's sponsor, and at the same time plaintiff executed and delivered to Harris her note for $25,000, bearing interest at the rate of 21%, and payable within one year. The note was guaranteed by Laurent's brother. As additional security, plaintiff delivered to Harris a stock certificate, representing her interest in the cooperative corporation, and an irrevocable stock power.

On November 2, 1982, 15 days before the loan became due and after plaintiff had paid interest for 11 months, plaintiff's attorneys sent a letter to Harris stating that the loan was usurious. Harris then sent plaintiff a check for the excess over the

Pl. won @ trial ct. on summary jud.

allowable interest on the loan. When the check was returned by her attorneys, Harris sent it to plaintiff once more, denominating it an unconditional tender made pursuant to law. She again rejected it and brought this action seeking judgment declaring that the loan was illegal because usurious, that the note and stock power were void and canceled, and directing that these documents and the stock certificate be returned to her along with all sums paid. Plaintiff moved for summary judgment and Special Term granted her the requested relief.

A divided Appellate Division, 110 A.D.2d 550, 488 N.Y.S.2d 164, reversed and remanded the action for trial. *← A.D.* Justice Bloom, writing for himself and Justice Carro, construed General Obligations Law § 5-519 as permitting a lender who tenders back the excess interest on a usurious loan to recover the principal and legal interest. Justice Asch concurred in that result but on different grounds. He viewed the transaction as one involving a purchase-money mortgage and thus exempt from the provisions of the usury laws. Justice Sandler, joined by Justice Lynch, dissented. Although he found the statutory language could be read as inconsistent with the expressed legislative intention of conforming the statute to prior judicial precedent, he believed that the amendment was not intended to overturn decisions holding that a tender back of excess interest does not entitle the lender to recover the underlying debt and unpaid lawful interest. In Justice Sandler's view of the case the lender was entitled to only lawful interest previously paid. We find no inconsistency between amended section 5-519 of the General Obligations Law and prior case law and concur in the dissenters' result. Accordingly, the order of the Appellate Division should be modified to grant plaintiff partial summary judgment declaring the note and stock power void and ordering these, as well as the stock certificate, returned to her, and directing defendants to pay plaintiff the excess over the lawful interest previously paid on the loan.

Preliminarily, Justice Asch's characterization of the transaction as a purchase-money mortgage must be addressed. Purchase-money mortgages constitute a narrow exception to the restrictions on interest found in the usury laws and thus if this transaction involved a purchase-money mortgage plaintiff might well have been bound by her agreement (see, Mandelino v. Fribourg, 23 N.Y.2d 145, 151, 295 N.Y.S.2d 654, 242 N.E.2d 823). Defendants did not raise this defense at Special Term. *Not a PMM* Apparently they never considered their transaction to be in the nature of a mortgage, and correctly so. A purchase-money mortgage is generally defined as "a mortgage executed at the time of purchase of the land and contemporaneously with the acquisition of the legal title, or afterward, but as part of the same transaction, to secure an unpaid balance of the purchase price" (38 N.Y. Jur., Mortgages and Deeds of Trust, § 7, at 25 [citing Boies v. Benham, 127 N.Y. 620, 28 N.E. 657]). Ms. Mensch, the lender in this case, was neither a seller of real property nor did she take back a mortgage to secure money borrowed to acquire any such property.

Turning to the main issue, the consequences of the lender's offer to tender back to plaintiff the amount of excess interest above the legally authorized rate she paid on this loan are governed by General Obligations Law § 5-519. It provides: "Every person who shall repay or return the money, goods or other things so taken, accepted or received, or the value thereof, *shall be discharged from any other or further forfeiture or penalty which he may have incurred under sections 5-511 or 5-513,* by taking or receiving the money, goods or other things so repaid, or returned, as aforesaid." (Emphasis added.) The dispute centers on the italicized words. Defendants contend that nullification of the usurious contract is one of the penalties provided by section 5-511[1] and thus the language of section 5-519 permits recovery of the principal and lawful interest if the excess is tendered to the borrower. Plaintiff counters that defendants' construction is inconsistent with judicial precedent and with the intention of the drafters of the legislation and, further, that such a construction permits easy avoidance of the proscriptions against excessive interest because any lender faced with a disavowal of a usurious loan could recover it, notwithstanding the illegality, merely by tendering the excess interest to the borrower.

Analysis starts with an understanding of General Obligations Law §§ 5-511 and 5-513. Section 5-511 deals with two types of lenders. First, referring to loans made by other than banks or savings and loan associations, it declares that all bonds, notes, contracts, deposits of goods, and the like arising within a usurious transaction are void. Thus, when a court deems a transaction to be usurious, it must declare the transaction and its supporting documents void, enjoin prosecution on them and order that all documents and collateral be canceled and surrendered. Second, section 5-511 provides that when the lender is a bank or savings and loan association, the usurious transaction is not void, but any interest thereon is forfeited. A penalty is also assessed: any excess interest paid by a borrower to the institution may be recovered from it in twice the amount paid. Section 5-513 provides that a borrower who is subject to a usurious transaction may bring an action to recover the excess interest paid on the loan.

Contrary to defendants' contentions, section 5-519's bar to further penalties or forfeitures after the tender of illegal interest does not foreclose a judicial determination that a usurious instrument is void, and that the underlying transaction and supporting documents have no legal force or binding effect. Such a determination is not just "another" penalty or forfeiture contained in sections 5-511 or 5-513 and it should not be confused with the penalties or forfeitures imposed by article 5 of the General Obligations Law. A penalty is commonly understood to be the exacting

---

1. 1. Section 5-511 provides:

Usurious contracts void

1. All bonds, bills, notes, assurances, conveyances, all other contracts or securities whatsoever, except bottomry and respondentia bonds and contracts, and all deposits of goods or other things whatsoever, whereupon or whereby there shall be reserved or taken, or secured or agreed to be reserved or taken, any greater sum, or greater value, for the loan or forbearance of any money, goods or other things in action, than is prescribed in section 5-501, shall be void, except that the knowingly taking, receiving, reserving or charging such a greater sum or greater value by a savings bank, a savings and loan association or a federal savings and loan association shall only be held and adjudged a forfeiture of the entire interest which the loan or obligation carries with it or which has been agreed to be paid thereon. If a greater sum or greater value has been paid, the person paying the same or his legal representative may recover from the savings bank, the savings and loan association or the federal savings and loan association twice the entire amount of the interest thus paid.

2. Except as provided in subdivision one, whenever it shall satisfactorily appear by the admissions of the defendant, or by proof, that any bond, bill, note, assurance, pledge, conveyance, contract, security or any evidence of debt, has been taken or received in violation of the foregoing provisions, the court shall declare the same to be void, and enjoin any prosecution thereon, and order the same to be surrendered and cancelled.

Section 5-513 provides:

Recovery of excess

Every person who, for any such loan or forbearance, shall pay or deliver any greater sum or value than is allowed to be received pursuant to section 5-501, and his personal representatives, may recover in an action against the person who shall have taken or received the same, and his personal representatives, the amount of the money so paid or value delivered, above the rate aforesaid.

of a sum of money as punishment for performing a prohibited act, or for not performing a required act (see, Black's Law Dictionary, at 1020 [5th ed 1979]), e.g., the payment of double the amount of excess interest required by section 5-511. A forfeiture is the loss of a right by the commission of a crime or fault (id., at 584), e.g., the forfeiture of interest provided in section 5-511. A legal determination that a transaction governed by section 5-511 is void is not a penalty or a forfeiture. It is no more than the implementation of a statutory expression of the familiar rule that illegal contracts, or those contrary to public policy, are unenforceable and that the courts will not recognize rights arising from them (McConnell v. Commonwealth Pictures Corp., 7 N.Y.2d 465, 469, 199 N.Y.S.2d 483, 166 N.E.2d 494; Sternaman v. Metropolitan Life Ins. Co., 170 N.Y. 13, 19, 62 N.E. 763, *rearg. denied* 170 N.Y. 616). The law leaves the parties to such agreements where it finds them (Hettich v. Hettich, 304 N.Y. 8, 105 N.E.2d 601; see generally, 21 N.Y. Jur. 2d, Contracts, §§ 147-186). Accordingly, section 5-519 does not prevent a declaration of the invalidity of the debt, notwithstanding the tender of excess interest improperly charged. The lender's tender may avoid future litigation but it cannot revive the void contract.

This conclusion is confirmed by the history of usury laws in this State and by judicial precedent. That historical background was thoroughly analyzed in Curtiss v. Teller, 157 App. Div. 804, 143 N.Y.S. 188, affd., 217 N.Y. 649, the leading case on the subject, and was reviewed by the Appellate Division below (110 A.D.2d 550, 553-556, 488 N.Y.S.2d 164). At the time *Curtiss* was decided, the civil usury laws were codified in article 25 of the General Business Law (Consol. Laws, ch. 20, L.1909, ch. 25). The *Curtiss* court stated that those statutes did two separate things, they "(1) declare[d] the usurious transaction void, and (2) provide[d] for forfeitures and penalties against the usurer" (Curtiss v. Teller, supra, 157 App. Div. pp 807-808, 143 N.Y.S. 188; see also, Bowery Sav. Bank v. Nirenstein, 269 N.Y. 259, 199 N.E. 211). In thus interpreting the statute, the court held that the tender-back provisions of section 376[2] would not save the lender "the money which he had actually advanced upon the usurious loan, together with interest thereon" (id., 157 App. Div. p. 817, 143 N.Y.S. 188). In 1963 section 376 was reenacted as section 5-519 of the General Obligations Law and the usury provisions of the General Business Law were consolidated into it, the sponsor of the legislation noting that no change in the existing law on the subject was intended (1963 N.Y. Legis Ann, at 103). Inasmuch as the recodification did not alter the words of the statute and was not intended to alter the effect or judicial interpretation of it, perforce, it did not change the consequences of a tender back of excess interest.

There was a significant change of the language of section 5-519 in 1965, however. . . .

The sole amendment to the General Obligations Law was the alteration of language in section 5-519. . . .

This alteration removed the words "acquitted" and "punishment" and added the phrase "under sections 5-511 or 5-513," the words prompting the present

---

2. General Business Law § 376 provided: "Return of excess a bar to further penalties. Every person who shall repay or return the money, goods or other thing so taken, accepted or received, or the value thereof, shall be acquitted and discharged from any other or further forfeiture, penalty or punishment, which he may have incurred, by taking or receiving the money, goods or other things so repaid, or returned, as aforesaid" (Recodified at General Obligations Law § 5-519 [L.1963, ch. 576]).

dispute, in order to distinguish the penalties of civil usury laws from the punishments of the criminal usury laws. . . .

The "present judicial interpretation" the amendment intended to reflect was the interpretation we affirmed in Curtiss v. Teller, 157 App. Div. 804, 143 N.Y.S. 188, *affd.*, 217 N.Y. 649, supra, namely, that a usurious transaction is void *ab initio,* and a return of excess interest cannot save to the lender the money actually advanced, or the interest due on the loan (see, id., p. 817, 143 N.Y.S. 188). Consequently, although defendants need not return the lawful interest plaintiff has already paid, they cannot recover either the money loaned or the interest remaining due in this transaction.

The order below should be modified to grant plaintiff partial summary judgment declaring the note and the stock power void and ordering their return together with the stock certificate; defendants should be ordered to return to plaintiff the excess over the legal interest paid on the loan, and the matter should be remitted to Supreme Court, New York County, for a determination of the amount due. As so modified, the order is affirmed, with costs. The certified question is answered in the negative.

Wachtler, C. J., and Meyer, Kaye, Titone and Hancock, J J., concur.

Alexander, J., taking no part.

NOTES AND QUESTIONS

1. The civil penalties for usury range from forfeiture of all interest and principal to loss only of the interest portion that exceeds the statutory maximum. The solution applied in Moran v. Kenai Towing and Salvage, Inc., supra p. 207, falls in between the two extremes: loss of all interest. Which of the various possible solutions is preferable and why? Is the solution imposed by statute in New York, as applied in Szerdahelyi v. Harris, overkill? Critical of the New York position is Berger, Adding Insult to Injury: How *In re Venture Mortgage Fund* Exposes the Inequitable Results of New York's Usury Remedies, 29 Fordham Urb. L.J. 2193 (2002), focusing on a New York case subsequent to Szerdahelyi v. Harris. What merit is there to the unique treatment in New York of banks and savings and loans, mentioned in the Szerdahelyi v. Harris opinion: interest forfeited, but not principal, plus a penalty of double the amount of excess interest?

2. In some states it is a felony to charge extremely high rates of interest: for instance, New York, over 25 percent per annum, N.Y. Penal Law, § 190.40 (McKinney 1999); and Colorado, over 45 percent per annum, Colo. Rev. Stat. Ann. § 18-15-104 (West 2004). In a number of other states usury is a misdemeanor. Would it not be preferable to eliminate all civil usury restrictions and let the market determine interest rates, subject only to criminal sanctions and, as in the *Feller* case, limits on unreasonable charges for interest likely to be substantially above the market?

(d)   Federal Preemption

Federal statutes and regulations have preempted some state usury laws. As a result, in most states, state usury restrictions no longer apply to first mortgage loans on residential real estate, including apartment building loans. This important preemption was imposed by Title V of the Depository Institutions Deregulation and Monetary Control Act of 1980, Pub. L. No. 96-221, 94 Stat. 132 (1980). As to mortgage usury laws, the act, as amended, provides in part, 12 U.S.C.A. §1735f-7a (2001):

> (a)(1) The provisions of the constitution or the laws of any State expressly limiting the rate or amount of interest, discount points, finance charges, or other charges which may be charged, taken, received, or reserved shall not apply to any loan, mortgage, credit sale, or advance which is—
>
> (A) secured by a first lien on residential real property, by a first lien on all stock allocated to a dwelling unit in a residential cooperative housing corporation, or by a first lien on a residential manufactured home;
>
> (B) made after March 31, 1980; and
>
> (C) [This subsection describes in detail the sorts of loans and lenders affected by the preemption. In effect, it extends to all significant lenders.]
>
> (b)(1) Except as provided in paragraph (2) . . . , the provisions of subsection (a)(1) of this section shall apply to any loan, mortgage, credit sale, or advance made in any State on or after April 1, 1980.
>
> (2) . . . the provisions of subsection (a)(1) shall not apply to any loan, mortgage, credit sale, or advance made in any State after the date (on or after April 1, 1980, and before April 1, 1983) on which such State adopts a law or certifies that the voters of such State have voted in favor of any provision, constitutional or otherwise, which states explicitly and by its terms that such State does not want the provisions of subsection (a)(1) to apply with respect to loans, mortgages, credit sales, and advances made in such State. . . .
>
> (4) At any time after March 31, 1980, any State may adopt a provision of law placing limitations on discount points or such other charges on any loan, mortgage, credit sale, or advance described in subsection
>
> (a)(1) of this section.
>
> (c) The provisions of subsection (a)(1) shall not apply to a loan, mortgage, credit sale, or advance which is secured by a first lien on a residential manufactured home unless the terms and conditions relating to such loan, mortgage, credit sale, or advance comply with consumer protection provisions specified in regulations prescribed by the Federal Home Loan Bank Board. . . .

NOTES AND QUESTIONS

1. In addition to its preemption of state usury laws, the 1980 Depository Institutions Act had other important features, including nationwide authorization of NOW accounts (interest-bearing checking accounts), relaxation of truth-in-lending requirements, and, as we have seen, considerable deregulation of the thrifts.

In explaining usury preemption, the Senate Report on the Deregulation Act spoke of the need "to ease the severity of the mortgage credit crunches of recent years and to provide financial institutions, particularly those with large mortgage portfolios, with the ability to offer higher interest rates on savings deposits." S. Rep. No. 96-368, 96th Cong., 1st Sess. 18 (1979).

On the 1980 Deregulation Act as it applies to usury, see Burke and Kaplinsky, Unraveling the New Federal Usury Law, 37 Bus. Law. 1079 (1982). The United States Treasury Department has promulgated regulations on preemption of state usury laws, 12 C.F.R. pt. 590 (2006).

2. Thirteen states elected to preserve usury restrictions after April 1, 1983 for residential first mortgage loans covered by the federal statute above. These states are: Colorado, Georgia, Hawaii, Idaho, Iowa, Kansas, Massachusetts, Minnesota, Nebraska, North Carolina, South Carolina, South Dakota, and Wisconsin. The federal preemption continues in the remaining states. Is it anomalous, in such states, that homeowners are no longer protected in their first mortgage borrowings, whereas business borrowers, who tend to be more streetwise, often may continue to derive usury protection?

4. Method of Amortization

Another common mortgage provision is the method of amortization, which describes the rate at which the borrower repays the loan balance. Prior to the 1930s, when most loans had short-term maturities, lenders did not press for interim principal reduction; although the borrower made periodic interest payments, the original debt usually remained intact until maturity. At maturity, the borrower would either repay the entire loan or renew the loan in part or full.

Since the 1930s, however, due largely to the influence of the FHA, most residential first mortgages have been *self-amortizing*, which requires periodic principal payments leading to the *gradual* elimination of the loan balance over the term of the loan. The more typical form of self-amortizing mortgage involves *level payment* debt service, that is, equal (usually monthly) debt service installments. Given this objective, the calculation of the (monthly) installment derives from a formula with three variables: original principal balance, the length of the loan, and the rate of interest. Tables that aid in the computation are readily available, for example, from banks and mortgage brokers. Table 2-2 is an example of such a table.

TABLE 2-2
Monthly Level Payments (Dollars) to Amortize $1000 Various Amortization Periods and Interest Rates
Term in Years

Interest Rate Percent	10	15	20	25	30
14.0	15.53	13.32	12.44	12.04	11.85
13.0	14.93	12.65	11.72	11.28	11.06
12.0	14.35	12.00	11.01	10.53	10.29
11.0	13.77	11.37	10.32	9.80	9.52
10.0	13.22	10.75	9.65	9.09	8.78 -
9.0	12.67	10.14	9.00	8.39	8.07
8.0	12.13	9.56	8.36	7.72	7.34

Problem: Compute the level payment required monthly to amortize a $40,000, 15-year mortgage at 13.0 percent interest; a $60,000, 30-year mortgage at 10.0 percent interest.

a) $40 \cdot 12.65 = $ _____

b) $60 \cdot 8.78 = $ _____

You should be aware of the changing relationship between interest and principal in the level payment mortgage; with each installment the interest component gets smaller while the amortization grows. Take, for example, a $50,000, 12 percent, 30-year mortgage, carrying monthly debt service of $514.50. Each installment of debt service goes first toward the payment of interest on the unpaid loan; whatever sum remains goes then into principal reduction. Allocation of interest and principal for the first three months and the final months appears in Table 2-3.

TABLE 2-3

Month	Installment	Interest	Principal	Principal Balance After Monthly Payment
1	$514.50	$500.00	$ 14.50	$49,985.50
2	514.50	499.86	14.64	49,970.86
3	514.50	499.71	14.79	49,956.07
—	—	—	—	—
—	—	—	—	—
—	—	—	—	—
360	514.50	5.00	509.50	0

Notice, also, how slowly amortization proceeds via the level payment mortgage. Table 2-4 shows the percent of unpaid debt remaining at five-year intervals on this hypothetical loan.

TABLE 2-4

Year	Principal Balance	Percentage of Original Balance
5	$48,830	97.66
10	46,710	93.42
15	42,855	85.71
20	35,845	71.69
25	23,120	46.24
30	0	0

The usual alternative to a *level payment* self-amortizing mortgage is the so-called *constant amortization* (declining payment) loan, which one sees more often in investment situations. This method of amortization requires equal amounts of principal reduction in each installment. Again using the example of a $50,000, 12 percent, 30-year mortgage, the schedule of debt service appears in Table 2-5. Over the thirty years, if the hypothetical mortgages go to term, the level payment mortgage will be far more costly. Why is that?

TABLE 2-5

Month	Installment	Interest	Principal	Principal Balance After Monthly Payments
1	$638.88	500.00	138.88	49,861.12
2	637.49	498.61	138.88	49,722.24
3	636.10	497.22	138.88	49,583.36
—	—	—	—	—
—	—	—	—	—
—	—	—	—	—
360	140.27	1.39	138.88	0

Since the income of many homebuying households tends to rise during the mortgage term, both in real and inflated dollars, this might argue for a mortgage whose debt service starts quite low and later steps up. (One close analogy is the life insurance policy calling for premium increases after three to five years in anticipation of the policyholder's greater income.) Such mortgage instruments, the *graduated payment* mortgage (GPM), now exist, although their use remains fairly limited. Because the monthly payments at the outset of the loan are lower than the amount necessary to amortize the loan on a fixed rate basis, this may result in negative amortization during the early years of the loan. Not every state permits that.

The "balloon" mortgage. As we have seen, mortgages are not always self-amortizing. A mortgage is said to have a "balloon" when regular debt service installments do not reduce the unpaid principal balance to zero. While mortgages are still occasionally written to require only interest payments for the entire term, more often the balloon mortgage carries a schedule of mortgage reduction lower than necessary to achieve self-amortization. For example, one might find a $50,000 mortgage calling for $2,000 amortization yearly, all due in fifteen years. This mortgage would have a $20,000 balloon. The balloon arrangement offers the property owner the great advantage of higher cash flow during the mortgage term. He must be ready, however, when the loan matures either to refinance it or pay off the balloon.

5. Casualty Insurance Requirement

Most all mortgage agreements include a provision requiring that casualty insurance be maintained on the mortgaged property, with a common requirement being that the mortgagor insure for the benefit of the mortgagee.[17] If the mortgagor insures for the benefit of the mortgagee and an insured loss occurs, the insured loss payment to the mortgagee reduces the amount of the mortgagee debt by the amount of the loss payment.

17. On casualty insurance requirements in mortgage agreements see Nelson & Whitman, Real Estate Finance Law §§ 4.13-4.16 (4th ed. 2002); Randolph, A Mortgagee's Interest in Casualty Loss Proceeds: Evolving Rules and Risks, 32 Real Prop., Prob. & Tr. J. 1 (1997).

The precise scope and meaning of casualty insurance requirements in mortgage agreements have been the frequent subject of litigation. *Omni Berkshire* is one such case and considers whether or not a mortgagor was required by the mortgage loan agreement to maintain insurance coverage against terrorism acts, a very costly form of coverage following the terrorism attacks of September 11, 2001.

Omni Berkshire Corp. v. Wells Fargo Bank

307 F. Supp. 2d 534 (S.D.N.Y. 2004)

CHIN, District Judge.

In this case, plaintiffs borrowed $250 million in 1998 (the "Loan") pursuant to an agreement (the "Agreement"), secured by five hotels. The Agreement required plaintiffs to obtain and maintain certain insurance, including "comprehensive all risk insurance" on the hotels as well as "such other reasonable insurance" as the lender might request. Prior to September 11, 2001, plaintiffs did not have separate insurance to cover damage from terrorist acts, for damage from terrorist acts was included in the "all risk" coverage. After September 11, 2001, however, insurance companies began excluding terrorist attacks from their "all risk" policies. Terrorism insurance was still available, principally in the form of separate, stand-alone policies at a substantial additional expense. Here, the servicing company for the Loan requested that plaintiffs obtain additional terrorism insurance, but plaintiffs refused, citing the cost. This lawsuit followed.

Two issues are presented: First, whether plaintiffs' obligation to maintain "comprehensive all risk insurance" requires it to continue to maintain terrorism coverage in the post-September 11, 2001 world, now that terrorism insurance is typically excluded from "all risk" policies; and second, assuming no such obligation existed, whether it was reasonable for the servicing company to require plaintiffs to obtain terrorism insurance under the "other reasonable insurance" clause.

The case was tried to the Court without a jury on July 21 and 22, 2003. For the reasons set forth below, I conclude that plaintiffs were not required to purchase terrorism insurance by virtue of the "all risk" clause, but that the servicing company acted reasonably in requesting additional terrorism insurance pursuant to the "other reasonable insurance" clause. Hence, judgment will be entered in favor of defendant. My findings of fact and conclusions of law follow.

BACKGROUND

A. THE FACTS

1. THE LOAN

Plaintiffs Omni Berkshire Corp., HCD Chicago Corp., HCD Houston Corp., HCD Dallas Corp., TRT Development Co. Dallas, and HCD Operating Co., L.P. (collectively, "Omni") own or operate certain hotels in the United States, Canada, and Mexico. On August 28, 1998, Omni entered into the Agreement with Secore

Financial Corp. (the "Lender"), for the Loan and Omni borrowed $250 million. (Ex. 1; Tr. 33–36).[1] The Loan was secured by five of Omni's hotels, located in New York City, Chicago, Houston, Dallas, and Irving, Texas. The outstanding balance of the Loan, at the time of trial, was approximately $230 million. (Ex. 247). The estimated full replacement costs of the pledged properties was $349 million. (Ex. 13). When the Loan closed, the five hotels were worth approximately $500 million. (Ex. 3, at p. S–54; Tr. 83). The hotels were cross-collateralized, meaning that the lender could look to all five properties for repayment of the Loan. (Tr. 70, 83–84). During the negotiations over the terms of the Loan, the subject of terrorism was never discussed. (*Id.* 40, 87).

Defendant Wells Fargo Bank, N.A. ("Wells Fargo") is the servicing company for the Loan, and is charged with administering the Loan and enforcing the terms of the Agreement. Wells Fargo succeeded Wachovia Bank ("Wachovia"), the original servicing company.

The Loan is one of a number of loans, totaling some $1.8 billion in principal amount, that have been securitized and offered to the public. Shares — or "certificates" — have been sold to members of the public pursuant to a prospectus. (Ex. 23; Tr. 218).

2. THE AGREEMENT

Section 6.1(a) of the Agreement requires Omni to "obtain and maintain" insurance for Omni and the five hotels. It requires eight specific listed coverages, including:

> comprehensive all risk insurance on the [five hotels] . . . in an amount equal to one hundred percent (100%) of the "Full Replacement Cost," . . . but the amount shall in no event be less than the outstanding principal balance of the Loan. . . . In addition, [Omni] shall obtain . . . flood hazard insurance . . . and . . . earthquake insurance.

(Ex. 1, §6.1(a)(i)). Although the Agreement contains some 19 pages of definitions, it does not define the phrases "comprehensive all risk insurance" or "all risk." (*See id.*, §1.1 (definitions)). The Agreement does not specifically refer to terrorism insurance or acts of terrorism. (*Id.; see* Tr. 250).

Section 6.1(a) also requires Omni to obtain and maintain:

> upon sixty (60) days' written notice, such other reasonable insurance and in such reasonable amounts as Lender from time to time may reasonably request against such other insurable hazards which at the time are commonly insured against for property similar to [each of the five hotels] located in or around the region in which the [hotel] is located.

(*Id.*, §6.1(a)(ix)).

3. OMNI'S INSURANCE

Since the Loan's inception, Omni has maintained comprehensive all risk insurance, at its own cost and expense. For 2002–2003, the annual premium for the all risk

---

1. References to "Ex." are to the joint trial exhibits received at trial. References to "Tr." are to the transcript of the trial on July 21 and 22, 2003.

policy was approximately $550,000, and for the 2003-2004 time period, the annual premium was just under $500,000. (Tr. 38–40; Exs. 14, 24). The comprehensive all risk policies obtained by Omni up until March 1, 2002, did not contain an exclusion for terrorist acts. (*E.g.,* Exs. 33, 202). In fact, Omni's policy at the time the Agreement was signed provided that "damage done by terrorists . . . is insured." (Ex. 33, at 000507; *see* Tr. 85).

As witnesses for both sides agreed, before 9/11, "all risk" policies covered damage caused by acts of terrorism; there was no exclusion for acts of terrorism. (Tr. 45–47, 135, 276, 322). Prior to 9/11, terrorism insurance was "a nonissue." (*Id.* 106). After 9/11, however, the insurance landscape changed: insurance companies, in general, began excluding damage from terrorist attacks from their "all risk" policies. (*Id.* 45, 48, 106, 136, 295–96). Terrorism insurance was available after 9/11, but it had to be obtained in the form of separate, stand-alone policies, and the premiums were high.

In the fall and summer of 2002 time frame, Omni obtained quotes for insurance for the hotels at more than a million dollars. Omni believed the prices were exorbitant and was unwilling to spend that much money. (*Id.* 58, 65, 66–67, 75–76, 121–24, 138, 153; Exs. 220, 222).

On March 1, 2002, when Omni renewed its all risk policy, the renewed policy contained an exclusion for acts of terrorism. (Tr. 49–50; Ex. 14, at p. U–GU–592).[2] Omni did not purposefully seek a policy that excluded terrorism coverage; when Omni sought to purchase insurance for the 2002–2003 time period by requesting bids, all of the proposed policies were submitted with terrorism excluded. Omni was unable to find an "all risks" policy that included coverage for acts of terrorism, with the exception of the limited $25 million in coverage. (Tr. 44–50; *see* Ex. 14).

4. THE DISPUTE

By letter dated July 11, 2002, when it was still the servicing company for the Loan, Wachovia advised Omni that Omni's insurance did not comply with the Agreement because the insurance excluded terrorist acts. (Tr. 42–43; Ex. 73). By letter dated July 26, 2002, Omni responded that it did not agree that the Agreement required terrorism insurance. (Tr. 52–53; Ex. 79). Nonetheless, Omni also stated that it had obtained quotes for terrorism insurance policies and determined that "such policies come at an *extremely* high cost." (Ex. 79 (emphasis in original)).

On August 5, 2002, Michael G. Smith, Omni's general counsel, spoke by telephone with Scott Husselbee of Wachovia about the insurance issue. (Tr. 54–55). Husselbee stated that he had not read the Agreement, that Wachovia had to tend to 9,000 loan agreements, and that Wachovia was unable to meet with all 9,000 borrowers to discuss the issue of terrorism insurance. (*Id.* 54–56).

The parties engaged in further discussion and exchanged additional correspondence. (*See, e.g.,* Exs. 35, 80, 82). After several months, Wells Fargo offered to accept less than the full replacement cost of the five hotels ($349 million) and even less than the loan balance ($230 million): it agreed to accept $60 million in coverage. (Tr. 234–36; *see* Exs. 13, 247). Wells Fargo thought it had reached an agreement with Omni, but was then advised by Omni representatives that the owner of Omni

---

2. There was a limited exception to the exclusion. If there was $25 million or less in damages from an act of terrorism, the damages were covered. If the damages exceeded $25 million, there was *zero* coverage. (Tr. 50–51, 75, 115–16).

did not want to spend the money for terrorism insurance. (Tr. 236–37). Omni commenced this lawsuit on September 13, 2002.

5. THE TRIA

On November 26, 2002, after this action was filed, the Terrorism Risk Insurance Act of 2002, Pub.L. 107–297, 116 Stat. 2322 (the "TRIA"), was signed into law. The TRIA prohibits exclusions for certain "Acts of Terrorism" from insurance policies for a limited time period during which insurers were required to notify their insured of the availability of and rates for insurance coverage for "Acts of Terrorism." The TRIA, however, defined an "Act of Terrorism" as an act of terrorism causing damage within the United States or to certain United States property located outside the country, "committed by an individual or individuals acting on behalf of any foreign person or foreign interest." *Id.* at 2323–24.

Hence, the TRIA does not apply to acts of domestic terrorism. Moreover, although it requires that insurance be made available for acts of terrorism committed by individuals acting on behalf of a foreign interest, it does not place any restrictions on the amount that insurers can charge for such insurance.

6. ALL RISK POLICIES AND TERRORISM INSURANCE

As noted, the Agreement does not define the phrases "comprehensive all risk insurance" or "all risk." (*See* Ex. 1, § 1.1 (definitions)). "All risk" insurance is property insurance that covers damage resulting from all risks other than those that are specifically excluded from coverage; if a risk is not specifically excluded, it is deemed covered.[3] Typical exclusions found in "all risk" policies are war, pollution, earthquake, and flood. (Tr. 37–38, 95–96, 99, 294–95). Over time, the standards of the insurance industry have changed in this respect. (*Id.* 104, 166, 250, 324). For example, in the mid to late 1990s, the "Y2K" exclusion was introduced to exclude damages resulting from the failure of computer systems to recognize the year 2000. (*Id.* 97). Another exclusion that has developed in recent years is a mold exclusion, excluding damage caused by mold in buildings. (*Id.* 97, 295). The development of the terrorism exclusion after 9/11 is yet another example of a change in industry standards. (*Id.* 295–96). Over time, "all risk" policies will vary. (*Id.* 104–05, 163).

The cost of terrorism insurance has decreased significantly since 2002. (Tr. 132–33, 177; *compare* Ex. 222 *with* Ex. 256). Many insureds, including a significant number of hotel owners, have purchased stand alone terrorism policies. (Tr. 147–48; Exs. 59, 68). . . .

As of July 8, 2003, Wells Fargo serviced 3632 loans. Of these, 2309 had terrorism insurance. (Ex. 332). In situations where Wells Fargo was itself the lender, it determined whether to require terrorism insurance on a case-by-case basis. (Tr. 226–27). Where Wells Fargo is the servicer and not the lender, it has proceeded on a categorical basis, requiring terrorism insurance across-the-board. (*Id.* 228). Wells Fargo has treated the situations differently because when it is the lender, its obligation is only to itself as lender, whereas in the situations where, as here, the

---

3. The name "all risk" is a misnomer, for an all risk policy does not cover *all* risks of loss, but only risks that are not specifically excluded. (Tr. 320–21, 341). *See Port Auth. of N.Y. & N.J. v. Affiliated FM Ins. Co.,* 311 F.3d 226, 234 (3d Cir.2002) ("[I]n the insurance industry, 'all risks' does not mean 'every risk'"); Barry R. Ostrager & Thomas R. Newman, *Insurance Coverage Disputes* § 21.04, at 1238 (12th Ed.2004).

loan is securitized, it has a fiduciary obligation to third parties — it must protect the interests of the certificate holders. (*Id.* 229).

During the pendency of this case, Omni obtained a quote for $60 million in terrorism coverage (both TRIA certified and non-certified) for the five hotels at a price of $316,000 for a year. (Tr. 72–73, 76–77; Ex. 227). This price was reasonable. (Ex. 334, ¶¶ 37–44; Ex. 335, at 4). Nonetheless, $316,000 is approximately 63% of the cost of Omni's all risk policy. (*Id.* 130). In addition, if the insurance is required, the cost would continue through the life of the Loan, *i.e.,* until 2008. (*Id.* 181).

B. PRIOR PROCEEDINGS

Omni commenced this action on September 13, 2002, seeking a determination that it was not required under the Agreement to obtain terrorism insurance. It immediately moved for a temporary restraining order and preliminary injunction to prevent Wells Fargo from "force-placing" the insurance. The motion was withdrawn by agreement of the parties.

Thereafter, the action was essentially held in abeyance as the parties engaged in discussions to resolve the matter and awaited action by Congress on the proposed terrorism legislation, which eventually was passed as the TRIA. When discussions between the parties failed, Omni renewed its motion for a preliminary injunction on March 19, 2003. By Memorandum Decision entered April 17, 2003, I concluded that Omni had not demonstrated a likelihood of success, but I granted the motion on other grounds. *Omni Berkshire Corp. v. Wells Fargo Bank, N.A.,* No. 02 Civ. 7378 (DC), 2003 WL 1900822 (S.D.N.Y. April 17, 2003).

The parties completed discovery. The case was tried on July 21 and 22, 2003. At the conclusion of the trial, I reserved decision. The parties thereafter submitted post-trial briefs.

DISCUSSION

The two matters for consideration are (a) the "all risk" clause and (b) the "other insurance" clause. I address each in turn.[4]

A. THE "ALL RISK CLAUSE"

The first issue is whether Omni was required, by virtue of the "all risk" clause of the Agreement (Ex. 1, §6.1(a)(i)), to purchase terrorism coverage after insurance companies started excluding acts of terrorism from "all risk" policies after 9/11. I hold that it was not.[5]

---

4. A threshold issue is the burden of proof: it is unclear whether Omni or Wells Fargo bears the burden of proof in this case. I need not decide the issue, for this case does not turn on who bears the burden of proof.

5. There is little case law on point. Two decisions involve similar situations, but they provide little guidance as they addressed only preliminary issues and were not final decisions on the merits. *See Four Times Square Assocs., L.L.C. v. Cigna Invs., Inc.,* 306 A.D.2d 4, 764 N.Y.S.2d 1 (1st Dep't 2003); *Philadelphia Plaza–Phase II v. Bank of America Nat'l Trust & Sav. Assoc.,* No. 3745, 2002 WL 1472337 (Pa. Ct. Comm. Pleas June 21, 2002).

Under New York law,[6] the key to contract interpretation is "the parties' reasonable expectations." *Sunrise Mall Assocs. v. Import Alley of Sunrise Mall, Inc.*, 211 A.D.2d 711, 621 N.Y.S.2d 662, 663 (2d Dep't 1995); *see VTech Holdings Ltd. v. Lucent Techs., Inc.*, 172 F.Supp.2d 435, 441 (S.D.N.Y.2001) ("the essence of contract interpretation . . . is to enforce a contract in accordance with the true expectations of the parties in light of the circumstances existing at the time of the formation of the contract") (internal quotations and citation omitted). To give effect to the parties' reasonable expectations, the court must "determine the parties' purpose and intent." *Sunrise Mall*, 621 N.Y.S.2d at 663. It must do so by looking at the language the parties chose to use, the contract as a whole, and the conduct of the parties. *Id.; Space Imaging Europe, Ltd. v. Space Imaging L.P.*, 38 F.Supp.2d 326, 334 (S.D.N.Y.1999).

If the language of a contract is ambiguous, the court may look to extrinsic evidence of the parties' intent. *Space Imaging*, 38 F.Supp.2d at 334. Extrinsic evidence may include evidence of trade usage. *United States Naval Inst. v. Charter Comm., Inc.*, 875 F.2d 1044, 1048–49 (2d Cir.1989) ("Usage and customs may be proved . . . to aid in interpretation of the words of the parties.") (quoting 3 A. Corbin, *Corbin on Contracts* § 556, at 240–42 (1960)); *Record Club of America, Inc. v. United Artists Records, Inc.*, No. 72 Civ. 5234(WCC), 1991 WL 73838, *10 (S.D.N.Y. April 29, 1991) ("When a trade usage is widespread, there is a presumption that the parties intended its incorporation by implication, unless the contract language negates it.") . . . .

There is little in terms of extrinsic evidence. As the parties agree, in 1998, when the Agreement was executed, all risk policies covered acts of terrorism because terrorism was not specifically excluded. When the parties negotiated the Agreement, terrorism insurance was a "nonissue," and there was no discussion of terrorism insurance. Hence, there is no direct evidence of what the parties intended because the subjects of terrorism insurance and whether the requisite "all risk" insurance had to cover terrorism were not discussed.

Nonetheless, there is some circumstantial evidence as to what the parties intended. The parties did not define "all risk" insurance at least in part because there was, and still is, a general understanding in the insurance industry as to the meaning of "all risk" insurance. It was commonly understood that the standard "risk" policy had evolved over time and that it could continue to evolve over time. The Y2K, mold, and terrorism exclusions are examples of exclusions that are now commonly found in "all risk" policies that did not exist some years ago.

Under these circumstances, if the parties had intended to require Omni to maintain for the life of the Agreement "all risk" insurance in the form that existed in August 1998, *i.e.*, that included terrorism insurance, they surely would have said so. Indeed, they would have re-written § 6.1(a)(i) of the Agreement to read in words or substance that Omni was required to maintain:

> comprehensive all risk insurance on the [five hotels] . . . in an amount equal to one hundred percent (100%) of the "Full Replacement Cost," *in the form that comprehensive all risk insurance exists today, i. e., August 28, 1998.*

---

6. The Agreement is governed by New York law. (Ex. 1, § 10.3(A)).

(Ex. 1, § 6.1(a)(i) (underlined language added)). That the parties did not include such or similar language suggests that the parties intended to require only what the industry generally accepted — knowing that the generally accepted all risk policy might evolve over time. *See Karabu v. Pension Benefit Guaranty Corp.*, No. 96 Civ. 4960 (BSJ), 1997 WL 759462, *13 (S.D.N.Y. Dec.10, 1997) (holding that reference in contract to "F.A.A.-approved maintenance program" referred to program "as it evolves over time, rather than as fixed on any particular date," because the industry understood the phrase "to refer to an evolving standard").

Other language in the Agreement also supports this interpretation. When the parties required Omni to maintain all risk insurance, they specifically required Omni to also obtain coverage for flood and earthquake. These were standard exclusions from all risk policies. Hence, when the parties wanted to deviate from the standard all risk policy to include coverage for risks traditionally excluded, like flood and earthquake, they included language in the Agreement to that effect. No such language was included for terrorism insurance. Again, at that time terrorism insurance was a "non-issue," but when the parties wanted to depart from the usual practice with respect to all risk coverage, they did so explicitly.

Finally, this is the only interpretation that makes sense. The argument that the parties intended a rigid, precise definition of "all risk" simply is not logical, for otherwise they would have included a definition of "all risk" insurance. Moreover, in § 6.1(a)(i), clearly the parties were bargaining for what was commercially reasonable and accepted in the trade — the common, everyday understanding of "all risk" and not some specific definition that deviated from the generally accepted. Indeed, after 9/11, Omni was unable to purchase an "all risk" policy without a terrorism exclusion. In addition, as discussed below, there was another provision of the Agreement to cover additional insurance that the lender might request.

Accordingly, I hold that the parties did not intend to require Omni to forever maintain "all risk" insurance precisely as it existed in 1998. Hence, in 2002, Omni was required only to purchase the generally accepted "all risk" policy, and it was not required by § 6.1(a)(i) to purchase a separate terrorism insurance policy.

B. THE "OTHER INSURANCE" CLAUSE

Even assuming the "all risk" clause did not require Omni to purchase a stand alone terrorism policy, the issue remains whether Wells Fargo acted reasonably in requiring Omni to purchase terrorism coverage under the "other insurance" clause of the Agreement. (Ex. 1, § 6.1(a)(ix)). I conclude that Wells Fargo acted reasonably in requiring Omni to obtain, as "other reasonable insurance," an additional $60 million in terrorism coverage.

First, Wells Fargo's concern that Omni's hotels are at risk is, unfortunately, reasonable. In the World Trade Center attacks on 9/11, one hotel was destroyed and two others were damaged. (Tr. 81–82). Omni itself has taken steps to upgrade security at its hotels. (Ex. 235; Tr. 82). The five hotels in question are located in New York, Chicago, and Texas, and surely there is some risk that they could be targeted. The Omni hotel in New York, for example, is located near a number of high-profile buildings. The Court also takes judicial notice of the bombing of a Marriot hotel in Jakarta, Indonesia, in August 2003, which resulted in at least 14 deaths and injuries to 150 others. (*See* Def. Post–Trial Mem., Ex. B).

Second, the record contains substantial proof that the owners of many hotels and other commercial properties have purchased terrorism insurance. (*See* Exs. cited at Def. Post–Trial Mem. at 11-12). These include the Marriott hotels, including hotels in Manhattan, Dallas, Houston, Chicago, and San Francisco (Exs. 302, 303, 304, 305; Tr. 246); the Westin hotel in Chicago (Ex. 307); the Omni hotel in the CNN Tower in Atlanta (Garcia Dep. 72–74); the Hilton hotels, including one in Chicago (Ex. 306; Tr. 220); the Boykin Lodging Co. hotels, including one in Chicago (Ex. 308); the Felcor Lodging LP hotels (Tr. 301, at 15); and the Gaylord hotels. (Ex. 309; Tr. 219–20).

Third, the cost of the $60 million in coverage that Wells Fargo agreed to accept is reasonable: approximately $300,000 per year. (Ex. 334, ¶¶ 37–44; Ex. 335, at 4). Indeed, the cost of terrorism insurance has dropped significantly since the months immediately after 9/11.

Fourth, the additional insurance would benefit not only Wells Fargo but Omni as well. As the broker who was consulted by Omni's broker opined: "[Omni's refusal] to buy terrorism insurance is worrisome to me, but more so, I am sure, for their lender. . . . But the risk has clearly heightened." She continued: "Rather than helping them keep fighting the lender (this has been going on for months — they've bought enough time), perhaps we should look at ways to alleviate the whole issue — and get them a quote they can accept. It will NOT be nothing. It WILL be something. But right now, they are spending hours and legal fees for what? No cover?" (Ex. 68).

Omni makes a number of arguments in support of its contention that Wells Fargo acted unreasonably, including, among others, the following: Wells Fargo proceeded on a blanket basis rather than on an individualized case-by-case basis; the hotels are cross-collateralized and their value far exceeds the outstanding balance of the loan; the cost of $316,000 for a terrorism policy is still 63% of the cost of an all risk policy; Wells Fargo failed to make a proper demand; and the Court should be looking at events in 2002 rather than at the state of affairs at the time of trial.

I have considered these arguments and they are rejected. The short answer is simply that in the post–9/11 world when so much more is at risk, it was reasonable for Wells Fargo to request, on behalf of its certificate holders, that Omni provide an additional $60 million in insurance coverage to account for the loss of terrorism coverage created when the insurance industry decided to exclude terrorism from all risk policies.

CONCLUSION

For the reasons set forth above, judgment will be entered in favor of Wells Fargo dismissing Omni's complaint, with prejudice. Omni shall have thirty days from today to obtain $60 million in terrorism insurance; if it fails to do so, Wells Fargo is free to force-place the insurance at Omni's expense.

E. ALTERNATIVE MORTGAGE INSTRUMENTS

We have already encountered alternatives to the fixed rate long-term mortgage, including the adjustable rate or variable rate mortgage and the graduated payment mortgage. There are many others, as mortgage originators seek to respond competitively to various borrower and investor preferences. The following excerpt illustrates the diversity in types of modern mortgages.

Levin and Roberts, Future Forms of Financing — Lending Devices Addressed to Inflation and Tight Money

American Bar Association, Real Prop. Prob. and Tr. Sec., Financing Real Estate During the Inflationary 80's at 31-51 (1981)

B.   SOME NEW FINANCING DEVICES

Various alternative mortgage instruments (AMIs) have been implemented or are being considered and refined to complement the FRM and to stimulate the real estate market in the United States. Many of these were initially developed for the residential market. They include the variable rate mortgage (VRM); graduate payment mortgage (GPM); graduated payment adjustable mortgage (GPAM); renegotiable rate mortgage (RRM); rollover mortgage (ROM), shared appreciation mortgage (SAM); price level adjusted mortgage (PLAM); deferred interest mortgage (DIM); and flexible loan insurance program mortgage (FLIP). These, along with equity participations, convertible mortgages, joint ventures, and loans with short terms and/or kicker interest, have become the principal means by which the institutional and noninstitutional lender have avoided the recent inflationary pattern and credit crunch in the commercial lending market.

C.   OBJECTIVES OF THE NEW DEVICES

The various AMIs serve lender and borrower interests in different ways. Some (such as the VRM, RRM, ROM, PLAM and SAM) offer the lender protection against inflation which may, in turn, allow a lender to charge initially a lower rate of interest, bringing new borrowers into the market. Other AMIs (such as GPMs, DIMS and FLIPS), offer payment schedules that are more affordable for borrowers, without really providing benefits to lenders except in the resulting stimulation of the market. A portfolio of SAMs, for instance, should bring increased yields proportional to inflation's impact on the cost of funds, thus easing disintermediation pressures on lenders, and making more funds available for mortgage lending even in inflationary periods. More plentiful mortgage funds may lead to a higher demand for the funds and hence for new construction, to the benefit, indirectly, of much of the economy. However, for the lender there is always the risk that yields on SAMS will be reduced if inflation in real property values slows or ceases.

   GPMs, on the other hand, do not improve a lender's cash flow or necessarily provide a hedge against inflation. But they do permit a borrower who projects a continuously rising cash flow to enter the market in anticipation of future income levels. The borrower's credit is an important factor here, as equity may be reduced by negative amortization in the early years of the loan. A lender may have to accept an increased risk of default in order to accommodate a borrower whose expectations are brighter than his current financial picture. . . .

II. THE VARIABLE RATE MORTGAGE AND DUAL RATE-VARIABLE RATE MORTGAGE

A. CHARACTERISTICS

A variable interest rate loan or mortgage is a long-term loan which increases or decreases with a referenced index that reflects changes in the cost of funds to the lender and/or the current market rate of interest. Future payments are not known at the time the loan is originated, but the interest rate could fall, along with the index, to the borrower's advantage. Because the lender is protected against inflation, a VRM can be less restrictive as to assumption and prepayment and can be offered for a longer term. . . .

Probably the best index one could use is a weighted average cost of funds to the lending institutions. A weighted average cost of funds is very stable, but has the disadvantage (from the borrower's point of view) of tending to move upward far more readily than downward. In the residential market, the FHA National Average Mortgage Rate would be a stable index. Other indices might include the CPI, the LIBOR, the prime rate and comparable AA utility bond or commercial paper rates. Some of these indices seem less suitable than others, because they reflect volatile short-term market conditions not directly related to the cost of mortgage funds.

Regardless of which index is chosen, the frequency of periodic adjustments is another important issue. The longer the intervals, the greater the stability and the probability that long-term trends will be reflected. To promote greater stability, a lender may require a minimum change in the index before requiring a corresponding change in the interest rate. . . .

The dual rate-variable rate mortgage is a loan which involves two distinct interest rates: a deferred short-term interest rate on the mortgage balance, and a current long-term interest rate on the principal payment. The short-term rate would reflect the current market interest rate. This provides the borrower with a payment plan that follows the projected income stream of the property and long term interest trends. It provides the lender with an overall yield reflecting short term interest rates, although the lender's cash flow may not keep up in the same fashion. . . .

III. GRADUATED PAYMENT MORTGAGE AND GRADUATED PAYMENT ADJUSTABLE MORTGAGE [CONTENTS OMITTED]

IV. RENEGOTIABLE RATE MORTGAGE AND ROLL-OVER MORTGAGE

A. CHARACTERISTICS

A renegotiable rate mortgage is a loan in which the payments are calculated on a long-term (e.g., twenty- or thirty-year) amortization schedule, with a short-term (e.g., five years) maturity or with frequent (e.g., every five years) mandatory rate adjustments. The short-term note may be secured by a long-term mortgage. The loan is renegotiated at the new interest rate (usually the then market interest rate) at the end of each designated period. The loan may be renewable either at the option of the borrower or of the lender. . . .

Canada has had experience with ROMs since the 1930s, but only since 1969 have ROMs come into widespread use. Under the terms set by law for government guaranteed (insured) mortgages, the ROM is renegotiated after a minimum of five years, with a twenty-five-year minimum amortization period. Borrowers may prepay up to 10 percent in each of the initial two years and the full amount thereafter without penalty. In 1976, the average interest rate of nongovernment insured mortgages in Canada was nearly 12 percent, while five-year term certificates paid over 10 percent. On the other hand, interest rates on five-year term certificates in June 1978 averaged 8¾ percent, while conventional single-family (roll-over) mortgages were priced just over 10 percent. Although relatively expensive, mortgage funds appear to be readily available in Canada.

In Canada, lenders are under no legal obligation to refinance the loan at the end of each five-year term, but experience has shown that they tend to do so for creditworthy borrowers. There is now some movement to the use of even shorter term loans, in an attempt to adjust the lenders' yield more precisely. The supply of mortgage credit is relatively uninterrupted, disintermediation pressures are reduced, and housing cycles seem slightly less pronounced than in this country. Nonetheless, caution must be used in drawing on the Canadian experience because of the obvious differences between Canada's economic and financial structures and those in the United States. . . .

V. Deferred Interest Mortgage

The DIM is a variant of the GPM, in which the lender defers a portion of the interest payments during the initial years and adds the amount of the deferred interest to the outstanding balance of the loan for payment in subsequent years. The terms of a DIM usually provide for a lower initial interest rate which is increased within five or ten years. In addition to the deferred interest, the lender may receive a fee upon resale of the residence. DIMs are a suitable form of mortgage in areas experiencing a rapid appreciation in home values and a high rate of turnover in the housing stock.

VI. The Flexible Loan Insurance Program

The FLIP is the brainchild of FLIP Mortgage Corporation in Flemington, New Jersey. This corporation packages the FLIP concept together with a computer program and markets the package to lenders. A FLIP is a type of GPM with a highly individualized payment program. On the purchase of a home, a buyer makes a down payment which is placed in an interest bearing account and takes out a loan, in effect, for the full purchase price. Each FLIP establishes a schedule of monthly deductions for principal and interest from the account to supplement the buyer's out-of-pocket payments on the loan. Consequently, it enables an initial reduction of the debt service until the exhaustion of funds in the account.

FLIPs were first tried in 1977 and proved popular with consumers. Nonetheless, their use has been hindered by lenders' reluctance to engage in highly leveraged residential transactions, and by a severely constricted secondary market. Since the introduction of FLIPs, neither FNMA nor FHLMC has been willing to purchase them.

VII. Tenants in Common Keeping Equity (Ticket)

The TICKET plan is a convenient form of financing the purchase of residential properties for buyers with limited funds to meet a seller's down payment requirements. Under the plan, an investor provides the buyer with the cash for the down payment and takes an interest as co-tenant of the property. The investor receives no debt service but shares in the gains or losses upon the sale of the property. The parties agree to sell or to refinance within five years. The buyer obtains financing for the balance of the purchase price from a third party lender. The investor's unsecured position as a co-tenant removes any problems of the buyer's compliance with the third party lender's restrictions on subordinate debt.

TICKET plans are offered in New Jersey by the Sterling National Realty Group. Ticket Corporation, the developer of the plan, is based in San Jose, California.

VIII. Contingent Interest Mortgages

A. CHARACTERISTICS

Contingent interest mortgages are established forms of financing which, singly and in combination with other AMI devices, will be widely used in the current inflationary economy. Normally the borrower must service debt at a stated interest rate, either fixed or variable, plus a contingent interest component comprised of a portion of the proceeds it derives from the property. Considerations such as the borrower's initial and projected income from the property, the terms of the borrower's leases with its tenants, and the type of property (office, retail, banking, apartment units, etc.) affect the terms of the contingent interest element. The method of computing contingent interest, what items are included or excluded, and the definition of various terms require careful consideration, negotiation and drafting.

B. COMPUTATION

Contingent interest may be based on a percentage of gross receipts or of net income. Under a gross receipts formula, all of the borrower's revenues can be swept into the computation prior to any adjustments for expenses or for receipts which merely reimburse the borrower as a landlord. From the lender's viewpoint this method is more reliable and administratively convenient than use of a net income or cash flow approach. The lender may encounter difficulties ascertaining and keeping account of excluded and included items under a net income formula. However, a borrower agreeing to pay his lender a percentage of gross receipts runs a very real risk in an inflationary economy that operating expenses may increase more quickly and in a greater amount than income, and that his net cash flow after debt service will actually diminish. It is submitted that devices intended to protect lenders from the ravages of inflation should not also result in exacerbating the effects of inflation on the expense side for the borrower. Net income determined on a cash basis enables the borrower to meet its debt service obligations when due, but also raises the possibility that the borrower may elect to defer receipt of payments to a subsequent accounting period. Net income determined on an accrual basis offers the lender the certainty that income will be included in net income for a current accounting period without manipulation by the borrower, but the borrower may be placed at a disadvantage because it may lack the funds to meet the amount of its obligation. . . .

IX. SHARED APPRECIATION MORTGAGE

A. CHARACTERISTICS

A SAM loan is generally defined as a loan which has a fixed interest rate set below the prevailing market rate over the term of the loan and contingent interest based upon a percentage of the appreciation of the property securing the loan payable at the earlier of maturity or payment in full of the loan or sale or transfer of the property. A SAM is the newest and probably most controversial of the AMIs now offered or under consideration in the United States and, therefore, will receive more extensive coverage in these materials than the AMIs and other devices previously discussed.

A SAM loan would call for equal monthly installments of principal and fixed interest in a sufficient amount to fully amortize the loan over a certain amortization period, although the term of the SAM would be shorter than its amortization period.

The contingent interest which is intended to compensate the lender for the differential between the market rate and the lower loan interest rate would be a portion of the net appreciated value of the property which is to be paid at the earlier of the maturity date, payment in full of the loan or the sale, transfer, disposition or further encumbrance of the property securing the loan.

The terms of a typical SAM might be:

(a) a below-market fixed interest rate; plus
(b) a rate of contingent interest (i.e., the percentage share of any appreciation) sufficient to produce an effective gross yield in excess of the yield on a conventional FRM;
(c) a short loan term, usually not more than ten years;
(d) a longer amortization period of twenty to thirty years;
(e) appreciation to be determined either by the actual sales price or by appraisal, allowing recovery by the borrower of the cost of capital improvements;
(f) a sizable prepayment penalty during the early years of the loan term;
(g) acceleration of the loan maturity upon sale, transfer or refinancing;
(h) a conservative loan to value ratio.

An alternative form of SAM might provide for a fixed interest rate over a longer term and for a periodic reappraisal of the property (e.g., every five years). The borrower would pay as interest to the lender an amount equal to a percent of the increase in value of the property over the last appraisal. This amount would be payable in cash or by the lender taking a note from the borrower in this amount at the original interest rate, with the same amortization rate and maturity date as the original loan or with increased amortization or an extended maturity date. If the property were sold, the mortgagee would receive its share of the excess of the sales price over the last appraisal. . . .

X.   The Price Level Adjusted Mortgage

A.   CHARACTERISTICS

A PLAM is a mortgage which provides for periodic increases or decreases in the principal amount due, based on appraisals or on a predetermined price level index. The goal is to periodically adjust the outstanding debt so that the debt keeps up with inflation while the nominal interest rate remains constant. The lender, therefore, does not charge an inflation premium in the stated interest rate in anticipation of the declining value of the dollar and the lender's actual yield on the loan would be approximately the same as stated, regardless of inflation. Actual payments would rise with the rate of inflation, but the initial payments, because there is no necessity to charge an inflation premium, would theoretically be much lower than those on an FRM.

In a PLAM, the borrower would negotiate a fixed interest rate, a schedule for adjustment of principal and an index or other method for revaluing the principal. Assuming that inflation amounted to 10 percent per year, on an annual adjustment plan the outstanding mortgage balance would be increased by a factor of 10 percent plus accrued interest called for under the terms of the mortgage, from which would be deducted the total payments paid by the borrower for that year. The mortgage balance would then be adjusted at the end of each year during the term of the loan.

PLAMs are used extensively in Brazil but not in the United States. They involve the same practical problems of selecting an index or an appraisal process as the VRM or SAM, and the practice of adjusting principal offers no advantages over the practice of adjusting interest, and may involve additional legal problems. . . .

NOTE

In addition to the alternative types of mortgage instruments described by Levin and Roberts, the ingenuity of the market has produced others, examples of which are the convertible ARM, a combination adjustable and fixed rate instrument permitting an ARM to be converted to a fixed rate at the borrower's option after a certain period of time; a convertible mortgage, with the lender having the option to convert all or a portion of its investment into an equity share at a later date; and a reverse annuity mortgage, permitting the borrower to draw on equity to make mortgage payments, a format attractive to many elderly homeowners as it not only provides needed funds following retirement but also makes it possible for them to continue living in their old home. For discussion of these options, see Mortgage Products for All Palates, 48 Mortgage Banking 94 (Oct. 1987); and Levy, Marks & Weller, Convertible Mortgages Lure Creative Investors and Owners, 18 Real Est. Rev., no. 4, p. 30 (1989). On reverse annuity mortgages see Reilly, Reverse Mortgages: Backing Into the Future, 5 Elder Law J. 17 (1997); Sawyer, Reverse Mortgages, An Innovative Tool for Elder Law Attorneys, 26 Stetson L. Rev. 617 (1996).

As we have seen in considering the secondary mortgage market, many alternative types of securities have been sold backed by pools of mortgages. The diversity of mortgage-backed securities reflects the appeal of mortgages, properly packaged, to a wide range of investors. These securities, in effect, are alternative forms of mortgage instruments.

F.   BASIC SECURITY TRANSACTIONS

The law of secured real estate transactions is a complex body of legal doctrine, often varying substantially from state to state. It includes a scattering of statutes and administrative regulations, much case law interpreting the statutes or applying common law principles, and at important points significant constitutional principles. All of this complexity and diversity exists in a market for land and land-related legal instruments that is increasingly national and even international in scope.

1. Forms of Security Devices

a. The Mortgage

We have already used the word "mortgage" repeatedly and have generally done so as a layman would — to describe a loan on real property. The lawyer knows better. A mortgage is not the loan itself, but a security interest in property given to an obligee (usually a lender) to secure the loan or, occasionally, some other obligation. Such other obligation might be the promise of the obligor to act as surety for the debts of a third person; in that instance the mortgage would be called a collateral security mortgage. The party who holds a mortgage is called the *mortgagee;* the party whose property is subject to a mortgage is called the *mortgagor.* Very often neither the mortgagee nor the mortgagor will be the original mortgaging parties, since the mortgage will have been sold or assigned or the mortgaged property will have been transferred. The mortgages dealt with in this text are mostly mortgages on real estate, not mortgages on personalty, which are called chattel mortgages. We shall learn, however, that real estate mortgages may be either fee mortgages or leasehold mortgages; the common law treatment of leaseholds as "chattels real" causes some blurring of the distinction between real and chattel mortgages.

What is the effect on a real estate mortgage of improvements made on the property after the mortgage becomes effective? What if a building is built or a new elevator or furnace installed in an existing building, do the improvements become part of the mortgage security? Assuming no exemption of future improvements in the mortgage, they are added to the security of the mortgage if considered fixtures and thereby treated as additions to the real property. However, a troublesome problem can arise as to mortgage priority if before an item became a fixture it was covered by a chattel mortgage. The Uniform Commercial Code deals with this problem and under some circumstances the chattel mortgage will have priority over the real estate mortgage as to the fixture. Further problems may also arise because of uncertainty over what is and is not a fixture.

Where a mortgage is given to secure a loan, the loan usually is evidenced by the obligor's note or bond, which accompanies the mortgage. Although the terms often are used interchangeably, technically a bond is a sealed instrument and a note is an unsealed instrument; until the 1966 repeal of the federal excise tax on corporate bonds mooted the difference, a corporate mortgagor could avoid the tax by issuing a note instead of a bond.

What does the mortgagee get when it receives a mortgage? The answer to that question has varied greatly over the course of centuries, but today, for most practical purposes, the mortgagee receives a lien[18] on the mortgagor's property as of the time that the mortgage is recorded. (Between the mortgaging parties, the lien is effective when the mortgage is executed and delivered, but since most disputes over priority involve third parties, the critical date is that of recordation.) In an earlier era, the mortgagee obtained title to the mortgagor's property subject to divestment if the debt were paid on the due or law day. Often this arrangement meant hardship for the mortgagor, for a late tender of payment, late even by so little as one day, would not bring a return of title unless the mortgagee volunteered to give it. In time, chancery intervened in behalf of defaulting mortgagors by letting them "redeem" the property from the mortgagee if they tendered payment within a reasonable period after the law day. This equitable right of redemption[19] grew into an implied term of every mortgage bargain, enforceable by a bill in equity.[20] This form of mortgagor protection is treated by the courts as immutable and not waivable by mortgagors.

Now the mortgagee faced hardship — the hardship of uncertainty — for it could not be sure, after default, when the title would indefeasibly vest. A late tendering mortgagor might yet persuade chancery that the tender was not unreasonably delayed. Taking the initiative, mortgagees began to petition the courts to cut off, or foreclose, the mortgagor's equity of redemption. In this way, the procedural remedy of foreclosure was born. The decree of foreclosure, which was issued some months after the law date and upon notice to the defaulting mortgagor, vested the mortgagee's title to the real estate security; prior to the decree redemption was possible, but after the decree, it was not.

If, when foreclosure occurred, the real estate was worth more than the mortgage debt, still another source of hardship remained for the mortgagor. Since foreclosure vested title in the mortgagee, the mortgagee stood to benefit, while the mortgagor stood to lose, from any surplus in property value. No restitution was necessary. By the early 1800s, state legislatures began to respond to the evident harshness of this situation; mortgagees who applied for a foreclosure decree were

---

18. Even in states where conveyancing practice still uses language in the mortgage instrument that signifies the transfer of legal title to the mortgagee, all that the mortgagee gets is a lien interest. At an earlier time, American courts differentiated between the interest of a mortgagee holding title and the interest of a mortgagee having a lien only; today, most of the differences have disappeared. There remains, however, one. In a few states, known as title states, the mortgagee has the continuing right to possession, as it does in England. In one or two other states, known as "hybrid" or "intermediate" theory states, the mortgagee is entitled automatically to possession immediately upon default. Everywhere else, the mortgagee must petition the court for the right possession — via a court appointed receiver — to protect the security from waste or dissipation of the rents; usually the petition is received and granted as part of a foreclosure proceeding.

19. Be sure not to confuse the equitable right of redemption, which the mortgagor holds until the default hardens into foreclosure, with the statutory right to redeem. The latter operates only after the equity of redemption is extinguished and entitles the mortgagor, in states where the right exists, to buy back the real estate from the purchaser at the foreclosure sale.

20. Redemption will normally be ordered by an equity court if the mortgagor alleges ability to pay whatever is due. The court then determines the precise amount due and sets a date, usually some months in the future, when the mortgagor must pay or, in most states, be foreclosed. Payment within the prescribed time discharges the mortgage. If the mortgagor defaults, others with interests in the land, including secured junior lenders, also may redeem to protect their interests from foreclosure.

The courts will not uphold or enforce any provision in the mortgage that attempts, through waiver by the mortgagor or otherwise, to eliminate or reduce the mortgagor's equitable right of redemption. This prohibition on "clogging the equitable right of redemption" has been rigorously adhered to since the seventeenth century. For consideration of the modern significance of the clogging principle, see Licht, The Clog on the Equity of Redemption and Its Effect on Modern Real Estate Finance, 60 St. John's L. Rev. 452 (1986). On clogging the equity of redemption also see Restatement of the Law Third, Property, Mortgages (1997), § 3.1 and the helpful Comment following that section.

ordered to sell the property at a public sale and to pay over to the mortgagor (and to any junior lienors) the surplus moneys from the sale, i.e., the moneys not needed to satisfy the claims of the foreclosing mortgagee. Sometimes, of course, the sales price fails to satisfy the debt, and this may give rise to further claim for a deficiency judgment. In a substantial majority of states, *foreclosure by judicial sale* has become the exclusive or generally used process, and it is available everywhere. The process as supplanted, which for obvious reasons became known as *strict foreclosure,* survives in only a few states as a permitted remedy.[21]

One other form of foreclosure deserves mention, for it does not depend upon judicial decree. Where the mortgage instrument gives the mortgagee the power, and state law does not prevent its exercise, a sale arranged for by the mortgagee may be held to transfer the interest of the defaulted mortgagor. A *mortgage with power of sale* grew out of the efforts of English lawyers to avoid Chancery; by the mid-1800s, statutes confirmed the practice, and today, in England, the practice prevails. It exists in over half the states. In England the sale may be held privately, the mortgagor being deemed protected sufficiently by the requirement that the sale must be "bona fide to a stranger and at a reasonable price." In the United States the sale is public and statutes regulate the conduct of the sale and the method of giving notice.

The purchaser in theory obtains the same rights in the property as would be acquired had the purchase been by a judicial sale, since the mortgagee is selling the title as it existed when the mortgage containing the power of sale was given. Nevertheless, the costlier, slower, and more cumbersome judicial sale is frequently preferred because it creates a permanent court record of the events leading to the transfer of the mortgagor's interest, while the purchaser at a nonjudicial sale may have only the recitals in his deed to establish the regularity of the title.

State law varies as to whether a mortgagee may bid at any sale that it conducts pursuant to the power of sale. Generally the mortgagee will be permitted to do so if the mortgage gives it the privilege or if the sale is actually conducted by a public officer. What arguments do you see for and against letting the mortgagee participate in the bidding?

If the sale results in surplus moneys, the foreclosing mortgagee will usually bring a bill of interpleader joining the mortgagor and junior lienors so that their rights to the surplus may be decided judicially.

b. The Trust Deed Mortgage (Deed of Trust)[22]

Many states, both in lien and title, recognize a device called a *trust deed* mortgage, which creates a three-party mortgage transaction. When the loan is made, the

21. Strict foreclosure, while not permitted in the original foreclosure proceeding, may sometimes be used to correct an error in the original proceeding. Take this example: X, who holds a first mortgage, obtains a foreclosure decree and bids in (i.e., purchases) the property at the public sale. Then X discovers that service on Y, who held a second mortgage or a subordinate judgment lien against the property, was omitted in the foreclosure action, so that Y's lien survives the decree. Rather than reinstitute the sale, X may be able to apply for a decree of *strict foreclosure* — upon notice to Y, of course — that would cut off Y's interest in the real estate and relegate Y to a claim against the mortgage proceeds. Whether the decree is granted or not would probably depend on the showing of the relationship between the value of the property and the sales price and on the circumstances of Y's non-service.

22. A trust deed should not be confused with the *land trust,* a device for concealing real estate ownership, which is especially popular in the Chicago area. Under the usual "Illinois" land trust, record title is held by a corporate trustee (a bank or title insurance company), but the trustee's powers are

borrower deeds the real estate security to a trustee, usually an institution specializing in that role. While the mortgage remains current, the trustee has few duties; mortgage payments go directly to the lender who is the trust beneficiary. At maturity, or whenever the loan is repaid, the trustee reconveys the property to its rightful owner. But if a default occurs, the trustee must arrange a public sale of the mortgagor's interest—much as would a mortgagee with power of sale. The trustee will usually conduct the sale and deed the property to the highest bidder. The trustee may not, however, acquire the property itself.

Assignment of the mortgage leaves the trust intact. The original lender transfers the note or other evidence of obligation. The assignee then becomes the trust beneficiary.

While the differences between the straight mortgage and the trust deed mortgage may have once been significant,[23] that no longer is so. Courts and legislatures recognize the functional identity between the two mortgage forms, and, in a lien state, for example, the rights and powers of the trustor-mortgagor do not end because he parts with legal title. Thus, the mortgagor retains the right to possession until a default occurs and there has been a public sale or appointment of receiver. The mortgagor may also sell, lease, or further mortgage the real estate, subject, of course, to the trust. Which of the two forms the lender uses depends mainly upon the custom within the state.

c. The Deed Absolute

Real estate security transactions sometimes involve the lender receiving from the borrower a deed absolute although the parties intended the transaction to be a mortgage. This disguised form of mortgage usually has been insisted upon by the lender as a condition to making the secured loan. There are different reasons for lenders insisting on such a disguised mortgage. For example, the lender may be attempting to hide a usurious transaction, to prevent the need for a foreclosure if the borrower defaults on the loan terms, or to avoid the borrower's post-foreclosure right of redemption in states permitting such a right. A good brief summary of the prevailing law on the deed absolute as a mortgage is incorporated in the section of the Restatement which appears below.

Restatement of the Law Third, Property, Mortgages (1997)

§ 3.2 The Absolute Deed Intended as Security

(a) Parol evidence is admissible to establish that a deed purporting to be an absolute conveyance of real estate was intended to serve as security for an obligation,

---

restricted by an unrecorded trust agreement whereby the beneficiary (and "real" owner) retains full powers of management and control. Advantages asserted for the land trust, in addition to privacy of ownership, are avoidance of probate, facilitation of multi-ownership, and insulation of the real estate from the claims of judgment creditors.

23. For a good discussion of these differences, see Bank of Italy National Trust & Savings Assn. v. Bentley, 20 P.2d 940 Cal. (1933).

and should therefore be deemed a mortgage. The obligation may have been created prior to or contemporaneous with the conveyance and need not be the personal liability of any person.

(b) Intent that the deed serve as security must be proved by clear and convincing evidence. Such intent may be inferred from the totality of the circumstances, including the following factors:

(1) statements of the parties;

(2) the presence of a substantial disparity between the value received by the grantor and the fair market value of the real estate at the time of the conveyance;

(3) the fact that the grantor retained possession of the real estate;

(4) the fact that the grantor continued to pay real estate taxes;

(5) the fact that grantor made post-conveyance improvements to the real estate; and

(6) the nature of the parties and their relationship prior to and after the conveyance.

(c) Where, in addition to the deed referred to in Subsection (a) of this section, a separate writing exists indicating that the deed was intended to serve as security for an obligation, parol evidence is admissible to establish that the writings constitute a single security transaction.

NOTES

1. Some states have statutes concerning deeds absolute as mortgages. See, e.g., Fla. Stat. Ann. § 697.01 (1994), which provides as follows:

(1) All conveyances, obligations conditioned or defeasible, bills of sale or other instruments of writing conveying or selling property, either real or personal, for the purpose or with the intention of securing the payment of money, whether such instrument be from the debtor to the creditor or from the debtor to some third person in trust for the creditor, shall be deemed and held mortgages, and shall be subject to the same rules of foreclosure and to the same regulations, restraints and forms as are prescribed in relation to mortgages.

(2) Provided, however, that no such conveyance shall be deemed or held to be a mortgage, as against a bona fide purchaser or mortgagee, for value without notice, holding under the grantee.

2. There also is considerable case law authority holding a deed absolute to be a mortgage when adequate proof is submitted that a mortgage was intended by the parties. The court's opinion in Moran v. Kenai, appearing in a previous section of this casebook, is one such case.

d. The Installment Land Contract

The installment land contract is a form of financing fairly frequently used in purchasing real estate, particularly low-cost tract housing and farm properties. The installment land contract is also referred to as a contract for deed, bond for deed, or long-term land contract. It should not be confused with the short-term contract of sale used for land sales in which the closing is customarily only 90 days or so from the time the sale contract is signed. This latter kind of contract, in which such matters as title search and examination and buyer seeking financing occur during the short executory period, is considered in some detail hereafter in Chapter Four.

The installment land contract normally remains executory for a long period, frequently ten to twenty years, and its principal purpose is to provide financing acceptable to the parties. Usually, when this device is used, the buyer has a poor credit rating, the seller is having difficulty in selling at a price acceptable to the seller, but the seller is willing to finance the purchase by an installment land contract in order to sell the property. In some respects, installment land contracts resemble purchase money mortgages, but in many states these contracts have advantages to sellers over purchase money mortgages, especially in available remedies if buyers default. These remedy advantages and the problems they raise are considered toward the end of this chapter.

When land is sold pursuant to an installment land contract, ordinarily the buyer takes possession and occupies the property throughout the contract period. Payment customarily is amortized, the buyer paying principal and interest installments similar to those required in many mortgage loan situations. Legal title remains in the contract seller during the contract period and typically is acquired by the buyer only when payment is completed. A deed is then delivered to the buyer. Commonly, the buyer agrees to pay property taxes on the parcel being purchased, insure the improvements, and maintain the property in good repair. The buyer's interest usually may be assigned without consent of the seller, and the seller's interest likewise may be transferred. Both buyer's and seller's interests normally may be mortgaged. A feature of most installment land contracts, which the parties at the time often consider desirable, is that the contracts are entered into and buyers acquire the right to possession quickly and with little if any transaction cost. Even down payments are usually lower than in most real estate sales.

A serious disadvantage of many installment land contracts is that buyers frequently are uninformed as to the obligations they are entering into and often are unrepresented by counsel. Even the protections that accrue to many buyers through third-party financing are absent. In third-party financing of real estate sales, lenders almost invariably take steps to determine adequacy of the security for loan purposes, and this can give at least assurance to buyers that it is safe to proceed with the purchase. Many installment land contract buyers are particularly vulnerable to fraudulent and unconscionable sales schemes, and even if they have legal rights of redress, may be too uninformed or fearful to seek legal help.

In their approaches to installment land contracts, it is evident that courts and legislatures are subject to two often opposing objectives: on the one hand, to encourage a form of financing that enables less creditworthy but often deserving persons to buy land, including homes and farms; and on the other, to prevent installment land buyers from being taken advantage of by sellers. The legal response to these opposing aims varies considerably among the states, but the trend is toward more protection of buyers. The risk in this trend is that the law will provide so much protection to buyers that sellers will refuse to sell to those less creditworthy but deserving. There are limits to the risks sellers are willing to assume. Sellers also are unlikely to enter into installment land contracts unless there are benefits unobtainable in other forms of conveyancing and financing.

NOTES

1. On installment land contracts see Nelson & Whitman, Real Estate Finance Law §§ 3.26-3.38 (4th ed. 2002); Restatement of the Law, Third, Property, Mortgages § 3.4 (1997); Nelson, The Contract for Deed as a Mortgage: The Case for the Restatement Approach, 1998 B.Y.U. L. Rev. 1111.

2. Quite a few states have now legislated to give the installment land contract buyer greater protection. For example, among statutory installment land contract requirements in Maryland, Md. Real Prop. Code Ann. §§ 10-102 to 10-107 (Michie 2003), are (1) that the contract shall be in writing, signed by all parties, and contain all terms; (2) the buyer shall be given a copy of the contract and shall have an unconditional right to cancel the contract until the copy is received; (3) the vendor shall record the contract within 15 days from its signing, otherwise the buyer may cancel; (4) unless the contract specifies an earlier date, the buyer may demand upon payment of 40 percent of the purchase price that he receive a deed on condition that he execute a purchase money mortgage for the unpaid balance and absorb specified closing expenses; and (5) the vendor shall furnish to the buyer periodic statements showing the unpaid contract balance and the disbursement of installment payments for such purposes as taxes, insurance, and debt service.

3. Congress has brought interstate land sales, often based upon installment contracts, within its regulatory ambit. Interstate Land Sales Full Disclosure Act, 15 U.S.C.A. §§ 1701-1720 (1998).

4. Courts and legislatures have also acted to relieve some of the harshness of the installment contract if the buyer defaults. Problems of contract default are considered later in this chapter.

PROBLEM

A practice engaged in by some installment land contract sellers is to conceal interest rates higher than the stated contract rate and sometimes even higher than third-party lenders would charge on second mortgages. This practice may help explain the installment contract's growing popularity in some states and deserves to be carefully understood. Consider the following illustration:

Seller wishes to sell property for $50,000. The property carries a $30,000 first mortgage bearing 8 percent interest and $2,780 annual debt service. Buyer can raise $4,000 in cash and must finance the balance of the purchase price. The parties enter into an installment contract:

Contract Price:	$50,000	
Down Payment:	$ 4,000	
Contract Balance:	$46,000	
Terms:	$ 5,814	yearly, which includes 12 percent interest on the unpaid contract balance

Now consider the first year's events. Buyer pays $5,814. From this payment, seller remits $2,780 to the holder of the first mortgage. This sum includes $2,400 interest

(0.8 × $30,000) and $380 principal. Notice, however, that seller is actually getting 12 percent interest on the first mortgage part of the contract price, which the bank has financed, as well as on the $16,000 of the contract price that seller has financed. In short, seller receives a 4 percent override on the bank's investment in the property.

For the first year, seller's *effective* return is not the contract's stated 12 percent, but a concealed 19.5 percent!

	Interest
$16,000 at 12 percent	$1,920
[$30,000 at 4 percent]	$1,200
Total	$3,120

Rate of Return $\dfrac{\$3{,}120}{\$16{,}000}$ = 19.5 percent

See if you can compute seller's effective interest return for the second year. Is it higher or lower than 19.5 percent? ~~lower — pays less interest.~~

Note, finally, that hidden interest charges occur only when the property has already been mortgaged and the mortgage rate is lower than the contract rate.

Do you see any relevance to our earlier discussion of leverage?

e. Miscellaneous Security Devices

Although we will examine them more fully later, both the lease (with and without an option to purchase) and the sale-and-leaseback are financing devices in which the lessor extends credit to the lessee and retains a security interest — his right to reenter in the event of default. To think of a lease as a financing device may seem odd, until one realizes that the lessor has given his tenant the use of an asset having a specific value for a finite term, on condition that the tenant return the asset unimpaired at the end of the term and pay "interest" on the asset value during the term of the lease. What makes the lease both a financing and security device is the landlord's reserved or statutory power to terminate the lease if the "debt service" is not paid. If this power did not exist, the landlord could sue only for damages for contract breach.

The sale-and-leaseback is a complex mortgage substitute that is becoming commonplace, especially where the assets have commercial value: industrial plants, office buildings, shopping centers, aircraft, etc.

2. Junior (or Secondary) Mortgage Financing

a. Conventional Second Mortgages

Second mortgages, those subordinate to outstanding first mortgages, are frequent forms of real estate financing and often necessary for many buyers or other owners if they are to acquire properties or build on them. If sufficient first mortgage financing cannot be obtained, a second mortgage may provide the needed added funds to make a transaction viable. The subordinate character of the second mortgage usually, although not always, means that it is riskier than the first mortgage on the same property. Because of this greater risk, a second mortgage typically carries a higher interest rate than the first mortgage to which it is subordinate. In particularly risky transactions, second mortgage interest rates may be so high as to encounter usury problems.

Many purchase money mortgages are second mortgages. The buyer can make a down payment and obtain a first mortgage, but still is short of what is needed to pay the purchase price. To make the sale, the seller then may be willing to take a purchase money mortgage for the balance due. There also are third-party lenders, nonsellers, that make second mortgage loans. These lenders include both individuals and institutions. In some communities, there are lawyers and accountants who act as intermediaries in arranging second mortgage loans, with individuals as lenders. Commercial finance companies are major institutional second mortgage lenders, as are many of the mortgage companies doing business in most communities. Banks and savings and loans also do a substantial volume of second mortgage lending, including loans secured by junior mortgages on homes when homeowners are in need of funds for such purposes as emergency medical expenses or children's college tuition.

Second mortgages include many of the same provisions as do first mortgages. However, the duration of second mortgages, their length until maturity, usually is shorter than that of the first mortgages to which they are subordinate. Second mortgages also may include such additional provisions as that the mortgagor will not consent to revising any terms in the first mortgage without consent of the second mortgagee; the second mortgagee may make any first mortgage payments in default and add these payment sums to the second mortgage debt; a first mortgage default shall constitute a default on the second mortgage; and the mortgagor will insure the property against fire, flood, and windstorm damage and in an amount sufficient to cover the amount owed under the first and second mortgages. Why these added second mortgage provisions and whom are they intended to benefit?

If in default, a second mortgage may be separately foreclosed, but the person taking title on foreclosure takes subject to the outstanding first mortgage.

Loans are occasionally made secured by third and even fourth mortgages, but such loans are rare today. They were more frequent earlier in this century.

b. The Wraparound Mortgage

The wraparound mortgage is a form of junior financing most frequently used when the borrower has an existing mortgage at an interest rate substantially below the present market rate and the borrower needs additional funding. A wraparound mortgage then commonly enables the borrower to acquire additional funding at lesser cost than the current market interest rate by sharing the benefit of the favorable existing mortgage with the wraparound mortgagee. The wraparound mortgagee, in effect, takes over responsibility for the existing first mortgage and, in return, makes a second mortgage loan to the borrower at a face amount totaling the remaining balance on the existing first mortgage plus the added amount being loaned the borrower. The wraparound mortgagee may or may not assume the first mortgage but is expected to make debt service payments on that mortgage.

The interest rate on the wraparound mortgage usually is below current market because the wraparound mortgagee is obtaining a benefit from the spread between the wraparound mortgage interest rate and the first mortgage interest rate.

NOTE

For a more detailed description of wraparound mortgages and the legal problems they may create see Madison et al, The Law of Real Estate Financing §§ 8.12-8.15 (2004); Lifton, Practical Real Estate in the 80's, Legal, Tax and Business Strategies, 390-396 (1983); St. Claire, Wraparound Mortgage Problems in Nonjudicial Foreclosures, 20 Real Est. L.J. 221 (1992); Zampano & Morrison, Is the Wrap Back? Renewed Interest in the Wraparound Mortgage in Installment Sales, 18 Real Est. L.J. 343 (1990); Note, Unwrapping the Wraparound Mortgage Foreclosure Process, 47 Wash. & Lee L. Rev. 1025 (1990).

3. Construction Financing

Most buildings and other major real estate improvements are constructed principally or entirely from loan funds, with the improved property as security for the loans. Because of the many risks and uncertainties in construction projects, construction financing is unusually complicated and frequently involves two lenders: a construction lender and a long-term or permanent lender. The latter is known as a takeout lender. The construction lender will finance the project through the construction stage; and if construction is satisfactorily completed, the construction lender will be paid in full and the long-term lender take over the financing. The reason for the two-lender process is specialization in real estate finance. Due to differences in risk, profit possibilities, and expertise, some types of lenders concentrate on construction loans and other types of lenders on long-term postconstruction loans. Commercial banks do much of the construction lending in the United States. They are attracted by the higher interest rates charged for such loans, despite the greater default risks involved. They also are attracted by the lesser inflation risk of these short-term loans and the greater origination and other fees earned from loans of these kinds. A variety of other lenders make takeout loans.

Construction loan funds are usually paid out in installments as construction progresses, borrowers thereby paying interest only as money is needed, and lenders making funds available only if construction is proceeding satisfactorily. Most construction lenders have developed very substantial expertise in monitoring construction as it proceeds and determining when conditions have been met justifying payment of the next loan installment. This expertise also is helpful, when and if there are defaults, in deciding whether or not the lender should negotiate workout arrangements with the borrower, take over possession, or foreclose, and, in the case of foreclosure, in deciding if the lender should acquire the property and complete construction.

Among the many contingencies involved in construction financing are whether work on the project being financed will proceed on schedule and whether it will meet anticipated costs and quality standards. Many factors can cause delay; for example, weather, material shortages, strikes, contractor errors, design problems, and borrower insolvency. Cost overruns are a frequent problem, too, as is work or material quality below what the lender, and perhaps the borrower, consider acceptable. Most long-term lenders prefer to avoid construction risks and generally are not staffed to evaluate or monitor the construction process. They prefer longer-term loans on completed projects and are willing to take lesser interest for what generally are more stable loans.

Construction loans are short-term, with full repayment normally due when construction is satisfactorily completed. The short-term character of these loans raises a serious concern for construction lenders: they want substantial assurance that the loans will be paid when due. Usually, the borrowers can pay only if they refinance with a long-term lender. To increase repayment possibilities, the practice has developed of construction lenders' refusing to make construction loans unless and until a commitment has been obtained from a long-term lender to provide long-term financing on proper completion of construction. Not only does this provide considerable assurance to construction lenders that they will be paid when their loans mature, but it also means that long-term lenders, expert at making such evaluations, have concluded that borrowers' titles are good, that surveys have been made disclosing no problems troublesome to lenders, and that the projects, if successfully completed, are economically sound. These conclusions by long-term lenders give further assurance to construction lenders that construction lending is justified.

Life insurance companies do much of the postconstruction lending on larger projects. Other lenders that do a substantial amount of postconstruction lending, following preconstruction commitments, are savings and loans, savings banks, and pension funds. There also are savings and loans and savings banks that make construction loans, and for a time in the recent past, there were real estate investment trusts that did considerable construction lending. Furthermore, some institutional lenders will make construction loans without prior takeout commitments, either expecting to provide the long-term financing themselves or hoping a long-term takeout lender can later be found. Such construction loans are most likely if projects are small, borrowers have particularly favorable credit ratings, or additional collateral is put up for the loans.

Typical construction loan terms state the loan amount, interest rate, supplemental fees payable to the lender, insurance coverage, and loan disbursement schedule and conditions. Also common is an agreement by the borrower to protect the construction lender's first lien on the land from superior mechanics' and materialmen's liens and all other liens or encumbrances that might be superior to the lender's lien. A further provision may be added that the borrower will comply with all obligations under the postconstruction loan commitment. Payments of principal in construction loans rarely are amortized. Some terms may be included as a supplemental agreement between the construction lender and borrower, setting forth in considerable detail when loan disbursements shall be made and the pre-disbursement requirements for each stage of the construction process, including lender approval procedures for change orders in work, materials, plans, and specifications.

A major construction lender preference is that the construction mortgage have priority over other mortgages and liens on the construction site. Obtaining and retaining first lien status is one means of reducing risks in the relatively high-risk field of construction lending. One common type of secured interest that construction lenders often want priority over is the purchase money mortgage. Developers often buy land with the intent to build on it; their sellers are aware of this intent; and the sale price reflects the land's development potential. To obtain a desired price, the seller of development land may be willing to help finance the developer's plans by taking back a purchase money mortgage and then subordinating this security to that of the construction lender. Only with such subordination may the construction lender be willing to make funds available for construction. But under such circumstances, does the construction lender take on a legal obligation to the seller to make certain that construction loan funds are used for intended construction purposes, thereby helping to protect the seller's security interest? The next case, Rockhill v. United States, deals with this problem. Other types of secured creditors that construction lenders usually wish to have lien priority over are contractors and suppliers of building materials. These essential participants in the construction process have available what generally are very favorable mechanics' or materialmen's liens. The upcoming case of Kemp v. Thurmond considers circumstances under which construction lenders may secure priority over those with mechanics' or materialmen's liens.

Rockhill v. United States

418 A.2d 197 (Md. 1980)

RODOWSKY, Judge.

This matter comes to us from the United States District Court for the District of Maryland under the Maryland Uniform Certification of Questions of Law Act.[1] It arises on a motion to dismiss a complaint. In essence we are asked whether, under Maryland law, a mortgage lender whose loan is for construction or repair purposes and who obtains lien priority by subordination, thereby owes a duty to the subordinating lienor to exercise care that the borrower applies the loan proceeds to the intended purposes of the loan. On the facts alleged, our answer is "no."

Eunice L. Rockhill and The Flag Harbor Corporation (Sellers), who have been designated as appellants, in November 1975 respectively conveyed two adjoining pieces of property in Calvert County to Neal E. Beachem and Mary E. Beachem (Borrowers). Sellers took back deeds of trust to secure payment of the unpaid balances of the purchase prices. The properties conveyed by Sellers included some frontage on the Chesapeake Bay and contained a small marina. In January 1977 the marina suffered extensive damage from ice and the area was subsequently declared a disaster area. Borrowers applied for and were granted a disaster loan from appellee, Small Business Administration (SBA). Sellers subordinated their purchase money deeds of trust to the lien securing the SBA loan by agreements with Borrowers dated November 4, 1977. On November 14, 1977 Borrowers executed deeds of trust upon the properties in favor of SBA to secure repayment of the disaster loan. Appropriate recording was effected. Thereafter Borrowers defaulted on the SBA loan. A petition to foreclose was filed on April 11, 1979. Sellers intervened as defendants in the foreclosure proceedings and counterclaimed for

---

1. Maryland Code (1974, 1980 Repl. Vol.), §§ 12-601 through 12-609 of the Courts and Judicial Proceedings Article.

a declaration that their purchase money deeds of trust were entitled to first lien status. When SBA moved to dismiss Sellers' counterclaim for failure to state a claim upon which relief could be granted, Sellers requested certification of that issue to this Court. In an opinion dated November 2, 1979 the United States District Court reviewed the allegations, determined that Maryland law governs[2] and concluded that certification should be granted. The certified question is:

Whether the allegations contained in the counterclaim of [Sellers], as reprinted in the statement of facts set out in the Court's opinion dated November 2, 1979 state a cause of action under Maryland law which, if proven, would entitle them to have the subordination agreement dated November 4, 1977, set aside and the priority of their liens restored?

The allegations set out in the opinion are that in August 1977 Borrowers approached Sellers, indicated that they were in the process of applying for an SBA disaster loan and stated that one of the loan requirements was that Sellers subordinate their liens on the properties to the deeds of trust to be executed for the benefit of SBA. Sellers executed the requested subordination agreements with Borrowers in reliance on the fact that Borrowers would use the loan funds to improve the properties and thereby increase their value. The terms of the loan authorization issued by SBA required Borrowers to use the loan proceeds for repairs and improvements on the properties and obligated SBA to distribute the funds as the work was completed. SBA did not properly inspect the progress of the work being performed, properly administer its loan, or properly disburse funds as the repairs were performed. As a result Borrowers used all the loan funds for their own benefit and not for the benefit of the properties.

The opinion determining to certify the question, in order precisely to delineate the issues, also states:

Rockhill and Flag Harbor have not alleged:

1) that the SBA expressly agreed or represented to [Sellers] that it would disburse the funds only as improvements or repairs were completed;

2) that [Sellers] signed or are a party to the SBA-Beachem loan arrangement;

3) that the SBA signed or is a party to the subordination agreement;

4) that the subordination agreement contains language which conditions its enforceability upon the SBA overseeing the use of the funds or distributing the funds only as the work progressed; or

5) that the subordination agreement contains language which limits [Sellers'] waiver of priority only to the amount of the loan which was actually used to repair or improve the property.

The general problem presented here has been addressed in a number of decisions. Typically the subordinating party is the owner of land who sells it, or makes a long term lease of it, to a developer who will require financing. An increase in the value of the property upon completion of the contemplated improvements is

---

2. Since the United States District Court has determined that Maryland law controls, the question contemplates that we consider SBA as if it were a private lender. Thus we do not consider whether any duties are imposed on SBA, relevant to this matter, under the laws of the United States.

anticipated, so that the owner may be offered an attractive purchase price or rental. The owner, in turn, assumes some of the risk of the venture by agreeing to an arrangement under which those who will more substantially finance the development obtain priority over a take-back purchase money mortgage, or obtain a lien on the lessor's reversionary interest.

The term "subordination" is used in at least two general senses in the cases of the type presented here. One aspect refers to the executory promise to subordinate to financing of a described type (hereinafter sometimes called a "subordination clause"). The term is also applied to the declaration or agreement which expressly manifests assent to the priority of a specific lien (hereinafter sometimes called a "subordination agreement"). Some subordination clauses contemplate the execution by the subordinator of a subordination agreement. Others are drafted with the object of effecting subordination without further documentation when a given loan falls within the description of the subordination clause ("automatic subordination").

If the borrower defaults and the seller is faced with both non-payment of this subordinated obligation and loss of his land, the search begins for a legal theory which will result in a reversal of the priorities. Because part of a seller's purpose in subordinating is to facilitate development of the property, the quest for relief has included focusing on whether the proceeds of the loan to which the seller subordinated were in fact utilized to enhance the value of the security. Legal theories which have received at least some judicial recognition and by which priority has been wholly or partially restored to the subordinating seller (or lessor) include:

1. A subordination agreement by which lender and seller are in privity and under which the lender expressly assumes a duty to supervise use by the borrower of the loan proceeds or to restrict their use to designated purposes;

2. Collusion by the lender with the borrower in a diversion of loan proceeds by the borrower from a purpose to which the borrower is obligated to the seller to apply them;

3. An automatic subordination clause under which the seller expressly conditions his subordination on use of the loan proceeds for a designated, limited purpose or on the performance of specified duties by the lender;

4. A condition or limitation which is implied in an otherwise unqualified subordination agreement, whether or not the lender is in privity with the seller under it, based upon a condition or limitation expressed in the subordination clause between seller and borrower; and

5. A judicial determination that the lender owes the seller a duty to exercise a degree of care (variously expressed) over the use of the loan proceeds based upon the relationship of the parties to the project and upon the expectations of the seller.

Theories 1 and 2 present what are considered to be the requirements for relief under the general rule. Here an express agreement between Sellers and SBA is not alleged. Nor is there any allegation that SBA in effect colluded with the Borrowers.

Similarly, theory 3 is not presented here. SBA does not assert an automatic priority based on compliance with an express condition in a subordination clause in the purchase money deeds of trust to Sellers.

Sellers, however, press decisions which have departed from the general rule. They begin their attack at the level of theory 4 and rely upon Miller v. Citizens Savings & Loan Ass'n., 248 Cal. App. 2d 655, 56 Cal. Rptr. 844 (1967). In that case the $95,000 purchase money deed of trust contained a clause subordinating its lien to one or more deeds of trust "'made primarily for the purpose of constructing improvements'" and provided that the proceeds of the preferred loan might be disbursed for a number of types of costs including offsite improvements, onsite improvements, escrow charges, insurance, loan costs and advertising. Construction loans totalling $349,500 were obtained to which the seller, without qualification, agreed with the lender to subordinate. The final loan disbursement of $26,341.30 was not utilized for a purpose described in the subordination clause of the purchase money deed of trust. In the seller's action challenging the priority of the construction deeds of trust, dismissal at the close of the plaintiff's case was reversed. It was held that the seller had presented a *prima facie* case for placing the last $26,341.30 of the construction loan advances behind the purchase money lien. The court reasoned that the unqualified subordination between seller and lender must be read together with the limited subordination clause of the purchase money deed of trust of which the lender had knowledge. These were said to be parts of a single agreement so that the limitations on use set forth in the latter were read into the former.

Miller was followed and extended in Middlebrook-Anderson Co. v. Southwest Savings & Loan Ass'n., 18 Cal. App. 3d 1023, 96 Cal. Rptr. 338 (1971), which is also pressed by Sellers here. In *Middlebrook* the seller entered into a contract to sell 28 lots to the borrower under an escrow arrangement. The escrow instructions specified a sale price of $365,000 of which $169,500 was deferred and to be secured by a purchase money deed of trust. "This deed was to be second and junior to a construction loan to be obtained at some later time by the buyers." Id. at 1026, 96 Cal. Rptr. at 339. During the pendency of the escrow the buyer-borrower advised the seller that the construction lender required its deed of trust to be recorded first. This was done. The construction lender disbursed $1,464,400 of which $300,000 was used for purposes other than construction. When the construction lender threatened foreclosure, the seller filed a complaint which included an allegation that the lender had "knowledge that the seller would subordinate its lien *on condition* the loan funds were to be used only for construction improvements." Id. at 1029, 96 Cal. Rptr. at 341 (Emphasis added). Dismissal on demurrer was reversed. The court's analysis was in terms of contract law.

> [T]he lender's claim to priority flows from the agreement between the seller and the buyer. It is only as a result of the seller's waiver of his statutory right to a first lien that the lender achieves priority. Thus, the lender is a third party beneficiary in the seller-buyer agreement, but only to the extent that it abides by the conditions of subordination. If the lender does not comply with the seller's conditions it does not achieve priority. Since one condition to priority is the proper use of the construction funds, the priority of the construction loan lien does not vest until such time as the funds are applied to the construction purpose. [Id. at 1033, 96 Cal. Rptr. at 344.]

The court then took a step beyond *Miller* and equated the priority effected by the order of recording with priority accomplished by a subordination agreement.

As we read both *Miller* and *Middlebrook,* a condition was implied in the subordination to the lender based upon a condition expressed in the subordination clause of the agreement between the seller and the borrower. In the matter at hand there is no subordination clause between Sellers and Borrowers which is alleged to have been the basis for obtaining the Sellers' subordination to SBA.[3] Rather, Sellers and Borrowers directly entered into the agreements subordinating specifically to the SBA loan. Those subordination agreements are unconditional and there is no other agreement relied upon from which a conditional or limited subordination can be implied.[4] It is therefore unnecessary for us to determine in this case whether Maryland law recognizes an implied condition as was done in *Miller* and *Middlebrook*.

Thus the issue resolves to whether there is a duty on the lender, enforceable by the seller, to see to the application of the loan proceeds where the purpose of the loan is to make improvements or repairs. As indicated above, the majority of courts have determined there is no such duty.

> The general rule throughout the United States is that where a landowner agrees to subordinate his fee interest to a mortgage lien for the purposes of obtaining a construction loan, without an express covenant from the mortgagee (or lessee-developer) to the landowner, to see to the application of the sums advanced, possible diversion of funds by the mortgagor-developer is a risk assumed by the landowner, unless the latter is able to demonstrate fraud or collusion between the mortgagor-developer and the mortgagee.

Grenada Ready-Mix Concrete, Inc. v. Watkins, 453 F. Supp. 1298, 1313 (N.D. Miss. 1978). [Discussion of cases in accord omitted.]

Sellers, however, rely on three decisions which reach a contrary result. Commercial Standard Insurance Co. v. Bank of America, 57 Cal. App. 3d 241, 129 Cal. Rptr. 91 (1976), held there was a duty owed by the lender to the surety on a performance bond posted by the builder under a construction contract with the owner who was the construction borrower. The lender had agreed with the owner

---

3. The original record certified by the Clerk of the United States District Court for the District of Maryland contains only that court's opinion and the certified question. A joint record extract has been submitted here which sets forth certain of the documents including both purchase money deeds of trust made by the Borrowers. The trust deed for the benefit of The Flag Harbor Corporation contains the following provision:

> That the Trustees hereunder shall be required, without the necessity of obtaining the prior consent or joinder of the deed of trust note holder, to subordinate *not more than approximately 50% of the property to any phase of development* of the said deed of trust to any bona fide construction and/or permanent loan, land acquisition, land development, or loans placed from time to time upon the subject property or any portion or portions thereof, without curtailment and at no cost to the Grantor.

The trust deed for the benefit of Eunice L. Rockhill is the same but for the italicized words.

4. Also included in the joint record extract is Sellers' counterclaim, paragraph 14 of which alleges in part:

> That the Plaintiffs' execution of the Subordination Agreements heretofore referred to was based entirely upon the representation that the SBA would properly administer its loan . . . to insure compliance with its loan provision.

At oral argument Sellers took the position that an express representation by an authorized representative of SBA is not required in order to state a cause of action. It is Sellers' position that a representation by the Borrowers, in a transaction which is structured as the one presented here, can be considered an implied representation of SBA. In support of the position Sellers referred to Cambridge Acceptance Corporation v. Hockstein, 102 N.J. Super. 435, 246 A.2d 138 (App. Div. 1968). Sellers' theory of implied representation is not substantially distinguishable from judicial recognition of a legal duty on the part of the lender, which is discussed, infra.

to disburse the loan funds to the contractor for work completed as evidenced by inspection reports supplied by the lender's employees. In litigation following the contractor's default, the surety's claim over against the lender was held good against demurrer. The court weighed policy considerations on the issue of imposition of the duty as claimed. It found the loss foreseeable, that imposition of a duty would cause the bank to exercise due care in future cases and that it would probably impose on the bank the burden of employing persons competent to evaluate the progress of construction. On the other hand, it considered the surety in as good a position as the lender to spread the risk of improper disbursement equitably throughout the construction industry. The balance was tipped in favor of imposing the duty because Cal. Civ. Code § 1714 (West 1973) provides: "Everyone is responsible . . . for an injury occasioned to another by his want of ordinary care or skill in the management of his property or person, except so far as the latter has, willfully or by want of ordinary care, brought injury upon himself." Because there was no public policy ground which clearly supported an exception to this statutory principle, the statute was applied to the lender. *Commercial Standard Insurance Company* is distinguishable in light of this California statute.

[handwritten margin note: NO statute here.]

Appellants also cite Cook v. Citizens Savings & Loan Ass'n, 346 So. 2d 370 (Miss. 1977). A builder's lien was held to attach to the funds realized by the construction lender on foreclosure because in "paying out construction funds, [lender] should have used reasonable diligence to see that the funds were actually used in payment of materials or other costs of construction. Southern Life Insurance Co. v. Pollard Appliance Co., 247 Miss. 211, 150 So. 2d 416 (1963)." Id. at 372. The reference to *Southern Life* makes clear that the court in *Cook* is referring to a rule of Mississippi mechanics' lien law under which "a construction mortgagee has preference over materialmen and laborers only to the extent that its funds actually go into the construction." Southern Life Insurance Co. v. Pollard Appliance Co., supra, 247 Miss. at 221, 150 So. 2d at 420.

The authority of *Cook* as support for the position of Sellers in the case at hand is greatly undermined by Grenada Ready-Mix Concrete, Inc. v. Watkins, supra. A ground lessor had "subordinated" to construction financing. In a diversity action injunctive and monetary relief was sought by the lessor based on an implied contractual duty of the lender and on an asserted equitable duty to avoid manifest injury to the subordinator where there had been a cost overrun of $114,998 on the $1,125,000 construction loan under which $1,090,115 had been disbursed. Application of the rule in Cook v. Citizens Savings & Loan Ass'n., supra, for the benefit of the lessor was specifically argued. The federal court was of the opinion that the Mississippi Supreme Court would adopt the majority rule because it had

> consistently followed what may fairly be regarded as a conservative view in supporting the priority of mortgagees who exercise ordinary care in the disbursement of their funds, even against the claims of unpaid materialmen or laborers-claimants who stand upon a much higher plane than would the subordinated landowner who contributes no materials or efforts to the construction job, and who has at his disposal a means for protecting his interests in any commercial venture by insisting upon the inclusion of protective language in the documents comprising the agreement. [Grenada Ready-Mix Concrete, Inc. v. Watkins, supra, 453 F. Supp. at 1314.]

As authority for a duty of loan supervision on SBA, Sellers stress Cambridge Acceptance Corp. v. Hockstein, supra,[5] a *per curiam* opinion of the Appellate Division of the Supreme Court of New Jersey which affirmed the Chancery Division, reported as Cambridge Acceptance Corp. v. American National Motor Inns, Inc., 96 N.J. Super. 183, 232 A.2d 692 (1967). There the ground lessor, the lessee and the lender entered into a subordination agreement which recited that lender "*has agreed to advance construction monies* to assist in the . . . construction of the aforementioned motel building . . . and [lessee] has agreed to execute and deliver its mortgage *as security for the construction loan. . . .*" Id. at 189, 232 A.2d at 695 (Emphasis in text). It appeared from a memorandum of loan agreement, to which the lessor was not a party, that the $100,000 loan was for the general corporate purposes of the lessee which was engaged in motel development at a number of locations. As construed by the appellate court, the documents did not stipulate that the lessor's subordination was limited to a lien for moneys advanced which were actually applied to construction. It read the documents as evidencing on the part of the lessor no more than "an expectation and intention that the construction [would] actually take place by use of the money borrowed." Cambridge Acceptance Corp. v. Hockstein, supra, 102 N.J. Super. at 438, 246 A.2d at 140. The court recognized the general rule and cited many of the cases in support thereof which are set forth above. Nevertheless, it affirmed a judgment in favor of the lessor, as defendant in an action to foreclose the mortgage, and said:

> While, under general principles of mortgage subordination law outlined above, a construction lender taking the benefit of a subordination is not a guarantor to the subordinator or liable to him for mere negligence in seeing to the appropriation of the moneys to the construction, we think plain principles of equity at least call for such a construction lender to make and administer the loan in the conventional manner of a construction lender rather than mask what is essentially a loan on the general credit and reliability of the borrower and the security of the land value as a construction loan, and act accordingly in disbursing the funds. [Id. at 440, 246 A.2d at 141.]

The lender in *Hockstein* had "never conceived this loan as, or undertook to administer it in the manner of a conventional construction loan." For these reasons it was held that the lender "is now equitably estopped from asserting the subordination in derogation of the owners' fee interest." Id. at 441, 246 A.2d at 141.

We do not view *Hockstein* as on all fours with the instant matter since there is no allegation that SBA internally considered the loan as one based on the general credit of Borrowers, and not as one for repairs. However, Sellers urge that the effect on them is the same as in *Hockstein,* since they allege that *none* of the loan proceeds improved the properties and enhanced their value, due to breach of duty by SBA.

Appellants' position in essence assumes the existence of standards of loan supervision in the construction lending field which are so basic that compliance with them can be said to be a legal duty or an implied condition of the subordination. The many cases which have rejected any duty, absent an express agreement between lender and subordinator, belie this assumption. On the other hand, the relatively few cases which have applied what we have ranked as theories 4 and 5 do

5. *Hockstein* has been followed in Fikes v. First Fed. Sav. & L. Ass'n., 533 P.2d 251 (Alaska 1975).

not represent a developing body of case law expanding the liability of lenders in this area. Cf. Phipps v. General Motors Corp., 278 Md. 337, 341, 363 A.2d 955, 957 (1976). *Hockstein* and the California decisions have generated substantially less than unanimous response. [Omission of cases cited.]

It should also be observed that there are policy considerations, rooted in other California statutes, which in part explain the California decisions discussed above. Cal. Civ. Proc. Code § 580b (West 1976) prohibits a deficiency judgment "after any sale of real property . . . under a deed of trust, or mortgage, given to the vendor to secure payment of the balance of the purchase price of real property. . . ."[6] See Middlebrook-Anderson Co. v. Southwest Savings & Loan Ass'n., supra, 18 Cal. App. 3d at 1037, 96 Cal. Rptr. at 347; Miller v. Citizens Savings & Loan Ass'n., supra, 248 Cal. App. 2d at 659,56 Cal. Rptr. at 848. Further, under Cal. Civ. Code § 3391(2) (West 1970) a contract cannot be specifically enforced against a promisor "[i]f it is not, as to him, just and reasonable." The Supreme Court of California has interpreted this provision to require that "an enforceable subordination clause must contain terms that will define and minimize the risk that the subordinating liens will impair or destroy a seller's security." Handy v. Gordon, 65 Cal. 2d 578, 581, 55 Cal. Rptr. 769, 770-71, 422 P.2d 329, 330-31 (1967). See Middlebrook-Anderson Co. v. Southwest Savings & Loan Ass'n., supra, 18 Cal. App. 3d at 1036, 96 Cal. Rptr. at 346.

The principal reason why the majority of courts decline to impose a duty on the lender, absent a contractual basis, is that it is within the power of the subordinator to refuse to subordinate if the terms of the subordination are not acceptable to him. We believe that reasoning remains valid. To find the existence of a legal duty where none is expressed in the contract has much the same effect as judicially rewriting the contract for the parties. In Jones v. John S. Stubbs & Associates, 243 Md. 480, 221 A.2d 361 (1966) we reversed the grant against the seller of specific performance of the subordination clause in a purchase money deed of trust in a situation which was not within its terms. We said that "the lower court lacked authority, by construction or otherwise, to read a condition into the agreement to subordinate that was not provided for therein." Id. at 484, 221 A.2d at 364.

In addition, the rule for which Sellers contend introduces an added element of uncertainty into real estate transactions. A construction mortgage which on the public record enjoys a first lien status under an unqualified subordination agreement can, under Sellers' contentions, be converted into a junior lien. This could occur for a variety of reasons, ranging from fraud, through cost estimating which proves to be too low, to classifying one or more particular payments to be for purposes which have not enhanced the value of the security. Many construction lenders are institutions which invest the savings of countless people, and which are required by law to limit mortgage investments to first liens. Their bargained for priority by subordination should not be subject to reordering dependent on the vagaries of proof under a vague standard.

To the extent that we have guidance from the General Assembly on this matter of policy, it points toward stability in these transactions. Maryland Code (1974),

---

6. We are not unmindful that the joint record extract reflects the purchase money deeds of trust in the instant matter provide that there shall be no personal liability on the part of the makers of the promissory notes and of the grantors of the deeds of trust, or their heirs or assigns.

§ 3-102 of the Real Property Article provides that any subordination agreement may be recorded. The express reference to subordination agreements was inserted in the recording statutes as part of the revision of the real property laws effected by Chapter 349, § 1 of the 1972 Laws of Maryland, which was prepared with accompanying comments by the Section of Real Property, Planning and Zoning Law of the Maryland State Bar Association. As to present § 3-102 the Section commented: "Subordination agreements have been specifically mentioned to negate an old New York case, Gillig v. Maass, 28 N.Y. 191, which held that subordination agreements could not constitute constructive notice in the absence of an express statutory provision." Expressly legislating to prevent the application of a decision from another jurisdiction which might prevent a recorded subordination agreement from operating as constructive notice gives some indication of a policy that the subordination agreement is the place to look for rights of priority and suggests that we should not reach out to disturb the legal effects of that instrument as written, based upon the results of a tracing of funds disbursed.[7]

For these reasons, we answer the certified question, "No."

CERTIFIED QUESTION ANSWERED AS ABOVE SET FORTH. COSTS TO BE PAID BY APPELLANTS.

NOTE AND QUESTIONS

In the *Middlebrook-Anderson* opinion, discussed in the *Rockhill* opinion, it is stated:

> It has been pointed out by many courts and commentators that as between the seller and the lender, the lender is by far in the better position to control the use of the loan proceeds and thereby prevent misappropriations by the developer. The lender can require documented evidence that expenses have been incurred and can corroborate this by on-site inspections. It is common for lenders to control disbursements, since they, too, have an interest in preventing misuse of loan proceeds. . . . The lender is in a far better position to absorb any loss since such contingencies may be provided for in its profit and loss estimates. Finally, allocation of the loss to the lender would encourage the parties to provide for the various contingencies by contract. [18 Cal. App. 3d at 1036-1037, 96 Cal. Rptr. at 346-347.]

Are these arguments convincing and should the *Middlebrook-Anderson* position be preferred to the result reached in the *Rockhill* case? If the *Middlebrook-Anderson* position is taken, should lenders be paid for assuming the added expense and risk of monitoring disposition of loan funds? If they should be paid, who should pay them?

---

7. At oral argument Sellers additionally suggested estoppel and third-party beneficiary theories. Apart from a knowledge of Sellers' general purpose for subordinating which is implicit in the asserted duty which we have rejected, there is no allegation that SBA knew Sellers were giving up their first lien position in reliance on SBA following any particular procedure. Nor does the counterclaim allege facts indicating that the parties to the SBA-Borrowers loan agreement intended to recognize Sellers as the primary party in interest and as the real promisee. Hamilton and Spiegel, Inc. v. Board of Education, 233 Md. 196, 200, 195 A.2d 710, 711-12 (1963).

Kemp v. Thurmond

521 S.W.2d 806 (Tenn. 1975)

COOPER, Justice. This is an action to enforce mechanics' and materialmen's liens upon a house and lot owned by E. C. Thurmond III and wife, Doris Thurmond. The issue now before the Court is which lien has priority—the lien of petitioners, Builders Supply Company, Inc., and K–T Distributors, Inc., who furnished materials used in the construction of the house, or the lien secured by a trust deed held by the respondent, The Martin Bank, Martin, Tennessee.

In January, 1971, E. C. Thurmond applied to The Martin Bank for a construction loan in the amount of $25,000.00 with the funds to be used in the construction of a dwelling on a one acre lot which Thurmond proposed to buy from his brother-in-law.

By May, 1971, Thurmond had acquired the lot and had secured a commitment from the First Federal Savings and Loan Association of Fulton, Kentucky, to The Martin Bank that First Federal would loan $25,000.00 on the Thurmond house, when it was completed. Thurmond then went to The Martin Bank where the arrangements for the construction loan were "finalized" and a note and trust deed were executed. The total amount to be loaned Thurmond by The Martin Bank was $25,000.00 and the money was to be made available as needed for construction and in relation to the work performed. The construction loan was to be paid from the proceeds of the permanent loan.

The trust deed, which was recorded on May 17, 1971, describes the Thurmond indebtedness to the bank as follows:

". . . To secure and make certain prompt payment of ($2,500.00) Two Thousand Five hundred and No/100 Dollars borrowed money: Evidenced by a promissory note of even date by the said E. C. Thurmond, III and wife, Doris B. Thurmond payable to the Martin Bank, Martin, Tennessee. Said note to be paid on demand with interest at the rate of 8% per annum.

"2. This deed of trust secures in addition to the original amount of said loan stated hereinbefore, all renewals and extension of said loan and the note evidencing it and such ADDITIONAL SUMS as thereafter may be loaned by The Martin Bank, Martin, Tennessee to the first party, or their successors in title, prior to the cancellation of this deed of trust said additional loans in no event to exceed $22,500.00 in addition to the original amount loaned. The additional advances are to be due and payable as provided in the notes evidencing same and bearing interest at the rate of_____percent per annum from date until paid, provided such note recites that the sum is to be secured by this trust."

In addition to the initial $2,500.00 loan, The Martin Bank loaned the Thurmonds $7,500.00 on June 18, 1971, $5,000.00 on August 11, 1971, and $10,000.00 on September 2, 1971, for a total of $25,000.00. These monies were used by Thurmond in constructing the house.

Petitioners' liens against the Thurmond property were perfected and relate to and date from the first visible commencement of work on the Thurmond house. T.C.A. § 64-1104. The exact date of commencement of work is not set out in the record. However, it is conceded by all parties that no materials had been delivered to the Thurmond property and no labor had been expended on the Thurmond house at the time the trust deed was executed and recorded and the initial

$2,500.00 was loaned the Thurmonds. It is also conceded that work was commenced on the property before the additional loans were made.

In determining whether advances made after the giving of a mortgage shall receive priority over intervening mechanics' liens, courts generally look to whether the mortgagee is under an obligation, pursuant to the terms of his agreement with the mortgagor, to advance the sum or sums called for by the instrument. Many courts, including this Court, "have recognized that where the making of the advances is obligatory upon the mortgagee or beneficiary, the lien of a mortgage or trust deed receives priority over mechanics' liens when the mortgage or deed has been recorded before the mechanic's lien attaches, despite the fact that advances are actually given subsequently to this time." Annot.: Mortgage-Mechanic's Lien — Priority, 80 A.L.R.2d 179, 191; Theilen v. Chandler, 9 Tenn. App. 345 (1928); Kingsport Brick Corp. v. Bostwick, 145 Tenn. 19, 235 S.W. 70 (1921). "In determining the priority of the lien of a party lending money under a trust deed and that of materialmen, it was wholly immaterial whether the party lending the money had advanced the entire amount at the time material was furnished if the obligation to advance the money existed." Theilen v. Chandler, 9 Tenn. App. 345 (1928).

Petitioners do not take issue with the above statement of applicable law, but insist that the Court of Appeals erred in finding that "it was an obligation on the part of The Martin Bank to make additional loans." The Martin Bank, in turn, insists that this Court is faced with a concurrent finding of fact by the chancellor and the Court of Appeals on the issue, and that the only question is whether there is any material evidence in the record to support the finding that The Martin Bank was under legal obligation to make additional loans up to $25,000.00.

While a finding of an obligation on the part of The Martin Bank to make additional loans to the Thurmonds may be implicit in the chancellor's holding that The Martin Bank's lien under the deed of trust included the advancements up to $25,000.00, the chancellor made no such specific finding. Absent this, we do not feel bound by the "concurrent finding of fact" rule, but have reviewed the record with a view of determining where the preponderance of evidence lies on the issue. On doing so, we find ourselves in agreement with the finding of the Court of Appeals that "The Martin Bank was under a legal obligation to make its advances, pursuant to its agreement with Thurmond to make those advances, so long as the work progressed. . . . Therefore, the lien (of The Martin Bank) is for the full amount of the recited amount to be advanced. The lien thereof relates back to the filing of the Trust Deed and it is superior to the appellant's lien."

The judgment of the Court of Appeals is affirmed. Costs in this Court are adjudged against the petitioners, Builders Supply, Inc., and K–T Distributors, Inc., and their surety.

Fones, C. J., and Henry, Brock and Harbison, JJ., concur.

NOTES AND QUESTIONS

1. Why would a lender ever make an optional future advances construction loan?
2. "In California, the courts have enunciated what, it has been said, may with propriety be denominated as the 'California rule,' which, although opposed elsewhere by authority of respectability, is also sustained by strong reason and eminent authority. The rule is that the lien of a mortgage does not operate to secure *optional*

advances made under the mortgage after the mortgagee has acquired actual notice of an encumbrance subsequent in point or time to his mortgage, so as to defeat or impair the rights of the subsequent encumbrancer. This rule is likewise applicable to trust deeds. To the extent of advances made without actual notice, the mortgage has priority over all liens subsequent to its execution. Recordation of the mortgage is notice to subsequent encumbrancers that it constitutes a lien to the sum therein named. If they desire so to do, they may ascertain the actual condition of the security and by notice to the holder of the prior mortgage prevent any additional encumbrance of the property for further advancements by giving notice of their liens, in which case they are entitled to have the senior mortgagee limited to the recovery of such advances as he has made under his mortgage prior to receipt of actual notice of the vesting of the junior liens, but if they do not give notice, their rights must be held subject to the mortgage to the full extent of advancements made. The rule does not apply where the provisions in the first mortgage makes it obligatory upon the mortgagee to make the advances, for it would be manifestly unsound to hold that actual notice of a subsequent mortgage would deprive the mortgagee of his lien for advances he is compelled to make. . . ." Oaks v. Weingartner, 234 P.2d 194, 196 Cal. App. (1951) (emphasis added).

(a) Mortgages usually provide that if the premises are not kept in good repair, or if the real estate taxes or hazard insurance premiums are unpaid, the mortgagee may make such repairs as it deems necessary "properly to preserve the property" or may pay such taxes or premiums, and any sums so paid "shall be a further lien" under the mortgage. Acting under this paragraph, will the mortgagee have made an optional or obligatory advance? Should the advance for repairs be treated differently from the advance for unpaid taxes?

(b) A junior mortgagee pays an overdue installment on a prior mortgage to prevent default and foreclosure. Is this optional or obligatory?

(c) Construction loan agreements usually provide for successive advances to coincide with stages of completion: for example, disbursement of 20 percent of the loan when foundation set; 20 percent when building roofed in; 20 percent when interior plaster set; 20 percent when certificate of occupancy issued; 20 percent thirty days later. Acting under this arrangement, as in Kemp v. Thurmond, supra, will the mortgagee always have made an optional or obligatory advance? If the subsequent lienor who is disputing the mortgagee's priority has furnished labor or materials to the site, will his ground be more solid than, let us say, a judgment creditor's?

3. What are the arguments for and against the rule (in California and in most other states) that protects even optional advances unless the senior lienor gets actual notice of the intervening claims? To subordinate the advance, why should it not suffice that the intervening claim be recorded before the advance is made?

4. A Florida statute (Fla. Stat. Ann. § 697.04 (Supp. 2006)), erases the common law distinction between obligatory and optional advances and protects all such advances against subsequent lienors from the time the mortgage is filed for record. It matters not that the advance is made with actual notice of the intervening claims. Cf. Silver Waters Corp. v. Murphy, 177 So. 2d 897, 900 (Fla. Dist. Ct. App. 1965). Michigan has a similar statute, Mich. Comp. L. Ann. § 565.901 and 565.902 (2006). What are the arguments for and against this type of statutory scheme?

5. Compare the treatment of future advances that appears in §§ 2.1 and 2.3 of Restatement of the Law, Third, Property, Mortgages (1997).

Skip to 189

§ 2.1 Future Advances

(a) A mortgage secures "future advances" if it secures performance of an obligation that comes into existence or is enlarged after the mortgage becomes effective.

(b) As between the parties to a mortgage, repayment of future advances will be secured by the mortgage if the parties have so agreed. The agreement need not be in the mortgage and need not be written. If a separate agreement for future advances is made at the time the mortgage becomes effective, but is unwritten, it will be enforceable only to the extent permitted by the Parol Evidence Rule.

(c) As against a person acquiring an interest in the mortgaged property subsequent to the mortgage, repayment of future advances will be secured only if an agreement of the kind described in Subsection (b) exists and

(1) the mortgage states that repayment of future advances is secured; or

(2) the person has other notice of the parties' agreement concerning future advances at the time the interest is acquired; or

(3) the mortgage states a monetary amount to be secured.

(d) If the mortgage states a monetary amount to be secured and makes no provision for future advances in excess of that amount, the total amount of the principal obligation secured by the mortgage may never exceed the stated amount, except as provided in Subsection (e) of this section.

(e) If the parties to the mortgage have agreed, in the mortgage (or otherwise, to the extent recognized under the Parol Evidence Rule) that the secured obligation includes the following items, the mortgage will secure their payment to the extent permitted by local law, notwithstanding that when added to the principal obligation they cause the total balance to exceed the stated amount:

(1) interest (including interest on amounts accruing as interest during previous periods and added to principal);

(2) costs of collection or foreclosure;

(3) attorneys' fees;

(f) A mortgage to secure repayment of future advances is valid whether or not any advances are made at the time the mortgage becomes effective.

§ 2.3 Priority of Future Advances

(a) If a mortgage secures repayment of future advances, all advances have the priority of the original mortgage. Whether or not the mortgage secures repayment of future advances, if the parties have agreed that the mortgage secures payment of interest, costs of collection or foreclosure, or attorneys' fees, these items have the priority of the original mortgage.

(b) Except as provided in Subsection (c), the mortgagor may at any time issue a notice to the mortgagee

(1) terminating the validity of the mortgage with respect to further advances; or

(2) subordinating the priority of the mortgage, as against intervening interests, with respect to further advances.

Such a notice is effective even if the termination or subordination with respect to further advances violates a contractual obligation of the mortgagor to draw further advances, but the mortgagor may be liable in damages for breach of such an obligation. Upon receipt of the notice, the mortgagee must provide the mortgagor with a certificate in recordable form stating that the notice has been received. If the notice provides for subordination of the mortgage with respect to further advances, the mortgagee may elect to treat it as terminating the validity of the mortgage with respect to such advances.

(c) The mortgagor may not issue the notice described in Subsection (b) above and any notice issued by the mortgagor is ineffective, if:

(1) a termination or subordination of further advances would unreasonably jeopardize the mortgagee's security for advances already made; or

(2) the further advances will benefit persons other than the mortgagor, and the mortgagee has a contractual duty to provide such benefit.

(d) Even if the mortgagor issues a notice under Subsection (b), the mortgage continues to secure, with its original priority, the items listed in Subsection (a) and any expenditures reasonably necessary for protection of the security (§ 2.2).

Note that § 2.3 makes no distinction between advances that the mortgagee is contractually obligated to make and those that are optional, in effect rejecting the obligatory-optional distinction.

But what purpose are subsections 2.3(b) and (c) intended to serve?

Haz–Mat Response, Inc., v. Certified Waste Services, Ltd.

910 P.2d 839 (Kan. 1996)

DAVIS, Justice:

This appeal comes before us upon our grant of review on two issues: (1) whether the removal of hazardous waste from landowners' property was an "improvement of real property" within the meaning of the mechanic's lien statute, K.S.A. 60-1101; and (2) whether a subcontractor not in privity with the owner of the property may initiate an action for unjust enrichment against the owner when the prime contractor fails or refuses to pay the subcontractor.

The trial court granted summary judgment to the defendant on both issues. The Court of Appeals affirmed the trial court's judgment that the plaintiff's removal of waste was not lienable under K.S.A. 60-1101 but reversed and remanded for consideration of the plaintiff's unjust enrichment claim. *Haz–Mat Response, Inc., v. Certified Waste Services, Ltd.,* 21 Kan.App.2d 56, 896 P.2d 393 (1995).

The material facts necessary for the resolution of the issues presented are largely undisputed. Defendant Coastal Refining and Marketing (Coastal) contracted with defendants Certified Supply Corporation (Certified) and Chief Supply Corporation (Chief) to dispose of up to 500,000 pounds of Coastal's hazardous waste located on Coastal's property in four containers: two above-ground emulsion breaking tanks, one API separator, and one in-ground tank. Certified and Chief subcontracted with plaintiff Haz–Mat Response, Inc., (Haz–Mat) to perform part of the work.

Problems arose during performance of the contract, and although Haz–Mat removed the waste from the storage tanks, it was not disposed of as required by the prime contract. Coastal hired other contractors to complete the work. Coastal refused to pay Certified and Chief, who in turn refused to pay Haz-Mat. Haz-Mat filed a mechanic's lien and thereafter filed suit against Certified, Chief, Coastal, and CIC Industries, the apparent owner of the real property on which Coastal conducted business. (Hereinafter, CIC and Coastal will be referred to simply as "Coastal.") In its petition, along with breach of contract claims against Chief and Certified, Haz–Mat asked for foreclosure of a mechanic's lien against Coastal. In the alternative, Haz–Mat asked for judgment against Coastal, Chief, and Certified on the theory of quantum meruit/unjust enrichment. In a separate claim, Haz–Mat asserted a fraud claim against Chief.

Coastal filed a summary judgment motion, claiming that hazardous waste removal would not support a mechanic's lien because the removal is not an improvement of real property. Coastal also claimed that a subcontractor may not recover against a property owner on the basis of unjust enrichment in the absence of privity of contract. On the basis of undisputed facts, the trial court granted Coastal summary judgment on both claims.

Haz–Mat then entered into a stipulation with Chief and Certified for dismissal of all other claims. The trial court dismissed in accord with the stipulation. Haz–Mat appealed. The Court of Appeals affirmed the trial court's ruling that Haz–Mat's activities under the circumstances of this case could not form the basis for a mechanic's lien. However, the Court of Appeals reversed the trial court, concluding that under the circumstances, Haz–Mat had a viable unjust enrichment claim against Coastal notwithstanding a lack of privity. 21 Kan.App.2d at 65–66, 896 P.2d 393. We granted petitions for review on both issues.

MECHANIC'S LIEN

The Court of Appeals concluded that the removal of hazardous material under the given facts did not constitute an "improvement of real property" within the meaning of K.S.A. 60–1101 and, therefore, was not lienable. As recognized by the Court of Appeals, the issue presented was a matter of first impression in this state.

We agree with the Court of Appeals' conclusion that the removal of hazardous waste in the circumstances of this case was not lienable; we also agree with some of the rationale provided for this conclusion. However, because this is a case of first impression, we choose to conduct our own analysis of the issues presented. Because this analysis involved the interpretation of a statute, our standard of review is unlimited. See *Todd v. Kelly*, 251 Kan. 512, 515, 837 P.2d 381 (1992).

Our mechanic's lien law is remedial in nature, enacted for the purpose of providing effective security to any persons furnishing labor, equipment, material, or supplies used or consumed for the improvement of real property under a contract with the owner. The theory underlying the granting of a lien against the property is that the property improved by the labor, equipment, material, or supplies should be charged with the payment of the labor, equipment, material, or supplies.

At the same time, a mechanic's lien is purely a creation of statute, and those claiming a mechanic's lien must bring themselves clearly within the provisions of the authorizing statute. *Kansas City Heartland Constr. Co. v. Maggie Jones Southport Cafe, Inc.*, 250 Kan. 32, 34, 824 P.2d 926 (1992). The statute must be followed strictly with regard to the requirements upon which the right to lien depends. *Schwaller Lumber Co., Inc. v. Watson*, 211 Kan. 141, Syl. ¶ 2, 505 P.2d 640 (1973). However, because the statute is remedial and designed for the benefit and protection of persons designated by the act, once a lien has been found to have attached, the law is to be liberally construed in favor of such claimant. *See Holiday Development Co. v. Tobin Construction Co.*, 219 Kan. 701, 704–05, 549 P.2d 1376 (1976).

K.S.A. 60–1103 provides that a subcontractor may obtain a mechanic's lien as provided for in K.S.A. 60–1101. K.S.A. 60-1101 states:

"Any person furnishing labor, equipment, material, or supplies used or consumed for the improvement of real property, under a contract with the owner or with the trustee, agent or spouse of the owner, shall have a lien upon the property for the labor, equipment, material or supplies furnished, and for the cost of transporting the same."

There is no dispute that Haz–Mat complied with all statutory requisites in filing its mechanic's lien, that it provided labor and materials used in the removal of hazardous waste on the owner's real property, and that it has not been paid under its subcontract. The question before the trial court and on appeal is whether Haz–Mat's waste-removal activities constituted an *improvement of real property*.

The phrase "improvement of real property" is not defined in the Kansas mechanic's lien statute. The only reported Kansas case interpreting the term "improvement" as used in our mechanic's lien statute is *Mark Twain Kansas City Bank v. Kroh Bros. Dev. Co.*, 14 Kan.App.2d 714, 717, 798 P.2d 511, *rev. denied* 248 Kan. 996 (1990). The question presented in *Mark Twain* was whether the architectural and engineering services provided by subcontractors constituted lienable labor resulting in an improvement to real property when construction was never commenced and there appeared no visible or physical manifestation of the subcontractors work on the property. *Mark Twain* held that the professional services provided were never used or consumed in any improvement of the real property within the meaning of K.S.A. 60–1101. The Court of Appeals relied in part on the earlier case of *Benner–Williams, Inc. v. Romine*, 200 Kan. 483, 485, 437 P.2d 312 (1968), wherein this court said: "In order for a mechanic's lien for labor and materials to attach, such items must be used or consumed for the improvement of real property, and thus become part of the realty itself."

Mark Twain concluded that there is a requirement of "[s]ome visible improvement" or some "visible effect on the real estate" "in order to put those who seek to acquire an interest in the land on notice that building has commenced on the property." 14 Kan.App.2d at 721, 798 P.2d 511. However, an examination of the cases relied upon by the Court of Appeals does not support the conclusion that there must be some visible effect on the real property for the activity to be lienable. *Mark Twain* further concluded that improvement is "generally defined as any physical addition made to real property that enhances the value of the land." 14 Kan.App.2d at 720, 798 P.2d 511. While this definition may be generally true, there is no requirement under our present law that there be a physical addition made to real property. Further, while the improvement will enhance the value of the land, it need not actually enhance the market value of the land. See 53 Am.Jur.2d, Mechanics' Liens § 2, p. 517. See also *Masterson v. Roberts*, 336 Mo. 158, 163, 78 S.W.2d 856 (1934) (the question of whether alteration of a building makes the property more valuable is a business decision the owner makes when he authorizes the work to be done and does not affect whether a mechanic's lien may attach).

While the Court of Appeals in this case discusses *Mark Twain*, it did not base its decision on *Mark Twain*. Instead, the Court of Appeals adopted the following dictionary definition of improvement: "A valuable addition made to property (usually real estate) or an amelioration in its condition, amounting to more than mere repairs or replacement, costing labor or capital, and intended to enhance its value, beauty or utility or to adapt it for new or further purposes." Black's Law Dictionary 757 (6th ed. 1990). Applying this definition, the Court of Appeals concluded that the removal of the waste under the circumstances of this case was not lienable in that removal was part of a maintenance program necessary in the normal course of Coastal's business. "The removal of the waste did not become a part of the property or enhance the value of the real estate because defendant would generate more waste to take its place." 21 Kan.App.2d at 62, 896 P.2d 393.

The phrase "improvement of real property" first appears in K.S.A 60–1101 in 1964. Other than in *Mark Twain,* the meaning of the term "improvement" used in K.S.A. 60–1101 has not been discussed or defined in Kansas. However, earlier Kansas cases not involving the precise issue we now address provide some guidance for the present statute. In *Hill v. Bowers,* 45 Kan. 592, 26 P. 13 (1891), the statute in question granted a lien for a person who furnished material for erecting any fence. The court held that it must appear not only that such material was purchased to be used for fencing, but it must also appear that the same was in fact so used as to become a part of the realty. *Mortgage Co. v. Weyerhaeuser,* 48 Kan. 335, 29 P. 153 (1892), involved the question of when time begins to run under the lien statute. The court held that it was not the placing of some material on lots later used in construction which started the time but that it was the digging of a cellar. "A lien for fixtures or machinery dates from the time they are furnished or put up, by the express words of the section." 48 Kan. at 344, 29 P. 153.

The labor, equipment, material, or supplies must by the express terms of the statute be used or consumed for the improvement of property. In *Seyb–Tucker Lumber and Implement Co. v. Hartley,* 197 Kan. 58, 415 P.2d 217 (1966), the last date material was furnished became important. It was determined that a certain gallon of turpentine was purchased for use in the construction but never used in the actual construction. In holding that the gallon purchased could not be the basis for a lien and relying on established Kansas law, the court concluded that " 'no lien can be allowed for material purchased for a building on the land of the owner unless it in fact goes into the building and becomes a part of the realty.' " 197 Kan. at 62, 415 P.2d 217 (quoting *Sash & Sales Co. v. Early et al,* 117 Kan. 425, 232 Pac. 232 [1925]). Similarly, in *Benner–Williams, Inc. v. Romine,* 200 Kan. at 485, 437 P.2d 312, the court held: "In order for a mechanic's lien for labor and materials to attach, such items must be used or consumed for the improvement of real property, and thus become part of the realty itself."

However, Kansas law does not require that an actual structure be built on the property. In *Benner–Williams,* a lien existed where the labor and materials were provided to remodel an existing residence. See 200 Kan. at 486, 437 P.2d 312. In *Southwestern Electrical Co. v. Hughes,* 139 Kan. 89, 93, 30 P.2d 114 (1934), this court determined that bringing in and grading dirt was a lienable activity in that it was an improvement in the property. In *Hughes,* this court concluded that grading was lienable where the evidence established that the lots were low and dirt had to be hauled in to grade up around the house and garage. The court noted that the grading necessary under the plan of construction was as essential as the building of steps to get up and down. The court held: "Dirt furnished for grading the lot as a necessary feature of the plan of construction of the building was a lienable item." 139 Kan. 89, Syl. ¶5, 30 P.2d 114.

The Court of Appeals in this case cited an Alabama case dealing with the definition of the term improvement. In *Mazel v. Bain,* 272 Ala. 640, 133 So.2d 44 (1961), the Alabama Supreme Court dealt with the question of whether clearing land, which included "pushing stumps and scrub oaks, raking and leveling the said lands" was an improvement on land under their statute which granted a lien to "every . . . person . . . who shall do or perform any work, or labor upon . . . any building or *improvement on land*." (Emphasis added.) 272 Ala. at 641, 133 So.2d 44. The Alabama Supreme Court adopted the Black's Law Dictionary definition of the improvement and held that the labor was lienable. Moreover, the court recognized that the determination of what activity was lienable under its statute depended upon an examination of the facts in each case. The court recognized that improvements meriting the protection of a lien under the statute may occur in unforeseen variety and, thus, the determination was to be made on the facts of each particular case. 272 Ala. at 641–42, 133 So.2d 44.

Another case dealing with the definition of improvement to real property is *Cates v. Hunter Engineering Co.*, 205 Ill.App.3d 587, 151 Ill.Dec. 133, 563 N.E.2d 1239 (1990). *Cates* is a products liability action involving an allegation of negligent design, assembly, and manufacture of a cold rolling mill, which was characterized as a machine. The question was whether the plaintiff's action was time barred under Illinois law, which provided in part that no action based upon tort may be brought against any person for an act or omission in the design, planning, supervision, observation, or management of construction, or construction *of an improvement to real property*, after 10 years elapsed from the time of such act or omission. 205 Ill. App.3d at 588, 151 Ill.Dec. 133, 563 N.E.2d 1239.

The question on appeal was whether the defendant had met its burden of establishing that the cold rolling mill was an *improvement to real property* within the meaning of the statute. *Cates* defined an "improvement" as an addition to real property amounting to more than mere repair or replacement and which substantially enhances the value of the property. The court concluded that the installation of the cold rolling mill was more than a "mere repair or replacement," that the installation substantially enhanced the value of the real property, and that the installation was, therefore, an improvement to real property under the statute. 205 Ill. App.3d at 588–90, 151 Ill.Dec. 133, 563 N.E.2d 1239.

From the above discussion, several observations may be drawn concerning the statutory construction of the phrase "improvement of real property" as used in K.S.A. 60–1101: (1) What is or is not an improvement of real property must necessarily be based upon the circumstances of each case; (2) improvement of the property does not require the actual construction of a physical improvement on the real property; (3) the improvement of property need not necessarily be visible, although in most instances it is; (4) the improvement of the real property must enhance the value of the real property, although it need not enhance the selling value of the property; (5) for labor, equipment, material, or supplies to be lienable items, they must be used or consumed and thus become part of the real property; (6) the nature of the activity performed is not necessarily a determining factor of whether there is an improvement of real property within the meaning of the statute; rather, the purpose of the activity is more directly concerned in the determination of whether there is an improvement of property which is thus lienable; and (7) the furnishing of labor, equipment, material, or supplies used or consumed for the improvement of real property may become lienable if established to be part of an overall plan to enhance the value of the property, its beauty or utility, or to adapt it for a new or further purpose, or if the furnishing of labor, equipment, material, or supplies is a necessary feature of a plan of construction of a physical improvement to the real property. Finally, consistent with the Court of Appeals' opinion in this case, Black's Law Dictionary's definition most closely reflects what is meant by use of the phrase "improvement of real property" in K.S.A. 60–1101: "A valuable addition made to real property (usually real estate) or an amelioration in its condition, amounting to more than mere repairs or replacement, costing labor or capital, and intended to enhance its value, beauty or utility or to adapt it for new or further purposes." Black's Law Dictionary 757 (6th ed. 1990).

Applying the above definition, we find no evidence in the record that the removal of the hazardous waste was part of an overall plan to improve the property or that removal would necessarily enhance the value of the real property. Removal would presumably allow the business to continue as it had before removal. There is no evidence that removal would adapt the property for new or further purposes. In fact, the evidence established that the same business would be conducted as before. We agree with the Court of Appeals that the removal was not lienable because it was part of a maintenance program that was necessary in the normal course of Coastal's business. The evidence fails as a matter of law to demonstrate that the removal was an "improvement of real property" within the meaning of K.S.A. 60–1101.

UNJUST ENRICHMENT

The Court of Appeals correctly notes that the question whether a subcontractor can recover from an owner on the basis of unjust enrichment or quantum meruit under the facts of this case is a question of law, with an unlimited scope of review. . . .

The sole basis for the trial court's decision that a claim for unjust enrichment would not lie was lack of privity between the owner, Coastal, and the subcontractor, Haz–Mat. Our past cases establish that recovery under quasi-contract or unjust enrichment is not prohibited simply because the subcontractor and the owner of the property are not in privity. This conclusion is consistent with the theory of quasi-contract and unjust enrichment, which does not depend on privity. See 66 Am. Jur.2d, Restitution and Implied Contracts § 2, pp. 943–44. . . .

In theory, the right to recover under unjust enrichment is governed by principles of equity. The obligation upon which the right to recover is based is created and imposed by law to prevent unjust enrichment at the expense of another. If the law is to allow the action based upon an implied-in-law contract between the owner and subcontractor, there must exist some special circumstances that would justify requiring the owner to pay. An examination of our past cases and further consideration of those cases set forth in Annot., 62 A.L.R.3d 288, convinces us that an essential prerequisite to such liability is the acceptance by the owner (the one sought to be charged) of benefits rendered under such circumstances as reasonably notify the owner that the one performing such services expected to be compensated therefor by the owner. In the absence of evidence that the owner misled the subcontractor to his or her detriment, or that the owner in some way induced a change of position in the subcontractor to his or her detriment, or some evidence of fraud by the owner against the subcontractor, an action for unjust enrichment does not lie against the owner by a subcontractor.

Although Haz-Mat submitted an affidavit stating that its president "believed" Coastal was responsible for the bill along with the prime contractor, Haz–Mat did not present any evidence nor did it claim that this supposed belief was based on any statement or promise by Coastal. We do not suggest that privity must be established or that a promise by the owner must be established in order for the plaintiff to have an unjust enrichment claim, but there must exist such special circumstances to warrant such an action. Here, no such circumstances existed.

The Court of Appeals concluded that unjust enrichment would lie because "plaintiff's removal work is not lienable under K.S.A. 60–1101" and an action in equity might be plaintiff's only available avenue. In reaching its conclusion, we believe the Court of Appeals placed too much emphasis on the position of the plaintiff and failed to emphasize that the basis of an unjust enrichment action involves a consideration of the circumstances surrounding the acceptance and retention of the benefit by the defendant. While the position of the plaintiff is always a factor to be considered, it is "the acceptance or retention by the defendant of the benefit under such circumstances as to make it inequitable for the defendant to retain the benefit without payment of its value" that is of critical importance in making a determination of whether such an action will lie. *J.W. Thompson Co.*, 243 Kan. at 512, 758 P.2d 738.

Holiday Development Co., 219 Kan. 701, 549 P.2d 1376, remains good law. Those factors set forth in that opinion should be considered when deciding whether there is a basis for an action for unjust enrichment. However, the *Holiday Development Co.* factors are not exhaustive. As we have concluded in this case, an essential prerequisite to such liability for unjust enrichment in a case between a subcontractor and owner not in privity is the acceptance, by the one sought to be charged, of benefits rendered under such circumstances as reasonably to notify him or her that the one performing such services expected to be compensated therefor by the one sought to be charged. Moreover, the undisputed facts fail to establish that Coastal misled Haz-Mat to its detriment, that Coastal in some way induced a change of position in Haz-Mat to its detriment, or that any fraud existed. Although on an entirely different basis, we conclude that the undisputed facts require affirmance of the trial court's decision that the theory of unjust enrichment was not available to Haz-Mat.

The judgment of the Court of Appeals is affirmed in part and reversed in part, and the judgment of the district court is affirmed.

NOTE ON MECHANICS' AND MATERIALMEN'S LIENS

Of major importance in construction, remodeling, and repair of real estate improvements are mechanics' and materialmen's liens, sometimes referred to as construction liens.[24] These liens are statutory, they are provided for in every state, and the statutes vary extensively among the states. Mechanics' and materialmen's liens are designed to increase payment prospects for those who provide labor and materials for real property improvements on credit, credit extension being the usual practice; and these liens normally protect contractors, subcontractors, laborers, architects, engineers, surveyors, landscapers, and providers of

24. On Mechanics' and materialmen's liens, see Nelson & Whitman, Real Estate Finance Law §§ 12.4 and 12.6 (2d ed. 1985); 3 Powell on Real Property §§ 38-10 to 38-19 (2005); Siegfried, Introduction to Construction Law ch. 4 (1987); and Note, Mechanics' Lien Priority Rights for Design Professionals, 46 Wash. & Lee L. Rev. 1035 (1989).

construction materials.[25] An underlying purpose of the liens is to aid real estate development by encouraging the credit extension necessary to most such development. No doubt, too, the lien statutes also reflect the political influence on legislatures of powerful contractor, building trades, and building supply interests who benefit from the liens. There is variation among the states as to what constitutes an improvement that can result in a mechanics' or materialmen's lien, the *Haz–Mat* case being an example of a more restrictive interpretation of what constitutes an improvement under an applicable state mechanics' and materialmen's lien statute.

Mechanics' and materialmen's liens give security protection to those who have supplied labor or materials for land improvements and who have not been paid. The liens are on the buildings or other structures being improved and generally on the underlying and nearby land as well.[26] In some states, the liens may not attach for small claims, such as any claim under $500.[27] The states vary as to whether or not lien claim payments may exceed the total owed by the property owner for unpaid labor and materials.[28]

25. E.g., Cal. Civ. Code Ann. § 3110 (West 1993):

Persons entitled to lien; agent of owner
   Mechanics, materialmen, contractors, subcontractors, lessors of equipment, artisans, architects, registered engineers, licensed land surveyors, machinists, builders, teamsters, and draymen, and all persons and laborers of every class performing labor upon or bestowing skill or other necessary services on, or furnishing materials or leasing equipment to be used or consumed in or furnishing appliances, teams, or power contributing to a work of improvement shall have a lien upon the property upon which they have bestowed labor or furnished materials or appliances or leased equipment for the value of such labor done or materials furnished and for the value of the use of such appliances, equipment, teams, or power whether done or furnished at the instance of the owner or of any person acting by his authority or under him as contractor or otherwise. For the purposes of this chapter, every contractor, subcontractor, sub-subcontractor, architect, builder, or other person having charge of a work of improvement or portion thereof shall be held to be the agent of the owner.

26. E.g., Texas Prop. Code Ann. § 53.022 (Vernon 1995):

Property to Which Lien Extends
   (a) The lien extends to the house, building, fixtures, or improvements, the land reclaimed from overflow, or the railroad and all of its properties, and to each lot of land necessarily connected or reclaimed.
   (b) The lien does not extend to abutting sidewalks, streets, and utilities that are public property.
   (c) A lien against land in a city, town, or village extends to each lot on which the house, building, or improvement is situated or on which the labor was performed.
   (d) A lien against land not in a city, town, or village extends to not more than 50 acres on which the house, building, or improvement is situated or on which the labor was performed.
27. E.g., Pa. Stat. Ann. tit. 49, § 1301 (Purdon 2001).
28. In most states, lien claims may exceed and be collectible in excess of the owner's contract liability, as the claimants have a direct claim on the property being improved. So unpaid subcontractors retain lien claims even though the owner has paid the prime contractor in full. Typical of statutes permitting such direct claims is Pa. Stat. Ann. tit. 49. § 1301 (Purdon 2001):

Every improvement and the estate or title of the owner in the property shall be subject to a lien . . . for the payment of all debts due by the owner to the contractor or by the contractor to any of his subcontractors for labor or materials furnished in the erection or construction, or the alteration or repair of the improvement. . . .

Illustrative of statutes generally limiting the owner's liability to no more than what the owner has contracted to pay is N.Y. Lien Law § 4 (McKinney 1993).

If labor is performed for, or materials furnished to, a contractor or subcontractor for an improvement, the lien shall not be for a sum greater than the sum earned and unpaid on the contract at the time of filing the notice of lien, and any sum subsequently earned thereon. In no case shall the owner be liable to pay by reason of all liens created pursuant to this article a sum greater than the

Statutes of the various states differ considerably as to how and when mechanics' and materialmen's liens attach, their duration, and their priorities. Depending on the state, the liens may become effective when construction on a project commences, whether construction is started by the lien claimant or someone else;[29] when the lien claimant commences its work on the project or initially provides materials for the project;[30] or when the lien claimant files or records its claim in a public office.[31] – NY In most states, commencement of work or supplying of materials, unless paid for in advance, establishes the time at which the liens attach. There are obvious difficulties for other creditors or potential creditors in determining precisely when these commencement acts occurred or even if they have occurred. But, for lien attachment purposes, as against a bona fide purchaser, some states consider that work has commenced only if it is reasonably apparent from an examination of the site.[32]

In recording act terms, the existence of mechanics' and materialmen's liens in most states may be off-record risks for some time, as the liens may not be disclosed by examination of public records. However, it is a common statutory requirement, where lien attachment requires no filing or recording in a public office, for such a filing or recording to be made at a later date for lien rights to be perfected or continued.[33] The later date for preserving the lien usually is a set time, often within a few months, after the lien claimant completes its work or the entire construction project is completed.

It is common for all established mechanics' and materialmen's liens on a particular site to have equal priority with one another, sharing pro rata if the property on foreclosure sale fails to bring enough to pay all of these liens.[34] But in some states, priority among mechanics' liens is determined by seniority in when the respective lien rights were established, as by the order of filing with a public officer.[35] However, as Kemp v. Thurmond and notes following indicate, advance payment construction mortgages usually have priority over mechanics' and materialmen's liens, even for loan moneys paid over by the lender after the mechanics' and materialmen's liens became effective.

If the mechanics' or materialmen's lien claimant is not paid, the lien may be enforced by a judicial proceeding brought to force sale of the property, the sale proceeds being used to pay the secured debt. This procedure is analogous to judicial foreclosure of a mortgage and is often referred to as a foreclosure action.[36] Lien foreclosure actions are rather infrequent, as most lien claimants are paid without resort to judicial enforcement or the liens are eliminated in foreclosures by mortgages with priority.

value or agreed price of the labor and materials remaining unpaid, at the time of filing notices of such liens, except as hereinafter provided.

29. E.g., Haw. Rev. Stat. Ann. §§ 507-41 and 507-46 (Michie 2006).

30. E.g., Iowa Code Ann. § 572.2 (West supp. 2006), and as construed by Iowa case law.

31. E.g., N.Y. Lien Law §§ 3 and 10 (McKinney 1993 & supp. 2006).

32. E.g., Minn. Stat. Ann. § 514.05 (West 2002).

33. E.g., Ky. Rev. Stat. § 376.080 (Michie 2005 supp.).

34. E.g., Ariz. Rev. Stat. Ann. § 33-1000 (West 2006). In a few states, however, some types of mechanics' and materialmen's liens have priority over others. E.g., Tenn. Code Ann. § 66-11-107 (2004), laborers' liens have priority over other mechanics' and materialmen's liens.

35. E.g., Iowa Code Ann. § 572.17 (West 1992).

36. E.g., Mich. Comp. Laws Ann. § 570.1117 (West 1996).

Mechanics' and materialmen's liens commonly do not attach to property of federal, state, or local governments.[37] The liens generally are protective measures for those who supply labor or materials for construction on private but not public lands. However, bonding protection often is required to protect those who supply labor or materials for public construction projects.[38] Prime contractors, under federal and state statutes, must provide bonds guaranteeing that all work and materials contracted for by the prime contractors will be paid. Subcontractors, laborers, and materials' suppliers are protected by this bonding. - *in gov't sites.*

The stop notice is another device that a minority of states, by statute, have authorized for enabling unpaid suppliers of construction work or materials to secure payment. If these unpaid suppliers follow requisite procedures, they may, by filing a stop notice, force payment to them of undisbursed construction loan funds still held by the construction lender or borrower. A stop notice is analogous to a garnishment and can be more effective than a mechanics' or materialmen's lien in obtaining payment, especially if, as is usually the case, the unpaid supplier's lien is subordinate to the construction lender's mortgage. A stop notice also can be a very effective move if the unpaid supplier believes that the developer is likely to misallocate construction loan funds that should be paid to the supplier. Stop notices are used principally in private construction projects, but some statutes permit them in government projects as well.[39] Further consideration of mechanics' and materialmen's liens as off-record risks under state recording acts is included in Chapter 5 of the casebook.

G.   TRANSFERS OF ENCUMBERED PROPERTY

A common occurrence in real estate markets is for the mortgagor to sell the land. What then happens to the mortgage? Often the mortgage is paid off by the mortgagor following the sale, the mortgagor usually using the sale proceeds to pay off the mortgage. But an alternative procedure is also often followed when the mortgagor sells the land. Under this alternative the old mortgage remains and the buyer takes over most or all of the mortgage payment obligations. There are different forms of takeover but the two most common are the buyer taking subject to the old mortgage and the buyer assuming the old mortgage. The legal implications and risks to the buyer and seller vary depending on which of these two takeover options they agree on. The differences between the assumption and takeover options and the implications of each are considered in the following hypothetical factual problem and questions.

Owner purchased a $50,000 tract two years ago. She financed her acquisition through First Bank by a $40,000 mortgage that has since been paid down to $35,000. Owner decides to sell; the best price she can get is still $50,000, this from an offeror who, happily for our hypothetical, happens to have $15,000 cash.

The usual choice in arranging the sale is between refinancing and mortgage takeover. In the former, buyer pays seller $15,000, and mortgages the property to

---

37. But cf. N.Y. Lien Law § 5 (McKinney 2006 Supp.).
38. E.g., Neb. Rev. Stat. § 52-118 (2004).
39. E.g., Cal. Civ. Code Ann. §§ 3156-3176.5 (West 1993 and Supp. 2006), private works; §§ 3179-3214 (West 1993 and Supp. 2006), public works (West 1993 Supp. 2006).

Second Bank for $35,000, which is used to pay off the original mortgage. Can you see the closing in which among the papers shuffled are seller's deed, buyer's $15,000 check, buyer's note and mortgage to Second Bank, Second Bank's check for $35,000 (made payable to whom?), and First Bank's release of mortgage?

If, on the other hand buyer takes over seller's mortgage, he gives seller the $15,000, takes seller's deed, and enters possession. But his possession and ownership are dependent upon his (or somebody's) keeping up the payments on First Bank's mortgage. If that mortgage incurs a default, buyer stands to lose the property. Also, there is another usual consequence to default: not only may the lender, by one or another procedure, take the security in satisfaction of his debt, he may also recover the deficiency from seller,[40] absent a release or a discharge, if the security does not bring as much as the debt. Hence, in a takeover transaction, seller is at risk of a concurrence of a decline in the value of the sold property and a default by her buyer, events which do tend to concur. One way of reducing that risk is to get the buyer not only to take the property *subject* to the bank's security interest, but also to have buyer promise seller that he, buyer, will maintain the payments. With such a promise, known as buyer's *assuming* the mortgage, seller can recover from buyer any deficiency liability imposed on seller by the lender.

Keeping in mind that the major variations are refinance or takeover, and that the two forms of takeover are "subject to" or "assumption," determine why the following statements are true:

a. The more the seller has paid off on principal, and the more the property has risen in value since the original First Bank loan, the more likely the parties will need to handle the deal by refinancing;

b. The seller will sometimes, but not always, try to insist — where the buyer can make the choice — that the deal be handled by refinancing instead of takeover;

c. The lower (higher) the market interest rate at the time of resale relative to the original mortgage interest rate, the more (less) likely that First Bank would prefer takeover to refinancing;

d. Where there is no difference between the terms of the existing mortgage and the mortgage available through refinancing, mortgage takeover is cheaper for the buyer;

e. The shakier the income prospects of the property, the less likely buyer will be willing to *assume* the mortgage;

f. First Bank would prefer that buyer *assume* the mortgage, rather than take *subject to.*

1. Mortgage Takeover: The Rights of the Grantor as Against the Grantee

The grantor of mortgaged land has no claim against a non-assuming grantee to personally pay the debt. But the land remains liable (as principal), not only to the claim of the mortgagee, but also — via subrogation — to the claim of the grantor who, facing personal liability, pays off the debt after a mortgage default.

---

40. This implies, of course, that the seller is or has been obligated on the mortgage debt. When will this not be the case?

When the mortgage is assumed, the grantor adds to its rights against the land, rights against the grantee personally. While the grantor certainly may sue for reimbursement after paying the debt, most courts also let the grantor recover from the delinquent grantee as soon as default occurs. The grantor may also have the right to compel an assuming grantee to exonerate it by paying the debt to the mortgagee.

2. *Mortgage Takeover: The Rights of the Mortgagee as Against the Assuming Grantee*

Schneider v. Ferrigno   SKIP.
147 A. 303 (Conn. 1929)

MALTBIE, J. This action is brought by the holders of a certain mortgage to recover upon a condition contained in a deed of the mortgaged premises to the defendant wherein he assumed and agreed to pay the mortgage. It was originally executed by Ethel M. Holmes Case to one Paradise, being a fourth mortgage for $15,475 upon certain premises owned by her. Paradise sold the note and mortgage to David Miller and Miller sold them to the plaintiff Baggish and to Samuel Schneider, who took title to his half interest in the name of his wife, the other plaintiff. Before he acquired his interest in the note and mortgage, Schneider purchased the equity of redemption, taking title subject to the mortgages upon the premises. Later he entered into negotiations with the defendant for the exchange of the premises for certain real estate owned by the defendant, but, when the terms came to be arranged, Schneider was unwilling to assume certain mortgages on the defendant's premises and to execute purchase-money mortgages to him, so he proposed to transfer his premises to a brother-in-law, Krawitzky, and then have him make the exchange. Accordingly he did transfer the premises to Krawitzky, who assumed and agreed to pay the mortgages upon it, including the one in suit, "as part consideration for this deed," and Krawitzky and the defendant then made the exchange, the defendant also assuming and agreeing to pay the mortgages on the premises Krawitzky conveyed to him. The defendant later lost title to the premises by reason of a strict foreclosure of an incumbrance prior to that held by the plaintiffs. The trial court decided for the defendant solely upon the ground that, in view of the fact that Schneider had not himself assumed payment of the mortgage upon the property, the break in the chain of assumptions prevented a recovery by the plaintiffs upon the assumption agreement in the deed to the defendant, and that he did not intend to make a contract for the benefit of the holders of the note and mortgage in suit.

The appellants seek many corrections in the finding, but, in the view we take of the case, none of them are material. The basic question presented is, "Can the holder of a mortgage make liable one who, upon acquiring title to the premises, has assumed and agreed to pay that mortgage, despite the fact that, in the chain of title from the original maker of the mortgage, some owner of the equity of redemption has not assumed and agreed to pay it?" Where such situations have come before the courts, in the absence of statutory provision, different conclusions have been reached. Those which deny a right of recovery advance various reasons. Wiltsie,

Mortgage Foreclosure (4th Ed.) § 246, states that such a conclusion is based upon the fact that there is no consideration for the assumption, but that can hardly be so; the agreement to assume is but one term in the contract by which the lands are acquired, and, if that contract as a whole is supported by a valuable consideration, it cannot be said that any one term lacks such support. Williston, Contracts, § 386, suggests as the basis for the conclusion that, where the grantor of the equity of redemption was not himself liable by reason of an assumption of the mortgage and hence had no interest in the assumption of it by his grantee, the only intelligent object which can be attributed to him is to guard against a supposed or possible liability on his part, and he cannot be assumed to have intended to confer a benefit upon the holder of the mortgage; but it is difficult to see why, if his object is assumed to be to protect himself against a possible liability, his mental attitude is any different than it would be, had he sought to protect himself against a definite liability fixed by his own agreement to pay the mortgage. The cases which deny liability, such as the leading case of Vrooman v. Turner, 69 N.Y. 280, 285, 25 Am. Rep. 195, do not seem fully to recognize the extent and force of the rule which permits a third party beneficiary to sue upon a contract as it has now been developed.

The controlling test now is, Was there any intent to confer a right of action upon the third party? Amer. Law Inst. Restatement, Contracts, §§ 133, 135; Byram Lumber & Supply Co. v. Page, 109 Conn. [256], 146 A. 293. If the grantor of the equity of redemption who has not assumed the mortgage has no object to protect himself, an intent to confer a right to sue upon the holder of the mortgage would be the most natural motive to assign to him in requiring his grantee to agree to pay it. It is true that difficulties might be encountered in an attempt to work out the problem upon the equitable doctrine whereby, as between a mortgagor and his grantee who assumes and agrees to pay the mortgage, the latter becomes the principal debtor and the former occupies the position of surety, at least as it is applied in many jurisdictions, but with us that principle applies only as between the mortgagor and the grantee of the equity of redemption, and does not of itself affect the right of the mortgagee. Savings Bank of Ansonia v. Schancupp, 108 Conn. 588, 592, 144 A. 36. As regards the latter, the basis of a recovery upon an agreement by a grantee of the equity of redemption to pay the mortgage is stated in Tuttle v. Jockmus, 106 Conn. 683, 689, 138 A. 804, 806, as follows: "The right of the mortgagee to bring an action upon an assumption of the mortgage by the grantee of the equity of redemption is ordinarily based upon the principle which permits a third party to bring an action upon a contract made for his benefit." . . .

The conclusion of the trial court that it was not the intention of the defendant to make a contract for the benefit of the holders of the note in suit we understand to refer to the intention which the law attributes to him by reason of the assumption of the mortgage under the circumstances of this case. Of course, the question is, What intent is disclosed by the terms of his agreement read in the light of the surrounding circumstances, not such actual intent as he may have entertained? Quinby Co. v. Sheffield, 84 Conn. 177, 193, 79 A. 179; Easterbrook v. Hebrew Ladies' Orphan Society, 85 Conn. 289, 295, 82 A. 561, 41 L.R.A. (N.S.) 615.

The trial court was in error in holding that the plaintiffs could not hold the defendant liable upon his assumption of the mortgage because of the break in the claim of assumptions due to Schneider's failure to assume it. As the case was decided solely upon this ground, we remand it for further proceedings according to law.

There is error, and new trial is ordered.

All the Judges concur.

NOTES AND QUESTIONS

1. The facts in *Schneider* are an example of the highly speculative practices prevailing in many markets, including real estate markets, during the 1920s, practices that contributed to the severe depression of the 1930s. However, even today speculation in heavily mortgaged real estate is common although it is extremely rare today for a land parcel to be encumbered with more than two mortgages.

2. Why apparently was Krawitzky inserted in the chain of title between Schneider and Ferrigno? This apparently was agreed to in advance by all three of them. Under the agreement, Krawitzky was expected to convey title immediately on to Ferrigno. Why did Schneider not convey directly to Ferrigno?

3. If the plaintiffs had successfully recovered payment of the debt from the mortgagor, Ethel Case, could she then have recovered the amount of that payment from Ferrigno as mortgage assumer?

4. For a more extended discussion of the legal concepts justifying mortgagee recovery from buyers who have assumed the seller's mortgage, including the concepts of third-party beneficiary and equitable subrogation, see Nelson & Whitman, Real Estate Finance Law, §§ 5.11-5.14 (3d ed. 2002).

First Federal Savings & Loan Assn. of Gary v. Arena

406 N.E.2d 1279 (Ind. App. 1980)

CHIPMAN, Judge.

CASE SUMMARY

First Federal Savings and Loan Association of Gary, (First Federal), appeals from a grant of summary judgment in favor of Michael and Grace Arena, (Arenas), in a foreclosure action brought by First Federal against the Arenas and their grantee, Sanford G. Richardson, as well as various lienholders.

First Federal asserts it was erroneous for the trial court to hold that altering the mortgages' interest rate was a material change which discharged the Arenas from personal liability on the mortgages. According to First Federal, a reservation of rights clause contained in the supplemental agreements to the mortgages executed by the Arenas and First Federal, permitted First Federal in its dealings with Mr. Richardson to increase the rate of interest on the mortgages without first affording the Arenas notice or obtaining their consent, while still retaining the Arenas' liability on the mortgages. The trial court, however, found the reservation of rights clause did not authorize First Federal to so act and entered judgment in favor of the Arenas.

We affirm the judgment of the trial court.

FACTS

On May 26, 1965, the Arenas executed a note, mortgage, and supplemental agreement with First Federal. The note provided for a loan of $32,000 at an interest rate of 5 ¾%, and the mortgage securing this note provided for advances of up to $6,400. March 11, 1966, the Arenas were granted an advance of $5,100, and in consideration, they executed a modification and extension agreement which provided they would owe a new balance of $36,664.81, and the interest rate would be increased to 6%. A separate note, mortgage, and supplemental agreement were also executed by the Arenas in relation to this advance.

March 10, 1969, the Arenas conveyed the real estate which was the subject of both the May 26, 1965 and March 11, 1966, mortgages to Sanford G. Richardson by warranty deed subject to the two mortgages to First Federal. The same day, without notice to or the consent of the Arenas, Mr. Richardson and First Federal entered into a modification and extension agreement, under the terms of which Richardson assumed both of the mortgages in question, and the time for payment was extended to twenty years; there was also a change in the interest rate from 6% to 7¼%. Thus, this agreement, signed only by Richardson and First Federal, was designed to be a modification of First Federal's earlier agreement with the Arenas by extending the time of payment and modifying the terms of payment to which the Arenas and First Federal had agreed.

After June 27, 1975, Richardson failed to make the payments due under the March 10, 1969, modification and extension agreement. As a result, a default on the mortgages and notes occurred and a suit in foreclosure was filed on behalf of First Federal against the Arenas, Richardson, and several lienholders. . . .

DECISION

Conclusion — By reason of an expressed provision to that effect in the supplemental agreements between the Arenas and First Federal, the Arenas were not released from liability upon extension of the mortgage in the agreement between Mr. Richardson and First Federal; however, this agreement not only extended the time for payment, but it also modified the terms of payment by increasing the interest rate. It is our opinion the trial court properly found the Arenas had not consented to such a change in interest rates and, therefore, were released from liability.[3] Arenas' grantee and First Federal could not modify the original mortgagors' agreement without the mortgagors' consent.

---

3. If the full amount due on foreclosure did not exceed the value of the property at the time of the execution of the Modification and Extension Agreement, it was proper for the trial court to completely discharge the Arenas. Mutual Ben. Life Ins. Co. v. Lindley, (1932) 97 Ind. App. 575, 183 N.E. 127; Stevens, Extension Agreements in the "Subject-To" Mortgage Situation, 15 U. Cin. L. Rev. 58 (1941). As a corollary, if the value of the land at the time of this agreement was less than the amount of the mortgage on the property, the Arenas should have remained liable to the extent of this difference.

Although it was improper for the trial court to hold there was a complete discharge without also holding the value of the land at the time of the March 10, 1969, agreement fully supported the mortgage loan, First Federal never raised any error regarding the extent to which the Arenas were discharged . . . ; consequently, we can only assume the amount due on foreclosure on March 10, 1969, would have been less than the value of the property at that time.

We note, since Mr. Richardson offered to purchase the real estate in question for $37,000, and the aggregate balance remaining unpaid when Mr. Richardson and First Federal executed the Modification and Extension Agreement was $33,393.83, it appears the value of the land, in fact, did exceed the amount due, and thus, a complete discharge would have been proper.

The focal point in this controversy is the meaning to be accorded a reservation of rights clause which appeared in the supplemental agreement executed by the Arenas when they obtained the initial mortgage and later secured the advance. The agreement provided:

> THE UNDERSIGNED, Michael Arena and Grace Arena, Husband and Wife, . . . , hereinafter referred to as the Mortgagor, hereby executes and delivers to FIRST FEDERAL SAVINGS AND LOAN ASSOCIATION OF GARY, . . . , hereinafter referred to as the Mortgagee, this Supplemental Agreement, pursuant to a Mortgage executed and delivered concurrently herewith, and this Supplemental Agreement is expressly made a part of said Mortgage, ...
> THE MORTGAGOR COVENANTS: . . . .
> 6. That in the event the ownership of said property or any part thereof becomes vested in a person other than the Mortgagor, the Mortgagee may, without notice to the Mortgagor, deal with such successor or successors in interest with reference to this mortgage and the debt hereby secured in the same manner as with the Mortgagor, and may forbear to sue or may extend time for payment of the debt, secured hereby, without discharging or in any way affecting the liability of the Mortgagor hereunder or upon the debt hereby secured;

First Federal asserts the reservation of rights language set out above permitted it, in dealing with Richardson, to increase the interest rate and extend the time of payment without first obtaining the Arenas' consent while still retaining their liability. Appellant takes the position that the portion of paragraph six providing for no discharge modified forbearing to sue and extending time for payment as well as dealing in the same manner as with the mortgagor; therefore, since the interest rate was increased when the Arenas were given their additional advance, according to First Federal, raising the interest rate in its agreement with Richardson would merely be dealing with him in the same manner as it had dealt with the Arenas and, consequently, should not result in a discharge.

The Arenas, on the other hand, contend the reservation of rights clause in the Supplemental Agreement made no reference to the alteration or modification of the interest rate but rather, referred only to an extension of the time for payment or the decision to forbear to sue.

While it is true paragraph six indicates First Federal could deal with successors in interest to the mortgage in the same manner as with the mortgagor, we hold the resolution of whether this meant First Federal and the Arenas' grantee would be permitted to increase the interest rate without affecting the Arenas' liability was a question of law for the trial court since the rules applicable to construction of contracts generally apply to the construction of an agreement whereby a purchaser of mortgaged premises assumes the payment of the mortgage. 20 I.L.E. Mortgages § 193. . . .

The essence of the appeal before us then is whether the trial court correctly concluded that as a matter of law, the scope of the reservation of rights clause found in paragraph six did not include altering or modifying the interest rate, and consequently, First Federal did not reserve the right to modify and increase the interest rate from 6% to 7¼% without the consent of the Arenas. We hold the trial court's entry of summary judgment in favor of Arenas was proper.

When the Arenas conveyed the real estate to Richardson subject to the existing mortgages to First Federal, the land became as to said parties, the primary source of funds for payment of the debt. Mutual Ben. Life Ins. Co. v. Lindley, (1932) 97 Ind. App. 575, 183 N.E. 127. No technical relation of principal and surety arose between the Arenas and their grantee from this conveyance, but an equity did arise which bears a close resemblance to the equitable rights of a surety. As a result, the Arenas assumed a position analogous to that of a surety, and the grantee became the principal debtor to the extent of the value of the land conveyed. Mutual Ben. Life Ins. Co. v. Lindley, supra; Warm, Some Aspects of the Rights and Liabilities of Mortgagee, Mortgagor and Grantee, 10 Temple L.Q. 116 (1936).

While a mortgagor in such a situation may consent in advance to future modifications or agree his liability will not be discharged by subsequent agreements between his grantee and the mortgagee, such clauses are to be strictly construed against the mortgagee, see Friedman, Discharge of Personal Liability on Mortgage Debts in New York, 52 Yale L.J. 771, 788 (1943), since it would be unjust to subject the mortgagor to a new risk or material change to which he has not consented. Consequently, a reservation of rights clause will not prevent a discharge of liability where the modification in question exceeds the scope of the consent in the clause. This should come as no surprise since the mortgagor occupies the position of a surety, and the law of suretyship provides that a surety is entitled to stand on the strict letter of the contract upon which he is liable, and where he does not consent to a variation and a variation is made, it is fatal, see American States Insurance Co. v. Floyd I. Staub, Inc., (1977) Ind. App., 370 N.E.2d 989; White v. Household Finance Corp., (1973) 158 Ind. App. 394, 302 N.E.2d 828; therefore, an agreement between the principals for a higher interest than called for by the original contract will, if made without the surety's consent, release him from all liability. 74 Am. Jur. 2d Suretyship § 47 (1974); see also 4 Am. Jur. 2d Alteration of Instruments § 55 (1962).

The fact First Federal dealt with the grantee shows it knew of the Arenas' conveyance, and knowing of this conveyance, it was incumbent upon First Federal not to deal with the grantee in such a manner as would jeopardize or alter the surety-principal relationship. Warm, Some Aspects of the Rights and Liabilities of Mortgagee, Mortgagor and Grantee, 10 Temple L.Q. 116 (1936). The modification and extension agreement in question provided Mr. Richardson would personally assume the mortgage debt and thus, inured to the benefit of First Federal, but at the same time, the terms of the Arenas' earlier mortgage were changed to the detriment of the Arenas. If this increase in the interest rate was beyond the scope of the reservation of rights clause, the Arenas were thereby discharged, and the grantee became the sole debtor on the mortgages.

We hold the trial court properly rejected First Federal's argument that by increasing the interest rate it was merely dealing with Mr. Richardson in the same manner as it had dealt with the Arenas, and therefore, according to paragraph six, the Arenas should not have been discharged.

While it is true paragraph six indicated First Federal could deal with successors in interest to the mortgage in the same manner as with the mortgagor, this provision did not say First Federal could do so with impunity. We agree with the trial court that the portion of this paragraph providing for no discharge only modified forbearing to sue or extending the time for payment; consequently, the mortgagor would not be discharged from liability if the mortgagee simply extended the time for payment of the debt or opted not to bring suit, but these were the only situations where the mortgagee knew to a certainty his actions in dealing with the grantee would not discharge the mortgagor. The reservation of rights clause in paragraph six did not apply to activities which allegedly came within the gambit of dealing in the same manner as with the mortgagor. At the risk of being redundant, we again note, paragraph six stated in part:

> 6. [T]he Mortgagee may, without notice to the Mortgagor, deal with . . . successors in interest with reference to this mortgage and the debt hereby secured in the same manner as with the Mortgagor, *and.* . . . (our emphasis)

The punctuation used clearly sets this portion of paragraph six apart from the remainder of the paragraph which then goes on to provide the mortgagee

> may forbear to sue or may extend time for payment of the debt, . . . , without discharging or in any way affecting the liability of the Mortgagor hereunder or upon the debt hereby secured.

In order to give the reservation of rights clause the expanded application urged by First Federal so that it also applied to dealing in the same manner as with the mortgagor, it would be necessary to ignore the punctuation used and the maxim that such clauses should be strictly construed against the mortgagee. Further, such a construction would change the reservation of rights provision from applying in two definite situations to an open-ended invitation to argue there was no discharge because the mortgagee either could have or in fact had dealt with the mortgagor in the same manner; the possible activities which arguably could then come within this clause's application would be indefinite.

We hold the construction of the supplemental agreement between the Arenas and First Federal was a question of law for the trial court, which correctly held paragraph six did not authorize First Federal and the Arenas' grantee to alter the terms of payment on the mortgage debt by increasing the interest rate without affecting the Arenas' liability.

Judgment affirmed

Miller, P. J., and Young, J., concur.

NOTES AND QUESTIONS

1. Why did Richardson apparently agree to the interest rate increase and to assume the mortgage? Did he not have a right to take subject to the mortgage at the old interest rate?

2. Why do you think First Federal sought recovery from the Arenas rather than proceeding further with the foreclosure suit it had filed?

3. Most states by statute or case law require that assumption of mortgage obligations be in writing. But some states apparently do not require that such obligations be in writing. The two statutes below are examples of the diversity among the states on the writing requirement. For case law providing further examples of such diversity see Case Note on Mortgage Assumption Formalities, Restatement of the Law Third, Property, Mortgages 348-349 (1997).

N.J. Stat. Ann. § 46:9-7-1 (2003)

§ 46:9-7-1. Express agreement required for assumption of mortgage debt

Whenever real estate situate in this State shall be sold and conveyed subject to an existing mortgage or is at the time of any such sale or conveyance subject to an existing mortgage, the purchaser shall not be deemed to have assumed the debt secured by such existing mortgage and the payment thereof by reason of the amount of any such mortgage being deducted from the purchase price or by being taken into consideration in adjusting the purchase price, nor for any other reason, unless the purchaser shall have assumed such mortgage debt and the payment thereof by an express agreement in writing signed by the purchaser or by the purchaser's acceptance of a deed containing a covenant to the effect that the grantee assumes such mortgage debt and the payment thereof.

Idaho Code Ann. § 9-506 (2004)

§ 9-506. Original obligations — Writing not needed — A promise to answer for the obligation of another, in any of the following cases, is deemed an original obligation of the promisor, and need not be in writing: . . .

3. Where the promise, being for an antecedent obligation of another is made . . . upon a consideration beneficial to the promisor, whether moving from either party to the antecedent obligation, or from another person.

STOP

to 533

H.   REMEDIES OF SECURED CREDITORS

1.   *Preforeclosure Rights*

Lifton, Real Estate in Trouble: Lenders Remedies Need an Overhaul

31 Bus. Law. 1927, 1931-1934 (1976)

Three different conceptual approaches to the mortgage and the mortgagee's rights to possession in case of default are embodied in state mortgage acts and judicial decisions. In the majority of states, even when the mortgage instrument uses language that signifies a transfer of title, the mortgagee only gets a lien or security interest in the property which can be activated by foreclosure sale. When a default occurs, unless the owner voluntarily turns over possession, the mortgagee has little hope of getting physical possession except through foreclosure proceedings.

A few title states, however, like the early common law, still treat the mortgage as a conveyance of the property to a lender to be returned to the borrower when the mortgage debt is discharged. In theory, the lender also gets the continuing right to possession which he agrees not to exercise unless there is a default. In another small group of so-called "intermediate" theory states, courts talk in terms of the right to possession being retained by the mortgagor until default, but after default automatically accruing to the mortgagee. Despite these theoretical differences, even in the title and intermediate states, modern courts are reluctant to grant a mortgagee physical possession of the property. And even where physical possession may be available, restraints on the mortgagee and the risks of possession may dissuade lenders from seeking it. In some jurisdictions, a mortgagee in possession may have minimum power over the property. It may not be compensated for its own management efforts or be able to recover money advanced for improving or maintaining the property during its possession.[41] The mortgagee in possession also may risk having to account to the owner under stringent rules of accounting for decisions on renting and operating the property if the owner later redeems the property.[42] As a result of these limitations, rather than seek physical possession to protect itself against the owner skimming off the income while the property deteriorates the lender will usually look to the traditional remedies granting constructive possession. These are contained in standard mortgage provisions for assignment of rents and for appointment of a receiver in case of default.

Generally, an assignment of rents can be activated in title, intermediate and some lien states by the mortgagee's serving notice on the tenants in the property to pay their rents to the mortgagee.[43] Although an assignment of rents is of no value in a property like a hotel, restaurant or theatre with daily operating income, it may be more effective in the case of a property with monthly tenants. Frequently, however, when the mortgagee attempts to activate an assignment of rents, the tenants will react to the conflicting demands for rent from the owner and the mortgagee by not paying rent to either until the issue is resolved in court. And many courts, particularly in lien states, are unwilling to deliver the rents to the mortgagee even if such action is warranted, preferring instead to appoint an independent receiver to collect and apply the rents.

Convincing the court to appoint a receiver, though, is not always easy. In some jurisdictions a provision in the mortgage for appointment of a receiver upon the mortgagee's demand is sufficient as a matter of course to get a receiver installed.[44] But in a few states it has been almost impossible to get a receiver appointed because of legislation enacted during the depression years to protect homeowners and farmers.[45] In between, are those courts which require proof that the security is impaired and sometimes also that the borrower is insolvent.[46] Courts differ

41. Although a mortgagee generally is entitled to credit for maintenance expenditures, credit for improvement is more difficult to recoup. See Osborne §§ 168, 169. This distinction may be very difficult to make in day-to-day management of a property.

42. Hall v. Goldsworthy, 136 Kan. 247, 14 P.2d 659 (1932); Osborne §§ 164, 167; 59 C.J.S. (2d) Mortgages §§ 305, 318, 336; See Pioneer Building & Loan Assn. v. Compton, 138 S.W.2d 884 (Tex. App. 1940) (mortgagor may recover from mortgagee for failure to perform its obligation to use reasonable diligence to rent the property). The mortgagee in possession may also face problems under the Interstate Land Act or the Securities & Exchange Act. Kaster, Hershman & Roegge, Realty Interests, Default and Resale, 52 Practising Law Institute (1975).

43. Freedman's Sav. & Trust Co. v. Shepherd, 127 U.S. 494 (1888); Osborne § 150. Some lien states view an assignment of rents as security for the loan which may not be activated short of foreclosure or appointment of a receiver. See Dime Savings Bank v. Altman, 275 N.Y. 62, 9 N.E.2d 778 (Ct. App. 1937), *reargument denied*, 275 N.Y. 545 (1937). Other jurisdictions treat it as an absolute assignment of rents and give the beneficiary mortgagee the right to the rents upon default. See Kinnison v. Guaranty Liquidating Corp., 18 Cal. 2d 256, 115 P.2d 450 (1941). See also In re Ventura-Louise Properties, 490 F.2d 1141 (9th Cir. 1974).

44. In Westchester County, for example, it may take no more than a week to get a receiver appointed. See Kaster, Hershman & Roegge, supra note 22, at 155, citing similar rapid appointment of a receiver in New York, California, and Washington.

45. 59 C.J.S.2d Mortgages § 656. In South Dakota a provision for consent to appointment of a receiver is against public policy and unenforceable. S.D. Compiled Laws Ann. § 44-8-7 (1967). Although in a foreclosure by judicial action, the court may appoint a receiver if authorized by law, the criteria for appointment are stringent. Id. § 21-21-2. See In re Federal Shopping Way, Inc., 457 F.2d 176 (9th Cir. 1972), discussing the Washington statute prior to its amendment in 1969. See also Investors Syndicate v. Smith, 105 F.2d 611 (9th Cir. 1939).

46. 3 Powell § 465, at 696.14; 59 C.J.S.2d Mortgages § 656. Some courts hesitate to appoint a receiver, even in the face of a mortgage provision for appointment which recites that "such appointment shall be made as a matter of absolute right to (lender) and without reference to the adequacy or inadequacy of the property mortgaged or to the solvency or insolvency of the mortgagor." 3 Powell, § 465, at 696.15.

considerably on what constitutes impairment and what is required to prove it. Where the court's criterion is replacement value rather than economic value, it is difficult to prove that the property is impaired unless the building is being so poorly maintained that physical inspection shows a sharp deterioration in value. Impairment may also be demonstrated where the economic values have plummeted dramatically; for example, where utilities are cut off because of nonpayment and large numbers of tenants are leaving.

The mortgagee may present expert testimony from the appraiser who made the original loan appraisal that because of the economic decline of the property—the failure to reach certain rental levels, for example—the present value of the property is less than the appraised value on which the loan was based. In the case of certain institutional lenders, the mortgagor may counter by noting that under state law the lender was prohibited from making a loan of more than 75 percent of the property's value[47] so that the economic value of the property had to fall more than 25 percent for the loan to be impaired. It is difficult for a lender to admit what is often true—that the original loan exceeded 75 percent of value, and therefore any significant loss of value endangers its mortgage.

The struggle to have a receiver appointed can take too much time, in the face of what appears to be obvious need. In the case of one apartment hotel in Miami, for example, after defaulting on a mortgage of $7,500,000, the owner sold the property for $12,000 in cash to two out-of-state speculators. A purchase of defaulted property with a yearly gross income of $4,000,000 for a cash price that low inevitably suggests that the purchaser has in mind quickly recouping the cash portion of his purchase price from any available funds, as well as taking advantage of whatever else he can milk from the property. The buyers of this property quickly retrieved their investment and more at the expense of the creditors. They purchased three Cadillac cars for $65,000 in due bills and entered into favorable long-term leases with members of their families. Yet, it took almost two months from the time the mortgagee requested the court to appoint a receiver to get a receiver appointed.

Finally, a receiver is too often chosen by the court because of his political connections or friendship rather than his managerial ability and real estate knowhow. And the award for a receiver's fees can eat up a good part of the property's income.

a. Mortgagee Taking Possession

Myers–Macomber Engineers v. M.L.W. Construction Corp.

414 A.2d 357 (Pa. Super. 1979)

WIEAND, Judge. Does a mortgagee who goes into possession of an incomplete condominium development upon default in the terms of a mortgage by the mortgagor owe a

---

47. Regarding loan-to-value ratios permitted to life insurance companies, see generally, Gunning & Roegge, Contemporary Real Estate Financing Techniques, 3 Prop., Probate & Trust J. 325 (1968). New York State, for example, limits its state chartered commercial and savings banks to making 75% loans on improved real estate. N.Y. Banking Law §§ 103(4), 235(6)(a) (McKinney Supp. 1971). National banks are limited to 90% of appraised value if the property is improved by a building and 66 ⅔% if unimproved. 12 U.S.C. § 371 (Supp. IV, 1974).

duty to use undistributed mortgage funds to satisfy the mortgagor's unpaid debts? The lower court held that a mortgagee in possession becomes a quasi trustee with a responsibility to satisfy outstanding, job related claims against the mortgagor. We disagree and reverse.

M.L.W. Construction Corporation was the owner and developer of a series of condominiums on a nineteen acre tract in East Pennsboro Township, Cumberland County. HNC Mortgage and Realty Investors agreed to lend construction money in the amount of $5,850,000.00, which sum was secured by a construction mortgage. After $2,900,000.00 had been advanced, the developer defaulted. HNC thereupon exercised the right given by the terms of the mortgage to assume control of the project as a mortgagee in possession. Subsequently, HNC foreclosed on its mortgage and purchased the incomplete development at sheriff's sale. The project was completed by a contractor employed by HNC.

The appellee, Myers–Macomber Engineers, had performed site–preparation work pursuant to a contract with M.L.W., for which it is owed an unpaid balance of $11,298.98. In this action of assumpsit appellee alleged that M.L.W. had breached its contract to pay for services rendered. M.L.W. did not contest the claim. In a separate count against HNC, appellee contended that the lender was liable for the value of engineering services on theories of unjust enrichment. The trial court submitted this issue to a jury, which returned a verdict in favor of appellee and against HNC for $11,000.00. Motions for new trial and judgment n.o.v. were denied, and judgment was entered on the verdict. HNC appealed.

"Mortgagee in possession" is a term applied to the special status of a mortgagee who has obtained possession of property from the mortgagor with the consent of the latter. See generally: 55 Am. Jur. 2d Mortgages §§ 184, 185, 193-196; Osborne, Mortgages §§ 160-176 (2d ed., 1970). Such consent is usually contained, as here, in the mortgage agreement. This remedy avoids the drastic step of foreclosure, while enabling the mortgagee to protect and preserve its security interest. The mortgagee does not thereby limit its right to foreclose, and, upon foreclosure, the mortgagee may purchase the property at sheriff's sale. Girard Trust Company v. Dempsey, 129 Pa. Super. 471, 476, 196 A. 593, 595 (1938). Frequently, foreclosure becomes necessary despite the salvage efforts of a mortgagee in possession. If the mortgagor should avoid foreclosure by paying off the mortgage debt while the mortgagee is in control of the property, however, the mortgagee must surrender possession to the mortgagor, for the mortgagor has retained his title to the real estate throughout the mortgagee's occupancy. Elliot v. Moffett, 365 Pa. 247, 74 A.2d 164 (1950); Malamut v. Haines, 51 F. Supp. 837 (M.D. Pa. 1943).

When a mortgagee goes into possession, he does not become the owner of the real estate. Provident Trust Co. of Philadelphia v. Judicial Building and Loan Asso., 112 Pa. Super 352, 171 A. 287 (1934); Malamut v. Haines, supra. Rather, he becomes a quasi trustee, managing the property for the benefit of the mortgagor, but at the same time protecting his own interest. Zisman v. City of Duquesne, 143 Pa. Super. 263, 18 A.2d 95 (1941); McNicholas' Appeal, 137 Pa. Super. 415, 9 A.2d 200 (1939). As a mortgagee in possession, his duty is to comport with the same standard of conduct as a prudent owner, i.e., he must manage the property in a reasonably prudent and careful manner so as to keep it in a good state of preservation and productivity. Landau v. Western Pennsylvania National Bank, 445 Pa. 217, 282 A.2d 335 (1971); Integrity Trust Co. v. St. Rita Building & Loan Asso., 317 Pa. 518, 177 A. 5 (1935). See also: Osborne, Mortgages § 168 (2d ed., 1970).

The mortgagee in possession has a duty to collect the rents and profits which accrue during his occupancy and apply them to the mortgage debt. Provident Trust Co. of Philadelphia v. Judicial Building & Loan Asso., supra. Moreover, the mortgagor is entitled to an accounting from his mortgagee who has taken possession. Landau v. Western Pennsylvania National Bank, supra; Winthrop v. Arthur W. Binns, Inc., 160 Pa. Super. 214, 50 A.2d 718 (1947).

The fiduciary duty of a mortgagee in possession, however, is owed only to the mortgagor. Thus, the mortgagee cannot be required to account to a second mortgagee for income received while the mortgagee was in possession, McNicholas' Appeal, supra; or to a creditor of the mortgagor, Supreme Council of the Royal Arcanum v. Susque Frozen Foods, 44 Northumberland L.J. 13 (1972). Similarly, a mortgagee in possession is not liable to a purchaser at sheriff's sale for taxes owed on the property. Fassitt v. North Tioga Building & Loan Asso., 133 Pa. Super. 146, 2 A.2d 499 (1938).

It follows that in the absence of a valid agreement by which the mortgagee has assumed or guaranteed payment of the mortgagor's debts, the mortgagee cannot be required to pay unsecured claims held by creditors of the mortgagor. Such creditors must look to the mortgagor upon whose credit they relied.

Appellee argues that the mortgagee will be unjustly enriched if it is permitted to retain the benefit of appellee's engineering work. Reliance is placed on the principle that when a person receives a benefit from another, and it would be unconscionable for the recipient to retain that benefit, the doctrine of unjust enrichment requires the recipient to make restitution. Binns v. First National Bank of California, Pennsylvania, 367 Pa. 359, 80 A.2d 768 (1951); DeGasperi v. Valicenti, 198 Pa. Super. 455, 181 A.2d 862 (1962); Restatement of Restitution, § 1; 66 Am. Jr. 2d Restitution and Implied Contracts § 3. See also: Roman Mosaic & Tile Co., Inc. v. Vollrath, 226 Pa. Super. 215, 313 A.2d 305 (1973). This equitable doctrine imposes on the recipient an obligation in the nature of quasi contract. L. Simpson, Contracts, § 5 at 5, (2d ed., 1965); A. Corbin, Contracts, § 19 at 44 (1963). The most significant requirement for recovery on quasi contract, however, is that the enrichment to the defendant *must be unjust*. Annot., 62 A.L.R.3d 288, 294 (1975).

In the instant case, appellant was not enriched unjustly. When appellant took possession of the condominium project it had already advanced to the developer the sum of $2,900,000.00. Included in the monies advanced was the entire amount budgeted for site preparation. Thus, it was not unjust that it received the benefit of such engineering work when it was compelled by the developer's default to take possession of the incomplete building project. Moreover, it does not appear that the mortgagee, after purchasing the real estate at sheriff's sale and employing its own contractor to complete the project, was able to dispose of the completed project at a profit.

The legislature in Pennsylvania has by statute provided the mechanics' lien as a means by which a contractor or subcontractor can obtain security for work done. Other security can be acquired by contract. If the right to file a mechanics' lien has been waived, if a contractor chooses to rely upon the personal credit of the party with whom he contracts, a court should not rewrite the contract of the parties or legislate a right to receive payment from a mortgagee who has been compelled to go into possession to preserve its security. Such a rule would do much to impair the availability of capital upon which the building industry so greatly depends. In any event, if additional remedy is needed, it should come from the legislature and should not be decreed by judicial fiat. East Penn Contracting Corp. v. Merchants National Bank of Allentown, 37 Leh. L.J. 268 (1977), aff'd, 254 Pa. Super. 613, 387 A.2d 114 (1978).

Reversed and remanded for the entry of judgment n.o.v. in favor of appellant.

NOTE

Apart from an agreement by the parties to the contrary, there is considerable authority giving the mortgagee right to possession of the mortgaged premises in those states that treat the mortgagee as having title rather than just a lien on the mortgaged land. In lien states, the mortgagor generally is considered to have the right to possession. However, in title states the parties usually agree that the mortgagor shall retain possession; but in both lien and title states, the mortgage may provide, as it did in the *Myers–Macomber* case, that if the mortgagor defaults, the mortgagee has the right to take over possession. The usual reasons for the mortgagee taking possession following default by the mortgagor are to protect and preserve the security or to acquire income from the property and apply it to the outstanding debt. The mortgagee, and perhaps the mortgagor as well, may prefer that the mortgagee assume possession than that a receiver do so. It is often hoped that if the mortgagee takes over possession, foreclosure will not be necessary, but by taking over possession the mortgagee ordinarily does not give up the right to foreclose later.

The mortgagee in possession has certain legal obligations to the mortgagor, who continues to hold a substantial interest in the property. The mortgagee must account to the mortgagor for rents and profits from the land and disposition of these rents and profits. The mortgagee may not commit acts of waste. There is uncertainty, however, as to how far the mortgagee may go in making repairs and improvements to the property, whether or not the mortgagee may recover for repairs and improvements made, and whether or not he or she may be compensated for the management of the premises.

What criteria do you believe should determine what repairs and improvements to the property mortgagees in possession may make, their right to reimbursement for repair and improvement costs and from whom, and whether or not they can be compensated for their management services?

b. Acceleration by Mortgagor Default

Most real estate mortgages provide for installment payments of principal and interest. They also usually provide that substantial default by the mortgagor gives the mortgagee the right to accelerate remaining payments and declare the entire mortgage debt immediately due and payable. The usual default resulting in acceleration is nonpayment of an installment payment when due. But acceleration clauses in mortgages may include default of other mortgagor obligations as justifying acceleration, such as mortgagor failure to pay property taxes on the mortgaged property or mortgagor failure to pay insurance premiums on that property.

Most all mortgages with acceleration clauses make acceleration optional with the mortgagee. If optional and the mortgagor defaults, for a valid acceleration to occur the mortgagee must provide adequate notice to the mortgagor that the option is

being exercised. As the upcoming *Webster Bank* case shows, extended communications between the mortgagee and mortgagor often occur following default by the
mortgagor and result in eventual controversy over whether the mortgagee had
accelerated or had only threatened to do so. Mortgagees' lawyers often do some
or all of the negotiating with mortgagors following default and should take care to
assure that any acceleration desired by their clients is clearly and unequivocally
communicated to the mortgagors following default.

Webster Bank v. Oakley

830 A.2d 139 (Conn. 2003)

NORCOTT, J.

The named defendant, Lorna T. Oakley, appeals from a judgment of strict
foreclosure rendered by the trial court in favor of the plaintiff, Webster Bank. In
this appeal, the defendant claims that the trial court improperly concluded that:
(1) the plaintiff clearly and unequivocally had exercised its option, under the
mortgage, to accelerate the defendant's loan; and (2) the federal Americans with
Disabilities Act (ADA), 42 U.S.C. § 12101 et seq., the federal Fair Housing Amendments Act of 1988 (FHAA), 42 U.S.C. § 360 et seq., and the state fair housing laws,
General Statutes § 46a–64b et seq., do not require a bank, which is foreclosing on a
mortgage loan that it has serviced, to accommodate a disabled mortgagor's inability
to make her loan payments. We disagree with the defendant, and we affirm the
judgment of the trial court.

The record reveals the following relevant facts and procedural history. In April,
1993, the defendant executed a thirty year mortgage deed and note on her condominium unit with a predecessor in interest of the plaintiff.[4] The principal amount
of the mortgage was $70,000, with a monthly payment of $495.46. The mortgage
agreement contained an acceleration clause that delineated a procedure to be
followed in the event of default by the borrower.[5] It also contained a nonwaiver
clause, which provided that "[a]ny forbearance by Lender in exercising any right or
remedy shall not be a waiver of or preclude the exercise of any right or remedy."

---

4. The plaintiff's predecessor in interest was the Bristol Mortgage Corporation, a wholly owned
subsidiary of the Bristol Savings Bank. In 1995, the Bristol Savings Bank merged with the plaintiff. With
the merger, the plaintiff acquired all of the assets of the Bristol Savings Bank. These assets included all
shares of, and assets owned by the Bristol Mortgage Corporation, which no longer is in existence and has
no interest in the debt between the plaintiff and the defendant.

5. The mortgage's acceleration clause provided in relevant part: "Lender shall give notice to
Borrower prior to acceleration following Borrower's breach of any covenant or agreement in this
Security Instrument. . . . The notice shall specify: (a) the default; (b) the action required to cure
the default; (c) a date, not less than 30 days from the date the notice is given to Borrower, by which the
default must be cured; and (d) that failure to cure the default on or before the date specified in
the notice may result in acceleration of the sums secured by this Security Instrument and foreclosure
or sale of the Property. The notice shall further inform Borrower of the right to reinstate after acceleration and the right to assert in court the non-existence of a default or any other defense of Borrower to
acceleration and foreclosure or sale. If the default is not cured on or before the date specified in the
Notice, Lender at its option may require immediate payment in full of all sums secured by this Security
Instrument without further demand and may invoke any of the remedies permitted by applicable law.
Lender shall be entitled to collect all expenses incurred in pursuing the remedies provided in this
paragraph . . . including, but not limited to, reasonable attorney's fees and costs of title evidence."

The defendant had worked as a social worker for the Connecticut department of children and families until March, 1999. In March, 1999, she stopped working because she had suffered from significant psychiatric disabilities, including severe depression, which rendered her unable to perform her work duties. She then took unpaid medical leave from her employment. Consequently, in September, 1999, the defendant defaulted on her mortgage obligations. At that point in time, she owed the plaintiff $2885.32 for payments past due since June of that year.

In September, 1999, the plaintiff sent to the defendant a default and cure letter dated September 13, 1999. This letter informed her that she had until October 13, 1999, to pay the total past due amount. The letter warned the defendant that if she did not pay the total amount due by October 13, the entire mortgage balance would be accelerated.[6] Subsequently, on October 14, 1999, the plaintiff sent another letter to the defendant advising her that, because it had not received the requested payment, the plaintiff considered the debt accelerated, and referred the matter to its attorney for collection.

Thereafter, the plaintiffs attorney sent to the defendant a letter dated October 19, 1999, informing her that she had until October 27, 1999, to cure the default by paying the amount owed, which at that time was $3501.09. The letter warned that failure to cure the default by that time potentially would result in foreclosure. That letter contained a clause stating that "[n]othing contained in this letter shall be deemed to be a waiver of any of the [plaintiff's] rights, remedies, or recourses available to it under the Note, the Mortgage, or any other documents executed with respect to this loan."

Subsequently, on November 17, 1999, the plaintiff filed this action against the defendant seeking foreclosure of the mortgage, immediate possession of the mortgaged premises, a deficiency judgment, and other equitable relief. As special defenses, the defendant asserted, inter alia, that the plaintiff was barred from foreclosure because: (1) the letters from the plaintiff and its attorney had failed to provide her with proper notice of the default and acceleration; and (2) the plaintiff, by not making a reasonable accommodation for the defendant's disabilities, had denied and interfered with her right to live in her dwelling under the FHAA, the ADA and § 46a–64b et seq. The defendant also sought recoupment and setoff, and she counterclaimed for damages on these, and other, grounds.

The plaintiff thereafter moved for summary judgment of strict foreclosure, which the trial court granted, over the defendant's objection, as to liability only. In its memorandum of decision, the trial court concluded that none of the subsequent communications to the plaintiff from the defendant constituted a waiver of the default and cure notice that had been communicated to her in the original September, 1999 letter.[8] The trial court also concluded that the reasonable accommodations provisions of the FHAA and § 46a–64b et seq., as well as the ADA, were not applicable to the enforcement of a mortgage. . . .

---

6. The letter explained acceleration to the defendant as "the entire principal balance, together with any accrued interest, late charges, escrow deficiencies, and/or legally collectible expenses will be immediately due and payable."

8. In a subsequent articulation of its decision, the trial court emphasized that the October 19, 1999 letter from the plaintiff's counsel specifically advised the defendant that nothing contained therein constituted a waiver of the plaintiff's rights and remedies under the mortgage and note.

THE PLAINTIFF'S CLEAR AND UNEQUIVOCAL EXERCISE OF ITS OPTION TO ACCELERATE THE MORTGAGE LOAN

The defendant's first claim presents a threshold issue in this appeal. The defendant contends that the trial court improperly concluded that the series of three letters sent by the plaintiff and its attorney constituted the requisite clear and unequivocal exercise of the mortgage's acceleration option. Specifically, the defendant claims that these letters do not constitute a clear and unequivocal exercise of the plaintiff's right to accelerate because, after she had received a letter from the plaintiff informing her that the loan had been accelerated, she then received a subsequent communication from the plaintiff's attorney that was phrased as a default and cure letter. The defendant, accordingly, contends that the loan was not accelerated properly because she never had received any communication of acceleration following her receipt of the default and cure letter from the plaintiff's attorney, which she claims the trial court improperly ignored.[9] . . .

We conclude that the trial court properly determined that the communications from the plaintiff and its attorney to the defendant constituted a clear and unequivocal exercise of the plaintiff's right to accelerate the defendant's mortgage loan.

"Notices of default and acceleration are controlled by the mortgage documents. Construction of a mortgage deed is governed by the same rules of interpretation that apply to written instruments or contracts generally, and to deeds particularly. The primary rule of construction is to ascertain the intention of the parties. This is done not only from the face of the instrument, but also from the situation of the parties and the nature and object of their transactions. . . . A promissory note and a mortgage deed are deemed parts of one transaction and must be construed together as such." (Citation omitted; internal quotation marks omitted.) *Citicorp Mortgage, Inc. v. Porto*, 41 Conn.App. 598, 602, 677 A.2d 10 (1996).

We note that, under the terms of the mortgage in the present case, <u>acceleration is an optional remedy</u> in the event of default by the borrower. See footnote 5 of this opinion. Accordingly, the rule articulated by the Appellate Court in *City Savings Bank of Bridgeport v. Dessoff*, 3 Conn.App. 644, 649, 491 A.2d 424, cert. denied, 196 Conn. 811, 495 A.2d 279 (1985), is applicable. In *City Savings Bank of Bridgeport*, the court concluded that "[t]he <u>general rule is that where the acceleration of the maturity of a mortgage debt on default is made optional with the mortgagee, some affirmative action must be taken by him evidencing his election to take advantage of the accelerating provision, and that until such action has been taken the provision has no operation.</u> *The exercise of the option should be made in a manner clear and unequivocal, so as to leave no doubt as to the mortgagee's intention. The option is effectively exercised by manifesting the fact in such manner as to apprise the mortgagor.* . . . Even a declaration may be a sufficient exercise of the option, but to be effective the declaration must be followed by an affirmative act toward enforcing the declared intention." (Citation omitted; emphasis added; internal quotation marks omitted.) Id. . . .

We conclude that, under the holdings in *Christensen v. Cutaia*, supra, 211 Conn. at 619–20, 560 A.2d 456, and *Northeast Savings, F.A. v. Scherban*, supra, 47 Conn.

---

9. The defendant also contends that the default and cure letter from the plaintiff's attorney did not comply properly with the prerequisites for foreclosure set forth in the mortgage because it provided less than thirty days to cure the default.

App. at 227–28, 702 A.2d 659, the plaintiff clearly and unequivocally exercised its option of accelerating the loan once the defendant had defaulted. The first letter provided ample warning to the defendant that, if she did not cure her default by October 13, the entire loan amount would be accelerated. After the defendant failed to cure her default, the plaintiff sent prompt notice to the defendant that it considered the debt accelerated, and that the matter had been referred to its attorney for collection. The very next communication to the defendant came five days later from the plaintiff's attorney. Thus, in our view, the defendant had ample awareness of the plaintiffs intentions with respect to acceleration of the debt.[10] Moreover, under this court's interpretation of nonwaiver clauses set forth in *Christensen v. Cutaia*, supra, at 620, 560 A.2d 456, the plaintiffs conduct in affording the defendant eight additional days to stave off the consequences of acceleration and foreclosure by curing the default cannot be construed as a waiver of its option to accelerate the mortgage loan. Indeed, a conclusion by this court that a lender, by giving a borrower one more opportunity to cure a default, has not clearly and unequivocally exercised its right to accelerate the debt, ultimately would militate against persons in the defendant's position; such a conclusion surely would eviscerate any inclination or incentive that a lender might have to extend any kind of generosity or flexibility to borrowers in default, on the eve of commencing litigation.

Moreover, the letter from the plaintiff's attorney was not contradictory, as the defendant claims, because beyond affording the defendant a few more days to cure her default, *it did not retract expressly the previous notice of acceleration.* Accordingly, the trial court properly concluded that the plaintiff's letters constituted a clear and unequivocal exercise of its option to accelerate the mortgage debt.

[The court then considers the discrimination claim of the defendant and holds against her on this claim too.]

c.   Transfer in Lieu of Foreclosure

Harbel Oil Company v. Steele

83 Ariz. 181, 318 P.2d 359 (1957)

JOHNSON, Justice. This is an appeal from a judgment in favor of Horace Steele and Ethel Steele, Texas Independent Oil Company, a corporation, Blakely Oil, Incorporated, a corporation, defendants-appellees, and against Harbel Oil Company, a corporation, plaintiff-appellant. The plaintiff-appellant will thereafter be

---

10. The defendant points out that, at her deposition, Lisa Siedlarz, the plaintiff's assistant vice president in charge of the residential legal department, testified that the October 19 letter from the plaintiff's attorney possibly could mean that the loan had not yet been accelerated. The defendant contends that this testimony is the "only evidence" in the record with respect to the October 19 letter from the plaintiff's attorney, and offers it in support of her claim that the trial court improperly concluded that nothing in the October 19 letter created a genuine issue of material fact. Inasmuch as construction of the mortgage, note and letters presents a question of law, we, however, conclude that Siedlarz's testimony is merely a speculative, and indeed, inadmissible legal opinion; see, e.g., *Sagamore Group, Inc. v. Commissioner of Transportation,* 29 Conn.App. 292, 299, 614 A.2d 1255 (1992) ("a witness is incompetent to offer a legal opinion except on the issue of foreign law"); and not, as the defendant contends, evidence that creates an issue of material fact.

referred to as plaintiff. The defendants-appellees, Horace Steele and Ethel Steele, will be referred to as defendants (Steele), and the defendant-appellee, Texas Independent Oil Company, a corporation, as defendant (Texas). It was agreed in the pretrial order that the defendant (Texas) is the successor in interest to the assets and liabilities of Texas Independent Oil Company, a copartnership, composed of the defendants (Steele). The parties further stipulated that defendant (Texas) and defendant Blakely Oil, Incorporated, a corporation, for the purpose of this proceeding, stand in the same position as the other defendants.

The material facts briefly stated are: Plaintiff had acquired a twenty-year lease of vacant land located in Phoenix, Arizona, from Dr. E. A. Cruthirds, for the purpose of erecting and operating a gasoline service station. In order to finance the construction thereof the defendants (Steele) agreed to loan plaintiff the sum of $10,000 which was to be repaid in monthly installments with interest. The cost of the station in excess of $10,000 was to be paid by plaintiff but the record is silent as to the actual cost. As security for the loan the parties executed four instruments: (1) an assignment of the Cruthirds lease for a term of four years and five months (or until the loan was repaid), (2) a sublease back to plaintiff, (3) a conditional sales and loan agreement (covered the equipment in the station), and (4) a products contract whereby plaintiff agreed to purchase the products of defendants (Steele).

The sublease provided that upon the failure of plaintiff to observe the terms and conditions of the Cruthirds lease and of the sublease, or to pay the monthly rent, then the defendants (Steele) may declare the sublease at an end and recover possession as if said premises were held by forcible detainer. The conditional sales and loan agreement provided that defendants (Steele), in case of default, shall be entitled, as its option, to take possession of the equipment and retain any monies paid as liquidated damages.

Thereafter, plaintiff was in default in the payment of rent under the sublease for the months of May, June and July, 1950, and in default of four monthly payments under the conditional sales and loan agreement (less than $500 having been paid). On July 7, 1950, defendant (Texas) served upon plaintiff a letter setting forth the above defaults, declaring the sublease at an end and requesting possession of the premises and equipment. On July 15, 1950, plaintiff voluntarily surrendered and defendant (Texas) took possession of the premises and equipment. Subsequently, defendant (Texas) made improvements to the premises and sub-leased to defendant, Blakely Oil, Incorporated.

On October 24, 1952, plaintiff by letter advised defendant (Texas) it desired to redeem the premises and its possession by full payment and satisfaction of the existing mortgage indebtedness upon defendant (Texas) rendering a complete accounting. No accounting was made and this suit was instituted.

The complaint seeks a finding that the instruments in question are a mortgage, for an accounting, and other related relief.

The trial court properly found from the admissions in the joint answer and the stipulations of the parties that said instruments were executed as security for the loan. However, plaintiff makes six assignments of error, all of which will be resolved upon a determination of the issue as to whether the trial court erred in holding the instruments to be a chattel mortgage, and that such mortgage had been foreclosed in compliance with section 62-527, A.C.A. 1939 (A.R.S. § 33-757).

The instruments having been admitted to be a mortgage we are not confronted with the question of whether documents which on their face appear absolute are in fact a mortgage. We are, however, presented with the issue of whether the mortgage in question is a real property mortgage or a chattel mortgage. The assignment of the Cruthirds lease to defendants (Steele) is the basic instrument securing the loan. One of the estates in land less than a freehold is an estate for years. Section 71-101, A.C.A. (A.R.S. § 33-201). Estates for years are chattels real. Section 71-103, A.C.A. 1939 (A.R.S. § 33-202). The assignment of the Cruthirds lease for a term of four years and five months (or more if the loan remains unpaid) is a chattel real. At common law a lease for years, being a chattel real, is personal property; and unless it has been modified by statute, a leasehold interest, though a chattel real, is personal property and subject to the rules governing personal property.

We do not think, as urged by plaintiff, it is necessary to determine the question of whether our legislature, in enacting the various statutes involving real property, intended to abolish the common law rule as applied to chattels real. The real question in issue is whether a leasehold estate for a term of years is an interest in real property capable of being transferred under the provisions of the statute, section 62-501, A.C.A. 1939 (A.R.S. § 33-701). This section provides as follows:

"Interest in real property mortgageable — Formalities in making — *Any interest in real property capable of being transferred may be mortgaged.* The mortgage can be created, renewed, or extended, only by writing, executed with the formalities required of a grant of real property, and may be acknowledged, certified and recorded, in like manner and with like effect." (Emphasis supplied.)

A leasehold estate for a term of years is an interest in land capable of being transferred. It possesses many characteristics of an ordinary chattel, and has some aspects of real property as it passes a present interest in land. . . .

We have held a statute must be interpreted in conformity with the language used by the legislature. Mayberry v. Duncan, 68 Ariz. 281, 205 P.2d 364. The language of section 62-501, supra, is not limited to real property but states any interest in real property capable of being transferred may be mortgaged. Although a chattel real is personal property it nevertheless transfers an interest in real property. Obviously the instruments in question constituted a real property mortgage within the purview of the statute. The related remedial statute, section 62-515, A.C.A. 1939 (A.R.S. § 33-721), requires that mortgages of real property shall be foreclosed by action in court. In Davis v. First Nat. Bank, 26 Ariz. 621, 229 P. 391, we held mortgages of real property may not be summarily foreclosed, but only by action in a court of competent jurisdiction.

Defendants contend there was a mutual agreement to rescind the sublease and surrender the premises. This argument and the cases cited relate to a landlord and tenant relationship, and is without merit as to defense to the requirement that a mortgage of real property shall be foreclosed by action in a court. Equity favors the right to redeem and will not deny the right except upon strict compliance with the steps necessary to divest it. Romig v. Gillett, 187 U.S. 111, 23 S. Ct. 40, 47 L. Ed. 97. . . .

The judgment is reversed and the case remanded for proceedings not inconsistent herewith.

Udall, C.J., and Phelps and Struckmeyer, JJ., concur.

Windes, J., dissents.

NOTES ON "DEED" IN LIEU OF MORTGAGE FORECLOSURE

1. Consider whether the court in the *Harbel* case misconstrued the statute that requires foreclosure by court action. Arguably, the statute does not cover the facts at issue here, even if the mortgage was of real property. In any event, Arizona is one of the few states that does not recognize a voluntary conveyance by the mortgagor of his equity of redemption when made to the mortgagee in accord and satisfaction of the mortgage debt. On the prevailing position as to the validity of deeds in lieu of foreclosure see Nelson & Whitman, Real Estate Finance Law § 6.18 (2002). Accepting a deed in lieu of foreclosure has definite advantages for the mortgagee, but the giving of the deed may also have some advantages for the mortgagor. What are these advantages? And what are the disadvantages? On balance, do you prefer Arizona's insistence upon court action?

2. Before a lender decides to take a deed in lieu of foreclosure, the circumstances of the particular situation should be carefully analyzed, as there can be both advantages and disadvantages to the lender by taking a deed rather than foreclosing. These advantages and disadvantages are considered in Boneparth, Taking a Deed in Lieu of Foreclosure: Pitfalls for the Lender, 19 Rl. Est. L.J. 338 (1991). See also Nelson & Whitman, Real Estate Finance Law § 6.18 (2002).

d. Workouts

Black, Loan Workout Strategies[48]

4 Prob. & Prop. 39 (March/April 1990)

The term "workout" as used in this article refers to the situation where the borrower and lender attempt to compromise their respective positions and rights so that, although neither party is going to receive the entire benefit of the original bargain, at least they are both in an acceptable position under the circumstances. The purpose of the loan workout will be to restructure the loan as an alternative to foreclosure, bankruptcy or litigation.

Although usage of the term "workout" has become commonplace in the daily practice of lawyers in many areas, there are those who have not yet been immersed in this type of practice. Familiarity with potential issues related to loan workouts is becoming increasingly important to practitioners in areas not previously affected by the economic downturn experienced in certain sections of this country. It is common to read headlines pronouncing "boom areas" such as Atlanta and Boston as the latest over-built markets destined for a real estate market crash. As these and other markets fall into an economic slump, more lawyers will be required to assist either borrowers or lenders in addressing the inevitable myriad of issues which arise as a result. . . .

48. On workouts, also see Friedrich, Workouts, 18 J. Rl. Est. Tax. 257 (1991); Roberts, Negotiating and Drafting the Workout Agreement, 3 Modern Real Estate Transactions 1393 (ALI-ABA 1987); Saft, Mortgage Workouts, 17 Real Est. Fin. J. 35 (2001); Golub, Making Workouts Work, 50 Urban Land no. 4, at 21 (1991); and Strauss, The Overlooked Loan Workout Issue: Others With Interests at Stake, 8 Rl. Est. Finance no. 3, at 44 (1991).

POSTURING FOR A WORKOUT

The typical workout situation occurs when a downturn in the market results in reduced value of rental income from a property, thereby severely impacting a borrower's ability to satisfy its loan obligations related to the property. The downturn in the market may result from overbuilding, failure or decline of a local major industry or an economic boom in a competing region which siphons away substantial portions of the local industry or labor supply. Increased price competition for the remaining tenants results, and rental price wars begin to drive property incomes down.

As revenues from the property decline, the borrower approaches the lender seeking assistance to keep the project viable. Because the project is experiencing financial difficulties, the borrower will desire to renegotiate the terms of the loan. The major points the borrower may want to renegotiate with the lender include writing off accrued interest or reducing future interest on the note, and a reduction in the principal amount of the promissory note.

At this point each side usually obtains legal counsel to provide advice during the negotiations. It is imperative from the start that each party candidly assess its strengths and weaknesses, from the economic and the legal perspectives, to determine their respective leverage abilities in the negotiations. Each party must also recognize that these negotiations may result in a range of alternatives, including foreclosure, a deed in lieu of foreclosure or a modification of at least some of the loan terms.

At all times during negotiations, each side should seek protection of the value of the collateral. The lender should try to protect the property's value to decrease the likelihood that the borrower will need to return to the lender with another loan modification request because of its inability to satisfy the loan obligations. The lender must also recognize that it may later own the property, and it is generally much easier to maintain, rather than to restore, property value. The borrower has an obvious incentive to maintain the property value because it has poured its money, time and expertise into the property and has an expectation of receiving compensation for such input. . . .

Saving troubled real estate projects through workouts will depend on the borrower and lender deciding that the benefits of a workout outweigh the alternatives. Successful workouts are based on individuals taking or not taking action based upon what they perceive to be their own self interest. Their perception of what action or non-action is in their best interest will be influenced largely by the economic conditions of each party to the workout and the general economic conditions impacting the marketplace. . . .

The borrower obviously will have more negotiating leverage in a workout if its principals have not previously executed personal guarantees, since the borrower's greatest leverage in renegotiating a troubled loan is that it will abandon the project if reasonable concessions are not made by the lender. Conversely, the borrower will have less leverage in negotiations if the personal assets of principals of the borrower can be reached to make up any deficiency. . . .

From the lender's perspective, however, if the lender is unsecured or undersecured, it should determine if the borrower has other assets available that may be pledged to secure a debt extension or modification. If the borrower has numerous creditors and limited assets, cooperation from the borrower may result in a secured position in additional collateral, ahead of other competing creditors. Although the transaction may be set aside as a preference under federal bankruptcy law if the borrower goes into bankruptcy within 90 days (or in the case of an insider, one year) of the pledge of additional collateral, the lender is in no worse a position than when it was originally unsecured or undersecured. Even when a borrower has no available assets, a workout may result in a long-term payout satisfied by the debtor's future earning capacity.

STAGES OF A DEPRESSED ECONOMIC CYCLE

Like all economic cycles, economic downturns have three distinct parts: a beginning, a middle and an end. To properly counsel a client as to strategies, the lawyer must know the stage of the economic cycle for the area in which the property is located. The lawyer also must understand the different issues associated with each stage of the cycle and the consequences for the borrower and the lender.

THE BEGINNING OF THE CYCLE

The most difficult period in which to consummate a workout is the beginning of the economic downturn. This period is the most embarrassing time for the borrower, since the project (which may be the borrower's pride and joy) appears to be a failure. The borrower will not want its peers, competitors, other lenders, tenants and trade contractors to know it is experiencing financial difficulties. The lender may not be sympathetic and may consider the problem to be limited to the particular borrower or to a limited number of projects.

The borrower, the lender and the borrower's personal and business acquaintances probably will not understand how many other people are affected by similar circumstances. For example, three years ago, at the beginning of the current economic downturn in Dallas, a major Dallas-based lender determined that it would not grant concessions to work out problem loans. As far as that lender was concerned, if their policy resulted in the lender obtaining possession of the property securing the loan, that was an acceptable alternative. That lender based its policy on the extreme price increases the local real estate market had just experienced, and believed that prices would soon escalate again, with the lender realizing a handsome profit. However, that lender became so overburdened by the overwhelming amount of real estate inventory acquired as a result of this policy that its entire operation was paralyzed and the lender was subsequently placed into receivership.

THE MIDDLE OF THE CYCLE

The middle of a depressed economic cycle represents not only the most likely time that a workout will succeed, but also the most likely time it will not succeed. This period is characterized by <u>many borrowers experiencing economic problems</u> and lenders being besieged by proposals for workouts.

A workout is most likely to succeed during this time because the borrower and the lender should finally understand the market conditions. The borrower can make proposals based on existing market conditions that should finally be stabilizing. During this same period, the lender may not be as strong as it originally was, since it will also be feeling the effects of the market depression in both its loan and asset portfolio. The lender has an increased incentive to try a loan restructuring with a borrower it trusts and has confidence in, rather than to add another property to an already over-swollen inventory.

Conversely, a workout is most likely to fail during this time because the lender may be less responsive to a borrower's requests. This unresponsiveness may be attributable to external and internal circumstances beyond its control. For example, the lender may be (1) under supervision or conservatorship by regulatory agencies; (2) subject to additional regulatory constraints; (3) incurring significant personnel changes as the inevitable witch-hunts for the real or imagined causes for the state of the lender's loan portfolio begin; (4) responding to workout requests and proposals only after extreme delays as a result of the additional approvals that have to be obtained by the regulatory authorities; and (5) overwhelmed by the number of projects that are in trouble, with inadequate staff to handle the volume of requests and problems.

Another reason that the workout is most likely to fail during this time is that the negative economy may have convinced the borrower that it is no longer worth the effort to continue fighting a battle with property values that continue to slide downward. The borrower may also be convinced that it is too expensive to continue to subsidize the property from other income or assets when there is no way of knowing the depth of the market's bottom. Consider, for example, the mind-set of a borrower who valiantly holds on and does everything it can to make its project work in the face of a market decline before approaching its lender for loan concessions. Also consider the borrower's position as the market continues to decline, due to factors beyond the borrower's control, after consummating a workout, resulting in the prior loan concessions being essentially worthless and new loan concessions being required. Multiply this cycle again and again as, over a period of only one or two years, the property loses as much as one-half its income stream. In an overbuilt market, this is a realistic scenario and it is common for borrowers to reach a point where, for both economic and psychological reasons, the borrower perceives that it is no longer worth continuing to fight the mounting losses.

THE END OF THE CYCLE

The end of an economic downturn is apparent. Bankruptcies and litigations proliferate during this period because lenders are grasping for all the monetary sources they can reach and borrowers are looking for someone, including lenders, to blame for their projects' failures. The end of an economic downturn is also indicated when there are fewer projects to be worked out, since most products have already been restructured to terms reflecting current market values. Any further restructuring to be achieved at this point is generally through bankruptcy and litigation.

TYPES OF WORKOUT PLANS

Although there are innumerable ways of modifying the terms of a loan to achieve a workout satisfactory to both lender and borrower, there are five basic forms that the workout may take. The following is a brief discussion of each form.

1.   REINSTATEMENT

One form a workout may take involves documentation that reinstates the defaulted loan, subject to terms which vary in some, if not most, respects from the original loan terms. The parties may agree to add terms that:

- grant the lender a profit participation or equity interest in the property;
- provide for interest "pay rates" and "accrual rates," with pay rates to be lower than accrual rates;
- require the borrower to provide additional collateral;
- contain cross-default provisions with other loans to the borrower; and
- provide personal liability for the borrower, its principals, or some third party guarantor.

In exchange for those concessions from the borrower to the lender, it is not uncommon for the reinstatement to provide the borrower relief involving (a) extension of the loan maturity, (b) additional funding for the project by the lender, (c) reduction or deferral of interest on the loan and (d) consent to otherwise prohibited secondary financing.

If the borrower has not provided a personal guarantee at the origination of the loan, a lender may request one during a workout. The borrower should guarantee the loan at this point only as a last resort, since it may lose significant bargaining leverage by granting this concession. As with the original loan negotiations, a borrower's goal in the workout negotiations should be to focus on continuing to limit its risk associated with the project and other originally pledged security. If the project is not successful because of increased interest rates, an economic recession or other factors, the borrower should retain the flexibility to re-analyze its level of commitment to the project.

Lenders commonly demand cross-collateralization as a condition to modify the loan terms. As with personal liability, if the borrower concedes to this demand, it will be losing future bargaining leverage. The loss of bargaining leverage results because the borrower is shifting its risk from the original investment in the project to include additional assets. If future circumstances result in further problems with the loan, the risk has been expanded from the original project to include other assets, and the borrower's decision to cut its losses and walk away from the project will have more drastic consequences.

Parties will often reach an agreement to reinstate an installment debt after acceleration but before foreclosure. In this event, the agreement normally requires the borrower to bring current all past due installments of principal and interest and pay the lender's expenses (including attorneys' fees) incurred in connection with the modification and reinstatement. Acceptance of payment of the past due debt amount and expenses, with no further clarification of the obligations between the borrower and the lender, may create uncertainties for each party with respect to their future legal relationship. For example, the acceleration may have triggered the running of the statute of limitations, or the lender's acceptance may have waived acceleration, with the obligation continuing as if no acceleration had occurred. . . .

2. Lender takeover of control

Lenders frequently demand that the borrower comply with various requirements that amount to an attempt to control certain aspects of the borrower's project. Lenders may dictate such stringent demands on the borrower in the workout that the lender gains rights typically associated with ownership of property. Examples of this type of conduct by the lender include:

- instructing the borrower which creditors to pay,
- determining which cash disbursements will be made to the borrower,
- dictating the amount the borrower can spend for tenant improvements,
- requiring the borrower to hire a project overseer or workout consultant selected by the lender,
- making recommendations to terminate certain employees,
- selecting contractors and management and leasing personnel, and
- setting leasing criteria.

The most famous case in this area is State National Bank of El Paso v. Farah Manufacturing Company, Inc. 678 S.W.2d 661 (Tex. Ct. App. 1984). This case generally is referred to as the case holding that a secured creditor may be liable to a debtor for wrongful "control" of the debtor. Lender's counsel must be cognizant of the concepts discussed in *Farah,* which involved a successful action by a borrower for affirmative recovery against a lender for damages alleged to have been caused by the lender during the lender's "control" of the borrower. After cessation of the lender's "control," the borrower regained its financial strength and began to generate profits.

There are four points on which the borrower's claim in *Farah* for wrongful "control" is grounded—no default by the borrower under the loan, fraud on the borrower by the lender, duress caused by the lender and interference by the lender with business relations. In addition to the recognized causes of action of fraud, duress and interference, to recover against the lender, the borrower must prove that these proximately caused the borrower's damage.

The interference with business relations claim was based on the facts that the lender had packed the board with directors of its own choice, forced the resignation of directors it disliked and forced the hiring of a consultant of its own choosing who sold off the company's assets to retire the lender's indebtedness prematurely. The jury verdict of $18.9 million was based on testimony that company suffered losses in that amount during the time that the lender's "consultant" was running the company.

3. Voluntary conveyance to the lender

In some instances, the borrower and lender may agree that the best resolution is for the borrower to voluntarily relinquish all control over the property and to transfer ownership to the lender. This transfer may be accomplished by a deed in lieu of foreclosure, which provides the lender with ownership of the property without undertaking the expenses and time delays associated with the foreclosure process.

Because a deed in lieu of foreclosure may cause the lender to be subjected to claims of subordinate lienholders and tenants, lender's counsel should thoroughly exercise due diligence efforts for lease and title examinations. Borrower's counsel should confirm that the borrower is <u>released from all liability and obligations under the loan, and that the lender assumes the borrower's obligations to third parties to the extent they relate to the project.</u>

Normally a borrower's willingness to relinquish possession voluntarily is dependent on the borrower's perception of the potential profit or loss from the project and concessions the lender is willing to make in return. Because it is to the lender's advantage to obtain possession and control as soon as possible to minimize decline in property value, a lender should promptly accomplish a transfer of title by deed-in-lieu or friendly foreclosure. This promptness also minimizes the lender's risk of liability for improper assertion of control.

4. SALE TO THIRD PARTY

A lender should consider alternatives to involuntary liquidation of assets and filing suit. Cooperation from the debtor in liquidating assets frequently results in more monetary consideration for the secured lender. Voluntary liquidation eliminates the inherent uncertainties of judicial and non-judicial foreclosures; it may also allow the secured lender to stay in the financing business and out of the operation of the debtor's business and all the attendant problems.

The borrower and lender may agree, in consideration of the lender agreeing to abstain temporarily in the exercise of its rights and remedies under the loan documents, that the borrower will place the property on the market for sale. Certain issues require agreement and documentation prior to marketing the property, such as the length of time the lender will wait for the property to sell before exercising its rights, the minimum price at which the borrower must sell if an offer is received, the sharing of or assistance with expenses until the property is conveyed, and the distribution of sales proceeds if a sale to a third party is consummated. The parties may agree to a distribution of the sale proceeds between the parties as their respective interests may appear (e.g., the lender is fully paid off and the borrower retains any balance), or in some other proportion agreed to by the parties (i.e., the lender may accept a payoff in some amount less than the full balance of principal and interest owed on the loan and the borrower may receive some amount from the property as compensation for its contribution of effort, expertise and capital).

5. THIRD PARTY COMPLETION

The previous strategies have focused primarily on completed projects. Construction loans pose unique problems because of the nature of the collateral. Common causes of problem construction loans include:

- dramatic downturns in the economy after the project is under way,
- budget overruns,
- contractor-caused delays,
- diversions of funds by the developer or general contractor,
- insolvency of the developer or general contractor,
- poor construction management,
- design defects, and
- force majeure.

Completion of the project is usually the best alternative, despite projections that the project will not generate sufficient income to satisfy the borrower's loan obligations, since cessation of construction generally causes even greater losses. The lender may not feel comfortable with the borrower completing construction and the borrower may agree that a third party acting in a receiver-type capacity will complete the project. In this situation, the borrower will obviously prefer to retain sufficient control over both the property and the third party to protect itself and its investment or, alternatively, will want a release of liability under the loan. The lender will want an assignment of all the borrower's rights in the project, including construction contracts, bonds and leases.

In a construction loan workout the overriding urgency, from the lender's point of view, is to get the project promptly completed and avoid a cessation of the work. A partially completed project on which work has stopped often has less market value than the loan proceeds funded up to that point, and buyers for a partially completed project are difficult to find even in a healthy market.

The previously discussed concept of protection of collateral is especially applicable in a construction loan workout. A dormant project is subject to weather damage, vandalism and theft, and if the cessation of construction continues, the contractors may desert to other projects. The cost of completing the improvements with new contractors can increase dramatically, because of the additional problems and risks those contractors may perceive and because they may realize the desperate nature of the situation and their negotiating advantage. The lender must be cognizant of these factors when selecting a workout strategy.

CONCLUSION

Lawyers who have not encountered a workout oriented practice may find themselves inundated with workouts as the real estate "boom/bust" cycle leaves ever widening ripples across the country in much the same manner as a stone dropped into a still pond. Familiarity with the issues to be considered is essential whether workouts already permeate the practice or are only on the horizon. It is also useful to keep the issues in mind even in a healthy market, for who knows what the future may hold for a particular loan.

2. Foreclosure

Mortgagor default may result in mortgagor loss of all interest in the mortgaged premises. A mortgage is a secured transaction and the secured lender has the right to satisfaction of the debt by resort to the security if the borrower is delinquent in paying the debt. The procedure whereby the mortgagor's interest in the mortgaged land is sold or taken over by the mortgagee in full or partial satisfaction of the outstanding obligation is known as foreclosure. There are detailed statutory procedures, with considerable variation from state to state, as to how foreclosures are to be carried out, but the usual procedure followed includes an auction sale, the property going to the highest bidder.

In a judicial foreclosure action it is important that the plaintiff join as defendants all persons whose interests in the mortgaged premises are subordinate to the plaintiff's interest. These commonly include, among others, the original mortgagor, the present owner of the property if it has been conveyed by the mortgagor, junior mortgagees and lien holders, and any additional persons, such as lessees or easement holders, who claim a less than fee interest in the land created subsequent to the mortgage. Failure to join any of these persons means that the foreclosure will not terminate their interest in the land. If a deficiency decree can be had in a foreclosure proceeding, still other parties may be joined who presently have no interest in the land but may be personally obligated for the mortgage debt, such as mesne transferees who assumed the mortgage before conveying the property, or guarantors of the debt. Persons whose interests are senior to those of the foreclosing plaintiff are normally not joined, as the foreclosure cannot terminate their interests. Thus a foreclosing second mortgagee normally will not join the first mortgagee. The usual plaintiff in foreclosure proceedings is the original mortgagee, but others may have foreclosure rights, including the assignee of a mortgage and the executor or administrator of a deceased mortgagee.

Foreclosure laws reflect efforts by the legal system to balance fairly the interests of debtors and creditors, but the resulting laws often fail to satisfy fully either group. The history of foreclosure laws is marked by many statutory and case law modifications seeking to adjust this balance, usually resulting in more favorable treatment of debtors.

a. Types of Foreclosure

Prather, Foreclosure of the Security Interest

1957 Univ. Ill. L. F. 420, 427-430

METHODS OF FORECLOSURE

After a default by the borrower, the lender or his successor in interest must seek to realize upon the real property security by selling or acquiring ownership of the land, at the same time extinguishing any equitable rights belonging to the borrower. The process is called foreclosure, which in its dictionary definition means "to shut out; exclude or bar."

In the early days of English mortgage law there was no necessity for foreclosure. The courts enforced the mortgage in accordance with its written terms, and a failure of the borrower to pay his debt when due simply extinguished all of his rights in the land. Because of the gradual development of a borrower's equitable right to redeem the land at a later date, however, foreclosure became necessary to extinguish the right.

Methods of foreclosure vary greatly from state to state. In some states foreclosure is quick and cheap; in others it is a long and expensive process.

Foreclosure procedures available for use must be sought under the laws of the state where the property is situated. While the diversity of state foreclosure laws is formidable, the most prevalent methods in use are foreclosure by sale in judicial proceedings, and foreclosure by exercise of a power of sale contained in the mortgage. . . . Although in some states one method is exclusive, in many states the mortgagee may elect which method he will pursue, including an election to proceed on the note alone, on the mortgage, or on both concurrently.

Strict Foreclosure. In jurisdictions which permit its use, strict foreclosure usually is one of several remedies, although ordinarily it is confined to cases where (1) the mortgagor is insolvent, (2) the mortgaged premises are not of sufficient value to pay the debt, and (3) there are no outside creditors or encumbrancers. The process begins with a complaint or a petition to foreclose. The complaint is brought against not only the owner but all persons who may have the right to redeem, including a spouse, tenants, and junior lien holders, if any. After summons either by personal delivery, or by publication and mailing of notice where personal summons is not possible, the defendants are given the opportunity to introduce defenses such as invalidity of the mortgage, prior payment, or failure of consideration.

After hearing any defenses, the court will determine if there has been a default and if the mortgagee has the right to foreclose. A decree or judgment is then entered, setting out the amount due to the lender, and specifying a period, ordinarily from two to six months, in which the borrower may redeem by payment of the amount due. The decree provides also that if the property shall not have been redeemed within the period specified, the borrower and all persons claiming under him shall be forever barred and foreclosed. As of the time the specified period expires, the mortgagee becomes the sole owner of the property. No sale of the premises is involved.

Some courts have called strict foreclosure a harsh remedy since it transfers the property to the mortgagee without a sale, the value appearing not to be taken into account.

Foreclosure by Sale in Judicial Proceedings. Under this method, the procedure is identical with that of strict foreclosure until the point that judgment or decree is about to be entered. At this time, the procedure becomes different, due to the widespread belief that if the land is sold at a public sale it might bring more than the mortgage debt, leaving something for the borrower. Although judicial sale predominates in most parts of the country, it later will be shown that in practical operation the theory seldom works out in accordance with the original purpose.

At the time of entering the decree, the court determines the amount due to the mortgagee. The decree provides that a specified period of notice shall be given to the public that the property is to be sold at public auction. The notice, usually by newspaper publication, must include a description of the property, the time, place, and terms of the sale, and the officer designated to conduct the sale. The officer usually is a master in chancery, a sheriff, or other officer appointed or authorized by the court.

The mortgagee customarily is permitted to bid at the auction, and in practice, the mortgagee almost invariably is the only or the highest bidder. If such bids are confined to the unpaid amount of the mortgage, the mortgagee may avoid parting with any cash. The bid price is merely applied to the mortgage debt.

Upon receiving a report of the auction, the court will determine the equity and propriety of the sale, and if it approves, the officer is ordered to execute either a deed to the purchaser or, as in Illinois, a certificate of sale. If the state law does not provide statutorily for a further period in which the borrower may redeem, the purchaser at this point becomes the sole and absolute owner of the land.

Foreclosure by Exercise of Power of Sale. In a great many states, a mortgage may be foreclosed without recourse to the courts, and the usual method is that of foreclosure by exercise of a power of sale contained in the security instrument. Power of sale mortgages are used primarily because they afford a less expensive as well as a more convenient and expeditious mode of foreclosure, and the mortgagor is not required to pay the greater expenses of a regular foreclosure action.

Foreclosure by power of sale specifically must be authorized in the mortgage instrument. Such clauses spell out what shall be considered a default, and, in the event of such default, confer power on the mortgagee (or trustee in the case of a trust deed) to sell the property after public notice at public auction.

Ordinarily personal notice of the proposed sale to the borrower is necessary, but certain states permit notice by advertisement. In order to be able to bid in at his own sale, the mortgagee or trustee must have expressly provided such authorization in the mortgage instrument, otherwise he is barred from the bidding. A deed is issued by the mortgagee as conductor of the sale to the highest bidder. Almost invariably this is the mortgagee himself. Again, while the equity of redemption is cut off by the process, statutory redemption may or may not be allowed, depending upon state statutory provisions. While the purchaser at the sale obtains immediate possession in states having no period of redemption, in states allowing a redemption period the majority allow the mortgagor to remain in possession, although the statute or the mortgage may contain different stipulations as to rents. To exercise the power of sale there is no need for the mortgagee to make entry. . . .

Lifton, Real Estate in Trouble: Lender's Remedies Need an Overhaul

31 Bus. Law. 1927, 1936-1941 (1976)

The usual way for the mortgagee to realize on its security is to foreclose on the property and see it sold to a third party or buy it in the foreclosure sale. The laws governing mortgage foreclosure are the outgrowth of efforts by the courts and legislatures to balance two competing claims: the secured lender's right to its security and the owner's right to whatever value the property has above the mortgage loan.

Under the common law rule, if the debtor failed to pay a mortgage on the due date, title would permanently vest in the mortgagee. Equity courts first developed the "equity of redemption" to give the debtor a period of time after the due date to pay the loan and redeem his property. When mortgagees complained that they were unable safely to convey title to a buyer without fear that the equity of redemption later would destroy the sale, the courts permitted them to "foreclose" the equity of redemption after notice and the expiration of a stated period of time. But this "strict foreclosure" did not protect the value in the property in excess of the mortgage from being wiped out. Thus, starting in the early 1800s, the concept evolved of selling the property in an open auction with appropriate safeguards to enable the owner to realize any value above the mortgage.

If real estate were traded in a ready auction market like listed securities, the foreclosure sale would have resolved the problem of the mortgagee's and owner's competing equities. The security would be sold on the market, the debt repaid to the lender and any excess returned to the owner. But real estate does not trade freely in an auction market. Most real estate buyers are not accustomed to all-cash purchases, and require the flexibility of face-to-face negotiation to tailor a transaction to meet the economic and tax needs of the parties. Under the best of circumstances it takes time and most often a knowledgeable broker to find a buyer for real property. Under the circumstances of a forced auction sale, it is almost impossible to find a buyer. As a result, in about 99 percent of public foreclosure sales the mortgagee ends up as the only bidder in the sale and buys the property in. An auction sale is particularly ineffective during periods of economic depression and collapsed real estate values. Yet, it is in periods of economic strain that large numbers of foreclosures occur and mortgagors get wiped out, eliciting the concern of voters, judges and legislators. And the courts and legislators have responded by formulating a variety of laws and procedures aimed at protecting the owner from losing his equity in the property.

A major consequence of this concern for the owner is that an action for foreclosure by judicial sale has to be tried as any other civil action. With inevitable discovery, trial calendar delays and other incidents of litigation it might take months or years to complete, particularly if the owner interposes counterclaims. Moreover, in a number of instances, judges have held off or threatened to hold off foreclosure by out-of-state mortgagees for long periods of time to force a settlement with local property owners or local mechanic lienors. In one case, the court found sufficient "sweat equity" deserving its protection in testimony that the owner had worked so diligently on the property that he suffered a heart attack! Finally, judicial foreclosure can be an expensive proceeding involving fees for attorneys, trustees and sheriffs.

A more effective foreclosure remedy, generally used in eighteen states, is a power of sale provision, giving the mortgagee or trustee the right to arrange the sale of the property after appropriate notice, usually by advertisement. Because it does not require judicial action, this method sharply reduces foreclosure time and costs. In addition, although to foreclose under a power of sale the lender may have to give up any claim to a deficiency judgment, it has the advantage of avoiding statutory rights of redemption. . . .

A major obstacle encountered by mortgagees in twenty-six states is the statutory "rights of redemption" which gives the owner and certain others having an interest in the property the right for a specified time after foreclosure to redeem the property from the purchaser in the foreclosure sale at the sales price. These statutes are intended as a threat to force the mortgagee and other potential bidders to bid the full value of the property of the foreclosure sale in order to preclude the owner from later seeking to redeem the property at the below-market sales price.

Redemption periods range from six months to as much as 18 months, and there is a split of authority as to whether the right can be waived. The statutes also differ regarding the rights of the purchaser during the redemption period. In some states the purchaser is denied title and possession of the property during the redemption period; the mortgagor stays in possession, collects the rents and operates the property. If the property has been abandoned, it may have to remain vacant during the redemption period. Other statutes give possession to the purchaser but mandate appointment of a receiver to collect the earnings during the period. In these cases, the purchaser does not get any cash flow from the property until termination of the redemption period.

Most states with statutory rights of redemption permit the purchaser to take possession and operate the property during the redemption period. Some, however, limit the redemption price to the face amount of the mortgage plus foreclosure costs, so that the purchaser is not reimbursed for managing the property or for money spent on property improvements. Under these circumstances, a practical purchaser will not take a chance on rehabilitating the property during the redemption period. In some states, even rents collected by the purchaser while in possession, must be deducted from the redemption price.

The effect of these statutes is to diminish the interest of outside bidders in the property. If the mortgagee buys in the property, it ties up the mortgagee's funds for long periods of time, making the procedure more costly and delaying the day when the mortgagee can safely undertake rehabilitation of the property. Yet, experience with the statutes demonstrates that statutory rights of redemption are almost never exercised.

The mortgagee which operates foreclosed property may face added problems. In some states operation of foreclosed properties will subject the mortgage lender's entire portfolio in the state to state tax. In other states a mortgagee operating foreclosed property may be required to qualify to do business in the state. This presents a problem if the mortgagee is an out of state bank which cannot legally qualify to do business in the state. Such a mortgagee may have to engage a trust company, which can qualify, to operate its property and make independent decisions as to leasing, selling, and capital improvements; decisions which should properly be made by the mortgagee. Alternatively, the mortgagee may use a subsidiary which, to be completely separate from the parent, may require different officers and employees. In both cases the lender must be concerned that if its insulation from the trust company or the subsidiary is not sufficient, it will be deemed to be doing business illegally which may mean loss of its ability to enforce its other securities in the state.

NOTES AND QUESTIONS

1. The centuries old equity of redemption right in common-law countries still is extensively recognized and relied on by courts when mortgagors default. The right also has long been protected against "clogging" by the parties themselves, including refusal of the courts to recognize an agreement in or created contemporaneously with the mortgage that impairs the mortgagor's right to redeem prior to foreclosure. On the mortgagor's equity of redemption and legal effect of the parties' efforts to limit it see Restatement of the Law Third, Property, Mortgages § 3.1, including the comment and notes following that section; and Licht, The Clog on the Equity of Redemption and Its Effect on Modern Real Estate Finance, 60 St. John's L. Rev. 452 (1986). The traditional rationale for the equity of redemption is debtor protection, including the need to protect mortgagors from being taken advantage of by more knowledgeable and financially stronger mortgagees. This rationale seems of questionable merit in many contemporary real estate transactions, particularly those involving most all commercial real estate mortgages. Marshall Tracht has advanced another rationale for the equity of redemption, fostering settlements. In his article, Renegotiation and Secured Credit: Explaining the Equity of Redemption, 52 Vand. L. Rev. 599-632 & 635 (1999), he has this to say as to the fostering settlements rationale:

> The equity of redemption requires that a period of time (determined by the foreclosure procedures of the jurisdiction) elapse between default and conversion of the collateral. This time factor is often discussed as an opportunity for the borrower to redeem the collateral, but this obscures a second crucial point. The foreclosure period

is a time for <u>negotiation between the borrower and lender</u>. It is commonplace for economic analyses of law to note that negotiation is not costless, but it is still relatively uncommon to focus on the need for time within which negotiations can take place. Successful negotiations require an opportunity for the parties to exchange information in a credible fashion. This bargaining process often involves sequential offers and responses calculated to communicate intentions and beliefs in a manner that simple statements of fact or intent cannot convey credibly. The equity of redemption, by compelling a period of delay between default and liquidation of the collateral, creates the time that may be needed for negotiations to succeed. . . .

In fact, the data supports the conclusion that the primary function of mortgage law, upon default, is to permit the extra-legal resolution of the situation, whether by refinancing and paying off the lender, selling the collateral, or negotiating a workout. <u>Foreclosure is a last resort, rarely used unless the</u> borrower has no equity to preserve and the parties find themselves unable to negotiate a resolution.

2. Strict foreclosure is more efficient and less costly to mortgagees than foreclosure by sale in judicial proceedings. However, because of its potential disadvantages to mortgagors strict foreclosure is not permitted in most states. A few states that permit strict foreclosure have, by statute, sought to reduce or eliminate its possible disadvantages to mortgagors. One such state is Connecticut and its statute, Conn. Gen. Stats. Ann. § 49-15 (2006 Supp.), provides in part as follows:

§ 49-15. Opening of judgments of strict foreclosure

(a) Any judgment foreclosing the title to real estate by strict foreclosure may, at the discretion of the court rendering the same, upon the written motion of any person having an interest therein, and for cause shown, be opened and modified, notwithstanding the limitation imposed by section 52-212a, upon such terms as to costs as the court deems reasonable; but no such judgment shall be opened after the title has become absolute in any encumbrancer.

Connecticut courts have relied on this statute in refusing strict foreclosure and requiring foreclosure by sale on a showing by the mortgagor or by a junior lienholder that the property has a market value that exceeds the amount of the mortgage. See, e.g., Brann v. Savides, 712 A.2d 963 (Conn. App. 1998); Fidelity Trust Co. v. Irick, 538 A.2d 1027 (Conn. 1988). However, despite the added protection that the Connecticut statute provides, presumably there are occasional parties entitled to the benefit of the statute who because they are not represented by counsel and are unsure of the statutory protection it provides are disadvantaged by the strict foreclosure that occurs.

3. To whom and when is foreclosure by exercise of power of sale likely to be more favorable than foreclosure by sale through judicial proceedings?

4. Under what circumstances might foreclosing plaintiffs in judicial foreclosure proceedings join as defendants persons whose interests are senior to those of the plaintiffs?

5. If a mortgage is in default, generally the mortgagee may either bring an action on the secured debt or foreclose, and in most jurisdictions may pursue these remedies concurrently or successively so long as the debt has not been fully satisfied. However, if the mortgagor also has a claim against the mortgagee concerning the property covered by the mortgage, problems can arise under the *single action*

doctrine that may prevent the mortgagee from obtaining full satisfaction of the debt. The single action doctrine, where applicable, requires that a defendant who is sued but has a claim arising out of the same transaction on which the suit is based must either file a counterclaim or lose that claim. The single action doctrine seeks to have related claims considered and resolved in one proceeding. A 1984 Missouri case illustrates how a mortgagee can lose his or her claim from failure to counterclaim as required. In Westoak Realty & Investment, Inc. v. Hernandez, 682 S.W.2d 120 (Mo. Ct. App. 1984), a builder-lender foreclosed under a power of sale but the sale left a deficiency; the builder-lender was then sued by the buyer-borrower for construction contract damages relative to the property in question, but defaulted; the builder-lender then brought an action on the note against the buyer-borrower for the deficiency. It was held that the builder-lender was barred from recovery on the note because the builder-lender failed, in the buyer-borrower's damage action, to counterclaim for the amount owed on the note.

6. A number of states in the past, particularly major farm states in depression periods, have enacted mortgage moratorium statutes temporarily suspending mortgagees' foreclosure rights or in other respects restricting mortgagees' rights when mortgagors are in default. An obvious form of debtor protection, often applicable only to agricultural properties, such statutes have commonly been held constitutional. However, the Supreme Court of Oklahoma has held a mortgage moratorium statute unconstitutional under the federal and state constitutions as impairment of obligation of contract. Federal Land Bank of Wichita v. Story, 756 P.2d 588 (Okla. 1988). In accord, under a somewhat similar statute, is Federal Land Bank of Wichita v. Bott, 240 Kan. 624, 732 P.2d 710 (1987).

b. Selected Foreclosure Problems

(1) Foreclosure Sale Terms and Conditions: Price Adequacy and Chilled Bidding

Manoog v. Miele

350 Mass. 204, 213 N.E.2d 917 (1966)

REARDON, Justice. This case involves a deficiency judgment and is here on the defendant's exceptions to the judge's refusal to give certain instruction to the jury and to his exclusion of a question during trial. The facts are as follow.

On December 4, 1958, the defendants executed a $45,000 note secured by a mortgage on certain parcels of real estate. They defaulted on this note in May, 1962. Following notice on October 5, 1962, of his intention to foreclose, the plaintiff took possession of the premises on October 23, 1962. On October 26, 1962, nineteen days before the foreclosure sale, the plaintiff Manoog entered into an agreement with one Barber for the purchase and sale of the property described in the mortgage. Under the agreement Barber gave Manoog a $2,000 deposit and contracted to purchase the premises from him for $45,000, subject however to the acquisition of title by Manoog at the foreclosure sale. Manoog described the contract purchase price of $45,000 as a "fair price for that property" on October 26, 1962. The agreement further provided that Manoog was to receive from Barber as part of the purchase price a ten year mortgage in the sum of $35,000 at six percent interest and was to pay a broker's commission. Manoog "talked" to the defendant Snow about the agreement before it was executed but did not then or later disclose the purchase price. Before the foreclosure sale Manoog permitted Barber to occupy the premises and to bring trucks upon the property. At the foreclosure sale held on November 14, 1962, there were seven or eight people in attendance, including Barber, and the auctioneer made a general solicitation for bids. Manoog, however, was the sole bidder and, when his bid of $40,000 was accepted, he gave the auctioneer a $2,000 deposit in accordance with the terms of the sale as advertised. Sometime thereafter Manoog sold the land to Barber for $45,000. In this action the jury assessed a deficiency of $5,488.67 against both defendants. This figure reflected the total of the unpaid balance of the note, unpaid interest thereon to the date of sale, taxes paid by Manoog, and the costs of sale, with credits to the defendants for rents received by the plaintiff prior to sale, and such amounts as they had prepaid for the real estate taxes.

1. The question which was put to the plaintiff and excluded was, "You expected to keep the $45,000.00 when you passed papers on that property without disclosing it to Snow or Miele?" There was evidence that the plaintiff had never disclosed to the defendants the details of his agreement with Barber. Since the plaintiff never in fact disclosed the price, whether or not he had intended to disclose it was of no importance. The question asked was thus immaterial and the judge did not err in excluding it.

2. The judge, in charging the jury on the responsibilities of the mortgagee in the circumstances described above, cited and quoted from West Roxbury Co-op Bank v. Bowser, 324 Mass. 489, 492, 87 N.E.2d 113, 115, where it was said, "It is familiar law that a mortgagee in exercising a power of sale in a mortgage must act in good faith and must use reasonable diligence to protect the interests of the mortgagor. . . . The burden is on the mortgagor (the defendants here) to prove that the mortgagee has failed in that duty. . . . When, as was the fact here, 'a mortgagee . . . is both seller and buyer, his position is one of great delicacy. Yet, when he has done his full duty to the mortgagor in his conduct of the sale under the power, and the bidding begins, in his capacity as bidder a mortgagee may buy as cheaply as he can, and owes no duty to bid the full value of the property as that value may subsequently be determined by a judge or a jury.'" The judge continued his charge, "Now, the defendants have introduced evidence and a fact that is not disputed is that prior to the foreclosure sale plaintiff made an arrangement with one Mr. Barber to sell the property to him at a price of $45,000. The defendant[s] . . . [claim] that under those circumstances there was a breach of the duty owed by the mortgagee in the mortgagee's conduct of the foreclosure sale. That is a question of fact that you will have to determine. It is not a question of law, but I can instruct you the defendant[s] . . . [argue] that you have a price differential there. . . . You are entitled to ask yourselves, also, these questions. Acting in good faith and with reasonable diligence, should Mr. Manoog have said to Mr. Barber when they were negotiating for a property, 'Look, the property is going to be sold at a foreclosure sale. Why don't you show up at the sale and bid for yourself?' Should he have refrained from entering into an agreement as a matter of good faith with Mr. Barber or were the terms of the agreement he entered into substantially different from the terms of the mortgage foreclosure itself so that it had no effect on the bidding? These are questions, Mr. Foreman, ladies and gentlemen, that you are going to have to decide and not questions of law upon which the Court can give you any instructions. So that with respect to the issues in the case, you must decide this issue. First, did the plaintiff

act in good faith and did he exercise reasonable diligence in the conduct of the foreclosure sale? If your answer is the Plaintiff did act in good faith and in the exercise of reasonable diligence in the conduct of the foreclosure sale, then you would be warranted in finding for the plaintiff. . . ." In addition to giving the portions of the charge quoted above, the judge had granted one of the requests of the defendants for instructions to the jury to the effect that "[t]he mortgagee, in foreclosing his mortgage has the duty of good faith and reasonable care to secure the highest price that the property can bring." The judge, however, denied the defendants' request that he charge the jury that the "[p]laintiff, as foreclosing mortgagee is a trustee for the benefit of all persons interested, including the Defendant[s]."

There was no necessity for the judge to go further than he did in delineating the obligations of the mortgagee in this instance. The principles drawn from the *West Roxbury Co-op Bank* case cited by the judge provided appropriate guidelines for the jury on the facts which had been laid before them. The sense of the charge given to the jury was that the duty of acting with good faith and reasonable diligence imposed on the mortgagee was a strict one. What the judge had to say about the mortgagee's duties placed them in their proper perspective before the jury. The jury would have been confused rather than assisted by the employment of the word "trustee" in the judge's charge, for there is no built-in magic in that word which would have added any more in the way of guidance than the judge conveyed without using it.

3. The defendants requested an instruction to the effect that "[t]he conduct of the Plaintiff in bidding $40,000.00 at the foreclosure sale, when prior to the sale he had entered into an agreement to sell the property for $45,000.00 constitutes bad faith." There was no error in refusing to give this instruction. The question which it raised was whether the defendants had "chilled" the sale. Lexington Trust Co. v. McCabe, 313 Mass. 733, 735, 49 N.E.2d 435. Whether a sale has been "chilled" is a complex question of fact which cannot be said to hinge solely upon the existence of a differential between the agreement price and the foreclosure sale price. See Cambridge Sav. Bank v. Cronin, 289 Mass. 379, 383, 194 N.E. 289.

A knowledgeable mortgagee should not be allowed to assume a position such that he preempts the field of bidders and discourages other potential bidders at a sale. He is not to be permitted to indicate in advance to other potential bidders that it is his intention to bid a price beyond a reasonable figure at the foreclosure sale unless they agree to buy the property from him at a reasonable price once he has bought the property at the foreclosure sale at a price which is unreasonably low. Such behavior by a mortgagee might result in a substantial deficiency to be later collected from the mortgagor. On the other hand, the law must not be such as to discourage a mortgagee from dealing prior to the foreclosure sale with persons who might otherwise not be interested in the property. A smaller deficiency to be met by the mortgagor may well be occasioned by a mortgagee's knowledge of the availability of a person who will purchase from the mortgagee subsequent to a mortgagee's acquisition of title at the foreclosure sale. See Dexter v. Shepard, 117 Mass. 480, 485-486.

In the instant case it appears that the mortgagee placed the property with a broker for sale. Having found a possible purchaser the mortgagee contracted to accept a purchase money mortgage at a reasonable rate of interest. In determining whether the mortgagee "chilled" the sale, as the defendants charged, it would have been relevant to inquire whether the purchaser could have procured similar financing elsewhere, whether the purchaser was a good or a bad credit risk, and whether the interest rate of six percent was more favorable than otherwise might have been expected from the nature of the premises. These are only some of the factors pertinent in an inquiry as to whether the mortgagee had in fact "chilled" the sale or whether, alternatively, he had so contracted with a purchaser as to be able himself to offer a price at the foreclosure sale which would most minimize the mortgagor's deficiency. The matter was adequately treated by the judge's charge which noted the existence of the price differential, the difference in the terms of the purchase sale agreement and the foreclosure sale, and their effect as a question of fact upon the plaintiff's duty of diligence and good faith.

4. The judge properly denied the defendants' request for a charge that the failure of the plaintiff to disclose to them that he had entered into a contract to sell the property for $45,000 constituted bad faith. The judge charged instead that this conduct was only one of several factors to be considered in a determination of whether there had been bad faith on the part of the mortgagee.

Exceptions overruled.

NOTES AND QUESTIONS

1. Why do you think that Barber agreed to purchase the land from Manoog, subject to Manoog acquiring title at the foreclosure sale, rather than purchasing the property himself at the foreclosure sale? - he didn't have the cash.

2. Considering that foreclosure sale transactions are forced auction sales, what is a proper price frequently has caused courts difficulty when fairness of the sales has been challenged. Mere inadequacy of price, assuming there has been no rigged bidding and all required statutory procedures have been followed, is generally not sufficient to upset a foreclosure sale. Yet, in extreme cases of price inadequacy, courts have invalidated such sales. For example, in Johnson v. Johnson Standard Life Insurance Co., 5 Ariz. App. 587, 429 P.2d 474 (1967), a foreclosure sale price of $5,000 for property worth $73,000 was set aside; and in Baskurt v. Beal, 101 P.3d 1041 (Alaska 2004), a foreclosure sale was voided when property with a fair market value of $225,000 was sold at a foreclosure sale for $26,781. The Alaska court in its opinion stated: "Generally, mere inadequacy of price is not sufficient by itself to require setting aside a foreclosure sale. However, if the inadequacy of the sale price is (1) 'so gross as to shock the conscience and raise a presumption of fraud or unfairness,' or (2) is coupled with other irregularities in the sale procedures, then invalidation of the sale may be justified." In Central Financial Services, Inc. v. Spears, 425 So. 2d 403 (Miss. 1983), a foreclosing mortgagee, who 12 days after the foreclosure sale resold the foreclosed land for 2½ times its foreclosure sale price, was required by the Mississippi Supreme Court to pay over his profit to the mortgagors on the grounds that the foreclosure price was unconscionably low.

Pearman v. West Point National Bank

887 S.W.2d 366 (Ky. App. 1994)

MILLER, Judge:

Harold Dean Pearman brings this appeal from a judgment and order of sale of real property dated March 9, 1993. We reverse.

The facts are clear. On February 25, 1992, West Point National Bank (the bank) brought the instant action against Pearman to enforce a judgment lien on real property. Ky.Rev.Stat. (KRS) 426.720. The lien resulted from a deficiency judgment in a foreclosure proceeding (Civil Action No. 91-CI-305) upon unrelated real property in the Hardin Circuit Court.

In the instant action, Pearman attacks the validity of the deficiency judgment. In this regard, it becomes necessary to examine the circumstances surrounding the foreclosure. In that action, a judgment and order of sale was entered on May 14, 1991. It concerned real property owned by Pearman located on North Wilson Road in Radcliff, Hardin County, Kentucky. The judgment was for $44,271.03, plus accrued interest. The property was appraised at a fair market value of $45,000.00. KRS 426.520. The realty was sold "at the courthouse door" by the master commissioner on July 12, 1991, with the bank being the sole bidder and purchaser at $31,000.00 — approximately two-thirds of the appraised value. The obvious purpose in bidding that amount was to avoid the equity of redemption provided in KRS 426.530. The master commissioner's report of sale was filed on the same day (July 12) with the clerk serving notice on July 15, 1991. Ky.R.Civ.P. (CR) 53.06. No exceptions were taken. The order and judgment confirming the sale and directing the master commissioner's deed was entered July 30, 1991. Therein, a deficiency was granted against Pearman in a sum exceeding $16,000.00. KRS 426.005. On the day before the deficiency judgment was entered (July 29), the bank contracted for sale of the property with certain third parties (Steve and Kevan Chung) for the appraisal of $45,000.00,[1] a sum in excess of Pearman's total indebtedness. After receiving the deed from the master commissioner, the bank conveyed the property to the Chungs.[2]

In defense of the present action, Pearman argues that his obligation to the bank was extinguished by the bank's action in purchasing and reselling the property, thus there is no deficiency and the judgment should not be allowed to stand. The circuit court commented that "[t]he bid at 2/3rds value will not pay off the indebtedness leaving a 'deficiency.' However, the Bank now owns the property which it can resell for its true market value (which will be at least the amount they originally loaned on it or more as banks seldom will loan 100% of its value). And that is what happened in this case. Even before the Court had confirmed the sale, the Bank had resold it for its true market value. (An appraised value of $45,000.00). In reality, there was no 'deficiency.'" The circuit court further noted that it has not been faced with a case where "a lending institution has sought to collect a 'deficiency judgment' wherein it was able to resell the property for the amount of the indebtedness." Nevertheless, on March 9, 1993, the circuit court upheld the deficiency judgment and entered the judgment and order of sale from which this appeal is taken.

Pearman contends that the circuit court committed reversible error by recognizing the validity of the deficiency judgment. We agree.

The circuit court relied upon *Kentucky Joint Stock Land Bank v. Farmers Exchange Bank*, 274 Ky. 525, 119 S.W.2d 873, 877 (1938), wherein the status of a mortgagee who purchased the collateral at a foreclosure sale was addressed. The Court stated:

[handwritten margin note: NO deficiency.]

---

1. Steve and Kevan Chung paid $10,000.00 in cash, and the bank financed the balance.
2. The master commissioner's deed to the bank bore the date of July 30, 1991, and showed a recordation date of August 14, 1991.

There might be *qualifying facts and circumstances* whereby one who may be liable for the originally secured debt might still have some remaining equity in the mortgaged property, even after sale; but whether so or not, there are certainly no such qualifying facts appearing in this record, even by the remotest intimation. On the contrary, the record presents only the usual case where a court ordered the sale of mortgaged property, and which order was executed by the court's commissioner in the usual and ordinary manner as prescribed by the law. The owner of the debt, secured by the lien ordered to be enforced, became the purchaser at an advanced price of more than fifty per cent above the appraised value of the property. The bidder later received a deed pursuant to the order of the court, and credited the indebtedness by the net amount of its bid. Under all the law that has been cited to us, and under all that we have been able to find — as well as in accordance with logic, justice and common sense — the sold security became exhausted upon its sale, in the circumstances and conditions outlined, and the vendee of the court's commissioner . . . obtained an unencumbered title, and which consequence follows whether the purchaser is the holder of the secured debt — and consequently the plaintiff in the proceedings wherein the mortgaged property was sold — or whether he be a stranger to the debt.

. . . In each case the purchaser — without some agreement or *conduct on his part creating a different result* — obtains the title to the judicially sold property free from the lien created by the enforced mortgage, notwithstanding the net proceeds of the sale were insufficient to extinguish the mortgage debt. (Emphases added.)

We do not perceive, as did the trial court, that this holding is fatal to Pearman's position. We construe *Kentucky Joint Stock* as holding that generally a mortgagee who purchases at his own judicial sale takes title free from any equity by one liable on the secured debt, except when "qualifying facts and circumstances" exist. *Id.* We believe there exists qualifying facts and circumstances in the instant action, such being that the bank contracted with third parties (the Chungs) to sell the mortgaged property *during the foreclosure action* and, in fact, ultimately sold same for an amount which would have wholly satisfied the debt owed by Pearman. More succinctly, we view the qualifying and distinguishing feature of this action as being that the bank contracted to sell the mortgaged property while the mortgagor-mortgagee relationship was yet in full force and effect. Such becomes a pivotal and consequential fact owing to the implied covenant of good faith and fair dealing in the mortgage contract.

In *Ranier v. Mount Sterling Nat'l Bank*, Ky., 812 S.W.2d 154, 156 (1991), the Court observed that "[i]n every contract, there is an implied covenant of good faith and fair dealing." We are bound to conclude that the mortgage contract in question contains such a covenant and that neither the loan delinquency nor the foreclosure process impaired its validity. *Cf.* Annot., 55 A.L.R.4th 1026 (1987). We believe the covenant imposed upon the bank the duty to act in a bona fide[3] manner throughout the foreclosure proceedings. It may reasonably be assumed that for an appreciable time before the contract of sale was entered into, the bank was aware of the Chungs' interest in Pearman's property and of their willingness to purchase it for $45,000.00. In any event, its failure to adopt a course that would have liquidated its customer's debt in the entirety and choosing instead to seize an advantageous

---

3. *Black's Law Dictionary* 177 (6th ed. 1990) defines "bona fide" as being "[i]n or with good faith; honestly, openly, and sincerely; without deceit or fraud. . . . Truly; actually; without simulation or pretense. Innocently; in the attitude of trust and confidence; without notice of fraud, etc. Real, actual, genuine, and not feigned." (Citations omitted.)

business opportunity was a breach of its good faith obligation. <u>Under these circumstances, we believe the bank should not be allowed to profit</u>. We conclude that the bank's breach of its duty of good faith and fair dealing resulted in effacement of the deficiency.

NOTES

1. The court in the *Pearman* case refers to Kentucky statutes that can benefit defaulting mortgagors by discouraging excessively low real property sale prices at foreclosure and other court ordered sales. The Kentucky statutes provide as follows:

Ky. Rev. Stat. Ann. (Michie 2005)

§ 426.520. Appraisal of real property before judicial sale
(1) Before any real property is to be sold under an order or judgment of a court, other than an execution, the commissioner or other officer selling the property shall have <u>it appraised, under oath, by two (2) disinterested</u>, intelligent housekeepers of the county, who may be sworn by the officer. If they disagree, the officer shall act as umpire. If only a part of a tract of land is sold, the part sold shall, after the sale, be revalued in like manner.

(2) The appraisal made shall be in writing, signed by the persons making it, and returned by the commissioner or officer to the court which made the order or rendered the judgment for the sale of the property. The appraisal shall be filed among the papers of the cause in which the judgment was rendered or the order made, and entered on the records of the court.

§ 426.530 Right of redemption — Manner of redeeming — Purchaser to receive writ of possession and deed.
(1) If real property sold in <u>pursuance of a judgment or order</u> of a court, other than an execution, does not bring <u>two-thirds of its appraised value,</u> the defendant and his representatives may redeem it within a year from the day of sale, by paying the original purchase money and ten percent (10%) per annum interest thereon.

Quite conceivably, except for these statutory provisions, the Bank in the *Pearman* case would have made an even lower bid, and probably would have prevailed as the only bidder.

2. Rigged bidding that resulted in criminal prosecution has occasionally taken place in some communities. An example of this that included organized crime participation was reported as follows in the *New York Times* on September 23, 1998.

The bidding could not have been more public: foreclosed houses auctioned off by a court-appointed referee on the very steps of the State Supreme Courthouse in Queens.

Federal prosecutors say that <u>for at least 10 years, a ring of real estate brokers and speculators, using bribes and threats to keep outsiders from competing, manipulated the bidding on as much as $50 million in property and replaced the auctions with a shadow system of their own.</u>

At the courthouse auctions, which were advertised in newspapers and open to members of the public, the ring members snapped up the most desirable properties with low-ball bids. Afterward, the members of the ring held secret, illicit auctions to determine who ultimately acquired the properties, prosecutors say. . . .

According to court papers, the bid-riggers designated one buyer for a given proper-ty, who in the absence of competing bidders would offer a low-ball price. After the public auction, the group would meet in secret, usually at the office of a ring member a few blocks away. There, they would hold a second auction for the property, at which the participants would submit written bids that more closely approached the fair market value of the property. The winning bids ranged from a few thousand dollars to as much as $50,000 more than the price paid at the first auction.

The high bidder at the secret auction would then reimburse the designated bidder from the official auction. And the difference between the two prices — for example, the $50,000 — would be split among the other participants and called a commission. Ultimately, the winning bidder would either sell the property for a quick profit or renovate it.

The *Times* report goes on to say that nonmembers of the bid-rigging group in attendance at the auctions who were possible bidders were discouraged from bid-ding by members paying them not to bid, demanding payment from a potential bidder to prevent any bid-rigging group member from bidding, or by other intimi-dating threats. The report adds that the bid-rigging scheme was ended by criminal prosecution of 35 bid-rigging group members, 9 of whom had pleaded guilty as of the date of the *Times* report.

Skip to
242

(2) *Constitutionality of Power of Sale Procedures*

Warren v. Government National Mortgage Assn.

611 F.2d 1229 (8th Cir. 1980), cert. denied, 449 U.S. 847 (1980)

McMANUS, District Judge. This is an appeal by Vivian Warren (plaintiff) from a final judgment in favor of Government National Mortgage Association (GNMA), holding no violation of her fifth amendment rights resulting from an extrajudicial foreclo-sure under a deed of trust. In her complaint, predicated principally under 28 U.S.C. § 1331 (federal question), plaintiff sought declaratory and mandamus relief.

Plaintiff and her husband[2] were the owners of a residence in Kansas City, Missouri, which they purchased in August of 1966 from the United States Depart-ment of Housing and Urban Development (HUD). As part of the purchase price, they executed a note, secured by a deed of trust, to the Federal National Mortgage Association (FNMA). Thereafter, by Congressional Act, FNMA was converted into GNMA, a private corporation wholly-owned by the federal government. 12 U.S.C. § 1716 et seq. Plaintiff's note and deed of trust were transferred and assigned to GNMA. The deed of trust included a "Power of Sale" clause[3] which in the event of

---

2. Plaintiff and her husband were separated at the time the action was filed and he was not an original party. Thereafter, by amendment, he was made a party defendant as a necessary party who would not join as plaintiff. (FRCP 19)(a). Summons was issued and served, and the husband defaulted.

3. The deed of trust was executed on "FHA Form No. 2139m (Revised August 1962)," which was then the standard printed form devised, approved and provided by the FHA for use in connection with federally insured loans on property situated in the State of Missouri. Compare 24 CFR § 203.17. The deed of trust form included the following pertinent language, referred to here as the "Power of Sale" clause:

NOW, THEREFORE, . . . if default be made in the payment of said note herein provided . . . then the whole of said note and interest thereon to date of foreclosure shall

default permitted the trustee to initiate an extrajudicial foreclosure sale in accordance with Missouri statutory procedures.[4]

In September of 1970, the successor trustee under the deed of trust — a private attorney retained by GNMA and not otherwise employed by the federal government — mailed a letter, first class not registered nor certified receipt, to the plaintiff and her husband, notifying them that GNMA deemed the payments on the note to be in default and that, as holder of the note, GNMA had elected to declare the entire principal due. The letter, therefore, demanded payment of the entire balance but contained no mention or threat of foreclosure by a trustee's sale. For whatever reasons,[5] plaintiff made no response to the letter.

Thereafter, GNMA foreclosed against plaintiff by causing the trustee to advertise in a newspaper, used almost exclusively for such legal notices, and to conduct a public sale, all in compliance with the power of sale clause in the deed of trust. GNMA was the purchaser at this sale.

After the foreclosure sale, plaintiff was notified by letter of the sale and demand was made for possession on or before October 26, 1970. She did not vacate the premises and GNMA brought an action for unlawful detainer in the Missouri Magistrate's Court, securing a judgment in that case on January 11, 1971. GNMA secured possession of the property by a writ of restitution on or about April 7, 1971.

Plaintiff's challenge rests essentially on her contention that she was denied fifth amendment due process rights to notice and hearing *prior* to the foreclosure sale.[6] We affirm on the basis of no federal government action.

The Due Process Clause of the Fifth Amendment to the United States Constitution provides that: "No person shall . . . be deprived of . . . property, without due process of law; . . . " It applies to federal government not private action, Public Utilities Comm'n v. Pollak, 343 U.S. 451, 461, 72 S. Ct. 813, 96 L. Ed. 1068 (1952); while the fourteenth amendment due process clause applies to the states, see, e.g., Moose Lodge No. 107 v. Irvis, 407 U.S. 163, 172-73, 92 S. Ct. 1965, 32 L. Ed. 2d 627 (1972); Shelley v. Kraemer, 334 U.S. 1, 13, 68 S. Ct. 836, 92 L. Ed. 1161 (1948). The standard for finding federal government action under the fifth amendment is the same as that for finding state action under the fourteenth amendment. See, e.g., Geneva Towers Tenants Org. v. Federated Mortgage Investors, 504 F.2d 483, 487 (9th Cir. 1974); Ponce v. Housing Authority of Tulare County, 389 F. Supp. 635, 648 (E.D. Cal. 1975). That standard is that there must exist "a sufficiently close nexus between the [government] and the challenged action of the regulated entity so that the action of the latter may be fairly treated as that of the [government] itself." Jackson v. Metropolitan Edison Co., 419 U.S. 345, 351, 95 S. Ct. 449, 453, 42 L. Ed. 2d 477 (1974).

---

become due and payable and this deed shall remain in force; and said Trustee or his successor . . . , at the request of the legal holder of the aforesaid note, may proceed to sell the property . . . at public vendue . . . to the highest bidder for cash, first giving twenty days public notice of the time, terms and place of sale and of the property to be sold by advertisement in some newspaper published in said Jackson County, Missouri, and upon such sale shall execute a deed conveying the property so sold to the purchaser thereof.

4. Missouri statutory law permits the extrajudicial foreclosure of deeds of trust, which in Missouri are commonly used as security agreements in lieu of mortgages. Rev. St. Mo. § 433.410 et seq. (1969).

5. The record indicates that plaintiff had only a fifth grade education and neither she nor her husband could read. In a related case, she testified that she couldn't remember ever receiving the letter. Cf. Warren v. GNMA, 521 S.W.2d 441, 442 (Mo. en banc 1975).

6. Plaintiff originally filed this suit alleging additionally that the Missouri statute authorizing such extrajudicial foreclosures violated the fifth and fourteenth amendments, and sought both a declaratory judgment voiding the sale and injunctive relief.

It is undisputed in this case that GNMA is a corporate entity, wholly-owned by the federal government, 31 U.S.C. § 846. It was created by the partition of the FNMA under the National Housing Act of 1968, 12 U.S.C. § 1716 et seq., and is under the management and control of the Secretary of HUD, 12 U.S.C. §§ 1723(a) and 1723a(d). It has no capital stock, 12 U.S.C. § 1717(a)(2)(A). The economic benefits and burdens of its administration inure to the Secretary of the Treasury, 12 U.S.C. § 1722. Moreover, under 12 U.S.C. § 1717(b)(1), it is authorized to purchase, service, sell or otherwise deal in mortgages insured under 12 U.S.C. §§ 1701-1750g by the Federal Housing Authority (FHA).[7] Thus, GNMA is not only wholly-owned by the federal government but it also operates under federal government authority.[8]

The parties stipulated that the courts of Missouri had never passed on the constitutional issues presented in the case, and the trial court determined that it was a proper cause for abstention and dismissed the case on that basis.

On appeal, this court affirmed the application of the abstention doctrine, but reversed the dismissal, directing the plaintiff to file a suit in state court, and directing that the case remain on the federal court docket until determination of the constitutional issues by the Supreme Court of Missouri. Warren v. GNMA, 443 F.2d 624 (8th Cir. 1971).

The Supreme Court of Missouri decided the fourteenth amendment issue against the plaintiff. Warren v. GNMA, 521 S.W.2d 441 (Mo. en banc 1975). The rationale for the decision is found in Federal National Mortgage Association v. Howlett, 521 S.W.2d 428 (Mo. en banc 1975) (decided the same day as the *Warren* case). The Missouri Court only discussed the fourteenth amendment constitutional question and stated:

> We hold that the foreclosure of the deed of trust on appellant's property was pursuant to the *contractual* provisions in the deed of trust and *not by authority of state law*. It follows that appellant's contention that state action was present on the theory that the power of sale exercised by the trustee was conferred by state statute is overruled. (Emphasis added).

The Missouri Supreme Court relied upon the reasoning and result in Bryant v. Jefferson Fed. Sav. & Loan Assoc., 166 U.S. App. D.C. 178, 509 F.2d 511 (D.C. Cir. 1974). After the *Warren* decision, similar result was reached in cases involving extrajudicial foreclosures. Charmicor, Inc. v. Deaner, 572 F.2d 694 (9th Cir. 1978); Northrip v. FNMA, 527 F.2d 23 (6th Cir. 1975); and Barrera v. Security Bldg. & Inv. Corp., 519 F.2d 1166 (5th Cir. 1975). These cases hold that the fact that state statutes regulate and govern the procedures to be followed in an extrajudicial foreclosure of real estate under power of sale clause contained in a mortgage or deed of trust does not establish that the foreclosure constituted state action.

Subsequent to the Missouri Supreme Court decision in *Warren,* this case was reactivated in the federal district court below, limited to the fifth amendment issues.

7. GNMA is authorized to deal only in mortgages or deeds of trust insured under federal programs and is not, unlike FNMA, authorized to deal in "conventional mortgages." Compare 12 U.S.C. §§ 1717 (a)(2)(A) & 1717(b)(1) with 12 U.S.C. § 1717(a)(2)(B) & 1717(b)(2). Thus, GNMA was authorized to deal in plaintiff's deed of trust in this case because that deed of trust was insured by FHA under § 203 of the National Housing Act, 12 U.S.C. § 1709.

8. Although the pertinent legislative history is somewhat unclear with respect to Congress' intent in bifurcating the old FNMA into two distinct corporate entities — FNMA and GNMA — in 1968, it is fairly certain that Congress was primarily motivated by "the emphasis of recent years of increased reliance on private sponsorship under our housing programs and participation by private enterprises in the financing and production of housing." H.R. Rep. No. 1585, 90th Cong., 2d Sess. reprinted in [1968] U.S. Code Cong. & Admin. News, pp. 2873, 2874. To that end, Congress decided to place the former FNMA's secondary market operation in a new privately owned corporation (with the continued designation FNMA) and its special assistance, management and liquidating functions in the new GNMA. Id., U.S. Code Cong., supra, at 2875; see also id., at 2943-48, 3004-09.

Thus, if considered purely as a matter of statutory and organizational form the new GNMA could perhaps be viewed as more "governmental" than its counterpart FNMA. We, however, read the legislative history to indicate Congress' intent as being essentially to dissociate as far as possible the newly created entities, however characterized as to form, from the federal government in regard to their respective secondary mortgage market functions.

In short, in terms of substance as opposed to form, we view the functions served by GNMA as being no more governmental than those served by the new FNMA, and accordingly we consider the cases holding the new FNMA's secondary mortgage market functions to be essentially "private action" as persuasive authority on the federal government action issue presented in this case. Compare Roberts v. Cameron–Brown Co., 556 F.2d 356, 358-60 (5th Cir. 1977); Northrip v. FNMA, 527 F.2d 23, 30-33 (6th Cir. 1975).

To recognize these relational facts, however, does not end the federal government action inquiry for, as was the case in Public Utilities Comm'n. v. Pollak, 343 U.S. 451, 72 S. Ct. 813, 96 L. Ed. 1068 (1952), the deciding issue in this regard is not simply whether GNMA is a government-owned or authorized corporation; rather, it is whether as such GNMA's foreclosure action pursuant to the contractoral power of sale clause in the deed of trust was so closely linked to federal government regulation that it can in actuality be viewed more as the action of the federal government itself than that of GNMA. Compare also Jackson v. Metropolitan Edison Co., 419 U.S. 345, 356-57 & n.16, 95 S. Ct. 449, 42 L. Ed. 2d 477 (1974).

In approaching the latter issue, we emphasize that the power of sale clause as contained in the deed of trust is a contractual power having its genesis in the deed of trust itself and as such exists independent of any statute otherwise governing it. Compare, e.g., FNMA v. Howlett, 521 S.W.2d 428, 432 (Mo. en banc) *appeal dismissed* 423 U.S. 909, 96 S. Ct. 210, 46 L. Ed. 2d 137 (1975); Warren v. GNMA, 521 S.W.2d 441 (Mo. en banc 1975). As a party to the contract, and even though it was a governmentally-owned and authorized entity, GNMA had a right to resort to its contractual remedies just as a purely private entity had. See Atlantic Mutual Ins. Co. v. Cooney, 303 F.2d 253, 259 (9th Cir. 1962). Accord Rex Trailer Co., Inc. v. United States, 350 U.S. 148, 151, 76 S. Ct. 219, 100 L. Ed. 149 (1956).

We therefore are of the general opinion that mortgage foreclosures through power of sale agreements such as the one at issue here are not in and of themselves power of a governmental nature. Compare Northrip v. FNMA, 527 F.2d 23, 31 (6th Cir. 1975); Byrant v. Jefferson Federal Savings and Loan Assoc., 166 U.S. App. D.C. 178, 180-81, 509 F.2d 511, 513-14 (D.C. Cir. 1974). The trial court implicitly recognized this when it concluded that "a wholly-owned government agency can enforce a valid *contractual* provision for foreclosure without running afoul of the constraints of the Fifth Amendment, under all circumstances in which the foreclosure of the same contract by a private lender would be held not to violate the requirements of due process." Warren v. GNMA, et al., Civil Action No. 19006-2, Memorandum Opinion and Judgment at p. 6 (W.D. Mo., February 12, 1979) [Designated Record on Appeal p. 117].

Plaintiff's major contention in this regard is that, all these considerations notwithstanding, federal government action is implicated in this case because the deed of trust form was specifically approved by HUD regulations, 24 CFR § 203.17, and therefore GNMA's foreclosure action pursuant to that deed of trust was by implication also specifically approved by HUD. If this court were to accept plaintiff's argument, every FHA guaranteed mortgage held either by GNMA, FNMA or a private lending agency would be placed in the same position of constitutional uncertainty simply by virtue of the fact that the mortgage form must also be approved by a federal agency under HUD regulations. Moreover, plaintiff's argument ignores the point that the central inquiry is not whether the form of the deed of trust is approved by federal regulations, but rather it is whether there exists a sufficiently close nexus between the government regulations and the challenged activity specifically at issue so that the challenged activity itself may be fairly treated as truly that of the federal government directly. Cf. Jackson v. Metropolitan Edison Co., 419 U.S. 345, 351, 95 S. Ct. 449, 42 L. Ed. 2d 477 (1974). Accord, Roberts v. Cameron-Brown Co., 556 F.2d 356, 358 (5th Cir. 1977), ["The government must be involved *with the activity* that causes the actual injury." (emphasis added)].

The challenged activity specifically at issue in this case is GNMA's extrajudicial foreclosure pursuant to the power of sale terms of the deed of trust, performed in accordance with Missouri laws. Plaintiff cites 24 CFR Pts. 200 & 203 generally as support for her argument that the Secretary of HUD, vicariously through GNMA, directly regulates GNMA's foreclosure procedures here. We find nothing in those general provisions, however, constituting direct federal government regulation of GNMA's servicing policies, including what methods it may use to protect its financial interest in the mortgage on default.

Concededly, the commissioner of the FHA is required to approve the form of the mortgage or deed of trust before it is eligible for FHA insurance under 24 CFR § 203.17, but that regulation does not dictate what foreclosure provisions are to be included in the deed of trust. Indeed, 24 CFR § 203.17(b), (c) and (d) explicitly set forth certain provisions which must be included in any mortgage or deed of trust approved under subpart 203. If the Secretary of HUD had intended to regulate the specific *method* of foreclosure to be adopted by an investor in an insured mortgage, the regulations would certainly have directly and expressly set forth that method in 24 CFR § 203.17.

Moreover, it is admitted in this case that the foreclosure of plaintiff's deed of trust was according to its own terms and under the extrajudicial foreclosure statutes of Missouri. There is nothing in the record to indicate that the powers otherwise exercisable by officers or employees of the federal government were in any way applied or used in this foreclosure of plaintiff's deed of trust. In fact, the foreclosure was conducted by the successor trustee strictly in accordance with Missouri law pursuant to his position as the contractually appointed trustee and not as a government employee.

Further, the only direct government involvement in the relations with the mortgagor or grantor of the deed of trust after default can be found in 24 CFR § 203.355. The regulation contemplates that if a claim is to be made under the mortgage insurance certificate then the mortgagee must take whatever steps, including foreclosure if and as permitted under state law, that are necessary to vest title to the property in either its name, or in the name of the commissioner. The rule, however, does not make explicit what specific foreclosure methods or procedures are to be adopted by the mortgagee. Thus, we view it as insufficient to conclude that the power of sale foreclosure methods at issue here were that of the federal government itself.

We conclude generally, therefore, that the federal government has neither mandated nor approved the method of foreclosure to be followed in the event of default; nor could it since the foreclosure procedures must accord with Missouri law. Since federal government regulation was not directly and substantially linked to the challenged foreclosure activity complained of by plaintiff and at issue here, no "federal government action" exists and plaintiff has no cognizable constitutional claim under the fifth amendment.

For the foregoing reasons, we affirm the judgment of the District Court. We need not reach waiver and other issues raised by plaintiff.

NOTES AND QUESTIONS

1. In your opinion was the possibility that many thousands of mortgages guaranteed by FHA would be "constitutionally uncertain" if the court held for plaintiff, a major consideration in the *Warren* court reaching the decision it did?

2. A U.S. Supreme Court case decided fifteen years after the decision in the *Warren* case creates doubts as to the continued validity of the law as set forth by the *Warren* court. This U.S. Supreme Court case is Lebron v. National Railroad Passenger Corp., 513 U.S. 374 (1995).

3. Some states have recently amended their power of sale foreclosure statutes to require efforts at notice which will increase the probability that those against whom foreclosure is sought will actually receive notice of the impending action. Illustrative of such statutes is Tex. Prop. Code Ann. §51.002 (Vernon Supp. 2005), now requiring notice by certified mail in addition to posting it on the courthouse door.

(3) Omitted Parties

Springer Corporation v. Kirkeby-Natus

80 N.M. 205, 453 P.2d 376 (1969)

NOBLE, Chief Justice. Kirkeby-Natus (hereafter termed Kirkeby) foreclosed its first mortgage covering 403 acres of lands securing an indebtedness of $521,458.11, bidding in the land for $323,625.00, and obtained a deficiency judgment for $197,833.11. Springer Corporation (hereafter termed Springer) held a second mortgage on 94.96 acres of the land mortgaged to Kirkeby, securing an indebtedness of $77,800.00. By reason of an abstractor's error, Springer was not made a party to the Kirkeby foreclosure. Springer then brought this action to foreclose its second mortgage. Kirkeby, in this suit, by counterclaim, was granted foreclosure of its first mortgage against Springer. Springer was held entitled to redeem from the Kirkeby foreclosure, within nine months after the date of the judgment in this case, but only upon payment of the full amount paid by Kirkeby for the entire 403 acres bought at the foreclosure sale — $323,625.00, plus $13,041.07, being the unpaid balance of the deficiency judgment. Springer has appealed. The cross-complainants have likewise appealed.

The trial court found that Kirkeby had received a credit of $184,792.04 on its deficiency judgment, leaving a balance of $13,041.07. Springer appears to contend that a greater credit should have been allowed but Findings 24 and 25, so determining, have not been attacked as being unsupported by the evidence and, accordingly, are binding on this court on appeal. Cooper v. Bank of New Mexico, 77 N.M. 398, 423 P.2d 431; Baca v. Gutierrez, 77 N.M. 428, 423 P.2d 617. Also, it is clear that the findings are amply supported by the proof.

It is settled in this jurisdiction that the rights of one who is not a party to a mortgage foreclosure action are not affected by any judgment rendered therein nor by a foreclosure sale pursuant thereto. Conway v. San Miguel County Board of Education, 59 N.M. 242, 282 P.2d 719; Mann v. Whitely, 36 N.M. 1, 6 P.2d 468. See also Annot., 134 A.L.R. 1490, 1492. Thus, the failure to join Springer, a junior lien holder, left its rights, including its equity of redemption, unaffected and unimpaired.

The fact that Springer was not a party to the Kirkeby foreclosure, however, does not deprive Kirkeby of the benefit of its judgment against those parties who were before the court in its foreclosure action. Mann v. Whitely, supra. The counterclaim in the instant case constituted a separate and independent action to foreclose the Kirkeby mortgage against the Springer rights. Kirkeby, relying on §§24-2-19 and 24-219.1, N.M.S.A. 1953, argues that Springer was only entitled to redeem within nine months from the date of sale held pursuant to the Kirkeby foreclosure.

It is clear to us that since Springer's rights, including its right of redemption, were not impaired or affected by the original Kirkeby foreclosure to which Springer was not a party, its right of redemption only accrues upon the entry of a judgment foreclosing its rights in a separate and independent action, or the judgment of the counterclaim in the instant case. John Hancock Mut. Life Inc. Co. v. Mays, 152 Kan. 46, 102 P.2d 984.

Relying on Green v. Dixon, 9 Wis. 532 (1859); 2 Wiltsie on Mortgage Foreclosure (4th Ed.) § 1071; and 2 Jones on Mortgages (8th Ed.) § 1375, Springer argues that because it was not made a party to the Kirkeby senior mortgage foreclosure proceeding, and because Springer's junior mortgage only covers some 95 acres out of the 403 acres securing the senior mortgage, it should be permitted to redeem from the Kirkeby sale pro tanto by paying only the pro rata part of the amount for which the property sold at the Kirkeby sale. We cannot agree.

This question is one of first impression in New Mexico and appears to have been resolved by relatively few courts of other jurisdictions. It is a general rule that a mortgage is an entire thing, and must be redeemed in its entirety, and that a mortgagee cannot be required to divide either his debt or his security. 2 Jones on Mortgages (8th Ed.) § 1372; Annot., 134 A.L.R. 1490, 1511. An exception pointed out by the author, supra, at § 1375, indicating that where an owner of the land has not been made a party to the foreclosure of the senior mortgage, and the senior mortgagee is the purchaser at the sale, the owner not made a party may redeem pro tanto upon the theory that the senior mortgagee, by such purchase, voluntarily severed his right and obtained an indefeasible title to part of the land and a defeasible title to another part, affords some color for the Springer argument. See also 2 Wiltsie on Mortgage Foreclosure (4th Ed.) § 1071; Monese v. Struve, 155 Or. 68, 62 P.2d 822. Our research discloses that the statement in Wiltsie has support only in Green v. Dixon, supra. 2 Jones on Mortgages, § 1375, states a similar exception, relying only on Green v. Dixon, supra, and Wilson v. Tarter, 22 Or. 504, 30 P. 499. The basis of these decisions and the exceptions stated in Wiltsie and Jones is criticized by the author in 2 Glenn on Mortgages (1943) § 299.1, who says the rule is objectionable because of a false premise, that is, it assumes that the senior mortgagee in his second independent action to require the junior lien holder to elect whether to redeem, is asking a favor of equity, and thus can be forced to accept a partial redemption as the price of equity. Glenn argues that, in fact, the senior mortgagee is not asking a favor, and that partial redemption should not be allowed merely because the junior encumbrancer happened to be omitted as a party in the first foreclosure. The exception to the general rule is likewise criticized in a note, 50 Harvard L. Rev. 990. See 25 Ill. L. Rev. 720. 2 Glenn on Mortgages, supra, at 1257, points out that the real relief of a partial encumbrancer lies in invoking the rule of marshalling by which the junior encumbrancer may require a senior mortgagee to exhaust his remedy against property other than that covered by the partial mortgage of the junior encumbrancer. That doctrine was applied in Hinners v. Birkevaag, 113 N.J. Eq. 413, 167 A. 209, at the instance of an omitted junior mortgagee, who established the relative values of the respective tracts in the subsequent independent action.

The Wisconsin Supreme Court, in Buchner v. Gether Trust, 241 Wis. 148, 5 N.W.2d 806, without reference to its earlier decision in Green v. Dixon, supra, appears to have rejected the reasoning of the earlier case. In *Buchner,* the court expressly said that the rights of a junior encumbrancer not made a party to the foreclosure of the senior mortgage are "unimpaired and unchanged by the defective foreclosure." The court further said: ". . . Except for the dictum in the *Winter* case, [Winter v. O'Neill, 241 Wis. 280, 5 N.W.2d 809] we discover no case holding that the rights of the junior claimant are improved or increased by the defect in the foreclosure proceedings. In accordance with quite elementary principles of justice, his position is preserved and equity will not permit that he suffer any disadvantage from the failure to include him as a party. It would be utterly unfair to do more than this."

The Supreme Court of Florida, in Quinn Plumbing Co. v. New Miami Shores Corp., 100 Fla. 413, 129 So. 690, 73 A.L.R. 600, discussed Green v. Dixon, supra, and specifically rejected the reasoning by which a junior encumbrancer, who was not a party to the foreclosure of the senior mortgage, is permitted to redeem pro tanto from the senior mortgage. In Key West Wharf & Coal Co. v. Porter, 63 Fla. 448, 58 So. 599, 610, Am. Ann. Cas. 1914A, 173, the Florida court said of the holder of a junior mortgage covering only a portion of the land held as security for a senior mortgage: ". . . Their portions of said land, as well as all the residue of said mortgaged tract, are bound for the payment of the whole of both mortgages; and the courts have no power to release any part of the land from the lien of the mortgages by affixing thereto a sum, less than the entire sum of the mortgages, which, when paid, shall release such part from the lien of the mortgages. . . ."

The only absolute right of a junior mortgagee, as against a senior mortgagee, is the right to redeem from the senior mortgagee. 3 Jones on Mortgages (8th Ed.) § 1781. The rights of an omitted junior encumbrancer remain precisely as they were before the proceedings were instituted to foreclose the first mortgage. They are neither enlarged nor diminished by the defective foreclosure. McGough v. Sweetzer, 97 Ala. 361, 12 So. 162, 19 L.R.A. 470.

The judgment appealed from must be reversed, however, and the cause remanded because the judgment provided that Springer should have a period of nine months from the date of the entry of the judgment in the instant case within which to redeem the property from the mortgage foreclosure sale in Cause No. A-12537 on the docket of the district court of Bernalillo County. Section 24-2-18, N.M.S.A. 1953, provides that no property shall be sold under a mortgage foreclosure proceeding until sixty days after the date of the entry of the foreclosure judgment. Section 24-2-19, N.M.S.A. 1953, gives a person entitled to redemption nine months from the date of such foreclosure sale within which to redeem therefrom. Construing the two statutory provisions together, as we must, it is apparent that a person entitled to redeem is thus given at least eleven months from the date of the foreclosure judgment within which to redeem. We have said that because Springer was not a party to the first foreclosure action, it will not be permitted to suffer any disadvantage from the failure to include it as a party. It is apparent that the judgment in the instant case shortened Springer's period of redemption by sixty days. This was error.

What we have said makes it unnecessary to discuss other questions argued or briefed. It follows that the judgment appealed from should be affirmed in all respects except that the judgment must be vacated and a new judgment entered granting Springer eleven months from the date of such judgment within which to redeem from the Kirkeby foreclosure sale.

It is so ordered.

Moise and Tackett, JJ., concur.

NOTES AND QUESTIONS

1. If a junior mortgagee is not joined as a defendant in a foreclosure action by the senior mortgagee, a Florida court in Miami-Dade County v. Imagine Properties, 752 So.2d 129 (Fla. App. 2000), held that the junior mortgagee retains a right of redemption and may redeem by paying the amount of the senior mortgage debt but need not pay the costs and expenses of the foreclosure action.

2. The mortgagor's interest commonly is called an equity of redemption, whether or not the mortgage is in default. The equity of redemption is to be distinguished from the statutory right to redeem, which arises after foreclosure by sale and permits the mortgagor to redeem for a specified period of time following the foreclosure sale or judgment. About half the states provide the statutory rights to redeem. Absent such statutory rights, defaulting mortgagors may redeem only until foreclosure sale or decree. Statutory rights of redemption can create sufficient uncertainty about future ownership so as to deter for many months alienation or development of the land.

3. Why should a senior mortgagee be permitted to foreclose the interest of a junior mortgagee? And why should a junior mortgagee of less land than that covered by the senior mortgage not be permitted to redeem pro tanto by paying the pro rata portion of what the property was sold for at foreclosure sale? Are the reasons given in the principal case satisfactory?

Como, Inc. v. Carson Square, Inc.

689 N.E. 2d 725 (Ind. 1997)

DICKSON, Justice.

The appellant-defendant, Como, Inc., appeals from the grant of summary judgment in favor of the appellee-plaintiff, Carson Square, Inc., in an action to terminate Como's leasehold interest in Carson Square Shopping Center in Indianapolis.

Between 1975 and February, 1993, the shopping center was owned by Carson Partners, subject to a mortgage held by American Fletcher National Bank and Trust Company n/k/a Bank One, Indianapolis, NA. In June, 1990, Como and Carson Partners entered into a five-year lease for a 20,000 square foot space in the shopping center which was to house Primo Catering and Banquet Hall, a catering business operated by Como. The lease was later amended to give Como two consecutive five-year options to renew. In February, 1991, Carson Partners defaulted on the mortgage. Bank One sought foreclosure on the shopping center, but neither named Como as a party to the foreclosure action nor notified Como of its commencement. A judgement of foreclosure was entered in February of 1993 and, on August 3, 1993, Bank One assigned its mortgage and judgment of foreclosure to Carson Square, which purchased the shopping center at a sheriffs sale the following day. This action resulted from the ensuing dispute between Como and Carson Square primarily regarding whether the foreclosure action terminated Como's leasehold interests.

trial   The trial court granted summary judgment in favor of Carson Square declaring that Como's lease was forever barred and foreclosed, that Como has no present rights or interest in the shopping center, that Como must deliver immediate possession to Carson Square, and that Como must pay Carson Square fair market value rent from the time Carson Square acquired the premises. The Court of Appeals reversed, holding that Como was denied due process by its exclusion from the foreclosure action, and that the foreclosure did not abolish Como's leasehold. *Como, Inc. v. Carson Square, Inc.*, 648 N.E.2d 1247, 1249 (Ind.Ct. App.1995). We granted transfer to review this issue.

However, of the four members of this Court able to participate in this case, two justices believe that the result reached by the Court of Appeals was correct, and two justices are of a contrary belief. This rare circumstance is anticipated in our rules which provide that in cases where the Supreme Court is evenly divided upon the proper disposition of the cause once transfer is granted, "transfer shall be deemed denied and the decision of the Court of Appeals shall be affirmed and becomes the law of the case." Ind.App. Rule 11(B)(5). This rule is intended to facilitate finality in a particular case, not to establish precedent on issues upon which this Court is evenly divided.

While our previous order granting transfer vacated the opinion of the Court of Appeals under Indiana Appellate Rule 11(B)(3), the effect of said decision upon the parties herein is now affirmed as the law of the case.

SHEPARD, C.J., and SULLIVAN and BOEHM, JJ., concur, noting that DICKSON and BOEHM, JJ., believe that the result reached by the Court of Appeals is correct and that SHEPARD, C.J., and SULLIVAN, J., believe that the opinion of the Court of Appeals is incorrect.

SELBY, J., not participating.

NOTES AND QUESTIONS

① In your opinion how should the Supreme Court of Indiana have decided the *Como* case and why? A different result on similar facts was the decision of an Oregon court. In Director of Veteran's Affairs v. Martin, 898 P.2d 230 (Or. App. 1995), a lessee of a lease entered into subsequent to a mortgage on the property was held not to be a necessary party in a foreclosure action and, although not named in the foreclosure proceeding, must give up possession to the purchaser at the foreclosure sale.

② A lease senior in time to a mortgage generally remains in effect following foreclosure, the person acquiring the property following the foreclosure becoming the lessor under the terms of the senior lease. A lease junior in time to a mortgage can be extinguished by foreclosure of the mortgage if the lessee is joined as a defendant in the foreclosure proceedings. Mortgagees sometimes intentionally do not join such junior lessees as foreclosure defendants. Why this conscious determination not to join junior lessees?

(4)   *Risks of a Junior Encumbrancer: Senior Lien Default*   SKIP

All mortgagees face some risk of loss when default occurs. The value of the security may not adequately cover the unpaid debt (which will include interest arrearages, curative advances, and foreclosure costs) and the mortgagor, even if personally liable, may be unable to pay the deficiency. The junior mortgagee, however, faces a special problem — that of "cover" — if default occurs in the senior mortgage. When the senior mortgagee sells the security under a power of sale or foreclosure decree, the junior mortgagee must look to the "surplus" proceeds of sale to realize anything on his security interest. As the following problems reveal, this is often, at best, a chancy prospect for the junior mortgagee — one, if at all possible, he would do well to avoid.

PROBLEMS

A owns a building that is appraised at $500,000 and is encumbered with two mortgages. X holds the first mortgage of $400,000. Y holds the second mortgage of $50,000. Assume X currently is owed $400,000 and Y is owed $50,000.

1. The first mortgage (but not the second mortgage) is in default. X forecloses and joins Y in the foreclosure action.

(a) At the foreclosure sale, X is prepared to make the opening bid. What amount might you suggest? How much new cash must X raise to bid $400,000?

(b) At the foreclosure sale, X has opened the bidding at $400,000. Except for Y, no other bidders appear. Y bids to protect his security interest. What amount might you suggest? How much new cash must Y raise to satisfy his bid?

(c) At the foreclosure sale, Z, a stranger, bids $430,000. In advising Y as to whether to continue the bidding, what factors would you weigh?

2. The second mortgage (but not the first mortgage) is in default. Y forecloses.

(a) Who should be joined in the foreclosure action?

(b) At the foreclosure sale, Y is prepared to make the opening bid. What amount might you suggest? How much new cash must Y raise to satisfy his bid?

3. The clauses below routinely appear in a junior mortgage.

§ 5567. Second Mortgage Clause.
This mortgage is subject and subordinate to ____ mortgage ____ given to secure the payment of ____ dollars and interest, recorded in the office of the ____, of the County of ____ in liber ____ of section ____ of mortgages, ____ now ____ prior lien ____ on said premises.

AND IT IS HEREBY EXPRESSLY AGREED, that should any default be made in the payment of any installment of principal or of the interest on ____ said prior mortgage, and should such installment of principal, of such interest remain upaid and in arrears for the space of ten days, or should any suit be commenced to foreclose ____ said prior mortgage, then the amount secured by this mortgage and the accompanying bond, shall become and be due and payable at any time thereafter at the option of the owner or holder of this mortgage.

AND IT IS HEREBY FURTHER EXPRESSLY AGREED, that should any default be made in the payment of any installment of principal, or of the interest on ____ said prior mortgage, the holder of this mortgage may pay such installment of principal, or such interest and the amount so paid, with legal interest thereon from the time of such payment, may be added to the indebtedness secured by this mortgage and the accompanying bond and shall be deemed to be secured by this mortgage and said bond, and may be collected thereunder. Modern Legal Forms § 5567 (Supp. 1967).

(a) Is the first mortgagee obligated to accept a tender made in behalf of the mortgagor pursuant to the third paragraph above?

(b) In the absence of the third paragraph above, would the junior mortgagee be privileged to make a tender if the mortgagor objected?

(c) If you represented the junior mortgagee, what provisions might you ask for, in addition to the standard clauses, to strengthen your client's status?

4. *Non-monetary Defaults:* Not every mortgage default results from the borrower's failure to pay his debt service installments currently. The typical loan agreement places other duties on the borrower (e.g., avoidance of waste, restoration of premises after casualty, payment of real estate taxes) that may lead to a default if the violation is not cured, and — more worrisome — certain other obligations (e.g., avoidance of insolvency, nontransfer of the mortgaged premises without the lender's consent) may lead to a default, with its attendant acceleration and foreclosure, that the junior lienor would be unable to cure.

Do you have any drafting or negotiating suggestions for placing the junior lienor somewhat less at peril under these circumstances?

3. *Postforeclosure Redemption Rights*

In about half the states, statutes provide for redemption after foreclosure for a period, varying among the states, from six months to two years.[48] These postforeclosure rights are often referred to as statutory redemption and are to be distinguished from preforeclosure equity of redemption rights. Those entitled to redeem after foreclosure include junior lienors as well as mortgagors and their successors. In most states the mortgagor has the right to possession during the period in which redemption is permitted. The amount that must be paid to redeem is usually the foreclosure sale price plus the expenses of foreclosure. Priorities exist for the right to redeem if more than one person has redemption rights, the mortgagor normally having the highest priority.

If a mortgagor or his successor redeems, junior liens are often considered to be revived. If a junior lienor redeems, he acquires the rights of the foreclosure sale purchaser and this interest can become a full title if no one with superior redemption rights redeems by the close of the redemption period. However, as illustrated by the next case, First Vermont Bank & Trust Co. v. Kalomiris, this is not true everywhere, and it may be necessary for the redeeming junior lienor to foreclose separately the mortgagor's interest in order to terminate all rights of the mortgagor.

The usual arguments in favor of postforeclosure redemption rights are that they tend to encourage higher prices for property when sold at foreclosure sale and to act as a corrective when foreclosure sale prices are inadequate in relation to real value. Also, these statutes can be of major benefit to mortgagors in temporary financial difficulties, such as farmers in a bad crop year. Among arguments against such statutes are that they increase the cost of the foreclosure process, including expensive delays to purchasers at foreclosure sale in obtaining possession and marketable title, and that postforeclosure redemption rights are unnecessary

---

48. On the states with postforeclosure redemption rights and cites to their statutes, see Nelson and Whitman, Real Estate Finance Law 772, note 2 (4th ed. 2002). Maine is the only eastern seaboard state with such a statute.

because infrequently exercised. However, consistent with Professor Tracht's discussion earlier of the advantages of the equity of redemption, the statutes can frequently be of benefit to each of the parties to a mortgage foreclosure proceeding by providing still further time for negotiation.

Frequently in statutory redemption states not only are there extended negotiations between the purchaser and the borrower after foreclosure but time-consuming delays due to efforts by the mortgagor to obtain the needed financing for redemption. But as is evident from the next case, the *Dalton* case, the mortgagor must be careful to comply with the timing and other requirements of the state's statutory redemption law as failure to comply with those requirements can result in loss of the right to redeem.

a. Effect of Redemption

Dalton v. Franken Const. Companies, Inc.

914 P.2d 1036 (N.M. App. 1996)

PICKARD, Judge.

1. Petitioner, Robert Hanford Dalton (Dalton), appeals the district court's determination that he did not timely exercise his statutory right of redemption of a property which had been sold at a judicial sale. Dalton argues that he substantially complied with the time requirements of NMSA 1978, Section 39–5–18(A) (Repl. Pamp.1991) to effect a redemption of the property. Dalton further argues that the equities of the case are such that the district court abused its discretion when it denied Dalton's petition for redemption. We affirm the decision of the district court.

FACTS

2. Dalton filed for bankruptcy on December 8, 1992. This stayed a foreclosure action which had been initiated against five properties owned by Dalton. The stay was lifted on March 2, 1994, and the properties were sold as separate parcels at a foreclosure sale on April 7, 1994. Each parcel was sold subject to Dalton's right of redemption. *See* § 39–5–18. However, because Dalton was a debtor in a Chapter 7 bankruptcy proceeding, the right of redemption was owned and controlled as an asset of the bankruptcy estate by the bankruptcy trustee (the Trustee). Dalton made an oral request after the April 7 sale that the Trustee abandon the right of redemption as an asset of the bankruptcy estate. The Trustee filed a notice of abandonment on June 2, 1994, which allowed Dalton to pursue redemption on his own behalf.

3. The Special Master's sale of April 7, 1994, was confirmed on April 12, 1994. Pursuant to agreement, Dalton had a two-month right of redemption. *See* NMSA 1978, § 39–5–19 (Repl.Pamp.1991) (redemption period may be shortened by prior agreement). The last day on which Dalton could redeem the properties was Monday, June 13, 1994. Four of the five properties that had been sold were redeemed by Dalton within the redemption period and are not the subject of this dispute. The fifth property (the property), the subject of this case, was purchased by Respondent Franken Construction Companies, Inc. (Franken).

4. Dalton was not able to obtain a loan commitment for the amount necessary to redeem the property until the afternoon of June 7, 1994, when the Bank of

Las Vegas (the Bank) conditionally approved a loan to cover the price of redemption. In exchange for the loan commitment, the Bank wanted assurances that the Bank would have a first and superior lien on the property and that the funds would be returned if the redemption bids were unsuccessful. Therefore, the loan proceeds were delivered to Dalton in a cashier's check with three payees: the district court clerk, Dalton, and the Bank itself. The check was delivered to the clerk's office on June 7, 1994, and held for deposit to the clerk's trust account on June 8, 1994.

5. On June 9, 1994, the Bank received a title insurance commitment which ensured that the Bank would be the first and superior lienholder on the property. However, the district judge was out of town, so the Bank's second concern — that the funds would be returned if the redemption was not approved — remained unsatisfied. When the district court clerk deposited the check, the Bank refused to endorse its own cashier's check. Thus, it could not be deposited into a trust account that the clerk opened in another bank and identified as proceeds for the redemption.

6. The district judge returned from out of town on June 13, 1994 — the last day of Dalton's redemption period. A Bank official contacted the judge regarding the assurances the Bank needed before it would endorse the check for deposit. The judge told the Bank to contact an attorney because it would not be proper for the judge to give any oral assurances or to prepare any written documents to that effect. Dalton's counsel, who did not practice in Las Vegas, faxed a motion and an order to the district court that afternoon. The documents were not filed, and the judge did not sign the order, because of a policy against filing or signing faxed copies. This policy was communicated to Dalton's attorney on June 13. The original motion and order were delivered to the court on June 14; the motion was filed and the judge signed and filed the order. The cashier's check was then redeposited and processed. The funds for the redemption were transferred into the clerk's trust account on June 17, 1994, four days after the June 13, 1994 deadline.

7. The district court concluded that Dalton "failed to timely exercise the right of redemption as required by law by failing to timely deposit the cash sum of $140,000.00 with the Clerk of the District Court." The district court reasoned that because the Bank refused to endorse the cashier's check, the check was not negotiable as cash and was therefore not in compliance with the statutory requirement that cash be deposited to effect a redemption. See § 39–5–18(A)(2). The district court refused to find or conclude that the equities favored Dalton.

DISCUSSION

1. SUBSTANTIAL COMPLIANCE

8. Dalton argues that he substantially complied with Section 39–5–18(A). In his requested findings of fact and conclusions of law, Dalton represents that the only reason that the Bank's requirement for assurance regarding the return of the funds was not satisfied on time was because the district judge was out of town. When the judge returned, he indicated that an order addressing the Bank's concerns would have to be prepared for his signature. Dalton's counsel faxed a prepared order to the judge's office. Dalton's substantial compliance argument is premised on his view that the judge indicated to him that the judge would sign the original order when he received it. However, the judge refused Dalton's requested finding to this

effect. The original order was received and signed by the judge on June 14, 1994, one day after the statutory period had expired.

9. Dalton contends that we should take a liberal view of his efforts to obtain the necessary funding to redeem the property. He contends that our decision in *Western Bank of Las Cruces v. Malooly*, 119 N.M. 743, 895 P.2d 265 (Ct.App.1995), expresses a public policy in favor of redemption. That is a misreading of *Malooly*. What we said there was that it would violate public policy "to prevent redemption that is in accordance with the statute." *Id.* at 749, 895 P.2d at 271. In other words, the statute establishes public policy, and the courts advance that policy by enforcing the statute. Nevertheless, Dalton is correct that he may prevail if he establishes substantial compliance with the statutory requirements. *See Lane v. Lane*, 121 N.M. 414, 419, 912 P.2d 290, 295 (App.1996), *cert. denied*, 121 N.M. 375, 911 P.2d 883 (1996). However, for the following reasons, Dalton's efforts did not rise to the level of substantial compliance.

10. Dalton contends that once the Bank's concerns were addressed by the judge's oral order, for all practical purposes the terms of the statute had been met. Only the "technicality" of release of the funds remained. However, Dalton misconstrues both the facts found by the district court and the statute. The district judge refused Dalton's requested finding to the effect that he had told Dalton that he would sign the order. *See Gallegos v. Wilkerson*, 79 N.M. 549, 551, 445 P.2d 970, 972 (1968) (refusal to make finding on a material issue is tantamount to ruling against the party with the burden of proof).

11. As for the statute, it provides in pertinent part:

> After sale of any real estate pursuant to [a] judgment or decree of any court, the real estate may be redeemed by the former defendant owner. . . .
>
>   2. by petitioning the district court in which the judgment or decree of foreclosure was entered for a certificate of redemption and by making a deposit of the amount [paid for the property at the foreclosure sale with ten percent interest per year and payment of all taxes, interest, and penalties] *in cash* in the office of the clerk of the district court. . . .

Section 39-5-18(A) (emphasis added). We interpret statutes by giving the words of the statute their ordinary, everyday meaning, *Western Bank of Las Cruces*, 119 N.M. at 746, 895 P.2d at 268, unless we discern clear and express legislative intent to the contrary, *Id.* Section 39-5-18 clearly states that persons seeking to redeem their property must deposit cash with the clerk of the district court. We see no reason to deviate as far from the express language of the statute in the instant case as Dalton's argument suggests.

12. Although we would agree that delivery to the court of a fully negotiable cashier's check would substantially comply with the statutory requirement of cash, the district court found that Dalton had not fulfilled even that requirement. The cashier's check could be negotiated only after endorsement by all three payees. But the Bank refused to endorse the check by June 13 and did not advise the court clerk until June 16 that the check would clear. Simply put, cash or its substantial equivalent was not available to repay Franken on June 13, 1994. Just as a personal check will not satisfy the statute even though there are sufficient funds in the account on which the check is drawn to cover the check, *see Weiner v. Eder*, 22 Ill.2d 408, 176 N.E.2d 777 (1961), an unendorsed cashier's check will not satisfy the statute, even though future endorsement may be predictable.

13. Dalton relies on the Utah case of *United States v. Loosley*, 551 P.2d 506 (Utah 1976), to support his argument that he substantially complied with the statute and is entitled to redeem the property. *Loosley* involved a tender of the correct amount due for the redemption one day before the redemption period expired. *Id.* at 508. The tender of payment was refused because payment was tendered without the judgment and affidavit of lien attached, as required by statute, and the payment was allegedly delivered to the wrong person. *Id.* at 507. The Utah Supreme Court declared that the mortgagor had acted in good faith and in substantial compliance with the redemption statute and was entitled to redeem. *Id.* at 508. The Utah court was persuaded by the fact that the foreclosure purchasers had waived their right to strict compliance by not objecting at a time when the redemptioners could have cured the defects. *Id.*

14. In contrast, in this case, Dalton's failure to timely tender the required payment in cash goes to the core of his obligation under the statute. It was not a timely tender of a cash payment as required by the statute. Dalton's failure to deposit cash with the district court clerk was more than merely a technical deficiency. *See Huston v. Lewis*, 818 P.2d 531, 536 n. 24 (Utah 1991) (characterizing *Loosley* as involving waiver of technical deficiencies). Nor is this case like *Advance-Rumely Thresher Co. v. Judd*, 104 Kan. 757, 180 P. 763 (1919), in which there was a slight deficiency in the amount tendered. *See id.* 180 P. at 765. Here, there was in effect no cash tender of most of the amount due. The redemption attempt was therefore not in compliance with the terms of Section 39–5–18(A)(2).

2. EQUITY

15. We consider next whether the district court abused its discretion when it declared that Dalton's redemption bid was unsuccessful under the circumstances of this case. Notwithstanding Dalton's lack of substantial compliance with the requirements of the redemption statute, Dalton contends that the district court erred in failing to apply equitable principles when it declined to find that cash was available as of June 13, 1994.

16. We disagree. In *Plaza National Bank v. Valdez*, 106 N.M. 464, 466, 745 P.2d 372, 374 (1987), our Supreme Court stated that equitable relief from the time limitations of the redemption statute would be entertained only upon "some showing of wrongful conduct on the part of the person against whom relief is sought." Here, there is not even an assertion of wrongful conduct by Franken. Even if there may be equitable grounds for relief other than those recognized in *Plaza National*, the facts here would certainly fall short.

17. The chief reason for denying equitable relief to Dalton is that he waited too long to take the necessary action. We first note that Dalton did not make a written request to the Trustee that the Trustee abandon the right of redemption. Second, Dalton's efforts to redeem the property did not begin until after the Trustee had abandoned the right of redemption as an asset of the bankruptcy estate on June 2, 1994. Evidence was adduced at trial that Dalton received word several days before the redemption rights were abandoned that the Trustee was likely to abandon these rights, and nothing would have prevented Dalton from inquiring about bank financing even earlier than that. Yet Dalton waited until after the Trustee had filed the notice of abandonment to begin to take the necessary steps to effectuate a redemption.

18. In addition, Dalton's arguments that factors beyond his control prevented him from providing cash by June 13, 1994, are not as persuasive as Dalton's recitation of the facts would seem to indicate. When the Trustee abandoned the right of redemption on June 2, 1994, Dalton knew that he was beginning the process of redemption late in the game. His margin for error with regard to procedural matters and processing delays was slim to none. Nevertheless, he allowed minor procedural matters to go unchecked, which contributed to the delay in obtaining and processing the necessary funds.

19. We do not agree that the equities of this case required the district court to grant the untimely redemption on grounds of fairness. As our Supreme Court said in *Richardson v. Pacheco,* 35 N.M. 243, 245, 294 P. 328, 329 (1930):

> the statute gives the mortgagor nine months in which to recover his property. . . . He who waits until the last day to seek out the purchaser takes the risk of missing him. It is effective action, not good intentions, that the statute calls for.

CONCLUSION

20. The decision of the district court is affirmed.

21. IT IS SO ORDERED.

NOTES AND QUESTIONS

1. In accord with the *Dalton* case is a later New Mexico case, Brown v. Trujillo, 88 P.3d 881 (N.M. App. 2004). In its opinion the court in that case states the following:

> In general, there are two situations in which a court will use its equitable powers to grant a debtor an extension of the redemption period. In the first type of situation, the debtor fulfills all of the requirements of the redemption statute, but redemption is not complete because of a clerical error or technical mix-up. . . . In the second type of situation, courts look for evidence of fraud, deceit, or collusion to justify the grant of a redemption period extension.

The Court then refused to permit an extension of the redemption period as the alleged misconduct by the purchaser was too trivial and there was "no indication that Debtor was ready, willing, and able to tender the proper amount within the redemption period, notwithstanding Purchaser's misconduct."

2. The New Mexico statute permitting the parties to shorten the redemption period, a shortening that the parties in the *Dalton* case had agreed to, provides as follows:

**N.M. Stat. Ann. § 39-5-19 (Michie 2003). Application;
shorter redemption period**
> . . . The parties to any such instrument [being foreclosed] may, by its terms, shorten the redemption period to not less than one month, but the district court may in such cases, upon a sufficient showing before judgment that redemption will be effected, increase the period of redemption to not to exceed nine months notwithstanding the terms of such instrument.

Are there justifiable policy reasons for this statute that probably motivated the legislature to adopt it or is it merely the result of lobbying pressure by politically powerful lender interests?

3. In states that permit postforeclosure redemption, more than one person with rights to redeem may wish to redeem. A problem then can arise as to which of these persons has a preferred right to redeem. The usual position is that if there are several junior lienors, seniority determines the preference. For example, a second mortgagee will be given redemption rights over a third mortgagee. The privilege of redemption may be given in successive periods to junior lienors in accord with their seniority. But if a junior lienor redeems, he may be subject to reredemption by a more senior party during the post-foreclosure period. See generally Durfee and Doddridge, Redemption from Foreclosure Sale — the Uniform Mortgage Act, 23 Mich. L. Rev. 825, 845 (1925); and 4 American Law of Property § 16.177 (Casner ed. 1952).

Why is it not inevitable that if a junior party chooses to redeem, the senior party with redemption rights will also choose to redeem? Why is it that some parties with redemption rights seek to redeem and others do not?

b. Federal Preemption

Skip to 264

United States v. Stadium Apartments, Inc.

425 F.2d 358 (9th Cir. 1970)

DUNIWAY, Circuit Judge: This case presents the question whether state redemption statutes should apply when the Federal Housing Authority (FHA) forecloses a mortgage which it has guaranteed. We hold that such statutes do not apply.

The federal statute here involved is Title VI of the National Housing Act, 12 U.S.C. §§ 1736-1746a. The stated objective of Title VI is "to assist in relieving the acute shortage of housing . . . available to veterans of World War II at prices within their reasonable ability to pay. . . ." 12 U.S.C. § 1738(a). The statute confers authority upon the Secretary (formerly the Commissioner) "to make such rules and regulations as may be necessary to carry out the provisions of this subchapter." 12 U.S.C § 1742. Such regulations were promulgated, and those that were in force in November 1949, when the mortgage here in question was executed and insured appear in the 1947 Supplement to the Code of Federal Regulations. (24 C.F.R. § 580 (1947 Supp.).) Citations to C.F.R. in this opinion are to the 1947 supplement.

The way in which the Act and regulations operated are well illustrated in this case. In 1949, appellee Stadium Apartments, Inc., desired to construct, under Title VI, an apartment house in Caldwell, Idaho. It applied to Prudential Insurance Company for a loan. Such a loan was eligible for insurance under 12 U.S.C. § 1743(a). The conditions for eligibility are set out in 12 U.S.C. § 1743(b). The mortgagor must be approved by the Secretary, who can impose certain regulations upon both the mortgagor and the property mortgaged. Certain terms of the mortgage are also prescribed. Application for approval was made, as required by 24 C.F.R. §§ 580.1-580.7. The FHA then issued a commitment of insurance, as required by 24 C.F.R. § 580.8. The mortgage was executed upon a form prescribed by FHA, and accepted for insurance. 24 C.F.R. §§ 580.10-580.37. The amount of the insured loan was $130,000. The mortgage contained this provision:

"The Mortgagor, to the extent permitted by law, hereby waives the benefit of any and all homestead and exemption laws and of any right to a stay or redemption and the benefit of any moratorium law or laws."

Stadium Apartments defaulted in 1966, and Prudential assigned the mortgage to the Secretary of Housing and Urban Development, pursuant to 12 U.S.C. § 1743(c). The Secretary paid Prudential the amount then due, as required by 12 U.S.C. § 1743(c). The United States then obtained a default judgment foreclosing the mortgage, 12 U.S.C. §§ 1713(k), 1743(f). The district judge, in spite of the foregoing provision, framed the foreclosure decree to allow for a one-year period of redemption, as provided by 2 Idaho Code § 11-402. The question is whether this was error.

Stadium Apartments, Inc. having defaulted, is not represented here. Because the question is of some importance, we were disturbed that the government had chosen to appeal this uncontested case, when hitherto the FHA has at times consented to decrees providing for post-sale redemption rights as required by state laws. We therefore determined, following the initial oral argument in which only government counsel appeared, that the Attorneys General of the states within our circuit and of the Territory of Guam should be invited to submit amicus curiae briefs. The State of California has done so, taking a position opposed to that advocated by the government. Washington, Arizona and Guam adopted California's view. We were also unsure that the government's position in this case comported with the policies of various federal lending agencies; hence, we requested information from the government regarding such policies, as well as relevant statistics on past lending practices. Armed with this information, and additional briefs, and having now had the benefit of further oral argument, we are more fully prepared to render our decision.

It is settled that the applicable law is federal. In a decision that has become a leading case on the question, United States v. View Crest Garden Apts., Inc., 9 Cir., 1959, 268 F.2d 380, 381, arising under the National Housing Act, Title II, 12 U.S.C. § 1707 ff. we held: "But we do find it to be clear that the *source* of the law governing the relations between the United States and the parties to the mortgage here involved is federal. (Citations omitted) . . . It is therefore equally clear that if the law of the State of Washington is to have any application in the foreclosure proceeding it is not because it applies of its own force, but because either the Congress, the FHA, or the Federal Court adopts the local rule to further federal policy." 268 F.2d at 382.

The first question is whether the Congress adopted state law in its definition of "mortgage" and "first mortgage." California argues that it did. The language relied upon appears in 12 U.S.C. § 1736(a), and reads: "The term 'mortgage' means a first mortgage on real estate, in fee simple, or on a leasehold (1) under a lease for not less than ninety-nine years which is renewable; or (2) under a lease having a period of not less than fifty years to run from the date the mortgage was executed; and the term 'first mortgage' means such classes of first liens as are commonly given to secure advances on, or the unpaid purchase price of, real estate, under the laws of the State in which the real estate is located, together with the credit instruments, if any, secured thereby."

We rejected California's argument in *View Crest*, supra, where identical language in 12 U.S.C. § 1707 was relied upon. We said: "The argument is that in adopting the state definition of 'first mortgage,' Congress intended to adopt *all* the incidents of the mortgage relation under state law including remedies on default and the appointment of receivers. That this is not the case is clear from reading section

1713 of the same Act which defines certain acts as being in default (part g) and sets out certain remedies that the FHA can pursue such as institution of foreclosure (part k) proceedings without reference to whether or not there is such a remedy for the default described in the State where the property is located. Moreover, there is no apparent reason for assuming that Congress is incorporating by reference certain duties under state law also meant to restrict the United States to the state remedies for breach of those duties. . . ." 268 F.2d at 382.

We proceeded to point out the convenience inherent in defining "first mortgage" in terms of local law, thus making available local recording acts, and continued: "A different set of factors come into play when the planning stage and the working stages of the agreement have been terminated. After a default the sole situation presented is one of remedies. Commercial convenience in utilizing local forms and recording devices familiar to the community is no longer a significant factor. Now the federal policy to protect the treasury and to promote the security of federal investment which in turn promotes the prime purpose of the Act — to facilitate the building of homes by the use of federal credit — becomes predominant. Local rules limiting the effectiveness of the remedies available to the United States for breach of a federal duty can not be adopted." 268 F.2d at 383.

We think that the validity of this approach is emphasized by the fact that the definition relied upon does *not* refer to state law in defining "mortgage"; it does so only in defining "first mortgage." And the statute now before us, like the statute considered in *View Crest,* defines default without reference to state law (12 U.S.C. § 1743(c)) and provides for remedies without reference to state law (12 U.S.C. § 1743(c)) and incorporating the provisions of § 1713(k). No other federal statute is relied upon.[3]

We conclude that the Congress did not adopt state redemption statutes as part of the federal law.

The second question is, did the FHA adopt those statutes? California says that it did, relying on two arguments. First, it points to the regulations. 24 C.F.R. § 580.18 provides: "The mortgage must contain a provision or provisions, satisfactory to the Commissioner, giving to the mortgagee, in the event of default or foreclosure of the mortgage, such rights and remedies for the protection and preservation of the property covered by the mortgage and the income therefrom, as are available under the law or custom of the jurisdiction." No similar provision exists for the mortgagor. Instead, 24 C.F.R. § 580.21 merely provides: "The mortgage may contain such other terms, conditions and provisions with respect to . . . foreclosure proceedings . . . and other matters as the Commissioner may in his discretion prescribe or approve." To be eligible for insurance the mortgage must be executed on a form approved by the Federal Housing Commissioner. (4 C.F.R. § 580.10.)

We cannot find in this language an adoption of state redemption statutes. If anything can be said for it, it is that § 580.21 permits a provision against such rights.

Second, California points to the waiver language contained in the mortgage, quoted above in our statement of facts, and particularly to the phrase "to the extent permitted by law." This phrase, California says, must refer to Idaho law, because (1) there is no other law to which it can refer and (2) the mortgage form was prepared for use in Idaho. The argument is buttressed by the contention that there are no

---

3. 28 U.S.C. § 2410(c) provides for a one-year post-sale right of redemption as a condition of jurisdiction over the United States when the United States is a junior lienor. This provision is made inapplicable to the National Housing Act by 12 U.S.C. § 1701(k).

federal homestead or exemption laws, or rights to a stay, or redemption or moratorium laws. . . . We agree that such laws are state laws, but the question is, what law is
referred to as permitting that their benefits be waived? It must be the law applicable
to this mortgage, which is, as we have seen, federal law. And there is no federal law
which says that FHA cannot condition its participation upon waiver of the benefit of
such state laws. The provision is in general terms, applicable in any state; it is
obviously not specifically adapted to Idaho law. We find the waiver provision merely
precautionary, and not an adoption of the local law.

Finally, we come to the third question: should the federal courts adopt the local
law granting a post-foreclosure sale right of redemption in those states where it
exists? Here, both authority and policy convince us that they should not.

Every federal appellate case dealing with the government's foreclosure remedy
under insured mortgages applies federal law to assure the protection of the federal
program against loss, state law to the contrary notwithstanding. Most of the cases
cite and apply the principles of *View Crest*. Many cases rely upon express provisions
in the mortgage that are in conflict with local law, but frequently couch the decision
in broader terms. Several of these cases involve appointment of a receiver pending
foreclosure. One such case holds that the government can collect and retain the
rents during the period of redemption (consented to by the government), contrary
to local Idaho law. . . .

Many cases simply rely on principles of federal law, in the absence of directly
applicable federal statutes or regulations.

Through all of these cases there runs a dominant rationale, that stated by us in
View Crest, supra — "Now [after default] the federal policy to protect the treasury
and to promote the security of federal investment which in turn promotes the
prime purpose of the Act — to facilitate the building of homes by the use of federal
credit — becomes predominant. *Local rules limiting the effectiveness of the remedies
available to the United States for breach of a federal duty can not be adopted.*" (268 F.2d at
383, emphasis added.)

California relies heavily upon two cases, United States v. Yazell, 1966, 382 U.S.
341, 86 S. Ct. 500, 15 L. Ed. 2d 404, and Bumb v. United States, 9 Cir., 1960, 276 F.2d
729. We are convinced that the facts of these two cases are distinguishable.

Here, too, we deal with the remedy, and as we have seen, in every such case
involving federally insured mortgages, the courts have applied federal law "for the
protection of the treasury and to promote the security of the federal investment."

Reasons of policy dictate the same result. In the first place, only 26 of the states
provide for post-foreclosure redemption. The periods of redemption vary widely.[4]

4. The following is a list, supplied by the government, of the state laws imposing post-foreclosure
redemption periods, other than Idaho, and the periods prescribed: "7 Alabama Code (Recomp. 1958)
727 (2 years); Alaska Statutes 09.45.190, 09.35.250 (1 year; 4 Ariz. Rev. Stat. 12-1282 (6 months); 3A Ark.
Stat. 1947 Ann. 30-440 (1 year); Cal. Code Civ. Proc. 725a (1 year); Colorado Rev. Stat. (1963) 118-9-
2 (6 months); 77 Ill. Ann. Stat. 18c (1 year); 4 Kan. Stat. Ann. 60-2414 (6 to 18 months); Kentucky Rev.
Stat. 426.220 (1 year); 14 Maine Rev. Stat. Ann. 6204 (1 year); Mich. Stat. Ann. 27A.3140, M.C.L.A.
§ 600.3140 (6 months); Minn. Stat. Ann. 580.23 (6 months); 29 Vernon's Ann. Mo. Stat. 443.410 (1 year);
7 Rev. Code Mont. 93-5836(2) (1 year); 1 Nev. Stat. 21.210 (1 year); 5 N. Mex. Stat. Ann. 24-2-19, 24-2-19.1
(9 months); 6 N. Dak. Cent. Code 32-19-18 (1 year); 1 Or. Rev. Stat. 23.560 (1 year); S.D. Comp. Laws
(1967) 21-52-1 et seq. (1 year); Tenn. Code Ann. 64-801 (2 years); Utah Rules Civ. Proc., Rule 69 (f)(3)
(6 months); 4 Vermont Stat. Ann. Title 12, App. III, Rule 39 (1 year); Rev. Code Wash. Ann. 6.24.140
(8 months or a year); Wyoming Stat. 1-480 (6 months).

Wisconsin proposes the foreclosure sale until a one year period for redemption after judgment has
expired. Wisconsin Stat. Ann. 278.10(2)."

So do other conditions to redemption and the rules governing right to possession, right to rents, making repairs, and other matters arising during the redemption period. . . . There is a split of authority as to whether the right of redemption can be waived. Similarly, there is a split of authority as to the right of the mortgagee to recover the value of improvements made during the redemption period. It would be contrary to the teaching of every case that we have cited to hold that there is a different federal policy in each state, thus making FHA "subject to the vagaries of the laws of the several states." Clearfield Trust Co. v. United States, 1943, 318 U.S. 363, 367, 63 S. Ct. 573, 575, 87 L. Ed. 838. Which policy is to be the federal policy, that of the states which do not provide for a period of redemption, or that of those which do? And if the policy is to be the latter, is it to embrace, in each state, all of the special rules applicable in that state alone? Is it to be expanded to establish a federal right of redemption in each state where none exists under local law?

In response to our request, the government has informed us of the views of federal agencies involved in the lending or insuring of funds for private housing purposes. These include, in addition to the Federal Housing Administration, the Farmers Home Administration of the Department of Agriculture, acting under 42 U.S.C. § 1471 ff., and the Veterans Administration, acting under 38 U.S.C. § 1800 ff. We quote the government's response: "The Farmers Home Administration, the Federal Housing Administration, and the Veterans Administration have informed us that their experience has indicated that the imposition of post-foreclosure-sale redemption periods makes the foreclosure remedy more costly and administratively time-consuming in those states whose local law so provides. Generally, the reasons given in support of this conclusion are . . . that existence of a post-sale period for redemption chills bidding at the foreclosure sale, forcing the United States to buy the property at the sale and to hold it (paying meanwhile the costs of maintenance) until the expiration of the period, when it finally can give good title to a purchaser." Additional reasons stated by the government are quoted [below].[7]

---

7. "The Farmers Home Administration has stated that where post-sale redemption periods have been imposed, the mortgaged property may, after sale and before expiration of the redemption period, 'stand unoccupied and unattended for considerable periods of time and consequently [may] deteriorate substantially in value, to the detriment of the financial interest of the United States and without concomitant benefit to any other party.' Similarly, the Veterans Administration reported to us that where a post-sale redemption period is imposed unless the former owner redeems timely, the mortgagee or his assignee are obligated to pay holding costs during the redemption period, i.e., taxes, public improvements, if any, the cost of repairs to preserve the security and the cost of hazard insurance premium when necessary. There is also for consideration the interest normally accruing on the outstanding investment. Moreover, many of these properties have been abandoned and must remain vacant during redemption periods. In many instances they are subject to extreme vandalism during these periods which is, of course, costly to the holder.

"Most pertinent to the present case, of course, were the comments of the Federal Housing Administration concerning foreclosures on multi-family projects like that involved here. The Federal Housing Administration reported to us: 'It is perhaps the normal situation to find any project in foreclosure to be in need of substantial repair. Many mortgagors, during a period of diminishing income, utilize the net income to keep the mortgage current as long as possible, keeping maintenance expenses to a bare minimum. When the evil day arrives that the income will no longer cover the mortgage payments, he falls into default, and the subject of the foreclosure action is a property which requires substantial expenditures to place it in properly habitable condition, and to make it attractive to the rental market. With the notable exception of Alabama, redemption statutes permit a foreclosure purchaser to receive from a redemptioner little more than the price bid at the foreclosure sale, so that a purchaser is well advised to keep rehabilitation expenses to an absolute minimum until the redemption period expires. As a practical matter, this delays the day when FHA, as such purchaser can safely embark on a program involving capital expenditures, thereby delaying the day when the property may be placed in condition for its best use and for advantageous sale which will reimburse the insurance fund for a portion of the loss incurred as a result of the mortgagor's default.'"

We do not find the policy arguments presented by California convincing. First, it is argued that the purpose of the redemption statutes is to force the mortgagee and others to bid the full market price at the sale. We assume that this is the purpose; we are not convinced that the statutes accomplish it. What third party would bid and pay the full market value, knowing that he cannot have the property to do with as he wishes until a set period has gone by, and that at the end of the period he may not get it, but instead may be forced to accept a payment which may or may not fully reimburse him for his outlays? In some states he cannot get possession. In some states if he does get possession and collects rents, they will be deducted from his reimbursement. . . . In some states, if he makes repairs, he will not be repaid for his outlays. These are precisely the problems which the federal government should not have to face. It is not in the real estate business. It should not have to hold and manage properties for any period longer than is absolutely necessary for it to get back its money. It should not be subjected to the risk that the property will deteriorate, and it should not be left with no means to protect itself against such losses.

Our doubts as to whether the statutes accomplish the purpose is reinforced by the fact that in many states, partly because of those statutes, real estate financing is almost exclusively secured by trust deeds with power of sale. This is certainly true in California, and the statutory right of redemption does not apply to such sales. One is tempted to inquire why, if public policy so strongly favors a post-sale period of redemption, the legislature has not applied it to sales under trust deeds? Perhaps it is because the redemption statute has, in some states, made the use of mortgages almost a dead letter.

Moreover, the policy of FHA is to bid the fair market value at the foreclosure sale. For this purpose, it has the property carefully appraised before bidding. See Book 2, Volume VII, Sec. 72926 of the FHA Manual. It is authorized by 12 U.S.C. § 1713(k) to "bid any sum up to but not in excess of the total unpaid indebtedness secured by the mortgage, plus taxes, insurance, foreclosure costs, fees, and other expenses. . . ." It bids fair market value for its own protection as well as that of the mortgagor and other lienors. It is limited to the amount specified because the objective is to recover its loss on the mortgage insurance, not to put the government in the business of buying and speculating in real property. Presumably, if the property is worth more, others will increase the bid, the government will be paid in full, and the excess will go to junior lien holders and, if there be sufficient funds, to the mortgagor.

It is also suggested that a purpose of the redemption statutes is to protect junior lienors. Perhaps. But if the objective of the statutes is to obtain bids equal to market value, and if as is argued, the bidding would be lower in the absence of the statutes, then junior lienors could more easily protect themselves in the latter situation. They could buy the property at the sale for less. It is always open to the junior lienors to protect themselves by bidding. They take with notice of the senior lien. Here, the government's judgment was for $93,804.97; its bid was $55,100. The court found the value of the property to be $58,000. The deficiency judgment is for $37,728.88. This is a singularly inappropriate case in which to be concerned about junior lien holders. They simply have no equity in the property. There is no evidence that second mortgagees or contractors are less willing to extend credit on the security of junior liens in the states that have no redemption statutes than they are in the states that do, or in California when the first lien is almost always secured by a trust deed rather than by a mortgage.

Nor is it accurate to say that the application of state redemption rights does not tie up government funds; as this case illustrates, it does do so. Under 12 U.S.C. § 1743(c) the mortgagee has the option of assigning the mortgage to the Secretary and being paid the full amount of the guarantee, instead of itself foreclosing. As might be expected, that is what Prudential did in this case. Why would any mortgagee do otherwise, when by so assigning it can receive the full benefit of the insurance without having to incur the expense and risk attendant upon foreclosure? Under the statute, Prudential received the full benefit of the insurance — government obligations equal to the then total value of the mortgage, in this case more than $90,000. If the redemption period applies, the government must wait a year to get its money back — and it may not then get it all, or even as much as it bid.

We conclude that the Idaho statute providing for right of redemption is not here applicable.

Finally, we note that the district court's decision did not purport to balance state and federal policies in allowing the period of redemption. Instead, it reasoned that Prudential (the original mortgagee) would have been subject to the redemption rights provided by state law, and that the United States could have no more rights than Prudential. Even assuming arguendo that Prudential would have been subject to state law, it does not follow that the federal government is limited to the remedies of the private mortgagee.

That portion of the judgment providing for a right and period of redemption is reversed and the matter is remanded to the district court with directions to modify the judgment in a manner consistent with this opinion.

ELY, Circuit Judge (dissenting): I respectfully dissent. The majority, with broad strokes, erases highly significant redemptive rights created by statute in the Territory of Guam and eight of the states comprising our Circuit as well as equitable rights of redemption hitherto applied by the courts of Hawaii. These rights are deeply rooted in history, founded on an equitable principle applied through centuries to protect the temporarily disadvantaged without working significant prejudice against his creditor. The approach which I take is made, not only in the interests of local mortgagors involved in the federal housing program, but also in the interests of the federal program itself. I do not dispute the fact that federal abrogation of state-created rights is often necessary for the protection of federal programs, but I have been unable to accept the majority's proposition that its dramatic result is here warranted by an overpowering motive of federal self defense. Time after time, the Congress of the United States has created programs through which private loans are guaranteed by the federal government. In not one of those programs has Congress ever prescribed that, in connection with those programs, state redemptive rights, either statutory or equitable, are eliminated. To me it is inconceivable that the members of Congress, when they enacted the many federal lending programs now extant, were either ignorant of, or blind to, the existence of state redemptive rights in foreclosure proceedings. When the Country's legislators have apparently deemed it unnecessary, in protecting the interests of the federal government, to strike down the states' rights in question, I think it presumptuous that a federal court should substitute its policy judgment to the contrary. My Brother Duniway's opinion, while written with his characteristic scholarship and technical precision, does not, insofar as I can see, demonstrate the existence of any controlling precedent requiring the conclusion which is reached. In this light, as well as in that of other considerations which I shall discuss, I respectfully submit that the majority's opinion constitutes an unnecessary intrusion into the legitimate local affairs of nine western states, and of the Territory of Guam, and moreover, represents an unwarranted judicial usurpation of federal legislative power.

I can accept the assumption that federal law is controlling. United States v. View Crest Garden Apts., Inc., 268 F.2d 380 (9th Cir. 1959).

But my proposition is that we should give effect to the pertinent and equitable state law by incorporating it into the federal program. The Supreme Court did exactly that with respect to a state coverture law in United States v. Yazell, 382 U.S. 341, 86 S. Ct. 500, 15 L. Ed. 2d 404 (1966), and our court did the same with respect to a state "bulk sale statute in Bumb v. United States, 276 F.2d 729 (9th Cir. 1960). The controlling criterion on the question is whether the state law can be given effect without either conflicting with federal policy or destroying needed uniformity in the pertinent federal law in its operation within the various states. United States v. Yazell, supra at 352, 86 S. Ct. 500. Thus, we should first reach an understanding of the purpose and effects of state redemption statutes.

The statutes can best be understood through a brief review of their historical development. The original method of mortgage foreclosure was known as strict foreclosure, a method whereby, on default, the mortgagee obtained a court decree awarding the mortgagor's interest in the security to the mortgagee. This offensive procedure was subject to severe defects, the most obvious of which was that the mortgagor faced the possibility of forfeiting all his equity in the property in the event that the property was worth more than the unpaid balance on the debt.

The harshness of strict foreclosure led to the concept of foreclosure by sale. Theoretically, the property was to be sold to the highest bidder with the mortgagee having first claim to the proceeds and the mortgagor obtaining his equity in the form of whatever surplus remained. This approach was expected to yield more even results by allowing the competitive market to set the value of the land instead of the "value" being set at the amount of the unpaid debt as was the fact under strict foreclosure. Unfortunately, this expectation was frustrated by reason of the immense advantages favoring the mortgagee at the sale. First, it was unnecessary for the mortgagee to raise and expend any cash up to the amount of the unpaid debt. Secondly, there would not often be an interested outside buyer, or junior lienholder with cash, at the precise time of the sale. Thus, the senior mortgagee was assured of being almost always the only bidder at the sale. The junior lienors, in particular, suffered under this method since their interests were cut off by judicial sale. Since they had no weapons with which to force the sale price above the amount of the senior's claim, they often realized nothing on their claims.

The response of many jurisdictions to the unsatisfactory results of the foreclosure-by-sale procedure was the adoption of a statutory redemption period. The basic design of statutory redemption consists of giving the mortgagor and those claiming under him (including junior lienors) the right to redeem the property from the purchaser at the sale within a specified period by paying, *not* the balance of the debt secured, but the price paid at the sale. The objective of the redemption right is that the mortgagee or other bidders, if any, shall bid not less than the fair market value of the land, since otherwise the purchaser risks being divested of the land by redemption at less than its market value.

The key to understanding the statutory redemption right lies in the proposition that the statute's operation is in the nature of a threat. When redemption is exercised, it is thereby evidenced that the mortgagee has not bid adequately at the sale and the statute has not had its intended effect. On the other hand, if the threat functions successfully and the mortgagee does bid adequately, then the mortgagor and junior lienors, if any, will have been satisfied to the full value of the property and there will be no reason for exercising the redemption right. If he bids the full market value of the property, then the mortgagee may rest secure in the knowledge that it will not be redeemed. See generally Durfee & Doddridge, Redemption From Foreclosure Sale, 23 Mich. L. Rev. 825, 827-834 (1925); Note, Redemption From Judicial Sales, 5 U. Chi. L. Rev. 625, 626 (1938).

With the foregoing as background, the relation of redemption statutes to the federal housing policies can be more clearly analyzed. The particular program involved here, War Housing Insurance, is only one of many administered under various Acts of Congress. This program, as the majority notes, is designed to stimulate housing for veterans; other programs are designed for rural housing, poverty relief, urban renewal, etc. All of the programs have as their basic goal the stimulation of construction by guaranteeing that lenders, contractors, and suppliers will not suffer losses on extending credit to builders and owners. Of course, some programs are more concerned with the owners and their need for housing than they are with the market for mortgages. This would be true, for instance, of a program designed to supply single-family housing while it would not be as crucial a consideration in the construction of multiple dwelling units. Thus, protection of the mortgagor's interests takes on greater or less significance depending on the type of program involved. It seems crystal clear to me, however, that the type of balancing involved in deciding what rights the mortgagor should have requires legislative attention to the entire scope of housing programs. I will deal with the Congress' role in this question later.

It seems no less clear to me that, disregarding the question of protection of the individual mortgagor, the goals of *any* federal housing program could not be served by the majority's decision. From the viewpoint of a mortgagor in a state with redemption provisions, and in the light of the majority's decision, it would be more desirable to finance privately than to finance through an FHA guaranteed mortgage. Even more important, potential junior lienors, such as contractors and suppliers, will be less willing to extend credit under these circumstances. Nor can junior lienors protect themselves, as the majority suggests, by bidding at the foreclosure sale. I have already explained that one reason for the existence of the redemption statutes is that the enormous leverage of the foreclosing mortgagee is not matched by junior lienors, who typically have very small cash reserves and never have the first "paid up" interest.

Thus one effect of the majority's decision will be to lower the attractiveness of FHA financing in states that have enacted redemption statutes. Other states have other methods of protecting both mortgagors and junior lienors that will not be matched in the redemption states.[1] Therefore, the uniformity among the states for which the Government argues cannot possibly be furthered by the majority's decision. Instead, uniformity would be furthered by conforming federal programs with state law.

---

1. Some states provide for a statutory appraisal and prohibit foreclosure for less than a percentage of that value, while other states depend on anti-deficiency legislation and upset prices. See Jones, Mortgages § 1611(a).

The Government, and also the majority, make several arguments designed to show that redemption statutes are neither important nor necessary. The first is that the statutes do not work because no third party will bid at the sale, knowing that he will be subject to redemption. The statutes, as I have tried to explain, are not the least bit concerned with the actions of third parties since they were necessitated by the observation that third parties do not ordinarily bid at foreclosure sales in any event. Instead of trying to stimulate bidding at the sale, they set up the more realistic possibility that the property will be redeemed if the mortgagee's bid is inadequate.

The majority also asserts that redemption rights are unimportant because most financing in modern times is accomplished through the use of trust deeds, which do not provide for redemption rights. There may be valid reasons for the distinction,[2] but we need not be concerned with them here. What is important is that the legislatures of the states have allocated certain rights to each method of financing with the result that a choice is available depending on the nature of the transaction and the needs of the parties. Once the parties have selected either method, they should accept all its consequences. Moreover, if redemption rights truly are of negligible importance, then it could be said that the Government has wasted much valuable time in pursuing a frivolous appeal!

The Government argues at one point that the policies of the redemption right are satisfied by the alleged practice of the FHA carefully to appraise the fair market value of the property and to make its bid accordingly at the foreclosure sale. It is interesting to note that the Government argues elsewhere that the effect of redemption statutes is to *depress* bidding at the sale. But it is even more interesting, and remarkable, that a federal statute expressly prohibits the agency from bidding more than the unpaid balance on the debt! 12 U.S.C. § 1713(k), as incorporation by 12 U.S.C. § 1743(f).

Even if we assumed that the FHA contravened the prohibitory statute and was in some way bound to continue its asserted practice, such unilateral action of the FHA could not satisfy the premise of the redemption statutes. That premise is that the fair market value is realizable only through the interplay of competing economic forces. This premise is not satisfied by judicial sale because of the demonstrated falsity of the assumption, made by the majority, that a third party will come in to force the price up to market value at the sale. The fact that competing economic forces are necessary is amply shown in the case at bar, since the value of the land was set by the court according to the testimony of one Government witness. This value was less than one-half the original purchase price and far below the unpaid balance on the debt. The Government obtained a deficiency judgment for the difference between the set value and the unpaid debt. The Government then proceeded to buy in the property at the sale for an amount *less than the market value set by the court.*

Remaining unconvinced by the argument that the redemption statutes are unimportant and unnecessary, I can turn to other contentions made by the majority. The first is that the Government should not be required to maintain the

2. Originally, the distinction lay in the conceptualistic notion that the grantor conveyed all his interest through the trust deed, so that, unlike a mortgagor, he had nothing on which to base a right of redemption. More recently, the distinction has been based on such facts as that creditors cannot obtain deficiency judgments when property is sold under a trust deed and that notice requirements are more extensive under trust deeds. See, e.g., Comment, Comparison of California Mortgages, Trust Deeds and Land Sale Contracts, 7 U.C.L.A. L. Rev. 83, 88 (1959); Comment, Trust Deeds: Suit Upon Note Before Security Has Been Exhausted, 20 Calif. L. Rev. 318, 321 (1932).

premises during the redemption period. The majority asserts that the FHA does not have the manpower or the funds to place and keep the property in good repair, especially since the expense of improvements made by the purchaser-mortgagee is not recoverable as part of the redemption price. The first answer to this argument is that some redemption statutes specifically include the cost of upkeep and repair in the redemption price. E.g., Cal. Code Civ. Proc. § 702. In addition, this is one element of redemption that could be molded to fit the Government's legitimate interests, as this court did in Clark Investment Co. v. United States, 364 F.2d 7 (9th Cir. 1966).

I note with some incredulity that the majority cites *Clark Investment* for the proposition that Idaho law requires deduction of collected rents from the redemption price. In *Clark Investment,* this court held that the Idaho law could not be applied to the United States when property is redeemed from it. That decision itself clearly shows that the right of redemption can be maintained without any harm to the FHA because the courts can tailor certain elements of redemption to the benefit of the United States.

Clark Investment also demonstrates that the FHA is not necessarily confined to the same risks and burdens that other financers face. For example, during the redemption period, it can actually make a profit on the property with no more burden on its manpower than any other purchaser would have. Moreover, there is no reason why the Government should not accept a large share of the risks mentioned by the majority. The very purpose of the entire federal housing program is to provide badly needed housing that could not otherwise exist. I cannot imagine why the United States would venture into such a program if it were not willing to accept risks, possibly even greater risks than would be accepted by the normal financing institution.

Nor am I persuaded that redemption periods inordinately tie up federal funds. Since the FHA is limited in its bid to the amount of the unpaid debt, it can expect to have property more valuable than that amount redeemed rather promptly. In the case of less valuable property, it will have to live with the fact that it is facing a loss, no matter what happens. One way in which this loss could be ameliorated would be to hold the property during the period of redemption, a period in which the agency can realize a valuable return on its money in the form of rents. If this is deemed to be too severe a burden upon the FHA, then the Congress is best equipped to recognize any such supposed burden and to relieve the agency from it.

Next, the Government argues, albeit weakly, that the issue is foreclosed by prior case law standing for the proposition that remedies under the federal housing programs must be uniform, without regard to the laws of the individual states. The cases cited by the Government do not support such a broad proposition. Principal reliance is on Clearfield Trust Co. v. United States, 318 U.S. 363, 63 S. Ct. 573, 87 L. Ed. 838 (1943), and United States v. View Crest Garden Apartments, 268 F.2d 380 (9th Cir. 1959). *Clearfield Trust* dealt with the question of what law should be applied to the case of a forged endorsement on a United States check. There, the Court noted that a single piece of commercial paper issued by the United States may easily be involved in several transactions in different states. Therefore, the possible confusions and uncertainty required a uniform rule that could be constructed by the courts. Here, we have a single transaction within a single state and there can be no uncertainty or divergence of results if the state law is applied.

View Crest Garden Apartments is much closer to the facts of this case, since it dealt with whether to apply state law in the appointment of a receiver after default on an FHA mortgage. The court relied principally on the distinction between the rights of the parties and the remedies available for the protection of those rights. After pointing out that Congress had adopted state laws for convenience in defining the rights of the parties, the court went on to note that after default the need for convenience had terminated and that the then paramount interest was furtherance of the policies of the act by attempting to insure certainty of return on the investment. In the opinion's bearing on our case, certain of its language is remarkably significant. That language is, "It is urged that to hold that federal law applie[d] would result in great hardship to mortgagors who would thereby be deprived of all rights under state law such as the right of redemption. We do not think that such a conclusion necessarily follows. A court confronted with that question could determine it by weighting the federal interest against the particular local policy involved. *If the considerations weighted by the court suggest an adoption of local law, such as the local rule on redemption, that could be done.*" Id. at 383 (emphasis added).

Although the court in *View Crest* evidently believed that redemption is more in the nature of a right than a remedy (or means of cutting off a remedy), I prefer not to rest on the conclusionary use of labels. Accepting the court's guidance that the involved interests should be weighed, I fail to see in what way the state interest conflicts with the true and most praiseworthy interests of the federal government. Certainly the minor inconveniences suffered by the FHA in managing the property is outweighed by the benefit to the national program in protecting the interests of contractors and suppliers. Therefore, we need not balance national interest against state interest but could simply give effect to all the policy considerations underlying both federal and state law.

Finally, I come to the Government's lame contention that the failure of Congress to provide for redemption rights is the equivalent of an express provision that state redemption laws should not be recognized. The logical absurdity of this argument is, of itself, sufficient to subvert the contention. But the abundant statutory and regulatory language apparently adopting state law in this context should not be overlooked. For example, the statutory definition of the rights of the United States itself provides that "the term 'first mortgage' means such classes of first liens as are commonly given to secure advances on, or the unpaid purchase price of, real estate, *under the laws of the State, in which the real estate is located, . . .*" 12 U.S.C. § 1707(a) (emphasis added). The regulations provide, "The mortgage must contain a provision or provisions, satisfactory to the Commissioner, giving to the mortgagee, in the event of default or foreclosure of the mortgage, such rights and remedies for the protection and preservation of the property covered by the mortgage and the income therefrom, *as are available under the law or custom of the jurisdiction.*" 24 C.F.R. § 580.18 (1968) (emphasis added). Even the waiver in the present mortgage, on which the Government relied so strongly in the court below, provides that it is effective "to the extent permitted by law." Surely, we must presume that this language refers to the law of Idaho, for the federal law contains no such corresponding provisions to be waived or to which the waiver could be applicable.

At the very least, it seems unusual for the Government to argue that congressional silence can be equated with express abrogation of state-created rights. It is especially significant that, as we were informed on oral argument, the FHA has introduced several bills to achieve the result reached here, but Congress has consistently refused to adopt this approach. The Supreme Court has stated on more than one occasion that rights should not be displaced or eliminated without the clearest legislative mandate. United States v. Shimer, 367 U.S. 374, 81 S. Ct. 1554, 6 L. Ed. 2d 908 (1961); Mitchell v. Robert De Mario Jewelry, Inc., 361 U.S. 288, 80 S. Ct. 332, 4 L. Ed. 2d 323 (1960). I could not hold that silence on the part of Congress can be taken to effect an abrogation of time-honored state rights, derived from the most exalted principles of equity and so carefully designed, not only for the protection of debtors and creditors alike, but also for the promotion of the general economic welfare of the public at large.

I would affirm.

NOTES AND QUESTIONS

1. Both the majority and dissenting opinions in the *Stadium Apartments* case are thorough and well reasoned. In your opinion how should the *Stadium Apartments* case have been decided and why?

2. The United States Supreme Court has made some effort to resolve the question of when state law should be adopted as federal law in cases in which the federal government is asserting or foreclosing a lien. In United States v. Kimbell Foods, Inc., 440 U.S. 715, 728-729 (1979), the Court set forth general tests for deciding whether or not to adopt state law in such lien cases:

> Undoubtedly, federal programs that "by their nature are and must be uniform in character throughout the Nation" necessitate formulation of controlling federal rules. [Citations omitted.] Conversely, when there is little need for a nationally uniform body of law, state law may be incorporated as the federal rule of decision. Apart from considerations of uniformity, we must also determine whether application of state law would frustrate specific objectives of the federal programs. If so, we must fashion special rules solicitous of those federal interests. Finally, our choice-of-law inquiry must consider the extent to which application of a federal rule would disrupt commercial relationships predicated on state law.

Perhaps because of their generality and ambiguity, the effect of the *Kimbell* tests has been spotty; some courts have been influenced by them, but other courts have ignored them.

3. The courts have taken different positions on federal preemption of state mortgage laws and there is considerable inconsistency among them in their reasoning and decisions. On the federal preemption problem considered by the *Stadium Apartments* and *Kimball* cases and a review of other relevant case law, see Nelson and Whitman, Real Estate Finance Law § 11.6 (4th ed. 2002). At one point Nelson and Whitman come to this conclusion about the problem:

> The question is fundamentally one of policy, and it ought to be resolved by the political branches — the Congress and the agencies that administer the programs. It is within their power to preempt state law by statute or regulation, and in some instances they have done so [citing, as an example, the Multifamily Mortgage Foreclosure Act, 12 U.S.C.A. §§ 3701-3717]. It makes little sense for federal judges to speculate about how obnoxious the state rule is to a federal program, when those who devised and

administer the program can decide for themselves and announce the extent to which state law should govern it. Unless they have done so, or the impairment of the program is obvious and egregious, state law should be followed by the courts. Id. at 147.

4. Deciency Judgments

A real estate mortgage transaction involves the transfer of an interest in land by the mortgagor to the mortagee as security for payment of a debt. The mortgagor has promised to pay the debt and has in addition provided the mortgagee with security to back up that promise. If the mortgagor defaults, the mortgagee generally can resort to the security through foreclosure, and if this fails to produce enough to pay the amount due, <u>the mortgagee usually can obtain a deficiency judgment against the mortgagor for the balance still owed</u>. Of course, if foreclosure produces more than what the mortgagor owes, the mortgagor is entitled to the excess. In case of default by the mortgagor, a mortgagee commonly may, but seldom will, sue on the debt without seeking resort to the security.

In some states deficiency judgments have been highly controversial and restrictions have been placed on mortgagees obtaining such judgments. These restrictions, many of them originating in the depression of the 1930s, reflect popular feeling that mortgage debtors who lose their homes or farms or other lands, especially in adverse economic times, have lost enough and should not be subject to further liability on the underlying debts. It is also felt that foreclosure sales frequently do not bring fair market prices, being forced sales often in depressed periods; hence their prices should not be the basis for determining deficiencies. <u>Deficiency judgment restrictions are mostly statutory</u> and take different forms, such as no deficiency judgment if a certain type of mortgage is foreclosed — a purchase money or nonjudicial power of sale mortgage, for example; or the deficiency may only be sought in a foreclosure proceeding; or the deficiency must be based on a separate determination of fair or reasonable value of the foreclosed property rather than on the foreclosure sale price. Antideficiency legislation varies considerably among the states, and many states have no serious deterrents to a mortgagee securing a deficiency judgment, plus accrued interest and foreclosure expenses, whenever a foreclosure sale price is insufficient to pay off the mortgage debt.

New York Real Property Actions and Proceedings Law

§ 1371 (McKinney 2006)

1. If a person who is liable to the plaintiff for the payment of the debt secured by the mortgage is made a defendant in the action, and has appeared or has been personally served with the summons, the final judgment may award payment by him of the whole residue, or so much thereof <u>as the court may determine to be just and equitable</u>, <u>of the debt remaining unsatisfied</u>, <u>after a sale of the mortgaged property</u> and the application of the proceeds, pursuant to the directions contained in such judgment, the amount thereof to be determined by the court as herein provided.

2. <u>Simultaneously with the making of a motion for an order</u> confirming the sale, provided such motion is made within ninety days after the date of the

consummation of the sale by the delivery of the proper deed of conveyance to the purchaser, the party to whom such residue shall be owing may make a motion in the action for leave to enter a deficiency judgment upon notice to the party against whom such judgment is sought or the attorney who shall have appeared for such party in such action. Such notice shall be served personally or in such other manner as the court may direct. Upon such motion the court, whether or not the respondent appears, shall determine, upon affidavit or otherwise as it shall direct, the fair and reasonable market value of the mortgaged premises as of the date such premises were bid in at auction or such nearest earlier date as there shall have been any market value thereof and shall make an order directing the entry of a deficiency judgment. Such deficiency judgment shall be for an amount equal to the sum of the amount owing by the party liable as determined by the judgment with interest, plus the amount owing on all prior liens and encumbrances with interest, plus costs and disbursements of the action including the referee's fee and disbursements, less the market value as determined by the court or the sale price of the property whichever shall be the higher.

3. If no motion for a deficiency judgment shall be made as herein prescribed the proceeds of the sale regardless of amount shall be deemed to be in full satisfaction of the mortgage debt and no right to recover any deficiency in any action or proceeding shall exist. . . .

move in 90 days

NOTES

1. The New York statute both confirms the mortgagee's right to a deficiency and limits the deficiency to the difference between the amount of claim and the "fair and reasonable market value," not to the difference between the amount of claim and the foreclosure sale price. In practically every state the mortgagee may obtain a judgment for a deficiency — usually without benefit of statute. Through the years, however, courts and legislatures have devised methods to protect the debtor from being victimized by superficial bidding at the sale. There are, of course, provisions for the giving of notice, the time, place, manner, and terms of conducting the sale. A court of equity may refuse to confirm a sale or may set it aside upon evidence of chilled bidding or upon a showing of inadequacy so gross as to "shock the conscience or raise a presumption of fraud or unfairness." See Ballentyne v. Smith, 205 U.S. 285 (1907). Where foreclosure is by power of sale, the mortgagee is not permitted to buy unless the mortgagor has given his consent or, under some statutes, a public officer conducts the sale. Nearly half the states allow the mortgagor (and junior lienors) to redeem from the foreclosure sale upon payment of the sale price plus specified interest; these *statutory rights to redeem,* dating back to the panic of 1837, were intended to dissuade a perfunctory bid on the theory that too low a price would invite redemption. (Since the redemption period may run six months or longer, redemption may cause the very lackluster interest on the part of potential bidders it was expected to prevent.)

The depression of the 1930s gave new impetus to the effort to protect mortgage debtors, for even in normal times the result of a forced sale does not usually reflect the "reasonable" market value of the property. Some states, like New York, abandoned the sale price as the presumptive measure of fair value and forced the mortgagee who was seeking the deficiency judgment to prove "fair and reasonable market value." Fine in theory, except during the 1930s no market existed. Wrestling with this conundrum, some lower courts went back to pre-depression values, until the New York Court of Appeals held that the statute intended to set up a new "equitable standard" in lieu of market value, in which market transactions, if any, were only one item. See Heiman v. Bishop, 272 N.Y. 83, 4 N.E.2d 944 (1936). The values found on the new test were said to approximate tax assessments. See Friedman, Personal Liability on Mortgage Debts in New York, 51 Yale L.J. 382, 396 (1942).

If property is sold at foreclosure for less than fair market value, the mortgagor, under the New York statute, is not entitled to be reimbursed for the difference between the fair market value and the mortgage debt. Evergreen Bank v. D & P Justin's, Inc., 152 A.D.2d 898, 544 N.Y.S.2d 244 (1989).

2. Military personnel are entitled to benefits of The Soldiers' and Sailors' Civil Relief Act of 1940, 50 U.S.C.A. app. §§ 501-591 (1990), now known as the Servicemembers Civil Relief Act, 50 U.S.C.A. §§ 501-596 (1990 & Supp. 2006). This law tolls the statute of limitations during military service, permits a mortgagor to reopen foreclosure after release from duty on proof of a meritorious defense, and authorizes a court to stay foreclosure or execution on a money judgment. Service personnel must be able to show, however, that military service has "materially affected" their ability to meet their debts or defend actions brought against them. On the Act, see Nelson and Whitman, Real Estate Finance Law §§ 8.9-8.11 (4th ed. 2002 and Supp. 2004).

3. Deficiency judgments are possible with strict foreclosure, as is illustrated by a Connecticut statute providing for a judicial valuation and deficiency judgment on motion after the time for redemption has expired. Conn. Gen. Stat. Ann. § 49-14 (1994).

Mid Kansas Fed. S&L v. Dynamic Development Corp.

167 Ariz. 122, 804 P.2d 1310 (1991)

OPINION

FELDMAN, Vice Chief Justice.

A construction lender held notes secured by first and second deeds of trust on a residential developer's property. The lender acquired title to the property at a trustee's sale on the second trust deed and thereafter brought an action against the developer for the balance due on the first notes. The court of appeals held that the lender was precluded from doing so under A.R.S. § 33-814(G)[1] and the rationale of our decision in Baker v. Gardner, 160 Ariz. 98, 770 P.2d 766 (1989).

We must determine whether the anti-deficiency statutes apply to a residential developer and whether a lender may recover the balance owing on the first notes after it has acquired title to the property at the foreclosure sale of its second deed of trust. Rule 23, Ariz. R. Civ. App. P., 17B A.R.S. We have jurisdiction under Ariz. Const. art. 6, § 5(3) and A.R.S. § 12-120.24.

---

1. Then codified as § 33-814(E).

FACTS AND PROCEDURAL HISTORY

A. FACTUAL BACKGROUND

Dynamic Development Corporation (Dynamic) is a developer that builds and sells residential and commercial property. In May 1985, Dynamic secured financing from Mid Kansas Federal Savings and Loan Association (Mid Kansas) for the construction of ten "spec" homes on lots Dynamic owned in a Prescott subdivision. The total loan, amounting to $803,250, was disbursed in the form of ten separate loans, each evidenced by a separate note and secured by a separate deed of trust on a single unimproved lot. Unable to complete construction with the amounts financed under the first notes, Dynamic obtained an additional $150,000 loan from Mid Kansas in January of 1986. This loan was evidenced by a single promissory note and a blanket deed of trust on the seven lots remaining unsold.

The first and second notes came due in the summer of 1986. Two more lots were sold and released from the liens. In the fall of 1986, Mid Kansas notified Dynamic that the five remaining properties would be sold at a trustee's sale if the total debt on the first and second notes was not paid. Dynamic was unable to pay the total balance due, but did sell one more lot prior to the trustee's sale and applied the proceeds to the second note.

Mid Kansas noticed a trustee's sale on the four remaining properties, each of which was by then improved by a substantially finished residence. At the time of the trustee's sale, Dynamic owed Mid Kansas approximately $102,000 on the second note and $425,000 on the four first notes. Originally, the sales on the first deeds were scheduled for the day after the sale on the second deed. On January 20, 1987, the second-position blanket deed of trust was foreclosed by the sale of the four parcels. Mid Kansas purchased the property with a credit bid of the balance owed on the second note. The four first-position sales were postponed and ultimately never held. Having thus acquired title to the property, Mid Kansas now seeks to waive the security of the first liens and sue for the balance due on the first notes.

B. PROCEDURAL BACKGROUND

Mid Kansas's amended complaint stated causes of action for recovery of the balance due under each of the four promissory notes. Mid Kansas moved for partial summary judgment on the four debt claims. The trial court granted the motion and entered judgment for Mid Kansas pursuant to Rule 54(b), Ariz. R. Civ. P., 16 A.R.S.

The court found that Dynamic was in default on the four construction notes in the principal amount of $425,250 plus interest at thirteen percent. The court rejected Dynamic's claim that Mid Kansas had "artificially created a deficiency and now seeks a deficiency judgment against the maker of the notes." The court determined that

under the holding of Southwest Savings and Loan v. Ludi, 122 Ariz. 226 [594 P.2d 92 (1979)], Plaintiff can maintain an action on these notes notwithstanding there was a Trustee's Sale instituted by Plaintiff on a separate deed of trust involving the [same] subject properties.

On appeal, Dynamic argued that Mid Kansas was prohibited from recovering on the promissory notes by the Arizona anti-deficiency statute, A.R.S. §33-814(G). After the release of our opinion in *Baker*, Dynamic filed a supplemental brief asserting that *Ludi* could no longer be read to permit a residential mortgage holder to waive its security and sue on the note. See Southwest Sav. & Loan Ass'n v. Ludi, 122 Ariz. 226, 594 P.2d 92 (1979). Dynamic argued that *Baker* prohibited any attempt to waive the security and sue on the note as a disguised action for deficiency. Therefore, Mid Kansas could not both foreclose the second deed by power of sale and elect to sue Dynamic on the first notes covering the same property.

The court of appeals reversed and remanded the case for entry of judgment for Dynamic. Mid Kansas Fed. Sav. & Loan Ass'n v. Dynamic Dev. Corp., 163 Ariz. 233, 787 P.2d 132 (Ct.App.1989). The court held that under *Baker,* Mid Kansas' attempt to waive the security and sue on the debt was an action for a deficiency, barred after a trustee's sale under §33-814(G). Judge Brooks concurred in the result, but argued that the case should have been decided according to the principles of merger and extinguishment, rather than under the anti-deficiency statute, because he was "not persuaded that a residential developer may claim the statutory protection against deficiency judgments afforded to homeowners under Baker v. Gardner." Id. at 239, 787 P.2d at 138 (Brooks, J., concurring).

Mid Kansas petitioned for review in this court, presenting the following issues for our consideration:

1. Whether commercial developers of residential property who borrow for business purposes are entitled to the benefit of Arizona's consumer anti-deficiency statutes, A.R.S. §§33-729(A) and 33-814(G).
2. Whether Arizona's anti-deficiency statutes apply when the encumbered properties are not actually used as residencies.
3. Whether a lender's election to waive its security and sue upon a construction loan note secured by a deed of trust constitutes an action for a deficiency prohibited by Arizona's anti-deficiency statutes, A.R.S. §§33-729(A) and 33-814(G).

DISCUSSION

A. THE APPLICABILITY OF THE ANTI-DEFICIENCY STATUTES

Arizona has two anti-deficiency statutes. A.R.S. §33-729(A) applies to purchase money mortgages and purchase money deeds of trust foreclosed judicially pursuant to the authority of A.R.S. §33-807(A). A.R.S. §33-814(G) applies to deeds of trust that are foreclosed by trustee's sale, regardless of whether they represent purchase money obligations. Both sections prohibit a deficiency judgment after sale of a parcel of "property of two and one-half acres or less which is limited to and utilized for either a single one-family or single two-family dwelling." A.R.S. §§33-729(A), 33–814(G).

Arizona also has an election of remedies statute within the general law applicable to mortgages. Under A.R.S. §33-722, a mortgagee can foreclose and seek a deficiency judgment or can sue on the note and then execute on the resultant judgment but cannot bring both actions simultaneously. See Washburn, The Judicial and Legislative Response to Price Inadequacy in Mortgage Foreclosure Sales, 53 S. Cal. L. Rev.

843, 928 (1980). The election statute is intended to protect the debtor from multiple suits and at the same time grant the creditor the benefit of the security.

The election statute alters the traditional common law rule that a holder of a note secured by a mortgage has the right to sue on the note alone, to foreclose on the property, or to pursue both remedies at once (although there may be only one recovery on the debt). See Paramount Ins., Inc. v. Rayson & Smitley, 86 Nev. 644, 472 P.2d 530, 533 (1970).[2] However, the reach of the statute, as applied to most mortgages, is quite limited. In Smith v. Mangels, 73 Ariz. 203, 207, 240 P.2d 168, 170 (1952), this court held the election statute does not preclude a subsequent foreclosure action after judgment on the debt, as is the case in some other states. See, e.g., Neb. Rev. Stat. §§ 25-2140 and 25-2143 (1989); N.Y. Real Prop. Acts. Law § 1301 (McKinney 1979); S.D. Codified Laws Ann. §§ 21-47-5 and 21-47-6 (1987).

In *Baker*, we held the election statute was limited by the subsequently enacted purchase money mortgage anti-deficiency statute, A.R.S. § 33-729(A), which barred the lender from waiving the security and suing on the debt. 160 Ariz. at 104, 770 P.2d at 772. In so holding, we joined the courts of California and North Carolina in finding that such an election is inconsistent with the anti-deficiency statutes, which limit the lender to recovery from the land itself. Id.

Baker held that the lender should not be allowed to circumvent the anti-deficiency statute by electing to sue the debtor on the note, thereby realizing any difference between the value of the real property and the amount owed on the debt. As our supplemental opinion pointed out, *Baker's* holding applies whenever the anti-deficiency statutes apply and therefore is not always limited to the purchase money situation. 160 Ariz. at 106-07, 770 P.2d at 774-75. Assuming that the deed of trust falls within one of the anti-deficiency statutes, an action for a deficiency is prohibited after a trustee's sale on any deed of trust and after judicial foreclosure on purchase money deeds of trust. See A.R.S. §§ 33-814(G) and 33-729(A). If a lender holds a non-purchase money deed of trust, he *may* recover a deficiency *if* he does so through an action for judicial foreclosure because A.R.S. § 33-729(A) applies only to purchase money liens. In this latter case, of course, the debtor receives the protections of judicial foreclosure, including a statutory redemption right.[3]

---

2. Under the statutory scheme, the provisions within the law of mortgages (chapter 6 of A.R.S. Title 33) are not applicable to deeds of trust unless the deed of trust is judicially foreclosed as a mortgage pursuant to A.R.S. § 33-807(A). See A.R.S. § 33-805. The election statute is within chapter 6. Therefore, the election statute is not applicable to deeds of trust foreclosed by trustee's sale, and there is no analogous statute within the law applicable to deeds of trust. Dynamic does not contend that the lender lost its common law right to elect among its remedies. See generally Universal Inv. Co. v. Sahara Motor Inn, Inc., 127 Ariz. 213, 215, 619 P.2d 485, 487 (Ct.App.1980) (deed of trust statute does not mandate foreclosure by trustee's sale, but allows option to foreclose as mortgage or bring action on debt).

3. In Arizona, the debtor has no right of statutory redemption after the deed of trust is foreclosed by trustee's sale. A.R.S. § 33-811(B). This is also the rule in California, where deficiency judgments are prohibited after foreclosure by trustee's sale. The following comments regarding the California statute inform our discussion of A.R.S. § 33-814(G):

> The {statute's} purpose . . . was to put nonjudicial enforcement of a deed of trust on a par with judicial foreclosure and sale. . . . [Prior to its enactment] . . . [c]reditors preferred private sale because it avoided a statutory period of redemption. By exercising the power instead of foreclosing judicially, the creditor could obtain a deficiency judgment as well as the enhanced proceeds of a redemption-free sale. This procedure allowed the creditor to bid in the property himself at an unfairly low price — or offer that opportunity to someone else — secure in the knowledge that any deficiency would be recoverable in a personal judgment against the principal. Comment, Exonerating the Surety: Implications of the California Antideficiency Scheme, 57 Cal. L. Rev. 218, 232 (1969).

Read together, therefore, the statutes enact the following scheme: when the holder of a non-purchase money deed of trust of the type described in A.R.S. 33-814(G) forecloses by non-judicial sale, the statute protects the borrower from a deficiency judgment. The lender therefore may not waive the security and sue on the note. *Baker*, 160 Ariz. at 106, 770 P.2d at 774. The holder may, however, seek to foreclose the deed of trust as if it were a mortgage, as allowed by § 33-814(E); if he does so, the debtor is allowed redemption rights under § 33-726 and 12-1281 through 12–1289 and is thus protected from low credit bids, but the holder may recover a deficiency judgment — the difference between the balance of the debt and the sale price — unless the note is a purchase money obligation. In the latter case, the borrower is protected by the mortgage anti-deficiency statute, A.R.S. § 33-729(A), which applies only to purchase money obligations. *Baker*, 160 Ariz. at 106, 770 P.2d at 774.

Thus, if under *Baker* and the facts of this case Dynamic is protected by an anti-deficiency statute, Mid Kansas could not elect to waive its security and sue on the first notes after having already chosen to proceed by trustee's sale under the second deed of trust.

B. PERSONS AND PROPERTIES INCLUDED WITHIN THE STATUTORY DEFINITIONS

Mid Kansas argues that neither Dynamic, as a developer, nor the property under construction is protected by an anti-deficiency statute. Neither of the statutes is limited to individual homeowners rather than residential developers. Rather, the statutes apparently protect any mortgagor, provided the subject property is a single one- or two-family residential dwelling on two and one-half acres or less.[4]

As we noted in *Baker*, both anti-deficiency statutes were enacted in 1971, along with several other laws designed to protect consumers. 160 Ariz. at 101, 770 P.2d at 769. As with virtually all anti-deficiency statutes, the Arizona provisions were designed to temper the effects of economic recession on mortgagors by precluding "artificial deficiencies resulting from forced sales." Id. (quoting Boyd and Balentine, Arizona's Consumer Legislation: Winning the Battle But . . . , 14 Ariz. L. Rev. 627, 654 (1972)). Anti-deficiency statutes put the burden on the lender or seller to fairly value the property when extending the loan, recognizing that consumers often are not equipped to make such estimations. See generally Spangler v. Memel, 7 Cal.3d 603, 102 Cal.Rptr. 807, 812-13, 498 P.2d 1055, 1060-61 (1972); Leipziger, Deficiency Judgments in California: The Supreme Court Tries Again, 22 U.C.L.A.L. Rev. 753, 759-61 (1975). Indeed, the articulated purpose behind A.R.S.

---

4. The statutes read as follows (relevant portions emphasized): A.R.S. § 33-729(A):

[I]f a mortgage is given to secure the payment of the balance of the purchase price, or to secure a loan to pay all or part of the purchase price, of *a parcel of real property of two and one-half acres or less which is limited to and utilized for either a single one-family or single two-family dwelling* . . . [there shall be no deficiency judgment] . . .

A.R.S. § 33-814(G):

If *trust property of two and one-half acres or less which is limited to and utilized for either a single one-family or single two-family dwelling* is sold pursuant to the trustee's power of sale, no action may be maintained to recover any difference between the amount obtained by sale and the amount of the indebtedness and any interest, costs and expenses.

§ 33-729(A) (and presumably behind its deed of trust counterpart, as we held in *Baker*) was to protect "homeowners" from deficiency judgments. See *Baker*, 160 Ariz. at 101, 770 P.2d at 769.

However, absent express limiting language in the statute or explicit evidence of legislative intent, we cannot hold that the statute excludes residential developers. Where the language of a statute is plain and unambiguous, courts must generally follow the text as written. *Mid Kansas*, 163 Ariz. at 238, 787 P.2d at 137 (citing State Farm Mut. Ins. Co. v. Agency Rent-A-Car, Inc., 139 Ariz. 201, 203, 677 P.2d 1309, 1311 (Ct.App.1983); cf. Ritchie v. Grand Canyon Scenic Rides, 165 Ariz. 460, 799 P.2d 801 (1990) (rule inapplicable where it would produce absurd result)). While we can infer that the legislature's primary intent was to protect individual home-owners rather than commercial developers, neither the statutory text nor legislative history evinces an intent to *exclude* any other type of mortgagor.[5] Indeed, the North Carolina Supreme Court decided to apply a similar anti-deficiency statute to a commercial borrower, finding that the statute expressed no intent to exclude commercial transactions and therefore that the court could not read in such an intent. Barnaby v. Boardman, 313 N.C. 565, 330 S.E.2d 600, 603 (1985). Therefore, we hold that so long as the subject properties fit within the statutory definition, the identity of the mortgagor as either a homeowner or developer is irrelevant.

In contrast to the lack of legislative limitation as to the type of mortgagor protected, there is specific textual expression as to the type of property protected. Both statutes require that the property be (1) two and one-half acres or less, (2) limited to and utilized for a dwelling that is (3) single one-family or single two-family in nature. In applying a statute, we have long held that its words are to be given their ordinary meaning, unless the legislature has offered its own definition of the words or it appears from the context that a special meaning was intended. State Tax Comm'n v. Peck, 106 Ariz. 394, 395, 476 P.2d 849, 850 (1970).

A.R.S. § 33-814(G) calls for the property to be "limited to" a single one- or two-family dwelling. The word "dwelling" is susceptible to several interpretations, depending on the context of its use. See 28 C.J.S. Dwelling (1941 and 1990 Supp.). However, the principal element in all such definitions is the "purpose or use of a building for human abode," meaning that the structure is wholly or partially occupied by persons lodging therein at night or *intended* for such use. Id.; see also Smith v. Second Church of Christ, Scientist, 87 Ariz. 400, 405, 351 P.2d 1104, 1107 (1960) (defining "dwelling" as "a building suitable for residential purposes").

The anti-deficiency statutes require not only that the property be limited to dwelling purposes, but also that it be "utilized for" such purposes. In Northern Arizona Properties v. Pinetop Properties Group, the court of appeals held that an investment condominium, which was occasionally occupied by the owners and occasionally rented out to third persons, fell within the statutory definition. 151 Ariz. 9, 725 P.2d 501 (Ct. App. 1986). In deciding that the statute applied to a dwelling used for investment purposes and not as the mortgagor's principal resi-dence, the court employed the definition of "dwelling" in Webster's Ninth New Collegiate Dictionary and in several housing codes as "a shelter . . . in which

---

5. We take notice of the fact that the legislature has included such a limitation in other statutory provisions. For example, A.R.S. § 33-806.01(D), which deals with a trustee's right to transfer his interest in trust property, applies only to trust property that is limited to and utilized for dwelling units and that is *not* used for commercial purposes.

people live." Hence, although the condominium was held as an investment, it was also used (utilized) as a dwelling. Id. at 12, 725 P.2d at 504.

In contrast to the *Northern Arizona Properties* case, the property in question here had never been used as a dwelling, and was in fact not yet susceptible of being used as a dwelling. There is a difference between property intended for eventual use as a dwelling and property utilized as a dwelling. We hold that commercial residential properties held by the mortgagor for construction and eventual *resale* as dwellings are not within the definition of properties "limited to" and "*utilized* for" single-family dwellings. The property is not utilized as a dwelling when it is unfinished, has never been lived in, and is being held for sale to its first occupant by an owner who has no intent to ever occupy the property. Cf. *Northern Arizona Properties* (mortgagors intended to occupy property occasionally and rent it out).

Therefore, we hold that by its terms, the anti-deficiency statute does not apply to Dynamic in this case and A.R.S. § 33-814(G) does not preclude Mid Kansas from waiving its security and bringing a debt action on the notes.[6]

C. THE DOCTRINE OF MERGER AND EXTINGUISHMENT

Because we hold that the anti-deficiency statute does not apply, we must reach the merger and extinguishment issue that is the basis of the concurring opinion in the court of appeals. Dynamic listed that issue for our consideration under Rule 23(c), Ariz. R. Civ. App. P., 17B A.R.S., as an issue not decided by the court of appeals but that would need to be addressed if the court of appeals' opinion were reversed.[7]

1.   Merger of Estates

As Dynamic has noted, the facts in this case provide the basis for two merger arguments. The first is the theory of merger of estates. Generally, when one person obtains both a greater and a lesser interest in the same property, and no intermediate interest exists in another person, a merger occurs and the lesser interest is extinguished. 3 R. Powell, The Law of Real Property § 459 (1990 Rev.). Thus, merger may occur when a mortgagee's interest and the fee title are owned by the same person. Id. The potential for merger arises whenever a mortgagee acquires the mortgagor's equity of redemption. However, even if a merger would otherwise occur at law, contrary intent or equitable considerations may preclude this result under appropriate circumstances. 2 L. Jones, The Law of Mortgages § 1080 (8th ed. 1928). This court has long recognized these general rules of merger of estates.

---

6. Because we conclude that Dynamic is not protected by the anti-deficiency statute, we do not reach the issue of whether Mid Kansas's action on the first notes would have constituted an action for deficiency under *Baker* or an action on an "independent obligation" under *Ludi*. In *Ludi*, as in *Baker*, two notes were secured by the same real estate. However, unlike *Baker*, the second note in *Ludi* was given to obtain a home improvement loan and therefore was "independent from" the first note, given to secure a purchase money deed of trust. *Ludi*, 122 Ariz, at 228, 594 P.2d at 94. We note that, in any case, *Ludi* is not in direct conflict with *Baker* because the lender in *Ludi* used a judicial proceeding to foreclose its first deed of trust before bringing an action on the second, non-purchase money obligation. Id. at 227, 594 P.2d at 93.

7. In its response, Dynamic characterizes this issue as one involving unjust enrichment and election of remedies. The doctrine takes into consideration a little of both, but is more properly characterized as merger and extinguishment.

Bowman v. Cook, 101 Ariz. 366, 419 P.2d 723 (1966); Hathaway v. Neal, 31 Ariz. 155, 251 P. 173 (1926).

We assume, therefore, no one arguing to the contrary, that when Mid Kansas acquired title on the foreclosure of its *second* lien, its rights under *that* lien were merged in the title. See *Bowman*, 101 Ariz. at 367, 419 P.2d at 724. The question before us, however, is somewhat different. Today we must consider if Mid Kansas's rights under the *first* lien were affected when it acquired title by foreclosure on its *second* lien.

2. Merger of Rights

Where the same mortgagee holds both a first and second mortgage on the mortgagor's land, and becomes the purchaser at the foreclosure sale of one of the mortgages, the question of merger of *rights*—often called extinguishment—arises. The merger of rights doctrine addresses the narrow question of whether the mortgagor's personal liability on the senior debt has been discharged. Wright v. Anderson, 62 S.D. 444, 253 N.W. 484, 487 (1934). The primary issue in the doctrine of merger of rights is whether the lender would be unjustly enriched if he were permitted to enforce the debt. See generally Burkhart, Freeing Mortgages of Merger, 40 Vand. L. Rev. 283, 382 (1987).

Although the mortgagee's purchase of the property at the foreclosure of the senior mortgage will not extinguish the debt secured by a junior mortgage, the reverse is true where the junior mortgage is foreclosed. If one holding both junior and senior mortgages forecloses the junior and purchases the property at the foreclosure sale, the long-standing rule is that, absent a contrary agreement, the mortgagor's personal liability for the debt secured by the first mortgage is extinguished. G. Nelson & D. Whitman, Real Estate Finance Law § 6.16, at 467 (2d ed. 1985). The rule has been followed for generations. . . .

The basis of the merger of rights doctrine is that the purchaser at a foreclosure sale of a junior lien takes subject to all senior liens. *Ren-Cen Club*, 377 N.W.2d at 434; *Wright*, 253 N.W. at 487; see also Burkhart, supra, 40 Vand. L. Rev. at 377. Although the purchaser does not become personally liable on the senior debt (as does an assuming grantee), the purchaser must pay it to avoid the risk of losing his newly acquired land to foreclosure by the senior lienholder. Therefore, the land becomes the primary fund for the senior debt, and the purchaser is presumed to have deducted the amount of the senior liens from the amount he bids for the land. *Tri-County Bank*, 449 N.W.2d at 541.[8] As the court in *Wright* explained, when the same mortgagee holds both the junior and senior mortgages on the land and buys at the foreclosure sale of the junior mortgage:

> The mortgagor . . . has an equitable right to have the land pay the mortgage before his personal liability is called upon and the purchaser will not be permitted to retain the land . . . and enforce the same against the mortgagor personally.

253 N.W. at 487. Similarly, the court in *Ren-Cen Club* noted that

---

8. In a transfer "subject to" the senior mortgage, the essence of the transaction is that "the transferee agrees, as between her and her transferor, that the debt is to be satisfied out of the land." Nelson & Whitman, supra, § 5.3, at 271.

[t]he indebtedness will be presumed to have been discharged so soon as the holder of it becomes invested with title to the land upon which it is charged, on the principle that a party may not sue himself at law or in equity. The purchaser is presumed to have bought the land at its value, less the amount of indebtedness secured thereon, and equity will not permit him to hold the land and still collect the debt from the mortgagor.

377 N.W.2d at 435 (quoting Belleville Savings Bank v. Reis, 136 Ill. 242, 26 N.E. 646, 647 (1891)(citations omitted)).

Thus, the merger of rights doctrine holds that the senior lien is merged into — or extinguished by — the title acquired by the lienholder when he acquires the mortgagor's equity of redemption under a sale on the junior lien. Of course, this rule comes into play only when the equity of redemption is extinguished. See *Wright*, 253 N.W. at 487; 2 Jones, supra, § 1080, at 514. Although the deed of trust is a relatively new instrument that postdates cases such as *Wright* and *Belleville,* we find the doctrine of merger and extinguishment even more compelling under a modern deed of trust statute, which cuts off the borrower's equity of redemption at the time of the trustee's sale. See A.R.S. § 33-811(B). In Patton v. First Federal Savings & Loan Ass'n, we commented on the unique features of the deed of trust that required a strict construction in favor of the borrower:

> Compared to mortgage requirements, the Deed of Trust procedures authorized by statute make it far easier for lenders to forfeit the borrower's interest in the real estate securing a loan, and also abrogate the right of redemption after sale guaranteed under a mortgage foreclosure. . . . [U]nder a Deed of Trust, the trustee holds a power of sale permitting him to sell the property out of court with no necessity of judicial action. The Deed of Trust statutes thus strip borrowers of many of the protections available under a mortgage. Therefore, lenders must strictly comply with the Deed of Trust statutes, and the statutes and Deeds of Trust must be strictly construed in favor of the borrower.

118 Ariz. 473, 477, 578 P.2d 152, 156 (1978).

As we have previously noted, even where a merger would otherwise occur at law, an express agreement between the parties that no merger shall occur often precludes such a finding by the court. Nelson & Whitman, supra, § 6.16, at 467 (citing Toston v. Utah Mortgage Loan Co., 115 F.2d 560 (C.C.A. Idaho 1940); Continental Title & Trust Co. v. Devlin, 209 Pa. 380, 58 A. 843 (1904); Van Woerden v. Union Improvement Co., 156 Wash. 555, 287 P. 870(1930)). Of course, where the mortgagee acquires title to the property through an involuntary conveyance, such as foreclosure, the parties obviously will not have formed a mutual intent concerning the continued enforceability of the debt. Burkhart, supra, 40 Vand. L. Rev. at 377.

However, such an intent may be implied under circumstances that would make a finding of merger inequitable to the parties. The dissent in Wright, for instance, argued that where the mortgagee paid the full value of the property without deducting the amount of the prior lien, the rule of merger should not apply. 253 N.W. at 489 (Polley, J., dissenting). This argument was adopted by a recent decision that allowed a bank to retain its claim for the unsecured deficiency remaining on the first mortgage even though the bank purchased the property at the foreclosure sale on the second mortgage. In re Richardson, 48 B.R. 141 (Bkrtcy. E.D. Tenn. 1985). The court found that the bank had not tried to take unfair advantage of the debtor because its bid had reflected the value of the property and the bank had, in addition, credited the debtors with the amount beyond the bid it received on reselling the property. Id. at 142. A different result would obtain where the mortgagee is permitted to keep land that is worth as much as the two mortgage debts and also allowed to collect on the senior debt. In the latter situation, the mortgagee would be unjustly enriched, and the merger doctrine is appropriately applied to destroy the senior debt. Nelson & Whitman, supra, § 6.16, at 467-68.

The facts in this case clearly illustrate and require application of the doctrine of merger and extinguishment; they also demonstrate that no equitable exception is appropriate here. Mid Kansas held the four first deeds of trust and the second blanket deed of trust on the four lots. Mid Kansas purchased all four pieces of property with a credit bid of the amount due on the second lien, $101,986.67. Mid Kansas thus acquired free and clear title to improved property apparently worth between $555,750 and $608,000.[9] Even accepting the lower figure, it is apparent that the sum of the junior and senior liens ($527,236.67 — exclusive of interest and costs) on the property at the relevant time — the date of the foreclosure sale — was probably less than the value of the property. Mid Kansas obviously tendered a credit bid that was discounted by the amount of the senior liens. Therefore, Mid Kansas would be unjustly enriched were we to allow it to acquire, for $100,000, property worth over $500,000 and also sue Dynamic for another $400,000 under the first notes. Mid Kansas does not contend that the property it acquired was worth less than the total owed on the first and second liens.

On these facts, we hold that the doctrine of merger and extinguishment applies. . . .

CONCLUSION

The anti-deficiency statute, A.R.S. § 33-814(G), does not apply to Dynamic in this case because the homes under construction were not utilized for single-family dwellings. We vacate the court of appeals' opinion and reverse the trial court's judgment. The case is remanded to the trial court for proceedings consistent with this opinion. On remand, the parties will have the opportunity to present evidence as to the value of the property at the time of the foreclosure sale. If the facts are as they appear on this record, equity will require no exception to the doctrine of merger and extinguishment. If Dynamic prevails, it will be eligible for its attorney's fees subject to Rule 21, Ariz. R. Civ. App. P., 17B A.R.S.

NOTES AND QUESTIONS

1. On policy grounds, can the Arizona scheme be justified for determining when creditors can obtain deficiency judgments and when not in mortgage and deed of trust situations? Why, for example, should purchase money mortgagors receive

9. The value of the properties, as listed on the IRS Statements of Acquisition or Abandonment of Secured Property filed by Mid Kansas, totalled $555,750. Mid Kansas submitted appraisals to the trial court estimating the value of the lots, if completed in accordance with the plans and specifications, at $608,000. Ironically, the IRS statements filed by Mid Kansas stated that the "borrower was not personally liable for repayment of the debt," although Mid Kansas attributes this to "clerical error" and has since "corrected" the forms.

special antideficiency protection? And should antideficiency protection ever be extended to developers and other business borrowers? How might the Arizona scheme be improved?

2. An argument against such mortgagor protection laws as antideficiency and postforeclosure redemption statutes is that these laws appreciably increase the cost of mortgage money to home buyers. See, for example, Meador, The Effects of Mortgage Laws on Home Mortgage Rates, 34 J. Econ. & Bus. 143 (1982). A subsequent study, however, concludes that from its data this cost increase is so limited as not to be statistically significant. Schill, An Economic Analysis of Mortgagor Protection Laws, 77 Va. L. Rev. 489, 500-515 (1991). Professor Schill advances the further argument in support of antideficiency and postforeclosure redemption laws that these laws function as a desired and desirable form of insurance for mortgagors. He concludes: "Mortgagors, especially those who live in states with volatile economies, may place a high value on mortgagor protections, such as an entitlement to be free from personal liability, the ability to remain in possession of the property during the foreclosure and redemption periods, or the ability to repurchase their homes within a certain period after the foreclosure sale." Id. at 500. He goes on to assert that mortgagor protection laws may also advance economic efficiency by reducing homebuying risks and increasing optimal levels of housing consumption. However, he adds, these laws should be narrowed to cover only those in need of protection — homebuyers and perhaps small businesses.

Referring to some of the more restrictive antideficiency legislation, the Powell treatise states: "[This legislation] is a recognition of the modern shift from viewing the mortgage as a personal relationship predicated upon acquaintance and the believed solvency of the borrower, to seeing it as an investment device largely handled by corporations. It is to be hoped that more states will enact similar statutes." 4 Powell on Real Property § 37.50 (1997). Do you agree that more states should enact legislation restricting mortgagees' rights to deficiency judgments?

3. For arguments strongly opposing unlimited deficiency liability of home mortgage borrowers following foreclosure and also proposing a statutory limit on such liability of 5 percent of the amount of debt owing at the time of foreclosure, see Mixon, Deficiency Judgments Following Home Mortgage Foreclosure: An Anachronism That Increases Personal Tragedy, Impedes Regional Economic Recovery, and Means Little to Lenders, 22 Texas Tech L. Rev. 1 (1991). Professor Mixon is especially concerned with the deficiency laws of Texas, but much of what he has to say is relevant to other states as well. He, of course, favors section 511(b) of the Uniform Land Security Interest Act providing that after foreclosure of a mortgage on property bought for individual use as a personal residence "there is no liability for a deficiency, notwithstanding any agreement." See Mixon and Shepard, Antideficiency Relief for Foreclosed Homeowners: ULSIA Section 511(b), 27 Wake Forest L. Rev. 455 (1992).

Extensive protection of defaulting mortgagors also is opposed in Hughes, Taking Personal Responsibility: A Different View of Mortgage Anti-Deficiency and Redemption Statutes, 39 Ariz. L. Rev. 117 (1997), which comes to this conclusion:

> Irrespective of the effectiveness, or lack thereof, of anti-deficiency legislation and statutory rights of redemption in providing financial and other relief for mortgagors, and without regard to who is best able to avoid or bear the risks of mortgage defaults, mandatory rules that provide these forms of borrower relief signal societal approval of

mortgagors' failure to honor their promises and to take responsibility for the burdens of their mortgage obligations. This signaling contributes to the moral impoverishment of individual mortgagors and, ultimately, to the moral impoverishment of our society at large.

A preferable and morally justifiable means of addressing our collective concern for the plight of mortgagors is 1) to require comprehensive and comprehensible disclosures to prospective borrowers, regarding the potential consequences of default, and 2) to require mortgagees to perform a borrower sophistication analysis as part of the loan qualification process. Mortgagees should not be permitted to make loans to borrowers who have not demonstrated the ability to understand the risks of the mortgage transaction, as described in the required disclosures. However, once a mortgagor has been appropriately qualified, and notified of the potential risks of a mortgage default, the mortgagee should be permitted to pursue foreclosure and, in applicable cases, a deficiency judgment, unimpeded by statutory rights of redemption and anti-deficiency legislation.

4. Many loans for large amounts on postconstruction income-producing properties, such as office buildings, often are nonrecourse. If a mortgage loan is nonrecourse, this means that the lender, in case of default, can obtain recovery of amounts due only from the security and may not sue the mortgagor on the underlying debt or seek a deficiency judgment against the mortgagor if the full amount due is not recovered in a foreclosure. In a nonrecourse mortgage loan, the lender is relying on income from the property rather than other income and assets of the borrower as the source of payment on the loan. The mortgage note may signify a nonrecourse loan by such language as "the borrower is not personally liable on this loan," or "in case of default, the lender shall have recourse only against the property secured by the mortgage."

Borrower nonrecourse immunity may be limited by agreement between borrower and lender but a court may hold a borrower personally liable to the lender for waste despite a nonrecourse provision in the loan agreement. What constitutes waste in this context has been liberally construed to include nonpayment of real property taxes. See, e.g., Travelers Insurance Co. v. 633 Third Associates, 973 F.2d 82 (2d Cir. 1992) & 14 F.3d 114 (2d Cir. 1994), involving nonpayment of real property taxes on a 41-story office building covered by a $145 million loan. For different degrees of borrower nonrecourse immunity and different kinds of nonrecourse loans, see Gregory M. Stein, The Scope of the Borrower's Liability in a Nonrecourse Real Estate Loan, 55 Wash. & Lee L. Rev. 1207 (1998).

Why do lenders ever agree to make nonrecourse loans?

-STOP-

5. *Bankruptcy Considerations*

Many mortgagors against whom foreclosure is being sought or recently has been obtained are insolvent and faced with the possibility or even probability of bankruptcy. Despite the protection provided by mortgagees holding security interests, bankruptcy can affect mortgagees' rights. This casebook is not the appropriate place to deal comprehensively and in detail with the relation of bankruptcy to the law of mortgages, but attention should be directed to some important respects in which bankruptcy can affect mortgage foreclosures. One respect is that bankruptcy proceedings may result in a stay of the mortgagee's right to initiate or continue foreclosure proceedings. These stays may be brief or lengthy but in some instances can last until the bankruptcy case is closed. Another important respect in which bankruptcy can affect mortgage foreclosures is that some mortgage foreclosure sales can be set aside as actually or constructively fraudulent if made within a year prior to the debtor's bankruptcy at a price that is not a fair equivalent for the property.

NOTE

For more extended discussion of bankruptcy stays pertaining to mortgage lenders' rights, see 4 Powell on Real Property, § 37.48[3] (1997); Lifton, Practical Real Estate in the 80s: Legal, Tax and Business Strategies 297-306 (2d ed. 1983); Murphy, The Automatic Stay in Bankruptcy, 34 Clev. St. L. Rev. 567 (1986); Bogart, Games Lawyers Play: Waivers of the Automatic Stay in Bankruptcy and the Single Asset Loan Workout, 43 U.C.L.A. L. Rev. 1117 (1996).

6. *Reforming Mortgage Foreclosure*

Mortgage foreclosure laws and practices are frequently criticized. Foreclosing lenders often complain about foreclosure costs and delays, defaulting mortgagors commonly object to low prices at foreclosure sales and high deficiency judgments, and junior creditors are prone to be critical of how their interests are treated by the foreclosure process. There have been many suggestions for reforming the process, but those by Professor Stark appearing below merit special attention because they rely heavily on data obtained by Professor Stark in an empirical study she made of foreclosures in a large metropolitan county, Cook County, Illinois, the county in which Chicago is located.

Stark, Foreclosing on the American Dream: An Evaluation of State and Federal Foreclosure Laws

51 Okla. L. Rev. 229, 229-231, 235-236, 247-250 (1998)

Approximately sixty-five million Americans own their homes and were able to purchase these homes with loans secured by real estate mortgages (in 1995 lenders loaned more than three trillion dollars secured by residential real estate).[2] The purchase of these homes represents the largest single financial investment that most individuals will make. In addition, individuals often experience a strong emotional attachment to their homes. Consequently, the prospect of losing one's home in a real estate foreclosure is both financially and emotionally devastating. On the other hand, in order to make this dream affordable it is important for lenders to

---

2. To get a sense of the amount of residential real estate foreclosures occurring recently in the United States, it should be noted that in the fourth quarter of 1996, one percent of this debt (i.e., $30 billion) was delinquent to such an extent that the mortgagee elected to foreclose upon the real estate mortgage which secured the debt. See Delinquencies on the Rise at Year-end, Mortgage Marketplace, Mar. 10, 1997, available in 1997 WL 7938104.

be able to provide financing for these purchases at rates which provide a profit to the lender but which borrowers can afford to pay. The more expensive the process to collect on bad debt, the higher the interest rates or loan fees to future borrowers because lenders pass along their collection costs to new borrowers. Recognizing these two sides of the coin, each state has enacted foreclosure laws which attempt to balance the interests of the defaulting borrower (protecting any equity she has in her property) with the interests of the lender and future non-defaulting borrowers (a foreclosure process which is as quick and inexpensive as possible).

Lenders charge that the foreclosure process in many states is too long and costly. Due to the federal government's role as the insurer of many real estate loans and provider of financing, Congress has also been concerned with the impact of disparate state foreclosure laws on the many programs administered by the federal government through its Department of Housing and Urban Development (HUD) and has enacted certain federal foreclosure laws which preempt state foreclosure laws in certain circumstances, with the goal of reducing the time it takes to foreclose on bad debts and to reduce the costs associated with the foreclosure process. In the meantime, borrowers and their proponents claim that the current state foreclosure laws are grossly unfair to borrowers. They claim that because third parties rarely attend real estate foreclosures, the foreclosing lender is able to bid less than the amount due to the lender at the foreclosure sale, recover the difference as a deficiency judgment against the borrower, and then resell the property for a profit.

While many have criticized the foreclosure laws as unfair and inefficient, few have collected data to test how fair and efficient foreclosure laws are in reality. This author has conducted an empirical study of judicial foreclosures in Cook County, Illinois (the Empirical Study)[3] to test the accuracy of the conflicting conventional wisdom with an eye towards utilizing the data collected to arrive at an approach which can further the legitimate interests of both lenders and borrowers. . . .

Two basic criticisms of the foreclosure process are that it is unfair and inefficient. These criticisms are based upon the assumption that third parties rarely bid at a foreclosure sale. As a result, the argument goes, the lender is able to bid far below the fair market value of the property, resell the property at a profit and sue the borrower for the difference between the amount bid and the final judgment amount. If this is how the foreclosure system routinely operates, the system would clearly be unfair to borrowers and seriously flawed. If third parties rarely bid at a

3. The author collected data with respect to every judicial foreclosure case filed in the Chancery Court of Cook County, Illinois, in July 1993 and July 1994, ascertaining the percentage of cases which were dismissed (through reinstatement, redemption, modification of the loan or bankruptcy filing) and collecting data on the cases which sold at a foreclosure sale, including any resales of property within one year of the foreclosure sale. . . .

Illinois requires a judicial foreclosure and provides for a seven month redemption period for residential properties which must be exercised before the sale, rather than after. 735 Ill. Comp. Stat. 5/15-1603(b)(1) (West 1993). Among the fifty states, the median period which passes prior to the judicial foreclosure sale is eight months and the median post-sale redemption period is six months for both judicial and nonjudicial sales.

The author's reform proposal is confined to the setting of foreclosures of non-income producing properties (i.e., "residential real estate"). There are many reasons for this limitation. First, the data collected in the Empirical Study came overwhelmingly from residential real estate. Second, the dynamics of commercial real estate are far different from residential real estate (the bankruptcy law protections widely differ in the commercial context) (chapter 11 laws are quite different from chapter 13), appraisals (a linchpin to the reform proposal) are more prone to variation in results in a commercial context than in a residential one, and the issue of measuring the borrower's equity in the property is more complicated in the commercial context.

foreclosure sale and the lender ends up with the property almost all of the time, then the foreclosure sale process is also inefficient since the sale's process is costly and time consuming with no corresponding gains to lenders or borrowers. As previously mentioned, one of the key purposes of the Empirical Study is to test which of these criticisms is well founded.

Assuming for the moment that third parties rarely bid at or close to the fair market value of the property at a foreclosure sale (prior studies and this study confirm this as fact), it is not difficult to speculate why this is the case. First, typical home purchasers may not even know that the property is for sale because no signs are posted on the property and the sale is not advertised in the real estate section of the newspaper (it is advertised in the legal section). Second, the bidder is not given the opportunity to inspect the property prior to bidding on it. Third, at the sale the bidder is customarily required to pay ten percent of the bid price immediately and the balance in forty-eight hours (making it impossible to finance the payment of the property with a conventional loan). Finally, in a number of jurisdictions, the mortgagor can redeem the property within six months or more after the foreclosure sale. These standard features of a foreclosure sale drive the typical home purchaser out of the market. To the extent that third parties come to a foreclosure sale and bid at the sale, they tend to be real estate investors who are experienced in investing in real estate and are either cash rich or enjoy a line of credit so that they can bid at the foreclosure sale and pay off the balance in forty-eight hours. These investors, commonly referred to as "scavengers," are aware that risks inhere in purchasing property in this manner (such as the inability to inspect the property prior to bidding at the foreclosure sale and the lack of warranties regarding the physical condition of the house) and will, consequently, only bid when they think they are bidding much less than the fair market value of the property.

Yet, the fairness issue is sometimes even more broadly construed. Some would criticize a foreclosure process in which a lender or a third party is able to bid any amount less than the fair market value of the property, even if this result occurred infrequently. The foreclosure sale should be reformed, according to those who hold this view, to make the sale commercially reasonable so that the amount bid reflects the fair market value, or the borrower should be able to recapture any gain made upon a resale within a short period of time after the foreclosure sale. When this article refers to a "fair" foreclosure process, it is not referring to a process where the defaulting borrower's interest is considered to the exclusion of the interests of the lender and all non-defaulting borrowers. A "fair" foreclosure system is one that attempts to balance the interest of lenders and all non-defaulting borrowers in an efficient foreclosure process against the interest of borrowers who default in a process which provides a true opportunity and means to protect any equity they have in the property in foreclosure. To the extent that the lender is not made whole through the foreclosure process, the lender will transfer those costs to all borrowers in the form of higher fees or interest rates and, consequently, lenders and non-defaulting borrowers share an interest in keeping the costs of the foreclosure process as low as possible. . . .

The data collected in the Empirical Study suggest a better way to handle residential real estate foreclosures — one which would better protect the borrower's equity in the property, if any, and would provide a more efficient process than is found in the fifty states or even in the federal procedures. This author recommends a bifurcated foreclosure process. Foreclosures would either be judicial strict foreclosures or judicial foreclosures with a required commercially reasonable sale of the property. After (i) the foreclosure action is filed and the mortgagor is served, and (ii) a ninety day reinstatement period has expired, the court[88] will order an appraisal of the value of the mortgage property which must be completed before the judgment of foreclosure.[89] If the amount of the appraisal reflects a value of the property which is less than the debt due on the date of the judgment of foreclosure plus a percentage of said judgment amount as set forth in the statute,[90] the property is deeded to the lender on the date of the judgment of foreclosure (i.e., a judicial strict foreclosure with no public sale). The statute would require the passage of a four month period from service of the mortgage before the judgment of foreclosure could occur and would give no discretion to a court to postpone the judgment date without agreement of the borrower and lender. The borrower would have a ninety day statutory right of reinstatement and a statutory redemption which can be exercised anytime before the expiration of said four month period.[91] There would be no right of redemption after the judgment of foreclosure.

If, however, the amount of the appraisal exceeds the judgment amount by more than the required specified percentage, then if the borrower failed to exercise the ninety day reinstatement right and failed to redeem within four months (and if any junior mortgagees fail to redeem within said four month period), the property must be sold in a manner which is commercially reasonable, and the borrower and any junior mortgagees would have no further redemption rights after the sale.

The purpose of requiring that the appraisal reflect a value of the property which is a specified percentage in excess of the judgment amount is to make certain that the borrower has sufficient equity in the property before requiring the lender to undergo the more expensive and time consuming commercially reasonable sales process. For example, if, after study, it becomes apparent that on average it costs a lender ten percent of the judgment amount to pay for performance of the commercially reasonable sale and the costs the lender incurs in carrying the property from the date of the judgment of foreclosure until the property sells, then unless the appraisal reflects a value of the property which exceeds ten percent of the judgment amount, the borrower does not have any true equity in the property worthy of requiring the more costly process of a commercially reasonable sale. Prior to reforming the foreclosure process, further data should be gathered to determine what these costs typically would amount to calculated as a percentage of the judgment amount and that figure should be applied in the statute as the amount by which the appraised value exceeds the judgment amount in order to require the commercially reasonable sale as opposed to a strict foreclosure.

Lenders would benefit from a reform which bifurcates the foreclosure process since the more expensive and commercially reasonable foreclosure process will only

88. The court rather than the lender should order the appraisal and the standards for how the appraisal should be prepared should be spelled out in the statute. . . .

89. The statute would permit a judgment of foreclosure within four months after service of summons, giving one month to obtain the appraisal.

90. The percentage set forth in the statute would be based upon studies collecting data on the median costs lenders incur to carry the property, the median time period for carrying property until it can be sold in a commercially reasonable manner, and the median costs of the sale of the property. The Illinois study roughly estimated this percentage at 14% based upon an assumed carrying time of six months and an assumed median resale price of $75,000. . . .

91. Any junior mortgagees would also be served and given an opportunity to redeem the property.

be required when an appraisal reflects that the borrower has sufficient equity in the property and the borrower still fails to reinstate or redeem the loan prior to the judgment of foreclosure (according to the data from the Empirical Study, this should rarely occur). When the appraisal reflects that the borrower has no equity in the property (which should be the majority of the cases which go to foreclosure sale according to the data from the Empirical Study), the lender will be able to take title to the property in a more cost efficient manner than is currently required in the fifty states.

While requiring an appraisal and sometimes a commercially reasonable sale appears to add to the costs of the foreclosure process, in light of the data collected in the Empirical Study, it should actually operate to reduce costs. Based upon surveys of appraisers in Chicago who handle residential real estate appraisals, the cost of the appraisal should typically run from $200 to $300 and can be prepared in a few days.[93] If the appraisal shows that the borrower has insufficient equity in the property, the property will be deeded to the lender on the date of judgment of foreclosure, thereby reducing the timing of the process by between four and five months (according to the Empirical Study, it took a median of nine months from the date the case was filed until the judicial sale was completed) and saving over five percent of the judgment amount in costs (based upon saving approximately four percent in accrued interest and advances which would otherwise accrue during the period from the judgment until the sale and saving approximately one percent of the judgment amount which would otherwise be expended in connection with costs to perform the public sale). In addition, allowing the lender to retake the property more quickly when the borrower has no equity in the property may also lead to less deterioration to the property, which commonly occurs during the foreclosure process.

Borrowers would benefit from this bifurcated process because it would require a commercially reasonable sale (and thus a bid price much more closely approximating the fair market value of the property) when the borrower has equity in the mortgaged property and is unable to protect its equity by reinstating the loan or paying off the loan prior to the foreclosure sale.[96] If the property is worth $100,000

---

93. The difference in cost is based upon how unique the house is that is being appraised. If there are many unique features to the house then the appraisal cost could increase to as high as $600. . . .

96. In some cases from the Empirical Study, resales of the property within one year after the foreclosure sale reflect that some borrowers failed to protect their significant equity in their property (some resales resulted in profits ranging from 32% to 326%). . . . One possible explanation is that some borrowers are too ill or otherwise incompetent to protect their interests in any of the ways that borrowers typically protect their equity such as through a sale of the property, refinance or reinstatement of the loan, or the filing of a bankruptcy action. It is important to require a commercially reasonable sale to protect such borrowers. It would also be helpful to require by statute that at the time the borrower is served with the summons, the borrower also be supplied with an explanation of the options available to a borrower in connection with the loan default. The exact wording of the form could be prescribed by statute and would encourage the borrower to seek legal counsel to advise the borrower on its options and to provide a summary of the options the borrower could consider such as exercising the right of reinstatement, attempting to refinance or sell the property before the redemption period expires, negotiating a loan work-out or deed-in-lieu of foreclosure with release of personal liability, and bankruptcy options. The Uniform Land Security Interest Act takes a similar approach and requires that the lender advise the borrower of various rights and options of the borrower (such as any rights to cure the default and how to do so, the possibility of a deed-in-lieu of foreclosure, any rights to sell the property subject to the debt or to refinance the debt) when the lender sends the notice of default and intent to perform a foreclosure sale of the property.

and the debt and sales costs together equal $90,000, the borrower's true equity in the property is ten thousand dollars. Under the proposed process, the property would sell for at or very near its market value of one hundred thousand dollars, the lender would be paid off due to the commercially reasonable sale, and the borrower would receive the net proceeds from the sale.[97] Under the proposed process, lenders and third parties will be less likely to reap large profits in the occasional situation where the borrower in fact has significant equity in the property but was unable to reinstate or redeem the loan before the foreclosure sale. Furthermore, since the costs to perform the appraisal are relatively minor (far less than the typical current sales costs in Illinois for the selling officer and costs to advertise the sale), it should not pose a barrier to the borrower being able to redeem the property prior to the judgment of foreclosure or prior to the commercially reasonable sale, if applicable. It is important for the law to require a commercially reasonable sale because the Empirical Study reflects that the optional foreclosure features are rarely utilized. In none of the cases examined in the Empirical Study did the borrower petition the court for any of the optional features allowed by the Illinois statute to make the foreclosure sale more commercially reasonable. Lenders in the cases in the study only petitioned for one feature, which related to having a private entity rather than the Cook County Sheriff's Office conduct the foreclosure sale (to reduce the costs of the foreclosure sale).

This proposal purposely leaves open the issue of recovering a deficiency, mainly because the bifurcated process should work on its own to protect the borrower's equity in the property. However, some states enact anti-deficiency legislation for reasons other than protecting the borrower's equity in the property (e.g., to prevent a double loss to the borrower when property values decline generally). Whether federal concerns should preempt a state's policies on this issue is beyond the scope of this article.

The proposed bifurcated foreclosure process would satisfy the federal government's desire for a quick and inexpensive process (the proposal would lead to a four month process in most cases without the costs associated with a sale of the property), but would at the same time provide a meaningful opportunity for the borrower to protect any equity it has in its property (by providing a judicial wake up call, a ninety day reinstatement period, a four month period to redeem, and a commercially reasonable sale if an appraisal reflects true equity in the property).

This author strongly urges Congress to replace the existing federal foreclosure laws and to enact any new federal foreclosure laws based upon the bifurcated foreclosure process outlined in this article and urges state legislators to consider revising their residential foreclosure laws along the lines of the proposal outlined in this article. Enactment of the reform proposal outlined in this article will promote the interests of the federal government and lenders in a uniform and inexpensive process and will simultaneously promote the legitimate interests of defaulting borrowers in a realistic opportunity to protect their equity in their investment.

---

97. The statute should require a process to notify the borrower that the borrower is entitled to this surplus amount and a procedure to collect this amount. Currently in Illinois, a borrower will not know when a surplus is bid unless the borrower is at the foreclosure sale. Based on anecdotes from those who represent lenders in the foreclosure process it appears that in a number of instances the borrower does not in fact claim the surplus amount (presumably due to not knowing that a surplus was bid and that it was entitled to it).

NOTE

Among other foreclosure reform proposals meriting serious consideration are those in the Uniform Nonjudicial Foreclosure Act, a uniform act prepared and approved by the National Conference on Uniform Laws. For a detailed discussion of this act see Nelson and Whitman, Reforming Foreclosure: The Uniform Nonjudicial Foreclosure Act, 53 Duke L.J. 1399 (2004). Due to failure of the states to adopt this or other uniform foreclosure acts and the adverse consequences of the extensive diversity among the states in their foreclosure laws, Nelson and Whitman propose that Congress work with the National Conference of Uniform Laws in drafting a uniform foreclosure law that Congress would adopt binding on all the states and that would create national consistency in the foreclosure process. Such a law, according to Nelson and Whitman, should also seek to add to the efficiency of the foreclosure process and aim particularly at lowering costs of the foreclosure process in ways beneficial to purchasers of securitized mortgages.

On other mortgage foreclosure reform proposals see Goldstein, Reforming the Residential Foreclosure Process, 21 Real Estate L.J. 286 (1993); Lifton, Real Estate in Trouble: Lender's Remedies Need an Overhaul, 31 Bus. Law. 1927 (1976); Madway and Pearlman, A Mortgage Foreclosure Primer: Part III, Proposals for Change, 8 Clearinghouse Rev. 473 (Nov. 1974).

7. Remedies for Breach of Installment Land Contracts

Installment land contract sellers may have a number of remedies available if buyers default, including self-help recovery of possession, forfeiture, rescission, specific performance, damages for breach of contract, or suit to recover possession. These remedies, in the context of a contract buyer's failure to close, are considered in Chapter Four. However, some remedy problems deserve emphasis here in the context of installment land contracts.

Breaches by installment land contract buyers often raise particularly difficult problems because such contract buyers at the time of breach may have been in possession for a long period of time; made substantial payments on the purchase price; may have made improvements in the property or committed waste, or both; and, with the passage of time, the market value of the property may have changed greatly from the contract price.

Courts and legislatures have had difficulty in shaping some remedies so as to provide fair treatment of both buyers and sellers. The forfeiture remedy, in particular, has caused concern, as it may result in buyers losing not only their interests in the property but all payments made as well, with consequent seller benefits that may be difficult to justify. Not surprisingly, equity principles have frequently been invoked by courts to qualify use of the forfeiture remedy. Statutes, too, in some states have sought to limit the forfeiture rights of installment land contract sellers. In a few states, installment land contract buyers, in default, are treated similarly to mortgagors, with much the same protections as are available to that favored class of debtors.

Carlson v. Hamilton

8 Utah 2d 272, 332 P.2d 989 (1958)

HENRIOD, Justice. Appeal from a judgment for money paid by plaintiff buyers to defendant sellers under a real estate contract which the former breached. Reversed. Costs to defendants.

The subject of the contract was a farm with a home situate thereon. The sale price was $22,000, with $1,000 annual installments, the purchasers to pay the taxes also. Such payments were met the first year, but plaintiffs failed to make payments the second year, notifying defendants that they would be unable to carry out the terms of the contract. Defendants advised plaintiffs that if they would pay the taxes and the interest the payment of the $1,000 principal would be forgotten for the time being. Even so, plaintiffs again indicated to defendants that they would not meet the commitments made under the contract. Under the circumstances defendants resumed possession of the property which at the time was not occupied by plaintiffs or anyone else.

Defendants did not sue for specific performance or for the arrearages resulting by plaintiffs' default, as defendants well may have done. Instead, they chose to take back the property and retain the amounts paid as liquidated damages, which the contract clearly provided they could do.

Plaintiffs brought suit to recover everything they had paid under the contract before default, being the sum of $6,680. The evidence indicated that considerable damage had been done to the house and property during the two years plaintiffs occupied them. The trial court made findings as to the amount of damage done and added it to a reasonable two-year rental value, concluding the plaintiffs had paid $2,119.94 more on the contract than defendants actually had been damaged. Plaintiffs were awarded judgment for that amount, apparently under the theory that in Perkins v. Spencer, 121 Utah 468, 243 P.2d 446, we determined that a defaulting buyer could require the return of all sums paid in over and above actual damage caused the seller.

Perkins v. Spencer is no authority for such doctrine. The spirit of that case calls for adhesion to a principle that equity historically has indulged, — that it abhors unconscionability shocking to such degree that the function of equity would be misconceived and misapplied by the enforcement of such unconscionability, even though it may have been the subject of contract.

Such unconscionability is obvious in the *Perkins* case, where, after a breach committed only four months after execution of the contract, an exaction of over 27% of the entire purchase price was attempted, — $2,725 where the price was $10,000, and where the seller demanded the entire balance of the price before conveying the property. In the instant case, the amount of damage that the contract said could be considered as liquidated damages was $2,119.94. Occupancy had been enjoyed a full two years. The bona fides of the sellers generously was demonstrated by a volunteered waiver of the principal for the time being if the buyers would but pay the taxes and interest. The amount of damages here was but 9½% of the purchase price, an amount that would exceed but little the real estate commission that would have to be paid on resale of the property that defendants took back without fault on their part, from those who caused all the difficulty by breaking the contract.

The two cases are poles apart, the one obviously being punctuated by unconscionability, the other appearing to call only for the exaction of a reasonably small percentage of the price for a breach that would cause delay for repairs, time lapse for re-sale, and possibly other times of damage susceptible of little but conjectural measurement.

People should be entitled to contract on their own terms without the indulgence of paternalism by courts in the alleviation of one side or another from the effects of a bad bargain. Also, they should be permitted to enter into contracts that actually may be unreasonable or which may lead to hardship on one side. It is only where it turns out that one side or the other is to be penalized by the enforcement of the terms of a contract so unconscionable that no decent, fair-minded person would view the ensuing result without being possessed of a profound sense of injustice, that equity will deny the use of its good offices in the enforcement of such unconscionability. We think no such case is presented here.

In Peck v. Judd [7 Utah 2d 420, 326 P.2d 712, 717,] Mr. Justice Worthen poignantly expressed the thought when he said "It is not our prerogative to step in and renegotiate the contract of the parties. . . . There is no reason why we should consider the vendee privileged . . . unless the conditions . . . are unconscionable . . . and . . . we should recognize and honor the right of persons to contract freely and to make real and genuine mistakes when the dealings are at arms' length." He pointed out also that buyers ofttimes reap a handsome harvest by the appreciation of real estate values, but that equity will not interfere to require the buyer to share such increment with the seller. "Courts of equity," he said, "should not interfere except when sharp practice or most unconscionable result is to be prevented."

McDonough, C.J., and Crockett, Wade and Worthen, J.J., concur.

NOTES AND QUESTIONS

1. Suppose that in Carlson v. Hamilton, seller had sued to cancel the installment contract because of buyer's default. Could buyer then claim successfully that the contract was an "equitable" mortgage for which foreclosure would be the only appropriate method for cutting off his interest? If yes, would buyer then be entitled to redemption prior to the decree? For what sum? If buyers did not have the moneys to redeem, would seller then be able to keep all moneys received?

2. Courts have become increasingly reluctant to enforce forfeiture provisions in installment land contracts. Among declared reasons for refusing to apply these clauses are that a forfeiture constitutes a penalty or unjust enrichment; enforcement would be unconscionable; a desire to grant buyers who are behind in their payments a right of repayment similar to a mortgagor's equity of redemption right; and waiver of the forfeiture right by the seller having accepted one or more late payments. For substantive limitations on forfeiture and alternatives to that remedy, see 15 Powell on Real Property § 840.03[6] (1997).

Also, some states have sought to ease the forfeiture hardship on installment contract buyers by statutes giving buyers a grace period following default in which to comply with the terms of the contract. Arizona is one such state, and its statute provides in part:

D. Forfeiture of the interest of a purchaser in the property for failure to pay monies due under the contract may be enforced only after expiration of the following periods after the date such monies were due:

1. If there has been paid less than twenty percent of the purchase price, thirty days.

2. If there has been paid twenty percent, or more, but less than thirty percent of the purchase price, sixty days.

3. If there has been paid thirty percent, or more, but less than fifty percent of the purchase price, one hundred and twenty days.

4. If there has been paid fifty percent, or more, of the purchase price, nine months.

E. For the purpose of computing the percentage of the purchase price paid under subsection D of this section, the total of only the following constitutes payments on the purchase price:

1. Down payments paid to the seller.

2. Principal payments paid to the seller on the contract.

3. Principal payments paid to other persons who hold liens or encumbrances on the property, the principal portion of which constitutes a portion of the purchase price, as stated under the contract.

Ariz. Rev. Stat. Ann. § 33-742 (2006).

One claimed advantage of installment land contracts is that they enable persons of modest means to buy their own homes, as little or no down payment usually is required. Forfeiture, a quick and simple method of termination in case purchasers default, is one of the attractions that installment land contracts have for sellers and makes them more willing to enter into such transactions. Do you think that grace periods seriously deter use of the installment land contract as a security device in the sale of real estate? Are such contracts subject to so much abuse and capable of creating so much hardship on buyers that with or without grace periods on default they should be prohibited? Is the best solution that provided by the Uniform Land Transactions Act §§ 3-102 3-501(1975), in which transactions intended to create security interests in land, including mortgages and installment land contracts, are generally treated similarly, with the same rights and remedies in case of default? And see Okla. Stat. Ann. tit. 16, § 11A (West 1999), that holds most installment land contracts to be mortgages.

3. Other ways in which states by statute have sought to protect the installment land contract purchaser are to permit the purchaser of residential property to secure a deed and purchase money mortgage after 40 percent or more of the purchase price has been paid, Md. Real Prop. Code Ann. § 10-105 (Michie 2003); to require judicial foreclosure and sale for the seller to recover possession on default if the purchaser has made payments for at least five years or has paid 20 percent or more of the purchase price. Ohio Rev. Code Ann. § 5313.07 (Page 2002).

4. In many jurisdictions, landlords may not lock-out or otherwise use self-help to dispossess tenants wrongfully holding over. The rationale for this position is that the courts will provide adequate relief, without the risks of violence or other encroachment on tenants' rights that may result from such self-help. On these landlord self-help restrictions, see 2 Powell on Real Property § 17,02[2] (2003); and Restatement

(Second) of Property, Landlord and Tenant §§ 14.1-4.3. Those states imposing self-help restrictions on landlords are likely to impose similar restrictions on installment land contract sellers using self-help to dispossess buyers in default who have lost the legal right to continued possession.

I. PREJUDICIAL TREATMENT OF SOME HOME BUYERS

Many home buyers and prospective home buyers are vulnerable to prejudicial treatment by lenders and also by real estate brokers and casualty insurers. Particularly vulnerable are low- and moderate-income persons unrepresented by a lawyer in negotiating mortgage terms and in some urban areas racial minorities attempting to purchase homes. Two of the more common forms of prejudicial treatment of home buyers are predatory lending and redlining. Predatory lending is a vague concept but basically consists of lenders taking undue advantage of home buyers with very limited financial resources and often with little understanding of the legal obligations they are incurring when entering into a mortgage loan.[1] Predatory lending has been particularly prevalent in mortgage lending to racial minorities in some sections of big cities, such as parts of the South Side and West Side of Chicago and parts of the Bronx in New York City. Redlining is a form of prejudicial treatment of prospective home buyers because of their race, ethnicity, or class.[2] The term's origin is the blatant practice that some lenders at one time followed of outlining in red on local maps, often visible to their customers, areas of cities

1. Unmasking the Predatory Loan in Sheep's Clothing: A Legislative Proposal 21 Harv. Blackletter L. J. 129, 130 (2005).

Part of the complexity associated with addressing predatory lending is the fact that it can take many forms and is therefore difficult to define consistently. Put simply, predatory lending is the situation where a mortgage broker or mortgage lender engages in fraudulent, deceptive or sharp practices to induce borrowers (often the elderly or minorities) to enter into "bad" loans. The loans are "bad" because they contain one or more of the following features: (i) the loan is overpriced (i.e., containing interest rates, fees, and closing costs that are higher than they should be in light of the borrower's credit and net income); (ii) there is no net economic benefit to the refinance (commonly referred to as "loan flipping"); (iii) the borrower cannot afford to make the payments on the loan and the lender is counting on the borrower's equity in the property to become whole after the borrower defaults (commonly referred to as "equity stripping"); and (iv) the loan contains a myriad of other exploitive terms that the borrower does not comprehend (for example, a large prepayment charge or paying for credit life insurance in one lump sum when the loan is likely to be refinanced soon).

On predatory lending see also Azmy and Reiss, Modeling a Response to Predatory Lending: The New Jersey Home Ownership Security Act of 2002, 35 Rutgers L.J. 645 (2004); Engel and McCoy, A Tale of Three Markets: The Law and Economics of Predatory Lending, 80 Tex. L. Rev. 1255 (2002); Hammond, Predatory Lending — A Legal Definition and Update, 34 Real Est. L.J. 176 (2005); Lopez, Using the Fair Housing Act to Combat Predatory Lending, 6 Geo. J. on Poverty L. & Pol'y. 73 (1999). Professor Stark, in her article quoted above, more fully discusses predatory lending and sets forth a proposed Mortgage Counseling Intervention Law that requires applicants of high-cost home loans to receive counseling on the pricing of the loan and frequently the loan's advisability.

2. On redlining and the related issue of housing discrimination, see 2 Nelson and Whitman, Real Estate Finance Law, § 11.5 (2002); Days, Rethinking the Integrative Ideal: Housing, 33 McGeorge L. Rev. 459 (2002); Duncan et al., Redlining Practices, Racial Resegregation and Urban Decay: Neighborhood Housing Services as a Viable Alternative, 7 Urb. Law. 510 (1975).

where the lenders would not make mortgage loans, usually areas occupied predominantly by racial minorities.[3]

Federal and state governments have made efforts to legally prevent the more egregious aspects of predatory lending and redlining.[4] But these efforts have encountered problems of appropriately balancing the interests of lenders and borrowers, determining the extent to which the federal government should intervene in imposing legal controls, and establishing a workable and effective enforcement system for the legal controls that are imposed.

The objective of this section is to highlight the prejudicial treatment of some home buyers, problem, provide examples of laws aimed at the problem, and to note some of the difficulties in satisfactorily resolving the problem. Prejudicial treatment of home buyers and the laws concerning it are far too complicated a subject to attempt comprehensive coverage here.

An article that provides a very thorough analysis and critique of predatory lending appears in Engel and McCoy, A Tale of Three Markets: The Law and Economics of Predatory Lending, 80 Tex. L. Rev. 1255 (2002). In their article, Professors Engel and McCoy conclude that the then current law on predatory lending was inadequate in many respects. They make the following very significant observations:

> For the most part, neither the states nor the federal government have comprehensive laws designed to redress predatory lending. Instead, victims of predatory lending currently must rely on a loose assortment of statutes and common-law rules that were not designed to address the devastating harm inflicted by predatory lenders. These remedies are rooted in traditional liberal notions of informed consent and free will. Consistent with that liberal ideology, under current remedies, predatory-lending contracts are generally enforceable except where fraud or nondisclosure has operated in some way that is inimical to free will. Barring this sort of culpable misrepresentation, however, the law normally does not question the substance of predatory-loan terms. . . .
>
> Contract law, disclosure, and consumer counseling fail because they place the onus on highly vulnerable victims to refrain from signing loans, rather than on the lenders and brokers who perpetrate these loans. Fraud laws and antidiscrimination laws are more formidable, but their scope is too narrow and enforcement is suboptimal. The other traditional response, price regulation, has extensive adverse effects on the availability of credit.
>
> Given these shortfalls, an effective remedy must accomplish several things. It must force predatory lenders and brokers to internalize the harm that they cause and create effective disincentives to refrain from making predatory loans. It must compensate victims for their losses and grant reformation of predatory loan terms. It must outlaw predatory practices in such a way that the law is understandable, violations can be easily proven, and lenders and brokers cannot evade their obligations. At the same time, it must avoid unnecessary price regulation and excessive constraints on legitimate subprime lending. It must furnish the private bar and victims with adequate incentives to

3. Other home buyers and prospective home buyers that have occasionally encountered prejudicial treatment by lenders and real estate brokers are the elderly, families with small children, and homosexual couples.

4. On the various federal statutes aimed at restricting some aspects of predatory lending or redlining, see Barron and Berenson, Federal Regulation of Real Estate and Mortgage Lending (4th ed.); 2 Nelson and Whitman, Real Estate Finance Law § 11.5 (2002 and 2004 pocket part).

bring predatory lending claims, while avoiding incentives toward spurious claims. And it must promote the adoption of best practices by the mortgage industry.[49]

Shortly after the Engel and McCoy article was published, New Jersey enacted the New Jersey Home Ownership Security Act of 2002, some current sections of which appear below. To what extent does the New Jersey Act appear to fill the shortfalls noted by Engel and McCoy? What further changes, if any, seem needed?

N. J. Stat. Ann. 46:10 B-25 (Supp. 2006)

Prohibited practices

a. No creditor making a home loan shall finance, directly or indirectly, any credit life, credit disability, credit unemployment or credit property insurance, or any other life or health insurance, or any payments directly or indirectly for any debt cancellation or suspension agreement or contract, except that insurance premiums or debt cancellation or suspension fees calculated and paid on a monthly basis shall not be considered financed by the creditor.

c. No creditor shall recommend or encourage default on an existing loan or other debt prior to and in connection with the closing or planned closing of a home loan that refinances all or any portion of that existing loan or debt.

d. No creditor shall charge a late payment fee in relation to a home loan except according to the following rules:

(1) The late payment fee may not be in excess of 5% of the amount of the payment past due.

(2) The fee may only be assessed by a payment past due for 15 days or more.

(3) The fee may not be charged more than once with respect to a single late payment. If a late payment fee is deducted from a payment made on the loan, and such deduction causes a subsequent default on a subsequent payment, no late payment fee may be imposed for such default. If a late payment fee has been once imposed with respect to a particular late payment, no such fee shall be imposed with respect to any future payment which would have been timely and sufficient, but for the previous default.

(4) No fee shall be charged unless the creditor notifies the borrower within 45 days following the date the payment was due that a late payment fee has been imposed for a particular late payment. No late payment fee may be collected from any borrower if the borrower informs the creditor that nonpayment of an installment is in dispute and presents proof of payment within 45 days of receipt of the creditor's notice of the late fee.

(5) The creditor shall treat each and every payment as posted on the same date as it was received by the creditor, servicer, creditor's agent, or at the address provided to the borrower by the creditor, servicer, or the creditor's agent for making payments.

e. No home loan shall contain a provision that permits the creditor, in its sole discretion, to accelerate the indebtedness. This provision does not prohibit acceleration of the loan in good faith due to the borrower's failure to abide by the material terms of the loan.

---

49. Engel and McCoy, A Tale of Three Markets: The Law and Economics of Predatory Lending, 80 Tex. L. Rev. 1255, 1298, 1317-1318 (2002). The article also proposes a detailed remedy, which it refers to as a suitability remedy, that would impose obligations on subprime home loan lenders to make home loans suitable to the needs of the borrower, with appropriate safeguards and sanctions.

f. No creditor shall charge a fee for informing or transmitting to any person the balance due to pay off a home loan or to provide a release upon prepayment. Payoff balances shall be provided within seven business days after the request.

Honorable v. Easy Life Real Estate System

100 F.Supp.2d 885 (N.D. Ill. 2000)

BUCKLO, District Judge.

This case poses, most centrally, the question of what is required to make out an "exploitation" theory of liability for racial discrimination in the sale of real estate. The plaintiffs here are African–Americans who sought to buy rehabbed homes offered for sale by the defendants in or near the predominantly black Austin area on the west side of Chicago, Illinois. They claim that the defendants' selling practices violated 42 U. S. C. §§ 1981–82 (civil rights), and 42 U.S.C. § 3604(b) (Fair Housing Act), by taking unfair advantage of unsophisticated first time buyers in a racially discriminatory way.[1] The defendants move for summary judgment, and I deny the motion.

I

During the period of the violations alleged in this case, Easy Life Real Estate System ("Easy Life") offered homes it represented to be fully rehabbed for sale to first time buyers at very low down payments. It targeted the 95% African–American community of Austin on the West side of Chicago, arranging for Federal Housing Administration ("FHA") insured loans from certain lenders. Easy Life's agents told Ruby Honorable that one home in Austin, which she eventually bought, was "the only one" she qualified for. They falsely told Shirley and Stekeena Rollins that an Austin house Easy Life was selling was really in adjacent Oak Park, and then, when that deception was discovered, that it was too late to back out of the deal, although it was not. Easy Life's agents did not allow negotiation on the price of homes. They gave the buyers the funds for their down payments, making it appear that the money was a gift from a relative. They paid off Ms. Honorable's outstanding debts. Easy Life encouraged plaintiffs to bring in family members as co-signers, and had buyers sign blank pieces of paper where an explanation for credit delinquency could be filled in later. Easy Life prevented or discouraged plaintiffs from inspecting the homes, which were very shabbily done and not properly rehabbed.

II

A

In these circumstances, the plaintiffs argue that Easy Life and the other defendants (1) exploited unsophisticated buyers in a dual, racially segregated housing market

---

1. The plaintiffs also sued under the federal racketeering statute, 18 U.S.C. § 1962 ("RICO"), as well as various state law causes of action. In a previous opinion, I certified the class with respect to the discrimination claims for liability purposes, dismissed the plaintiffs' RICO and state law fraud claims, and limited the injunctive relief they might seek for the remaining state law claims, leaving this essentially as a discrimination case. *See Honorable v. Easy Life Real Estate System,* 182 F.R.D. 553 (N.D.Ill.1998) (laying out in more detail the identity of the parties and the background to this case).

by taking wrongful advantage of a situation created by socioeconomic forces tainted by racial discrimination. In doing these things, according to the plaintiffs, the defendants also (2) intentionally discriminated against African–American home buyers by deliberately targeting them with predatory sales practices, committing "reverse redlining." The Fair Housing Act also allows for (3) disparate impact liability, but that is not at issue here. The defendants ask for summary judgment because the law requires that for exploitation theory liability, they must be shown to have "market power," enough influence to shape the market, but their expert testimony shows that the defendants did not have market power in the relevant market.

Under the "exploitation" theory, as the Seventh Circuit explains it, the plaintiffs argue that:

> As a result of racial discrimination there existed two housing markets . . . , one for whites and another for blacks, with the supply of housing available in the black market far less than the demand. Defendants entered the black market selling homes for prices far in excess of their fair market value and far in excess of prices which whites pay for comparable homes in the white market and on more onerous terms than whites similarly situated would encounter. . . .

Clark v. Universal Builders, 501 F.2d 324, 328 (7th Cir.1974) (*Clark I*). To establish "exploitation" liability, the plaintiffs must show that (1) as a result of racial segregation, dual housing markets exist, and (2) defendant sellers took advantage of this situation by demanding prices and terms unreasonably in excess of prices and terms available to white citizens for comparable housing. *Clark v. Universal Builders, Inc.*, 706 F.2d 204, 206 (7th Cir.1983) (*Clark II*). Here (1) is not in dispute. Rather, the defendants argue that (2) is not true, that they could not have done what the plaintiffs allege because they lacked market power.

The defendants' claim that exploitation requires market power is derived from its reading of *Clark II*, where the Seventh Circuit held that this theory of liability "does not eliminate questions about how a business can set its prices above a reasonable level. In the absence of collusion, or a situation of a business having sufficient market power of its own, it is difficult to understand how a business could retain its market share against non-exploiting competitors." 706 F.2d at 212 n. 8. The plaintiffs there "presented no plausible explanation of how defendants could have charged unreasonable prices in the face of a market for housing which showed no indicia of being monopolized or uncompetitive. In other words, there [was] no adequate explanation of how the defendants could have obtained the market power to do what they [were] accused of doing." *Id.* at 211.

The language quoted by the defendants, however, does not support the claim that exploitation liability requires market power in the traditional sense of a large enough share of the market. What the Seventh Circuit requires, rather, is an economically credible explanation of how an exploiter can stay in business charging above-market prices. *Clark II* suggests that this could be established in at least three ways: by a showing of (1) collusion, (2) market power based in market share, or (3) some other basis not there offered by the plaintiffs. The Seventh Circuit does not make market power necessary for exploitation liability, as is shown by the explanatory qualification at 706 F.2d at 212 n. 8, cited by the defendants themselves. Market power based in market share is just one way to show the mechanism by which the exploitation occurs. A plaintiff may show others.

B

The plaintiffs do not argue that the defendants colluded with anyone else to raise prices in the relevant market. They rather argue that there was a mechanism other than possession of market power through which the defendants charged African–American home buyers housing prices unreasonably in excess of what white buyers were charged. The plaintiffs say that this case "involves much more than . . . excess pricing"; it also involves "a pattern of deception and misrepresentation targeted at first time home buyers in the overwhelmingly minority Austin community." In particular, the evidence in the record shows that the defendants "were deliberately depriving buyers of truthful information necessary to take meaningful advantage of competitive alternatives" by "grooming buyers who were totally dependant on Easy Life."

According to the plaintiffs, then, the defendants were able to exploit African–Americans by carving out a noncompetitive enclave in the market. Whether or not the defendants had market power in the relevant market, they were able to retain their market share and persist in these practices while charging above-market prices by, in effect, taking the unsophisticated, first-time minority buyers who had the misfortune to fall into their clutches out of the competitive market by deceptively making these buyers wholly dependant upon them for the mechanics and where-withal of home-buying, controlling their access to potential properties, loans, down payments, attorneys, and all their information. Their theory tracks the analysis of Professor Hanson and Douglas Kysar, who argue that "market outcomes frequently will be heavily influenced, if not determined, by the ability of one actor to control the format of information, the presentation of choices, and, in general, the setting within which market transactions occur," allowing some to "exploit those tendencies for gain." Jon G. Hanson & Douglas A. Kysar, *Taking Behavioralism Seriously: The Problem of Market Manipulation*, 74 N.Y.U. *L.Rev.* 630, 635 (1999). This is what the plaintiffs argue happened here. In the *Clark* cases, by contrast, there was no such evidence of markets being distorted by deception-driven dependency on the seller, and thus *Clark II* is distinguishable.

This is a novel, innovative and serious argument. Courts have been reluctant to assume consumers are too ignorant and benighted to fend for themselves merely because they are poor. *See, e.g., Miller v. Civil City of South Bend*, 904 F.2d 1081, 1098 (7th Cir.1990), *rev'd on other grounds by Barnes v. Glen Theatre*, 501 U.S. 560, 111 S.Ct. 2456, 115 L.Ed.2d 504 (1991) ("The robust paternalism and class consciousness that once permitted such a distinction have lost their legitimacy.") (free speech context). However, this is not a case where a court makes unwarranted presumptions that people lack the information, confidence, and experience to be "normal" consumers. Here the plaintiffs themselves argue that they were thus limited. Therefore, I do no more than take the plaintiffs at their word. That is not class snobbery or paternalism.

More deeply, the economic theories that imply that market prices are efficient, thus beneficial for consumers, presuppose that consumers are informed, markets are competitive, and the costs of making transactions are not excessively burdensome. To produce theoretical equilibrium, neoclassical economics in fact assumes *perfect* information, *perfect* competition, and *no* transaction costs, among other idealizations. But these assumptions must be relaxed, and perhaps, ultimately replaced, if economic theory is to have any application to what happens in actual markets.[2] In the ordinary case, the assumptions are roughly approximately true, or it would be a miracle if the theory had any degree of predictive or explanatory power. However, if these conditions fail to obtain to a sufficient degree, even the rough efficiency of the market outcome can no longer be presumed. The conclusion (that markets are efficient) no longer follows from the premises.

Housing markets in particular, even in the ordinary case, may well be several steps removed from the standard assumptions because of the special characteristics of the product and the complexity of the transaction. Professor Eskridge argues that research shows that "homebuyers usually do not engage in wealth-maximizing behavior but, instead, act like 'satisficers.' They search for alternatives until they find one that is 'good enough,' rather than 'best.'" William N. Eskridge, *One Hundred Years of Ineptitude: The Need for Mortgage Rules Consonant with the Economic and Psychological Dynamics of the Home Sale and Loan Transaction*, 70 *Va. L.Rev.* 1083, 1114 (1984) (internal citations omitted). Eskridge notes that although "satisficing . . . generally yield[s] good results for low-cost decisions, it may be a poor strategy for high-cost decisions such as buying and financing a home. A bad decision made on insufficient information costs the homebuyer thousands of dollars." *Id.* First time homebuyers are less likely to shop around because of stress. *Id.* at 1116 (internal citations omitted). Moreover, even in the ordinary case, "the formally integrated transaction," combining all the financial aspects of homebuying into a package, means that "shopping is curtailed and rational decisionmaking made more difficult." *Id.* at 1126 (internal citations omitted).

When this situation is combined with evidence of racially discriminatory market manipulation by control of information and all aspects of the transaction in a context where the homebuyers are arguably especially vulnerable to manipulation, the plaintiffs have come forward with evidence that the business practices of the defendants might well have distorted the markets enough to enable them to stay in business while charging above market rates to their selected clientele.

Moreover, the defendants do not really challenge this claim. They might have argued that the plaintiffs had not shown that Easy Life's customers really had no other options once Easy Life got hold of them, but, as explained below, the defendants merely assume that ordinary, "rational" consumers would have had other options and taken them. An undefended assumption, even if it is part of an economic theory, is not enough to carry a summary judgment motion in the face of

---

2. Recent research has pointed towards developing a new approach to the application of economics that treats these deviations from standard assumptions systematically. *See* generally Richard H. Thaler, *Quasi–Rational Economics* (1991). The term "quasi-rational" refers to the fact that people's actual behavior departs from that of the "rational actor" posited by standard economic models. The recent development of "behavioral" law and economics attempts to apply a more realistic set of assumptions. *See Behavioral Law and Economics* (Cass R. Sunstein ed.1999); Symposium, *The Legal Implications of Psychology: Human Behavior, Behavioral Economics, and the Law*, 51 *Vand. L.Rev.* 1495 (1998).

Judge Posner contends that behavioral law and economics is "merely a set of challenges to the theory-builders" rather than a theory itself. Richard A. Posner *Rational Choice, Behavioral Economics, and the Law*, 50 *Stan. L.Rev.* 1551, 1560–61 (1998). This is fair enough, at least so far, but that does not mean the criticisms are not valid. More fundamental discussions of the limits of economic rationality can be found in Jon Elster, *Sour Grapes: Studies in the Subversion of Rationality* (1983) and Elizabeth S. Anderson, *Value in Ethics and Economics* (1993).

competent evidence that the assumption is false. The defendants rest their case for summary judgment on the proposition that the plaintiffs must show that they had market power. They do not adequately consider any other ways that the defendants could get away with selling houses at noncompetitive rates, such as the market distortion theory. The defendants, therefore, have waived this response.

The defendants' direct attempt to deal with the plaintiffs' market distortion argument is to argue, first, that under the plaintiffs' theory, "any seller of the home at the market price would be guilty of exploitation." This would "revolution-ize the economic structure in Austin, resulting in the flight of businessman and service providers to avoid claims of exploitation based on race." The defendants thus recycle the argument that attempts to enforce civil rights legislation will backfire, harming the people it is supposed to benefit as businesses flee to avoid lawsuits. They offer no evidentiary or legal support for this ancient and disreputable proposition.

Second, the defendants argue that the plaintiffs' theory opens unlimited vistas of liability. This represents a misunderstanding. For the plaintiffs' theory to succeed, the plaintiffs must show that (1) the prices charged were systematically above-market; this could not be presumed merely from a showing that the market was distorted;[3] (2) the purported exploiters deliberately subverted the conditions for market competition by closing off access to alternatives and information, deceptive-ly making naive and unsophisticated people dependant on them; this could not be shown from the mere existence of imperfect competition; and (3) there was racial discrimination involved in this exploitative process. The defendants' hypothetical African–American Austin homeowner offering his own home for sale at the market rate would, therefore, be safe.

C

I here consider whether the defendants could prevail on their chosen terms. Did Easy Life have market power in the relevant market anyway? The defendants argue that for market power, Easy Life, as a matter of law, must have had at least a 35% market share in the relevant market, referring to the Federal Trade Commission's Horizontal Merger Guidelines, which state that firms with a market share below 35% are presumed to be unable to exercise market dominance. *See also Valley Liquors, Inc., v. Renfield Importers, Ltd.*, 678 F.2d 742 (7th Cir.1982) (*Valley I*) (antitrust), *and* 822 F.2d 656 (7th Cir.1987) (*Valley II*) (same).

The plaintiffs respond that antitrust standards do not apply in a discrimination context. Antitrust laws are meant to encourage vigorous competition, promote economic efficiency, and maximize consumer welfare. *MCI Communications Corp. v. American Tel. & Tel. Co.*, 708 F.2d 1081, 1113 (7th Cir.1983). The FHA, by contrast, "is concerned with ending racially segregated housing." *Southend Neighborhood Improvement Assoc. v. County of St. Clair*, 743 F.2d 1207, 1210 (7th Cir.1984). Sections 1982 (no racial discrimination in housing) and 1981 (same for contracts) are

---

3. The plaintiffs' evidence of overpricing is mainly that the condition of the houses was too awful to bear the tariff Easy Life charged. This is circumstantial, but it is not defeated by the defendants' claim that the price was efficient because it was the price charged in the market, a question-begging argument unless the presuppositions of efficiency are demonstrated in the face of the plaintiffs' challenge.

likewise civil rights laws. Where the goals differ, the plaintiffs say, so should the standards.

But the defendants are correct that, in the absence of some other mechanism, which, in this subsection, I assume for the sake of argument is lacking, the defendants would not have the "capability," required by *Clark II*, 706 F.2d at 212, to affect prices without market power. The antitrust standard for market share is not addressed to narrow antitrust concerns of efficiency as opposed to nondiscrimination, but to what courts have held to be required by economic theory to affect price in an otherwise competitive market. If the defendants cannot affect price, they cannot exploit minorities by discriminatory pricing.[4] So, setting aside other novel mechanisms such as the market distortion argument discussed above, the plaintiffs must show that the defendants had market power in the relevant market. This does not go to whether the defendants committed illegal discrimination under some other theory than the exploitation theory, as discussed below.

The defendants argue that the relevant market is all available residences in the predominantly African–American areas of Chicago and its suburbs.[5] They offer expert testimony by economists at Lexecon, Inc., a research firm that provides economic analyses for legal purposes, that Easy Life's market share of "all African–American residents" in the greater Chicago area was approximately 4.1 percent. Even in the Austin market, the defendants' analysis indicates that its market share was only between 6 and 10.5 percent. Lexecon concludes that there were no significant barriers to market entry even in Austin, where at least 25 other sellers of homes operated during the period of the alleged violations, and at least six other firms were rehabbing homes. The plaintiffs object that the Lexecon analysis understates Easy Life's market shares by 100%, because it treats Home Mortgage Disclosure Act figures referring to single family homes, defined as one-unit to four-unit properties, as if the figures represented only single-unit properties. The corrected figures nonetheless do not push the figures up to the 35% market share.

I agree with the plaintiffs, however, that their own experts' analyses have generated a triable issue of fact as to whether the defendants had market power. First, the defendants' argument that the relevant geographical market is all the predominantly African–American residential areas of Chicago presumes that rational and informed buyers, facing above-market prices for decrepit properties in Austin, would look elsewhere. However, Lexecon does not justify the assumption that the plaintiff class is well enough described by the ideal rational actor picture as would be required to make this story work. The plaintiffs, on the other hand, specifically dispute the claim, presenting expert testimony that members of the class are, rather, especially unsophisticated, uninformed, naive, vulnerable, and easily prey to misrepresentation and pressure of the sort that they contend the defendants committed. A rational jury might find that the members of the class, because of

4. On the plaintiffs' own market distortion theory, the markets are not otherwise competitive; the discriminatorily created dependency is what serves the function of market-share based market power in the standard theory.

5. The defendants also say that "the proper definition of the relevant market includes all residential options available to African–Americans . . . in Chicago and its suburbs." As we do not have legally segregated housing, and African–Americans, at least in theory, can live anyplace they can afford, that would mean the relevant market is the whole Chicagoland area. However, the defendants' expert study restricted its analysis to the predominantly African–American areas, on the unfortunately plausible assumption that in a housing market as segregated as Chicagoland, many predominantly white areas are not in practice reasonably available to African–Americans.

their special characteristics and the defendants' conduct, would be unlikely to substitute housing outside of Austin. There is, therefore a jury question about whether the geographical limits of the relevant market is Austin or a wider area.

Second, there is a material issue about whether the defendants exceeded the 35% requirement for market power. The plaintiffs offer expert testimony that Easy Life dominated the rehabbed homes market in Austin, listing or selling 63% of the rehabbed homes in Austin during the time in question. The Lexecon analysis does not directly address whether the rehabbed homes market in Austin is the relevant product market. The argument that rational buyers would substitute cheaper homes offered by others outside Austin for more expensive homes offered by Easy Life in Austin suggests that Lexecon would say the same thing about rehabbed as opposed to nonrehabbed homes, in Austin or elsewhere, as standard economic analysis would imply.

But, as explained, standard economic analysis may not apply to the plaintiff class in anything like the straightforward way that Lexecon assumes. The plaintiffs offer evidence that Easy Life's customer base may have been attracted to home ownership in Austin specifically by the prospect of obtaining a rehabbed property (perhaps on the assumption that they could afford nothing else), and so a rational finder of fact could conclude that Easy Life controlled more than 35% of the relevant product and geographical market so understood. These empirical arguments based in the plaintiffs' concrete circumstances cannot be defeated by a one-size-fits-all use of economic theory where the applicability of its fundamental assumptions to the facts at hand are put in question by competent evidence in the case.

III

Even if I were to accept the defendants' arguments about market power, there is an alternative reason why summary judgment cannot be granted. The defendants' motion is directed solely to the exploitation theory. It does not address the plaintiffs' intentional discrimination claims about "reverse redlining." Redlining is the practice of denying the extension of credit to specific geographic areas due to the income, race, or ethnicity of its residents.[6] Reverse redlining is the practice of extending credit on unfair terms to those same communities. See S.Rep. No. 103–169, at 21 (1993), *reprinted in* 1994 U.S.C.C.A.N. 1881, 1905; *see also Reverse Redlining: Problems in Home Equity Lending,* before the Senate Committee on Banking, Housing, and Urban Affairs, 103rd Cong. 243–471 (1993).

These sort of practices come within the ambit of the Fair Housing Act; *see NAACP v. American Family Mut. Ins. Co.,* 978 F.2d 287, 301 (7th Cir.1992) (discriminatory denials of insurance and discriminatory pricing), which is to be read broadly. Courts have construed the statute to cover "mortgage 'redlining,' insurance redlining, racial steering, exclusionary zoning decisions, and other actions by individuals or governmental units which directly affect the availability of housing to minorities." *Southend Assoc.,* 743 F.2d at 1209–10 & n. 3 (citing cases). The law is "violated by discriminatory actions, or certain actions with discriminatory effects,

---

6. The term was derived from the actual practice of drawing a red line around certain areas in which credit would be denied. *United Companies Lending Corp. v. Sargeant,* 20 *F.Supp.* 2d 192, 203 n. 5 (D.Mass.1998).

that affect the availability of housing." *Id.* at 1210. If so, the law would also prohibit reverse redlining. Although sections 1981 and 1982 are narrower, *id.*, they may be construed to prohibit some or all of the practices of which the plaintiffs produce evidence here; the defendants have at least waived the right to argue the contrary here by failing to do it.

IV

In sum, the plaintiff's have indicated a mechanism whereby the defendants might have exploited minority homebuyers in Austin by discriminatorily creating dependency and distorting the housing market. The plaintiffs have also raised a triable issue of fact about whether the defendants had market power in the relevant market because the special characteristics of the plaintiff class could have inhibited the substitution that would have widened the relevant market and diluted the defendants' market share. Finally, the defendants do not address the plaintiffs' arguments based on an intentional discrimination rather than an exploitation theory. Therefore I DENY the defendants' motion for summary judgment.

NOTES AND QUESTIONS

1. Two federal statutes that impose restrictions on redlining, statutes referred to in the Honorable v. Easy Life Real Estate System opinion, are the Civil Rights Act and the Fair Housing Act. Sections of these acts appear below. There are other federal statutes that at least in part are aimed at the redlining problem. Among them are the Home Mortgage Disclosure Act, 12 U.S.C.A. §§ 2801 et seq., the Community Reinvestment Act of 1977, 12 U.S.C.A. §§ 2901 et seq., and the Equal Credit Opportunity Act, 15 U.S.C.A. §§ 1691 et seq.

2. Some states also have anti-redlining statutes, see e.g., Cal. Health & Safety Code, §§ 35800 et seq. (West 1999); N.J. Stat. Ann. 17:16 F1 to 17:16 F-11 (2001).

3. Despite existing anti-redlining laws, prejudicial treatment of prospective home buyers because of their race, ethnicity, or class still is common and extensive. Why is this so and what more can and should the legal system do to prevent such prejudicial treatment?

Civil Rights Act

42. U.S.C.A. (2003)

§ 1981. Equal rights under the law

(a) Statement of equal rights

All persons within the jurisdiction of the United States shall have the same right in every State and Territory to make and enforce contracts, to sue, be parties, give evidence, and to the full and equal benefit of all laws and proceedings for the security of persons and property as is enjoyed by white citizens, and shall be subject to like punishment, pains, penalties, taxes, licenses, and exactions of every kind, and to no other.

(b) "Make and enforce contracts" defined

For purposes of this section, the term "make and enforce contracts" includes the making, performance, modification, and termination of contracts, and the enjoyment of all benefits, privileges, terms, and conditions of the contractual relationship.

(c) Protection against impairment

The rights protected by this section are protected against impairment by nongovernmental discrimination and impairment under color of State law.

§ 1982. Property rights of citizens

All citizens of the United States shall have the same right, in every State and Territory, as is enjoyed by white citizens thereof to inherit, purchase, lease, sell, hold, and convey real and personal property.

Fair Housing Act

45 U.S.C.A. (2003)

§ 3601. Declaration of policy

It is the policy of the United States to provide, within constitutional limitations, for fair housing throughout the United States.

§ 3603. Effective dates of certain prohibitions

(a) Application to certain described dwellings

Subject to the provisions of subsection (b) of this section and section 3607 of this title, the prohibitions against discrimination in the sale or rental of housing set forth in section 3604 of this title shall apply:

(1) Upon enactment of this subchapter, to —

(A) dwellings owned or operated by the Federal Government;

(B) dwellings provided in whole or in part with the aid of loans, advances, grants, or contributions made by the Federal Government, under agreements entered into after November 20, 1962, unless payment due thereon has been made in full prior to April 11, 1968;

(C) dwellings provided in whole or in part by loans insured, guaranteed, or otherwise secured by the credit of the Federal Government, under agreements entered into after November 20, 1962, unless payment thereon has been made in full prior to April 11, 1968: *Provided,* That nothing contained in subparagraphs (B) and (C) of this subsection shall be applicable to dwellings solely by virtue of the fact that they are subject to mortgages held by an FDIC or FSLIC institution; and

(D) dwellings provided by the development or the redevelopment of real property purchased, rented, or otherwise obtained from a State or local public agency receiving Federal financial assistance for slum clearance or urban renewal with respect to such real property under loan or grant contracts entered into after November 20, 1962.

(2) After December 31, 1968, to all dwellings covered by paragraph (1) and to all other dwellings except as exempted by subsection (b) of this section.

(b) Exemptions

Nothing in section 3604 of this title (other than subsection (c)) shall apply to —

(1) any single-family house sold or rented by an owner: *Provided,* That such private individual owner does not own more than three such single-family houses at any one time: *Provided further,* That in the case of the sale of any such single-family house by a private individual owner not residing in such house at the time of such sale or who was not the most recent resident of such house prior to such sale, the exemption granted by this subsection shall apply only with respect to one such sale within any twenty-four month period: *Provided further,* That such bona fide private individual owner does not own any interest in, nor is there owned or reserved on his behalf, under any express or voluntary agreement, title to or any right to all or a portion of the proceeds from the sale or rental of, more than three such single-family houses at any one time: *Provided further,* That after December 31, 1969, the sale or rental of any such single-family house shall be excepted from the application of this subchapter only if such house is sold or rented (A) without the use in any manner of the sales or rental facilities or the sales or rental services of any real estate broker, agent, or salesman, or of such facilities or services of any person in the business of selling or renting dwellings, or of any employee or agent of any such broker, agent, salesman, or person and (B) without the publication, posting or mailing, after notice, of any advertisement or written notice in violation of section 3604(c) of this title; but nothing in this proviso shall prohibit the use of attorneys, escrow agents, abstractors, title companies, and other such professional assistance as necessary to perfect or transfer the title, or

(2) rooms or units in dwellings containing living quarters occupied or intended to be occupied by no more than four families living independently of each other, if the owner actually maintains and occupies one of such living quarters as his residence.

(c) Business of selling or renting dwellings defined

For the purposes of subsection (b) of this section, a person shall be deemed to be in the business of selling or renting dwellings if —

(1) he has, within the preceding twelve months, participated as principal in three or more transactions involving the sale or rental of any dwelling or any interest therein, or

(2) he has, within the preceding twelve months, participated as agent, other than in the sale of his own personal residence in providing sales or rental facilities or sales or rental services in two or more transactions involving the sale or rental of any dwelling or any interest therein, or

(3) he is the owner of any dwelling designed or intended for occupancy by, or occupied by, five or more families.

§ 3604. Discrimination in the sale or rental of housing and other prohibited practices

As made applicable by section 3603 of this title and except as exempted by sections 3603(b) and 3607 of this title, it shall be unlawful —

(a) To refuse to sell or rent after the making of a bona fide offer, or to refuse to negotiate for the sale or rental of, or otherwise make unavailable or deny, a dwelling to any person because of race, color, religion, sex, familial status, or national origin.

(b) To discriminate against any person in the terms, conditions, or privileges of sale or rental of a dwelling, or in the provision of services or facilities in connection therewith, because of race, color, religion, sex, familial status, or national origin.

(c) To make, print, or publish, or cause to be made, printed, or published any notice, statement, or advertisement, with respect to the sale or rental of a dwelling that indicates any preference, limitation, or discrimination based on race, color, religion, sex, handicap, familial status, or national origin, or an intention to make any such preference, limitation, or discrimination.

(d) To represent to any person because of race, color, religion, sex, handicap, familial status, or national origin that any dwelling is not available for inspection, sale, or rental when such dwelling is in fact so available.

(e) For profit, to induce or attempt to induce any person to sell or rent any dwelling by representations regarding the entry or prospective entry into the neighborhood of a person or persons of a particular race, color, religion, sex, handicap, familial status, or national origin.

(f)(1) To discriminate in the sale or rental, or to otherwise make unavailable or deny, a dwelling to any buyer or renter because of a handicap of—

(A) that buyer or renter,

(B) a person residing in or intending to reside in that dwelling after it is so sold, rented, or made available; or

(C) any person associated with that buyer or renter.

(2) To discriminate against any person in the terms, conditions, or privileges of sale or rental of a dwelling, or in the provision of services or facilities in connection with such dwelling, because of a handicap of—

(A) that person; or

(B) a person residing in or intending to reside in that dwelling after it is so sold, rented, or made available; or

(C) any person associated with that person.

(3) For purposes of this subsection, discrimination includes—

(A) a refusal to permit, at the expense of the handicapped person, reasonable modifications of existing premises occupied or to be occupied by such person if such modifications may be necessary to afford such person full enjoyment of the premises except that, in the case of a rental, the landlord may where it is reasonable to do so condition permission for a modification on the renter agreeing to restore the interior of the premises to the condition that existed before the modification, reasonable wear and tear excepted.

(B) a refusal to make reasonable accommodations in rules, policies, practices, or services, when such accommodations may be necessary to afford such person equal opportunity to use and enjoy a dwelling; or

(C) in connection with the design and construction of covered multi-family dwellings for first occupancy after the date that is 30 months after September 13, 1988, a failure to design and construct those dwellings in such a manner that—

(i) the public use and common use portions of such dwellings are readily accessible to and usable by handicapped persons;

(ii) all the doors designed to allow passage into and within all premises within such dwellings are sufficiently wide to allow passage by handicapped persons in wheelchairs; and

(iii) all premises within such dwellings contain the following features of adaptive design:

(I) an accessible route into and through the dwelling;

(II) light switches, electrical outlets, thermostats, and other environmental controls in accessible locations;

(III) reinforcements in bathroom walls to allow later installation of grab bars; and

(IV) usable kitchens and bathrooms such that an individual in a wheelchair can maneuver about the space.

(4) Compliance with the appropriate requirements of the American National Standard for buildings and facilities providing accessibility and usability for physically handicapped people (commonly cited as "ANSI A117.1") suffices to satisfy the requirements of paragraph (3)(C)(iii).

(5)(A) If a State or unit of general local government has incorporated into its laws the requirements set forth in paragraph (3)(C), compliance with such laws shall be deemed to satisfy the requirements of that paragraph.

(B) A State or unit of general local government may review and approve newly constructed covered multifamily dwellings for the purpose of making determinations as to whether the design and construction requirements of paragraph (3)(C) are met.

(C) The Secretary shall encourage, but may not require, States and units of local government to include in their existing procedures for the review and approval of newly constructed covered multifamily dwellings, determinations as to whether the design and construction of such dwellings are consistent with paragraph (3)(C), and shall provide technical assistance to States and units of local government and other persons to implement the requirements of paragraph (3)(C).

(D) Nothing in this subchapter shall be construed to require the Secretary to review or approve the plans, designs or construction of all covered multifamily dwellings, to determine whether the design and construction of such dwellings are consistent with the requirements of paragraph (3)(C).

(6)(A) Nothing in paragraph (5) shall be construed to affect the authority and responsibility of the Secretary or a State or local public agency certified pursuant to section 3610(f)(3) of this title to receive and process complaints or otherwise engage in enforcement activities under this subchapter.

(B) Determinations by a State or a unit of general local government under paragraphs (5)(A) and (B) shall not be conclusive in enforcement proceedings under this subchapter.

(7) As used in this subsection, the term "covered multifamily dwellings" means—

(A) buildings consisting of 4 or more units if such buildings have one or more elevators; and

(B) ground floor units in other buildings consisting of 4 or more units.

(8) Nothing in this subchapter shall be construed to invalidate or limit any law of a State or political subdivision of a State, or other jurisdiction in which this subchapter shall be effective, that requires dwellings to be designed and constructed in a manner that affords handicapped persons greater access than is required by this subchapter.

(9) Nothing in this subsection requires that a dwelling be made available to an individual whose tenancy would constitute a direct threat to the health or safety of other individuals or whose tenancy would result in substantial physical damage to the property of others.

§ 3605. Discrimination in residential real estate-related transactions

(a) In general

It shall be unlawful for any person or other entity whose business includes engaging in residential real estate-related transactions to discriminate against any person in making available such a transaction, or in the terms or conditions of such a transaction, because of race, color, religion, sex, handicap, familial status, or national origin.

(b) "Residential real estate-related transaction" defined

As used in this section, the term "residential real estate-related transaction" means any of the following:

> (1) The making or purchasing of loans or providing other financial assistance —
>
>> (A) for purchasing, constructing, improving, repairing, or maintaining a dwelling; or
>>
>> (B) secured by residential real estate.
>
> (2) The selling, brokering, or appraising of residential real property.

(c) Appraisal exemption

Nothing in this subchapter prohibits a person engaged in the business of furnishing appraisals of real property to take into consideration factors other than race, color, religion, national origin, sex, handicap, or familial status.

§ 3615. Effect on State laws

Nothing in this subchapter shall be construed to invalidate or limit any law of a State or political subdivision of a State, or of any other jurisdiction in which this subchapter shall be effective, that grants, guarantees, or protects the same rights as are granted by this subchapter; but any law of a State, a political subdivision, or other such jurisdiction that purports to require or permit any action that would be a discriminatory housing practice under this subchapter shall to that extent be invalid.

CHAPTER THREE

Basic Tax Considerations of the Real Estate Transaction

The Internal Revenue Code has done even more than Quia Emptores to revolutionize real estate transactions. So common an event as the sale or purchase of a family or vacation home is fraught with tax considerations, even though more compelling matters of personal preference and need usually control the choice. For transactions in which the primary purpose is not to provide housing for the taxpayer, tax factors are essential to the investment decision: to sell or not to sell, to invest or not to invest, to buy or to lease, to pay all cash or to finance, to sell for all cash or to give credit to the buyer, and so forth. Moreover, the choice of organizational form and the financial terms and legal structure of the transaction may determine whether the investor achieves his or her tax objectives. The real estate lawyer can no more remain ignorant of taxes than can the physician of antibiotics (or, for that matter, of taxes).

Over the years, real estate investments have been subject to a wide range of tax policies and tax changes can have a dramatic impact on the real estate market. During the early 1980s, for example, tax shelters that took advantage of heavy leverage and accelerated depreciation made real estate investment vastly more attractive than many investment options that were far more economically productive. The Tax Reform Act of 1986 (TRA) changed the tax landscape more extensively than did any occurrence since Congress enacted the Internal Revenue Code of 1954. To provide for reduction of the ceiling rate from 50 to 28 percent,[1] and to do so in a revenue-neutral fashion, Congress had to greatly enlarge the income base on which tax rates are levied. This meant the repeal or tightening of a broad range of "preferential" items — credits, deductions, and exemptions, which had become imbedded in the Code. In curtailing these benefits, Congress hammered real estate investment especially hard. Commercial properties lost as much as half of their value in many markets, and the collapse of real estate values played an important role in the savings and loan crisis that cost the federal government over $200 billion.

At the heart of nearly all tax planning are two ideas: pay as little as possible; and hold off on paying it for as long as possible. For real estate investors, the first idea — pay as little as possible — is intimately wrapped up in the rules for recovering the acquisition cost of real property (that is, depreciation deductions), and the ability to

---

1. The top rate has been increased several times since then, first to 31 percent and then to 39.6 percent.

use those depreciation deductions to offset income generated by the real property and/or outside income. The ability to avoid tax this way has been dealt with through three major sets of rules: at-risk rules, passive activity loss rules, and depreciation recapture, each of which we will be addressing. The second idea, pay as late as possible, is at the heart of numerous tax strategies, including installment sales, deferred payment, and section 1031 exchanges.

A. COST RECOVERY (DEPRECIATION) AND TAX CREDITS

1. Cost Recovery (Depreciation)

Depreciation is a means of allocating the cost of an asset over the years of its projected useful life. If an asset is subject to wear and tear, wasting, or obsolescence, its owner's net worth is gradually reduced by the declining value of the property. For both accounting and taxation purposes, the basic aim of cost recovery is to calculate more accurately the owner's net income or loss during each year of the asset's use, by recognizing the asset's economic attrition as it occurs, rather than delaying recognition until the property is disposed of or scrapped.

Beyond its tax accounting role, the allowance for depreciation can become a powerful incentive to develop and acquire property. When Congress sought to stimulate the economy with the 1981 passage of the Economic Recovery Tax Act (ERTA), it introduced "Accelerated Cost Recovery System (ACRS)," which enabled taxpayers to write off in 15 years, rather than the 40 years under prior law, the cost of newly built real estate improvements. Through the interplay of the *Crane* rule — which adds to the property's adjusted basis any bona fide mortgage used to acquire the property — and the pre-TRA exemption from the at-risk rules — which meant that nonrecourse and recourse mortgages could generate the same loss deductions — the real estate investor was able to obtain through tax benefits alone (with little monetary risk) an after-tax yield that was hugely attractive whether the property was economically sound or not.

As early as 1984, Congress began to have second thoughts about ERTA's role as a real estate stimulant,[2] and, two years later, TRA repealed the use of ACRS for post-1986 real estate investments. The recovery period for property placed in service after 1986 is 27.5 years for residential rental property and 39 years for nonresidential property. Worse still, TRA required the investor to use straight-line depreciation in every case.[3]

For properties placed in service prior to 1987, each of the prior systems remains in force. To illustrate the differing impact on real estate of the pre-ERTA, ERTA,

---

2. That year, Congress lengthened the cost recovery period to 18 years and in 1985 added a nineteenth year.

3. TRA loosened the straight-line method in one respect: the taxpayer need not account for salvage value. I.R.C. § 168(b)(3). TRA also provided for the optional use of a 40-year straight-line write-off both for residential and nonresidential properties. I.R.C. § 168(g)(2). Few investors are likely to find this option attractive, except perhaps those seeking to avoid the alternative minimum tax.

and TRA rules, a $1 million all-cash investment in a commercial property placed in service on January 1 would produce a maximum first-year cost recovery as follows:

Pre-ERTA (1980)	$ 50,000
ERTA (1981)	$120,000
TRA (1987)	$ 30,400

a. Depreciation Methods

Problem: On January 1st, X places in service an apartment house costing $3 million, the construction price allocated between land $500,000 and building $2.5 million. Compute the cost recovery allowance for the first and second year by the straight-line method, and by the double and 175 percent declining balance methods.

Straight-line depreciation: At present, straight-line depreciation is the only cost recovery method available to real estate investors. The computation is made by applying a constant multiple to a constant balance. The cost of residential real estate can currently be recovered over 27.5 years, and salvage value can be ignored. Only the $2.5 million cost allocated to the building is recoverable. X multiplies that cost by the reciprocal of the recovery period — in the case of a 27.5-year period, approximately 3.64 percent ($2,500,000 × .0364 = $91,000). The depreciation for the second and each succeeding year remains unchanged.

Double declining balance: From 1954 until 1981, the Code permitted the owner of newly built rental real estate to elect, as an alternative to the straight-line method, the declining balance form of accelerated depreciation. In the case of apartments, double (or 200 percent) declining balance was the most favorable treatment allowed. The computation is made by applying a constant multiple to a changing balance. Under double declining balance, the constant multiple is equal to twice the straight-line rate for the given asset. During this era, new apartments could be written off over 40 years (estimated useful life). Thus, the constant multiple is 5 percent (2 × .025). This percentage is multiplied by the undepreciated balance[4] — in our example, $2.5 million in the first year — to result in an allowance of $125,000. In the second year this process is repeated; since the undepreciated balance has declined to $2,375,000, the product also declines ($2,375,000 × .05 = $118,750). In succeeding years the drop continues; if charted, the depreciation would resemble a hyperbolic curve. After a number of years, the taxpayer would benefit by switching to straight-line depreciation, a move the Code permitted.

175 percent declining balance: During the ERTA era, the depreciation tables for real estate allowed a 15-year cost recovery period, and the 175 percent declining balance method of depreciation.[5] The computation theory is the same as for double declining balance — that is, a constant multiple applied to a changing balance, except that (a) the constant multiple is 1.75 times the straight-line rate

---

4. Taxpayers using the declining balance methods do not account for salvage value in computing depreciation. This is because of the impossibility, under this method, of reducing the basis to zero.

5. Double declining balance was permitted for low-income rental housing. I.R.C. of 1954, § 168 (b)(2)(A), (3)(A).

and (b) under ERTA's 15-year cost recovery period, the straight-line rate became 6.67 percent. Thus, the first year's allowance is $291,812 ($2,500,000 × .0667 × 1.75).[6] The second year's allowance is $257,751.

b. Depreciation Recapture

"Recapture" is a means of preventing taxpayers from transforming ordinary income into capital gains, which are taxed at a lower rate.[7] Suppose that the taxpayer has taken $100,000 in cost recovery deductions prior to his sale of the property. The $100,000 reduction in adjusted basis will lead to the first $100,000 of gain at the time of sale. The cost recovery deductions, however, offset ordinary income, whereas the reciprocal gain would enjoy the more favorable capital gains treatment. The Code repairs this asymmetry by taxing — that is, recapturing — gains attributable to basis reduction as ordinary income.

Recapture has taken several forms since it entered the Code in the early 1960s. These variations reflect how long the property was held prior to sale, whether it qualified as either residential property or low-income housing, which tended to enjoy more benign treatment, and to whom the property was transferred. The basic approach respecting real property has been to "recapture" — that is, to treat as ordinary income — only the excess of depreciation actually taken over the allowances that straight-line depreciation would have produced during the holding period.[8] Today, recapture is broader, in that all gain attributable to depreciation must typically be recaptured and is taxed at a 25 percent rate.

2. Tax Credits

a. The Rehabilitation Tax Credit

To qualify for the one-time rehabilitation tax credit, a building must have been (1) "substantially rehabilitated," (2) placed in service before the beginning of the rehabilitation, and (3) left with at least 75 percent of its preexisting external walls intact.[9] In addition, unless the building is a certified historic structure, it must have been placed in service for the first time at least 30 years before the rehabilitation began.[10] A building has been "substantially rehabilitated" only if "qualified

---

6. The ERTA tables rounded off the first year's cost recovery to $300,000.

7. TRA evened the capital gains and ordinary income tax rates, but subsequent increases in the top rate on ordinary income and reductions in the capital gains tax rate have revived the differential. As of 2006, long-term capital gains (gains on assets held for more than one year) are taxed at either a 5 percent or 15 percent rate, depending on the taxpayer's tax bracket.

8. I.R.C. § 1250. I.R.C. § 1245, which deals with recapture for non-realty assets, reaches all depreciation previously allowed. The Code similarly taxed the depreciated-related gain on all nonresidential properties placed in service between 1981 and 1986, except where straight-line depreciation was used. I.R.C. § 1250(c), 1250(d)(11), 1245(a)(1).

9. I.R.C. § 48(g)(1)(A).

10. I.R.C. § 48(g)(1)(B).

rehabilitation expenditures" during a two-year period selected by the taxpayer in accordance with the Regulations are both greater than the adjusted basis of the property and greater than $5,000.[11]

If a building qualifies, only that portion of its basis that is attributable to "qualified rehabilitation expenditures" is eligible for the credit.[12] This amount is then multiplied by the "rehabilitation percentage" to obtain the amount of the credit.[13] The present credit percentage is 20 percent for the rehabilitation of certified historic structures and 10 percent for the rehabilitation of nonhistoric structures originally placed in service at least 30 years ago. As with all tax credits, the taxpayer may subtract the amount of the rehabilitation tax credit from the amount of tax that he would otherwise owe.

In the case of historic structures, the credit extends both to residential and nonresidential buildings, but as to nonhistoric structures, the credit remains limited to nonresidential buildings. The taxpayer's basis in a qualified building must be reduced by the full amount of the credit claimed.

b. Low-Income Housing Credit (LIHC)

One of the few new preferences appearing in the 1986 TRA was the low-income (rental) housing credit. This credit replaced certain earlier tax incentives designed to stimulate the private production of rental housing for the poor.[14] The LIHC provides a dollar-for-dollar reduction in tax liability for taxpayers who develop rental housing for households with incomes less than or equal to 60 percent of the area median income. The amount of the credit depends on the number of low-income housing units produced.

The details of the credit are so complex as to be almost discouraging. Once mastered, however, the credit is remarkably generous. For example, in the case of 1987 expenditures for new construction and rehabilitation, the investor was entitled to a credit of 9 percent annually for ten years, equivalent to a subsidy whose present value was 70 percent of the qualifying outlays.[15] Four-percent, ten-year credits (present value: 30 percent) were available where qualifying existing housing was acquired or where the new construction and rehabilitation were financed with tax-exempt bonds or similar federal subsidies.[16] The law requires the Treasury to adjust the credit percentage to reflect changes in construction and rehabilitation costs to preserve the present value (70 or 30 percent) of the credit.[17] These adjusted percentages apply to projects as they come on line. For example, for projects placed in service in January 1990, the credit percentages were 8.89 and 3.81.[18]

---

11. I.R.C. § 48(g)(1)(C).

12. I.R.C. § 48(a)(1)(E).

13. I.R.C. § 48(a)(2)(F)-(c)(2).

14. These earlier incentives included preferential cost recovery and recapture rules, the § 167(k) five-year amortization of rehabilitation expenditures, and the special treatment of construction period interest and taxes.

15. I.R.C. § 42(b)(1).

16. Id.

17. I.R.C. § 42(b)(2).

18. P.H., Fed. Taxes 2nd, 424.01.

To receive the credit, the taxpayer must target no fewer than 20 percent of the units in the project to low-income families (those whose income is 50 percent or less of area median gross income) — known as the 20-50 test — or no fewer than 40 percent of the project units to slightly higher-income families (those whose income is 60 percent or less of area median gross income) — known as the 40-60 test.[19] Moreover, the gross rent charged to tenants in units eligible for the credit may not exceed 30 percent of the qualifying income for a family of its size.[20] Finally, TRA allocates a state-by-state ceiling on the volume of credit available under this program.[21]

Once the project qualifies, all of the construction, rehabilitation, or acquisition costs attributable to the low-income units benefit from the credit.[22] As the taxpayer receives credit, this reduces the property's adjusted basis. Stringent credit recapture rules apply if the taxpayer violates the rental rules upon which the credit depends.[23]

3.   The Concept of Tax Shelter

Consider a real estate investment by an individual named Iris. She purchases land and a building for $1 million, providing $100,000 of her own capital and borrowing the other $900,000 through a 9 percent 30-year self-liquidating mortgage from a commercial bank; annual mortgage payments are roughly $86,900. The property generates $350,000 in income per year, and has direct costs (utilities, maintenance, trash collection, repairs, real estate taxes, and so forth) of $250,000 per year, leaving $100,000 in cash available to cover the mortgage payments of $86,900. The remaining $13,100 — called "cash flow after financing" or CFAF — is available for Iris to use.

She does not necessarily get to keep all the money she makes, of course. Iris will have to pay income taxes, both state and federal. Our discussions will focus on federal taxation for two reasons: first, federal income taxes are generally much larger than state income taxes; and second, many state income tax systems are directly or indirectly patterned on federal income taxes.

How much income tax does Iris owe, however? To figure this out, we need to know Iris's marginal tax rate and the taxable income from the project. Assume for the moment that Iris's marginal tax rate is 70 percent (as it was, at the top rate, in the early 1980s). But what is Iris's taxable income? The $13,100 CFAF generated by the property is only a starting point, and two major adjustments have to be made to get from this point to taxable income.

First, some of the money that Iris paid out during the year is not deductible as an expense on her taxes. Her mortgage payment consists of two basic components: interest, which is the charge she pays for using the lender's money, and principal, which is repayment of the borrowed funds. Interest is a real expense and can be deducted in calculating taxable income. However, if you borrow or repay money, that is not income or expense: upon borrowing you have additional assets

---

19. I.R.C. § 42(g)(I).
20. I.R.C. § 42(g)(2).
21. I.R.C. § 42(h).
22. The eligible basis may be reduced, however, in a building containing non-low-income units whose average quality exceeds that of the qualifying low-income units. I.R.C. § 42(d)(3).
23. I.R.C. § 42(j).

(the money) but also a matching liability (the debt), so your wealth hasn't changed. When you repay, you have less cash, but also less debt, so again you have no change in wealth. So, Iris was not taxed on the $900,000 when she borrowed it, nor can she deduct the loan principal each year as she repays it. Of her $86,900 in payments, approximately $6,150 was principal repayment and cannot be deducted. Since we already subtracted this from her income (when we subtracted the total debt payment), we must add it back, raising her taxable income to $13,100 + $6,150 = $19,250.

The second major adjustment is depreciation, or cost recovery. When a business buys things that it uses currently, those are expenses that are currently deductible. But when a business buys an asset with a long economic life, it is required to deduct the cost of acquisition over the life of the asset. Consider a company that spends $35,000 to purchase a truck that is expected to last five years, and can be sold for scrap for $5,000 at the end of that period. The company might be required to spread out the $30,000 cost of the truck ($35,000 acquisition cost less $5,000 salvage value at the end of its useful life), counting only $6,000 of the purchase price as a deduction each year for the truck's expected five-year life.

Iris's building is a long-lived asset which presumably is wearing out over time. Accordingly, she should be able to deduct the cost of the building over its expected economic life. This is depreciation, or cost recovery. Note that land does not wear out; only buildings and other improvements do. So only the cost of the building, and not the cost of the land, can generate depreciation deductions. Assuming the value of the land was $200,000, and the value of the building was $800,000, she can deduct that $800,000 acquisition cost over a period defined by the tax code. Assume for the moment that the tax code permits the deduction in equal amounts over 15 years (similar to the tax treatment permitted under the 1981 tax code) without regard to any salvage value; she can deduct $800,000/15 = $53,333 each year. This leaves her with taxable income of $19,250 − $53,333 = −34,083.

Why this difference between Iris's cash flow and her reported income? Note that the adjustments for principal amortization and depreciation reflect differences between the actual cash flow that Iris experiences and the tax treatment she receives. Loan amortization required her to use cash, but did not generate a deduction. Depreciation, on the other hand, did not use any cash but was deductible.

These calculations can be summarized:

Gross Income	$350,000	
less: Operating Expenses	−250,000	
equals: Net Operating Income	$100,000	(Also called "Cash Flow before Financing")
less: Debt Service Payments	−86,900	
equals: Cash Flow after Financing	$ 13,100	
plus: Principal Amortization	6,150	
less: Depreciation deduction.	−53,333	
equals: Taxable Income (Loss)	($34,083)	

An alternative way of saying the same thing is that Iris has income, after operating expenses, of $100,000. She can then deduct the interest she paid on her mortgage and the depreciation of the improvements to calculate her taxable income:

Gross Income	$350,000
less: Operating Expenses	−250,000
equals: Net Operating Income	$100,000 (Also called "Cash Flow before Financing")
less: Mortgage Interest	−80,750
less: Depreciation Deduction	−53,333
equals: Taxable Income (Loss)	($34,083)

The critical point is that Iris has $13,100 in cash available at the end of the year, but that she can report to the government a *loss* of $34,083. Assuming she can use this loss to offset other income, she would actually get to reduce her total tax bill by .70 × $34,083 = $23,858, even though the property generated a positive cash flow.

To summarize, if the taxable loss generated by the property can be used to offset other taxable income, it will reduce her income taxes by $23,858. Meanwhile, she also has $13,100 in cash generated by the property, for a cash return of $36,958 for the year. Based on her initial investment, this is a cash-on-cash return of $36,958/ $100,000, or nearly 37 percent.[24]

Why does Iris receive such beneficial tax treatment, declaring a loss when the property seems to have generated a profit? The critical element is the depreciation deduction, which is deductible on her taxes even though it did not require any expenditure of cash from operations. In this example, Iris was permitted to use an unrealistically fast depreciation period of 15 years, allowing her to deduct 1/15th of the purchase price of the improvements each year for 15 years even though the improvements are likely to last much longer than that. (The tax code has sometimes permitted accelerated depreciation schedules like this (or even faster), although under the current tax code nonresidential real property must be depreciated over 39 years.) This depreciation deduction sheltered all of the income generated by the property from any tax burden. Even after offsetting the income from the project, the depreciation deduction created a further loss that could be used by Iris to shelter income she may have earned elsewhere.

There is a slight countervailing factor — loan amortization — which used cash without generating a deduction, but loan amortization is normally quite small in the early years of a loan. To the extent that the depreciation deduction exceeds loan amortization, income from the project (and potentially other income) can be sheltered from income taxes.

From this example, we can grasp two key realities of real estate investment. First: Whenever cost recovery exceeds mortgage amortization, tax-sheltered income results; in fact, the amount of tax-sheltered income equals the excess of cost

---

24. Of course, this cash-on-cash return for the first year is only a starting point for analyzing the quality of the investment. Iris will also be concerned with the likelihood that the property will appreciate over time, the taxes she may owe upon the sale of the property, and a host of other factors.

recovery over amortization (in our example: $53,333 − $6,150 = $47,183; $13,100 of this shelter is used to eliminate the taxes on the cash that Iris earned from the investment this year, while the remaining $34,083 offsets outside income she would otherwise have to pay tax on). This assumes that no other tax provisions prevent Iris from applying her loss to shelter outside income, a matter addressed in detail below. Second: A tax loss — available to offset taxable income from other sources — can coexist with positive cash flow to the investor.

Do not conclude, however, that tax-sheltered income forever escapes taxation. The reckoning occurs if, and when, the asset is disposed of in a taxable transaction, such as a sale, taxable exchange,[25] or mortgage foreclosure.[26] (No reckoning occurs if the taxpayer holds the property unto death.) The depreciation deductions taken by the taxpayer reduce the basis in the property, increasing the gain upon sale.

In our example, Iris had an initial basis of $1 million (her acquisition cost). Each year, she must reduce her basis by the $53,333 in depreciation deductions that she takes. So, if Iris were to resell the property after six years for $1 million — the exact cost that she paid — she would have a gain of $320,000. (The sale price ($1 million) less the basis ($1 million minus prior depreciation of 6 × $53,333).) Iris would realize a taxable gain measured, in effect, by the accumulated cost recovery enjoyed during the holding period. But even if she must someday report and suffer taxes on previously deferred income, the taxpayer has received the equivalent of an interest-free loan from the Treasury in the amount of the deferred taxes. And if the gain on sale is taxed at a capital gains rate that is lower than the ordinary income tax rate she would have paid each year, then she also reduces the total amount of tax that she pays.

The collapse of tax shelter. When property is held free and clear, the owner receives tax-sheltered income until the depreciable basis is reduced to zero. But if the property is mortgaged, an untaxed stream of cash depends on the continuing surplus of cost recovery over amortization. Should amortization ever exceed cost recovery, the owner will have earned taxable income that is not reflected in cash. Most taxpayers would regard this prospect bleakly.

This "negative" tax shelter is most likely to occur in either of two situations. First, when accelerated declining balance depreciation methods were used, the depreciation deduction would decline each year, potentially dropping below the amount of loan amortization after several years. Second, even with straight-line depreciation, negative shelter can result late in the life of a self-amortizing loan, when amortization becomes a much bigger part of the loan payment. The size of the "negative" tax shelter is measured by the same formula we used a moment ago, that is, cost recovery less mortgage amortization. One way to ensure indefinite tax shelter is to use straight-line cost recovery and obtain a mortgage with constant amortization at a level below that of the cost recovery. But this invites other problems. Constant amortization may mean that the early installments of debt service will greatly exceed those for a level payment mortgage; otherwise the mortgage either cannot amortize itself or must be written over a much longer term (often not possible). Furthermore, the owner who fails to maximize the first year's tax shelter dilutes the advantage of tax deferral.

---

25. Like-kind exchanges can extend income deferral; I.R.C. § 1031. For further discussion, see the text at pages 341–356 infra.

26. See, e.g., Commissioner v. Tufts, 461 U.S. 300 (1983).

Faced with a collapsing tax shelter, the taxpayer should explore two options: (1) sell or exchange the property; or (2) refinance the mortgage. The first option is self-evident, although the owner's desire to sell is no guarantee of a favorable market response; moreover, the sale will itself engender taxability. Sometimes, the taxpayer will be able to achieve a tax-free exchange, more infra,[27] with beneficial results. The taxpayer who elects the second option and refinances the mortgage will be seeking initially lower amortization. (Query: Without reducing the principal balance, how can this be achieved?) But, as in the case of a sale or exchange, refinancing may not be possible or propitious when tax factors make it urgent: Prepayment may be barred or expensive; interest rates may have risen; mortgage money may be unavailable; or the property may not support the terms sought. In short, the investor who decides to maximize tax-sheltered income must recognize both the inherent risks and the uncertainty of successful counter tactics.

If this example seems unrealistic, be assured that deals with even worse economics than this one could be highly profitable for investors under the tax laws that were in effect in the 1970s and 1980s. The combination of rapid depreciation (which generated large losses for tax purposes) and high marginal tax rates (which made tax savings very valuable to the investor) resulted in deals that could be highly profitable to investors even though, if there were no taxes at all, they would have lost money. Much of the tax system applicable to real estate investments today can be traced directly back to the need to stop the use of depreciation deductions to shelter outside, unrelated income.

B.   LIMITS ON THE DEDUCTIBILITY OF EXPENSES

1.   Congress's Assault on the Real Estate Tax Shelter

a.   Extension of At-Risk Rules to Real Estate Activity

In 1976 Congress added § 465 to the Code to prevent individuals and certain closely held corporations from deducting losses that exceeded the taxpayer's economic investment in the activity generating the loss. The provisions of § 465 — known as the at-risk rules — applied to a broad range of activities associated with tax-shelter investment, such as equipment leasing, oil and gas exploration, and the production and distribution of motion picture films or video tapes. Pointedly, § 465 did not apply to real estate activity other than to the holding of mineral property. However, the 1986 TRA partly removed real estate's favored status.

The at-risk principles are easily explained, although — as with so much of tax law — lawyer ingenuity and transactional complexity often muddy the outcome. Suppose that a taxpayer acquires property (for example, a co-tenancy interest in an airplane subject to an equipment lease) for which she pays $1 million: $100,000 in cash and $900,000 in the form of a nonrecourse purchase money mortgage. Under the at-risk rules, the taxpayer would be able to deduct only the first $100,000

27. See pages 341–356 infra.

of losses generated by her investment. This measures the amount economically at risk, in the sense that if the venture collapsed, the taxpayer would lose her $100,000 but have no further exposure. Any additional tax losses would be placed in a "suspense account" awaiting one of several events: (1) the taxpayer might contribute additional cash or cash equivalents; (2) the taxpayer might assume part of the debt; (3) the investment might generate taxable income; or (4) the investment might be disposed of at a gain. As the investment turned "profitable" or the taxpayer invested new equity or assumed part of the debt, previously nondeductible losses could then be used. Section 465, in short, sought to stanch some of the revenue drain that the *Crane* rule[28] and a spirited tax shelter industry had opened up. During its decade-long (1976-1986) immunity from the at-risk rules, real estate had become the preferred tax-shelter investment.

Even after TRA, however, §465 does not cover all nonrecourse real estate financing. The present law immunizes real estate investors from the at-risk rules where they have obtained qualified nonrecourse financing.[29] This exception applies if the mortgage lender is (1) not "related" to the taxpayer; (2) not the seller of the property or someone "related" to the seller; and (3) not a person who is paid a fee with respect to the taxpayer's investment in the property, for example, the promoter. The exception also applies where a governmental entity has made the nonrecourse loan or has guaranteed it. A further exception allows the nonrecourse loan to qualify, even if it came from a related person, if the terms of the loan were commercially reasonable — that is, based on a written unconditional promise to pay on demand, or at a specified time, a definite sum of money at a market rate interest — and on substantially the same terms as loans involving unrelated persons.

Example (1): O purchases an apartment building for $10 million. O pays $500,000 in cash and gives back to the seller, an unrelated individual, a $9.5 million nonrecourse, purchase money mortgage. The terms of the mortgage are "commercially reasonable." O would be deemed to have only $500,000 at risk because the financing has come from the seller. O would be able (subject, of course, to the passive activity restraints, infra) to write off losses of that magnitude.

Example (2): Assume the same facts as in Example (1), except that the seller is a governmental entity. O would he deemed to have the entire $10 million at risk, even though the mortgage is nonrecourse.

Example (3): Assume the same facts as in Example (1), except that O borrows the $9.5 million to acquire the property through a governmentally guaranteed loan, or from either a governmental or unrelated lender. Without having to show that the terms of the mortgage are "commercially reasonable," O would be deemed to have the entire $10 million at risk, even though the mortgage is nonrecourse.

---

28. In Crane v. Commissioner, 331 U.S. 1 (1947), the Court held that nonrecourse debt incurred to acquire property could be included in the amount of the taxpayer's basis in that property.

29. I.R.C. §465(b)(6).

Example (4): Assume the same facts as in Example (1), except that O borrows the $9.5 million from a related person and the interest rate is significantly below (or above) the market rate on comparable loans by qualified persons. Almost certainly, the mortgage terms are not "commercially reasonable," and O would be deemed, initially, to have only $500,000 at risk.

Example (5): Assume the same facts as in Example (2). Six months later, the mortgage principal unchanged, O sells the property subject to the mortgage to P, an unrelated person. P pays $10.5 million for the property, including $1 million in cash. P would be deemed to have the entire $10.5 million at risk.

Complicating the enforcement of § 465 has been uncertainty over the amount of investment considered at risk. The Code defines "at-risk" as the amount of money and the adjusted basis of other property contributed by the taxpayer to the activity and, as to any amounts borrowed for the contribution, those loans for which the taxpayer is personally liable or has pledged other property (to the property's fair market value) as security for repayment: moreover, any borrowed contribution cannot come from a related person or from someone having an interest in the venture. In the effort to finesse § 465, promoters have invented an array of credit devices that give the appearance of risk, if not the full reality; the Service and the Tax Court have had their hands full in dealing with these ploys.

Because real estate investments so often are held in partnership,[30] one must also be familiar with the loss-limitation rules of subchapter K and their interplay with § 465. Section 704(d) allows partners to write off their distributive share of partnership losses only to the extent of the adjusted basis of their interest in the partnership—in partnership talk, the so-called "outside basis." Without unraveling any of the complexities of subchapter K, we can say that a real estate partner must now satisfy both the § 704(d) basis and the § 465 at-risk requirements, in addition to those of § 469 (passive activity), before she will enjoy loss deductibility.[31]

b. Limited Deductibility of Passive Activity Losses and Credits

TRA also introduced § 469[32] and its concept of passive activity, which limits the use of losses incurred in trade or business activities in which the taxpayer does not materially participate, including rental activities. Losses from these "passive activities" may only be used to offset income from other passive activities, and not from other investment income or income from other trade or business activities.

30. Because of changes to subchapter S, an S corporation has become a more attractive vehicle for real estate activity.
31. When the real estate partnership has borrowed on a nonrecourse basis, quite usual when the partnership acquires property financed with a purchase money mortgage, both the partnership and the partners, separately, will be deemed borrowers for the purpose of determining whether the mortgage is to be treated as qualified nonrecourse financing. Under this two-step procedure, the partnership must first establish that, as to the entity, the debt qualifies; then, each partner, as to herself, must make a similar showing. I.R.C. §§ 465(b)(C), 49(a)(1)(D), (E)(1).
32. I.R.C. § 469.

Section 469 is inordinately complex,[33] as well as especially harsh. The Code defines "passive activity" to include the conduct of any trade or business in which the taxpayer does not materially participate.[34] In addition, any rental activity falls within § 469, except where the taxpayer provides substantial services, such as those associated with an inn or hotel.[35] Accordingly, both the occasional rental of a one-family house (property held for the production of income) and a 50-story office building (trade or business property) are treated as a passive activity. So, too, is any investment in the form of a limited partnership interest.[36]

Although the taxpayer-owner will continue to report income and expenses in the usual way, should operating losses occur, § 469 limits their deductibility to the income generated by the taxpayer's other passive activities. Any unused losses must then be carried forward, available to offset any income from the subsequent years' passive activity. If the taxpayer disposes of his entire interest in a passive activity in a fully taxable transaction to an unrelated party, any residual losses attributable to that activity, including disposition losses, shed their passive activity character, and may be used to offset nonpassive activity income.[37]

Example: A owns a limited partnership interest whose distributive share of the firm's loss in 2002 is $20,000. In that year A has no passive activity income and must carry forward the $20,000 loss. In 2003 A sells her limited partnership interest and incurs a $5,000 loss. In that year A has $3,000 of passive activity income from other sources. A in 2003 can deduct the $20,000 of carry-forward loss and the $2,000 of current excess passive activity loss against A's nonpassive activity income.

What does it mean for a taxpayer to "materially participate" in the activity, such that the income or losses will not be categorized as passive? The taxpayer's participation must be "regular, continuous and substantial."[38] The determination of whether a particular taxpayer has met this standard can be complex and is covered by extensive regulations.[39] While other situations may be difficult to categorize, however the regulations provide that a taxpayer is deemed to have materially participated if (1) the taxpayer participated in the activity for more than 500 hours during the year; or (2) was substantially the only participant.

Section 469 does not require that rental activities be treated as passive if the real property business exception applies, which depends on the satisfaction of two tests. First, more than one-half of the personal services performed by the taxpayer must be performed in real property trades or businesses in which the taxpayer materially participates.[40] Second, the taxpayer must perform more than 750 hours of services in real property trades or businesses in which the taxpayer materially participates.[41]

---

33. The § 469 regulations are more than 130 pages long.
34. I.R.C. § 469(c)(1).
35. Temp. Reg. § 1.469-1T(e)(3)(ii).
36. I.R.C. § 469(h)(2).
37. I.R.C. § 469(g).
38. I.R.C. § 469(h)(1).
39. Treas. Regs. § 1.469-5T.
40. I.R.C. § 469(c)(7)(B)(i).
41. I.R.C. § 469(c)(7)(B)(ii).

Section 469 applies to individuals, estates, trusts, closely held C corporations (five or fewer individuals owning directly or indirectly more than 50 percent of the stock), and personal service corporations. An investment in an S corporation is a passive activity if the corporation conducts a trade or business in which the taxpayer does not materially participate. Somewhat more liberal rules apply to rehabilitation and low-income rental housing investments.

Section 469 does contain a modest exception for rental ventures in which the individual taxpayer "actively participates" in management, even though an agent may handle the day-to-day affairs.[42] Active participation is a lower standard than "material" participation. This exception allows the taxpayer to offset the first $25,000 of rental losses against other forms of income. Even this limited privilege, however, phases out ratably for taxpayers whose adjusted gross income exceeds $100,000, disappearing altogether when AGI reaches $150,000.

> *Example:* A owns and actively manages an apartment house that in 2003 suffers a $40,000 operating loss. In that year, A has adjusted gross income of $120,000. A may deduct $15,000 (60 percent × $25,000) of the passive activity loss against other income.

You should note that income from investments in securities, such as stock dividends and bond interest, is not passive income, notwithstanding the investor's inactive stance. This is portfolio income, which, like earned income from wages and salaries, may no longer be sheltered by passive activity losses.[43] To prevent the use of limited partnerships to circumvent the passive activity loss rules, the partnership in preparing its return must separately state any portfolio income.

(1)   The Interplay Between Tax Credits and Passive Activity

Although Congress may well have intended to provide a receptive tax climate both for historic preservation and investment in low-income rental housing, the passive activity rules have a limiting effect. The rules curtail not only the deduction of losses but also the use of tax credits. Any tax credit generated by a passive activity (other than foreign tax credits) may offset only the tax attributable to passive income. Unused credits, just as unused losses, enter a suspense account where they are carried forward as an offset against future years' passive source income.

To describe the passive activity treatment of tax credits is too forbidding. However, against the backdrop of the passive activity rules, the following groups of investors appear to be best suited to take advantage of housing tax credits:

1. any taxpayer with sufficient passive income to absorb the passive activity credit;
2. limited partnerships of individual investors who are each allocated approximately $7,750[44] of credits yearly;
3. widely held corporations (not subject to the passive activity rules).

---

42. I.R.C. § 469(i).
43. I.R.C. § 469(e)(1).
44. This assumes that the taxpayer's marginal rate is 31 percent (.31 × $25,000).

Novogradac and Fortenbach, The Low-Income Housing Tax Credit, Tax Notes 113-121 (Jan. 1, 1990), provides a more detailed analysis.

c. The Alternative Minimum Tax

Real estate investors, in calculating their taxes (and after-tax investment return), must be aware of the alternative minimum tax, which Congress first imposed in 1969 to prevent higher income taxpayers from avoiding their "fair share" of tax liability. The alternative minimum tax is payable only to the extent that it exceeds the taxpayer's "regular tax."[45] In calculating the alternative tax, the taxpayer must determine an alternative tax base through a series of upward adjustments to the taxpayer's regular tax base. A flat 24 percent rate is then applied to the alternative tax base.[46]

Upward adjustments relating to real estate include the following:

1. Cost recovery is recalculated using the straight-line method and a 40-year recovery period for all properties placed in service after 1986;[47]
2. In the case of individual taxpayers, real property taxes are nondeductible unless they qualify as business or investment expenses;[48]
3. Tax-exempt interest receipts in newly issued private activity bonds are included (examples include bonds financing sewage disposal facilities, solid waste disposal facilities, and qualified multifamily residential rental projects);[49]
4. The charitable deduction is reduced by valuing the contribution of appreciated capital gain property (including real estate) at its adjusted basis.[50]

Of further moment to individual taxpayers, miscellaneous itemized deductions,[51] state and local income taxes, and part of the medical expense deduction are excluded in calculating alternative minimum taxable (AMT) income.[52] Itemized items that remain deductible include qualified residence interest, qualifying investment interest, and casualty and theft losses.

Once determined, the alternative minimum tax base is then reduced by a $40,000 exemption[53] ($30,000 in the case of a single individual and $20,000 in the case of a married person filing a separate return). It is this base to which the alternative 24 percent rate is applied. The taxpayer then pays the higher of the regular or the alternative minimum tax.

45. I.R.C. § 55(a),(c).
46. I.R.C. § 55(b). TRA had previously set the rate at 21 percent for noncorporate taxpayers.
47. I.R.C. § 56(a)(1).
48. I.R.C. § 56(b)(1).
49. I.R.C. § 57(a)(5).
50. I.R.C. § 57(a)(6).
51. I.R.C. § 67.
52. I.R.C. § 57(b)(1).
53. The exemptions are subject to a phase-out provision. For a married couple filing jointly, the phase out begins at $150,000 of adjusted gross income. The exemption is reduced by 2 percent for every $2,500 of adjusted gross income over the threshold amount; I.R.C. § 55(d)(3).

The effect of the AMT is to render tax deductions or credits useless to the taxpayer beyond the point at which the AMT exceeds the regular tax that would be owed. This makes the tax calculations for a developer or investor more complex because the tax consequences on any given transaction are likley to depend on the overall tax position the taxpayer is in at the end of the given year. Moreover, to the extent that tax deduction or credits reflect policy decisions by Congress, intended to channel capital into desired uses, the AMT undercuts these policies.

The AMT is becoming an important issue in tax debates because the triggers for the AMT are not indexed for inflation. As a result, it is applying to a rapidly escalating number of taxpayers. See, e.g., R. Jason Griffin, Comment, The Individual Alternative Minimum Tax: Is It Touching People That It Shouldn't Be?, 4 Hous. Bus. & Tax. L.J. 259 (2004). Congress has held the expansion of the AMT in check through a number of one-year patches, such as the Tax Increase Prevention and Reconciliation Act of 2005, which increased exemptions to keep the AMT from applying to millions of middle-class taxpayers through the end of 2006. Whether similar short-term patches or a more comprehensive revision to the AMT is enacted will be a critical decision that will affect tax planning in every arena, including real estate.

As we have noted, the heyday of the real estate tax shelter ended in 1986. The repeal of accelerated cost recovery for real estate investments, based upon a 19-year cost recovery period, and its replacement with mandatory straight-line depreciation, based upon either a 27.5- or 31.5-year (now 39-year) cost recovery period, dramatically shrank the spread between cost recovery and mortgage amortization upon which tax shelter depended. Coupled with enactment of the passive activity rules, which cover all real estate rental properties, and the limited extension of the at-risk rules to real estate nonrecourse mortgages, the present law discourages the formation of newly formed real estate tax shelters that are programmed to incur large first-year tax losses. This does not mean, of course, that tax shelters are a historical footnote. Rather, the conception of tax shelter as it relates to real estate has changed from that of a venture designed to generate large spillover tax losses into one that may well show taxable income from the very outset, yet generate a cash flow, some part of which remains sheltered.

Let us return to the example that began this section. Although the investment generated cash for Iris of $13,100 in the first year, the taxable income from the investment was negative. Even if Iris cannot use the loss to offset taxes otherwise owed on outside (nonpassive) income, the depreciation deduction still prevents her from having to pay any current taxes on the $13,100 she earns from her investment this year.

C. CLASSIFICATION OF REAL PROPERTY

The taxability of real estate investment and transfer depends initially upon the purpose for which the property is held. With respect to real property, the Code contains four general purposes: (1) property held as a personal residence, (2) property held for the production of income, (3) property held for use in a trade or business, and (4) property held primarily for sale to customers.

1. *Property Held as a Personal Residence*

In general, expenses incurred in owning a home are not tax deductible, because they are not incurred for the purpose of generating income. However, the federal tax code has one massive subsidy for home ownership, in the form of the home mortgage interest deduction.

Taxpayers may deduct interest paid on acquisition indebtedness and home equity indebtedness secured by a qualified residence.[54] Acquisition indebtedness refers to debt, up to $1 million (or $500,000 for a married taxpayer filing separately), incurred in acquiring, constructing, or substantially improving the residence, and includes any refinancing of that debt.

The Code defines home equity indebtedness as any indebtedness other than acquisition indebtedness for which a qualified residence is security. Two further limits exist: (1) the amount of home equity indebtedness cannot exceed the residence's fair market value, less any unpaid acquisition indebtedness (when the home equity loan is incurred); (2) only the first $100,000 of home equity indebtedness generates an interest deduction ($50,000 for a married taxpayer filing separately).[55]

Example (1): X buys a home in 2000 for $200,000 and later spends $40,000 in capital improvements. X gives the seller a $160,000 purchase money mortgage and gives a lender a $20,000 second mortgage to finance the improvements. X has $180,000 of acquisition indebtedness.

Example (2): The facts are the same as in Example (1), except that in 2003, when the combined mortgage balance has dropped to $140,000, X refinances the two mortgages into a single $140,000 lien. X has $140,000 of acquisition indebtedness.

Example (3): The facts are the same as in Example (2), except that the amount of the refinanced mortgage is $210,000. X has $140,000 of acquisition indebtedness. X also has $70,000 of home equity indebtedness, provided that the residence's fair market value is at least $210,000.

Example (4): The facts are the same as in Example (3), except that in 2005, when the balance of the refinanced mortgage is $180,000, X takes out a second mortgage in the amount of $50,000. At this juncture, X would have $110,000 of remaining acquisition indebtedness, and $120,000 of home equity indebtedness, provided that the residence's fair market value is at least $230,000. X can deduct the interest on all $110,000 of the acquisition indebtedness, but can deduct the interest on only $100,000 of the home equity indebtedness.

54. I.R.C. § 163(h)(3)(A).
55. I.R.C. § 163(h)(3)(C).

Note, finally, the distinction between repairs on one's residence, which can neither be deducted nor capitalized, and (substantial) improvements, which are nondeductible but can support acquisition indebtedness and be capitalized.

Although losses on disposition are nonrecognized, any gain realized on the sale or exchange of a personal residence would normally be taxable[56] as capital gain, since the Code regards one's residence as a capital asset.[57] However, § 121 provides that gain on the sale or exchange of a principal residence may be excluded from gross income, up to a limit of $250,000 for an individual or $500,000 for a qualified married couple. To take advantage of this exclusion, the taxpayer must have used the property as his or her primary residence for periods aggregating at least two years out of the five years preceding the sale or exchange. The exclusion may be used repeatedly, but not more than once every two years. Partial exceptions to these last two rules may be available if sale was caused by a change in the taxpayer's place of employment, health, or unforeseen circumstances.[58]

Before leaving the topic of taxpayer residence, we should mention that a personal residence sometimes may be used partially for business purposes, thus entitling a taxpayer to deductions for depreciation and maintenance expenses for the business part of the premises. This option led to such widespread taxpayer abuse, as well as to such uncertainty over whether the business use of one's home would make the related expenses deductible, that Congress imposed strict limits for a qualifying home office under TRA. The rules were further tightened by the Supreme Court decision in Commissioner v. Soliman,[59] which held that a home office is a principal place of business only if (1) the most important activities connected with the business take place in the home office, or (2) the taxpayer is required to spend most of his or her working hours in the home office. This standard, which eliminated the home office deduction for millions of taxpayers, was relaxed by the Taxpayer Relief Act of 1997. The 1997 amendments reinstated the pre-*Soliman* rule: a home office can be a principal place of business if it is used for the administrative or management activities of the taxpayer's trade or business, provided there is no other fixed location where the taxpayer conducts substantial administrative or management activities.

In any event, the home office deduction is limited to the excess of the gross income attributable to the business activity over the sum of the deductions already allowable to the home office portion of the dwelling (for example, for property taxes and qualified residence interest) and the deductions allowable to the trade or business within the home office portion.[60]

2. *Property Held for the Production of Income (Investment Property)*

Prior to the 1986 Tax Reform Act, investment property came in two principal forms: property that currently was nonincome producing, such as raw land held for

---

56. I.R.C. § 61(a)(3).
57. I.R.C. § 1221.
58. I.R.C. § 121(c)(2)(B); Regs. § 1.121-3(B).
59. Commissioner v. Soliman, 112 S. Ct. 701 (1993), *rev'g* 935 F.2d S2 (4th Cir. 1991), which affirmed 94 T.C. 20 (1990).
60. I.R.C. § 280A(c)(5).

future use or appreciation, and property that was income producing but not used in the taxpayer's trade or business, such as a one-family house or a vacation home whose owner had rented it out. Under TRA, the rental property becomes a passive activity subject to § 469's loss deductibility rules.

For investment property (not used in the taxpayer's trade or business) real estate taxes and mortgage interest are deductible, the latter item treated as investment interest and subject to the limitations of § 163(d). The owner may continue to deduct all the ordinary and necessary expenses incurred in managing, conserving, or maintaining the property. Moreover, the taxpayer has a limited election under § 266 to deduct or to capitalize "carrying costs,"[61] so a taxpayer with no current income against which to offset tax, interest, and other deductions, may apply these outlays to increase the basis in the property, lowering the eventual gain on disposition of the property.

If the asset is depreciable, unless the owner's use of the property is "not engaged in for profit,"[62] depreciation must be taken.[63] Current production of income is not essential for the asset to be depreciable. To qualify, the owner need only show that the purpose in holding the property was acquisition of current or future income.[64]

Section 183, which limits the deductibility of expenses from activities "not engaged in for profit" typically concerns the owners of resort condominiums who hire out their units to transient renters.[65] To determine whether the activity is "not for profit," the statute provides that unless a rental activity earns a profit in any two of five consecutive years, the taxpayer must overcome a presumption of a § 183 not-for-profit activity.[66] Where the owner fails to overcome the presumption, deductions are available in the following order: (1) the "as-of-right" deductions for property taxes, investment interest, and casualty losses; (2) § 212 deductions, exclusive of depreciation; (3) depreciation. However, the aggregate deductions may not exceed the property's rental income, except that the taxpayer is entitled to the "as-of-right" deductions regardless of rental income.[67]

The deductibility of investment- or business-related losses must also be tested against the at-risk and passive activity rules, or I.R.C. §§ 465 and 469.

---

61. If the property is unimproved, interest, taxes, and all other carrying costs may be capitalized. Treas. Reg. § 1.266-1(a),(b)(1). If the parcel is improved, however, only specified carrying charges, which do not include real estate taxes, may be capitalized as a matter of right. Id.

62. I.R.C. § 183.

63. I.R.C. § 167(6).

64. William C. Herrmann, 17 T.C. 903, 907 (1951), acq., 1952-1 C.B. 2. "The term 'production of income' under Section 212 [deduction of all ordinary and necessary expenses] is . . . not confined to recurring income but applies as well to gains from the disposition of property." This broad definition has been held to be applicable under § 167, and therefore there is no difference between property held for investment and property for the production of income. George W. Mitchell, 47 T.C. 120 at 128, acq., 1967-1 C.B. 2.

65. If the owner or related persons occupy the unit for more than 14 days annually (or 10 percent of the "fair rental" days, whichever is greater), the activity is personal and the owner must prorate the property's aggregate expenses, beyond the real estate taxes, interest, and casualty losses — items otherwise deductible — to reflect the percentage of personal use. I.R.C. § 280A(d),(e).

66. Treas. Reg. § 1.183-2(b) specifies nine factors that bear on the taxpayer's motive or intent to carry on the activity for profit despite its nonprofitable record. These factors include the time and effort expended, the expertise of the taxpayer's advisors, the businesslike manner of the taxpayer's bookkeeping, the likelihood of future appreciation, and the element of personal pleasure or recreation.

67. Treas. Reg. § 1.183-1(b).

The sale or exchange of property held for the production of income is a capital transaction.[68] Capital loss deductions are limited, however, either to the extent of capital gains (in the case of corporations), or to capital gains plus a maximum of $3,000 against other taxable income (in the case of noncorporate taxpayers).[69]

3. Property Held for Use in a Trade or Business

It can sometimes be vexatious to distinguish this category from a property held for investment. In general, rental apartments, offices, and stores, which involve some ongoing management, are regarded as trade or business property, even when the owner is an accountant or lawyer. By contrast, the occasional letting out of a room in one's home, or the fixing up of an inherited house for eventual resale, would be deemed an investment, rather than a trade or business.[70]

In holding trade or business property, the taxpayer may deduct "trade or business" expenses,[71] interest,[72] taxes,[73] and depreciation.[74] Operating losses also are deductible[75] except as limited by the passive activity rules, supra.

In defining capital asset, § 1221(2) excludes property used in the taxpayer's trade or business.[76] Instead, trade or business assets held for more than one year are treated as § 1231 property,[77] which means that gains and losses on the disposition of trade or business property are treated differently. If the taxpayer's § 1231 gains for any taxable year exceed the § 1231 losses for the year, the net gains are treated as long-term capital gains.[78] Conversely, if the year's transactional losses exceed the year's gains, the net losses receive ordinary loss treatment.[79] If there is any

---

68. I.R.C. § 1221.

69. I.R.C. §§ 165(f), 1211. The taxpayer may utilize the capital loss carryover provisions of I.R.C. § 1212.

70. 2 Guerin, Taxation of Real Estate Dispositions § 16.17 (1982). Decisional law is muddled. Compare Grier v. United States, 120 F. Supp. 395 (D. Conn. 1954), *aff'd per curiam*, 218 F.2d 603 (2d Cir. 1955), with Leland Hazard, 7 T.C. 372 (1946), acq., 1946-2 C.B. 3. In *Grier*, taxpayer had inherited a one-family house that was being rented. When he sold the house at a loss, taxpayer sought to qualify the event as a [§ 1221] capital loss, because the Code then made it advantageous for him to do so. Over the commissioner's vigorous opposition, the court agreed with the taxpayer's designation. In *Hazard*, decided a few years earlier, the Tax Court had held that the rental by a lawyer of his former residence constituted a trade or business to him, which permitted him to obtain § 1231 treatment of his loss. The irony of *Grier* is that the commissioner's argument was consistent with his acquiescence in *Hazard*. Lest you conclude that the overriding principle is "taxpayer always wins," examine McNeill v. Commissioner, 251 F.2d 863, 866 (4th Cir. 1958).

71. I.R.C. § 162(a).

72. I.R.C. § 163(a).

73. I.R.C. § 164.

74. I.R.C. § 167(a)(1).

75. I.R.C. § 165(a), (c)(1).

76. I.R.C. § 1221(2).

77. I.R.C. § 1231(b)(1).

78. I.R.C. § 1231(a)(1).

79. I.R.C. § 1231(a)(2).

unabsorbed loss, the taxpayer can use the carryover provisions of § 172,[80] which are far more generous than the capital loss carryover provisions of § 1212.[81] However, to counter a tax-avoidance ploy, whereby a taxpayer would aggregate § 1231 losses in year 1 and gains in year 2 — rather than combining them in a single year, causing capital gains to absorb ordinary losses — Congress now requires the taxpayer to "recapture" net § 1231 losses incurred during the five-year period preceding a taxable year in which the taxpayer enjoys § 1231 gains.[82] The following illustrates § 1231 recapture.

> *Example:* In 2003, taxpayer has a net § 1231 loss of $50,000. In 2004, taxpayer has a net § 1231 gain of $70,000. Taxpayer would treat $50,000 as ordinary income (the recaptured portion of the gain) and $20,000 as long-term capital gain.

During the holding period, property used in a trade or business receives the same tax treatment as property held for the production of income, with the technical difference that (trade or business) expenses are deductible under § 162[83] rather than under § 212 (expenses for the production of income) and with the more substantive difference that trade or business interest expenses are fully deductible, whereas investment interest is deductible only to the extent of the taxpayer's net investment income.[84]

4. *Property Held Primarily for Sale to Customers*

Property held "primarily for sale to customers in the ordinary course of [the taxpayer's] trade or business" is discussed separately because, like trade or business assets, it is excepted from the § 1221 definition of capital asset.[85] Unlike trade or business assets, however, which are also excepted by § 1221 but advantageously treated under § 1231, all property held primarily for sale to customers is an "ordinary" asset and any sale or exchange transaction will result in ordinary income (or loss), rather than a capital gain (or loss) which is normally taxed at a lower rate.

During the holding period prior to sale, the taxpayer may deduct "trade or business" expenses, interest, state and local taxes, and, as permitted by the passive activity rules, any operating losses. The allowance for depreciation, however, does not apply to property held primarily for sale to customers, unless the property also is used to produce current income.[86]

---

80. I.R.C. § 172.
81. I.R.C. § 1212.
82. I.R.C. § 1231(c).
83. I.R.C. § 162.
84. I.R.C. § 163(d).
85. I.R.C. § 1221(1).
86. Compare Camp Wolters Enterprises, 22 T.C. 737, 754 (1954), *aff'd*, 230 F.2d 555 (5th Cir. 1956), *cert. denied*, 352 U.S. 826 (1956), with I.T. 1342, I-1 C.B. 169 (1922).

Taxpayers whose activity makes their income subject to ordinary gains treatment are called "dealers," as distinguished from "investors" — taxpayers able to utilize §§ 1221 or 1231. Owners who subdivide their property before sale are almost certainly dealers,[87] unless they can qualify the transaction under the more liberal, but tricky, provisions of § 1237.[88]

The courts have been deluged with disputes (and, perhaps, will be once again) involving taxpayers who were not confirmed dealers (or, if confirmed dealers, engaged in an unusual activity) but tagged by the Service as a dealer in the transaction at hand. Consider how you would decide the following illustrative cases:

1. Homebuilder acquires 28-acre tract for intended subdivision, but resells 16-acre portion to commercial buyer after deciding not to develop residentially. Ordinary income or capital gains?[89]
2. Building supply company acquires customer's unsold houses in settlement of account and makes a further profit on their sale. Ordinary or capital gains?[90]
3. An investor in rental real estate, forced to raise funds to pay off a debt, sells 14 homes one year, 31 the next, and 12 the following year. Ordinary income or capital gains?[91]
4. A dealer sets up a separate investment account, in which he places a small multi-family dwelling. A few years later the building is sold. Ordinary income or capital gains?[92]
5. Taxpayer acquires land for development, but upon learning of condemnation threat, transfers the property to his investment holding company. Condemnation ensues a few months later. Ordinary income or capital gains?[93]

One point of confusion centered on the word "primarily," which forms part of the § 1221(1) phrase. In the following decision, the United States Supreme Court tried to settle its meaning.

---

87. Palos Verdes Corp. v. United States, 201 F.2d 256 (9th Cir. 1952).

88. I.R.C. § 1237. This section permits a noncorporate owner, who is not currently a dealer, to subdivide (but not substantially improve) a parcel and report part, and perhaps all, of the gains from the sale of the lots, as long-term capital gain. For a more detailed discussion, including sample tax computations and an opinion that § 1237 may booby trap the taxpayer, see Anderson, Tax Planning of Real Estate 203-211 (7th ed. 1977). See also Gerald Robinson, Federal Income Taxation of Real Estate § 12.05[2][b] (2006).

89. See Maddox Construction Co. v. Commissioner, 54 T.C. 1278 (1970) (held: capital gain); cf. also Frank H. Taylor and Son, Inc., 32 T.C.M. 362 (1973).

90. See, e.g., Thompson Lumber Co., 43 B.T.A. 726 (1941) (held: capital gain). But cf. Houston Endowment, Inc. v. United States, 606 F.2d 77, 81 (1979).

91. Sec McGah v. Commissioner, 210 F.2d 769, 771 (9th Cir. 1954) (held: capital gain).

92. Compare Jones v. Commissioner, 209 F.2d 415 (9th Cir. 1954) (held: ordinary income for three properties; capital gain for fourth property, a house purchased for taxpayer's mother and held for six years); Rollingwood Corp. v. Commissioner, 190 F.2d 263 (9th Cir. 1951).

93. Case v. United States, 633 F.2d 1240 (6th Cir. 1980) (held: capital gain).

Malat v. Riddell[94]

383 U.S. 569 (1966)

PER CURIAM. Petitioner was a participant in a joint venture which acquired a 45-acre parcel of land, the intended use for which is somewhat in dispute. Petitioner contends that the venturers' intention was to develop and operate an apartment project on the land; the respondent's position is that there was a "dual purpose" of developing the property for rental purposes or selling, whichever proved to be the more profitable. In any event, difficulties in obtaining the necessary financing were encountered, and the interior lots of the tract were subdivided and sold. The profit from those sales was reported and taxed as ordinary income.

The joint venturers continued to explore the possibility of commercially developing the remaining exterior parcels. Additional frustrations in the form of zoning restrictions were encountered. These difficulties persuaded petitioner and another of the joint venturers of the desirability of terminating the venture; accordingly, they sold out their interests in the remaining property. Petitioner contends that he is entitled to treat the profits from this last as capital gains; the respondent takes the position that this was "property held by the taxpayer primarily for sale to customers in the ordinary course of his trade or business," and thus subject to taxation as ordinary income.

The District Court made the following finding: "The members of [the joint venture], as of the date the 44.901 acres were acquired, intended either to sell the property or develop it for rental, depending upon which course appeared to be most profitable. The venturers realized that they had made a good purchase price-wise and, if they were unable to obtain acceptable construction financing or rezoning . . . which would be prerequisite to commercial development, they would sell the property in bulk so they wouldn't get hurt. The purpose of either selling or developing the property continued during the period in which [the joint venture] held the property."

The District Court ruled that petitioner had failed to establish that the property was not held primarily for sale to customers in the ordinary course of business, and thus rejected petitioner's claim to capital gain treatment for the profits derived from the property's resale. The Court of Appeals affirmed, 347 F.2d 23. We granted certiorari (382 U.S. 900) to resolve a conflict among the courts of appeals with regard to the meaning of the term "primarily" as it is used in § 1221(1) of the Internal Revenue Code of 1954.

The statute denies capital gain treatment to profits reaped from the sale of "property held by the taxpayer primarily for sale to customers in the ordinary course of his trade or business." (Emphasis added.) The respondent urges upon us a construction of "primarily" as meaning that a purpose may be "primary" if it is a "substantial" one.

As we have often said, "the words of statutes — including revenue acts — should be interpreted where possible in their ordinary, everyday senses." Crane v. Commissioner, 331 U.S. 1, 6. And see Hanover Bank v. Commissioner, 369 U.S. 672, 687-688; Commissioner v. Korell, 339 U.S. 619, 627-628. Departure from a literal reading of statutory language may, on occasion, be indicated by relevant internal

---

94. Footnotes omitted.

evidence of the statute itself and necessary in order to effect the legislative purpose. See, e.g., Board of Governors v. Agnew, 329 U.S. 441, 446-448. But this is not such an occasion. The purpose of the statutory provision with which we deal is to differentiate between the "profits and losses arising from the everyday operation of a business" on the one hand (Corn Products Co. v. Commissioner, 350 U.S. 46, 52) and "the realization of appreciation in value accrued over a substantial period of time" on the other. (Commissioner v. Gillette Motor Co., 364 U.S. 130, 134.) A literal reading of the statute is consistent with this legislative purpose. We hold that, as used in § 1221(1), "primarily" means "of first importance" or "principally."

Since the courts below applied an incorrect legal standard, we do not consider whether the result would be supportable on the facts of this case had the correct one been applied. We believe, moreover, that the appropriate disposition is to remand the case to the District Court for fresh fact-findings, addressed to the statute as we have now construed it.

Vacated and remanded.

Mr. Justice Black would affirm the judgments of the District Court and the Court of Appeals.

Mr. Justice White took no part in the decision of this case.

On remand, the trial court found that the primary purpose of the project had been to develop rental property. As a result, the taxpayer was entitled to treat the income as capital gain.

Except for its effort at definition, the Supreme Court in *Malat* offers lower courts little help in resolving the disputes between taxpayer and commissioner over "dealer" classification. As a result, the case law remains in disarray, as evidenced below.

Byram v. Commissioner

705 F.2d 1418 (5th Cir. 1983)

GEE, Circuit Judge.

"If a client asks you in any but an extreme case whether, in your opinion, his sale will result in capital gain, your answer should probably be, 'I don't know, and no one else in town can tell you.'"[1]

Sadly, the above wry comment on federal taxation of real estate transfers has, in the twenty-five years or so since it was penned, passed from the status of half-serious aside to that of hackneyed truism. Hackneyed or not, it is the primary attribute of truisms to be true, and this one is: in that field of the law—real property tenure—where the stability of rule and precedent has been exalted above all others, it seems ironic that one of its attributes, the tax incident upon disposition

---

1. Comment, Capital Gains: Dealer and Investor Problems, 35 Taxes 804, 806 (1957), quoted in 3B Mertens, Law of Federal Income Taxation § 22.138 n.69 (Zimet & Weiss rev. 1958); Biedenharn Realty Co. v. United States, 509 F.2d 171, 175 (5th Cir. 1975), *rev'd en banc*, 526 F.2d 409 (5th Cir. 1976), *cert. denied*, 429 U.S. 819, 97 S. Ct. 64, 50 L. Ed. 2d 79 (1976); Thompson v. Commissioner, 322 F.2d 122, 123 n.2 (5th Cir. 1963); Cole v. Usry, 294 F.2d 426, 427 n.3 (5th Cir. 1961).

of such property, should be one of the most uncertain in the entire field of litigation. But so it is, and we are called on again today to decide a close case in which almost a million dollars in claimed refunds are at stake. Doing so requires us to survey the development of this law in our circuit and to consider what application here, if any, the recent decision in Pullman-Standard v. Swint, 456 U.S. 273, 102 S. Ct. 1781, 72 L. Ed. 2d 66 (1982), is to find.

FACTS

The trial court, sitting without a jury in this taxpayer's suit for refund, found the following facts:

During 1973, John D. Byram, the taxpayer, sold seven pieces of real property. Mr. Byram was not a licensed real estate broker, was not associated with a real estate company which advertised itself, and did not maintain a separate real estate office. He advertised none of the seven properties for sale, nor did he list any of them with real estate brokers. To the contrary, all of the transactions were initiated either by the purchaser or by someone acting in the purchaser's behalf.

None of the properties sold was platted or subdivided. Byram devoted minimal time and effort to the sales in question, occupying himself chiefly with his rental properties. Byram's income for 1972 and 1973 included substantial amounts of rental income and interest income.

The district court's findings do not reflect the following additional facts, which apparently are not disputed by the parties. From 1971 through 1973, Byram sold 22 parcels of real property for a total gross return of over $9 million and a net profit of approximately $3.4 million. The seven properties at issue in this case sold for approximately $6.6 million gross, resulting in a profit of approximately $2.5 million. Six of the seven properties were held by Byram for periods ranging from six to nine months, intervals just exceeding the then-applicable holding periods for long-term capital gains. The seventh property had been held for two years and six months.

Although, as noted above, Mr. Byram received substantial rent and interest income in 1973, nevertheless his rental activities for that year resulted in a net tax loss of approximately $186,000. He received rental income from only one of the seven properties sold in 1973. The record does not reflect the exact relative amounts of income attributable to the sales in question and Byram's other activities.

Certain facts are disputed by the parties. The government asserts in its brief that Byram had entered into contracts to sell at least three of the seven properties in issue before he actually acquired them. Byram first responds that the record reflects only two such instances, not three; and at oral argument the government appeared to concede the point. As to those two transactions, Byram asserts that he acquired the right to purchase the properties by executing a contract before he entered into a contract to sell them; it was only closing on the purchases that postdated his contracts to sell. Finally, the government asserts, and Byram denies, that by virtue of Byram's civic activities in Austin, Texas, Byram's business of selling real estate was well-known in the community.

Based on its subsidiary findings indicated, the district court made ultimate findings that Byram held each of the seven properties for investment purposes and not primarily for sale to customers in the ordinary course of his trade or business. Judgment was therefore entered granting Byram the capital gains treatment that he sought. The government brought this appeal.

. . . Profits derived from the sale of "capital assets," known as "capital gains," are entitled to favorable tax treatment under the Internal Revenue Code (the "Code"). See 26 U.S.C. §§ 1201, 1202. The term "capital asset" is defined in relevant part as "property held by the taxpayer," not including property held "primarily for sale to customers in the ordinary course of [the taxpayer's] trade or business." Id., § 1221. The district court found that Byram "was not engaged in the real estate business" during the relevant years and that each of the seven properties in issue was held "for investment purposes and not primarily for sale to customers in the ordinary course of [Byram's] trade or business." Accordingly, the district court held that Byram was entitled to treat the profits from his 1973 sales as capital gains and ordered an appropriate refund. Our first task is to decide the correct standard by which to review the district court's principal finding[3] that Byram's holding purpose was for investment rather than for sale. The choice of a standard will determine the outcome of many cases; if the issue is treated as factual, the district court's decision is final unless clearly erroneous, F.R.C.P. 52(a), but if a question of law is presented, we may decide it *de novo*.

The question whether the characterization of property as "primarily held for sale to customers in the ordinary course of [a taxpayer's] trade or business" is an issue of fact or one of law has engendered tremendous controversy and conflict both in this[4] and in other[5] circuits. Recognizing the conflict in our own cases, a panel recently attempted to resolve it by breaking the statutory test down into its component parts,

---

3. In Suburban Realty Co. v. United States, 615 F.2d 171 (5th Cir.), *cert. denied*, 449 U.S. 920, 101 S. Ct. 318, 66 L. Ed. 2d 147 (1980), we recognize that the Code definition of "capital asset" gives rise to at least three inquiries:

   1. was taxpayer engaged in a trade or business, and, if so, what business?
   2. was taxpayer holding the property primarily for sale in that business?
   3. were the sales contemplated by taxpayer "ordinary" in the course of that business?

Id. at 178 (footnote omitted).

In many situations, these questions are analytically independent. For example, it will oftentimes be beyond dispute that a taxpayer is engaged in the real estate business with respect to certain properties, yet other properties may not be held primarily for sale in that business, or particular sales may be outside its ordinary scope. See, e.g., Wood v. Commissioner, 276 F.2d 586 (5th Cir. 1960); Maddux Construction Co. v. Commissioner, 54 T.C. 1278 (1970). However, in the present case the three statutory questions tend to merge into one, because the existence of a business, Byram's holding purpose, and the "ordinariness" of sales must all be determined by characterization of the same transactions. Moreover, because we decide below that Byram's holding purpose must be treated as an issue of fact, and that the district court's finding is not clearly erroneous, the holding below must be left undisturbed and we need not address related questions arguably posed by the statute.

4. See *Suburban Realty*, 615 F.2d at 180, collecting cases treating the issue as one of law, e.g., Houston Endowment, Inc. v. United States, 606 F.2d 77, 83 (5th Cir. 1979); United States v. Winthrop, 417 F.2d 905, 910 (5th Cir. 1969); Galena Oaks Corp. v. Scofield, 218 F.2d 217 (5th Cir. 1954); and another line of cases treating the question as essentially factual, e.g., United States v. Burket, 402 F.2d 426, 429 (5th Cir. 1968); Thompson v. Commissioner, 322 F.2d 122, 127 (5th Cir. 1963).

5. Three other circuit courts of appeals treat the issue as one of fact. Philhall Corp. v. United States, 546 F.2d 210 (6th Cir. 1976); Brown v. Commissioner, 448 F.2d 514 (10th Cir. 1971); Municipal Bond Corp. v. Commissioner, 382 F.2d 184 (8th Cir. 1967). Two circuits treat it as a question of law, following our cases that so hold. Turner v. Commissioner, 540 F.2d 1249 (4th Cir. 1976); Jersey Land & Development Corp. v. United States, 539 F.2d 311 (3d Cir. 1976). In other circuits, the issue is apparently unsettled. Compare Sovereign v. Commissioner, 281 F.2d 830 (7th Cir. 1960) (fact question) with Hansche v. Commissioner, 457 F.2d 429 (7th Cir. 1972) (treats question as open); compare Estate of Segel v. Commissioner, 370 F.2d 107 (2d Cir. 1966) (applies clearly erroneous standard) with In re Joseph Kanner Hat Co., 482 F.2d 937 (2d Cir. 1973) (bankruptcy case; dicta that de novo review applies). See also Cruttenden v. Commissioner, 644 F.2d 1368 (9th Cir. 1981) (open question); Parkside, Inc. v. Commissioner, 571 F.2d 1092, 1095 n.5 (9th Cir. 1977) (only one panel member accepts position that issue is one of fact).

see note 3, *supra*, some of which we held "are predominantly legal conclusions or are 'mixed questions of fact and law,' whereas others are essentially questions of fact." Suburban Realty, 615 F.2d at 180 (footnote omitted). . . .

Though the characterization of issues as ones of law or fact may be difficult in some cases, the present case is not one of them. . . .

The purpose for holding property, like the purpose for maintaining a seniority system at issue in *Swint*, is a question of intent and motive.[9] As such, it is a question of pure fact, and is neither a question of law nor a mixed question of law and fact. See 456 U.S. at 287, 102 S. Ct. at 1789, 72 L. Ed. 2d at 79. The factors usually cited to justify plenary review of holding purpose are the same factors that the Court found unpersuasive in determining the proper standard of review in *Swint*. For example, both issues involve a consideration of all facts and circumstances, with emphasis on particular significant factors. Compare James v. Stockham Valves & Fittings Co., supra note 6 (relevant considerations under Title VII) with *Suburban Realty*, 615 F.2d at 176, 182-85 (factors relevant to holding purpose under the Code). Similarly, both issues require the district court to use a reasoning process in analyzing the facts and to apply certain legal standards in making its finding. See note 9, *supra*. Resolution of either issue can determine the outcome of a case. None of those considerations affected the *Swint* Court's conclusion that the issue of discriminatory intent is neither a question of law nor a mixed question of law and fact, but is a pure question of fact. We see no reason to subject a district court's determination of holding purpose to a different standard of review than that applied to a district court's finding of discriminatory intent. The district court's finding in the present case that Byram held his property for investment rather than for sale to customers in the ordinary course of his business must be accepted unless it is clearly erroneous.

The record and the district court's findings of fact indicate that in determining Byram's holding purpose, the court considered all the factors this court has called "the seven pillars of capital gains treatment":[10]

(1) the nature and purpose of the acquisition of the property and the duration of the ownership; (2) the extent and nature of the taxpayer's efforts to sell the property; (3) the number, extent, continuity and substantiality of the sales; (4) the extent of subdividing, developing, and advertising to increase sales; (5) the use of a business office for the sale of the property; (6) the character and degree of supervision or control exercised by the taxpayer over any representative selling the property; and (7) the time and effort the taxpayer habitually devoted to the sales.

9. We have uniformly held that the statutory exception for property "held" for sale to customers, 26 U.S.C. § 1221, requires an inquiry into a taxpayer's intent. See, e.g., *Suburban Realty*, 615 F.2d at 182-85; Biedenharn Realty Co. v. United States, 526 F.2d 409, 422-23 (5th Cir.) (en banc), *cert. denied*, 429 U.S. 819, 97 S. Ct. 64, 50 L. Ed. 2d 79 (1976). Moreover, the fact that the taxpayer's subjective state of mind is not controlling and objective inquiry must be made by the court does not render the issue any less one of intent or any less factual. See Commissioner v. Duberstein, 363 U.S. 278, 286, 290-91, 80 S. Ct. 1190, 1199, 4 L. Ed. 2d 1218, 1225, 1228 (1960).

10. In application, these "pillars" have come more nearly to resemble the walls of a maze. See, e.g., *Suburban Realty*, 615 F.2d 171; *Biedenharn Realty*, 526 F.2d 409.

United States v. Winthrop, 417 F.2d 905, 910 (5th Cir. 1969). Recent cases have placed particular emphasis on four of these factors, noting that frequency and substantiality of sales is the most important factor, and that improvements to the property, solicitation and advertising efforts, and brokerage activities are also especially relevant considerations. *Biedenharn Realty*, 526 F.2d at 415-16; *Suburban Realty*, 615 F.2d at 176. At the same time, it has been repeatedly emphasized that these factors should not be treated as talismans. *Winthrop*, 417 F.2d at 911. Rather, "each case must be decided on its own peculiar facts. . . . Specific factors, or combinations of them, are not necessarily controlling." *Biedenharn Realty*, 526 F.2d at 415 (quoting Thompson v. Commissioner, 322 F.2d 122, 127 (5th Cir. 1963)).

The district court found most of the *Winthrop* factors absent in Byram's case. Byram made no personal effort to initiate the sales; buyers came to him. He did not advertise, he did not have a sales office, nor did he enlist the aid of brokers. The properties at issue were not improved or developed by him. The district court found that Byram devoted minimal time and effort to the transactions.[11] The government does not contend that any of these findings are clearly erroneous. Rather, the government argues that the frequency and substantiality of Byram's sales, together with the relatively short duration of his ownership of most of the properties, establishes that Byram intended to hold the properties for sale in the ordinary course of his business. In light of our decision regarding the standard of review, the government's argument must be that the district court clearly erred in finding these factors outweighed by the other relevant evidence. We cannot reasonably say that the district court's finding that Byram held his properties for investment was clearly erroneous.

The record reveals that during a three-year period, Byram sold 22 parcels of real estate for over $9 million, netting approximately $3.4 million profit.[12] Though these amounts are substantial by anyone's yardstick, the district court did not clearly err in determining that 22 such sales in three years were not sufficiently frequent or continuous to compel an inference of intent to hold the property for sale rather than investment. Compare *Suburban Realty*, 615 F.2d at 174 (244 sales over 32-year period); *Biedenharn Realty*, 526 F.2d at 411-12 (during 31-year period, taxpayer sold 208 lots and twelve individual parcels from subdivision in question; 477 lots were sold from other properties). This is particularly true in a case where the other relevant factors weigh so heavily in favor of the taxpayer. "[S]ubstantial and

---

11. This factor has been slighted in recent cases, not because it is unimportant, but because it was irrelevant to our consideration of the activities of large corporate organizations. See, e.g., *Suburban Realty*, 615 F.2d 171; *Houston Endowment*, 606 F.2d 77; *Biedenharn Realty*, 526 F.2d 409. However, in a case like the present one, where the government seeks to show that an individual taxpayer is holding property for sale in a certain business, the quantum of that individual's activity becomes very relevant. Long before the proliferation of tests and factors engulfed the capital gains field, this court made the common sense observation that the word "business" means "busyness; it implies one is kept more or less busy, that the activity is an occupation." Snell v. Commissioner, 97 F.2d 891, 892 (5th Cir. 1938); see also Stern v. United States, 164 F. Supp. 847, 851 (E.D. La. 1958) ('[A] court should not be quick to put a man in business . . . simply because he has been successful in earning extra income through a hobby or some other endeavor which takes relatively small part of his time.'), *aff'd*, 262 F.2d 957 (5th Cir.), *cert. denied*, 359 U.S. 969, 79 S. Ct. 880, 3 L. Ed. 2d 836 (1959). The district court was entitled to give great weight to Byram's time and effort devoted to sales in determining whether he held his property for sale in the ordinary course of his business.

12. Although only the seven sales completed in 1973 are at issue in this case, prior years' activities are relevant to the characterization of the 1973 transactions. See Thompson v. Commissioner, 322 F.2d 122, 127 (5th Cir. 1963).

frequent sales activity, standing alone, has never been held to be automatically sufficient to trigger ordinary income treatment." *Suburban Realty*, 615 F.2d at 176. Moreover, Byram's relatively short holding periods for some of the properties do not tip the balance in favor of the government. Ranging from six to nine months, these periods exceeded the then-applicable threshold for long-term capital gain treatment. In establishing those thresholds, Congress clearly expressed its intent that sales of otherwise qualified capital assets held for six to nine months be accorded capital gains treatment. To avoid frustration of that intent, a court should avoid placing too much weight on duration of ownership where other indicia of intent to hold the property for sale are minimal.

Mr. Byram has presented us with a close case. Had we been called upon to try or retry the facts, perhaps we would have drawn different inferences than did the district court. However, *Swint* has relieved us of that duty. Our review of the evidence convinces us that the district court was not clearly erroneous in finding that Byram held his properties for investment and not for sale in the ordinary course of his trade or business. . . .

NOTES AND QUESTIONS

1. Compare Bramlett v. Commissioner, 960 F.2d 526 (5th Cir. 1992), decided for the taxpayers, who relied heavily upon *Byram*. Taxpayers had formed Mesquite East, as a joint venture, to hold title to undeveloped acreage, and Town East, a corporation, to develop the property. Before any development began, Mesquite East sold the acreage to Town East at a substantial markup, and Town East thereafter sold off the acreage, after installing streets, storm drainage, sanitary sewer and water lines, to unrelated third parties. The Tax Court treated Town East as an extension of the joint venture, since the same four taxpayers were the owners, in proportionate shares, of both the joint venture and the corporation. Accordingly, the entire profit from the land sales, including the markup on the Mesquite East to Town East transfer, would have been taxed as ordinary income. The Fifth Circuit reversed, finding that common ownership by itself did not make the corporation an agent of the joint venture, and that the protection of limited liability afforded by the corporation was a substantial business reason for creating the corporation. See also Phelan v. Commissioner, T.C.M. 2004-206, 88 T.C.M. 223 (2006).

2. Also compare Goodman v. United States, 390 F.2d 915 (Ct. Cl. 1968), decided against the taxpayers. The Goodmans were New York City lawyers who specialized in real estate law. Their practice gave them opportunities to buy and sell realty for their own account, as well as for clients and associates. They were not licensed real estate brokers. During the three tax years in question, the Goodmans sold 32 different realty interests. Of these, 15 had been held less than six months, and only five had been held as long as five years. In each instance, the taxpayers' investment was that of a minority membership within the ownership syndicate. The taxpayers' net income from the sale or disposal of their real estate interests during this period exceeded by roughly one-third their net income from the practice of law. To the trier of fact, this evidence demonstrated that the taxpayers bought and held the various property interests primarily for sale to customers.

3. *Goodman* illustrates the professional taxpayer who also "invests" heavily in real estate. Why should it matter that the Goodmans earned more from real estate than

from the practice of law? Suppose that the taxpayers' major source of income had been legal fees: Would this change the result? Should it? Compare *Goodman* with Robert L. Adam, 60 T.C. 996 (1973), where taxpayer, a full-time CPA, obtained capital gains treatment on nine resales of property over a four-year period.

4. Does the Code discriminate against taxpayers whose livelihood comes partly from real estate investments? Suppose that the Goodmans had invested in corporate securities, including real estate corporations, and had churned their portfolio with the same frequency and profitability; would their gains be taxed at ordinary or capital rates? Does the §1221 phrase "primarily for sale to *customers*" explain satisfactorily the differing treatment of real estate and corporate securities? Cf. M. Chirelstein, Federal Income Taxation 339 (6th ed. 1991).

5. Even taxpayers who are real estate dealers may still seek investor status as to occasional properties. See, for instance, Richard Pritchett, 63 T.C. 149 (1975), where taxpayer real estate broker held investment properties in his own name and used partnerships or corporations for his regular dealings. In according capital gains treatment to the taxpayer's "investments," the court stressed the absence of advertising or subdivision, and the relatively long holding periods.

6. Section 1236 offers the securities dealer (for instance, underwriter, floor specialist) a method to insulate his securities "investments" from §1221(1) status. The dealer must elect before the close of the day on which the securities were acquired whether to hold the property as an investment. He is bound by the election. What are the merits of a similar election in the real estate field?

7. *Malat* involved a taxpayer who claimed a "dual purpose" in acquiring the property. A related situation is that of a taxpayer whose purpose changes after acquisition. In a typical scenario, taxpayer acquires investment property, but after a number of years (and corresponding appreciation of the property) decides to sell the property much as a dealer might—by subdivision, improvements, heavy advertising, or the use of brokers. The taxpayer may then claim that he has done so merely to *liquidate* the investment most feasibly and at the best price, and that he did not intend to enter into the subdivision business. For contrasting results, compare Estate of Josephine Clay Simpson, 21 T.C.M. 371 (1962), with Winthrop v. Tomlinson, 417 F.2d 905 (5th Cir. 1969). Suppose that taxpayer has paid $1 million for property, that he can resell it for $2 million without subdivision and sales promotion, and that his "liquidation" activity will net $3.5 million. Does the Code allow an allocation of gain between investment and dealership activity? Answer: No. However, courts have permitted taxpayers to treat one portion of their property as investment and another portion of the same property as "held primarily for sale to customers." See Frank H. Taylor & Son., Inc. v. Commissioner, 32 T.C.M. 362 (1973).

8. A closely related situation arises when a long-term owner of an apartment building decides to convert the project to a cooperative or condominium and sell off the units individually. Is there any way for the taxpayer to avoid §1221(1)? See Gangi v. Comm'r, T.C. Memo. 1987-561 (taxpayers involved in rental real estate business realized capital gains, not ordinary income, by sale of condominium units in connection with the termination of the rental business); John Delaney, When Will the Liquidation-of-Investment Theory Apply to a Sale of Condominium Units?, 71 J. Taxn. 45 (1989).

9. Where several taxpayers share interests in the same real property, as in *Goodman,* must they all be treated alike, that is, as dealers, or nondealers? Cf. Riddell

v. Scales, 406 F.2d 210, 212 (9th Cir. 1969); Tibbals v. United States, 362 F.2d 266, 278 (Ct. Cl. 1966). Suppose that X, a dealer, owns a controlling interest in the X corporation; will X's status taint the corporation's? Same result if X owns a controlling interest in a partnership? Cf. Royce W. Brown, 54 T.C. 1475 (1970), *aff'd*, 488 F.2d 514 (10th Cir. 1971); contra C. Frederick Frick, 31 T.C.M. 286 (1972).

10. Further readings include Jeffery D. Moss, Keys to Avoiding "Dealer" Status for Real Estate Investors—Planning and Structuring for Bifurcation of Gain, 33 Mi. Real Prop. Rev. 76 (2006); David Lloyd Forney, Comment, Appellate Review of Dealer Status in Realty Sales Under I.R.C. § 1221, 45 U. Pitt. L. Rev. 847 (1984); William A. Friedlander, To "Customers": The Forgotten Element in Characterization of Gains on Sales of Real Property, 39 Tax L. Rev. 31 (1983).

D. TAX STRATEGY: HOW TO POSTPONE TAXES ON THE SALE OF REAL PROPERTY

1. The Installment Sale

The buyer rarely pays all cash when acquiring real property. If buyer borrows entirely from third parties (such as a commercial lender), the seller will receive full cash for his equity. Often, however, the seller will extend purchase money financing for some (perhaps the entire) part of the unpaid price. Absent the installment sale provisions of the Code, first enacted in 1954, full gain realization might result in serious hardship for the seller who agrees to accept the buyer's liabilities in lieu of cash.

Section 453, the installment sale provision, was significantly amended in 1980. Although the 1980 amendments resulted from a custom-tailored set of proposals intended to simplify the treatment of installment sales,[95] more recent changes have both added new layers of complexity and restricted the benefits from installment reporting. The principal features of the present law include:

1. no ceiling on the percentage (formerly "no more than 30 percent") of the selling price that the seller may receive in the taxable year of the sale;
2. no requirement that the seller receive a minimum of two installment payments, as to which confusion once existed. A sale is now eligible for installment reporting even when there is only a single installment—that is, one lump sum made in a taxable year subsequent to that in which the sale occurs;
3. a requirement that the taxpayer elect out of the provisions of § 453 if she does not wish to report an eligible sale on the installment basis; otherwise, § 453 treatment is now automatic, reversing the section's once elective feature (query: under what circumstances might the taxpayer wish to report her entire gain in the year of the sale?);
4. a bar against installment reporting for dealers both in real and personal property;

95. Installment Sales Revision Act of 1980, 96th Cong., 2d Sess. (1980).

5. an exception to this bar, however, as to dealers who sell residential lots, time-share rights, and farm property, if the dealer elects to pay interest on the deferred tax liability arising from the use of the installment method;[96]

6. full recognition of depreciation recapture income in the year of the sale, even if the seller receives no principal payments in that year;[97]

7. a requirement that the seller pay interest on the deferred tax liability as to any outstanding installment obligations whose balance at the close of the taxable year exceeds $5 million.[98]

The underlying mechanics of installment sale reporting remain unchanged, however. These mechanics are illustrated below.

a. Definitions

If a transaction qualifies as an installment sale under § 453, gain is realized and taxable only as the seller actually receives the sales proceeds. The installment method does not apply to losses.

Selling Price: This is the total consideration agreed upon for the property. It includes cash, the buyer's notes, other property received by the seller, and the amount of any mortgage being transferred with the real estate, whether the buyer assumes the mortgage or takes subject to it. The selling price is not reduced by sales commissions or other expenses of sale.[99]

Gross Profit: This is the selling price less the adjusted basis; the latter is increased (except for dealer sales) to include commissions, attorney's fees, and other sales expenses.[100]

Contract Price: In most cases, this equals the seller's cash equity in the property and is the amount the seller will eventually receive in cash, including payment on the buyer's notes, or in other property. In addition, any excess of mortgage over basis will be included in the contract price.[101]

Gross Profit Ratio: This is the ratio of the gross profit to the contract price.[102]

Payments Received in the Taxable Year: The § 453 calculation is based upon the payments received in the taxable year. These payments are best considered in terms of the initial year and each subsequent year. In the first taxable year, the payments

---

96. I.R.C. § 453(1). The amount of interest, geared to the applicable federal rate, covers the period from the date of the sale to the dates on which the year's installment payments are received.

97. I.R.C. § 453(i). Any recapture income so recognized is added back to the basis of the property for the purpose of determining the gross profit and the gross profit ratio.

98. I.R.C. § 453A(c). The taxpayer must calculate and pay interest yearly on the amount of deferred tax liability. The deferred tax liability for any obligation is the amount of the unrecognized gain at the year-end, multiplied by the maximum rate of tax then in effect. Interest is geared to the underpayment rate in effect under § 6621(a)(2), but applies only to that fraction of the taxpayer's installment obligations that exceeds $5 million. A "de minimis" exception covers installment obligations arising from the transfer of any property whose sale price does not exceed $150,000.

99. Reg. § 15A.453-1(b)(2)(ii).

100. Reg. § 15A.453-1(b)(2)(v).

101. Reg. § 15A.453-1(b)(2)(iii).

102. Reg. § 15A.453-1(b)(2)(i).

would include cash or other property (for instance, the notes of someone other than the buyer) received by the seller at or before the closing, together with any principal reduction payments (but not of interest) made on the buyer's note during the year. In addition, where the buyer takes over an outstanding mortgage whose balance exceeds the seller's basis in the property, the excess of mortgage over basis will be deemed a first year's payment. After the first taxable year, only the principal reduction payments on the buyer's notes would be subject to the § 453 calculation.

Although the buyer's notes, ordinarily, are not regarded as payments until reduction or disposition occurs, if the seller receives a demand note, or a readily tradable corporate or governmental obligation, the face amount of the note or obligation will be includable in income at the very outset.[103] Also, if a taxpayer sells depreciable property to a controlled entity, for example a corporation in which he owns directly or indirectly more than 50 percent of the value of the outstanding stock, all payments to be received shall be treated as received in the initial year, unless the taxpayer can overcome the presumption that tax avoidance informed the sale.[104]

b. Illustrations

Mortgage Less Than the Seller's Basis. On September 1, 2003, X, a nondealer and calendar year taxpayer, sells property that has $300,000 basis and is subject to a $250,000 mortgage for $400,000. The terms are $50,000 cash; $250,000 by the buyer taking over the first mortgage, and $100,000 by the buyer giving back a note and second mortgage. The buyer makes a note reduction payment of $40,000 on December 1, 2003 and also makes a $50,000 principal payment on the first mortgage before the end of 2003. Assume no recapture income.

What is the seller's 2003 taxable gain? This is an installment sale, without regard to the percentage of the selling price that X receives in the year of sale, so long as some part of the unpaid price is received after 2003. X must elect out of § 453 to avoid installment treatment.

The taxpayer reports as 2003 income all payments received in 2003 multiplied by the gross profit ratio (the ratio of the gross profit to the contract price). Here, the gross profit ratio is two-thirds: $100,000 (gross profit)/$150,000 (contract price). The total 2003 payments received are $90,000: $50,000 cash and $40,000 note reduction. (We ignore the buyer's $50,000 payment on the existing first mortgage.) Therefore, in 2003, the seller's taxable gain is $60,000 (2/3 times $90,000). The two-thirds gross profit ratio will also govern all future payments.

Mortgage Exceeds the Seller's Basis. In the problem above, assume that the seller's basis is $220,000. What is the seller's 2003 taxable gain?

First, to determine the payments received in 2003, we must include the $30,000 excess of mortgage balance ($250,000) over the adjusted basis ($220,000). This will increase the payments that X receives in 2003 to $120,000.

103. I.R.C. § 453(f)(4).
104. I.R.C. § 453(g).

Moreover, the transfer of property subject to a mortgage in excess of basis also changes both the calculation of contract price and, derivatively, the gross profit ratio. In this instance, in calculating contract price, we add the $30,000 mortgage excess to the $150,000 value of X's equity. Thus, the recalculated contract price is $180,000. Here, gross profit is also $180,000: $400,000 selling price minus $220,000 adjusted basis. The gross profit ratio, therefore, rises to 100 percent, and X in 2003 must report as a taxable gain the entire $120,000 of payments received. All future years' payments received will also be fully taxed. One can state categorically that whenever property having a mortgage balance in excess of basis is the subject of an installment sale, the gross profit ratio becomes 100 percent. Can you explain why?

c. The Related Parties Ploy

Prior to certain 1980 amendments to § 453, taxpayers could arrange a win-win situation, one enabling them to gain the benefit of deferred taxation while effectively receiving the full cash value for their equity. To achieve this result, the owner of appreciated property would first enter into an installment sale with a close family member (contract 1). The related purchaser, shortly afterwards, would then resell the property for all cash to the ultimate buyer (contract 2). Since the related purchaser would start with a stepped-up basis (his purchase price), the gain or loss from the contract 2 resale would consist only of the fluctuation in value, usually minimal, between the two contracts. The initial seller, however, would achieve gain deferral under contract 1 until the related purchaser actually made the installments provided for under the contract, even though the family unit, which would include the initial seller, had full use of the cash received under contract 2. Thus, after the related party's resale, all appreciation would be realized within the related group but gain recognition might be deferred for a considerable time.[105]

Under current law, an installment sale to a related person[106] that is followed, within two years,[107] by a second disposition of the same property triggers an acceleration of the payments received by the original seller, to the extent that additional cash and other property flows into the related group.[108] The following illustrates this treatment:

Example: On September 1, 2003, X, a nondealer and calendar year taxpayer, sells property that has a $300,000 basis and is subject to a $250,000 mortgage to his son, XS, for $400,000. The terms are: no cash down; $250,000 by the buyer taking over the

---

105. In addition to spreading out the gain, the seller might also receive some estate planning benefits, since the value of the installment obligation would then be frozen for estate tax purposes. Any subsequent appreciation in the value of any property acquired by reinvestment of the proceeds from the "installment" sale would not affect the seller's gross estate, since the value of the "replacement" property would no longer be included in the seller's gross estate. 96th Cong., 2d Sess., U.S. Sen., Comm. on Fin., Rpt., Installment Sales Revision Act of 1980, pp. 12-13.

106. In applying the resale rules, the Code defines "related persons" under the relationship rules of § 267(6) and the stock attribution rules of § 318(a); I.R.C. § 453(f)(1).

107. The two-year period is suspended during the time the related buyer substantially lessens his risk of loss as to the property by holding a put, making a short sale or any other transaction, or when another person holds a right to acquire the property; I.R.C. § 453(e)(2).

108. I.R.C. § 453(e)(2).

first mortgage; and $150,000 by XS giving back an unsecured note, all due in ten years. On January 2, 2004, XS resells the property to Y, an unrelated person, for $400,000. Y takes over the $250,000 first mortgage and pays XS $150,000 in cash.

Prior to the amendment, X could postpone recognition of the $150,000 gain for ten years, until XS repaid the note. Under the present law, X would be required to report the entire gain in 2004, the taxable year in which the second disposition occurred.[109]

Congress has further limited the use of § 453 for installment sales of depreciable property to controlled entities—for example, where a taxpayer sells depreciable property to a corporation in which she owns directly or indirectly more than 50 percent of the value of the outstanding stock; I.R.C. §§ 453(8), 1239(b). In such a case, the transferor must report in the year of the disposition all future payments to be received as well as the current payments, unless she can establish that tax avoidance was not one of the principal reasons for the transaction.

d.   Disposition of the Buyer's Installment Obligation

The 1980 Revision Act treated more clearly the seller's sale or other disposition of the buyer's installment obligation, an event that had caused some earlier uncertainty. The following example illustrates the issue and the present treatment.

Example: Taxpayer sells property with a basis of $25,000, for $50,000. Taxpayer receives $10,000 in cash and the buyer's $40,000 note. Prior to receiving any payment on the note, Taxpayer sells the note for $32,000. What is the taxpayer's gain on the note disposition?

  Taxpayer's gross profit ratio is 50 percent ($25,000/$50,000), creating a $20,000 basis in the $40,000 note. The sale of the note for $32,000 results in a $12,000 gain, recognized in the taxable year of the disposition.[110]

The seller also derives income if she disposes of the buyer's obligation other than by sale or exchange, for example, through a gift or dividend distribution. (Transfers at death are expressly excluded.)[111] The seller's income would then be measured by the excess of the obligation's face value over its basis—in the above example, $20,000.

What continued to cause some uncertainty, even after the 1980 Revision Act, was the question of when a disposition had occurred. The seller might, for example, pledge the installment obligation as security for a loan, rather than selling or discounting the note, and some courts treated the pledge differently from a sale, and not as a recognition event. United Surgical Steel Co. v. Commissioner, 54 T.C. 1214 (1970), *acq.*, 1971-2 C.B. 3; Schaeffer v. Commissioner, T.C.M. 1981-27. In an effort to resolve this matter, the 1986 Tax Reform Act added a mind-boggling layer of complexity to § 453, but the tax bar quickly persuaded Congress that its solution was both numbing and unworkable. This led in 1988 to a simple declaration that if

---

109. In the case of a second disposition that is not sale or exchange, the fair market value of the property disposed of is treated as the amount realized for this purpose. I.R.C. § 453(e)(4).

110. I.R.C. § 453B.

111. I.R.C. § 453B(c).

the seller pledged the installment obligation, the net loan proceeds would be treated as a payment received.[112]

Other situations where the issue of disposition has arisen include:

a. substitution of the buyer's note and mortgage for a land contract between the seller and buyer (no disposition: Rev. Rul. 55-5, 1955-1 C.B. 331).
b. transfer of the buyer's note to the seller's grantor trust (disposition, unless grantor deemed to have retained ownership under trust rules: Rev. Rul. 81-98, 1981-1 C.B. 40).
c. buyer's issuance of a new note to replace the original installment obligation, in settlement of a lawsuit (nondisposition: Akira Kutsunai, 83,182 PH Memo TC).

Section 453B and the Treasury Regulations also list several other disposition and nondisposition events. The former includes cancellation of the obligation; the latter includes transfers between spouses or incident to a divorce, contribution to or distribution from a partnership, and various corporate organization and reorganization situations.

2. The Deferred Payment Method

In some instances of an installment sale, the taxpayer cannot readily determine gross profit and, derivatively, the gross profit ratio because of the indeterminacy of the selling price. This situation arises when the contractual right to full payment is contingent upon future events, or the fair market value of the buyer's obligations is not readily ascertainable.

Prior to 1980, sellers in such situations could use the "deferred payment" method to report their gain. Under this approach, whose authority derived from a reading of § 1002, the taxpayer asserted that until the contingency was entirely removed or the value of the buyer's obligations fully ascertainable, the amount of realized gain — an essential element of recognized gain — could not be measured. Thus, the first receipts of cash (or other property) from the buyer would be treated as a return of capital — a nontaxable event — to be applied in reduction of basis. Not until recovery was complete, that is, not until the basis was reduced to zero, would taxability begin. Thereafter, all receipts would be taxable. The Regulations accepted this approach in principle,[113] although the taxpayer would still have to persuade the Commissioner and the courts of the indeterminacy of the selling price. See, for instance, Jones v. Commissioner, 60 T.C. 663 (1973), *nonacq.*, 1980-1 C.B. 2, *rev'd and remanded*, 524 F.2d 788 (9th Cir. 1975), *on remand*, 68 T.C. 837 (1977), *aff'd*, 617 F.2d 536 (9th Cir. 1980).

Congress, in 1980, sought to curtail use of the deferred payment method. Section 453(j) directs the Secretary of the Treasury to issue regulations for "ratable basis recovery" in transactions where the gross profit or the total contract price (or both) cannot be readily ascertained. The ensuing regulations distinguish between two

112. I.R.C. § 453A(d).
113. Treas. Regs. § § 1.453-4,6.

situations. Where the buyer's obligations bear a fixed amount, a cash method seller must treat as an amount realized in the year of sale the obligations' fair market value, which shall be considered as worth no less than the fair market value of the property sold (less other consideration received); an accrual method taxpayer may make some adjustment to reflect any contingency as to when payments are to be made. But under no circumstances will an installment sale for a fixed amount obligation be considered an "open transaction."[114]

In the second situation, where the seller's *right* to repayment is contingent upon future events, the Regulations provide for "ratable basis recovery." This technique is described in extensive detail, which does not warrant restatement here.[115] Deferred payment thus remains an option of sorts, but its use has become far more limited, and where available, its benefits are also more limited.

3. Tax-Free Exchanges Under § 1031

Section 1031 has become an increasingly popular vehicle for real estate tax deferral. Although the section was first intended chiefly to permit tax-free replacements of tangible personal property (for example, industrial machines), § 1031's broad compass, the courts' readiness to construe the section generously, along with the Treasury's effort to provide easily followed roadmaps, all have given real estate operators an option for gain deferral that is often worth exploring.

Section 1031(a) provides for nonrecognition of gain or loss when the taxpayer exchanges property held for productive use in a trade or business or for investment solely for "like-kind" property held either for productive use in a trade or business or for investment. When these conditions are met, nonrecognition is required. Various forms of property are excluded from § 1031(a) treatment, however, even if the purpose for which the property is held satisfies the Code. Chief among the excluded categories are stocks, bonds, and partnership interests. Because it does not meet the qualifying purpose requirement, a private residence or dealer property would not be eligible for § 1031(a) treatment either.

Whether the exchanged properties, if otherwise qualifying, are also "like-kind" is sometimes uncertain.[116] The Regulations state that "like-kind" refers to the nature and character of property and not to its grade or quality, and give some surprising illustrations: improved real estate for unimproved real estate; a leasehold of a fee with 30 years or more to run, for a fee interest in real estate.[117] The Code now provides that real property located in the United States and real property located outside the United States are not property of like kind.[118]

114. Reg. § 15A.453-1(d)(2).
115. Reg. § 15A.453-1(c).
116. In 1989, the Senate failed to adopt a House-approved provision that would have narrowed considerably the like-kind standard. Under the House amendment, § 1031 would have applied only to exchanges of property "similar or related in service or use," the § 1033 standard for the replacement property that qualifies an involuntary conversion for tax deferral.
117. Treas. Reg. § 1.1031(a)-1(b).
118. I.R.C. § 1031(h).

§ 1031. Exchange of property held for productive use or investment

(a) Nonrecognition of gain or loss from exchanges solely in kind

(1) In general No gain or loss shall be recognized on the exchange of property held for productive use in a trade or business or for investment if such property is exchanged solely for property of like kind which is to be held either for productive use in a trade or business or for investment.

(2) Exception This subsection shall not apply to any exchange of—

(A) stock in trade or other property held primarily for sale,

(B) stocks, bonds, or notes,

(C) other securities or evidences of indebtedness or interest,

(D) interests in a partnership,

(E) certificates of trust or beneficial interests, or

(F) choses in action.

For purposes of this section, an interest in a partnership which has in effect a valid election under section 761(a) to be excluded from the application of all of subchapter K shall be treated as an interest in each of the assets of such partnership and not as an interest in a partnership. . . .

(b) Gain from exchanges not solely in kind If an exchange would be within the provisions of subsection(a), of section 1035(a), of section 1036(a), or of section 1037(a), if it were not for the fact that the property received in exchange consists not only of property permitted by such provisions to be received without the recognition of gain, but also of other property or money, then the gain, if any, to the recipient shall be recognized, but in an amount not in excess of the sum of such money and the fair market value of such other property.

(c) Loss from exchanges not solely in kind If an exchange would be within the provisions of subsection(a), of section 1035(a), of section 1036(a), or of section 1037(a), if it were not for the fact that the property received in exchange consists not only of property permitted by such provisions to be received without the recognition of gain or loss, but also of other property or money, then no loss from the exchange shall be recognized.

(d) Basis If property was acquired on an exchange described in this section, section 1035(a), section 1036(a), or section 1037(a), then the basis shall be the same as that of the property exchanged, decreased in the amount of any money received by the taxpayer and increased in the amount of gain or decreased in the amount of loss to the taxpayer that was recognized on such exchange. If the property so acquired consisted in part of the type of property permitted by this section, section 1035 (a), section 1036(a), or section 1037 (a), to be received without the recognition of gain or loss, and in part of other property, the basis provided in this subsection shall be allocated between the properties (other than money) received, and for the purpose of the allocation there shall be assigned to such other property an amount equivalent to its fair market value at the date of the exchange. For purposes of this section, section 1035 (a), and section 1036 (a), where as part of the consideration to the taxpayer another party to the exchange assumed (as determined under section 357 (d)) a liability of the taxpayer, such assumption shall be considered as money received by the taxpayer on the exchange. . . .

a. The Mechanics of § 1031

Problem A: X owns an apartment building that he has held for investment. The adjusted basis is $1 million. The building's fair market value is $5 million. Y owns a ranch with a fair market value, also of $5 million. X wishes to acquire the ranch, which Y is willing to sell at its market value.

If X were to sell the apartment building to a third person, let us say, Z, for $5 million, he would suffer a net capital gain of $4 million (assuming no recapture), on which his federal capital gains tax would come to $600,000 (assuming the 15 percent rate). (X must also consider state and local income taxes.) However, if X exchanged the building directly for Y's ranch, and held the ranch for a qualifying purpose, § 1031(a) would require nonrecognition. The acquired property would receive a substituted basis of $1 million.[119]

Since Y, presumably, wants to cash out his equity, he will not wish to retain the apartment building and will resell it (shortly) to a third person, Z, for $5 million. Do you see, as to Y, that § 1031(a) does not apply to the X-Y exchange?

If you are wondering whether, as to X, § 1031(a) covers this three-corner deal, in which Y serves mainly as a conduit between X and Z, the *Biggs* case, following, should supply the answer.

Problem B: X owns an apartment building that he has held for investment. The adjusted basis is $1 million. The building's fair market value is $5 million. Y owns a ranch with a fair market value of $4 million. In order to complete an exchange between X and Y, Y agrees to pay $1 million in cash.

Section 1031(a) does not qualify this exchange because X has not received solely like-kind property. The nonqualifying property, cash, is called "boot," and § 1031 (b) handles exchanges, otherwise qualifying, that involve the receipt of boot. This section provides that gain, if any, shall be recognized in the amount of any money, and the fair market value of any nonqualifying property, received by the taxpayer; in our example, X must recognize a $1 million net capital gain. The remaining $3 million of gain would enjoy deferral.

Despite the $1 million gain recognition, X's basis in the ranch becomes $1 million — as it was in Problem A. Section 1031(d) commands a substituted basis ($1 million) in the newly acquired property decreased by the amount of any money received ($1 million) and increased by the amount of any gain recognized ($1 million). To test whether this outcome is sound, calculate X's ultimate gain if he were to resell the ranch at the $4 million acquisition value.

Purchase money notes would be regarded as a cash equivalent on this exchange, and X would be taxed on their fair market value, subject to § 453 treatment as an installment sale. Note, however, that if the exchange is one that would otherwise result in a nonrecognized loss to the taxpayer, the receipt of money or "other property" does not result in partial recognition.[120]

---

119. I.R.C. § 1031(d).
120. I.R.C. § 1031(r).

Problem C: X owns an apartment building that he has held for investment. The adjusted basis is $1 million. The building's fair market value is $5 million, but the building is subject to a $2 million mortgage. Y owns a ranch with a fair market value of $3 million. X and Y exchange their properties.

The amount of any mortgage liability attached to the transferred property, which the transferee either assumes or takes subject to, is treated as boot and, thus, as potentially taxable under § 1031(b).[121] Accordingly, in our example, X must recognize a $2 million gain on the exchange. The remaining $2 million of gain would enjoy deferral.

The basis calculation would again result in a post-exchange basis of $1 million for the ranch. From X's vantage, Y's $2 million mortgage takeover is viewed as the equivalent of "money received," so that X must first adjust his $1 million substituted basis downward by $2 million to reflect the boot before adjusting it upward in the same amount to reflect gain recognition. Once more, to test the soundness of this result, what is X's gain if he were to resell the ranch at the $3 million acquisition value?

Consider, also, the effect of a mortgage takeover on Y's basis for the apartment house, if Y were to qualify his leg of the transaction under § 1031. To make this calculation, assume that Y's basis in the ranch prior to the exchange was $1.5 million.

Often mortgages or other boot will be present on both sides of the transaction. Try to work through the following problem.

Problem D: X owns an apartment building that he has held for investment. The adjusted basis is $1 million. The building's fair market value is $5 million, but the building is subject to a $2 million mortgage. Y owns a ranch that he has held for investment. The adjusted basis is $1.5 million. The ranch's fair market value is $4 million, but the ranch is subject to a $1.5 million mortgage. X and Y exchange the two properties. X receives $500,000 in cash.

What is X's recognized gain? ($1 million)
What is Y's recognized gain? (zero)
What is X's post-exchange basis in the ranch? ($1 million)
What is Y's post-exchange basis in the apartment building? ($2.5 million)

b.   The Three-Cornered Exchange

Biggs v. Commissioner

---

632 F.2d 1171 (5th Cir. 1980)

HENDERSON, Circuit Judge. The Commissioner of Internal Revenue appeals from the decision of the United States Tax Court holding that a transfer of real property effected by the taxpayer, Franklin B. Biggs, constituted an exchange within the meaning of § 1031 of the Internal Revenue Code of 1954. We affirm.

---

121. Treas. Reg. § 1.1031(6)-1(c).

The numerous transactions which form the subject of this suit are somewhat confusing and each detail is of potential significance. Thus, it will be necessary to recount with particularity the facts as found by the Tax Court.

Biggs owned two parcels of land located in St. Martin's Neck, Worcester County, Maryland (hereinafter referred to as the "Maryland property"). Sometime before October 23, 1968, Biggs listed this property for sale with a realtor. The realtor advised Biggs that he had a client, Shepard G. Powell, who was interested in purchasing the property.

Biggs and Powell met on October 23, 1968 to discuss Powell's possible acquisition of the Maryland property. Biggs insisted from the outset that he receive real property of like kind as part of the consideration for the transfer. Both men understood that Biggs would locate the property he wished to receive in exchange, and Powell agreed to cooperate in the exchange arrangements to the extent that his own interests were not impaired.

On October 25, 1968, Biggs and Powell signed a memorandum of intent which provided, in pertinent part, the following:

> I. PURCHASE PRICE: $900,000 NET to SELLERS. . . .
> c. $25,000.00 down payment at signing of contract. . . .
> d. $75,000.00 additional payment at time of settlement, which shall be within ninety
> (90) days after contract signing, making total cash payments of $ 100,000.00.
> II. MORTGAGE:
> a. Balance of $800,000.00 secured by a first mortgage on Real Estate to SELLERS at
> a 4% interest rate; 10 year term. . . .

The memorandum contained no mention of the contemplated exchange of properties. Upon learning of this omission, Biggs' attorney, W. Edgar Porter, told Powell that the memorandum of intent did not comport with his understanding of the proposed transaction. Powell agreed to have his attorney meet with Porter to work out the terms of a written exchange agreement.

Biggs began his search for suitable exchange property by advising John Thatcher, a Maryland real estate broker, of the desired specifications. Subsequently, Biggs was contacted by another realtor, John A. Davis, who had in his inventory four parcels of land located in Accomack County, Virginia, collectively known as Myrtle Grove Farm (hereinafter referred to as "the Virginia property"). Biggs inspected the property, found it suitable, and instructed Davis to draft contracts of sale.

As initially drawn, the contracts named Biggs as the buyer of the Virginia property. However, at Porter's suggestion, they were modified to describe the purchaser as "Franklin B. Biggs (acting as agent for syndicate)." The contracts were executed on October 29th and 30th, 1968, and contained the following terms:

Paid on execution of contract	$ 13,900.00
Balance due at settlement	115,655.14
Indebtedness created or assumed	142,544.86
Total — Gross Sales Price	$272,100.00

Upon signing the contracts, Biggs paid $13,900.00 to the sellers of the Virginia property. Because Powell was either unable or unwilling to take title to the Virginia property, Biggs arranged for the title to be transferred to Shore Title Company, Inc. (hereinafter referred to as "Shore"), a Maryland corporation owned and controlled by Porter and certain members of his family. However, it was not until December 26, 1968 that the purchase was authorized by Shore's board of directors. On January 9, 1969, prior to the transfer to Shore, Biggs and Shore entered into the following agreement with respect to the Virginia property:

1. At any time hereafter that either party hereto requests the other party to do so, Shore Title Co., Inc. will and hereby agrees to convey unto the said Franklin B. Biggs, or his nominee, all of the above mentioned property, for exactly the same price said Shore Title Co., Inc. has paid for it, plus any and all costs, expenses, advances or payments which Shore Title Co., Inc. has paid or will be bound in the future to pay, over and above said purchase price to Shore Title Co., Inc., in order for Shore Title Co., Inc., to acquire or hold title to said property; and it [is] further agreed that at that time, i.e. when Shore Title Co., Inc. conveys said property under this paragraph and its provisions, the said Franklin B. Biggs, or his nominee will simultaneously release or cause Shore Title Co., Inc. to be released from any and all obligations which the latter has created, assumed or become bound upon in its acquisition and holding of title to said property.

2. All costs for acquiring or holding title to said property by both the said Shore Title Co., Inc. and Franklin B. Biggs, or his nominee shall be paid by the said Franklin B. Biggs, or his nominee at the time of transfer of title under paragraph numbered 1 hereof.

On or about the same date, the contracts for the sale of the Virginia property were closed. Warranty deeds evidencing legal title were delivered to Shore by the sellers. Biggs advanced to Shore the $115,655.14 due at settlement and, by a bond secured by a deed of trust on the property, Shore agreed to repay Biggs. Shore also assumed liabilities totalling $142,544.86 which were secured by deeds of trust in favor of the sellers and another mortgagee. Biggs paid Thatcher's finder's fee and all of the closing costs.

On February 26, 1969, Shore and Powell signed an agreement for the sale by Shore of the Virginia property to Powell or his assigns. Payment of the purchase price was arranged as follows:

Upon execution of the agreement	$ 100.00
Vendee assumed and covenanted to pay the following promissory notes, all secured by deeds of trust on Virginia property:	
To Shore Savings & Loan Association	58,469.86
To those from whom Shore acquired the Virginia property	84,075.00
To Franklin B. Biggs	115,655.14
Balance due at settlement	13,900.00
Total purchase price	272,200.00

The next day, February 27, 1969, Biggs and Powell executed a contract which provided that Biggs would sell the Maryland property to Powell or his assigns upon the following terms:

Cash, upon execution	$ 25,000.00
Cash, at settlement	75,000.00
First mortgage note receivable from Mr. Powell	800,000.00
Total	$900,000.00

The contract further stated:

Sellers and Purchaser acknowledge the existence of a Contract of Sale dated February 26th, 1969, between Shore Title Co., Inc., Vendor-Seller; and Shepard G. Powell or Assigns, Vendee-Purchaser, copy of which is attached hereto and made a part hereof, whereby that Vendor has contracted to sell and that Vendee has agreed to buy from that Vendor at and for the purchase price of Two Hundred Seventy Two Thousand Two Hundred Dollars ($272,200.00) . . . [the Virginia property]. As a further consideration for the making of this Contract of Sale . . . for the sale and purchase . . . of . . . [the Maryland property] the said Shepard G. Powell or Assigns, for the sum of One Hundred Dollars ($100.00) in cash, in hand paid, receipt whereof is hereby acknowledged, does hereby bargain, sell, set over and transfer unto said Franklin B. Biggs all of the right, title and interest of the said Shepard G. Powell or Assigns in and to said Virginia property and said Contract of Sale relating thereto, upon condition that the said Franklin B. Biggs assumes and covenants to pay (which he hereby does) all of the obligations assumed by the said Shepard G. Powell under the aforesaid Contract of Sale between him and Shore Title Co., Inc.; and said Franklin B. Biggs hereby agrees to hold Shepard G. Powell or Assigns harmless from any liability under any and all of said obligations on said Virginia property, and the said Shepard G. Powell and said Franklin B. Biggs do hereby jointly and separately agree to execute and deliver any and all necessary papers to effect delivery of title to said Virginia property to said Franklin B. Biggs and to relieve said Shepard G. Powell from any and all obligations assumed by him thereon.

On the same date, Powell and his wife assigned their contractual rights to acquire the Maryland property to Samuel Lessans and Maurice Lessans. The Lessanses, in turn, sold and assigned their rights to acquire the Maryland property to Ocean View Corporation (hereinafter referred to as "Ocean View"), a Maryland corporation, for $1,300,000.00 by an agreement dated May 22, 1969. The purchase price was comprised of $150,000.00 to be paid into escrow at the time the contract was signed, an $800,000.00 note executed by Ocean View in favor of Biggs at the time of settlement, a $250,000.00 note from Ocean View to the Lessanses, and a $100,000.00 note from Ocean View to the real estate agents at closing.

Ocean View was incorporated on May 21, 1969. At the first meeting of its board of directors, the corporation was authorized to acquire the Maryland property and, also, to quit-claim any interest it might have in the Virginia property. It is undisputed, though, that neither the Lessanses nor Ocean View had any interest whatsoever in that property.

On May 24, 1969, Shore executed a deed conveying all of its right, title and interest in the Virginia property to Biggs. Powell and his wife, the Lessanses and Ocean View all joined in executing the deed as grantors, despite their apparent lack of any cognizable interest in the property. This instrument provided that:

> [T]he said Shore Title Co., Inc., a Maryland corporation, executes this deed to the Grantee herein for the purpose of conveying the . . . Virginia property hereinafter described by good and marketable title, subject to the assumption by the Grantee herein of the obligations hereinafter referred to, and all of the other Grantors herein join in the execution of this deed for the purpose of releasing and quit-claiming any interest in and to the property described herein and for the purpose of thereby requesting Shore Title Co., Inc. to convey said property to the Grantee herein in the manner herein set out. . . .

By the same deed, Biggs agreed to assume and pay the notes in favor of the mortgagee and the owners from whom Shore had acquired the Virginia property, in the total sum of $142,544.86. On May 29, 1969, Biggs executed a deed of release in favor of Shore indicating payment in full of the $115,655.14 bond.

On May 26, 1969, Biggs and his wife, Powell and his wife and the Lessanses sold the Maryland property to Ocean View. Contemporaneously, Ocean View executed a mortgage in the face amount of $800,000.00 in favor of Biggs. Also on this date, all of the contracts were closed. Ocean View received the deed to the Maryland property and Biggs accepted title to the Virginia property.

Biggs reported his gain from the sale of the Maryland property on his 1969 federal income tax return as follows:[1]

Selling price of Maryland property	$900,000.00	100.00%
Exchange — Virginia property	298,380.75[a]	33.15%
Boot	$601,619.25	66.85%
Selling price Maryland property	$900,000.00	
Basis-date of exchange	186,312.80	
Gain	$713,687.20	
Not recognized-exchange		
(Sec. 1031 I.R.C.) 33.15%	236,587.31	
Taxable gain	$477,099.89	53.011%

[a] Such figure included finders' fees and legal costs incident to the acquisition of the Virginia property.

Biggs elected to report the transaction under the installment sales provision of § 453 of the Code. The Commissioner issued a notice of deficiency based upon his determination that there was no exchange of like-kind properties within the meaning of § 1031. The Tax Court disagreed, and ruled in favor of Biggs.[2]

---

1. Biggs admits that, even if the transaction qualifies as a § 1031 exchange, he used an incorrect method to calculate the gain to be recognized.
2. The Tax Court opinion is reported at 69 T.C. 905 (1978).

Section 1031 provides, in pertinent part, that the gain realized on the exchange of like-kind property held for productive use or investment shall be recognized only to the extent that "boot" or cash is received as additional consideration. The Commissioner does not deny that Biggs fully intended to carry out an exchange that would pass muster under § 1031. It was undoubtedly for this purpose that Biggs insisted from the beginning of his negotiations with Powell that he receive property of like kind as part of the consideration for the transfer of the Maryland property. Cf. Alderson v. C.I.R., 317 F.2d 790 (9th Cir. 1963). However, as this court made clear in Carlton v. United States, 385 F.2d 238 (5th Cir. 1967), the mere intent to effect a § 1031 exchange is not dispositive. Indeed, the Commissioner's primary contention is that, under the authority of our holding in *Carlton*, Biggs failed to accomplish an exchange because the purchaser, Powell, never held title to the Virginia property.

The facts on which *Carlton* was decided parallel those which we now consider in several respects. Carlton, the taxpayer, wished to trade a tract of ranch land for other property of a similar character in order to obtain the tax benefits afforded by § 1031. This intent was made explicit in the negotiations and resulting option contract entered into by Carlton and General, a corporation which desired to purchase the ranch property. Carlton proceeded to locate two parcels of suitable exchange property, negotiate for the acquisition of this property, and pay a deposit on each parcel. General executed the actual agreements of sale and then assigned its contract rights to purchase the exchange property to the taxpayer. However, the crucial factor which distinguishes *Carlton* from the instant case is that General actually paid cash for the ranch property which Carlton then used two days later to purchase the exchange property. A panel of this court held that the receipt of cash transformed the intended exchange into a sale:

> [W]hile elaborate plans were laid to exchange property, the substance of the transaction was that the appellants received cash for the deed to their ranch property and not another parcel of land. The very essence of an exchange is the transfer of property between owners, while the mark of a sale is the receipt of cash for the property.

385 F.2d at 242 (footnote and citations omitted).

Although the payment and receipt of cash was the determinative factor, the court went on to cite additional reasons to support its holding of a sale, rather than an exchange:

> Further, General was never in a position to exchange properties with the appellants because it never acquired the legal title to either the Lyons or the Fernandez property. Indeed, General was not personally obligated on either the notes or mortgages involved in these transactions. Thus it never had any property of like kind to exchange. Finally, it cannot be said that General paid for the Lyons and Fernandez properties and merely had the properties deeded directly to the appellants. The money received from General by the appellants for the ranch property was not earmarked by General to be used in purchasing the Lyons or Fernandez properties. It was unrestricted and could be used by the appellants as they pleased.

385 F.2d at 242-243. The Commissioner maintains that this language in *Carlton* establishes as an absolute prerequisite to a § 1031 exchange that the purchaser have

title to the exchange property. We do not agree with this interpretation. The *Carlton* decision was based on the aggregate circumstances discussed therein and, as we have noted, the most significant of these was the receipt of cash by the taxpayer. In the present case, the transfer of the Maryland property and the receipt of the Virginia property occurred simultaneously, and the cash paid to Biggs at the closing constituted "boot." Also in contrast to the facts found in *Carlton*, Powell, as contract purchaser, did "assume [ ] and covenant [ ] to pay . . . promissory notes, all secured by deeds of trust on the Virginia property," plus the balance due at settlement. We cannot ignore the legal obligations and risks inherent in this contractual language, even though Powell was subject to such risks only for a short period of time. Also, the unrestricted use of funds which was a problem in *Carlton* is of no concern here because Biggs received cash only upon the closing of all transactions.

Thus, we are left with the sole consideration that Powell never acquired legal title to the Virginia property. Yet, if we were to decide, as the Commissioner urges, that this factor alone precludes a § 1031 exchange, we would contravene the earlier precedent established by this court in W. D. Haden Co. v. C.I.R., 165 F.2d 588 (5th Cir. 1948). *Haden* also involved a multi-party exchange in which the purchaser, Goodwin, never held title to the exchange property. However, since Goodwin had contracted to purchase the property, the court held that the taxpayer had effected a like-kind exchange, stating that the purchaser "could bind himself to exchange property he did not own but could acquire." 165 F.2d at 590.

Our resolution of the title issue is also tangentially supported by language contained in the Ninth Circuit's recent opinion in Starker v. United States, 602 F.2d 1341 (9th Cir. 1979). Briefly stated, the *Starker* facts involved a transfer of the taxpayer's real property to the purchaser, Crown Zellerbach Corp., in exchange for the corporation's promise to acquire other real property in the future and convey it to the taxpayer. The government argued that this arrangement did not qualify for § 1031 treatment because the transfers were not simultaneous and, alternatively, the contract right received by the taxpayer was personal property and, hence, not like-kind to the real property he had conveyed. The Ninth Circuit disagreed and, in response to the latter argument, stated:

> This is true, but the short answer to this statement is that title to real property, like a contract right to purchase real property, is nothing more than a bundle of potential causes of action: for trespass, to quiet title, for interference with quiet enjoyment, and so on. The bundle of rights associated with ownership is obviously not excluded from section 1031; a contractual right to assume the rights of ownership should not, we believe, be treated as any different than the ownership rights themselves. Even if the contract right includes the possibility of the taxpayer receiving something other than ownership of like-kind property, we hold that it is still of a like-kind with ownership for tax purposes when the taxpayer prefers property to cash before and throughout the executory period, and only like-kind property is ultimately received.

602 F.2d at 1355. Of course, we need not, and do not, express either acceptance or disapproval of the ultimate holding in *Starker*. However, the Ninth Circuit's discussion of the title versus right-to-purchase problem is, we believe, consistent with our own analysis.

We must also reject the Commissioner's assertions that the Tax Court applied the so-called "step-transaction doctrine" incorrectly, and that the transactions which occurred here were in substance a sale for cash of the Maryland property and an unrelated purchase of the Virginia property. The step-transaction doctrine was articulated in Redwing Carriers, Inc. v. Tomlinson, 399 F.2d 652 (5th Cir. 1968):

> [A]n integrated transaction may not be separated into its components for the purposes of taxation by either the Internal Revenue Service or the taxpayer. (Citation omitted.) In Kanawha Gas and Utilities Co. v. Commissioner, 5 Cir. 1954, 214 F.2d 685, 691, our Court through Judge Rives said:
>
>> In determining the incidence of taxation, we must look through form and search out the substance of a transaction. . . . [cases cited] This basic concept of tax law is particularly pertinent to cases involving a series of transactions designed and executed as parts of a unitary plan to achieve an intended result. Such plans will be viewed as a whole regardless of whether the effect of so doing is imposition of or relief from taxation. The series of closely related steps in such a plan are merely the means by which to carry out the plan and will not be separated.

399 F.2d at 658. The Tax Court found that the many transactions leading to the ultimate transfers of the Maryland and Virginia properties were part of a single, integrated plan, the substantive result of which was a like-kind exchange. This finding is amply supported by the evidence. Biggs insisted at all times that he receive like-kind property as part of the consideration for the transfer of the Maryland property. Powell agreed to this arrangement and assured Biggs of his cooperation. Biggs was careful not to contract for the sale of the Maryland property until Powell had obtained an interest in the Virginia land. When he and Powell did enter into an agreement of sale on February 26, 1969, the exchange was made an express condition of the contract. Biggs also avoided the step which was fatal to the taxpayer's intended exchange in *Carlton;* i.e., he did not receive any cash prior to the simultaneous closings of the properties on May 26, 1969. Under these circumstances, the Tax Court correctly determined that all transactions were interdependent and that they culminated in an exchange rather than a sale and separate purchase.

Finally, we examine the Commissioner's claim that Shore was serving as an agent for Biggs throughout the transactions, and that the accomplishment of the intended exchange was thereby precluded. Admittedly, the exchange would have been meaningless if Shore, acting as Biggs' agent, acquired title to the Virginia property and then executed the deed conveying title to Biggs. For, in essence, Biggs would have merely effected an exchange with himself. Cf. Coupe v. C.I.R., 52 T.C. 394 (1969). However, while the Tax Court refused to find, in contrast to its decision in *Coupe,* that Shore acted as an agent for the purchaser, Powell, it also specifically determined that Shore was not an agent of Biggs. Rather, Shore accepted title to the Virginia property, albeit at Biggs' request, merely in order to facilitate the exchange. We believe that this is an accurate characterization of Shore's role in the transactions. Consequently, we reject the Commissioner's agency notion also.

Undoubtedly, the exchange of the Maryland and Virginia properties could have been more artfully accomplished and with a greater economy of steps. However, we must conclude on the facts before us that the taxpayer ultimately achieved the intended result. Accordingly, the decision of the Tax Court is affirmed.

NOTES AND QUESTIONS

1. *Delayed exchanges.* In Starker v. United States, referred to in the *Biggs* opinion, the court allowed § 1031 treatment despite the fact that the second party received five years to find suitable exchange property. Because the second party was contractually bound to perform within that five-year period, the court viewed taxpayer's contractual entitlement to a property to be "named later" as equivalent to ownership thereof for purposes of effectuating a like-kind exchange. *Starker* exchanges became widespread, but the Tax Reform Act of 1984 has greatly curtailed the opportunity to delay selection of the second property. Section 1031(a)(3) requires that the exchange property be identified within 45 days of the day on which the taxpayer gives up the property to be relinquished or that the exchange property be received by the earlier of either 180 days after the transfer of the taxpayer's property or the due date (including extensions) of the taxpayer's return for that year.

2. The Treasury has issued regulations to cover the 1984 amendments on deferred exchanges. Under these rules, the taxpayer can satisfy the 45-day limit for identifying the replacement property only if he has designated the property in a signed written document that he has sent within that period to an unrelated person involved in the exchange. This writing may be the signed exchange agreement. The document must describe the replacement property unambiguously (legal description or street address), but the taxpayer may identify more than one property or replacement property. The rules limit the maximum number of properties the taxpayer may identify either to three (of any value) or to any number of properties as long as their aggregate fair market value does not exceed 200 percent of the value of the relinquished properties. If the taxpayer exceeds these limits, he is deemed not to have identified any replacement properties except to the extent that he completes the exchange before the end of the *identification* period or receives before the end of the *exchange* period replacement property constituting 95 percent of the aggregate fair value of all identified properties.

The taxpayer will satisfy the 180-day exchange period only if the replacement property is substantially the same property he has already identified. The regulations give the following example:

> B transfers real property X to C on May 17, 1991. Real property X, which has been held by B for investment, is unencumbered and has a fair market value on May 17, 1991, of $100,000. . . . In the exchange agreement, B identifies real property P as replacement property. Real property P consists of two acres of unimproved land and has a fair market value of $250,000. . . . On October 3, 1991, at B's direction, C purchases 1½ acres of real property P for $187,500 and transfers it to B, and B pays $87,500 to C. The fair market value of the portion of real property P that B has received ($187,500) is 75 percent of the fair market value of real property P. . . . B is considered to have received substantially the same property as identified.

Treas. Reg. § 1.1031(k)-1.

3. After the seller has transferred his property, he typically is unwilling to rely on the buyer's unsecured promise to transfer the like-kind replacement property in the future. Thus, a seller will require some type of security for, or guaranty of, the buyer's obligation to transfer the like-kind replacement property. In addition, a seller will often receive interest (or a "growth factor") to compensate him for the period between the transfer of his property and the receipt of the replacement property. Finally, in some transactions, the buyer may be unwilling or unable to acquire the replacement property. In such cases, the delayed exchange may be facilitated by an intermediary.

The seller's legitimate concerns in these matters pose a dilemma, for the rules provide that the taxpayer in a deferred exchange may be forced to recognize gain or loss if he actually or constructively receives money or other property before he actually receives the like-kind replacement property. This would occur, for example, if the transferor has the unrestricted right to demand that the transferee pay cash in lieu of acquiring and transferring the replacement property, even if the demand is never made and both the identification and receipt of replacement property satisfy the deferred exchange rules. The regulations set forth four safe harbors, the use of which will result in a determination that the taxpayer is not in actual or constructive receipt of money (absent an unrestricted right to receive money or other property):

Safe Harbor 1: The obligation to transfer the replacement property may be secured by cash or a cash equivalent held in a qualified escrow account or qualified trust. The escrow holder or trustee must be an unrelated party,[122] and the taxpayer's rights to utilize the cash generally must be limited until after all identified replacement property is received or the identification period ends without the identification of a replacement property;

Safe Harbor 2: The obligation to transfer the replacement property may be secured by (a) a mortgage, deed of trust, or other security interest; (b) a standby letter of credit; or (c) a third-party guarantee;

Safe Harbor 3: An unrelated intermediary may be used to facilitate the deferred exchange by agreeing both to acquire the relinquished property from the taxpayer, and to acquire and transfer the replacement property to the taxpayer;

Safe Harbor 4: The taxpayer may receive interest or other growth factor with respect to the deferred exchange, provided that the right to receive the interest is limited as indicated in Safe Harbor 1.

---

122. Related parties include persons who "act as the taxpayer's agent (including, for example, by performing services as the taxpayer's employee, attorney, or broker)." Treas. Reg. § 1.1031(a)-3(k)(1). However, a person is not treated as the taxpayer's "agent" and, thus, may serve as an intermediary if (1) the services performed by the agent are concerned with implementing a § 1031 nonrecognition exchange or (2) services performed by the agent are "routine financial services" performed for the taxpayer by a "financial institution." Treas. Reg. § 1.1031(a)-3(k)(2). It would appear that the rules shove attorneys from the field of "qualified intermediaries," while promoting the position of banks, escrow companies, title companies, and other financial institutions. Tax Notes, June 4, 1990, at 1154.

4. *The expanded boundaries of § 1031.* Several private letter rulings demonstrate how sellers and their advisors have expanded § 1031's horizons:

Swap for new building financed with seller's dollars. Retailing Corp. wants to sell its $20 million headquarters, in which it has a basis of $5 million, and move into a larger, custom-designed facility that will cost in the vicinity of $40 million. Venture Partnership wants to buy Retailing's buildings, but Retailing wants to avoid a federal income tax bill by structuring the deal as a tax-deferred exchange.

1. Venture enters into a long-term lease of suitable land chosen by Retailing. The 30-year lease is assignable and allows the original or successor lessee to purchase the land at any time after year five of the lease.
2. Venture will build a new building on the leased land to Retailing's specifications. Retailing has the right to approve all contracts, contractors, costs, modifications, and so forth.
3. Venture is required to contribute a minimum amount of cash to the project (itself borrowed from the project's architect, one of the partners of Venture). The lion's share of the cost of building the new structure will come from a nonrecourse construction loan from Retailing Corp. to Venture.
4. When the building is complete, Venture Partnership swaps its building and lease for Retailing's free-and-clear building. Venture repays enough of the construction loan from Retailing to even things out. In this example, Venture would repay about $20 million of the construction loan.

Letter Ruling 9149018 concludes that although Retailing acted as both a lender and exchanging party, the deal was a valid tax-deferred exchange under § 1031. Basic reason: Venture Partnership retained the risks of ownership and had cash at risk until the new building was completed.

Remainder interest swapped for fee-simple interest. Frank and Xavier, both unrelated, own a remainder interest and a life interest respectively in the same piece of investment property. Xavier wants the whole ball of wax, and Frank is amenable as long as he doesn't pay a current tax on the gain.

1. Using a qualified intermediary arrangement, Frank enters into a sales agreement with Xavier, then assigns the agreement to GoBetween (the intermediary). In turn, GoBetween will acquire suitable replacement property identified by Frank and deliver title to the new investment property to Frank.

Letter Ruling 9143053 concludes that Frank's remainder interest is like-kind to the fee interest, as long as both properties are held for investment.

Standby letter of credit to assure performance in a three-way exchange. Golf Course wants to enlarge by swapping its North Forty for Mr. Smith's South Fifty, a piece of property contiguous to the golf course. Developer wants to buy North Forty, and Mr. Smith wants to sell his South Fifty.

1. Golf Course grants Developer an exclusive, renewable option to acquire North Forty by (1) purchasing South Fifty and improving it to Golf Course's specifications, and (2) exchanging it for North Forty. The initial option term ends five days after the IRS issues a favorable ruling on the

transaction. The option is to be exercised by Developer delivering written notice that it intends to consummate the exchange.

2. When Developer exercises its option, Golf Course will transfer to it the title to North Forty. Developer will pay some cash and also will deliver a standby letter of credit (LOC) to assure it will deliver the replacement property, improved as per Golf Course's specifications, within the 180-day statutory replacement limit.

Letter Ruling 9141018 concludes that the standby LOC met all the regulatory requirements: (1) Golf Course can only draw on it in the event of Developer's failure to supply replacement property on a timely basis, and (2) the LOC is non-negotiable and nontransferable. Although the amount to be paid under the LOC wasn't fixed (it was equal to the agreed-upon value of North Forty, less cash Developer had expended improving South Forty), the I.R.S. ruled that this did not bar tax-deferred exchange treatment.

5. *Tenancy-in-common investments.* Partnership interests are excepted from the like-kind exchange provisions of § 1031. So, while a partnership as a whole can exchange its real property under § 1031, no individual partner can conduct a 1031 exchange of her partnership interest for other partnership interests or interests in real property. As a result, some investors started to turn to ownership as tenants-in-common (TIC) so that their individual interests could be exchanged. Often the investor will create an intermediate pass-through entity, such as a single-member limited liability company, to hold the TIC interest in order to obtain the benefits of limited liability. Rev. Proc 2002-22 provides an opportunity for TIC co-owners to secure private letter rulings that their relationship will not be deemed a partnership for tax purposes if certain conditions are met. This has dramatically increased interest in TIC ownership, and helped to fuel the growth of an industry devoted to helping taxpayers execute like-kind exhanges. See, e.g., Terence Floyd Cuff, Section 1031 Exchanges Involving Tenancies-in-common, *in* Tax Planning for Domestic & Foreign Partnerships, LLCs, Joint Ventures & Other Strategic Alliances 2006, 704 PLI/Tax 107 (Practicing Law Institute 2006); Alvin Robert Thorup, TIC or Treat: How Tenant-in-Common Real Estate Sales Can Avoid the Reach of the Securities Laws, 34 Real Est. L.J. 422 (2006).

6. *Related-party exchanges.* Congress in 1989 amended § 1031 to limit its use in related-party exchanges.[123] The problem Congress sought to cure is illustrated below:

Example: A owns property with a $150,000 basis, worth $1 million. An unrelated party wants to buy the property, but A wants to avoid the gain. B, a related party, owns like-kind property with a $900,000 basis, also worth $1 million. A and B exchange their properties. Neither A nor B is taxed on the trade. Shortly afterwards, B sells the newly acquired property to the unrelated party, and establishes a $100,000 gain — the

---

123. I.R.C. § 1031(f). For the purposes of this section, a related party would cover any of the relationships listed under § 267(b) or § 707(b)(1). These include:

— family members (brothers and sisters, spouse, ancestors, and lineal descendants);
— a corporation and a more-than-50 percent shareholder;
— two corporations that are members of the same controlled group;
— two controlled partnerships;
— tax-free transfer to controlled partnership.

difference between the $1 million selling price and the substituted $900,000 basis. A is not taxed on her potential $850,000 gain as long as she continues to hold the property.

The 1989 amendment imposes a two-year waiting period before the related party B can sell the property without penalty. If either related party to the exchange sells or disposes of the property exchanged in less than two years, both parties must recognize any gain or loss that § 1031 would otherwise defer. A's recognition would occur in the tax year of the later disposition, not in the year of the related-party exchange. In the illustration above, if B's resale occurred within two years, A also would be required to report a taxable gain.

The amendment also kicks in if the related parties reverse the transaction: B sells first to the unrelated party, who then exchanges the property with A within the two-year period. Here, too, A would be required to recognize the $850,000 gain; the exchange would not qualify for § 1031 nonrecognition.

The two-year waiting period is extended if either party is protected so as to substantially diminish his risk of loss. Thus, if B were to grant the unrelated party a two-year option to purchase the exchanged property for $1 million, the subsequent exercise of the option would trigger A's gain recognition. A broader net would also catch any exchanges that are "part of a transaction (or series of transactions) structured to avoid the purposes of the [related parties] subsection."[124] However, involuntary conversions (§ 1033) and dispositions made after the death of either party can occur without penalty.

7. *Minimization of boot.* Typically in an exchange, the two properties are not exactly equal in value, and at least one party receives some boot. To minimize the amount of boot, one author suggests the exchange of fee simple interests for residual interests, as in the following:

> *Example:* Lee T. Gator, an attorney, owns an office building that has a $1.5 million fair market value and is unencumbered. Gator's basis in the building is $500,000. Gator uses some of the building for his law offices and rents to other attorneys. Gator has decided to retire and would like to exchange his building for investment property, while avoiding any income tax on his realized gain.
>
> Judge Knott, one of Gator's tenants, would like to acquire Gator's building. Knott owns an apartment building that has a $2.5 million fair market value and is unencumbered. Knott's basis in his building is $1.75 million. Like Gator, Knott would like to defer gain recognition.
>
> To minimize the gain that must be recognized, Gator exchanges his office building for a remainder interest in Knott's apartment building. Gator's remainder interest will be subject to a five-year estate for years in the apartment building that Knott will reserve for himself. If the exchange occurred during August 1989 (imputed 10 percent annualized interest rate), the present value of Gator's remainder interest would be 62.0921 percent of the property's fair market value or $1,552,302.50. Thus, Gator would give Knott $52,302.50 worth of boot, and the Judge would recognize that much of his realized gain. However, Gator's $1 million of realized gain, and almost $700,000 of Knott's realized gain, would not be recognized under § 1031.

Rigall, Three Ways to Reduce Boot in Like-Kind Exchanges, 72 J. Tax. 20, 22 (1990).

---

124. I.R.C. § 1031(f)(4).

CHAPTER FOUR
Contracts of Sale

There are usually two major steps to a land sale transaction: first, a contract of sale, and later a closing. In sales of single-family homes, the closing typically is two or three months after the contract is entered into. The contract describes the property being sold and such terms as price, closing date, and quality of title being conveyed, which normally is marketable title. The buyer often will make a down payment to the seller, also known as an earnest money payment, when the contract of sale is signed. In residential sales this payment commonly is 10 percent. On entering into a sales contract, the buyer is considered to have equitable title, legal title passing at the closing.

During the executory interval, the time between the contract date and the closing date, the buyer usually seeks financing and typically also has a title examination made to determine if the seller has the title promised the buyer. As we have seen, most land sales are financed, at least in part, with borrowed money obtained by the buyer from a lending institution, the loan secured by the land being purchased. Before signing the contract of sale, the buyer usually has not lined up financing. Financing usually is sought during the executory interval, it then being clear that the buyer can acquire the property and on what terms. If the title examination discloses defects, the buyer notifies the seller and the seller ordinarily has until closing to perfect title in accord with whatever quality of title has been promised in the contract.

At the closing, the seller typically delivers a deed to the buyer and the buyer pays the balance of the purchase price to the seller, the lending institution making funds available so that this payment can be made. At the closing, too, each party may be required to satisfy the other that additional conditions in the contract, such as contracted-for title, have been met. If the parties are represented by legal counsel in the transaction, counsel in all probability will also attend the closing.

In some important aspects, the law of land sale contracts departs from contract law principles you have encountered in other law school courses. As you work through this chapter, be alert to these departures and give thought to why they exist and whether or not they are merited. Also, note that many buyers and sellers of land are not represented by legal counsel prior to or at the time of contracting to purchase. Lawyers often are not retained until later. As you go through the chapter, consider which of the litigated problems that arose would probably have been avoided if lawyers had been involved in negotiating the contract of sale. Of course, some parties do not retain legal counsel even during the executory interval. Where this is apparent, would any further problems that emerged likely have been prevented if there had been representation by a lawyer after the contract date?

There is considerable variation, by geography and transaction type, among the sorts of writings which appear sequentially as a real estate transaction moves toward consummation. Normal papering of a simple deal might involve: (1) the seller's listing agreement, (2) a brief "offer to purchase" or "binder" signed only by the buyer and accompanied by his deposit (or perhaps an even briefer "deposit receipt" signed only by the broker), and (3) a formal contract signed by both buyer and seller. Or perhaps after the listing agreement, the broker will obtain the buyer's signature to a detailed contract, which will then be submitted to the seller for signing, and then the parties will meet to prepare escrow instructions. A binder may include sufficient essential contract terms to possibly be held an enforceable contract. In negotiation of big real estate deals, the parties often execute a preliminary document called a letter of intent or memorandum of agreement that sets forth what terms are settled and what terms are still to be negotiated. In some cases, these preliminary documents have been held binding contracts, unresolved terms considered details to be later negotiated. The basic issue is whether the parties intended to be bound by the document, but this can be a difficult interpretive question.

A. STATUTE OF FRAUDS PROBLEMS

All states in this country long have had Statutes of Frauds applicable to transfers of interests in real property. The New York statute appearing below is a fairly typical example of such a statute. In interpreting Statutes of Frauds and adding supplemental case law on the writing requirement every state has an extensive body of case law, the case law frequently differing from state to state in what meets the writing requirement or under what circumstances no writing may be required for a legally enforceable real property sales contract.[1] The two cases included in this section of the case book are examples of important Statute of Frauds problems that often have been litigated. Kovarik v. Vesely considers what documents may be considered in determining compliance with the Statute of Frauds and Holman v. Childersburg Bancorporation, Inc. considers part performance, a widely recognized exception to the writing requirement.

Kovarik v. Vesely

3 Wis. 2d 573, 89 N.W. 2d 279 (1958)

Action by the plaintiffs Emil H. Kovarik, Jr., and Lorraine Mary Kovarik, his wife, to recover from the defendants George Vesely, Sr., Viola Vesely, his wife, and Henry Gardner a $4,000 down payment made by the plaintiffs to the defendants pursuant to contract on the purchase of land. The defendants Vesely counter-claimed for specific performance of the contract.

The contract was in writing dated July 6, 1956, and was drafted in the form of an offer to purchase by the Kovariks with an acceptance of such offer, such offer and acceptance being incorporated in one document. The purchase price was stated to be

1. For more extended discussion of the Statute of Frauds in real estate sales transactions, see Stoebuck & Whitman, Property 704-723 (3d ed. 2000). See also Braustein, Remedy, Reason and the Statute of Frauds, 1989 Utah. L. Rev. 383, and O'Connell, Boats Against the Current: The Courts and the Statute of Frauds, 47 Emory L.J. 253 (1998).

$11,000, of which $4,000 was paid by the Kovariks to Gardner, real estate broker for the Veselys. The contract provided that the $7,000 mortgage was payable in the form of a "$7,000 purchase money mortgage from the Fort Atkinson Savings & Loan Ass'n." The following special condition appeared in the body of the offer to purchase: "This offer is contingent upon buyer's ability to arrange above described financing."

The Kovariks shortly after entering into the contract made a written application to the Fort Atkinson Savings & Loan Association for the $7,000 mortgage loan on the premises being purchased. Kovarik testified that the terms and conditions of the loan were not inserted in this application at the time it was signed by him. Therefore, it may be assumed that they were inserted by the association after such signing of the application and before the same was acted upon. There is no claim made on this appeal that the insertion of such terms was not authorized by the Kovariks.

On August 10, 1956, the Kovariks learned that the association had rejected their loan application, a fact then already known to the defendants. On the same day Kovarik demanded return of the $4,000 down payment from Gardner. Gardner informed Kovarik that the latter would have to see Vesely about the matter because Gardner had no authority to pay back the $4,000. Kovarik then also on that day asked Vesely for the return of the money. Vesely refused such demand and suggested that Kovarik employ a lawyer.

The Kovariks then employed Attorney Williamson as their counsel who on August 17, 1956, conferred with a member of the law firm retained by the Veselys. The latter tendered the abstract of title to Mr. Williamson and advised him that the Veselys were willing to take back a first mortgage on the same terms and conditions as the Fort Atkinson Savings & Loan Association. Attorney Williamson refused such tender of the abstract, and in behalf of his clients also rejected the proposal with respect to the Veselys accepting the $7,000 first mortgage as payment of the balance of the purchase price.

Under date of September 9, 1956, the Kovariks instituted action to recover the down payment and the Veselys counter-claimed for specific performance. The action was tried to the court without a jury and the trial judge under date of June 14, 1957, filed a memorandum opinion reciting the facts and determining the legal issues in favor of the defendants. . . . [lwr ct.]

. . . [F]ormal findings of fact and conclusions of law were entered in conformity with the trial judge's memorandum opinion. Finding of Fact No. 5 reads as follows:

> That the buyers applied for a loan from the Fort Atkinson Savings & Loan Association in the amount of Seven Thousand Dollars, which loan would run for fifteen years and bear interest at the rate of five percent per annum, payable monthly, and it further provided for monthly payments of Eight Dollars per thousand or Fifty-six Dollars per month to apply first upon the interest and the balance upon the principal plus one-twelfth of the taxes based upon the preceding year for the term of fifteen years, and these terms of financing were satisfactory to the buyers.

Judgment was entered August 21, 1957, dismissing the plaintiff's complaint, and decreeing specific performance of the contract as prayed for in the counterclaim. The judgment requires the Kovariks to execute a $7,000 note and mortgage to the Veselys upon the purchased premises, the terms of such note and mortgage being those set forth in Finding of Fact No. 5. From such judgment the plaintiffs have appealed.

CURRIE, Justice. . . . The three issues confronting the court on this appeal are:

(1) Is the contract of purchase and sale, which was entered into between the plaintiff buyers and the defendant sellers, void because of failure to comply with the statute of frauds (sec. 240.08, Stats.)?

(2) How are the words of the contract, "This offer is contingent upon buyer's ability to arrange above described financing," to be construed?

(3) Was the offer of the defendant sellers to accept a $7,000 mortgage upon the same terms as those set forth in the prior loan application to the Fort Atkinson Savings & Loan Association timely made?

It is the contention of counsel for the buyers that the contract fails to comply with the statute of frauds because the terms of the $7,000 mortgage are not set forth therein. On the other hand, it is the position of the attorneys for the sellers that such mortgage terms were set forth in the written loan application which the buyers signed and filed with the Fort Atkinson Savings & Loan Association, and that such application, although a separate writing, constitutes part of the "memorandum" of purchase and sale.

The general rule is that the memorandum required by the statute of frauds may consist of several writings. [Citations omitted.] It is also not essential to the validity of such memorandum that a particular writing shall have been made with the intention that it constitute a memorandum of the contract. Restatement, 1 Contracts, p. 286, sec. 209.

The fact that the buyers mortgage loan application came into existence subsequent to the date on which the contract was signed by the parties is also immaterial. . . . Annotation 85 A.L.R. 1184, 1193.

In Kelly v. Sullivan, [252 Wis. 52, 30 N.W.2d 209], this court held that, when separate writings are necessary to spell out a memorandum of sale and they do not refer on their face to the same transaction, they cannot be construed together to constitute the memorandum required by the statute unless physically annexed to each other. In the *Kelly* case the separate writing particularly relied upon was unsigned by the defendant seller, who was the party sought to be charged. The New York court of appeals in the recent case of Crabtree v. Elizabeth Arden Sales Corp., [305 N.Y. 48, 110 N.E.2d 551], has held that the separate writings, even though one or more are unsigned, are sufficient to constitute the required memorandum, provided that when read together they appear to refer to the same transaction, or the connection between them and the transaction can be established by parol testimony. In so holding, the New York court in effect overruled a number of earlier New York decisions to the contrary. It is unnecessary for us to go that far in the instant case in order to hold that the loan application constitutes part of the memorandum of sale. We do not consider that Kelly v. Sullivan, supra, rules the instant case, because here the loan application is a separate writing subscribed by the Kovariks who are the parties against whom it is sought to enforce the contract.

We experience no difficulty in determining that the loan application to the Fort Atkinson Savings & Loan Association is a separate writing which is to be construed together with the original contract of the parties, and that together they constitute a sufficient memorandum to comply with sec. 240.08, Stats.[2] Kenner v. Edwards Realty & F. Co., 1931, 204 Wis. 575, 581, 236 N.W. 597.

---

2. Wis. Stat. § 240.08 (1967), cited by the court, voids only contracts of sale of which there is no memorandum signed *by the seller.* — EDS.

Counsel for the buyers also contend that the contract falls within the statute of frauds because the offer made in behalf of the sellers, to accept a $7,000 first mortgage having the same terms as stated in the loan application to the Fort Atkinson Savings & Loan Association, was made verbally and not in writing. The evidence of such offer is material on the issue of whether the event had occurred which removed the stated contingency from the plaintiff's offer to purchase. Proof of the occurrence of such event is not required to be part of the statutory memorandum. For example, let us suppose that, instead of the Fort Atkinson Savings & Loan Association having rejected the buyer's loan application, its chief executive officer had verbally informed both the buyers and the sellers that such application had been approved by the association and the loan granted, and the buyers had then refused to conclude the purchase of the premises. It is clear that in such a situation the buyers would not be permitted to assert that the contract was void under the statute of frauds because the association had verbally granted their loan application instead of doing so in writing. [The court then also held against the buyer on other issues raised.]

Judgment affirmed.

Holman v. Childersburg Bancorporation, Inc.,

852 So.2d 691 (Ala. 2002)

WOODALL, Justice.

Danita Kim Holman and her husband, D. Mark Holman, appeal from a summary judgment in favor of First Bank of Childersburg ("the Bank"), Childersburg Bancorporation, Inc. ("the Corporation"), and Byron Louie Henry, an officer of the Bank at the time of the underlying transaction, in the Holmans' action alleging breach of an agreement to release a tract of land from a mortgage lien. We affirm.

Events material to this dispute began in 1995, when the Holmans borrowed $275,000 from the Bank in connection with the purchase of approximately 16 acres of real property. The loan was secured by a mortgage on that property. Subsequently, the original 16-acre tract was subdivided into three tracts—tract I, tract II, and tract III. The Holmans allege in their complaint that in 1997 they and Henry reached an oral agreement regarding the disposition of some of the property. Under the alleged agreement, the Holmans would sell tract I. The parties agree that a portion of the sale proceeds were to be paid to the Bank to satisfy the mortgage on tract I. The Holmans allege that the Bank also agreed—in exchange for $175,000 of the purchase price of tract I—to execute an instrument releasing *tract II* from the mortgage lien, to enable the Holmans to obtain a construction loan to build a residence on tract II "when the time came that [the Holmans] wanted to build the house."

In May 1997, tract I was sold, and the Holmans paid the Bank $175,000. On May 7, 1997, the Bank executed a "Partial Release," releasing tract I from the mortgage lien. Subsequently, the Holmans began constructing a house on tract II. However, title searches conducted on or about July 2, 1998, December 11, 1998, and July 25, 2000, revealed to the Holmans that, as of the last date, no mortgage release had been recorded as to tract II. The Holmans allege that, as of December 11, 2000, the date the Holmans filed this action, the defendants were disclaiming any knowledge of an oral agreement to release tract II from the mortgage lien.

On December 11, 2000, the Holmans sued Henry and the Corporation. Their complaint, as eventually amended to include the Bank (the Corporation, the Bank, and Henry are hereinafter referred to collectively as "the defendants"), contained counts alleging (1) breach of a contract to release tract II from the mortgage lien, (2) negligence/wantonness, (3) fraudulent misrepresentation, (4) fraudulent suppression, (5) slander of title, and (6) civil conspiracy. A seventh count, added by amendment, was against the Corporation and the Bank for negligent hiring, training, and supervision of Henry. The complaint alleged that the property had been devalued and depreciated by the acts of the defendants. The complaint sought compensatory and punitive damages.

The defendants answered the last amended complaint, asserting affirmative defenses, including the Statute of Frauds. The Bank counterclaimed against the Holmans for amounts allegedly due on their notes with the Bank. Subsequently, the defendants moved for a summary judgment.

On November 2, 2001, the trial court entered a summary judgment for the defendants on various grounds. More specifically, it concluded that the breach-of-contract claims were barred by the Statute of Frauds and that the tort claims were barred by the applicable statutes of limitations. On May 7, 2002, the trial court, on the Bank's motion, dismissed the Bank's counterclaims against the Holmans.

From that judgment, which constituted the final disposition of all the claims asserted in this action, the Holmans appealed. On appeal, the Holmans argue, among other things, that the trial court erred in holding (1) that the Statute of Frauds barred the breach-of-contract claims, and (2) that the statutes of limitations barred the tort claims.

I. BREACH-OF-CONTRACT CLAIMS

. . . Alabama's Statute of Frauds provides, in pertinent part:

> "In the following cases, every agreement is void unless such agreement or some note or memorandum thereof expressing the consideration is in writing and subscribed by the party to be charged therewith or some other person by him thereunto lawfully authorized in writing:
> ". . . .
> "(5) Every contract for the sale of lands, tenements or hereditaments, or of any interest therein, . . . unless the purchase money, or a portion thereof is paid and the purchaser is put in possession of the land by the seller. . . ."

Ala.Code 1975, § 8-9-2(5). This section "requires that all contracts for the sale of real property be in writing and be signed by the party against whom the contract is asserted. The writing must also contain a recital of the consideration supporting the contract." *Pickard v. Turner,* 592 So.2d 1016, 1020 (Ala.1992). "[I]t is clear that an agreement to release lands from the effect of a mortgage is an agreement for the transfer of real property and thus falls within the Statute of Frauds." *Casey v. Travelers Ins. Co.,* 585 So.2d 1361, 1363 (Ala.1991).

The Holmans do not dispute that the alleged agreement is subject to the Statute of Frauds. They contend, however, that they have sufficiently established that a release, or a commemorative writing, *exists.*

A. EVIDENCE OF AN AGREEMENT

In this connection, the Holmans submitted the affidavit of Dennis Abbott, their former legal counsel. Abbott stated, in pertinent part:

"On or about August 29, 1997, I was contacted by the [Holmans] to close a construction loan on [tract II]. I was told by the [Holmans] that there was no payoff amount for this tract and that they had previously entered into an agreement with [the Bank] to the effect that if they sold [tract I] and their personal residence and paid [the Bank] certain agreed upon amounts, the Bank would, in turn, release [tract II], with no additional consideration so that the [Holmans] could obtain a construction loan. On or about August 29, 1997, I contacted Louie Henry to confirm the payoff amount and/or release agreement. Mr. Henry informed me that the Bank had, in fact, agreed to release [tract II] with no additional consideration. He acknowledged to me that he was aware that the Holmans were going to build a house on that tract and that the Bank had entered into an agreement several months prior thereto that it would release [tract II] for no additional consideration conditioned on the sale of [tract I] and the payment of $175,000.00 to the Bank. . . . I informed Mr. Henry that a title search revealed that [tract II] had not been released. He advised me to prepare a partial mortgage release and send it to him and that he would execute it and file it of record. Based on these representations, I closed the construction loan on the property and mailed the partial mortgage release to Mr. Henry.

On or about July 2, 1998, I was again contacted by the [Holmans] to close a second mortgage on [tract II] to enable [them] to complete construction of their residence. Title work done at that time revealed that [tract II] had still not been released from the original mortgage to [the Bank]. I contacted [the Bank] at that time and received assurances that the failure to release the property was merely an oversight and that if a partial mortgage release was again sent to the Bank, it would be executed and filed of record. Based on these representations, I closed the second mortgage on [tract II] and mailed another partial mortgage release to [the Bank].

On or about December 11, 1998, I was again contacted by the [Holmans] to close a second mortgage on [tract II]. The prior second mortgage was to be paid off and additional funds were being borrowed by the [Holmans]. Title work performed at the time revealed the existing second mortgage and also revealed that [the Bank] had still not released [tract II] from the original mortgage. I obtained a payoff on the existing second mortgage and contacted [the Bank] concerning its failure to release [tract II] as agreed. I again received assurances from the Bank that the failure to release the property was merely an oversight and that if I would send yet another partial mortgage release, it would be executed and filed for record. To the best of my knowledge and belief, I insisted that a partial mortgage release be faxed to the Bank and that the release be signed and faxed back to me for my file so that I could be assured at that time that the mortgage would be released. To the best of my knowledge, this was done and an executed copy of the partial mortgage release was faxed to my office. Based on the repeated assurances from [the Bank], the transaction was closed with a check being sent to pay off the existing second mortgage holder and an original partial mortgage release being sent to [the Bank] for execution and recordation.

I had no other dealings with the [Holmans'] property until on or about July 25, 2000. The [Holmans] contacted me and informed me that the second mortgage was being refinanced and that title work done by another attorney revealed that [tract II] had never been released from the original . . . mortgage. Subsequently, I contacted [the Bank] and was advised that Louie Henry no longer worked for the Bank. I talked with another bank official and was advised that the Bank was not in a position to execute and file a release. . . .

> On or about August 1, 2000, I talked with Louie Henry by telephone. The only property we discussed was [tract II] where the [Holmans'] residence was located. Henry assured me at that time that the Bank had agreed to release [tract II] from the original mortgage and that, in his best judgment, he had actually signed the partial mortgage release. He further stated that he did not know why the release had not been recorded or why the Bank was now refusing to release the property."

The Holmans contend that this affidavit, "at the very least, establishes an issue of fact regarding the existence of the [Bank's] release of the subject property." Holmans' Brief, at 21. They argue, in other words, that the defendants have *admitted* to an agreement to execute and record a release, and that, therefore, they are *estopped* to deny its existence. We disagree with this contention.

To be sure, "a party may be equitably estopped to raise the Statute of Frauds as a defense under certain limited circumstances." *Pate v. Billy Boyd Realty & Constr., Inc.*, 699 So.2d 186, 192 (Ala.Civ.App.1997). However, this Court "has made clear that a party *cannot* create an 'estoppel bar to raising the Statute of Frauds merely because a party admits, *either judicially or extrajudicially*, the existence of or the substance of an oral contract within the Statute.'" *Rice v. Barnes*, 149 F.Supp.2d 1297, 1302 (M.D. Ala.2001) (emphasis added) (quoting *Pate*, 699 So.2d at 192). This is so, because "to enforce an oral contract against a party merely because he or she admitted to its existence and substance . . . is likely to promote perjury. Instead of admitting to the contract, the breaching party would be tempted to deny the agreement in order to escape liability." *Darby v. Johnson*, 477 So.2d 322, 327 (Ala.1985); see also *Durham v. Harbin*, 530 So.2d 208, 212–13 (Ala.1988).

Despite the statements in Abbott's affidavit, neither an original nor a copy of the partial release relating to tract II has surfaced in this action. Neither has any writing evidencing the alleged agreement between the Bank and the Holmans for the release of tract II in exchange for $175,000 of the sales price of tract I been produced. Moreover, to the extent that Henry's alleged assurances regarding the understandings of the parties constitute "admissions," they do not, as a matter of law, create a bar to the operation of the Statute of Frauds.

The Holmans next contend that the Statute of Frauds does not bar their action, because, they insist, they have "met the partial performance exception requirements to the Statute of Frauds." Holmans' Brief, at 24. We also disagree with this contention.

B. PARTIAL PERFORMANCE

Section 8-9-2(5) expressly excepts from its operation purchasers who pay "the purchase money, or a portion thereof," and who are consequently "*put in possession of the land by the seller.*" (Emphasis added.) Construing the predecessor to § 8-9-2, this Court has stated:

> Unless the facts bring the case within one of the statutory exceptions, if the parol agreement between the two parties for the purchase of real estate from a third person 'involves a purchase by, or in the name of, one party and a subsequent transfer, conveyance, or vesting of an interest in the property to or in the other party, the statute of frauds applies.' 37 C.J.S., Frauds, Statute of, § 119, subsec. b, p. 614.

If, however, the contract has been fully performed, by the seller putting the purchaser in possession under the contract and the purchaser paying the seller a part or all of the purchase price, the contract is valid and is saved by the exception.

Talley v. Talley, 248 Ala. 84, 87, 26 So.2d 586, 589 (1946). Although this Court has suggested that the exception would apply to oral agreements to release realty from a mortgage lien, see *Casey v. Travelers Ins. Co.,* 585 So.2d 1361, 1364 (Ala.1991), the Holmans have not met the "possession" requirement.

In that connection, this Court explained:

The possession requirement of the 'part performance exception' to the requirement of a writing in land sales contracts was addressed in *Houston v. McClure,* 425 So.2d 1114 (Ala.1983). In that case, we reversed a summary judgment entered in a specific performance suit because there was a factual issue as to whether the acts of possession in the case were 'referable exclusively to the contract.' This requirement is mentioned in *Hagood v. Spinks,* 219 Ala. 503, 122 So. 815 (1929), in which the Court said:

'To take a case out of the statute of frauds . . . upon the ground of part performance, the acts of possession must be clear and definite, and referable exclusively to the contract, and by authority of the vendor. The existence of the contract and its terms should be established by competent proof to be clear, definite, and unequivocal in all its terms. If its terms, or the necessary acts of part performance, are not sustained by satisfactory proof, specific performance will not be decreed.' (Citations omitted [in *Smith*].)

219 Ala. at 504, 122 So. at 816. The meaning of 'referable *exclusively to the contract'* was discussed in *Jones v. Jones,* 219 Ala. 62, 121 So. 78 (1929). The Court stated as follows:

'The cases also hold that the possession of the purchaser must be exclusively referable to the contract . . . "that is to say, it must be such possession that an outsider, knowing all the circumstances attending it save only the one fact, the alleged oral contract, would naturally and reasonably infer that some contract existed relating to the land, of the same general nature as the contract alleged" (36 Cyc. 660). . . .'

219 Ala. at 63-64, 121 So. at 78. The *Jones* Court went on to say that

'. . . the possession must be referable to the promise and not to some domestic relationship of the vendor and vendee. 36 Cyc. 660, note 77. Where the person having the legal title to land is in possession, it is well established that such possession will be referred to the legal title. Here, the title being in the father, and both father and son being in possession, the law refers the possession to the father.' (Citations omitted [in *Smith*].)

"219 Ala. at 64, 121 So. at 78. The Court went further in adopting the following excerpt:

'In 36 Cyc. 660, is the following: "If the possession * * * could be accounted for just as well by some other right or title actually existing in the vendee's favor, or by some relation between him and the vendor other than the alleged oral contract, it is not such a possession as the doctrine requires."'

Smith v. Smith, 466 So.2d 922, 924–25 (Ala.1985) (emphasis added; footnote omitted). Elsewhere, this Court explained that " " " [t]he acts of part performance must . . . be such as would *not be done* but for the [alleged oral contract]." " " *Quinlivan v. Quinlivan,* 269 Ala. 642, 645, 114 So.2d 838, 840 (1959) (emphasis added) (quoting *Gibson v. Bryant,* 267 Ala. 97, 99, 100 So.2d 32, 34 (1958)). The exception applies only where " " " the acts of part performance *cannot be explained* consistently with *any other contract* than the one alleged." " " 269 Ala. at 645, 114 So.2d at 840 (quoting *Gibson,* 267 Ala. at 99, 100 So.2d at 34) (emphasis added).

It is clear from the discussion in *Smith* that the part-performance exception cannot apply in this case. This is so because the Holmans were *never out of possession* of tract II at any relevant time. On the contrary, they have been *in exclusive possession* of tract II since 1995, the date they purchased of the original 16-acre undivided parcel. In other words, they were in possession of tract II for approximately two years before it was created from the larger parcel, and for two years before it became the subject of an alleged oral agreement. See *Talley v. Talley,* 248 Ala. 84, 88, 26 So.2d 586, 589 (1946) ("payment and possession must concur to save the purchase from the grasp of the statute"). Clearly, the Holmans were not put in possession of tract II by the alleged oral agreement.

. . . The Holmans' construction of a residence on land to which they undisputedly had legal and physical possession would not inevitably lead an "outsider" to conclude that the alleged oral contract existed. The facts of this case clearly fail to satisfy the part-performance requirement. Consequently, the trial court did not err in holding that the Statute of Frauds barred the breach-of-contract claims.

II. TORT CLAIMS

The Holmans also contend that the trial court erred in holding that the applicable statutes of limitations barred their negligence/wantonness and other tort claims. The Bank, on the other hand, argues that the negligence/wantonness claims are also barred by the Statute of *Frauds.* More specifically, it states:

> There is not much left to say about [the negligence/wantonness claims], because the result is dictated by our argument as to [the breach-of-contract claims]. The *only duty alleged . . . in this case* is predicated upon an alleged contractual duty to release land from a mortgage; thus, the [Holmans'] claims of negligence are actually claims arising in contract.

Brief of First Bank of Childersburg, at 21 (emphasis added). We agree that the Statute of Frauds also bars the negligence/wantonness claims. Indeed, it is this alleged duty, and the breach thereof, that underlies *all* the tort claims.

As a general rule, "[i]f the proof of a promise or contract, *void under the statute of frauds,* is essential to maintain the action, there may be no recovery." *Pacurib v. Villacruz,* 183 Misc.2d 850, 861, 705 N.Y.S.2d 819, 827 (N.Y.Civ.Ct.1999) (emphasis added); see also *Dwight v. Tobin,* 947 F.2d 455, 460 (11th Cir.1991); *McDabco, Inc. v. Chet Adams Co.,* 548 F.Supp. 456, 458 (D.S.C.1982) (it is a "well accepted doctrine that one cannot circumvent the Statute of Frauds by bringing an action in tort, when the tort action is based primarily on the unenforceable contract"); *Weakly v. East,* 900 S.W.2d 755 (Tex.Ct.App.1995). This is so, because, "[i]f a plaintiff was allowed to recover the benefit of a bargain already barred by the statute of frauds, the statute of frauds would become meaningless." *Sonnichsen v. Baylor University*, 47 S.W.3d 122, 127 (Tex.Ct.App.2001). "Thus, the statute of frauds bars a [tort] claim when a plaintiff claims as damages the *benefit of the bargain* that he would have obtained had the promise been performed." *Id.* (emphasis added).

This Court has not expressly applied or rejected the general rule. . . . The issue is squarely presented in this case. The Holmans' recovery — whether under the breach-of-contract theory or under any of the tort theories — turns on the existence of an oral promise to record a release as to tract II, the proof of which is barred by the Statute of Frauds. This conclusion is illustrated by brief analyses of the allegations and arguments underlying the Holmans' various tort claims, with reference to the allegations of the breach-of-contract claims.

A. NEGLIGENCE/WANTONNESS

The basis for the Holmans' negligence/wantonness claims is that the defendants "had a *duty* to execute the appropriate documents and to take the necessary steps and action required to sign, file and/or record said documents in an effort to finalize and complete the agreements made between the parties," and that they "*breached said duty* by negligently and/or wantonly failing to sign, file and/or record the appropriate documents *necessary to release Tract Two*." (Emphasis added.) As a result, the Holmans allege, they "are greatly restricted in the free enjoyment, use and disposition of their property." They also allege that "the property has been greatly devalued and depreciated," and that they "have been unable to refinance the property without being forced to pay the unreasonable, arbitrary and capricious amount demanded by [the] defendants." Otherwise stated, the Holmans' argument is that the "duty" the defendants owed was to honor the alleged oral agreement to release Tract II, and the only "breach" was their failure to honor that agreement. In that connection, the Holmans argue that the defendants' "negligent and wanton conduct" consisted of their "refus[al] to provide a mortgage release of the subject Tract II." Holmans' Brief, at 31. Clearly, proof of the existence of the alleged oral agreement "is essential," *Pacurib*, 183 Misc. at 861, 705 N.Y.S.2d at 827, to their negligence/wantonness claims. If the Bank did not promise to release tract II, it owed no duty to do so.

B. FRAUD

Counts three and four purported to allege claims of fraud. In count three, the Holmans alleged that the defendants "represented to [them] . . . that defendants had agreed to release. . . . Tract Two from the Mortgage, and that defendants would execute a partial mortgage release . . . so that [the Holmans] could obtain a construction mortgage to build a house thereon." These representations, the Holmans allege, "were false, and [the Holmans] relied on said representations to their detriment." Similarly, count four alleged that the defendants "knew *at the time of contracting* with the [Holmans], and at different stages *throughout the life of the contract,* that Tract Two [was] not and/or [was] never intended to be released from the Mortgage." (Emphasis added.) "These facts were material," the Holmans alleged, "and defendants had an obligation to disclose said facts to [the Holmans]." Counts three and four alleged damages in terms identical to those alleged in counts one and two. The Holmans also argue:

The facts of the instant case clearly reveal that the [Holmans] fully expected the Defendants to file the release for the two acre parcel upon which they built their home. It was not until July/August 2000 that they began to believe that the Defendants had misrepresented or suppressed facts to them concerning the release and that the Defendants had no intention of performing on their agreement to release [tract II]."

Holmans' Brief, at 33.

Unless the Bank had, in fact, *promised,* as the Holmans alleged in *count one,* to release tract II upon payment of $175,000, there could be no misrepresentation or fraudulent concealment, as alleged in counts three and four. Thus, *here,* the facts underlying the fraud claims merely *duplicate* those underlying the breach-of-contract claims.[2] . . .

. . . Summary judgment was properly entered for the defendants. That judgment is therefore affirmed.

Affirmed.

MOORE, C.J., and HOUSTON, SEE, LYONS, BROWN, HARWOOD, and STUART, JJ., concur.

JOHNSTONE, J., concurs in the rationale in part and concurs in the judgment.

JOHNSTONE, Justice (concurring in the rationale in part and concurring in the judgment).

But for two exceptions, I concur in the rationale. Because the exceptions do not affect the result, I also concur in the judgment.

My first exception to the rationale is that the main opinion misses the point of the Holmans' very first argument. Their first argument is that enforcement of the agreement by the Bank to release the mortgage on tract II is not barred by the Statute of Frauds, § 8-9-2(5), Ala.Code 1975, since the agreement is, in fact, "in writing and subscribed by the party to be charged therewith" as required by that statute and that, because this writing has been lost or destroyed, *it may be proved by secondary evidence* consisting of the affidavit of the Holmans' former lawyer Dennis Abbott. The Holmans aptly cite Rule 1004(1), Ala. R. Evid., which allows proof of lost or destroyed documents by secondary evidence. The reason the Holmans' argument to this effect fails is that the particular secondary evidence they have submitted does not constitute substantial evidence of the fact they seek to prove — the existence of a writing memorializing the agreement.

The statements in the Abbott affidavit that most tend to prove the existence of such a writing read:

> *To the best of my knowledge and belief,* I insisted that a partial mortgage release be faxed to the Bank and that the release be signed and faxed back to me for my file so that I could be assured at that time that the mortgage would be released. *To the best of my knowledge,* this was done and an executed copy of the partial mortgage release was faxed to my office." (Emphasis added.)

The affiant's qualifying his statements by saying that they are to the best of his knowledge and belief, or to the best of his knowledge, deprives them of the probative value essential to constitute substantial evidence in opposition to the motion

---

2. On appeal, the Holmans do not argue that they have alleged, or offered evidence of, *promissory* fraud. Thus, cases recognizing a promissory-fraud exception to the Statute of Frauds, see, e.g., *US Diagnostic v. Shelby Radiology, P.C.,* 793 So.2d 714 (Ala.2000), need not be considered.

for summary judgment. *Florence Bldg. & Inv. Ass'n v. Schall,* 107 Ala. 531, 534, 18 So. 108, 109 (1894) ("[T]hey deposed merely that it was correct and true 'to the best of their knowledge and belief.' . . . [)]

My second exception to the rationale is that I respectfully disagree with the statement that, "[t]his Court has not expressly applied or rejected the general rule," 852 So.2d at 699, that "[a]s a general rule, '[i]f the proof of a promise or contract, *void under the statute of frauds,* is essential to maintain the action, there may be no recovery.'" 852 So.2d at 699 (quoting *Pacurib v. Villacruz,* 183 Misc.2d 850, 861, 705 N.Y.S.2d 819, 827 (N.Y.Civ.Ct.1999)) (emphasis added in main opinion). In *Hinkle v. Cargill, Inc.,* 613 So.2d 1216, 1220 (Ala.1992), this Court said:

> Cargill argues that a fraud action cannot be based on the breach of an unwritten contract that is void under the Statute of Frauds. As the above-cited authorities show, however, the Statute of Frauds does not bar proof of a fraud committed by means of a promise that ordinarily could not be enforced as a contractual promise because of the Statute of Frauds. Furthermore, 'it is well settled in Alabama that fraud may be predicated upon a breach of contract which is void, because not in writing, where the contract was made for the purpose of perpetrating the fraud.'

Caron v. Teagle, 408 So.2d 494, 496 (Ala.1981).

Likewise, in *US Diagnostic v. Shelby Radiology, P.C.,* 793 So.2d 714 (Ala.2000), this Court affirmed a money judgment in favor of a plaintiff on a claim of promissory fraud based on an oral promise which was void by operation of the Statute of Frauds.[5] While I agree with the main opinion that we should adopt the general rule and that we should not countenance tort actions based on promises void by operation of the Statute of Frauds, we should not do so without recognizing *Hinkle, supra, U.S. Diagnostic, supra,* and their ancestors and any progeny and overruling them to the extent that they allow promissory fraud actions or other tort actions dependent entirely on promises void by operation of the Statute of Frauds.

NOTES

1. Part performance is a well-established concept that will justify judicial enforcement of oral agreements to convey interests in land despite the writing requirements of the Statute of Frauds. In some states, such as Alabama, part performance is statutorily authorized; in most states it is solely a caselaw concept. Many courts hold that part performance is made out if the alleged buyer is in possession and has made payment to the ostensible seller or, alternatively, is in possession and has made substantial improvements to the property. But here, too, courts vary in what acts are sufficient for part performance, some holding that possession is enough, others requiring possession plus payment and improvements. Tenants claiming oral

---

5. While the Holmans do not characterize their fraudulent misrepresentation claim as "promissory fraud," they plead all of the essential elements of that species of promissory fraud recognized by *US Diagnostic, supra,* and the record contains substantial evidence tending to prove those elements. The character of a pleading is determined and interpreted from its essential substance, and not from its descriptive name or title. *Ex parte Alfa Mutual General Ins. Co.,* 684 So.2d 1281, 1282 (Ala.1996) (quoting *Union Springs Tel. Co. v. Green,* 285 Ala. 114, 117, 229 So.2d 503, 505 (1969)). Notwithstanding the lack of explication in the Holmans' briefs, I am concerned that part of the text of the main opinion is inconsistent with our previously published cases, as I discuss in this special writing.

agreements to buy pose special problems as they already are in possession and making payments. Improvements they make also may be referable to their enjoyment of the premises as tenants. For example, in Lebowitz v. Mingus, 100 A.D.2d 816, 474 N.Y.S.2d 748 (1984), it was held that expenditures of $50,000 by a tenant in renovating and improving a Manhattan apartment in which she lived was not unequivocally referable to an oral contract to sell the apartment.

If criteria for part performance are met by the party seeking the benefits of an oral contract, evidence will then be admissible to prove the terms of the oral agreement. Proving part performance is a preliminary step to proving what was agreed to.

2. Statute of Frauds language is similar in many of the states. Typical is this general language in the Florida statutes, covering, among other transactions, conveyancing of land interests and contracts to sell such interests:

Fla. Stat. Ann. (West 1984)

689.01. How real estate conveyed
   No estate or interest of freehold, or for a term of more than 1 year, or any uncertain interest of, in or out of any messuages, lands, tenements or hereditaments shall be created, made, granted, transferred or released in any other manner than by instrument in writing, signed in the presence of two subscribing witnesses by the party creating, making, granting, conveying, transferring or releasing such estate, interest, or term of more than 1 year, or by the party's agent thereunto lawfully authorized, unless by will and testament, or other testamentary appointment, duly made according to law; and no estate or interest, either of freehold, or of term of more than 1 year, or any uncertain interest of, in, to or out of any messuages, lands, tenements or hereditaments, shall be assigned or surrendered unless it be by instrument signed in the presence of two subscribing witnesses by the party so assigning or surrendering, or by the party's agent thereunto lawfully authorized, or by the act and operation of law. No seal shall be necessary to give validity to any instrument executed in conformity with this section. . . .

Fla. Stat. Ann. (West 2000)

725.01. Promise to pay another's debt, etc.
   No action shall be brought whereby to charge any executor or administrator upon any special promise to answer or pay any debt or damages out of her or his own estate, or whereby to charge the defendant upon any special promise to answer for the debt, default or miscarriage of another person or to charge any person upon any agreement made upon consideration of marriage, or upon any contract for the sale of lands, tenements or hereditaments, or of any uncertain interest in or concerning them, or for any lease thereof for a period longer than 1 year, or upon any agreement that is not to be performed within the space of 1 year from the making thereof, . . . unless the agreement or promise upon which such action shall be brought, or some note or memorandum thereof shall be in writing and signed by the party to be charged therewith or by some other person by her or him thereunto lawfully authorized.

3. Although the dispute in *Holman* was between borrower and lender, the issue was the satisfaction of the Statute of Frauds relating to transfers of interest in real property. However, in the wake of a wave of "lender liability" lawsuits in the 1980s and 1990s, some jurisdictions adopted Statutes of Frauds (sometimes called Credit

Agreement Acts) pertaining directly to lenders and credit agreements. These statutes were generally designed to protect lenders from (actual or alleged) oral promises, representations or modifications made by loan officers. See, e.g., Sidney W. DeLong, Placid, Clear-seeming Words: Some Realism about the New Formalism (With Particular Reference to Promissory Estoppel), 38 San Diego L. Rev. 13, 48–50 (2001); Todd C. Pearson, Limiting Lender Liability: The Trend Toward Written Credit Agreement Statutes, 76 Minn. L. Rev. 295 (1991).

4. Another exception to the Statute of Frauds recognized in many states is estoppel, a concept applied to justify the enforceability of an oral contract when necessary to prevent an unconceivable loss to one of the parties to the contract. On this exception to the Statute of Frauds, see Sterk, Estoppel in Property Law, 77 Neb. L. Rev. 756, 759-769 (1998).

— STOP —

B. LAND DESCRIPTIONS

Land descriptions are being considered in this coverage of contracts of sale because these preliminary conveyancing instruments should include complete and accurate descriptions of the property being sold. Unfortunately, however, descriptions used are not always what they should be, and appellate opinions back through the years include many cases challenging the validity of contracts of sale because incomplete or inaccurate descriptions, or questioning the boundaries of properties covered by sale contracts. Generally, the same land description methods and judicial approaches to ambiguities apply whether the description appears in a contract of sale, deed, mortgage, or other type of legal instrument. Land description errors can arise from a variety of causes, including inaccurate surveys, incorrect designations by sellers in showing land to buyers, and copying errors by typists combined with failure to proofread carefully what typists have copied. Once a description error is made in a legal instrument, such as a deed, it is often replicated in subsequent instruments, unless the error is apparent from the face of the instrument or unless a new survey takes place. The tendency is to copy descriptions from prior instruments transferring interests in the same land parcel. Note that the adequacy of land descriptions is one kind of title problem dealt with by the various forms of title protection discussed in Chapter Five.

Suppose S sells part of his ranch to B, a developer; B takes possession of his new property. He then sets concrete markers at each of its four corners, marks off the interior into streets that he dedicates to the public and into lots that he sells and that are promptly built up by his buyers. As time passes, the lots become the subject of the usual sorts of devolutionary and intervivos transfer, and each of them accumulates a reasonable amount of ownership complexity; a mortgage or an easement, or a power of termination for condition broken, a tax lien, and so on.

Then somebody takes a closer look at the deed from S to B. It appears that some sort of mistake was made, for B has located each of the four concrete markers nine feet west of the spot where it apparently should have been to mark the boundaries of the property apparently conveyed by S to B in the original deed. Furthermore, the street dedications and all the conveyances of the lots were prepared in relation to the description in the original deed rather than by reference to the concrete markers, but all the lots were physically laid out with reference to the markers. What a mess; everybody's driveway is where his neighbor's rumpus room should be. Every owner's actual occupancy encroaches on a neighbor; every owner is in turn encroached upon.

There are several ways out. One is to have all the owners, the friendly folks in the neighborhood (*and* the banks, municipalities, absentee owner's, unborn heirs, etc.) execute the necessary quitclaims and releases to conform ownership to occupancy. This, of course, they will do, if they can be found; if they are all that nice (if a municipality, for example, can quit claim in the face of a taxpayer's suit objection that all sales of municipal property must be by competitive bidding); and if too large a strain is not put on the generosity of one of the owners who recognizes that he only encroaches to the extent of an overwide driveway while his encroaching neighbor is, inter alia, a very expensive subsurface utility distribution pipe.

Failing a neighborhood concordat, the law of adverse possession may do the job, if time has run, if necessary tackings are permitted, and if each adverse claimant had the required state of mind during the possessory period. And even if the requirements for the acquisition of adverse title are not met, the possession-confirming body of law dealing with the establishment of boundaries by acquiescence or practical location can in some cases be invoked to cure discrepancies between instrumented lines and occupied ones.

The following sections center on two other approaches. First of all, if it is a particular reading of the deed from S to B that gives rise to the mess, perhaps a different reading will dispel it. Second, even if the reading that gives rise to the difficulty is the true one, perhaps it is legally permissible to show that S and B really meant that B was to have the markered area, even though the conveyance described something nine feet off. Accordingly, these sections present material on conventional methods of boundary description, and on legal techniques for resolving error and ambiguity, whether by interpretation or by conforming a document's erroneous or ambiguous description to true intention otherwise ascertained.

As to the latter problem, the material will be more of the same — rules of interpretation based on presumed intent, statute of frauds, parol evidence rule, and the like. These doctrines, however, will be extra sharply focussed; where-do-you-draw-the-line is, in boundary cases, not entirely metaphorical.[3]

1. Boundary Description Methods

A new property description originates with a subdivision. If an owner of a tract wishes to transfer the *entire* tract, he is most likely to convey by using the description under which he acquired the property. However, if a *portion* of the tract needs to be designated, as for intervivos or testamentary gift, listing with a broker, or for describing a bargain between owner and a buyer, a new description has to be created.

Boundary descriptions are operational statements; they tell the reader "Go to such and such a place, look for some markers or make some measurements at various orientations, and when you are finished, you will have traced out on the

---

3. On land descriptions and boundaries see Friedman on Contracts and Conveyances of Real Property, ch. 10 (7th ed. 2005). For a comprehensive collection of cases on descriptions, see Annot., Specificity of Description of Premises As Affecting Enforceability of Contract to Convey Real Property — Modern Cases, 73 A.L.R. 4th 135 (1989).

ground that which I am trying to describe." More technically, a description, to have legal effect, is supposed to be one with which a competent surveyor can identify a particular tract of land to the exclusion of all other tracts.

a. Metes and Bounds Descriptions

O owns Blackacre, which he believes to be a 160-acre tract, squarely oriented north and south, bounded on the west by the neighboring Smith property, on the north by a road. On Blackacre is a single spectacular oak tree — known to all the world as the Eastern Oak — located exactly 660 feet from O's west boundary and 1320 feet south of the road.

O bargains to transfer the northwest 40 acres of the tract to B. It is easy to work out a description of the 40 acres, in part because of the happy location of the oak, and in part because two sides of the tract to be conveyed run along the exterior boundaries of O's tract.

"Beginning at the Eastern Oak, thence 660 feet West to the J. B. Smith property, thence North to the Ross Road, thence along the road East 1320 feet, thence South 1320 feet, thence West to the place of beginning, containing 40 acres, all located approximately 5 miles Northwest of Tuba City, Wayne County, Illinois."[4]

This description is made up of a sequence of *calls,* operational instructions to the reader as to how to trace out on the ground the lines that bound the intended tract. Walking through the calls we have:

First Call: **From the Eastern Oak 660 feet West to the J. B. Smith property.** This call begins with a *monument* — the Eastern Oak. If an owner does not have a *natural monument* so happily located, he may set up a stake, an *artificial monument,* at the desired location. It would be even simpler to set an artificial monument at the southeast corner of the carved out area, phrasing the description from that.

The monument call is followed by a *distance* — 660 feet; a *course* — west; and an *adjoiner* — the J. B. Smith property. Since course and distance have been called from the oak, the adjoiner call is really not needed in this case to locate the terminus of the first line (but the possible uses of an apparently surplus adjoiner call should become clear later). If the distance call were omitted, so that the description read, "From the Eastern Oak to the J. B. Smith property," then somehow the property line of the Smith tract would have to be located. Assuming for now that "the J. B. Smith property" means what J. B. Smith owns, rather than what he in fact occupies, the likely way to find out Smith's boundaries is by examining the property description in the deed by which neighbor Smith acquired ownership. But query: If the distance call were omitted, how would the Smith line be located for the purposes of O's deed if the deed by which Smith acquired his land described his western boundary as "the West line of the tract adjoining on the East"?[5]

Second Call: **Thence [from the point located as per first call] North to the Ross Road.** This call has a course and an indication to the road; the latter can be conceived of as a monument in its physical existence, or as an adjoiner if conceived of as something owned by someone other than the grantor (more on roads later).

---

4. The description could have started elsewhere, ignoring the oak: "Beginning at the intersection of the East line of the Smith property and the Ross Road, thence East 1320 feet, thence South 1320 feet, thence West 1320 feet, thence North 1320 feet to the place of beginning."

5. Cf. the business usage: "Don't call us, we'll call you."

Third Call: **Thence [from the point located as per second call] along the road East 1320 feet.** This contains a double course indication: *East* and *along the road,* and a distance indication.

Fourth Call: **Thence [from point indicated by third call] South 1320 feet.** This indicates a course and a distance. Would it be better if the grantor set a concrete marker at the southeast corner of the tract, and called, "Thence to the concrete marker?"

Fifth Call: **Thence [from point indicated by fourth call] West to the place of beginning.**

Sixth Call: **Containing 40 acres.** This is a call for quantity.

Seventh Call: **All located approximately 5 miles Northwest of Tuba City, Wayne County, Illinois.** This, of course, is the anchorage of the description and probably ought to have been mentioned first; it tells where the starting point, Eastern Oak, is to be found.

b. Description by Fractional Part

It would simple for O to convey the square tract to B by stating: "The N.W. ¼ of my farm." For application, this requires (a) anchorage of "my farm," (b) a decision as to whether "N.W. ¼" means a square in the corner or a tract marked off by a diagonal between the north and west boundaries (usually the former). It is also important that somebody representing owner remember the above conveyance. Otherwise, when the S.W. corner is later sold it might be described as "the S.W. 40 acres of my farm." This would create difficulties if upon measurement it was discovered that the western half of the farm contained 70 or 90 acres.

c. Description by Government Survey

The tract for B which we are considering might be described as follows: "the N.W. ¼ of the N.W. ¼ of section 6, Township 3 North Range 2 West of the Third Principal Meridian, containing 40 acres," which, to the initiate, will indicate that a United States government survey is being used to anchor the description of the new tract, that the property is somewhere in Illinois, and that maybe a mistake has been made.

Much of the land in the United States has been public land of the United States government at one time or another (major exceptions are land in the original colonies, Texas, and some southwestern states where Spanish grants were honored). In preparing public lands for management and for fractionated transfer to myriad private owners, it was necessary to describe them. By a succession of statutes starting before 1800, the Congress directed the division of public land into *sections,* one mile on a side, containing 640 acres. Congress did not instruct the Bureau of Land Management to send out surveyors to look for elm trees in Kansas with which to anchor the description of the public land sections; rather the survey took reference points from longitude and latitude. The surveyors were instructed to locate on the ground and mark by monuments a series of some 35 points, e.g., for central Illinois: lat. 38° 28' 27" N, long. 89° 08' 54" W; for Colorado, Kansas, Nebraska, South Dakota, and Wyoming, a single point; for Oklahoma, yet another (with lat. 36° 30' 50" N, which should recall the Missouri Compromise) and so on. From each such monumented point the line of longitude was conceptually extended on the ground as "Principal Meridian." Each Principal Meridian was named or numbered for convenient subsequent reference; e.g., the Third for central Illinois, the Sixth for Colorado, the Choctaw (or Indian) for Oklahoma. Each line of latitude was similarly projected from the point as a *base line*. From these lines, a grid was built of *townships*,[6] each six miles square, and within each township 36 *sections*, each one mile square. All of this was to be accomplished by measurements on the ground, and the placement of monuments (stakes, cement markers, plates set into rock) to mark the township, and section, and sometimes quarter-section corners.

Once the survey was made, in any subsequent transaction with respect to land covered by the survey, one could speak of such and such a section, know that the ground was monumented to enable its location, and know that it consisted of 640 acres squarely oriented north and south; or at least that would be true if the survey were ideal.

Lapses from the ideal were inevitable, and one lapse was inherent. The townships were supposed to be a gridded succession, north and south, east and west, of six-mile-square areas covering the major part of the United States. However, the curvature of the earth and the convergence of longitudes toward the North Pole is such that a township could be six miles square, or it could be oriented north-south, but it couldn't be both. Thus suppose you start at the anchor point for the Third Principal Meridian; go six miles west, then six miles north, then return east to the meridian, and then go south back to the starting point. You will not have described a six-mile-square area; because of longitudinal convergence, the southern boundary of the tract just described will be 50-some feet longer than the northern boundary—50 feet being the approximate amount of longitudinal convergence at Illinois latitudes for each six miles of progress toward the Pole.

Accommodation for this tension between the desire for squareness and the desire to use longitudes as township boundaries was incorporated into the system; for our purposes it is only necessary to note that neither desire won out completely and therefore that there are many townships that do not consist of the ideal six-mile square with its ideal 36 sections, each one mile square and containing 640 acres.

There were additional deviations. The surveys, often made years apart, had to be fit into each other's monuments, and this fitting had to take into account not only the curvature-correction patterns just noted but also the inevitable inaccuracies caused by measuring instrument variation, terrain difficulties, haste induced by the presence of nearby hostiles, and natural or larcenous disappearance[7] or shifting of monuments. It would then happen that a surveyor working to create a proper six-mile-square township could not fit this to the monuments of neighboring surveys; he was then instructed to normalize as many sections as possible, working from south to north, and east to west—hence the remark above that Section 6 presents special problems. There is a uniform convention for numbering the sections within

6. More formally "Congressional Township," to be distinguished from the New England township, a governmental unit.

7. "[In Lebanon] we saw rude piles of stones standing near the roadside, at intervals, and recognized the custom of marking boundaries which obtained in Jacob's time. There were no walls, no fences, no hedges—nothing to secure a man's possessions but these random heaps of stones. The Israelites held them sacred in the old patriarchal times and these other Arabs, their lineal descendants, do so likewise. An American, of ordinary intelligence, would soon widely extend his property, at an outlay of mere manual labor, performed at night, under so loose a system of fencing as this." From Innocents Abroad, by Samuel Clemens.

a township; since *6* is always the section in the northwest corner of a township, it is likely to be monumented other than for a square 640 acres; hence a description reading "N.W. ¼ of N.W. ¼ of *Sec. 6 containing 40 acres*" makes you wonder.[8]

The description by government survey that heads this subsection is a fractional part description and also contains an acreage call.

d. Description by Plat Reference

"Tracts 7 and 8 of J. B. Miller's Subdivision of the N.W. ¼ of Section 6, Township 3 North, Range 2 West of the Third Prime Meridian, recorded in Registry of Deeds Book 17, etc."

A private owner may, as did the government, decide to break up his lands into tracts of various sizes and shapes for one or another management or disposition purpose. He then causes a map or plat to be made in which, after anchoring the exterior limits of the area being mapped, the several portions of the area are mapped in *their* exterior dimensions, and receive designations ("Lot 2," "Tract 1," etc.) that are thereafter convenient for use. In usual course, the map descriptions will be anchored by monumentation (a stake, a marking in a sidewalk, etc.), but the map itself will be a form of metes and bounds description, showing footages, areas, orientations, and adjoiners. With luck the monumentation and the map will be consistent.

Platting, of course, is most usual with respect to subdivision of once-rural land for sale to residents of the growing city. The plat will show streets, parks, etc. Its registration and approval are key points in public regulation of land planning.

e. Multiple Descriptions — "Being" Clauses

It is common to find a description that uses:

(a) *a lot number,* which requires reference to a plat with a metes and bounds description;

(b) *a separate metes and bounds description with complex calls,* e.g., "hence (from the oak tree) south 45° 13' east 4500 feet along the Smith property line to the elm tree";

(c) *an adjoiner description;*

(d) *an area designation;* and, to top it all off,

(e) *"being" clauses,* which might involve such notations as "Being the same premises" — or "Being the north 50 acres of those same premises" — "conveyed to Jones by Green by deed recorded Deed Book 47, Page 118. . . ."

---

8. When the northwest quarter of the northwest quarter of a section is described as containing 40 acres, one further inquiry is suggested. It is common to have roads and highways laid out on section lines. Since the tract under description has section lines for both its northern and western boundaries, if chunks have been taken off the section for roads along each line, there won't be 40 acres left for the northwest corner. In our initial illustration, of course, there was a road on the north line, but none on the west.

This latter clause, of course, calls for the descriptions in the recorded deed, which in turn might contain a being clause.

f. Plane Coordinates

There is increasing use of a plane coordinate system of boundary description, stimulated by the United States Coast and Geodetic Survey and validated by enabling legislation in a number of states. The Coast and Geodetic Survey has a series of stations scattered around the country, and any spot in the United States can be *described* by reference to a conceptual grid of lines running north and south, east and west, from the several stations. Any spot thus described can also be *located* at any time in the future by an elementary surveying technique using any three of the stations as monuments. Obviously, this is more permanent and precise monumentation than "neighbor Wilson's fence." Descriptions using this system call for points thus: "Coordinates North 1, 470, 588; East 416, 239," and give a reference to the particular survey on which the coordinates are based.

2. *Professionals and Boundary Descriptions*

a. The Lawyer

Once involved in boundary litigation, an attorney errs if he does not supplement his law school education on the topic with a short noncredit course from his experts. At any level of practice, attorneys who must use descriptions for their paper work can probably function perfectly well in transaction planning by having a reasonable proofreading system to verify a secretary's copy of someone else's description. After all, if Blackacre has been bought and sold and mortgaged and devised for a hundred years on the basis of a particular legal description used in instrument after instrument, chances are pretty good that the next transaction in Blackacre can be handled with the same description. And if Blackacre, by the march of progress, gets turned into Blackacre Terrace, descriptions of the now-subdivided lots will be prepared by surveyors rather than the subdivider's attorney; a lot buyer's attorney will rely on the survey rather than make up his own verbalization of the exterior lot lines of his client's purchase.

If the attorney does choose to concern himself with the old or new description that is at the base of his transaction, he can, even in the office, perform some checks.

Anyone who knows that north is at the top of the page and who can use a protractor can draw a map from a metes and bounds description. Some common errors in descriptions, however, will produce unmappability—as where four boundary lines are described running in order east, south, west and south, the last south being a transcriber's mistake for an intended north. Some errors map out into suspiciously odd shapes, as where, through number transposition, there is a misstatement of the angle at which two lines are to be projected. These can be caught in the office.

Some errors can be caught only by going to the site. Any layman can follow some of the description's directions by pacing off: if the description calls for projection of a line 50 feet from a road, and after 40 feet of pacing you run into a neighbor's back fence, a problem is raised.

Finally, there are errors that cannot be discovered without a surveyor's talents and instruments.

How many of these verifying operations ought a prudent attorney perform or have performed? There is no substantial body of case law in point or other authority from which a standard of conduct can be drawn, but the attorney's duties are presumably in large part a function of the bar's usual behavior in his area.

b. The Surveyor

In preventing mistakes in conveyancing it is not uncommon to have surveys precede the closing for purposes of running the lines from the description to the ground and also for noting visible third party intrusions, wires, pipes, and the like. The surveying firm that originally prepares a plat, one of whose lots is being transferred, normally is able to do transfer surveys more expeditiously than a newcomer. In the event of a mistake in which a surveyor is involved, there are of course possibilities of his being liable in some circumstances.

3. Ambiguous Descriptions

Westpoint Marine, Inc. v. Prange

812 N.E.2d 1016 (Ill.App. 2004)

Justice STEIGMANN delivered the opinion of the court:

In September 1999, plaintiff, WestPoint Marine, Inc., was leasing 500 feet of riverfront property from defendant Mary A. Prange, pursuant to a lease agreement that contained a provision granting WestPoint Marine an option to buy the property should Prange decide to sell it. The leased riverfront property was part of Prange's farm. On September 25, 1999, Prange entered into a contract to sell the Prange farm (including the riverfront property leased by WestPoint Marine) to defendant Pool 24 Tug Service, Inc.

In November 1999, WestPoint Marine filed a complaint seeking specific performance of the option-to-buy provision of its lease agreement with Prange. Following an October 2002 bench trial, the trial court denied WestPoint Marine's complaint for specific performance.

WestPoint Marine appeals, arguing that the trial court's decision was against the manifest weight of the evidence. We disagree and affirm.

I. BACKGROUND

In December 1993, Prange and her husband, William Prange (who is now deceased), entered into a lease with Grantz's Marine Service, Inc. The lease provided that (1) Grantz's Marine would "lease with an option to buy approximately five hundred (500) feet of river frontage" for 25 years, for the purpose of fleeting barges; and (2) the river frontage "is located in Calhoun County, on the right descending bank of the Illinois River, just below Hardin, IL. (approximately mile 20)." In February 1996, Grantz's Marine assigned the lease to WestPoint Marine.

The lease also provided, in pertinent part, as follows:

> "In the event [the Pranges] desire to sell or otherwise dispose of all or any portion
> of the river frontage below Hardin[,] IL., and have received a bona fide offer for the
> same, [s]ellers shall notify Steven F. Grantz in writing, and thereafter Steven F. Grantz
> shall have fifteen (15) days within which to purchase the river frontage at the price,
> terms, and conditions as is offered by the proposed purchaser."

In a September 27, 1999, letter, Prange's realtor, Jean Hagen, notified WestPoint
Marine's president, Kevin Jennings, that the entire Prange farm was going to be sold
to Pool 24 Tug Service, pursuant to the terms of a sales contract, a copy of which was
attached. On October 12, 1999, Jennings replied to Hagen via facsimile. The cover
page of the facsimile transmission stated, in pertinent part, "Please accept this as my
meeting, my comittment [sic] to express my intent to purchase before your deadline. I am looking forward to reaching final terms and conditions as soon as possible
in order to assist Ms. Prange in reaching her goals and time requirements." The two
pages that followed were in the form of a letter from Jennings to Prange and Hagen,
and set forth various conditions of Jennings' proposed purchase. The section
entitled "Description of Property," stated, in pertinent part, as follows: "The
property to be sold is located at Hardin, Illinois[,] and is described as the Mary Jo
Prange property, just south of Hardin, Illinois." In the section entitled "Price" the
letter stated, "[t]he proposed purchase price shall be negotiated in good faith
based upon appraisal by an independent third party."

At the October 2002 bench trial, the trial court admitted in evidence Prange's
deposition. Prange stated that she owned approximately 1,000 feet of riverfront
property. When asked if she knew the distance or the size of the area leased to
WestPoint Marine, she replied as follows:

> "It covered the 500 feet. Our property at that time was marked in lots on the river
> frontage, each was 50 foot and it began in the middle of lot 16 and 17. And they were
> further south from that by probably four lots. Then from that point, you could mark
> the 500 and they were just about at the same location each time."

She acknowledged that at times, WestPoint Marine used more than 500 feet of
riverfront property, and no one took umbrage at it.

Jennings testified at trial that when he sent Hagen the facsimile expressing his
intent to exercise the option to buy, he was not certain whether he would be buying
just the riverfront property or the whole Prange farm. When asked whether he
"wanted to exercise [his] option to purchase the property that [h]e had leased,"
Jennings responded, "yes." Jennings estimated that between 30 and 45 days during
any given year, WestPoint Marine used more than 500 feet of Prange's riverfront
property. Jennings also explained that WestPoint Marine's floating buoys were tied
off to trees on the riverfront property. Jennings estimated that it used up to 200 feet
inland, depending on water levels.

Jennings identified WestPoint Marine's exhibit No. 5 as a map showing the
location of the 500 feet of riverfront property that WestPoint Marine was leasing.
The trial court admitted the exhibit for demonstrative purposes only, after sustaining
Prange's objection to the exhibit on the ground of insufficient foundation.

At the conclusion of the trial, the trial court granted the parties additional time to file written arguments.

In July 2003, the trial court entered an order denying WestPoint Marine's complaint for specific performance. The order stated that the court found "[t]hat the lease agreement which [WestPoint Marine] alleges also creates a[n] 'option to buy' does not contain a description of the property specific enough for which specific performance should be granted."

This appeal followed.

II.   WESTPOINT MARINE'S CLAIM THAT THE TRIAL COURT'S DECISION WAS AGAINST THE MANIFEST WEIGHT OF THE EVIDENCE

WestPoint Marine argues that the trial court's decision was against the manifest weight of the evidence. We disagree.

Parties to a contract are not entitled to specific performance as a matter of right. Instead, the remedy of specific performance is granted in the exercise of the trial court's sound discretion. *Butler v. Kent*, 275 Ill.App.3d 217, 226, 211 Ill.Dec. 737, 655 N.E.2d 1120, 1126 (1995). "[C]lear, explicit[,] and convincing evidence is required to support a grant of specific performance," and where testimony is conflicting in a bench trial, the trial court's factual findings will not be disturbed unless they are against the manifest weight of the evidence. *Butler*, 275 Ill.App.3d at 227, 211 Ill. Dec. 737, 655 N.E.2d at 1126.

A contract for sale of real estate cannot be enforced by a court unless it contains the essential contract terms, including (1) the names of the buyer and seller; (2) a description of the property; (3) the sales price or the means of determining the price, and the terms and conditions of the sale; and (4) the signature of the party to be charged. *Kane v. McDermott*, 191 Ill.App.3d 212, 217, 138 Ill.Dec. 541, 547 N.E.2d 708, 712 (1989). In addition,

> "[t]he contract's terms must be so certain and unambiguous that the court can require the specific thing contracted for be done. Where the terms of a contract are ambiguous or where the writing is capable of more than one construction, parol evidence is admissible to explain or ascertain what the parties intended. However, parol evidence may not be used to supply missing terms. [Citation.] The court should not make a new contract for the parties." *Kane*, 191 Ill.App.3d at 217, 138 Ill.Dec. 541, 547 N.E.2d at 712.

"A description of property is sufficiently definite if it will enable a surveyor, by aid of extrinsic evidence, to locate the property." *Kane*, 191 Ill.App.3d at 217, 138 Ill.Dec. 541, 547 N.E.2d at 712.

WestPoint Marine contends that the trial court's finding that the property was not defined with enough specificity to grant specific performance was against the manifest weight of the evidence because there was "no evidence presented that the location of the property was disputed by any party." However, the issue is not whether the location of the property was disputed; rather, the issue is whether the contract, pursuant to which the trial court was asked to grant specific performance, identified the property with sufficient specificity.

In this case, the following evidence supports the trial court's finding that the property was not sufficiently defined in the lease: (1) the lease described the property only as "approximately" 500 feet of riverfront property at "approximately mile 20" "just below Hardin"; (2) the 500 feet of riverfront property used by WestPoint Marine fluctuated to some extent; (3) when Jennings attempted to exercise the option to buy, he was not certain what he would be buying; and (4) no agreement existed as to how far inland WestPoint Marine's lease extended. Reviewing the evidence under the appropriate standard of review, we conclude that the court's finding was not against the manifest weight of the evidence.

In so concluding, we note that this case is distinguishable from *Kane*. In that case, the crop lease that contained an option-to-buy provision contained a legal description of the property at issue. *Kane*, 191 Ill.App.3d at 217, 138 Ill.Dec. 541, 547 N.E.2d at 712. Here, the lease does not contain anything resembling a legal description of the property subject to the option-to-buy provision. It does not indicate the precise location or the dimensions of either the Prange farm or the 500 feet of river-front property leased by WestPoint Marine.

III. CONCLUSION

For the reasons stated, we affirm the trial court's judgment.

Affirmed.

APPLETON, J., concurs.

COOK, J., dissents.

Justice COOK, dissenting:

I respectfully dissent and would reverse the judgment of the trial court, remanding with instructions that the option to purchase be honored.

Prange owns a 49–acre tract of land on the west bank of the Illinois River, south of Hardin, Illinois. It appears the tract is primarily used for barge fleeting operations. In 1993, the Pranges entered into a 25–year lease with Grantz's Marine Service, Inc., covering "approximately five hundred (500) feet of river frontage," and giving Grantz's Marine a first option to purchase the leased premises. That lease was assigned to WestPoint Marine in 1996. On September 24, 1999, Pool 24 Tug Service, Inc., submitted an offer to purchase the 49–acre tract, "subject to cancellation of present lease on the riverfront of said property." (The lease provides that "In the event the river frontage is sold to another party, the purchaser will be obligated to honor the terms and conditions of this lease.") On September 27, Prange's agent notified WestPoint Marine of the pending contract, advising that "you, under the articles of the agreement, have fifteen (15) days within which to purchase the property as stated in the enclosed contract or forfeit your interests."

The lease agreement clearly provides WestPoint Marine with an option to purchase. WestPoint Marine and its predecessor have performed their obligations under the lease for more than 10 years. The majority now makes a new contract for the parties, deleting the option to purchase, a substantial right that the optionee had bargained for and paid for. If the option to purchase is invalid because the legal description in the lease is insufficient, is the lease also invalid? The majority should disclaim any intention to make its holding *res judicata* in any future action filed by Pool 24 Tug Service, Inc., seeking to invalidate the lease.

Where the facts are not in dispute, the existence and interpretation of a contract are questions of law that the trial court may decide on a motion for summary judgment and that we may review independently. *Pokora v. Warehouse Direct, Inc.*, 322 Ill.App.3d 870, 875, 256 Ill.Dec. 367, 751 N.E.2d 1204, 1209 (2001). The case cited by the majority for the proposition that parties to a contract are not entitled to specific performance as a matter of right and that deference should be given the trial court's factual findings is distinguishable, involving a complicated calculation of the amount due plaintiff for the "net fair market value" of his interest in the Village Green Investment Corporation. *Butler,* 275 Ill.App.3d at 225, 211 Ill.Dec. 737, 655 N.E.2d at 1125–26.

The trial court found that the lease agreement "does not contain a description of the property specific enough for which specific performance should be granted." How can that be? This lease agreement was executed in 1993, and the leased premises have been used continuously since that time. Perhaps in 1993 there could have been a dispute as to what property had been leased, but that is no longer possible. The law is clear that a lease need not contain a specific description of the property. "[A] defective description of land may be aided by the conduct of the parties, such as, that the vendor put the purchaser in possession of the premises intended to be conveyed." *Hayes v. O'Brien,* 149 Ill. 403, 413, 37 N.E. 73, 75 (1894). There is no dispute that a surveyor could stake out WestPoint Marine's existing operation. That is all that is required.

The majority ignores the holding of *Kane,* upon which it purportedly relies. *Kane* involved a farm lease of property in sections 8, 21, and 29, but the plaintiff sought to enforce the option only as to a part of the property in section 29. The exercise of the option in *Kane* said simply that the plaintiff was exercising the option granted in section 7 of the lease. Section 7 of the lease said simply that the plaintiff had "'first option to purchase any part or all of the land farmed by the tenant.'" *Kane,* 191 Ill.App.3d at 214–15, 138 Ill.Dec. 541, 547 N.E.2d at 710. This court *rejected* the argument that the property was insufficiently described in the option. "A description of property is sufficiently definite if it will enable a surveyor, by aid of extrinsic evidence, to locate the property. Any reference to ownership or other matters which would make the description definite will be considered to locate the property." *Kane,* 191 Ill.App.3d at 217, 138 Ill.Dec. 541, 547 N.E.2d at 712.

The majority decision is consistent with Justice Steigmann's dissent in *Crawley v. Hathaway,* 309 Ill.App.3d 486, 242 Ill.Dec. 677, 721 N.E.2d 1208 (1999), but we should follow the *Crawley* majority opinion. In that case, an agreement to buy a portion of a farm, "100 Acres More or less, 83 acres of pasture & timber and 19 acres of tillable ground" was held to be a sufficient description. *Crawley,* 309 Ill.App.3d at 487, 242 Ill.Dec. 677, 721 N.E.2d at 1209. The land is sufficiently described in the writings when that description will enable a surveyor, with the aid of extrinsic evidence, to locate the property. *Crawley,* 309 Ill.App.3d at 490, 242 Ill.Dec. 677, 721 N.E.2d at 1211, citing *Thomas v. Moore,* 55 Ill.App.3d 907, 911, 12 Ill.Dec. 898, 370 N.E.2d 809, 811–12 (1977). *Crawley* cited other cases. A description of the property only as "my farm" was deemed sufficient because the description could be made certain by the aid of extrinsic evidence and the property located. *Werling v. Grosse,* 76 Ill.App.3d 834, 841, 32 Ill.Dec. 399, 395 N.E.2d 629, 634 (1979). A letter that did not specify the subject property was sufficient where the surrounding facts and circumstances served to identify the subject matter of the letter as the premises in question. *Moore v. Pickett,* 62 Ill. 158, 161 (1871). "Moreover, parol evidence is admissible to identify the subject matter of the contract or memorandum. It is not necessary in contracts for the sale of real estate that it should be so described as to admit of no doubt as to what it is." *Callaghan v. Miller,* 17 Ill.2d 595, 599, 162 N.E.2d 422, 424 (1959).

There is a strong tendency for the courts to sustain a legal description if at all possible, since it is apparent that the parties intended for something to be conveyed or they never would have been involved in the transaction. J. Cribbet, Principles of the Law of Property 157 (1962). The majority here trashes the intent of the parties by its insistence that the lease "indicate the precise location or the dimensions of either the Prange farm or the 500 feet of riverfront property" (op. 286 Ill.Dec. at 4, 812 N.E.2d at 1019.), a specificity requirement that is disavowed by the cases. Just as an offer to sell "my farm," is sufficient, an offer to purchase "the property I lease" is sufficient.

Questions are presented when the owner of a tract leases out a portion of that tract with an option to purchase. Certainly the lessee should not be allowed to frustrate the lessor's later attempt to sell the entire tract by insisting that the leased portion be split off. On the other hand, the lessor should not be allowed to render the option nugatory merely by attaching additional land to the part under option. *The Retreat v. Bell*, 296 Ill.App.3d 450, 456, 231 Ill.Dec. 119, 695 N.E.2d 892, 896 (1998). WestPoint Marine acted appropriately here by offering to take the entire tract, or the portion it leased, as Prange chose. Prange will not be prejudiced whether WestPoint Marine or Pool 24 Tug Service, Inc., purchases the property.

NOTES

1. In Sterling v. Taylor, 6 Cal. Rptr. 3d 836 (Cal. App. 2003) the court considers the adequacy of a contract of sale that described the properties by street number. In holding the description sufficient the court's opinion includes the following:

Taylor [one of the defendants] contends that the description in the writings of the SMC Properties—"808 4th Street," "843 4th Street" and "1251 14th Street"—was insufficient to satisfy the statute of frauds. Early authorities might support this position.

The distinction between an inadequate description and defective description or between terms that are ambiguous and the lack of a description is not easily ascertainable. As Corbin states, "A study of the almost innumerable cases that have passed upon the sufficiency of a description will make it apparent that a description regarded as sufficient by one court has often been held insufficient by another." (Corbin, *supra*, § 22.12, p. 754.) Corbin goes on, "it is agreed by all that there must be some descriptive identification of the particular tract of land. But if the court is convinced that no fraudulent substitution of property is being attempted and that the land actually agreed upon has been clearly established by all the evidence, including the written memorandum, the surrounding circumstances, and the oral testimony, little time should be wasted in listening to argument that the written description is inadequate." (*Id.* at § 22.12, pp. 754–755.) . . .

It is not necessary to define precisely the identification of property necessary to satisfy the statute of frauds, for the descriptions in the writings in this case, lacking only the city and state, are adequate. Sterling has proffered parol evidence to specify the city in which the properties are located. Corbin states, "A tract of land can be sufficiently described by street and number or by a special name conferred upon the place by its owner or by the community. Oral evidence is admissible to prove ownership of the tract and also to show its location in a particular city or county." (Corbin, *supra*, § 27.12, p. 759, fns. omitted.) And Williston says, "'Descriptions of real property, omitting the town, county, or state where the property is situated, have been held sufficient where the deed or writing provides other means of identification.'" (Williston, *supra*, § 29:20, pp. 574–575, fn. omitted, quoting *Flegel v. Dowling* (1909) 54 Or. 40, 102 P. 178.)

Based on the descriptions of the properties in the writings, the location of the parties, the place of the transaction and the name of the seller (Santa Monica Collection), it is reasonable to assume that the properties in question were located in Santa Monica, California. Under these circumstances, and under the modern authorities, the description is sufficient to comply with the statute of frauds, and parol evidence is admissible to assist in the necessary identification of the properties and specifically, the city and state in which the properties are located. The writings, along with the parol evidence, constitute sufficient identification of the properties to avoid summary judgment. . . .

There are many cases contra to Sterling v. Taylor. See, e.g., Key Design, Inc. v. Moser, 983 P.2d 653 (Wash. 1999), in which the court said: "We will not overturn an established rule unless the party challenging it makes a clear showing that the rule is incorrect and harmful."

2. *Accurate description misunderstood by the parties.* Problems can arise even with descriptions free of error and ambiguity. In Hill-Shafer Partnership v. Chilson Family Trust, 165 Ariz. 409, 799 P.2d 810 (1990), the complex legal description in a contract of sale was complete and accurate but described a larger parcel than the parties had bargained for and believed was being conveyed. Neither party fully understood the terminology of the description and they both misunderstood what area was being described. The contract price was $620,500. The buyer sought specific performance and the seller rescission of the contract. Held for the seller on the grounds of no mutual assent, the opinion stating:

> We disagree with the court of appeals' conclusion that the preciseness of a legal description, as a matter of law, prevented a rescission based on a misunderstanding. Any reasonable view of the evidence inevitably leads to the conclusion that there was no meeting of the minds and no enforceable contract was formed. We conclude that the trial court properly granted summary judgment in favor of the seller. [165 Ariz. at 476, 700 P.2d at 817.]

3. Ambiguous land descriptions were particularly common in the early years of settlement, especially in regions not covered by government surveys. Crude descriptions were satisfactory for the times. In New England, for instance, many land parcels in rural areas are still held pursuant to metes and bounds descriptions that probably can no longer be located because essential monuments have disappeared. These often are parcels that have remained in the same family for generations, and no one has insisted on a survey that would provide a more accurate description. An extreme example of an early defective description, defective to the point of being ludicrous, is the one set forth below that appears in the records of a Connecticut probate court. Give some thought to how a party who holds a deed or mortgage with such a description or who is a devisee of land so described would go about perfecting title. Note again that what makes this description highly unusual is its many questionable calls, but instruments with at least one questionable call of the sort appearing below are not all that infrequent in New England instruments on which current land claims are based. The description is this:

> Commencing at a heap of stones about a stone's throw from a certain small clump of alders, near a brook running down off from a rather high part of the ridge, thence by a straight line to a certain marked white birch tree about two or three times as far from a

jog in the fence going around said ledge and the "Great Swamp" so called, thence in line of said lot in part and in part by another piece of fence which joins onto said line, and by an extension of the general run of said fence to a heap of stones near a surface rock, thence aforesaid to the "Horn" so called and passing around the same aforesaid, as far as possible, to the "Great Bend" so called, and from thence to a squarish sort of jog in another fence so on to a marked black oak tree with stones around it and thence by another straight line in about a contrary direction and somewhere about parallel with the line around by the "Great Swamp" to a stake and stone mounds not far off from an old Indian trail, thence by another straight line on a course diagonally parallel, or nearly so, with "Fox Hollow" run, so called, to a certain marked yellow oak tree on the off side of a knoll with flat stone laid against it, thence after turning around in another direction and by a sloping straight line to a certain heap of stones which is found by pacing just 18 rods more from the stump of the big hemlock tree where Philo Blake killed the bear, thence to the corner begun at by two straight lines of about equal length which are to be run in by some skilled and competent surveyor so as to include the area and acreage as herein set forth.

Cribbet and Johnson, Principles of the Law of Property

210-212 (3d ed. 1989)

The cases on legal description are legion but a "feel" for the judicial construction problem may be obtained by a look at ten canons of construction. They are as follows.

1. The construction prevails which is most favorable to the grantee, i.e., the language of the deed is construed against the grantor. If the deed contains two descriptions, the grantee can select that which is most favorable to him. This canon is based on the presumption that the grantor drafted the deed and, if an ambiguity has resulted, he has only himself to blame. As in insurance law, where the policy is typically construed against the insurer, this canon is frequently the unstated premise in a case otherwise inexplicable.[76]

2. If the deed contains two descriptions, one ambiguous and the other unambiguous, the latter prevails in order to sustain the deed. This is not so likely to happen with modern, short form deeds but with the old, prolix instruments it was not uncommon.

3. Extrinsic evidence will be allowed to explain a latent ambiguity but a patent ambiguity must be resolved within the four corners of the deed.[77] This old chestnut has lost much of its validity but it still must be reckoned with. It was based on the idea that if the defect was latent (not apparent to the parties when the deed was drafted) evidence of surrounding circumstances should be admitted to clarify intent, but if it was patent (apparent on the face of the document) the parties must have been aware of it when the deed was executed and no extrinsic evidence is necessary. It has long been clear that this canon is easily controlled by the determination of what is latent or patent and many writers have called for abolition of the distinction.[78]

---

76. See Hall v. Eaton, 139 Mass. 217, 29 N.E. 660 (1885) which makes little sense on any other basis.
77. Walters v. Tucker, 281 S.W.2d 843 (Mo. 1955).
78. McBaine, The Rule Against Disturbing Plain Meaning of Writings, 31 Cal. L. Rev. 145 (1943). In a footnote it is pointed out that the distinction "is gradually disappearing" and the hope is expressed that the time will soon come "when it will be of interest only to students engaged in tracing the history of law through periods of formalism to a period of realism."

4. Monuments control distances and courses; courses control distances; and quantity is the least reliable guide of all.[79] In a metes and bounds description, it is relatively easy to start with a known monument (the side of a road, a stream, a rock, etc.), move in a stated direction or course for a set distance, and end up with an impossible description because one of these elements is in error. This canon tries to set up a priority of reliability, based on presumed intent of the parties. Most monuments would be difficult to mistake so they are probably identified correctly. A course, "northerly at a 90° angle," is more certain than a distance, "thence eighty feet," since most people cannot measure distances with any degree of accuracy with the naked eye. Quantity, which is always hard to estimate, logically brings up the end of the list.

5. Useless or contradictory words may be disregarded as mere surplusage. The difficulty with this canon is patent. Which are the useless or contradictory words? Nonetheless, it states a useful truth since many prolix, confusing descriptions can be pared down to meaningful size to sustain a deed.

6. Particular descriptions control over general descriptions, although a false particular may be disregarded to give effect to a true general description. Any more questions?

7. A description, insufficient in itself, may be made certain through incorporation by reference. This is a particularly useful canon since it enables shorthand reference to be made to involved descriptions in other documents. It can create major merchantability problems, however, if the instrument referred to is not recorded and hence not available for title search.

8. If an exception in a deed is erroneously described, the conveyance is good for the whole tract and title to all of the land passes. Frequently, the grantor will convey Blackacre "except for" a described area. If the description of the exception is faulty, it could be argued that the entire deed should fail but this canon would sustain the larger grant at the expense of the grantor who made the error.

9. When a tract of land is bound by a monument which has width, such as a highway or a stream, the boundary line extends to the center, provided the grantor owns that far, unless the deed manifests an intention to the contrary.[80] The converse of this canon would lead to undesirable policy results. Suppose A, who owns to the center of a highway, conveys to B, but the description uses the edge of the road as one boundary. Years pass and the highway is vacated so that the easement of public use is removed. At this point, the narrow strip of land becomes valuable due to the discovery of oil or a change in the direction of urban growth. Who owns the strip? If the parties thought of it at all, they probably intended to transfer whatever land the grantor owned since the retention of a strip under an existing highway would be unreasonable. To prevent endless litigation over narrow strips and gores of land, the courts, in general, have followed the rule stated above.

10. A description in a deed includes the appurtenances to the tract even though they are not specifically mentioned in the deed.[81] Normally, only that portion of the land passes to the grantee which is specifically described in the deed. However, there are interests in the land which are appurtenant to the described tract in such a way that they have no existence apart from their parasitical attachment to the host

---

79. Pritchard v. Rebori, 135 Tenn. 328, 186 S.W. 121 (1916).
80. Bowers v. Atchison, T. and S.F. Ry. Co., 119 Kan. 202, 237 P. 913, 42 A.L.R. 228 (1925).
81. Stockdale v. Yerden, 220 Mich. 444, 190 N.W. 225 (1922).

premises. Thus, if A owns Blackacre and has an access road across Whiteacre to the highway, a conveyance of Blackacre to B will include the appurtenant easement even though not described in the conveyance. . . .

A study of the canons will reveal that they overlap in their statements of law and that some of them are contradictory. Moreover, it should be clear that any one of them will yield to a clear manifestation of intent, which is always the courts' major guideline. Even so, they serve a useful purpose, if only as a point of departure, and do give some degree of predictability in an uncertain area of the law.

NOTES AND QUESTIONS

1. *Reformation and the bona fide purchaser.* A seller who mistakenly over-conveys, or a buyer who mistakenly receives an underconveyance, cannot obtain reformation against a bona fide purchaser. This is the rule in some cases. As a practical matter, how likely is it that one will be able to acquire the status of bona fide purchaser where a mistakenly described conveyance is involved? Keep in mind that a buyer of real property is charged with notice of the rights of persons in *possession* of the premises.

2. *Deed calls for quantity.* People often talk about land values in terms of property in a downtown area selling for $250,000 a front foot, or of undeveloped property off to the southeast of a growing city selling at $15,000 an acre; and land sale prices are sometimes figured, say, at so much an acre. Someone buying Blackacre for its historic value qua Blackacre is not the same legal-economic fellow as the buyer who sees its lovely elms as bulldozeable impediments to his carving it up into the largest number of resaleable lots permitted by zoning laws.

Suppose Blackacre is sold as such, but is conceived by the parties and priced as so many acres permitting so many lots or as carrying such an agricultural production quota as is permitted by federal statutes. Then Blackacre turns out to have more or less acres than had been assumed as the basis of the bargain.

Parol evidence can be used to prove the basis of the bargain, and the regular remedy pattern comes into play — rescission or reformation, breach of warranty, price abatement or enhancement for overage and underage, etc. See 3 Corbin, Contracts § 604.

The fact that a quantity call is used as a part of a property description does not mean that the transaction was premised on a quantity.

C.   LEGAL EFFECT OF ADVERSE OCCUPANCY

Adverse possession or acquiescence in boundaries may result in the processing party acquiring valid legal title even though the deed or other evidence of title was unduly vague or the parties claiming title were mistaken as to where the true boundary was located. Zeglin v. Gahagen is an example of a case in which the court recognized the corrective effect of such adverse occupancy if it continues for a sufficient number of years.

Zeglin v. Gahagen

812 A.2d 558 (Pa. 2002)

OPINION

Justice SAYLOR

In this appeal involving a boundary dispute, the question presented is whether privity of estate between succeeding landowners is required to support tacking periods of ownership to form the requisite twenty-one-year period under acquiescence theory.

Appellants, Frank and Tammy Zeglin, and Appellees, Sean and Kimberlee Gahagen, own adjoining properties in Windber, Paint Township, Somerset County. The Zeglins purchased in 1977 from Cora Murphy, who, together with her late husband, had owned the property since 1937. The Gahagens bought from Margaret Swincinski in 1989, who had acquired the parcel in 1979 from the previous owners since 1972.

In 1995, the Gahagens employed a professional to survey their property and learned that their deed described a boundary on the Zeglins' side of a line marked by a row of bushes, utility pole, and fence that had been added by the Zeglins. The surveyor therefore concluded that the Gahagens' property extended over such visible line, and this was confirmed in a subsequent survey commissioned by the Zeglins. The Gahagens notified the Zeglins that a portion of their driveway encroached on their land, removed the bushes, and constructed a retaining wall adjacent to the surveyed boundary. The Zeglins responded by filing a complaint against the Gahagens sounding in ejectment and trespass and claiming ownership up to the line previously demarcated by the bushes, utility pole, and fence. In furtherance of this position, the Zeglins relied, *inter alia,* on the doctrine of acquiescence in a boundary, alleging that their occupancy and possession, together with that of their predecessors in title, for a period of more than twenty-one years established the visible line as the legal boundary. The Gahagens filed an answer and counterclaim.

In March of 2000, following a non-jury trial, the common pleas court issued a *decree nisi* in favor of the Zeglins, which it later made final. In accompanying opinions, the court summarized the acquiescence doctrine as follows:

> an occupation up to a fence on each side by a party or two parties for more than 21 years, each party claiming the land on his side as his own, gives to each an incontestable right up to the fence, whether the fence is precisely on the right line or not; and this is so although the parties may not have consented specifically to the fence in question.

Zeglin v. Gahagen, No. 369 Civ.1999, *slip op.* at 4 (C.P. Somerset Feb. 10, 2000) (Gibson, J.) ("Common Pleas Court Opinion") (quoting *Berzonski v. Holsopple,* 28 Som. Leg. J. 342, 358 (1973) (Coffroth, P.J.)). The court identified as the basis for the principle public policy favoring peace and the repose of titles. It reasoned that, for a period of more than twenty-one years, the Zeglins, the Gahagens, and their predecessors in interest had recognized and acquiesced in a boundary line demarcated by the hedgerow (and also highlighted by the fence maintained by the Zeglins through a portion of that time period). Although the Zeglins had occupied the property for only eighteen years prior to the Gahagens' actions, the court permitted them to tack the period of ownership by the Murphys, despite the fact that Cora Murphy had not specifically and formally conveyed her purported interest in the disputed tract to the Zeglins in the written deed. As pertains to tacking under the doctrine of adverse possession, the court recognized the requirement in Pennsylvania of privity of estate, namely, a higher degree of relation than that of mere grantor and grantee of a main parcel, generally comprised of specific and formal conveyance of the predecessor's interest in the disputed tract where the transfer is between unrelated parties. *See* Common Pleas Court Opinion, *slip op.* at 15 (quoting *Baylor v. Soska*, 540 Pa. 435, 438–39, 658 A.2d 743, 744–45 (1995)). The common pleas court found, however, that Pennsylvania courts had distinguished acquiescence in a boundary by applying the less rigorous requirement of privity of possession to claims predicated on such theory. *See id.* at 5 ("Pennsylvania courts have adopted the view that succeeding owners of property are bound by the fences that were accepted and recognized by former owners even without any other privity or formal transfer of the area possessed adversely." (citing *Berzonski*, 28 Som. Leg. J. at 358)).

On the Gahagens' appeal, the Superior Court reversed in a published decision. *See Zeglin v. Gahagen*, 774 A.2d 781 (Pa.Super.2001). At the outset, it acknowledged the limitations on appellate review pertaining to matters of equity. *See id.* at 783 ("'Our scope [and standard] of review in matters of equity [are] narrow and limited to determining whether the findings of fact are supported by competent evidence, whether an error of law has been committed or whether there has been a manifest abuse of discretion'" (citation omitted; interlineations in original)). The court determined, however, that, just as in the case of adverse possession, privity of estate is an essential prerequisite to employment of tacking to perfect a claim under acquiescence theory. *See id.* at 784–85 (citing *Plott v. Cole*, 377 Pa.Super. 585, 596, 547 A.2d 1216, 1222 (1988)). Accordingly, the Superior Court held that the common pleas court erred by permitting the Zeglins to tack the period of the Murphys' ownership based on privity of possession alone. *See id.*

Presently, the Zeglins argue that privity of estate as a prerequisite to tacking is inappropriate to, and contrary to the doctrine of, acquiescence in a boundary, since an underlying premise of such theory is that the evidence of longstanding acquiescence in a physical boundary by adjoining property owners will control over contrary deed calls. The Zeglins distinguish *Plott v. Cole*, cited by the Superior Court, as allowing for creation of privity by "other acts," and not solely by references culled from a deed. The Gahagens concede that the privity of estate requirement has not expressly been attached by Pennsylvania courts in acquiescence cases, but contend that such a requirement would alleviate confusion among landowners.

The establishment of a boundary line by acquiescence for the statutory period of twenty-one years has long been recognized in Pennsylvania.[1] Two elements are prerequisites: 1) each party must have claimed and occupied the land on his side of the line as his own; and 2) such occupation must have continued for the statutory period of twenty-one years. *See Jedlicka v. Clemmer*, 450 Pa.Super. 647, 654, 677 A.2d 1232, 1235 (1996); *Plott*, 377 Pa.Super. at 594, 547 A.2d at 1221. As recognized by the Superior

---

1. *See Reiter v. McJunkin*, 173 Pa. 82, 84, 33 A. 1012 (1896) ("After 21 years of occupancy up to a fence on each side as a line fence, it is not material to inquire whether the fence is on the right line or not."); *see also Dimura v. Williams*, 446 Pa. 316, 319, 286 A.2d 370, 371 (1972); *Brown v. McKinney*, 9 Watts 565, 567 (Pa.1840); *Martz v. Hartley*, 4 Watts 261, 262–63 (Pa.1835); *accord Schimp v. Allaman*, 442 Pa.Super. 365, 369, 659 A.2d 1032, 1034 (1995) ("a boundary line may be proved by a long-standing fence without proof of a dispute and its settlement or compromise" (citation omitted)).

Court and the common pleas court, the doctrine functions as a rule of repose to quiet title and discourage vexatious litigation. *See id.* at 592, 547 A.2d at 1220.

Although the elements are simply stated, courts have had difficulty tracing the theoretical underpinnings of the acquiescence precept.[2] In Pennsylvania, courts frequently have distinguished the doctrine from adverse possession, *see, e.g., Niles v. Fall Creek Hunting Club, Inc.,* 376 Pa.Super. 260, 267, 545 A.2d 926, 930 (1988); *Inn Le'Daerda, Inc. v. Davis,* 241 Pa.Super. 150, 163 n. 7, 360 A.2d 209, 215 n. 7 (1976), and in recent cases have categorized it, under the umbrella of "consentable boundaries," with a separate theory premised on dispute and compromise.[3] An examination of the decisional law demonstrates, however, that the doctrinal roots of acquiescence are grounded in adverse possession theory,[4] indeed, occupancy with open manifestations of ownership throughout the statutory period will generally satisfy the traditional elements of adverse possession.[5] Decisions involving acquiescence are frequently distinguishable from adverse possession cases only in that possession in the former are often based on a mistake as to the location of property

2. *See generally* HERBERT THORNDIKE TIFFANY, THE LAW OF REAL PROPERTY § 1159 (1975 & Supp. 2001) ("The decisions of a particular court [concerning acquiescence in boundaries] are not infrequently lacking in entire consistency, one with another, and occasionally the judicial discussion of the subject is such as to leave us somewhat in doubt as to the exact position of the court on the question."); Annotation, *Fence as a Factor in Fixing Location of Boundary Line — Modern Cases,* 7 A.L.R.4th 53, 59 (1981 & Supp.2002) ("It has been said that the doctrine of boundary by acquiescence is in chaotic condition." (citation omitted)).

3. *See also Corbin v. Cowan,* 716 A.2d 614, 617 (Pa.Super.1998); *Sorg v. Cunningham,* 455 Pa.Super. 171, 178, 687 A.2d 846, 849 (1997); *Plauchak v. Boling,* 439 Pa.Super. 156, 165, 653 A.2d 671, 675 (1995).

The earlier decisions generally reserved the terms "consentable line" and "consentable boundary" for the dispute and agreement paradigm. *See Culver v. Hazlett,* 13 Pa.Super. 323, 328 (1900) (describing "consentable line" as "a technical term, the basis of which is a dispute between adjoining owners and the compromise of such a dispute by a line agreed upon between them" (citing *Perkins v. Gay,* 3 Serg. & Rawle 327 (Pa. 1817))); *accord Beals v. Allison,* 161 Pa.Super. 125, 129, 54 A.2d 84, 86 (1947); *Ross v. Golden,* 146 Pa.Super. 417, 423, 22 A.2d 310, 313 (1941); *Miles v. Pennsylvania Coal Co.,* 245 Pa. 94, 95, 91 A. 211, 212 (1914); *Newton v. Smith,* 40 Pa.Super. 615, 619 (1909). Nevertheless, despite the distinction between acquiescence and consentable line theories, courts used the term "consent" loosely in acquiescence cases, *see, e.g., Dimura,* 446 Pa. at 319, 286 A.2d at 370–71, and ultimately the "consentable boundaries" rubric emerged to cover both theories, apparently in *Niles,* 376 Pa.Super. at 267, 545 A.2d at 930.

4. *See, e.g., Reiter,* 173 Pa. at 84, 33 A. at 1012 ("The maintenance of a line fence between owners of adjoining lands by their acts, up to which each claims and occupies, is a concession by each of the open, adverse possession by the other of that which is on his side of such division fence, which after twenty-one years will give title, though subsequent surveys may show that the fence was not exactly upon the surveyed line."); *Brown,* 9 Watts. at 567 ("A possession claim[ed] as [one's] own is in law and reason adverse to all the world — and as much so as if he has never heard of an adverse claim as if he had always known of it."); *Adams v. Tamaqua Underwear Co.,* 105 Pa.Super. 339, 342, 161 A. 416, 417 (1932); *Culver,* 13 Pa.Super. at 328–29 (noting that adverse possession is the foundation for recognized or "claim-to" line theories); *accord Penn v. Ivey,* 615 P.2d 1, 4 n. 4 (Alaska 1980) ("It is well recognized that a fence, as a matter of law, is 'one of the strongest indications of adverse possession.'" (citing cases)).

5. *See generally Baylor,* 540 Pa. at 438, 658 A.2d at 744 (delineating the elements of adverse possession as actual, continuous, exclusive, visible, notorious, distinct, and hostile possession of the land for twenty-one years). Notably, hostility, as a requirement of adverse possession, does not denote ill will, but rather, the intent to hold the property against the record title holder. *See Vlachos v. Witherow,* 383 Pa. 174, 176, 118 A.2d 174, 177 (1955); *accord* William Sternberg, *The Element of Hostility in Adverse Possession,* 6 TEMPLE L.Q. 207, 208 (1932) (stating that "a person is in hostile possession when he acts with reference to the land in the same way that the owner would act"). Moreover, "acquiescence" in the context of disputed boundaries "denotes passive conduct on the part of the lawful owner consisting of failure on his part to assert his paramount rights or interests against the hostile claims of the adverse user." Edward G. Mascolo, *A Primer On Adverse Possession,* 66 CONN. B.J. 303, 312–13 (Aug. 1992); *see also id.* at 313 (noting that, "in the case of acquiescence, the use or occupancy of the premises is hostile to and against the interests of the title owner"); *accord Cremer v. Cremer Rodeo Land and Livestock Co.,* 192 Mont. 208, 627 P.2d 1199, 1201 (1981) (distinguishing acquiescence from permission).

lines. *See generally* Annotation, *Adverse Possession Involving Ignorance or Mistake as to Boundaries — Modern Views,* 80 A.L.R.2d 1171, 1173 (1961 & Supp.2002).[6]

This confluence between acquiescence and adverse possession principles militates against the Zeglins' position, in light of this Court's determination, presently recognized by both the Superior Court and the common pleas court, that privity of estate is a prerequisite to tacking under adverse possession theory. *See Baylor,* 540 Pa. at 441, 658 A.2d at 746 (holding that "the only method by which an adverse possessor may convey the title asserted by adverse possession is to describe in the instrument of conveyance by means minimally acceptable for conveyancing of realty that which is intended to be conveyed").

Even so, the contrary analysis reflected in the Somerset County decisions is noteworthy and merits further consideration, Prior to *Baylor,* in the decision presently relied upon by the common pleas court, President Judge Coffroth made the case that the lesser standard of privity of possession should govern tacking successive periods of adverse possession, at least in boundary controversies. He reasoned that:

> [t]he circumstances of unified use, and physical transfer of possession of the disputed tract, and continued adverse use thereof and of the conveyed tract as an incorporated and unified whole, show that the parties intended to transfer not only the title to the conveyed tract, but also the possession to the disputed area whose use was integrated with the conveyed tract, notwithstanding the omission from the deed of any mention of the disputed area.

Berzonski, 28 Som Leg. J. at 370. Further, he described privity of possession as "the almost universal rule" supporting tacking in the boundary dispute context. *See id.* at 367 (citing 3 AM.JUR.2D ADVERSE POSSESSION § 80 (Supp.2002).[7,8] With regard to

---

6. Mistake, however, does not in and of itself negate application of adverse possession in Pennsylvania. *See Schlagel v. Lombardi,* 337 Pa.Super. 83, 486 A.2d 491, 494 (1984) (noting that "most jurisdictions 'deem the animus of the possessor irrelevant'[;] . . . Pennsylvania follows the majority view" (quoting *Lyons v. Andrews,* 226 Pa.Super. 351, 351–60, 313 A.2d 313, 316–17 (1973))). In this regard, the Maryland Court of Appeals has elaborated as follows:

> The modern trend and the better rule is that where the visible boundaries have existed for the period set forth in the Statute of Limitations, title will vest in the adverse possessor where there is evidence of unequivocal acts of ownership. In this view it is immaterial that the holder supposed the visible boundary to be correct or, in other words, the fact that the possession was due to inadvertence, ignorance, or mistake, is entirely immaterial.

Tamburo v. Miller, 203 Md. 329, 100 A.2d 818, 821 (1953).

7. The citations to secondary authorities employed by President Judge Coffroth are updated here.

8. As summarized by one commentator:

> At the present time, making allowance for contrary rulings still apparently adhered to in a few jurisdictions, the cases, especially the later ones, run generally to the effect that in order to permit the tacking of successive adverse possessions of vendor and purchaser of an area not within the premises as described in the deed or contract but contiguous thereto, the composite fact to be established is the intended and actual transfer or delivery of possession of such area to the grantee or vendee as successor in ownership or claim.

Annotation, *Tacking Adverse Possession of Area Not Within Description of Deed or Contract,* 17 A.L.R.2d 1128, 1131–32 (2002); *see also* HERBERT T. TIFFANY AND BASIL JONES, TIFFANY REAL PROPERTY § 1207 (3d ed. 2002) ("There is sufficient privity for this purpose, it would seem, when the use[ ] is, exercised, for the benefit of neighboring land, by successive owners or possessors of such land, between whom there exists some legal relation other than that of disseisor and disseisee."); *id.* at § 1146 ("This privity may be based upon contract, estate, or blood relationship, or upon any connecting relationship which will prevent a break in the adverse possessions and refer the several possessions to the original entry, and for this purpose no written transfer or agreement is necessary[;] [o]f course, there must be a transfer of a possessory right initially, in order that the

Pennsylvania, President Judge Coffroth observed that both this Court's decision in *Scheetz v. Fitzwater*, 5 Pa. 126 (1847), and the Superior Court's in *Stark v. Lardin*, 133 Pa.Super. 96, 1 A.2d 784 (1938), approved tacking on such terms, where there was no valid written transfer of the grantor's adverse possession of the disputed area to the subsequent owner. *See Berzonski*, 28 Som. Leg. J. at 369;[9] *accord Lenihan v. Davis*, 152 Pa.Super. 47, 49–50, 31 A.2d 434, 435 (1943).

Berzonski nonetheless acknowledged a contrary line of Superior Court authority, exemplified by *Masters v. Local Union No. 472, United Mine Workers*, 146 Pa.Super. 143, 22 A.2d 70 (1941), which implemented a requirement of privity of estate to support tacking without mention of *Scheetz* or *Stark*. The court, however, criticized *Masters'* reasoning as predicated on the erroneous assumption that landowners would generally lay claim to only part of the land that they possess or occupy,[10] and observed that in another line of cases, the Superior Court persisted in the idea that an intent to convey more than the premises actually described in a deed could be inferred from acts or circumstances apart from the deed itself. *See Berzonski*, 28 Som. Leg. J. at 372–73 (citing *Gerhart v. Hilsenbeck*, 164 Pa.Super. 85, 89, 63 A.2d 124, 126–27 (1949)). Based on these latter decisions, President Judge Coffroth concluded that "Pennsylvania has joined or rejoined the main stream of authority and validates . . . that privity may be established by oral agreement." *Id.* at 374.

Subsequent Pennsylvania cases generally followed *Masters* without reference to the view of a majority of jurisdictions as embodied in the reasoning of President Judge Coffroth. *See Glenn v. Shuey*, 407 Pa.Super. 213, 225, 595 A.2d 606, 612 (1991); *Wittig v. Carlacci*, 370 Pa.Super. 584, 589–90, 537 A.2d 29, 32 (1988); *Plott*, 377 Pa. Super. at 596, 547 A.2d at 1222; *Castronuovo v. Sordoni*, 357 Pa.Super. 187, 193–94,

---

transferee be entitled to claim a tacking of the transferor's possession."); 3 AM.JUR.2D ADVERSE POSSESSION § 79 (2002) (stating that "if one adverse claimant, by agreement, surrenders possession to another, and the acts of the parties are such that the two possessions actually connect, leaving no interval for the constructive possession of the true owner to intervene, the two possessions are blended into one, and the running of the limitation period on the right of the true owner to reclaim the land is continued").

9. In *Scheetz*, 5 Pa. at 132, the Court specifically indicated that "possession may be passed without title" and "[a] proprietor who occupies his neighbour's land as a part of his farm, may certainly transfer his possession of the whole by a conveyance of the farm."

10. The *Masters* reasoning has been similarly criticized in the commentary, as, for example, in the following passage from an annotation:

In *Masters v. Local Union* No. 472, . . . it was held that "the insurmountable difficulty" confronting defendant in making out title by adverse possession to the area on which the buildings stood was that in title by adverse possession to the area on which the buildings stood was that in neither "the deed" to the association nor in the deed from the latter's trustee in bankruptcy to the defendant was there "any conveyance" of the rights acquired by the grantor by possession. . . . The court quoted as controlling the language of *Zubler v. Schrack*, (a case not on its facts within the scope of this annotation, nor at all similar to the ones here dealt with) to the effect that "each succeeding occupant must show title under his predecessor, so as to preserve a unity of possession," a statement which it seems would be erroneously construed to mean that such "title" must be transferred by a deed, or by a deed describing the land subsequently in controversy. In fact, somewhat strangely, because not supporting the position taken by the court in the *Masters* Case, the court therein quoted from the opinion rendered in the *Schrack* Case, in the subsequent appeal in 46 Pa. 67, that "an adverse possession begun and continued for a time, in order to be available to a successor, must be transferred to such successor in some lawful manner. This is true as that property can only be rightfully acquired with the assent of its owner, or vested by operation of law." The latter language, it will be observed, is clearly open to the construction that the "adverse possession" need not be transferred by a deed describing the premises held adversely, but simply "in some lawful manner."

Annotation, *Tacking Adverse Possession*, 17 A.L.R.2d at 1178–79.

515 A.2d 927, 930–31 (1986). Nevertheless, prior to *Baylor,* courts continued to note an "other circumstances exception" based on *Scheetz* and *Stark. See, e.g., Glenn,* 407 Pa.Super. at 226 n. 6, 595 A.2d at 613 n. 6; *Wittig,* 370 Pa.Super. at 589–90, 537 A.2d at 32; *Castronuovo,* 357 Pa.Super. at 193, 515 A.2d at 931.[11] In *Baylor,* however, this Court dismissed the portion of the privity rules permitting the tacking based on acts or circumstances extrinsic to written deeds, reasoning that:

> [i]nterested parties have a right to discern from the record the state of the title of any parcel of land. If tacking were to be permitted because of vague, undefined "circumstances," there could and most likely would be no way for one not a party to the conveyance to know this. But the law mandates that a person asserting a claim of adverse possession make this assertion openly and notoriously to all the world. There must be no secret that the adverse possessor is asserting a claim to the land in question. If the adverse possessor's claim is to be passed on to a successor in title, therefore, there must be some objective indicia of record by which it can be discerned with some degree of certainty that a claim of title by adverse possession is being made and that the duration of this claim has been passed on to a successor in title.

Id. at 440, 658 A.2d at 745–46 (citation omitted).

Although *Baylor* was a boundary case, it proceeded on the theory of adverse possession, as opposed to acquiescence. While we recognize that this is a fine basis for distinction given the relatedness of these doctrines, strict application of *Baylor's* holding in the acquiescence paradigm would eliminate tacking in cases involving successive owners and mistaken boundaries, which would appear to be the prevailing set of circumstances in this line of decisions. *See* Annotation, *Tacking Adverse Possession,* 17 A.L.R.2d at 1131. Indeed, perhaps for this reason, Pennsylvania and other courts have previously suggested the application of more flexible rules in the acquiescence paradigm.[12]

As President Judge Coffroth aptly observed, the reason why privity of estate should not be deemed necessary to support tacking in this setting is, simply, because a prospective purchaser will see the fence or similar marking; given its "obvious presence as apparent boundary," he is therefore put on notice to inquire about its origin, history, and function. *See Berzonski,* 28 Som. Leg. J. at 361 ("After 21 years, the chips will be allowed to fall where they may, for reasons of equity and peace.").

---

11. Part of the confusion in the cases results from the fact that courts have employed the definition of privity of possession, *see* 3 AM.JUR.2D ADVERSE POSSESSION § 79 ("Privity of possession is a succession of relationship to the same thing, whether created by deed or by other act, or by operation of law."), in defining privity of estate. *See, e.g., Baylor,* 540 Pa. at 438–39, 658 A.2d at 744–45 (citations omitted); *see also supra* note 10.

12. *See, e.g., Plauchak,* 439 Pa.Super. at 170, 653 A.2d at 677–78; *Mayor and Town Council of New Market v. Armstrong,* 42 Md.App. 227, 400 A.2d 425, 433–34 (1979) (indicating that "color of title [is] not necessary for tacking to provide continuity of possession of land, provided the land in question [is] contiguous to that described in a deed, and that lands both titled and untitled were part of a close, apparent by reason of physical boundaries such as fences or hedges." (citations omitted)); *accord* 11 C.J.S. BOUNDARIES § 86 (Aug. 2002) ("Recognition and acquiescence of one owner may be tacked to that of a succeeding one, and privity of estate between successive owners is not necessary to permit of a technical tacking of their periods of holding to make out the statutory period." (footnotes omitted)); *cf. Howard v. Kunto,* 3 Wash.App. 393, 477 P.2d 210, 215 (1970) (characterizing the requirement of privity as merely "a judicial recognition of the need for some reasonable connection between successive occupants so as to raise their claim of right above status of the wrongdoer or the trespasser"), *overruled on other grounds, Chaplin v. Sanders,* 100 Wash.2d 853, 676 P.2d 431 (1984).

Accordingly, we find the majority view (requiring only privity of possession) better suited to claims brought under a theory of acquiescence in a boundary. We hold, therefore, that tacking is permitted in such context upon sufficient and credible proof of delivery of possession of land not within (but contiguous to) property described by deed of conveyance, which was previously claimed and occupied by the grantor and is taken by the grantee as successor in such interest.

The order of the Superior Court is reversed, and the case is remanded for reinstatement of the final decree of the common pleas court.

D. QUALITY

1. Caveat Emptor

As recently as the 1950s there was a reasonably coherent body of law dealing with seller's responsibilities to buyer as to structures on the sold premises. The law was "caveat emptor": the warning to the buyer was generally, "Guard yourself at all times," and particularly, "Look before you sign," "Don't assume, ask," and "Get it in writing."

One could find in the authorities a whole series of propositions that made up the "caveat emptor" system. They were all derived from the general bodies of contract and tort law, and as you read below a selection from the more important of the rules you will find nothing startling. To be sure, you ought to doubt whether there ever was a time and place where every proposition listed was rigidly applied to defeat every disappointed buyer, and you ought to recognize that some of the propositions have been weakened in recent years in their general applicability, whatever may be true about land sales. Nevertheless, here are propositions that defeated many a buyer in many a case.

NOTE: CAVEAT EMPTOR AS A SYSTEM OF PROPOSITIONS

1. *Promissory obligations of the seller: seller has contractual quality responsibilities only to the extent that he makes express warranties in contract of sale or deed.*

(a) There are no implied warranties of quality in the sale of real estate.

(b) Seller's oral promises preceding the contract of sale are unavailing to buyer because of the parol evidence rule.

(c) Seller's oral promises preceding the contract of sale are made unenforceable by the statute of frauds.

(d) Seller's oral promises between contract of sale and deed are unavailing to buyer because not supported by consideration.

(e) Express warranties in the contract of sale but not contained in the deed are unavailing to buyer because of the doctrine of merger. (This is a variant of the parol evidence rule.)

(f) An express quality warranty in the deed inures only to the grantee and does not run with the land.

(g) The remedy for breach of an express quality warranty is damages, not rescission.

(h) Breach of an express quality warranty does not subject the warrantor to liability for consequential damages, particularly personal injury damages.

2. *Duties of the seller not to misrepresent.* Here is a sampling of propositions from the tort law of misrepresentation: innocent, negligent, and intentional:

(a) *Nondisclosure:* (1) Seller has no duty to disclose any quality defect detectable by inspection. (2) Seller has no duty to disclose a concealed defect unless buyer proves that the defect is actually known to seller. (3) Seller has no duty to disclose a concealed defect known to him unless he knows that buyer is unaware of the defect and that the buyer would regard the defect as material.

(b) *Intentional misrepresentation:* (1) Seller's words are an unenforceable oral promise, rather than a duty-laden representation of fact. (2) Seller's quality affirmation is a mere opinion. (3) Buyer's inspection shows he does not rely on the representation. (4) Buyer's opportunity to inspect shows that he has no right to rely on the representation.

(c) *Agency problems:* (1) A real estate broker is not authorized to make quality representations to prospective purchasers. (2) Seller who authorizes a broker to make quality representations is not liable for intentional misrepresentations made by the agent.

(d) *Regulatory statutes:* Statutory duties imposed on seller by building codes or like regulatory statutes do not run to buyer.

(e) *Remedies:* (1) Buyer's remedy for misrepresentation is restricted to rescission. (2) A buyer who, after discovering a defect, keeps up mortgage payments while deciding on a course of action, has waived the tort. (3) The statute of limitations runs from the date of the tort, not the date of its discovery.

When it came to purchase of new homes from builder-vendors, all the rules that denied buyer protection unless he had it in writing got their bite from the fact that the instrumentation of the transaction was in the hands of the seller. In one of the last significant cases that reaffirmed the one-time nationwide rule that there were no implied warranties in the sale of a new home, Steiber v. Palumbo, 219 Ore. 479, 347 P.2d 978 (1959), the court noted that the transaction's documents did not contain any mention at all of the structure being sold.

Caveat emptor has recently been nationally undercut in a common law process that is still under development. This legal change also should come as no surprise to persons who have studied recent products law and recent landlord-tenant decisions.

You must note that we are dealing systematically only with private remedies for disappointing housing, and not with building codes, criminal statutes, conditional public subsidy programs, antitrust laws, and myriad other institutional and governmental constraints on the housing seller. The prophylaxis of a tightly administered building code might be enormously more protective to buyers than the opportunity to engage in expensive, time-consuming, nerve-frazzling, common law litigation — even if successful. And it may be that a vigorous, innovative, competitive housing supply industry would be the best protection of all.

Stambovsky v. Ackley[9]

169 A.D.2d 254, 572 N.Y.S.2d 672 (1991)

RUBIN, Justice.

Plaintiff, to his horror, discovered that the house he had recently contracted to purchase was widely reputed to be possessed by poltergeists, reportedly seen by

---

9. Note that this case was litigated in 1991 not 1691. — Eds.

defendant seller and members of her family on numerous occasions over the last nine years. Plaintiff promptly commenced this action seeking rescission of the contract of sale. Supreme Court reluctantly dismissed the complaint, holding that plaintiff has no remedy at law in this jurisdiction.

The unusual facts of this case, as disclosed by the record, clearly warrant a grant of equitable relief to the buyer who, as a resident of New York City, cannot be expected to have any familiarity with the folklore of the Village of Nyack. Not being a "local," plaintiff could not readily learn that the home he had contracted to purchase is haunted. Whether the source of the spectral apparitions seen by defendant seller are parapsychic or psychogenic, having reported their presence in both a national publication ("Readers' Digest") and the local press (in 1977 and 1982, respectively), defendant is estopped to deny their existence and, as a matter of law, the house is haunted. More to the point, however, no divination is required to conclude that it is defendant's promotional efforts in publicizing her close encounters with these spirits which fostered the home's reputation in the community. In 1989, the house was included in a five-home walking tour of Nyack and described in a November 27th newspaper article as "a riverfront Victorian (with ghost)." The impact of the reputation thus created goes to the very essence of the bargain between the parties, greatly impairing both the value of the property and its potential for resale. The extent of this impairment may be presumed for the purpose of reviewing the disposition of this motion to dismiss the cause of action for rescission (Harris v. City of New York, 147 A.D.2d 186, 188-189, 542 N.Y. S.2d 550) and represents merely an issue of fact for resolution at trial.

While I agree with Supreme Court that the real estate broker, as agent for the seller, is under no duty to disclose to a potential buyer the phantasmal reputation of the premises and that, in his pursuit of a legal remedy for fraudulent misrepresentation against the seller, plaintiff hasn't a ghost of a chance, I am nevertheless moved by the spirit of equity to allow the buyer to seek rescission of the contract of sale and recovery of his downpayment. New York law fails to recognize any remedy for damages incurred as a result of the seller's mere silence, applying instead the strict rule of caveat emptor. Therefore, the theoretical basis for granting relief, even under the extraordinary facts of this case, is elusive if not ephemeral.

"Pity me not but lend thy serious hearing to what I shall unfold" (William Shakespeare, Hamlet, Act I, Scene V [Ghost]).

From the perspective of a person in the position of plaintiff herein, a very practical problem arises with respect to the discovery of a paranormal phenomenon: "Who you gonna call?" as the title song to the movie "Ghostbusters" asks. Applying the strict rule of caveat emptor to a contract involving a house possessed by poltergeists conjures up visions of a psychic or medium routinely accompanying the structural engineer and Terminix man on an inspection of every home subject to a contract of sale. It portends that the prudent attorney will establish an escrow account lest the subject of the transaction come back to haunt him and his client—or pray that his malpractice insurance coverage extends to supernatural disasters. In the interest of avoiding such untenable consequences, the notion that a haunting is a condition which can and should be ascertained upon reasonable inspection of the premises is a hobgoblin which should be exorcised from the body of legal precedent and laid quietly to rest.

It has been suggested by a leading authority that the ancient rule which holds that mere non-disclosure does not constitute actionable misrepresentation "finds proper application in cases where the fact undisclosed is patent, or the plaintiff has equal opportunities for obtaining information which he may be expected to utilize, or the defendant has no reason to think that he is acting under any misapprehension" (Prosser, Law of Torts § 106, at 696 [4th ed., 1971]). However, with respect to transactions in real estate, New York adheres to the doctrine of caveat emptor and imposes no duty upon the vendor to disclose any information concerning the premises (London v. Courduff, 141 A.D.2d 803, 529 N.Y.S.2d 874) unless there is a confidential or fiduciary relationship between the parties (Moser v. Spizzirro, 31 A.D.2d 537, 295 N.Y.S.2d 188, *aff'd.*, 25 N.Y.2d 941, 305 N.Y.S.2d 153, 252 N.E.2d 632; IBM Credit Fin. Corp. v. Mazda Motor Mfg. (USA) Corp., 152 A.D.2d 451, 542 N.Y.S.2d 649) or some conduct on the part of the seller which constitutes "active concealment" (see, 17 East 80th Realty Corp. v. 68th Associates, — A.D.2d —, 569 N.Y.S.2d 647 [dummy ventilation system constructed by seller]; Haberman v. Greenspan, 82 Misc. 2d 263, 368 N.Y.S.2d 717 [foundation cracks covered by seller]). Normally, some affirmative misrepresentation (e.g., Tahini Invs., Ltd. v. Bobrowsky, 99 A.D.2d 489, 470 N.Y.S.2d 431 [industrial waste on land allegedly used only as farm]); Jansen v. Kelly, 11 A.D.2d 587, 200 N.Y.S.2d 561 [land containing valuable minerals allegedly acquired for use as campsite] or partial disclosure (Junius Constr. Corp. v. Cohen, 257 N.Y. 393, 178 N.E. 672 [existence of third unopened street concealed]; Noved Realty Corp. v. A.A.P. Co., 250 App. Div. 1, 293 N.Y.S. 336 [escrow agreements securing lien concealed]) is required to impose upon the seller a duty to communicate undisclosed conditions affecting the premises (contra, Young v. Keith, 112 A.D.2d 625, 492 N.Y.S.2d 489 [defective water and sewer systems concealed]).

Caveat emptor is not so all-encompassing a doctrine of common law as to render every act of non-disclosure immune from redress, whether legal or equitable. "In regard to the necessity of giving information which has not been asked, the rule differs somewhat at law and in equity, and while the law courts would permit no recovery of *damages* against a vendor, because of mere concealment of facts *under certain circumstances,* yet if the vendee refused to complete the contract because of the concealment of a material fact on the part of the other, equity would refuse to compel him so to do, because equity only compels the specific performance of a contract which is fair and open, and in regard to which all material matters known to each have been communicated to the other" (Rothmiller v. Stein, 143 N.Y. 581, 591-592, 38 N.E. 718 [emphasis added]). Even as a principle of law, long before exceptions were embodied in statute law (see, e.g., UCC 2-312, 313, 314, 315; 3-417 [2][e]), the doctrine was held inapplicable to contagion among animals, adulteration of food, and insolvency of a maker of a promissory note and of a tenant substituted for another under a lease (see, Rothmiller v. Stein, supra, at 592-593, 38 N.E. 718 and cases cited therein). Common law is not moribund. *Ex facto jus oritur* (law arises out of facts). Where fairness and common sense dictate that an exception should be created, the evolution of the law should not be stifled by rigid application of a legal maxim.

The doctrine of caveat emptor requires that a buyer act prudently to assess the fitness and value of his purchase and operates to bar the purchaser who fails to exercise due care from seeking the equitable remedy of rescission (see, e.g., Rodas v. Manitaras, 159 A.D.2d 341, 552 N.Y.S.2d 618). For the purposes of the instant motion to dismiss the action pursuant to CPLR 3211(a)(7), plaintiff is entitled to every favorable inference which may reasonably be drawn from the pleadings

(Arrington v. New York Times Co., 55 N.Y.2d 433, 442, 449 N.Y.S.2d 941, 434 N.E.2d 1319; Rovello v. Orofino Realty Co., 40 N.Y.2d 633, 634, 389 N.Y.S.2d 314, 357 N.E.2d 970), specifically, in this instance, that he met his obligation to conduct an inspection of the premises and a search of available public records with respect to title. It should be apparent, however, that the most meticulous inspection and the search would not reveal the presence of poltergeists at the premises or unearth the property's ghoulish reputation in the community. Therefore, there is no sound policy reason to deny plaintiff relief for failing to discover a state of affairs which the most prudent purchaser would not be expected to even contemplate (see, Da Silva v. Musso, 53 N.Y.2d 543, 551, 444 N.Y.S.2d 50, 428 N.E.2d 382).

No. it is not apparent.

The case law in this jurisdiction dealing with the duty of a vendor of real property to disclose information to the buyer is distinguishable from the matter under review. The most salient distinction is that existing cases invariably deal with the physical condition of the premises (e.g., London v. Courduff, supra [use as a landfill]; Perin v. Mardine Realty Co., 5 A.D.2d 685, 168 N.Y.S.2d 647 *aff'd.* 6 N.Y.2d 920, 190 N.Y.S.2d 995, 161 N.E.2d 210 [sewer line crossing adjoining property without owner's consent]), defects in title (e.g., Sands v. Kissane, 282 App. Div. 140, 121 N.Y.S.2d 634 [remainderman]), liens against the property (e.g., Noved Realty Corp. v. A.A.P. Co., supra), expenses or income (e.g., Rodas v. Manitaras, supra [gross receipts]) and other factors affecting its operation. No case has been brought to this court's attention in which the property value was impaired as a result of the reputation created by information disseminated to the public by the seller (or, for that matter, as a result of possession by poltergeists).

Where a condition which has been created by the seller materially impairs the value of the contract and is peculiarly within the knowledge of the seller or unlikely to be discovered by a prudent purchaser exercising due care with respect to the subject transaction, nondisclosure constitutes a basis for rescission as a matter of equity. Any other outcome places upon the buyer not merely the obligation to exercise care in his purchase but rather to be omniscient with respect to any fact which may affect the bargain. No practical purpose is served by imposing such a burden upon a purchaser. To the contrary, it encourages predatory business practice and offends the principle that equity will suffer no wrong to be without a remedy.

Defendant's contention that the contract of sale, particularly the merger or "as is" clause, bars recovery of the buyer's deposit is unavailing. Even an express disclaimer will not be given effect where the facts are peculiarly within the knowledge of the party invoking it (Danann Realty Corp. v. Harris, 5 N.Y.2d 317, 322, 184 N.Y.S.2d 599, 157 N.E.2d 597; Tahini Invs., Ltd. v. Bobrowsky, supra). Moreover, a fair reading of the merger clause reveals that it expressly disclaims only representations made with respect to the physical condition of the premises and merely makes general reference to representations concerning "any other matter or things affecting or relating to the aforesaid premises." As broad as this language may be, a reasonable interpretation is that its effect is limited to tangible or physical matters and does not extend to paranormal phenomena. Finally, if the language of the contract is to be construed as broadly as defendant urges to encompass the presence of poltergeists in the house, it cannot be said that she has delivered the premises "vacant" in accordance with her obligation under the provisions of the contract rider.

To the extent New York law may be said to require something more than "mere concealment" to apply even the equitable remedy of rescission, the case of Junius Construction Corporation v. Cohen, 257 N.Y. 393, 178 N.E. 672, supra, while not precisely on point, provides some guidance. In that case, the seller disclosed that an official map indicated two as yet unopened streets which were planned for construction at the edges of the parcel. What was not disclosed was that the same map indicated a third street which, if opened, would divide the plot in half. The court held that, while the seller was under no duty to mention the planned streets at all, having undertaken to disclose two of them, he was obliged to reveal the third (see also, Rosenschein v. McNally, 17 A.D.2d 834, 233 N.Y.S.2d 254).

In the case at bar, defendant seller deliberately fostered the public belief that her home was possessed. Having undertaken to inform the public at large, to whom she has no legal relationship, about the supernatural occurrences on her property, she may be said to owe no less a duty to her contract vendee. It has been remarked that the occasional modern cases which permit a seller to take unfair advantage of a buyer's ignorance so long as he is not actively misled are "singularly unappetizing" (Prosser, Law of Torts § 106, at 696 [4th ed. 1971]). Where, as here, the seller not only takes unfair advantage of the buyer's ignorance but has created and perpetuated a condition about which he is unlikely to even inquire, enforcement of the contract (in whole or in part) is offensive to the court's sense of equity. Application of the remedy of rescission, within the bounds of the narrow exception to the doctrine of caveat emptor set forth herein, is entirely appropriate to relieve the unwitting purchaser from the consequences of a most unnatural bargain.

Accordingly, the judgment of the Supreme Court, New York County (Edward H. Lehner, J.), entered April 9, 1990, which dismissed the complaint pursuant to CPLR 3211(a)(7), should be modified, on the law and the facts and in the exercise of discretion, and the first cause of action seeking rescission of the contract reinstated, without costs.

Judgment, Supreme Court, New York County (Edward H. Lehner, J.), entered on April 9, 1990, modified, on the law and the facts and in the exercise of discretion, and the first cause of action seeking rescission of the contract reinstated, without costs.

All concur except Milonas, J.P. and Smith, J., who dissent in an opinion by Smith, J.

SMITH, Justice (dissenting).

I would affirm the dismissal of the complaint by the motion court.

Plaintiff seeks to rescind his contract to purchase defendant Ackley's residential property and recover his down payment. Plaintiff alleges that Ackley and her real estate broker, defendant Ellis Realty, made material misrepresentations of the property in that they failed to disclose that Ackley believed that the house was haunted by poltergeists. Moreover, Ackley shared this belief with her community and the general public through articles published in Readers' Digest (1977) and the local newspaper (1982). In November 1989, approximately two months after the parties entered into the contract of sale but subsequent to the scheduled October 2, 1989, closing, the house was included in a five-house walking tour and again described in the local newspaper as being haunted.

Prior to closing, plaintiff learned of this reputation and unsuccessfully sought to rescind the $650,000 contract of sale and obtain return of his $32,500 down payment without resort to litigation. The plaintiff then commenced this action for that relief and alleged that he would not have entered into the contract had he been so advised and that as a result of the alleged poltergeist activity, the market value and resaleability of the property was greatly diminished. Defendant Ackley has counter-claimed for specific performance.

"It is settled law in New York that the seller of real property is under no duty to speak when the parties deal at arm's length. The mere silence of the seller, without some act or conduct which deceived the purchaser, does not amount to a concealment that is actionable as a fraud (see Perin v. Mardine Realty Co., Inc., 5 A.D.2d 685, 168 N.Y.S.2d 647, *aff'd.*, 6 N.Y.2d 920, 190 N.Y.S.2d 995, 161 N.E.2d 210; Moser v. Spizzirro, 31 A.D.2d 537, 295 N.Y.S.2d 188, *aff'd.*, 25 N.Y.2d 941, 305 N.Y.S.2d 153, 252 N.E.2d 632). The buyer has the duty to satisfy himself as to the quality of his bargain pursuant to the doctrine of caveat emptor, which in New York State still applies to real estate transactions." London v. Courduff, 141 A.D.2d 803, 804, 529 N.Y.S.2d 874, *app. dism'd.*, 73 N.Y.2d 809, 537 N.Y.S.2d 494, 534 N.E.2d 332.

The parties herein were represented by counsel and dealt at arm's length. This is evidenced by the contract of sale which, inter alia, contained various riders and a specific provision that all prior understandings and agreements between the parties were merged into the contract, that the contract completely expressed their full agreement and that neither had relied upon any statement by anyone else not set forth in the contract. There is no allegation that defendants, by some specific act, other than the failure to speak, deceived the plaintiff. Nevertheless, a cause of action may be sufficiently stated where there is a confidential or fiduciary relationship creating a duty to disclose and there was a failure to disclose a material fact, calculated to induce a false belief. County of Westchester v. Welton Becket Assoc., 102 A.D.2d 34, 50-51, 478 N.Y.S.2d 305, *aff'd.*, 66 N.Y.2d 642, 495 N.Y.S.2d 364, 485 N.E.2d 1029. However, plaintiff herein has not alleged and there is no basis for concluding that a confidential or fiduciary relationship existed between these parties to an arm's length transaction such as to give rise to a duty to disclose. In addition, there is no allegation that defendants thwarted plaintiff's efforts to fulfill his responsibilities fixed by the doctrine of caveat emptor. See London v. Courduff, supra, 141 A.D.2d at 804, 529 N.Y.S.2d 874.

Finally, if the doctrine of caveat emptor is to be discarded, it should be for a reason more substantive than a poltergeist. The existence of a poltergeist is no more binding upon the defendants than it is upon this court.

Based upon the foregoing, the motion court properly dismissed the complaint.

NOTE AND QUESTIONS

In 1995, after the *Stambovsky* case was decided, the following statute pertaining to disclosures in real estate transactions was enacted in New York:

New York Real Property Law, (McKinney 2006)

§ 443-a. Disclosure obligations

1. Notwithstanding any other provision of law, it is not a material defect or fact relating to property offered for sale or lease, including residential property regardless of the number of units contained therein, that:

(a) an owner or occupant of the property is, or was at any time suspected to be, infected with human immunodeficiency virus or diagnosed with acquired immune deficiency syndrome or any other disease which has been determined by medical evidence to be highly unlikely to be transmitted through occupancy of a dwelling place; or

(b) the property is, or is suspected to have been, the site of a homicide, suicide or other death by accidental or natural causes, or any crime punishable as a felony.

2. (a) No cause of action shall arise against an owner or occupant of real property, or the agent of such owner or occupant, or the agent of a seller or buyer of real property, for failure to disclose in any real estate transaction a fact or suspicion contained in subdivision one of this section.

(b) Failure to disclose a fact contained in subdivision one of this section to a transferee shall not be grounds for a disciplinary action against a real estate agent or broker licensed pursuant to this article.

Why do you believe this statute was enacted, and how would it apply to a haunted house situation similar to that in the *Stambovsky* case? Why was the haunted house situation not expressly referred to in the statute?

Roberts, Disclosure Duties in Real Estate Sales and Attempts to Reallocate the Risks

34 Conn. L. Rev. 1 (2001)

II.   THE SELLER'S DUTY TO DISCLOSE DEFECTS

A.   *The Old Rule: Caveat Emptor*

The doctrine of caveat emptor, ("let the buyer beware"), has long governed sales of real property.[1] Under this doctrine, sellers of real property had no duty to apprise the buyer of defects in the condition of the property.

While even caveat emptor did not protect a seller who affirmatively misrepresented the condition of the property, the huge impact of this rule was that it allowed a seller to remain silent. As long as the seller did not lie, he had no duty to disclose defects in the property to a purchaser. . . .

The doctrine of caveat emptor found support in the nineteenth century concept of rugged individualism. A seller need not disclose all that she knew in a business transaction because, in a free market, the diligent should not be deprived of the fruits of superior skill and knowledge lawfully acquired. The law was not asked to stand in loco parentis to buyers in order to protect them in the business dealings with other business people. Thus, the maxim of caveat emptor was derived from the political philosophy of laissez-faire, which mandated that a "buyer deserved whatever he got if he relied on his own inspection of the merchandise and did not extract an express warranty from the seller." The courts were not sympathetic to a buyer who was not diligent. The law expected the buyer to protect himself and use his own observations to discern the condition of the property before sale. . . .

---

1. This doctrine originated in the sixteenth century and has also applied to the sale of goods. Walton H. Hamilton, *The Ancient Maxim of Caveat Emptor,* 40 YALE L.J. 1133, 1156-69 (1931). Although abandoned under the Uniform Commercial Code with respect to the sale of goods, the doctrine persisted regarding sales of real property. Leo Bearman, Jr., *Caveat Emptor in Sales of Realty — Recent Assaults Upon the Rule,* 13 VAND. L. REV. 541, 561 (1961).

The doctrine of caveat emptor was followed in the United States until the middle of the twentieth century. Within the last forty years, however, the law has taken a sharp turn. Courts and legislatures have imposed ever increasing duties on sellers to disclose to prospective buyers information about the property being sold.

B.   *The Common Law Duty to Disclose Defects*

1.   *Jurisdictions Imposing the Duty*

a.   General Parameters

Under the modern trend, a seller cannot keep silent and leave the buyer to her own devices to discover defects. Most jurisdictions impose on the seller a duty of disclosure in certain situations. Generally, the seller must disclose a defect that is known to him, not observable to the prospective buyer, and is "material" or materially affects the value of the property.

California exemplifies the broad duty on sellers to disclose defects. The general rule can be summarized:

> where the seller knows of facts materially affecting the value or desirability of the property . . . and also knows that such facts are not known to, or within the reach of the diligent attention and observations of the buyer, the seller is under a duty to disclose them to the buyer.[18]

A breach of this duty of disclosure gives the buyer a cause of action for both rescission and damages. . . .[19]

b.   Types of Defects Requiring Disclosure

The affirmative duty to disclose defects is quite broad. The majority of litigation has involved the failure to disclose defects concerning the physical condition of the property such as termite infestations, foundation problems, and a myriad of other conditions. Other cases deal with the failure to disclose defects regarding subjective

---

18. *Id.* (quoting Lingsch v. Savage, 29 Cal. Rptr. 201, 204 (Ct. App. 1963)). A similar rule exists even in those states that allow the duty to disclose to be waived. For example, in Ohio, a seller may be liable for nondisclosure of a latent defect where the seller is under a duty to disclose facts and fails to do so. Miles v. McSwegin, 388 N.E.2d 1367, 1370 (Ohio 1979) (reasoning that nondisclosure, coupled with the hidden nature of termite infestation, entitled appellees to rely upon appellant's prior representation with regard to the overall soundness of the property); Brewer v. Brothers, 611 N.E.2d 492, 494 (Ohio Ct. App. 1992) (stating that nondisclosure will become the equivalent of fraudulent concealment when it becomes the duty of a person to speak so that the party with whom he is dealing may be placed on equal footing with him).

19. *Shapiro*, 76 Cal. Rptr. 2d at 107 (citing Karoutas v. HomeFed Bank, 283 Cal. Rptr. 809, 811 (Ct. App. 1991)). When jurisdictions enact a general duty for sellers' disclosure, they are attempting to comport with the general expectations of buyers. Buyers expect property to be in good condition unless it is obvious that it is not. The duty to disclose implies a representation on the part of the seller that the property is as good as it looks. Having, in effect, made these statements concerning the property, a seller is then under a duty to correct or reveal any inconsistencies he knows about or suffer the consequences.

or psychological conditions of the property such as the fact that a gruesome crime was committed there.[39] . . .

c. Materiality

Courts impose limits on what defects the seller must disclose. Most courts use a standard of materiality. Encompassed in this standard is the acknowledgment that a seller need not disclose every minor defect in the property, even though this may be of interest to the buyer. . . . The materiality of a nondisclosure is not determined subjectively by measuring how it would have affected the buyer's personal decision to purchase.

Instead, courts will look at the effect upon the objective value of the property in the market. For example, California courts use three considerations in determining materiality, "the gravity of the harm inflicted by nondisclosure, the fairness of imposing a duty of discovery on the buyer as an alternative to compelling disclosure, and its impact on the stability of contracts if rescission is permitted."[50] Defects "are material if they would have a significant and measurable effect on market value."[51]

d. Knowledge of the Parties

The seller must actually know of a defect materially affecting the value of the property before a duty is imposed on her to disclose it to the buyer. The seller has no duty to affirmatively inspect her premises in search of problems yet unknown. In other words, the seller is not a guarantor of the condition of the property, but is only responsible for disclosing what is known to her. . . .

e. Legal Theory of Recovery: Fraud

Even though no affirmative misrepresentation has been made, the legal theory of fraud is used by the courts to impose liability on a seller who has remained silent

---

39. . . . In *Reed v. King*, 193 Cal. Rptr. 130 (Ct. App. 1983), a seller failed to disclose that the property being sold had been the site of a multiple murder. *Id.* at 130. The court of appeal held that the psychological impact of these murders on the property could materially affect the property's value. *Id.* at 133. If so, the seller, who was aware of the crime that had occurred some ten years earlier, was under a duty to disclose this information. Therefore, the court reversed the trial court's granting of a demurrer. *Id.* Because the buyer could not reasonably anticipate that such a murder had occurred on the property, the buyer was under no duty to inquire into such an occurrence. *Id.*

Following this decision and with the advent of widespread fear regarding the stigma of property whose previous owners had AIDS or HIV, some twenty-nine states passed so-called psychological impact property statutes. Ronald Benton Brown & Thomas H. Thurlow III, *Buyers Beware: Statutes Shield Real Estate Brokers and Sellers Who Do Not Disclose that Properties Are Psychologically Tainted*, 49 OKLA. L. REV. 625, 626-28 (1996). These statutes provide protection to sellers and brokers "involved with psychologically impacted property." *Id.* at 628. In general, these statutes both remove the duty to disclose enumerated psychologically impacting events which may have occurred on the property and take away any cause of action a buyer might have against a seller or broker regarding such stigmatization. *Id.* These statutes make these events "not a material fact," and they therefore need not be disclosed. *Id.*

50. *Reed*, 193 Cal. Rptr. at 132.

51. Shapiro v. Sutherland, 76 Cal. Rptr. 2d 101, 107 (Ct. App. 1998) (internal citation omitted). Florida courts use the same test focusing on the relationship between the undisclosed fact and the value of the property. *Billian*, 710 So. 2d at 987 (quoting Johnson v. David, 480 So. 2d 625, 629 (Fla. 1985)).

and failed to disclose a defect in the property.[61] The seller who has lived in the home is thought to have knowledge of the condition of the property superior to that of the buyer. A duty to disclose defects to the buyer arises from this superior knowledge. The seller's silence is, therefore, the equivalent of an affirmative representation or fraud, also known as "negative fraud."

2. *Jurisdictions Imposing No Common Law Duty to Disclose Defects*

Not all jurisdictions have imposed on the seller a duty to disclose defects. For example, New York still adhere to the doctrine of caveat emptor and imposes on a seller no duty to disclose latent defects to a buyer.[70]

Massachusetts is in accord. "Homeowners who sell their houses are not liable for bar nondisclosure in circumstances where no inquiry by a prospective buyer imposes a duty to speak."[71] There must be some affirmative act of concealment by the seller. Similarly, Indiana, Alabama, and Minnesota impose no duty to disclose. . . ."

C. *Statutory Disclosure Duties*

Many states have imposed a statutory duty on sellers to disclose defects in the property. Generally, the defects that require disclosure are those that are material and unobservable to the prospective buyer. As with the common law disclosure duty, there is no liability where the seller had no knowledge of the defect or based his belief on professional or public reports provided to him and used ordinary care in obtaining the information. The Pennsylvania statute requires that "[a] seller must disclose to a buyer all known material defects about [the] property being sold that are not readily observable."[80] Similarly, a Delaware statute provides "a seller transferring residential real property shall disclose, in writing, to the buyer . . . all material defects of that property that are known at the time the property is offered for sale or that are known prior to the time of final settlement."[81] New Jersey has a statute specifically dealing with disclosure of off-site conditions.[82]

61. *See* Schnell v. Gustafson, 638 P.2d 850, 852 (Colo. Ct. App. 1981). A seller of real estate has a duty to disclose to his purchaser a known latent defect and his "failure to disclose amounts to concealment, making him vulnerable to a suit based upon fraud." *Id.* (quoting Cohen v. Vivian, 349 P.2d 366, 367 (Colo. 1960)).

70. Stambovsky v. Ackley, 572 N.Y.S.2d 672, 675 (App. Div. 1991) ("New York law fails to recognize any remedy for damages incurred as a result of the seller's mere silence, applying instead the strict rules of caveat emptor."). However, in *Stambovsky*, the court carved out an exception and allowed the buyer to rescind the contract because the seller himself had created the defect. *Id.* at 676. . . . *See also* Couch v. Schmidt, 613 N.Y.S.2d 511, 512 (App. Div. 1994) (holding that a seller has no duty to speak in an arm's length transaction and mere silence is not actionable as fraud); London v. Courduff, 529 N.Y.S.2d 874, 875 (App. Div. 1988) (holding that allegations that vendor failed to disclose that a vacant lot has been used as a landfill were insufficient to uphold a cause of action for fraud).

71. Solomon v. Birger, 477 N.E.2d 137, 142 (Mass. App. Ct. 1985).

80. PA. STAT. ANN. tit. 68 § 1025 (West Supp. 2001).

81. DEL. CODE ANN. tit. 6, § 2572 (1999).

82. New Residential Construction of Off-Site Conditions Disclosure Act, N.J. STAT. ANN. § 46:3C-1 to -12 (West Supp. 2001). The duty to disclose is to inform the buyer that lists of certain off-site conditions are available in the Municipal Clerk's office. *Id.* § 46:3C-8.

Generally speaking, the disclosure statutes supplement, but do not supercede, the common law disclosure duties. For example, in California, the statutory disclosure statement does not relieve the seller of the common law duty of disclosure if the common law duty is beyond the matter specified in the statutory form.[83] Conversely, the specific disclosure requirements of the statute can go beyond the common law duty. Therefore, in California, the statutory and common law disclosure duties run concurrently, but they are not identical. It seems clear that the legislature has not simply rubber-stamped the common law.

Many states do not have statutory disclosure rules.[86]

D. *Consequences of Disclosure Duties*

The effect of the demise of the doctrine of caveat emptor has been substantial. Under caveat emptor, the burden was on the buyer to become informed about the condition of the property. That burden has now been shifted to the seller. The seller must provide to the buyer all relevant information in his possession that materially affects the value of the property. Although the burden has not been shifted if a defect is readily observable to the buyer, a litigation averse seller would probably not wish to rely on this exception. . . .

NOTES AND QUESTIONS

1. For additional discussion of the decline of caveat emptor see Pancak et al., Residential Disclosure Laws: The Further Demise of Caveat Emptor, 24 Real Est. L.J. 291 (1996); and Lefcoe Property Condition Disclosure Forms: How the Real Estate Industry Eased the Transition from Caveat Emptor to "Sellers Tell All," 35 Real Prop., Prob. & Tr. J. 193 (2004). See also Tomcho, Commercial Real Estate Buyer Beware: Sellers May Have the Right to Remain Silent, 70 S. Cal. L. Rev. 1571 (1997),

---

83. The specification in the disclosure form of particular matters to disclose is not intended to limit or abridge any common law obligation for disclosure which otherwise exists. CAL. CIV. CODE § 1102.8 (West Supp. 2001). . . .

86. The following jurisdictions have no statutory disclosure rules for sellers of real property: Alabama, Arizona, Arkansas, Colorado, Connecticut, Florida, Kansas, Louisiana, Massachusetts, Minnesota, Missouri, Montana, Nevada, New Jersey, New York, Pennsylvania, South Carolina, Utah, Vermont, Washington, D.C., West Virginia and Wyoming.

Georgia seems to impose a disclosure duty where there is a suppression of a material fact and the particular circumstances of the case give rise to an obligation to communicate. See GA. CODE ANN. § 23-2-53 (Harrison 1999).

Maine has an approach which applies only to brokers. The Real Estate Brokerage License Act was passed in Maine in order to regulate the activities of real estate brokers. See ME. REV. STAT. ANN. tit. 32, §§ 13061-13069. The regulation included the formation of the Maine Real Estate Commission, which passed rules pursuant to the Brokerage License Act. See id. § 13062. These rules created a duty to disclose and require a broker to disclose "all material defects pertaining to the physical condition of the property." Id. § 13273. A failure to disclose this type of information is then actionable as common law fraud. See id. These regulations only apply to land sales which utilize a broker and have no effect on sales by property owners. See id.

Several other states have followed Maine's model, including Kentucky and Mississippi. For more information, see Robert M. Washburn, *Residential Real Estate Condition Disclosure Legislation*, 44 DE PAUL L. REV. 381 (1995).

discussing the widespread retention of caveat emptor in commercial real property sales law. Is this retention justified and, if so, why?

2. As was considered in Chapter One of the casebook there also are disclosure obligations on real estate brokers in many states.

2. *Implied Warranty*

In the sale of (new homes) in most American states, the doctrine of caveat emptor has been largely replaced and buyers are protected by implied warranties of fitness and habitability. This is a relatively new doctrine in the United States for the sale of homes, first appearing in the late 1950s and steadily spreading ever since; its rate of adoption has been particularly rapid for a new real property concept that is largely the creation of judicial case law. Implied warranty doctrine as it relates to housing sales is still evolving and there is a question as to how far it will be extended — whether it will become widely applicable to used home purchases, for example — and what defenses to implied warranty claims will be available to builder-vendors.

Albrecht v. Clifford
767 N.E.2d 42 (Mass. 2002)

Present: Marshall, C.J., Greaney, Ireland, Spina, Cowin, Sosman, & Cordy, JJ.
Cordy, J.

In 1993, Peter L. Albrecht and Margaret Page Albrecht bought a newly constructed single-family home with nine fireplaces from Alfred G. Clifford, an architect and general contractor. Several years later, the Albrechts learned that there were defects in the fireplaces and chimneys in another house that Clifford had built in their neighborhood. Consequently, they retained an inspector who found similar defects in the Albrechts' home. The Albrechts filed a complaint in the Superior Court asserting claims against Clifford for breach of contract (Counts I and II), breach of an implied warranty that the residence was constructed in a good and workmanlike manner (Count III), fraud and deceit (Count IV), negligent misrepresentation (Count V), and violation of G.L. c. 93A (Count VI). A judge in the Superior Court allowed Clifford's motion for summary judgment on all the Albrechts' claims. They appealed. We transferred the appeal to this court on our own motion to consider whether an implied warranty arises out of a contract for the sale of a newly constructed residence by a builder-vendor. We conclude that there is such a warranty but affirm the entry of summary judgment for the defendant on statute of limitations grounds. We affirm the judge's summary judgment rulings on the Albrechts' contract claims on other grounds.

1. Background.

In March, 1992, Clifford began construction of a single-family home on property he owned in Newbury (residence). In September, 1993, the Albrechts decided to buy the residence, and with the assistance of experienced and capable counsel, negotiated the terms of the sale with Clifford, including certain express warranties. On September 16,

1993, the Albrechts and Clifford executed a standard form purchase and sale agreement (agreement). Exhibit A to the agreement set forth the express warranties that Clifford and the Albrechts agreed would survive the delivery of the deed for one year, including: "all systems, e.g., plumbing, electrical, heating, fireplaces and chimneys etc., will work properly"; "the entire premises is built according to municipal and state regulations, including building, zoning, health, safety, electrical and plumbing codes"; and "the premises have been constructed in a good and workmanlike manner." However, this express warranty provision required the Albrechts to give Clifford written notice of any defects within one year of the delivery of the deed. On October 26, 1993, the Albrechts bought the residence from Clifford for $595,000. They moved in on December 23 1993, but never used any of the fireplaces.

In December, 1996, the Albrechts were told by a neighbor that the fireplaces and chimneys in their home, also built by Clifford, were defective. The Albrechts hired a mason whose inspection of the home led him to conclude that the Albrechts' fireplaces and chimneys were also defective. The Albrechts sent two letters to Clifford asking him to repair the defects, but Clifford and the Albrechts were unable to agree on a solution. On February 6, 1998, the Albrechts filed this lawsuit. During the litigation that ensued, the Albrechts retained an expert who concluded that the chimneys, fireboxes, dampers, flues, and smoke chambers were "not constructed in a good and workmanlike manner" and did not comply with the State building code.[5]

2. IMPLIED WARRANTY OF HABITABILITY.

In 1964, the Supreme Court of Colorado was the first court in the country to abandon the doctrine of caveat emptor and hold that a builder-vendor of a completed residential home impliedly warrants that it complies with applicable building code requirements, is built in a workmanlike manner, and is suitable for habitation. *Carpenter v. Donohoe,* 154 Colo. 78, 83–84, 388 P.2d 399 (1964). Since the decision in *Carpenter,* the majority of jurisdictions have similarly abandoned the doctrine of caveat emptor,[6] and adopted implied warranties of habitability or good workmanlike quality in the sale of newly constructed houses.[7] Although we have abandoned

---

5. The judge noted that "[Clifford and the realtor] are not in agreement that all of the chimney and fireplace defects claimed exist or even that they are all 'defects.'"

6. "Caveat emptor, which traditionally has applied to sales of real estate, developed at a time when a buyer and seller were in equal bargaining positions. They were of comparable skill and knowledge and each could protect himself in a transaction." *Chandler v. Madsen,* 197 Mont. 234, 238, 642 P.2d 1028 (1982). However, "[i]n the sale of new residential dwellings, the doctrine of caveat emptor has properly been eroded by the winds of contemporary realities." *Atherton Condo. Apartment–Owners Ass'n Bd. of Directors v. Blume Dev. Co.,* 115 Wash.2d 506, 517, 799 P.2d 250 (1990). See *David v. B & J Holding Corp.,* 349 So.2d 676, 678 (Fla.Dist.Ct.App. 1977), quoting *Gable v. Silver,* 258 So.2d 11, 17 (Fla.Dist.Ct. App.1972) (abandoning doctrine "brings the law much closer to the realities of the market for new homes than does the anachronistic maxim of caveat emptor"); *Hines v. Thornton,* 913 S.W.2d 373, 375 (Mo.Ct.App.1996), quoting *Smith v. Old Warson Dev. Co.,* 479 S.W.2d 795, 801 (Mo. 1972) ("The caveat emptor rule as applied to new houses is an anachronism patently out of harmony with modern home buying practices").

7. The expansion of implied warranties has resulted in a blurring of the "[t]he distinction, if any, between an implied warranty of habitability and an implied warranty of good quality and workmanship . . . in decisional law throughout the country." *Council of Unit Owners of Breakwater House Condominium v. Simpler,* 603 A.2d 792, 795 (Del.1992). A number of courts use both "habitability" and "good workmanlike quality" to describe the scope of the implied warranty. See *Roper v. Spring Lake Dev. Co.,* 789 P.2d 483, 485 (Colo.Ct.App.1990) (contractual responsibilities of builder of new house include buyer's right to home that is built in "workmanlike manner and one that is suitable for habitation"); *Elden v. Simmons,* 631 P.2d 739, 741 (Okla. 1981) ("the builder-vendor of a new home impliedly warrants that the

the doctrine of caveat emptor in the context of residential leases and held that such leases carry with them an implied warranty of habitability,[8] until today, we have not adopted such a warranty in the sale of new homes.

There are a number of important policy considerations that have led other jurisdictions to adopt the type of implied warranty urged on us in this case. An implied warranty assures that consumers receive that for which they have bargained, an objectively habitable home, see *Miller v. Cannon Hill Estates, Ltd.*, 2 K.B. 113, 120–121, 1931 WL 26626 (1931); it protects purchasers from structural defects that are nearly impossible to ascertain by inspection after the home is built, see *Christensen v. R.D. Sell Constr. Co.*, 774 S.W.2d 535, 538 (Mo.Ct.App.1989); and it imposes the burden of repairing latent defects on the person who has the opportunity to notice, avoid, or correct them during the construction process, see *Duncan v. Schuster–Graham Homes, Inc.*, 194 Colo. 441, 444, 578 P.2d 637 (1978). See also *Hines v. Thornton*, 913 S.W.2d 373, 375 (Mo.Ct.App.1996) ("The cause of action is directed to structural defects that a builder-vendor has the opportunity to observe but fails to correct; defects that, through the construction process, become latent and not subject to discovery by inspection").

These sound policy reasons lead us to adopt an implied warranty of habitability that attaches to the sale of new homes by builder-vendors in the Commonwealth.[9] The adoption of such a warranty is also consistent with the protections that our law affords consumers in other contexts. See *Boston Hous. Auth. v. Hemingway*, 363 Mass. 184, 293 N.E.2d 831 (1973) (implied warranty of habitability in residential leases); *George v. Goldman*, 333 Mass. 496, 131 N.E.2d 772 (1956) (implied warranty in construction contracts to do workmanlike job and use reasonable skill). See also G.L. c. 106, § 2–314 (implied warranty of merchantability for goods). Its purpose is to protect a purchaser of a new home from latent defects that create substantial questions of safety and habitability. While the scope of this warranty must be left largely to case-by-case determination, a home that is unsafe because it deviates from fundamental aspects of the applicable building codes, or is structurally unsound, or

---

new home is or will be completed in a workmanlike manner and is or will be reasonably fit for occupancy as a place of abode"); *Elderkin v. Gaster*, 447 Pa. 118, 128, 288 A.2d 771 (1972) ("builder-vendor impliedly warrants that the home he has built and is selling is constructed in a reasonably workmanlike manner and that it is fit for the purpose intended — habitation").

Other courts have limited the warranty to one of "habitability." Some of those courts define "habitability" as substantial compliance with all building and housing codes. *Carpenter v. Donohoe*, 154 Colo. 78, 83–84, 388 P.2d 399 (1964). Others define it in more general terms. See *Goggin v. Fox Valley Constr. Corp.*, 48 Ill.App.3d 103, 106, 8 Ill.Dec. 271, 365 N.E.2d 509 (1977) (new home must keep out elements and provide inhabitants with reasonably safe place to live, without fear of injury to person, health, safety, or property); *Aronsohn v. Mandara*, 98 N.J. 92, 104, 484 A.2d 675 (1984) (habitability "synonymous with suitability for living purposes; the home must be occupiable").

Courts have defined "good workmanlike quality" as "the quality of work that would be done by a worker of average skill and intelligence." *Nastri v. Wood Bros. Homes*, 142 Ariz. 439, 444, 690 P.2d 158 (Ct.App.1984). In *Dixon v. Mountain City Constr. Co.*, 632 S.W.2d 538, 541 (Tenn.1982), the court recognized an implied warranty that "the workmanship and materials used by the builder-vendor in the construction of a dwelling will meet the standard of the trade for homes in comparable locations and price range."

8. In *Boston Hous. Auth. v. Hemingway*, 363 Mass. 184, 293 N.E.2d 831 (1973), we held that "in a rental of any premises for dwelling purposes, under a written or oral lease, for a specified time or at will, there is an implied warranty that the premises are fit for human occupation." *Id.* at 199, 293 N.E.2d 831. The landlord impliedly warrants that there are no "latent [or patent] defects in facilities vital to the use of the premises for residential purposes and that these essential facilities will remain during the entire term in a condition which makes the property livable." *Id.*, quoting *Kline v. Burns*, 111 N.H. 87, 92, 276 A.2d 248 (1971).

9. We are not called on here to decide whether a second or subsequent purchaser may state a claim for breach of this implied warranty against the builder within the applicable statute of limitations.

fails to keep out the elements because of defects of construction, would breach the implied warranty we adopt today.

This implied warranty is independent and collateral to the covenant to convey, and survives the passing of title to and taking possession of the real estate. It cannot be waived or disclaimed, because to permit the disclaimer of a warranty protecting a purchaser from the consequences of latent defects would defeat the very purpose of the warranty.[10]

This implied warranty does not make the builder an insurer against any and all defects in a home, impose on the builder an obligation to deliver a perfect house, or protect against mere defects in workmanship, minor or procedural violations of the applicable building codes, or defects that are trivial or aesthetic. Its adoption is not intended to affect a buyer's ability to inspect a house before purchase, to condition the purchase on a satisfactory inspection result, or to negotiate additional express warranties.

To establish a breach of the implied warranty of habitability a plaintiff will have to demonstrate that (1) he purchased a new house from the defendant-builder-vendor; (2) the house contained a latent defect; (3) the defect manifested itself only after its purchase; (4) the defect was caused by the builder's improper design, material, or workmanship; and (5) the defect created a substantial question of safety or made the house unfit for human habitation. In addition, the claim must be brought within the three-year statute of limitations and the six-year statute of repose set forth in G.L. c. 260, § 2B.[11]

The motion judge concluded that the Albrechts' claim for relief under a theory of implied warranty failed because no such cause of action had been recognized in Massachusetts. Having recognized such a warranty, we now apply the principles just announced to the record on summary judgment.

The Albrechts are purchasers of a newly constructed home from a builder-vendor, and the defects about which they complain were discovered after they purchased the residence. In addition, based on their expert's affidavit, the Albrechts have adequately demonstrated, for purposes of summary judgment,[12]

---

10. The implied warranty that we establish here does not apply to the purchase or sale of unfinished homes, where the parties may choose to waive or disclaim all warranties.

11. General Laws c. 260, § 2B, provides: "Action of tort for damages arising out of any deficiency or neglect in the design, planning, construction or general administration of an improvement to real property . . . shall be commenced only within three years next after the cause of action accrues; provided, however, that in no event shall such actions be commenced more than six years after the earlier of the dates of (1) the opening of the improvement to use; or (2) substantial completion of the improvement and the taking of possession for occupancy by the owner." This statute is appropriately applied to an implied warranty of habitability because such a warranty is an obligation imposed by law and is "imposed apart from and independent of promises made and therefore apart from any manifested intention of parties to a contract." W.L. Prosser & W.P. Keeton, Torts § 92, at 656 (5th ed. 1984). Compare *Anthony's Pier Four, Inc. v. Crandall Dry Dock Eng'rs, Inc.*, 396 Mass. 818, 822, 489 N.E.2d 172 (1986) ("Because the standard of performance is set by the defendant['s] promises, rather than imposed by law, an express warranty claim is and generally has been understood to be an action of contract, rather than of tort"), with *Klein v. Catalano*, 386 Mass. 701, 720, 437 N.E.2d 514 (1982) (G.L. c. 260, § 2B, applies to implied warranty by architect to exercise required standard of care because to hold otherwise would frustrate legislative purpose of "limit[ing] the liability of architects, engineers, contractors, or others involved in the design, planning, construction, or general administration of an improvement to real property").

12. The standard of review of a ruling on a motion for summary judgment is "whether, viewing the evidence in the light most favorable to the nonmoving party, all material facts have been established and the moving party is entitled to a judgment as a matter of law." *Miller v. Mooney*, 431 Mass. 57, 60, 725 N.E.2d 545 (2000). "For a grant of summary judgment to be upheld, the moving party must establish that

that there are genuine issues of disputed fact about whether the defects were caused by the builder's improper design and workmanship, and whether they created a substantial question of safety.[13]

Whether the Albrechts can adequately demonstrate that the defects were "latent" is more questionable. Latent defects are conditions that are hidden or concealed, and are not discoverable by reasonable and customary observation or inspection. Black's Law Dictionary 429, 887 (7th ed. 1999). The defects in this case, however, were in some measure readily observable. In concluding that the fireplaces and chimneys were defective, the Albrechts' expert did not have to dismantle them or any other part of the residence. He merely made observations and measurements of the materials and components (e.g., hearths, fireplace boxes, dampers, flues, smoke chambers) that were readily accessible.[14] Admittedly, some of the observations (e.g., smoke chambers, flues, and chimney interiors) were more difficult than others (hearths, fireplace boxes, and dampers), and were made with the assistance of video equipment. Whether the discovery and correction of the obvious defects would have led to the discovery of those which were more difficult to observe is a close question on summary judgment, but is one that we need not resolve. We conclude, as the motion judge did, that even assuming a cause of action for the violation of an implied warranty, the Albrechts were barred from pursuing this claim because of their failure to raise it within the three-year statute of limitations.

3. STATUTE OF LIMITATIONS.

The Albrechts bought the residence on October 26, 1993, moved in on December 23, 1993, and filed their complaint on February 6, 1998, more than four years later. The motion judge concluded that, absent tolling of the applicable statutes of limitations, the claims for fraud and deceit (Count IV), negligent misrepresentation (Count V), and G.L. c. 93A (Count VI) were time barred.[15] He also concluded that the statutes were not tolled in the circumstances of this case. We agree.

To defeat Clifford's motion for summary judgment, the Albrechts sought to invoke the discovery rule. "The rule, which operates to toll a limitations period until a prospective plaintiff learns or should have learned that he has been injured, may arise in three circumstances: where a misrepresentation concerns a fact that was 'inherently unknowable' to the injured party, where a wrongdoer breached some duty of disclosure, or where a wrongdoer concealed the existence of a cause of action through some affirmative act done with the intent to deceive." *Patsos v. First Albany Corp.*, 433 Mass. 323, 328, 741 N.E.2d 841 (2001), citing *Protective Life Ins. Co. v. Sullivan*, 425 Mass. 615, 631–632, 682 N.E.2d 624 (1997).

---

there are no genuine issues of material fact, and that the nonmoving party has no reasonable expectation of proving an essential element of its case." *Id.*

13. Based on observations and measurements of the nine fireplaces and two chimneys, the expert rendered his opinion that "the numerous defects and code deviations are significant and potentially hazardous."

14. The expert concluded, among other things, that the combined depths of the fireboxes and hearths were too small, the dampers were too small, the flue liners were too small, and the walls around these components were not thick enough, all in violation of the State building code.

15. The judge applied the three-year statute of limitations in G.L. c. 260, §§ 2A, 2B, to Counts IV and V and the four-year statute of limitations in G.L. c. 260, § 5A, to Count VI.

We treat as a single argument the Albrechts' contention on appeal that there was no reason that they "knew or should have known" about the alleged defects, and the motion judge's conclusion that the alleged defects were not "inherently unknowable." See *Williams v. Ely*, 423 Mass. 467, 473 n. 7, 668 N.E.2d 799 (1996), and cases cited ("inherently unknowable" standard is no different from and is used interchangeably with the "knew or should have known" standard). "[T]o the extent that any misrepresentation concerns a fact which was 'inherently unknowable' by the plaintiffs at the time it was made and at the time of the sale . . . a cause of action for deceit in the sale of real estate accrues when a buyer learns of the misrepresentation or when the buyer reasonably should have learned of the misrepresentation." *Friedman v. Jablonski*, 371 Mass. 482, 485–486, 358 N.E.2d 994 (1976). "Inherent unknowability is not a fact, but rather a conclusion to be drawn from the facts." *Melrose Hous. Auth. v. New Hampshire Ins. Co.*, 402 Mass. 27, 31–32 n. 4, 520 N.E.2d 493 (1988) (question of inherent unknowability is properly for court to answer in case tried to master and without jury). Plaintiffs who assert that their cases should not be barred by the statute of limitations have the burden of demonstrating that they did not know of the defect within the statute of limitations and that "in the exercise of reasonable diligence, they should not have known." *Friedman v. Jablonski, supra* at 487, 358 N.E.2d 994.

The Albrechts claim that the purported defects were inherently unknowable and that they did not have any reason to suspect that there was a problem until December, 1996, when neighbors told them about their own problems with their fireplaces and chimneys. The motion judge concluded from the undisputed facts that the Albrechts' claims were not "inherently unknowable":

> "[T]he defects alleged were readily seen on an inspection conducted sometime after December of 1996. Such an inspection equally as well could have been conducted in 1993 when the Albrechts moved in. Similarly, the mere use of at least some of the nine fireplaces should have signalled a problem, if there was one. And perhaps most obviously, charges that the hearths were the wrong size or the fireboxes not deep enough presented situations that were in plain sight and discoverable by simple measurements."

Whether the defects were inherently unknowable or not, we conclude that on the record of undisputed facts, the Albrechts cannot meet their burden of demonstrating that "in the exercise of reasonable diligence, they should not have known" of them. *Friedman v. Jablonski, supra*. It was not reasonable as a matter of law for the Albrechts neither to inspect[16] nor to use the fireplaces when they knew the express warranty on the fireplaces and chimneys, which they had negotiated, lasted only one year. This conclusion is also implicit in the judge's conclusion that the defects were not "inherently unknowable" in the circumstances of this case. The statutes of limitations were therefore not tolled and the Albrechts' claims for fraud and deceit, negligent misrepresentation, and violation of G.L. c. 93A were filed after the applicable statutes of limitations had expired. For the same reason, the three-year

---

16. The Albrechts contracted for a prepurchase inspection of the residence that was limited to "readily accessible areas of the building" and "to visual observations only." The inspection report specifically stated that: "The report is not a compliance inspection or certification for past or present governmental codes or regulations of any kind." The inspection did not require the inspector to ignite a solid fuel fire or observe the interior of the fireplaces or flues.

statute of limitations provided in G.L. c. 260, § 2B, expired on the claim for breach of the implied warranty of habitability announced in today's decision.

4. BREACH OF CONTRACT CLAIMS (COUNTS I & II).

The Albrechts allege in Count I of their complaint that Clifford breached the terms of the purchase and sale agreement because "the Residence delivered to the Albrechts at or about the time of delivery of the deed was not completed in accordance with the requirements of the contract and is in violation of certain building laws." In Count II of their complaint, the Albrechts allege that Clifford breached the terms of the express warranty contained in Exhibit A to the purchase and sale agreement by failing "to complete the construction of the Residence in a good and workmanlike manner and in accordance with all applicable Massachusetts building laws and regulations." The judge entered summary judgment on Count I because it was based on a paragraph of the purchase and sale agreement (paragraph 9), that did not survive the Albrechts' acceptance of the deed but merged with it. The judge dismissed Count II as barred by the parties' own limitation period as set forth in the warranty itself. We agree with both of these conclusions.

Acceptance of a deed ordinarily merges all obligations in the purchase and sale agreement, except for those specified in the deed itself. *McMahon v. M & D Bldrs., Inc.,* 360 Mass. 54, 59, 271 N.E.2d 649 (1971). Consistent with this rule of merger, the agreement in this case expressly states that: "The acceptance of a deed by the BUYER . . . shall be deemed to be a full performance and discharge of every agreement and obligation herein contained or expressed, except such as are, by the terms hereof, to be performed after the delivery of said deed."

There is an exception to this general rule when a home builder agrees to undertake an obligation, such as constructing or repairing a building on the property, that is in addition or collateral to the conveyance of the deed. See *McMahon v. M & D Bldrs., Inc., supra* at 60, 271 N.E.2d 649 ("the plaintiffs' acceptance of the deed operated as a merger or waiver only to the extent of precluding any claim that the title which the defendant conveyed did not satisfy the requirements of the agreement").[17]

The Albrechts contend that paragraph 9 of the agreement created an obligation that was collateral to the conveyance of the deed and, as such, constituted a contractual warranty that the residence would comply with the applicable building codes. This contention is incorrect. Paragraph 9 of the agreement states that:

> "Full possession of [the residence] . . . is to be delivered at the time of the delivery of the deed, said premises to be then (a) fully completed in accordance with the requirements hereof, and (b) not in violation of any building, planning, health . . . or zoning laws. . . . The Buyer and its consultants shall be entitled personally to inspect

---

17. See also *Holihan v. Rabenius Bldrs., Inc.,* 355 Mass. 639, 642, 246 N.E.2d 638 (1969), quoting *Lipson v. Southgate Park Corp.,* 345 Mass. 621, 625–626, 189 N.E.2d 191 (1963) ("The deed merely conveyed the premises but it did not constitute performance of an agreement which provided for the erection of a building 'in a careful, workmanlike, and substantial manner' and the use of 'new and . . . best' materials in its construction"); *Lipson v. Southgate Park Corp., supra* at 625, 189 N.E.2d 191 ("A jury could find that an agreement, containing detailed plans and specifications for the erection of a dwelling, is not ordinarily included in a deed and that the acceptance of the deed was only conclusive of the [conveyance of land]").

said premises prior to the delivery of the deed in order to determine whether the condition thereof complies with the terms of this *or any* other clause hereof."

This paragraph is not a warranty. Rather, it describes some of the conditions on which the Albrechts could have refused to purchase the residence. The agreement provided that if Clifford had been unable to provide good title, convey or deliver possession of the residence, or "if at the time of the delivery of the deed the premises do not conform with [the agreement's] provisions"—including paragraph 9—he had up to thirty days to use reasonable efforts to remedy any of these problems. If he failed to fix any problems within that time, the agreement would have become void. We agree with the judge that Count I of the Albrechts' complaint fails because paragraph 9 is not a contractual warranty that survived the Albrechts' acceptance of the deed.

The warranties that were to survive the acceptance of the deed were identified in Exhibit A of the agreement. However, those warranties expressly survived the acceptance of the deed for only one year. The Albrechts did not notify Clifford of their problems with the chimneys and fireplaces until May 20, 1997, more than three years after they accepted the deed. We therefore agree that Count II, breach of the express warranties in Exhibit A of the agreement, is barred by the parties' own limitation period.

Judgment affirmed.

NOTES AND QUESTIONS

1. In 1988, a statute was passed in New York providing for implied warranties that new homes sold are free of latent defects. New York Gen. Bus. §§ 777-777a (McKinney Supp. 1996). The statute limits the time span of the warranties but gives subsequent purchasers remedies for warranty breach. In part, the New York act states:

§ 777

6. "Owner" means the first person to whom the home is sold and, during the unexpired portion of the warranty period, each successor in title to the home and any mortgagee in possession. Owner does not include the builder of the home or any firm under common control of the builder.

§ 777-a. . . . a housing merchant implied warranty is implied in the contract or agreement for the sale of a new home and shall survive the passing of title. A housing merchant implied warranty shall mean that:

a. one year from and after the warranty date the home will be free from defects due to a failure to have been constructed in a skillful manner;

b. two years from and after the warranty date the plumbing, electrical, heating, cooling and ventilation systems of the home will be free from defects due to a failure by the builder to have installed such systems in a skillful manner; and

c. six years from and after the warranty date the home will be free from material defects.

2. Unless the contract or agreement by its terms clearly evidences a different intention of the seller, a housing merchant implied warranty does not extend to:

a. any defect that does not constitute (i) defective workmanship by the builder or by an agent, employee or subcontractor of the builder, (ii) defective materials supplied by the builder or by an agent, employee or subcontractor of the builder, or (iii) defective design provided by a design professional retained exclusively by the builder; . . . or

b. any patent defect which an examination ought in the circumstances to have revealed, when the buyer before taking title or accepting construction as complete has examined the home as fully as the buyer desired, or has refused to examine the home. . . .

4. An action for damages or other relief caused by the breach of a housing merchant implied warranty may be commenced prior to the expiration of one year after the applicable warranty period, as described in subdivision one of this section, or within four years after the warranty date, whichever is later. . . . The measure of damages shall be the reasonable cost of repair or replacement and property damage to the home proximately caused by the breach of warranty, not to exceed the replacement cost of the home exclusive of the value of the land, unless the court finds that, under the circumstances, the diminution in value of the home caused by the defect is a more equitable measure of damages.

On the New York statute, see Note, New York's Implied Merchant Warranty for the Sale of New Homes: A Reasonable Extension to Reach Initial Owners?, 1990 Colum. Bus. L. Rev. 373; and Note, The New York Housing Merchant Warranty Statute: Analysis and Proposals, 75 Cornell L. Rev. 754 (1990).

Examples of other statutes providing for statutorily created implied warranties by builders protecting home purchasers are Minn. Stat. Ann. §§ 327A.01 to 327A.08 (West 2004 and Supp. 2006); and N.J. Stat. Ann. §§ 46B-1 to B-20 (West 2003).

2. Construction lenders run a risk of being held liable under implied warranties of quality if the lenders are co-joint venturers with builders or owners and share ownership or profits and losses. There is some authority holding construction lenders who are not co-joint venturers liable in negligence for defectively built homes. The lead case for such lender liability, with little subsequent support, is Connor v. Great Western Savings and Loan Association, 60 Cal. 2d 850, 73 Cal. Rptr. 369, 447 P.2d 609 (1968). In the *Connor* case, the majority took the position that since the developers' lender had sufficient power over the construction process through control over loan funds, it had a duty to exercise reasonable care to prevent the construction and sale of seriously defective homes to home buyers. The *Connor* case was a 4-3 decision and there were strong dissents. For an extended discussion of the case and its impact, see 7 Powell on Real Property § 938.10 (1991). Shortly after the *Connor* case was decided, the California legislature passed a statute limiting lender liability, Cal. Civ. Code § 3434 (West 1997):

A lender who makes a loan of money, the proceeds of which are used or may be used by the borrower to finance the design, manufacture, construction, repair, modification or improvement of real or personal property for sale or lease to others, shall not be held liable to third persons for any loss or damage occasioned by any defect in the real or personal property so designed, manufactured, constructed, repaired, modified or improved or for any loss or damage resulting from the failure of the borrower to use due care in the design, manufacture, construction, repair, modification or improvement of such real or personal property, unless such loss or damage is a result of an act of the lender outside the scope of the activities of a lender of money or unless the lender has been a party to misrepresentations with respect to such real or personal property.

3. Can implied warranties be waived by disclaimer clauses in agreements between home buyers and builder-vendors? Some courts have said yes if the waiver language is clear and free from doubt. G-W-L, Inc. v. Robichaux, 643 S.W.2d 392 (Tex. 1982), held that the following language constituted an effective waiver: "no . . . warranties, express or implied, in addition to said written instruments." It "could not be clearer," the Texas Supreme Court said, and added, "The parties to a contract have an obligation to protect themselves by reading what they sign." 643 S.W.2d at 393. But another court has insisted that for a valid disclaimer the buyer actually must have known of the waiver when the contract was entered into, and boilerplate clauses, however worded, are ineffective for that purpose. Crowder v. Vandendeale, 564 S.W.2d 879, 881 (Mo. 1978). Also, many courts will strictly construe disclaimer clauses against the builder-vendor. E.g., Petersen v. Hubschman Constr. Co., Inc., 76 Ill. 2d 31, 43, 389 N.E.2d 1154, 1159 (1979). In Nastri v. Wood Bros. Homes, Inc., 142 Ariz. 439, 690 P.2d 158 (Ariz. App. 1984), a disclaimer clause in an original purchaser's agreement with builder was held not to preclude an implied warranty action against the builder by a subsequent purchaser for latent construction defects. The *Nastri* court considered the attempted disclaimer void as to an innocent subsequent purchaser. There obviously is a strong but not universal tendency for courts to take a proconsumer approach to disclaimer clauses in home sale agreements, home buyers being considered consumers acquiring what are to them very expensive items, so meriting special protection.

4. In Bullington v. Pazangio, 45 S.W.3d 834 (Ark. 2001), the court held that an express warranty of workmanship and proper construction did not constitute waiver of an implied warranty of habitability and proper construction.

5. If an agreement for sale of an interest in commercial real property includes an "as is" clause, in effect a form of disclaimer, does this eliminate seller responsibility for physical defects in the property? In PBS Coals, Inc. v. Burnham Coal Co., 558 A.2d 562 (Pa. Super. 1989), the transferee of coal mining properties asserted that the cost of correcting polluted water drainage from the mine site should be borne by the transferor. Neither buyer nor seller was aware of the pollution situation when the transfer agreement was entered into. The sale agreement provided that the transferee would accept the properties "as is." The court held that the as is clause put the buyer on notice that there may be liabilities attendant to the purchase and that the as is language prevented any implied warranties from attaching. "While the harshness of placing the risk of loss in such a situation on an inexperienced consumer has sometimes been avoided by the courts, the facts of this case do not present us with a basis of relieving PBS [the transferee] of the burden here. The individuals who signed this agreement are seasoned businessmen who can safely be presumed to be familiar with terms of common usage in business transactions." 558 A.2d at 564. Would it have made a difference to the Pennsylvania court if the seller was aware of the condition at the time the contract was entered into but the buyer was not?

The result in *PBS Coals* has been questioned, the argument being advanced that environmental protection issues are so important that a broader range of criteria other than the commercial nature of a transaction should be considered in determining whether or not as is clauses shift responsibility for environmental risks. See Note, An "As Is" Provision in a Commercial Property Contract: Should It Be Left As Is When Assessing Liability for Environmental Torts?, 51 U. Pitt. L. Rev. 995 (1990).

6. In T&E Industries v. Safety Light Corp., 123 N.J. 371, 587 A.2d 1249 (1991), it was held that a purchaser of a radium-contaminated industrial site could recover clean-up costs, and maintenance costs until clean up, from a remote predecessor in title that had polluted the site. Plaintiff was unaware of the pollution or pollution risk at the time of purchase. The current property owner, it was held, could successfully assert an action based on strict liability for abnormally dangerous activity. The doctrine of caveat emptor would not apply to bar recovery. And by merely signing an "as is" contract, a purchaser ignorant of the abnormally dangerous condition would not assume risks from that condition, the court said.

7. In addition to disclaimer clauses, other defenses that may be successfully raised against a home buyer's assertion of implied warranty breaches include statutes of limitations, limited express warranties, reasonable care shown in construction, and proof that defects are so minor as not to be covered by the warranty. These defenses are discussed in Note, Implied Warranties in New Home Sales — Is the Seller Defenseless?, 35 S.C.L. Rev. 469 (1984).

3. Express Warranty

Many contracts for the sale of real property contain express warranties as to the quality of the premises being sold. However, ambiguity in warranty terms often leads to conflict and litigation, even when the contract is in writing. Recovery on asserted oral warranties may be especially difficult, as the oral statements relied upon may be considered merely expressions of opinion, not promises; and if promises, they may be unenforceable under the Statute of Frauds.

Garriffa v. Taylor

675 P.2d 1284 (Wyo. 1984)

CARDINE, Justice. This is an appeal from an action to recover damages for breach of an express warranty. Judgment was entered in favor of plaintiffs-appellees in the amount of $1,650, the cost of installing a septic tank, plus court costs, for a total judgment of $1,692.75.

We will reverse.

FACTS

The appellants sold a house to the appellees. Approximately nineteen months after appellees had moved into the house, they replaced the septic tank and sent the bill for the cost of replacement to appellants with a request for payment. Appellants refused payment and this suit was initiated.

Appellants had lived in the house for five years prior to the time of sale. Prior to that time, appellant, Maria Garriffa, had lived in the house for ten years with her parents, the previous owners. The house was at least forty years old. The preprinted real estate listing form had a category entitled sewerage. Above this the real estate agent had typed "Septic." These forms are prepared from information provided by the sellers. While the appellees were looking at the property, Mrs. Taylor asked Mrs. Garriffa where the septic tank was located. Mrs. Garriffa indicated that the tank was located north of the house. Mrs. Taylor also asked Mrs. Garriffa if the tank had been pumped; Mrs. Garriffa replied that they had not pumped the tank but that they had used chemicals to keep the system working properly. Appellees testified that there were some problems with the sewerage system several months after they moved into the house, but nothing was done.

Nineteen months after taking possession and occupying the house, the appellees contacted a septic tank sales and service company to pump the tank. When they dug into the area north of the house, they did not find a septic tank. However, they found two pipes running out of the house. At the end of the pipes appellees testified that there was an accumulation of rocks, dirt, and debris. The appellees then employed a contractor who installed a new septic tank. Appellees did not notify appellants concerning any of this until after the installation of the septic tank. They then forwarded them the bill, which appellants refused to pay. Appellees contend that there was an express warranty by the appellants that the property had a septic sewer system and that this warranty was breached because no septic system existed. Therefore, they contend that appellants are liable for the cost of installing the septic tank.

Appellants raised several issues for review, however, we need only address one to dispose of this case — whether or not there was an express promise or warranty enforceable against the appellants regarding the existence and durability of a septic system.

Contracts for the sale and purchase of land may include an express warranty on the sellers' part as to the physical quality or condition of the property.

> . . . It has been held that such an express warranty of quality is governed by the common law principles applicable to warranties of quality in the sale of goods. . . . 77 Am. Jur. 2d Vendor and Purchaser § 336.

An express warranty is created by any affirmation of fact made by the seller to the buyer which relates to the goods and becomes a part of the basis of the bargain. 67 Am. Jur. 2d Sales § 442. The primary question is whether there were any affirmations of fact or promises which amounted to an express warranty or whether the representations were merely opinions. General Supply and Equipment Co., Inc. v. Phillips, Tex. Civ. App., 490 S.W.2d 913 (1972). The standard generally used is that:

> . . . [W]hen a seller asserts a fact of which the buyer is ignorant, and the buyer relies on the assertion, the seller makes an express warranty; but, when the seller merely states his opinion or his judgment upon a matter of which the seller has no special knowledge, . . . then the seller's statement does not constitute an express warranty. . . . Lovington Cattle Feeders, Inc. v. Abbott Lab., 97 N.M. 564, 642, P.2d 167, 170 (1982). See also, Scovil v. Chilcoat, Okl., 424 P.2d 87 (1967).

In order for an express warranty to exist, there must be some positive and unequivocal statement concerning the thing sold which is relied upon by the buyer and which is understood to be an assertion concerning the items sold and not an opinion. Maupin v. Nutrena Mills, Inc., Okl., 385 P.2d 504 (1963). A representation which expresses the seller's opinion, belief, judgment, or estimate does not constitute an express warranty. Scheirman v. Coulter, Okl., 624 P.2d 70 (1980). It is important to consider whether the seller asserts a fact about which the buyer is ignorant or whether he merely states an opinion or judgment upon a matter of which the seller has no special knowledge and upon which the buyer might be expected to have an opinion or to exercise his own judgment. Carpenter v. Alberto Culver Co., 28 Mich. App. 399, 184 N.W.2d 547 (1970). All the circumstances surrounding a sale are to be considered in determining whether there was an express warranty or merely an expression of opinion. Lovington Cattle Feeders, Inc. v. Abbott Lab, supra; Price Brothers Co. v. Philadelphia Gear Corp. 649 F.2d 416 (6th Cir. 1981), *cert. denied* 454 U.S. 1099, 102 S. Ct. 674, 70 L. Ed. 2d 641.

The question of whether an express warranty exists is for the trier of fact. Scheirman v. Coulter, supra. In the absence of special findings of facts, the reviewing court must consider that the judgment carries with it every finding of fact which is supported by the evidence. Hendrickson v. Heinze, Wyo., 541 P.2d 1133, 1135 (1975). However, where nonconflicting evidence admits of only one conclusion, a contrary conclusion cannot stand. Wyoming Farm Bureau Mutual Ins. Co. v. May, Wyo., 434 P.2d 507 (1967).

In this case there is not a conflict in evidence; therefore, we must look at the undisputed facts in relation to the requirements necessary for an express warranty. There was uncontradicted testimony by the real estate agent that the phrase, "Septic" on the real estate listing agreement is interpreted as meaning that it does not have city sewer, "[i]t has some sort of a septic system." There was also testimony by appellee that appellant had stated that there was a septic system located north of the house and that they had not had any difficulty with the system. There was no testimony presented that they had had problems with the system, knew of any present difficulties, or that they had information which they did not disclose. Appellee testified concerning the septic system:

"Q.   (*By Mr. Tate*) You said on your direct examination you didn't look at the system when you bought it; is that correct?
"A.   We looked at what we could see.
"Q.   You can't look at a sewage system when you buy an old house.
"A.   That's true.
"Q.   It would be pretty impractical.
"A.   That's right.
"Q.   And if the Garriffas never dug that system up, they really wouldn't know what was under there themselves either.
"A.   They wouldn't know what was under the ground, no."

We do not find that these statements were sufficient to form an express warranty concerning the septic sewerage system. The house was at least forty years old. Appellants stated that they had never had any problem with the septic system and that the tank had not been pumped. There was no testimony contradicting these statements. The statements were very general. They related to appellants' experience in the house. Appellants were not dealers of septic systems, nor were they people who had a special knowledge about these matters. Guess v. Lorenz, Mo. App., 612 S.W.2d 831 (1981). Representations of fact which are capable of determination are warranties, but the mere expression of an opinion is not. Young & Cooper, Inc. v. Vestring, 214 Kan. 311, 521 P.2d 281 (1974).

We find that these statements merely expressed the sellers' opinions and beliefs concerning the septic system and did not constitute an express warranty. If both parties are free from fault, there is no compelling reason to require the seller, instead of the purchaser, to bear the loss. Cook v. Salishan Properties, Inc., 279 Or. 333, 569 P.2d 1033 (1977). Appellees purchased a forty-year-old house not connected to the city sewer. Sewage was moved from the house by a septic system installed forty years earlier. What kind of system was installed forty years earlier we do not know. We do know that these systems do not last forever. When, more than a year after purchase of the house, this system did not function as expected, appellees, without demand or notice to appellants, employed a contractor of their choice and installed a new septic tank. They now ask that appellants be required to pay for that new septic tank. That was not their bargain. Because appellants' statements did not constitute an express warranty, we will reverse with instructions to the trial court to enter a judgment in accordance with this opinion.

NOTES AND QUESTIONS

1. Federal agencies that insure or guarantee mortgage loans are directed by Congress to require warranties of quality by builders or sellers of new homes financed by these insured or guaranteed mortgage loans. 12 U.S.C.A. § 1701j-1 (2001), applicable to HUD; and 38 U.S.C.A. § 3705 (2001), applicable to the Veterans Administration. The warranty requirements in the two statutes are very similar.

2. Should there be a legal requirement that all sales contracts for new housing being sold to persons who intend to live in the housing include government specified warranties of quality? If not, why not?

3. *Warranties of title.* When the closing occurs, the seller transfers title to the buyer, typically by a deed. Deeds usually include one or more of these covenants or warranties of title: seisin; right to convey; against encumbrances; general warranty; quiet enjoyment; further assurance. A full warranty deed includes all of these covenants, a special warranty deed includes one or more of them but not all. A deed without covenants or warranties of title is called a quit claim deed, and such deeds are frequent with grantors who are donors or are terminating a claim against a land title. A quit claim deed transfers whatever interest, if any, the grantor has in the property.

Covenants in contracts of sale as to title are no longer binding after closing. But these covenants can be and commonly are perpetuated by new covenants or warranties of title in the deed.

— STOP —

E.   RISK OF LOSS FROM DAMAGE DURING THE EXECUTORY INTERVAL

Bixby, The Vendor-Vendee Problem: How Do We Slice the Insurance Pie?

19 The Forum 112-114 (1983)

An executory contract for real property involves an agreement to sell property with a subsequent transfer of title. Between the time of the agreement and transfer of title, damage to the property may occur. The parties can contractually agree [on] who is to bear the risk of loss. In the absence of contractual agreement, the courts have developed three primary rules to allocate risk of loss between vendor and vendee.

The first rule leaves the risk of loss on the vendor until title passes. After a loss a vendee may elect to complete the contract or rescind it. There may be an additional election to abate the price. Placing the risk on the vendor has been called the "Massachusetts" rule. It has been followed in only a few states.

The second rule places the risk of loss on the vendee after the contract has been signed. This rule is based on the 1801 English case, Paine v. Meller. The vendee is considered to have all the indicia of ownership except title, that is, he is the equitable owner. This rule is referred to as the doctrine of "equitable conversion." Although in many instances the vendee may have possession of the property, the doctrine of equitable conversion does not require possession. Risk of loss shifts to the vendee immediately. Limited exceptions occur if the vendor for some reason was not in a position to convey title.

The equitable conversion rule is followed by a majority of American jurisdictions despite being severely criticized for placing a substantial burden on a vendee (risk of loss) without corresponding benefits. The continuing vitality of the equitable conversion rule is probably due to the presence of insurance. There is a reasonable probability the vendor had a preexisting property insurance policy. American courts almost uniformly impose a trust on the proceeds of the vendor's insurance policy for the benefit of the vendee in states following the equitable conversion rule. This is consistent with the asserted layman's concept that insurance runs with the property. The English accomplished the same result by statute when their courts refused to give the vendee the benefit of a vendor's insurance.

The third common law rule focuses on possession of the property. The person in possession bears the risk of loss until title is transferred. It is asserted the possession test is preferable because it places the risk of loss on the party likely to have the most interest in protecting the property. The possession test was adopted in the Uniform Vendor and Purchaser Risk Act promulgated by the National Commissioners on Uniform State Laws. This act has been adopted in eleven states. The possession rule is also used in the more recent Uniform Land Transaction Code. . . .

The foregoing risk of loss rules for executory real estate transfers are relatively straightforward. It is the judicial effort to provide insurance coverage to a person who is not a party to the insurance contract which creates most problems in vendor-vendee situations. In trying to give an uninsured the benefit of insurance on a case by case basis, courts have rejected certain principles of insurance. While these insurance principles are often tested in other situations, the vendor-vendee cases seem to trigger more conflicts more often.

The insurance principles often ignored by courts in deciding vendor-vendee cases include: the insurance policy is a personal contract; insurance is intended to provide indemnity; insurance covers the insurable interest of the insured; an insurer is subrogated to the rights of its insured; and loss is determined as of the date of the occurrence.

Skelly Oil Co. v. Ashmore

365 S.W.2d 582 (Mo. 1963) (en banc)

HYDE, Judge. [In March 1958, defendant-sellers were the owners of improved business premises. The premises were subject to a $7200 mortgage and were leased to a tenant through 1961 at a rental of $150 per month.

Defendants, that same March, agreed to sell the premises, subject to the lease but free of the mortgage, to Skelly Oil Company for $20,000. Skelly, owning premises adjacent to those in the suit, planned at some later date to combine the tracts for a gas station. The closing was set for April 16, 1958. On April 7, 1958, the building on the lot was destroyed by fire without fault of either party. Seller had a $10,000 insurance policy, and, according to its terms, the insurance company paid off the $7200 mortgage and gave the $2800 balance to defendants. Plaintiffs sued for a decree compelling defendants specifically to perform but seeking an abatement in the purchase price of $10,000 as the amount of the insurance policy proceeds. The trial court decreed plaintiffs' requested relief; defendants appealed. The opinion states the facts, dismisses defendants' contention that there was no enforceable contract, and continues:]

The contract of sale here involved contained no provision as to who assumed the risk of loss occasioned by a destruction of the building, or for protecting the building by insurance or for allocating any insurance proceeds received therefor. When the parties met to close the sale on April 16, the purchaser's counsel informed vendors and their attorneys he was relying on Standard Oil Co. v. Dye, 223 Mo. App. 926, 20 S.W.2d 946, for purchaser's claim to the $10,000 insurance proceeds on the building. . . . It is stated in 3 American Law of Property, § 11.30, p. 90, that in the circumstances here presented at least five different views have been advanced for allocating the burden of fortuitous loss between vendor and purchaser of real estate. We summarize those mentioned: (1) The view first enunciated in Paine v. Meller (Ch. 1801, 6 Ves. Jr. 349, 31 Eng. Reprint 1088, 1089) is said to be the most widely accepted; holding that from the time of the contract of sale of real estate the burden of fortuitous loss was on the purchaser even though the vendor retained possession. (2) The loss is on the vendor until legal title is conveyed, although the purchaser is in possession, stated to be a strong minority. (3) The burden of loss should be on the vendor until the time agreed upon for conveying the legal title, and thereafter on the purchaser unless the vendor be in such default as to preclude specific performance, not recognized in the decisions. (4) The burden of the loss should be on the party in possession, whether vendor or purchaser, so considered by some courts. (5) The burden of loss should be on vendor unless there is something in the contract or in the relation of the parties from which the court can infer a different intention, stating "this rather vague test" has not received any avowed judicial acceptance, although it is not inconsistent with jurisdictions holding the loss is on the vendor until conveyance or jurisdictions adopting the possession test. . . .

We do not agree that we should adopt the arbitrary rule of Paine v. Meller, supra, and Standard Oil Co. v. Dye, supra, that there is equitable conversion from the time of making a contract for sale and purchase of land and that the risk of loss from destruction of buildings or other substantial part of the property is from that moment on the purchaser. Criticisms of this rule by eminent authorities have been set out in the dissenting opinion of Storckman, J., herein and will not be repeated here.

We take the view stated in an article on Equitable Conversion by Contract, 13 Columbia Law Review 369, 386, Dean Harlan F. Stone, later Chief Justice Stone, in which he points out that the only reason why a contract for the sale of land by the owner to another operates to effect conversion is that a court of equity will compel him specifically to perform his contract. He further states: "A preliminary to the determination of the question whether there is equitable ownership of land must therefore necessarily be the determination of the question whether there is a contract which can be and ought to be specifically performed *at the very time when the court is called upon to perform it.* This process of reasoning is, however, reversed in those jurisdictions where the 'burden of loss' is cast upon the vendee. The question is whether there shall be a specific performance of the contract, thus casting the burden on the vendee, by compelling him to pay the full purchase price for the subject matter of the contract, a substantial part of which has been destroyed. The question is answered somewhat in this wise: equitable ownership of the vendee in the subject matter of the contract can exist only where the contract is one which equity will specifically perform. The vendee of land is equitably entitled to land, therefore the vendee may be compelled to perform, although the vendor is unable to give in return the performance stipulated for by this contract. The non sequitur involved in the proposition that performance may be had because of the equitable ownership of the land by the vendee, which in turn depends upon the right of performance, is evident. The doctrine of equitable conversion, so far as it is exemplified by the authorities hitherto considered, cannot lead to the result of casting the burden of loss on the vendee, since the *conversion depends upon the question whether the contract should in equity be performed.* In all other cases where the vendee is treated as the equitable owner of the land, it is only because the contract is one which equity first determines should be specifically performed.

"Whether a plaintiff, in breach of his contract by a default which goes to the essence, as in the case of the destruction of a substantial part of the subject matter of the contract, should be entitled to specific performance, is a question which is answered in the negative in every case except that of destruction of the subject matter of the contract. To give a plaintiff specific performance of the contract when he is unable to perform the contract on his own part, violates the fundamental rule of equity that . . . *equity will not compel a defendant to perform when it is unable to so frame its decree as to compel the plaintiff to give in return substantially what he had undertaken to give* or to do for the defendant.

"The rule of casting the 'burden of loss' on the vendee by specific performance if justifiable at all can only be explained and justified upon one of two theories: first, that since equity has for most purposes treated the vendee as the equitable owner, it should do so for all purposes, although *this ignores the fact that in all other cases the vendee is so treated only because the contract is either being performed or in equity ought to be performed;* or, second, which is substantially the same proposition in a different form, the specific performance which casts the burden on the vendee is an incident to and a consequence of an equitable conversion, whereas in all other equity relations growing out of the contract, the equitable conversion, if it exists, is an incident to and consequence of, a specific performance. Certainly nothing could be more illogical than this process of reasoning." (Emphasis ours.)

For these reasons, we do not agree with the rule that arbitrarily places the risk of loss on the vendee from the time the contract is made. Instead we believe the Massachusetts rule is the proper rule. It is thus stated in Libman v. Levenson, 236 Mass. 221, 128 N.E. 13, 22 A.L.R. 560: When "the conveyance is to be made of the whole estate, including both land and buildings, for an entire price, and the value of the buildings constitutes a large part of the total value of the estate, and the terms of the agreement show that they constituted an important part of the subject matter of the contract . . . the contract is to be construed as subject to the implied condition that it no longer shall be binding if, before the time for the conveyance to be made, the buildings are destroyed by fire. The loss by the fire falls upon the vendor, the owner; and if he has not protected himself by insurance, he can have no reimbursement of this loss; but the contract is no longer binding upon either party. If the purchaser has advanced any part of the price, he can recover it back. Thompson v. Gould, [supra] 20 Pick. [37 Mass.] 134, 138. If the change in the value of the estate is not so great, or if it appears that the buildings did not constitute so material a part of the estate to be conveyed as to result in an annulling of the contract, specific performance may be decreed, *with compensation for any breach of agreement,* or relief may be given in damages." (Emphasis ours.) . . . An extreme case, showing the unfairness of the arbitrary rule placing all loss on the vendee, is Amundson v. Severson, 41 S.D. 377, 170 N.W. 633, where three-fourths of the land sold was washed away by the Missouri River (the part left being of little value) and the vendor brought suit for specific performance. Fortunately for the vendee, he was relieved by the fact that the vendor did not have good title at the time of the loss, although the vendor had procured it as a basis for his suit. However, if the vendor had then held good title even though he did not have the land; the vendee would have been required to pay the full contract price under the loss on the purchaser rule. (Would the vendee have been any better off if the vendor had good title from the start but did not have the land left to convey?) The reason for the Massachusetts rule is that specific performance is based on what is equitable; and it is not equitable to make a vendee pay the vendor for something the vendor cannot give him.

However, the issue in this case is not whether the vendee can be compelled to take the property without the building but whether the vendee is entitled to enforce the contract of sale, with the insurance proceeds substituted for the destroyed building. We see no inequity to defendants in such enforcement since they will receive the full amount ($20,000.00) for which they contracted to sell the property. Their contract not only described the land but also specifically stated they sold it "together with the buildings, driveways and all construction thereon." While the words "Service Station Site" appeared in the caption of the option contract and that no doubt was the ultimate use plaintiff intended to make of the land, the final agreement made by the parties was that plaintiff would take it subject to a lease of the building which would have brought plaintiff about $6,150.00 in rent during the term of the lease. Moreover, defendants' own evidence showed the building was valued in the insurance adjustment at $16,716.00 from which $4,179.00 was deducted for depreciation, making the loss $12,537.00. Therefore, defendants are not in a very good position to say the building was of no value to plaintiff. Furthermore, plaintiff having contracted for the land with the building on it, the decision concerning use or removal of the building, or even for resale of the entire property, was for the plaintiff to make. Statements were in evidence about the use of the building and its value to plaintiff made by its employee who negotiated the purchase but he was not one of plaintiff's chief executive officers nor possessed of authority to bind its board of directors. The short of the matter is that defendants will get all they bargained for; but without the building or its value plaintiff will not.

We therefore affirm the judgment and decree of the trial court.

Eager, Leedy and Hollingsworth, J.J., concur.

Storckman, J., dissents in separate opinion filed.

Westhues, C.J., and Dalton, J., dissent and concur in separate dissenting opinion of Storckman, J.

STORCKMAN Judge (dissenting). . . . I cannot assent to the holding that the plaintiff is entitled to specific performance on any terms other than those of the purchase contract without reduction in the contract price. . . .

The evidence is convincing that Skelly Oil Company was buying the lot as a site for a service station and that in so using it they not only wanted the Jones's lease terminated but intended to tear down and remove the building in question. The contract documents support this conclusion. Both the option and the letter of acceptance refer to the contract as a "service station site" and contain escape clauses permitting Skelly to avoid the purchase agreement if proper permits could not be obtained or if zoning laws prohibited such use. From the time the option was first granted on July 31, 1957, through its various extensions, until the letter of March 4, 1958, Mr. Busby, Skelly's real estate representative, was cooperating with and urging Mr. Ashmore and his attorney to secure a termination of the Jones's lease (which was on the entire property) even to the extent of filing an ejectment suit against the lessee. Then after the fire Skelly's legal department prepared as one of the closing documents an agreement to be executed by the Ashmores and the Jones for mutual cancellation of the lease. The purchase contract calls for an assignment of the Jones's lease by the Ashmores to Skelly and its honoring the lease; but, at the request of Mr. Busby, the Ashmores on April 17, 1958, with the approval of their attorney, executed and delivered to Mr. Busby the mutual cancellation agreement. This conduct is consistent with its prior activities, but is inconsistent with plaintiff's present contention that the building and its rental under the lease represented a substantial part of the consideration for the purchase of the real estate.

Count 1 of the petition is for specific performance in accordance with the terms of the purchase contract; Count 2 seeks a declaration that the defendants hold the $10,000 insurance proceeds in trust for the benefit of the plaintiff and that the defendants be required to pay the proceeds to the plaintiff or that the amount thereof be applied in reduction of the purchase price of the property. Count 2 alleges that the concrete block, single-story building which was used as a grocery store was totally destroyed by fire, that the defendants collected the insurance thereon, and that "said building was a valuable appurtenance on said real estate worth more than $10,000.00 and that its destruction reduced the value of said real estate more than the sum of $10,000.00."

In spite of the issue made by Count 2 as to effect of the destruction of the building upon the value of the real estate, the trial court refused to permit cross-examination of plaintiff's witness to establish that the purpose and intent of Skelly was to remove the building from the premises when the lease was terminated, and the court rejected defendants' offer of proof to the same effect. In this equity action the testimony should have been received. It did not tend to vary or contradict the written contract but dealt with an issue made by plaintiff's petition based on a partial destruction of the subject matter subsequent to the acceptance of the option. Nevertheless, there was other evidence from which it could be reasonably inferred that the use of the real estate as a filling station site necessitated the removal of the building. Mr. Ashmore testified that he originally asked $27,000 for the property but reduced his price on Mr. Busby's representation that the improvements had no value to Skelly and that Skelly would be glad to have Mr. Ashmore remove them.

The plaintiff introduced no evidence of the market value of the property before or after the fire in support of the allegations in Count 2. The amount paid by the insurance company is of little or no benefit as evidence of the actual value of the building because of the valued policy law of Missouri which provides that in case of the total destruction of a building by fire, insurance companies shall not be permitted to deny that the property insured was worth at the time of issuing the policy or policies the full amount for which the property was insured. Sections 379.140 and 379.145, R.S. Mo. 1959, V.A.M.S. Defendants' evidence tended to prove that the real estate was worth more as a site for a service station after the fire than before and that the value of the real estate after the fire was in excess of $20,000.

The claim of neither party is particularly compelling insofar as specific performance in this case is concerned. The destruction of the building by fire, its insurance, and the disposition of the insurance proceeds were matters not contemplated by the parties and not provided for in the purchase contract documents. Skelly's representative did not know that Mr. Ashmore carried insurance on the building until after the fire, and he then told Mr. Ashmore that despite the fire the deal would be closed on the agreed date. Skelly's present claims are an afterthought inconsistent with its conduct throughout the negotiations and prior to the closing date.

In short, as to both Skelly and the Ashmores, the destruction of the insured building was a fortuitous circumstance supplying the opportunity to rid the property of a vexatious lease, to dispose of the building, and at the same time resulting in a windfall of $10,000. And the problem, in fact the only seriously contested issue between the parties, is which of them is to have the advantage of this piece of good fortune. Skelly contracted to pay $20,000 for the property. If it is awarded the $10,000 windfall, it will receive a $20,000 lot for $10,000. If the Ashmores retain the $10,000, they will in fact have realized $30,000 for a piece of property they have agreed to sell for $20,000.

In claiming the proceeds of the Ashmores' fire insurance policy, Skelly did not contend that the value of the real estate as a service station site had decreased. After learning of the fire and the existence of the insurance policy, Skelly's counsel did some research and, as he announced when the parties met in Joplin to close the deal, Skelly was relying on a case he had found, Standard Oil Company v. Dye, 223 Mo. App. 926, 20 S.W.2d 946. And in its basic facts the case admittedly is quite similar to this one although there were no attendant circumstances such as we have in the present case. The doctrine of [this case] laboriously evolved from Paine v. Meller, (1801) 6 Ves. Jr. 349, 31 Eng. Reprint 1088, is "that a contract to sell real property vests the equitable ownership of the property in the purchaser, with the corollary that any loss by destruction of the property through casualty during the pendency of the contract must be borne by the purchaser." The twofold rationale of this doctrine is a maxim that "equity regards as done that which should have been done," from which it is said the "vendor becomes a mere trustee, holding the legal title for the benefit of the purchaser or as security for the price." 27 A.L.R.2d 444, 448, 449. All of the experts and scholars seem to agree that this doctrine and its rationale is misplaced if not unsound. . . . As to the maxim, Williston said, "Only the hoary age and frequent repetition of the maxim prevents a general recognition of its absurdity." 4 Williston, Contracts, § 929, p. 2607. As to the corollary, Williston points out that while the purchaser may have an interest in the property, it is equally clear that the vendor likewise has an interest, and as for the vendor's being a trustee for the purchaser observes, "However often the words may be repeated, it cannot be true that the vendor is trustee for the purchaser." 4 Williston, Contracts, § 936, p. 2622. See also Pound, The Progress of The Law — Equity, 33 Har. L.R. 814, 830.

Nevertheless, adapting this doctrine and following a majority opinion in another English case, Rayner v. Preston, (1881) L.R. 18 Ch. Div. 1 (CA), the rule as stated in the Dye case has evolved: "Where the purchaser as equitable owner will bear the loss occasioned by a destruction of the property pending completion of the sale, and the contract is silent as to insurance, the rule quite generally followed is that the proceeds of the vendor's insurance policies, even though the purchaser did not contribute to their maintenance, constitute a trust fund for the benefit of the purchaser to be credited on the purchase price of the destroyed property, the theory being that the vendor is a trustee of the property for the purchaser." Annotation 64 A.L.R.2d 1402, 1406. Many jurisdictions have modified or do not follow this doctrine, some take the view that the vendor's insurance policy is personal to him, and Parliament has enacted a statute which entirely changes the English rule. 4 Mo. L.R. 290, 296. The rule is not as general as the annotator indicated, and as with the rule upon which it is founded, all the experts agree that it is unsound, their only point of disagreement is as to what the rule should be. . . .

Professor Williston was of the view that the risk of loss [pending transfer of legal title] should follow possession (4 Williston, Contracts §§ 940, 942), and that view has been written into the Uniform Vendor and Purchaser Risk Act 9C U.L.A., p. 314 and 1960 Supp., p. 82. Eight states have adopted that act and four of those, California, New York, South Dakota, and Oregon, are listed among the fifteen jurisdictions said by the A.L.R. annotator (64 A.L.R. 1406) to follow the Dye case. . . .

Vance is of the opinion that a rule of "business usage" should be adopted, but he ruefully adds, "Here we have another instance in which business usage substitutes the insurance money for the insured property, despite the general rule that the two are not legally connected; and, as usual, the courts are sluggishly following business." Vance, Insurance § 131 p. 781. Dean Pound assails Vance's contention that the insurance money is any part of the thing bargained for and he also vigorously attacks the theory that the vendor is a trustee for the vendee. 33 Har. L.R., 1. c. 829, 830. . . .

Automatic application of the doctrine that "equity regards that as done which ought to be done," in the circumstances of this case, begs the question of *what ought to be done.* Because the insurance proceeds may be a windfall to those legally entitled does not necessarily mean that justice will be accomplished by transferring them elsewhere. The substance of the purchase contract and the use to which the property is to be put must be considered. A resort to equity should involve a consideration of other equitable principles or maxims such as the equally important maxims that "equity follows the law" and "between equal equities the law will prevail."

A valid legal excuse is a sufficient reason for refusal of specific performance. . . . Destruction of a particular thing upon which the contract depends is generally regarded as a legal excuse for nonperformance. . . .

If plaintiff's contention is that there has been a substantial failure or impairment of the consideration of the contract by reason of the destruction of the building, then I do not think that the Ashmores should be entitled to specific performance, and because of the theory of mutuality it would seem that Skelly would not be entitled to specific performance unless it was willing to perform its legal obligations under the purchase contract as drawn. We would not be justified in making a new contract for the parties to cover the building insurance, and a court of equity will not decree specific performance of a contract that is incomplete, indefinite or uncertain. . . . Nor can the courts supply an important element that has been omitted from the contract. . . .

If the subject matter of the purchase contract was not as well or better suited to Skelly's purpose after the fire than it was before, then it appears from the authorities above discussed that Skelly could avoid the contract entirely or that it could clearly establish the amount and manner in which it was damaged. What would the situation be if the building had not been insured or for only a small amount? The fact that the building was insured and the amount thereof are hardly determinative of Skelly's alleged injury.

But Skelly did not after the fire or in this action elect to abandon the contract although the Ashmores gave it the opportunity to do so rather than to sell at the reduced price. It is quite evident that Skelly has received one windfall as the result of the fire in that the lease is terminated and the site can be cleared at less cost. It has not shown itself to be entitled to another, the one now legally vested in the Ashmores. Ideally the purchase contract should be set aside so that the parties could negotiate a new one based on the property in its present condition. But the contract by its election to take title has foreclosed this possibility. . . . As the opinion stands, the adoption of the Massachusetts rule is more imaginary than real. The equitable conversion theory is *applied*, not the Massachusetts rule.

The opinion simply awards the *proceeds* of the fire insurance policy. It does not, and could not on the evidence in the present record, ascertain the compensation or damages, if any, to which Skelly is entitled by reason of the destruction of the building. Evidence of this sort was excluded by the trial court. Count 2 of the plaintiff's petition claims the insurance proceeds on the theory of a trust fund as a matter of law and that seems to be the basis of the majority opinion's award of the insurance fund to the purchaser. This is the antithesis of the Massachusetts rule which contemplates the ascertainment of the amount of compensation or damages that will assure the vendee receiving the value for which it contracted, and no more. . . .

Although the entire court now seems to be in agreement that the theory of equitable conversion should not be adopted and that the equitable rules which should govern are those that require an allowance of compensation or damages to fit the particular case, nevertheless a majority of the court have concurred in an opinion which makes the amount of insurance proceeds the yardstick. This is the rejected doctrine of equitable conversion regardless of the name given to it. . . .

NOTES AND QUESTIONS

1. If, as the dissent states, one or the other parties is going to receive a $10,000 windfall, why not resolve the problem by splitting the windfall sum and awarding each party $5,000?

2. The Uniform Vendor and Purchaser Risk Act covers loss during the executory interval. It has been adopted by these states: California, Hawaii, Illinois, Michigan, Nevada, New York, North Carolina, Oklahoma, Oregon, South Dakota, Texas, and Wisconsin. Section 1 of the Act provides:

> Any contract hereafter made in this State for the purchase and sale of realty shall be interpreted as including an agreement that the parties shall have the following rights and duties, unless the contract expressly provides otherwise:
>
> (a) If, when neither the legal title nor the possession of the subject matter of the contract has been transferred, all or a material part thereof is destroyed without fault of the purchaser or is taken by eminent domain, the vendor cannot enforce the contract, and the purchaser is entitled to recover any portion of the price that he has paid;
>
> (b) If, when either the legal title or the possession of the subject matter of the contract has been transferred, all or any part thereof is destroyed without fault of the vendor or is taken by eminent domain, the purchaser is not thereby relieved from a duty to pay the price, nor is he entitled to recover any portion thereof that he has paid.

3. *Specific performance with abatement.* Following a loss during the executory interval, the buyer may be entitled to specific performance of the sale contract with abatement. This right is described as follows in Brush Grocery Kart v. Sure Fine Market, 47 P.3d 680, 685-686 (Colo. 2002):

> Where a vendee is entitled to rescind as a result of casualty loss, the vendee should generally also be entitled to partial specific performance of the contract with an abatement in the purchase price reflecting the loss. Where the damage is ascertainable, permitting partial specific performance with a price abatement allows courts as nearly as possible to fulfill the expectations of the parties expressed in the contract, while leaving each in a position that is equitable relative to the other. *Lucenti*, 423 N.Y.S.2d 886, 399 N.E.2d at 923-24 (applying common law rule allowing partial specific enforcement with price abatement for casualty loss in order to effectuate substance of parties agreement). Partial specific performance with a price abatement has long been recognized in this jurisdiction as an alternative to rescission in the analogous situation in which a vendor of real property is unable to convey marketable title to all of the land described in the contract. *See Murdock v. Pope*, 156 Colo. 7, 396 P.2d 841 (1964) (collecting cases into the nineteenth century); *cf.* § 38-30-167.

4. *Risk following possession.* In *Skelly Oil*, seller's tenant was in possession at the time of the fire; buyer bought subject to that tenant's rights, the tenant had not yet given a red rose or otherwise attorned to the buyer. How would a rule that the risk follows the possession be applied?

5. *Equitable conversion.* Whether the concept of equitable conversion is question-begging or question-solving as applied to executory interval fires, it is, in either case, unnecessary. There is plenty of contract doctrine to do any legal job that needs doing in these cases. The relevant contract doctrines (frustration, impossibility,

independent conditions, implied conditions and promises, failure of consideration, etc.) are supposedly bottomed on intent, and so the premises of our free society require them to be honored in determining disputes between free actors in a free land-money exchange. Those same premises require that results not be derived from a depersonalization of the parties into "owner" and "not owner" via property doctrine. It has never been suggested that concepts of equitable conversion would control an explicit agreement between the parties as to their relations in the event of an interim fire.

Anyway, Skelly Oil started the transaction involved in the principal case by acquiring an option on the site, although Skelly had picked up the option (converted it into a bilateral contract) before the fire. Who in the world, other than a considerable number of courts (see A.L.R. 1225 (1926)), would say that a fire during the period of an otherwise enforceable but as yet unexercised option would leave the optionee remediless — remediless in spite of the fact that the jurisdiction would award to a bilateral contract buyer a post-fire specific performance decree with abatement for insurance proceeds? The concept of equitable conversion is involved here, but it does not fully serve the optionee, partly because of the unsatisfactory and derided concept of mutuality.

However, determining whether buyer or seller is owner or equitable owner of Blackacre during the executory interval is important for many legal purposes whether or not fire loss allocation ought to be one of them. The characterization is central in determining — or at least describing — the relations of the buyer and seller not with each other, but with third persons.

For example, after Blackacre is under contract to buyer, does a creditor of the seller reach seller's interest in Blackacre by levy on Blackacre or by garnisheeing buyer? The law of a state provides that the real property of an intestate deceased descends to his heirs but that his personalty shall devolve on his personal administrator for distribution according to a statutory formula; S dies intestate, who gets what? Does the date of contract or deed measure the holding period of "property" for Internal Revenue Code purposes? In the next case, a seller's relation to his insurance company turns on whether or not he continued, after contract, to be the "owner." This is, of course, just an elementary refresher of the point that questions of "ownership" for buyer and seller are numerous.

Yet it is surprising that the questions just posed are answered in terms of ownership. At any given moment in the United States there are thousands of properties in executory interval, the buyers and sellers of which are netted into the complex of legal relationships between Blackacre and the world of third persons. The surprise is that the intestacy statutes, or the Internal Revenue Code, or the Bankruptcy Act or whatever body of law controls the particular relationship rarely deals specifically with the executory interval phenomenon and leaves it to be disposed of by the larger generalizations of ownership.

Finally, practical aspects of executory interval planning for a land transaction may involve these third party relationship questions as importantly as buyer-seller problems inter se. But the problems are as much those of creditors' rights and taxation as they are of land transfer, and it is to the former categories of instructional organization that we consign them.

6. *Other executory interval changes: Rezoning and eminent domain.* Steinway and Sons contracted to buy from two separate tract owners, intending, as was known to both sellers, to use the tracts as a unit for construction of a business building and

adjacent warehouse. After contract and before closing, a rezoning of one of the tracts precluded the intended use. Steinway was held excused as to the rezoned tract but not as to the other. Anderson v. Steinway & Sons, 178 A.D. 502, 165 N.Y.S. 608, *aff'd,* 221 N.Y. 639, 117 N.E. 575 (1917); Biggs v. Steinway & Sons, 229 N.Y. 320, 128 N.E. 211 (1920).

An eminent domain taking of all or part of the land during the executory interval presents problems closely analogous to those of destruction by fire or otherwise. Both eminent domain and rezoning cases can be argued against the buyer in common law terms of equitable conversion and by conventional property principles; but they have a special pro-buyer doctrinal feature. In the usual contract for the sale of land, the buyer is excused if seller cannot, at closing, supply him with a deed carrying *marketable title* to the land. A fire loss will not be regarded as clouding seller's title, but a post-contract zoning change or eminent domain might be so regarded. Mixing this extra doctrinal feature with the equitable conversion and contract principles has of course produced a pattern of results for rezoning and condemnation cases fully as incoherent as that of the fire cases described in *Skelly Oil.* See Friedman, Contracts and Conveyances of Real Property § 4.10 (4th ed. 1984).

Bixby, The Vendor-Vendee Problem: How Do We Slice the Insurance Pie?

19 The Forum 112, 127-128 (1983)

As a preliminary matter the courts should abandon the doctrine of equitable conversion as it applies to the allocation of risk of loss between vendor and vendee for destruction of real property in the executory period. The Massachusetts rule or the possession rule of the Vendor and Purchaser Risk Act is more logical. Even with the adoption of a more logical risk of loss rule, the desire of courts to provide insurance to someone not insured will continue to create conflicts with insurance principles. Consideration might be given to legislation which would give either vendor or vendee the benefit of the other's insurance. Attorneys and others involved in the transfer of real property should consider the conflict between risk of loss rules and insurance principles in drafting sales documents.

Recognizing that problems will still arise, the following guidelines for handling vendor-vendee cases are suggested.

1. The cases involving a single policy are the most difficult. (a) In states following the equitable conversion rule, the trust doctrine will undoubtedly continue to be used to give the vendee the benefit of a vendor's insurance. The trust doctrine should be recognized as a counterbalance to the harshness of the equitable conversion risk of loss rule. (b) In states following the Massachusetts rule or the possession rule for allocating risk of loss, there is less justification for imposing the trust doctrine. Cases such as Long v. Keller, [104 Cal. App. 3d 312, 163 Cal. Rptr. 532 (1980), court refused to give vendee the benefit of vendor's insurance] should be followed. (c) Efforts to impose a trust for the benefit of a vendor when insurance is purchased by the vendee should be scrutinized carefully and generally should be rejected absent strong equitable considerations. (d) In the absence of a trust doctrine, courts may still negate subrogation by a vendor's insurer by interpreting the intent of the executory sales contract.

2. The double coverage cases are less troublesome. (a) In double coverage cases when there is no overlap between policies the courts should follow the underlying risk of loss rule and permit subrogation. An exception would be where subrogation is waived by the sales agreement. (b) In double coverage situations where there is an "overlap" among policies, the courts should be flexible. Nonetheless, the courts should not prorate between policies unless there is at least a partial identity between or among the named insureds or designations historically considered equivalent to an "insured," such as a mortgagee.

QUESTION

Do Bixby's recommendations merit adoption, and if so, why?

F. TIME OF PERFORMANCE

Kasten Construction Co. v. Maple Ridge Construction Co.

245 Md. 373, 226 A.2d 341 (1967)

HORNEY, Judge. The question presented by this appeal is whether the Maple Ridge Construction Company (Maple Ridge), as buyer, is entitled to require the Kasten Construction Company (Kasten), as seller, to specifically perform a contract in which settlement for the sale for certain building lots was to have been made in sixty days but the time was not stipulated as being of the essence.

The contract of sale, dated December 4, 1964, provided for the sale and purchase of a tract of land in Section 4 of the Maple Ridge Subdivision in Anne Arundel County consisting of thirty-four "finished" lots designated as 20-A and 20-B through 36-A and 36-B. The contract further provided that Maple Ridge was to have an option to purchase ninety-four other lots in the subdivision within twelve months from the date of the contract of sale and was given the first refusal to purchase approximately five hundred of the remaining lots in Sections 3 and 4. Subsequently, when financing difficulties were encountered, the settlement date was extended in writing to on or before March 19, 1965, but again time was not stated to be of the essence. Maple Ridge had requested a longer extension, but it was refused by Kasten and later requests for extensions were also refused.

Although Kasten in the interim between the making of the contract of sale and the extended settlement date had bulldozed several of the streets or roads and stabilized them with gravel, it had made little progress toward providing Maple Ridge with the finished or completed lots it needed to begin constructing homes. No agreement had been made between Kasten and the County with respect to street and drainage easements and there had been delays in connection with the construction of the curbs and gutters and the installation of public utilities. And while a proposed agreement and bond was completed by the County department of public works on March 3, 1965 and delivered to Kasten promptly, it was never executed and returned. Moreover, although Kasten recorded a deed of "covenants, restrictions and conditions" purporting to cover Sections 3 and 4 of Maple Ridge, which it was agreed was required before the houses to be thereafter constructed would be eligible for FHA financing, Maple Ridge was never consulted or afforded an opportunity to participate in formulating the specifications contained in the restrictions. Maple Ridge, however, in addition to engaging an architect to prepare plans for houses to be constructed in the development and the renting of a trailer to be used on location as an office at a total outlay of $12,000, had continued trying to obtain the type of financing it hoped to get before the extended settlement date expired without having to use such of the personal funds of its president as were available to the corporation. In the meantime the settlement date came and went and neither party made a demand on the other. But when Maple Ridge notified Kasten five days after the expiration of the extension that it had applied for a title examination and it would take about three weeks to complete it, Kasten in turn notified Maple Ridge that the contract of sale had expired, as had the extension, and that it considered the contract null and void and no longer in force. Subsequent negotiations were unsuccessful and this suit for specific performance was brought.

On the evidence and the exhibits produced at the hearing, the chancellor, having found that although the buyer was dilatory in making the necessary financial arrangements and in applying for a title examination, it had tendered full performance of the terms of the contract within a reasonable time after the expiration of the extended settlement date; that the seller, besides acting as if time was not of the essence, had been somewhat lackadaisical in the performance of its part of the contract; and that the seller had suffered no loss that could not be compensated by the payment of interest, decreed specific performance of the contract of sale.

On appeal, Kasten, claiming that the chancellor erred in decreeing specific performance, contends that its refusal to grant further extensions was clear indication that time was of the essence and should therefore have been inferred from the circumstances. Maple Ridge, however, claiming that a specified date for settlement did not mean that the parties intended time to be of the essence, contends that it was not and that the delay in making settlement was reasonable under the circumstances.

In a case involving specific performance, where the intention of the parties is always the controlling factor, the general rule is that time is not of the essence of the contract of sale and purchase of land unless a contrary purpose is disclosed by its terms or is indicated by the circumstances and object of its execution and the conduct of the parties. Of course, one may lose his right to specific performance by gross laches and unreasonable delay in paying the purchase money. Ordinarily, however, time is held to be of the essence only when it is clear that the parties have expressly so stipulated or their intention is inferable from the circumstances of the transaction, the conduct of the parties or the purpose for which the sale was made. . . . Applying these tests to the facts of this case, we think the chancellor was correct in decreeing that Maple Ridge was entitled to specific performance. Under the circumstances, it was not necessary to regard the stipulation fixing the original and extended times for payment of the purchase price as imposing a condition requiring strict and punctual compliance in order to entitle the buyer to specific performance. . . . Nor, even though the buyer was somewhat neglectful in not paying the balance of the purchase money on the day it was due, can it be said that the delay, particularly in view of the fact that the seller was in no hurry to perform its part of the contract, was unreasonable. . . . In any event, the buyer was required to compensate the seller for whatever loss it sustained by the payment of interest. Moreover, the mere fixing of a particular date for the completion of a contract for the sale and purchase of land is not regarded as being of the essence with respect to payment but treats the provision as formal rather than essential.

Although the seller relies principally on Stern v. Shapiro, 38 Md. 615, 114 A. 587 (1921), Doering v. Fields, 187 Md. 484, 50 A.2d 553 (1947), and Levy v. Baetjer, 198 Md. 240, 81 A.2d 644 (1951), to support the claim that the chancellor erred in granting specific performance, all of these cases are distinguishable on the facts from the case at bar. In *Stern*, the provision that the down payment was to be forfeited in the event settlement was not made within the time specified, warranted the inference that time was of the essence. Here, a forfeiture was neither provided nor contemplated. In *Doering*, the buyers not only made no effort to settle within the agreed time, but despite an extension were still unable to pay the balance of the purchase money at the expiration of the extended period. Here, although the extended time had expired, the president of the corporate buyer had tendered full performance within a reasonable time thereafter. In *Levy*, the express provision that time was of the essence was held not to have been waived by the extension of the settlement date. Here, the very absence of the essentialness of time without more distinguishes that case from this.

The further claim that the presence of a stipulated settlement date in the contract of sale impels an inference that time was to be of the essence is likewise without merit. In Soehnlein v. Pumphrey, it was said (at p. 338 of 183 Md., at p. 845 of 37 A.2d): "The accepted doctrine is that in the ordinary case of contract for the sale of land, even though a certain period of time is stipulated for its consummation, equity treats the provision as formal rather than essential, and permits the purchaser who has suffered the period to elapse to make payments after the prescribed date, and to compel performance by the vendor notwithstanding the delay, unless it appears that time is of the essence of the contract by express stipulation, or by inference from the conduct of the parties, the special purpose for which the sale was made, or other circumstances surrounding the sale." . . . When there has been a delay, as there was in this case, the important question is whether it was reasonable. The chancellor found that it was and we cannot say that he erred in so doing.

Decree affirmed; appellants to pay the costs.

NOTES

1. A uniform act coverage

1. Uniform Land Transactions Act:

§ 2-302. [Time of Performance; Time of Essence]
> (a) If the contract does not fix the time for performance,
>> (1) the time for performance is a reasonable time after the making of the contract and tender must be at a reasonable hour and after reasonable notice to the other party of intention to tender; and
>> (2) either party may fix a time for performance if the time is not unreasonable and is fixed in good faith.
> (b) Except as provided in subsection (d), even though the contract specifies a particular time for performance, the failure of one of the parties to tender his

performance at the specified time does not discharge the other party from his duties under the contract unless:

    (1) the failure to perform, under the circumstances, is a material breach, or

    (2) the contract explicitly provides that failure to perform at the time specified discharges the duties of the other party.

(c) The phrase "time is of the essence" or other similar general language does not of itself provide explicitly that failure to perform at the time specified discharges the duties of the other party.

(d) If the contract specifies a particular time for performance, either party, by reasonable and good faith notice to the other before that date, may specify effectively that failure to perform on the specified date will discharge him from his own duties under the contract.

(e) If the contract specifies a particular time for performance, and a failure to tender performance at the specified time does not discharge the other party (subsections (b) and (d)):

    (1) the time for performance is a reasonable time thereafter; and

    (2) the rules of subsection (a) as to time for tender and fixing of time for performance apply.

This uniform act has been adopted by no jurisdiction.

2. *Buyer tender.* If a buyer sues for specific performance, must the buyer pay the full price into the registry of the court at the time the action is commenced?

Consider the practical remarks of Judge Crockett on the validity of an insufficient funds check as a tender. The following is from his concurring opinion in Sieverts v. White, 2 Utah 2d 351, 356, 273 P.2d 974, 977 (1954):

Though the practice may not be one to be commended, it is not uncommon, in various types of financing of business transactions, to write a check with the expectation of transferring funds or credit from one account to another, or arranging credit with the bank, or depositing money to cover commitments, if and after, a check is accepted. If such a check were refused there would be no practical use of arranging for the money or credit to cover it. This might entail considerable inconvenience, difficulty or even hardship, to no useful purpose. Serious injustices might result if the offeree in such a transaction could defeat proof of tender simply by showing that the offeror had not sufficient funds in the bank to cover the check at the time it was offered.

The offeree, of course, has a right to reject the tender by check when it is made. This is perfectly proper if he states the ground of his objection, but it is only reasonable that the person making a tender has a right to know the ground of the objection, so that if it be well taken he may protect himself by conforming thereto within the required time. If the offeree has failed to state an objection, or objects on other grounds, it would be manifestly unfair to permit him to defeat proof of tender by check on the sole ground that there were not sufficient funds to cover the check at the time the tender was made, because the offeror may have arranged for payment of the check if it had been accepted. This reasoning is reflected in our statute which requires the person to whom a tender is made to "specify any objection" he has thereto or be "deemed to have waived it."

3. *Waiver.* Each party may waive the other party's obligation when time is of the essence. In Evelyn v. Raven Realty, 215 Md. 467, 138 A.2d 898 (1958), the court held that in order to take advantage of seller's waiver of a time condition, the buyer must be able to show that he could have performed at the essential date.

4. On time of performance in real estate sales contracts see the extended coverage in Stoebuck & Whitman, The Law of Property 756-763 (3d ed. 2000).

G. MARKETABLE TITLE

Most contracts for the sale of real property provide expressly or by implication that the seller will convey a marketable title to the buyer. Unless it is clear that the parties intend a different type of title, it is generally implied that the seller will provide a marketable title to the buyer even though the contract does not expressly so state. The concept of marketable title is a rather vacuous one but developed due to the need for such a concept given the frequent uncertainty at the time the contract of sale was entered into as to what if any defects may exist in the seller's title. A marketable title need not be a perfect title and very long-shot possibilities of valid claims being successfully asserted against the seller's title will not make a title unmarketable. But a perfect title may not be a marketable title if there is sufficient chance that the validity of the seller's title will be litigated. Moreover, some nontitle restrictions on land use have been held will make the title unmarketable, for example, lack of public access to the land parcel in question. Some real property contracts of sale do not include an obligation on the seller to provide marketable title. A common alternative is that the seller will provide a title that a reputable title insurance company will insure, but as most title insurance companies insure marketable title, indirectly the marketable title obligation on the seller exists. Another common exception to marketable title in contracts of sale is that the seller will provide marketable title but with certain designated exceptions, such as an outstanding mortgage that the buyer is assuming or taking subject to.

Abstract definitions of marketable title appear in many judicial opinions, treatises on property law, or law review articles. One such, that appears in 14 Powell on Real Property, pp. 81-121 (2005), is as follows:

> A title is marketable if it meets the reasonable judgment standard applied by the courts. If a reasonable person — knowing the facts about seller's title including its chain of title, encumbrances against it and any opposing claims of ownership — would accept the title without hesitation, then the title is marketable. [citing many cases]

However, it should be recognized that there is extensive case law as to whether or not particular factual situations constitute marketable title. Abstract definitions are of limited help in resolving many questions as to whether or not a marketable title obligation has been satisfied in particular factual situations.

Voorheesville Rod & Gun v. E.W. Tompkins

626 N.E.2d 917 (N.Y. 1993)

HANCOCK, Judge.

The first issue in this case is whether the subdivision regulations of the Village of Voorheesville apply to a conveyance of a portion of a parcel of land where it is intended by the parties to the transaction that the lands shall remain undeveloped. If the regulations apply, then the primary issue is whether defendant seller's failure to seek subdivision approval before the transfer renders the title unmarketable. We conclude that the Village's subdivision regulations apply to this sale of property. But we further hold that defendant's refusal to seek the subdivision approval here does not cause the title to be unmarketable. Because no provision in the contract requires defendant to obtain subdivision approval and the only basis for plaintiff's specific performance claim is its failed assertion of unmarketable title, we reverse, deny plaintiff's summary judgment motion for specific performance, and dismiss the complaint.

I

On January 15, 1986, plaintiff Voorheesville Rod & Gun Club, Inc., signed a standard preprinted contract with defendant E.W. Tompkins Company, Inc., to purchase a portion of defendant's property located in the Village of Voorheesville, Albany County, for $38,000. The contract specified that the property would be conveyed by warranty deed subject to all covenants, conditions, restrictions and easements of record, and also to zoning and environmental protection laws, "provided that this does not render the title to the premises unmarketable." The property to be conveyed consisted of 24.534 acres of undeveloped land used for recreational purposes. The parties agree that plaintiff buyer did not intend to change the existing condition or use of the property after the purchase.

On August 23, 1986, prior to the revised closing date, plaintiff's attorney sent defendant's attorney a copy of the Village of Voorheesville's subdivision regulations and requested that defendant comply with them. Defendant did not seek subdivision approval. Defendant sent plaintiff a time-of-the-essence notice, demanded a closing on August 29, 1986, and notified plaintiff that if it did not close, that would be considered an anticipatory breach of contract. When plaintiff failed to close, defendant canceled the contract and returned plaintiff's $5,000 deposit. On September 4th, plaintiff informed defendant that the cancellation was unacceptable because defendant's failure to obtain subdivision approval had rendered the title unmarketable and, for that reason, plaintiff's financing bank was unwilling to close. Plaintiff then sought the requisite approval from the Village of Voorheesville Planning Commission. The Commission denied the application, stating that the subdivision regulations required that the application be submitted "by the [property] owner or an agent of the owner."

Plaintiff commenced this action on September 12, 1986, for specific performance or damages for breach of contract and then moved for partial summary judgment seeking specific performance. Supreme Court ordered that the contract be specifically performed by defendant and directed that defendant apply to the Village for subdivision approval and close on the subject property within a reasonable time after approval. The court held that defendant's failure to obtain subdivision approval made the title unmarketable and relieved plaintiff from closing until the approval was obtained (*Voorheesville Rod & Gun Club v. Tompkins Co.,* 141 Misc.2d 38, 532 N.Y.S.2d 699).

The Appellate Division affirmed, stating that the sale of a portion of defendant's real property subjected the sale to the subdivision regulations of the Village of Voorheesville, even though development of the land was not then contemplated.

The Court concluded that defendant's refusal to obtain subdivision approval rendered the title unmarketable, particularly because it appeared that plaintiff "would be 'plagued by zoning problems'" (*Voorheesville Rod & Gun Club v. Tompkins Co.*, 158 A.D.2d 789, 791, 551 N.Y.S.2d 382).

Thereafter, plaintiff moved in Supreme Court for an order compelling defendant to file the subdivision application and convey the property. Noting that the subdivision application had been made and approved, Supreme Court directed defendant to transfer the property. Then the parties stipulated to discontinue all causes of action interposed in the pleadings except plaintiff's claim for specific performance of the contract. This Court granted defendant leave to appeal from the stipulation, deemed a judgment, bringing up for review the prior nonfinal Appellate Division order pursuant to CPLR 5602(a)(1)(ii).

II

The preliminary issue is whether the Village's subdivision regulations apply at all under the circumstances presented. If they do not, that is the end of the matter and we do not reach the separate question of whether defendant's refusal to obtain subdivision approval rendered the title to the property unmarketable. Thus, we must first interpret the Village's Land Subdivision Regulations, which provide in pertinent part:

"Article II: *Definitions*

* * * * * *

"*Subdivision:* means the division of any parcel of land into two or more lots, blocks, or sites, with or without streets or highways and includes re-subdivision.

* * * * * *

"Article III: *Procedure in Filing Subdivision Applications*
"Whenever any subdivision of land is proposed to be made, and before any contract for the sale of, or any offer to sell any lots in such subdivision or any part thereof is made, and before any permit for the erection of a structure in such proposed subdivision shall be granted, the subdivider or his duly authorized agent shall apply in writing for approval of such proposed subdivision."

Defendant maintains that, pursuant to article III, subdivision approval is required only in instances where building or development is contemplated; and because no development of the subject property was intended, the regulations do not apply in this case. This claim is not persuasive. It is undisputed that defendant was selling only a portion of its property; therefore, the subject property transfer constituted a subdivision within the meaning of article II of the regulations. Article III clearly requires subdivision approval "[w]henever any subdivision of land is proposed" and before any sales contract is executed. Contrary to defendant's interpretation, merely because article III requires subdivision approval, *inter alia*, "before any permit for the erection of a structure in such proposed subdivision shall be granted", it does not follow that subdivision approval is necessary *only* when a building permit will be sought (*see, Matter of Esposito v. Town of Fulton Planning Bd.*, 188 A.D.2d 779, 591 N.Y.S.2d 254). Indeed, defendant's interpretation would effectively limit the purpose of the regulations to controlling building on individual parcels of property. Such an interpretation is contrary to the Village's broader policy, as stated in article I of the regulations, to "consider land Subdivision Plats as part of a plan for the orderly, efficient and economical development of the Village", which means, among other things, that "all proposed lots shall be so laid out and of such size as to be in harmony with the development pattern of the neighboring properties". Clearly, the stated policy of the regulations is that subdivision approval should be acquired for any proposed subdivision, not just those to be immediately developed.

III

Given that the subdivision regulations apply, we turn to the main issue: whether lack of subdivision approval constitutes a cloud on the title which renders the title unmarketable. It is undisputed that the contract is silent as to the specific issue of subdivision approval. Thus nothing in the contract imposes upon defendant the affirmative obligation of obtaining subdivision approval.[1] Rather, paragraph 4 of the contract, entitled "Existing Conditions", provides that the property would be conveyed by warranty deed

> "subject to all covenants, conditions, restrictions and easements of record. *Subject also to zoning and environmental protection laws;* any existing tenancies; * * * and any state of facts which an inspection and/or accurate survey may show, *provided that this does not render the title to the premises unmarketable*" (emphasis added).

As stated, plaintiff was to purchase the property subject to zoning laws, which are closely related to subdivision regulations (*see generally, Matter of Golden v. Planning Bd.,* 30 N.Y.2d 359, 372, 334 N.Y.S.2d 138, 285 N.E.2d 291; 2 Anderson, New York Zoning Law and Practice § 21.02 [3d ed.]). This requirement conforms to the well-settled rule that "where a person agrees to purchase real estate, which, at the time, is restricted by laws or ordinances, he will be deemed to have entered into the contract subject to the same [and] [h]e cannot thereafter be heard to object to taking the title because of such restrictions" (*Lincoln Trust Co. v. Williams Bldg. Corp.,* 229 N.Y. 313, 318, 128 N.E. 209; *see, Pamerqua Realty Corp. v. Dollar Serv. Corp.,* 93 A.D.2d 249, 251, 461 N.Y.S.2d 393; 3 Warren's Weed, New York Real Property, Marketability of Title, § 8.07 [4th ed.]; Annotation, *Zoning or Other Public Restrictions On the Use of Property as Affecting Rights and Remedies of Parties to Contract for the Sale Thereof,* §§ 3, 5[b], 39 A.L.R.3d 362, 370, 376).

The only limitation that the contract places upon plaintiff's duty to purchase the property subject to zoning laws is when the application of such laws would render title to the property unmarketable. It was not necessary for the contract to specify that a marketable title was required because, in the absence of a stipulation to the contrary, it is presumed that a marketable title is to be conveyed (*see, Regan v. Lanze,*

---

1. To the extent that plaintiff now claims—distinct from its argument that lack of subdivision approval renders the title unmarketable—that defendant has an implied good-faith contractual duty to obtain subdivision approval as a precondition of performing the contract, this issue was not raised by plaintiff in its summary judgment motion papers and thus is not preserved for our review.

We also note that this is not a case where the seller is seeking specific performance of a contract to compel a buyer to purchase property lacking subdivision approval or where a municipality is trying to block such a conveyance, and we do not address such situations here.

40 N.Y.2d 475, 482, 387 N.Y.S.2d 79, 354 N.E.2d 818; *Laba v. Carey,* 29 N.Y.2d 302, 311, 327 N.Y.S.2d 613, 277 N.E.2d 641; 3 Warren's Weed, *op. cit.,* Marketability of Title, § 1.01). Accordingly, the issue reduces to whether the lack of subdivision approval constitutes a defect in the title which makes it unmarketable.

The test of the marketability of a title is "whether there is an objection there to such as would interfere with a sale or with the market value of the property" (*Regan v. Lanze,* 40 N.Y.2d 475, 481, 387 N.Y.S.2d 79, 354 N.E.2d 818, *supra*). A marketable title is "a title free from reasonable doubt, but not from every doubt" (*id.,* at 482, 387 N.Y.S.2d 79, 354 N.E.2d 818). We have said that a "purchaser ought not to be compelled to take property, the possession or title of which he may be obliged to defend by litigation. He should have a title that will enable him to hold his land free from probable claim by another, and one which, if he wishes to sell, would be reasonably free from any doubt which would interfere with its market value" (*Dyker Meadow Land & Improvement Co. v. Cook,* 159 N.Y. 6, 15, 53 N.E. 690). As can be seen from these definitions, marketability of title is concerned with impairments on title to a property, i.e., the right to unencumbered ownership and possession, not with legal public regulation of the use of the property (*see, Lincoln Trust Co. v. Williams Bldg. Corp.,* 229 N.Y. 313, 318, 128 N.E. 209, *supra;* 5A Warren's Weed, *op. cit.,* Title, § 1.01; *compare,* 3 Warren's Weed, *op. cit.,* Marketability of Title, §§ 1.01, 2.01, *with* § 8.07). Accordingly, a zoning ordinance, existing at the time of the contract, which regulates only the use of the property, generally is not an encumbrance making the title unmarketable (*see, Lincoln Trust, supra,* at 318, 128 N.E. 209; *Anderson v. Steinway & Sons,* 178 App.Div. 507, 513, 165 N.Y.S. 608, *affd.* 221 N.Y. 639, 117 N.E. 575; *Pamerqua Realty Corp. v. Dollar Serv. Corp.,* 93 A.D.2d 249, 251, 461 N.Y.S.2d 393, *supra;* 3 Warren's Weed, *op. cit.,* Marketability of Title, § 8.07; 1 Rasch, New York Law and Practice of Real Property § 22.61 [2d ed.]).

Where, however, a contract expressly provides that the seller warrants and represents that, upon purchase, the property will not be in violation of any zoning ordinance, the purchaser "is entitled to demand that the vendor rectify the same or return any moneys paid on account" (*Pamerqua Realty Corp.,* 93 A.D.2d 249, 251, 461 N.Y.S.2d 393, *supra; see, Artstrong Homes v. Vasa,* 23 Misc.2d 608, 201 N.Y.S.2d 138 [Meyer, J.]; 3 Warren's Weed, *op. cit.,* Marketability of Title, § 8.07; 1 Rasch, *op. cit.,* § 22.61). Contrary to plaintiff's claim, the present case does not fall within this exception to the general rule. Defendant did not warrant or represent that it would obtain subdivision approval; rather, plaintiff agreed to purchase the property subject to the zoning laws. In effect, plaintiff is attempting to add a term to the contract after the deal has been made. Thus, although defendant's failure to obtain subdivision approval was a violation of the regulations which were in effect when the parties contracted, such violation did not make the title unmarketable (*see, Lincoln Trust, supra,* 229 N.Y. at 318, 128 N.E. 209; *Pamerqua Realty Corp.,* 93 A.D.2d 249, 251, 461 N.Y.S.2d 393, *supra;* 3 Warren's Weed, *op. cit.,* Marketability of Title, § 8.07; 1 Rasch, *op. cit.,* § 22.61).[2]

We recognize, as noted by the courts below, the increasing sophistication of municipalities regarding subdivision regulation and their ability to prevent the

---

2. Since it is undisputed that plaintiff did not intend to develop or further partition the parcel but only to continue its recreational use, there is no basis for any claim that the property would be "plagued by zoning problems".

purchaser from developing property as allowed by the zoning laws until the requisite subdivision approval is obtained (*see, Delaware Midland Corp. v. Incorporated Vil. of Westhampton Beach*, 79 Misc.2d 438, 445, 359 N.Y.S.2d 944, *affd. on opn. below*, 48 A.D.2d 681, 369 N.Y.S.2d 378, *affd. on opn, at Sup. Ct.* 39 N.Y.2d 1029, 387 N.Y.S.2d 248, 355 N.E.2d 302 ["Implicit in the power to control subdivisions is the authority to prevent illegal development by denial of permission to build"]; *see also*, Village Law § 7–714; Town Law § 268; *Matter of Golden v. Planning Bd.*, 30 N.Y.2d 359, 372, 334 N.Y.S.2d 138, 285 N.E.2d 291, *supra; cf., Freundlich v. Town Bd.*, 73 A.D.2d 684, 422 N.Y.S.2d 215, *affd.* 52 N.Y.2d 921, 437 N.Y.S.2d 664, 419 N.E.2d 342 [property may not be sold pursuant to invalid sales map without approval of planning board]). The solution for avoiding such problems, however, is not for the courts to expand the conditions which render title unmarketable, thereby altering the concept of marketability of title, but for the parties to real estate contracts to include specific provisions dealing with the duty to obtain subdivision approval.

Accordingly, the judgment appealed from and the order of the Appellate Division brought up for review should be reversed, with costs, plaintiff's motion for partial summary judgment should be denied, and defendant's cross motion for summary judgment dismissing the complaint should be granted.

KAYE, C.J., and SIMONS, TITONE, BELLACOSA and SMITH, JJ., concur.

LEVINE, J., taking no part.

Judgment appealed from and order of the Appellate Division brought up for review reversed, etc.

NOTES AND QUESTIONS

1. What might plaintiff have insisted on at the contract drafting stage that would have avoided the result in the *Voorheesville Rod* case?

2. If the implied good faith argument had been timely raised how do you believe the New York Court of Appeals would have ruled on that argument?

3. *The meanings of marketable title.* A seller who contracts to sell Blackacre generally assumes an obligation to convey a "marketable title"; this note will treat the main aspects of that concept. To some extent, we will deal with matters more fully developed in Chapter Five in conjunction with recording, quiet title actions, and the like.

Marketable title disputes readily group into two categories: what kind of ownership in Blackacre seller is committed to transfer to buyer; what kind of proof of that ownership buyer must be given.

(a) What kind of ownership in Blackacre is seller committed to transfer to buyer? What seller is selling will seldom be described simply as "Blackacre with appurtenances," but it is useful to start with the obligation entailed by so simple a subject-matter description. Blackacre having been described as subject, seller is obligated to pass a fee simple absolute in those premises, and the fee must be free of *encumbrances*. In its largest meaning, encumbrances include, inter alia, leases, liens (mortgage, tax, etc.), marital rights, easements, private use restrictions, or encroachments (Blackacre must not be encroached upon by a neighbor's structure even if the structure unlawfully encroaches; buyer is not to be regarded as having to buy the law-suit for its removal. Blackacre's structures must not unlawfully encroach on a neighbor.)

Seller's title obligation having been defined as "Blackacre in fee simple absolute free of encumbrances," three sorts of disputes arise. The first picks up all the substantive law of property, mortgages, creditor's rights, etc. Did the document by which the seller acquired Blackacre pass fee simple absolute or some lesser estate? Was a mortgage satisfied by payment to the mortgagee after the mortgagee had assigned? And so on.

Another sort of dispute involves the question of what kind of language serves to cut down how much of seller's normal obligation. Thus, a seller, having leased the premises before entering the contract of sale, will of course only promise to sell Blackacre "subject to lease." Suppose the closing is delayed, that the lease expires during the delay period, and that seller renews the lease during that period. Or seller may sell "subject to easements": Does this excuse seller if it is discovered that there is an encroachment by a neighbor that hasn't lasted quite long enough to have become a prescriptive easement? Of course, allied to these cases are those involving the use of extrinsic evidence to cut down seller's obligation, and evidence of mistake to avoid it.

Finally, it turns out that there are some kinds of use interferences that define out as easements or encroachments, and thus as encumbrances, but that nevertheless ought not be regarded as violations of seller's marketable title obligation. This third category of marketable title disputes centers on classifying use encumbrances as violative or not. Thus, suppose that seller promises expressly or impliedly to convey Blackacre free of encumbrances and that Blackacre is described in the contract by a metes and bounds description that extends to the center of the public street that abuts Blackacre and that provides its access to the outside world. The street is an easement; it's an easement on Blackacre as described, but its presence nevertheless does not cause seller to lack marketable title. The rule just announced proceeds from the premise that the street is beneficial, so that any reasonable buyer ought to be pleased with its presence. You can readily imagine disputes as to whether the burden of a particular street exceeds its benefits. Just as buyer is deemed to have assented to a beneficially encumbering easement, so also he is usually deemed to have assented to *easements* and *encroachments,* whether or not beneficial, that were visible upon an inspection of the premises. Seller will argue that if the buyer went out to the premises and saw overhead wires or the like, he obviously was willing to assent to take subject to those wires if he didn't insist on an express clause obligating seller to get rid of them before closing. Buyer will, of course, argue that he obviously expected seller to make the usual encumbrance-free transfer, inasmuch as seller didn't expressly except the wires from his contract obligation. The cases fall on both sides of this dispute. For the seller, there are cases that require the buyer to take subject to encumbrances that were seen even though not excepted. There are also cases that excuse seller for visible encumbrances whether or not seen by buyer in the particular case.

(b) What kind of proof of ownership must seller furnish to buyer? Seller ownership of Blackacre free of flaws is one thing; proof of that ownership another. Taking the easiest case, suppose that seller is in possession of Blackacre and that visual and seismographic inspection of the premises discloses no hint of adverse interests. Suppose further that seller is the grantee of Blackacre in fee simple absolute by a recorded deed, the grantor of which in turn was the grantee of a recorded deed and so on all the way back to the first transaction in which Queen Isabella deeded the property to Miles Standish. Nevertheless, *if* the deed to seller was a forgery and *if* seller had taken possession the day before the inspection as a disseizor vi et armis, seller would not be the owner of Blackacre. Therefore as part of the marketable title requirement must seller as a regular matter furnish proofs to buyer that the deed to him was not a forgery? Or that none of the other deeds were? Or that a recorded deed dated 1876, which recites no consideration, was in fact delivered so as to pass title by gift? Or that all the grantors were sane? And so on.

These cases, generally, are those in which both record and possession facts suggest that seller is the true unencumbered owner of Blackacre, and the law is that seller on that state of appearances has satisfied his obligation to prove his title unless buyer has some colorable information to suggest that the record and possession appearances are invalid.

The reverse case is one in which seller really does own Blackacre, but the necessary record regularity is lacking. Thus, record title to a strip on the edge of Blackacre is in X, but seller and his predecessors have been in full adverse possession of the strip for 126 years. *Or,* the last recorded deed to Blackacre has as its grantee, George W. Jonhson, and the seller's name is George W. Johnson. Would a buyer's lawyer advise his client to pay George W. Johnson for Blackacre, when George W. Jonhson is clearly the record owner? Suppose an affidavit can be obtained from the grantor in the recorded deed that he intended to convey to George W. Johnson, and that he delivered possession to George W. Johnson? This would make buyer's lawyer feel somewhat better in allowing the deal to close, but then he'd worry about the fact that although he trusts the grantor (a nice old man) and has his affidavit, how will the situation appear when his buyer-client, say five years hence, becomes a seller of Blackacre?

In most cases of this sort, where record appearances *to some degree* belie ownership, but the seller *to some degree* can prove ownership, the seller really does own Blackacre. He can establish this with varying delays and amounts of expense by getting affidavits, releases from the apparent record interest holder, and finally by an action to quiet title. Which steps he will have to take, if any, for which kinds of flaws will be developed at Chapter Five infra.

Yet, in a case in which buyer contends that record flaws deprived seller of marketable title, why can't seller simply prove that he owns Blackacre in that very proceeding, and thus defeat buyer's damage action or sustain his own? *Query:* In a proceeding for specific performance of a contract to buy Blackacre, brought by George W. Johnson as seller against the buyer, with an adjudication for plaintiff on a finding that he, George W. Johnson, was the true owner, would this adjudication bind true owner George W. Jonhson, who appears after buyer has reluctantly complied with the decree and who sues to eject buyer? The fact that no res judicata effect can be given to the seller-buyer proceedings against the record claimant is the commonly asserted ground for denying record supplementation by proof in such proceedings (at least, where there is more color to the potential record claim than arises from a probable typographical transposition).

The last paragraph suggests that there is a kind of dispute generated by the face of the record that the court can resolve in buyer-seller litigation. It may be that seller is the true owner of Blackacre in light of all the deeds of record only if such and such a statute really docked all the tails in North Carolina. No fact being in dispute, there is no need for res judicata to bar against future claims by the tenant in tail, and the stare decisis effect of the holding will adequately protect a buyer forced to comply with his contract of purchase. Where the dispute arises from construction of a particular instrument, categorization of the issue as one of fact or law largely determines its resolvability in buyer-seller proceedings.

On the point of the last paragraph, however, it may be that the buyer-seller deal will be interpreted as not requiring buyer to stay tied up in the transaction until legal uncertainties are resolved, even if that resolution would provide adequate protection against potential future adverse claimants.

4. The Regan v. Lanze opinion, referred to by the court in the *Voorheesville Rod & Gun* case, extensively elaborated on marketable title as follows:

> A marketable title has been defined as one that may be freely made the subject of resale. It is one which can be readily sold or mortgaged to a person of reasonable prudence, the test of the marketability of a title being whether there is an objection thereto such as would interfere with a sale or with the market value of the property. The law assures to a buyer a title free from reasonable doubt, but not from every doubt, and the mere possibility or suspicion of a defect, which according to ordinary experience has no probable basis, does not demonstrate an unmarketable title. "If 'the only defect in the title' is 'a very remote and improbable contingency,' a 'slender possibility only,' a conveyance will be decreed."
>
> To be sure, a purchaser is entitled to a marketable title unless the parties stipulate otherwise in the contract. Except for extraordinary instances in which it is very clear that the purchaser can suffer no harm from a defect or encumbrance, he will not be compelled to take title when there is a defect in the record title which can be cured only by a resort to parol evidence or when there is an apparent encumbrance which can be removed or defeated only by such evidence. [Case citations in the above quotations are omitted.]

5. *Some administrative problems.* Contract or custom will provide that seller furnish or buyer procure the proofs of seller's title during the executory interval. Buyer's attorney is expected to get to the title examination with reasonable diligence and to notify seller's attorney promptly of any flaws discovered. There are many cases in which buyer's interim behavior is held to have waived a flaw in seller's title or to have waived any time-of-the-essence requirements on seller to have title in proper shape by the closing date.

6. Although sellers commonly contract to sell marketable title, the contracts normally are valid even though the sellers had no title or only defective title when contracting. What is significant is their title on closing, the time they have contracted to provide marketable title, if this is the quality of title promised. As one court has explained: ". . . a person may enter into a valid contract to sell real estate to which he has no title, provided he is able to carry through with the transaction after the final payment is made or tendered." English v. Sanchez, 796 P.2d 236, 238 (N.M. 1990).

7. In supplementing statutes and judicial case law on titles, half the states also have title standards approved by the conveyancing bar, usually a state bar association committee or section, that are used as guides in determining whether or not titles are marketable. Connecticut was the first state to have statewide title standards, the Connecticut Bar Association adopting a set of standards in 1938. Extensively relied on title standards now are in effect in about 20 states. Title standards are not government enacted or declared laws, and are not binding on courts. However, they are a form of privately created law generally followed by lawyers and on occasion cited by courts in their opinions, and hence have much the same effect as laws

created by governments. In these respects they resemble such other forms of privately created law as bar association codes of ethics, where not adopted as formal rules of court, and opinions of bar association professional ethics committees.

H. SELLER'S REMEDIES FOR BREACH BY BUYER

The usual formula for determining seller's damages if buyer defaults and seller seeks damages is the difference between the contract price and the market value of the property at the time of buyer breach. As with most general legal propositions, there may be reasons for courts not to follow this formula. There may, for example, be a valid liquidated damages clause in the sale contract, the market may have declined substantially shortly after the breach, the market value on the breach date may be too speculative, or the seller may have failed adequately to mitigate damages. In addition to damages based on the difference between contract price and market value on the breach date, many modern courts also will allow the seller consequential or incidental damages for added expenses or losses incurred by the seller arising from the buyer's breach.

Jones v. Lee

971 P.2d 858 (N.M.App. 1998)

DONNELLY, J.

Ihn P. Lee and Philomena Lee (Buyers) appeal from judgments determining that they breached a contract to purchase an Albuquerque, New Mexico, residence and awarding compensatory and punitive damages to Sam P. Jones and Sharon A. Jones (Sellers), and compensatory damages to Sonja Waldin and The Vaughn Company, Inc. (Broker–Agents). Buyers raise four issues on appeal: (1) whether the trial court erred in determining the applicability and measure of damages to be awarded to Sellers for breach of a real estate contract; (2) whether the trial court's award of consequential and special damages was proper and supported by substantial evidence; (3) whether the trial court erred in awarding punitive damages; and (4) whether the trial court erred in finding that Buyers were required to pay a broker's commission to Broker–Agents. Affirmed in part and reversed in part.

FACTS AND PROCEDURAL BACKGROUND

Following negotiations between the parties, on June 25, 1994, Buyers entered into a written real estate contract wherein they agreed to purchase Sellers' residence for $610,000. Sellers had listed the property for sale with Metro 100 Realtors. The purchase agreement entered into between Buyers and Sellers also listed Broker–Agents as Sellers' agents. Several weeks after signing the purchase agreement and tendering $6000 in earnest money, Buyers informed Sellers they were unable to consummate the agreement because of financial reasons. Buyers submitted a proposed termination agreement, dated August 23, 1994, to Sellers, whereby Buyers offered to void the contract in return for forfeiting their $6000 earnest money deposit.

Sellers rejected the proposed termination agreement and when it became clear that Buyers were not going to honor the purchase agreement, Sellers relisted the property for sale. Sellers ultimately sold the property in November 1994 to another purchaser for $540,000, $70,000 below the contract price originally agreed upon by the defaulting Buyers.

On April 12, 1995, Sellers filed suit against Buyers, seeking damages for breach of the real estate purchase agreement. Buyers filed several counterclaims against Sellers and a third-party claim against Broker–Agents. The counterclaims and third-party claim alleged, *inter alia,* that Sellers and their Broker–Agents misrepresented the fact that Waldin and The Vaughn Company were acting as agents for Sellers; that Sellers and their Broker–Agents were guilty of fraud; that Sellers and their Broker–Agents were negligent; that the contract should be declared void; and that Broker–Agents were guilty of unfair trade practices. Broker–Agents also filed a counterclaim against Buyers asserting that, as third-party beneficiaries, they were entitled to recover their real estate commission on the sale.

Following a bench trial, the trial court dismissed Buyers' counterclaims against Sellers and the third-party claims against Broker–Agents. The trial court adopted findings of fact and conclusions of law and entered a judgment in favor of Sellers, awarding them $70,000 in damages for the loss resulting from the resale of the realty at a lower price; $300 for a heating warranty required to be furnished the new buyers; $1433 for a solar inspection required by the new buyers; $126 for a consultation on the solar system required by the new buyers; $2250 for interest payments on the first and second mortgages until resale; $17,156, plus gross receipts tax, for a broker's commission; $11,000 for architect and contractor fees incurred on a home Sellers had planned to build following the sale of their home; and $10,172 for interest claimed to have been lost by Sellers on the net proceeds of the contract sale price. The compensatory and special damages awarded by the trial court totaled $112,748.94. In addition to the compensatory and special damages listed above, the trial court also awarded $33,000 in punitive damages, together with costs and prejudgment interest. The total damages awarded to Sellers amounted to $157,118.94, plus court costs.

In a separate judgment, the trial court also awarded Broker–Agents the sums of $18,300, plus $1,017.94 gross receipts tax, for their loss of the commission and $16,448 in attorney fees, together with gross receipts tax thereon.

DISCUSSION

I. APPLICABILITY AND MEASURE OF DAMAGES

Buyers argue that the trial court erred in awarding compensatory and special damages to Sellers and that it utilized an incorrect measure in calculating the amount of damages to be awarded. On appeal, a reviewing court will not overturn the trial court's findings of fact or award of damages if there is substantial and competent evidence to support such determination, or unless it is clearly demonstrated that the trial court employed an incorrect measure of damages. *See Ranchers Exploration & Dev. Corp. v. Miles,* 102 N.M. 387, 390, 696 P.2d 475, 478 (1985); *Wirth v. Commercial Resources, Inc.,* 96 N.M. 340, 346, 630 P.2d 292, 298 (Ct.App.1981).

If a purchaser defaults on a contract to purchase realty, as a general rule, the seller has three alternative remedies. The sellers may (1) seek relief in equity for rescission, (2) offer to perform and bring an action for specific performance, or (3) elect to retain the realty and file suit seeking an award of damages. *See Van Moorlehem v. Brown Realty Co.,* 747 F.2d 992, 994 (10th Cir.1984); *see also* 12 *Thompson on Real Property* § 99.14(b) (David A. Thomas ed., 1994 & Supp.1996). Here, Sellers elected to sue for damages. Where a party elects to sue for damages resulting from a breach of land sale contract, the burden is on that party to present competent evidence to support such claim for damages. *See Bennett v. Price,* 692 P.2d 1138, 1140 (Colo.Ct.App. 1984). The rationale underlying the award of damages in a breach of contract case is to compensate the non-defaulting party with just compensation commensurate with his or her loss. *See Construction Contracting & Management, Inc. v. McConnell,* 112 N.M. 371, 378, 815 P.2d 1161, 1168 (1991); *Allen v. Allen Title Co.,* 77 N.M. 796, 798, 427 P.2d 673, 675 (1967).

Buyers accurately note that New Mexico follows the "loss of the bargain" rule in determining damages resulting from a purchaser's breach of a contract to buy realty. *See Aboud v. Adams,* 84 N.M. 683, 688–89, 507 P.2d 430, 435–36 (1973). The "loss of the bargain" rule, recognized in *Aboud,* has been reaffirmed by our Supreme Court in *Hickey v. Griggs,* 106 N.M. 27, 30, 738 P.2d 899, 902 (1987), and *Wall v. Pate,* 104 N.M. 1, 2, 715 P.2d 449, 450 (1986). . . .

Buyers argue that the trial court erred in calculating compensatory damages of $70,000 solely by determining the difference between the contract price agreed upon by the parties and the subsequent resale price of the property, without determining the fair market value of the property at the time of the breach. The parties stipulated that the fair market value on August 23, 1994, was $610,000; thus, Buyers argue that Sellers did not sustain any compensatory damages because "at the time of the breach . . . they held property worth exactly the same amount as the contract price[.]"

Buyers are correct that in order to apply the loss of the bargain rule, the trial court must determine the value of the property at the time of the breach and compare that amount with the contract price. *See Aboud,* 84 N.M. at 689, 507 P.2d at 436; *see also* 5 Arthur L. Corbin, *Corbin on Contracts* § 1098A, at 535 (1964) (where purchaser defaults on purchase of realty, "the vendor's damages are the full contract price minus the market value of the land at date of breach and also minus any payment received").

In *Aboud* our Supreme Court addressed an analogous situation to that presented here, observing:

> [T]he loss of the bargain rule was not properly applied as there was no finding made of the market value of the land in question at the time of the breach. The trial court simply took the difference between "what the Adams had agreed to pay and what he later sold [the property] for[.]"

Aboud, 84 N.M. at 689, 507 P.2d at 436. The *Aboud* Court, quoting from 55 Am.Jur. *Vendor and Purchaser* § 526, at 920, further observed:

> "[I]n this country in the case of a private sale of land, the right of the vendor to resell on account of the [purchaser's default] and recover any deficiency arising on the resale is generally denied."

84 N.M. at 689, 507 P.2d at 436. Due to the trial court's failure to determine the market value of the property at the time of the breach, the Court in *Aboud*

remanded the case to the trial court to expressly determine the market value, noting:

> While a subsequent sale is evidence of the market value at the time of breach, it is not conclusive and the court must properly establish the market value at such time. Thus, evidence of the resale price is properly admitted as one of the factors in determining market value.

Id. (citation omitted).

Where the market value at the time of the breach is the same as the contract price, the sellers are generally limited to the recovery of only nominal damages or forfeiture of any earnest money, unless the sellers have established that they have also incurred special damages resulting from such breach. . . . *See generally* 5 Corbin, *supra,* § 1098A, at 535 ("Costs of making a resale may be allowed as consequential damages.").

In the instant case, like *Aboud,* there was no finding determining the date of breach or the market value of the property at the time of the breach. These determinations are essential factors in applying the loss of the bargain rule and in calculating the amount of general damages resulting from a purchaser's breach of a real estate contract. Thus, we conclude that the cause must be remanded for adoption of express findings of fact in accordance with the rule.

We noted above that the parties stipulated to the fair market value of the property on August 23, 1994. Also, while the date agreed upon for closing is generally the time for measuring the property's value at the time of the breach, *see* 14 Richard R. Powell, *Powell on Real Property* ¶ 882[2], at 81–218 (Patrick J. Rohan, former rev. ed.1998), during oral argument on appeal, Sellers stated that the breach occurred on August 23, 1994, when Buyers tendered a proposed termination agreement.

The general rule is that stipulations are ordinarily binding on the parties absent fraud, mistake, improvidence, material change in circumstances, or unless equitable considerations require otherwise. *See Barker v. Barker,* 93 N.M. 198, 199, 598 P.2d 1158, 1159 (1979); *Esquibel v. Brown Constr. Co.,* 85 N.M. 487, 490, 513 P.2d 1269, 1272 (Ct.App.1973). *See generally* 4 Richard A. Lord, *Williston on Contracts* §§ 1, 2 (1974).

As indicated in *Aboud,* 84 N.M. at 689, 507 P.2d at 436, a subsequent sale of land may be considered evidence of the market value at the time of breach and should be considered with other evidence bearing on the issue. It is unclear from the appellate record, including our questioning and the attorneys' answers at oral argument, for what purpose and to what effect the parties agreed to the stipulation before the trial court concerning market value. It shall be for the trial court on remand to determine what effect to give the stipulation and to otherwise determine the market value at the time of breach, to compare that to the contract sale price, and to calculate general damages, if any.

II.   AWARD OF SPECIAL DAMAGES

Buyers also challenge the trial court's award of special damages. Special damages may be awarded by the fact finder in a breach of contract case if the damages are shown to have resulted as the natural and probable consequence of the breach and, at the time of the formation of the contract, the breaching party reasonably knew or should have anticipated from the facts and circumstances that the damages would probably be incurred. *See Camino Real Mobile Home Park Partnership v. Wolfe,* 119 N.M. 436, 443, 446, 891 P.2d 1190, 1197, 1200 (1995) (party found to have breached contract is liable for general damages and special or consequential damages reasonably foreseeable as a result of the breach); *Wall,* 104 N.M. at 2, 715 P.2d at 450 (special damages may be awarded if the loss was foreseeable by breaching party at time of contracting). The parties are presumed to have contemplated the ordinary and natural incidents or consequences of nonperformance of the contract. *See E & B Specialties Co. v. Phillips,* 86 N.M. 331, 333, 523 P.2d 1357, 1359 (1974). *See generally* Restatement (Second) of Contracts § 351(1) (1981).

1. SOLAR SYSTEM AND HEATING WARRANTY

Buyers challenge the trial court's special damages award of $1433 for an inspection of the solar system, $126 for a consultation on the solar system, and $300 for a heating warranty incident to the resale of the residence. The trial court found that these damages were reasonably foreseeable by a person in Buyers' situation when the contract was formed. We agree. Whether a situation is reasonably foreseeable is generally a question of fact to be determined by the fact finder from the evidence and circumstances. As observed in *Camino Real Mobile Home Park Partnership,* 119 N.M. at 446, 891 P.2d at 1200, the foreseeability of damages rule "anticipates an explicit or tacit agreement by the defendant 'to respond in damages for the particular damages understood to be likely in the event of a breach[.]'" (Quoting *Wall,* 104 N.M. at 2, 715 P.2d at 450.) Here, although the purchase agreement between Buyers and Sellers did not specifically require an inspection of the solar system or consultation regarding its effectiveness, nevertheless, Paragraph 15 of the residential purchase agreement indicated that Sellers, at closing, would see to it that the heating and solar system would be "in the same condition as of the date of acceptance, normal wear and tear excepted and subject to the provisions of Paragraphs 10 and 12" of the agreement. Since the contract contemplated that an inspection would be made of the solar and heating systems, and these are major components of the residence, there was evidence in the record from which the trial court could reasonably determine that inspection of these systems and consultation with a specialist concerning such systems would be a reasonably foreseeable requirement imposed by a future purchaser. Similarly, our review of Paragraph 10 of the real estate sales agreement indicates the existence of evidence from which the trial court could find that Sellers may be required to pay for a heating warranty from a future purchaser. Paragraph 10 is a paragraph in the form contract indicating a list of warranties, the costs of which are sometimes borne by the sellers. The existence of this list in the contract is evidence upon which the trial court could find that the cost of the warranty was reasonably foreseeable.

2. INTEREST

After Buyers' default, Sellers relisted the property for sale and continued making payments on the first and second mortgages on the property until the subsequent sale. Sellers presented evidence that the interest payments on the mortgages totaled $4500. The trial court found that the mortgage interest that Sellers continued to pay on their residence following the breach by Buyers was foreseeable. However, the trial court acknowledged that Sellers enjoyed the benefit of the continued occupancy of the residence and therefore reduced this award of interest by one-half.

The trial court correctly determined that Sellers may be entitled to damages resulting from the payment of mortgage interest due to Buyers' breach of contract to purchase realty because such damages were reasonably foreseeable. Where a buyer defaults on a residential purchase agreement, thus forcing the seller to replace the property on the market for sale, the lapse of time between the original closing date and a subsequent sale may give rise to the incurring of special damages by the seller. *See Shaeffer v. Kelton,* 95 N.M. 182, 187, 619 P.2d 1226, 1231 (1980) (after default by purchaser plaintiff may recover interest payments on construction loan for period plaintiff sought to locate another buyer); *see also Karakehian v. Boyer,* 900 P.2d 1273, 1281 (Colo.Ct.App.1994) (interest on first and second mortgages held foreseeable as damages).

Buyers also challenge the trial court's award of $10,172 for interest alleged to have been lost on the net proceeds of the sale of the property. The trial court computed this award by determining a reasonable rate of interest that Sellers could have obtained for the four-month period between Buyers' breach and resale to the new buyers on the full purchase price contained in the real estate purchase agreement, less closing costs and repayment of mortgages. Buyers contend that interest computed in this way amounts to double recovery under *Van Moorlehem,* 747 F.2d at 994. On this record, we cannot tell whether double recovery or indeed any improper recovery will result if the award of $10,172 is allowed to stand. We note that the trial court's award of prejudgment interest ran only from the date of trial, and not from the date the claim accrued, and is proper for an award of prejudgment interest under NMSA 1978, § 56–8–3 (1983). *See Sunwest Bank v. Colucci,* 117 N.M. 373, 377, 872 P.2d 346, 350 (1994). It is unclear from the record whether the trial court's award of prejudgment interest was under Section 56–8–3 or NMSA 1978, § 56–8–4 (1993). Upon remand, the trial court is directed to reconsider the award of $10,172 in light of *Van Moorlehem* and in relation to its award, if any, of compensatory damages and prejudgment interest.

3.   FEES INCIDENT TO SEPARATE LOT

The trial court also awarded $11,000 special damages for architect's and contractor's fees incurred by Sellers in planning to build a new home on a lot acquired by Sellers in 1992.

Sellers' response to Buyers' request for admissions conceded that prior to 1995, Sellers did not notify Buyers of the existence of the lot purchased by them in December 1992. Sellers admitted at trial that they did not know whether Buyers were aware of Sellers' strained financial status or the fact that they had previously purchased a lot on which they contemplated constructing a new house. In preparation for the construction of a new house, Sellers hired an architect and consulted with a contractor, thereby incurring expenses for $9000 and $2000 respectively. Sellers admitted that they had originally paid $150,000 for the lot and subsequently sold it for $194,000. We agree with Buyers that there is insufficient evidence in the record to establish that the architect's and the contractor's expenses incurred by them prior to the execution of the 1995 purchase agreement were reasonably foreseeable to Buyers when the parties executed the agreement. *See Wall,* 104

N.M. at 2, 715 P.2d at 450 (special damage arising from breach of contract must be expenses which are not expected to occur regularly to other plaintiffs and which are shown to have been within the contemplation of the parties at the time of the formation of the contract). As such, Sellers are not entitled to recover their claim for these fees.

III. AWARD OF PUNITIVE DAMAGES

The trial court awarded punitive damages against Buyers for their conduct in attempting to persuade Sellers to agree to terminate the contract. The trial court found, among other things:

> 23. [Buyers] and their family members engaged in acts of extremely poor judgment toward [Sellers] in their efforts to persuade [Sellers] to agree to a termination of the contract. One of these acts, [Buyers'] and their son's attempting to contact Mrs. Jones at her house, reasonably frightened Mrs. Jones but did not intimidate [Sellers] into agreeing to termination of the contract.
>
> 24. [Buyers] made misrepresentations of fact regarding their financial situation in their efforts to persuade [Sellers] to agree to a termination of the contract.
>
> 25. At the time of their breach of the contract, [Buyers] had approximately $577,000 in a checking account, and earned income of more than $16,000.00 per month, plus bonuses.
>
> 26. [Buyers'] failure to consummate the contract to purchase was wanton, utterly reckless and in utter disregard of their contractual obligations, and was sufficient to warrant the imposition of punitive damages. [Buyers'] conduct evidenced such a cavalier attitude toward their own obligations and the harm inflicted on [Sellers] as to establish their intent to harm [Sellers].
>
> 27. An equitable and reasonable award of punitive damages is $33,000.00.

Buyers argue that the punitive damage award is unsupported by substantial evidence and is incorrect as a matter of law because it was linked to an incorrect computation of compensatory damages. Absent proof that the conduct of a party resulting in a breach of contract was malicious, fraudulent, oppressive, or recklessly committed, with a wanton disregard of the other party's rights, an award of punitive damages is improper. *See McConnell*, 112 N.M. at 375, 815 P.2d at 1165; *see also* UJI 13–861 NMRA 1998; *Albuquerque Concrete Coring Co. v. Pan Am World Servs., Inc.*, 118 N.M. 140, 143, 879 P.2d 772, 775 (1994). Because the purpose of punitive damages is to punish and deter improper conduct, there must be some evidence of a culpable mental state on the part of the party who has caused the breach. *See McConnell*, 112 N.M. at 375, 815 P.2d at 1165. Thus, absent a showing that the breaching party intended to inflict harm on the non-breaching party or conduct which violates community standards of decency, the actions of the breaching party will not serve as a basis for an award of punitive damages. *See id.*

In explaining the punitive damages award, the trial court stated that the award was "approximately a third of the compensatory damages." The trial court found that Buyers "made intentional misrepresentations of fact to Norwest Mortgage regarding [Buyers'] financial ability to close the transaction in order to be relieved of their obligation under the contract" and that "[a]t the time of their intentional breach, [Buyers] had sufficient capital and income to finance the purchase of the property."

Our review of the record indicates a factual basis from which the trial court could properly assess punitive damages against Buyers. The trial court found that the conduct of Buyers included acts intended to persuade Sellers to agree to terminate the agreement. Additionally, despite Sellers' request that Buyers communicate with them through their attorneys or Broker–Agents, Buyers attempted to contact them directly and, on one occasion, severely frightened Mrs. Jones by pounding on the front door of the residence so forcibly that the lock on the door to the residence had to be replaced.

Because the trial court, in assessing the award of punitive damages against Buyers, stated that it based the award of punitive damages, in part, on its computation of compensatory damages, and we have determined that the award of compensatory damages was not calculated on the "loss of the bargain rule," we remand the issue of the award of punitive damages to the trial court for the adoption of additional findings of fact and conclusions of law concerning the amount, if any, of punitive damages, after the trial court calculates its award of damages, if any, based on loss of the bargain.

IV. REAL ESTATE COMMISSION

The trial court awarded special damages to Sellers for Broker–Agents' commission owed by them in the amount of $18,300, plus gross receipts tax. Buyers claim they have no obligation to pay a real estate commission to Broker-Agents because Broker–Agents did not have a written listing agreement for the property, as required by NMSA 1978, § 47–1–45 (1949). We find this argument unpersuasive. It is undisputed that Sellers entered into a written listing agreement with Metro 100 Realtors, Inc. The trial court properly found that Broker–Agents were the subagents of Sellers. Buyers admitted that Waldin was an agent for The Vaughn Company. Moreover, the listing agreement signed by Sellers stated that the broker could list the property on the multiple listing index and "may offer subagency to other brokers . . . [i]n return for procuring a purchaser for the property [and] Broker shall pay 3% of [the] sales price plus applicable gross receipts tax to the Subagent." While Buyers correctly note that agreements for the sale of realty must be in writing, there is no requirement that agreements between brokers to share commissions be in writing. Moreover, such authority was expressly contained in the original listing agreement and in the real estate sales agreement executed by Buyers. See Hapsas Realty Inc. v. McCoun, 91 N.M. 659, 660, 579 P.2d 785, 786 (1978). In Otero v. Buslee, 695 F.2d 1244, 1250–51 (10th Cir.1982), the court observed that New Mexico follows the rule that a broker is entitled to his or her commission even if the purchaser, after signing a real estate purchase agreement, defaults on the contract. See also Hayes v. Reeves, 91 N.M. 174, 178, 571 P.2d 1177, 1181 (1977); Stewart v. Brock, 60 N.M. 216, 225–26, 290 P.2d 682, 687 (1955). See generally Sonja A. Soehnel, Annotation, Modern View as to Right to Real Estate Broker to Recover Commission from Seller–Principal Where Buyer Defaults Under Valid Contract of Sale, 12 A.L.R. 4th 1083 (1982).

We affirm the trial court's award of the real estate commission, plus gross receipts tax to Broker–Agrents. However, our review of the record indicates that the trial court in entering a separate judgment for Broker–Agents duplicated a similar award included in the judgment awarded to Sellers. Thus, on remand, the trial court should enter an amended judgment directing that the commission earned by Broker–Agents be paid by Sellers to Broker–Agents out of the amount of damages recovered by Sellers.

CONCLUSION

For the reasons discussed herein, the cause is remanded for redetermination of the amount of compensatory and special damages, and/or the award of punitive damages, consistent with the matters discussed herein. On remand, in accordance with the written real estate agreement, the trial court should also award Sellers and Broker–Agents appropriate attorneys' fees for their services incident to this appeal.

It is so ordered.

NOTE

In Roesch v. Bray, 46 Ohio App. 3d 49, 545 N.E.2d 1301 (1988), the seller was awarded damages following default by the buyer of a sale contract. Damages were based on the difference between the contract price and the market value of the property at the time of breach. But the latter value was determined by the sale price obtained by the seller one year after the breach. This sale price was considered a fair estimate of value a year earlier because in the interim period the market was slow. However, the appellate court refused to award seller damages for expenses during the year between breach and sale, including payment for utilities, insurance, real estate taxes, yard maintenance, and advertising. These expenses, it was said, are "incidental to ownership." Arguably, some or all of these expenses should have been the basis for awarding damages to the seller, if it had been shown that seller had made consistent and reasonable efforts to sell following the breach. Certainly, a breaching buyer should not be obligated to pay seller's carrying costs for more than a reasonable time following breach.

Uzan v. 845 UN Ltd. Partnership

778 N.Y. Supp. 2d. 171 (2004)

MAZZARELLI, J.

This appeal presents the issue of whether plaintiffs, who defaulted on the purchase of four luxury condominium units, have forfeited their 25% down payments as a matter of law. Because the governing purchase agreements were a product of lengthy negotiation between parties of equal bargaining power, all represented by counsel, there was no evidence of over-reaching, and upon consideration of the fact that a 25% down payment is common usage in the new construction luxury condominium market in New York City, we hold that upon their default and failure to cure, plaintiffs forfeited all rights to their deposits pursuant to the rule set forth in *Maxton Builders, Inc. v. Lo Galbo*, 68 N.Y.2d 373, 509 N.Y.S.2d 507, 502 N.E.2d 184.

FACTS

In October 1998, Defendant 845 UN Limited Partnership (sponsor or 845 UN) began to sell apartments at The Trump World Tower (Trump World), a luxury condominium building to be constructed at 845 United Nations Plaza. Donald Trump is the managing general partner of the sponsor. Plaintiffs Cem Uzan and

Hakan Uzan, two brothers, are Turkish billionaires[1] who sought to purchase multiple units in the building.

In April 1999, plaintiffs and an associate executed seven purchase agreements for apartments in Trump World. Only four of those units (the penthouse units) are the subject of this lawsuit and appeal. As relevant, Cem Uzan defaulted on contracts to buy two penthouse units on the 90th floor of the building, and Hakan defaulted on contracts to purchase two other penthouse units on the 89th floor.[2]

The building had not been constructed when plaintiffs executed their purchase agreements. In paragraph 17.4 of those contracts, the sponsor projected that the first closing in the building would occur on or about April, 1, 2001, nearly two years after the signing of the agreements.

The condominium offering plan included a section titled "Special Risks to be Considered by Purchasers," which stated:

> Purchasers will be required to make a down payment upon execution of a Purchase Agreement in an amount equal to 10% of the purchase price, and within 180 days after receipt of the executed Purchase Agreement from Sponsor or 15 days after Purchaser receives a written notice or amendment to the Plan declaring the Plan effective, whichever is earlier, an additional down payment equal to 15% of the purchase price. . . .

Once construction was completed, the building's offering plan was amended to require a 15% down payment. Notably, both the original and the amended offering plans prominently disclosed the sponsor's right to retain the *entire down payment* should there be an uncured default.

NEGOTIATIONS PRECEDING EXECUTION OF THE PURCHASE AGREEMENTS

Plaintiffs were represented by experienced local counsel during the two-month-long negotiation for the purchase of the apartments. There were numerous telephone conversations between counsel, and at least four extensively marked-up copies of draft purchase agreements were exchanged. In consideration for plaintiff's purchase of multiple units, the sponsor reduced the aggregate purchase price of the penthouse units by more than $7 million from the list price in the offering plan for a total cost of approximately $32 million. Plaintiffs also negotiated a number of revisions to the standard purchase agreement, including extensions of time for payment of the down payment. As amended, each purchase agreement obligated plaintiffs to make a 25% down payment: 10% at contract, an additional 7½% down payment twelve months later, and a final 7½% down payment 18 months after the execution of the contract. At no time did plaintiffs object to the total amount required as a non-refundable down payment.

---

1. In an unrelated action, plaintiffs were found to have defrauded Motorola, Inc. Out of approximately $1 billion in connection with a deal to develop a cellular telephone network in Turkey (*see Motorola Credit Corp. v. Uzan,* 274 F.Supp.2d 481, 490–492 [S.D.N.Y. 2003]). Plaintiffs are subject to various orders in the federal action restraining their assets, and they are subject to arrest if they attempt to enter the United States (*id.*).

2. The transactions for three of the seven total units closed In July of 2001. Antonio Betancourt, an associate of the Uzans, purchased two units on the 59th floor of the building, and plaintiff Cem Uzan purchased a unit on the 80th floor.

There were other significant amendments to the standard purchase agreement which benefitted plaintiffs. These included: (1) rights to terminate the contracts if the closing had not occurred by December 31, 2003; (2) rights to advertise the units for resale prior to closing; (3) conditional rights to assign the purchase agreements to a third party; and (4) the right of each brother to terminate his contracts if the sponsor terminated the purchase agreements for the other brother's units. It is noted that according to counsel for the sponsor, the right to assign the purchase contracts prior to closing had not been granted to any other purchaser of a unit at Trump World. Also, at plaintiffs' urging, the sponsor added language to the purchase agreements agreeing not to install machinery on the roof that would cause noise or vibration in the apartments.

The executed purchase agreements provide, at paragraph 12(b), that:

> [u]pon the occurrence of an Event of Default . . . [i]f Sponsor elects to cancel . . . [and [i]f the default is not cured within . . . thirty (30) days, then this Agreement shall be deemed canceled, and Sponsor shall have the right to retain, as and for liquidated damages, the Down payment and any interest earned on the Down payment.

Plaintiffs paid the first 10% down payment installment for the penthouse units on April 26, 1999 when they signed the purchase agreements. They paid the second 7½% installment in April 2000, and the third 7½% installment in October 2000. The total 25% down payment of approximately $8 million was placed in an escrow account.

DEFAULT, FAILURE TO CURE, AND THIS ACTION

On September 11, 2001, terrorists attacked New York City by flying two planes into the World Trade Center, the city's two tallest buildings, murdering thousands of people. Plaintiffs, asserting concerns of future terrorist attacks, failed to appear at the October 19, 2001 closing, resulting in their default. By letter dated October 19, 2001, plaintiffs' counsel stated:

> [W]e believe that our clients are entitled to rescind their Purchase Agreements in view of the terrorist attack which occurred on September 11 and has not abated. In particular, our clients are concerned that the top floors in a "trophy" building, described as the tallest residential building in the world, will be an attractive terrorist target. The situation is further aggravated by the fact that the building bears the name of Donald Trump, perhaps the most widely known symbol of American capitalism. Finally, the United Nations complex brings even more attention to this location.

That day 845 UN sent plaintiffs default letters, notifying them that they had 30 days to cure. On November 19, 2001, upon expiration of the cure period, the sponsor terminated the four purchase agreements.

Plaintiffs then brought this action. They alleged that Donald Trump had prior special knowledge that certain tall buildings, such as Trump World, were potential targets for terrorists. Plaintiffs also alleged that Trump World did not have adequate protection for the residents of the upper floors of the building. In their first cause of action, plaintiffs averred that the sponsor's failure to advise prospective purchasers of the specific risks of a terrorist attack on Trump World, and to amend the offering plan to describe these risks, constituted common-law fraud and deceptive sales practices pursuant to General Business Law § 352. Plaintiffs' second claim is that the same acts constituted violations of General Business Law §§ 349 and 350. The third cause of action sought a declaratory judgment that the down payment was an "unconscionable, illegal and unenforceable penalty." The IAS court dismissed plaintiffs' first two claims in a March 2002 order not on appeal.

MOTIONS FOR SUMMARY JUDGMENT

After exchanging discovery and conducting various depositions, plaintiffs moved for summary judgment on their third cause of action, arguing that forfeiture of the down payments was an unenforceable penalty. In support of their motion, plaintiffs submitted an attorney's affirmation to which were annexed: the pleadings, correspondence between counsel, the IAS court's order denying dismissal of the declaratory judgment cause of action, and certain news articles and promotional materials about the Trump World Tower.

Defendant opposed the motion and cross-moved for summary judgment, asserting that defaulting vendees on real estate contracts may not recover their down payments. Defendant submitted the affidavits of Donald Trump, Leonard Ritz, Esq. and Ian Silver, Esq., two associates at the sponsor's law firm, Marilyn Weitzman, president of a nationwide real estate consulting firm headquartered in New York City, and Michael Martin, a consultant to the Trump Corporation.

Defendant also included the offering plan, the purchase agreements, Cem Uzan's 2000 purchase agreement for an apartment at 515 Park Avenue (with a 25% down payment provision), various correspondence between the parties, excerpts from the deposition testimony of Hakan Uzan, Jeffrey M. Diamond and Donald Trump, studies regarding the Manhattan real estate market, and an estimation of the sponsor's damages as of March 31, 2003. Defendant's submissions contain substantial evidence of the common usage of a 20–25% down payment in the preconstruction luxury condominium market.

THE ROLE OF THE 25% DOWN PAYMENT

In his affidavit in support of the cross motion, Donald Trump stated that he sought 25% down payments from pre-construction purchasers at the Trump World Tower because of the substantial length of time between contract signing and closing, during which period the sponsor had to keep the units off the market, and because of the obvious associated risks. Trump also affirmed that down payments in the range of 20% to 25% are standard practice in the new construction luxury condominium submarket in New York City. He cited three projects where he was the developer, The Trump Palace, 610 Park Avenue and Trump International Hotel and Tower, all of which had similar down payment provisions. Trump also noted that,

> [i]n new construction condominium projects, purchasers often speculate on the market by putting down initial down payments of 10% and 15% and watching how the market moves. If the market value increases, they will then make the second down payment. If the market prices drop, they may then walk away from their down payment. . . .

Both Weitzman and Martin stated, based upon research detailed in their affidavits, that the volatility of individual real estate transactions increases with the size of the unit involved, and that price swings for three- and four-bedroom units, such as the penthouse units plaintiffs sought to purchase here, were greater than for smaller apartments.

Defendant also presented a compilation of sixteen recent condominium offering plans, all of which required down payments of either 20% or 25% of the purchase price for the unit. Fourteen of the sixteen offering plans required 25% down payments. Further, defendant provided proof that in July 2001, plaintiff Cem Uzan closed on the purchase of an apartment on the 80th floor of Trump World after making a 25% down payment, and that he had previously purchased another apartment at 515 Park Avenue, also with a 25% down payment provision.

THE ORDER APPEALED

After hearing oral argument on the motion, the IAS court granted defendant partial summary judgment, finding that plaintiffs forfeited the portion of their down payment amounting to 10% of the purchase price, pursuant to *Maxton Builders, Inc. v. Lo Galbo*, 68 N.Y.2d 373, 509 N.Y.S.2d 507, 502 N.E.2d 184, *supra*. The court held that the remainder of the down payment was subject to a liquidated damages analysis to determine whether it bore a reasonable relation to the sponsor's actual or probable loss. Defendant appeals from that portion of the order which denied it full relief.

DISCUSSION

More than a century ago, the Court of Appeals, in *Lawrence v. Miller*, 86 N.Y. 131 [1881], held that a vendee who defaults on a real estate contract without lawful excuse cannot recover his or her down payment. It reaffirmed this holding, in *Maxton, supra*, again in 1986. The facts of *Lawrence* are common to real estate transactions, and parallel those presented here. In that case, plaintiff made a $2000 down payment on the purchase of certain real estate, and then defaulted. The seller refused to extend plaintiff's time to perform the contract, retained the down payment, and ultimately sold the property to another purchaser. In plaintiff's subsequent action for a refund of the down payment, the Court of Appeals affirmed a judgment dismissing the complaint, stating:

> To allow a recovery of this money would be to sustain an action by a party on his own breach of his own contract, which the law does not allow. When we once declare in this case that the vendor has done all that the law asks of him, we also declare that the vendee has not so done on his part. And then to maintain this action would be to declare that a party may violate his agreement, and make an infraction of it by himself a cause of action. That would be ill doctrine.

(*Lawrence*, 86 N.Y. 131, 140.)

For over a century, courts have consistently upheld what was called the *Lawrence* rule and recognized a distinction between real estate deposits and general liquidated damages clauses.[3] Liquidated damages clauses have traditionally been subject to judicial oversight to confirm that the stipulated damages bear a reasonable proportion to the probable loss caused by the breach. By contrast, real estate down payments have been subject to limited supervision. They have only been refunded upon a showing of disparity of bargaining power between the parties, duress, fraud, illegality or mutual mistake (*see Cipriano v. Glen Cove Lodge # 1458*, 1 N.Y.3d 53, 769 N.Y.S.2d 168, 801 N. E.2d 388).

In *Maxton,* plaintiff had contracted to sell defendants a house, and accepted a check for a 10% down payment. When defendants canceled the contract and placed a stop payment on the check, plaintiff sued for the down payment, citing the *Lawrence* rule. Defendants argued that plaintiff's recovery should be limited to its actual damages. In ruling for the vendor, the Court of Appeals identified two legal principles as flowing from *Lawrence.* First, that the vendor was entitled to retain the down payment in a real estate contract, without reference to his actual damages. Second, the "parent" rule, upon which the first rule was based, that one who breaches a contract may not recover the value of his part performance.

The Court noted that the parent rule had been substantially undermined in the 100 years since *Lawrence.* Many courts had rejected the parent rule because of criticism that it produced a forfeiture "and the amount of the forfeiture increases as performance proceeds, so that the penalty grows larger as the breach grows smaller" (*Maxton,* 68 N.Y.2d 373, 379, 509 N.Y.S.2d 507, 502 N.E.2d 184 [cite omitted]).

The Court also noted that since *Lawrence,* the rule of allowing recovery of down payments of not more than 10% in real estate contracts continues to be followed by a "majority of jurisdictions," including in New York (*Maxton,* 68 N.Y.2d at 380, 509 N.Y.S.2d 507, 502 N.E.2d 184). Thereafter, the court noted the long and widespread reliance on the *Lawrence* rule in real estate transactions, and it concluded that, based upon notions of efficiency and avoiding unnecessary litigation, the rule should remain in effect (*id.* at 381, 509 N.Y.S.2d 507, 502 N.E.2d 184).

After acknowledging that "[R]eal estate contracts are probably the best examples of arms length transactions," the Court broadly concluded:

> Except in cases where there is a real risk of overreaching, there should be no need for the courts to relieve the parties of the consequences of their contract. **If the parties are dissatisfied with the rule of [*Lawrence*], the time to say so is at the bargaining table.**

(*Maxton,* 68 N.Y.2d 373, 382, 509 N.Y.S.2d 507, 502 N.E.2d 184 [emphasis supplied].)

The *Maxton/Lawrence* rule has since been followed by this Court as well as the other departments to deny a refund of a down payment when a default has occurred. . . .

Further, other departments have specifically applied the *Maxton/Lawrence* rule, where, as here, a real estate down payment of greater than 10% of the purchase price is at issue. . . .

Applying the reasoning of these cases to the facts of the instant matter, it is clear that plaintiffs are not entitled to a return of any portion of their down payment. Here the 25% down payment was a specifically negotiated element of the contracts. There is no question that this was an arm's length transaction. The parties were sophisticated business people, represented by counsel, who spent two months at the bargaining table before executing the amended purchase agreements.

Further, the record evidences that it is customary in the pre-construction luxury condominium industry for parties to price the risk of default at 25% of the purchase price. . . .

Accordingly, the order of the Supreme Court, New York County (Alice Schlesinger, J.), entered July 21, 2003, which, to the extent appealed from, denied defendant 845 UN Limited Partnership's motion for summary judgment, should be reversed, on the law, with costs, defendant's motion granted and the complaint dismissed. The Clerk is directed to enter judgment in favor of defendant-appellant dismissing the complaint as against it.

Order, Supreme Court, New York County (Alice Schlesinger, J.), entered July 21, 2003, reversed, on the law, with costs, defendant-appellant 845 UN Limited Partnership's motion for summary judgment granted and the complaint dismissed. The Clerk is directed to enter judgment in favor of defendant-appellant dismissing the complaint as against it.

NOTES AND QUESTIONS

1. In your opinion were the seller's loss prospects too speculative in the *Uzan* case to justify the buyers' losing their 25 percent down payment?

2. Some courts have held that a seller is entitled to retain a 10 percent down payment following default by the buyer if there is a liquidated damage clause in the contract of sale. One such case is Kraft v. Michael, 166 Pa. Super. 57, 70 A.2d 424 (1950), in which the court relied on a contract liquidated damages clause in holding that seller was entitled to a 10 percent down payment even though the seller later sold the house to a third party at a somewhat higher price than provided for in the defaulted contract.

3. A Washington statute, Wash. Rev. Code Ann. § 64.04.005 (West Supp. 2006), provides as follows:

64.04.005. Liquidated Damages — Earnest Money Deposit — Exclusive Remedy — Definition

(1) A provision in a written agreement for the purchase and sale of real estate which provides for liquidated damages or the forfeiture of an earnest money deposit to the seller as the seller's sole and exclusive remedy if a party fails, without legal excuse, to complete the purchase, is valid and enforceable, regardless of whether the other party incurs any actual damages. However, the amount of liquidated damages or amount of earnest money to be forfeited under this subsection may not exceed five percent of the purchase price.

(2) For purposes of this section:

(a) "Earnest money deposit" means any deposit, deposits, payment, or payments of a part of the purchase price for the property, made in the form of cash, check, promissory note, or other things of value for the purpose of binding the purchaser to the agreement and identified in the agreement as an earnest money deposit, and does not include other deposits or payments made by the purchaser; and

(b) "Liquidated damages" means an amount agreed by the parties as the amount of damages to be recovered for a breach of the agreement by the other and identified in the agreement as liquidated damages, and does not include other deposits or payments made by the purchaser.

(3) This section does not prohibit, or supersede the common law with respect to, liquidated damages or earnest money forfeiture provisions in excess of five percent of the purchase price. A liquidated damages or earnest money forfeiture provision not meeting the requirements of subsection (1) of this section shall be interpreted and enforced without regard to this statute.

Why the 5 percent limit on forfeitures?

Smith v. Mady

146 Cal. App. 3d 129, 194 Cal. Rptr. 42 (1983)

SCHAUER, Presiding Justice. Defendants, who were defaulting purchasers under an agreement to buy real property from plaintiff sellers, appeal from a judgment after a non-jury trial. On appeal the question presented is whether a defaulting buyer of realty is entitled to credit, against consequential damages charged to buyer, an increased price obtained by the seller upon a quick resale.

The essential facts are not in dispute. In September of 1980, plaintiffs and defendants entered into a written agreement by which defendants were to purchase respondent plaintiffs' residence for a purchase price of $205,000. The sales escrow was to close in early December of 1980. However, defendants defaulted and the sale did not take place. On December 7, 1980, within a few days after the expected close of escrow and breach by defendants, plaintiffs entered into another contract to sell the property to third parties. Under this second sales agreement, the purchase price was $215,000. The second sale proceeded to close in February of 1981.

The instant lawsuit was commenced on December 5, 1980, for breach of the first sales contract. Upon trial the court recognized that there were no "benefit-of-the-bargain" damages under Civil Code section 3307[1] since the purchase price in the rapid resale established that the value of the property at the time of the breach was in excess of the property price of the earlier sale. However, the trial court found consequential damages under Civil Code section 3300,[2] suffered by sellers for cost of insurance, gardening, property taxes, utilities and encumbrance interest payments incurred between the default and the subsequent sale. The trial judge declined to offset the consequential damages with the increased resale proceeds, remarking upon the separate character of the resale transaction in comparison with the sale to defendants which gave rise to the breach. A judgment for plaintiffs in the sum of $2,648.34[3] was entered and this appeal followed.

1. Civ. Code § 3307 provides: "The detriment caused by the breach of an agreement to purchase an estate in real property, is deemed to be the excess, if any, of the amount which would have been due to the seller, under the contract, over the value of the property to him."
2. Civ. Code § 3300 provides: "For the breach of an obligation arising from contract, the measure of damages, except where otherwise expressly provided by this Code, is the amount which will compensate the party aggrieved for all the detriment proximately caused thereby, or which, in the ordinary course of things, would be likely to result therefrom."
3. The sales contract between plaintiffs and defendants provided for reasonable attorneys' fees for the prevailing party in litigation arising out of the agreement, and the trial court awarded plaintiffs such fees in the sum of $750, in addition to the $2,648.34. Since plaintiffs are not prevailing parties in view of the reversal on this appeal, the award of attorneys' fees for trial and appeal services is left to the trial court on the remand. (Schoolcraft v. Ross (1978) 81 Cal. App. 3d 75, 82, 146 Cal. Rptr. 57.)

The sole issue is whether a defaulting purchaser of real property is entitled to credit, against damages from his default, the increase in proceeds of a subsequent, but rapid, resale at a higher price. We resolve the issue in the affirmative and reverse.

Under the provisions of Civil Code, section 3307, "The detriment caused by the breach of an agreement to purchase an estate in real property, is deemed to be the excess, if any, of the amount which would have been due to the seller, under the contract, over the value of the property to him." But the view that this section is exclusive, and precludes other consequential damages occasioned by the breach, was rejected in Royer v. Carter (1951) 37 Cal. 2d 544, 550 [233 P.2d 539]. Under Civil Code, section 3300, other damages are recoverable, usually embracing the out-of-pocket expenses lost by failure of the transaction. (Wade v. Lake County Title Co. (1970) 6 Cal. App. 3d 824 at p. 830, 86 Cal. Rptr. 182.)

The Supreme Court in *Royer* (at p. 550 [233 P.2d 539]) stated that: ". . . the vendee's breach may make it necessary for the vendor to incur *additional expenses* to realize the benefit of his bargain . . . [and] [w]hen such *additional expenses* are the natural consequence of the breach, they may be recovered in addition to those provided for in section 3307." (Italics added.) The *Royer* opinion deals specifically with the expenses which the innocent vendor would incur in a second sale. More recent cases have shed further light on the scope of "additional expenses" which *Royer* sanctioned.

In Allen v. Enomoto, 228 Cal. App. 2d 798, 803-805 [39 Cal. Rptr. 815], the court allowed the vendor's out-of-pocket expenses for fire insurance, mortgage interest and real property taxes on the subject property. The award was premised on a finding that the vendor had continued diligently to attempt to resell the subject property and that the resale was made within the shortest period of time possible. The unspoken premise of such a holding is that the vendor (who still wishes to sell the property) actually has had to pay out-of-pocket expenses proximately caused by the vendee's breach. (Abrams v. Motter (1970) 3 Cal. App. 3d 828 at pp. 849-850, 83 Cal. Rptr. 855, footnote omitted.)

In both *Abrams* and Sutter v. Madrin (1969) 269 Cal. App. 2d 161, 74 Cal. Rptr. 627, it was recognized that ". . . resale . . . should be made with reasonable diligence to qualify the vendor to an allowance . . ." (id. at p. 169, 74 Cal. Rptr. 627) for consequential damages incurred after the breach. Additionally, both cases acknowledged that a vendor's continued ownership after a purchaser's default may have a "use" value which should be offset against expenses of the continuing ownership. (Id. at p. 168, 74 Cal. Rptr. 627; Abrams v. Motter, supra, 3 Cal. App. 3d at p. 850, 83 Cal. Rptr. 855.)

The facts in *Sutter* differ somewhat from the instant case in that the *Sutter* defaulting purchaser was seeking restitution of a portion of his deposit under the real estate sales contract. However, we find the fundamentals reviewed in *Sutter* to be equally applicable here. Also pertinent is ". . . the line of cases beginning with Freedman v. Rector etc. of St. Matthias Parish, 37 Cal. 2d 16 [230 P.2d 629, 31 A.L.R.2d 1], which have allowed recovery to a defaulting vendee in order to prevent the vendor from being unjustly enriched as a result of the vendee's default, even where the defaults has been willful. [Citations omitted.] As indicated by these cases the underlying purpose of the *Freedman* doctrine is to prevent the unjust enrichment of the seller at the expense of the buyer by requiring the former to refund to the latter payments made under the contract in excess of damages suffered by the seller." (Branche v. Hetzel (1966) 241 Cal. App. 2d 801 at p. 807, 51 Cal. Rptr. 188.)

The principle we draw from the precedents is that a vendor of real property is not to be ". . . placed in a better position by the buyer's default. This result is directly prohibited by section 3358 of the Civil Code."[4] [Citations omitted.]

Although it is well settled in the foregoing authorities that damages under Civil Code section 3307 for the difference between the contract price and property value may be insufficient to give the vendor the benefit of his bargain and he is entitled also to resale expenses and some costs of continued ownership, he should not be permitted to receive a windfall at the purchaser's expense. We discern no reason to deprive the defaulting purchaser of benefitting from a higher price on resale after continued ownership by seller while crediting the purchaser, as required under *Abrams* and *Sutter,* with the value of use to the seller during continued ownership.

In cases where the resale at a higher price occurs at a time much more distant from the breach than here, the vendor may show a lower property value at the moment of breach as well as increased costs of continuing ownership. However, in the case at bench the resale took place within a few days after the breach and established the value of the property at the time of breach. Realistically, the vendors here had sold their property to defendants at a price lower than the then value of the real estate. Sellers argue that the damages awarded only place them in the same position they would have been in had the defendants performed the contract, but a sufficient response is that had defendants performed plaintiffs would be in a worse position. By the resale sellers have obtained a $10,000 increment which is more than sufficient to absorb the $2,648.34 in increased costs of continuing ownership.

Inasmuch as under *Abrams* and *Sutter* the vendor has an obligation to resell promptly in order to obtain consequential damages and the resale price may fix the property value as a basis for Civil Code section 3307 damages, we are impelled to conclude that there is no inherent separateness in the original sale and subsequent resale transactions. The increased resale price should not be disregarded in considering an offset to consequential damages awarded to a vendor against a defaulting purchaser of real property.

The judgment is reversed and the cause remanded.

Johnson and Paez, J.J., concur.

NOTES

1. The Smith v. Mady type of offset can be applied if there is sufficient appraisal evidence of an increase in value of the property at time of trial but there has as yet been no sale at an appreciated price over the contract price. Askari v. R&R Land Co., 179 Cal. App. 3d 1101, 225 Cal. Rptr. 285 (1986).

---

4. Civ. Code, § 3358 provides; "Except as expressly provided by statute, no person can recover a greater amount in damages for the breach of an obligation, than he could have gained by the full performance thereof on both sides."

2. For a seller to recover loss-of-bargain damages for buyer default, seller must promptly seek to mitigate damages. In Spurgeon v. Drumheller, 174 Cal. App. 3d 659, 220 Cal. Rptr. 195 (1985), the court justified this requirement as follows:

> For the reason that no loss of bargain damages are available to a seller if there is a resale at the same or a higher price than the contract price, the law imposes on the seller of the property the duty to exercise diligence and to make a resale within the shortest time possible. . . . "Whether the resale is made one, two or three months later, or whether it be a year or more, it should be made with reasonable diligence to qualify the vendor to an allowance of an off-set against the vendee's claim for restitution of money paid." (Citation omitted.)

174 Cal. App. 3d at 665, 220 Cal. Rptr. at 198.

I. BUYER'S REMEDIES FOR BREACH BY SELLER

Mokar Properties Corp. v. Hall
179 N.Y.S.2d 814 (1958)

BOTEIN, Presiding Justice. This appeal is from an order of Special Term denying a motion by defendants which sought primarily to dismiss the complaint for failure to state a cause of action and on the ground that the claim was released. The complaint, grounded on the alleged failure to convey real property, sets forth three causes of action.

The first cause, against the individual defendants Lawrence and Melville Hall, alleges that they contracted in writing to sell to plaintiff two parcels of real estate in Manhattan improved with apartment houses. In the contract, a copy of which was annexed to the complaint, the Halls represented that they were record owners of the properties and that they would give title such as a responsible title company would approve and insure. Plaintiff paid $25,000 down on the signing of the contract and agreed to pay an additional $145,000 on the closing of title, the balance being subject to outstanding mortgages.

The contract provided that the purchaser agreed to deliver to the sellers' attorneys, at least seven days before the date fixed for closing title, a written statement of objections to title which the purchaser believed made title unmarketable. Pursuant to this provision, the Halls were timely notified prior to the date fixed for closing that the Title Guaranty & Trust Company required documents indicating the regularity of the transfer of the property in question from Melhar Realty Company, Inc., the previous record owner, to the Halls, who owned two-thirds of its corporate stock. Alleged consideration for the transfer was cancellation of an outstanding debt owed to the Halls by the corporation. The Halls were required by the title company either to show the unanimous consent of the stockholders to the transfer or to bring an action to bar any claim by Mathesius, the remaining stockholder; to provide proof of the solvency of the corporation at the time of conveyance so that the transfer would not be subject to attack by creditors; and to obtain a clearance on taxes chargeable against the corporation on dissolution.

It is further alleged that on the date set for closing, plaintiff tendered $145,000 as provided in the contract. However, the Halls failed to produce any of the documents required by the contract, or to provide any of the necessary instruments and assurances in connection with objections to title, and failed to tender the deed to the premises. The contract provided:

"In the event that the seller is unable to convey title in accordance with the terms of this contract, the sole liability of the seller will be to refund to the purchaser the amount paid on account of the purchase price and to pay the net cost of examining the title, which cost is not to exceed the charges fixed by the New York Board of Title Underwriters, and upon such refund and payment being made this contract shall be considered cancelled."

Two weeks after the closing date, defendants repaid to plaintiff the sum of $25,862.50, representing the down payment on the contract plus costs of title examination; but plaintiff claims to have lost the benefit of its bargain and seeks additional damages of $50,000.

. . . It is defendants' position that the complaint itself alleges that they were unable to convey marketable title, so that with the return of the deposit and the payment of the costs of examining title, their liability under specific contract provisions came to an end. . . .

Plaintiff, on the other hand, has alleged that the defaults of the Halls were willful and deliberate, and that the objections to title were such as were created by the defendants and could have been avoided or cured by them. . . .

Upon failure of a vendor to convey real property as required by contract, the damages recoverable by a purchaser are dependent to some extent on the cause of the failure. Where the vendor has acted in good faith but is unable to give good title, the purchaser may recover only the amount he has already paid on the purchase price, together with necessary expenses incurred pursuant to the contract, such as costs for investigating title and reasonable attorney's fees. [Citations omitted.] Where the vendor acts in bad faith or willfully disregards the contract, the purchaser may also be entitled to recover for the loss of his bargain. [Citations omitted.] Of course, the parties to a contract may agree to extend or restrict the liability consequent upon a breach; or they may agree that no damages will be payable at all once the status quo ante has been restored.

The contract in this case purported to limit the liability of the vendor to refund of the amount payable on account of the purchase price and payment of the net costs of examining title. But such restriction was to be applicable only "[i]n the event that the seller is *unable* to convey title in accordance with the terms of this contract" (emphasis supplied). A limitation condition on such inability contemplates the existence of a situation beyond the control of the parties. Implicit in such a limitation is the obligation to act in good faith. A party under circumstances such as have been alleged cannot exculpate himself from liability by reliance on a condition precedent when his own conduct is the cause of the nonperformance of that condition. . . . The vendor is under a duty to take affirmative action to convey a marketable title according to his contract of sale (Smith v. Browning, 225 N.Y. 358, 122 N.E. 217). If the vendor has contracted to convey, knowing that there are circumstances that will render it impossible to do so, or if he is able with the reasonable expenditure of money and effort to remedy defects in title and neglects or refuses to do so, he has not acted in good faith; and he cannot then limit his damages by shielding himself behind such self-created or easily scaled barriers.

The complaint having alleged that the default of the defendants was willful and deliberate, a triable issue is raised as to whether in fact defendants acted in good faith or whether their alleged inability to convey marketable title was due entirely to circumstances beyond their control. If defendants were unable or made no effort to obtain the consent of the remaining stockholder because they had transferred the corporate property to themselves without full disclosure of its value; if they were unable to show proof of the solvency of the corporation because they had stripped it of all its assets; and if they were unable to obtain tax clearances because they had willfully failed to meet their tax obligations, it could be found that they were undertaking to convey a title which, when they entered into the contract, they themselves knew they had rendered unmarketable. They should then be required to remedy the defects rather than to terminate the contract, or failing that, respond in damages, as sought in this complaint. In the event of an ordinary breach of an agreement to convey, the contractual provision defining and limiting the vendor's liability would govern. The allegations of willful and deliberate default in this case make inapplicable here the general rule that a reasonable contractual provision for a compensation in lieu of damages difficult of ascertainment will be upheld.

[The order was affirmed insofar as it denied the motion to dismiss the first cause of action.]

NOTES AND QUESTIONS

1. *The doctrine of Flureau v. Thornhill.* The limitation of liability clause in the principal case restates the doctrine of Flureau v. Thornhill, sometimes called the English rule.

Flureau, 96 Eng. Rep. 635, 2 W. Bl. 1078 (1776), holds that the buyer's recovery for seller's breach through inability to make title is confined to money back plus transaction expenses, but both *Flureau* and Bain v. Fothergill, L.R. 7 H.L. 158 (1874), in which the House of Lords put its approval on the Common Pleas decision in *Flureau,* contain dicta subjecting seller to the usual loss-of-bargain damages where his breach is a result of willfulness or bad faith, and the dicta have been converted into holdings in later cases.

Does the *Flureau* decision, in its special favoring treatment of real estate sellers over other types of contracting parties, comport with a theory that common law decisions, in whatever doctrinal form expressed, represent skillful efforts by wise judges to adapt rules of law to emergent social needs, or with a theory that such decisions are conscious or unconscious effectuations of the interests of dominant social or economic classes? The briefly reported facts of this case, decided Easter term, 1776, simply disclose a seller and buyer, not otherwise described, of a leasehold worth about £250 sold at an auction, and the principal dispute seems to be not about the issue for which the case is famous, but rather whether buyer could recover for losses sustained when some government securities that he sold to raise cash for his purchase went up in value after he sold them, so that he wound up without the leasehold and with depreciated cash on his hands.

Flureau seems to lay down an aberrational rule of damages, but maybe it simply effectuates well-established contract principles concerning mutual mistake of fact, or impossibility of performance, or even the rule of Hadley v. Baxendale — ". . . one reason for the rule lay in the fact that in England a contract for sale of real estate was closed almost directly. But in the United States, long-term options are given, as well as long-term executory contracts, so that while in England there was practically no fluctuation in the value of realty during the short time necessary for the closing of the contract, there may be considerable change in the value of the property under American practices." Carnahan, The Kentucky Rule of Damages for Breach of Executory Contracts to Convey Realty, 20 Ky. L.J. 304, 314 (1932).

2. U.S. states are divided on the damage rule, exemplified in the *Flureau* case; some permit the buyer to recover loss of bargain damages, some permit only the more limited Flureau type damages. On buyer damages for breach by seller see Stoebuck & Whitman, Property 726-727 (3d ed. 2000), which also asserts that there is no satisfactory justification for the Flureau type limitations. Are Stoebuck and Whitman correct? Are there justifiable reasons for limiting the good faith seller's damages and, if so, what are they?

Ruble v. Reich

611 N.W.2d 844 (Neb. 2000)

McCORMACK, J.

NATURE OF CASE

This is a breach of contract action brought by Tim D. Ruble and Karen L. Ruble to recover damages for a breach of a real estate purchase agreement by Harold Reich. Reich denied the Rubles' claim and brought a third-party complaint against Tim Francis and Woods Bros. Realty, Inc. (Woods Bros.), alleging that if there was a breach, any damages are the responsibility of Francis and Woods Bros. The county court found that Reich had breached the contract and awarded the Rubles damages. The county court also found in favor of Francis and Woods Bros. On appeal, the district court affirmed the judgment of the county court. Reich appealed, and on our own motion, we removed the matter to our docket pursuant to our authority to regulate the caseloads of this court and the Nebraska Court of Appeals.

BACKGROUND

In May 1996, Reich listed his residence located at 4345 F Street in Lincoln, Nebraska, with Woods Bros. Francis, a real estate broker for Woods Bros., marketed the property.

At some point in May or June, the Rubles contacted Jackie Taylor, a mortgage loan officer with Commercial Federal Bank, and obtained preapproval for a loan, allowing the Rubles to determine the price range of a home they could afford.

On July 28, 1996, the Rubles, through their real estate agent, executed a written offer to purchase Reich's residence for $83,000. The relevant sections of the offer for purposes of this case are set forth below. Paragraph 2 of the offer stated in part:

Buyer is to negotiate a new loan or shall assume the existing mortgage or deed of trust. . . . If processing of the loan or assumption has not been completed by the lending agency by the closing date specified elsewhere in this agreement, the time limit shall be automatically extended until the lending agency has, in the normal course of its business, advised either approval or rejection. . . . If this offer is not contingent on the sale of real estate owned by Buyer and the lender requires as a condition of granting the loan that the real estate owned by the Buyer be sold, then Seller shall have the option to declare this agreement null and void unless further written agreement between Buyer and Seller is obtained.

Paragraph 2A stated in part that the

[b]alance shall be paid in cash, or by cashier's check at time of delivery of deed, contingent upon Buyer's ability to obtain a loan, secured by first mortgage or deed of trust, on above described Property [4345 F Street] in the amount of $62,500. The loan is to be . . . conventional.

Under "Other Provisions," the offer stated that the purchase is "contingent upon Buyers' property at 3134 NW 7th, Lincoln, closing escrow. (This property is currently under contract)." the offer also stated that closing was to occur "on August 31, 1996 or within 0 days after loan approval, whichever shall last occur." On July 29, acting through Francis, Reich accepted the Rubles' offer, thereby creating a contract between the parties.

As stated in the purchase agreement, the loan the Rubles were applying for was a conventional loan for $62,500 from Commercial Federal Bank. The purchase price for Reich's residence was $83,000. The Rubles intended to use the money they would get from the equity in the sale of their residence at 3134 N.W. 7th Street as a downpayment on the purchase of Reich's residence.

Sometime in the middle of August, the Rubles realized they would not be able to close on August 31, 1996, because of a problem with the sale of their residence at 3134 N.W. 7th Street. On August 16, Reich received a telephone message which Francis had left on Reich's answering machine. The message indicated that the Rubles would not be able to close on August 31. After the telephone message on August 16, Reich and Francis had no contact until the middle of September when Francis left another telephone message for Reich asking whether the Rubles could move into Reich's residence prior to the upcoming closing date. Upon receiving the message, Reich called Francis and told him that he did not want to proceed with the closing. On September 26, the Rubles closed on the sale of their residence at 3134 N.W. 7th Street and were ready to close on the purchase of Reich's residence on the same day. The closing on the sale/purchase of Reich's residence did not occur.

The Rubles subsequently filed suit against Reich in county court alleging that on September 26, 1996, they were advised of their loan approval and that on that date, they were ready, willing, and able to close on the purchase of Reich's residence, and that Reich failed to close on September 26, thereby breaching the contractual obligations in the agreement. The Rubles' petition sought to recover various items of special damages. Reich denied the allegations against him in his answer, and subsequently, he filed a third-party complaint against Francis and Woods Bros. alleging that any breach of the purchase agreement and any damages resulting therefrom were caused by the acts and omissions of Francis and Woods Bros.

The county court entered an order finding that Reich had breached the purchase agreement and awarded the Rubles the following damages: $307.82 for hotel rooms; $4,650 for house rental fees; $500 for earnest money; $435 for loan and inspection fees; and $263.81 for truck rental fees. As to the third-party complaint, the county court found in favor of Francis and Woods Bros. and dismissed the third-party complaint. Reich motioned for a new trial, which was overruled. Reich timely appealed to the district court, which affirmed the judgment of the county court in all respects. . . .

ASSIGNMENTS OF ERROR

Reich assigns that the district court erred in affirming the county court's (1) finding that the contract between the parties obligated Reich to close on the sale of his house on a date later than the closing date stated in the contract, (2) awarding damages because a substantial portion of the damages was not actually suffered by the Rubles, and (3) finding that Francis and Woods Bros. did not breach their fiduciary duty to Reich. . . .

ANALYSIS

BREACH OF CONTRACT

The Rubles contend that final loan approval did not occur until their home at 3134 N.W. 7th Street closed because it was at this point that Commercial Federal Bank was willing to fund the loan. . . .

In this case, we are concerned with the phrase "loan approval" as used in the agreement. We determine that the phrase "loan approval" is unambiguous because it cannot be fairly interpreted in more than one way. . . .

When we construe the terms of the contract as a whole, it is apparent that the Rubles' loan approval was contingent on the sale of their residence at 3134 N.W. 7th Street. The Rubles had not closed on the sale of their residence on August 31, 1996, so pursuant to the agreement, the closing date on the sale/purchase of Reich's residence was automatically extended until the Rubles obtained loan approval. Reich was obligated to close after August 31.

DAMAGES

A suit for damages arising from breach of a contract presents an action at law. In a bench trial of a law action, the trial court's factual findings have the effect of a jury verdict and will not be disturbed on appeal unless clearly wrong. *Bachman v. Easy Parking of America*, 252 Neb. 325, 561 N.W.2d 369 (1997). . . .

Reich argues that the Rubles should not be awarded the full $775 a month they paid for rent because the evidence shows that the Rubles did not suffer damages of $775 per month. Reich relies on the testimony of Karen Ruble, wherein she stated that while the Rubles were renting, they did not have to pay the monthly mortgage payments they would have had to pay if the closing on Reich's residence had occurred. Karen Ruble also testified that the Rubles' mortgage payment to Commercial Federal Bank was "going to be like $630." Of this amount, approximately $130 would have been applied toward taxes and insurance and the balance would have been applied to principal and interest. Reich contends that this evidence establishes that by renting, the Rubles avoided $630 per month in mortgage payments and that therefore, their actual damages in house rental fees were only $145 per month ($775 less $630) for 6 months for a total of $870, rather than $4,650 as awarded by the county court.

In a breach of contract case, the ultimate objective of a damages award is to put the injured party in the same position the injured party would have occupied if the contract had been performed, that is, to make the injured party whole. *Radecki v. Mutual of Omaha Inc. Co.*, 255 Neb. 224, 583 N.W.2d 310 (1998); *Vowers & Sons, Inc. v. Strasheim*, 254 Neb. 506, 576 N.W.2d 817 (1998).

Damages, like any other element of a plaintiff's cause of action, must be pled and proved, and the burden is on the plaintiff to offer evidence sufficient to prove the plaintiff's alleged damages. *World Radio Labs. v. Coopers & Lybrand*, 251 Neb. 261, 557 N.W.2d 1 (1996).

The Rubles sufficiently proved that they incurred house rental payments of $775 per month for 6 months. The question becomes whether the district court erred in failing to reduce the amount awarded by the county court for rent payments because the Rubles would have had to pay mortgage payments in lieu of the rent payments if the contract had not been breached.

In measuring damages for a breach of contract, any cost or other loss that is avoided by the injured party's not having to perform is deducted from the amount of damages incurred. Restatement (Second) of Contracts § 347(c) (1981). This court has also held:

> In considering the amount of damages in breach of contract cases, the trier of fact, in applying the general rule on damages, must also bear in mind that generally speaking the losses sustained by reason of the breach or the gains prevented are both actual and consequential damages. Of necessity this requires consideration of the concepts of mitigation on the part of the nondefaulting party and *savings realized through the breach.*

(Emphasis supplied.) *Wells Fargo Alarm Serv. v. Nox-Crete Chem.*, 229 Neb. 43, 47, 424 N.W.2d 885, 889 (1988).

Karen Ruble testified that the total monthly mortgage payment on Reich's residence would have been $630 and that of this amount, $130 would have been applied toward taxes and insurance and $500 would have been applied toward principal and interest. We cannot conclude that the $500 per month that would have been applied toward principal and interest is equivalent to $500 paid toward a rent payment such that it should be reduced from the Rubles' damages award. A $500 payment that is applied toward principal and interest has benefits, such as building equity and creating tax deductions, that a $500 rent payment does not have. The Rubles, in making rent payments instead of mortgage payments, were denied these benefits. Therefore, we conclude that $500 of the $630 a month that the Rubles would have paid in mortgage payments should not be deducted from the damages award. However, the $130 of the monthly mortgage payment that would have been applied toward taxes and insurance was savings realized through the breach and should have been deducted from the damages. Karen Ruble also testified that the first mortgage payment on Reich's residence would not have been due until a month later than their first rent payment. Therefore, the $130 should not be deducted from the first month's rent payment. The Rubles' house rental damages are modified as follows: $775 for the first month, and $645 per month ($775 less $130) for the other 5 months of rent payments, for a total of $4,000 awarded for house rental payments. The other damages awarded by the county court and affirmed by the district court remain unchanged. . . .

CONCLUSION

The purchase agreement between the parties obligated Reich to close after the date specified in the agreement, August 31, 1996, if the Rubles did not have loan approval as of that date. The Rubles did not receive loan approval until September 26, and Reich's failure to close on this date was a breach of the contract. The Rubles are entitled to $775 for the first month, and $645 per month ($775 less $130) for the other 5 months of rent payments, for a total of $4,000 awarded for house rental payments. The other damages awarded by the county court and affirmed by the district court remain unchanged. The district court's decision upholding the county court's dismissal of the third-party complaint against Francis and Woods Bros. is affirmed.

AFFIRMED AS MODIFIED.

NOTE

Among other consequential damages for which a buyer may recover damages if the seller breaches are title examination costs, loss of profits from an established business operated by buyer on the property, loss of favorable financing due to interest rate increases, and loss of a profitable resale of the property. See generally Friedman on Contracts and Conveyances of Real Property 7-22 & 23 (7th ed. 2005). Specific performance also is a remedy generally available to the buyer if the seller breaches and the seller had title to the property.

CHAPTER FIVE

Title Protection

This chapter is concerned with the scope and methods of land title protection in the United States. Alternative means of title protection are critically analyzed and attention is centered on some of the more important problem areas. Considerable statutory material is dealt with, as basic legal policies in this field are frequently set by statute and an understanding of what these statutes do and are expected to do is essential. Included within the concept of title protection are devices not only for safeguarding title interests once acquired, but also for compensating in cases of loss of actual or apparent title rights. Title protection can also entail steps to clear defective titles once defects are apparent. This chapter stresses the two principal means of land title protection currently relied on in the United States: the recording acts and title insurance. These devices are cornerstones of the prevailing system by which American land titles are made comparatively safe and secure.

Title protection in the United States works well enough to enable intensive land development by a great variety of public and private interests. But American title protection is complex and costly, with some degree of uncertainty in almost every title. The margin of uncertainty can be substantially eliminated in most instances, but at present this can be an expensive and long drawn out process. Through reform of the law and of institutional procedures, greater efforts should be made to reduce the system's deficiencies. This chapter considers some of the prospects for achieving such a goal.

One reason for the complexity and cost of American title protection is the complexity of our land title law. The great diversity of legal interests in land permitted by our legal order makes the unraveling and appraising of outstanding legal interests in any particular land parcel difficult and expensive. In part this is inherent in the nature of land, particularly in an advanced modern society where much of the wealth is in private hands. Land parcels are valuable and permanent, and most of them can be used simultaneously by different persons. They also are ideal forms of security for extension of credit and, especially at the local government level, a major source of tax income. Increasingly, too, they are the subject of government regulation and subsidy. These factors have led to wide dispersal of legal rights in individual land parcels. Most parcels have had a complex title history, with termination of some old interests often in doubt and present rights frequently divided among owners, lenders, users, and government instrumentalities.

Continued reliance on the recording acts as the basis of title protection also contributes to cost and complexity. Reasonably well suited to a newly settled, sparsely populated rural nation, the recording acts have become less and less satisfactory as American title histories have lengthened, the number of parcels has increased, and the volume of public land records, notably in urbanized areas, has multiplied at an enormous rate. Recording act weaknesses have been compounded by the fact that maintaining public records essential to the system has been almost entirely a function of local government, the least effective and innovative level of American government. Further complications result from the public records not being the sole source of title data under the recording acts. A miscellany of private records, including unrecorded original instruments, may be relevant considerations, and so may the physical condition of the land itself and the character of its occupation, insofar as these factors indicate the existence of unrecorded interests. Other off-record information may also be significant. Even the state of mind of purchasers becomes important: when they took did they have actual notice of unrecorded interests? Patchwork legal changes and development of new title service groups, especially the title insurance companies, have helped in adapting the recording acts to changed circumstances; but these have been more palliatives than cures. Torrens registration, a system of title protection potentially more satisfactory than recording, has failed to catch hold in the United States, and its future prospects here are doubtful, for recording is so well established that a major shift to Torrens would hurt too many interests.

The American law of title protection has an important impact on a number of different groups, each having somewhat different interests in title protection, and consequently different and even conflicting views as to what ends title protection laws should serve. These include persons who own or think they own land interests; those desirous of buying land interests or lending on the security of such interests; unpaid creditors of persons owning land interests; professional title searchers and examiners; insurers of land titles; and government agencies that maintain public records pertaining to land titles. There are others, but these groups are the most obvious and most directly concerned. They further comprise subgroups, whose interests in title protection and title protection laws may be in conflict. For example, title insurers and lawyers in private practice compete for work, and more than one person may make claim to the same or overlapping ownership rights in the same land parcel.

Most ends that title protection laws serve tend to benefit some groups and harm others, benefit and harm usually being expressed in monetary terms as title protection normally is conceived of in those terms. Some possible ends are these:

1. A fast, accurate, and inexpensive means of ascertaining the legal status of the title to any particular land parcel;
2. Land titles in every community generally certain enough so as not to impede the marketability of land interests or deter land development;
3. Encouragement of land marketability by protecting bona fide purchasers without notice;
4. Protection of interests in land of those person whose interests are known or readily ascertainable;
5. Protection of interests in land of those persons unable adequately to protect themselves, such as person under disability and those unaware that they own land interests;
6. Assurance of compensation to those who have suffered losses in land transactions without fault on their part but through the bad faith or negligence of others;

7. No government out-of-pocket expenditures on land title records for privately held land interests beyond what is necessary for effective performance of government tax and regulatory functions; and

8. Fair compensation to those performing title protection services.

NOTE

It is comparatively simple to determine what ends title protection laws should further in the best interests of any one group. But how should a legislature or court resolve the questions and priorities of ends when dealing with title protection problems? Whose ends should they seek to serve? If your answer is the public interest, or the community at large, what does this mean in the title protection context, and how should a legislature or court approach the diversity of worthy interests and the ends that would best serve each, as listed above? If these questions cannot be satisfactorily answered in the abstract, consider them as they relate to the legal problems raised in succeeding chapters.

A. THE RECORDING ACTS[1]

Fundamental to title protection in the United States are the recording acts, statutes in effect in every state. The term "recording acts" has a variety of meanings, but here it is used in a narrow sense common to discussions of real property law. It means only those statutes that provide for land conveyancing records to be maintained by recorders of deeds (or equivalent public officials) and that establish priorities among successive purchasers of land interests. Under some circumstances these acts reverse the common law rule that priority among successive purchasers of land interests from the same grantor is dependent on priority in time of execution. Although they differ in detail, all the recording acts provide for (1) centralized filing of documents creating or transferring land interests, (2) maintenance of systems of public records, consisting primarily of copies of the filed documents, and (3) priorities for those interests appearing in the public records against those that do not.

Public land records provided for by the recording acts are generally maintained in the office of a designated public official of the county where the lands are located. In many states this official bears the title of county recorder of deeds. Most of the records maintained in recorders' offices are open for public inspection and are the principal source of land title data sought by professional searchers. But records

---

1. On recording acts generally see Patton & Palomar on Land Titles, ch. 1 (3d ed. 2003); 16 Powell on Real Property, ch. 82 (2000); Stoebuck & Whitman, Property §§ 11.9-11.11 (3d ed. 2000); Thompson on Real Property, ch. 92 (2d ed. 1994); Curtis, Simplifying Land Transfers: The Recordation and Marketable Title Provisions of the Uniform Simplification of Land Transfers Act, 62 Or. L. Rev. 363 (1983); Mattis, Recording Acts: Anachronistic Reliance, 25 Rl. Prop., Prob. & Tr. J. 17 (1990); Schechter, Judicial Lien Creditors Versus Prior Unrecorded Transferees of Real Property: Rethinking the Goals of the Recording System and Their Consequences, 62 S. Cal. L. Rev. 105 (1988); Sweat, Race, Race-Notice and Notice Statutes: The American Recording System, 3 Prob. & Prop. 27 (May/June 1989).

kept pursuant to the recording acts are not the only sources of information about land titles; and, on theories of notice or priority irrespective of notice, interests not apparent from an examination of these records may be outstanding and superior to any others. Such interests may be ascertainable from other public records, including court and tax records, and from an examination of the premises. Title examinations frequently involve inspection of these other sources, but some outstanding land interests still may not be uncovered, nor may any reasonable kind of search prove successful. The existence of such interests is an off-record risk that usually cannot be eliminated, although through title insurance or other means the risk may be passed on to someone else. However, known title defects, including interests with priority under the recording acts, frequently can be eliminated by such means as purchase of outstanding claims, passage of time and operation of limitations or curative acts, and suits to quiet title. Professional title searchers and examiners who negligently fail to locate title defects or report on them may be liable in tort or contract.

American recording acts were highly developed by the close of the colonial period.[2] In their early evolution they were probably influenced by English legislation, by the statute of enrollments and registry acts for the counties of Middlesex and York, and by English judicial decisions that purchasers with notice of unregistered conveyances were not protected by the registration statutes. But a general system of recording never developed in England as it did in the United States, and original title instruments kept in private hands had been the main sources relied on in title examinations of English lands. Registration somewhat similar to that provided for by the American Torrens system has, however, largely replaced this so-called title deeds system in England.

It is conventional to classify American recording acts into three main groups, emphasizing the varied significance of notice and the act of recording. The three types are often referred to as race, notice, and race-notice statutes. Under the race-type statute, a purchaser who records has priority over any interest then unrecorded, whether or not the purchaser had notice of the unrecorded interest when he took. In other words, the race to the recorder's office determines who prevails.

 Under a notice-type statute, a purchaser takes priority over all prior unrecorded interests of which he had no notice when he took. Once such a purchaser takes title, it is advisable for him to record in order to protect himself from subsequent purchasers, but he need not record to be protected against prior but unrecorded interests of which he had no notice. Race-notice-type statutes are similar to notice statutes, except that for a purchaser under a race-notice statute to prevail over a prior unrecorded interest of which he had no notice when he took, he must record before the prior unrecorded interest holder does. Thus, under a race-notice statute, the subsequent uninformed purchaser is not accorded automatic protection against a prior unrecorded but recordable interest, as is the case under the notice statute. The term race-notice is applied to statutes so designated because under them both the race and the notice are material to determination of priority.

Several states, Louisiana, North Carolina, and Delaware, have race statutes applicable to conveyances generally; a few other states have them for mortgages. Of the

---

2. On the history of the recording acts, see 14 Powell on Real Property § 82.01[1] (1999).

remaining states, about half have notice statutes and half have race-notice statutes.[3] Arizona, Illinois, and Massachusetts are among the notice states; and California, Michigan, and New York among the race-notice ones.

Filing for record under the recording acts is not essential to validity of an unrecorded but recordable instrument. Such an instrument is valid between the parties and is effective as against subsequent takers not protected by the recording acts. When recording act priorities do not apply, then priority among successive conflicting interests in the same land parcel normally is determined by the common law preference for the interest senior in time of execution.

Public records kept pursuant to the recording acts also have evidentiary value in judicial proceedings. In many states the recorded copies of instruments are primary evidence, with no requirement that the original be produced or accounted for. In other states contents of an instrument may be proven from the recorded copy, but only after accounting for the original.

The recording acts, with their stress on readily accessible public land records and priorities for interests appearing in these records, have been largely responsible for creating enough certainty in American land titles to meet the needs of a highly developed industrial society extensively based on private property rights. But there are serious weaknesses in the recording acts that have resulted in more title uncertainty than is necessary and high costs of title protection to minimize the risks inherent in the system. Weaknesses in the recording acts include: the extensive and complex searches that must be made, both on and off record, to determine the apparent state of a title; inefficiently maintained and indexed public records; the risk of outstanding title interests that cannot be ascertained from any reasonable search; and limited effectiveness of recording due to possible errors by recorders and chain of title restrictions on search obligations. What was no doubt a very good system in earlier days when title histories were short and searches comparatively easy is now a cumbersome and expensive procedure, particularly in highly urbanized communities. Following are representative recording acts, including examples of race, notice, and race-notice statutes.

Washington Revised Code Annotated

(2005)

§ 65.08.070.   *Real property conveyances to be recorded.* A conveyance of real property, when acknowledged by the person executing the same (the acknowledgment being certified as required by law), may be recorded in the office of the recording officer of the county where the property is situated. Every such conveyance not so recorded is void as against any subsequent purchaser or mortgagee in good faith and for a valuable consideration from the same vendor, his heirs or devisees, of the same real

---

3. For a state by state listing of recording acts and their classification as race, race notice, or notice enactments, see Recording Acts in the 50 States, 3 Prob. and Prop. 31 (May/June 1989). Some of these classifications may be open to question. See also Patton and Palomar on Land Titles, §§ 6-8 (3d ed. 2003 and Supp. 2006).

property or any portion thereof whose conveyance is first duly recorded. An instrument is deemed recorded the minute it is filed for record.

race

Florida Statutes Annotated

(2003)

§ 695.01.   *Conveyances to be recorded.* (1) No conveyance, transfer or mortgage of real property, or of any interest therein, not any lease for a term of 1 year or longer, shall be good and effectual in law or equity against creditors or subsequent purchasers for a valuable consideration and without notice, unless the same be recorded according to law; nor shall any such instrument made or executed by virtue of any power of attorney be good or effectual in law or in equity against creditors or subsequent purchasers for a valuable consideration and without notice unless the power of attorney be recorded before the accruing of the right of such creditor or subsequent purchaser.

race-notice

Arkansas Statutes Annotated

(2003)

§ 18-40-102.   *Lien attaches when recorded.* Every mortgage of real estate shall be a lien on the mortgaged property from the time it is filed in the recorder's office for record, and not before. The filing shall be notice to all persons of the existence of the mortgage.

Indiana Code Annotated

(Burns 2006, Supp. 2006)

32-21-4-1.   *Location of recording — First in time priority.*
      (a) The following must be recorded in the recorder's office of the county where the land is situated:
         (1) A conveyance or mortgage of land or of any interest in land.
         (2) A lease for more than three (3) years.
      (b) A conveyance, mortgage, or lease takes priority according to the time of its filing. The conveyance, mortgage, or lease is fraudulent and void as against any subsequent purchaser, lessee, or mortgagee in good faith and for a valuable consideration if the purchaser's, lessee's, or mortgagee's deed, mortgage, or lease is first recorded.

NOTES AND QUESTIONS

1. Without reference to interpretive judicial opinions, it is not always possible to determine with accuracy whether a particular recording act falls in the race, notice, or race-notice group. But from the statutory language appearing above, how do you think each of the enactments is classified?

2. What are the advantages and disadvantages of each of the three types of recording acts? On balance, which type is preferable? Should the answer vary depending on whether a locality is within a metropolitan area or is outside such an area and is largely rural or small town? Under a race-type statute, are titles more certain? For a detailed study concluding that notice statutes are preferable, see Mattis, Recording Acts, Anachronistic Reliance, 25 Rl. Prop., Prob. Tr. J. 17 (1991).

3. A period following delivery during which a purchaser could record and still have priority over a subsequent purchaser was at one time provided for in the recording acts of a number of states, and earlier, in some of the American colonies. The period of grace varied from five days to two years. Webb, The Law of Record of Title § 7 (2d ed. 1891). Due to the retroactive effect of recordation, persons buying interests in land were always in danger of being subject to unrecorded interests of which they had no notice. The reason for grace periods apparently was poor communication and slow mail service, which meant that instruments executed in England and other distant places would be long delayed in reaching the office of the locality where the land was located. Most grace period recording act provisions have been repealed. On early recording act provisions of this kind see Hackman, Time for Recording Title Instruments, 19 Lawyer & Banker 12, 16 (1926). Similar grace periods with retroactive effect upon filing in the public records are still fairly prevalent for mechanics' and materialmen's liens.

1. Administration

Assembly and maintenance of public records upon which effective operation of the recording acts depends is the administrative responsibility of local government, principally of the counties in most parts of the United States. When documents are submitted for recordation, employees of the recorder's office accept them, note the time of initial filing, copy the documents, bind the copies in large books, and index each copy in some manner that will facilitate location of it. Originals are normally returned to the persons who submitted them for recordation, usually transferees or their representatives. Index and document books are permanently stored, usually on open shelves, available for inspection during regular office hours by members of the public. Except for a few localities where past collections have been destroyed by fire or other holocaust, and apart from occasional pilfering or negligent failure to properly copy or store, recorders' offices normally contain copies of all documents recorded since the early days of settlement in the community. In much of the United States the earliest recorded document pertaining to any particular land parcel is likely to be a patent from the federal government, an instrument similar to a deed, issued when the parcel passed from the federal domain into private hands.

There are approximately three thousand counties or their functional equivalents in the United States. This means that not only is administration of public land records heavily decentralized, but there are inevitable variations in the details and caliber of administration. Some counties do a good job, some a very poor job; and the quality and methods of operation tend to vary with population size, number of land parcels in the county, local real estate activity, competence of local government personnel, and nature of state statutory provisions pertaining to public land records. As is to be expected, public recorders' offices differ greatly in the volume of documents handled and in the size of their document accumulations. In the great metropolitan counties these offices are vast and busy places housing large staffs of employees, the hundreds of thousands of new recordings which come in annually, and tremendous collections of past recordings maintained for public inspection. At the other extreme are offices in sparsely settled rural communities with relatively few land transactions. These offices may have only a few dozen document books, and a total of only two or three new recordings a day may be unusually heavy. Quite clearly, many of the operational problems of such offices are very different from those in metropolitan or even middle-sized communities.

Although sets of public records and the officials who process and maintain them are essential to the administration of a recording act system, private skill groups have developed that are also essential to a workable recording act system. These include groups that use the public records, or information gleaned from such records, to sell services to their customers or clients, for example, abstracters, lawyers, and title insurers, who, as part of their own work, commonly prepare and maintain private land records, in large part summaries or evaluations of relevant public records. Such records include abstracts prepared and sold by abstract companies and the title plant compilations maintained by many title insurers and abstracters. The manufacturers of data processing equipment constitute another essential skill group. These companies are increasingly being called on to help devise methods of data storage and retrieval for both public and private land record offices. And manufacturers' research staffs, in their work on more efficient means of handling masses of data, are influencing the probable future of land title search and examination.

Title insurance is sufficiently important so that it is considered separately in this chapter. However, it should be underscored at this point that private title insurance as it has developed in the United States is built upon the recording acts and systems of public land records. In determining exceptions to insurance coverage of any particular land title, title insurers' ultimate sources of data are primarily the public land records. This is true even of those companies maintaining their own title plants.

In the United States there are three major forms of title search and examination, each dominated by a different skill group or combination of skill groups.[4] In the first, lawyers in private practice make both searches and examinations and provide their clients with title opinions, usually in writing. These opinions ordinarily state who has title, indicate whether or not title is marketable, and describe any defects.

Under the second form of search and examination, lawyers in private practice do the examining and provide their clients with opinions but do not search the public records. Searching is done by professional abstracters who prepare written summaries of the titles to individual land parcels as disclosed by the public records. These summaries, or abstracts as they are called, are histories of the titles to particular parcels. An abstract has a series of entries, normally arranged chronologically, each

---

4. For the results of a bar association survey of forms of title search and examination in different sections of the country, see Dansby, Survey of Lawyers' Current Role in the Title Insurance Process, 3 Prob. and Prop. 43 (Sept./Oct. 1989). The Dansby article also includes a state by state listing of a majority of states as to prevalence of title insurance and how extensively private lawyers are utilized in title searches and examination.

entry a synopsis of or excerpt from a recorded document or other public record relevant to the land title in question. To the extent that the abstract is an accurate and complete reflection of the public records, it will have an entry for every step in the public record history of the title: every deed, mortgage, will, judicial decree, or other instrument or event bearing on the title and appearing in the public records will be referred to in a separate abstract entry. By carefully examining these entries a competent lawyer can determine the nature of the record title, including its current marketability. The companies that prepare abstracts are staffed by specialists in title searching, although few abstracters are lawyers. Many title insurance companies originally started as abstract companies, and some of the insurers still prepare and sell abstracts.

The third major form of title search and examination is one in which both search and examination functions are performed by a title insurance company as preliminary steps to issuance of title insurance policies. When a policy is ordered, company employees assemble and evaluate data requisite to insurability. Those employees who search rarely are lawyers; those who examine often are.

In counties where there is not enough title work to justify title company search and examination staffs, some companies, on request, will issue policies based on opinions of expert title lawyers in private practice. Thus title insurance is fairly frequent even under lawyer or lawyer-abstracter forms of title search and examination.

In recent years, the practice has increased of title insurance company agents, who are not company employees, making searches and examination for title companies and then issuing title insurance policies for the companies if the agents conclude that the titles are acceptable for insurance purposes. Many of these agents are lawyers in private practice, but many are nonlawyer abstracters or title searchers. The use of agents in this manner is an effort by the title insurers to expand market and reduce costs. Another not uncommon practice in some communities is for lawyers or title insurance companies to contract with outside title searchers to make title searches for them but not examinations. These searchers are independent contractors and most are nonlawyers. Many law firms also assign their employed paralegals to title searching work.

In many rural and small-town communities in the United States, other than in the Far West, title searches and examinations are still largely monopolized by law firms and abstracters. However, where title insurance companies have moved into both title insurance searching and examination by their own employees, there has been considerable displacement of private practitioners of law in performing one or both of these functions. In some communities, especially most major metropolitan centers, this displacement is almost complete, and the title work of lawyers in private practice is largely restricted to clearing defective titles and negotiating with title insurers to limit the scope of coverage exceptions and otherwise expand coverage. The shift away from title work has had important implications for the private practice of law, as at one time such work was a major source of income to lawyers in all parts of the United States. This loss of title searching and examination illustrates the vulnerability of lawyers in private practice to competition from specialized, high volume businesses and professions. Other occupations that have been particularly effective in cutting in on the work of private law firms include collection agencies, banks in their probate and trust work, and accountants dealing with tax matters.

NOTES AND QUESTIONS

1. As one would expect, there are different ways of going about title work and differences of opinion over which procedures are best. The following two excerpts illustrate points of view on scope and emphasis in abstracting and examining.

Bermond, Standardization of Abstracting, 38 Title News 10, 11-12 (Oct. 1959): "Some of the abstracts submitted to me for examination . . . are merely outlines or chains of title, little more than an index or list of the matters appearing of record. Others are virtual copies of everything on the public records. The former is, of course, too little. The latter, too much. What the examiner needs, and all he needs or desires is an abstract of the essential and intrinsic facts and information on record sufficient to base an intelligent opinion on the title.

"No matter how useful such undertaking may be at the local level, the full advantages of such organized efforts toward standardization cannot be realized without the establishment of a state-wide system. It is true that some abstracting problems may be inherent to particular locations, but the bulk of all of the problems are present, and the answers are the same all over any one state. . . .

"Most important of the causes of overmeticulous abstracting and title examination is fear. The fear may be of two sorts — First, we may be afraid of ourselves, lacking confidence in our own ability or judgment as to what is a proper conclusion on some point — Second, we may be afraid of what the next abstracter or examiner will require. It is from this latter type of fear that a vicious circle arises. No abstracter or examiner wants his reputation injured by having the next abstracter or title examiner call attention to something, however non-meritorious, that he has over-looked or disregarded. Unless some means of escape are provided, the type of pattern for abstracting and title examination will tend to be established in any community by those who raise the most objections irrespective of their triviality or lack of merit. Standardization is the most obvious cure for this. Fear that our own judgment may be wrong is quickly dispelled if we can find our particular question already answered in a standard upon which our fellow abstracters and examiners, including recognized specialists, have agreed as a rule of practice."

McQuiston, Scope of the Abstract: Investigations Aside From the Abstract, 14 Okla. L. Rev. 437, 454-455 (1961): "Purpose of title examination is to assist the client in making a real estate deal. Title opinions should not be composed to display the examiner's profound knowledge of the law nor to point out ignorance of those who have dealt with the title before. Of course, the examiner should make reasonable and necessary requirements. Sometimes an intelligent client experienced in real estate affairs will complete the deal without requiring expenditure of unusual title clearance costs, provided the title is safe, although not strictly marketable. This practice is pointed out in a recent article concerning the title opinion [Mosburg, Title by Adverse Possession, 13 Okla. L. Rev. 125 (1960).] Experienced clients, it is pointed out, are careful to have and demand a thorough examination and, although at times they act independently of their lawyer, their judgment is always based on a clearly analyzed title as shown in the examiner's written opinion. The writer of the article believes it is the examiner's duty to set forth possible defects that raise a reasonable question of safety or marketability, and particularly, it is essential to call the client's attention to the possibility of unabstracted prior claims such as unrecorded rights of persons in possession, encroachments, unfiled mechanics' and materialmen's liens, unmatured installments of special assessments not certified by the abstract and to warn of the necessity of investigating governmental zoning regulations applicable to the particular property.

"Conversely, the author states, if an examiner were so inclined he could point out numerous pitfalls against which even a bona fide purchaser has no adequate safeguard, such as the possibility of forgery, non-delivery of deeds, undisclosed minority or incompetency of grantors, false recitals of identity or marital status. These are risks a client always takes unless he chooses to purchase a policy of title insurance. In such cases the law of averages is overwhelmingly in favor of safety of the title. Calling these things to the client's attention would merely create a sense of insecurity, so it is recommended that the opinion be silent as to such matters."

2. In many states, abstracters are licensed. See, e.g., Kan. Stat. Ann. § 58-2801 (2005); Mo. Stat. Ann. §§ 94.110 & 94.360 (1998). On abstracter licensing see Eckhardt, Abstracter Licensing Laws, 28 Mo. L. Rev. 1, 54-55 (1963), in which the author has this to say:

> From the point of view of the general public it would be desirable if all abstracters were financially responsible, had adequate plants, were professionally competent, had regulated fees, and were liable to anyone relying on the abstract to his damage, with limitation running from the date of injury. As a practical matter, this ideal is unattainable, and it becomes a matter of balancing the potential for good against the potential for evil in the particular proposal. As a rule this will turn upon an analysis of the plant requirement and its related grandfather clause: Will the proposed act tend to bring all plants up to an adequate level, or will it tend to create a monopoly and perpetuate an inadequate plant?
>
> Further, from the public point of view, will the act be so stringent that in some counties no one will provide abstracting services? Inferior abstract service is better than no abstract service at all. The problem is not the same as with legal and medical services, because one can drive to a lawyer or doctor in the next county, but abstracting necessarily must be done locally.
>
> The question from the point of view of the abstracter is really two or more questions, because abstracters fall into several groups, each with different interests at stake. A majority of abstracters can and do meet the minimum requirements any licensing act might impose, viz., they are financially responsible (frequently by insuring the risk), have adequate plants, and are managed by competent personnel. They would like a license act in order to improve their weaker fellows, and to give the industry the prestige and status they think will come with licensing. They are sincere in believing there will be improvement both as to personnel and as to plant, and minimize or ignore the monopolistic tendency of some acts.
>
> On the other hand, many in the upper group of abstracters fear that any regulatory legislation will open the door to other regulation they do not desire, such as a schedule of maximum fees. They are not opposed to an abstracters' board of examiners composed of high-grade abstracters, but do fear what a board of political hacks might do (the political climate of course will vary from state to state and from time to time).
>
> Those abstracters who could not meet some or all of the basic requirements have a vital interest in defeating any license act, unless by grandfather clauses or otherwise their continuance in business is assured. This group is not represented in published discussions of the question because many of them are not active in or even members of their state and national associations.

3. In much of the United States, titles are customarily examined back to their inception in the federal government. However, in the older eastern sections of the

nation, such lengthy checking frequently is not done. In the East it is customary to examine transactions back for only a set period of years, commonly sixty years, and perhaps thereafter to a warranty deed. Why this more limited examination? What added risks, if any, are incurred in not checking back further?

4. Why do you think that preparation of abstracts of title has not generally become a local government service performed on a fee basis by government employees? Does it not make sense for those who maintain the public records to prepare abstracts of them? Some states authorize by statute recorders of deeds or other local officials to make and sell abstracts. See, for example, 55 Ill. Comp. Stat. Ann. § 5/3-5039 (2005); and Wis. Stat. Ann. § 59.44(3)(2000). However, a little of the abstract preparation market has been taken over by public authorities.

5. A good summary of problems encountered in abstract examination appears in Kubicek and Kubicek, Selected Topics in Examination of Abstracts of Title, 26 Drake L. Rev. 1 (1976-1977).

2. *Protection Provided*

a. Recordable Instruments

The trend has been to broaden the recording acts by increasing the kinds of conveyancing instruments that are recordable and as such can give constructive notice and priorities. Most title instruments are recordable: deeds, mortgages, leases, contracts of sale, options, grants of easements, etc. Wills and short-term leases are common but not universal exceptions. At one time, instruments pertaining only to equitable interests in land were not recordable in many states, but this has been changed almost everywhere. However, considerable variation exists among the states concerning the recordability of certain kinds of instruments peripheral to modern recording classifications, including affidavits and assignments of interests relating to land.

Before an instrument is entitled to be recorded, certain statutory prerequisites usually must be met. A widespread requirement is that a deed, mortgage, or other instrument creating, transferring, or terminating interests in land must be acknowledged before a notary public or other designated official, and the states differ on what essential statements the acknowledgment must contain. An alternative to acknowledgment commonly provided is the right to have a subscribing witness to execution of the instrument prove the validity of the instrument and its execution by declarations before an authorized official.[5] In most states instruments not properly acknowledged or proven are not entitled to constructive notice even if accepted by a recorder and placed of record. But some states have curative acts that fully validate such instruments as recordable after they have been in the proper records for a certain number of years.[6] And, generally, unacknowledged and unproven instruments are valid between the parties, their privies, and those with

---

5. See, for example, Or. Rev. Stat. §§ 93.440 and 93.480 (2005).

6. See, for example, Cal. Civ. Code Ann. § 1207 (West 1982), providing that the defective instrument will impart notice if of record for one year. Many such curative statutes require that the defective instrument be in the records for five or ten years before it has recording effect. Also see the discussion of curative acts, infra.

actual notice. A few states have requirements that each deed presented for recording shall contain prescribed information about the grantee; and there are statutory provisions that before a deed may be recorded, taxes on the property involved must be paid and the ownership change noted in the tax assessment books.[7] Failure to meet these latter requirements generally does not prevent the instrument from giving constructive notice if placed of record.

NOTES AND QUESTIONS

1. Why do you think many states do not provide for the recording of probated wills or short-term leases?

2. If unacknowledged and unproven deeds are valid between the parties and their privies, why should they not be recordable? The following statutory provision has been enacted in this or comparable form in a minority of states. Is such a provision desirable?

"Deeds, mortgages and other instruments of writing relating to real estate shall be deemed, from the time of being filed for record, notice to subsequent purchasers and creditors, though not acknowledged or proven according to law; but the same shall not be read as evidence, unless their execution be proved in the manner required by the rules of evidence applicable to such writings, so as to supply the defects of such acknowledgment or proof." 765 Ill. Comp. Stat. Ann. §5/31 (West 2001).

3. In Prudential Insurance Co. of America v. Holliday, 191 Neb. 144, 214 N.W.2d 273 (1974), two of three co-owners of a ranch mortgaged their undivided two-thirds interest but one of the mortgagors did not acknowledge the instrument. The mortgage was recorded and the court held the recording to be constructive notice only as to the interest of the co-owners who had acknowledged the instrument.

4. Mass. Gen. Laws Ann. c. 183, §6 (West 2003) provides: "Every deed presented for record shall contain or have endorsed upon it the full name, residence and post office address of the grantee and a recital of the amount of the full consideration thereof in dollars or the nature of the other consideration therefor, if not delivered for a specific monetary sum. The full consideration shall mean the total price for the conveyance without deduction for any liens or encumbrances assumed by the grantee or remaining thereon. All such endorsements and recitals shall be recorded as part of the deed. Failure to comply with this section shall not affect the validity of any deed. No register of deeds shall accept a deed for recording unless it is in compliance with the requirements of this section."

What is the purpose of this section?

b. Purchasers and Creditors

For subsequent takers to be entitled to priority under the recording acts as against prior unrecorded interest holders, they must have paid for their land

---

7. Md. Real Prop. Code Ann. Real Property § 3-104 (Michie Supp. 2005). And see Wash. Rev. Code Ann. § 82.45.090 (West Supp. 2006), requiring that before a conveyance or sale instrument is accepted for recording, any tax due on sale of such real estate shall be paid.

interest; and payment must have been substantial in relation to the value of the interest acquired. Donees as subsequent takers are not protected by the recording acts;[8] and in some states certain classes of creditors are not protected even though they have acquired interests in particular land parcels. However, a number of statutes expressly include creditors, or at least designated kinds of creditors, and universally mortgagees are included as protected subsequent takers.

~ Skip to 490

Horton v. Kyburz

53 Cal. 2d 59, 346 P.2d 399 (1959)

SCHAUER, Justice. In this action to have defendant declared the constructive trustee for plaintiff of an undivided one half interest in real property, plaintiff appeals from a judgment which decrees that he has no interest in such property. Plaintiff alleged and the trial court found facts sufficient to raise a constructive trust under the view of Notten v. Mensing (1935), 3 Cal. 2d 469, 473-477 [1-6], 45 P.2d 198, and Ryan v. Welte (1948), 87 Cal. App. 2d 897, 901-903 [4-6], 198 P.2d 357; i.e., plaintiff's father and step-mother orally agreed that all their property would go to the survivor for life and that the survivor would will such property one half to plaintiff and one half to those relatives of the step-mother whom she chose; in reliance on the oral agreement the spouses put their property in joint tenancy and plaintiff's father forebore to make any testamentary or other disposition of his property to members of his own family which would have been effective in the event the step-mother survived him, which she did; the step-mother took the subject realty as surviving joint tenant, conveyed it to herself and defendant, her relative, as joint tenants, and on her death defendant took as surviving joint tenant. But defendant alleged and the trial court found that he gave "good and valuable consideration" for the conveyance and took as a bona fide purchaser.

Plaintiff urges that as a matter of law defendant is not a bona fide purchaser because (1) there is no evidence that he gave consideration adequate to cut off plaintiff's equity, because (2) the evidence establishes that defendant took with constructive notice of plaintiff's equity, and because (3) there was no agreement between defendant and plaintiff's step-mother that defendant would receive *all* the subject property on her death but rather defendant alleged and the trial court found that defendant gave "good and valuable consideration" for the agreement of plaintiff's step-mother to convey "a joint tenancy interest" which plaintiff asserts, is only a one half interest. Plaintiff also contends that the trial court erred (4) in admitting, over objection, evidence of assertedly "self-serving" oral declarations of plaintiff's deceased step-mother, (5) in admitting, over objection, the will of plaintiff's step-mother, which states that she devises her entire estate to defendant, and (6) in rejecting evidence of the value of the subject realty shortly before the institution of this action, offered on the issue of adequacy of the consideration given by defendant.

8. Colorado is an exception to this. In Colorado donees are protected by the recording acts. Colo. Rev. Stat. § 38-35-109 (West 2005 Supp.). See Recording Acts — Colorado Protects Donees — Suggested Revision of the Colorado Act, 41 U. Colo. L. Rev. 290 (1969).

We have concluded that plaintiff's contentions, considered (as they must be) on the basis of facts found by the trial court from conflicting evidence, do not impel reversal.

Plaintiff is the son of Robert and Annie Horton, who were divorced prior to 1916. In 1916 Robert married Elizabeth. They remained married until Robert's death in 1931. There was no issue of their marriage. Robert throughout his life had a close and affectionate relationship with plaintiff, and plaintiff often visited Robert and Elizabeth in their home.

In 1930 Robert and Elizabeth purchased and took up residence on the subject property, a ranch of 223 acres. During their marriage they had orally agreed that all property owned by either of them would go to the survivor for life and the survivor on his or her death would will such property one half to plaintiff and one half to those relatives of Elizabeth whom she might select.[2] In reliance on their oral agreement they put all their property, including the subject ranch, in joint tenancy and Robert made no will or other disposition of his property to any members of his own family in the event Elizabeth should survive him. On February 18, 1930, he made a will which would have devised the entire ranch to plaintiff if Elizabeth had predeceased Robert.

Defendant is Elizabeth's grandnephew. She took defendant into her home in 1932, when he was four years old, and their relationship was similar to that of mother and son.

From the time of Robert's death until 1949 Elizabeth leased the ranch for grazing purposes for $125 a year. In 1948 Elizabeth sold 63 acres of the ranch to the United States government for $50 an acre.

On February 15, 1954, without plaintiff's knowledge Elizabeth conveyed the ranch to defendant and herself as joint tenants. She caused this deed to be recorded on February 19, 1954. The trial court found

> That said conveyance . . . was made for good and valuable consideration in that prior to 1954 ["About the end of '49" and "Quite a few times" thereafter, according to defendant's testimony] said Elizabeth A. Horton informed defendant, Norvin R. Kyburz, that if said Norvin R. Kyburz would maintain and improve said real property during the lifetime of said Elizabeth A. Horton that she would convey to him a joint tenancy interest in said real property; that for more than seven (7) years prior to the death of said Elizabeth A. Horton on October 11, 1956, said Norvin R. Kyburz did improve and maintain said property.[4] . . . That at no time prior to the filing of the

2. The evidence of this oral agreement is as follows: Plaintiff testified that on January 18, 1931, the day following his father's death, plaintiff and his wife, at Elizabeth's request, called at the home of plaintiff's aunt and uncle (Robert's brother) where Elizabeth was visiting. There Elizabeth told plaintiff, in the presence of his wife, aunt, and uncle, that "The reason I wanted to see you was, your father and I had an agreement that if he died first, I was to have the use of all the property until I died; and then it was to be divided to — his half was to go to you, and I could leave my half to anyone I wished, on my side of the family. . . . Now, it won't do you any good to start any trouble, because all the property is in joint tenancy, and that is the way it is going to be." Plaintiff's wife, uncle, and aunt gave substantially similar testimony. Also plaintiff, his wife, and his aunt each testified that Robert, prior to his death, had made statements to the effect that "I am going to give this ranch to Vincent [plaintiff] when I die."

4. Defendant testified that before 1949 he had done some work in maintaining and repairing the ranch property and other property of Elizabeth; that "About the end of '49 [when defendant was 21 years of age] she said if I would continue helping her with her maintaining her places and the ranch, she would leave them to me"; that thereafter Elizabeth repeated the substance of this statement "Quite a few times" and defendant from time to time worked on Elizabeth's property and contributed some of his money to its improvement and maintenance; that in 1954 "She told me as long as I was putting part of my

plaintiff's complaint herein did . . . defendant, have any knowledge that said plaintiff claimed any right, title or interest in and to said real property. . . . That defendant . . . is a bona fide purchaser of said real property . . . and to enforce against said defendant the oral agreement made and entered into between [Robert and Elizabeth] . . . would be harsh, oppressive and unjust.

Sufficiency of Consideration paid by Defendant to Elizabeth. Plaintiff urges that because "This entire proceeding is one in equity and involving equitable considerations" defendant, to establish his position as bona fide purchaser, must show not merely that he gave value for the conveyance but that he gave "adequate consideration" in the sense that such adequacy is necessary to obtain specific performance of a contract. To uphold this contention would appear to contravene rules of contract and real property law long established in this state. When the Legislature in 1872 enacted as code law the familiar rule (Civ. Code, § 3391) that "Specific performance cannot be enforced against a party to a contract . . . 1. If he has not received an *adequate* consideration for the contract . . ." (italics added) it also dealt with subjects pertinent to the present action by enacting the following rules:

"No implied or resulting trust can prejudice the rights of a purchaser . . . of real property for value and without notice of the trust." (Civ. Code, § 856.)

"Any benefit conferred, or agreed to be conferred, upon the promisor, by any other person, to which the promisor is not lawful entitled, or any prejudice suffered, or agreed to be suffered, by such person, other than such as he is at the time of consent lawfully bound to suffer, as an inducement to the promisor, is a good consideration for a promise." (Civ. Code, § 1605.) The term "good consideration" in section 1605 is equivalent to the term "valuable consideration." (Aden v. City of Vallejo (1903), 139 Cal. 165, 168, 72 P. 905, rejecting the earlier view, expressed in Clark v. Troy (1862), 20 Cal. 219, 224, that "A good consideration is such as that of blood, or of natural affection. A valuable consideration is such as money or the like.") The Clark case refused to accept the contention, similar to that advanced by the present plaintiff, that the expression "valuable consideration" in the former Conveyancing Act did not mean "only that amount of money, or its equivalent, which would support a contract at common law — that is, one dime or one cent" but rather meant "such a consideration as would support an executory contract in a Court of Equity" (at page 222 of 20 Cal.), and held that "The inadequacy of price is a circumstance proper to be considered in determining the question of good faith, but it will not the less fall within the legal definition of a valuable consideration, however disproportionate it may be to the value of the land" (at page 224 of 20 Cal.).

This remained the rule under the 1872 enactment of section 1107 of the Civil Code, which provides that "Every grant of an estate in real property is conclusive

---

money in on the ranch that she would protect me too, that she would give me a joint tenancy deed and that is when she went to Judge Mundt."

Judge Albert H. Mundt testified that in 1954, while he was engaged in the private practice of law, Elizabeth asked him to draw a joint tenancy deed of the ranch to herself and defendant; that "I suggested to her that it would not be in her best interest to do so in that it was taking control of the property from her and putting it at least partially in control of her nephew. She informed me at that time that she not only wanted to do so but was obligated to do so because she had agreed with him previously that if he would assist her and maintain that property and other properties that she would convey the property to him in joint tenancy and upon her death he would get all of it. And she told me that he had complied with his agreement and that he had done certain work the nature and extent of which I do not recall."

against the grantor, also against everyone subsequently claiming under him, except a purchaser . . . who in good faith and for a valuable consideration acquires a title . . . by an instrument that is first duly recorded." (See Civ. Code, §5; Cain v. Richmond (1932), 126 Cal. App. 254, 260, 14 P.2d 546; cf. United States v. Certain Parcels of Land (U.S. Dist. Ct., S.D. Cal., C.D. 1949), 85 F. Supp. 986, 1006, footnote 17.)

It has been pointed out that "The recording laws were not enacted to protect those whose ignorance of the title is deliberate and intentional, nor does a mere nominal consideration satisfy the requirement that a valuable consideration must be paid. Their purpose is to protect those who honestly believe that they are acquiring a good title, and who invest some substantial sum in reliance on that belief." (Beach v. Faust (1935), 2 Cal. 2d 290, 292, 40 P.2d 822.) But here there is evidence that defendant gave more than "mere nominal consideration." He testified that he and Elizabeth did the following work on the ranch:

> Well, we fixed the fences. We put in the northeast fence which was about a little over a quarter of a mile, and I built the northwest fence. It is about a quarter of a mile, about ready to fall down, and a couple of cross fences. We had three wells drilled. We paid fifty percent apiece . . . on the wells. Put an aluminum roof on the barn and jacked it up and poured a foundation on the north end of it and pillars through the middle and through the south end. We run water to the corral and across the road; put in pressure pumps and separator house. We knocked the front of it off and rebuilt that, reroofed it; put a foundation in the front of it and put a cement floor in it. We built a three-car garage out of aluminum; and the clearing of the land and the reservoir around the hill; and the seeding of the south side; and there is about an acre of permanent pasture besides the brush clearing and burning and stuff that we had done before that.

Defendant paid for half the roofing and half the cost of bulldozers to clear part of the land. He bought the seed, pump, and sprinkler pipe for the permanent pasture. The clearing of brush and repair of fences were done prior to 1949. The wells were drilled in 1954 and 1955. The record is silent as to just when the rest of the work was done, but it can be inferred that it was after 1949 because from the time of Robert's death until 1949 Elizabeth "leased [the ranch] out for cattle grazing," and after 1949 defendant "started running stock on it."

Plaintiff argues that defendant could have done little work on the ranch after the making of the 1949 agreement because from September, 1949, until September, 1953, he was in the armed services and thereafter he worked full time at various jobs. These circumstances were for the appraisal of the trier of fact; they do not show as a matter of law that defendant's contribution to the maintenance and improvement of the realty was barely nominal. Plaintiff further argues that work of defendant done after the 1954 conveyance by Elizabeth to herself and defendant as joint tenants could not have been consideration for such conveyance since defendant was co-owner of the property. But the consideration for which Elizabeth bargained and which defendant gave was *continued* help in maintaining the property, not help merely until Elizabeth should convey a legal interest in the property to defendant.

Also pertinent to the subject of consideration is plaintiff's attack on the trial court's refusal to admit evidence that in 1956, shortly after Elizabeth's death and shortly before the institution of this action, defendant agreed to sell the ranch (then reduced to 160 acres) for $950 an acre. The trial court took the position that evidence of value in 1956 was not relevant. It appears that evidence of the value of the property in 1956, when defendant received full legal title as surviving joint tenant, would be relevant to the question of "inadequacy of price [which] is a circumstance proper to be considered in determining the question of good faith" necessary to constitute defendant a bona fide purchaser (Clark v. Troy (1862), supra, 20 Cal. 219, 224), but that exclusion of the evidence was not prejudicial because had it been received it would have required interpretation by other evidence to connect it controllingly with value in 1954 (when Elizabeth executed the joint tenancy deed to herself and defendant). Furthermore, insofar as relates to the reasonableness of the original oral offer made by Elizabeth to defendant in 1949, the value in 1956 would be entitled to little, if any, weight. It will be recalled that there was evidence that in 1949 Elizabeth ceased to rent the ranch (then comprising 223 acres) for $125 a year and sold 63 acres of it to the United States government for $50 an acre. This 63 acres apparently had some connection, not adequately explained, with construction of Folsom Dam. The finding of the trial court, as hereinabove mentioned, is that "prior to 1954 said Elizabeth . . . informed defendant . . . that if [defendant] . . . would maintain and improve said real property during the lifetime of said Elizabeth A. Horton that she would convey to him a joint tenancy interest in said real property; that for more than seven (7) years prior to the death of said Elizabeth A. Horton on October 11, 1956, said Norvin R. Kyburz did improve and maintain said property."

Concerning the value of the ranch the following may also be mentioned: In the course of a colloquy as to admissibility of evidence of its value in 1956, defendant's counsel remarked, "the court may well take judicial notice of the fact that in this particular area that we are concerned here with that there has been a vast increase in property values owing to Folsom dam being erected or construction there and in the past six or seven years." The court replied, "Yes, what I had in mind when I was inquiring of Mr. Paras [plaintiff's counsel], value — " and Mr. Paras interjected a comment on the consideration allegedly given by defendant. From the foregoing colloquy it is not apparent whether the court felt that it could take judicial notice of the rising value of the ranch for its bearing on defendant's good faith, but it does at least appear that the matter was brought to its attention.

Plaintiff cites Bank of Ukiah v. Gibson (1895), 109 Cal. 197, 200, 41 P. 1008, for the proposition that a mere promise of the purchaser is not value within the rule which protects a bona fide purchaser. The proposition is generally sound (Davis v. Ward (1895), 109 Cal. 186, 189-190, 41 P. 1010; Rest. Trusts 2d (1959), § 302) but it does not necessarily control the factual situation here. At the time of plaintiff's attack on the conveyance, the contract was fully executed; any implied promise of the purchaser-defendant to render services and assist in maintaining the ranch had been performed; at least some services had been rendered which were accepted by Elizabeth as full performance.

Evidence Assertedly Establishing that Defendant was Put on Notice of Plaintiff's Claim. Plaintiff urges that the following testimony of defendant shows that defendant had constructive notice of plaintiff's interest, i.e., that defendant had "actual notice of circumstances sufficient to put a prudent man upon inquiry as to a particular fact" and "by prosecuting such inquiry, he might have learned such fact" (Civ. Cod, § 19):

Q. Norvin, during the time that you lived with your aunt [great aunt Elizabeth], did your aunt ever say anything to you about . . . plaintiff Vincent Horton getting any of her property?

A. No sir.

Q. Did you ever have any conversation with her concerning the possibility of his coming in on any of the property?

A. Between '55 and '56 she brought it up one day that if anything happened to her that she didn't want my mother or her sister to come in on the will or anything. And I brought it up about did she think that Vincent would ever try to come in.

Q. I see. You asked her if she thought that Vincent would ever come in?

A. Yes, sir.

Q. What was her answer?

A. She didn't think he would. . . .

Q. May I ask why you asked that question?

A. Because Vincent was the only one on the other side that I thought would have anything to say about it or — well, that is the only one we ever saw.

Q. Can you tell me what made you think that he might have anything to say about it?

A. No, I don't — he was the only one I could think of.

Q. Just occurred to you to ask that question about Vincent, is that correct?

A. Well, it came up that spur of the moment. It was over —

Q. You brought it up?

A. I brought it up about Vincent but she started about the other party.

Q. Was this after 1953 when you had this conversation?

A. '53? It was '49.

Q. This conversation concerning Vincent was in '49?

A. Oh, '55 and '56.

Q. '55 and '56?

A. Yes, sir.

Q. I see. It was after your father had died?

A. He died in '53.

Q. You indicated that he died in '53 and this conversation took place afterwards?

A. '55, yes sir.

Q. And is that the only conversation you ever had with your aunt concerning Vincent Horton?

A. Yes.

The foregoing conversation held after Elizabeth had executed and caused recordation of the joint tenancy deed to herself and defendant in 1954, and after defendant had furnished some consideration for the conveyance, does not as a matter of law show that defendant was put on notice of plaintiff's equitable claim. It shows that defendant was concerned with the possibility that plaintiff might assert some claim but neither the conversation alone nor the conversation coupled with the rather small and indefinite, but valuable consideration which defendant gave for the ranch shows that defendant deliberately remained ignorant of a state of facts as to which he should have been put on notice.

Plaintiff's Claim that Defendant was at Most a Bona Fide Purchaser of a One Half Interest in the Ranch. Defendant alleged and the trial court found that prior to 1954

Elizabeth agreed that if defendant would maintain and improve the ranch "she would convey to him a joint tenancy interest in said real property." Since "A joint interest is one owned by two or more persons in equal shares . . ." (Civ. Code, § 683) plaintiff argues that under the agreement between Elizabeth and defendant Elizabeth undertook to convey and defendant gave consideration for only a one half interest in the ranch; plaintiff says that Elizabeth did not agree not to sever the joint tenancy and urges that the joint tenancy deed did not convey to defendant the one half interest which Elizabeth had orally agreed with Robert was to go to plaintiff.

Judge Mundt, however, testified that when (in 1954) Elizabeth asked him to prepare the joint tenancy deed she said that she had agreed with defendant "that she would convey the property to him in joint tenancy and upon her death he would get all of it" and defendant testified that Elizabeth said "if I would continue helping her with her maintaining her places and the ranch, she would leave them to me." The foregoing testimony supports the view the defendant gave consideration for Elizabeth's promise not merely to put the ranch in joint tenancy with defendant but also to leave it in joint tenancy so that the right of survivorship would operate. The trial court stated that "I think everyone has been telling the truth in this case. . . . I believe all the folks in the case." It is apparent that the case was tried on the theory that defendant claimed as bona fide purchaser of the entire interest in the ranch, and that if the trial court had specifically found concerning the present contention of plaintiff its finding would have been adverse to plaintiff and in accord with the above quoted testimony of Judge Mundt and defendant. Therefore, under familiar rules of appellate review, we must reject plaintiff's argument that the judgment decreeing that defendant is the owner of the ranch and plaintiff has no interest in it is not supported by the allegation and finding that Elizabeth agreed to convey to defendant a joint tenancy interest. . . .

While on the record it may seem to some of us that, were we triers of fact, we might have reached findings differing in some respects from those declared by the trial judge, we recognize that we did not see and hear the witnesses and, hence, on conflicting evidence have neither right nor power to disagree with the trier of fact.

For the reasons above stated the judgment is affirmed.

NOTES AND QUESTIONS

1. Why should not donees or those paying nominal consideration be protected as subsequent takers? Is there sufficient merit to the valuable consideration requirement to justify its retention? Can it be justified as bolstering the notice requirement on the theory that in many situations the meager consideration paid indicates that the transferees involved must have had notice?

2. Suppose that a subsequent taker without notice makes a partial payment and then becomes aware of a prior unrecorded interest. What should be the respective rights of the prior and subsequent interest holders?

In Seguin v. Maloney-Chambers Lumber Co., 198 Ore. 272, 253 P.2d 252, 256 P.2d 514 (1953), X conveyed standing timber to A. This instrument of conveyance was not recorded. Later X contracted to convey to B the land on which the trees were located, including the timber previously sold to A. B paid $5,000 toward the purchase price, the balance to be paid in installments, and B to receive a deed upon all payments being made. When B contracted to buy and when he paid the $5,000, he was unaware of the conveyance from X to A. But before B made any further payments, he was informed of the timber conveyance from X to A. In a quiet title proceeding brought by B against A, the court held that A's interest in the timber was superior to B's, except that B was declared to have a lien on the standing timber minus the value of timber cut and removed by B.

Why should A receive the timber and B, in essence, receive back his payment? Why should not B receive the timber but be required to pay A for the value of the timber as of the contract date or date of partial payment, minus payments by B before B obtained notice? What criteria should resolve this question? Is this one of those legal problems in which one solution is no more appealing than another, hence the court must act arbitrarily? Should the proportion of the contract price paid by B before notice be an important consideration? Should it make any difference whether the subsequent taker's interest is legal or equitable?

(3) Under these facts, should A have a cause of action of any kind against X or B? Assume the transactions occurred in the following chronological order:

X-A, mortgage delivered

X-B, deed delivered

B-C, deed delivered

X-B, deed recorded

B-C, deed recorded

X-A, mortgage recorded

Assume that B is a donee from X who knew of the X-A mortgage when he took delivery of his deed, but that C is a bona fide purchaser who paid the full value of the property and was unaware of the X-A mortgage when taking delivery. Does your answer vary depending on whether the applicable recording act is a race, race-notice, or notice one?

If two deeds from the same grantor to different grantees, the deeds having the same descriptions, are recorded on the same day, which will prevail?

c. Notice from Recording

The recording of an instrument does not necessarily mean that constructive notice of its contents will be held to exist. Even though an instrument is recordable and filed for record by someone entitled to protection of the recording act, it is possible under some circumstances that the instrument will not be given recording effect. It may, for instance, be outside the chain of title of some persons who may acquire an interest in the parcel involved, and recording is generally not constructive notice to such persons. Although an instrument may have been filed for record, a public official may have been negligent and as a result the instrument was never placed of record or indexed, or it may have been inaccurately transcribed onto the records or inaccurately indexed. In some states these circumstances prevent an instrument from having recording effect. Courts and legislatures often take the position that although an instrument is filed or placed of record, it should not be constructive notice if it is impossible to find the instrument in the public records or if it can be found only by an unduly burdensome search. A common counter judicial or legislative policy is to protect those who have made a reasonable effort to record. Under the recording system, interests of those who record are frequently inconsistent with those of persons obligated to search, and in various situations a choice between the two must be made. In close cases, some courts and legislatures tend to favor those who record and others those who must search.

Kiser v. Clinchfield Coal Corp.
200 Va. 517, 106 S.E.2d 601 (1959)

WHITTLE, Justice. On October 26, 1951, Clinchfield Coal Corporation, hereinafter called Clinchfield, filed a bill in chancery against Mont B. Kiser, et al., alleging title to the coal and minerals underlying a tract of 117 acres of land in Dickenson county. . . . The bill further alleged Mont B. Kiser and his lessees (appellants here) were mining coal and trespassing upon said land.

Upon the filing of the bill the court entered an order restraining the trespass until the case could be heard on its merits.

Appellants demurred to the bill, and without waiving their demurrer, answered the same. Depositions were taken, and upon a hearing, the circuit court on October 4, 1957, entered a decree overruling the demurrer, adjudging Clinchfield to be the owner of the mineral estate in the 117 acres. . . . A commissioner was appointed to ascertain the damages resulting from the alleged trespass. From this decree appellants appeal.

The record and briefs were voluminous, and there are some contentions made which we do not deem of sufficient merit to be considered. The material questions for decision are . . . .

III. Was Clinchfield entitled to a decree adjudging it the owner of the mineral estate underlying the 117-acre tract of land? . . .

Question No. III challenges Clinchfield's right to the mineral estate in the 117-acre tract. The record discloses that in 1884 the land here involved was a part of a large tract consisting of some 1400 acres owned in fee simple by James M. Kiser, father of Schofield, which is the common source of title of all parties to this controversy.

On January 31, 1884, James M. Kiser and wife conveyed the 117 acres by deed in fee simple to their son Schofield. There was no exception of the mineral estate. This deed was not recorded until November 30, 1888 and, as hereinafter pointed out, was never acknowledged by James M. Kiser. In the meantime, on December 7, 1887, James Kiser and wife, together with certain of their children not here involved, conveyed the mineral estate and certain timber to Tazewell Coal and Iron Company.

The evidence discloses that after the deed of 1884 to Schofield Kiser was executed, he held possession of the surface until December 12, 1891, when he executed a deed for the 117 acres to James M. Kiser and wife, which contained the following exception, "with the exception of the coal and minerals" and certain timber.

Thus, at the time of the conveyance of 1887 of the mineral estate by James M. Kiser and wife to the Tazewell company, Schofield was in possession of the surface of the land, and under the common law rule stated in Chapman v. Chapman, 91 Va. 397, 21 S.E. 813, his possession was sufficient to charge Tazewell with notice of Schofield Kiser's deed. However, by statute enacted by the General Assembly of January 15, 1900, the common law rule was abrogated by adding a proviso to the recording statute (Acts of Assembly 1899-1900, p. 89) to the effect that mere possession shall not be notice to subsequent purchasers for valuable consideration. Norfolks & P. Traction Co. v. C. B. White & Bros., 113 Va. 102, 73 S.E. 467; Code of 1950, § 55-96. This was the law in effect on August 7, 1902, when Tazewell Coal and Iron Company executed two deeds to the land in question, one conveying to William Patrick an undivided three-fourths interest in the mineral estate, and the other conveying to L. C. Ware an undivided one-fourth interest in the mineral estate.

Thereafter, by mesne conveyances, the mineral estate passed to Clinchfield, at which time the proviso that mere possession shall not be notice to subsequent purchasers for valuable consideration was in effect. Thus, this proviso applied to all purchasers of the mineral estate since the enactment of the statute abrogating the rule in the *Chapman* case, and mere possession by Schofield or Mont Kiser since the effective date of the statute constituted no notice of Schofield's deed.

The record clearly discloses that Clinchfield in good faith, for valuable consideration, purchased in 1907 the mineral estate embraced in the deed from James M. Kiser to Tazewell, relying upon said deed and the recorded chain of title by subsequent conveyances from Tazewell and its successors in title. Therefore, if Clinchfield so purchased without notice of Schofield Kiser's deed, then Schofield's deed was and is void as to Clinchfield's deed of purchase.

Further, the record discloses that the only certificate of acknowledgment, or any other proof of execution of the deed by James M. Kiser to Schofield Kiser on January 31, 1884, appears to be a certificate of Jessie Wampler, a notary public, certifying the privy examination and acknowledgment of Elizabeth Kiser, wife of the grantor. Nowhere is it shown that James M. Kiser acknowledged the deed; therefore the deed was not duly admitted to record as to him. §§ 2500, 2501, Code 1887; now §§ 55-106 and 55-113, Code 1950.

It is argued by counsel for appellants that the attorney for Clinchfield who examined the title to the mineral estate prior to purchase must have had actual notice of Schofield's deed. It will be remembered that the deed from James M. Kiser to Schofield was not filed for recordation until after the conveyance of the coal and minerals by the deed from James M. Kiser to Tazewell, and an attorney examining the record as to the title to the mineral estate would not be called upon to look for the recordation of adverse conveyances in the name of James M. Kiser subsequent to the date of the recordation of the duly acknowledged deed from James M. Kiser to the Tazewell Coal and Iron Company. The deed to Schofield Kiser was not recorded until four years and ten months after its execution, and ten months after the recordation of the deed to the Tazewell company. See Bowman v. Holland, 116 Va. 805, 83 S.E. 393.

In order for a deed and its recitals to operate as constructive notice to a bona fide purchaser of land it must be a link in the purchaser's chain of title. No purchaser is chargeable with constructive notice of all matters of record but only with such as the title deeds of the estate refer to or put him on inquiry about. Lewis v. Barnhart, 145 U.S. 56, 12 S. Ct. 772, 36 L. Ed. 621; Flanary v. Kane, 102 Va. 547, 46 S.E. 312.

It was not incumbent upon Clinchfield's attorney to search the record for adverse conveyances by James M. Kiser recorded after the recordation of the Tazewell Coal and Iron Company's deed.

Appellants further contend that even if Mont Kiser's paper title to the mineral estate is not good as against Clinchfield, he has title to the same by adverse possession by reason of Schofield's possession. This is not true under the circumstances here involved. After the severance of the surface estate from the mineral estate, color of title to the mineral estate alone and possession of the surface estate not held adversely, is not sufficient. Mont Kiser has shown no occupancy or use of any part of the mineral estate such as would constitute actual possession, and there is no merit in this contention. Clevinger v. Bull Creek Coal Co., Inc., 199 Va. 216, 219, 220, 98 S.E.2d 670, 672, 673; 58 C.J.S. Mines and Minerals § 157, page 329.

The record title exhibited by Clinchfield shows that it has a good recorded paper title to the mineral estate which was conveyed by the deed of December 7, 1887 from James M. Kiser to Tazewell Coal and Iron Company, and the evidence shows that it has exercised acts of exclusive ownership over the same and is therefore the owner of the mineral estate in the 117 acres in controversy.

For the reasons stated the decree appealed from is affirmed.

NOTES AND QUESTIONS

1. One of the links in Clinchfield's chain of title was weak: Tazewell was junior in time and not protected by the recording acts because it was on notice of Schofield Kiser's interest. Should this not have prevented Clinchfield from prevailing in the principal case?

2. What could Clinchfield have done to have discovered the Schofield Kiser interest and interests derived from him? Should Clinchfield have been obligated to search for and discover these interests?

3. The Virginia statute on possession, originally enacted in 1900, states the following: "The mere possession of real estate shall not, of itself, be notice to purchasers thereof for value of any interest or estate therein of the person in possession." Va. Code Ann. § 55-96A.1 (2003). The statute is a very unusual one and presumably was enacted to benefit an important Virginia industry, coal mining.

4. Do you favor the Massachusetts or Vermont position or the one preferred by the court, as these positions are described in this excerpt from the opinion in Woods v. Garnett, 72 Miss. 78, 84-87, 16 So. 390, 391-392 (1894)?

> When a conveyance is made to one who fails to record his deed until after another has received and recorded a conveyance from the grantor, but with notice of the first deed, what are the rights of the first grantee against a purchaser from the second, where such purchaser, having no actual knowledge of the facts, buys after the record of prior deed? This question is determined by a construction of our registry act; for at the common law a second purchaser of the fee could take nothing, since by the first conveyance the grantor would have divested himself of all his estate and would have nothing to convey. Basset v. Nosworthy, 2 White & T. Lead. Cas. Eq. 1, and note; Co. Litt. 290f, note 13. By our registry act, it is declared that the instruments thereby required to be recorded

NY rule: chain of title reasoning doesn't matter.

"shall be void as to all creditors and subsequent purchasers for valuable consideration without notice, unless they shall be acknowledged or proved, and lodged with the clerk of the chancery court of the county, to be recorded, in the same manner that other conveyances are required by this act to be acknowledged or proved and recorded; but the same as between the parties and their heirs, and as to all subsequent purchasers with notice, or without valuable consideration, shall nevertheless be valid and binding." Code 1880, § 1212; code 1892, § 2457. "Every conveyance, convenant, agreement, bond, mortgage and deed of trust shall take effect as to all subsequent purchasers for a valuable consideration, without notice, and as to all creditors, only from the time when delivered to the clerk to be recorded." Code 1880, § 1213; Code 1892, § 2458. In Massachusetts and Vermont it is held that a purchaser is not bound to examine the record after the date of a recorded conveyance, to discover whether the grantor therein has made another conveyance prior in time, but junior in record, but may safely purchase from the grantee in the first recorded conveyance, if he, the purchaser, has not actual notice of the prior deed, and no notice of the facts which make it his duty to prosecute inquiry. Connecticut v. Bradish, 14 Mass. 296; Trull v. Bigelow, 16 Mass. 406; Morse v. Curtis, 140 Mass. 112, 2 N.E. 929; Day v. Clark, 25 Vt. 397. And this is said to be the more reasonable rule by the annotators of the Leading Cases in Equity (Le Neve v. Le Neve, 2 White & T. Lead. Cas. Eq. 180), and by Mr. Jones (1 Jones, Mortg. § 574). The decided weight of authority is, however, to the contrary, though Mr. Jones cites none of them as supporting the contrary rule except the New York decisions. . . . The question has never been decided in this state, though in Harrington v. Allen, 48 Miss. 492, there is a doctrine in which Judge Simrall, mistaking the facts of his case, seems to favor the Massachusetts rule. The decisions in Massachusetts and Vermont, while resulting in practically the same end, proceed on irreconcilable and opposite principles. In Massachusetts it is ruled that the purchaser from the grantee in the deed junior in date, but senior in record, need not examine the records after the date of registration of the conveyance to his grantor. Morse v. Curtis, 140 Mass. 112, 2 N.E. 929. In Vermont it is held that he is bound by the constructive notice afforded by the registration of the first deed, that it is notice to him of the fact that a deed prior to that of his grantor had been made, but it is not notice that his grantor had notice of the first deed; and so the conveyance to the first purchaser from the second grantee is preferred in Vermont, not because the purchaser is himself a purchaser without notice, for the registration of the prior deed is notice of its existence, nor because his grantor was a purchaser without notice, for that may or may not be true, but because the purchaser did not know that his grantor was not a bona fide purchaser; and thus, under the Vermont decisions, one may secure protection, as though he were a bona fide purchaser, when neither he, nor any one under and through whom he derives title, was in fact such purchaser. This rule has no recognition except in Vermont, so far as we have discovered. We think the Massachusetts decisions are erroneous, because they hold that one not bound by the registry law is protected by it. But for the registry law, where one has conveyed his title, he has nothing left to convey to another, and that other, with or without notice of the prior conveyance, would get nothing, for his grantor had nothing to convey. Now, the statute comes, and provides that, though a conveyance of the class named in the statute may be made, it shall, as to certain persons, viz. creditors and purchasers without notice, be valid only from a certain time, viz. the time when it is filed for record. In other words, the operation of the unrecorded conveyance is suspended until it shall be recorded as against creditors and purchasers without notice, and where recorded it does not operate by relation as against such persons from the day of its execution, but is effectual only from and of the date of its delivery for record. But where filed for record it has full scope and effect against the world. One who buys after that event can find no protection in the statute, for its terms have been complied with by the holder of the adverse title. It is no answer to say that it is inconvenient to the purchaser to examine a long and voluminous record, made after the record of the title of his grantor. To this the sufficient reply is that, but for the registry acts, he would not have even the protection which such records afford, but would deal at his peril with his grantor, and secure only such title as he might assert. If that grantor had good title because a purchaser for value, without notice, that is a defense to his vendee; but if such grantor was not such purchaser, then the validity of the title he conveys must depend upon the character of his vendee; and, if such vendee is not a bona fide purchaser under the common law or the statute, we cannot perceive from what source a principle can be deduced which will afford him protection. It seems clear to us that one who buys an estate cannot invoke the protection of the registry act as against a deed recorded under such act at the time of his purchase.

5. If subsequent takers are on actual or constructive notice of instruments, they generally are considered on constructive notice of matters referred to in the instruments pertaining to the titles in question. If the recitals are indefinite or incomplete but suggest that prior claims against a title may exist, subsequent takers generally are considered on notice of what reasonable inquiry would disclose. Statutes in some states have sought to narrow the notice scope of recitals in instruments. For example, N.Y. Real Property Law § 291e (McKinney 2006), provides in part:

> 1. This section applies to any language, contained in a conveyance of real property in this state, which (a) excepts or reserves a part of any or all parts of the described premises which have been or may have been previously conveyed, or previously contracted to be sold or exchanged, by the grantor or by a previous owner, or (b) otherwise indicates that the premises or some part or parts thereof have been or may have been previously conveyed or that a contract has been or may have been previously made for the sale or exchange of all or some part or parts thereof, or (c) indicates that only such part of the premises described is intended to be conveyed as the grantor, or a previous owner, has not previously conveyed or has not previously contracted to sell or exchange, and, in any of the cases described in this subdivision, fails to identify the premises previously conveyed or contracted to be sold or exchanged in any other manner than by indicating that a conveyance or contract has previously been made or indicating the fact or possibility that one or more conveyances or contracts have been or may have been previously made.
>
> 2. An exception, reservation or recital described in subdivision one of this section is (a) void as against a subsequent purchaser in good faith and for a valuable consideration, who has no other notice of the identity of the premises to which it refers, and (b) ineffective to give notice to such subsequent purchaser of the previous conveyance or contract so referred to or create any duty of inquiry with respect thereto, unless, in either case, such previous conveyance or contract is sufficient to identify the premises to which the exception, reservation or recital refers and is recorded as provided in this article before the recording of the instrument by which the subsequent purchaser acquires his estate or interest.

Why do you think this statute was enacted? What ends does it further?

6. In In re Ryan, 851 F.2d 502 (1st Cir. 1988), it was held that an improperly witnessed mortgage instrument, actually put of record in a Vermont recorder's office, did not provide constructive notice of the mortgage. The opinion relies heavily on an 1869 Vermont Supreme Court case interpreting the Vermont recording act as requiring two witnesses for a mortgage to be entitled to recording. The

mortgage in question had only one witness. The First Circuit reversed a bankruptcy court ruling that one witness was sufficient to give the mortgage constructive notice. The bankruptcy court reasoning, with which the First Circuit disagreed, was that the Vermont Supreme Court quite likely would no longer follow its 1869 precedent, as this would be "formalism to an extreme." The First Circuit also held that the properly recorded assignment of the mortgage in question, an assignment that included the requisite two witnesses, did not put subsequent purchasers on inquiry notice of the defectively witnessed mortgage because the assignment was outside the chain of title, thus no constructive notice of the mortgage.

Another case requiring strict compliance with legal requirements is Waicker v. Banegura, 745 A.2d 419 (Md. 2000). In that case a judgment lien was indexed by the county court clerk's office under the name Baneguna, rather than the correct name, Banegura. The result of this misindexing, the court held, was that it failed to provide constructive notice to a subsequent lien holder or purchaser without actual notice of the judgment lien. So, in the *Waicker* case, the subsequent lien takes priority over the misindexed lien. A more liberal case as to legal formalities is In re Williams, 584 S.E.2d 922 (W.Va. 2003). Deeds of trust acknowledged by an unauthorized notary were recorded in that case and the court held that the recording, despite the acknowledgment by an improper person, constituted constructive notice for purposes of determining priority in a bankruptcy proceeding, provided no improper benefit was obtained by the notary or any party to the instrument and no harm resulted.

7. Would the recording act system be much more efficient today if the record keeping and record retention were principally performed by state agencies rather than county agencies? *Yes!*

Cross, The Record "Chain of Title Hypocrisy"

57 Colum. L. Rev. 787, 787-796 (1957)

Anyone reading part of the mass of recording act cases in almost any American jurisdiction will be confronted with the "chain of title" rationale often invoked to resolve priority between competing claimants to interests in land. The assertion is that a subsequent purchaser[1] will have priority over an earlier claimant to the same title unless the antecedent claim is revealed within the "chain" of the title which the subsequent purchaser believes he is getting. The conception has been evolved apparently to effect some practical protection by the recording acts. These acts commonly provide that an instrument shall be ineffective against certain competing claimants unless the direction of the statute is followed. The statute may make the instrument "void" as to the competitor or may state that if the statutory direction is followed the record of an instrument shall be notice to all the world. The chain of the title concept is commonly used without regard to the possible importance of the particular form of statute.

---

1. "Subsequent purchaser" is here used generically to include any person who by the force of the applicable recording act may be able to assert its protection, and it is assumed that he has the necessary qualities, e.g., actual good faith and payment of valuable consideration.

I. THE RECORD CHAIN OF TITLE CONCEPT

From the rule that all conveyances are "innocent" it must follow that a current claimant can prevail only if he can establish that ownership has in fact passed from the sovereign (theoretically) through his predecessors to himself, and hence that there is a chain or sequence of transactions ending in him. The record chain of title concept has an additional connotation, that of defining the length of each link in the sense of fixing the period of time for search in the records against a particular owner. Rather than strictly a chain of transfers it connotes a chain of owners or persons interested in the title. The typical statute says nothing of chain of title — it appears by a judicial gloss which has done much to conceal the inadequacy of the protection afforded by the acts. Consequently the needed corrections are not pressed.

Chain of title has been used in a geographical sense to disqualify, as not part of the chain to tract one, an instrument having the primary function of conveying tract two, even though as between the parties it creates rights in tract one and specifically so states.[5] The term had also been used to narrow the operative effect of record "notice to the whole world" (in some of the statutes), thus permitting disregard of the "wild deed" from a person who, so far as the records reveal, had no interest in the land.[6] This discussion has no principal concern with these two uses of the term.

From the practical necessities of search in the public records has evolved the meaning definitive of the length of each link. This is the method to determine whether a prospective vendor has the interest he purports to have, the records are examined to discover the sequence of transfers which support his assertion of title. Unless the origin of his title is known the search must extend backwards in time looking for the record of a conveyance to the vendor; then continuing backwards, search is made for the record of the instrument in which the vendor's grantor was the grantee, and continuing similarly as to each predecessor until the transfer from the sovereign is discovered, or in older states, far enough back until an apparently firm "root" is located. In an earlier time this must have involved thumbing through the actual volumes of the record, but since indexing has been directed by the legislatures, the initial search for the person has been in the indexes. The history of transfer now discovered, the process is reversed and search is made to determine what each of the various owners did with or to the title during the period of his apparent ownership. As to each owner there should be a small overlap in time, i.e., the search is made from the day before execution of the deed to him (not the day of recording) until the day after recording of the deed from him (not the day of execution). Thus the length of the respective links is identified. A transaction by the then owner fairly discoverable of record within the duration of his link is in the

---

5. This meaning is involved in Glorieux v. Lighthipe, 88 N.J.L. 199, 96 Atl. 94 (1915) (restrictive covenant affecting lot 1 in deed to lot 2 — not in chain of title). Contra, Finley v. Glenn, 303 Pa. 131, 154 Atl. 299 (1931) (easement on lot 1 in favor of lot 2 created in deed to lot 2 — in chain of title).

Professors Merrill and Philbrick believe the "chain" is narrow. 2 Merrill, Notice §981 (1952); Philbrick, Limits of Record Search and Therefore of Notice, 93 U. Pa. L. Rev. 125, 169 (1944) (this article is in three parts, id. at 125, 259, 391). Mr. R. G. Patton does not agree. 4 American Law of Property § 17.24 (Casner ed. 1952). Compare the analysis of Bowman v. Holland, 116 Va. 805, 83 S.E. 393 (1914) in Note, Title Search in Virginia, 26 Va. L. Rev. 385 (1940), with MacKenzie, Examining for Conveyances by a Grantor after He Has Conveyed Title of Record, 26 Va. L. Rev. 831 (1940).

6. 4 American Law of Property § 17.17 (Casner ed. 1952).

chain of title, but all other transactions, though reflected in the records in fact, are not in the chain of title.[8] Under this approach the prospective purchaser has no concern with instruments thus determined to be out of the chain of title. Professor Philbrick asserts this is the proper meaning of the term.[9] Mr. R. G. Patton has concurred.[10] And where search or examination is made directly from the public records this meaning is apparently adopted to control the extent of search.

Since it is not now practicable to search in the actual record or transcription books, if it ever was for long, this then is the resulting proposition: A prospective purchaser can be confident he will get good title from his vendor if an examination of the indexes in the indicated manner, and a study of the transactions thereby discovered, reveal a chain of title without infirmity. But is this so? I suggest that to assert that such a "chain of title" assures ownership in the vendor is sheer hypocrisy.

II.   The Infirmities of Chain of Title Reasoning

A. *The Immateriality of the Index.*   The most glaring weakness stems from the rule that a grantee has established his position and barred a subsequent purchaser from the protection afforded by the recording act when the prior grantee has merely "filed" or "lodged" his instrument with the recording officer for record, without regard to what that officer does about transcribing it or making an index to the transcription. Nearly as fatal is the proposition that the grantee is secure against subsequent parties if the instrument is transcribed though not indexed at all or indexed in a misleading manner.

It is asserted that application of the chain of title approach is essential to accomplish the purpose of protection for the subsequent purchaser. Without denying the accuracy of this assertion, it may be observed that twenty-six states have decisions not overruled which hold that filing or lodging with the recording officer fulfills the grantee's duty, or that the subsequent purchaser gets no protection from the lack or

---

8. "Chain of title" notice seems to be a one-way street—forward in time only, not backward even though the persons in the chain may initially be discoverable only by the "backward" search. Thus an instrument *in favor of* or *to* the record owner can be ignored. Philbrick, supra note 5, at 170 n. 146. This is reasonable when the instrument is in his favor as creditor or mortgagee, as in Pyles v. Brown, 189 Pa. 164, 42 A. 11 (1899) or Veazie v. Parker, 23 Me. 170 (1843). The searcher is not interested in any such position, but is it equally reasonable when the instrument is a deed which *might* be his necessary title deed? To illustrate: search against M to learn his source of title before 1920 when he conveyed to N. In 1918 M's name appears in the index as mortgagee—irrelevant; in 1917 he appears as grantee—relevant? In 1915 he appears as grantee from the real source of his title, and if search could run forward from 1915, in 1917 the searcher would be looking for deeds from M, not to him. Going backward in time, the reverse is true. Nonetheless the rule applied in the Veazie case, supra, was believed by the Texas court to answer the question of notice from the 1917 deed (in effect), and it could be ignored. Frank v. Heidenheimer, 84 Tex. 642, 19 S.W. 855 (1892).

The chain has a certain ephemeral quality in another "wild deed" problem. Suppose V contracts to sell to P, and P mortgages to M. The mortgage is recorded but the contract is not. Then A buys P out, pays V the balance due on the contract, receives and records the deed from V. A though he knows nothing in fact of the mortgage to M takes subject to it; his chain of title includes P and hence he must search for P's transactions. Simonson v. Wenzel, 27 N.D. 638, 147 N.W. 804 (1914). However, if A conveys to B who knows nothing of P, B as a bona fide purchaser for value will apparently take free of M's mortgage. Although it is in A's chain of title it is not in B's. Cf. Fullerton Lumber Co. v. Tinker, 22 S.D. 427, 118 N.W. 700 (1908) (rejection of this argument *because* of tract indexing).

9. Philbrick, supra note 5 (passim), particularly at 167, 179.

10. 4 American Law of Property § 17.19 (Casner ed. 1952).

inaccuracy of an index, and four more states have cases in which one or the other of these propositions is stated.

Under typical statutes the normal steps in recording are these: (1) filing the instrument with the recording officer and payment of the required fees; (2) notation by the officer in an entry or reception book if there is one, or preliminary entry in an index book; (3) actual transcription in the appropriate record book; (4) completion of the index(es) to the record; and (5) return of the instrument by the officer. Completion of these steps can be called full recording.[17] The cases cited above recognize that a prior grantee must start the recording process before a subsequent purchaser buys if he is to prevail against the subsequent purchaser, but in concluding that full recording is not required, the courts reason that, as recording is for the protection of the subsequent purchaser, he should bear the burden of the officer's inadequate performance. The applicable statute may provide that an instrument is void unless "lodged" or "filed" with the officer, or it may provide that an instrument is deemed recorded from the moment it is filed for record. The literal interpretation of the statute preserves as near as may be the grantee's position at common law. The factual patterns have varied, as the footnotes indicate. In some situations the instrument was still held by the officer, but there was no clue in the books to its existence; in others the instrument had been returned but the recording process was not completed; in others the instrument had been lost; in others the transcription was inaccurate. The rule of immateriality of the index has an understandable origin, even though it may not have current rationality. The need for an index apparently was not fully appreciated at first, and after the enactment of the recording acts, additional, independent statutes were passed directing the recording officer to prepare indexes to the records then in existence and henceforth to make indexes contemporaneously with the recording. The gap in time between the enactments fostered analysis of them separately.

From the standpoint of the recording process stated above the instruments are not really recorded. Of course some courts wisely so hold, and require more than mere "filing" with the officer; a few also conclude that indexing is a necessary part of recording. But wherever these positions, stated in the preceding paragraphs, are maintained, the record chain of title cannot reveal with certainty what the subsequent purchaser will get.

B. *The Time Element.* Even if there is full recording there are two situations in which the time element—the length of the link in the record chain—is particularly important: first, where the prior grantee's deed is recorded after the subsequent purchaser's deed is recorded; and second, where the prior grantee's deed is recorded before the grantor acquired the title which he purports to convey to the subsequent purchaser (the estoppel by deed or after-acquired title problem). Discussion of these problems can be simplified by use of symbols identifying X as the common grantor; A as the prior grantee with B and C as successors under A;

---

17. There is inevitably an interval of time between the beginning and end of the process; careful search should reveal the existence of instruments in the officer's hands not yet transcribed or indexed. See Perkins v. Strong, 22 Neb. 725, 36 N.W. 292 (1888). This of course can be burdensome if hundreds or thousands of instruments are filed in a single day.

and R as the subsequent purchaser with S and T as successor under R. A diagram may be helpful:

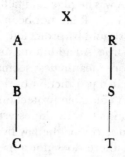

Thus the X-A transaction is prior in time of occurrence to the X-R transaction, and the A-B-C chain is prior in time of origin to the R-S-T chain.

1. The subsequent purchaser who records first. No problem in chain of title analysis arises when X is owner and conveys to A who records his deed before X conveys to R. The chain of title problem is presented when R records before A, but A records before the R-S transaction occurs. Even here there is no unresolved problem if R is within the protection of the recording act, because the title he secures with the aid of the act as a bona fide purchaser for value can be passed to S even though S knows of A's deed. However, when R knows of A's claim he is not protected by the act, and the question arises, can S who subsequently takes in actual good faith assert that he is protected by the act against A? Here the adoption or rejection of chain of title reasoning is crucial.

The practical mechanics of search are such that as to the period during which A records his deed, S will be searching for conveyances from R, having abandoned X as grantor on discovery of the X-R deed of record. Since, according to the rationale, the X-A deed is not reasonably discoverable by S, he should take free of it. This may be called the Massachusetts view, whose object is protection of the subsequent purchaser. The contrary result may be called the New York view. In the latter, chain of title reasoning is believed not to be persuasive and emphasis is on protection of the prior grantee, A, when he has done all the statute specifically requires him to do. This is to record his deed; if he does not, the statute says certain persons are protected; if he does, no claimant getting into the picture thereafter (as S does) can get any protection from the statute. Difficulty of discovery is irrelevant. It is just unfortunate that the statute does not afford a greater practical protection to the subsequent purchaser. The New York view apparently finds acceptance in ten states and is the majority view.

2. The estoppel by deed situation. In the estoppel by deed area a preliminary distinction must be drawn. The operative effect of the estoppel by deed doctrine may be merely to prevent X from claiming title against his estoppel grantee, A (to whom X has "conveyed" before receiving title himself); or it may be that the title when secured by X automatically inures or passes to A. The latter approach, the inurement doctrine, is primarily important here. The competing claimants are A, the estoppel grantee, and R, to whom X conveyed after receiving title. Limiting his examination by the chain of title search, R will not discover A's deed in the record because as to the period of time in which A's deed is recorded R will be looking for conveyances by X's grantor not by X. Again, the recording statutes typically are

silent. If as a matter of law the title is in A and he has recorded, he can assert that there is nothing in the usual statute by which he can be deprived of his title. The basic counter argument is that A was negligent in failing to discover from the record that X apparently had no title, while R has not been negligent and the spirit of the recording act requires that he should be protected. This may usually be true but it can hardly be said to be always true. An additional argument that the X-A deed is a nullity and recording is therefore meaningless seems to be an exaggeration. If the inurement doctrine is the rule in a jurisdiction by decision only (or if the estoppel by deed operates only to give A equitable protection against X), there may be fair reason to nullify it when it conflicts with the asserted protection given R by the statute. But if the inurement doctrine is the law by statute and the recording act does not specifically nullify it, there does not appear to be persuasive reason to prefer R through a claimed but unexpressed policy. It is asserted that the inurement doctrine in a majority of states gives way to the protection of the recording act for the subsequent purchaser, nonetheless there are several states where it has not given way, although the point was argued. These include, surprisingly enough, Massachusetts, which is strong on chain of title reasoning in the A against S controversy discussed above, as well as several other states in which it is held that the title inures to A, no point being made of recordation, although in most cases A's deed was promptly recorded.

If in either of these last two situations A's priority is found, certainly it cannot be said that the chain of title passing from vendor back through A will establish the validity of the vendor's (X's) title!

NOTE

On the chain of title concept, see also Stoebuck & Whitman, The Law of Property 894-898 (3d ed. 2000).

Note, The Tract and Grantor-Grantee Indices

47 Iowa L. Rev. 481, 481-485 (1962)

A practical and convenient means of locating records which an owner of property must rely upon to prove his title and which a prospective purchaser must depend upon when making a title search is an indispensable part of a workable system of recordation. Therefore, it is not surprising to discover that statutory provisions providing for some system of indexing which affords a history of ownership of land and which discloses instruments or encumbrances affecting title to real property have been enacted in every state. There are currently two types of indices in use: (1) the grantor-grantee index, and (2) the tract index. This should not be interpreted as meaning that a dual system of indexing has always been present in the United States, for under the land owned by the English, French, Mexican, and Spanish governments on the North American Continent, there were no numbered tract systems in existence which could serve as a basis for land description. This was, of course, directly related to the fact that a competent survey had never been made of the land owned by these countries. Under these circumstances, even tax levies had to be against the owners of the land rather than against the land itself. Therefore, it was only logical that when some system of indexing was finally adopted the alphabetical or grantor-grantee system of indexing was selected. Nevertheless, even after the United States Government acquired the land formerly held by foreign countries in what is now the United States and adequate Government surveys had been undertaken and completed, the grantor-grantee system of indexing was still retained as the basis of land description. However, it was gradually discovered that the grantor-grantee system of indexing was inadequate in many respects. This led several states to enact statutes establishing a tract or numerical system of indexing. Nevertheless, even those states which adopted the tract system of indexing retained the alphabetical system of indexing which they had established at an earlier date.

Under the grantor-grantee or alphabetical index, pages are assigned in the index to each letter of the alphabet. As an instrument is received at the recorder's office, it is first recorded and then indexed under the name of the granting party on the appropriate page of the index. In addition, the county recorder is usually required to make notations on the grantor's page which disclose the name of the other party to the transaction, the book and page of the record where this particular transaction can be found, a description of the property, the date when the instrument was executed, the date when the instrument was filed for recordation, and the nature of the instrument. These same notations are then made as the transaction is indexed under the name of the grantee or the receiving party. After both steps have been completed, the instrument is considered to have been properly indexed.

Under the tract indexing system each parcel of land in a certain area is assigned a separate page in the index and every subsequent transaction affecting this property will be noted thereon. Under the tract system of indexing, a "parcel of land" means any geographical unit of land which has been surveyed and platted, such as sections, blocks, and lots. In addition to describing the property, the tract index also discloses the character of the instrument which affects the title to the property, the date of the execution of the instrument, the date of the filing of the instrument for recordation, and the names of the parties to the transaction. Under this system, therefore, *all* the instruments which affect the title to a particular parcel of realty will be noted on one page of the index. For this reason and innumerable others, the uniform adoption of the tract index has been urged by many legal scholars. However, the reaction of the respective state legislatures to this proposal apparently has not been enthusiastic. This fact has led one respected scholar to exclaim: "Nevertheless, it is a rebuke to legislators, and to the legal profession, that . . . the courts must determine priorities on the basis of an outmoded and generally unused system of indices." However, in view of the persistence of this course of action and the likelihood that a jurisdiction will retain its grantor-grantee system of indexing even if it adopts the tract index, a comparison of the advantages offered by the two different systems when applied to established doctrines in the law of property would appear to be appropriate.

I. Relation of Indexing to Recordation

In property law, an index is generally defined as a means provided for pointing out or indicating where the record to a certain parcel of realty may be found. The implication created by such a definition is that <u>an index constitutes no part of the record</u>. Nevertheless, a split of authority exists on the issue whether indexing is in fact necessary to complete recordation. The prevailing view is that an index forms no part of the record. Therefore, <u>the instrument filed constitutes constructive notice of its existence from the time it is delivered to the county recorder even though the recorder fails to index it</u>. A great number of the decisions which support this view rely on the construction of the applicable state statutes in that recordation and indexing are usually provided for in separate sections of the state code. Therefore, the courts rationalize that had the legislators intended the index to be an indispensable part of the record without which the record would not impart constructive notice of its contents, they would have either provided for indexing in the same section of the code which provided for recordation or they would have specifically stated in the statutes that indexing was necessary to complete recordation.

The minority view considers indexing to be an essential part of recordation without which the record does not impart constructive notice of its contents. In some instances, state statutes are directly responsible for this view in that they expressly state that without indexing, the act of recordation is incomplete. However, the consideration of one of the fundamental purposes of the recording acts — affording protection to the subsequent purchaser — in conjunction with the state statute which requires indexing is the most common source of justification for this view. Accordingly, if this view were to be accepted, in many instances the record would be considered of no effect when there had been either an absence of indexing or improper indexing even though the complaining party had not relied on the index. This view is consistent with the result which is reached in all instances involving the filing of instruments and their transcription to the permanent record. This rule persists because a system of recording is not based on whether there is an actual search of the records but, rather, on whether proper documents have been provided so that *if* a party decides to make a title search, a complete record will be at his disposal. Regardless of the fact that the minority rule is based upon one of the underlying purposes of recordation, it is clear that the rule cannot solve all the problems which arise in the area of indexing. In the case of Barney v. McCarty some of these problems were faced by the Iowa Supreme Court. The plaintiff had acquired the mortgage which the county recorder had not indexed until twelve years after the time the plaintiff had presented his mortgage for recording. During this twelve-year period, the property in question was sold to the defendants who claimed to be purchasers for value without notice. On an appeal to the Iowa Supreme Court, the court affirmed the trial court's refusal to render a foreclosure decree ordering a sale of the property involved to repay the mortgage held by the plaintiff and pointed out that that Iowa code expressly required the filing of the instrument, the copying of the instrument into the record book, and the indexing of the instrument. Relying on the purposes for the establishment of a system of recordation, the court interpreted the legislative intent as requiring the indexing of an instrument before there could be valid recordation. Such a result <u>undoubtedly places upon a grantee the burden of maintaining some surveillance over the actions of the county recorder until he records and properly indexes an instrument</u>. It is obvious that the decision reached by the court in the *Barney* case affords a subsequent purchaser more protection than he receives under the rule that indexing is not essential to complete recordation in that in this instance, the *grantee* of the property rather than the subsequent purchaser suffers for the mistakes of the county recorder. Although a burden is undoubtedly imposed upon a grantee under this rule, nevertheless, the grantee is in a much better position to ensure the sufficient indexing of his instrument than is the subsequent purchaser. Requiring him to ensure that the instrument is indexed would not be harsh in view of the fact that a subsequent purchaser ordinarily would have no notice whatsoever of the prior transaction and could acquire none by investigating the index.

Another related problem is present in those jurisdictions which follow the rule that indexing is essential to recordation in that the courts usually conclude that recordation is complete only when there has been "sufficient" or "proper" indexing. Generally, the courts have considered an entry in an index "sufficient" or "proper" if it is complete enough to direct a searcher to the record, even though some detail required by statute to be indexed has been omitted or incorrectly reported. In view of the fact that an index is the only practical source for examining the state of the title to realty and, therefore, relied upon by all title examiners, the index should logically be made an essential part of the record without which the record does not impart constructive notice of the existence of an instrument. The adoption of a statute requiring this procedure would not only afford more security to land titles, but would also ensure greater protection of subsequent purchasers.

NOTES AND QUESTIONS

1. As a matter of policy, should the chain of title limitations on constructive notice of recorded instruments be legally inapplicable in any county that has a public tract index whether or not that index is made an essential part of the record by statute or case law? Should it be inapplicable if a private tract index for recorded land transactions in the county is maintained by a private abstract company or title insurer and used in preparing abstracts or passing on applications for insurance?

2. Who should be preferred in defective indexing cases: parties who record or subsequent takers who are obligated to search the records? Should it make any different that, although they rarely make later checks to determine if indexing has taken place, parties who record have it within their power to do so?

A New Jersey case, Howard Savings Bank v. Brunson, 244 N.J. Super. 571, 582 A.2d 1305 (1990), held against the party whose document, a mortgage, was misindexed, stating:

> Obviously, one effect of finding a duty in the mortgagee to see that his instrument is properly indexed will be that the mortgagee will be required to conduct "run down" searches or to employ some other similar mechanism for ensuring that his interest is properly indexed. Yet such a practice is seen as making good business sense anyway. [244 N.J. Super. at 579, 582 A.2d at 1309.]

The court in *Howard Savings Bank* reasoned that the New Jersey statutes requiring recording and indexing indicate a fundamental purpose of providing notice to subsequent parties in interest and the indices should be considered part of the record so as to fulfill this purpose. The alternative to relying on the indices would be a page by page examination of all recorded instruments for as far back as the search extended. This the court considered far too burdensome and costly.

3. In literally applying relevant statutory language, a recent Pennsylvania Supreme Court opinion, First Citizen National Bank v. Sherwood, 879 A.2d 178 (Pa. 2005), concludes that a properly recorded mortgage results in constructive notice of the mortgage even though the mortgage was indexed under the wrong name. Two judges dissented and argue that the majority position is illogical and state that "If proper recordation alone gives the world constructive notice of a mortgage, then there is no need to index the mortgages at all—recordation without indexing must suffice. Surely the legislature did not intend this absurd result."

4. The prevailing position is that those who file instruments for recording assume the risk that the recorder's office will fail to transcribe or will accurately transcribe so that subsequent purchasers are on constructive notice only of instruments as copied into the public records. Patton & Palomar on Land Titles § 64 (3d ed. 2003). Risk is often allocated differently in defective transcription cases from defective indexing cases: commonly to the person filing for record if there is an error in transcription, to the subsequent purchaser if there is an indexing error. How can such differences be justified? In both kinds of situations should not risk be on the same person?

5. Until an instrument filed for record has been transcribed by the recorder's office, the original is kept in the recorder's possession, available for examination by those searching titles. Transcription usually takes place within a few days. After transcription the original normally is returned to the party who filed it for record.

How long should the original be constructive notice if kept in the recorder's possession and not transcribed? In Whalley v. Small, 25 Iowa 184 (1868), a deed of trust was filed for record in 1842 and apparently through inadvertence never transcribed but kept in the recorder's office. In 1860, the grantor of the deed of trust conveyed the property and the grantee and subsequent takers through him were unaware of the deed of trust when they acquired their interests. In litigation over the title the Iowa Supreme Court held that the subsequent purchasers did not take subject to the deed of trust. In its opinion the court said at 189-190:

> In the nature of things, there must, of necessity, exist a period of time between the filing and recording. The law designs that during such reasonable time that may so intervene, the filing shall be notice of the instrument. But certainly, it would be extending great indulgence to officers and parties whose duty it is to record and procure the recording of the instrument, to give them more than a quarter of a century, the time which expired in this case, to record and index the instrument after it is filed, and yet, to hold that during all of this long period the deed, slumbering forgotten in some out-of-the-way receptacle of the recorder's office, operates as notice to the world of its contents, while at the same time the very parties who claim under it are ignorant of its existence. Such an interpretation of the law would defeat its very object.
>
> The filing fixes the time from which the notice of the instrument commences, under the presumption that reasonable diligence will be exercised to comply with the other directions of the law made for its lawful registration. Within what time this must be done, it is not for us now to determine, further than to hold, that a quarter of a century cannot be considered a reasonable or proper time to permit the instrument to lie unrecorded, and that the filing cannot be considered as imparting notice during this long period.

6. In many jurisdictions, if the copy of an instrument properly of record is destroyed or disappears, it continues to give constructive notice. A major risk, of course, is destruction of public records by fire or other natural calamity; and there have been instances in which substantially all recorded instruments in a county have been lost when the structure in which they were stored was destroyed. Some states have legislation, often referred to as burnt record acts, specifically directed to this problem. Often these acts were passed following major holocausts and provide procedures for accommodating to the massive record losses that occurred. For example, see Ill. Laws 1871-1872, at 652-662, a burnt records act passed in 1872 after the Chicago Fire of 1871; and Cal. Stat. 1906, Extra Sess., cc. 52-59, at 70-82, enacted following the San Francisco Earthquake of 1906.

Section 1 of the Illinois Act, 765 Ill. Comp. Stat. Ann. § 45/1 (2001), provides:

> Whenever it shall appear that the records, or any material part thereof, of any county in this state have been destroyed by fire or otherwise, any map, plat, deed, conveyance, contract, mortgage, deed of trust, or other instrument in writing affecting real estate in such county, which has been heretofore recorded, or certified copies of such, may be re-recorded; and in recording the same the recorder shall be deemed and taken as the date of the record thereof. And copies of any such record, so authorized to be made under this section, duly certified by the recorder of any such county, under his seal of office, shall be received in evidence, and have the same force and effect as certified copies of the original record.

Under this section of the Illinois act, there is no obligation to re-record, and a subsequent purchaser takes subject to the recorded interest even if the record has been destroyed and not re-recorded. Gammon v. Hodges, 73 Ill. 140 (1874). But in Kentucky Coal & Timber Development Co. v. Conley, 184 Ky. 274, 211 S.W. 734 (1919), a duty was placed on a grantee to record his deed when the recorded copy was destroyed in a fire. Failure to record within a reasonable time resulted in the instrument being treated as though never recorded, and a subsequent purchaser without notice was held to have superior title. The court considered this "a case calling for the application of the rule that where the loss must fall on one of two innocent parties, it will be put on him whose negligence has made the loss possible."

7. Unless she has made a search of the public records, should a subsequent taker be preferred by the recording acts to a prior unrecorded interest holder? Unless she has actually relied on the public records, is the subsequent taker deserving of the acts' protection? What if the motive of the subsequent taker in not examining the public records is to avoid the risk of actual notice from discovery of instruments put of record that do not give constructive notice, such as defectively acknowledged deeds?

8. An Arizona statute provides as follows:

> Any document evidencing the sale, or other transfer of real estate or any legal or equitable interest therein, excluding leases, shall be recorded by the transferor in the county in which the property is located and within sixty days of the transfer. In lieu thereof, the transferor shall indemnify the transferee in any action in which the transferee's interest in such property is at issue, including costs, attorney's fees and punitive damages. [Ariz. Rev. Stat. Ann. § 33-411.01 (West 2006)]

Why does the Arizona statute obligate recording by the transferor rather than the transferee? Under what kinds of situations may the statute result in liability of the transferor to the transferee?

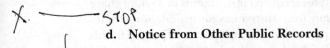

d. Notice from Other Public Records

There are many kinds of public records pertaining to land titles other than those records required by the recording acts.[9] In no state are all these records centralized in one place, but some states have gone much farther than others in the degree of centralization provided for. In some states, the offices of recorders of deeds contain not only conveyancing records but a number of other kinds of land title records as well. Important land title records can also be found in public offices of various court clerks (for judicial records pertaining to land) and county treasurers (for property tax records evidencing tax liens on land).

In the course of their title searching, professional title searchers customarily check through public records other than those that the recording acts say must be kept. It is also customary in the course of their work for professional searchers to go to public offices other than those of recorders of deeds. Local variations exist in the broadness and intensity of these searches. As will be shown in the materials on title insurance, large abstract and title insurance companies often facilitate their title searches by duplicating many of the public land records for a particular county and keeping them on their own premises in more easily searchable form. These private collections of public records are known in the trade as title plants.

In considering different kinds of public records, special attention should be given to why the records are required and whom they are intended to benefit. In particular, what effect do the records have on land titles; and what inducement is there for prospective transferees of land interests to have the records searched?

Lane and Edson, Land Title Recordation Systems: Legal Constraints and Reforms[10]

II-25 (1978)

A recurring complaint of title searchers is that they cannot limit their searching efforts to the records lodged in the recording office, but must also examine the records maintained in numerous other public offices. How many other public offices need to be visited varies with each state, and often with each county within a state. A thorough search of title might necessitate visits to the county offices of the tax assessor and sheriff, to the offices of the clerks of the county court of general jurisdiction and of the county probate court, to the offices of the city tax assessor

---

9. You are reminded again of the narrow meaning here given to the term "recording acts." See the introductory comments at the beginning of this chapter. Note that the term is occasionally given a different usage by legal authorities, and some or all of the statutes authorizing other kinds of public records also sometimes are referred to as recording acts.

10. A report prepared for the U.S. Department of Housing and Urban Development, pursuant to a contract with Booz, Allen & Hamilton, Inc. Footnotes omitted.

and health department, to the office of the clerk of the city court of general jurisdiction, to the office of the clerk of the federal district court, and to state offices at the state capital with responsibility for the collection of state taxes and for corporate status. The principal events reflected in the documents that these offices maintain of concern to the title searchers are those directly affecting the property (such as lis pendens filings and unpaid real estate taxes), and those directly affecting the property owner with possible consequences on his title. Except for real estate taxes and special assessments, most of these documents are indexed only under an individual's or business name, as, for example, a defaulting taxpayer, a deceased owner, or a defendant to a judicial action.

Two common problems face title searchers seeking information about these kinds of events. One is the physical distance between the county recorder's office where the land conveyancing documents are maintained and the offices housing these other records. The distances and relative inconveniences vary, of course. In one suburban Philadelphia county, the recorder's office and the office of the county registrar of wills are on the same floor in the same building; in the next county, they are in different buildings separated by two miles of clogged urban streets. The relevant state offices are usually in the state capital which may be across the state. The separateness of these records and their different physical locations cause the process of title searching to take longer and cost more than if the records were integrated. The maintenance costs of private title plants must also be increased because of the more difficult logistics in continually collecting documents from so many different locations.

Another serious problem is that, except for real estate taxes and special property assessments, these records are indexed by the names of the individual or business property owners. Finding the correct names in voluminous name indexes can be difficult because of inadequate alphabetization and multiple and variant names. We need to take a closer look at this latter problem.

Whitehurst v. Abbott

225 N.C. 1, 33 S.E.2d 129 (1945)

Special proceeding for the sale of land for partition by Ada V. Whitehurst and others against Henry D. Abbott. From an adverse judgment, plaintiff appeals.

New trial.

Special proceedings for the sale of land for partition in which defendant filed answer denying the alleged title of plaintiffs and pleading sole seizin and adverse possession under color for more than twenty years. The answer having raised issues of fact, the cause was transferred to the civil issue docket of Camden County Superior Court for trial.

John L. Hinton, a resident of Pasquotank County, died testate in January 1910, and on January 29, 1910 his will was probated in common form in Pasquotank County. A copy of the will was certified to and recorded in the office of the clerk of the Superior Court of Camden County.

The will devised the lands of testator to his wife and his children other than J. C. Hinton who predeceased the testator. No provision was made in the will for the widow and children of the deceased son.

At the time of his death the testator owned a tract of land in Camden County known as the Abbott Ridge Farm containing 324 acres. On August 12, 1910, R. L. Hinton, son of the testator, purchased the interest of the other devisees and took deed therefor which was duly registered in the Camden County registry.

On September 30, 1918, the widow and children of J. C. Hinton, deceased, filed a caveat to the will of John L. Hinton. No notice of lis pendens was filed in Camden County or indexed or cross-indexed in the lis pendens docket in the office of the clerk of the Superior Court in Pasquotank County.

On July 24, 1919, R. L. Hinton, while the hearing on the caveat was pending, conveyed the Abbott Ridge Farm in Camden County to one T. G. McPherson.

On January 10, 1920, judgment was entered in the caveat proceedings sustaining the caveat on the grounds of mental incapacity and undue influence and declaring the will null and void. On appeal to this Court the judgment was affirmed. In re Hinton's Will, 180 N.C. 206, 104 S.E. 341. The judgment declaring the will null and void was not certified in Camden County and no marginal entry was made on the certified copy of the will as recorded in Camden.

On December 4, 1923, McPherson conveyed to defendant Henry D. Abbott that part of the Camden County farm which is described in the complaint and is the subject matter of this action.

When the cause came on for hearing in the court below, the jury, by their answers to the issues submitted, found that T. G. McPherson and H. D. Abbott were each purchasers for value and without notice of the claim of plaintiffs. There was judgment on the verdict decreeing that plaintiffs have no right, title, or interest in the land in controversy and plaintiffs appealed. . . .

BARNHILL, Justice. R. L. Hinton was a devisee, executor, and propounder of the will of John L. Hinton. He purchased the interest of the other devisees in the Camden County property. He and the other devisees were dealing inter partes in the property of the estate. He conveyed the land after the caveat was filed. Any claim that he was an innocent third party and that his deed, executed pendente lite, conveyed a good title is without substance. To hold otherwise would open the door for parties to litigation to convey the subject matter of the litigation pending a hearing and thus render the court powerless to enforce its own decrees. Newbern v. Hinton, 190 N.C. 108, 129 S.E. 181.

As to T. G. McPherson, grantee of R. L. Hinton, a different question arises. Had he purchased before the filing of the caveat unquestionably under our decisions his title would have been unassailable. G.S. § 31-39: Newbern v. Leigh, 184 N.C. 166, 113 S.E. 674, 26 A.L.R. 266; Whitehurst v. Hinton, 209 N.C. 392, 184 S.E. 66; Anno. 26 A.L.R. 270. But such is not the case. He acquired title to the property in Camden after the filing of the caveat from one of the devisees who was directly affected by the proceedings then pending in Pasquotank, the county in which the original will was probated. Is he charged with constructive notice of the claim of plaintiffs?

At common law a pending suit was regarded as notice to all the world. The complaint or cross-complaint, as the case might be, was the lis pendens and any person dealing with the property pendente lite was bound by the judgment rendered. Massachusetts Bonding & Insurance Co. v. Knox, 220 N.C. 725, 18 S.E.2d 436, 138 A.L.R. 1438; 34 Am. Jur. 363.

The ever-increasing volume of litigation rendered this common-law rule so harsh and burdensome upon abstracters that the Legislature intervened and adopted the modifying Acts now incorporated in Article 11, Chapter 1, General Statutes of

North Carolina. Now the pending action does not constitute notice as to land in another county until and unless notice thereof is filed in the county in which the land is located. G.S. § 1-116 et seq.; Collingwood v. Brown, 106 N.C. 362, 10 S.E. 868; Spencer v. Credle, 102 N.C. 68, 8 S.E. 901.

When a will is probated in common form, any interested party may appear and enter a caveat. G.S. § 31-32. But a caveat is an in rem proceedings. In effect it is nothing more than a demand that the will be produced and probated in open court, affording the caveators an opportunity to attack it for the causes and upon the grounds set forth and alleged in the caveat. It is an attack upon the validity of the instrument purporting to be a will and not an "action affecting the title to real property." The will and not the land devised is the res involved in the litigation. Prospective purchasers were held to notice that probate jurisdiction was in Pasquotank County and if they acquired title without ascertaining the status of the proceedings in that county they did so at their peril. Hence the lis pendens statute has no application. So contend the appellants.

Thus we are called upon to decide the force and effect of the lis pendens statute as it related to a caveat proceedings.

The registration statute, G.S. § 43-18, modifies the common-law rule of lis pendens. Its purpose is to stabilize titles by requiring recordation of all deeds, mortgages, or other paper writings which transfer or encumber the title to land. Our lis pendens statute, above cited, is designed to supplement the registration law and to provide a simple and readily available means of ascertaining the existence of adverse claims to land not otherwise disclosed by the registry. Notice under the Act is required to give constructive notice to prospective purchasers when the claim is in derogation of the record. Insurance Co. v. Knox, supra.

The effect of lis pendens and the effect of registration are in their nature the same thing. They are only different examples of the operation of the rule of constructive notice. One is simply a record in one place and the other is a record in another place. Each serves its purpose in proper instances. They are each record notices upon the absence of which a prospective innocent purchaser may rely.

Bearing this broad general purpose in mind it would seem to be apparent that the Legislature intended the term "action," as used in G.S. § 1-116, to embrace all judicial proceedings affecting the title to real property or in which title to land is at issue.

Naturally proceedings in court are divided into various classifications. Each class has its own particular label. But the word "action," when unqualified, is an inclusive term and connotes all judicial proceedings of a civil nature maintained and prosecuted for the purpose of asserting a right or redressing a wrong. When qualified, as in the statute, by the term "affecting the title to real property," it includes and embraces all such proceedings wherein the title to real property is at issue.

Such is a caveat. Though not an adverse proceedings in the ordinary sense, interested parties are notified and given an opportunity to be heard. Legal rights are at stake and the issues raised are tried as in other civil actions.

While in one sense the will is the res involved in the caveat proceedings, it is quite clear that any final decree entered therein will directly affect the title to the land devised. The probated will constitutes a muniment of title unassailable except in a direct proceedings. G.S. § 31-19. It operates as a conveyance of title to the land devised. Any action or proceedings contesting its validity directly assails the validity of such conveyance and necessarily involves the title. Hence the filing of notice under the lis pendens statute is essential to give constructive notice to those who are not directly interested in the proceedings. McIlwrath v. Hollander, 73 Mo. 105, 39 Am. Rep. 484.

But lis pendens notice under the statute is not exclusive. Nor is it designed to protect intermeddlers. When a person acquires an interest in property pending an action in which the title thereto is at issue, from one of the parties to the action, with notice of the action, actual or constructive, he is bound by the judgment in the action just as the party from whom he bought would have been. This rule seems to be universal and is considered by all the courts to be absolutely necessary to give effect to the judgments of the courts because, if it was not so held, a party could always defeat the judgment by conveying in anticipation of it to some stranger and the claimant would be compelled to commence a new action against him. Rollins v. Henry, 78 N.C. 342; Jarrett v. Holland, 213 N.C. 428, 196 S.E. 314.

"Our statute on the subject . . . only purports to deal with constructive notice and its effect on subsequent purchasers, but, where one buys from a litigant with full notice or knowledge of the suit and of its nature and purpose and the specific property to be affected, he is concluded or his purchase will be held ineffective and fraudulent as to decree rendered in the cause and the rights thereby established. Griswold v. Miller, 15 Barb. [N.Y.] 520; Corwin v. Bensley, 43 Cal. 253-262; Wick v. Dawson, 48 W. Va. 469-475, 37 S.E. 639; 25 Cyc. p. 1425; Bennett on Lis Pendens, p. 319." Morris v. Basnight, 179 N.C. 298, 102 S.E. 389, 391.

Plaintiffs offered evidence tending to show that when the court proceedings was being heard at the January Term, 1919, McPherson was present in court and that he talked about the case in the presence of his son and his brother, all prior to the time he purchased. Upon this evidence, which is uncontradicted, plaintiffs duly requested the court to give a peremptory charge on the second issue which is as follows: "Did T. G. McPherson purchase the lands in controversy for value and without notice of plaintiff's claim?"

The court declined to give the requested instruction. Instead it charged the jury that the burden rested upon the plaintiffs to show that McPherson "did not purchase it for value and that at the time he, T. G. McPherson, had notice of plaintiff's claim to the land in question" and that if they failed to so find they should answer the second issue "Yes." In this there was error prejudicial to the plaintiffs.

As heretofore stated a party directly interested in judicial proceeding affecting the title to real property cannot convey a good title to the res pendente lite. Even so, the grantee acquires a good title provided he purchases (1) for value, and (2) without notice, actual or constructive. Both conditions must appear. Hence the absence of either is fatal.

The uncontroverted evidence tends to show and it seems to be admitted that Hinton conveyed to McPherson pendente lite. This being true, his deed was ineffective and fraudulent as against the final decree in the pending action. Upon such showing plaintiffs were entitled to judgment, certainly as against McPherson, unless it should be made to appear that he purchased for value and without notice. This is an affirmative defense and he who claims to be a bona fide purchaser for value without notice so as to avoid the defective character of his deed has the burden of proving that fact. Hughes v. Fields, 168 N.C. 520, 84 S.E. 804; King v. McRackan, 168 N.C. 621, 84 S.E. 1027, affirmed on rehearing, King v. McRackan, 171 N.C. 752, 88 S.E. 226; 27 R.C.L. 737.

The conditions under which defendant acquired title are on this record immaterial. At that time there was no presumptively valid will of record operating as a muniment of title. It had been annulled by decree of court. It protects a purchaser only until vacated. G.S. § 31-19. It follows that his title rests squarely upon the title possessed by his grantor.

If McPherson was an innocent purchaser for value, his deed to defendant conveyed title in fee to the land therein described. Conversely if McPherson purchased with notice, then immediately upon the entry of the final decree in the caveat proceedings invalidating the will, the plaintiffs, as heirs-at-law of J. C. Hinton, by operation of law, became seized and possessed of an undivided interest in the Camden County land. From that instant they were tenants in common with McPherson. His deed to defendant thereafter executed conveyed only such interest as he possessed and the vested interest of plaintiffs can be defeated only by twenty years' adverse possession pleaded by defendant.

But defendant insists that even though, at the time he purchased, the will was void, the certified copy thereof filed in Camden County was still of record without any notation or entry that would operate as notice to him of the judgment entered in Pasquotank County and that he had the right to rely on this record as a valid link in his chain of title. We cannot so hold. *why ?*

Whatever may be the effect of Chap. 108, P.L. 1921, the rights of the parties to this action accrued prior to its enactment and are to be controlled by the law as it existed before the effective date of that statute.

At that time it was the original will as probated in the county in which the testator resided at the time of his death that constituted the muniment of title as to all land devised. C.S. § 4145. Ownership under the will in nowise is made dependent upon the certified copy directed to be recorded in the county where the land lies. C.S. § 4163. The only purpose of the certified copy disclosed by the pertinent statute was to give information to abstracters and to direct their attention to the source of title — the will as originally probated. Hence when the original will was annulled by judicial decree the certified copy ceased to have any force and effect for any purpose.

Nor is defendant protected by the provisions of Sec. 2 of the 1921 statute. At the time of its enactment the final decree had been entered. There was no valid will of record. If McPherson purchased with notice title had vested in plaintiffs. The Legislature was without authority to divest them of their title and revest it in McPherson. It is not to be presumed that the General Assembly so intended. In any event the Act cannot be so construed. Section 17, 19, Art. I, N.C. Const.

It follows that there must be a new trial in accord with this opinion. It is so ordered.

New trial.

NOTES AND QUESTIONS

1. The North Carolina lis pendens statutes, N.C. Gen. Stat. §§ 1-116 to 1-120.1 (2005), are fairly typical of such enactments in many of the states. They provide as follows:

§ 1-116 *Filing of notice of suit.* (a) Any person desiring the benefit of constructive notice of pending litigation must file a separate, independent notice thereof, which notice shall be cross-indexed in accordance with G.S. 1-117, in the following cases:
 (1) Action affecting title to real property;

(2) Actions to foreclose any mortgage or deed of trust or to enforce any lien on real property; and

(3) Actions in which any order of attachment is issued and real property is attached.

(b) Notice of pending litigation shall contain:

(1) The name of the court in which the action has been commenced or is pending;

(2) The names of the parties to the action;

(3) The nature and purpose of the action; and

(4) A description of the property to be affected thereby.

(c) Notice of pending litigation may be filed:

(1) At or any time after the commencement of an action pursuant to Rule 3 of the Rules of Civil Procedure; or

(2) At or any time after real property has been attached; or

(3) At or any time after the filing of an answer or other pleading in which the pleading party states an affirmative claim for relief falling within the provisions of subsection (a) of this section.

(d) Notice of pending litigation must be filed with the clerk of the superior court of each county in which any part of the real estate is located, not excepting the county in which the action is pending, in order to be effective against bona fide purchasers or lien creditors with respect to the real property located in such county.

§ 1-116.1. *Service of notice.* In all actions as defined in G.S. § 1-116 in which notice of the pendency of the action is filed, a copy of such notice shall be served on the other party or parties. . . .

§ 1-117. *Cross-index of lis pendens.* Every notice of pending litigation filed under this article shall be cross-indexed by the clerk of the superior court in a record, called the "Record of Lis Pendens" to be kept by him pursuant to G.S. 2-42(6).

§ 1-118. *Effect on subsequent purchasers.* From the cross-indexing of the notice of lis pendens only is the pendency of the action constructive notice to a purchaser or incumbrancer of the property affected thereby; and every person whose conveyance or incumbrance is subsequently executed or subsequently registered is a subsequent purchaser or incumbrancer, and is bound by all proceedings taken after the cross-indexing of the notice to the same extent as if he were made a party to the action. For the purposes of this section an action is pending from the time of cross-indexing the notice.

§ 1-119(a). *Notice void unless action prosecuted.* The notice of lis pendens is of no avail unless it is followed by the first publication of notice of the summons or by an affidavit therefor pursuant to Rule 4(j)(1)c of the Rules of Civil Procedure or by personal service on the defendant within sixty days after the cross-indexing. . . .

§ 1-120. *Cancellation of notice.*—The court in which the said action was commenced may, at any time after it is settled, discontinued or abated, on application of any person aggrieved, on good cause shown, and on such notice as is directed or approved by the court, order the notices authorized by this article to be cancelled of record, by the clerk of any county in whose office the same has been filed or recorded; and this cancellation must be made by an endorsement to that effect on the margin of the record, which shall refer to the order.

§ 1-120.1 *Article applicable to suits in federal courts.* The provisions of this Article shall apply to suits affecting the title to real property in the federal courts.

On lis pendens generally, see Nelson & Whitman, Real Estate Finance Law § 7.13 (4th ed. 2002); 14 Powell on Real Property, ch. 82A (1999).

2. In their detailed requirements, lis pendens statutes vary somewhat from state to state. For example, a common requirement is that for lis pendens to apply, descriptive information concerning the suit must be filed with a designated public official who maintains sets of records readily accessible to persons examining land titles. But statutes differ as to which public official shall be responsible for accepting and maintaining lis pendens records. Some states follow the North Carolina requirement that it be the clerk of the general court of first instance in the county where the land is located; for example, Fla. Stat. Ann. § 148.23(1)(a) (West 2006). Other states provide that it be the recorder of deeds; for example, Cal. Civ. Proc. Code § 405.20 (West 2004). And in some, no special filing of notice is necessary, service of summons charges third persons with notice of pendency of suit. One such statute is Ohio Rev. Code Ann. §§ 2703.26 to 2703.27 (Page 1999), but only as to suits brought in the county where the land is located. Some states place a time limit on the effectiveness of lis pendens notices. In New York, for example, the effective notice period is three years. N.Y. Civ. Prac. Law § 6513 (McKinney 1980).

3. One rationale for lis pendens is that it prevents parties to litigation from avoiding the effects of a possible adverse judgment by conveying out during pendency of the proceedings. So in most states the filing of a lis pendens can have consequences only for subsequent takers of interests in the land involved. Those who acquire their interests prior to filing of the lis pendens are generally unaffected by the litigation unless made parties. However, in some states, those who acquire interests in the land prior to the litigation, but fail to record prior to filing of the lis pendens, have also been held bound by any judgment as though they had taken subsequent to the lis pendens filing. See Bristol Lumber Co. v. Dery, 114 Conn. 88, 157 A. 640 (1932); and Jones v. Jones, 249 Miss. 322, 161 So. 2d 640 (1964). What justification can there be for making such prior unrecorded transferees subject to lis pendens doctrine?

4. There have been serious challenges recently to lis pendens statutes as providing inadequate notice and hearing opportunities and thereby violating procedural due process. On this problem see Note, Connecticut's Lis Pendens Shapes Up: Williams v. Bartlett, 16 Conn. L. Rev. 413 (1984); and Note, A Proposal for Reformation of the Iowa Lis Pendens Statute, 67 Iowa L. Rev. 289 (1982).

A Connecticut statute, § 52-325(a) & (b), seeks to shield lis pendens from constitutional attack. The statute permits a property owner against whose property a lis pendens has been filed to seek a preliminary court order that there is no probable cause for the action to which the lis pendens pertains. A prompt court hearing on the issue is then held. If no probable cause is found, the court must cancel the lis pendens notice. This cancellation is only as to the lis pendens, it is not a determination as to the title claim being asserted. For a New York statute that appears to have the same objective of shielding lis pendens from due process attack, see N.Y. CPLR § 6501 (Supp. 2006).

5. The limited effect of lis pendens is discussed as follows in 5303 Realty Corp. v. O & Y Equity Corp., 64 N.Y.2d 313, 315-316, 476 N.E.2d 276, 278 (1984):

A notice of pendency, commonly known as a "lis pendens," can be a potent shield to protect litigants claiming an interest in real property. The powerful impact that this device has on the alienability of property, when conjoined with the facility with which it may be obtained, calls for its narrow application to only those lawsuits directly affecting title to, or the possession, use of enjoyment of, real property. Consequently, a suit to specifically perform a contract for the sale of stock representing a beneficial ownership of real estate will not support the filing of a notice of pendency.

↳ NOLP for coops

**First Federal Savings & Loan Assn.
of Miami v. Fisher**

60 So. 2d 496 (Fla. 1952)

CHAPMAN, Justice. On September 16, 1939, a final decree of divorce and property settlement was entered in the Circuit Court of Dade County, Florida, in the case of Freda Y. Fisher v. Porter G. Fisher. The following pertinent provisions are set out in the final decree: . . .

"Ordered, adjudged and decreed that the bonds of matrimony heretofore and now existing between complainant, Freda Y. Fisher, and the defendant, Porter G. Fisher, be and the same are hereby forever dissolved, and that the complainant and defendant are hereby divorced one from the other, a vinculo matrimonii; and it is hereby further . . . ?

"Ordered, adjudged and decreed that the agreement heretofore entered into by and between the complainant and defendant herein, dated September 11, 1939, providing for the matters of custody of the child, P. Graham Fisher, his maintenance, the matters of alimony and property settlements, be and the same *is hereby in all respects approved.* . . ."

The following stipulations signed by Freda Y. Fisher and husband, Porter G. Fisher, were before the Court at the time of the entry of the divorce decree and property settlement on September 16, 1939, to wit:

> It is stipulated by and between the undersigned complainant and defendant and their respective solicitors in the above styled cause that, if a final decree of divorce is entered, said decree shall contain the following provisions. . . .
>
> 6. Defendant is also to maintain the house at 531 49th Street, Miami Beach, Florida for a home for the complainant and her son. . . .
>
> 7. *In the event defendant dies or remarries, then, in that event the defendant's interest in the house shall be conveyed to the son P. Graham Fisher.* . . .

Some two or three months after the date of the decree, on November 13, 1939, Porter G. Fisher remarried and the second wife was Alma F. Fisher. On July 19, 1946, Porter G. Fisher and wife, Alma F. Fisher, made, executed and delivered their promissory note in the sum of $10,400 payable to the First Federal Savings and Loan Association of Miami. Simultaneously with the execution and delivery of the aforesaid promissory note they secured the payment thereof by execution of a mortgage to the Federal Savings Bank, which described the home owned by Porter G. Fisher located at 531 49th Street, Miami Beach, Florida. The mortgage was duly recorded in the office of the Clerk of the Circuit Court of Dade County, Florida. The home described in the mortgage supra was in the possession of Freda Y. Fisher and son, Porter G. Fisher, Jr., when the note and mortgage were executed by the husband, Porter G. Fisher, Sr., and the second Mrs. Fisher (Alma F. Fisher). It appears that the first Mrs. Fisher and son occupied the home pursuant to the divorce stipulations made a part of the final decree.

The Federal Savings and Loan Association, on February 9, 1949, filed foreclosure proceedings on the mortgage given it by Porter G. Fisher and wife, Alma F. Fisher. The proceedings progressed to a final decree, when the property was sold by a Special Master, and a Special Master's deed was executed conveying the residential property supra to the First Federal Savings and Loan Association. On June 25, 1950,

Freda Y. Fisher filed in her divorce suit her motion for a final decree for arrears in support and also to enforce the provisions of paragraph 7 of the stipulations, to wit: "7. In the event defendant dies or remarries, then, in that event, the defendant's (Porter G. Fisher's) interest in the house shall be conveyed to the son P. Graham Fisher." The Chancellor below heard the parties on the motion and other appropriate pleadings and entered its order requiring Porter G. Fisher to convey his right, title and interest in the home occupied by Freda Y. Fisher and son situated at 531 49th Street, Miami, Florida, in accordance with the provisions of Section 7 supra of the stipulations signed by the parties when the divorce decree was entered. On May 25, 1951, Porter G. Fisher and wife, Alma F. Fisher, executed and delivered to Porter G. Fisher, Jr., a deed to the described property, pursuant to an order or decree of the Court below. It was recorded among the public records of Dade County, Florida, on June 4, 1951.

On August 15, 1951, Porter G. Fisher, Jr., filed in the Circuit Court of Dade County, Florida, his suit to quiet title as against the First Federal Savings and Loan Association and alleged that the Special Master's deed acquired by it through the foreclosure of its mortgage was subject to, inferior and subservient to the title conveyed to Porter G. Fisher, Jr., by his father, Porter G. Fisher, Sr., and wife, Alma F. Fisher, and said conveyance was a cloud which created doubt and suspicion as to the true fee simple title held and owned by Porter G. Fisher, Jr. That the title conveyed by the Special Master to the Federal Savings and Loan Association was made with full knowledge and notice of the provisions described in Section 7 of the divorce stipulation, which was approved and confirmed by the final decree of divorce. Section 7 thereof could have been ascertained by an examination of the final decree of divorce duly recorded among the public records of Dade County, Florida. Also, Freda Y. Fisher and son, Porter G. Fisher, Jr., were in the open, adverse and continuous possession of the home and were residing therein prior and subsequent to the date of giving the note and mortgage to the Savings Association. The Chancellor, by an appropriate decree, cancelled the Special Master's deed to the First Federal Savings and Loan Association as a cloud upon title as held by Porter G. Fisher, Jr. The Federal Savings and Loan Association appealed.

On this appeal counsel for the appellant Association contend that provision 7, supra, of the marriage agreement, which as approved and confirmed by the terms of the final decree of divorce entered between Freda Y. Fisher and husband Porter G. Fisher, Sr., was legally insufficient to constitute notice, implied or constructive, of the claims and interest of Porter G. Fisher, Jr., in and to the described property, although Fisher, Sr., had not lived or resided in the home from 1939 until giving the mortgage on July 16, 1946. He remarried within ninety days after the divorce decree was entered. It was the Chancellor's conclusion that the divorce decree and divorce stipulation were legally sufficient to constitute lawful notice of the interest of Porter G. Fisher, Jr., in and to the described property.

In the case of Sapp v. Warner, 105 Fla. 245, 141 So. 124, 143 So. 648, 144 So. 481, we held that notice is of two kinds: actual and constructive. Constructive notice has been defined as notice imputed to a person not having actual notice, for example: such as would be imputed under the recording statutes to persons dealing with property subject to those statutes. Actual notice is also said to be of two kinds: first, express, which includes what might be called direct information and, second, implied, which is said to include notice inferred from the fact that the person had means of knowledge, which it was his duty to use and which he did not use, or as it is sometimes called implied actual notice. Constructive notice is a legal inference, while implied notice is an inference of fact, but the same facts may sometimes be used to prove both constructive and implied actual notice. The foregoing rule has been reaffirmed by this Court. See Rinehart v. Phelps, 150 Fla. 382, 7 So. 2d 783.

The record reflects that Porter G. Fisher, Sr., under the terms of the divorce agreement, was to provide his first wife and son with a home and furnishings. It is not disputed that they lived in the original home of the parties located at 531 49th Street, Miami. It is not contended that P. Graham Fisher, Sr., ever lived in the home after the divorce decree, but married again within approximately three months thereafter. If the appellant had made inquiry as to the possession of the property upon which it later made a loan of $10,400 and accepted a mortgage, the fact would have developed that P. Graham Fisher, Sr., was not in possession of the property but the possession thereof was in his divorced wife. Under these circumstances we are forced to hold that the appellant failed to exercise, in the acceptance of the note and mortgage that degree of care as the law imposed upon it.

Another theory of the case is that the appellant, by searching the records in the office of the Clerk of the Circuit Court of Dade County, Florida, would have found the divorce decree and property settlement appearing upon the record, and a provision thereof which is viz.: "Ordered, adjudged and decreed that the agreement heretofore entered into by and between the complainant and defendant herein, dated September 11, 1939, providing the matters of custody of the child, P. Graham Fisher, his maintenance, the matters of alimony and property settlements, be and the same is hereby in all respects approved. . . ."

It is our view and conclusion that the decree appealed from should be and it is hereby affirmed on the authority of Sapp v. Warner, supra.

Affirmed.

Terrell, Roberts and Mathews, JJ., concur.

 Sebring, C.J., and Thomas and Hobson, JJ., dissent.

NOTES AND QUESTIONS

1. Is there any difference between constructive notice and implied notice, as those terms are used by the court in the principal case? And if there is a difference, does it serve any useful function to make such a distinction?

2. Judgments that create or declare interests in land are generally considered binding on subsequent takers of the land parcels involved. A broad range of judicial proceedings may result in judgments of this kind: suits to quiet title, eminent domain takings, mortgage foreclosures, divorce proceedings, and will contests being but a few. By statute, judgments for money can in most states create liens on land owned by the judgment debtor; and such liens are also binding on subsequent takers, provided that the necessary statutory formalities are followed. One common requirement for a judgment to be binding on subsequent takers of land interests is that it be made a matter of public record in the county where the land is located. Docketing in that county's court records or filing with its recorder of deeds is the usual means of giving a judgment this broader effect.

3. In many states, the requirements for federal court judgment liens are the same as those for liens of state court judgments. The federal statute authorizing this conformity, 28 U.S.C.A § 1962 (1994), provides:

Every judgment rendered by a district court within a State shall be a lien on the property located in such State in the same manner, to the same extent and under the same conditions as a judgment of a court of general jurisdiction in such State, and shall cease to be a lien in the same manner and time. This section does not apply to judgments entered in favor of the United States. Whenever the law of any State requires a judgment of a State court to be registered, recorded, docketed or indexed, or any other act to be done, in a particular manner, or in a certain office or county or parish before such lien attaches, such requirements shall apply only if the law of such State authorizes the judgment of a court of the United States to be registered, recorded, docketed, indexed or otherwise conformed to rules and requirements relating to judgments of the courts of the State.

In most states, liens of federal judgments can arise only if docketed or put of record in some public office in the county where the land is situated. However, 28 U.S.C. § 1962 does not apply to judgments not resulting in judgment liens but otherwise affecting land titles. Thus in Norman Lumber Co. v. United States, 223 F.2d 868 (4th Cir. 1955), the court held that an eminent domain judgment entered by a United States District Court in North Carolina did not have to be docketed and indexed in the office of a state court clerk in the county where the land was situated, even though a North Carolina statute so required. Not only was the judgment valid without compliance with the state statute, but it created rights in the condemnor superior to those of a purchaser without actual notice who bought from the condemnee some years later. In its opinion at 872, the court of appeals said:

> "Whether docketing and cross indexing of federal judgments of condemnation with state court records should be required as a condition of validity as against subsequent purchasers from the condemnee is a matter for Congress, and, so far, Congress has not seen fit to take action with regard to the matter."

How could the purchaser from the condemnee in the *Norman Lumber Company* case have determined if title had been taken by proceedings brought in a federal court? Should Congress require docketing and cross indexing of federal judgments of condemnation with state court records? Why do you think Congress has not done so?

4. As land titles frequently pass by devise or descent, title searches often must be made in the records of probate or other courts that have jurisdiction over administration of decedents' estates. Laws concerning wills, intestate succession, and the formalities of estate administration are, of course, important to land title search and examination. A host of troublesome legal problems can arise in connection with succession to real property interests by death.

United States v. Union Central Life Insurance Co. *Skip to 528*

368 U.S. 291, 82 S. Ct. 349, 7 L. Ed. 2d 294 (1961)

Opinion of the Court by Mr. Justice BLACK. . . . Robert G. Peters, Jr., and his wife, of Oakland County, Michigan, failed to pay their 1952 federal income taxes. In January 1954 an assessment for this delinquency was filed in the Internal Revenue Collectors' Office at Detroit, Michigan, at which time a lien arose "in favor of the United States upon all property" of the two delinquent taxpayers.[1] Some 10 months

---

1. Sections 3670 and 3671 of the Internal Revenue Code of 1939, in effect at that time.

after the Government's tax lien arose, Mr. and Mrs. Peters executed a mortgage on real property they owned in Oakland County to secure an indebtedness to the respondent Union Central Life Insurance Company. They defaulted in payment of the mortgage, and Union Central filed this action to foreclose in the Circuit Court of Oakland County, joining the United States as a party defendant because of its asserted lien.

The company claimed priority for its mortgage over the earlier created federal lien because no notice of the federal lien had been filed with the register of deeds in Oakland County as then required by Michigan law.[2] For this alleged priority the company relied on § 3672(a)(1) of the 1939 Internal Revenue Code, as amended, providing that a federal tax lien shall not be valid as against any mortgagee until notice has been filed "In the office in which the filing of such notice is authorized by the law of the State or Territory in which the property subject to the lien is situated, whenever the State or Territory has by law authorized the filing of such notice in an office within the State or Territory." The Government, however, claimed that Michigan had not "authorized" filing within the meaning of the statute and that the case should be governed by § 3672(a)(2) which provides that "whenever the State . . . has not by law authorized the filing of such notice in an office within the State," the notice may be filed in "the office of the clerk of the United States district court for the judicial district in which the property subject to the lien is situated." Since the federal lien had been filed in the District Court months before the mortgage was executed and filed in the county register of deeds' office, the Government claimed that its lien had priority. The Government's contention that Michigan had not "authorized" a state office for filing the federal tax notice was based on the fact that the Michigan law purporting to authorize such filing expressly required that a federal tax lien notice contain "a description of the land upon which a lien is claimed," even though the form long used for filing federal tax lien notices in the District Courts throughout the United States does not contain a description of any particular property upon which the lien is asserted. In support of its contention the Government pointed to the fact that in 1953 the Michigan Attorney General ruled that federal tax lien notices not containing such a description are not entitled to recordation, and it is stipulated that from the time of that ruling, up to 1956,[3] "it was the policy of the office of the Register of Deeds for said County of Oakland not to accept for recording notices of Federal tax liens which did not contain a legal description of any land."

Because the United States had not filed a notice complying with the Michigan law, the Michigan Circuit and Supreme Courts held the federal lien to be subordinate to the mortgage, 361 Mich. 283, 105 N.W.2d 196. While this holding is in accord with Youngblood v. United States, 141 F.2d 912 (C.A. 6th Cir.), it conflicts with United States v. Rasmuson, 253 F.2d 944 (C.A. 8th Cir.). In order to settle this conflict and because of the importance of the question in the administration of the revenue laws, we granted certiorari. 365 U.S. 858.

The Michigan requirement that notice of the federal tax lien be filed in Michigan is, of course, not controlling unless Congress has made it so, for the subject of federal taxes, including "remedies for their collection has always been conceded

---

2. Act 104, Public Acts of Michigan of 1923, repealed April 13, 1956, by Act 107, Public Acts of Michigan of 1956.

3. Act 104 was repealed April 13, 1956.

to be independent of the legislative action of the States." United States v. Snyder, 149 U.S. 210, 214. While § 3672(a)(1) unquestionably requires notice of a federal lien to be filed in a state office when the State authoritatively designates an office for that purpose, the section does not purport to permit the State to prescribe the form or the contents of that notice. Since such an authorization might well result in radically differing forms of federal tax notices for the various States, it would run counter to the principle of uniformity which has long been the accepted practice in the field of federal taxation. Moreover, a required compliance with Michigan law would mean that the federal tax lien would be superior to all those entitled to notice only as to the property described in the notice even though § 3670 broadly creates a lien "upon all property and rights to property, whether real or personal, belonging to" a taxpayer. This language has been held to include in the lien all property owned by the delinquent taxpayer both at the time the lien arises and thereafter until it is paid.[4] It seems obvious that this expansive protection for the Government would be greatly reduced if to enforce it government agents were compelled to keep aware at all times of all property coming into the hands of its tax delinquents. Imposition of such a task by the Michigan law could seriously cripple the Government in the collection of its taxes, and to attribute to Congress a purpose so to weaken the tax liens it has created would require very clear language. The history of § 3672 belies any such congressional purpose.

In 1893 this Court decided in United States v. Snyder, 149 U.S. 210, that the federal tax lien could be enforced against bona fide purchasers who had no notice of the lien, despite a state law attempting to defeat the lien unless it has been recorded. In order to grant relief from the *Snyder* rule, Congress in 1914 passed an Act requiring, much as the provision here in question did, that the tax liens should not be "valid as against any mortgagee, purchaser, or judgment creditor" until notice was filed with the clerk of an appropriate District Court, or, whenever a State authorized such filing, in the office of a county recorder of deeds.[5] This statute was amended in 1928 by adding that the lien would not be valid until notice was filed "*in accordance with the law of the State or Territory* in which the property subject to the lien is situated, whenever the State or Territory has by law provided for the filing of such notice. . . ."[6] (Emphasis supplied.) Following this in United States v. Maniaci, 36 F. Supp. 293, *aff'd*, 116 F.2d 935, both a United States District Court and a Court of Appeals refused to enforce a federal tax lien on Michigan property because the notice of lien, although filed both in a District Court and in the office of the proper Michigan register of deeds, did not contain the description of the property required by Michigan law. In this holding emphasis was placed on the clause added in 1928, requiring notice to be filed "in accordance with the law of the State or Territory in which the property subject to the lien is situated. . . ."

Less than two years after the *Maniaci* holding Congress again amended the lien notice provisions, struck out "in accordance with the law of the State or Territory" and substituted the language in the section here controlling that notice was not valid until filed "In the office in which the filing of such notice is authorized by the law of the State or Territory."[7] The reports of the House and Senate Committees

---

4. Glass City Bank v. United States, 326 U.S. 265.

5. 37 Stat. 1016.

6. 45 Stat. 876.

7. 56 Stat. 957, § 3672(a)(1) of the Internal Revenue Code of 1939, as amended.

reporting this amendment point strongly to a purpose to get away from the ruling in the *Maniaci* case and make it clear that, while notice of a federal lien must be filed in a state office where authorized by a State, the notice is sufficient if given in the form long used by the Department "without regard to other general requirements with respect to recording prescribed by the law of such State or Territory."[8] The Department never accepted the *Maniaci* case and its practice has been to use forms which do not contain a particular description of any property owned by a delinquent taxpayer. The notice provisions were once more amended in the 1954 Code, this time providing that the notice shall be valid if in the Department form "notwithstanding any law of the State or Territory regarding the form or content of a notice of lien."[9] The House Report stated that this amendment was merely "declaratory of the existing procedure and in accordance with the long-continued practice of the Treasury Department."[10]

The Michigan law authorizing filing only if a description of the property was given placed obstacles to the enforcement of federal tax liens that Congress had not permitted, and consequently no state office was "authorized" for filing within the meaning of the federal statute. It was therefore error for the Michigan courts to fail to give priority to the Government's lien here, notice of which had been filed in the District Court in accordance with federal law.

The judgment of the Michigan Supreme Court is reversed and the cause is remanded to that court for proceedings not inconsistent with this opinion.

Reversed and remanded.

Mr. Justice Douglas dissents.

NOTES AND QUESTIONS

1. Why does the U.S. Internal Revenue Service oppose a requirement that it include land descriptions in its tax lien notices? And why did the Michigan authorities favor such descriptions in federal government tax lien notices?

2. The Uniform Federal Tax Lien Registration Act is now in effect in Michigan, Mich. Comp. Laws Ann. §§ 211.661 to 211.687 (1998 & Supp. 2006-2007), and provides in part:

Section 2.
   This act shall apply only to federal tax liens and to other notices of federal liens which under any act of Congress or any regulation adopted pursuant to an act of Congress are required or permitted to be filed in the same manner as notices of federal tax liens.

Section 3.
   (1) Notices of liens, certificates, and other notices affecting federal tax liens or other federal liens shall be filed pursuant to this act.
   (2) Notices of liens upon real property for obligations payable to the United States and certificates and notices affecting the liens shall be filed in the office of the register of deeds of the county in which the real property subject to the liens is situated.

8. H.R. Rep. No. 2333, 77th Cong., 2d Sess. 173. See also S. Rep. No. 1631, 77th Cong., 2d Sess. 248.
9. Section 6323(b) of the Internal Revenue Code of 1954.
10. H.R. Rep. No. 1337, 83d Cong., 2d Sess. A406-A407.

Section 5. . . .

(4) Upon request of any person, the filing officer shall issue his or her certificate showing whether there is on file, on the date and hour stated, any notice of lien, certificate, or notice affecting any lien filed under this act or former Act No. 162 of the Public Acts of 1967, naming a particular person, and if a notice or certificate is on file, giving the date and hour of filing of each notice or certificate.

Almost every state now provides by statute for local filing of federal tax liens. See generally 5 Powell on Real Property § 39.05[1] (1998).

3. For many years considerable dissatisfaction with federal tax lien laws has existed. By passage of the Federal Tax Lien Act of 1966, 80 Stat. 1125, Congress sought to alleviate some of this dissatisfaction. Among other lien law changes made by the 1966 act, the Internal Revenue Code of 1954 was amended to give priority over federal tax liens to certain categories of claims or property interests, even though the claims or interests were created after filing of federal tax lien notices. Included in this list of "superpriority" claims are liens of general real estate taxes, liens for special assessments on real estate, and some mechanics' liens. 26 U.S.C.A. § 6323(b)(6) and (7) (2002).

4. Liens on real property for unpaid local and state general property taxes and special assessments can generally be determined from public records, and these records are regularly checked in the course of title examinations. In some places, such tax liens are entered in separate tax lien records; in some, an examination of tax assessment and payment records must be made. When unpaid, other local and state taxes can result in liens on real estate, and the existence of these liens can be ascertained from examining public records. Examples of such liens are N.Y. Tax Law § 692(d) (McKinney 1999), income tax lien; and Va. Code § 58.1-908 (2003), estate tax lien.

5. In addition to public records of tax liens, lis pendens, judgment liens, and priorities created by other judicial determinations, additional interests in or claims against particular land parcels may be discovered by searching public records other than conveyancing records kept pursuant to the recording acts. Of major importance are mechanics' and materialmen's liens, a public record of which generally is required sooner or later to validate or continue validation of these liens. Among other public records that may disclose claims against land are records of attachments of real property that may be made at the commencement of certain judicial proceedings, e.g., Me. Rev. Stat. Ann. tit. 14, §§ 4451 and 4454 (2003).

6. Why do you think that all public records pertaining to land titles in each county, or at least a cross-reference to such records, are not centralized in one public office so as to facilitate title searching? What public records do you think should be so centralized that frequently are not?

e. Off-Record Risks

All legally protected land interests are not apparent from a search of public records. Under many circumstances, title interests are recognized as valid even though their existence or validity is not disclosed by these records. Even bona fide purchasers without actual notice can be subordinated to off-record interests, often but not always on the grounds that they have constructive notice.

Person acquiring interests in land are generally obligated to examine physically the premises for indications of interests inconsistent with the record title. Inquiry of parties in possession may be required, especially if their right to possession does not appear of record. Further inquiry should be made if there is evidence of land use incompatible with the title as shown by the public records. If transferees fail to examine adequately the premises before they take, they are put on notice of what a reasonable examination would have disclosed. In some states, mechanics' and materialmen's liens may be created without first being put of public record, and for a period of time may bind even subsequent transferees. Merely because a land transaction appears of record and seems to be valid does not necessarily mean that it is valid or has created any legally recognized land interests. The underlying instrument may have been forged, never delivered when necessary, executed by a person without legal capacity, or for some other reason be void. Putting a void instrument of record generally has no effect as a validating act.

The above are just a few of the many off-record risks to land titles. Although they rarely cause losses to persons acquiring interests in land, these risks are a sufficient threat so that purchasers and lenders commonly take some precautions to avoid them, and they are major inducements to the acquisition of title insurance.

Miller v. Green

264 Wis. 159, 58 N.W.2d 704 (1953)

Prior to November 4, 1950, the defendant, Mary Green, owned a farm of 63 acres located in Pierce county. During November, 1949, she rented the farm to the plaintiff, Eugene M. Miller, for the year of 1950. He raised a crop thereon during the season of 1950. On November 4, 1950, Mrs. Green and the plaintiffs, Eugene M. Miller and his wife, made a land contract by the terms of which the latter agreed to buy the farm for $3,500, $400 having been paid as earnest money.

On November 29, 1950, the defendant, W. E. Hines, paid Mrs. Green $500 toward the purchase price of the same farm. On the next day Mrs. Green executed a deed conveying the farm to Hines. The deed was delivered on December 1, 1950, and recorded in the office of the register of deeds on the same day. Later Hines paid the balance of the purchase price, $3,300.

The Miller land contract was not recorded until March 7, 1951.

The action was commenced on March 8, 1951, to set aside the deed to W. E. Hines and Avis Hines, and for specific performance on the part of Mrs. Green of her agreement to convey to plaintiffs.

Judgment dismissing the complaint was entered on June 16, 1952. Plaintiffs appeal. . . .

CURRIE, Justice. Defendants Hines claim that their title under their deed is superior to the land contract interest of the plaintiffs inasmuch as their deed was recorded first. Section 235.49, Stats., provides as follows:

"Every conveyance of real estate within this state hereafter made (except patents issued by the United States or this state, or by the proper offices of either) which shall not be recorded as provided by law shall be void as against any subsequent purchaser in good faith and for a valuable consideration of the same real estate or any portion thereof whose conveyance shall first be duly recorded."

The question at issue on this appeal is whether the defendants Hines qualify under the foregoing statute as subsequent purchasers *"in good faith."* Plaintiffs contend that the defendants Hines do not so qualify because the plaintiffs were in possession of the premises on November 29, 1950, when the defendant W. E. Hines paid Mrs. Green $500 toward the purchase price of the farm, and that such possession constituted constructive notice of the plaintiff's rights under their land contract. This makes it necessary to review the evidence bearing on such possession by the plaintiffs, or either of them.

Approximately 40 acres of the 63-acre tract was cultivated land and the remainder was pasture and woods. The buildings on the farm consisted of a small log house, a barn, and some sheds, which were in a dilapidated condition; the house was unlivable; and such buildings had not been used for many years. The plaintiff Eugene M. Miller had leased the entire 63-acre tract for the crop season of 1950 and had grown crops on the cultivated 40 acres and had grazed livestock on the remaining portion. The crop had been harvested prior to November, 1950, and the livestock had been removed when cold weather came about November 22, 1950. However, starting November 4, 1950 (the date that the Millers contracted to purchase this farm tract), Miller's father, in behalf of the Millers, hauled between 59 and 60 loads of manure to the farm. First the manure was spread over the land, but then after a snowstorm came it was piled on a pile about 100 feet from the road, such pile being about 60 feet long and several feet high. Such hauling of manure was taking place on November 29, 1950 (the date that the defendants Hines made the $500 down payment on the purchase price), and continued until about December 8 or 9, 1950. Also in November, prior to the snowstorm, approximately 2 acres of land had been plowed by Miller, which plowed land was plainly visible from the abutting highway before the snowstorm.

The Hines farm was located about one half mile from this 61-acre tract, although the distance by highway was about one and one half miles. Part of the tract was visible from the Hines home. The defendant W. E. Hines testified that he knew that the plaintiff Eugene M. Miller had leased the tract for the crop season of 1950, but denied that he drove past the tract on the abutting highway during November, 1950, and denied having seen the plowing of the land, the hauling of the manure, or the manure pile on the land, although he admitted finding the manure pile there the following spring.

The general rule is that possession of land is notice to the world of whatever rights the possessor may have in the premises. The reason underlying this rule is well stated in Pippin v. Richards, 1911, 146 Wis. 69, 74, 130 N.W. 872, 874:

> The theory of the law is that the person in possession may be asked to disclose the right or title which he has in the premises, and the purchaser will be chargeable with the actual notice he would have received, had he made inquiry. Mateskey v. Feldman, 75 Wis. 103, 43 N.W. 733; Brinkman v. Jones, supra [44 Wis. 519]. In Frame v. Frame, 32 W. Va. [463], at page 478, 9 S.E. [901] at page 907 (5 L.R.A 323), the court said: "The earth has been described as that universal manuscript, open to the eyes of all. When, therefore, a man proposes to buy or deal with realty, his first duty is to read this public manuscript; that is, to look and see who is there upon it, and what are his rights there. And, if the person in possession has an equitable title to it, he is as much bound to respect it, as if it was a perfect legal title evidenced by a deed duly recorded."

An apt statement of this general principle of possession being constructive notice is stated in State v. Jewell, 1947, 250 Wis. 165, at page 171, 26 N.W.2d 825, at page 828, 28 N.W.2d 314:

> The possession of real estate is generally considered constructive notice of rights of the possessor, whether the possession is sought to be used for the purpose of charging a purchaser with notice of an outstanding equity, or whether it is sought to charge a subsequent purchaser with notice of an unrecorded instrument and thereby defeat his right to protection under the recording acts. It is so held in the United States courts and in 28 states of the Union. 55 Am. Jur. [Vendor and Purchaser] 1087, sec. 712, and cases cited.

The rule with respect to possession of a tenant constituting notice of any rights claimed by such tenant is stated in 5 Tiffany, Real Property, Third Ed., p. 73, sec. 1291:

"It has been decided in a number of states that, by the possession of a tenant under a lease, a purchaser is chargeable with notice, not only of the tenant's rights under the lease, but also of any right which he may have not under the lease, as, for instance, under an agreement by the lessor to sell the property to him."

The authorities generally hold that in order that possession may constitute constructive notice such possession must be "open, visible, exclusive and unambiguous." Ely v. Wilcox, 20 Wis. 523, Wickes v. Lake, 25 Wis. 71; and 55 Am. Jur., Vendor and Purchaser, p. 1090, sec. 716. It will thus be seen that the requirements as to the type of possession that will constitute constructive notice are practically identical with the requirements of the type of possession necessary to constitute adverse possession. In view of the fact that the farm buildings were unusable, the plowing of the 2 acres of land after November 4, 1950, and the hauling of the manure practically every day throughout November were acts which not only were "open and visible," but also "exclusive and unambiguous." They were the customary acts of possession which could be exercised as to unoccupied farm lands at such time of year. Surely they would have been sufficient to have constituted acts of adverse possession, and it would appear that the rule as to acts of possession necessary to constitute constructive notice to a purchaser is no more strict. Wickes v. Lake, supra, is authority for the principle that actual residence on the land is not required in order to have sufficient possession to constitute constructive notice.

In George v. Stansbury, 1922, 90 W. Va. 593, 111 S.E. 58, both the plaintiff and defendants claimed title to a city lot. The plaintiff, during 1919, had maintained a garden on the lot, and the following year, although he did not have a garden there, he permitted the owner of a nearby lot who was excavating for a building to haul a large quantity of dirt from the excavation and dump it on the lot so as to fill a low place. It was during this second year that the defendants purchased the premises and obtained a deed which they recorded, while the plaintiff's title was not recorded. The West Virginia court held that the gardening during the one season, followed by the permitting of the dirt to be hauled in and dumped the second year, constituted sufficient possession to be constructive notice to the defendants of plaintiff's rights, and plaintiff was held to have the superior title. If hauling dirt onto a vacant lot constitutes sufficient possession to be constructive notice to a subsequent purchaser, surely hauling manure onto farm land, as in the instant case, should be held to be equally effective to constitute constructive notice.

In Lyman v. Russell, 1867, 45 Ill. 281, plaintiff purchased some farm land but did not record his deed. The defendants claimed under a subsequent mortgage executed by plaintiff's vendor. The question was whether there was such "actual, open, notorious and visible possession" of the lands by plaintiff as to constitute constructive notice to the subsequent mortgagees. Plaintiff's act of possession consisted of plowing some of the land in view of all who passed along the adjoining highway. The Illinois court held that the plaintiff's possession was sufficient notice to put a subsequent purchaser on inquiry, and should operate as notice of plaintiff's rights.

The learned trial court in the instant case apparently was of the opinion that, in order for the plaintiff Eugene M. Miller's possession of the premises to have been constructive notice to the defendants Hines that Miller claimed rights of ownership therein, there must have been some change in the type of his possession after November 4, 1950 (the date the Millers entered into the contract to purchase), and his possession prior thereto. This is very apparent from finding No. 5 of the findings of fact made by the trial court, such finding reading as follows:

> That the plaintiff, Eugene M. Miller, continued in possession of said premises, and continued to pasture livestock thereon until about November 22, 1950, when it was necessary to remove them because of the weather, and continued to make such use of the tillable land on said premises as the weather permitted during the month of November, 1950. That the defendant, W. E. Hines knew at that time of the oral lease between the plaintiff, Eugene M. Miller, and the defendant, Mary Green, for the 1950 season. That there was nothing in the use to which the land was put by the plaintiff, Eugene M. Miller, to indicate to the defendant, W. E. Hines, that [there] had been a change in the status of said plaintiff with relation to said land.

In other words the trial court found that there was possession of the premises by Millers from November 4, 1950, through to the end of that month, but there was no change in the type of possession. Apparently it was the theory of the trial court that the defendants Hines could assume, because of such lack of change in the character of possession, that the possession after November 4, 1950, was that of a tenant and not of a purchaser. The authorities, however, clearly establish that no such change in the character of possession is necessary.

8 Thompson on Real Property (Permanent Edition), p. 413, sec. 4516, states:

"If the tenant changes his character by taking an agreement to purchase, or he has this right under his lease and exercises his option to purchase, his possession amounts to notice of his equitable title as purchaser."

To the same effect see Anderson v. Brinser, 1889, 129 Pa. 376, 404, 11 A. 809, 18 A. 520, 521, 6 L.R.A. 205, wherein the Pennsylvania court stated:

> Knowledge of the existence of a lease will, of course, give constructive notice of all its provisions; but the possession, apart from the lease, we think, should be treated as notice of the possessor's claim of title, whatever that claim may be, for the lease may be but the first of two or more successive rights acquired by the tenant. While in the occupancy under a lease for years, the tenant may have purchased under articles, and entitled himself to an equity; or, indeed, he may have purchased the legal estate in fee, and failed to record his deed. Would it be supposed that a knowledge of the precedent lease would dispense with the duty of inquiry, and entitle a subsequent grantee to the

protection of an innocent purchaser? . . . In Sugden on Vendors, (volume 1, 6th Amer., from 10th London, Ed., p. 265, § 22,) it is expressly stated, and numerous authorities are cited in support of the statement, that if a tenant, during his tenancy, changes his character by having agreed to purchase the estate, his possession amounts to notice of his equitable title as purchaser.

It is our considered judgment that the acts of possession on the part of the plaintiff Eugene M. Miller throughout the remainder of the month of November, 1950, following the purchase of the tract by the Millers on November 4, 1950, constituted constructive notice to all the world which required a subsequent purchaser to make inquiry as to what rights, if any, the plaintiff Eugene M. Miller claimed to have in the premises. Subsequent purchasers could not safely assume, without inquiry, as did the defendants Hines, that, because Miller had theretofore been a tenant for the season, there had been no subsequent change in his rights from that of a tenant to that of a purchaser.

Judgment reversed and cause remanded with directions to enter judgment as prayed for in plaintiffs' complaint.

NOTES AND QUESTIONS

1. In most all jurisdictions, purchasers of interests in land are on constructive notice of what an examination of the premises would disclose as to the title. There are statutory exceptions, however, in a few states. For example, Va. Code § 55-96 (2003), which states: "The mere possession of real estate shall not, of itself, be notice to purchasers thereof for value of any interest or estate therein of the person in possession." This statute was important to the court's decision in Kiser v. Clinchfield Coal Corp., supra. Another example is a New Mexico statute, N. M. Stat. Ann. § 14-9-3 (2003): "Possession alone based on an unrecorded executory real estate contract shall not be construed against any subsequent purchaser, mortgagee in good faith or judgment lien creditor either to impute knowledge of or to impose the duty to inquire about the possession or the provisions of the instruments." Why do you think these two statutes were passed?

2. Many courts have been reluctant to impute notice of an unrecorded title when acts of occupation are not exclusive, continuous, or readily apparent. There is a similar reluctance when the acts of occupancy occurred some considerable time in the past. Compare Miller v. Green with these cases holding that the indicated acts of occupancy did not constitute notice of the occupiers' titles: Sanford v. Alabama Power Co., 256 Ala. 280, 54 So. 2d 562 (1951), continuous occupation of the surface plus mining operations many years earlier (contest over mineral rights); Anderson v. Barron, 208 Ga. 784, 69 S.E.2d 874 (1952), infrequent visits to vacant land, posting no trespassing signs, occasional cutting and removal of timber, and payment of taxes; Burlew v. City of Lake Forest, 104 Ill. App. 3d 800, 433 N.E.2d 353 (1982), building and retaining a fence; Hosier v. Great Notch Corp., 23 N.J. Misc. 1, 40 A.2d 196 (1944), planting and harvesting a corn crop; Paganelli v. Swendsen, 50 Wash. 2d 304, 311 P.2d 676 (1957), earlier construction of improvements and posting for sale signs; and Fohn v. Title Ins. Corp. of St. Louis, 529 S.W.2d 1 (Mo. 1975), advertising signs, not indicative of ownership, posted on the premises.

8. Why should a purchaser ever be on notice of what an examination of the premises would disclose? In all of these cases, is not the difficulty caused by the willful or negligent conduct of the prior owner in failing to record, and should not the prior owner therefore be responsible for failing to perform this simple act?

Martinique Realty Corp. v. Hull

64 N.J. Super. 599, 166 A.2d 803 (App. Div. 1960)

FREUND, J.A.D. Plaintiff, the purchaser of a leasehold interest in a 55-apartment building in Passaic, commenced this suit against the tenants of one of the apartments for damages for the non-payment of rent allegedly due and owing under the terms of a five-year written lease. Defendants asserted the defense of payment, claiming that the entire rent for the term of the lease had been paid in advance to the former lessor, plaintiff's vendor, and that plaintiff purchased subject to all of defendants' rights as lessees. No basic facts being in issue, the Law Division granted defendants' motion for summary judgment on the ground that plaintiff was chargeable with notice of defendants' rights in and to the apartment, as created between defendants and plaintiff's assignor. Plaintiff files the instant appeal from that determination.

The apartment building in question was formerly owned by The Martinique, a New Jersey corporation. On August 5, 1957 the corporation entered into a five-year lease with defendants for a 1 1/2 room apartment. The gross rental, including security deposit, was $8,450, the rent payable at the rate of $130 per month. Defendants immediately delivered to the landlord a check in the amount of $130, and on August 15, 1957, apparently in accordance with an oral arrangement, the entire rental balance was paid in advance by defendants in the form of a check for $8,320.

On or about October 22, 1957, at the lessor's suggestion, defendants agreed to exchange their apartment for a larger one in the same building. Since the rent on the larger apartment was $150 a month, it was agreed that defendants would make up the difference in annual installments of $240, besides providing additional security of $100. Accordingly, a new lease was executed; its terms ignore the prior advance payment and simply provide that rent will be paid to the landlord over a five-year term, commencing December 1, 1957 and terminating October 31, 1962, in the gross sum of $9,000, payable "in equal monthly installments of $150 in advance on the first day of each and every calendar month during said term." Both the additional security deposit of $100 and the sum of $240, covering the additional rental for the calendar year beginning December 1, 1957, were paid by check to the landlord. A letter dated October 23, 1957 was received by defendants from the lessor's agent, acknowledging the rent prepayment and the $240 annual payment arrangement. Defendants took possession of their new apartment in November 1957.

Subsequently, on December 16, 1957, The Martinique sold and conveyed title to the premises to Cambrian Estates, Inc., a New York corporation, taking back, at the same time, a long-term lease covering the apartment building. On April 29, 1958, the lease-hold interest of The Martinique was sold to the present plaintiff, a separate and distinct corporation. At the time of purchase, plaintiff caused an uneventful search to be made at the office of the Passaic County Clerk. (The Hulls did not record their lease until July 16, 1958.) It apparently relied upon its vendor's silence and its reading of paragraph 45(a) of the Martinique-Cambrian leaseback agreement of December 16, 1957, providing that "the lessee shall not without the prior written consent of the Lessor with respect to any lease now in existence or any renewal or extension thereof of any space demised to any tenant, accept prepayment of rent in excess of one month prior to its due date."

In May of 1958 plaintiff mailed rent statements to all of its tenants. Defendants, having learned for the first time that ownership of the leasehold had changed hands, refused to tender any rent by reason of their prepayment.

Plaintiff's contention on this appeal is two-fold. It argues, first, that as the transferee of the leasehold interest, it was entitled to the benefit of all of the covenants between its predecessor and the Hulls. Secondly, it urges that it had a right to rely upon the terms of defendants' lease as written, and that the prepayment of rent is therefore no bar as such prepayment was inconsistent with the terms of the lease; further, that it had no notice, at the time of purchase, of defendants' advance payments, and that it was not, under the principle of Feld v. Kantrowitz, 98 N.J. Eq. 167, 130 A. 6 (Ch. 1925), aff'd, 99 N.J. Eq. 847, 132 A. 657 (E. & A. 1926), and 99 N.J. Eq. 706, 134 A. 920 (Ch. 1926), required to make inquiry of each tenant as to the latter's interest in the property outside of the written lease. Defendants respond by questioning the applicability of the *Feld* case, arguing that plaintiff was under a duty to make inquiry respecting the rights of lessees under their tenancies and that failure to make such inquiry charges plaintiff with notice of such rights. They further contend that the payment of rent by a tenant to his landlord in advance of the time stipulated in the lease for its payment is a discharge pro tanto from the claim of the lessor, and therefore a valid defense against the assignee of the lessor's interest.

Plaintiff is confronted at the outset by the specific statutory provision that the rights of a lessee of real estate for a term of years vis-à-vis his lessor survive the passing of the lessor's interest to another by assignment or otherwise. R.S. 46:8-3, N.J.S.A.; 51 C.J.S. Landlord and Tenant § 44(2), p. 567. This is but an illustration of the general rule that the assignee of a contract right takes subject to all defenses valid against his assignor. N.J.S. 2A:25-1, N.J.S.A. While it may be contended that the applicability of these sections is limited by the penalties inherent in our recording act, R.S. 46:22-1 et seq., N.J.S.A., embracing leases for a term exceeding two years, N.J.S.A. 46:16-1(a), the statute requires, however, that the prevailing purchaser be bona fide in nature.

An essential characteristic of the bona fide purchaser is his lack of notice of the interest of the unrecorded or late-recorded party. It is long settled that the purchaser of a lessor's interest in property has a duty to make inquiry as to the extent of the rights of any person in open, notorious and exclusive possession of the premises; if this duty is not discharged, then notice is imputed to the purchaser of all facts which a reasonably prudent inquiry would have revealed. [Citations omitted.] Such inquiry must be made of the tenant in possession, and if inquiry is made only of the former lessor, the tenant will not be precluded from asserting against the purchaser such rights as he possessed against the lessor. Arcade Realty Holding Corp v. Hildinger, 6 N.J. Misc. 1055, 1058, 144 A. 25 (Ch. 1928).

Moreover, it has been held, in a situation strikingly parallel to the one at hand, that the duty of inquiry is not discharged when an intending purchaser of a leasehold merely examines the written lease which the occupant has signed with the owner of record. The purchaser assumes at his peril that the instrument accurately defines the rights of the occupant. Caplan v. Palace Realty Co., N.J. 110 A. 584 (Ch. 1920). Vice-Chancellor Learning stated unequivocally in the latter case that:

> If the purchaser is content to rely upon the representations of the landlord, either express or implied, to the effect that the writing contains . . . . an accurate statement of the terms actually agreed upon, and fails to inquire of the tenant touching those facts . . . the purchaser's rights as against the tenant can rise no higher than those which were in fact enjoyed by the landlord under that instrument, and any right of reformation of the instrument for fraud or mistake which the tenant may have enjoyed against the landlord may in like manner be enjoyed against the purchaser.

(110 A., at p. 585).

Plaintiff contends, however, that the duty of inquiry has been severely restricted, if not eliminated entirely, in cases involving a multi-tenanted office or apartment building. Reliance is placed exclusively on the opinions in Feld v. Kantrowitz, supra. There, an attorney, a tenant in a small office building, claimed that he had acquired, under an unrecorded assignment, an option to purchase a one-sixth interest in the building. The defendant, who had entered into a contract to purchase the entire property without notice of plaintiff's option and without making inquiry of the tenant, claimed status as a bona fide purchaser and asserted that defendant's unrecorded option was extinguished. The vice-chancellor took cognizance of the doctrine of inquiry notice but held that it did not apply to the situation before him. He reasoned that since an office building or apartment house is constructed for the very purpose of creating numerous tenancies, a purchaser should be able to assume that the occupants of the offices or apartments possess the designated status of tenants. Therefore, he concluded, "under these circumstances, to change a prospective purchaser with notice of any right, title, or interest of one of the tenants, beyond the right of tenancy, would be absurd." 98 N.J. Eq., supra, at p. 169, 130 A., at p. 7. He further discussed the rule that to put the purchaser on inquiry notice, the tenant must be in exclusive possession, and concluded that the interest of one of numerous tenants of a large building does not satisfy the exclusivity requirement. The vice-chancellor's decision was affirmed on the sole ground that he had applied the proper procedural principles in denying plaintiff a preliminary injunction; the Court of Errors and Appeals expressly disclaimed any examination of the merits of the litigation. 99 N.J. Eq. 847, 849, 132 A. 657, (E. & A. 1926). Subsequently, the cause came on for final hearing, at which time the vice-chancellor reiterated his position, further stating that Caplan v. Palace Realty Co., supra, "does not, so far as my reading of the opinion reveals, refer in any way to the constructive notice arising from tenancy in a building such as the one involved in the case at bar." 99 N.J. Eq., supra, at p. 707, 134 A., at p. 920.

The precise holding in Feld would seem to be clearly distinguishable from the instant fact situation in that defendants are not herein asserting any interest "beyond the right of tenancy," that is, beyond a demand for recognition of the precise terms of their tenancy. To apply Feld to the instant situation would be to contravene the general rule that possession and occupancy of the premises by the tenant amount to notice of his advance payment of rent, and that such prepayment — honestly made, and in the absence of special circumstances putting the tenant on notice that he is prejudicing the rights of third parties — will protect the tenant against further liability for such rent to the landlord and all successors to his interest. 52 C.J.S. Landlord and Tenant § 535, p. 348; 32 Am. Jur., Landlord and Tenant, § 461, p. 378. Boteler v. Leber, 112 N.J. Eq. 441, 164 A. 572 (Ch. 1933), cited by plaintiff, is not opposed to this view. The court in *Boteler* left open the question of whether notice would affect the rights of the parties. Furthermore, the lease was expressly subordinated to the mortgage, thereby insulating the mortgagee's rights to the rents upon default.

On the other hand, we cannot in all candor overlook indications in the language of *Feld* broad enough to encompass the instant case, namely: (1) the vice-chancellor's statement (98 N.J. Eq., supra, at p. 172, 130 A., at p. 8), that he might decide differently if "dealing with the right of a tenant as such, even in this kind of a building, *that appears in his lease.*" (Emphasis added.) Evidence of the prepayment of the Hulls did not, as we have noted, appear in their lease; and (2) the attempt to distinguish the *Caplan* case on the ground that a multi-tenanted building was not there involved, leaving the implication that the purchaser of such a building can justifiably rely exclusively on the tenants' leases as written.

We must therefore consider, to the extent it bears on the present appeal, the question which we left open in Schnakenberg v. Gibraltar Savings and Loan Assn., 37 N.J. Super. 150, 158, 117 A.2d 191, 196 (App. Div. 1955): "Whether the rights of a tenant in possession and the duties of a purchaser of realty vary with the size and character of the building . . . ."

At least with respect to the details of a tenant's *leasehold* arrangement with his landlord, we are convinced that the purchaser's duty of inquiry does not vary with the number of tenants occupying the property. The arguments advanced in favor of such a correspondence are of dubious validity. Inquiry notice is an equitable doctrine designed to effect a distribution of precautionary burdens in a situation involving two "innocent" parties. American Law of Property, § 17.11, pp. 565-66. We see little merit in plaintiff's insistence that it would be exceedingly onerous to require inquiry of every tenant in a multi-tenanted building. The statement in *Feld,* 98 N.J. Eq., supra, at p. 169, 130 A., at p. 7, that it "would be absurd" to hold that "one contemplating the purchase of one of the great office buildings in the metropolitan district would be under a duty to personally interview every one of the hundreds of tenants occupying the offices thereof" ignores the very practical and effective device of the written communication. The duty to inquire is discharged by the exercise of due diligence or reasonable prudence, see Clawans v. Ordway B. & L. Assn., 112 N.J. Eq. 280, 284, 164 A. 267 (E. & A. 1933), and what such an inquiry fails to reveal is not further protected by the mere continued possession of the tenant. 4 American Law of Property, § 17.12, p. 576. Under certain circumstances, written inquiry may be sufficient to discharge that duty.

We need not dwell upon the statement in *Feld* that no single occupant of a multi-tenanted building is in such exclusive possession as to warrant the invoking of the purchaser's duty of inquiry. For the period of his lease, the lessee is considered the exclusive owner and occupier of the demised premises. Longi v. Raymond-Commerce Corp., 34 N.J. Super. 593, 600, 113 A.2d 69 (App. Div. 1955). That the demised premises consist of one apartment rather than an entire building should not be of consequence. This is not a situation involving the interests of the various family occupants of a single house. See Rankin v. Coar, 46 N.J. Eq. 566, 22 A. 177, 11 L.R.A. 661 (E. & A. 1890); Annotation, 2 A.L.R.2d 857 (1948).

Each apartment in the building under consideration is an entirely separate habitational unit, evidenced by a separate landlord-tenant arrangement.

We expressly refrain from a determination as to whether a purchaser's duty of inquiry extends to collateral interests of the lessee which are independent of his tenancy. We note, however, that the majority rule appears to extend the inquiry notice doctrine to cover certain collateral interests of the lessee, such as an option to purchase, see Annotations, 17 A.L.R.2d 331 (1951), 27 A.L.R.2d 1112 (1954), though perhaps not a claim of ownership of the fee. See Annotation, 74 A.L.R. 355, 357 (1931).

In any event, plaintiff, having failed to fulfill its duty of inquiry with respect to defendants' rights under their tenancy, is subject to the prior effective discharge by the latter of their rental obligations. Caplan v. Palace Realty Co., supra.

Judgment affirmed.   *Skip to 537*

QUESTIONS

1. What kind of written inquiries directed by a purchaser or mortgagee to the many tenants of a large building do you think might satisfy the court in the principal case that the purchaser or mortgagee was entitled to protection as a bona fide taker against tenants with unrecorded leases? Do you think it would make a difference if the structure involved were a large office building with many individual tenants rather than a large residential apartment house?

2. What do you think of the result in the following case? A went into possession of a farm as a tenant and later purchased from B, the owner, but failed to record the deed. Subsequently, B offered to sell the land to C. C inquired of A, the party in possession, as to what interest he had in the premises, and A said that he had a deed from B. C then checked the public records and, of course, found no record of such a deed. He asked B about the conveyance to A, and B denied that there ever had been a conveyance to A. C then purchased the farm from B, accepting delivery of a deed. In a contest between A and C, the court held for C, taking the position that C was a bona fide purchaser without notice of the deed from A to B. In its opinion, the court said: "Under all the circumstances shown here, we think, as did the Chancellor, that Alexander [C] made such inquiry as was reasonable and that the rule as to notice from possession did not apply so as to give priority to Gregory's [A's] deed." Gregory v. Alexander, 51 Tenn. App. 307, 316, 367 S.W.2d 292, 297 (1962).

Hadrup v. Sale

201 Va. 421, 111 S.E.2d 405 (1959)

MILLER, Justice. In this suit appellants, A. Hadrup, and W. C. Spratt and W. C. Spratt, Jr., partners, trading as Fredericksburg Pipe and Supply Company, assignees of A. Hadrup, seek to enforce a mechanic's lien taken out by them upon a house and lot owned by Thomas Battaile Sale, Jr., and Margaret B. Sale, appellees. From a decree of October 24, 1958, that declared the mechanic's lien to be invalid, we granted an appeal.

Some months prior to July 9, 1956, Hadrup entered into a contract with Normandy Village, Incorporated, owner of numerous lots in a residential subdivision known as

Normandy Village, to do the plumbing and heating work in the building erected on lot 67, section 4. On July 9, 1956, Hadrup assigned in writing to W. C. Spratt and W. C. Spratt, Jr., partners, all sums of money due him under his contract.

Appellants, on July 29, 1957, filed in the appropriate clerks' office a memorandum of mechanic's lien in the sum of $1,265 for plumbing and heating work done by Hadrup on the house and lot. However, lot 67 had been purchased on March 19, 1957, by appellees from Normandy Village, Incorporated. Appellees' deed was duly recorded but appellants had no actual knowledge of the sale until the day their lien was filed in the clerk's office.

About the time appellants filed their mechanic's lien, many other similar liens were filed against lots in the subdivision owned by Normandy Village, Incorporated, and its numerous grantees. Seven separate suits for various amounts were instituted by mechanic's lien claimants against Normandy Village, Incorporated, and other lot owners in the subdivision, and holders of liens on the lots.

By decree of January 10, 1958, these seven suits, in which numerous liens and claims of varying dignities and priorities were asserted against the same defendants and subject matter, were consolidated into a single cause and referred to a special commissioner to take evidence and report upon the inquires set out in the decree.

The inquiry pertinent to this appeal follows: "The validity of the mechanic's liens which have been asserted in these causes against the properties standing in the names of the parties hereto."

After hearing voluminous testimony from numerous witnesses and considering many exhibits, the commissioner reported that the work on the building on lot 67 was completed during the second week of August, 1957, and the mechanic's lien filed by appellants on the 29th day of July, 1957, was a valid lien against the house and lot in the sum of $1,265, with interest from July 27, 1957.

Exceptions were filed to the commissioner's report, and in an opinion that ruled upon the exceptions, the court found that no work was done by Hadrup on the house and lot bought by appellees on March 19, 1957, subsequent to their purchase, and that by the change of ownership on March 19, 1957, the work on the building was then "otherwise terminated" within the meaning of § 43-4, Code 1950. As appellants did not file their lien within sixty days after March 19, 1957, the lien was held invalid. In its opinion the court said:

> . . . Any work that Hadrup did on the house must have been done for the prior owner before 19 March, 1957, and Hadrup's lien against Sale's house should have been filed within sixty days after 19 March, 1957 whether the house was finished or not. When there is a change of ownership, that is notice to contractors and workmen who do no further work on the house, that the statute has begun to run and the lien even on an unfinished house must be filed within the limitation period from the date of sale.

In the decree which conformed to the opinion, the court held that appellants' mechanic's lien was invalid.

Appellants' assignment of error is that the court erred when it held that the sale and conveyance of the house and lot by Normandy Village, Incorporated, to appellees "otherwise terminated" the work on the building within the meaning of § 43-4, Code 1950.

The material part of that section follows:

"A general contractor, in order to perfect the lien given by the preceding section, shall file at any time after the work is done and the material furnished by him and before the expiration of sixty days from the time such building, structure, or railroad is completed, or the work thereon otherwise terminated . . . ."

The question presented is solely one of law. It is: Did the conveyance of the house and lot "otherwise terminate" the work upon the building and make it necessary for Hadrup and his assignees to file their lien within sixty days of the date of sale?

No Virginia case has been cited to us nor have we found one that decides the specific question. The trial court relied upon and cited Bolton v. Johns, 1847, 5 Pa. 145, 47 Am. Dec. 404, and note. However, in that case the statute construed was materially different from our statute.

The effect of a conveyance of the property upon the right to assert a mechanic's lien is dependent upon the character of the mechanic's lien statute in force in the particular jurisdiction.

"The determination of what effect a conveyance of the real estate has upon the right to assert a mechanic's lien depends upon the kind of statute in existence in the particular jurisdiction. Under statutes which provide that the claimant shall, upon giving or filing notice, have a lien upon the property, a sale of it in good faith before the notice of lien is given or filed prevents the acquisition of any lien. On the other hand, under statutes which recognize the right to a lien from the date of the contract or the time of the commencement of the building or other improvement, or from the beginning of the performance of the labor or the furnishing of material for which the lien is claimed, a lien which has thus attached is not affected by a change of ownership during the progress of the work. This rule applies to property which is sold to a municipal corporation. Where there has been a change of ownership, a purchaser is chargeable with notice that a lien might attach to the property for the improvements. A purchaser before the time for filing a lien on the property has expired may be required to pay such lien although in purchasing he relies upon the representations of the vendor that the contractor's claims against the property have all been paid in full." 36 Am. Jur., Mechanic's Liens, § 217, p. 140.

In Thorn v. Barringer, 73 W. Va. 618, 621, 81 S.E. 846, 847, in construing and applying mechanic's lien statutes somewhat similar to ours, the court said:

"Under our law Thorn's lien attached to the property, for all materials furnished by him under the contract and used in the building, as of the time that his furnishing the materials and the use of them began. Cushwa v. Improvement [Loan & Building] Association, 45 W. Va. 490, 32 S.E. 259 . . . ."

One purchasing premises on which buildings are in process of erection must take notice of any mechanic's lien right that has attached prior to his purchase. He must inquire what contracts are in course of execution on a property he is about to buy. He must further inquire what has been done and may be done under any such contracts that he finds. "A party purchasing premises on which buildings are in the process of erection, having knowledge of the same, is bound to make inquiry as to the rights of parties furnishing materials or performing work thereon, and is charged with constructive, if not actual notice of their lien." Phillips on Mechanics' Liens, sec. 227. "The fact that the work is in progress, is a notice to all of the rights of the mechanic,

and all conveyances made during that time are made subject to the mechanic's rights."
Rockel on Mechanics' Liens, sec. 150. . . .

Of like import is Boisot, Mechanics' Liens (1897), §§ 312-316.

It should be observed that § 43-4 provides that the general contractor, to perfect
his lien, shall file his memorandum "at any time after the work is done and
materials furnished by him and before the expiration of sixty days from the time
such building . . . is completed, or the work thereon otherwise terminated." Burks,
Pleading and Practice, 4th ed. § 459, p. 891. This language, when fairly construed,
means that an inchoate lien attaches when the work is done and materials furnished
which may be perfected within the specified time. Wallace v. Brumback, 177 Va. 36,
41, 12 S.E.2d 801. There is nothing in the statute to indicate that the work on the
building is "otherwise terminated" by a mere sale. Such a construction would
impose an undue hardship upon the contractor and is not in keeping with the
language or spirit of the statute.

The mechanic's lien asserted by appellants is declared to be valid. That portion
of the decree of October 24, 1959, which held it to be invalid is reversed and the
cause remanded for the entry of a decree not in conflict with the views herein
expressed.

Reversed and remanded.

NOTES ON MECHANIC'S AND MATERIALMEN'S LIENS AS TITLE RISKS

1. For a period of time during and after construction, in some states, priority by
statute is given to mechanics' and materialmen's liens over the interests of
subsequent bona fide purchasers or encumbrancers of the land, whether or not,
apparently, the bona fide purchasers or encumbrancers knew or could have known
of the liens when they acquired their interests. See, e.g., Franks v. Wood, 217 Ark. 10,
228 S.W.2d 480 (1950); Starek v. TKW, Inc., 410 So. 2d 35 (Ala. 1982), but a fee
purchaser of an existing structure, as distinct from a new one, has priority; and
Lenexa State Bank v. Dixon, 221 Kan. 238, 559 P.2d 776 (1977), dictum citing in
support Warden v. Sabins, 36 Kan. 165, 12 P. 520 (1887). And see Ohio Rev. Code
Ann. §§ 1311.13 and 1311.14 (Page 2002), with certain exceptions for property
improvement mortgages.

Is it good policy to give such benefits to the construction and building supply
industries? Where mechanics' and materialmen's liens are off-record risks, how can
prospective purchasers or mortgagees protect themselves from the possible existence of such liens? Prior to the time the liens are put of record, how can these
parties even determine whether or not liens of this kind exist? On mechanics' and
materialmen's liens also see Note, ch. 2, p. 276.

2. Following the concept of due process enunciated in such cases as Snaidach v.
Family Finance Corp., 395 U.S. 337, 89 S. Ct. 1820, 23 L. Ed. 2d 349 (1969) and
Fuentes v. Shevin, 407 U.S. 67, 92 S. Ct. 1983, 32 L. Ed. 2d 556 (1972), the
Connecticut mechanics' lien statute was held unconstitutional in Roundhouse
Construction Corp. v. Telesco Masons Supplies Co., Inc., 168 Conn. 371, 362 A.2d
778 (1975), *vacated and remanded,* 423 U.S. 809 (1975), *reaff'd,* 170 Conn. 155, 365
A.2d 393, *cert. denied,* 429 U.S. 889 (1976). The Connecticut Supreme Court, in

concluding that the mechanics' lien procedures provided for in its state's enact-ments did not meet constitutional due process requirements, stated:

> Under Connecticut procedure, the party claiming the lien is not required to post any bond or provide any surety to protect the owner of the property subjected to the lien against damages from an unsupportable lien. . . . The filing and perfection of the lien may be done by a claimant entirely ex parte, without authorization, supervision or control by a judicial officer. . . . Most conspicuously absent from the Connecticut procedure is any provision whatsoever for any sort of a timely hearing, either before or after the recording of the lien, which would give the property owner an opportunity to be heard or require the lienor to justify his lien. The statutes allow the lien to continue for two years without any further action on the part of the lienor, during which time the owner of the property is without recourse in the courts to contest the merits of the claim underlying the lien. . . . The plaintiff argues that the "taking" of the property under a mechanic's lien statute is de minimis. It is true that the depriva-tion which results from the filing of a mechanic's lien is not as obvious or as great as the dispossession of property under the statutes struck down in the *Snaidach* and *Fuentes* cases, but the recording of a mechanic's lien, while it does not prevent alienation of the property, does, as a practical matter, severely restrict the opportunity for and possibility of its alienation.

Following the decision in the *Roundhouse Construction Corp.* case, the Connecticut legislature extensively revised its mechanics' lien statutes in an effort to meet the Court's constitutional objection. Conn. Gen. Stat. Ann., §§ 49-33 to 49-40a (1994 & Supp. 2006).

Considerable law review commentary on constitutionality of various mechanics' lien statutes came along soon after *Snaidach, Fuentes,* and *Roundhouse Construction Corp.* Examples are Annual Survey of Oklahoma Law, 6 Okla. City Univ. L. Rev. 575-580 (1981); Frank and McManus, Balancing Almost Two Hundred Years of Economic Policy Against Contemporary Due Process Standards — Mechanics' Liens in Maryland After *Barry Properties,* 36 Md. L. Rev. 733 (1977); Note, Constitu-tionality of Mechanics' Liens Statutes, 34 Wash. & Lee L. Rev. 1067 (1977); Note, The Colorado Mechanics' Lien Statute: Is Due Process Provided?, 49 U. Colo. L. Rev. 127 (1977); and Comment, The Constitutional Validity of Mechanics' Liens Under the Due Process Clause — A Reexamination after *Mitchell* and *North Georgia,* 55 B.U.L. Rev. 263 (1975). Some states have revised their mechanics' lien statutes to provide greater due process protection. Two such statutory revisions are discussed in Comment, Nebraska Remakes the Mechanic's Lien: An Analysis of the Nebraska Construction Lien Act, 16 Creighton L. Rev. 128 (1982); and Note, Liens: Mechanics' and Materialmen's Liens: Conforming to New Statutes and the Bankruptcy Code, 36 Okla. L. Rev. 722 (1983).

NOTE ON OTHER OFF-RECORD RISKS

In addition to bona fide purchasers' off-record risks considered above, there are a scattering of other off-record risks they may run. Examples of some of these appear below. In no instance was the risk apparent from the face of the record, and yet the off-record interest was held paramount to that of the subsequent bona fide purchaser without notice. Chances of loss from such risks, however, are very slight, for incidents that could lead to these kinds of loss occur infrequently. Furthermore, as to some of the risks, most prevailing case law is favorable to bona fide purchasers without notice, following the strong judicial preference for these innocent takers. This preference commonly is exerted quite independently of the recording acts, and the trend in the cases seems to be toward further extending the immunity of bona fide purchasers. When bona fide purchasers are claiming through instruments asserted to be invalid, they are more likely to prevail if the court labels the instrument voidable instead of void. Their chances are also increased if the court finds negligent or dilatory conduct on the part of the other side or those through whom it is claiming. Although these off-record risks rarely cause losses to persons acquiring interests in land, they are a sufficient threat so that purchasers and lenders commonly take some precautions to avoid them, and the risks are major inducements to acquisition of title insurance. When loss occurs, it often is total, adding to the attraction of title insurance. Examples of these miscellaneous off-record risks are these:

(a) Incapacity of a grantor. A grantor in the bona fide purchaser's chain of title did not have the legal capacity to convey because mentally ill or feeble-minded, so the transfer was held invalid. Erickson v. Bohne, 130 Cal. App. 2d 553, 279 P.2d 619 (1955); Beavers v. Weatherly, 250 Ga. 546, 299 S.E.2d 730 (1983); and Dewey v. Allgire, 37 Neb. 6, 55 N.W. 276 (1893). Contra Brown v. Khoury, 346 Mich. 97, 77 N.W.2d 336 (1956).

(b) Defrauding of a grantor. A grantor in the bona fide purchaser's chain of title was tricked into signing a mineral deed when he thought he was signing a mineral lease. As a result of this "fraud in the execution," the court held the instrument void, passing nothing to the grantee or to bona fide purchasers from the grantee. Hauck v. Crawford, 75 S.D. 202, 62 N.W.2d 92 (1953). Contra Marlenee v. Brown, 21 Cal. 2d 668, 134 P.2d 770 (1943); and Dixon v. Kaufman, 79 N.D. 633, 58 N.W.2d 797 (1953).

(c) Forgery of an instrument. A forged or altered instrument in the bona fide purchaser's chain of title prevents the bona fide purchaser from acquiring a valid interest. Martin v. Carter, 400 A.2d 326 (D.C. 1979); Prater v. Prater, 208 Miss. 59, 44 So. 2d 582 (1949); and Mosley v. Magnolia Petroleum Co., 45 N.M. 230, 114 P.2d 740 (1941).

(d) No delivery of an instrument. An instrument in the bona fide purchaser's chain of title was never delivered because the grantee surreptitiously removed the deed from the glove compartment of the grantor's automobile, so no interest passed to the grantee or to a bona fide purchaser from the grantee. Watts v. Archer, 252 Iowa 592, 107 N.W.2d 549 (1961). Similar result when an escrow agent improperly gave up possession of a deed contrary to the terms of the escrow agreement. Blakeney v. Home Owners' Loan Corp., 192 Okla. 158, 135 P.2d 339 (1943).

(e) No acknowledgment of an instrument. An instrument in the bona fide purchaser's chain of title was not acknowledged and hence was void by the law of the controlling state. A notary public apparently filled out the acknowledgment blanks, so that on its face the instrument appeared to have been properly executed. But the notary was not present at the execution of the instrument and the grantor never made any acknowledgment statements to the notary. Dixon v. Kaufman, 79 N.D. 633, 58 N.W.2d 797 (1953).

(f) Subsequent probated will. Heirs of a decedent conveyed land to a bona fide purchaser and later a will was probated leaving the land to someone other than the conveying heirs. The devisee under the will was held to take as against the bona fide purchaser. Reid's Administrator v. Benge, 112 Ky. 810, 66 S.W. 997 (1902); and Barnhardt v. Morrison, 178 N.C. 563, 101 S.E. 218 (1919). Contra Eckland v. Jankowski, 407 Ill. 263, 95 N.E.2d 342 (1950).

(g) Pretermitted after-born child. Devisee under a will, subsequent to probate, borrowed money secured by a deed of trust on the devised land. Years later, an after-born and pretermitted child of the testator brought suit to determine title to the land and was held to have an interest superior to the holder of the trust deed, even though the trust deed holder had been unaware of the child's interest when the loan was made and security accepted. Conroy v. Conroy, 130 Tex. 508, 110 S.W.2d 570 (1938). Accord Chicago B. & Q.R. Co. v. Wasserman, 22 F. 872 (1885).

(h) Prior adverse possession. A record owner of land lost title to it as the result of adverse possession by a neighbor. Thereafter the record owner sold the land to a bona fide purchaser. The bona fide purchaser acquired no title to the land even though at the time of purchase the adverse possessor was not occupying the land and an examination of the premises would have disclosed no indication of the adverse possessor's claim to the land. Mugaas v. Smith, 33 Wash. 2d 429, 206 P.2d 332 (1949); accord: Taylor v. Tripp, 330 N.W.2d 542 (S.D. 1983).

As to each type of off-record risk illustrated above, what could a title searcher do to determine if a prior off-record interest exists? Would any of these search efforts be so costly that it would be unreasonable to expect them to be made?

On the subject of this note see Straw, Off-Record Risks for Bona-Fide Purchasers of Interests in Real Property, 72 Dick. L. Rev. 35 (1967). — STOP —

3. Eliminating Title Defects

Title defects, whether based on actual or potential claims and whether of record or not, may be eliminated in a variety of ways, one of the more common of which is through the passage of a prescribed period of time and operation of a statute of limitations or similar type statute that cuts off previously existing rights. Another common means is litigation, particularly the suit to quiet title, that can result in a decree clearing the title of some or all of its defects. Besides litigation, the defective title holder often has additional options for clearing his title, including, among others, such possibilities as buying up outstanding title interests; paying off lien or encumbrance claims; securing affidavits resolving troublesome questions of heirship, marital status, or identity of parties in the chain of title; surveying the premises so as to correct land description uncertainties; and recording a new instrument that rectifies errors in one that was previously recorded. On occasion, too, statutory changes in the substantive law may eliminate present or prospective title defects; for example, statutes abolishing dower. In rare instances, substantive statutory modifications in real property rights are even made for the express purpose of clearing title to a particular land parcel.

a. Statutes of Limitations, Adverse Possession, and Curative Acts

Legislatures have long attempted to make land titles more certain and to simplify the process of title search by enactments that cut off stale nonpossessory title claims.

Such enactments are usually classified as statutes of limitations. There has also been a long history of legislation that seeks to make titles more certain by validating defective instruments or transactions. The defects concerned are usually defects of form and until validated make the instruments or transactions partially or completely ineffectual. These latter kinds of statutes are commonly classified as curative acts, although not always clearly distinguishable from those labelled as statutes of limitations.[11] Adverse possession statutes also frequently operate to clear titles when the adverse holder has a questionable or clouded title, as he often does in adverse possession situations. Adverse possession statutes also frequently operate to clear titles when adverse holders have questionable or clouded titles, as commonly they do. Perhaps the major justification for retaining the adverse possession concept in modern property law is its very useful function of eliminating stale actual or potential possessory claims against land titles. Without the adverse possession concept, it frequently would be very difficult to resolve many title problems, or those benefiting from title claims often would be receiving hard-to-justify windfalls.

Weekes v. Rumbaugh

144 Neb. 103, 12 N.W.2d 636 (1944)

NUSS, District Judge. This action was commenced by appellee on April 11, 1942, to foreclose a mortgage executed and delivered November 12, 1926, and filed on November 23, 1926. By its terms the mortgage was due on November 3, 1929, but interest had been paid thereon November 24, 1933, to November 3, 1933. The original mortgage was never refiled nor was a copy thereof ever filed. On May 15, 1940, the defendant, appellant here, bought the land in question for value. Since more than ten years elapsed after the maturity of the mortgage debt before the action was brought the defendant claimed the action was barred by the statute of limitations, specifically Section 20-202, Comp. St. 1929. The trial court ruled against defendant and he appealed.

The mortgage was by its terms due on November 3, 1929. It was therefore barred on November 3, 1939, and the defendant below acquired good title, relieved of the lien of the mortgage, by his purchase for value on May 15, 1940, unless the period of limitation was postponed, extended or tolled by the payment of interest on November 24, 1933. The defendant claims that the amendment of 1925 (Laws 1925, Ch. 64) to Section 6 of the code of civil procedure, Section 20-202, Comp. St. 1929, did so bar the mortgage and the lien and that he acquired a title therefor free and relieved of the said lien.

The plaintiff on the other hand contends that under the decision of this court in Steeves v. Nispel, 132 Neb. 597, 273 N.W. 50, the amendment of 1925 was invalidated or circumscribed so that the payment of interest tolled the ten year period. There is no allegation that the amendment of 1925 was or is unconstitutional, nor is it claimed that the *Nispel* case so held. The amendment is therefore presumed to be constitutional. "The basic principle which underlies the entire field of legal concepts pertaining to the validity of legislation is that by enactment of legislation, a

11. For efforts to distinguish statutes of limitations and curative acts, see Basye, Clearing Land Titles 36-37 (2d ed. 1970); and Simes and Taylor, The Improvement of Conveyancing by Legislation 17, 37 (1960).

constitutional measure is presumed to be created. In every case where a question is raised as to the constitutionality of an act, the court employs this doctrine in scrutinizing the terms of the law. In a great volume of cases the courts have enunciated the fundamental rule that there is a presumption in favor of the constitutionality of a legislative enactment." 11 Am. Jur. 776, sec. 128.

In State v. Adams Express Co., 85 Neb. 25, 122 N.W. 691, 693, 42 L.R.A., N.S., 396, it is said: "In making the investigations we start with the presumption that the statute in question is a valid and constitutional exercise of legislative power. [Citations omitted.] In [Davis v. State, 51 Neb. 301, 70 N.W. 984] the rule is well stated as follows: 'Every legislative act comes before this court surrounded with the presumption of constitutionality, and this presumption continues until the act under review clearly appears to contravene some provision of the Constitution.'"

The burden of proof of the invalidity of any statute is therefore upon the one so claiming. "In consequence of the general presumption in favor of the validity of acts of the legislature and desires of the courts in resolving all doubts in favor of their validity, the rule has become established that courts will not search the constitution for express sanction or for reasonable implication to sustain a legislative enactment; the successful assailant must be able to point out the particular provision that has been violated and the ground on which it has been infringed." 11 Am. Jur. 795, sec. 132, and many cases cited.

The question relative to the constitutionality of the act must be presented to the trial court else it cannot be considered by this court. Howarth v. Becker, 128 Neb. 580, 259 N.W. 505; State v. Knudtsen, 121 Neb. 270, 236 N.W. 696; Mergenthaler Linotype Co. v. McNamee, 125 Neb. 71, 249 N.W. 92. In the first two cases above cited this court applied the rule notwithstanding that the person claiming the invalidity of the statute was successful in the district court. Thus in the case of Howarth v. Becker, supra [128 Neb. 580, 259 N.W. 506], it was said:

> The appellee contends that the trial court rightfully denied the application for two reasons, first, that the Moratory Act, section 20-21, 159, Comp. St. Supp. 1933, is unconstitutional. . . .
>
> We have carefully examined the record in this case and we fail to find that the unconstitutionality of section 20-21, 159, Comp. St. Supp. 1933, was pleaded or presented to the trial court for determination. This court has consistently held that in order for this court to consider the question of the constitutionality of a statute, it must first be raised and placed in issue in the trial court. First Trust Co. v. Glendale Realty Co., 125 Neb. 283, 250 N.W. 68; Bell v. Niemann, 127 Neb. 762, 257 N.W. 69. We therefore hold that the question whether the Nebraska Moratory Act violates the Nebraska Constitution is not determinable in this court on this appeal for the reason that it was not presented to the district court in this case.

For the foregoing reasons any question relative to the constitutionality of the amendment of 1925 cannot be considered, and this court must presume for the purpose of this proceeding, that the amendment is valid and constitutional.

The question then arises as to the proper consideration to be given to the amendment in question. It is entirely clear, as established by an overwhelming array of authorities, that the cardinal principle of construction or interpretation of a statute is to arrive at and give effect to the intention of the legislature. 25 R.C.L. 960. City of Lincoln v. Nebraska Workmen's Compensation Court, 133 Neb. 225, 274 N.W. 576; Kearney County v. Hapeman, 102 Neb. 550, 167 N.W. 792.

Since the act in question is clearly remedial it is well to call attention to several other pertinent rules, to wit: "In construing a remedial statute three things must be considered, viz., 'the old law, the mischief and the remedy.'" Clother v. Maher, 15 Neb. 1, 16 N.W. 902. See also City of Lincoln v. Nebraska Workmen's Compensation Court, supra. Further, a remedial statute is to receive a liberal construction to carry into effect the purposes for which it was enacted. City of Lincoln v. Nebraska Workmen's Compensation Court, supra; State v. Fremont, E. & M.V.R. Co., 22 Neb. 313, 35 N.W. 118; Becker & Degen v. Brown, 65 Neb. 264, 91 N.W. 178. And that a statute of doubtful meaning should be construed, if reasonably possible, so as to carry out the purpose and intention of the legislature, and when this purpose is manifest it will prevail over a seeming conflict in the language. City of Lincoln v. Nebraska Workmen's Compensation Court, supra. State v. Ure, 91 Neb. 31, 135 N.W. 224.

With these rules in mind we proceed to a discussion of the law in question. Prior to the amendment of 1925 (Laws 1925, Ch. 64) to Section 6 of the code of civil procedure, that section provided that an action for the recovery of the title or possession of lands, tenements or hereditaments, "or for the foreclosure of mortgages thereon," could only be brought within ten years after the cause of action shall have accrued. Sec. 8507, Comp. St. 1922. By construing the above section with certain other sections, as this court held in Teegarden v. Burton, 62 Neb. 639, 87 N.W. 337, and McLaughlin v. Senne, 78 Neb. 631, 111 N.W. 377, should be done, the ten year period was extended under Section 22 of the code (Sec. 8522, Comp. St. 1922) by part payment, written acknowledgment of debt or promise to pay. It was likewise postponed by Section 7 of the code, (Sec. 8518, Comp. St. 1922) in favor of any person "under any legal disability"; under Section 17 (Sec. 8519, Comp. St. 1922) in favor of any person "within the age of twenty-one years, insane or imprisoned." Again, it was tolled by Section 20 of the code (Sec. 8520, Comp. St. 1922) against any person "out of state, or shall have absconded or concealed himself." It is thus seen that the basic ten year period provided in Section 6 of the code could be postponed almost indefinitely for a variety of reasons, not one of which necessarily appeared on the face of the record. In the course of time a great many old unreleased mortgages accumulated on the records and clouded the titles. Since it was possible to extend the basic ten year period in the various ways above mentioned an examiner of titles in such case was compelled to assume that an old unreleased mortgage had been tolled in one of the ways mentioned and was still in effect.

On the contrary, in the case of mechanics liens, every one dealing with any land knew that when the period of two years had elapsed the lien could be disregarded with impunity and would cast no cloud upon the title. Goodwin v. Cunningham, 54 Neb. 11, 74 N.W. 315; Green v. Sanford, 34 Neb. 363, 51 N.W. 967. Although the two year period for the foreclosure of mechanic's liens was only one-fifth of the basic ten year period for the foreclosure of mortgages, that period had proved entirely satisfactory for many years and there has apparently never been any attempt to change it. If a definite period of limitation, not subject to extension for any reason, was satisfactory and desirable in the case of mechanics liens, there can be no reason why the same or a similar unqualified provision would not be equally desirable as to mortgages.

Evidently with some such thought the legislature in 1925 amended Section 6 of the code above mentioned by clarifying when the cause of action should be deemed to accrue. It provided that such cause should be assumed to accrue, "at the last date of the maturity of the debt or other obligation secured thereby, as stated in, or as ascertainable from the record of such mortgage. . . ." Later in the amendment it was provided:

> At the expiration of ten years from the date the cause of action accrues on any mortgage as is herein provided, such mortgage shall be presumed to have been paid, and the mortgage and the record thereof shall cease to be notice of the mortgage as unpaid and the lien thereof shall then cease absolutely as to subsequent purchasers and encumbrancers for value; said period of ten years shall not be extended by non-residence, legal disability, partial payment, or acknowledgment of debt.

Bearing in mind the old law, the mischief and the remedy, there can be no doubt that the legislature intended by the above to fix a definite unconditional period of limitation which could be extended only as therein provided by a refiling of the mortgage or a sworn copy thereof. Clearly the legislature intended to bar all mortgages where, on the face of the record, the cause of action accrued more than ten years previously, and that, regardless of anything which might formerly have tolled or extended the period. Only by making the period completely immune from being extended for any reason except as provided in the act would the law serve any useful purpose. See 17 Nebraska Law Bulletin, 137, 144. This being true the law should be so construed as to subserve the legislative purpose. The words of the act: "shall not be extended by non-residence, legal disability, partial payment, or acknowledgment of debt," should not receive a narrow or strict interpretation, but should be broadly and liberally construed to exclude every method or manner of tolling the statute, unless the mortgage is refiled or a sworn copy thereof filed.

The beneficial features of this legislation so overwhelmingly outweigh the trifling inconvenience to holders of mortgages that no reason can be conceived of why the amendment should be strictly construed.

As applied to this case the words "partial payment" in the act clearly include payments of principal and interest. The notes in question provided for the payment of a certain amount of money as principal and a certain amount or rate of money as interest. The principal and interest together at any given time constituted the indebtedness. The payment of principal or of interest which does not pay and satisfy the entire indebtedness is clearly a partial payment and, therefore, within the very terms of the law. Consequently the period of limitations in this case was not extended or tolled by the partial payment of interest and the lien of the mortgage was barred.

The case of Steeves v. Nispel, supra, relied on by plaintiff does not sustain her. It merely held that unrecorded written extension agreements are not included under any of the terms, "Non-residence, legal disability, partial payment, or acknowledgment of debt," in the amendment of 1925, and therefore, such written extension agreement will toll the ten year period. It seems to the writer of this opinion that the court in that case gave to the amendment of 1925 and the terms just quoted altogether too strict and narrow an interpretation and application. The writer believes that the legislative intent is entirely clear that as against purchasers and lienors for value, nothing should toll the ten year period unless the mortgage is refiled or a copy thereof filed. However, whether the writer's criticism is or is not valid, the *Nispel* case goes as far in restricting the operation of the amendment as the court is disposed to go. It does not justify the additional restriction upon the act sought to be imposed herein. While the 1925 amendment may not, in specific terms, exclude written promises or extension agreements from tolling the period, it does, expressly and specifically, prohibit "partial payments" from so extending it.

It is unnecessary to consider the effect of the 1941 amendment, Laws 1941, c. 35, since the mortgage in question was fully barred many months before that amendment was adopted.

The judgment of the district court is reversed and the action dismissed.

Reversed and dismissed.

NOTES

1. Certain kinds of claimants commonly are exempted from adverse application of statutes of limitation. Those often favored in this way are persons under legal disability, holders of future interests prior to rights becoming possessory, spouses with inchoate dower or curtesy rights, and federal and state governments. In addition, in many states, certain events can stop the running of the statutory period to the disadvantage of those who would otherwise benefit. Part payment of an overdue mortgage debt is an example of such a tolling of the limitations period. One result of these exempting and tolling preferences so far as land titles are concerned is to make statutes of limitations much less effective as title clearance and protection devices for those claiming interests in land against which old, stale claims are outstanding. Owners wishing to sell or mortgage may find that they do not have marketable title because of such claims. Decades of adverse possession may even be ineffectual to create good title.

A trend has long been apparent to cut down on exceptions to the running of limitations periods. One approach has been to eliminate the exceptions, at least in some situations. The Nebraska statute construed in Weekes v. Rumbaugh illustrates this. Another way of dealing with limitations exceptions is to place an absolute time limit on how long the exception may extend running of the period. An Oregon statute, for instance, does this:

> If, at the time of the cause of action accrues, any person entitled to bring [certain actions, including those for the recovery of real property] is within the age of 18 years or insane, the time of such disability shall not be a part of the time limited for the commencement of the action; but the period within which the action shall be brought shall not be extended more than five years by any such disability, nor shall it be extended in any case longer than one year after such disability ceases.

Or. Rev. Stat. § 12.160 (2005).

Still another way of weakening exceptions is to require an additional recording or a judicial proceeding to keep excepted interests alive. This approach has also been used more broadly to limit interests not treated as exceptions. The marketable title acts have incorporated this re-recording approach. Another is the following Iowa statute, Iowa Code Ann. § 614.15(1):

> In all cases where the holder of the legal or equitable title or estate to real estate situated within this state, prior to July 1, 1991, conveyed the real estate or any interest in

the real estate by deed, mortgage, or other instrument, and the spouse failed to join in the conveyance, the spouse or the heirs at law, personal representatives, devisees, grantees, or assignees of the spouse are barred from recovery unless suit is brought for recovery within one year after July 1, 1980. But in case the right to the distributive share has not accrued by the death of the spouse making the instrument, then the one not joining is authorized to file in the recorder's office of the county where the land is situated, a notice with affidavit setting forth affiant's claim, together with the facts upon which the claim rests, and the residence of the claimants. If the notice is not filed within two years from July 1, 1991, the claim is barred forever. Any action contemplated in this section may include land situated in different counties, by giving notice as provided by section 617.13.

2. The following Oklahoma statute, Okla. Stat. Ann. tit. 16, § 4 (West 1953, Supp. 1976-1977), was held constitutional in Saak v. Hicks, 321 P.2d 425 (Okla. 1958):

. . . a deed relating to the homestead shall be valid without the signature of the grantor's spouse, and the spouse shall be conclusively deemed to have consented thereto, where the same shall have been duly recorded in the office of the county clerk of the county where the real estate is situated for a period of ten (10) years prior to a date six (6) months after the effective date thereof, and thereafter when the same shall have been so recorded for a period of ten (10) years, and no action shall have been instituted within said time in any court of record having jurisdiction seeking to cancel, avoid or invalidate such deed relating to the homestead by reason of the alleged homestead character of the real estate at the time of such conveyance.

3. One means of making titles more certain, as well as to make many fee titles more marketable, is to limit the time that certain kinds of land interests may be valid. An example is Minn. Stats. Ann. § 500.20 (West Supp. 2006), that, with some exceptions, limits covenants, conditions, or restrictions affecting land to 30 years after their creation. In addition, § 500.20 makes such interests ineffectual and they may be wholly disregarded if they become of no benefit to those in whose favor they are to be performed.

4. All American states have adverse possession statutes, a form of statute of limitations that can result in the adverse holder acquiring unencumbered title to the land. In many instances the adverse holder has a defective title and his adverse possession for the statutory period results in the claims against his title being terminated. Although state adverse possession statutes differ considerably in the details of their coverage, this North Carolina enactment is typical:

No action for the recovery or possession of real property, or the issues and profits thereof, shall be maintained when the person in possession thereof, or defendant in the action, or those under whom he claims, has possessed the property under known and visible lines and boundaries adversely to all other persons for twenty years; and such possession so held gives a title in fee to the possessor, in such property, against all persons not under disability.

N.C. Gen. Stat. § 1-40 (2005).

In some states the period of time required to make out title by adverse possession is shortened if the adverse holder also has a claim of title that although defective is sufficient to constitute color of title. The following are illustrative of such statutes:

735 Ill. Comp. Stat. Ann. § 513-109 (West 2000)

Payment of taxes with color of title. Every person in the actual possession of lands or tenements, under claim and color of title, made in good faith, and who for 7 successive years, continues in such possession, and also, during such time, pays all taxes legally assessed on such lands or tenements, shall be held and adjudged to be the legal owner of such lands or tenements, to the extent and according to the purport of his or her paper title. All persons holding under such possession, by purchase, legacy or descent, before such 7 years have expired, and who continue such possession, and continue to pay the taxes as above set forth so as to complete the possession and payment of taxes for the term above set forth is entitled to the benefit of this Section.

Fla. Stat. Ann. (West 2002)

§ 95.16

(1) When the occupant, or those under whom he claims, entered into possession of real property under a claim of title exclusive of any other right, founding the claim on a written instrument as being a conveyance of the property, or on a decree or judgment, and has for 7 years been in continued possession of the property included in the instrument, decree, or judgment, the property is held adversely. If the property is divided into lots, the possession of one lot shall not be deemed a possession of any other lot of the same tract. Adverse possession commencing after December 31, 1945, shall not be deemed adverse possession under color of title until the instrument upon which the claim of title is founded is recorded in the office of the clerk of the circuit court of the county where the property is located.

In a few states, only persons with color of title may successfully acquire title by adverse possession. E.g., N.M. Stat. Ann. § 37-1-22 (2002).

Dennen v. Searle

149 Conn. 126, 176 A.2d 561 (1961)

KING, Associate Justice. On September 18, 1941, Mary A. Searle conveyed a tract of land in Windsor to her four children as tenants in common. These children comprised the three plaintiffs in this action, Rena L. (Searle) Dennen, Ralph B. Searle and Inez C. Searle, and also Elbert A. Searle, the deceased husband of Mildred Beebe Searle, the defendant in this action. Although Mary A. Searle reserved a life estate in herself, this need not be considered, since she apparently died prior to the execution of the instrument here in controversy.

On June 21, 1948, all four children joined in the execution of an unartfully drawn instrument which is styled "Agreement" and which purports to change the rights and interests of the cotenants inter se and to convey to others certain remainder interests in the land. This instrument remained unrecorded until May 19, 1953. The defendant's husband died intestate on May 10, 1953, leaving, as those entitled to his estate, the defendant and her two children, Milton C. and Enid L. Searle. See General Statutes, §§ 46-12, 45-274. The defendant knew nothing of the agreement until after her husband's death. The plaintiffs are in possession of the property and claim that their rights in it are those purportedly given them under the agreement. The defendant and her two children, at some undisclosed time after her husband's death but prior to February 19, 1955, executed a mutual distribution of the estate of her husband wherein all of his interest in the tract question was set to her. No claim is made that this mutual distribution was executed prior to the effective date of the validating act hereinafter discussed.

The plaintiffs brought this action to quiet title under General Statutes, § 47-31. They alleged possession in themselves and such other rights and interests in the property as were purportedly given them by the agreement, and also that the defendant claimed rights in the property adverse to them. They asked for a judgment determining her rights in the property and settling the title thereto. Since none of the remaindermen other than the defendant were made parties, their rights cannot be authoritatively determined, and we confine our consideration to the rights of the plaintiffs and the defendant in the property. The remaindermen should have been made parties, and we decide this case only because, as hereinafter appears, our construction of the agreement and our determination of the claims of law made in respect to it deprive the remaindermen of nothing. See cases such as Auchincloss v. City Bank Farmers Trust Co., 136 Conn. 266, 273, 70 A.2d 105.

The plaintiffs claim their interests in the property solely under and by virtue of the agreement, which they claim is a valid deed. The defendant asserts that the agreement is inoperative as a deed for a number of reasons. . . .

The defendant also claims that even if the instrument is a deed, it is inoperative for lack of any seal. Since there is no seal, the instrument fails to conform to the requirements as to the due execution of a conveyance of realty as set forth in General Statues, § 47-5, and on its face is inoperative as a deed. See Savings Bank of New Haven v. Davis, 8 Conn. 191, 212; Howe v. Keeler, 27 Conn. 538, 555; Bickart v. Sanditz, 105 Conn. 766, 772, 136 A. 580. The plaintiffs claim that this defect was cured by subsequent validating acts. At the legislative sessions of 1949, 1951 and 1953, acts were enacted, in substantially identical language, validating properly recorded conveyances which were defective because of the absence of a seal. None purported to validate a conveyance unless the conveyance had been recorded nor in fact did it. Mangusi v. Vigiliotti, 104 Conn. 291, 295, 132 A. 464. The agreement was recorded May 19, 1953, so that it was validated, if validation was possible, by the 1953 validating act, which, as a special act, took effect upon its approval by the governor on June 30, 1953. General Statutes, § 2-32. The defendant claim that the validating act could not affect her, since its operative date was subsequent to that of her husband's death and at the moment of his death his interest vested in those entitled to his intestate estate, that is, the defendant and his heirs at law, the two children. See General Statutes, §§ 46-12, 45-274; Parlato v. McCarthy, 136 Conn. 126, 133, 69 A.2d 648; O'Connor v. Chiascione, 130 Conn. 304, 306, 33 A.2d 336, 148 A.L.R. 169; Ziulkowski v. Kolodziej, 119 Conn. 230, 233, 175 A. 780, 96 A.L.R. 1065; 2 Locke & Kohn, Conn. Probate Practice § 266.

"What the Legislature may prescribe it may dispense with, and it may cure by subsequent act an irregularity of nonobservance of requirements which it originally might have dispensed with, provided that vested rights have not intervened." Sanger v. City of Bridgeport, 124 Conn. 183, 186, 198 A. 746, 748, 116 A.L.R. 1031. Since the requirement of a seal was prescribed by statute, there can be no question of the right of the General Assembly to cure the defect arising from the omission of a seal, as between the parties of the instrument. Ibid. Thus, if the agreement had been recorded, and its validation had occurred, before the death of Elbert A. Searle, the deed would have been effectually validated. He could have had no equitable justification for objecting to the validation. The question arises as to what equities this defendant has which her husband lacked. At the moment of his death, a one-third interest in his interest in the property vested in her. She paid nothing for it. She did nothing in reliance on the state of the record title. She was not a creditor of her husband's estate. Her position is not that of a bona fide purchaser for value, or even of a purchaser for value with notice. She has no equities other than those he had. See cases such as Finnegan v. LaFontaine, 122 Conn. 561, 568, 191 A. 337; Sanford v. DeForest, 85 Conn. 694, 698, 84 A. 111; Green v. Abraham, 43 Ark. 420, 425. In short, she could not by the mere act of inheritance gain interests, legal or equitable, in the property greater than those of the person from whom she inherited. Shadden v. Zimmerlee, 401 Ill. 118, 125, 81 N.E.2d 477. Her interest, to be sure vested at the time of her husband's death, but her interest was a one-third interest in his interest, with whatever infirmities his interest had, including the possibility of validation of the deed. First School District v. Ufford, 52 Conn. 44, 49; Watson v. Mercer, 8 Pet. 88, 33 U.S. 88, 110, 8 L. Ed. 876. The 1953 validating act was effective to cure the lack of a seal in the deed. . . .

The court correctly held that the defendant's interest in the property in question is limited to the remainder interest granted her under the final dispositive clause of the deed; that this interest is defeasible by the exercise of the power of sale given the surviving cotenants; and that neither she nor the other distributees of the estate of Elbert A. Searle acquired, either by descent or distribution, any interests in the property which survived the validation of the deed.

There is no error.

NOTES

1. The curative act held applicable in the principal case provides:

> Any deed, lease or other instrument made for the purpose of conveying, leasing or affecting real property, or pertaining to or affecting any interest therein, and recorded in the land records of the town in which such land is located, which deed, lease or other instrument was not sealed by the parties, or any of them; any deed, lease or other instrument made for the purpose of conveying, leasing or affecting real property, or pertaining to or affecting any interest therein, recorded in the land records of the town in which such land is located, the acknowledgment of which was not completed, or was erroneously taken or recited, or was taken by a person not having authority to take such acknowledgment or where the authority of the person taking such acknowledgment was not stated or authenticated, or where no acknowledgment by the parties, or any of them, to such deed, lease or instrument was taken, is validated. [1953 Conn. Spec. Laws c. 26, § 7, at 1035.]

Why do you think the Connecticut legislature passed this kind of curative act rather than repealing the seal and acknowledgment requirements?

Note that subsequent to the above 1953 act, the Connecticut legislature at various times has updated validations by a series of similar statutes. This practice of updating validations by a series of comparable curative acts has occurred in a number of states.

2. Some curative acts apply to defective instruments as they become of record for a set number of years. The following is illustrative of a broad statute of this kind:

> When any owner of land the title to which is not registered, or of any interest in such land, signs an instrument in writing conveying or purporting to convey his land or interest, or in any manner affecting or purporting to affect his title thereto, and the instrument, whether or not entitled to record, is recorded, and indexed, in the registry of deeds for the district wherein such land is situated, and a period of ten years elapses after the instrument is accepted for record, and the instrument or the record thereof because of defect, irregularity or omission fails to comply in any respect with any requirement of law relating to seals, corporate or individual, to the validity of acknowledgment, to certificate of acknowledgment, witnesses, attestation, proof of execution, or time of execution, to recitals of consideration, residence, address, or date, to the authority of a person signing for a corporation who purports to be the president or treasurer or a principal officer of the corporation, such instrument and the record thereof shall notwithstanding any or all of such defects, irregularities and omissions, be effective for all purposes to the same extent as though the instrument and the record thereof had originally not been subject to the defect, irregularity or omission, unless within said period of ten years a proceeding is commenced on account of the defect, irregularity or omission, and notice thereof is duly recorded in said registry of deeds and indexed and noted on the margin thereof under the name of the signer of the instrument and, in the event of such proceeding, unless relief is thereby in due course granted. [Mass. Gen. Laws Ann. c. 184, §24 (West 1991).]

3. In Sabasteanski v. Pagurko, 232 A.2d 524 (Me. 1967), the Maine Supreme Court refused to apply a validating act retroactively, stating:

> The curative statute was clearly designed to have retrospective application but such statutes must be carefully construed so as not to violate constitutional requirements: "There can be no doubt that Legislatures have the power to pass retrospective statutes, if they affect remedies only. Such is the well settled law of this State. But they have no constitutional power to enact retrospective laws which impair vested rights, or create personal liabilities." [Citations omitted.] . . . [Quoting with approval] Patton on titles, Vol. 1, page 273, Sec. 83 wherein it is stated: "But because of the constitutional protection to vested rights, curative acts are inoperative, as to all innocent third persons who acquired their rights before enactment of the statutes."
>
> Applying the law as thus stated to the facts of the instant case it follows that plaintiff was first to receive and record a valid deed of the three-acre parcel and as a third-party purchaser with vested rights, his title cannot be destroyed by the validating statute. [524 A.2d at 525-526.]

b. Suits to Quiet Title

Title to land can be adjudicated in a number of different kinds of proceedings, but the most important in many American states is the suit to quiet title. Suits of this sort are frequently brought to clear and thereby protect titles when owners wish to sell or mortgage, when defects been discovered that make the titles unmarketable and less valuable, and when easier title clearance means are inadequate for the job. Only a small percentage of these proceedings are contested, either because the defendants' claims are of such dubious value as not to be worth the bother or, if service is by publication, so old and remote that the defendants, who may not even know they have claims, never receive actual notice of suit. The title clearance possibilities of suits to quiet title differ considerably from state to state. In a few states, broad in rem proceedings are provided for that can generally purge titles of all defects, if the suits are not successfully defended. More typically, however, requirements of personal service, relative ease of direct or collateral attack, and severe restrictions on who can bring such proceedings have greatly limited the potential of suits to quiet title. Both legislatures and courts have generally been reluctant to increase the title clearing effectiveness of the suit to quiet title device. Concern over summary deprivation of defendants' rights has apparently been the principal reason for this reticence. Constitutional considerations have occasionally been crucial, although it is clear that rather strongly pro-plaintiff quiet title legislation can be devised that will withstand constitutional attack.

Berry v. Howard

33 S.D. 447, 146 N.W. 577 (1914)

POLLEY, J. The record in this case shows that one Eberhart Thomson died intestate, on the 3d day of March, 1904, and that, at the time of his death, he was seized in fee of a 120-acre tract of land in Brown county; that, in 1905, this land was sold by the treasurer of the county for the taxes thereon; that, no redemption having been made from said sale, a treasurer's deed, purporting to convey the said land to the purchaser at the said tax sale, was issued on the 25th day of March, 1908; and thereafter, on the 11th day of May, 1908, the grantee in said treasurer's deed conveyed the said premises to the appellant in this action. The respondent is the administrator of the estate of the said Thomson, and this action, commenced within less than three years after the issuance of said deed, is brought for the purpose of having the said tax deed canceled and title to the premises in controversy quieted in the estate of the plaintiff's intestate. The case has been once before this court, upon an appeal from an order overruling a demurrer to plaintiff's complaint (Berry v. Howard, 26 S.D. 29, 127 N.W. 526, Ann. Cas. 1913A, 994) where plaintiff's right to maintain the action in his representative capacity is sustained; and it is conceded that said premises belong to the said estate, unless the title thereto was divested by the tax deed to defendant's grantor, and certain court proceedings that will be hereinafter noticed.

It is claimed by the respondent that there were numerous defects and informalities in the various proceedings leading up to the issuance of the tax deed, which render the deed voidable; but, in the view we take of the case, it will be unnecessary to consider more than one of these defects. Respondent's intestate was never married, but left surviving him, as his sole heirs at law, a sister and three brothers, to wit, Mary A. Hall, Halver Roass, Ole Silerud, and Martin Bjekness. At the time of, prior to, and ever since the death of the said Thomson, his said sister, Mary A. Hall, lived on land adjoining the land of Thomson; and it was at her house that he lived, and where he died. The trial court found as a fact that, upon the death of said Thomson, on the 3d day of March, 1904, the said Mary A. Hall took possession of, and remained in possession of, the said premises until after respondent was appointed administrator of Thomson's estate, on the 29th day of December, 1908, when he took possession thereof. Prior to the issuance of the tax deed upon which appellant bases his claim of title, his grantor undertook to serve the notice required by section 2212 of the Pol. Code. The notice attempted to be served in this instance was addressed as follows: "To Eberhart Tomson, otherwise known as Eberhart Thomson, the owner, person in possession and in whose name the S. 1/2 of the S.E. 1/4 and N.W. 1/4 of the S.E. 1/4, Sec. six (6), in township one hundred twenty-seven (127) north, range sixty-five (65) west 5th P. M., in Brown county, South Dakota, is taxed, and to all other persons in interest." Then follows the regular statutory notice of expiration of period of redemption and issuance of tax deed. This notice was served by the sheriff of Brown county, as the agent of the holder of the said tax sale certificate, upon one Martin C. Hall, who is a son of the said Mary A. Hall, and resided with her on land adjoining the disputed premises. It was also published in a legal newspaper in that county for the statutory length of time.

It is contended by the respondent, and the trial court so held, that this did not constitute service of the notice of issuance of tax deed as is required by said section 2212. In our opinion the court was correct in so holding. The contents and manner of service of the notice of the issuance of a tax deed has been the subject of consideration by this and other courts in the past. [Citations omitted.]

Section 2212 designates the person upon whom notice of the issuance of tax deed must be served. It names two classes of persons upon whom service may be made and is in the alternative. It must be served "upon the owner . . . of the land so sold, and upon the person in possession of such land or town lot unredeemed, and also upon the person in whose name the land is taxed." It is optional with the holder of the certificate whether he serve the owner of the land or the person in possession thereof; but it is imperative, in all cases, that he serve one or the other of them and that he also serve the person in whose name the land is taxed. This gives the holder of the certificate the option: First, of serving the owner of the land, and also the person in whose name it is taxed; or, second, he may serve the person in possession and also the person in whose name the land is taxed. Of course, if the land is taxed to an "unknown" owner, then the notice cannot be served upon the person in whose name it is taxed, there being no such person to serve. In this case, Eberhart Thomson, the person in whose name the land was taxed, being dead, service on him could not be made; and, having been dead at the time the land was assessed for taxation, it should be treated as though it were a case where the land were taxed to an unknown owner. This is the rule adopted in Iowa under a similar statute: "As there was no person in existence to whom the land was assessed and taxed, the situation may be said to be analogous to that where lands are assessed and taxed under the heading as to ownership of 'unknown.'" Grimes v. Ellyson, 130 Iowa 286, 105 N.W. 418. The affidavit of service of the notice upon Martin C. Hall contains the averment that he was then in possession of the land; but, as the notice was not addressed to him, and as he was in no wise mentioned therein as the party who was to be affected by such notice, the service upon him was a nullity. Woods v. Hardy, supra. And, moreover, the court found that at this identical time the land was in the possession of Mary A. Hall. No attempt ever having been made to serve her as the party in possession, the notice, in order to have had any validity whatever, must have been served in one of the ways pointed out by the statute upon the owners of the land; but, as we have already seen, Mary A. Hall, Halver Roass, Ole Silerud, and Martin Bjekness were the owners of the land at the time of the attempted service of the notice; and, although Mary A. Hall lived upon land adjoining the premises to be affected by the notice, no attempt was ever made to serve her or to give notice to either of the other owners. Therefore the treasurer was wholly without jurisdiction to issue the deed.

But this deed, though irregularly issued and subject to cancellation, was yet color of title; and appellant, for the purpose of putting outstanding claims, if any existed against the disputed premises, at rest, immediately after he acquired his interest therein, commenced an action in the circuit court for Brown county, under the provisions of chapter 81, Laws of 1905. Said action was not only brought for the purpose of quieting the title to the real property involved in this action, but included a large number of segregated tracts situated in Brown county and was against a large number of persons who were named as defendants, and against the heirs, devisees, legatees, executors, administrators, and creditors of any deceased person, or persons, who might have, or claim to have, any interest in any of the described premises adverse to the claims of the plaintiff in that action. Said action was prosecuted to final determination, and decree therein was entered on the 11th day of September, A.D. 1908. This decree purports to quiet the title to the disputed premises in the appellant as against all the world, with the exception of the said Mary A. Hall and Martin C. Hall; and it is now urged by the appellant that, although the said tax deed may have been insufficient to bar a recovery in this action, such recovery is barred by the said decree.

In that action, the said Mary A. and Martin C. Hall were made defendants by name and were served personally with the summons and complaint. They both appeared and answered in the case: but upon the filing of their answers, the appellant, upon his own motion, and at his own costs, caused the dismissal of the said action as to those two defendants, and the decree entered in said action does not purport to quiet the appellant's title as against either of them. This left the one-fourth interest in the disputed premises, inherited from the said Eberhart Thomson by Mary A. Hall, undetermined, and, as to her, the said decree is not a bar or any hindrance to the assertion of her claim to a one-fourth interest in the said premises in this action. As to the interests of the other three heirs of Eberhart Thomson, a more difficult question is presented, and one that will require careful analysis of chapter 81, Laws of 1905. If they were in fact parties defendant to the said action, then the plaintiff is barred from the assertion of any claims on their behalf in this action, and such an attempt would be a collateral attack on said judgment and cannot be maintained.

From the language used in said act, its scope is as broad as it can well be made. The action which a claimant to an interest in real property is authorized by this law to maintain is virtually against all the world, and may determine every conceivable interest adverse to plaintiff, and against all claimants — whether known or unknown.

But there are some limitations that must be observed. In order to make one a party defendant to such action he must be named as such and served with a summons by some method pointed out by the Code, unless his name cannot, by the exercise of due diligence, be ascertained.

Neither of the said owners (Halver Roass, Ole Silerud, or Martin Bjekness) was made defendant by name; and therefore whether they were parties defendant to the suit depends upon whether proper diligence was exercised in the attempt to ascertain their names. Service of the summons in said action was made by publication, and the affidavit of the plaintiff therein, upon which the order of publication was issued, was received in evidence and is made a part of the record on the appeal in this action. This affidavit sets out, in great detail, the effort made by appellant to learn the whereabouts of certain of the named defendants as well as the names of others unknown. This effort consisted of inquiry of various parties in Brown county, an examination of the county records of that county, and some correspondence; but it is a significant fact that no inquiry was made of the said Martin C. Hall, whom appellant claims was in possession of the disputed premises, nor of Mary A. Hall, whom the court found as a fact to be in possession of said premises. Both these parties were named as defendants, both were served, and both answered. While neither of these answers appear in the record, it may be assumed that the answer of Mary A. Hall, who is the owner of a one-fourth interest in said land, set out her source of title. This must have suggested inquiry which, if made by appellant, would certainly have led to the identification and probable location of the other owners — thus enabling appellant to have made them parties by name and give them notice of the pendency of the action. Instead of doing this, appellant dismissed his action as to those two defendants and made no effort whatever to have their interests, if any, determined. This leads to the inference that the appellant did not desire to have the title to the disputed premises determined in said action, and that the said heirs of Eberhart Thomson were not parties to the said action, and the court was wholly without jurisdiction to adjudicate their rights.

"Due diligence," as used in section 2 of chapter 81, Laws of 1905, has the same meaning as it does where used in section 112, Code Civ. Proc., and requires the same good faith effort on the part of the plaintiff in an action prosecuted under said chapter 81 to ascertain the name of a party who is to be divested of his interest in real property as said section 112 does to ascertain his whereabouts. This court has indicated the character of effort that is required by section 112, and, as it is a matter of vital import in proceedings under chapter 81, we reiterate and quote at length from what we said in Grigsby v. Wopschall, 25 S.D. 564, 127 N.W. 605, 37 L.R.A. (N.S.) 206: "While, in this class of cases, it is not necessary that all possible or conceivable means should be used to ascertain the whereabouts of a defendant, still it is necessary that the affidavit for publication should show that all reasonable means have been used to discover the whereabouts of defendant, to the end that he may receive actual notice of the pendency of the suit against him. This is what is meant by the term 'due diligence.' In Coughran v. Markley, 15 S.D. 37, 87 N.W. 2, it is very aptly stated: 'Judgments which exclude persons from any interest or lien upon land should not be rendered without actual notice, when by the exercise of reasonable diligence actual notice can be given. There should be either actual notice or an honest and reasonable effort to give it. The statute contemplates, and trial judges should invariably require, that the party who institutes the suit shall in good faith make every reasonable effort to not only ascertain that the defendant cannot be served within the state, but to ascertain his whereabouts, in order that copies of the summons and complaint may reach him through the mails or otherwise.' Where a defendant, on whom service by publication is sought, has recently left the state, plaintiff should ascertain the place where he last resided, and it is also incumbent upon plaintiff to ascertain whether such defendant left any relatives or agents or other business associates in such vicinity, and, if so, inquiry should be made of them, as persons presumed to be most likely to know the present whereabouts of such defendant. Failing to find such relatives, agents, or business associates, inquiry should be made of the nearest and most immediate neighbors of such defendant as persons also presumed to be likely to know the whereabouts of such defendant. Inquiry of the postmaster at the last-known post office address of such defendant might readily lead to the discovery of his whereabouts. The affidavit for publication should show that all reasonable inquiry has been made of persons likely or presumed to know the whereabouts of the person sought to be notified by publication. Near neighbors might know of near relatives of defendant who resided in some other locality who could furnish the desired information. It is the use of all such reasonable means of this character that constitutes 'due diligence.' The affidavit should show that such sources of inquiry have been reasonably pursued and exhausted. Inquiries made of persons in a distant part of the county, or state, 20, 50, 100, or more miles from the locality where defendant last resided, who are not personally acquainted with and did not know defendant, are wholly worthless and wholly immaterial to establish 'due diligence.' Such persons are not likely or presumed to know the whereabouts of defendant." The record does not show that the defendant made any such good-faith effort to ascertain the names and location of the owners of the disputed premises as would authorize the court to adjudicate their rights as unknown owners. He not only failed to exercise reasonable diligence in ascertaining and bringing before the court all parties in interest, but he dismissed his action as to such parties as disclosed an interest in this particular piece of land. By doing this, he withdrew said premises from consideration of the court and left the court without jurisdiction to determine any of the interests therein; and, the court not having such jurisdiction in said action, the decree entered therein did not affect the title to the premises in question and is no bar to the maintenance of this action.

Nothing said herein is to be taken as an expression of opinion as to the constitutionality or unconstitutionality of chapter 81 of the Session Laws of 1905. The law as it stands not having been complied with, it is not necessary to pass upon the validity of the law itself. Neither is anything said herein to be taken as an expression of opinion as to whether or not chapter 81, Laws of 1905, authorizes a party to have litigated, in one action, claims to separate tracts of land, plaintiff's title to which is derived from different sources, and where no community of interest exists between the several defendants.

At the beginning of the trial, the appellant objected to any further proceedings in the action until the respondent had paid or tendered to appellant all taxes, interest, and penalties, legal costs and expenses, as provided by section 2214, Pol. Code. The objection was overruled, and this ruling is urged as error by appellant. The court followed the provision of section 2225, Pol. Code, by ascertaining the amount to which appellant was entitled by reason of taxes paid and expense incurred on account of the land in controversy. Appellant was awarded judgment and given a lien on the premises for this amount. There was no error in this. Pettigrew et al. v. Moody, 17 S.D. 275, 96 N.W. 94.

This necessarily leads to the conclusion that the trial court was right, and the order and the judgment appealed from are affirmed.

American Land Co. v. Zeiss

219 U.S. 47, 31 S. Ct. 200, 55 L. Ed. 82 (1911)

As a result of the conditions caused in San Francisco by the great calamity of earthquake and fire, which befell that city in April, 1906, an extraordinary session of the legislature of California was convoked. One reason stated for the call was the necessity of providing for restoring the record title to land in San Francisco. An act to accomplish that purpose became a law upon its approval on June 16, 1906.

The Circuit Court of Appeals has certified the issues involved in a pending cause, the determination of which rests upon the validity of the statute just referred to. The pertinent facts arising on the record of the cause are stated in the certificate, and are hereafter set forth. The purpose contemplated is to obtain instructions as to whether the act in question "is violative of the Fourteenth Amendment of the Constitution of the United States," and whether by virtue of a decree rendered by the Superior Court of the city and county of San Francisco, referred to in the recital of facts, the American Land Company "has been deprived of its property without due process of law."

The following are the facts recited in the certificate:

The appellant as complainant in the court below brought its bill in equity against the appellee to remove a cloud from its title to real property and to quiet its title thereto. The bill alleges on April 10, 1908, and at all the times prior thereto referred to in the bill, George H. Lent and Mary G. Coggeshall were severally the owners in fee simple of two adjacent lots of land in San Francisco, which lots are described in the bill. The lots and others similarly situated are known as City Slip and Water Lots. Under the provisions of an act of the legislature of the State of California, approved March 5, 1851 (Stats. of 1851, page 764), the State leased this property to the city of San Francisco for the term of ninety-nine years. The appellee is alleged to be the owner of the unexpired portion of this lease as successor in interest of the city's right, and to be entitled to the possession thereof until March 26, 1950. The bill alleges that the appellee has no right whatever other than this right of possession and occupation; that notwithstanding the premises, the appellee claims to be the owner in fee simple of said lands under a judgment and decree of the Superior Court of the State of California in and for the city and county of San Francisco, made and entered December 19, 1906, in a proceeding entitled "Louis Zeiss, plaintiff, vs. All persons claiming any interest in, or lien upon the real property herein described, or any part thereof, defendant;" that said proceeding was brought under an act of the legislature of the State of California, entitled "An Act to provide for the establishment and quieting of title to real property in case of the loss or destruction of public records," approved June 16, 1906; that said claim of the appellee under said decree is without right, and said decree is void; that in the complaint in that proceeding the appellee, after properly setting forth the destruction of the records, alleged that he was the owner in fee simple, free of incumbrance, of the lands which are described in the bill in this case, and that he prayed for a decree of the Superior Court adjudging his title to be as set forth by him; that at the time of filing his complaint he filed his affidavit setting forth the character of the estate, the source of his title, his possession, and stating that he had made no conveyance of the land, that there were no liens on it, and that he did not know and that he had never been informed of any other person who claimed or may claim any interest or lien upon the property, or any part thereof, adversely to him. The affidavit contained no averment that inquiry of any kind had been made to ascertain whether such adverse claim did exist. It is shown in the bill that in said proceeding under said act of the legislature, summons was published in the Law Recorder for the space of two months, and was also posted on the land, and that after the period of publication of the summons the appellee herein obtained a decree of the court as prayed for by him. The bill further alleges that although the appellant's grantors were at all times citizens and residents of California, not seeking to evade but ready to accept service of summons, and easily reached for that purpose, no service was made upon them, nor did they in any way receive notice of the pendency of the action, nor did they gain any knowledge of the existence of the decree until more than a year after its entry. A demurrer was interposed to the bill in the court below for want of equity, which demurrer was sustained by the court and the bill was dismissed.

Mr. Chief Justice WHITE, after making the foregoing statement, delivered the opinion of the court. Although not objecting to an answer to the questions, nevertheless the American Land Company, which was the appellant below, suggests at bar a want of power to reply to the questions for a twofold reason: First, because the certificate on its face indicates that the court below was not in a state of mind which required the instruction of this court, but was merely desirous of provoking a direct decision by this court, to avoid the delay and the public inconvenience which otherwise might result. Second, because the certificate is so broad as simply to refer the whole case to this court for decision instead of presenting definite propositions of law for solution. While it may be that these suggestions find possible support, considering the record in a detached way, we think when the certificate is considered as a whole and the subject with which it deals is properly weighed the suggestions are without merit. We therefore pass to a consideration of the questions propounded.

It is apparent that the substantial considerations involved in the questions certified are embraced in the following, *a*, the authority of the State to deal with the subject with which the statute is concerned; *b*, upon the hypothesis of the existence of power, the sufficiency of the safeguards provided in the statute; *c*, upon the like hypothesis the adequacy of the proceedings had in the particular cause with which the certificate deals. We shall consider these subjects separately.

As to the power of the State. The conditions which led to the legislation in question were stated by the Supreme Court of California in Title Document Restoration Co. v. Kerrigan, Judge, 150 California, 289, 305. The court said:

> It is also a matter of common knowledge that in the city and county of San Francisco, at least, if not in other counties, the disaster of April last worked so great a destruction of the public records as to make it impossible to trace any title with completeness of certainty. That some provision was necessary to enable the holders and owners of real estate in this city to secure to themselves such evidence of title as would enable them, not only to defend their possession, but to enjoy and exercise the equally important right of disposition, is clear.

As it is indisputable that the general welfare of society is involved in the security of the titles to real estate and in the public registry of such titles, it is obvious that the power to legislate as to such subjects inheres in the very nature of government. This being true, it follows that government possesses the power to remedy the confusion and uncertainty as to registered titles arising from a disaster like that described by the court below. We might well pursue no further the subject of the power of the State to enact the law in question, and thus leave its authority to depend upon the demonstration necessarily resulting from the obvious considerations just stated. As, however, the question of power is intimately interwoven with the sufficiency of the procedure adopted, and as a clear comprehension of the scope of the power will serve to elucidate the question of procedure, we shall briefly refer to some of the leading cases by which the elementary doctrine of power over the subject of titles to real estate and the application of that doctrine to a case like the one in hand is settled beyond question. That a State has the power, generally speaking, to provide for and protect individual rights to the soil within its confines and declare what shall form a cloud on the title to such soil was recognized in Clark v. Smith, 13 Pet. 195. So, also, it is conclusively established that when the public interests demand the law may require even a party in actual possession of land and claiming a perfect title to appear before a properly constituted tribunal and establish that title by a judicial proceeding. Such was the method employed by the United States in settling as between itself and claimants under Mexican grants the title to property in California. Barker v. Harvey, 181 U.S. 481; Mitchell v. Furman, 180 U.S. 402; Botiller v. Dominguez, 130 U.S. 238; More v. Steinbach, 127 U.S. 70.

The question of what authority a State possesses over titles to real estate, and what jurisdiction over the subject it may confer upon its courts, received much consideration in Arndt v. Griggs, 134 U.S. 316. It was there held that, even as to ordinary controversies respecting title to land arising between rival claimants, the State possessed the power to provide for the adjudication of titles to real estate not only as against residents, but as against non-residents, who might be brought into court by publication. In the course of the opinion the court said (p. 320):

> It [the State] has control over property within its limits; and the condition of ownership of real estate therein, whether the owner be stranger or citizen, is subject to its rules concerning the holding, the transfer, liability to obligations, private or public, and the modes of establishing titles thereto. It cannot bring the person of a non-resident within its limits — its process goes not out beyond its borders — but it may determine the extent of his title to real estate within its limits; and for the purpose of such determination may provide any reasonable methods of imparting notice. The well-being of every community requires that the title to real estate therein shall be secure, and that there be convenient and certain methods of determining any unsettled questions respecting it. The duty of accomplishing this is local in its nature; it is not a matter of national concern or vested in the general government; it remains with the State; and as this duty is one of the State, the manner of discharging it must be determined by the State, and no proceeding which it provides can be declared invalid, unless it conflict with some special inhibitions of the Constitution, or against natural justice.

Manifestly, under circumstances like those here presented, the principle applies with equal force in the case of unknown claimants. Undisclosed and unknown claimants are, to say the least, as dangerous to the stability of titles as other classes. This principle received recognition and was applied in Hamilton v. Brown, 161 U.S. 256, where it was held to be competent for a State to make provision for promptly ascertaining, by appropriate judicial proceedings, who has succeeded to property upon the death of a person leaving such property within the State. It was said (p. 275):

> If such proceedings are had, after actual notice by service of summons to all known claimants, and constructive notice by publication to all possible claimants who are unknown, the final determination of the right of succession, either among private persons, as in the ordinary administration of estates, or between all persons and the State, as by inquest of office or similar process to determine whether the estate has escheated to the public, is due process of law; and a statute providing for such proceedings and determination does not impair the obligation of any contract

contained in the grant under which the former owner held, whether that grant was from the State or from a private person.

The application of the doctrine of governmental power as just stated, to a condition like the one here in question was aptly pointed out by the Supreme Court of Illinois in Bertrand v. Taylor, 87 Illinois, 235, where, in considering the Illinois Burnt Record Act, the court said:

> It was demanded as a matter of safety in a great emergency. It was not calculated to take any reasonable being by surprise. It was known throughout the civilized world that a large part of the city of Chicago had been destroyed by fire and that the records of courts and the records of deeds were all destroyed. This naturally commanded the attention of all reasonable persons everywhere, and called upon them to attend and see what means would be adopted to mitigate the evils and dangers incident to the destruction. This legislation was not done in a corner, but before the observation of a civilized world. We cannot doubt the power of the general assembly to pass the act.

The Supreme Court of California, in the *Kerrigan* case, supra, addressing itself to the same subject, pertinently observed (pp. 313, 314):

> Applying the principles which have led the courts in cases like Arndt v. Griggs, 134 U.S. 316, and Perkins v. Wakeham, 86 California, 580, to sustain judgments quieting titles against non-residents upon substituted service, why should not the legislature have power to give similar effect to such judgments against unknown claimants where the notice is reasonably full and complete? The validity of such judgments against known residents is based upon the ground that the State has power to provide for the determination of titles to real estate within its border, and that, as against non-resident defendants or others, who cannot be served in the State, a substituted service is permissible, as being the only service possible. These grounds apply with equal force to unknown claimants. The power of the State as to titles should not be limited to settling them as against persons named. In order to exercise this power to its fullest extent, it is necessary that it should be made to operate on all interests, known and unknown. As was said by Holmes, C.J., in Tyler v. Judges of the Court of Registration, 175 Massachusetts, 71, in speaking of a statute which, in the particular under discussion, was similar to ours: "If it does not satisfy the Constitution, a judicial proceeding to clear titles against all the world hardly is possible; for the very meaning of such a proceeding is to get rid of unknown as well as known claimants — indeed, certainty against the unknown may be said to be its chief end — and unknown claimants cannot be dealt with by personal service upon the claimant."

The power exerted by the act being then clearly within the legislative authority, we are brought to consider whether the lawful power was manifested in such a manner as to cause the act to be repugnant to the Fourteenth Amendment. And this brings us to the second proposition heretofore stated, viz:

The adequacy of the safeguards which the statute provides. As no complaint is made concerning the provisions of the statute relating to the designation of and notice to known claimants, we put that subject out of view and address ourselves to the provisions relating to unknown claimants or claims. The action which the statute authorizes may be brought by "Any person who claims an estate of inheritance, or for life in, and who is by himself or his tenant, or other person, holding under him, in the actual and peaceable possession of any real property" situated in a county where "the public records in the office of a county recorder have been lost or destroyed, in whole or in any material part, by flood, fire or earthquake." In the caption of the complaint the statute requires that the defendants shall be described as "all persons claiming any interest in or lien upon the real property herein described, or any part thereof." The summons is required to contain a description of the property affected by the suit and to be directed to "all persons claiming any interest in or lien upon the real property herein described, or any part thereof." The summons is to be published at least once a week for two months, and the defendants are commanded to appear and answer within three months after the first publication of the summons. A copy of the summons is required to be posted in a conspicuous place on each separate parcel of the property described in the complaint within fifteen days after the first publication of the summons. At the time of filing the complaint a notice of the pendency of the action, giving among other things a particular description of the property affected thereby, must be recorded in the office of the recorder of the county in which the property is situated, and it is made the duty of the recorder to enter, "upon a map or plat of the parcels of land, to be kept by him for that purpose, on the part of the map or plat representing the parcel or parcels so described a reference to the date of the filing of such notice and, when recorded, to the book and page of the record thereof." In considering the statute we are bound by the construction affixed to it by the Supreme Court of the State, and therefore treat as embraced within its terms that which the highest court of the State has declared the statute exacts, either expressly or by necessary implication. In the *Kerrigan* case, supra, it was held that the result of the provisions of the statute was "to require the complainant to designate and to serve as known claimants all whom, with reasonable diligence, he could ascertain to be claimants," a construction which, in effect declared that the statute prohibited the omission of a known claim or claimant, upon the conception that the rights of such claim or claimant would be foreclosed by the general designation and notice prescribed for unknown claimants. And in Hoffman v. Superior Court, 151 California, 386, where the doctrine of the *Kerrigan* case was reiterated and applied, the court, after holding that the statute requires the plaintiff in his affidavit to allege in terms "that he does not know and has never been informed" of any adverse claimants whom he has not specifically named, pointed out that failure of the plaintiff to make inquiry or to avail himself of knowledge which would be imputed to him because of facts sufficient to put him on inquiry as to the existence of adverse claims would be available "in any subsequent attack upon the decree, upon the ground that there was extraneous fraud of the plaintiff in making a false affidavit to obtain jurisdiction."

It is to be born in mind that it has been settled (Griffith v. Connecticut, 218 U.S. 563, and cases cited) that the Fourteenth Amendment does not operate to deprive the States of their lawful power, and of the right in the exercise of such power to resort to reasonable methods inherently belonging to the power exerted. On the contrary, the provisions of the due process clause only restrain those arbitrary and unreasonable exertions of power which are not really within lawful state power, since they are so unreasonable and unjust as to impair or destroy fundamental rights.

It is to be observed that the statute not only requires a disclosure by the plaintiff of all known claimants, but moreover at the very outset contains words of limitation that no one not in the actual and peaceable possession of property can maintain the action which it authorizes. No person can therefore be deprived of his property under the statute unless he had not only gone out of possession of such property and allowed another to acquire possession, or if he had a claim to such property or an interest therein, had so entirely failed to disclose that fact as to enable a possessor to truthfully make the affidavit which the statute exacts of a want of all knowledge of the existence of other claimants than as disclosed in his affidavit. Besides, it is to be considered that the statute, as construed by the California court, imposed upon the one in possession seeking the establishment of an alleged title the duty to make diligent inquiry to ascertain the names of all claimants. Instead, therefore, of the statute amounting to the exertion of a purely unreasonable and arbitrary power, its provisions leave no room for that contention. On the contrary, we think the statute manifests the careful purpose of the legislature to provide every reasonable safeguard for the protection of the rights of unknown claimants and to give such notice as under the circumstances would be reasonably likely to bring the fact of the pendency and the purpose of the proceeding to the attention of those interested. To argue that the provisions of the statute are repugnant to the due process clause because a case may be conceived where rights in and to property would be adversely affected without notice being actually conveyed by the proceedings is in effect to deny the power of the State to deal with the subject. The criterion is not the possibility of conceivable injury but the just and reasonable character of the requirements, having reference to the subject with which the statute deals. The doctrine on this subject was clearly expressed by the Court of Appeals of New York in In re Empire City Banks, 18 N.Y. 199, 215, where, speaking of the right of a State to prescribe in a suitable case for constructive service, it was said:

> Various prudential regulations are made with respect to these remedies, but it may possibly happen, notwithstanding all these precautions, that a citizen who owes nothing, and has done none of the acts mentioned in the statutes, may be deprived of his estate without any actual knowledge of the process by which it has been taken from him. If we hold, as we must, in order to sustain this legislation, that the constitution does not positively require personal notice in order to constitute a legal proceeding due process of law, it then belongs to the legislature to determine in the particular instance whether the case calls for this kind of exceptional legislation and what manner of constructive notice shall be sufficient to reasonably apprise the party proceeded against of the legal steps which are taken against him.

And in accordance with this view, the Supreme Court of California, in the *Kerrigan* case, pointed out that the statute furnished all the safeguards for which, in reason, it could have been expected to provide consistently with the condition dealt with. The court said (p. 312):

"Where, as here, the summons describing the nature of the action, the property involved, the name of the plaintiff, and the relief sought, is posted upon the property, and is published in a newspaper for two months, and a *'lis pendens'* containing the same particulars is recorded in the recorder's office and entered upon the recorder's map of the property, we cannot doubt that, so far as concerns the possible claimants who are not known to the plaintiff, the notice prescribed by the act is as complete and full as, from the nature of the case, could reasonably be expected."

The case of Ballard v. Hunter, 204 U.S. 241, is instructive on this feature of the case. In that case a judgment of the Circuit Court of Arkansas was affirmed which sustained the validity of a sale of lands for levee taxes. The Arkansas statute authorized the proceedings which had resulted in the sale, upon constructive publication against non-residents and unknown owners. Lands of Josephine Ballard were sold under the statutory proceeding, she not having knowledge of the existence of the suit or of the fact that the taxes had been assessed against her property. In the course of the opinion the court, speaking through Mr. Justice McKenna, said (p. 261):

> It is said, however, that Josephine Ballard was not made a defendant in the suit, though the records of the county showed that she was an owner thereof. But the statute provided against such an omission. It provided that the proceedings and judgment should be in the nature of proceedings in rem, and that it should be immaterial that the ownership of the lands might be incorrectly alleged in the proceedings. We see no want of due process in that requirement, or what was done under it. It is manifest that any criticism of either is answered by the cases we have cited. The proceedings were appropriate to the nature of the case.
>
> It should be kept in mind that the laws of a State come under the prohibition of the Fourteenth Amendment only when they infringe fundamental rights. A law must be framed and judged of in consideration of the practical affairs of man. The law cannot give personal notice of its provisions or proceedings to every one. It charges every one with knowledge of its provisions; of its proceedings it must, at times, adopt some form of indirect notice, and indirect notice is usually efficient notice when the proceedings affect real estate. Of what concerns or may concern their real estate, men usually keep informed, and on that probability the law may frame its proceedings; indeed, must frame them, and assume the care of property to be universal, if it would give efficiency to many of its exercises. This was pointed out in Huling v. Kaw Valley Railway & Improvement Company, 130 U.S. 559, where it was declared to be the "duty of the owner of real estate, who is a non-resident, to take measure that in some way he shall be represented when his property is called into requisition; and if he fails to give notice by the ordinary publications which have been usually required in such cases, it is his misfortune, and he must abide the consequences." It makes no difference, therefore, that plaintiffs in error did not have personal notice of the suit to collect the taxes on their lands or that taxes had been levied, or knowledge of the law under which the taxes had been levied.

While we are of opinion that the views just stated demonstrate the want of merit in the contention that the statute, because of the insufficiency of its requirements, was repugnant to the Fourteenth Amendment, a consideration of a provision of the general law of California, which by the construction of the Supreme Court of California is incorporated into the statute under consideration, would lead to the same result. Thus, in the *Hoffman* case, 151 California, 386, 393, the court said:

> In this connection it is proper to say that in determining whether or not due process of law is afforded, other statutes applicable to the proceeding may be considered. The provisions of § 473 of the Code of Civil Procedure apply in such cases. Any person interested in the property and having no actual notice of the decree, may come in at

any time within a year after its rendition and by showing that he has not been personally served with process and stating facts constituting a good defense to the proceeding — that is, facts sufficient to show that he has a valid adverse interest in the property — he may have the decree vacated, as to him and be allowed to answer to the merits.

The right conferred by § 473 of the code, it is to be observed, is an absolute right, although the section declares that the court may impose "such terms as may be just." Holiness Church v. Metropolitan Church Association (Cal. App.), 107 Pac. Rep. 633; Gray v. Lawlor, 151 California, 352.

Under this construction it might well be held, if it were necessary to do so, as establishing a rule of limitation which it was in the power of the State to prescribe, in view of the circumstances to which the limitation was made applicable. See Tyler v. Judges, 175 Massachusetts, 71, and State v. Westfall, 85 Minnesota, 437. See also Illinois cases concerning the power to fix a short period of limitations to meet a disaster like the one to which the statute in question relates, collected in Gormley v. Clark, 134 U.S. 346, 347.

These views dispose of all the contentions concerning the repugnancy of the statute to the Fourteenth Amendment which we think it necessary to separately consider. In saying this we are not unmindful of a multitude of subordinate propositions pressed in the voluminous brief of counsel and which were all in effect urged upon the Supreme Court of California in the *Kerrigan* and *Hoffman* cases and were in those cases adversely disposed of, and which we also find to be without merit. Some of them we briefly refer to. We do not think it is important to determine the precise nature of the action authorized by the statute, since the method of procedure which was prescribed was within the legislative competency. So, also, we do not deem it important to discuss what constitutes a judicial proceeding, since the statutory proceeding provided by the act was within the authority of the State to enact, and that it was judicial in character has been expressly determined by the court of last resort of the State. Indeed, not only these, but all contentions proceed upon a misconception as to the legislative authority of the State and the effect thereon of the due process clause of the Constitution of the United States. The error which all the propositions involved was pointed out in Twining v. New Jersey, 211 U.S. 78, where, speaking by Mr. Justice Moody, the court said:

> Due process requires that the court which assumes to determine the rights of parties shall have jurisdiction (citing cases) and that there shall be notice and opportunity for hearing given the parties, (citing cases). Subject to these two fundamental conditions, which seem to be universally prescribed in all systems of law established by civil countries, this court has, up to this time, sustained all state laws, statutory or judicially declared, regulating procedure, evidence and methods of trial, and held them to be consistent with due process of law.

3. The adequacy of the proceedings pursued in the case referred to in the certificate. As there is no claim that fraud, actual or constructive, was employed by Zeiss in obtaining the judgment complained of, and the proceedings conformed to the California statute, the considerations previously stated entirely dispose of this question.

It follows that both of the questions certified must be answered in the negative. And it is so ordered.

Comment, Enhancing the Marketability of Land:
The Suit to Quiet Title

68 Yale L.J. 1245, 1265, 1277, 1283 (1959)

THE SUIT TO QUIET TITLE

The modern suit to quiet title is a statutorily authorized proceeding designed to establish a title's status by adjudicating the validity of adverse interests in real property. The suit may be in rem or quasi-in-rem; in either case, the court obtains jurisdiction to adjudicate all interests in the land at issue through its control of that land. When the suit is in rem, unknown parties served by publication may be bound by the decree. When the suit is quasi-in-rem, on the other hand, a decree can bind only those parties named by the petitioner's complaint and served process either actually or constructively.[102] . . .

The principal objective of the quiet-title suit should be to restore the saleability of titles impaired by known or record defects. In addition, the suit should impart commercial respectability to interests acquired through adverse possession — interests which are not recognized under today's recording systems, and which rarely command more than a fraction of their actual value. The suit should further protect ostensibly clear titles against the multitudinous unrecordable and misrecorded claims which repeatedly emerge to destroy the peaceful use and possession of land. Succinctly, then, the goal sought for the modernized suit to quiet title is a proceeding available to almost any interest-holder in which all adverse claims can be marshaled, examined and settled by a court whose decree, once rendered and docketed, is both the exclusive and conclusive determinant of title. To attain this objective, a new type of authorizing statute is needed. . . .

The basic problem, then, is convincing lawmakers not of their authority to adopt in rem legislation but of the need therefor. Almost half the present quiet-title statutes are essentially adversary — requiring personal jurisdiction or the joinder of known nonresident claimants — and are not founded solely on judicial control over the res. Underlying these statutes is a marked legislative disinclination to authorize a decree which would conclusively settle the rights of unjoined, unnotified and unrepresented parties. But obtaining personal jurisdiction over or joining unknown interest-holders is patently impossible. Their claims must accordingly be expunged ex parte or allowed to emerge at any time to subvert a previously rendered judgment. The choice is between an in personam or quasi-in-rem decree, which is worth little as a title determinant, and an in rem proceeding, which binds all adverse claimants despite possible inequities. . . .

NOTES AND QUESTIONS

1. What are the inequities of broad suit to quiet title statutes, such as the one involved in American Land Co. v. Zeiss, that can clear all title defects? Should all

---

102. Whether an action is in personam, in rem, or quasi-in-rem involves an unsettled area of the law which has generated incessant controversy. See Mullane v. Central Hanover Bank & Trust Co., 339 U.S. 306, 313 (1950); Cook, The Powers of Courts of Equity (pts. 1-3), 15 Colum. L. Rev. 37, 106, 228 (1915); Fraser, Actions in Rem, 34 Cornell L.Q. 29 (1948); Walsh, Development in Equity of the Power To Act In Rem, 6 N.Y.U.L.Q. Rev. 1 (1928). . . .

statutes apply only to situations in which some holocaust has destroyed the public land records or should they be more generally applicable?

2. Many errors in land titles are not sufficiently serious to justify the time and expense of clearing them by suits to quiet title or other judicial proceedings; so less involved and less costly corrective devices may be used instead, including affidavits. Lawyers and title insurers, in determining marketability issues, often will accept affidavits by knowledgeable persons to explain apparent gaps in chains of title or clear other seeming title deficiencies. Issues that examiners frequently are willing to resolve by affidavit include questions of family history relating to titles—such as relevant births, deaths, survivors, and marital status—and questions of identity, for example, whether or not the same person conveyed out as earlier took title when there is a slight disparity in the public records between the name of a grantee and that of the next succeeding grantor. Title examiners also may accept affidavits alleging facts bearing on other significant title matters, including the acquisition of homestead rights and obtaining of title by adverse possession.

Affidavits pertaining to land titles have, however, posed problems as to their recordability and admissibility in evidence. In a number of states they may not be recorded so as to give actual or constructive notice of the allegations they contain; and they are considered hearsay, thus may not be admitted in evidence before courts. On hearsay grounds, recitals of fact in deeds and other conveyancing instruments also have been held inadmissable evidence. But there is something of a trend to expand the recordability and evidentiary value of affidavits bearing on land titles, of which these Connecticut and Wisconsin statutory provisions are indications:

Conn. Gen. Stat. Ann. § 47-12a (West Supp. 2006)

Affidavit of facts relating to title or interest in real estate

(a) An affidavit, which states facts relating to the matters named in subsection (b) of this section and which may affect the title to or any interest in real estate in this state, and which is made by any person having knowledge of the facts or competent to testify concerning them in open court, may be recorded in the land records of the town in which the real estate is situated. If so recorded, and if the affiant is dead or otherwise not available to testify in court, then the affidavit, or a certified copy of it, is admissible as prima facie evidence of the facts stated in it, so far as those facts affect title to real estate in any action involving the title to that real estate or any interest in it.

(b) The affidavits provided for in this section may relate to the following matters: Age, sex, birth, death, capacity, relationship, family history, heirship, names, identity of parties, marital status, possession or adverse possession, adverse use, residence, service in the armed forces, conflicts and ambiguities in description of land in recorded instruments, and the happening of any condition or event which may terminate an estate or interest.

(c) Every affidavit provided for in this section shall include a description of the land, title to which may be affected by facts stated in the affidavit, and shall state the name of the person appearing by the record to be the owner of the land at the time of the recording of the affidavit. The town clerk shall index the affidavit in the name of that record owner.

Wis. Stat. Ann. § 706.09 (West, 2001)

(1) *When conveyance is free of prior adverse claim.* A purchaser for a valuable consideration, . . . and his successors in interest, shall take and hold the estate or interest purported to be conveyed to such purchaser free of any claim adverse to or inconsistent with such estate or interest, if such adverse claim is dependent for its validity or priority upon: . . .

(i) *Facts not asserted of record.* Any fact not appearing of record, but the opposite or contradiction of which appears affirmatively and expressly in a conveyance, affidavit or other instrument of record in the chain of title of the real estate affected for 5 years. Such facts may, without limitation by noninclusion, relate to age, sex, birth, death, capacity, relationship, family history, descent, heirship, names, identity of persons, marriage, marital status, homestead, possession or adverse possession, residence, service in the armed forces, conflicts and ambiguities in descriptions of land in recorded instruments, identification of any recorded plats or subdivisions, corporate authorization to convey, and the happening of any condition or event which terminates an estate or interest.

Which of the above two statutes do you consider preferable, and what weaknesses are implicit in each statute as set forth?

4. Liability of Title Searchers and Examiners

For failure to do their work satisfactorily, professional title searchers and examiners may be liable in tort or contract. To their customers, and in some places even to others who rely on such work or for whose benefit it is carried on, this can be an additional form of protection. Abstracters, lawyers, and title insurance companies are the professionals most commonly involved, and carelessness is the usual reason for their unsatisfactory work. Risks of misconduct by search and examination professionals are spread by bonding or malpractice insurance, the latter also known as errors and omissions insurance.

NOTES AND QUESTIONS

1. In Florida, abstracters owe a duty of care in abstract preparation not only to the person with whom they contracted to provide the abstract, often the seller of the land, but also to the intended beneficiary of the contract for abstracting services, who is often the purchaser of the property. First American Title Insurance Co. v. First Title Service Co., 457 So. 2d 467 (Fla. 1984). But this liability to the beneficiary exists only if the abstracter knows or should know of the intended use by the beneficiary, and the Florida Supreme Court has specifically declined to extend an abstracter's liability more broadly to include all persons who foreseeably rely to their detriment on a negligently prepared abstract. Abstract Corp. v. Fernandez Co., 458 So. 2d 766 (Fla. 1985). Other courts have refused to extend the abstracter's liability to those who have not contracted for the abstracter's services. For example, Calamari v. Grace, 98 A.D.2d 74, 469 N.Y.S.2d 942 (1983). For arguments against the narrow privity position as applied to lawyers' negligence, see Note, Attorney

Negligence in Real Estate Title Examination and Will Drafting: Elimination of the Privity Requirement as a Bar to Recovery by Foreseeable Third Parties, 17 New Eng. L. Rev. 955 (1981-1982).

2. With the abstracter's liability in the principal case compare the title insurer's liability in Jarchow v. Transamerica Title Insurance Company, . . . infra.

3. Lawyers engaged in title searching and examination may be liable for negligent conduct in carrying out such work. See Note, Attorney Negligence in Real Estate Title Examination and Will Drafting: Elimination of the Privity Requirement as a Bar to Recovery by Forseeable Third Parties, 17 New Eng. L. Rev. 955 (1982); and Annot., Liability of Attorney for Negligence in Connection With Investigation or Certification of Title to Real Estate, 59 A.L.R. 3d 1176 (1974). Lawyers also are obligated to make disclosure to their clients of any defects discovered in the Title examination. See Comment, Liability of an Attorney for Negligence in Title Examination — Failure to Disclose Information to the Client, 13 J. Legal Prof. 263 (1988). Lawyer malpractice is more comprehensively considered in R. Mallen and J. Smith, Legal Malpractice (3d ed. 1989); D. Stern and J. Felix-Retzke, A Practical Guide to Preventing Legal Malpractice (1983); and Annot., What Constitutes Negligence Sufficient to Render Attorney Liable to Person Other Than Immediate Client, 61 A.L.R. 4th 464 (1988).

Should lawyers be liable if in title examinations they make errors of judgment concerning the law? Suppose a lawyer passes a title as marketable that a court later holds is unmarketable? Assume the lawyer was aware of all the relevant facts but misinterpreted or misapplied what turns out to be the controlling rule of law pertaining to the title point that resulted in the title being held unmarketable? Should the lawyer then be liable for negligence? What if the mistake was due to the lawyer's ignorance of a lead case or a clearly applicable title standard? Should a lawyer-specialist be held to a different standard of care from that of a lawyer who only occasionally examines titles?

4. In Owen v. Neely, 471 S.W.2d 705 (Ky. 1971), a damage action was brought against a lawyer by his client for a description error not noted in the lawyer's title opinion. However, the lawyer's certificate to the effect that the title was merchantable was expressly made "subject to any information that would be revealed by an accurate survey of the real estate." In its opinion, the court said:

> We are of the opinion that a lawyer certainly may protect himself by reservations and disclaimers expressly set forth in a certificate of title, but only if he has no reasonable grounds to suspect the actual existence of defects not mentioned. The average layman is not familiar with and ordinarily does not understand legal descriptions, and if his lawyer, accidentally or otherwise, receives information that should reasonably put him on notice of a defect we think it is his duty to investigate or report it to his client.

5. Another liability source that may be available to a grantee is the grantor. If the title turns out to have been defective at the time of transfer, the grantee took by warranty deed, and the defect was not expressly exempted from covenant coverage by the deed's terms, the grantee may be able to recover against the grantor for breach of the deed's covenants for title. Warranty deeds are discussed in Chapter Four at page 419 supra. Many states, by statute, provide for short form warranty deeds that result in some or all of the covenants for title being implied by inclusion in the granting clause of language to the effect that the grantor warrants the

conveyed premises. See, for example, Ill. Ann. Stat. c. 30, § 8 (Smith-Hurd Supp. 1991). Many owners' title insurance policies will continue even after conveyance to protect the grantor for liability under title covenants.

B. TITLE INSURANCE[12]

In most parts of the United States, including nearly all metropolitan areas, title insurance is a major form of title protection. It is an American innovation and little such insurance is written outside the United States.[13] The first American title insurance company was formed in 1876, and by World War II some title insurance was being written on lands in most all parts of the United States, with well-established companies in nearly all big cities. But the great expansion of this kind of coverage has come mostly since the mid-1940s, a period marked by extensive real estate activity, a tremendous volume of new subdivisions, and a vast number of new conveyances and mortgages. Title insurance has grown in both absolute and relative terms, for it has gradually cut in on other forms of title protection, particularly title search and examination by lawyers in private practice. In a number of big cities private practitioners of law have been eliminated from both title search and examination; and in some areas, notably in the Far West, this has happened in many middle- and small-sized cities as well. In these communities the title work of the private bar is reduced largely to occasional efforts at curing title defects that title companies will not insure or negotiating with title insurers to waive minor defects. But in all of New England and in much of the Midwest and South outside large metropolitan centers, private law firms still do a great deal of title examination work, and in some communities they do title searching as well.

There are several major types of title insurance operations. In one the title company determines whether or not to insure, based on the title opinion of a lawyer in private practice, whose opinion is forwarded to the company for decision on insuring. The lawyer or an abstracter does the search, and the lawyer examines the title data and gives the opinion. In another, title company employees do the search and examination and then determine whether or not to insure, in many places using a company title plant for the search. A title plant consists principally of duplicate copies of public records pertaining to all land parcels in a particular county, arranged and indexed to enable accurate and speedy searching of titles for individual parcels. Most highly developed plants are in counties with large populations. In a third type of operation, non-employee agents of the company, lawyers or nonlawyers, make the search and examination and determine whether or not the company will insure. In some instances, the searching is farmed out to independent contractors, who report back to the agents. The agents are authorized to issue company policies, usually without further clearance from the company. Within

---

12. On title insurance generally, see Burke, Law of Title Insurance (3d ed. 2000 & Ann. Supps.); Palomar, Title Insurance Law (2005); Powell, The Law of Real Property, ch. 92 (1999); Thompson on Real Property, ch. 93 (2d ed. 2002). For discussion of title insurance in a somewhat earlier era, see Johnstone, Title Insurance, 66 Yale L.J. 492 (1957).

13. A modest amount of title insurance is now being written on real property in other countries, supplementing government coverage of registered titles. On this insurance, see Palomar, Title Insurance Law, ch. 22 (2004).

limits, some agents may even settle claims. The agent format has become much more common in recent years.

The phenomenal growth of title insurance is attributable to a series of factors. For one thing, the big national lenders, especially the life insurance companies, like the relatively standardized coverage given by mortgagees' policies wherever written. This makes it easier for these large volume operators to determine the acceptability of mortgages originated for them or that they purchase in the secondary market. They also like the risk insurance feature. Demand for title insurance by national lenders is probably the single most significant reason for expansion in this type of title protection since World War II. Another reason for title insurance growth is that in many large metropolitan areas public records pertaining to land have become so voluminous and difficult to search that only specialists with a large volume of title work can operate efficiently. And only the mass volume operator can afford a comprehensive title plant, an essential to maximum efficiency in many big counties. Still another reason why title insurance has expanded so is that, being businesses, title companies have vigorously and successfully promoted their services, whereas their lawyer and Torrens competitors have been ineffective at such promotion, until recently lawyers in private practice even being prohibited from advertising.

Title insurance differs from most other kinds of insurance in that it does not insure against future risks but only against those existing at the time coverage is obtained. Further, it is issued only after a careful title search and examination and excludes any risks of substance disclosed by this process. As a result, loss ratios are low, with principal risks being negligence in search and examination and relatively rare defects not apparent from customary public record searches. Only one premium is paid for title insurance, and this includes a charge for search and examination if made by the title company. It is common, at the time land is sold, for a title company to issue two separate policies of insurance for which separate premiums are paid: one policy to the mortgagee and the other to the purchasing owner. Owners' policies do not cover grantees from the insured; if a buyer wishes coverage, a new policy must be ordered and paid for, even though the seller was covered. Mortgagees' policies usually cover assignees. In addition to fee owners and mortgagees, long-term lessees and holders of valuable oil and gas rights frequently obtain title insurance coverage.

1. Administration

Many title insurance companies are licensed to do business in a number of states, and a few, directly or through subsidiaries, operate nationally. In recent years the big companies have been strengthening their national positions by buying up local and regional companies. Many title companies have branch offices and agencies located at various points throughout the area in which they do business. Orders are accepted at all these outlets, while searches and examinations are made only at some. Companies that will insure in reliance on title opinions of lawyers in private practice usually will accept only opinions of lawyers experienced in title work whose work they trust, and the companies maintain lists of such lawyers.

There are considerable differences geographically within the United States in title insurance rates. When title insurance companies issue coverage in reliance on the opinion of a lawyer, the basic risk premium rate in some places may be as low as

$2.50 per thousand dollars of coverage for a mortgagee's policy and $3.50 per thousand dollars of coverage for an owner's policy, with somewhat lower rates common for coverage in excess of $100,000 per parcel. In many places basic rates are higher, as much as double or more in some localities. Charges are, of course, considerably greater if the title company also does the searching and examining, a common practice if the company maintains its own title plant in the area. Lower rates may prevail if an owner's policy is issued simultaneously with a mortgagee's policy or if the insurer has recently issued a policy on the same property. It is the usual practice of title companies, when insuring a particular piece of property for a very large amount of money, to reinsure with other companies, thereby spreading the risk. This is not only sound business practice but in some states is required by law.

An alternative to the typical commercial title insurer is the bar-related form of insurance organization, a title company owned and operated by the lawyers in a state, generally those lawyers active in title work.[14] Essentially these organizations are efforts by the practicing bar to counter the competition of the traditional kind of commercial title company and to divert to lawyers engaged in title work some of the insurance profits from title coverage. There are eight of these bar-related companies, and most of them write policies in only one state. The first of the bar-related title insurers was the Florida Lawyer's Title Guaranty Fund, established in 1947. Nationally, the percentage of title insurance written by bar-related insurers is small, but in some states it is sizable. The commercial insurers have in the past been strongly opposed to bar-related insurers, but this opposition has greatly diminished in recent years.

Zerwick, Creation and Maintenance of a Title Plant

34 National Capital Area Realtor 11 (No. 1, 1966)

. . . Actually, there are many kinds of title plants. They vary in the way different title men get hold of the title evidence that go into the plant; they vary in the kind of books or indexes that are used; and they vary in the classification or organization of this title evidence. And, so far as I know, no one has satisfactorily proved that one type of plant is superior to all others. Indeed, title men find an abiding joy in parrying all evidence that might indicate that any system other than their own has anything to offer them.

One group of title men really uses the public recording offices as their title plant. Each title search is a laborious sifting through of the offices of the recorder, the tax collector, the city assessor, and the clerks of the various courts—perhaps municipal, state, county and even federal. He, the title searcher, brings back to his own shop a digest of all the information in the public title plant which evidence and [sic] arguments or diminishes the title he is to reflect. With this information at hand,

14. On bar-related title insurers see Burke, Law of Title Insurance § 1.02[B] (2000 & Ann. Supps.); Palomar, Title Insurance Law § 2.6 (2005); Rooney, The Role of the Lawyer As a "Member" of a Bar Guaranty Fund, in A.B.A., Sec. of Real Prop., Prob. & Tr. L., Title Insurance: The Lawyer's Expanding Role 334 (1985); Natl. Assn. of Bar-Related Title Insurers, Bar-Related Title Insurance (1986); Payne, Title Guaranty Funds: Symptom, Cure or Nostrum?, 46 Ind. L.J. 208 (1971); Rooney, Bar-Related Title Insurance: The Positive Perspective, 1980 S. Ill. U.L.J. 263.

he analyzes and organizes it into an abstract, or a report of title, or a policy of title insurance, thus placing the information in the hands of the persons who are buying a lot, or borrowing money on the security of a parcel of real estate, or initiating a condemnation for public use, or simply furnishing information to an investor.

Other title people don't wait until a specific search is called for to go to the public records. They build and maintain a plant of their own. And that plant is a good plant to the extent that it exactly reflects or duplicates the original records at the courthouses and the city hall. The only difference at all is in the way those records are organized and indexed. The private title plant is economic to the extent that it improves the speed and accuracy with which a single title may be examined.

There are two extremes: the completely public records and a private plant embracing a reflection of *every* public record. Between the two lie all the title plants in the country.

Many title people omit some of the courthouse information — some of the information which is ultimately necessary in their final searches. They do a part of each final title search among the records at the source, work with the original documents, though they may create and maintain an index even to these records in their own private plant. . . .

The volume of public records is almost beyond the imagination of people not engaged in their use. In the last year before the County of Los Angeles started to microfilm its records, they bound and placed on reference shelves *each day* an average of 135 volumes of 450 pages each. That is about 35,000 heavy tomes a year. They were recording 4,500 instruments a day at that time (1958). Today the daily average is over 6,000.

. . . Private plants are not mere copies of the public records, but a re-organization of them. The basic information obtained must be exactly the same. But in the private plant there are two general classifications only — a classification by description of real estate which supplants the Grantor-Grantee Indexes and in which every instrument describing real estate is filed in such a manner that the searcher finds it through or by means of that description; and a classification by name, for those instruments which contain no description of property, like a judgment for money, a change of name, or an incorporation.

Thus the title searcher in the private plant quite often looks in but two places — a single tract or location index, and a single name index. Contrast this with the public records where there may be as many as twenty places or more where a search must be made. . . .

The creation of a title plant is a sort of crash maintenance project. A title plant is actually created as it is maintained. The tremendous job of bringing together the records from the beginning of the history of a county is merely a telescoping of the daily maintenance job — of doing what might ordinarily have accumulated over a hundred years, in as little as a year's time. . . .

. . . A title plant is never complete. It is never finished. It grows and changes with every market transaction involving real estate. The figures of speech which might be applied to it are many. As it refines the system of public records, it becomes the safety deposit vault of the land system of the community. Its facilities are a transportation system, a pipe line system accommodating the flow of title evidence. . . . It is largely manned by small, independent individuals and businesses making their living in a free economy by industry and service not duplicated, to my knowledge, elsewhere in the world.

Robinson, The Organization and Operation of Title Plants[15]

Due to the recording acts and related laws presently in force, a search of every lender and every purchaser is extremely prudent. But such searches can be highly complicated and difficult. The question then becomes: what can be done to make land title searches efficient and economical?

First, consider the principal public officials who maintain records that may affect titles to real estate:

1. Recorder of deeds, by whatever name or title he may have in a particular jurisdiction.

2. Clerks of the various municipal, county, state and federal courts in the area in which the real estate is located.

3. Officers of the various municipalities and the county clerk, county treasurer, county assessor or other public official charged with the responsibility of maintaining records pertaining to general taxes, street assessments, sewer assessments, special charges for city services and other special taxes and levies.

A title searcher must draw on records maintained by all these officials, and on occasion others as well, if those who order title examinations are to be adequately protected. In a sparsely-populated county in a state where tract indices are maintained by the recorder, searches can readily be made directly from the public records; but in most metropolitan areas a complete title plant is needed for quick and thorough searching. Surprisingly sophisticated record-keeping systems are also found in offices of abstracting firms and title companies in many small and medium-sized communities throughout the nation.

In organizing and operating a title plant, several basic problems are encountered: how to obtain recorded data from the various public offices, a procedure commonly referred to as the "take-off"; how to index and arrange this data once obtained; and how to use plant data most advantageously after a plant has been set up.

TAKE-OFFS

There are only a few ways in which take-offs are made. Either some kind of photocopy is made of relevant documents, or a typewritten or longhand copy or abstract is prepared of each such document. Photographing all recorded instruments and reproducing copies 80 percent of original size is now a common practice, as is microfilming.

THE TRACT BOOK SYSTEM

The method of indexing data in title plants may be one of several. The oldest and the one most generally used is to maintain and keep up to date a set of bound or loose-leaf tract index books, with a separate page or "account" for each parcel showing its title history. Accounts are arranged in alphabetical order by platted

---

15. This article was written especially for this casebook by James W. Robinson, formerly Secretary of the American Land Title Association, Washington, D.C.

subdivision name, followed by unplatted accounts in section, township and range number order, or in some other logical sequence for communities not covered by the rectangular survey system. Each transaction involving a parcel of land is then posted to the appropriate account, the index entry commonly showing the names of grantor and grantee, type of instrument, date of the instrument and its date of recording, and the book and page number or other filing designation of where a copy of the original document can be found. To facilitate title searches, subdivision accounts are usually broken down into lots, sectional accounts into quarter-sections. If microfilm copies of recorded instruments are part of a title plant, a punch card system can now be used to make both index and tab card entries. Each microfilm copy is inserted in a tab card with aperture. As microfilm becomes available, an operator using a typewriter card punch does two simultaneous jobs; typing and punching. As the tract index entry is being typed, identical information is also punched onto the aperture card. This is an example of the increased efficiency that mechanization is making possible in relation to land titles.

CARD INDEX SYSTEM

The card index system substitutes a card or cards for a page in the tract index. These cards are filed and posted in the same manner as the tract books are arranged. The advantage to a card system is its ease of handling and reproduction when titles are consolidated or split. However, cards readily become defaced, misfiled, or lost.

FOLDER SYSTEM

Under this system a separate document folder is maintained for each parcel of land. Every folder contains an up-to-date index to all transactions of record for which there is a legal description tying it to the parcel in question. Many plants also include in the folder photocopies of indexed documents, so that most of what is needed for a title examination is included in one package. Folders are filed and numbered in an order that simplifies locating them, frequently in accord with their geographic locality, such as subdivision, block and lot.

NAME INDICES

Every complete title plant must have a "name" or "general" index file. All recorded instruments that cannot be indexed by legal description, such as money judgments against individuals that may create liens on land, are noted in one central index. In some areas a Soundex System of indexing names is used for maximum efficiency in locating names that are spelled differently but sound alike. In other areas the practice of posting and searching only the verbatim spelling of names in recorded instruments is followed.

ELECTRONIC STORAGE AND RETRIEVAL

Title companies have been experimenting with electronic storage and retrieval equipment as a means of indexing information relating to land titles. Portions of entire title plants (judgment indices, delinquent tax records, standard policy exceptions, etc.) have already been stored in computers and are in daily use in a few of the larger companies. . . . The industry is a long way from push button title insurance, but investigation of the possibilities of electronic storage and retrieval is under continuing study.

SUPPLEMENTAL DATA

In addition to the indices described above, and variations and combinations of these indexing systems, every abstract or title insurance company has accumulated a vast amount of internal material, developed as a by-product of the public records, which may expedite investigation of titles to real estate. This material consists of such items as tract opinions (title findings covering subdivisions and other large tracts of land), previously issued policies, corporate documents (charters and bylaws), starter files, subdivision atlases and other detailed maps, official surveys, legal opinions, affidavits and other memoranda, court decisions, government regulations and a cross-reference system for converting street addresses to legal descriptions. All these are part of the title plant and are regularly used.

JOINT TITLE PLANTS

Whether or not a title or abstract company finds it profitable to maintain a title plant depends not only on the volume of recorded instruments and the quality of the records kept by public officials in a particular county, but also on the extent of competition. In a county with more than one title or abstract company, each company, if it is to maintain a complete plant, must duplicate the work and expense of its competitors for only a fraction of the available business. To avoid this costly repetition, a recent development in several large communities (Denver, Dallas, and Los Angeles) is a joint venture in which several title companies form a separate corporation to organize and maintain a single title plant, owned and used by all participating firms. . . .

THE OPERATION OF TITLE PLANTS

Regardless of what system or combination of systems are employed to develop and index information, it is in the use of the title plant that all the installation and maintenance work finds fulfillment. The search operations described below will be performed by persons with different titles, depending upon local terminology. In a small operation, one person might perform several or all of the functions. But generally here is what happens when an order is placed for a title insurance policy or an abstract of title:

A "caption writer" determines that the legal description on the application is valid and can be identified and reconciled with descriptions incorporated in the title plant records. He also determines the period of time to be searched, usually back to a previous policy or abstract.

A "chain man" compiles a list of all recorded documents that during the period to be searched were posted against the described property in the basic index.

A "name searcher" compiles a list of all current items (judgments, probate matters, mechanic's liens, etc.) posted against the names of the individuals appearing in the chain of title for the search period.

A "tax searcher" records the year, purpose, and amount of any unpaid general property taxes and special assessments shown against the property.

These different work sheets are then assembled in a file and assigned for examination to a highly-trained, experienced employee or officer of the firm. Upon going over the file, he may order additional documentation to fill in apparent gaps or deficiencies. He may, for instance, ask for a full copy of certain original instruments, a survey or physical inspection of the premises, or an affidavit on some dubious factual point. But once satisfied that the file is sufficiently complete, he will prepare the abstract or, if a title insurance policy has been ordered, a preliminary report of title, to be followed at a subsequent time by the policy of insurance. A further step, after closing of a real estate transaction, may be a later date search to reflect recording of the deed or mortgage and any mortgage releases.

SUMMARY

A title plant is a gigantic consolidated bookkeeping system, compiled from many sources, reflecting pertinent matters pertaining to land titles as disclosed principally by public recording act, judicial and tax records. Given the present scattered, often poorly indexed and sometimes incomplete nature of public land records, privately owned and operated title plants are helpful and frequently essential to accurately and quickly determine the record ownership of real property in the United States. In many counties, especially those in and around large cities, it is doubtful if the surge of homebuying, road building, office and commercial construction and subdivision of lands, which has characterized the present century, could have been accomplished under prevailing laws had it not been for the development and use of private plants. And title plants everywhere have tended to cut the cost of title searches and examinations.

2. *Protection Provided*

Title insurance protects the insured from loss as the result of title deficiencies not excepted by the policy. Most policies contain a number of exceptions: any material defects uncovered by the insurer in its search of the particular title, and certain risks that, in standard printed clauses, the insurer excludes in all coverage of the kind in question. For an added premium, there are companies that will provide extended coverage by eliminating some of their standard exceptions. State insurance regulations in some states control the kinds of extended coverage permitted.

Most title policies insure the title against both record and off-record claims, subject, of course, to stated exceptions. Coverage of off-record risks is desired by many knowledgeable insureds because of the difficulty, often the impossibility, of ascertaining that such risks exist. However, one type of policy, sometimes referred to as a title guarantee, insures only the record title. The policy states, in essence, that the insured has good record title, subject to any listed exceptions, and then obligates the company to pay any losses incurred by the insured should the record title be otherwise. It provides not only protection against negligence in search and examination of the public records, but guarantees that the record title is as represented, thus protecting against non-negligent search and examination errors. This limited form of policy was extensively written at an earlier stage in the evolution of title insurance.

Many insurers insist that at the time of policy issuance, an owner insure for the full value of the fee and a mortgagee for the full amount of the mortgage. Additional coverage is not required by the policy if subsequently the value of the property goes up, although if this happens, the owner may deem it wise to increase the face amount of the policy, which normally can be done by paying an added premium. If the owner substantially improves the property after he insures, some policies make him a coinsurer, providing he does not adequately increase the amount of coverage. As a coinsurer, he must bear some of the risk of loss.

In addition to protecting against title deficiencies, title insurance policies commonly provide certain benefits in case of litigation. These benefits usually include a commitment by the insurer, at its cost, to defend the insured in litigation over the title based on any claim not excepted by the policy. Failure of the insurer to defend can result in it being obligated to pay defense counsel retained by the insured.

As is true of other kinds of insurance, the scope of title insurance coverage is determined in large part by standard provisions in the insurers' policies. All companies use printed policy forms and their terms are often borrowed from state or national trade association approved documents. Of special importance have been the title policy forms developed and approved by the American Land Title Association, a national association of commercial title insurance companies, abstracters, and title lawyers, including counsel for large lending institutions. This association's forms, particularly its standard mortgagee's policies, have been widely adopted by title insurers. They are periodically revised.

NOTE

"Title insurance is a relatively simple business. In theory it should be a no loss coverage since properly researched, a title examination should result in the reporting of all defects and encumbrances. The problem is that title plants (i.e. the compilation of historical real estate transfers and related information) are not always absolutely correct, people make mistakes in keeping title plants up to date or do not evaluate the data available properly, and when it comes to real estate transactions there is always ample room for fraud and misrepresentations." Zucaro, The Title Insurance Industry, p. 3, based on remarks made January 28, 1992, to the Association of Insurance Financial Analysts and distributed by Old Republic International Corporation.

POLICY NO.:
SPECIMEN

LOAN POLICY OF TITLE INSURANCE
Issued by
Fidelity National Title Insurance Company

Any notice of claim and any other notice or statement in writing required to be given to the Company under this Policy must be given to the Company at the address shown in Section 17 of the Conditions.

COVERED RISKS

SUBJECT TO THE EXCLUSIONS FROM COVERAGE, THE EXCEPTIONS FROM COVERAGE CONTAINED IN SCHEDULE B, AND THE CONDITIONS, FIDELITY NATIONAL TITLE INSURANCE COMPANY, a California corporation (the "Company") insures as of Date of Policy and, to the extent stated in Covered Risks 11, 13, and 14, after Date of Policy, against loss or damage, not exceeding the Amount of Insurance, sustained or incurred by the Insured by reason of:

1. *Title being vested other than as stated in Schedule A.*

2. *Any defect in or lien or encumbrance on the Title. This Covered Risk includes but is not limited to insurance against loss from*

   (a) *A defect in the Title caused by*

      (i) *forgery, fraud, undue influence, duress, incompetency, incapacity, or impersonation;*

      (ii) *failure of any person or Entity to have authorized a transfer or conveyance;*

      (iii) *a document affecting Title not properly created, executed, witnessed, sealed, acknowledged, notarized, or delivered;*

      (iv) *failure to perform those acts necessary to create a document by electronic means authorized by law;*

      (v) *a document executed under a falsified, expired, or otherwise invalid power of attorney;*

      (vi) *a document not properly filed, recorded, or indexed in the Public Records including failure to perform those acts by electronic means authorized by law; or*

      (vii) *a defective judicial or administrative proceeding.*

   (b) *The lien of real estate taxes or assessments imposed on the Title by a governmental authority due or payable, but unpaid.*

   (c) *Any encroachment, encumbrance, violation, variation, or adverse circumstance affecting the Title that would be disclosed by an accurate and complete land survey of the Land. The term "encroachment" includes encroachments of existing improvements located on the Land onto adjoining land, and encroachments onto the Land of existing improvements located on adjoining land.*

3. *Unmarketable Title.*

4. *No right of access to and from the Land.*

OWNER'S POLICY OF TITLE INSURANCE
Issued by
Fidelity National Title Insurance Company

Any notice of claim and any other notice or statement in writing required to be given the Company under this Policy must be given to the Company at the address shown in Section 18 of the Conditions.

COVERED RISKS

SUBJECT TO THE EXCLUSIONS FROM COVERAGE, THE EXCEPTIONS FROM COVERAGE CONTAINED IN SCHEDULE B, AND THE CONDITIONS, FIDELITY NATIONAL TITLE INSURANCE COMPANY, a California corporation (the "Company") insures, as of Date of Policy and, to the extent stated in Covered Risks 9 and 10, after Date of Policy, against loss or damage, not exceeding the Amount of Insurance, sustained or incurred by the Insured by reason of:

1. *Title being vested other than as stated in Schedule A.*

2. *Any defect in or lien or encumbrance on the Title. This Covered Risk includes but is not limited to insurance against loss from*

   (a) *A defect in the Title caused by*

   (i) *forgery, fraud, undue influence, duress, incompetency, incapacity, or impersonation;*

   (ii) *failure of any person or Entity to have authorized a transfer or conveyance;*

   (iii) *a document affecting Title not properly created, executed, witnessed, sealed, acknowledged, notarized, or delivered;*

   (iv) *failure to perform those acts necessary to create a document by electronic means authorized by law;*

   (v) *a document executed under a falsified, expired, or otherwise invalid power of attorney;*

   (vi) *a document not properly filed, recorded, or indexed in the Public Records including failure to perform those acts by electronic means authorized by law; or*

   (vii) *a defective judicial or administrative proceeding.*

   (b) *The lien of real estate taxes or assessments imposed on the Title by a governmental authority due or payable, but unpaid.*

   (c) *Any encroachment, encumbrance, violation, variation, or adverse circumstance affecting the Title that would be disclosed by an accurate and complete land survey of the Land. The term "encroachment" includes encroachments of existing improvements located on the Land onto adjoining land, and encroachments onto the Land of existing improvements located on adjoining land.*

3. *Unmarketable Title.*

4. *No right of access to and from the Land.*

5. The violation or enforcement of any law, ordinance, permit, or governmental regulation (including those relating to building and zoning) restricting, regulating, prohibiting, or relating to

    (a) the occupancy, use, or enjoyment of the Land;

    (b) the character, dimensions, or location of any improvement erected on the Land;

    (c) the subdivision of land; or

    (d) environmental protection

    if a notice, describing any part of the Land, is recorded in the Public Records setting forth the violation or intention to enforce, but only to the extent of the violation or enforcement referred to in that notice.

6. An enforcement action based on the exercise of a governmental police power not covered by Covered Risk 5 if a notice of the enforcement action, describing any part of the Land, is recorded in the Public Records, but only to the extent of the enforcement referred to in that notice.

7. The exercise of the rights of eminent domain if a notice of the exercise, describing any part of the Land, is recorded in the Public Records.

8. Any taking by a governmental body that has occurred and is binding on the rights of a purchaser for value without Knowledge.

9. The invalidity or unenforceability of the lien of the Insured Mortgage upon the Title. This Covered Risk includes but is not limited to insurance against loss from any of the following impairing the lien of the Insured Mortgage

    (a) forgery, fraud, undue influence, duress, incompetency, incapacity, or impersonation;

    (b) failure of any person or Entity to have authorized a transfer or conveyance;

    (c) the Insured Mortgage not being property created, executed, witnessed, sealed, acknowledged, notarized, or delivered;

    (d) failure to perform those acts necessary to create a document by electronic means authorized by law;

    (e) a document executed under a falsified, expired, or otherwise invalid power of attorney;

    (f) a document not properly filed, recorded, or indexed in the Public Records including failure to perform those acts by electronic means authorized by law; or

    (g) a defective judicial or administrative proceeding.

10. The lack of priority of the lien of the Insured Mortgage upon the Title over any other lien or encumbrance.

11. The lack of priority of the lien of the Insured Mortgage upon the Title

    (a) as security for each and every advance of proceeds of the loan secured by the Insured Mortgage over any statutory lien for services, labor, or material arising from construction of an improvement or work related to the Land when the improvement or work is either

        (i) contracted for or commenced on or before Date of Policy; or

        (ii) contracted for, commenced or continued after Date of Policy if the construction is financed, in whole or in part, by proceeds of the loan secured by the Insured Mortgage that the Insured has advanced or is obligated on Date of Policy to advance; and

    (b) over the lien of any assessments for street improvements under construction or completed at Date of Policy.

5. The violation or enforcement of any law, ordinance, permit, or governmental regulation (including those relating to building and zoning) restricting, regulating, prohibiting, or relating to

   (a) the occupancy, use, or enjoyment of the Land;

   (b) the character, dimensions, or location of any improvement erected on the Land;

   (c) the subdivision of land; or

   (d) environmental protection

   if a notice, describing any part of the Land, is recorded in the Public Records setting forth the violation or intention to enforce, but only to the extent of the violation or enforcement referred to in that notice.

6. An enforcement action based on the exercise of a governmental police power hot covered by Covered Risk 5 if a notice of the enforcement action, describing any part of the Land, is recorded in the Public Records, but only to the extent of the enforcement referred to in that notice.

7. The exercise of the rights of eminent domain if a notice of the exercise, describing any part of the Land, is recorded in the Public Records.

8. Any taking by a governmental body that has occurred and is binding on the rights of a purchaser for value without Knowledge.

9. Title being vested other than as stated Schedule A or being defective

   (a) as a result of the avoidance in whole or in part, or from a court order providing an alternative remedy, of a transfer of all or any part of the title to or any interest in the Land occurring prior to the transaction vesting Title as shown in Schedule A because that prior transfer constituted a fraudulent or preferential transfer under federal bankruptcy, state insolvency, or similar creditors' rights laws; or

   (b) because the instrument of transfer vesting Title as shown in Schedule A constitutes a preferential transfer under federal bankruptcy, state insolvency, or similar creditors' rights laws by reason of the failure of its recording in the Public Records

       (i) to be timely, or

       (ii) to impart notice of its existence to a purchaser for value or to a judgment or lien creditor.

12. The invalidity or unenforceability of any assignment of the Insured Mortgage, provided the assignment is shown in Schedule A, or the failure of the assignment shown in Schedule A to vest title to the Insured Mortgage in the named insured assignee free and clear of all liens.

13. The invalidity, unenforceabiltty, lack of priority, or avoidance of the lien of the Insured Mortgage upon the Title

    (a) resulting from the avoidance in whole or in part, or from a court order providing an alternative remedy, of any transfer of all or any part of the title to or any interest in the Land occurring prior to the transaction creating the lien of the Insured Mortgage because that prior transfer constituted a fraudulent or preferential transfer under federal bankruptcy, state insolvency, or similar creditors' rights laws; or

    (b) because the Insured Mortgage constitutes a preferential transfer under federal bankruptcy, state insolvency, or similar creditors' rights laws by reason of the failure of its recording in the Public Records

        (i) to be timely, or

        (ii) to impart notice of its existence to a purchaser for value or to a judgment or lien creditor.

14. Any defect in or lien or encumbrance on the Title or other matter included in Covered Risks 1 through 13 that has been created or attached or has been filed or recorded in the Public Records subsequent to Date of Policy and prior to the recording of the Insured Mortgage in the Public Records.

The Company will also pay the costs, attorneys' fees, and expenses incurred in defense of any matter insured against by this Policy, but only to the extent provided in the Conditions.

IN WITNESS WHEREOF, FIDELITY NATIONAL TITLE INSURANCE COMPANY has caused this policy to be signed and sealed by its duly authorized officers.

Fidelity National Title Insurance Company

SEAL

SPECIMEN
Countersigned

10. Any defect in or lien or encumbrance on the Title or other matter included in Covered Risks 1 through 9 that has been created or attached or has been filed or recorded in the Public Records subsequent to Date of Policy and prior to the recording of the deed or other instrument of transfer in the Public Records that vests Title as shown in Schedule A.

The Company will also pay the costs, attorneys' fees, and expenses incurred in defense of any matter insured against by this Policy, but only to the extent provided in the Conditions.

IN WITNESS WHEREOF, FIDELITY NATIONAL TITLE INSURANCE COMPANY has caused this policy to be signed and sealed by its duly authorized officers.

Fidelity National Title Insurance Company

SEAL

SPECIMEN
Countersigned

27-031-06 (6/06)

ALTA Owner's Policy (6/17/06)

SCHEDULE A

Name and Address of Title Insurance Company:

Policy No.:
Loan No.:
Address Reference: PROPERTY STREET, [County], [State]

Amount of Insurance: $
Premium: $

Date of Policy:

1.   Name of Insured:

     Name

2.   The estate or interest in the Land that is encumbered by the Insured Mortgage is:

     A Fee

3.   Title is vested in:

     Names

4.   The Insured Mortgage and its assignments, if any, are described as follows:

     Paragraphs are inserted here.

5.   The Land referred to in this policy is described as follows:

     SEE EXHIBIT "A" ATTACHED HERETO AND MADE A PART HEREOF

6.   This policy incorporates by reference those ALTA endorsements selected below:

     —— 4-06   (Condominium)
     —— 4.1-06
     —— 5-06   (Planned Unit Development)
     —— 5.1-06-
     —— 6-06   (Variable Rate)
     —— 6.2-06   (Variable Rate-Negative Amortization)
     —— 8.1-06   (Environmental Protection Lien) Paragraph b refers to the
                   following state statute(s):
     —— 9-06   (Restrictions, Encroachments, Minerals)
     —— 13.1-06   (Leasehold Loan)
     —— 14-06   (Future Advance-Priority)
     —— 14.1-06   (Future Advance-Knowledge)
     —— 14.3-06   (Future Advance-Reverse Mortgage)
     —— 22-06   (Location) The type of improvement is a FILL IN, and the street
                   address is as shown above.

THIS POLICY VALID ONLY IF SCHEDULE B IS ATTACHED

ALTA Loan Policy (6/17/06)

SCHEDULE A

Name and Address of Title Insurance Company:

Policy No.:
Address Reference: PROPERTY STREET, [County], [State]

Amount of Insurance:	$
Premium:	$

Date of Policy:

1. Name of Insured:

    BUYER

2. The estate or interest in the Land that is insured by this policy is:

    A Fee

3. Title is vested in:

    BUYER

4. The Land referred to in this policy is described as follows:

    SEE EXHIBIT "A" ATTACHED HERETO AND MADE A PART HEREOF

THIS POLICY VALID ONLY IF SCHEDULE B IS ATTACHED

ALTA Owner's Policy (6/17/06)

LEGAL DESCRIPTION

EXHIBIT "A"

THE LAND REFERRED TO HEREIN BELOW IS SITUATED IN THE COUNTY OF [FILL IN], STATE OF [FILL IN], AND IS DESCRIBED AS FOLLOWS:

[Legal description]

APN:

ALTA Loan Policy (6/17/06)

Policy No.

LEGAL DESCRIPTION

EXHIBIT "A"

THE LAND REFERRED TO HEREIN BELOW IS SITUATED IN THE COUNTY OF [FILL IN], STATE OF [FILL IN], AND IS DESCRIBED AS FOLLOWS:

[Legal description]

APN:

ALTA Owner's Policy (6/17/06)

SCHEDULE B

EXCEPTIONS FROM COVERAGE

Except as provided in Schedule B - Part II, this policy does not insure against loss or damage, and the Company will not pay costs, attorneys' fees, or expenses that arise by reason of:

PART I

1.   Paragraphs are inserted here.

SCHEDULE B

PART II

In addition to the matters set forth in Part I of this Schedule, the Title is subject to the following matters, and the Company insures against loss or damage sustained in the event that they are not subordinate to the lien of the Insured Mortgage:

1.   Paragraphs are inserted here.

ALTA Loan Policy (6/17/06)

Policy No.

SCHEDULE B

EXCEPTIONS FROM COVERAGE

This policy does not insure against loss or damage, and the Company will not pay costs, attorneys' fees, or expenses that arise by reason of:

1.   Paragraphs are inserted here.

ALTA Owner's Policy (6/17/06)

EXCLUSIONS FROM COVERAGE

The following matters are expressly excluded from the coverage of this policy, and the Company will not pay loss or damage, costs, attorneys' fees, or expenses that arise by reason of:

1. (a) Any law, ordinance, permit, or governmental regulation (including those relating to building and zoning) restricting, regulating, prohibiting, or relating to
   (i)   the occupancy, use, or enjoyment of the Land;
   (ii) the character, dimensions, or location of any improvement erected on the Land;
   (iii) the subdivision of land; or
   (iv) environmental protection;
   or the effect of any violation of these laws, ordinances, or governmental regulations. This Exclusion 1(a) does not modify or limit the coverage provided under Covered Risk 5.
   (b) Any governmental police power. This Exclusion 1(b) does not modify or limit the coverage provided under Covered Risk 6.

2. Rights of eminent domain. This Exclusion does not modify or limit the coverage provided under Covered Risk 7 or 8.

3. Defects, liens, encumbrances, adverse claims, or other matters
   (a) created, suffered, assumed, or agreed to by the Insured Claimant;
   (b) not Known to the Company, not recorded in the Public Records at Date of Policy, but Known to the Insured Claimant and not disclosed in writing to the Company by the Insured Claimant prior to the date the Insured Claimant became an Insured under this policy;
   (c) resulting in no loss or damage to the Insured Claimant;
   (d) attaching or created subsequent to Date of Policy (however, this does not modify or limit the coverage provided under Covered Risk 11, 13, or 14); or
   (e) resulting in loss or damage that would not have been sustained if the Insured Claimant had paid value for the Insured Mortgage.

4. Unenforceability of the lien of the Insured Mortgage because of the inability or failure of an insured to comply with applicable doing-business laws of the state where the Land is situated.

5. Invalidity or unenforceability in whole or in part of the lien of the Insured Mortgage that arises out of the transaction evidenced by the Insured Mortgage and is based upon usury or any consumer credit protection or truth-in-lending law.

6. Any claim, by reason of the operation of federal bankruptcy, state insolvency, or similar creditors' rights laws, that the transaction creating the lien of the Insured Mortgage, is
   (a) a fraudulent conveyance or fraudulent transfer, or
   (b) a preferential transfer for any reason not stated in Covered Risk 13(b) of this policy.

7. Any lien on the Title for real estate taxes or assessments imposed by governmental authority and created or attaching between Date of Policy and the date of recording of the Insured Mortgage in the Public Records. This exclusion does not modify or limit the coverage provided under Covered Risk 11(b).

CONDITIONS

1. DEFINITION OF TERMS

The following terms when used in this policy mean:

(a) "Amount of Insurance": The amount stated in Schedule A, as may be increased or decreased by endorsement to this policy, increased by Section 8(b) or decreased by Section 10 of these Conditions.

(b) "Date of Policy": The date designated as "Date of Policy" in Schedule A.

(c) "Entity": A corporation, partnership, trust, limited liability company, or other similar legal entity.

(d) "Indebtedness": The obligation secured by the Insured Mortgage including one evidenced by electronic means authorized by law, and if that obligation is the payment of a debt, the Indebtedness is the sum of
(i) the amount of the principal disbursed as of Date of Policy;
(ii) the amount of the principal disbursed subsequent to Date of Policy;
(iii) the construction loan advances made subsequent to Date of Policy for the purpose of financing in whole or in part the construction of an improvement to the Land or related to the Land that the Insured was and continued to be obligated to advance at Date of Policy and at the date of the advance;
(iv) interest on the loan;
(v) the prepayment premiums, exit fees, and other similar fees or penalties allowed by law;
(vi) the expenses of foreclosure and any other costs of enforcement;
(vii) the amounts advanced to assure compliance with laws or to protect the lien or the priority of the lien of the Insured Mortgage before the acquisition of the estate or interest in the Title;
(viii) the amounts to pay taxes and insurance; and
(ix) the reasonable amounts expended to prevent deterioration of improvements; but the Indebtedness is reduced by the total of all payments and by any amount forgiven by an Insured.

(e) "Insured": The Insured named in Schedule A.

(i) The term "Insured" also includes
(A) the owner of the Indebtedness and each successor in ownership of the Indebtedness, whether the owner or successor owns the Indebtedness for its own account or as a trustee or other fiduciary, except a successor who is an obligor under the provisions of Section 12(c) of these Conditions;
(B) the person or Entity who has "control" of the "transferable record," if the Indebtedness is evidenced by a "transferable record," as these terms are defined by applicable electronic transactions law;
(C) successors to an Insured by dissolution, merger, consolidation, distribution, or reorganization;
(D) successors to an Insured by its conversion to another kind of Entity;
(E) a grantee of an Insured under a deed delivered without payment of actual valuable consideration

EXCLUSIONS FROM COVERAGE

The following matters are expressly excluded from the coverage of this policy, and the Company will not pay loss or damage, costs, attorneys' fees, or expenses that arise by reason of:

1. (a) Any law, ordinance, permit, or governmental regulation (including those relating to building and zoning) restricting, regulating, prohibiting, or relating to
    (i)   the occupancy, use, or enjoyment of the Land;
    (ii)   the character, dimensions or location of any improvement erected on the Land;
    (iii) the subdivision of land; or
    (iv)   environmental protection;
    or the effect of any violation of these laws, ordinances, or governmental regulations. This Exclusion 1(a) does not modify or limit the coverage provided under Covered Risk 5.
    (b) Any governmental police power. This Exclusion 1(b) does not modify or limit the coverage provided under Covered Risk 6.
2. Rights of eminent domain. This Exclusion does not modify or limit the coverage provided under Covered Risk 7 or 8.
3. Defects, liens, encumbrances, adverse claims, or other matters:
    (a) created, suffered, assumed, or agreed to by the Insured Claimant;
    (b) not Known to the Company, not recorded in the Public Records at Date of Policy, but Known to the Insured Claimant and not disclosed in writing to the Company by the Insured Claimant prior to the date the Insured Claimant became an Insured under this policy;
    (c) resulting in no loss or damage to the Insured Claimant;
    (d) attaching or created subsequent to Date of Policy (however, this does not modify or limit the coverage provided under Covered Risk 9 and 10); or
    (e) resulting in loss or damage that would not have been sustained if the Insured Claimant had paid value for the Title.
4. Any claim, by reason of the operation of federal bankruptcy, state insolvency, or similar creditors' rights laws, that the transaction vesting the Title as shown in Schedule A, is
    (a) a fraudulent conveyance or fraudulent transfer; or
    (b) a preferential transfer for any reason not stated in Covered Risk 9 of this policy.
5. Any lien on the Title for real estate taxes or assessments imposed by governmental authority and created or attaching between Date of Policy and the date of recording of the deed or other instrument of transfer in the Public Records that vests Title as shown in Schedule A.

CONDITIONS

1. DEFINITION OF TERMS

The following terms when used in this policy mean:

(a) "Amount of Insurance": The amount stated in Schedule A, as may be increased or decreased by endorsement to this policy, increased by Section 8(b), or decreased by Sections 11 and 12 of these Conditions.

(b) "Date of Policy": The date designated as "Date of Policy" in Schedule A.

(c) "Entity": A corporation, partnership, trust, limited liability company, or other similar legal entity.

(d) "Insured": The Insured named in Schedule A.

(i) The term "Insured" also includes

(A) successors to the Title of the Insured by operation of law as distinguished from purchase, including heirs, devisees, survivors, personal representatives, or next of kin;

(B) successors to an Insured by dissolution, merger, consolidation, distribution, or reorganization;

(C) successors to an Insured by its conversion to another kind of Entity;

(D) a grantee of an insured under a deed delivered without payment of actual valuable consideration conveying the Title

(1) if the stock, shares, memberships, or other equity interests of the grantee are wholly-owned by the named Insured,

(2) if the grantee wholly owns the named Insured,

(3) if the grantee is wholly-owned by an affiliated Entity of the named Insured, provided the affiliated Entity and the named Insured are both wholly-owned by the same person or Entity, or

(4) if the grantee is a trustee or beneficiary of a trust created by a written instrument established by the Insured named in Schedule A for estate planning purposes.

(ii) With regard to (A), (B), (C), and (D) reserving, however, all rights and defenses as to any successor that the Company would have had against any predecessor Insured.

(e) "Insured Claimant": An Insured claiming loss or damage.

(f) "Knowledge" or "Known": Actual knowledge, not constructive knowledge or notice that may be imputed to an Insured by reason of the Public Records or any other records that impart constructive notice of matters affecting the Title.

(g) "Land": The land described in Schedule A, and affixed improvements that by law constitute real property. The term "Land" does not include any property beyond the lines of the area described in Schedule A, nor any right, title, interest, estate, or easement in abutting streets, roads, avenues, alleys, lanes, ways, or waterways, but this does not modify or limit the extent that a right of access to and from the Land is insured by this policy.

(h) "Mortgage": Mortgage, deed of trust, trust deed, or other security instrument, including one evidenced by electronic means authorized by law.

(i) "Public Records": Records established under state statutes at Date of Policy for the purpose of imparting constructive notice of matters relating to

conveying the Title

(1) if the stock, shares, memberships, or other equity interests of the grantee are wholly-owned by the named Insured,

(2) if the grantee wholly owns the named Insured, or

(3) if the grantee is wholly-owned by an affiliated Entity of the named Insured, provided the affiliated Entity and the named Insured are both wholly-owned by the same person or Entity;

(F) any government agency or instrumentality that is an insurer or guarantor under an insurance contract or guaranty insuring or guaranteeing the Indebtedness secured by the Insured Mortgage, or any part of it, whether named as an Insured or not;

(ii) With regard to (A), (B), (C), (D), and (E) reserving, however, all rights and defenses as to any successor that the Company would have had against any predecessor Insured, unless the successor acquired the Indebtedness as a purchaser for value without Knowledge of the asserted defect, lien, encumbrance, or other matter insured against by this policy.

(f) "Insured Claimant": An Insured claiming loss or damage.

(g) "Insured Mortgage": The Mortgage described in paragraph 4 of Schedule A.

(h) "Knowledge" or "Known": Actual knowledge, not constructive knowledge or notice that may be imputed to an Insured by reason of the Public Records or any other records that impart constructive notice of matters affecting the Title.

(i) "Land": The land described in Schedule A, and affixed improvements that by law constitute real property. The term "Land" does not include any property beyond the lines of the area described in Schedule A, nor any right, title, interest, estate, or easement in abutting streets, roads, avenues, alleys, lanes, ways or waterways, but this does not modify or limit the extent that a right of access to and from the Land is insured by this policy.

(j) "Mortgage": Mortgage, deed of trust, trust deed, or other security instrument, including one evidenced by electronic means authorized by law.

(k) "Public Records": Records established under state statutes at Date of Policy for the purpose of imparting constructive notice of matters relating to real property to purchasers for value and without Knowledge. With respect to Covered

Risk 5(d), "Public Records" shall also include environmental protection liens filed in the records of the clerk of the United States District Court for the district where the Land is located.

(l) "Title": The estate or interest described in Schedule A.

(m) "Unmarketable Title": Title affected by an alleged or apparent matter that would permit a prospective purchaser or lessee of the Title or lender on the Title or a prospective purchaser of the Insured Mortgage to be released from the obligation to purchase, lease, or lend if there is a contractual condition requiring the delivery of marketable title.

2. CONTINUATION OF INSURANCE

The coverage of this policy shall continue in force as of Date of Policy in favor of an Insured after acquisition of the Title by an Insured or after conveyance by an Insured, but only so long as the Insured retains an estate or interest in the Land, or holds an obligation secured by a purchase money Mortgage given by a purchaser from the Insured, or only so long as the Insured shall have liability by reason of warranties in any transfer or conveyance of the Title. This policy shall not continue in force in favor of any purchaser from the Insured of either (i) an estate or interest in the Land, or (ii) an obligation secured by a purchase money Mortgage given to the Insured.

3. NOTICE OF CLAIM TO BE GIVEN BY INSURED CLAIMANT

The Insured shall notify the Company promptly in writing (i) in case of any litigation as set forth in Section 5 (a) of these Conditions, (ii) in case Knowledge shall come to an Insured of any claim of title or interest that is adverse to the Title or the lien of the Insured Mortgage, as insured, and that might cause loss or damage for which the Company may be liable by virtue of this policy, or (iii) if the Title or the lien of the Insured Mortgage, as insured, is rejected as Unmarketable Title. If the Company is prejudiced by the failure of the Insured Claimant to provide prompt notice, the Company's liability to the Insured Claimant under the policy shall be reduced to the extent of the prejudice.

4. PROOF OF LOSS

In the event the Company is unable to determine the amount of loss or damage, the Company may, at its option, require as a condition of payment that the Insured Claimant

furnish a signed proof of loss. The proof of loss must describe the defect, lien, encumbrance, or other matter insured against by this policy that constitutes the basis of loss or damage and shall state, to the extent possible, the basis of calculating the amount of the loss or damage.

5. DEFENSE AND PROSECUTION OF ACTIONS

(a) Upon written request by the Insured, and subject to the options contained in Section 7-of—these Conditions, the Company, at its own cost and without unreasonable delay, shall provide for the defense of an Insured in litigation in which any third party asserts a claim covered by this policy adverse to the Insured. This obligation is limited to only those stated causes of action alleging matters insured against by this policy. The Company shall have the right to select counsel of its choice (subject to the right of the Insured to object for reasonable cause) to represent the Insured as to those stated causes of action. It shall not be liable for and will not pay the fees of any other counsel. The Company will not pay any fees, costs, or expenses incurred by the Insured in the defense of those causes of action that allege matters not insured against by this policy.

(b) The Company shall have the right, in addition to the options contained in Section 7 of these Conditions, at its own cost, to institute and prosecute any action or proceeding or to do any other act that in its opinion may be necessary or desirable to establish the Title or the lien of the Insured Mortgage, as insured, or to prevent or reduce loss or damage to the Insured. The Company may take any appropriate action under the terms of this policy, whether or not it shall be liable to the Insured. The exercise of these rights shall not be an admission of liability or waiver of any provision of this policy. If the Company exercises its rights under this subsection, it must do so diligently.

(c) Whenever the Company brings an action or asserts a defense as required or permitted by this policy, the Company may pursue the litigation to a final determination by a court of competent jurisdiction, and it expressly reserves the right, in its sole discretion, to appeal from any adverse judgment or order.

real property to purchasers for value and without Knowledge. With respect to Covered Risk 5(d), "Public Records" shall also include environmental protection liens filed in the records of the clerk of the United States District Court for the district where the Land is located.

(j)"Title": The estate or interest described in Schedule A.

(k) "Unmarketable Title": Title affected by an alleged or apparent matter that would permit a prospective purchaser or lessee of the Title or lender on the Title to be released from the obligation to purchase, lease, or lend if there is a contractual condition requiring the delivery of marketable title.

2. CONTINUATION OF INSURANCE

The coverage of this policy shall continue in force as of Date of Policy in favor of an Insured, but only so long as the Insured retains an estate or interest in the Land, or holds an obligation secured by a purchase money Mortgage given by a purchaser from the Insured, or only so long as the Insured shall have liability by reason of warranties in any transfer or conveyance of the Title. This policy shall not continue in force in favor of any purchaser from the Insured of either (i) an estate or interest in the Land, or (ii) an obligation secured by a purchase money Mortgage given to the Insured.

3. NOTICE OF CLAIM TO BE GIVEN BY INSURED CLAIMANT

The Insured shall notify the Company promptly in writing (i) in case of any litigation as set forth in Section 5 (a) of these Conditions, (ii) in case Knowledge shall come to an Insured hereunder of any claim of title or interest that is adverse to the Title, as insured, and that might cause loss or damage for which the Company may be liable by virtue of this policy, or (iii) if the Title, as insured, is rejected as Unmarketable Title. If the Company is prejudiced by the failure of the Insured Claimant to provide prompt notice, the Company's liability to the Insured Claimant under the policy shall be reduced to the extent of the prejudice.

4. PROOF OF LOSS

In the event the Company is unable to determine the amount of loss or damage, the Company may, at its option, require as a condition of payment that the Insured Claimant furnish a signed proof of loss. The proof of loss must describe the defect, lien, encumbrance, or other matter insured against by this policy that constitutes the basis of loss or damage and shall state, to the extent possible, the basis of calculating the amount of the loss or damage.

5. DEFENSE AND PROSECUTION OF ACTIONS

(a) Upon written request by the Insured, and subject to the options contained in Section 7 of these Conditions, the Company, at its own cost and without unreasonable delay, shall provide for the defense of an Insured in litigation in which any third party asserts a claim covered by this policy adverse to the Insured. This obligation is limited to only those stated causes of action alleging matters insured against by this policy. The Company shall have the right to select counsel of its choice (subject to the right of the Insured to object for reasonable cause) to represent the Insured as to those stated causes of action. It shall not be liable for and will not pay the fees of any other counsel. The Company will not pay any fees, costs, or expenses incurred by the Insured in the defense of those causes of action that allege matters not insured against by this policy.

(b) The Company shall have the right, in addition to the options contained in Section 7 of these Conditions, at its own cost, to institute and prosecute any action or proceeding or to do any other act that in its opinion may be necessary or desirable to establish the Title, as insured, or to prevent or reduce loss or damage to the Insured. The Company may take any appropriate action under the terms of this policy, whether or not it shall be liable to the Insured. The exercise of these rights shall not be an admission of liability or waiver of any provision of this policy. If the Company exercises its rights under this subsection, it must do so diligently.

(c) Whenever the Company brings an action or asserts a defense as required or permitted by this policy, the Company may pursue the litigation to a final determination by a court of competent jurisdiction, and it expressly reserves the right, in its sole discretion, to appeal from any adverse judgment or order.

6. DUTY OF INSURED CLAIMANT TO COOPERATE

(a) In all cases where this policy permits or requires the Company to prosecute or provide for the defense of any action or proceeding and any appeals, the Insured shall secure to the Company the right to so prosecute or provide defense in the action or proceeding, including the right to use, at its option, the name of the Insured for this purpose. Whenever requested by the Company, the Insured, at the Company's expense, shall give the Company all reasonable aid (i) in securing evidence, obtaining witnesses, prosecuting or defending the action or proceeding, or effecting settlement, and (ii) in any other lawful act that in the opinion of the Company may be necessary or desirable to establish the Title or any other matter as insured. If the Company is prejudiced by the failure of the Insured to furnish the required cooperation, the Company's obligations to the Insured under the policy shall terminate, including any liability or obligation to defend, prosecute, or continue any litigation, with regard to the matter or matters requiring such cooperation.

(b) The Company may reasonably require the Insured Claimant to submit to examination under oath by any authorized representative of the Company and to produce for examination, inspection, and copying, at such reasonable times and places as may be designated by the authorized representative of the Company, all records, in whatever medium maintained, including books, ledgers, checks, memoranda, correspondence, reports, e-mails, disks, tapes, and videos whether bearing a date before or after Date of Policy, that reasonably pertain to the loss or damage. Further, if requested by any authorized representative of the Company, the Insured Claimant shall grant its permission, in writing, for any authorized representative of the Company to examine, inspect, and copy all of these records in the custody or control of a third party that reasonably pertain to the loss or damage. All information designated as confidential by the Insured Claimant provided to the Company pursuant to this Section shall not be disclosed to others unless, in the reasonable judgment of the Company, it is necessary in the administration of the claim. Failure of the Insured Claimant to submit for examination under oath, produce any reasonably requested information, or grant permission to secure reasonably necessary information from third parties as required in this subsection unless

6. DUTY OF INSURED CLAIM-ANT TO COOPERATE

(a) In all cases where this policy permits or requires the Company to prosecute or provide for the defense of any action or proceeding and any appeals, the Insured shall secure to the Company the right to so prosecute or provide defense in the action or proceeding, including the right to use, at its option, the name of the Insured for this purpose. Whenever requested by the Company, the Insured, at the Company's expense, shall give the Company all reasonable aid (i) in securing evidence, obtaining witnesses, prosecuting or defending the action or proceeding, or effecting settlement, and (ii) in any other lawful act that in the opinion of the Company may be necessary or desirable to establish the Title, the lien of the Insured Mortgage, or any other matter as insured. If the Company is prejudiced by the failure of the Insured to furnish the required cooperation, the Company's obligations to the Insured under the policy shall terminate, including any liability or obligation to defend, prosecute, or continue any litigation, with regard to the matter or matters requiring such cooperation.

(b) The Company may reasonably require the Insured Claimant to submit to examination under oath by any authorized representative of the Company and to produce for examination, inspection, and copying, at such reasonable times and places as may be designated by the authorized representative of the Company, all records, in whatever medium maintained, including books, ledgers, checks, memoranda, correspondence, reports, e-mails, disks, tapes, and videos whether bearing a date before or after Date of Policy, that reasonably pertain to the loss or damage. Further, if requested by any authorized representative of the Company, the Insured Claimant shall grant its permission, in writing, for any authorized representative of the Company to examine, inspect, and copy all of these records in the custody or control of a third party that reasonably pertain to the loss or damage. All information designated as confidential by the Insured Claimant provided to the Company pursuant to this Section shall not be disclosed to others unless, in the reasonable judgment of the Company, it is necessary in the administration of the 27-041-06 (6/06) claim. Failure of the Insured Claimant to submit for examination under oath, produce any reasonably requested information, or grant permission to secure reasonably necessary information from third parties as required in this subsection, unless prohibited by law or governmental regulation, shall terminate any liability of the Company under this policy as to that claim.

7. OPTIONS TO PAY OR OTHERWISE SETTLE CLAIMS; TERMINATION OF LIABILITY

In case of a claim under this policy, the Company shall have the following additional options:

(a) To Pay or Tender Payment of the Amount of Insurance or to Purchase the Indebtedness.

(i) To pay or tender payment of the Amount of Insurance under this policy together with any costs, attorneys' fees; and expenses incurred by the Insured Claimant that were authorized by the Company up to the time of payment or tender of payment and that the Company is obligated to pay; or

(ii) To purchase the Indebtedness for the amount of the Indebtedness on the date of purchase, together with any costs, attorneys' fees, and expenses incurred by the Insured Claimant that were authorized by the Company up to the time of purchase and that the Company is obligated to pay.

When the Company purchases the Indebtedness, the Insured shall transfer, assign, and convey to the Company the Indebtedness and the Insured Mortgage, together with any collateral security.

Upon the exercise by the Company of either of the options provided for in subsections (a)(i) or (ii), all liability and obligations of the Company to the Insured under this policy, other than to make the payment required in those subsections, shall terminate, including any liability or obligation to defend, prosecute, or continue any litigation.

(b) To Pay or Otherwise Settle With Parties Other Than the Insured or With the Insured Claimant.

(i) to pay or otherwise settle with other parties for or in the name of an Insured Claimant any claim insured against under this policy. In addition, the Company will pay any costs, attorneys' fees, and expenses incurred by the Insured Claimant that were authorized by the Company up to the time of payment and that the Company is obligated to pay; or

(ii) to pay or otherwise settle with the Insured Claimant the loss or damage provided for under this policy, together with any costs, attorneys' fees, and expenses incurred by the Insured Claimant that were authorized by the Company up to the time of payment and that the Company is obligated to pay.

Upon the exercise by the Company of either of the options provided for in subsections (b)(i) or (ii), the Company's obligations to the Insured under this policy for the claimed loss or damage, other than the payments required to be made, shall terminate, including any liability or obligation to defend, prosecute, or continue any litigation.

8. DETERMINATION AND EXTENT OF LIABILITY

This policy is a contract of indemnity against actual monetary loss or damage sustained or incurred by the Insured Claimant who has suffered loss or damage by reason of matters insured against by this policy.

(a) The extent of liability of the Company for loss or damage under this policy shall not exceed the least of

(i) the Amount of Insurance,

(ii) the Indebtedness,

(iii) the difference between the value of the Title as insured and the value of the Title subject to the risk insured against by this policy, or

(iv) if a government agency or instrumentality is the Insured Claimant, the amount it paid in the acquisition of the Title or the Insured Mortgage in satisfaction of its insurance contract or guaranty.

(b) If the Company pursues its rights under Section 5 of these Conditions and is unsuccessful in establishing the Title or the lien of the Insured Mortgage, as insured,

(i) the Amount of Insurance shall be increased by 10%, and

(ii) the Insured Claimant shall have the right to have the loss or damage determined either as of the date the claim was made by the Insured Claimant or as of the date it is settled and paid.

(c) In the event the Insured has acquired the Title in the manner described in Section 2 of these Conditions or has conveyed the Title, then the extent of liability of the Company shall continue as set forth in Section 8(a) of these Conditions.

prohibited by law or governmental regulation, shall terminate any liability of the Company under this policy as to that claim.

7. OPTIONS TO PAY OR OTHERWISE SETTLE CLAIMS; TERMINATION OF LIABILITY

In case of a claim under this policy, the Company shall have the following additional options:

(a) To Pay or Tender Payment of the Amount of Insurance.

To pay or tender payment of the Amount of Insurance under this policy together with any costs, attorneys' fees, and expenses incurred by the Insured Claimant that were authorized by the Company up to the time of payment or tender of payment and that the Company is obligated to pay.

Upon the exercise by the Company of this option, all liability and obligations of the Company to the Insured under this policy, other than to make the payment required in this subsection, shall terminate, including any liability or obligation to defend, prosecute, or continue any litigation.

(b) To Pay or Otherwise Settle With Parties Other Than the Insured or With the Insured Claimant.

(i) To pay or otherwise settle with other parties for or in the name of an Insured Claimant any claim insured against under this policy. In addition, the Company will pay any costs, attorneys' fees, and expenses incurred by the Insured Claimant that were authorized by the Company up to the time of payment and that the Company is obligated to pay; or

(ii) To pay or otherwise settle with the Insured Claimant the loss or damage provided for under this policy, together with any costs, attorneys' fees, and expenses incurred by the Insured Claimant that were authorized by the Company up to the time of payment and that the Company is obligated to pay.

Upon the exercise by the Company of either of the options provided for in subsections (b)(i) or (ii), the Company's obligations to the Insured under this policy for the claimed loss or damage, other than the payments required to be made, shall terminate, including any liability or obligation to defend, prosecute, or continue any litigation.

8. DETERMINATION AND EXTENT OF LIABILITY

This policy is a contract of indemnity against actual monetary loss or damage sustained or incurred by the Insured Claimant who has suffered loss or damage by reason of matters insured against by this policy.

(a) The extent of liability of the Company for loss or damage under this policy shall not exceed the lesser of

(i) the Amount of Insurance; or

(ii) the difference between the value of the Title as insured and the value of the Title subject to the risk insured against by this policy.

(b) If the Company pursues its rights under Section 5 of these Conditions and is unsuccessful in establishing the Title, as insured,

(i) the Amount of Insurance shall be increased by 10%, and

(ii) the Insured Claimant shall have the right to have the loss or damage determined either as of the date the claim was made by the Insured Claimant or as of the date it is settled and paid.

(c) In addition to the extent of liability under (a) and (b), the Company will also pay those costs, attorneys' fees, and expenses incurred in accordance with Sections 5 and 7 of these Conditions.

(d) In addition to the extent of liability under (a), (b), and (c), the Company will also pay those costs, attorneys' fees, and expenses incurred in accordance with Sections 5 and 7 of these Conditions.

9. LIMITATION OF LIABILITY

(a) If the Company establishes the Title, or removes the alleged defect, lien or encumbrance, or cures the lack of a right of access to or from the Land, or cures the claim of Unmarketable Title, or establishes the lien of the Insured Mortgage, all as insured, in a reasonably diligent manner by any method, including litigation and the completion of any appeals, it shall have fully performed its obligations with respect to that matter and shall not be liable for any loss or damage caused to the Insured.

(b) In the event of any litigation, including litigation by the Company or with the Company's consent, the Company shall have no liability for loss or damage until there has been a final determination by a court of competent jurisdiction, and disposition of all appeals, adverse to the Title or to the lien of the Insured Mortgage, as insured.

(c) The Company shall not be liable for loss or damage to the Insured for liability voluntarily assumed by the Insured in settling any claim or suit without the prior written consent of the Company.

10. REDUCTION OF INSURANCE; REDUCTION OR TERMINATION OF LIABILITY

(a) All payments under this policy, except payments made for costs, attorneys' fees, and expenses, shall reduce the Amount of Insurance by the amount of the payment. However, any payments made prior to the acquisition of Title as provided in Section 2 of these Conditions shall not reduce the Amount of Insurance afforded under this policy except to the extent that the payments reduce the Indebtedness.

(b) The voluntary satisfaction or release of the Insured Mortgage shall terminate all liability of the Company except as provided in Section 2 of these Conditions.

11. PAYMENT OF LOSS

When liability and the extent of loss or damage have been definitely fixed in accordance with these Conditions, the payment shall be made within 30 days.

12. RIGHTS OF RECOVERY UPON PAYMENT OR SETTLEMENT

(a) The Company's Right to Recover

Whenever the Company shall have settled and paid a claim under this policy, it shall be subrogated and entitled to the rights of the Insured Claimant in the Title or Insured Mortgage and all other rights and remedies in respect to the claim that the Insured Claimant has against any person or property, to the extent of the amount of any loss, costs, attorneys' fees, and expenses paid by the Company. If requested by the Company, the Insured Claimant shall execute documents to evidence the transfer to the Company of these rights and remedies. The Insured Claimant shall permit the Company to sue, compromise, or settle in the name of the Insured Claimant and to use the name of the Insured Claimant in any transaction or litigation involving these rights and remedies.

If a payment on account of a claim does not fully cover the loss of the Insured Claimant, the Company shall defer the exercise of its right to recover until after the Insured Claimant shall have recovered its loss.

(b) The Insured's Rights and Limitations

(i) The owner of the Indebtedness may release or substitute the personal liability of any debtor or guarantor, extend or otherwise modify the terms of payment, release a portion of the Title from the lien of the Insured Mortgage, or release any collateral security for the Indebtedness, if it does not affect the enforceability or priority of the lien of the Insured Mortgage.

(ii) If the Insured exercises a right provided in (b)(i), but has Knowledge of any claim adverse to the Title or the lien of the Insured Mortgage insured against by this policy, the Company shall be required to pay only that part of any losses insured against by this policy that shall exceed the amount, if any, lost to the Company by reason of the impairment by the Insured Claimant of the Company's right of subrogation.

(c) The Company's Rights Against Noninsured Obligors

The Company's right of subrogation includes the Insured's rights against noninsured obligors including the rights of the Insured to indemnities, guaranties, other policies of insurance, or bonds, notwithstanding any terms or conditions contained in those instruments that address subrogation rights.

The Company's right of subrogation shall not be avoided by acquisition of the Insured Mortgage by an

obligor (except an obligor described in Section 1(e)(i)(F) of these Conditions) who acquires the Insured Mortgage as a result of an indemnity, guarantee, other policy of insurance, or bond, and the obligor will not be an Insured under this policy.

13. ARBITRATION

Either the Company or the Insured may demand that the claim or controversy shall be submitted to arbitration pursuant to the Title Insurance Arbitration Rules of the American Land Title Association ("Rules"). Except as provided in the Rules, there shall be no joinder or consolidation with claims or controversies of other persons.

Arbitrable matters may include, but are not limited to, any controversy or claim between the Company and the Insured arising out of or relating to this policy, any service in connection with its issuance or the breach of a policy provision, or to any other controversy or claim arising out of the transaction giving rise to this policy. All arbitrable matters when the Amount of Insurance is $2,000,000 or less shall be arbitrated at the option of either the Company or the Insured. All arbitrable matters when the Amount of Insurance is in excess of $2,000,000 shall be arbitrated only when agreed to by both the Company and the Insured. Arbitration pursuant to this policy and under the Rules shall be binding upon the parties. Judgment upon the award rendered by the Arbitrator(s) may be entered in any court of competent jurisdiction.

14. LIABILITY LIMITED TO THIS POLICY; POLICY ENTIRE CONTRACT

(a) This policy together with all endorsements, if any, attached to it by the Company is the entire policy and contract between the Insured and the Company. In interpreting any provision of this policy, this policy shall be construed as a whole.

(b) Any claim of loss or damage that arises out of the status of the Title or lien of the Insured Mortgage or by any action asserting such claim shall be restricted to this policy.

(c) Any amendment of or endorsement to this policy must be in writing and authenticated by an authorized person, or expressly incorporated by Schedule A of this policy.

(d) Each endorsement to this policy issued at any time is made a part of this

9. LIMITATION OF LIABILITY

(a) If the Company establishes the Title, or removes the alleged defect, lien or encumbrance, or cures the lack of a right of access to or from the Land, or cures the claim of Unmarketable Title, all as insured, in a reasonably diligent manner by any method, including litigation and the completion of any appeals, it shall have fully performed its obligations with respect to that matter and shall not be liable for any loss or damage caused to the Insured.

(b) In the event of any litigation, including litigation by the Company or with the Company's consent, the Company shall have no liability for loss or damage until there has been a final determination by a court of competent jurisdiction, and disposition of all appeals, adverse to the Title, as insured.

(c) The Company shall not be liable for loss or damage to the Insured for liability voluntarily assumed by the Insured in settling any claim or suit without the prior written consent of the Company.

10. REDUCTION OF INSURANCE; REDUCTION OR TERMINATION OF LIABILITY

All payments under this policy, except payments made for costs, attorneys' fees, and expenses, shall reduce the Amount of Insurance by the amount of the payment

11. LIABILITY NONCUMULATIVE

The Amount of Insurance shall be reduced by any amount the Company pays under any policy insuring a Mortgage to which exception is taken in Schedule B or to which the Insured has agreed, assumed, or taken subject, or which is executed by an Insured after Date of Policy and which is a charge or lien on the Title, and the amount so paid shall be deemed a payment to the Insured under this policy.

12. PAYMENT OF LOSS

When liability and the extent of loss or damage have been definitely fixed in accordance with these Conditions, the payment shall be made within 30 days.

13. RIGHTS OF RECOVERY UPON PAYMENT OR SETTLEMENT

(a) Whenever the Company shall have settled and paid a claim under this policy, it shall be subrogated and entitled to the rights of the Insured Claimant in the Title and all other rights and remedies in respect to the claim that the Insured Claimant has against any person or property, to the extent of the amount of any loss, costs, attorneys' fees, and expenses paid by the Company. If requested by the Company, the insured Claimant shall execute documents to evidence the transfer to the Company of these rights and remedies. The Insured Claimant shall permit the Company to sue, compromise, or settle in the name of the Insured Claimant and to use the name of the Insured Claimant in any transaction or litigation involving these rights and remedies.

If a payment on account of a claim does not fully cover the loss of the Insured Claimant, the Com-pany shall defer the exercise of its right to recover until after the Insured Claimant shall have recovered its loss.

(b) The Company's right of subrogation includes the rights of the Insured to indemnities, guaranties, other policies of insurance, or bonds, notwithstanding any terms or conditions contained in those instruments that address subrogation rights.

14. ARBITRATION

Either the Company or the Insured may demand that the claim or controversy shall be submitted to arbitration pursuant to the Title Insurance Arbitration Rules of the American Land Title Association policy and is subject to all of its terms and provisions. Except as the endorsement expressly states, it does not (i) modify any of the terms and provisions of the policy, (ii) modify any prior endorsement, (iii) extend the Date of Policy, or (iv) increase the Amount of Insurance.

15. SEVERABILITY

In the event any provision of this policy, in whole or in part, is held invalid or unenforceable under applicable law, the policy shall be deemed not to include that provision or such part held to be invalid, but all other provisions shall remain in full force and effect.

16. CHOICE OF LAW; FORUM

(a) Choice of Law: The Insured acknowledges the Company has underwritten the risks covered by this policy and determined the premium charged therefor in reliance upon the law affecting interests in real property and applicable to the interpretation, rights, remedies, or enforcement of policies of title insurance of the jurisdiction where the Land is located.

Therefore, the court or an arbitrator shall apply the law of the jurisdiction where the Land is located to determine the validity of claims against the Title or the lien of the Insured Mortgage that are adverse to the Insured and to interpret and enforce the terms of this policy. In neither case shall the court or arbitrator apply its conflicts of law principles to determine the applicable law.

(b) Choice of Forum: Any litigation or other proceeding brought by the Insured against the Company must be filed only in a state or federal court within the United States of America or its territories having appropriate jurisdiction.

17. NOTICES, WHERE SENT

Any notice of claim and any other notice or statement in writing required to be given to the Company under this policy must be given to the Company at Fidelity National Title Insurance Company, Attn: Claims Department, Post Office Box 45023, Jacksonville, Florida 32232-5023.

("Rules"). Except as provided in the Rules, there shall be no joinder or consolidation with claims or controversies of other persons. Arbitrable matters may include, but are not limited to, any controversy or claim between the Company and the Insured arising out of or relating to this policy, any service in connection with its issuance or the breach of a policy provision, or to any other controversy or claim arising out of the transaction giving rise to this policy. All arbitrable matters when the Amount of Insurance is $2,000,000 or less shall be arbitrated at the option of either the Company or the Insured. All arbitrable matters when the Amount of Insurance is in excess of $2,000,000 shall be arbitrated only when agreed to by both the Company and the Insured. Arbitration pursuant to this policy and under the Rules shall be binding upon the parties. Judgment upon the award rendered by the Arbitrator(s) may be entered in any court of competent jurisdiction.

15. LIABILITY LIMITED TO THIS POLICY; POLICY ENTIRE CONTRACT

(a) This policy together with all endorsements, if any, attached to it by the Company is the entire policy and contract between the Insured and the Company. In interpreting any provision of this policy, this policy shall be construed as a whole.

(b) Any claim of loss or damage that arises out of the status of the Title or by any action asserting such claim shall be restricted to this policy.

(c) Any amendment of or endorsement to this policy must be in writing and authenticated by an authorized person, or expressly incorporated by Schedule A of this policy.

(d) Each endorsement to this policy issued at any time is made a part of this policy and is subject to all of its terms and provisions. Except as the endorsement expressly states, it does not (i) modify any of the terms and provisions of the policy, (ii) modify any prior endorsement, (iii) extend the Date of Policy, or (iv) increase the Amount of Insurance.

16. SEVERABILITY

In the event any provision of this policy, in whole or in part, is held invalid or unenforceable under applicable law, the policy shall be deemed not to include that provision or such part held to be invalid, but all other provisions shall remain in full force and effect.

17. CHOICE OF LAW; FORUM

(a) Choice of Law: The Insured acknowledges the Company has underwritten the risks covered by this policy and determined the premium charged therefor in reliance upon the law affecting interests in real property and applicable to the interpretation, rights, remedies, or enforcement of policies of title insurance of the jurisdiction where the Land is located.

Therefore, the court or an arbitrator shall apply the law of the jurisdiction where the Land is located to determine the validity of claims against the Title that are adverse to the Insured and to interpret and enforce the terms of this policy. In neither case shall the court or arbitrator apply its conflicts of law principles to determine the applicable law.

(b) Choice of Forum: Any litigation or other proceeding brought by the Insured against the Company must be filed only in a state or federal court within the United States of America or its territories having appropriate jurisdiction.

18. NOTICES, WHERE SENT

Any notice of claim and any other notice or statement in writing required to be given to the Company under this policy must be given to the Company at Fidelity National Title Insurance Company, Attn: Claims Department, Post Office Box 45023, Jacksonville, Florida 32232-5023.

NOTES AND QUESTIONS

1. Each of the above two policy forms has been approved by the American Land Title Association for use by title insurance companies.

2. What are the major differences between the above two policies, and why do you think the differences exist?

Smith and Lubell, Real Estate Financing: Protecting the Lender with Title Insurance

5 Real Est. Rev. No. 1, at 14 (1975)

THE NATURE OF TITLE INSURANCE

It may be of some interest and value to consider briefly just what title insurance is. Certainly, it bears little resemblance to other types of insurance, such as life or casualty insurance.

Life insurance insures a risk which is certain to occur in the future, that is, the death of the insured, although with term insurance the risk may not necessarily occur within the period insured. Possibly this form of insurance should more appropriately be categorized as "death" insurance. The premium is usually paid in periodic installments, but the insurance may be purchased with a single lump-sum premium.

Casualty or hazard insurance protects against loss due to a future contingency, such as fire, windstorm, flood, personal injury, or the like, which may or may not occur. It is almost always in the nature of term insurance.

Unlike the foregoing two forms of insurance, title insurance protects against the risk of a state of facts that may exist at the time the insurance is obtained. That risk is the possibility of a defect in title. Title insurance much resembles a warranty, since it protects against possible defects in the product. In this case the product is title to a particular parcel of real property. Title insurance is invariably single-premium insurance. The protection which it affords is available so long as the party who is insured has any interest in the particular real estate, either directly or under a contingent liability, such as that of the grantor (seller) under a warranty deed.

Title insurance also differs from other forms of insurance in that an extremely high percentage of the "premium" for title insurance is attributable to the cost of examination of the title to be insured. The expense thus covers risk avoidance rather than risk assumption. While it is true that with virtually all forms of insurance a part of the premium covers the assessment of a particular underwriting risk (e.g., medical or fire underwriting), the percentage of the premium used to determine the existence of risks is much greater in the case of title insurance than in any other form of insurance. . . .

In real estate financing, it is customary for the borrower to pay all costs and expenses in connection with the closing of the loan. Therefore, it is not surprising that title insurance premiums and charges are almost universally paid by the mortgagor rather than the mortgagee. Since the mortgagor is paying for title insurance for the benefit of the lender, it is appropriate to allow the mortgagor to select the title insurer for the loan transaction. The mortgagor makes his selection subject to the lender's requirements that the insurer be acceptable to the lender and that the amount of the risk not exceed that which the lender is willing to accept from the specific title insurer. If the amount of the insurance required by the lender exceeds the amount which the lender is willing to accept from the primary insurer, it is not necessary that a different insurer be selected. However, it is then customary to obtain reinsurance from qualified insurers. Generally, these reinsuring title companies are selected by the primary title insurance company, subject to the lender's approval, but upon occasion the lender will designate the reinsurer. In practice, it is unusual for the borrower to choose title reinsurers for the risk. . . .

The title insurance policy insures the title to the property as it appears in the required local recording offices. Consequently, it insures both the validity and priority of the lien of the lender's mortgage or deed of trust as it appears of record. The policy of title insurance also affords protection against

- Forgeries;
- Defects in execution of documents;
- Defects in legal proceedings; and
- Defective legal process.

This protection is not available on the basis of an abstract and attorney's opinion, when used as an alternative to title insurance. The attorney for a national lender who was wrestled with the difficulties presented by a missing heir appearing fifty years ago in the chain of title can appreciate the assistance and comfort which a title insurance binder affords by virtue of its coverage of this gap in the chain of title. It is this acceptance by title insurers of minor title defects on the basis of local experience that has influenced national lenders, as much as almost anything else, to require title insurance in preference to other title evidence.

National lenders lack familiarity with purely local problems and practices. Therefore, they must rely on title insurance with respect to purely local matters, such as those relating to surveys (e.g., encroachments) and matters which are revealed by an inspection of the property. . . .

There is an increasing trend toward furnishing a variety of affirmative insurances of title risks by endorsement, in each case for an appropriate additional premium. Where such additional insurance is a proper matter for title insurance coverage, the benefit of such insurance is one which should be made available to the national lender who is otherwise not in a position to assess the risk involved because of a lack of familiarity with local conditions.

NOTES

1. The coverage of title insurance policies is discussed in Burke, Law of Title Insurance, chs. 2, 5, 9, and 10 (2000 and Ann. Supps.; Palomar, Title Insurance Law chs. 4-9 (2005).

2. Beasley, Standard Endorsements for Extra Coverage, in Practicing Law Institute, Real Estate Law and Practice Course Handbook Series No. 251, at 135 (1984), describes such extra coverage as follows:

Although the title policy gives extensive coverage for title-related matters, many situations occur where coverage must be tailored or extended to cover a specific problem. It is possible to tailor the title policy to meet an insured's specific problem in what could be termed various standard categories through endorsements. An endorsement gives specific affirmative insurance against loss or damage arising by reason of an incident occurring or perhaps, in some circumstances, an incident not occurring. The endorsement adds coverage to the policy or, in some limited circumstances, the endorsement does not actually add coverage as much as it affirms the existence of coverage. . . .

Some endorsements, zoning as an example, affirmatively assure the insured that the property can be used for a specific purpose and that the improvements meet the requirements of the zone planning or building codes. Endorsements have been created for use with the ALTA policy form which was created and adopted by the American Land Title Association. Other states, through various title organizations, have created endorsements either for use with the ALTA policies or for use with specific policies issued in the state, such as the Oregon Land Title Association, California Land Title Association, New York Board of Title Underwriters, or others.

Among endorsements available throughout most of the United States are those protecting against loss from special assessments, mechanics' liens that may have priority over mortgage loans under certain circumstances, encroaching easements, covenants that may impair a mortgage loan, and zoning restrictions. An added premium may be required for these endorsements. Sample policy endorsements appear in A.B.A., Sec. of Real Prop., Prob. & Tr. L., Title Insurance, The Lawyer's Expanding Role 159-184 (1985). In Somerset Savings Bank v. Chicago Title Insurance Co., 649 N.E.2d 1123 (1995), no endorsement existed and the court held no coverage by the title insurance company for failure of a state agency to issue a building permit. The policy provided protection from defects in, or liens or encumbrances on, title. This coverage, the court held, affords no protection for governmentally imposed impediments on the use of the land or for impairments in the value of the land.

3. Mechanics' liens can be particularly troublesome to title insurers and their insureds, especially in relation to construction loans. A special ALTA Construction Loan Policy is available and often used for construction loan coverage, but mechanics' liens under this policy are generally covered by a special endorsement, the form of which varies depending on the law of the state in which the property is located. This mechanics' lien coverage, under the current ALTA Construction Loan Policy, is discussed in Jordan, What You Should Know About Mechanics' Lien Coverage, 68 Title News no. 4 at 5 (Sept.-Oct. 1989).

4. In some instances, title insurers are willing to negotiate with applicants for insurance, or with their counsel, to expand coverage beyond what normally is offered. See Cooney, Protecting Your Client: Negotiating Residential Title Insurance Coverages, 5 Prob. and Prop. 48 (May/June 1991).

Title insurers are becoming increasingly reluctant to insure mechanics' liens because of the high risk, and in the currently depressed real estate environment some insurers are doing so only in exceptional circumstances. Bohan, Managing the Risk of Mechanic's Lien Coverage, 8 Practical Real Estate Lawyer 43, 53 (July 1992). Bohan, one of the leading title insurance executives in the East, also states: "Most title insurers probably believe that it is not an appropriate function of title insurers to insure lenders or property owners against risk of loss or damage from unrecorded mechanics' liens. In almost every case, this coverage is largely provided on a casualty basis by the title insurer." Id.

5. Why are claims arising out of operation of federal bankruptcy, state insolvency, or similar creditors' rights laws expressly excluded from most title insurance policy coverage?

Note, Iowa's Prohibition of Title Insurance — Leadership or Folly?

33 Drake L. Rev. 683, 695-701 (1983-1984)

IV. CRITICISMS OF TITLE INSURANCE

Title insurance policies traditionally appeared "to be intentionally worded so as to obfuscate [their] true meaning and to confuse all but the select few truly knowledgeable insurance gurus in existence." Although the forms have been greatly simplified, and the language made more understandable, most consumers still do not understand their policies. They purchase the policy wanting the protection they believe it affords them, but are totally unaware of its dimensions and limitations. The typical title insurance purchaser not only does not understand the policy he purchases, but he is also totally without knowledge about available sellers and the services they offer.

Since real estate transactions are a rare occurrence in a typical property purchaser's life, there is no incentive for him to develop even a basic knowledge of title insurance. A basic lack of interest, and a desire not to slow down the transfer process usually lead the purchaser to delegate the selection of a title insurer to his attorney, banker, or real estate broker. Being unfamiliar with property law, and trusting the real estate professional's judgment, the purchaser usually accepts his recommendations without ever seeking out alternatives.

Due to the purchaser's nonparticipation in the selection of a title insurer, the market is an ineffective control on the industry, and the demand for owner's title insurance does not change significantly with changes in policy prices. When the purchase of title insurance becomes an integral step in real estate transactions, as it has in most states, consumer demand becomes highly inelastic, and the effectiveness of price competitiveness between sellers diminishes entirely.

The commercial title insurance industry operates as an oligopoly. There are only about ninety title insurers writing title insurance policies today, and over one-half of the title insurance written in this country is written by the nation's four largest title insurers. Although competition between title insurance companies is fierce, this competition does not manifest itself in premium rates which differ significantly within a geographic market. In many states, this lack of rate competition is forced upon the title insurance companies by state regulations setting the premium rates. In other areas, title insurers have formed state-sanctioned rating bureaus to gather industry loss data, and set uniform statewide rates.

As a result of the purchaser's lack of participation in the purchase of title insurance and the general unavailability of price competition, companies that have wished to increase their market share have been unable to do so by reducing prices or by improving coverage or services. Instead, the companies' competitive efforts have been channeled toward those individuals or institutions who would be advising the purchaser at the closing stages of the transaction: the brokers, the bankers, and the attorneys. The result is a system of "reverse competition," whereby the insurance companies compete for the recommendations of real estate professionals rather than for the business of the actual consumer. "Reverse competition" has often taken the form of payments to the real estate professional, in the form of rebates, commissions, fees, or kickbacks, and are *far in excess* of the payment justified by the work performed. As a result, the consumer pays a much higher premium than he would pay in a purely competitive situation.

These real estate professionals are, at least theoretically, in the best possible position to seek out the best policy at the best price, since they are constantly in the market for title insurance and have the business knowledge and facilities to investigate available policies. But because the title insurance companies solicit the real estate professional's referrals by providing him with more benefits or compensation than their competitors, "reverse competition" raises rather than lowers the premium price. The concern of the real estate professional is shifted thereby from looking after the best interests of the real estate purchaser he is advising to finding the title insurance company who will provide him the best return for his referral. When lenders receive a commission for referring a customer to a title insurance company, the incentive is strong to recommend its purchase even in cases where no title defect is suspected. Eventually, title insurance becomes a virtual requirement to obtaining a mortgage. In many parts of the country, lending institutions will no longer rely on the title opinions of local attorneys, and title insurance has become a necessity.

Perhaps the biggest controversy with regard to title insurance centers on the premium charged. The premium is typically derived by estimating the allowance needed by the company to cover the costs of operation, the required statutory reserves, the insured risks, and the property needs of the insurer. Title insurance rate structures, however, lack uniformity, and make evaluation and comparison difficult. . . . An overwhelming portion of premium costs is expended by the title insurance companies for expenses, overhead and commissions. The agent, for example, may retain as much as fifty percent of the premium as his commission for soliciting and processing the order and issuing the policy. The costs of the title search and examination, if done by the title insurer, also make up a large part of the company's operating expenses.

Only a small portion of the premium is actually used to pay for losses due to risks insured by the policy. Estimates of this "loss ratio" industry-wide are generally between five and ten percent. . . .

The face amount of a title insurance policy is the maximum amount payable under the policy. Whenever a claim is paid under a title insurance policy, the amount paid is deducted from the face amount of the policy, thereby reducing the amount of future coverage available to the insured. Legal expenses, however, are not deducted. The payment of a claim on a loan policy may be made to the lender without consent from or notice to the property owner. When the policy's face value has been decreased, an additional premium must be paid by the insured in order to maintain full coverage.

A similar problem occurs because of the effects of inflation. With property values increasing, the size of possible losses caused by title defects increase, but since few title insurance policies have built-in inflation clauses, the coverage under the policy does not keep pace, and the amount of coverage erodes. Consequently, to counter inflation, additional premiums must be purchased periodically. This is a trap that an unwary homeowner could easily fall into.

Another common criticism of the title insurance industry is that a lender's policy does not protect the interests of the purchaser/borrower, even though in most areas he is the party who is required to pay the premium. "While a lender's title insurance policy relates both to the lien of the mortgage and to the quality of the landowner's title, it does not do so for the benefit of the landowner. . . ."

Title insurance seeks to insure against only a limited number of title risks. The extensive exclusions and exceptions dilute considerably the coverage actually received. . . .

V. THE BENEFITS OF TITLE INSURANCE

Despite the problems caused by the inadequacies of title insurance coverage, however, the industry continues to expand because it does provide a very useful service to consumers. For a one-time premium, which is nominal when compared with the loss that the insured *could* sustain, the insured purchases "peace of mind." Since public records have become more complex, and the frequency of property transfers has greatly increased, the possibilities that the title search might overlook a cloud on the title, or that hidden defects might exist, have increased dramatically. Recovery against the title searcher, abstract company, or the attorney who gave the title opinion for loss of title due to defects is possible only when negligence can be proven, and even then, is limited by the financial situation of the negligent party. Title insurance provides "greater and longer economic accountability than the individual lawyer . . . and covers a number of risks which a search does not disclose and which therefore are excluded from the attorney's liability." Immediate or remote grantors also may desire protection since recovery may be sought from them based on the covenants of title contained in the purchaser's warranty deed, although such recovery may be barred, or may be subject to severe limitations.

The cost of the policy would be easily recaptured by the insured if the company defends him in a single title challenge action, and if the defense is unsuccessful, the title insurance company, not the insured, must suffer the loss, if it is covered under the policy. Without title insurance protection, the property owner must pay the expenses for defending his title whether he is successful or not, and additionally, must sustain the financial loss caused by the loss of title. . . .

Title insurance companies also tend to give the consumer a break when it appears that charging a full premium would be a windfall for the company. Discounted rates are often available when the company issues a new policy after an interest has been transferred or refinanced, and also when an abstract of the title has been previously compiled. Also, the problem caused by underinsurance tends to be greatly mitigated by the fact that "title losses rarely amount to more than a fraction of the coverage."

NOTES AND QUESTIONS

1. How much the insured will recover if there is a loss covered by a title insurance policy may depend on the property's valuation date. The most common position, apparently, is to measure the insured's loss based on the property's value when the title defect was discovered, although there is authority for using the date of purchase by the insured, the date on which the insured contracted to sell the property, or the date on which the title actually failed. A case holding the appropriate valuation date to be the date of defect discovery is Hartman v. Shambaugh, 96 N.M. 359, 630 P.2d 758 (1981), noted in 12 N.M.L. Rev. 833 (1982), in which Note cases following other valuation theories are discussed. Which theory of valuation do you consider preferable and why?

2. Although title insurance losses are small compared to most other types of insurance losses, title insurers' losses as a percentage of their current operating costs have been increasing, and this has been causing concern to the title insurance industry. Major types of losses are plant searching and abstract procedure; examination and opinion errors; basic covered risks, with fraud and forgery being particularly high; closing or escrow procedure errors; and special risk coverage, with mechanics' lien losses being a substantial but declining cause of loss. See Little et al., Claims — A Crisis — What We Can Do About It, 62 Title News No. 6, at 7 (1983); and Jensen and McCarthy, Title Industry Reports Record Losses, 61 Title News No. 12, at 6 (1982). Earlier loss data appear in American Land Title Association, The Title Industry, White Papers vol. 1, c. 4 (1976), reprinted in 56 Title News No. 6, at 9 (1977).

3. Agents, many of them nonlawyers, are now widely authorized to issue title insurance policies for their title insurance company principals. Most insurers have extensive agent networks, and insurer success often is seen as largely dependent on the number and geographical distribution of agents. Where fraud occurs, it often results from agent embezzlement of escrow funds or an agent issuing policies without listing encumbrances or liens known to the agent. The fraud problem has become sufficiently serious for the insurers to set up risk management programs involving their agents, programs that involve such steps as canceling agencies with poor risk records, more carefully investigating before authorizing new agencies, closer field supervising of agents, and tighter auditing and cash management of agents. The agent fraud problem is discussed more fully in Kelly, Agent Defalcation — An Underwriter's Challenge, 70 Title News no. 3, at 4 (June 1991); Junkermann, Risk in the Title Insurance Industry, 68 Title News no. 4, at 4 (Dec. 1989); and Rain, The Changing Partnership, 68 Title News no. 4, at 5 (Dec. 1989). Lawyer title insurance agents also can be faced with conflict of interest problems. These problems are discussed in Note, Conflict of Interest: Attorney As Title Insurance Agent, 4 Georgetown J. Legal Ethics 687 (1991).

4. If a title insurer indemnifies an insured, the insurer is subrogated to the rights of the insured against third persons. For a case in which such subrogation rights were held to exist, see Commonwealth to Use of Willow Highlands Co. v. Maryland Casualty Co., 373 Pa. 602, 97 A.2d 46 (1953). There a notary public had falsely certified to acknowledgement of a mortgage when signatures of the borrowers were forgeries. Insured paid the mortgagee for its loss under a title policy, and the insurer was then held subrogated to the insured's rights against the notary and his surety.

5. Some within the title insurance industry are concerned that a number of title insurers are threatened with eventual insolvency from lack of adequate loss reserves. Growing loss trends and increased competition are underlying problems affecting profitability and the need for greater loss reserves. The threat is becoming more severe as the industry becomes concentrated in fewer and fewer companies. Within a few years, it is asserted, title insurance for 80 to 90 percent of the nation's real estate is likely to be provided by only three or four companies, and failure of any one of these could have far-reaching consequences. What is needed, it is claimed, is stiffer and more consistent state laws mandating higher reserves, as well as a willingness within the industry to face up more realistically to responsible reserve needs. See Gregory, Mitchell and Zucaro, Title Insurance: A Time to Address Financial Stability Issues (1990), a publication of Old Republic Title Insurance

Group, Inc. See also Zucaro, The Title Insurance Industry, based on remarks made on January 28, 1992, to the Association of Insurance Financial Analysts and distributed by Old Republic International Corporation.

First National Bank & Trust Co. of Port Chester v. New York Title Insurance Co.

171 Misc. 854, 12 N.Y.S.2d 703 (Sup. Ct. 1939)

ALDRICH, J. The plaintiff brings this action to recover under a policy of title insurance issued by the defendant, covering the interest of the plaintiff as mortgagee upon certain real property to the extent of $8,400. The defendant pleads various defenses and a counterclaim for the cancellation or reformation of the policy. Many of the important facts of the case are not disputed.

In September, 1935, Max Karnowsky and Abe Karnowsky were, and had been for some thirty years, copartners engaged in the plumbing and heating business under the name of Karnowsky Brothers. They were indebted to the bank upon firm notes, indorsed by the partners individually, to the extent of $4,575. These notes were overdue. Prior to that time the partners had been the owners of certain real property known as 358 Willett avenue, in the village of Port Chester. Some time in August, 1935, the Karnowskys transferred the Willett avenue property to one Ike Nathan, a relative by marriage. This transfer came to the attention of the officers of the bank. The notes were turned over to the attorneys for the bank and an action commenced thereon. Conferences developed between the bank and its attorneys and the Karnowskys and their attorney. The Willett avenue property was subject to a first mortgage of $2,800 held by a third party. After some negotiations the Karnowskys agreed with the bank that the Willett avenue property should be reconveyed by Nathan to the Karnowskys, that the bank would take an assignment of the existing first mortgage for $2,800, that the Karnowskys would give an additional mortgage for $5,600, and that such two mortgages would be consolidated as one, the time of payment extended, etc. Out of the new mortgage there was to be paid all pending taxes and interest on the property; the balance was to be used in payment of the notes held by the bank. The plaintiff, having in mind the consummation of this arrangement, applied to the defendant for a policy of title insurance upon its interest as proposed mortgagee. The title was examined by the defendant and approved subject to certain exceptions not now material and the defendant company indicated its willingness to insure the title of the plaintiff accordingly.

The transfer of the title was consummated on September 30, 1935. The closing took several hours. The preparation of the papers and the handling of the closing was attended to by an attorney representing the title company, who later took care of recording the documents. By the transaction the property was conveyed back to the Karnowskys. The first mortgage of $2,800 was assigned to the bank. The new mortgage of $5,600 was executed and delivered to the bank. The consolidation agreement between the Karnowskys and the bank was duly executed. The papers were promptly recorded. The proceeds of the new mortgage were used for the payment of the notes and the other purposes indicated. The notes were surrendered and the action then pending on the notes was discontinued.

In accordance with its arrangement the title company issued its policy of title insurance, dated September 30, 1935, whereby it insured the plaintiff against all loss or damage not exceeding $8,400 "which the insured shall sustain by reason of any defect in the title of the insured to the estate or interest described in Schedule A hereto annexed, affecting the premises described in said schedule, or by reason of the unmarketability of the title of the insured described in said schedule to, or in said premises, or because of liens or incumbrances against the same at the date of this policy," subject to certain exceptions mentioned in Schedule "B," or excepted by the conditions of the policy. By Schedule "A," subdivision 1, the estate or interest insured by the policy was stated to be "Interest as mortgagee." By Schedule "A," subdivision 2, the description of the property the title to, or an interest in which was thereby insured, was the Willett avenue property. By Schedule "A," subdivision 3, the deed or other instrument by which the title or the interest thereby insured was vested in the insured was stated to be the assignment of the $2,800 mortgage, the new mortgage for $5,600 and the consolidation agreement. The excepted objections to title, etc., contained in Schedule "B," did not include any specification of any possible invalidity of the mortgage because in violation of the Bankruptcy Act against preferences.

On January 20, 1936, a petition for involuntary bankruptcy was filed against Max Karnowsky and Abraham Karnowsky, individually and as copartners doing business as Karnowsky Brothers. On February 5, 1936, they were duly adjudicated bankrupts accordingly by the District Court in the Southern District of New York. A trustee in bankruptcy was thereafter duly appointed. The trustee instituted an action in the District Court to set aside the $5,600 mortgage held by the bank on the ground that it was a preference. Issue was joined by the bank by the service of an answer containing a general denial. The bank gave notice to the title company of the institution of the action and demanded that the title company defend the suit. It appears that the title company, through the attorneys for the bank, defended the action under a disclaimer and subsequently paid the expenses of defending the case, without prejudice to the disclaimer. The case came on for trial in the District Court. On July 27, 1937, the court made its formal decision, containing findings of fact and conclusions of law, as a result of which judgment was directed setting aside the $5,600 mortgage upon the ground that it constituted a preference in violation of the Bankruptcy Law. Judgment was entered upon that decision on July 27, 1937, cancelling the $5,600 mortgage and the consolidation and extension agreement made thereunder. The first mortgage of $2,800 held by the plaintiff was validated to the extent of the full amount, with interest from August 1, 1937. No appeal was taken from that judgment. The plaintiff brings this action to recover the loss which it claims to have sustained under the policy. The amount demanded by the plaintiff in the complaint was $4,884.08. Upon the trial it was conceded that a final dividend to the plaintiff upon its claim as a general creditor for the amount by which it had been deprived of the benefits of the mortgage, amounting to $577.43, had been paid to the plaintiff through the bankruptcy court. The amount which the plaintiff claims is, therefore, $4,306.65. The bookkeeping statements presented on behalf of the plaintiff establish this amount as the paper loss. The defendant raises various objections to any recovery by the plaintiff.

First. The defendant contends that the policy cannot, in any event, be construed to cover the hazard of a loss sustained by the plaintiff by reason of the fact that the mortgage of $5,600 was declared invalid under the Bankruptcy Law. With this contention the court cannot agree. The title company knew that a new mortgage of $5,600 was to be given. It knew that the proceeds of that loan were to be used to pay the notes. It was fully acquainted with the general nature of the proposed transaction. It never indicated in the negotiations any intention not to cover this risk. There was never any oral agreement between the bank and the title company that the risk should not be covered by the policy. The policy insured the bank as mortgagee. The $5,600 mortgage was specifically included under Schedule "A." This particular risk was not excluded under Schedule "B." The policy, by its terms, insured against any loss or damage by reason "of any defect in the title of the insured to the estate or interest described." On the face of the policy it includes this particular defect in the title to the $5,600 mortgage. In accordance with the general rule, doubts and ambiguities, if any, contained in a policy of title insurance are to be resolved in favor of the insured, where the contract is drawn up by the insurer. (62 C.J. 1056 § 18; Marandino v. Lawyers T.I. Corp., 156 Va. 696; 159 S.E. 181; Broadway Realty Co. v. Lawyers T. Ins. & T. Co., 226 N.Y. 335, 337.) The policy, by its foregoing terms, certainly does not exclude the hazard of an attack on the mortgage under the Bankruptcy Law. There is no ambiguity on the face of the policy with respect to these provisions. But if there were such an ambiguity it would have to be resolved against the defendant which drew the contract. Subdivision 13 of the condition of the policy provides as follows: "Defects and incumbrances . . . created, suffered, assumed or agreed to by the insured . . . are not to be deemed covered by it." The invalidity of the mortgage because of preference was certainly a defect in the title of the bank to the mortgage insured. The words "assumed or agreed to" had reference to some particular defect or incumbrance assumed or agreed to by the bank by the title conveyance to it or by some collateral agreement made by the bank with reference to that specific subject-matter. Such words do not apply here. The word "created" had reference to some affirmative act on the part of the bank itself. The bank took the mortgage but it did not create the defect. That was created by operation of law. Such a clause does not protect the defendant from the very act insured against, which was the taking of the mortgage. . . .

Third. The defendant argues that the insured has not sustained any loss or damage within the meaning of the policy. The reasoning seems to be that because the plaintiff held certain notes before the mortgage was given, the adjudication by a decree of the Federal court did nothing more than put the plaintiff where it had been previously. This contention also must be overruled. What the defendant insured was the validity of the mortgage. By the policy (Conditions, subd. 2) a claim for damages arose: "(IV.) When the insurance is upon the interest of a mortgagee, and the mortgage has been adjudged by a final determination in a court of competent jurisdiction to be invalid, or ineffectual to charge the premises described in this policy." That is exactly the situation which has arisen here. The policy insured a first lien to the extent of $8,400. By the decree of a competent court that lien was limited to the amount of $2,800. The word "loss" is a relative term. Failure to keep what a man has or thinks he has is a loss. To avoid a possible claim against him; to obviate the need and expense of professional advice, and the uncertainty that sometimes results even after it has been obtained, is the very purpose for which the owner seeks insurance. To say that when a defect subsequently develops he has lost nothing and, therefore, can recover nothing, is to misinterpret the intention both of the insured and the insurer. (Empire Development Co. v. Title G. & T. Co., 225 N.Y. 53, 59, 60.) Under such a policy the insurer is liable for the actual loss sustained. (Montemarano v. Home Title Ins. Co., 258 N.Y. 478.) A leading case on the precise point is Foehrenbach v. German American T. & T. Co. (217 Penn. St. 331; 66 A. 561). In that case the plaintiff supposed that he was the owner of the entire interest in certain real property. He applied to the defendant for title insurance. The policy was issued. Subsequently others claimed an interest in the premises. They brought an action in which it was held that the plaintiff possessed only a half interest and not the whole of the property. The trial court dismissed his complaint against the title company, upon the ground that he had lost nothing. Upon appeal the plaintiff was awarded judgment in his favor. It was said that "failure to keep that which one has is loss." Also, "the estate or interest of the insured which was covered by the policy was that of owner in fee of the entire property, and any defect in title which reduced his interest below that point was, it seems to us, just that much loss, or damage, for which he was entitled to be indemnified." That decision is directly applicable here. Applying these principles, the plaintiff here certainly sustained a loss and damage within the meaning of the policy. The following figures, conclusively established by the plaintiff, show the bookkeeping loss:

Original total of both mortgages		$ 8,400.00
Less payments through amortization		426.88
Unpaid principal of mortgages at date of decree		$ 7,973.12
Credits chargeable against bank		
Balance in escrow account	$ 29.20	
Due from trustee on accounting as per decree	106.37	
Received from agent's rent account	153.47	
By mortgage validated by decree	2,800.00	
		−3,089.04
Loss or damage to date of decree		$ 4,884.08
Less bankruptcy dividend on claim of $4,884.08		577.43
Net loss and damage		$ 4,306.65

The foregoing figure would not necessarily be the amount of a recovery to which the plaintiff would be entitled. The title company did not guarantee the payment of the debt. It did not insure the adequacy of the security. We must, therefore, consider the value of the property which stood as security for the $8,400 mortgages. That property after recovery by the trustee in bankruptcy was sold for $5,900. That, however, was obviously a forced sale. The bankruptcy proceeding had to be closed up. The evidence shows that the trustee was pressing the agent to get some customer at some price. The defendant offered testimony upon this trial that the fair value in July, 1937, was $5,650 but that testimony is not convincing, when considered in connection with the income and other pertinent factors. The witness for the plaintiff gave a value of $9,000. In order to cover the entire loss of the plaintiff, the property, even allowing $500 for the expenses of a possible foreclosure, needed only a value of $8,473.12. The court is satisfied, and it will be found as a fact, that the actual value of the property prior to and at the time of the decree was

$9,000. As a matter of fact, the property was more than paying its way when the mortgage of $5,600 was declared invalid. It has more than paid its way since that time. Under the circumstances, to say there would have been a foreclosure is purely speculation. The value of the underlying property is not the sole index of the worth of a mortgage. The ascertainment of such value is a matter of the exercise of reasonable judgment after an intelligent and honest canvass of all factors relevant to the particular security. (Matter of New York Title & Mortgage Co., 277 N.Y. 66.) So considered, the mortgage was reasonably worth the face thereof. If the plaintiff is entitled to recover anything, it is entitled to a judgment for $4,306.65, with interest from the date the invalidity was adjudged. . . .

Fifth. The defendant pleads as a defense that provision of the policy which reads as follows (Conditions, subd. 5): "Any untrue statement made by the insured, or the agent of the insured, with respect to any material fact; any suppression of or failure to disclose any material fact; any untrue answer, by the insured, or the agent of the insured, to material inquiries before the issuing of this policy, shall void this policy."

It is upon the facts of this case, in the light of these provisions of the policy, that the litigation must be finally determined. The general principles applicable to such a subject-matter are substantially well settled. A title policy is one of insurance, so that it is governed for purposes of construction by the rules applicable to other insurance contracts. (62 C.J. 1056, § 14; De Carli v. O'Brien, 150 Ore. 35; 41 P.[2d] 411.) In accordance with the general rule, an innocent misrepresentation of a fact material to the risk will avoid a policy of title insurance. (62 C.J. 1058, § 25; Union Trust Co. v. Real Estate T. Co., 27 Pa. Co. Ct. 187.) Where a title insurance policy so provides, the suppression of a material fact will void the policy. (62 C.J. 1058, § 27; Rosenblatt v. Louisville Title Co., 218 Ky. 714; 292 S.W. 333.) A failure by the insured to disclose conditions affecting the risk, of which he is aware, makes the contract voidable at the option of the company. (Stipcich v. Metropolitan Life Ins. Co., 277 U.S. 311.) Concealment of material facts by the insured is a defense. (Vaughan v. United States T. G. & I. Co., 137 App. Div. 623.) The same rule is laid down in other cases. (Phillips v. U.S.F.&G. Co., 200 App. Div. 208; *aff'd.*, 234 N.Y. 618; Town of Hamden v. American Surety Co., 93 F.[2d] 482; Raebeck v. Title Guarantee & T. Co., 229 App. Div. 727; Sebring v. Fidelity-Phoenix Fire Ins. Co., 255 N.Y. 382.) What is material under such circumstances has been the subject of judicial consideration. In Geer v. Union M.L. Ins. Co. (273 N.Y. 261) the court said (p. 266) that the question in such case is not whether the insurance company might perhaps have decided to issue the policy even if it had been apprised of the truth; the question is whether failure to state the truth where there was duty to speak prevented the insurance company from exercising its choice of whether to accept or reject the application upon a disclosure of all the facts which might reasonably affect its choice, and (p. 269) the question in such case is not whether the company might have issued the policy even if the information had been furnished; the question in each case is whether the company has been induced to accept an application which it might otherwise have refused, as any misrepresentation which defeats or seriously interferes with the exercise of such a right cannot truly be said to be an immaterial one. Materiality is a matter of degree and a misrepresentation through concealment of a fact is material where it appears that a reasonable insurer would be induced thereby to take action which he might not have taken if the truth had been disclosed (p. 272).

Tested by these rules, the disposition of this case seems clear. Without considering controverted matters, the undisputed proof with respect to certain of the subject-matter shows both an affirmative misrepresentation and a misrepresentation through non-disclosure on the part of the plaintiff. There was a specific misrepresentation with respect to one material fact. It is undisputed that the financial condition of Karnowsky Brothers was substantially the same at the time of the adjudication in bankruptcy as at the time when the mortgage was given. The officers of the plaintiff, upon the trial, claimed a thorough understanding on their part of the underlying facts with reference to the financial situation of the debtors. The claims allowed in bankruptcy aggregated $13,313.86. Of this total $4,884.08 was the claim of the plaintiff arising through the invalidity of the mortgage; $3,341.44 was the claim of Mutual Trust Company, concerning which both the plaintiff and the defendant were informed at or before the time of the closing, $1,490 was a claim on a second mortgage which covered certain real property of the bankrupts at 26-28 Rollhaus place, such mortgagees having disclaimed the security and having elected to stand as general creditors. This item was not considered as an unsecured claim by either plaintiff or defendant. Technically it was not an unsecured claim at that time. These three items aggregate $9,715.52. The balance of $3,598.34 represented unsecured claims of general creditors. It appears that the attorney for Karnowsky Brothers in the discussion with an officer of the bank stated that the merchandise creditors totaled about $3,000. The attorney for the bank in his conference with the attorney for the title company does not appear to have stated the figures on such claims. He told them about the plaintiff bank and Mutual Trust Company claims and testified that with these exceptions he told the attorney for the title company "the general creditors were very small, very few." At the closing the attorney for the title company was given to understand by those present that the general creditors were very few and the amount inconsequential or negligible. Three thousand dollars is a substantial sum of money. There was a misstatement on that material subject.

There was a non-disclosure of various material matters. The bank failed to disclose the fact that it had in its files two credit statements from Karnowsky Brothers, one under date of October 18, 1933, and one under date of October 2, 1934. Referring, for a moment, to the second one, it appears that this statement was returned to Karnowsky Brothers when originally received by the bank "due to the irregularity appearing on the face of the same." The Karnowskys sent it back without correction. Neither the fact of the existence of the statement or its return by the bank with the expression quoted were made known to the title company. That there was at least one irregularity appearing on the face of the statement is certain. Under notes payable to banks the debtors listed $3,800. The claims of the bank itself, without considering the Mutual Trust Company, were in excess of that amount. The statement also discloses a gross overvaluation, among others, of the Willett avenue property. It was estimated at $25,000, when not even the officers, who claimed to be familiar with real estate values, have suggested any value in excess of $9,000. In connection with other circumstances, this statement had additional importance. By the statement certain premises at 407 North Main street were given an estimated value of $35,000, with mortgages of $10,850. In March, 1935, there came to the attention of the bank the fact that this property had been conveyed to one Markel. An estimated equity of some $24,000 thereby disappeared from the assets of the debtors. The fact of the conveyance known to the bank was not disclosed to the defendant. At the time of the mortgage the four months' period in which to attack the conveyance of March had expired under the Bankruptcy Law. The bank officers were fully familiar with the fact that the debtors were crowded for lack of cash. There was no disclosure to the defendant that a $24,000 unexplained departure of assets had occurred. If the explanation be that the value as estimated was grossly overstated, then the fact that the debtors had overstated was material to the defendant. If the explanation be that the property was conveyed without consideration, then it indicated a willingness on the part of the debtors to dispose of their property in such fashion and such willingness was a material matter from the standpoint of the defendant. If the explanation be that an additional consideration was paid and devoted to other purposes, then the disposition thereof was unknown. That also was material. If there be no explanation, and the record gives none, then the fact of the conveyance itself, in the light of the preceding statement, was of the utmost importance from the standpoint of the defendant. The bank knew that the deposit account of Karnowsky Brothers in the bank had been closed many months previously. The fact of the closing was not communicated to the defendant. The bank also knew that prior to the closing that account had been repeatedly overdrawn for a period of at least a year. That fact was not disclosed. On the contrary, the representation was made to the title company that Karnowsky Brothers had been customers of the bank for many years and that the bank thought very well of them. A comparison of the two financial statements also shows that the incumbrances upon 407 North Main street had increased from $7,500 on October 18, 1933, to $10,850 on October 2, 1934, and that the incumbrances upon 26-28 Rollhaus place had increased from $10,500 on the first date to $15,000 on the second date. The statements afford no adequate explanation of such increases aggregating $7,850. Nor does it appear what became of the money. This information was not disclosed by the bank. From the various facts above referred to various other inferences of the same nature might very well be drawn. It is sufficient to say that the record shows conclusively that there was not a full and frank disclosure by the bank to the defendant of all of the material information in the possession of the bank with respect to the risk to be insured against. For that reason, the complaint must be dismissed upon the merits. It will be so adjudged.

Sixth. The defendant pleads also a counterclaim for cancellation or reformation of the policy. This amounts to nothing more than a repetition of the various matters pleaded as a defense, and to which a reference has been made. The policy has an independent status so far as it applies to the $2,800 mortgage still in existence. The defendant is not entitled to rescission on the theory of a material misrepresentation, etc. It has neither repaid, tendered or offered to return the premium paid for the policy. Nor is there any basis for a reformation. There is nothing to indicate that by mutual mistake of both parties, or by a mistake of the defendant and fraud of the plaintiff, etc., the policy was drawn to cover a risk which the defendant did not intend to insure. So far as appears, the policy was drawn in the form that both parties intended it to be. There is nothing about it to be reformed. The counterclaim is dismissed upon the merits . . . . .

NOTES AND QUESTIONS

1. Can a large bank be expected to coordinate the activities of its personnel so as to avoid the risk of unintended misrepresentation and concealment concerning the

financial affairs of its mortgagors? To what extent should bank employees who negotiate and close mortgages covered by title insurance be expected to acquire information about mortgagors from bank files and other bank employees, and turn over this information to the title insurer?

2. The usual black letter requirement for valid insurance is that the insured must have an insurable interest in the thing insured; otherwise, the transaction is an illegal wager. Does and should title insurance meet this insurable interest requirement? Suppose at the time a title policy is issued the insured and insurer both incorrectly believe that the insured has a valid interest in a parcel of land. Can the insurer successfully refuse to pay out when it is later discovered that the insured never had any interest in the parcel and seeks to recover for a total loss under his policy? On insurable interest in property, see generally Keeton and Widiss, Insurance Law §§ 3.4-3.5 (1988); and 4 Appleman, Insurance Law and Practice cc. 109 and 110 (1941 & Supp. 1990).

3. It is commonly stated in title insurance cases, as in insurance cases generally, that ambiguities and uncertainties are construed against the insurer. Should this be done if, as is commonly the case, the insured is a knowledgeable institutional lender, such as a bank or a life insurance company?

4. A title policy clause excluding from coverage "defects known to the insured claimant" was held not to apply to assignees of the original insured mortgagee when assignees took without notice of the defects, although the defects apparently were known by the original insured when it took out the policy. Southern Title Insurance Co. v. Crow, 278 So. 2d 294 (Fla. Dist. Ct. App. 1973).

L. Smirlock Realty Corp. v. Title Guarantee Company

52 N.Y.2d 179, 418 N.E.2d 650 (1981)

JASEN, J. This appeal presents a question of first impression for our court. At issue is whether a policy of title insurance will be rendered void pursuant to a standard misrepresentation clause found therein as a result of the insured's failure to disclose a material fact which was a matter of public record at the time the policy was issued.

In November, 1967, the Town of Hempstead condemned and thereby acquired title to certain property on and adjacent to the premises known as 31-39 Carvel Place, which is located in Inwood, Long Island. At that time, the premises were owned by Bass Rock Holding, Inc. (Bass Rock), a corporation controlled by Helen and Anthony De Giulio. The Bass Rock property was improved by a warehouse and access to and from the property was over three public streets: Carvel Place to the north of the premises and St. George Street and Jeanette Avenue to its east. The principal loading docks for the warehouse were located at the easterly end of the building with direct access from St. George Street and Jeanette Avenue. In addition, there was an alleyway along the northern side of the warehouse connecting the Carvel Place entrance to these loading docks. However, clearance along this passageway was quite limited and trucks would often strike the warehouse building when attempting to maneuver down this alleyway. Because of this, the Carvel Street entrance was of little value as an access route for the warehouse facility.

The Bass Rock property was heavily indebted and in 1968 there was a default in mortgage payments. A foreclosure proceeding was instituted in the early part of

1969. It was at about this time that Gerald Tucker, general counsel for one of the mortgagees in the foreclosure proceeding, indicated an interest in the property and negotiations were commenced with the De Giulios with a view toward the eventual purchase of the Bass Rock property. Soon thereafter, the plaintiff corporation was formed by Tucker and a group of associated investors.

It was also around this time, according to the testimony of Abraham Lee, Special Counsel for the Town of Hempstead, that Lee telephoned Tucker to inform him that a portion of the Bass Rock property had been condemned by the town, and should be excluded from the foreclosure proceeding. Lee testified that he identified the condemned parcel as "abutting on Carvel Place," but that Tucker stated that he was not interested and would proceed with the foreclosure action anyway. The parcel in question subsequently was identified in the record as the town's damage parcel 8-6, taken for street alignment purposes.

Sometime after Tucker spoke with Lee, Tucker and Joseph Tiefenbrun, the attorney retained by plaintiff, met with the Bass Rock attorney to discuss the details of the sales contract. At this meeting, Tucker was informed that, although the exact location of the property involved was uncertain, Bass Rock was entitled to a $5,000 to $6,000 condemnation award from the Town of Hempstead. As a result of this discussion, the contract was amended to include a clause assigning "any condemnation award affecting the premises then due or to be due in the future" to the plaintiff. It was agreed that the necessary information concerning this condemnation would be provided at the title closing. On April 25, 1969, the sales contract was executed by Bass Rock and the plaintiff. The purchase price was set at $600,000.

On May 14, 1969, title was closed. During the closing, and in the presence of defendant's title closer, Tucker and Mrs. De Giulio discussed the condemnation award referred to in the sales contract. In fact, Mrs. De Giulio sketched an outline of the condemned property on the Bass Rock title survey. The parcel marked by Mrs. De Giulio was adjacent to the southwest corner of the Bass Rock property, but it was not part of nor did it affect any access route to the warehouse.

After title closed, defendant issued plaintiff a title policy covering the warehouse property. The policy contained the following clause insuring access to public streets: "Notwithstanding any provisions in this paragraph to the contrary, this policy, unless otherwise excepted, insures the ordinary rights of access and egress belonging to abutting owners." It should be noted that no exception was listed in the policy for any condemnation affecting Carvel Place, St. George Street or Jeanette Avenue.

At the time the property was purchased, plaintiff leased the entire premises to Pan American World Airways, Inc. In addition, plaintiff had spent an additional $95,000 above the purchase price in order to improve the premises for its new tenant. Unfortunately, it was soon discovered that the title search had failed to reveal that the roadbeds of St. George Street and Jeanette Avenue and a portion of the property along Carvel Place had been condemned by the Town of Hempstead two years prior to plaintiff's acquisition of the property. It was apparent that the defendant's title searchers simply failed to check the master card on file at the Nassau County Clerk's office covering the applicable section and block which would have revealed these condemnations.

By 1971, plans for urban development in the Town of Hempstead required the closing down of the warehouse access routes at St. George Street and Jeanette Avenue, thereby rendering the property valueless. As a result, Pan American quit the premises and plaintiff eventually lost 31-39 Carvel Place in a foreclosure sale. Plaintiff then commenced the present action against the defendant seeking to recover $600,000 in damages pursuant to its title insurance policy based on the defendant's failure to discover the condemned roadbed property.*

In its answer, defendant pleaded an affirmative defense based on the following standard provision in its policy:

"MISREPRESENTATION

"Any untrue statement made by the insured, with respect to any material fact, or any suppression of or failure to disclose any material fact, or any untrue answer by the insured, to material inquiries before the issuance of this policy, shall void this policy." According to defendant, plaintiff, through its agent Tucker, had knowledge prior to the closing of the town's condemnation as a result of his conversation with Lee. Defendant asserted that plaintiff's failure to divulge this knowledge to the defendant was a "failure to disclose [a] material fact" which rendered the title policy void.

At the end of a nonjury trial, Trial Term dismissed plaintiff's claim. Finding that plaintiff, through Tucker, had knowledge of the condemnations prior to the issuance of the policy which it failed to disclose to the defendant, Trial Term concluded that the policy was nullified.

On appeal, a unanimous Appellate Division, 70 A.D.2d 455, 421 N.Y.S.2d 232, affirmed, but for reasons somewhat different than those expressed at Trial Term. The Appellate Division determined that although Tucker had been alerted by Lee as to the taking along Carvel Place of damage parcel 8-6, this fact offered no basis for the further inference, one apparently drawn by Trial Term, that Tucker also had knowledge of the condemnation of the roadbeds at St. George Street and Jeanette Avenue. Thus, the Appellate Division found that Tucker only had knowledge prior to the closing of the Carvel Place taking and of the condemnation of the small adjacent parcel at the southwest corner of the property which was identified at the closing by Mrs. De Giulio. According to the Appellate Division, the crucial issue of the case was whether "this knowledge concerned a material fact, the concealment of which was tantamount to a misrepresentation sufficient to permit defendant to void its title policy" (70 A.D.2d, at p. 461, 421 N.Y.S.2d 232).

In addressing this issue, the court below defined materiality in terms of "whether the suppression deprived the insurer of its freedom of choice in determining whether to accept or reject the risk upon full disclosure of all the facts which might reasonably affect that choice." (70 A.D.2d at p. 462, 421 N.Y.S.2d 232). The court went on to state (at p. 463, 421 N.Y.S.2d 232) that materiality "extends to any information that might have been revealed had further inquiry followed the initial disclosure of the suppressed facts." The court found that information regarding the condemnation of damage parcel 8-6 at Carvel Place was not itself material in that that taking had little, if any, effect on the value of the property. However, because disclosure of the Carvel Place taking, revealed to Tucker prior to closing, would have caused the defendant to check the appropriate public records and inevitably

---

*.As a second cause of action, plaintiff alleged that defendant was negligent in conducting its title search by failing to discover the public records of the condemnations. The Appellate Division held that this second cause of action properly was dismissed because any claim of negligence in the title search merged into the subsequently issued title policy pursuant to the express terms of the certificate of title. Inasmuch as no appeal was taken by plaintiff from this determination, we do not concern ourselves here with plaintiff's second cause of action in negligence.

led to the discovery of the St. George Street and Jeanette Avenue condemnations, the Appellate Division concluded (70 A.D.2d, at p. 463, 421 N.Y.S.2d 232) that "no title insurance company with knowledge of [these] facts would have insured ingress and egress over streets already condemned for an urban renewal project." Therefore, inasmuch as Tucker's failure to disclose the information acquired in his conversation with Lee deprived the defendant of its "freedom of choice in determining the nature, scope and extent of the risk it would assume," the Appellate Division held (at p. 464, 421 N.Y.S.2d 232) that the suppression of the information regarding the Carvel Place condemnation was "material as a matter of law and would preclude recovery on the policy." We reverse.

At the outset, we note our agreement with the court below that information concerning the condemnations of damage parcel 8-6 adjacent to Carvel Place and the St. George Street and Jeanette Avenue roadbeds was material. It is manifest that revelation of this information certainly would have affected defendant's choice of insuring the risk covered by the policy issued to plaintiff. (See Vander Veer v. Continental Cas. Co., 34 N.Y.2d 50, 356 N.Y.S.2d 13, 312 N.E.2d 156; Geer v. Union Mut. Life Ins. Co., 273 N.Y. 261, 7 N.E.2d 125; Travelers Ins. Co. v. Pomerantz, 246 N.Y. 63, 158 N.E. 21; see, generally, 5A Warren's Weed New York Real Property, Title Insurance, § 2.08.) However, contrary to the view expressed by the Appellate Division, the mere existence of knowledge of a material fact on plaintiff's part does not end the analysis. Rather, in order to ascertain whether the policy has been voided, a further determination must be made as to whether plaintiff was under a duty to disclose this information to defendant. (Geer v. Union Mut. Life Ins. Co., 273 N.Y. 261, 7 N.E.2d 125, supra; Sebring v. Fidelity-Phoenix Fire Ins. Co. of N.Y., 255 N.Y. 382, 174 N.E. 761.) In order to make that determination, we first must examine the nature of the agreement entered into by the parties and the respective expectations and obligations of the insured and insurer which arise out of a policy of title insurance.

By definition, title insurance involves "insuring the owners of real property . . . against loss by reason of defective titles and encumbrances thereon and insuring the correctness of searches for all instruments, liens or charges affecting the title to such property." (Insurance Law, § 46, subd. 18; see also, § 438.) Or, as one lower court has expressed it, "[a] policy of title insurance means the opinion of the company which issues it, as to the validity of the title, backed by an agreement to make that opinion good, in case it should prove to be mistaken and loss should result in consequence to the insured." (First Nat. Bank & Trust Co. of Port Chester v. New York Tit. Ins. Co., 171 Misc. 854, 859, 12 N.Y.S.2d 703.) Essentially, therefore, a policy of title insurance is a contract by which the title insurer agrees to indemnify its insured for loss occasioned by a defect in title. (See 9 Appleman, Insurance Law and Practice, § 5201; 13 Couch, Insurance [2d ed.], § 48:108.)

Beyond its purely contractual aspects, however, the unique nature of a title insurance transaction was quickly recognized by the courts. In Empire Dev. Co. v. Title Guar. & Trust Co., 225 N.Y. 53, 59-60, 121 N.E. 468, this court noted: "To a layman a search is a mystery and the various pitfalls that may beset his title are dreaded but unknown. To avoid a possible claim against him; to obviate the need and expense of professional advice, and the uncertainty that sometimes results even after it has been obtained is the very purpose for which the owner seeks insurance." Rather than being treated merely as a contract of indemnity, title insurance was viewed as being more in the nature of a covenant of warranty against encumbrances under which "mere knowledge of a defect [in title] by the insuring owner would not constitute a defense." (Empire Dev. Co. v. Title Guar. & Trust Co., supra, at p. 61, 121 N.E. 468; Maggio v. Abstract Tit. & Mtge. Corp., 277 App. Div. 940, 98 N.Y.S.2d 1011.)

Interestingly, in response to the decision in the *Empire Dev. Co.* case, title companies adopted as a standard provision in their policies the very misrepresentation clause at issue on this appeal. (See 5A Warren's Weed New York Real Property, Title Insurance, § 2.08.) To date, however, this court has not been presented with an opportunity to examine the effect to be given to this clause in terms of imposing an obligation on the insured to disclose information to the insurer. Moreover, although at least one lower court has recognized the validity of this misrepresentation clause based on the insured's failure to divulge information to its insurer (Glickman v. Home Tit. Guar. Co., 15 Misc. 2d 167, 178, N.Y.S.2d 281, *aff'd.*, 8 A.D.2d 629, 185 N.Y.S.2d 756), other courts of this State which have addressed the issue of an insured's obligation to reveal information to its title insurer have held that the policy was voided by the insured's failure to disclose only in instances where there was evidence of intentional concealment on the part of the insured and the undisclosed information concerned a matter not of public record. (Vaughan v. United States Tit. Guar. & Ind. Co., 137 App. Div. 623, 122 N.Y.S. 393; First Nat. Bank & Trust Co. of Port Chester v. New York Tit. Ins. Co., 171 Misc. 854, 12 N.Y.S.2d 703, supra; cf. Sullivan v. Tomgil Bldg. Corp., 46 Misc. 2d 613, 260 N.Y.S.2d 465.)

One Federal court, addressing a provision identical to that found in the defendant's policy, stated that the clause "must be given a common sense application and, considering the nature of title insurance transactions, a duty to speak could be found only if the insurance applicant had actual knowledge of certain defects or encumbrances. Further, misrepresentation could be found only if one charged with such a duty to speak intentionally failed to disclose the information." (Lawyers Tit. Ins. Corp. v. Research Loan & Inv. Corp., 361 F.2d 764, 768.) In a like manner, other jurisdictions which have addressed similar clauses have required a showing that the insured had actual knowledge of the title defect which was intentionally concealed from the insurer. Moreover, these cases indicated, either expressly or by implication, that the title policy would only be voided in instances where the undisclosed information was not discoverable by the insurer by reference to publicly filed records. (Collins v. Pioneer Tit. Ins. Co., 629, F.2d 429; Rosenblatt v. Louisville Tit. Co., 218 Ky. 714, 292 S.W. 333; Fohn v. Title Ins. Corp. of St. Louis, 529 S.W.2d 1 [Mo.]; Pioneer Nat. Tit. Ins. Co. v. Lucas, 155 N.J. Super. 332, 382 A.2d 933, *aff'd.*, 78 NJ. 320, 394 A.2d 360; Laabs v. Chicago Tit. Ins. Co., 72 Wis. 2d 503, 241 N.W.2d 434; Bush v. Coult, 594 P.2d 865 [Utah]; see 9 Appleman, Insurance Law and Practice, § 5205; 7 Powell, Real Property, Title Insurance, par. 1037.)

We agree with the view expressed by these cases. Therefore, we hold that a policy of title insurance will not be rendered void pursuant to a misrepresentation clause absent some showing of intentional concealment on the part of the insured tantamount to fraud. Moreover, because record information of a title defect is available to the title insurer and because the title insurer is presumed to have made itself aware of such information, we hold that an insured under a policy of title insurance such as is involved herein is under no duty to disclose to the insurer a fact which is readily ascertainable by reference to the public records. Thus, even an intentional failure to disclose a matter of public record will not result in a loss of title insurance protection.

In so holding, we merely recognize the practical realities of the transaction involved. As mentioned earlier, title insurance is procured in order to protect against the risk that the property purchased may have some defect in title. The emphasis in securing these policies is on the expertise of the title company to search the public records and discover possible defects in title. Thus, unlike other types of insurance, the insured under a title policy provides little, if any, information to the title company other than the lot and block of the premises and the name of the prospective grantor. Armed with this information, the title company then can search the various indices and maps to ascertain the state of title to the property. Indeed, it is because title insurance companies combine their search and disclosure expertise with insurance protection that an implied duty arises out of the title insurance agreement that the insurer has conducted a reasonably diligent search. (McLaughlin v. Attorneys' Tit. Guar. Fund, 61 Ill. App. 3d 911, 18 Ill. Dec. 891, 378 N.E.2d 355; Shotwell v. Transamerica Tit. Ins. Co., 16 Wash. App. 627, 628-631, 558 P.2d 1359, *aff'd.*, 91 Wash. 2d 161, 588 P.2d 208; see 9 Appleman, Insurance Law and Practice, § 5213.) This duty may not be abrogated through a standard policy clause which would, if given the effect urged by defendant, place the onus of the title company's failure adequately to search the records on the party who secured the insurance protection for that very purpose. (See Empire Dev. Co. v. Title Guar. & Trust Co., 225 N.Y. 53, 121 N.E. 468, supra.)

Of course, an intentional failure by the insured to disclose material information not readily discernible from the public records will render the policy void. For instance, where the insured secures title insurance with knowledge that there exists some hidden defect in title, such as a forged deed, incapacity of the grantor, or the existence of an unrecorded easement (see, generally, 5A Warren's Weed New York Real Property, Title Insurance, § 2.04) and the insured conceals that information from the title insurer, then such a failure to disclose will result in nullification of the policy.

In this case, there was no showing that plaintiff's agent, Tucker, intentionally failed to disclose the information concerning the Carvel Place condemnation. In fact, it would appear that defendant was at least put on notice as to the existence of condemnations affecting the Bass Rock property by the recital in the sales contract assigning all condemnation awards to plaintiff and by the discussion of the condemnation of the small southwest parcel which took place at the closing. In any event, it is undisputed that the existence of the St. George Street and Jeanette Avenue condemnations was readily ascertainable from the public records available at the Nassau County Clerk's office. Defendant, having failed to avail itself of this information, now attempts to avoid its obligation under the policy by claiming that plaintiff failed to disclose material information concerning title to the property. However, because plaintiff was under no duty to disclose this publicly available information to defendant, the policy will not be rendered void pursuant to the misrepresentation provision found therein.

Finally, defendant's answer contained a counterclaim premised upon an agreement entered into between the parties whereby the defendant advanced certain moneys in plaintiff's behalf for taxes and expenses attributable to plaintiff's attempt to secure a condemnation award from the Town of Hempstead. Pursuant to that agreement, plaintiff was to repay defendant the amounts so advanced subject to a setoff of any sums found due to plaintiff under its title policy. Inasmuch as plaintiff offers no basis for overturning the judgment rendered in defendant's behalf on this counterclaim, we do not disturb that award. Of course, payment of the amounts owing under this counterclaim must await a determination of the amount due plaintiff as damages under its title policy.

Accordingly, the order of the Appellate Division should be modified, with costs to plaintiff, to the extent of reversing the dismissal of plaintiff's first cause of action and remitting the case to Supreme Court, Nassau County, for a trial on the issue of plaintiff's damages. As so modified, the order should be affirmed.

Cooke, C.J., and Gabrielli, Jones, Wachtler and Fuchsberg, JJ., concur.

Meyer, J., taking no part.

Order modified, with costs to plaintiff, and the case remitted to Supreme Court, Nassau County, for a trial on the issue of plaintiff's damages in accordance with the opinion herein and, as so modified, order affirmed.

NOTE

In subsequent proceedings on the issue of damages, plaintiff was awarded $593,850, plus interest, and also compensation for counsel fees and maintenance expenditures. L. Smirlock Realty Corp. v. Title Guarantee Co., 97 A.D.2d 208, 469 N.Y.S.2d 415 (1983), *aff'd.*, 63 N.Y.2d 955, 473 N.E.2d 234 (1984).

Jimerson v. First American Title Ins. Co.

989 P.2d 258 (Colo. App. 1999)

Opinion by Judge CRISWELL.

Second third-party plaintiff, Glen Edwin Jimerson (seller), appeals from the summary judgment entered by the trial court in favor of second third-party defendant, First American Title Company (title company). We affirm.

The material facts are undisputed. Seller conveyed his home to a buyer by means of a general warranty deed. Prior to that conveyance, the title company had provided a commitment for a title insurance policy, and after the closing, it had issued its policy naming the buyer as the insured.

Approximately one year after the sale, seller's brothers filed a complaint against the buyer claiming an interest in the property. The buyer, through an attorney provided by the title company, answered the complaint and asserted a third-party claim against seller. The buyer claimed that seller had violated the warranties in the deed that had warranted the buyer's quiet and peaceable possession of the property.

Seller answered the buyer's complaint, filed a cross-claim against the brothers, and asserted his own third-party claims for negligence and negligent misrepresentation against the title company. Seller's claims of negligence were premised on the fact that the commitment for title insurance had not disclosed the brothers' alleged interest in the property.

The title company moved for summary judgment with respect to the claims brought by seller. The trial court concluded that it owed no duty to seller and, therefore, that it was not liable to him. Hence, that court granted the title company's motion and certified its order as a final judgment under C.R.C.P. 54(b). It is from that judgment that seller appeals.

Summary judgment is a drastic remedy and should be granted only if the moving party demonstrates that there does not exist a genuine factual controversy over a material issue and it is clearly shown that the moving party is entitled to a judgment as a matter of law. *Churchey v. Adolph Coors Co.,* 759 P.2d 1336 (Colo.1988). A court rendering summary judgment does not engage in fact finding, so our review of the trial court's ruling is *de novo. Aspen Wilderness Workshop, Inc. v. Colorado Water Conservation Board,* 901 P.2d 1251 (Colo.1995).

I.

Seller first contends that the title company owed him a duty that arose from a contract between him and the title company. Although the exact nature of the duty asserted by seller is unclear, we disagree with his contention that any contractual duty was owed to him.

When it issued its commitment for title insurance, the title company offered to issue a title insurance policy to the buyer upon the satisfaction of certain conditions, one of which was the payment of a premium. The terms of the title commitment specifically noted that the title company's "only obligation" was "to issue" the policy to buyer and that, once the policy was issued, its obligation under the commitment would be satisfied. Hence, even if it be assumed that seller's payment of the premium, as called for by the commitment, gave rise to some contractual arrangement between seller and the title company, so that seller could enforce the obligations established by the commitment, that obligation was wholly performed when the title company issued the title insurance policy to the buyer in the form called for by the commitment.

Further, the title company did not assume any obligation to seller by virtue of the title insurance policy itself. Although the policy was not made a part of this record, the terms of the commitment make clear that the buyer and a lender were to be the only insureds under the policy and the only persons to whom any obligation was owed.

Contrary to seller's assertion, the mere fact that he paid the policy premium did not make him a party to the policy nor create obligations not expressly provided for in that instrument. *See First American Title Insurance, Co. v. Willard,* 949 S.W.2d 342 (Tex.App.1997) (act of paying title insurance premium does not make payor a party to the insurance contract).

Likewise, seller was not a third-party beneficiary of the insurance policy. That policy was issued for the sole benefit of the buyer and the lender, and none of the documents placed in the record, including those attached to seller's response to the title company's motion for summary judgment, discloses any facts which demonstrate that the title company intended seller to benefit directly from the policy issued to the buyer. *See E.B. Roberts Construction Co. v. Concrete Contractors, Inc.,* 704 P.2d 859 (Colo.1985).

II.

Seller also contends that, even if the title company owed him no contractual obligations, it nevertheless is liable to him under the theory of negligent misrepresentation because of the failure of both the commitment and the policy to note the existence of the claimed interest of his brothers. Again, we disagree.

A professional supplier of information may be liable for its negligence to a person with whom it has no contractual relationship, providing that supplier of information knows that the recipient of the information will provide it to that person or knows that the information is to be used to influence a transaction. *Wolther v. Schaarschmidt,* 738 P.2d 25 (Colo.App.1986). *See generally* Restatement (Second) of Torts § 552 (1977).

However, liability will attach only if the third party's losses stem from that party's justifiable reliance on the information. *Mehaffy, Rider, Windholz & Wilson v. Central Bank,* 892 P.2d 230 (Colo.1995). *See Stagen v. Stewart-West Coast Title Co.,* 149 Cal. App.3d 114, 196 Cal.Rptr. 732 (1983) (title company liable only if person for whose guidance information is supplied justifiably relied on information).

Here, seller alleged that he and the buyer had entered into a contract of purchase and sale of the property in question; that he then engaged the title company to provide a title insurance commitment; and that, thereafter, the transaction was closed in accordance with the parties' contract. At that time, he conveyed the property to buyer by general warranty deed, warranting his title to the property, and the title insurance policy was then issued.

Under seller's allegations, it is clear that he had assumed the obligation to convey good title to buyer before the title commitment was issued by the title company. His later conveyance by warranty deed was simply the fulfillment of his previously assumed obligation, which had been created before the issuance of the commitment.

Given these circumstances, therefore, even if we assume that information contained in a commitment to issue a title insurance policy can furnish the basis for a negligent misrepresentation claim by someone other than those designated as insureds under that commitment, it is clear that, here, seller did not reasonably rely upon any such information in conveying the property to the buyer. He had assumed that obligation before the title company furnished any information to either of the parties to the transaction.

The judgment is affirmed.

NOTE

On parties to whom the insurer may be liable for failure to search or disclose see Palomar, Title Insurance Law § 12.9 (2005).

Brown's Tie & Lumber Co. v. Chicago Title Co. of Idaho

115 Idaho 56, 764 P.2d 423 (1988)

BAKES, Justice.

This case involves a defaulted land sales agreement and an erroneous reporting of title to real property that allegedly caused damage to the seller. The plaintiff, Brown's Tie & Lumber Company (Brown's Tie), contracted to sell the Quality Inn Motel in Boise, Idaho, to a group of Californians, whose interest as buyers was bought out by Terrance R. Batt. Chicago Title Company of Idaho (Local), one of the defendants here, acted as the closing agent for the sale, and was also designated as the trustee under Brown's Tie's deed of trust. In February 1981, Batt defaulted and Brown's Tie directed Local to proceed with foreclosure and to issue a commitment to insure title to the purchaser at the foreclosure sale. Early the next month, Local issued a foreclosure report and commitment for title insurance. In issuing the commitment, Local acted as agent for Chicago Title Insurance Company (National), the other defendant here. Thereafter, Local gave the required notice of a trustee's sale scheduled for August 3, 1981.

After the statutory time for curing the default had expired, Batt and Brown's Tie began negotiating a consensual cure agreement. Because a feature of the agreement was Batt's promise to cure unauthorized encumbrances against the property, Brown's Tie, in late July 1981 prior to accepting the cure, contacted an employee of Local to receive an update on all encumbrances upon the property. Local advised Brown's Tie that no subsequent liens or encumbrances had been recorded, when in fact Batt had recorded a deed of trust subsequent to issuance of the commitment without the knowledge or consent of Brown's Tie. This instrument, which the parties have termed the Hoback deed of trust, was in the amount of $880,000. Acting upon this information from Local, Brown's Tie decided not to foreclose and allowed Batt to cure.

In August 1981, Batt again defaulted, and Brown's Tie again ordered foreclosure proceedings. Local's foreclosure report and commitment for title insurance failed to report or disclose Batt's deed of trust. A second foreclosure sale was scheduled for January 7, 1982. However, in early November, Local discovered the unreported deed of trust and notified Brown's Tie of its existence. Brown's Tie thereupon made a written claim to Local and National under the title insurance commitment for damages caused by their failure to discover and report the deed of trust, and for damages that might result from any delayed foreclosure sale. Local and National responded with a joint letter dated November 5, 1981. In it they neither admitted nor denied liability. They stated that if the January foreclosure sale were not postponed, Local would resign as trustee, and the title policy given at the sale would include an exception for the deed of trust which Local had initially failed to disclose. Brown's Tie alleges it had no reasonable alternative but to allow postponement of the foreclosure sale. The foreclosure sale was then re-set for March 15, 1982.

Meanwhile, Batt filed bankruptcy proceedings in California, and as a result, the March 1982 foreclosure sale was vacated by a bankruptcy court's restraining order. Brown's Tie contends that the defense of the bankruptcy action was tendered to Local and National, but both rejected the defense. After filing briefs and attending a hearing, Brown's Tie was eventually able to reach a settlement with the bankruptcy trustee. The settlement provided that the foreclosure sale would be allowed to proceed, and that the property would be encumbered by an option in favor of the trustee to purchase the motel on or before May 10, 1982.

Eventually, Brown's Tie, through realtor Paul B. Larsen, was able to obtain a binding sale agreement from a third party by July 23, 1982, and the transaction closed on September 1, 1982, with financing terms for $2.8 million. Thereafter, Brown's Tie demanded compensation from Local and National for damages incurred as a result of the failure to discover Batt's deed of trust. Brown's Tie argues that at no time have Local or National admitted insurance coverage or liability for damages. Brown's Tie's claim was denied by defendants.

Brown's Tie then filed suit, alleging breach of contract, negligence, negligent misrepresentation, breach of fiduciary duty, insurer's bad faith, and unfair claim settlement practices. Brown's Tie sought as damages alleged losses resulting from the delay in the sale of the motel, including operating expenses or losses during the period of delay. Brown's Tie submitted the affidavit of a realtor, Paul B. Larsen, who stated "that had plaintiff regained clear title to the Quality Inn on August 3, 1981, the property could have been sold to other buyers for approximately $2.8 million on or about October 1, 1981."

This certified appeal comes from an entry of partial summary judgment in which the district court essentially said that Brown's Tie had an action in contract, not tort. Brown's Tie assigns error to the dismissal of its claims of negligence, negligent misrepresentation, and insurer's bad faith. Brown's Tie also challenges the trial court's order in limine which excluded evidence of operating expenses and losses during the alleged period of delay, and evidence relating to a hypothetical sale which would have occurred earlier but for the failure to discover and report Batt's deed of trust.

I.

Defendants assert that the trial court properly dismissed plaintiff's tort claims. They cite the case of Anderson v. Title Ins. Co., 103 Idaho 875, 655 P.2d 82 (1982), and argue that the contracts for title insurance and policies are the source of the duties between the parties, not negligence principles. We agree.

In *Anderson*, the purchasers of real property sought to bring an action in negligence against a title insurance company which had failed under a policy of title insurance to except a properly recorded conveyance. The negligence action was pursued despite the fact that the insurer had tendered the full amount of the policy, such amount equaling the purchase price of the land in question. The substance of the purchaser's argument was as follows:

> Appellants contend that a title insurance company is liable in tort for failure to discover the conveyance of a portion of purchasers' land to the State of Idaho. Appellants argue that the practice in Idaho is that parties generally buy title insurance and rely on the insurance rather than an abstract of title. Before a purchaser buys property he orders a preliminary title report which tells him that the policy will insure against all encumbrances except those specifically listed in the report. Appellants argue that the purchaser is relying on the title insurer in the same manner in which he would rely on an abstractor of title and therefore the insurer has the same obligation as an abstractor and is liable in tort for errors or omissions.

Id., at 876, 655 P.2d at 83. The *Anderson* court rejected this argument, noting that the insurance company had not purported to act as anything other than a title insurance company and had not assumed any duties in addition to that of issuing a policy of title. Ford v. Guarantee Abstract and Title Company, Inc., 220 Kan. 244, 553 P.2d 254 (1976), a case in which a title insurance company had acted as an escrow agent, was held distinguishable. *Anderson*, supra, 103 Idaho at 877, 655 P.2d at 84.

To fall outside the rule of *Anderson*, it must be shown that the act complained of was a direct result of duties voluntarily assumed by the insurer in addition to the mere contract to insure title. As we explain below in our discussion of damages, negligence liability will not be imposed upon a title insurer absent these additional circumstances because title insurance only insures against damage resulting from defects in the insurer's title in the property, and does not represent that the contingency insured against will not occur.

In the instant case, Local has acted as closing agent, as trustee, and as agent for the insurer, National. There are essentially two acts of Local's which form the basis of Brown's Tie's negligence and negligent misrepresentation claims: the first is the July 1981 verbal update of encumbrances by Local; the other is the second commitment for title insurance issued in September 1981, which failed to report the $880,000 Hoback deed of trust.

With regard to the first act, the verbal update in July of 1981, neither the Brown's Tie–Batt deed of trust nor the Idaho Trust Deeds Act, I.C. §§ 45-1502 et seq., establishes a duty on the part of Local to provide such updates. Further, as insurer, Local had fulfilled all of its obligations under its first commitment for title insurance and had, in fact, accurately reported the status of title to the Quality Inn. Because the verbal update was not given pursuant to Local's role as trustee, the *Anderson* rule applies barring any cause of action based upon negligence for this act. Further, the act does not fall within the Restatement (Second) of Torts § 552 because separate consideration was not given for the verbal update.[1]

As to the second commitment for title insurance, which failed to note the Hoback deed of trust, it clearly was an action taken pursuant to Local's role as insurer and agent for National. Thus, *Anderson* is directly applicable and plaintiffs' theories based upon negligence were properly dismissed.

Brown's Tie urges that the holding in *Anderson* does not apply since I.C. § 41-2708 (1)(b) was not in force at that time. The statute provides:

41-2708. Determination of insurability — Prohibited risks — Rebates. —
(1) Insurability. No title insurance on real property in the state of Idaho shall be issued unless and until the title insurer or its agent: . . .
    (b) Has caused to be made a search and examination of the title and a determination of insurability of title in accordance with sound title underwriting practices. . . .

Brown's Tie suggests that the above language creates a duty on the part of title insurers to conduct a reasonable search of title before issuing a policy. We disagree.

Unlike similar statutes of sister states,[2] section 41-2708(1) of the Idaho Code does not mandate a "reasonable search" of title. It provides only that "a search and examination of the title" shall be made. We find it significant that the Idaho legislature, unlike other states, has chosen to omit the word "reasonable." It has long been the rule in Idaho that only abstractors of title may be found negligent, see

1. This cause of action has never been recognized in Idaho and we do not, by today's opinion, intend to do so. We simply note that even if Idaho did recognize the rule, the facts of this case would not fall within it. We reserve the question whether Idaho will permit recovery under negligent misrepresentation for another day.

2. See Alaska Stat. § 21.66.170; Fla. Stat. § 627.7845; Kan. Stat. Ann. § 40-235; Nev. Rev. Stat. § 692A.220; N.M. Stat. Ann. § 59A-30-11; Tenn. Code Ann. § 56-35-129; and Utah Code Ann. § 31A-20-110.

Merrill v. Fremont Abstract Co., 39 Idaho 238, 227 P. 34 (1924), and this Court has never deviated from the rule. See e.g., *Anderson*, supra. A familiar rule of statutory construction provides that a statute will not be construed so as to overturn long-established principles of law "unless an intention to do so plainly appears by express declaration or necessary or unmistakable implication, and the language employed admits of no other reasonable construction." Doolittle v. Morley, 77 Idaho 366, 372, 292 P.2d 476, 481 (1956).

No such intention plainly appears from the face of I.C. § 41-2708(1). Rather, as the trial court below wrote in its well-reasoned memorandum decision:

> [A]llegations of negligent performance of duties under I.C. § 41-2708 simply characterize a form of breach. Theories of malpractice sounding in negligence may be necessary where there is no contractual duty or contractual standard existent upon which to measure performance. Here, however, the duty or standard of performance is set forth by contract — the foreclosure reports and title insurance commitments — and measurement of performance can be fully accomplished by reference to the contracts. Any malpractice becomes a form of breach, rather than a separate claim for relief or cause of action.

We hold that I.C. § 41-2708 does not create a duty in tort upon the part of title insurers to conduct a reasonable search and inspection of title. Further, we hold that Brown's Tie has not averred circumstances which would avoid the rule of *Anderson*, which is controlling in this appeal; accordingly, we affirm the trial court's dismissal of Brown's Tie's negligence claims. Also, the dismissal of the negligent misrepresentation count is affirmed for the reasons stated above.

II.

Brown's Tie also appeals from the trial court's dismissal of its allegation of insurer's bad faith in settling claims. See, e.g., White v. Unigard, 112 Idaho 94, 730 P.2d 1014 (1986). Brown's Tie asserts that when the Hoback deed of trust was disclosed, it immediately made a claim for coverage and damages for delay under the insurance commitment. Brown's Tie argues that Local and National jointly threatened to change the terms of the title policy by inserting an exception for the Hoback deed of trust unless Brown's Tie agreed to a delay in the foreclosure sale.

The Brown's Tie–Batt deed of trust, which was drafted by counsel for Brown's Tie, specifically granted Local the power to delay the foreclosure sale and recognized its statutorily imposed notice obligations as trustee. See I.C. § 45-1505. The action of Local in delaying the scheduled foreclosure sale after discovering the Hoback deed was clear that trust deed from title at the judicial sale, and therefore was a proper exercise of its powers as trustee and cannot form the basis for an insurer's bad faith claim.[3]

Brown's Tie also argues that when the California bankruptcy trustee filed a complaint to stop the sale scheduled pursuant to the second commitment, both Local and National rejected the tender of defense, even though, Brown's Tie argues, they were the cause of the delay that allowed the bankruptcy to complicate

---

3. We note that Brown's Tie's breach of contract and breach of fiduciary duty actions remain viable in the court below and are not before this Court on the instant interlocutory appeal.

the foreclosure proceedings. However, defendants did not agree to defend such actions. The policy which was incorporated by reference into the commitments provides:

3. Defense and Prosecution of Actions — Notice of Claim to Be Given by an Insured Claimant. —

(a) The Company, at its own cost and without undue delay, shall provide for the defense of an insured in all litigation consisting of actions or proceedings commenced against such insured . . . *to the extent that such litigation is founded upon an alleged defect, lien, encumbrance, or other matter insured against by this policy.*" (Emphasis added.)

Brown's Tie reads defendants' duties too broadly. The bankruptcy action in California arose from the voluntary action of Batt in seeking bankruptcy protection, and was not litigation ". . . founded upon an alleged defect, lien, encumbrance, or other matter insured against by this policy." Defense of such action was not covered by the commitment or the policy. We therefore affirm the trial court's dismissal of the insurer's bad faith claim.

III.

Next, we address the propriety of the trial court's order in limine, which excluded evidence of business losses allegedly incurred during the period of delay and also evidence purporting to establish the terms of a sale which Brown's Tie could have negotiated but for the delay.

These damages were properly excluded. Under general contract principles, consequential damages are not recoverable unless they were specifically contemplated by the parties at the time of contracting:

"The damages for which compensation is sought need not have been precisely and specifically foreseeable," but only "*such* as were reasonably foreseeable and within the contemplation of the parties at the time they made the contract." Suitts v. First Sec. Bank of Idaho, N.A., 110 Idaho 15, 22, 713 P.2d 1374, 1381 (1985) (emphasis in original.)

Lost profits are generally not recoverable in contract unless there is something in that contract that suggests that they were within the contemplation of the parties and are proved with reasonable certainty. Nelson v. World Wide Lease, Inc., 110 Idaho 369, 378, 716 P.2d 513, 522 (Ct. App. 1986).

Here, the parties specifically agreed upon the extent of possible liability of Local and National. The commitment for title insurance provides:

3. Liability of the Company under this Commitment shall be only to the named proposed Insured and such parties included under the definition of Insured in the form of policy or policies committed for and only for actual loss incurred in reliance hereon in undertaking in good faith (a) to comply with the requirements hereof, or (b) to eliminate exceptions shown in Schedule B, or (c) to acquire or create the estate or interest or mortgage thereon covered by this Commitment. *In no event shall such liability exceed the amount stated in Schedule A for the policy or policies committed for and such liability is subject to the insuring provisions,* the Exclusions from Coverage and the

Conditions and Stipulations of the form of policy or policies committed for in favor of the proposed Insured which are hereby incorporated by reference and are made a part of this Commitment except as expressly modified herein. (Emphasis supplied.)

The parties, as is reflected in the commitments, did not contemplate "actual loss" to broadly encompass all damages, including lost profits, causally related to a defect in title. The insurer has agreed to compensate for actual loss incurred in clearing or removing unexpected encumbrances not to exceed the amount stated in Schedule A. The business success is not what has been insured, only the title. Such has been explained in Appleman's respected treatise on insurance law:

The purpose of title insurance is to protect a transference of real estate from the possibility of a loss through defects that may cloud the title. One of the reasonable expectations of a policyholder who purchases title insurance is to be protected against the defects in his title which appear of record. It has aptly been pointed out that a title insurance policy does not insure the value of any particular property, or even the property at all, but rather insures the title against defects that may damage the insured's interest in the property. Nevertheless, while a title insurer assumes the risk of losses due to a defective title, and distributes losses among all those subject to same risk, a policy of title insurance does not represent that the contingency insured against will not occur.

9 Appleman, Insurance Law and Practice § 5201, pp. 8–9 (1981).

We hold that under the terms of the commitments for title insurance, the subsequent policy "actual loss" does not include those damages which were the subject of the trial court's order in limine. We therefore affirm the court's exclusion of those uncontemplated damages.

The decision below is affirmed in all respects.

Costs to respondents; no attorney fees on appeal.

Shepard, C.J., and Huntley, J., concur.

NOTES AND QUESTIONS

1. Would a better solution in *Brown's Tie* have been to hold the insurer liable in tort for negligence, a liability that could be expressly waived in the insurance contract but was not? Would not this position better protect most home buyers and other ill-informed title insurance applicants but enable more knowledgeable applicants to negotiate for lower rates if negligence is waived? Also, should a title insurer be liable for negligence in searching only if it voluntarily agrees to assume this risk, as the court holds, or be permitted to exculpate itself from liability for search or examination errors by contract with insureds? And is it a reasonable construction of the Idaho statute to hold that no reasonable search is required by title insurers?

2. In a case similar to *Brown's Tie*, the Montana Supreme Court, in Lipinski v. Title Insurance Company, 655 P.2d 970, 974 (1982), three judges dissenting, states:

Although title insurance applicants are interested in obtaining insurance coverage, their primary interest is in what the examination discloses. For this they rely on the title companies to tell them of any risks. Risks usually covered by title insurance policies include errors in the title examination, including the negligent failure to note a title defect. A title company, as insurer, owes its clients the duty of conducting a title search with reasonable care.

The Montana Supreme Court, in another split decision, reiterated its position that a title insurer has a duty to conduct a diligent search for title defects, as distinct from merely insuring the title, and may be liable for negligent failure to locate and notify the insured of title defects that are reasonably ascertainable. Malinak v. Safeco Title Insurance Company, 661 P.2d 12 (Mont. 1983).

The Supreme Court of Nebraska had this to say in its opinion in Heyd v. Chicago Title Insurance Company, 218 Neb. 296, 303, 354 N.W.2d 154, 158 (1984), an action charging an insurer with negligence in title searching and examination:

> We now hold that a title insurance company which renders a title report and also issues a policy of title insurance has assumed two distinct duties. In rendering the title report the title insurance company serves as an abstractor of title and must list all matters of public record adversely affecting title to the real estate which is the subject of the title report. When a title insurance company fails to perform its duty to abstract title accurately, the title insurance company may be liable in tort for all damages proximately caused by such breach of duty. A title insurance company's responsibility for its tortious conduct is distinct from the title insurance company's responsibility existing on account of its policy of insurance. Different duties and responsibilities imposed on the title insurance company, therefore, can be the basis for separate causes of action — one cause of action in tort and another in contract.

In a later decision, Tess v. Lawyers Title Ins. Corp., 557 N.W.2d 696 (Neb. 1997), the Supreme Court of Nebraska stated that a title insurer could be liable for negligence in failure to set forth in its preliminary title report certain title restrictions not of record but of which the insurer was aware. However, for such liability to exist the party for whom the preliminary report was prepared must have relied on the preliminary title report in closing the sale transaction.

3. In White v. Western Title Ins. Co., 40 Cal. 3d 870, 710 P.2d 309 (1985), the California Supreme Court held a title insurer liable for breach of contract and negligence for failure to locate and report water rights appearing in public records. The preliminary title report stated that it "is issued solely for the purpose of facilitating the issuance of title insurance and no liability is assumed thereby." This statement was held ineffective to relieve the insurer from negligence liability: "A title company is engaged in a business affected with the public interest and cannot, by an adhesory contract, exculpate itself from liability for negligence." [40 Cal. 3d at 884, 710 P.2d at 315-316.]

4. It is common for title companies to be relied on not just for insurance coverage but for information as to the state of a title. Buyers and lenders are among those who make use of title companies for title opinion purposes. In an effort to limit title company liability for inaccuracies in these preliminary title reports, the following California statute, Cal. Ins. Code Ann. § 12340.11 (West 2005), was enacted in 1981:

> "Preliminary report," "commitment," or "binder" are reports furnished in connection with an application for title insurance and are offers to issue a title policy subject to the stated exceptions set forth in the reports and such other matters as may be incorporated by reference therein. The reports are not abstracts of title, nor are any

of the rights, duties or responsibilities applicable to the preparation and issuance of an abstract of title applicable to the issuance of any report. Any such report shall not be construed as, nor constitute, a representation as to the condition of title to real property, but shall constitute a statement of the terms and conditions upon which the issuer is willing to issue its title policy, if such offer is accepted.

5. Title insurance companies, for some insurance applications, contract with abstract companies or others to make title searches and prepare title reports, the reports relied on by the insurers in determining whether or not to insure and the terms of the insurance policies issued. These title report preparers may be liable to the title insurance companies for breach of contract or negligence if the reports are inaccurate and as a result the insurer is responsible to the insured for damages. For cases so holding see Fidelity National Title Insurance Company v. Tri-Lakes Title Co., Inc., 968 S.W.2d 727 (Mo. App. 1998); and Fidelity National Title Insurance Company v. First New York Title & Abstract Ltd., 707 N.Y.S.2d 112 (2000).

Jarchow v. Transamerica Title Insurance Company

48 Cal. App. 3d 917, 122 Cal. Rptr. 470 (1975)

. . . In early June 1970, real estate broker Melvin A. Jarchow and building contractor William A. Canavier and their wives ("Plaintiffs") became interested in a three-acre parcel of real property located in the city of Placentia owned by Mr. and Mrs. LaBorde. Although the property was improved with a single family residence, plaintiffs felt it could be developed into a boat, trailer, and camper storage facility. They contacted Transamerica Title Insurance Company ("Defendant") and requested the title officer in the Fullerton branch to search the state of the record title and furnish them with a preliminary report. In searching the title, defendant's employees discovered an easement from Frank F. Hill and Kate L. Hill (the LaBordes' predecessors in interest) to Pete J. Perez and Annie Perez ("Perez Easement"), which had been recorded on November 28, 1960. The deed purported to convey to the Perezes a 20-foot easement for ingress and egress purposes across the northern boundary of the subject property. But for some inexplicable reason, reference to the recorded Perez Easement was omitted from the Preliminary Title Report furnished the plaintiffs. However, the report did indicate that in 1958, when the Hills conveyed the subject property to LaBordes, they had reserved a 20 × 395 foot easement for ingress and egress ("Hill Easement") across the northern boundary of the subject property.

After receiving the preliminary report, there were discussions between plaintiffs and Transamerica as to whether defendant would eliminate the Hill Easement as an exception to coverage and proceed to insure plaintiffs against the Hill Easement in the event the plaintiffs purchased the property. The escrow/title officer consulted with her superiors and obtained authorization to do so.

As a result of the title search and the conversations with the defendant, plaintiffs promptly entered escrow with the LaBordes. Transamerica acted as escrow holder and also acted as title insurer with the understanding it would provide a standard form title insurance policy insuring title in the name of the buyers and insuring the LaBordes' security interests as holders of the first trust deed.

On August 27, 1970, the escrow closed and Transamerica issued the title policy.[1] The policy did *not* list the Hill Easement as one of the items excluded from coverage. Nor was the Perez Easement mentioned.

Within a few days after they took possession of the property, plaintiffs were informed that Perez claimed an easement for ingress and egress across their property. The Perezes owned the land immediately to the north of the subject parcel and Perez claimed that he has been using the 20-foot strip for access to his duplex residence since 1954; he also claimed that he had a deed from Hill which he acquired in 1960 which gave him easement rights over the northern strip of plaintiffs' property—a strip 20 feet wide and variously described as being from 132 feet to 263 feet long.[2]

Upon being advised of Perez' claims, plaintiffs contacted Transamerica and requested the company to take action to establish plaintiffs' title against the threat presented by the Perez Easement. Transamerica refused to initiate any action upon the plaintiffs' behalf, taking the fatuous position that it had no obligation to plaintiffs under the title policy since the Perez Deed had been excluded from coverage—notwithstanding the fact that the Perez Easement was not even mentioned in the exclusionary provisions of the policy.

After receiving the negative response from Transamerica, plaintiffs filed their initial complaint wherein they sought quiet title and injunctive relief against the Perezes and damages and attorney fees against Transamerica. Transamerica filed a cross-complaint to reform the policy, claiming that a mistake had been committed by the escrow/title officer in preparing the typing instructions in that the Hill Easement should have been excepted from coverage.

Pending the trial of the first action, plaintiffs applied for and obtained approval of their proposed Site Development Plan for the storage facility from the city of Placentia. However, development of the property was conditional; Perez had notified the city that he had a deed which he claimed gave him a right to use the strip; plaintiffs' proposed plan would have blocked the access to the Perez property with a building; one of the conditions imposed by the city because of the Perez Deed was to keep that access open. Although they received approval of their plan, plaintiffs decided not to proceed with it because of the clouds on the title.

While the trial on the complaint and cross-complaint was pending, plaintiffs filed the supplemental complaint seeking general and punitive damages on the basis of the aforesaid tort theories. It was stipulated that the material allegations thereof would be deemed denied without the necessity of Transamerica filing a formal answer thereto. It was also agreed that a bifurcation occur, with the action on the complaint and cross-complaint having priority.

---

1. The policy issued to the plaintiffs was prepared on a California Land Title Association Standard Coverage Policy Form; in essence, it provided that Transamerica insured the plaintiffs and the LaBordes against loss or damage in the sum of $72,000, together with any costs, attorney fees and expenses which the company may be obligated to pay and which the insureds sustain by reason of any defect in or lien or encumbrance on the title of the subject land as disclosed by the public records; excluded from coverage were all interests, claims, liens or easement which were not disclosed by the public records.

2. Both the Hill Easement and the Perez Easement were 20 feet wide and each overlapped the other so far as they affected the plaintiffs' land. However, at one time, the Hills owned all or most of the tract of which the Perez parcel and plaintiffs' parcel were a part. Consequently, the Hills had reserved a long strip to provide access to their other parcels to the west of Perez.

The Court Trial

The first trial went on intermittently over a period of three months. At the conclusion thereof, the court handed down a Memorandum Decision and Findings of Fact and Conclusions of Law. Before entering judgment, the court amended the findings on two or three occasions. The material findings follow: The Perezes had no right, title or interest in the subject property by virtue of the deed from Hill or otherwise; in 1958, the Hills conveyed the subject parcel to the LaBordes and reserved the 20-foot strip for purposes of ingress and egress for the benefit of some other land they then owned; the deed containing the reserved easement was recorded; the use of the strip by Perez was with the consent of LaBordes, plaintiffs' predecessor in interest; said consent was subject to revocation by LaBordes and the plaintiffs; the consent had been revoked by the LaBordes' sale of the real property to the plaintiffs and by the plaintiffs' action in serving a notice of revocation upon Perez when they acquired the property; at the time Transamerica conducted its title search preparatory to the issuance of the preliminary report and at the time the plaintiffs' escrow closed on August 27, 1970, the Perez Deed of November 1960 and the Hill Easement of 1958 were both of record; the Perez Deed, being a void conveyance, was excluded from coverage under the Transamerica policy; however, Transamerica was negligent in preparing the preliminary report; Transamerica knew or should have known that plaintiffs would rely on the title search as evidenced by the preliminary report; the escrow/title officer discovered the existence of the Perez Deed before the preliminary report was prepared; Transamerica negligently failed to disclose the existence of the Perez Easement in the preliminary report; as a result of the negligence of Transamerica, plaintiffs temporarily lost the use of the strip from August 27, 1970 to May 1, 1973 and were entitled to $172 damages as a result thereof; plaintiffs also retained counsel and were entitled to attorney's fees in the sum of $7,184 to quiet title to the Perez Deed; however, Transamerica was *not* obligated to take legal action upon the plaintiffs' behalf to eliminate the Perez Easement;[3] as to the Hill Easement, it constituted a cloud on the title until May 1, 1973 (Transamerica obtained a quitclaim deed from Hills' successor-in-interest during the course of the first trial) and was insured against under the terms of the title policy; consequently, there was until May 1, 1973 a cloud or defect on the title insured against under the Transamerica policy; the Hill Easement, being a cloud on the title, resulted in *substantial damages*[4] to plaintiffs until removed in 1973; however, the property sustained no compensable detriment (e.g., from loss of use) despite the cloud created by the Hill Easement for two reasons: (1) Transamerica removed the cloud by obtaining a quitclaim deed from the Hills' successor-in-interest during the trial, and (2) plaintiffs failed to mitigate their damages since they did not develop the property pending the trial, although they could have done so; and finally, Transamerica was not entitled to reformation of the policy inasmuch as it had knowledge of the Hill Easement and agreed to insure against it.

---

3. This finding is wrong as a matter of law. (See Discussion, infra.)

4. In his initial findings, the trial judge inadvertently found the plaintiffs suffered *no damages* as a result of the defect in the title resulting from the Hill Easement; however, prior to instructing the jury and prior to entry of judgment, the trial judge modified or corrected the findings and found plaintiffs suffered *substantial damages* as a result of the cloud created by the Hill Easement.

THE JURY TRIAL

In October 1973, the jury trial commenced. The testimony on the liability issue was understandably repetitive of that introduced in the first trial. However, extensive testimony was presented on the proximate cause and damage issues, particularly with reference to the distress and anguish experienced by plaintiffs from the time they learned of the clouds on the title until the time the same were extinguished — a period in excess of two and one-half years.

Canavier, age 53, suffered from a prior heart condition; he experienced tension and nervousness in being required to engage in court litigation for a period in excess of two and one-half years; his doctor prescribed Valium; the worry from tension created by the litigation caused him extreme stress; he worried over his wife's condition and her reaction to the litigation; and Transamerica's refusal to proceed against Perez caused him great emotional anguish.

Mrs. Canavier testified to the following effect: After discovering the existence of the Perez Deed and after determining that Transamerica intended to do nothing about it, she became extremely nervous; she was unable to sleep and worried constantly over the litigation, the money situation, and what they would do with the property; she was also worried about the effect the litigation would have on her husband's heart condition; her observations of her husband's distress posed a worry to her over possible loss of security for herself and her daughter in the event her husband died; she was in constant turmoil over Transamerica's refusal to clear title to the property; she was worried about the coplaintiffs (the Jarchows) who put most of their savings into the project; she was constantly concerned about the paying of attorney fees and litigation costs; they had to continue payments on the property although its status and future remained clouded due to the litigation; she was shocked when she learned Transamerica refused to clear title and she was greatly disturbed about the mistake Transamerica made because she felt when you employ an expert in title matters you should receive a clear title; the litigation was long and costly; it took over two and one-half years to clear the title and their financial resources were being depleted in payments; the prospect of going to court disturbed her greatly; she was humiliated and embarrassed by having to discuss in public her private feelings and all the problems encountered with the property during the course of the litigation.

Jarchow, age 61, testified to the following effect: He was unable to sleep during the pendency of the litigation; he and his wife had put all of their reserve savings in the property; his wife was required to return to work after discovery of the Perez Easement; the burden of continuing to make payments on the subject property and the financial hardship imposed by litigation expenses was a constant source of worry; he was constantly concerned about the outcome of the litigation inasmuch as he had invested everything he had in the property and he was not at all certain as to whether the title would ever be straightened out; he was shocked about Transamerica's failure to honor the title policy and its failure to report the clouds on the title; he was humiliated by his wife having to go back to work and being compelled to go to a psychiatrist; his wife would awake at night and sob and moan and worry over the pending litigation; his emotional distress resulted, at least in part, from Transamerica's failure to sue Perez or otherwise eliminate the easement.

Mrs. Jarchow testified that since the litigation had commenced she suffered from loss of sleep and had to go back to work; their finances were declining; the worry over the attorney's fees was constant; she felt their security was gone as a result of the continued litigation; her blood pressure rose and she did not feel well; inasmuch as they had invested most of their savings in the property, she had been required to neglect her teeth; she was worried over her husband's health and the attorney's fees and court costs; she was amazed to learn of Transamerica's mistake and shocked when it refused to correct its error; she could not believe they purchased an insurance policy for the purpose of protecting them and then received no protection from the insurer.

A court appointed psychiatrist testified to the following effect: While the plaintiffs were deeply concerned about their investment being impaired and their supposed inability to develop the property because of the litigation, he was of the opinion that the litigation aggravated the symptoms, as did Transamerica's failure to honor its contractual commitments; in short, many of the plaintiffs' symptoms were directly attributable to the litigation and Transamerica's blatant refusal to clear the title.

After both sides rested, the court read its Findings of Fact and Conclusions of Law (as amended) to the jury and the jury was instructed it was bound thereby.

Special interrogatories were propounded to the jury. The jury answered that Transamerica did *not* act maliciously toward plaintiffs, did *not* defraud plaintiffs, and did *not* act outrageously towards the plaintiffs. Consequently, no punitive damages were awarded. However, the jury did expressly find, in answering the special interrogatories, that the plaintiffs' emotional distress was legally caused by defendant's negligence in failing to disclose the Perez Deed in the preliminary report and by defendant's conduct with regard to the cloud created by the Hill Easement. The jury also found that *not* all of the emotional distress suffered by the plaintiffs was caused by failure to proceed with the planned development of the real property; in other words, the jury impliedly found that the emotional distress suffered by the plaintiffs was caused by the defendant's negligence and bad faith and the resultant worry and anguish flowing from Transamerica's utter failure to provide a good title or to do anything to correct its errors in connection with the search it made, the preliminary report it prepared, and the policy it issued.

EMOTIONAL DISTRESS

. . . Transamerica asserts that California law tracks the majority common law rule: Damages for emotional distress will not be awarded in an action for negligence unless that distress resulted directly from, or manifested itself in, physical injury. The rule requires physical "impact or injury," thus limiting the number of situations in which mental distress damages, occasioned by "merely negligent" behavior, may be recovered. (2 Harper & James, The Law of Torts (1956), § 18.4, pp. 1031-1032; 4 Witkin, Summary of Cal. Law (8th ed. 1974) § 548, pp. 2815-2816.) But American jurisdictions have been far from uniform in their application of the foregoing rule.

Those courts which have strictly applied the "impact or injury" standard have offered a variety of reasons for doing so. Four have received particular attention: (1) Emotional distress not so severe as to result in physical injury is too trivial a harm to merit recognition and remedy. (2) Mental distress is an injury which may easily be feigned and, without the impact or injury requisite, courts would be inundated with fraudulent claims. (3) Such injuries are too difficult to measure in dollar amounts, and courts should refrain from imposing speculative judgments on defendants.

(4) In most cases where physical impact and injury are absent, the casual link between a defendant's negligent act and a plaintiff's distress is sufficiently attenuated so that courts should refuse to adjudicate negligence actions alleging only mental distress damages; in other words, the proximate cause problem makes it nearly impossible for courts to place articulable limits on defendants' liability. (Rest. 2d Torts, § 436A, com.; 2 Harper & James, The Law of Torts (1956) § 18.4, pp. 1032-1034; Prosser, Law of Torts (4th ed. 1971) § 54, pp. 327-328.)

But application of the "impact or injury" rule — which denies court access to arguably injured parties — has resulted in a jurisprudential conflict of no small proportions. A fundamental principle of our system of justice is that for every wrong there is a remedy (e.g., an injured party should be compensated for all damage proximately caused by a wrongdoer); and departure from this principle may be justified only by the most compelling considerations. (Crisci v. Security Ins. Co., 66 Cal. 2d 425, 433, 58 Cal. Rptr. 13, 426 P.2d 173.) Since application of the "impact of injury" requirement constitutes a significant departure from the aforestated maxim, it has been the object of much criticism by both jurists and scholars.

The argument that emotional distress is a trivial injury is an antiquated concept which the advance of modern psychology has repudiated; research has shown that mental trauma can be just as debilitating as physical paralysis. (Pound, Interpretations of Legal History (1923) p. 120.) Fraudulent claims are not likely to be eliminated by application of the rule, since the slightest impact, or the most attenuated of physical injuries have been found sufficient to satisfy the rule's requirement. (Battalla v. State, 10 N.Y.2d 237, 219 N.Y.S.2d 34, 176 N.E.2d 729.) Further, the California Supreme Court has observed that "the possibility that fraudulent assertions may prompt recovery in isolated cases does not justify a wholesale rejection of the entire class of claims in which that potentiality arises." (Dillon v. Legg, 68 Cal. 2d 728, 736, 69 Cal. Rptr. 72, 77, 441 P.2d 912, 917.) Nor does the problem of speculative damages (given the current sophistication of the medical profession) present any greater problem in mental distress cases than it does, for example, in personal injury cases involving pain and suffering. (See Battalla v. State, supra, 10 N.Y.2d 237, 219 N.Y.S.2d 34, 176 N.E.2d 729; 59 Geo. L.J. 1237.) And, finally, the proximate cause problems raised by mental distress cases are really no greater than those which arise in many negligence actions involving physical injury. (See Prosser, Law of Torts (4th ed. 1971) § 54, pp. 327-328.)[8] But the fact that this causation problem has so often been used as a justification for the "impact or injury" requirement merely serves to point up the fundamental concern which underlies the reluctance of many courts to recognize a cause of action in negligence for emotional distress. . . .

. . . From the preceding discussion, it necessarily follows that the only valid objection against recovery for mental distress is the danger of fraudulent claims. This problem should be confronted and resolved by rules of proof rather than by imposition of limits on the negligence action itself. (See Prosser, Law of Torts (4th ed. 1971) § 54, p. 328.) . . .

---

8. It should be noted that a number of states specifically have rejected the "impact or injury" rule and have permitted recovery for negligently inflicted emotional distress. (Rodriques v. State, 52 Hawaii 156, 472 P. 2d 509; Battalla v. State, supra, 10 N.Y.2d 237 219 N.Y.S.2d 34, 176 N.E.2d 729; see also 59 Geo. L.J. 1237.)

In 1967, in Crisci v. Security Ins. Co., supra, 66 Cal. 2d 425, 58 Cal. Rptr. 13, 426 P.2d 173, the court expressly rejected strict application of the common law "impact or injury" requirement and suggested a new standard when it stated: "[I]t is settled in this state that mental suffering [including nervousness, grief, anxiety and worry] constitutes an aggravation of damages when it naturally ensues from the act complained of" and that "[s]uch awards are not confined to cases when the mental suffering award was in addition to an award for personal injuries," but may be recovered in cases where tortious conduct constituted an interference with property interests alone. In so holding, the court reasoned that where an actionable claim has resulted in substantial damages, apart from emotional distress, the danger of fictitious claims is greatly reduced: "other damages," be they to the plaintiff's person or to his property, provide the court with a sufficient guarantee of genuineness of the claim to accord redress for the emotional injury. (P. 433, 58 Cal. Rptr. 13, 426 P.2d 173.)[10] . . .

We conclude that the "impact or injury" rule is no longer strictly applied in California, and that courts may adjudicate negligence claims for mental distress when sufficient guarantees of genuineness are found in the facts of the case — e.g., when the plaintiff has suffered *substantial damage* apart from the alleged emotional injury.[11] . . .

Applying the aforestated standard, we have concluded that Transamerica's negligent act — its failure to list the Perez Deed on plaintiffs' preliminary title report — substantially damaged plaintiffs' financial and property interests in the amount of $7,270 ($170 for loss of use and $7,100 in attorney's fees). Such damages provide sufficient guarantees of the genuineness of plaintiffs' emotional distress claim to satisfy the *Crisci* standard. Having determined the plaintiffs' cause of action is not deficient for its failure to meet the common law "impact or injury" test, we next must measure plaintiffs' case against traditional negligence analysis to insure that a cause of action in negligence was adequately set forth.

Actionable negligence involves three elements: (1) a legal duty to use due care; (2) breach of that duty; and (3) the breach as proximate (legal) cause of the resulting injury. (4 Witkin, Summary of Cal. Law (8th ed. 1974) § 488, p. 2749.)

When a title insurer presents a buyer with both a preliminary title report and a policy of title insurance, two distinct responsibilities are assumed. In rendering the first service, the insurer serves as an abstractor of title — and must list *all* matters of public record regarding the subject property in its preliminary report. . . . The duty imposed upon an abstractor of title is a rigorous one: "An abstractor of title is hired because of his professional skill, and when searching the public records on behalf of a client he must use the degree of care commensurate with that professional skill . . . the abstractor must report all matters which affect his client's interests

10. In *Crisci*, plaintiff suffered $91,000 in financial injury (presumably, in part, the property interest interfered with was the right to use these funds) when defendant-insurer failed to accept a reasonable settlement offer from an injured third party and exposed plaintiff to liability well beyond the limits of her insurance policy. The court found this substantial injury justified an accompanying award of $25,000 for emotional distress.

11. We note that the Supreme Court has yet to permit recovery for negligently inflicted emotional distress where the mental injury was the only damage caused by the defendant's wrongful conduct. Though endorsement of such an action seems to be the logical end product of the decisional trends in this area, we set forth no such rule in this case. As discussed, infra, the instant case involves substantial financial injury and thus resolution of this case may be had based upon the specific standard articulated in *Crisci*.

and which are readily discoverable from those public records ordinarily examined when a reasonably diligent title search is made." . . . Similarly, a title insurer is liable for his negligent failure to list recorded encumbrances in preliminary title reports. . . .

It is undisputed that Transamerica breached its duty. The Perez Deed was a recorded instrument; Transamerica had actual knowledge of it at the time the preliminary title report was issued. Transamerica was duty-bound to report all matters which could affect plaintiffs' interest in the subject property. Defendant failed to list an encumbrance of record and, in doing so, breached its duty to plaintiffs.

Turning to the causation issue a defendant's conduct is the proximate legal cause of a plaintiff's injury if it is a substantial factor in bringing about the harm suffered . . . ; but the proximate cause attributed to defendant's act *need not* be the sole cause of the harm. (Prosser, Proximate Cause in California, 38 Cal. L. Rev. 369, 379-380.) But for Transamerica's failure to report the Perez Deed, plaintiffs would not have suffered distress when they learned of its existence. It was entirely foreseeable that plaintiffs would suffer mental anguish and distress when they were apprised of defendant's negligence since they relied on the preliminary report before purchasing the property.

When a title insurer breaches its duty to abstract title accurately, it is liable, in tort, for all the damages proximately caused by said breach. (Civ. Code, § 3333.) Since the "impact or injury" requirement presents no bar to plaintiffs' complaint — and the elements of an action for negligence have successfully been set forth — the trial court acted with propriety in determining that a cause of action for negligently inflicted emotional distress was pleaded and proved.[13]

BAD FAITH

Transamerica next contends that plaintiffs' supplemental complaint failed to state a cause of action for breach of the title insurance policy's implied covenant of good faith and fair dealing, and argues that the trial court erred in denying its motion for judgment on the pleadings. Defendant maintains that it withheld none of the policy's benefits from plaintiffs; it had no duty to quiet title with regard to the Perez Deed and it fulfilled its policy obligations regarding the Hill Reserved Easement when it obtained a quitclaim deed during the course of the trial.

Every contract contains an implied in law covenant of good faith and fair dealing; this covenant provides that neither party will interfere with the rights of the other to receive the benefits of the agreement. . . . Breach of the covenant provides the injured party with a tort action for "bad faith," notwithstanding that the acts complained of may also constitute a breach of contract. . . . The cause of action is applicable to all insurance contracts, including policies of title insurance. . . .

Since a primary consideration in purchasing insurance is the peace of mind and security it will provide when the contingency insured against arises . . . , an insured

---

13. Plaintiffs might have also stated an action herein for negligent misrepresentation. (See Hawkins v. Oakland Title Ins. & Guar. Co., supra, 165 Cal. App. 2d 116, 126, 331 P.2d 742; Williams v. Polgar, 391 Mich. 6, 215 N.W.2d 149; cf. Hale v. George A. Hormel & Co., . . . 121 Cal. Rptr. 144.)

may recover for any emotional distress suffered as a result of an insurer's bad faith, as well as any other detriment proximately resulting from the breach. . . .[14]

The gravamen of the supplemental complaint is that defendant failed to take affirmative action to remove the clouds cast upon plaintiffs' title by the Perez Deed and Hill Reserved Easement. We conclude that Transamerica's refusals to attempt to remove these encumbrances were acts of bad faith which breached the policy's implied covenant of good faith and fair dealing.

In determining what benefits or duties an insurer owes his insured pursuant to a contract of title insurance, the court may not look to the words of the policy alone, but must also consider the reasonable expectations of the public and the insured as to the type of service which the insurance entity holds itself out as ready to offer. . . .

Transamerica issued plaintiffs a standard form title policy (California Land Title Assn. Standard Coverage Policy #4000 — 1963, amended 1969). Paragraph four (4) of the policy's conditions and stipulations provides, in pertinent part, as follows: "The Company, at its own cost and *without undue delay* shall provide (1) for the defense of the Insured in all litigation consisting of actions . . . commenced against the Insured . . . ; or (2) *for such action as may be appropriate to establish the title . . . as insured,* which litigation . . . is founded upon an alleged defect, lien or encumbrance insured against by this policy. . . ." (Emphasis added.)

This provision of the title policy sets forth two obligations of the insurer: (1) To defend the insured's tile if a third party claims, in a judicial proceeding, an interest insured against by the policy, and (2) in the event that a third party claimant chooses not to litigate his claim, to take affirmative action (by filing an action to quiet title or by offering to compromise the third party's claim) to provide the insured with title as stated in the policy. . . .

The case law regarding a title insurer's bifurcated obligation to seek judicial determination of insured-against title defects deals almost exclusively with the duty to defend.[15] Here, however, we have a third party claimant who did not find it necessary to sue the insureds to exercise his claimed right — he instead persuaded the city planning commission to impose restrictions on plaintiffs' development which would insure that he would continue to enjoy his asserted easement. . . .

In determining whether the insurer's duty to defend has matured, courts, after looking at the nature and kind of risk covered by the policy, must decide whether a *potential* of liability for indemnity under the title insurance policy is raised at the time the defense is requested. If possible liability exists, the title company is duty bound to defend the insured in a quiet title action. Failure to provide a defense under such circumstances gives rise to a cause of action in tort for bad faith. . . .[16] The rule regarding an insurer's duty to defend really can take no other form; otherwise the insured would be required to finance his own defense and then, only if he is successful, hold the insurer to its promise by means of a second suit for reimbursement. If this construction were followed, a basic reason for the purchase

---

14. To recover for mental distress injuries an insured need not show that defendant's conduct was outrageous or otherwise intentional; mere indefensible unfair treatment is enough to justify recovery (Gruenberg v. Aetna Ins. Co., supra, 9 Cal. 3d 566, 580, 108 Cal. Rptr. 480, 510 P.2d 1032.)

15. This is not surprising, since an insured is almost always in possession of the subject property and a third party encumbrancer must seek adjudication of his claimed right if it is to be exercised at all.

16. It should be noted that the insurer has an alternative to assuming the defense of its insured when the issue of coverage is unclear; it may file a declaratory relief action to test its duty. (State Farm Mut. Auto. Ins. Co. v. Allstate Ins. Co., 9 Cal. App. 3d 508, 527, 88 Cal. Rptr. 246.)

of insurance would be defeated: instead of having purchased insurance against the trauma and financial hardship of litigation, the insured will have found that he has purchased nothing more than a lawsuit. . . .

In applying the aforestated rules to the instant case, we must conclude that defendant breached its duty to take affirmative action to provide plaintiffs with a clear title as to both the Perez Deed and the Hill Reserved Easement.

The trial court erred in its findings of fact and conclusions of law (in the first trial) when it ruled that Transamerica owed plaintiffs no duty to quiet title in regard to the cloud created by the Perez Deed. The trial court reasoned that since the Perez Deed was void ab initio, and not covered by the indemnity provisions of the policy, Transamerica's duty to quiet title on plaintiffs' behalf in regard to the Perez Easement never matured. But this reasoning erroneously assesses defendant's duty retrospectively.

It is the rule that "the duty to defend [the obverse of defendant's duty in the present case] . . . does not turn upon the ultimate adjudication of coverage but upon facts known to the insurer at the inception of the third party's suit against its insured." . . .[18]

. . . When plaintiffs requested that defendant remove the cloud created by the Perez Deed, they reasonably expected that Transamerica would honor their request by filing a quiet title action, pursuant to the obligation the company had assumed under paragraph four (4) of the policy's conditions and stipulations. When Transamerica refused it acted in bad faith and breached the policy's implied covenant of good faith and fair dealing.

In the course of determining whether Transamerica acted in bad faith in failing to take affirmative action in regard to the Hill Easement, two questions are raised: (1) Did plaintiffs give defendant sufficient notice of the existence of that encumbrance to give rise to a duty to quiet title; and (2) did plaintiffs suffer substantial enough injury as a result of the breach to justify an emotional distress award?

A duty to defend (or quiet title) arises when the insurer is notified of the existence of a defect. . . . And the duty to defend is fixed by the facts which the insurer learns, not only from the insured, but from the complaint and other sources as well. . . .

Transamerica conceded it had actual knowledge of the existence of the Hill Reserved Easement at the time it issued its preliminary title report. When plaintiffs requested that Transamerica quiet title in regard to the Perez Deed, defendant further admits that there was some confusion as to the relationship between the Perez and Hill interests and that, at one point, both were thought to be the same easement interest. When plaintiffs apprised the insurer that title to the strip

---

18. It is an oversimplification to assert that the duties to defend and to quiet title are precisely equivalent. The duty to defend arises only after a third party claimant has filed an action against the insured; in such circumstances it is plain that the insured's title is subject to a real cloud. However, the kindred duty to quiet title does not, and should not, arise in every situation in which the insured requests his insurer to act: there must be present in the facts and circumstances of the case some indicia that the encumbrance with which the policy holder is concerned is a genuine cloud upon his title. (Note, however, that should the insurer decide that the alleged cloud is illusory, it must bear the risk of its decision, and may, subsequently, be found to have acted in bad faith.) (Comunale v. Traders & General Ins. Co., supra, 50 Cal. 2d 654, 660, 328 P.2d 198.)

In the present case such indicia were present: The Perez claim was recognized by the city planning commission (to the extent that they imposed certain restrictions on plaintiffs' development); hence, Perez' claim, in fact, encumbered plaintiffs' property and constituted an actual cloud on their title.

of land claimed pursuant to the Perez Deed was in dispute (since defendant knew that the Hill Reserved Easement also concerned at least a part of that same strip), Transamerica was effectively notified that the Hill Easement constituted a potential cloud on plaintiffs' title-as-insured. Hence, when Transamerica refused to take any action to remove the cloud, it breached its covenant of good faith and fair dealing.

A number of California decisions have suggested that the bad faith breach of an insurance agreement must result in "substantial damages" apart from those due to mental distress before an award for the emotional injury may be made. . . . Here, Transamerica maintains that plaintiffs did not suffer substantial damage because of the Hill Easement and, that therefore, a cause of action for bad faith infliction of emotional distress could not be stated.

But the Hill Easement was inextricably tied to the Perez Easement dispute and as such constituted a substantial cloud upon plaintiffs' property (and thus did substantial damage) until it was removed.

It appears that Hill reserved an easement interest in the plaintiffs' parcel (when initially conveyed in 1958) for the benefit of other of his parcels in the same tract (these did not include the Perez parcel). Several years after the aforementioned conveyance, Hill gave a deed to Perez which purported to convey an easement interest in the Hill Reserved Easement. When litigation commenced concerning the validity of the Perez Deed, the question of to what extent the Hill Easement still encumbered the subject property was inevitably raised. Thus, the legal fees paid by plaintiffs in prosecution of their quiet title action against Perez were, secondarily but necessarily, incurred to determine the effect of the Hill Easement upon their title. In addition, the pendency of the lawsuit constituted demands upon plaintiffs' time, energies and financial resources. These various burdens are sufficient evidence of real and substantial injury to satisfy the substantial damage standard set forth in *Crisci*. Defendant's contention that substantial damages were not incurred in regard to the Hill reservation because the injury suffered was not compensated by the trial court in the first proceeding is of no moment in light of our preceding discussion: substantial damages in this context need not be compensable. Consequently, plaintiffs were properly awarded damages for emotional distress for Transamerica's bad faith breach of the title policy.

Transamerica claims that it neither breached the covenant of good faith, nor substantially injured plaintiffs, because during the course of the first trial (to quiet title) it obtained a quitclaim deed of the Hill Easement. This argument has no merit. Defendant consistently refused to quiet title on plaintiffs' behalf in regard to a claim admittedly covered by the policy—forcing plaintiffs to bring suit and endure the trauma and financial hardship of litigation—and then sought to avoid bad faith liability for their delay by finally delivering to the insureds the benefit of their policy. This argument lacks integrity; if such a course of conduct were endorsed, an insurer's duty to clear title would not exist in fact, but only in form.

Defendant knew of the existence of the Hill reservation, its close connection with the Perez Deed, and admitted that the Hill Easement was covered by the policy—yet still refused to assume its duty to quiet title. This court must conclude that plaintiffs' supplemental complaint adequately set forth an emotional distress claim for bad faith breach of the title insurance agreement, and that the trial court's denial of defendant's motion for judgment on the pleadings was proper. . . .

SUFFICIENCY OF THE EVIDENCE

Defendant argues that its motion for judgment notwithstanding the verdict (Code Civ. Proc. § 629), should have been granted by the trial court since the jury's awards of $50,000 to each of the plaintiffs were not supported by substantial evidence. Transamerica contends that the primary cause of plaintiffs' mental distress was their unreasonably perceived inability to develop the property. At the first trial the court found that the property could have, in fact, been developed in spite of the problems created by defendant's negligence and bad faith. The court therefore concluded that Transamerica was not liable for damages flowing from the failure to develop, and defendant contends that the record is silent as to emotional distress experienced for any other reason. We disagree. . . .

The record is replete with evidence that much of plaintiffs' distress was attributable to causes other than the delay in the development of their property. Each of the plaintiffs testified that he had experienced emotional distress (e.g., loss of sleep, anxiety, worry, tension and nervousness) because of concern over the litigation necessitated by Transamerica's negligence and bad faith, and the attorney's fees incurred therein. Both Canavier and Jarchow testified they were distressed and frustrated over defendant's refusal to fulfill its contractual obligations. Mrs. Jarchow was upset because the title insurance policy the plaintiffs had purchased appeared to be worthless. In addition, two psychiatrists testified that each of the plaintiffs was under emotional stress which had been engendered (at least secondarily) by the traumas attendant to the bringing of the present lawsuit. This sound, solid evidence satisfies the substantial evidence rule. . . .

EXCESSIVE DAMAGES

Where a jury award is so grossly disproportionate as to raise a presumption of passion or prejudice an appellate court is duty-bound to modify the award. . . . However, in searching the record for evidence of passion or prejudice, the reviewing court must be mindful that the trial court's determination should be accorded great weight. . . .

Transamerica argues that since the amount awarded plaintiffs for their property and financial injuries ($170 and $7,100) was small relative to the amount awarded for emotional distress, the latter award was excessive. However, in light of the tortious acts committed by Transamerica (notably the repeated acts of bad faith), it is likely that the greatest portion of plaintiffs' injuries would take the form of emotional distress (e.g., vexation, tension, frustration, and worry). As this court has previously noted, "there is no fixed or absolute standard by which to compute the monetary value of emotional distress." . . . Plaintiffs were required to suffer through years of litigation and frustration because of defendant's tortious acts. An award of $50,000 per plaintiff for over three years of anxiety and mental discomfort does not strike this court as being excessive nor motivated by passion or prejudice.

Finally, plaintiffs contend that they are entitled to attorney's fees on appeal. Contrary to their contention, the subject title insurance policy *does not* contain an attorney's fees provision for the benefit of the insurer, and, therefore cannot contain a reciprocal provision for the insureds' benefit. Consequently, plaintiffs are not entitled to an award of fees on appeal.

The judgment is affirmed.

Gardner, P.J., and Tamura, J., concur.

NOTES AND QUESTIONS

1. Most title insurance policies contain provisions to the effect that the insurer shall provide for the defense of the insured in litigation challenging the title which has been insured. Such a covenant to defend may even create an obligation on the insurer to initiate proceedings to protect the insured's title if the insured may otherwise lose his asserted interest. For example, in Lawyers Title Insurance Corp. v. McKee, 354 S.W.2d 401 (Tex. Civ. App. 1962), a covenant to defend was construed as obligating the insurer to bring proceedings adjudicating the insured's title when the insured was out of possession and in peril of losing his asserted interest through adverse possession by a third-party claimant. If the insurer breaches its duty to defend, the insured may retain his own counsel to handle the litigation and the insured's reasonable litigation expenses so incurred must be paid by the insurer. For the insurer to become obligated under its covenant to defend, the insured must promptly notify the insurer of any claim against the title, including litigation alleging a defect in the title.

If the insured elects to take over his own title defense, however, assuming no prior breach of the covenant to defend by the insurer, the insured waives his rights under the policy to have litigation expenses paid for by the insurer. Thus, in Buquo v. Title Guarantee and Trust Co., 20 Tenn. App. 479, 482, 100 S.W.2d 997, 998 (1936), the Tennessee Court of Appeals, Eastern Section, stated:

> With respect to the right and duty of defendant to defend actions brought against complainant, the insured, the certificate provides as follows:
>
>> The Title Guaranty & Trust Company of Chattanooga will, and shall have the right, at its own cost, to defend the party guaranteed in all actions of ejectment or other proceedings founded upon a claim of title or encumbrance prior in date to this certificate and not excepted therein. In case any person having an interest in this certificate shall receive notice or have knowledge of any such action or proceedings, it shall be the duty of such person at once to notify the company thereof in writing, and secure to it the right to defend the action. Unless the company shall be so notified within ten days, then all liability of this company in regard to the subject matter of such action or proceeding shall cease and be determined.
>
>> We think this clause of the certificate is to be construed as requiring the company, upon notice in writing, to defend such action. However, we think the party guaranteed, in the absence of any notice from the company that it insists upon its right to defend the action, could waive this benefit under the certificate and assume the defense of the action, employing attorneys of his own selection. While the company is interested in the defense of such an action to the extent of the amount of its liability to its insured, the insured might have, and often would have, as much or more at stake than the company. For this reason insured might, in some cases, prefer to conduct the defense himself even though entitled to this benefit under the terms of the certificate.

On the insurer's defense duty, see Pedowitz, The Title Insurer's Obligation to Defend the Insured, reprinted in Practicing Law Institute, Real Estate Law and Practice Course Handbook Series No. 251, at 587 (1984).

2. Differences of opinion can exist as to whether or not a title policy covers a particular claim of loss. What should a title insurer do to protect itself against contract and tort liability if an insured notifies it of a claim against the title, and the insurer believes in good faith that the title is not insured against such a claim? Does it make a difference if suit has been brought against the insured on the claim? What should the insurer do if it believes the policy insures against the alleged defect but that the claim is frivolous and cannot be proven? In the *Jarchow* case, would a declaratory relief action by the insurer to determine the issue of its liability have protected it adequately against emotional distress damage suffered by the insureds because of insurer's delay in defending or perfecting title?

3. With or without the impact requirement, is negligent infliction of emotional distress a form of injury readily feigned? If such injuries can be readily feigned, do adequate legal protections exist to prevent unjustified recoveries for emotional distress in defective title cases?

4. A Missouri statute, Mo. Ann. Stat. § 375.420 (Vernon 2002), provides as follows:

> In any action against any insurance company to recover the amount of any loss under a policy of automobile, fire, cyclone, lightning, life, health, accident, employers' liability, burglary, theft, embezzlement, fidelity, indemnity, marine or other insurance except automobile liability insurance, if it appears from the evidence that such company has refused to pay such loss without reasonable cause or excuse, the court or jury may, in addition to the amount thereof and interest, allow the plaintiff damages not to exceed twenty percent of the first fifteen hundred dollars of the loss, and ten percent of the amount of the loss in excess of fifteen hundred dollars and a reasonable attorney's fee; and the court shall enter judgment for the aggregate sum found in the verdict.

In Missouri, on facts similar to those in the *Jarchow* case, what do you think the insured parties would have recovered? Would this result be preferable to that in *Jarchow*?

5. On title insurer tort liability there are more recent cases in accord with the *Jarchow* case. E.g., Parker v. Ward; 614 So.2d 975 (Ala. 1992); Bank of California v. First American Title Insurance Co., 826 P.2d 1126 (Alaska 1992); and Shada v. Title & Trust Co. of Fla., 457 So.2d 553 (Fla. App. 1984). There also are later cases contra to *Jarchow* on title insurer tort liability. E.g., Mickam v. Joseph Louis Palace Trust, 849 F.Supp. 516 (1993), also holding title insurer not liable in tort to third parties; and Walker Rogge, Inc. v. Chelsea Title & Guaranty Co., 562 A.2d 208 (N.J. 1989), but concluding that a title insurer may be liable in tort to the insured if the insurer provides the insured with an abstract in addition to a title policy. By statute, the law of California is now contra to *Jarchow* on the tort liability issue. Cal. Ins. Code §§ 12340.11 (West 2005), and construing the statute, see Rosen v. Nations Title Ins. Co., 66 Cal. Rptr. 2d 714, 720 (Cal. App. 1997). The relevant California statutory provision is set forth in the casebook just prior to the *Jarchow* opinion.

In an article on title insurer tort liability the author, a lawyer specializing in title insurance matters, has this to say in opposition to the *Jarchow* position on title insurer tort liability:

> None of the public policy arguments for imposing tort liability is so compelling as to justify departure from the general rule that an insurance company's obligation to its

insured is governed by the policy contract. Although title insurance policies are contracts of adhesion, so too are most other insurance policies, as well as other important consumer contracts, such as mortgage loan documents. More important, the standard policy forms provide practical benefits far beyond any protection that an owner or mortgage lender could ever obtain through a title abstract or an attorney opinion. It is for this very reason that title insurance now has supplanted these other devices to protect against the risk of title defects. Although the title insurance company's liability under the policy is limited to the amount of insurance purchased, this limitation is neither unfair to the policy holder, nor is it a bargain that a court should describe as unconscionable.

In areas outside real estate, experience teaches that tort remedies are an inefficient means of compensating accidental injuries. This is illustrated by the many efforts at tort reform in automobile accident and medical malpractice cases. Indeed, a reform frequently suggested in these cases is to replace the fault-based tort remedy with no-fault insurance. Within the realm of real estate, title insurance already has supplanted the older, fault-based remedies that a purchaser or mortgage lender had against a title attorney or abstractor.

From a historical perspective, *Jarchow* and similar cases represent tort reform in reverse. Deciding on public policy grounds that an insured's no-fault remedy under a title insurance policy is inadequate, these cases permit the insured to recover in tort. This remedy imposes upon insurance companies duties they did not undertake; confers upon insureds benefits for which they did not bargain; and superimposes on an efficient insurance remedy the inefficient, uncertain, and anachronistic remedies that apply most appropriately to forms of title protection long out of favor in the real estate market.

In reversing *Jarchow,* the California legislature displayed prudent recognition of the harmful consequence that might flow from the imposition of a tort remedy. The California statute and the contract-view cases, such as *Walker Rogge,* are not anti-consumer, they merely follow the familiar principle that courts should enforce insurance contracts as written unless the transaction is so unfair that enforcement would be unconscionable. Absent an unconscionable bargain — which is not present in title insurance policies — there is no justification for courts to engraft a tort remedy onto a fundamentally reasonable insurance system for managing the risk of title defects.

Davis, More Than They Bargained For: Are Title Insurance Companies Liable in Tort for Undisclosed Title Defects?, 45 Cath. U. L. Rev. 71, 106-107 (1995).

3. *Regulation of Title Insurers*[16]

Title insurers are less rigorously regulated by the state than most other kinds of insurers. Their relatively low loss ratios no doubt are an important reason for this. Nonetheless, state statutes and regulations do impose some meaningful organizational and financial restrictions on title insurers similar to those applicable to insurers generally. Among the government controls that have had an impact on the operations of title insurers include antitrust legislation and restrictions on

16. On regulation of title insurance companies, see Burke, Law of Title Insurance, chs. 14-16 (3d ed. 2000 & Ann. Supps.); Palomar, Title Insurance Law, chs. 15, 18, & 21 (2005).

unauthorized practice of law. Efforts initiated by bar associations to enforce unauthorized practice of law restrictions have narrowed somewhat the range of services offered by title insurers, particularly the drafting of customers' security and conveyancing instruments.[17]

Johnstone, Land Transfers: Process and Processors

22 Val. U. L. Rev. 493, 512–513 (1988)

Title insurers are subject to government regulation, largely at the state level, but this control generally is less restrictive than that pertaining to most other kinds of insurers. One set of insurer regulations is designed to protect policy holders by safeguarding company solvency and the ability to pay insured losses that may occur. Nearly all states have one or more statutes directed at protecting the solvency of title insurers by such means as reserve or guaranty funds for paying policy claims, minimum paid-in capital requirements, and reinsurance or co-insurance requirements for coverage of single large risks. Even without these statutory forms of protection, one powerful title insurance customer group, the large lenders, would probably force a considerable degree of insurer solvency protection for policy holders. Another form of government control of title insurers is rate regulation, and about half the states impose some kind of control over premium rates charged by title insurers, although rate requests are rarely denied. Other types of title insurer regulations imposed by some states are a requirement that policy forms be approved by a state agency; [and] prohibitions on writing other kinds of insurance including mortgage insurance. . . . Prevailing state regulation of title insurance is sufficient for the federal McCarran-Ferguson Act [15 U.S.C.A. §§ 1011 et seq. (1997)] to apply and exempt this form of insurance from the federal antitrust laws, but ancillary activities of title insurers, such as escrow services, title searches and examinations, and presumably operation of joint title plants, are subject to the federal antitrust laws.

Another federal statute of relevance to title insurers is the . . . Real Estate Settlement Procedures Act [12 U.S.C.A. §§ 2601-2617 (2001)] prohibiting referral fees and fee splitting in real estate settlement service transactions. This provision, although favored by many title insurers, is a major competitive restriction on the insurers' efforts to attract referral business. Unauthorized practice of law proscriptions also have been held applicable to title companies in the drafting of legal documents, providing title opinions when insurance has not been applied for, and providing escrow and closing services. In recent years, however, there have been very few reported unauthorized practice cases involving title companies, which indicates greater forbearance by both the bar and the courts, and probably, as well, some reluctance by title insurers and their agents to perform tasks they believe would be contested as illegal behavior. Unauthorized practice relative to title companies has become, if not a dead issue, a quiescent one.

---

17. On title insurers and the unauthorized practice of law, see Burke, Law of Title Insurance, ch. 16 (3d ed. 2000 and Ann. Supps.); Payne, Title Insurance and the Unauthorized Practice of Law Controversy, 53 Minn. L. Rev. 423 (1969); and Brossman and Rosenberg, Title Companies and the Unauthorized Practice Rules: The Exclusive Domain Reexamined, 83 Dick. L. Rev. 437 (1979).

NOTES AND QUESTIONS

1. What purposes are served by each of the statutory sections below, and why do you think they were passed?

215 Ill. Comp. Stat. § 155/4 (2000)

(a) Every title insurance company licensed or qualified to do business in this State shall, within 30 days after the effective date of this Act or within 30 days after incorporated or licensed to do business, whichever is later, deposit with the Department, for the benefit of the creditors of the company by reason of any policy issued by it, bonds of the United States, this State or any body politic of this State in amounts as specified in subsection (b). The bonds and securities so deposited may be exchanged for other such securities. No such bond or security shall be sold or transferred by the Director except on order of the circuit court or as provided in subsection (d). As long as the company depositing such securities remains solvent, the company shall be permitted to receive from the Director the interest on such deposit.

(b) Every title insurance company shall deposit bonds or securities in the sum of $50,000 plus $5,000 for each county, more than one, in which the real estate, upon which such policies are issued, is located, to maximum deposit of $500,000. Every title insurance company guaranteeing or insuring titles to real estate in counties having 500,000 or more inhabitants shall deposit securities with the Department in the sum of $500,000. Any title insurance company having deposited $500,000 in securities with the Department shall be entitled to guarantee or insure titles in any or all counties of the State.

N.J. Stat. Ann. § 17:24-7 (West 1994)

[Title insurance companies] shall not be permitted to write any new contracts guaranteeing payment of principal and interest of bonds and mortgages. . . .]

Fla. Stat. Ann. § 627.7841 (West 2005)
Casualty title insurance prohibited

A title insurance policy or guarantee of title may not be issued without regard to the possible existence of adverse matters or defects of title.

2. Since 1987 a state agency, the Iowa Finance Authority, through its Title Guaranty Division, has been authorized to offer and operate a self-sustaining program of title guaranties on Iowa real property, in effect a form of title insurance. Iowa Code Ann. § 16.91 (West 2005). Iowa had been the only state that prohibited title insurance from being written in the state. But title insurance on real property interests in Iowa may be purchased out of state. On title insurance in Iowa see Palomar, Title Insurance Law § 1.5 (2005).

3. In Land Title Company of Alabama v. State ex rel. Porter, 292 Ala. 691, 299 So. 2d 289 (1974), it was charged that title examinations and commitments for title insurance by a title insurer constitute the unauthorized practice of law. The court held that the conduct in question was not the unauthorized practice of law, that a title insurer must be permitted to review public records in determining whether or not to insure, and that the commitments were not title opinions but binders to issue title policies. However, it has been held that title companies may not draft deeds and other conveyancing instruments, nor may they conduct real estate closings at which title company employees give legal advice or express opinions as to the effect

of legal documents. See, e.g., Coffee County Abstract and Title Co. v. State ex rel. Norwood, 445 So. 2d 852 (Ala. 1984). Contra on title company drafting of deeds and legal instruments, Bar Assn. of Tenn. v. Union Planters Title Guarantee Co., 46 Tenn. App. 100, 326 S.W.2d 767 (1959). See generally, Annot., Title Examination Activities by Lending Institution, Insurance Company, or Title and Abstract Company, As Illegal Practice of Law, 85 A.L.R. 2d 184 (1962).

4. Large commercial banks are showing some interest in acquiring and operating title insurance companies. For arguments against banks being permitted to own title companies, including risks of conflict of interest and the possibility that policies would be written on more of a casualty basis with consequent decline in the quality of titles, see Palomar, Bank Control of Title Insurance Companies: Perils to the Public That Bank Regulators Have Ignored, 44 Sw. L.J. 905 (1990).

Christie, Antitrust Update

62 Title News No. 7, at 21 (1983)

There are, of course, in this industry [title insurance] and others many cooperative or joint activities that are beneficial and without antitrust risk as long as properly structured and conducted. In addition . . . I would refer to some other longstanding and promising new activities which fall in this category. One is the joint title plant which has for many years been utilized in various locations around the country. Another would be the cooperative development of computer systems for use in the title insurance industry. The benefit to the public in terms of an improved product and the potential for cost-saving through the avoidance and duplicate facilities and efforts has led antitrust law enforcers to give general blessing to these kinds of activities. Nevertheless, in each case care must be taken to assure that the joint effort is not undertaken or conducted for the purpose of eliminating competition and the arrangement must contain no restrictions on the activities of the participants which unreasonably restrain competition or create unreasonable barriers to entry for other competitors. The precise legal requirements demanded by the antitrust laws would depend, of course, on the specifics of the project involved and the market setting in which it occurs, but these possibilities need not necessarily be foreclosed by the legal requirements of the antitrust laws.

Another form of permissible joint activity is, of course, participation in industry trade associations at the ALTA, state or local level. These associations serve legitimate and useful functions not only for the members but for the public as well. As a result, involvement in such organizations is not only permissible but should be encouraged. However, those who are involved and do attend should constantly have in mind that the context in which they are operating calls for some discretion in connection with association business as well as in a purely social context. . . .

Because of the changing rules in antitrust doctrines applicable to the title insurance business and the increasing costs associated with any involvement in antitrust litigation — not to mention the more stringent penalties for any violation — the development of increased corporate sensitivity concerning possible antitrust problems will be beneficial to the underwriters concerned as well as to the industry as a whole. That development might take the form of improving the channels of communication between operating people and the company's law department. Seeing the potential for a problem and discussing it in advance with company counsel will tend to avoid lots of down-the-road difficulty.

How do you do that? The best approach might well vary from company to company but I would offer some suggestions. Consider the development of a company compliance manual which would discuss the law, speak in practical terms of dos and dont's and spell out the appropriate source within the company for the resolution of any questions. Such a manual ought to be comprehensible to operating people rather than a theoretical exercise and ought to address rather specifically the kinds of situations that may give rise to antitrust problems as might be encountered during the ordinary course of business. Consider occasional meetings in the field between company lawyers and operating people to discuss issues as they arise in a practical everyday sense. Consider an occasional antitrust audit by company counsel designed to isolate areas of concern before they become litigation problems. . . .

NOTES

1. The McCarran-Ferguson Act, 15 U.S.C.A. §§ 1011 et seq. (1997), exempts insurers from the federal antitrust laws to the extent their activities are the business of insurance, are regulated by state law, and do not constitute a boycott, coercion, or intimidation. All states impose regulations on insurers. Title insurance is the business of insurance within the meaning of the McCarran-Ferguson Act. Commander Leasing Co. v. Transamerica Title Insurance Co., 477 F.2d 77 (10th Cir. 1973). However, the provision of escrow services by title insurance companies has been held not to fall within the business of insurance exemption of the federal antitrust laws. United States v. Title Insurance Rating Bureau of Arizona, Inc., 700 F.2d 1247 (9th Cir. 1983).

2. It has been alleged that unjustified price discrimination among different classes of insurers and unjustified price fixing exist in the title insurance industry. This, it is asserted, results in inflated title insurance costs to insureds. Uri, The Title Insurance Industry: A Reexamination, 17 Real Est. L.J. 313 (1989). Uri recommends enhanced competition in the title insurance industry by prohibiting industry rating bureaus; repeal of the McCarran-Ferguson Act, thereby making insurance subject to the federal antitrust laws; and allowing title companies to put new rates in effect without approval of state insurance departments. John Christie, who wrote the article excerpted above, vigorously takes issue with Uri in Christie, The Title Insurance Industry: A Reexamination Revisited, 18 Real Est. L.J. 354 (1990). Christie favors state regulation of insurance and argues that industry rating bureaus, where they exist, are created and licensed by the state and that insurance rates filed by the bureaus are adequately scrutinized by state regulators to determine whether rates are excessive or unfairly discriminatory.

C. REFORMING THE SYSTEM

The prevailing American system of land title protection, the recording acts backed up by title insurance, is cumbersome and costly. There have been many efforts to reform the system. Some are rather modest, such as curative acts, statutes of limitations, and tract indexes. But several more significant reforms have been proposed, each with some adoption in the United States. These include marketable title acts; major restructuring of land record keeping and retrieval, with extensive use of electronic recording; and Torrens registration. The first two of these reforms seek to improve the present prevailing system; Torrens registration entails substituting a different system, title certification, for recording. All of these reforms seek to make the process of title protection more efficient and titles more certain. The remainder of this chapter considers these more significant reforms.

Among the troublesome policy issues bearing on reforms in the land title protection system are what kinds of land rights, if any, should be sacrificed to more efficient title search and examination; who should bear the out-of-pocket costs of reform in the land title protection system and, if the system is to be subsidized by the government, which level of government should do the subsidizing; what degree of state or national uniformity in title protection procedure and coverage is desirable; and whether integrated public land record systems should be set up with stored information usable for many different purposes, of which title examination would be but one.

1. Marketable Title Acts[18]

These acts seek to reduce the scope of title searches and examinations, thereby simplifying title work. Acquisition and evaluation of title data are made easier and some efforts to clear titles of defects become unnecessary because some potential claims that otherwise would be defects are invalidated. Marketable title acts also make titles more certain by eliminating certain kinds of title risks. However, the benefits of marketable title acts come at a cost. Some of the land interests that are terminated by the acts conceivably should not be terminated or are terminated in many instances without those holding such interests being aware of the termination when it occurs.

In 1919, Iowa adopted the first act generally called a marketable title act.[19] A number of other states, many in the Midwest, have since passed similar legislation.[20] Marketable title acts borrow elements of both statutes of limitations and curative acts but ordinarily apply more broadly than these other statutes.

---

18. On marketable title acts generally, see Patton & Palomar on Land Titles § 563 (3d ed. 2003); 14 Powell on Real Property § 82.04 (2005); Simes & Taylor, Improvement of Conveyancing by Legislation (1960); Stoebuck & Whitman, Property § 11.12 (3d ed. 2000); Barnett, Marketable Title Acts — Panacea or Pandemonium?, 53 Cornell L. Rev. 45 (1967); Note, The Marketable Record Title Act and the Recording Act: Is Harmonic Coexistence Possible?, 29 U. Fla. L. Rev. 916 (1977).

19. 1919 Iowa Acts. c. 270.

20. Statutes often referred to as marketable title acts are in effect in California, Connecticut, Florida, Illinois, Indiana, Iowa, Kansas, Michigan, Minnesota, Nebraska, North Carolina, North Dakota, Ohio, Oklahoma, South Dakota, Utah, Vermont, Wisconsin, and Wyoming. See Stoebuck & Whitman, Property 900 (3d ed. 2000).

Basye, Trends and Progress — The Marketable Title
Acts

47 Iowa L. Rev. 261, 261–267 (1962)

I. PERSPECTIVE

"For avoiding all fraudulent conveyances, and that every man may know what estate or interest other men may have in any houses, lands, or other hereditaments they are to deale in. . . ." In so reciting, the first recording act adopted in America[1] suggested the duality in purpose and effect, and the unattained goal, that characterize the recording system to this day.

The colonists clearly understood that they were requiring every person acquiring an interest in land to record his conveyance. And, as the penalty for noncompliance, they were willing to impose loss of the interest intended to be acquired. But under the recording acts, as they have persisted to our time, the prospective purchaser of a piece of land need only take a deed from the seller and record it. That deed, if in proper form, will operate as an effective transfer, and the timely recording of it will preserve the interest received. But the purchaser is not interested merely in receiving an instrument of conveyance. He also wishes to be certain that the seller owns the interest purportedly transferred to him. He also wants to know that by the conveyance he will fully succeed to the seller's former ownership and thereby become able to market it himself later on. He can ascertain this only by examining the recorded evidence of all transfers up to and including the one by which his seller acquired title from his predecessor. Thus the recording system serves in dual capacities: (1) it performs a conveyance function; and (2) it preserves the written evidence by which we are enabled to appraise titles. Our entire system of conveyancing and title security, rooted in the American tradition, is predicated upon the assumption that a prospective purchaser can determine whether a seller has a good title by examining its history from the public records. Actually this is not completely possible, but the assumption is one upon which we must necessarily rely if we are to deal in land at all.

Mere statement of this dual function of recordation points unerringly to the shortcomings of the recording system in fulfilling its larger purposes in our time. Any modern system of land transfer must achieve economy, expediency, and security. Titles must be maintained in a sufficiently marketable condition to coincide with our current conception of land as a commodity that moves freely and easily in commerce. Certainly they cannot be permitted to become impaired and impeded by the functioning of the conveyancing machinery itself. That these objectives are not attained by any of the conveyancing and title assurance methods founded upon the recording system has become apparent to all thoughtful observers. Instead, for over half a century there has been ever increasing dissatisfaction with our system of transferring land. On a mounting scale real estate transactions have grown unnecessarily slow, unduly expensive, and needlessly uncertain. With the passage of years and the lengthening of chains of title, the process of appraising marketability has become progressively more cumbersome. The machinery employed for these purposes has become altogether inadequate for the needs of our time.

---

1. An act of the Massachusetts Bay Colony of 1640. See 4 American Law of Property § 17.4 (Casner ed. 1952); Haskins, The Beginnings of the Recording System in Massachusetts, 21 B.U. L. Rev. 281 (1941).

The inefficiency of this institution which has served us for 300 years might suggest that we throw the system overboard immediately and start afresh. Until twenty years ago we heard earnest advocation that we adopt the Torrens system of title registration. Even if we grant that this system has merit, it does not now appear to be acceptable in this country. In fact its use has been abolished in some states after an extended period of trial. Our one hope of bringing about simplicity would appear to be in a thorough overhauling and renovating of our present system. It has become increasingly clear that this can be accomplished only through enactment of systematic, comprehensive legislation.

In very recent years several states, striving to achieve the benefits of a simpler system for conveyancing procedure, have thoughtfully worked out one or more pieces of legislation which are the heart of any such legislative program. The measures are appropriately called marketable title legislation. So far ten states have adopted marketable title acts and many others are giving serious consideration to them. This type of legislation is rapidly gaining favor and proving to be highly effective. In fact, it bids fair to be the most successful expedient for promoting simplicity in land transfers in this country since the introduction of the Torrens system.

It is the thesis of this Article that the basic ideas involved in the acts, as improved upon and adapted to local conditions, should become, and promise to become, a permanent and universal feature of our recording systems.

Brief analyses are offered of the generic problems and the acts' general approach to their solution. The particular statutes and the several interesting decisions that have arisen under them are discussed. And lastly, the precise terms and application of such legislation are considered in connection with the provisions of the model act prepared under the auspices of the Section of Real Property, Probate and Trust Law of the American Bar Association.

II. THE PROBLEMS STATED

A. GENERALLY

Ever since the establishment of a recording system in America we have assumed that the recording of an instrument disclosing an interest in A would give constructive notice of A's interest to all the world and, moreover, that it would continue to do so for all eternity unless that interest were sooner transferred or extinguished. That assumption is still basic to our recording system today.

So long as transfers of land remained few, so long as the history of a title was confined to a short expanse of time, examinations and appraisals of titles were relatively simple. But each successive transfer, whether by private instrument, by judicial proceedings or by operation of law, not only extends the length and scope of search but also requires a more intricate appraisal in order to ascertain the present status of land ownership. One may estimate the mounting proportion with which the labor and difficulty in examining a title varies with the number of transfers. Considering the number of long descriptions and the number and length of judicial proceedings, perhaps it would be fairly accurate to say that the task increases according to the square of the number of transfers.

A solution must be found. One can be found if we scrutinize with all possible openness of mind the actual performance of our conveyancing system as we find it today.

The essential reasons for the present inefficiency are fairly obvious. They may be enumerated as follows: (1) the increased burden of search; (2) the economic waste in repetitive examinations; (3) the development of overmeticulous title examination inherent in the system itself; (4) the failure of statutes of limitations to accomplish their intended purpose; and (5) the lack of effective legislation to redefine and promote marketability in reasonable ways.

B.   BURDEN OF SEARCH

As ownership of land passes from one person to another, not only does the period of title search become greater but the number of instruments and proceedings which constitute the chain of title also increases. Both factors add progressively to the burden of search; both factors increase the possibility of error which results in unmarketable titles. Each transfer in the chain of title tends to make the job of the conveyancer more difficult and burdensome. We see the recording system slowly but inevitably bogging down of its own weight.

C.   REPETITIVE EXAMINATIONS

Probably none of the pioneers who had a hand in originating our recording system envisaged the monumental task that title examiners would face after the passage of just one century of transfers. Every time that land is bought and sold, it becomes the burdensome task of some examiner to trace the title back to its origin and pass judgment anew upon each link in the chain. How much longer can we continue to justify this practice? How insurmountable will be the complications half a century hence, or even a quarter of a century hence!

Our recording system from its very beginning contemplated that a person having a permanent or long-term interest in land should be able to preserve that interest by merely recording proper notice of it. In addition to complete ownership, interests of this kind include easements, leases, mortgages, and also all kinds of future interests. Purchasers of land normally understand that they must take subject to these outstanding interests because they appear somewhere in the record history of the title. But we must not lose sight of the fact that their present existence can only be determined by a search of the whole title throughout the entire period of its history. We have previously felt that owners of interests of this kind should be able to protect themselves by one recording, especially if the interest is of a non-possessory kind. Repeated examinations thus become endlessly necessary under our existing systems.[8]

D.   OVER-METICULOUS TITLE EXAMINATION

Every title examiner owes a duty to his client to advise him truly and conscientiously as to whether he believes the title which he intends to buy is a marketable one. On the subject of marketability an individual examiner is likely to advise the purchaser not only as to what he believes concerning its freedom from attack as a practical

---

8. The Massachusetts Judicial Council recently drew and precisely stated the contrary conclusion: "Today, after 300 years the need of re-recording of evidence to bring the document within the reach of a reasonable period of search is like the original need of recording." See Report of Judicial Council of Massachusetts, Improving Our Land Title Recording System 20, 22 (32d Rep. 1956).

matter but also as to what a future examiner may say concerning it. He cannot justifiably ignore defects of which another might demand correction. Each appraisal of title tends to err on the side of caution and conservatism, with the result that trivialities are overemphasized. Thus the entire process tends to become dominated by overabundant caution and ultrameticulous judgments. "Unlike water, all conveyances seek the highest level," is the picturesque way one writer has described this legal phenomenon. Title examiners are not to be unduly criticized for their punctilious observance of minutiae. The basic difficulty lies in the mechanical operation of the system itself. Its very nature demands satisfaction of whatever doubtful questions appear in titles.

Until a few years ago no attempt had ever been made to set up any standards to be followed by title examiners. Gradually it was felt that if certain standards could be laid down in advance, they could accomplish much to dispel fears that opinions of future examiners would be at variance with present appraisals. Knowledge as to how others will treat certain recurring problems will increase the confidence with which present opinions can be rendered. Thus far real estate title standards have been adopted in twenty-two states on a statewide basis and in several other communities on a county or city level. Lawyers in these states unhesitatingly attest their value. Title Standards committees in most states have been actively engaged in improving or extending their standards to make them function ever more efficiently to accomplish a job that has long needed to be done. A by-product of these title standards is that committees working with them become alert to the need for legislation to bring about needed improvements in local property law, and they have become increasingly instrumental in supporting needed statutory changes. Iowa has, for example, long been a leader in both movements.

E. SHORTCOMINGS OF STATUTES OF LIMITATIONS

Statutes of limitations have long occupied an essential and important place in property law. They express a policy that is designed to promote repose and give security to possession of land coupled with acts of ownership. They operate in two ways: first, by punishing an owner who fails to assert his right within a prescribed period of time; and, second, by quieting the title of one who consistently asserts his rights during a prescribed period of time. It is true that land is occasionally acquired by wrongful dispossession followed by adverse possession for the requisite length of time to confer title. But the vast majority of cases of adverse possession have their origin in an intended transfer of title which is ineffective merely for failure to comply with some formality of conveyancing.

Despite the beneficial effects produced by the application of statutes of limitations in individual cases, the importance of these statutes for providing a good record title is not so great as might be supposed. First, there is no device for registering a title acquired by adverse possession. Second, statutes of limitations do not ordinarily operate against owners of future interests, persons under disabilities, the state or other governmental units. Hence, conventional statutes of limitations do not and cannot achieve their full usefulness as a means of providing a record marketable title.

Notwithstanding the foregoing observations on the limited effects of statutes of limitations, they do in some respects have certain virtues in promoting marketable titles. Limitations apply not alone to cases of adverse possession; they can be made to apply equally well to all manner of nonpossessory rights. Judgments, mechanics' liens, mortgages, deeds of trust, land contracts, options, notices of lis pendens are all cases in point. How should statutes of limitations affect these interests?

We have long been accustomed to the rule which declares that a judgment shall cease to be a lien after the expiration of a fixed number of years. In other words the mere passage of time extinguishes the interest and does so absolutely, irrespective of disabilities or other factors which might ordinarily suspend or extend the running of the statute. We know that the same principle applies in the case of mechanics' liens. If notice of a mechanic's lien is filed but no suit is commenced within the statutory period thereafter, the notice of lien ceases to have any significance. It is extinguished as an interest, either actual or potential. To determine marketability, one need only examine the record with a calendar before him. That treatment should be extended to as many kinds of interests as possible without unduly prejudicing the rights of others.

F. REDEFINING MARKETABILITY BY LEGISLATION

The orthodox definition of marketable title is one free of all reasonable doubt, one which a reasonably prudent person would be willing to accept. Stated another way, a marketable title is one which does *not* contain a defect, outstanding interest or claim which may conceivably operate to defeat or impair the owner's title. This negative concept of marketability has become an implied invitation for courts to declare a title unmarketable if an examiner has entertained any doubt whatever in his mind with respect to it. A moment's reflection will convince us that we have been more concerned in the past with unmarketability of titles than with marketability. And too often unmarketability may depend upon some technical error or irregularity in an instrument many years old giving rise only to an apparent claim or interest that no court in the world would sustain.

We have long needed to replace this negative approach by a positive one which will make marketability of a title depend upon its condition during a recent interval of time rather than upon technical defects which may have occurred in the distant past. So long as we continue to rely on our recording system to perform its function in the conveyancing process, some such method is fundamental to the maintenance of any degree of simplicity.

THE MODEL MARKETABLE TITLE ACT

As part of the work product of a joint research undertaking on conveyancing reform by the American Bar Association's Section of Real Property, Probate and Trust Law, and the University of Michigan Law School, a Model Marketable Title Act has been developed. It is based in considerable part on the Michigan Marketable Title Act[21] and to some extent on an Ontario act,[22] and has substantially influenced the form of marketable title acts in a number of states. As drafted by Professor Lewis M. Simes and his assistant, Clarence B. Taylor, the Model Act provides as follows.

21. 1945 Mich. Pub. Acts No. 200.
22. Ontario Investigation of Titles Act, Ont. Rev. Stat. c. 186 (1950).

Model Marketable Title Act[23]

Section 1. *Marketable Record Title.* Any person having the legal capacity to own land in this state, who has an unbroken chain of title of record to any interest in land for forty years or more, shall be deemed to have a marketable record title to such interest as defined in Section 8, subject only to the matters stated in Section 2 hereof. A person shall be deemed to have such an unbroken chain of title when the official public records disclose a conveyance or other title transaction, of record not less than forty years at the time the marketability is to be determined, which said conveyance or other title transaction purports to create such interest, either in (a) the person claiming such interest, or (b) some other person from whom, by one or more conveyances or other title transactions of record, such purported interest has become vested in the person claiming such interest; with nothing appearing of record, in either case, purporting to divest such claimant of such purported interest.

Section 2. *Matters to Which Marketable Title Is Subject.* Such marketable record title shall be subject to:

(a) All interests and defects which are inherent in the muniments of which such chain of record title is formed; *provided*, however, that a general reference in such muniments, or any of them, to easements, use restrictions or other interests created prior to the root of title shall not be sufficient to preserve them, unless specific identification be made therein of a recorded title transaction which creates such easement, use restriction or other interest.

(b) All interest preserved by the filing of proper notice or by possession by the same owner continuously for a period of forty years or more, in accordance with Section 4 hereof.

(c) The rights of any person arising from a period of adverse possession or user, which was in whole or in part subsequent to the effective date of the root of title.

(d) Any interest arising out of a title transaction which has been recorded subsequent to the effective date of the root of title from which the unbroken chain of title of record is started; *provided*, however, that such recording shall not revive or give validity to any interest which has been extinguished prior to the time of the recording by the operation of Section 3 hereof.

(e) The exceptions stated in Section 6 hereof as to rights of reversioners in leases, as to apparent easements and interests in the nature of easements, and as to interests of the United States.

Section 3. *Interests Extinguished by Marketable Title.* Subject to the matters stated in Section 2 hereof, such marketable record title shall be held by its owner and shall be taken by any person dealing with the land free and clear of all interests, claims or charges whatsoever, the existence of which depends upon any act, transaction, event or omission that occurred prior to the effective date of the root of title. All such interests, claims or charges, however denominated, whether legal or equitable, present or future, whether such interests, claims or charges are asserted by a person sui juris or under a disability, whether such person is within or without the state,

---

23. The Model Act, with commentary, appears in Simes and Taylor, The Improvement of Conveyancing by Legislation 6–16 (1960).

whether such person is natural or corporate, or is private or governmental, are hereby declared to be null and void.

Section 4. *Effect of Filing Notice or the Equivalent.*

(a) Any person claiming an interest in land may preserve and keep effective such interest by filing for record during the forty-year period immediately following the effective date of the root of title of the person whose record title would otherwise be marketable, a notice in writing, duly verified by oath, setting forth the nature of the claim. No disability or lack of knowledge of any kind on the part of anyone shall suspend the running of said forty-year period. Such notice may be filed for record by the claimant or by any other person acting on behalf of any claimant who is (1) under a disability, (2) unable to assert a claim on his own behalf, or (3) one of a class, but whose identity cannot be established or is uncertain at the time of filing such notice of claim for record.

(b) If the same record owner of any possessory interest in land has been in possession of such land continuously for a period of forty years or more, during which period no title transaction with respect to such interest appears of record in his chain of title, and no notice has been filed by him or on his behalf as provided in Subsection (a), and such possession continues to the time when marketability is being determined, such period of possession shall be deemed equivalent to the filing of the notice immediately preceding the termination of the forty-year period described in Subsection (a).

Section 5. *Contents of Notice; Recording and Indexing.* To be effective and to be entitled to record the notice above referred to shall contain an accurate and full description of all land affected by such notice which description shall be set forth in particular terms and not by general inclusions; but if said claim is founded upon a recorded instrument, then the description in such notice may be the same as that contained in such recorded instrument. Such notice shall be filed for record in the registry of deeds of the county or counties where the land described therein is situated. The recorder of each county shall accept all such notices presented to him which describe land located in the county in which he serves and shall enter and record full copies thereof in the same way that deeds and other instruments are recorded and each recorder shall be entitled to charge the same fees for the recording thereof as are charged for recording deeds. In indexing such notices in his office each recorder shall be entitled to charge the same fees for the recording thereof as are charged for recording deeds. In indexing such notices in his office each recorder shall enter such notices under the grantee indexes of deeds under the names of the claimants appearing in such notices. Such notices shall also be indexed under the description of the real estate involved in a book set apart for that purpose to be known as the "Notice Index."

Section 6. *Interests Not Barred by Act.* This Act shall not be applied to bar any lessor or his successor as a reversioner of his right to possession on the expiration of any lease; or to bar or extinguish any easement or interest in the nature of an easement, the existence of which is clearly observable by physical evidence of its use; or to bar any right, title or interest of the United States, by reason of failure to file the notice herein required.

Section 7. *Limitations of Actions and Recording Acts.* Nothing contained in this Act shall be construed to extend the period for the bringing of an action or for the doing of any other required act under any statutes of limitations, nor, except as herein specifically provided, to affect the operation of any statutes governing the effect of the recording or the failure to record any instrument affecting land.

Section 8. *Definitions.* As used in this Act:

(a) "Marketable record title" means a title of record, as indicated in Section 1 hereof, which operates to extinguish such interests and claims, existing prior to the effective date of the root of title, as are stated in Section 3 hereof.

(b) "Records" includes probate and other official public records, as well as records in the registry of deeds.

(c) "Recording," when applied to the official public records of a probate, or other court, includes filing.

(d) "Person dealing with land" includes a purchaser of any estate or interest therein, a mortgagee, a levying or attaching creditor, a land contract vendee, or any other person seeking to acquire an estate or interest therein, or impose a lien thereon.

(e) "Root of title" means that conveyance or other title transaction in the chain of title of a person, purporting to create the interest claimed by such person, upon which he relies as a basis for the marketability of his title, and which was the most recent to be recorded as of a date forty years prior to the time when marketability is being determined. The effective date of the "root of title" is the date on which it is recorded.

(f) "Title transaction" means any transaction affecting title to any interest in land, including title by will or descent, title by tax deed, or by trustee's, referee's, guardian's, executor's, administrator's, master in chancery's, or sheriff's deed, or decree of any court, as well as warranty deed, quitclaim deed, or mortgage.

Section 9. *Act to Be Liberally Construed.* This Act shall be liberally construed to effect the legislative purpose of simplifying and facilitating land title transactions by allowing persons to rely on a record chain of title as described in Section 1 of this Act, subject only to such limitations as appear in Section 2 of this Act.

Section 10. *Two-Year Extension of Forty-Year Period.* If the forty-year period specified in this Act shall have expired prior to two years after the effective date of this Act, such period shall be extended two years after the effective date of this Act.

NOTES AND QUESTIONS

1. Would the Model Act be constitutional if the exceptions section, §6, were omitted?

2. Marketable record title provisions, derived from the Model Marketable Title Act, are included as part of the Uniform Simplification of Land Transfers Act, an act approved in 1976 by the National Conference of Commissioners on Uniform State Laws. No dramatic new innovative proposals are contained in the act, but it does include in one concise and well-drafted document many provisions that would, if adopted, improve the conveyancing, recording, and lien laws of the average state. The prefatory note to the act describes in the following words what the act is trying to accomplish:

The purposes of the Act include the furtherance of the security and certainty of land titles, the reduction of the costs of land transfers, the balancing of the interests of all parties in the construction lien area, and the creation of a more efficient system of public land records. . . .

The high cost of real estate transfers has been seen by many analysts in recent years as being a substantial cause of the pricing of housing out of the reach of a large segment of the American public and of discouraging new investment in construction. This Act embodies a number of reforms designed to limit these costs. The required period of title search has been shortened through the adoption of marketable record title provisions similar to those which have proved successful in over a dozen states. The scope of the search has been further reduced by almost entirely eliminating those interests which can be asserted to those stated on the official record or of which a purchaser has actual knowledge. Wasteful formalities have been made unnecessary.

Considerable attention is paid to the mechanics of the recording system and to the divison of functions among the various participants in the process. Persons presenting documents for recording are required to give detailed information to enable the recording officer to index the documents correctly. The recording officer is given discretion in the development of systems for modernization and automation of recording operations and is given the responsibility for moving toward a system of at least limited geographic indexing. At the same time, in anticipation of the eventual computerization of the recording system, the recording office is relieved of all responsibility for making conclusions about the legal effects of documents submitted for recording. The office of state recorder is created to allow for coordination and sharing of experience in the modernization of recording practices.

Lane and Edson, Land Title Recordation Systems: Legal Restraints and Reforms[24]

II–53 to II–60 (1978)

. . . Marketable title acts have spawned considerable commentary, most of it favorable, but some highly critical. What follows is a summary of the principal issues and concerns that have been expressed about marketable title acts.

1. Constitutionality—The principal constitutional problem (principally under state constitutions) arises out of the retroactive aspect of a marketable title act. This is the problem: The parties to interests in land created and recorded prior to the enactment of the marketable title act have formed a reasonable expectation that the interests will have the characteristics attributable to them under the then operative laws, of which one characteristic is an indefinite duration, subject only to the then applicable statutes of limitations. Then along comes the marketable title act which can cut off these interests through the passage of time, unless the holder of the interest makes a new recording, a factor he never counted on and, as a practical matter, may never even learn about. Because their interests have been diminished through legislation, the holders of these interests can claim a deprivation of their property by government action, a substantive due process violation, and under some circumstances, an impairment of the obligation of their contract rights.

Constitutional challenges on legislation of this nature are generally resolved by balancing the injury to the person against the public purposes sought to be achieved. The greater the injury, the more immediate and important the public

---

24. A report prepared for the U.S. Department of Housing and Urban Development, pursuant to a contract with Booz, Allen & Hamilton, Inc.

purpose must be, although only rarely will a public purpose be admitted to justify a total deprivation of personal property rights.

Since the drafters of the marketable title acts were fully aware that courts take this approach to the constitutional issues presented by retroactive legislation, they sought to reduce the injury to persons by providing them with an opportunity of preserving their interests through a second recording. By this device, the effect of the marketable title act on the individual claiming an interest subject to being extinguished by the act could be said to be only that of imposing one additional requirement, that of recording a notice of his claim. This is similar to the requirements of the recording acts that have always been upheld by the courts. Those persons whose interests on the date that the marketable title act was passed were as old or older than the time period adopted by the act, were given two years or so to record their notices. Others had longer periods of time in which to record since their interests would be extinguished only after the 30 or 40 year period adopted by the act. With the individual injury reduced in this manner, and given the unquestionable public benefit from having shorter title searches and more secure titles, one court has specifically upheld the marketable title act enacted in its state, and a number of other decisions have been handed down applying the marketable title acts without questioning their validity.

Nevertheless, some commentators have expressed a concern for the constitutionality of these acts. Professor Payne believes that there is a risk that the means by which the older interests are extinguished, without even an attempt to provide notice to the holders of the interests, could be held by a court to deprive them of their procedural due process rights. . . .

2. Fairness — Consideration of the constitutionality of marketable title acts raises into focus the fairness of these laws, notwithstanding their apparent constitutionality. The critics of marketable title acts have stressed these problems.

Take, for example, the problem of future interests. Suppose a grantor conveys land to A for his life, with the remainder to B. Under this conveyance, B or his heirs will automatically acquire title upon A's death. After a couple of years, A conveys to C with a deed purporting to convey the full fee simple title. The 30 or 40 years of the marketable title act now pass so that the conveyance from A to C becomes the root of title. The remainder interest in B and his heirs is extinguished unless B and his heirs record their remainder interest sometime after the root of title. How really practical is that? B and his heirs have never heard of the marketable title act, and do not likewise know about A's conveyance to C. A probably intended to cut off B's interest when he used a deed purporting to convey a fee simple interest to C, so neither A nor C can be counted on to tell B of his jeopardy. . . .

Even without fraud on anyone's part, so-called "wild deeds," deeds outside the chain of title, do happen from time to time and a marketable title act can cause title to be awarded to the party with the less good claim if . . . respective claims were to be evaluated on the merits. Take a simple example: A grantor conveys a fee simple interest to A in 1930, and he conveys the same fee simple interest to B in 1931. Each deed is recorded at the time of its conveyance. In a dispute between A and B in 1940, A would prevail under the recording acts. In 1972, however, B would prevail under the marketable title act because his 1931 deed will have ripened into a mature root of title. . . .

When all is said and done, it seems that, despite our best efforts, some instances of gross unfairness can and will happen under marketable title acts. But given the infrequency with which instances of unfairness have actually occurred in states with marketable title acts for many years, the risk of unfairness can be fairly viewed as far less important than the immediate and substantial public benefits arising out of the marketable title acts.

3. Term of years in the act — The designated time period in enacted marketable title acts ranges from 20 to 50 years. If the period is too long, the principal benefits of the act will not be achieved. For example, a 50-year statute accomplishes little by way of shortening the period of title searching in an area where the customary period of searching is 60 years. On the other hand, if the period is too short, too many outstanding legal interests will have to be re-recorded, and the possibility of unfairness to those who neglect to re-record their interests and the inducement for fraud will increase. A short period would also strengthen the case of proponents for exceptions when the act is being considered by the legislature.

The Model Marketable Title Act prepared by Professor Simes elected a 40-year period, while USLTA shortens this to a 30-year period. Professor Payne supports the 30-year period with the interesting observation that it would eliminate most Depression-period conveyancing documents that were "awash with defective tax sales, foreclosures and the like." However, he also noted that any shorter period would be unacceptable to the mortgage lending industry.

4. Who benefits and what interests are protected by the act? — The original Iowa marketable title act and the Minnesota act by judicial interpretation were limited to owners claiming a fee simple title. Neither the Model Act nor USLTA contains this limitation, but both apply to all interests in land, whether total or partial. However, the drafters of the Model Act anticipated that it would be primarily holders of fee simple interests who would claim the benefits of the act.

Unlike the recording statutes, the benefits of the marketable title acts are not limited to bona fide purchasers for value. The acts are available to all persons holding or claiming protected interests in land, although, as discussed immediately below, some acts require the claimant to be in possession. However, the benefits of the marketable title act drafted by the Alabama Law Institute under the guidance of Professor Payne (but not yet enacted) would be limited to bona fide purchasers for value on the rationale that, by casting the statute in the same mold as a recording act, its constitutionality becomes unassailable.

5. Possession as a condition to claiming benefits of the act — A couple of the enacted marketable title acts permit only title holders in actual possession of the property to claim the benefits of the act. The purpose of this requirement is to provide a means for resolving the "wild deed" problem where each of two claimants can demonstrate a chain of title beginning in an unrelated, but matured root of title. As between these two claimants, the marketable title act will operate to extinguish the interest of the party not in possession, without regard to whose root of title is more recent.

There are several objections to requiring the prerequisite of possession. One is that the act becomes inapplicable to unoccupied land where no one can be said to be in possession. This could be the case with timber holdings and unfenced rangeland. Professor Simes also rejected possession as a condition to the availability of the benefits of the Model Marketable Title Act, first, because it violated his basic [tenet] that all title disputes should be resolved on the basis of what appears in the public records, without inquiry into facts and circumstances existing beyond the record, and second because he believed that two independent chains of title would occur too infrequently to justify much concern.

6. Exclusions from the act—Commentators on marketable title acts have identified the number of interests in land exempted from the operation of the acts as a principal deficiency. An analysis of each of these exemptions from the act needs to be made to evaluate the justification for the exclusion, to measure the extent to which that exempted interest could, if successfully asserted against the owner, interfere with his use and enjoyment of his property and security of his title, and to determine whether assurance of the non-existence of the exempted interest can be formed only by extending the title search back in time beyond the root of title.

The Model Marketable Title Act drafted by Simes includes four exceptions. They are:

— any easement on the property that is observable by inspection.
   This exemption refers primarily to utility lines and railroads that pass over the surface of property. No one who visits a site can fail to observe these easements or be misled by the absence of a recorded notice within the time period of the act; yet, to deny an exception to the utility companies and railroads would impose a major burden on them of recording and re-recording notices. In the case of overhead wires, this could apply to every land parcel in a city. It is less clear whether the exception would include an access easement. It may depend on the extent of traffic over the easement or whether, even in the absence of traffic, there are readily observable tell-tale marks of an easement such as a worn path or a paved walkway.
— any interest acquired by adverse possession in which some part of the period of possession was subsequent to the root of title.
   This exemption is necessary because the marketable title acts are not intended to adversely affect the rights of persons claiming title by adverse possession unless the entire period of adverse possession preceded the root of title. This exception does not affect title searching anyway, since adverse possession cannot be discovered from the records.
— any interest of the United States.
   Only the federal government can effectively cut off an interest it has in property, and Congress has not seen fit to do so. Making explicit this exception only restates what the law would be anyway, but it has the advantage of warning people of the risk.
— the interests of a lessor upon the termination of a lease.
   This is intended to protect the lessor of a lease extending over the period of time of the marketable title act from the risk that his lessee might convey a fee simple interest to a third party. Alone among Simes' recommended exceptions, this one is probably not necessary since it is unlikely that a long-term lessee would try to convey a fee simple interest, or that his grantee would accept it when the record shows the lessor as owning the property. Further, the lessor would probably receive notice in plenty of time to take corrective action from the cessation of his rental payments or other events affecting the use or condition of the property.

In actuality, most of the enacted title acts have lengthened the list of exceptions to include one or more of the following interests:

— the interests of the state, county, city or other political subdivision.
— all easements and other interests held by utilities and railroads.

— mineral interests and water rights.
— possibilities of reverter, rights of entry for conditions broken, and restrictive covenants.
— mortgages and other security interests.
— remainders and reversions.

NOTES AND QUESTIONS

1. Which, if any, of the marketable title act exceptions referred to in the report immediately above, other than those appearing in the Model Act, do you consider desirable? Why?

2. Exceptions can seriously hamper the effectiveness of marketable title acts. As a commentator on the North Carolina act has said: "Unfortunately, the quest to assure victory for the marketable title legislation resulted in the loss of major battles to vested interests and the concession of numerous and broad exceptions to the thirty-year limitation." Note, 52 N.C.L. Rev. 211, at 221 (1973). The North Carolina exceptions even include "deeds of trust, mortgages and security instruments or security agreements duly recorded and not otherwise unenforceable," and certain covenants restricting property to residential use. N.C. Gen. Stat. § 47B-3(11)&(13) (2005).

Wichelman v. Messner
250 Minn. 88, 83 N.W.2d 800 (1957)

MURPHY, Justice. Action to determine adverse claims and to obtain possession of certain realty by Melvin Wichelman against Fred Messner, Independent Consolidated School District No. 81 of Sibley County, Victor Glaeser, and John Glaeser. The Glaesers have interests identical to plaintiff but, having refused to join plaintiff's action, they were joined as defendants. The trial court determined the fee simple interests to be an undivided 627/648 in plaintiff, an undivided 14/648 in John Glaeser, and an undivided 7/648 in Victor Glaeser. From the judgment, defendants Fred Messner and Independent Consolidated School District No. 81 appeal.

On July 6, 1897, H.F. Hoppenstedt conveyed a parcel out of Lot 4 of his farm in Sibley County, 10 rods by 16 rods, to defendant school district's predecessor by a warranty deed, regular in form except for the following provisions:

". . . provided nevertheless and on condition however, that said premises shall be used and occupied as and for a school house site and school grounds and that whenever such occupancy and use of the same shall cease and terminate said premises shall revert to said parties of the first part, their heirs and assigns and again become a part of and belong to Lot No. 4 above described. And the said H.F. Hoppenstedt one of the parties of the first part for himself and his heirs, executors and administrators. . . ."

The defendant school board closed the school on the site on August 16, 1946, and since that date had not used the premises for school purposes. Following a vote on May 20, 1952, by the members of the school district to sell the school land, bids were solicited. Plaintiff, on September 24, 1952, submitted a bid of $1,356 which was not accepted. Subsequently, the school district by warranty deed sold and conveyed the premises to defendant Messner, the present owner of the original Hoppenstedt farm, for $1,650.

Plaintiff then solicited the Hoppenstedt heirs and received from them releases and quitclaim deeds for which he paid each various amounts from a minimum of $1 to a maximum of $10. Prior to the commencement of this action, no form of reentry had been attempted, nor had there been any notice filed pursuant to M.S.A. § 541.023. The school district remained in possession until the sale to Messner.

At the trial the defendants contended that the original conveyance from Hoppenstedt to the school district was a fee simple on condition subsequent, while the plaintiff contended that the deed expressed a determinable fee which would vest title automatically without the necessity of reentry upon discontinued use of the property for school purposes. The distinctions between these two estates are discussed at length in Consolidated School District No. 102, Washington County v. Walter, 243 Minn. 159, 66 N.W.2d 881. Since we hold that § 541.023 applies with equal force to both a determinable fee and a fee upon condition subsequent, further discussion of that issue is unnecessary.

We think this case is controlled by § 541.023 which specifically relates to conditions and restrictions contained in old documents.

As to the operative provisions of this act, subd. 1 states:

> As against a claim of title based upon a source of title, which source has then been of record at least 40 years, no action affecting the possession or title of any real estate shall be commenced by a person, . . . after January 1, 1948, to enforce any right, claim, interest, incumbrance or lien founded upon any instrument, event or transaction which was executed or occurred more than 40 years prior to the commencement of such action, unless within 40 years after such execution or occurrence there has been recorded in the office of the register of deeds [the required notice]. . . .

In the same subdivision the statute discusses generally the kind of interest which might be extinguished by failure to file the required notice. It states: " . . . If such notice relates to *vested or contingent rights* claimed under a *condition subsequent or restriction* it shall affirmatively show why such *condition or restriction* is not, or has not become nominal so that it may be disregarded under the provisions of Minnesota Statutes 1945, Section 500.20(1)." (Italics supplied.)

Subd. 2, with reference to application of the act, states: "This section shall apply to every right, claim, interest, incumbrance or lien founded upon any instrument, event or transaction 40 years old at the date hereof, or which will be 40 years old prior to January 1, 1948, except those under which the claimant thereunder shall file a notice as herein provided prior to January 1, 1948."

Subd. 4 provides for the manner of filing and recording the notices with the register of deeds and registrar of titles.

Subd. 5 states that any claimant under any instrument, event, or transaction barred by the provisions of: ". . . this section shall be conclusively presumed to have abandoned all right, claim, interest, incumbrance or lien based upon such instrument, event or transaction; and the title in the name of any adverse claimant to the real estate which would otherwise be affected thereby shall not be deemed unmarketable by reason of the existence of such instrument, event or transaction. . . ."

The plaintiff contends that this statute was intended to eliminate "purely technical grounds of objection to the title" and was not intended to affect a substantial interest in real property. Counsel amici curiae for the plaintiff have by able arguments and briefs contended that the act by its own terms may properly be invoked "only by one who owns a separate and complete source of title which has been of record at least 40 years and for that period not subject to the adverse claim to be barred." They argue further that "The fundamental purpose and intent of this statute and its predecessors was and is to make secure and marketable those titles whose claims have been of record a substantial period of time, i.e., at least 40 years, as against *adverse claims* not asserted or otherwise preserved by the notice of claim." Stating the same proposition and amplifying it so as to include the precise situation involved in this suit, they argue that:

". . . the 40-year recorded source of title which is to be protected and stabilized is a *separate* source of title of record for at least 40 years and during all of that time free of the defect or adverse claim which is asserted — not a title predicated wholly upon the instrument which contains the right or condition to be barred or extinguished."

They argue that the title of the school district was not a source of title within the protection of the statute, asserting that for 40 years its interest was subject to the condition stipulated in the deed and consequently not a source of title adverse for 40 years, but only during the period from the time the school board decided not to use the property for school purposes, until this action was brought.

The defendants assert that the limiting conditions set forth in the conveyance express a condition subsequent or restriction within the meaning of subd. 1 of the act and that the interest is conclusively presumed to have been abandoned by reason of the failure to record notice of interest as provided by subds. 4 and 5 of the act.

As will appear from the discussion to follow, much of what we say goes beyond the immediate issues raised by the appeal. This is explained by the fact that counsel amici curiae have voiced concern as to the impact of the Marketable Title Act, § 541.023. In deference to them and the considerable segment of the bar for whom they speak, we have attempted to express our views as to all the points raised. Consequently, the opinion is necessarily extended.

1. In construing the 40-year statute we are required by § 645.16 to "ascertain and effectuate the intention of the legislature" and among other matters are to consider the occasion and necessity for the law; the circumstances under which it was enacted; the mischief to be remedied; and the object to be attained, as well as the consequences of a particular interpretation. We are required by § 645.17 to keep in mind that the legislature does not intend a result that is absurd, impossible of execution, or unreasonable; that the legislature does not intend to violate the Constitution of the United States or of this state; and that the legislature intends to favor the public interest as against any private interest.

We must further keep in mind that this particular statute is an amendment of the so-called 50-year statute enacted in 1943, later amended in 1945, and again amended by L. 1947, c. 118, which is now § 541.023. The act must be construed in light of the significant fact that the legislature referred to the type of interest with which we are here concerned by making it applicable to "vested or contingent rights claimed under a condition subsequent or restriction." 17 Dunnell, Dig. (3 ed.) § 8936(b), et seq.

2. Moreoever, the expressed policy of the legislature that "ancient records shall not fetter the marketability of real estate" is itself a source of law which "should not only be construed and applied liberally, but . . . should be accepted as a new point of departure for the process of judicial reasoning." 17 Dunnell, Dig. (3 ed.) § 8959, notes 47 and 48. "The Legislature has the power to decide what the policy of the law shall be, and if it has intimated its will, however indirectly, that will should be recognized and obeyed."

3. We are asked to define the term "claim of title based upon a source of title, which source has been of record at least 40 years" and to identify the particular estate in land which the legislature intended to protect by the provisions of the act. In doing so we may consider the relation of § 541.023 to kindred statutes governing the subject of estates in land. 82 C.J.S., Statutes, § 365.

4. It is plain from the wording of the statute itself that the legislature intended to relieve a title from the servitude of provisions contained in ancient records which "fetter the marketability of real estate." It is also clear from the plain wording of the act that it intended the provisions to benefit a title so as to relieve it from the restriction of "vested or contingent rights" derived from events or documents granting a "condition subsequent or restriction" which occurred more than 40 years prior to the commencement of the action.

5. Applying this language to estates in real property, as defined by §§ 500.01 and 500.02, the obvious conclusion is that the legislature intended this act to apply to a fee simple ownership. In Minnesota, estates in lands are divided into estates of inheritance, estates for life, estates for years, and estates at will and by sufferance. § 500.01. Under the definition of § 500.02, "Every estate of inheritance shall continue to be termed a fee simple, or fee; and every such estate, *when not defeasible or conditional,* shall be a fee simple absolute or an absolute fee." (Italics supplied.) Since a fee simple ownership is an estate of inheritance which may be defeasible or conditional, it is the estate which benefits by the sanctions of the act. It is clear that the act was intended to relieve the fee from old conditions and restrictions which § 500.02 by definition recognizes. See, 41 Minn. L. Rev. 232. The Iowa Marketable Title Act (Iowa Code 1950, § 614.17, I. C.A.), uses the phrase "record title" to describe the title benefited. While it is uncertain what interpretation will be given to the term "title" in that act, it has been suggested that the meaning of this term is fee simple title. See, Comment, 2 Drake L. Rev. 76, 81.

6. It is important for us to note here that the statute expressly includes "vested or contingent rights claimed under a condition subsequent or restriction" among the interests which will be barred if the statutory notice is not filed. It must therefore follow that the word "title" includes not only the fee simple absolute but also the defeasible fees (§§ 500.02 and 500.07).

7. It is manifest from the express policy stated by the legislature that "ancient records shall not fetter the marketability of real estate," that by specific reference to conditions subsequent or restrictions, whether mature or immature, the legislature intended to bar these lesser interests which conflict with the fee, it being the

expressed intention of the legislature that those interests which have substantial value may be preserved by recordation.

8. The fee simple defeasible is defined in Restatement, Property, § 16, as follows: "An estate in fee simple defeasible is an estate in fee simple which is subject to a special limitation (defined in § 23), a condition subsequent (defined in § 24), an executory limitation (defined in § 25) or a combination of such restrictions." By interpreting the phrase "a claim of title based upon a source of title" as a recorded fee simple ownership as defined by § 500.02, a reasonable result follows. The fee simple estate is exempted from the clogs which impair its marketability. If such outstanding interests are not considered important enough to register, no action may be commenced upon them. Under this interpretation as pointed out by 41 Minn. L. Rev. 232, 234, ". . . lessors, remaindermen and owners of defeasible fees will not be barred by owners of lesser interests who would lack the fee simple title necessary to invoke the act."

9. As was observed with reference to the Iowa act (McClain, General Limitation of Real Estate Actions, 6 Iowa L. Bull. 77, 88), this measure is limited in its applications to cases in which the proper showing is or can be made and its application to each particular state of facts is to be determined as those facts arise. We may assume that the legislature has provided in general terms the conditions to which the act applies, leaving to the court the problem of determining the precise situations which come within its general provisions. Aside from the observations set forth hereafter which relate to continuing estates discussed in the briefs and arguments, we do not undertake to announce a general interpretation which might be understood to apply to each precise situation which might arise with reference to the myriad problems which grow out of transactions relating to real estate. In this decision we are limiting our holding to the question of whether the Minnesota Marketable Title Act permits the record owner of a fee simple title, as defined by § 500.02, to be relieved from the burdens and restrictions outstanding against such fee, where the fee title itself is predicated upon the instrument which contains the right or condition to be extinguished.

10. Counsel amici curiae for the plaintiff assert that the act raises serious questions as to the status of the relative rights of parties on all instruments of record more than 40 years and makes specific reference to certain continuing interests in real estate. In considering this objection we must continue to keep in mind that the statute should be given a reasonable construction in light of its stated purpose that "ancient records shall not fetter the marketability of real estate." Although the language of the statute is general, it may be limited in its operation to cases which may be said to fall within the mischief intended to be remedied.

50 Am. Jur., Statutes, § 307, states: ". . . Such general words and phrases must be construed as limited to the immediate objects of the act, however wide and comprehensive they may be in their literal sense. These rules are particularly applicable where they are necessary to prevent absurd or futile results."

There are cases in which we may imply exceptions to the general provisions of the statute without being subject to the criticism of having entered the legislative field. This is particularly true where the exceptions are necessary to give effect to legislative intent.

". . . In this connection, it has been declared that where the whole context and the circumstances surrounding the adoption of an act show a legislative intention to make an exception to the general terms of the act, the exception will be recognized by the courts." 50 Am. Jur., Statutes, § 432.

These principles will be applied in the following interpretation of the statute as it may relate to the various interests which counsel amici curiae for plaintiff feel might be extinguished by the interpretation for which the defendants contend. . . .

Mortgages: Recorded mortgages (securing monetary obligations payable over a term of at least 40 years), which are not barred by other statutes and which the fee owner has assumed or taken "subject to," are exempt from the requirement of filing notice under certain circumstances. Mortgages which are represented by a current active relationship with the fee owner are implicitly exempt from the requirement of filing notice. The mortgagor's affirmative act of making periodic payments to the mortgagee, when coupled with the terms of the recorded mortgage, is conclusive notice and recognition of the mortgagee's "living interest." Such an interest should be contrasted with possibilities of reverter and conditions subsequent which are of indefinite duration. The legislature may have properly assumed that these latter interests, having generally outlived the reasons for their creation, may be for the benefit of persons now deceased or successors who are disinterested in the observance of restrictions and conditions and that the interests consequently impede the full economic use of property and are contrary to public policy. As to such interests the filing of a written notice is essential to establish why the "condition or restriction is not, or has not become nominal" and that it has not been abandoned. Mortgages, on the other hand, are of definite duration; are an active relationship between persons currently interested in the performance of the mortgage agreement; facilitate the use and development of property; and are not against public policy. Current active mortgages are not "ancient records" which "fetter the marketability of real estate." Notice and recognition of the recorded mortgage as a valid living interest is inherent in the active relationship between the fee owner and the mortgagee. The filing of notice within the 40-year period after the creation of the mortgage, however, would provide more security to the mortgagee since he would not have to rely on having a sufficiently current and active relationship (a fact question) to preserve his right.

Leases: The fear that leasehold interests might ripen into ownership by reason of the Marketable Title Act is likewise unwarranted. See, § 504.03. Since under the interpretation we have given to the term "claim of title based upon a source of title," as meaning recorded fee simple ownership, owners of lesser interests in real estate lack the fee simple title necessary to invoke the protection of the act. 41 Minn. L. Rev. 232.

Remainder interests: The plaintiff argues that the interpretation contended for by the defendants would operate to defeat the interests of remaindermen and in support of his argument proposes this hypothetical situation: "By decree or conveyance, a life interest is vested in A in 1910 with remainder to B upon expiration of such life estate. A goes into and retains possession for more than 40 years. In 1955 he decides to claim adversely to B or his heirs and assigns on the basis of this case and so notifies B. B sues to determine adverse claims, although he is not yet in possession." On this state of facts they suggest A would prevail because he owned an adequate source of title and B's only basis of claim is a document which was of record for more than 40 years.

It seems clear to us that it would be unreasonable and inconsistent with the statute's purpose to include within the meaning of the word "title" the term for years and the life estate and thus compel the reversioner or remainderman to file the statutory notice or be barred. It cannot be seriously argued that the holder of the life estate or his tenant would have an estate of inheritance which would permit him to invoke the protection of the act. "Only those who possess a title which complies with the conditions of the statute are qualified to invoke its aid." Lytle v. Guilliams, 241 Iowa 523, 529, 41 N.W.2d 668, 672, 16 A.L.R.2d 1377. The legislature does not intend a result that is unreasonable; and it does not intend to violate the Minnesota or United States Constitutions. § 645.17 (1, 3).

11. We conclude that, taking § 541.023 as a whole and construing the language used in it in light of the object and purpose which the legislature intended to accomplish, the term "source of title" must refer to *recorded fee simple ownership*, an estate which under § 500.02 may be "defeasible or conditional." It is the latter type of ownership, particularly, which may be impaired by stale conditions and restrictions which affect its marketability, and it is clear that the legislature intended to require those owning interests in old conditions and restrictions which burden such ownership to record notice of the continued existence of such rights or permit extinguishment of them.

12. The Marketable Title Act is a comprehensive plan for reform in conveyancing procedures and encompasses within its provisions the collective sanctions of (a) a curative act, (b) a recording act, and (c) a statute of limitations. It is a curative act in that it may operate to correct certain defects which have arisen in the execution of instruments in the chain of title. It is a recording act in that it requires notice to be given to the public of the existence of conditions and restrictions, which may be vested or contingent, growing out of ancient records which fetter the marketability of title (see, Klasen v. Thompson, 189 Minn. 254, 248 N.W. 817). It is as well a statute of limitations in that the filing of a notice is a prerequisite to preserve a right of action to enforce any right, claim, or interest in real estate founded upon any instrument, event, or transaction which was executed or occurred more than 40 years prior to the commencement of the action, whether such claim or interest is mature or immature and whether it is vested or contingent.

13. Curative statutes are a form of retrospective legislation which reach back on past events to correct errors or irregularities and to render valid and effective attempted acts which would be otherwise ineffective for the purpose the parties intended, particularly irregularities in conveyancing requirements. They operate to complete a transaction which the parties intended to accomplish but carried out imperfectly. Basye, Clearing Land Titles, §§ 201, 204. Such curative acts do not impair the obligation of contract. Ross v. Worthington, 11 Minn. 438, Gil. 323. Retrospective legislation in general, however, will not be allowed to impair rights which are vested and which constitute property rights. Seese v. Bethlehem Steel Co., D.C., D. Md., 74 F. Supp. 412, 417, *affirmed*, 4 Cir., 168 F.2d 58; Fuller v. Mohawk Fire Ins., Co., 187 Minn. 447, 450, 245 N.W. 617, 618.

14. Statutes of limitations are based on the theory that it is reasonable to require that stale demands be asserted within a reasonable time after a cause of action has accrued. See Basye, Clearing Land Titles, § 52. In Baker v. Kelley, 11 Minn. 480 at page 493, Gil. 358 at page 371, we said:

> . . . Statutes of limitation . . . prescribe a period within which a right may be enforced, afterward withholding a remedy for reasons of private justice and public policy. It would encourage fraud, oppression and interminable litigation, to permit a party to

> delay a contest until it is probable that papers may be lost, facts forgotten, or witnesses dead. A limitation law is intended to prevent this, and such a law is uniformly held valid.

See, also, Bachertz v. Hayes-Lucas Lumber Co., 201 Minn. 171, 275 N.W. 694.

The constitutional prohibitions against retrospective legislation do not apply to statutes of limitation, "for such a statute will bar any right, however high the source from which it may be deduced, provided that a reasonable time is given a party to enforce his right." Meigs v. Roberts, 162 N.Y. 371, 378, 56 N.E. 838, 840; Day, Curative Acts and Limitations Acts, 9 U. of Fla. L. Rev. 145, 152; Basye, Clearing Land Titles, § 206; Opinion of the Justices, N.H., 131 A.2d 49. This requirement of a reasonable time within which to assert the right, however, means that the holder of a future interest ordinarily cannot be barred by the operation of statutes of limitation until a reasonable time after he acquires the right to maintain an action to acquire possession. Simes and Smith, Law of Future Interests, §§ 1962; 1963; Basye, Clearing Land Titles, § 55.

15. What may be a reasonable time depends upon the sound discretion of the legislature in the light of the nature of the subject and purpose of the enactment, and we have said that "the courts will not inquire into the wisdom of the exercise of this discretion by the legislature in fixing the period of legal bar, unless the time allowed is manifestly so short as to amount to a practical denial of justice." Hill v. Townley, 45 Minn. 167, 169, 47 N.W. 653, 654; Note, 33 Minn. L. Rev. 54.

16. It is apparent from the recordation provisions of the 40-year statute which we are considering that the legislature did not intend to arbitrarily wipe out old claims and interests without affording a means of preserving them and giving a reasonable period of time within which to take the necessary steps to accomplish that purpose. The recordation provisions of the act provide for a simple and easy method by which the owner of an existing old interest may preserve it. If he fails to take the step of filing the notice as provided, he has only himself to blame if his interest is extinguished. "The constitutionality of imposing this duty would seem to have been settled beyond question by the decisions sustaining retroactive recording statutes." Scurlock, Retroactive Legislation Affecting Interests in Land, Mich. Legal Studies, p. 82; Klasen v. Thompson, supra. . . .

17. A period of nine months was provided to file the required notice. Lesser periods than this have been held reasonable. . . .

Moreover it should be kept in mind that the Bar of Minnesota had knowledge of the enactment of this legislation. See, Reprint of Program Talks from Annual Meetings, 1947, 1948, Section of Real Property Law, Minnesota State Bar Association. It was aimed at an important legal reform. See Maloney, Comments on Minnesota Laws, 30 Minn. L. Rev. 32; Brehmer, Limitations of Actions, 30 Minn. L. Rev. 23; 32 M.S.A. p. 388. . . .

18. It has been argued that § 541.023 is unconstitutional by reason of the fact that in the first sentence of subd. 1 the clause: "As against a claim of title based upon a source of title, which source has then been of record at least 40 years" is so vague and ambiguous as to render it meaningless. . . .

. . . It is a cardinal rule of construction that, rather than pronounce a statute unconstitutional and void, the court will draw inferences from the evident intent of the legislature. State ex rel. Foot v. Bazille, 97 Minn. 11, 106 N.W. 93, 6 L.R.A., N.S., 732. Extreme caution should be exercised by courts before declaring a statute void and it should be upheld unless it is so uncertain and indefinite that, after exhausting all rules of construction, it is impossible to ascertain the legislative intent. See, Anderson v. Burnquist, 216 Minn. 49, 11 N.W.2d 776.

19. The policy expressly stated by the act itself that ancient records shall not fetter the marketability of real estate must be a rule and guide in determining the meaning of the term "source of title" as used in the statute. Applying this rule so as to determine the kind of "title" whose marketability the legislature desires to promote, we conclude that by use of the term "claim of title based upon a source of title," the marketability of which might be impaired by a condition subsequent or restriction, the legislature had in mind the recorded fee simple title which may be a defeasible or conditional estate as defined by § 500.02.

20–21. The plaintiff has contended that the term "source of title" is susceptible of so many varying and conflicting definitions that it is meaningless. Citing B. W. & Leo Harris Co. v. City of Hastings, 240 Minn. 44, 59 N.W.2d 813, he asserts that the grantee in a stray or interloping deed might become "the absolute owner" of property. We do not think the statute lends itself to an interpretation to the effect that title may be founded on a stray, accidental, or interloping conveyance. Its object is to provide, for the recorded fee simple ownership, an *exemption* from the burdens of old conditions and restrictions which at each transfer of the property interfere with its marketability. The statute does not operate to provide a foundation for a new title. But, in view of the persuasive arguments of the counsel amici curiae, it may be of benefit to examine more closely the objects which the statute seeks to accomplish.

For § 541.023 to operate in a particular case to extinguish any interest, two basic requirements are necessary. First, the party desiring to invoke the statute for his own benefit must have a requisite "claim of title based upon a source of title, which source has then been of record at least 40 years," (i.e., a recorded fee simple title). Secondly, the person against whom the act is invoked must be one who is "conclusively presumed to have abandoned all right, claim, interest . . ." in the property (subd. 5).

There are three classes of persons against whom no one can invoke the act. They are (1) those persons who seek to enforce any right, claim, interest, encumbrance, or lien founded upon any instrument, event, or transaction which was executed or occurred *within* 40 years prior to the commencement of the action; (2) those persons who seek to enforce a claim founded on any such instrument or event which was executed or occurred *over* 40 years prior to the commencement of the action, *if they have filed proper notice* within 40 years of the execution or occurrence of the instrument, event, or transaction upon which it is founded; and (3) those excepted by subd. 6 of the act, which includes persons in possession. . . .

22. We must reject the construction suggested by counsel amici curiae for plaintiff that the 40-year period does not begin to run in favor of a determinable fee or a fee subject to a condition subsequent until after a breach of the restriction. Applying that construction to the facts of the instant case, where the restrictions were created in 1897 and broken in 1946, the 40-year period would not expire until 1986; and if a restriction were created in 1800 and not breached until 2000, the 40-year period would not expire until the year 2040. Some other statute of limitations, or adverse possession, or laches would probably operate within 40 years after breach and § 541.023 would be unnecessary. The economic reason for which the original grantor imposed the restriction in either of these cases would probably

have ceased long before its breach; yet unless it is breached the restriction has an indefinite duration. We may assume that in enacting this statute the legislature adopted the view that such a restriction on the fee is probably so scattered among numerous heirs and assignees that it is almost impossible to locate them. In the case before us the plaintiff who purchased quitclaims from the heirs was himself unable to acquire the total interest. Outstanding interests of this nature are likely to have merely nuisance value 40 years after their creation. They are the type of clogs at which the provisions of the act are aimed. Obviously the policy of preventing ancient records from fettering the marketability of the fee is frustrated by the construction contended for by the plaintiff.

23. Plaintiff asserts that Messner did not have a sufficient "source of title" to invoke the act. The term "source of title" must be interpreted in light of the stated policy of the act that "ancient records shall not fetter the marketability of real estate." We cannot agree with the argument of the plaintiff that the act can only be invoked by one who owns "a separate and complete source of title which has been of record at least 40 years and for that period is not subject to the adverse claim to be barred." If the Minnesota Marketable Title Act contained the same provision as the Indiana Law (Burns' Ind. Stat. Ann. § 2–632) there would be some force to his contention. That statute provides: ". . . This section shall mean that the record title owner shall have a marketable title of that interest in the real property which the muniments of his title purport to convey to him." One writer has said that this provision expressly excepts interests created by provisions of limitations contained in the muniments of title of the record owner. The Minnesota Act (M.S.A. § 541.023, subd. 1) is entirely different in that it specifically refers to "vested or contingent rights claimed under a condition subsequent or restriction" as evils intended to be eliminated in attaining the goal of free alienability of land. The plaintiff fails to point out, under the construction he suggests how the statute would be of any real value in fostering the marketability of a fee title. It seems to us that the provision in the Indiana act defeats in large measure the very purpose of this type of legislation which is intended to relieve a chain of title from the accumulated burdens of old conditions and restrictions set forth in provisions contained in instruments making up the chain of title. . . .

26. It appears further that the constitutionality of the Minnesota statute is preserved by the provisions exempting persons in "possession of real estate" from the requirement of filing notice and allowing persons not in possession a reasonable time to file statutory notice. See, Aigler, Constitutionality of Marketable Title Acts, 50 Mich. L. Rev. 185; 38 Minn. L. Rev. 285; Hammon v. Hatfield, 192 Minn. 259, 256 N.W. 94. . . .

30. An examination of the various marketable title acts indicates that they were intended to operate as statutes of limitation to bar all interests, including vested future interests, if proper notice is not filed, as well as to correct irregularities that can be reached by pure curative statutes. The language of our statute itself supports this view. Basye, Clearing Land Titles, § 171, et. seq.

Yielding to the demand to solve the problems created by restrictions unlimited in time, a number of marketable title acts have been passed by various states. Such limiting statutes are considered vital to all who are engaged in or concerned with the conveyance of real property. They proceed upon the theory that the economic advantages of being able to pass uncluttered title to land far outweigh any value which the outdated restrictions may have for the person in whose favor they operate. These statutes reflect the appraisal of state legislatures of the "actual economic significance of these interests, weighed against the inconvenience and expense caused by their continued existence for unlimited periods of time without regard to altered circumstances." Trustees of Schools of Township No. 1. v. Batdorf, 6 Ill. 2d 486, 492, 130 N.E.2d 111, 115; see, 43 Ill. L. Rev. 90. They must be construed in the light of the public good in terms of more secure land transactions which outweighs the burden and risk imposed upon owners of old outstanding rights to record their interests.

Reversed.

The opinion filed herein August 10, 1956, is hereby withdrawn and the foregoing opinion is substituted in lieu thereof.

NOTES AND QUESTIONS

1. In 1959, subsequent to the *Wichelman* decision, an additional subsection was added to the Minnesota Marketable Title Act. As amended, Minn. Stat. Ann. § 541.023 (West Supp. 2006), provides as follows:

> Subd. 7. *Source of title.* For the purposes of this section, the words "source of title" as used in subdivision 1 hereof shall mean any deed, judgment, decree, sheriff's certificate, or other instrument which transfers or confirms, or purports to transfer or confirm, a fee simple title to real estate, including any such instrument which purports to transfer, or to confirm the transfer of a fee simple title from a person who was not the record owner of the real estate. However, any such instrument which purports to transfer, or to confirm the transfer of, a fee simple title from a person who was not the record owner of the real estate to the grantee or transferee named in such instrument shall be deemed a source of title "of record at least 40 years" within the meaning of subdivision 1 only if, during the period of 40 years after it was recorded, the following two conditions are fulfilled: (1) another instrument was recorded which purports to transfer a fee simple title from said grantee or transferee to another person and (2) no instrument was recorded which purports to be or confirm a transfer of any interest in the real estate by or from whoever was the record owner in fee simple immediately before the commencement of said period of 40 years. The purpose of the next preceding sentence is to limit the effect of erroneous descriptions or accidental conveyances.

What weaknesses in the act do you think this section was intended to correct?

2. In a 5-4 decision in 1982, the United States Supreme Court upheld as constitutional, under the United States Constitution, the Indiana Dormant Mineral Interests Act. Texaco, Inc. v. Short, 454 U.S. 516 (1982). The Indiana Act provides that certain mineral interests shall lapse and revert to the surface owner if the mineral interest is not used for a period of 20 years and the mineral interest owner, prior to the end of the 25-year period or a 2-year grace period after the Act's effective date, fails to record in the local county recorder's office a statement of claim. The recording or re-recording provision resembles similar provisions in most general marketable title acts; and the *Texaco* case is supportive authority for these latter acts being constitutional. The majority upheld the act, under the U.S. Constitution, against taking, due process, impairment of contract, and equal protection challenges. Brennan, in dissent, argued that the statute, for acceptable

due process, should have provided for advance notice of forfeiture to the mineral owners.

3. The Iowa Marketable Title Act was held constitutional in Presbytery of Southeast Iowa v. Harris, 226 N.W.2d 232 (Iowa 1975). A dissent to that opinion, at page 244, declares:

> Because § 614.24 does far more than simply bar claims, and in effect divests persons of their existing property interests, it cannot in the end be justified as a mere statute of limitations. Accordingly, the question must be whether the statutory procedure designed to forestall divestiture comports with constitutional guarantees of due process. The statute contains no provision for notice. Statutory enactment alone was evidently deemed sufficient notice for those persons whose interests in property would be affected. I am not persuaded that manner of notice is "such as one desirous of actually informing . . . might reasonably adopt to accomplish it" (the constitutional standard for due process). Mullane v. Central Hanover Bank & Trust Co., 339 U.S. 306, 315. . . . Moreover, I am frankly unable to reconcile recent decisions broadening the due process rights of persons possessing interests in personalty with the procedural burdens placed on persons under § 614.24 to take affirmative action to protect their interests in realty. [Citing Snaidach v. Family Finance Corp., 395 U.S. 337 (1969), and Fuentes v. Shevin, 407 U.S. 67 (1972), among other cases.]

4. Is the court's argument convincing that a stray deed may not be a source of title within the meaning of the Minnesota Act? What would be the result if there are two independent chains of title going back of record over forty years? How does the Model Marketable Title Act dispose of the stray deed and multiple chain of title problems?

5. Over 60 lawyers and law firms throughout Minnesota appeared and filed amici curiae briefs in the *Wichelman* case because of the obvious potential effect the case would have on the state's land titles. Basye, Clearing Land Titles 417 (2d ed. 1970). These lawyers are listed in the reports of the opinions.

2.   *Torrens Registration*

In much of the world outside the United States, including England and a number of Commonwealth countries, land title registration is the prevailing form of title protection and the registered title the principal source of title data.[25] Registered titles, often referred to as Torrens titles,[26] are provided for by statute

---

25. On land title registration in the United States, see Burke, American Conveyancing Patterns, ch. 5 (1978); 14 Powell on Real Property, ch. 83 (2000); 11 Thompson on Real Property § 92.10 (2d ed. 2002); McCormack, Torrens and Recording: Land Title Assurance in the Computer Age, 18 Wm. Mitchell L. Rev. 61 (1992).

26. In the United States, the term Torrens commonly is used to designate any land title registration system in which a binding title determination of each registered title is made by a public official. However, some commentators, particularly in England, consider Torrens as but one of several registration systems differing in detail from one another, and they classify the English system as separate from the Torrens system followed in Australia, the United States, and most of Canada. For an analysis consistent with this latter usage and one that compares the English and Torrens systems, see Simpson, Land Law and Registration 76-80 (1976). Different types of land registration systems are also discussed in Burke, American Conveyancing Patterns 103-107 (1978).

in ten American states,[27] but in no state is registration compulsory, and no community has a majority of its parcels registered. Registration apparently is heaviest in the Honolulu area, with about 40 percent of the island of Oahu in Torrens; and it is fairly substantial in and around Chicago, Minneapolis-St. Paul, and Boston, although little used elsewhere. The period of greatest support for Torrens registration in the United States was earlier in this century, but interest faded and half of the states that had Torrens statutes have repealed them or let them expire.[28] Torrens in the United States received a major blow when, in 1990, Illinois repealed its Torrens Act, 765 Ill. Comp. Stat. Ann. §§ 40/1 to 40/2 (2001). Under the repealer no additional land may be registered; most types of legal instruments pertaining to existing registered land may no longer be registered; all certificates of title to registered land shall gradually be recorded and subject to the recording act; and after certificate recording, title to the lands involved shall be conveyed or encumbered in the same manner as title to unregistered lands. As the accumulations of American land title records become ever more massive, and as revolutionary new ways of dealing with storage and retrieval of such accumulations continue to be made, a shift over to Torrens or some derivative of it may become necessary and desirable. The successful use of land title registration in many countries with problems similar to our own conceivably is a portent of what the United States too may ultimately find is the most effective title system for its needs. Support for an expanded use of Torrens by American states keeps surfacing, usually from law professors. Title insurers obviously are concerned about this threat to their business.

a. Administration

Under land title registration systems, the title is registered, rather than possible evidences of title being recorded or registered. Registration involves periodic determinations by public officials as to the state of the title, and these determinations are generally binding. So, with certain exceptions, the various interests in a particular parcel of land may be ascertained by examining the registration certificate that has been issued for that parcel. In the United States, where Torrens statutes are in effect, land title registration is a county responsibility and the counties employ title examiners to make the requisite determinations. However, when a title is first being brought within the Torrens system in the United States, a judicial proceeding similar to a suit to quiet title must be brought; hence, initial registration is a judicial function. Appeal to the courts from the decisions of title examiners also may be available. Advantages commonly claimed for registration are that it is potentially a less cumbersome system and hence potentially a faster, cheaper, and more certain means of title protection. Needless to say, the American title insurance companies, and to some extent the practicing bar, challenge the claims of superiority made for Torrens over the American recording system.

---

27. Colorado, Georgia, Hawaii, Massachusetts, Minnesota, North Carolina, Ohio, Pennsylvania, Virginia, and Washington.

28. California, Illinois, Mississippi, Nebraska, New York, North Dakota, Oregon, South Carolina, South Dakota, Tennessee, and Utah.

Patton, Evolution of Legislation on Proof of Title to Land

30 Wash. L. Rev. 224, 228–235 (1955)

Apparently the earliest method of proving title to land was by actual occupancy—not necessarily a complete or exclusive occupancy but nevertheless that form which precluded other use of the land. This was the basis, and the extent, of land ownership by the American Indians, both as tribes and as families. It has been the criterion among all nomadic people. It has a preferential status in the establishment of private ownership when the nomads changed their way of life and effected permanent settlements.

Some of the earliest legislation of the United States provided for the survey and sale of its public lands, and restricted the private acquisition of land from the government in other than the surveyed rectangular subdivisions of the survey. However it was necessary to recognize the possessory titles of pioneers who had settled on public land in advance of the making of the surveys. This was done by the enactment of numerous townsite acts which provided a legal procedure for proof of rights thus acquired and the issuance of patents to the respective settlers. Thus their possessory titles were changed to documentary or legal titles.

Possessory titles are recognized by the courts when they protect a first trespassing squatter against acts of a subsequent trespasser. They are given priority over the claims of the conventional title holder when the latter has lost his right to judicial assistance by reason of acts which raise an estoppel or for failure to act within a period of time which the courts or the legislature have fixed as a limitation of action. In these cases the holder of the possessory title may by court action secure a documentary title in the form of a judgment which confirms a title acquired by estoppel or by adverse possession. . . .

Just as experience has improved our methods of locating and marking the boundaries of any particular parcel of land and the terms by which it may be accurately described, it is reasonable to assume that experience may have also produced an improved method of indicating to anyone interested therein the ownership of that parcel of land and particularly of enabling the owner to furnish ready proof of his title and the exact items of encumbrance thereon. The purchaser of an automobile or a lender taking automobile paper as security encounters no hazards of title requiring risk insurance: the auto license amounts to a certificate of ownership. The same is true of a passbook issued by a savings bank or a certificate of stock issued by a corporation. Sir Richard Torrens, then plain Richard Torrens, could have well obtained from the latter a suggestion of the applicability of the certificate system to land ownership. Not being a banker, but instead having spent much of his life as a customs officer before being appointed Registrar General of South Australia (and thus in charge of the registration of all instruments affecting title to real estate in the province), his earlier experience with the ship registry system led him to wonder why the title to a tract of land could not be registered the same as the title to a ship. The system with which he was comparing the land records which had come under his supervision was that provided by the English Merchants Shipping Law. Under it, a page in the registry is given to each ship, and on it appears the name and description of the ship, the name of the owner, and from time to time liens or encumbrances and releases. A duplicate of the page in the form of a certificate is given to the owner, and that is the evidence of his ownership in any part of the world. If ownership is divided, each owner is given a certificate for his share. To make a transfer, the certificate holder executes an assignment of a part or all of his interest, the assignment and the certificate are sent to the registry office, whereupon the certificate is cancelled, the page closed, and a new page is opened for the new owner or owners, and new certificates are issued. At no time is there outstanding more than one certificate for the same interest and it is not necessary to go back of any outstanding certificate nor to examine any page other than that currently in force. In view of its success as applied to such valuable property as ships, not only in England but in other ship registries, why might not the system be applied to real estate? The new Registrar General set about the drafting of legislation to that effect and had the satisfaction of seeing it enacted, not only locally but in many jurisdictions of the British Empire. During the twentieth century the system has been incorporated into the legal system of several American states, Hawaii, the Philippines and the Dominican Republic, and the name of Mr. Torrens has come into the language both as a verb (to torrens a title) and as an adjective (a torrens title).

Proof of title from the original title deeds served very well in England for several centuries; but at a time when land transfers other than by succession at death were very few. Then instrument registration served fairly well in the United States as well as in Australia and other British possessions so long as settled communities were small enough that questions of notice and bona fides were infrequent. But with the present increases in property values, number of transactions, and volume of records, something better is needed than a mere registration of instruments under which every transaction is at the risk of the investor — buyer, mortgagee or lessee, as the case may be — and where any interest is acquired subject to all defects in the entire chain of title which have not been barred by limitation. What is needed is not a mere registration of instruments but a registration of title. That a "torrens title" is of this character has been well stated in the following quoted paragraphs:

> The basic principle of this system is the registration of the title to land instead of registering, as the old system requires, the evidence of such title. In the one case, only the ultimate fact or conclusion that a certain named party has title to a particular tract of land is registered, and certificate thereof delivered to him. In the other case, the entire evidence from which the proposed purchasers must, at their peril, draw such conclusion is registered.
>
> The official certificate will always show the state of the title and the person in whom it is vested. The basic principle of the system is the registration of the title to the land, instead of registering, as under the old system, the evidence of such title.
>
> That registration of title is in the abstract to be preferred to registration of assurances may at once be conceded, for the former aims at presenting the intending purchaser or mortgagee with the net result of former dealings with the property, while the latter places the dealings themselves before him, and leaves him to investigate them for himself. In one case he finds, so to speak, the sum worked out for him; in the other, he has the figures given him, and has to work out the sum for himself.

Like the metric system in comparison with our current non-decimal system of weights and measures, there can be no doubt that a certificate system of evidencing land titles would have been vastly superior to the recording system, and would have obviated much litigation and much of the unfairness and financial loss reflected in title decisions. Had it been inaugurated at the inception of colonial and proprietary titles, or even at the time of patenting of the public lands of the states and of the

United States to settlers and purchasers, the patents could have been exchanged for certificates of title as is done in the provinces of Western Canada. But where instead the title to a tract of land has first been the subject of recording, as is the case in Eastern Canada and in the United States, there necessarily exists the hazard as to ownership and encumbrance which has already been mentioned as incident to titles covered by most of the recording acts, greater or less depending upon the type of the act. Without going into detail as to these hazards, the fact that they exist, and that the public is fully aware of the fact, is amply demonstrated by the size of various title insurance companies and the large percentage of the titles in many communities for which the owners consider insurance to be necessary. In order therefore to adapt a certificate system to proof of title in the United States, the most important feature of the authorizing statutes are those sections which outline a method for a conclusive determination as to ownership and encumbrance so that these items may be reflected in the first certificate of title. After issuance of that first certificate the matter is as simple as transferring or mortgaging corporation stock or a ship, the usual deed of conveyance serving the same purpose as an assignment or a bill of sale respectively. For issuance of that first certificate the status of a title cannot here be determined by an administrative office. Both in the original proceeding and in any subsequent proceeding in relation to a registered or "torrensed" title, any question which is exclusively judicial in character must be determined by the court. However this is an advantage rather than otherwise in that the title is thus kept at all times in the form of an adjudicated title rather than one merely presumptively good.

Accordingly in the United States the transfer of a title from the recording-act system to the certificate system must be by a judicial proceeding affirmative in character but nevertheless resembling a suit to quiet title — an action in which the court will be given jurisdiction of all parties, both known and unknown, who could by any possibility assert an adverse right or claim, and in which the court can determine the holder of the fee title, the holder of all subordinate titles or interests with their conditions and limitations, and all existing liens upon or rights in the land.

The proceeding is conducted under the close supervision of an officer of the court, designated in the acts as an Examiner of Titles, but clothed with all the powers of a referee. The initial application of the claimant must be checked by him as to form and must receive his endorsed approval before it can be filed. He must then examine the title records with the aid of an abstract or search furnished by the applicant; the premises must be inspected or surveyed for the purpose of determining all occupancies; the examiner-referee files a report showing all deviations from a direct chain of title in the applicant free of encumbrance and free from occupancy by other than the applicant (i.e., a report showing the record ownership of all interests in the land, all liens thereon, all possible claimants of interest or liens as shown by the records, the occupancies, or the admissions found in the application). The report further recommends (requires) certain parties as defendants, being all the parties necessary to an adjudication, on proper evidence at the subsequent hearing, that the applicant or applicants, as the case may be, hold the fee title to the premises, and as to exactly what interests, claims or liens are subsisting against the property.

This done, the burden then shifts to the attorney for the applicant. He prepares a petition for summons in which he must list under appropriate subdivisions all defendants named by the Examiner; or as to any found to be deceased, the parties who, per evidence to be produced by him at the hearing for a finding of fact in the courts' decree, have succeeded as heirs or devisees to ownership of the interest or claim of the decedent. On the basis of the petition, and any evidence required by the judge or the Examiner, there is entered an order for summons pursuant to which the clerk of court issues a summons addressed to said parties and to "parties unknown claiming any right, title or interest" in the land there described. The attorney attends to securing service of the summons on each and every defendant in the manner prescribed by statute as to the particular types of defendants (resident, non-resident, those who cannot be located), and upon the "parties unknown" by publication. All of the acts are meticulous in the matter of observing due process of law and in the main they conform, in this respect, to the "burnt record acts."

If an answer is filed, the issue is tried in the same manner as in any other land title case, in some states by a special land court and in others by the general trial court. In case of a default of appearance by the defendants, no decree is entered "pro confesso" but evidence must be produced to substantiate every claim of the applicant which is not affirmatively corroborated by the earlier report of the Examiner. Whether the hearing is conducted by the Examiner as referee or by the judge, it appears to be the usual practice to receive in evidence the Examiner's report and incidental thereto, by reference, all the records upon which it is based.

If it is found that the applicant lacks title to the land involved or to any portion thereof, the court must dismiss the application in toto or as to the portion to which the applicant is unable to prove title from the records or otherwise. As to the portion of the land to which the applicant proves title, usually the entire tract described in his application, the court enters a decree with appropriate findings of fact upon which to base paragraphs adjudicating that the title is in the applicant, either free from encumbrance or subject to specified items including rights of dower or courtesy or a statutory substitute and ordering that the Registrar of Titles enter a certificate of title in line with the adjudication upon the forthwith filing with him of a certified copy of the decree. The form of the certificate is prescribed by statute; and the latter also provides for issuance of a copy which is no different except for endorsement across its face of the words "Owner's Duplicate." A mortgagee's or a lessee's duplicate may be had also at a slight charge. The original certificate is retained by the Registrar and is bound with others in numerical order in a book designated as a register.

After entry of the first certificate, the matter of filing mortgages, judgments, attachments, mechanics' lien claims, notices of lis pendens and the like is substantially the same as for filing similar claims against a certificate of stock. The instrument is given a document number, retained by the Registrar and noted in considerable detail on the certificate of title in his register. Instruments discharging such claims are similarly filed and memorialized.

Voluntary transfers of title are effected in substantially the same manner as transfers of corporate stock: the Owner's Duplicate and the deed are filed with the Registrar; he makes appropriate entries in his indices and reception book and endorses a cancellation across the face of both the duplicate and the certificate in the register; if the deed is for all the land covered by the certificate, he enters a new certificate to the grantee (and issues a new Owner's Duplicate) for that land; if the deed is for a part only of the land described in the certificate, he enters a new certificate and an Owner's Duplicate to the grantee for the part described in the deed, and a residue certificate and duplicate for the unconveyed portion in favor of the registered owner named in the cancelled certificate.

In case of an involuntary transfer — devise, descent, execution sale, mortgage foreclosure, etc. — there arises a purely judicial question which the Registrar as a member of the administrative division of the tri-partite state government may not determine. The matter must be presented to the court by petition in a "proceeding subsequent to registration." If an issue can be made as to the granting of the order requested, notice must be given to all parties adversely interested. The notice may be by summons, order to show cause or other written notice depending upon the applicable statute. But if the issue is one which the court may properly determine without notice of the hearing, no notice need be given and an order to the Registrar is entered pro forma.

Conclusiveness of the certificates of title is safeguarded not only by expiration of the periods within which to reopen a proceeding or to appeal from an order or decree but also by a limitation statute as to any contest, six months under most of the torrens statutes. No one appears to have suffered from the shortness of the period and it obviates all necessity of examining the original proceeding six months after entry of the decree or registration. Not but that, as in the case of any judgment, a decree may be set aside for fraud. However this ground attack need not concern a purchaser or mortgagee in that it is not available as against a bona fide purchaser without notice. In fact, the conclusiveness of the certificate is so strong that the certificate prevails when issued to a bona fide purchaser on the basis of a forged deed. So long however as the registered owner takes proper care of his duplicate there is no danger from this source in that a deed, or a purported deed, from him is inoperative and cannot be filed with the Registrar unless accompanied by the Owner's Duplicate. In case of loss or destruction of that instrument, the situation is the same as when a bond or a stock certificate is lost — no transaction regarding it is possible until there is a replacement. In the case of a title certificate this is accomplished by an order of court addressed to the Registrar, and entered only after ample testimony to establish the loss or destruction.

The superiority of the certificate system of evidencing title to land has been ably summarized in decisions of the courts among which are the following:

"The purpose of the judgment is to create a judgment in rem perpetually conclusive. Other proceedings in rem may determine the status of a ship or other chattel that is transient; this legislation provides for a decree that shall conclude the title to an interest that is as lasting as the land itself."

"The purpose of the Torrens law is to establish an indefeasible title free from any and all rights or claims not registered with the Register of Titles, with certain unimportant exceptions, to the end that any one may deal with such property with the assurance that the only rights or claims of which he need take notice are those so registered."

And these statements are particularly significant in contrast with one found in a case antedating the Torrens statutes and necessarily involving a titled based upon the recording act, that "it is impossible in the nature of things that there should be a mathematical certainty of good title."

Barnett, Marketable Title Acts — Panacea or Pandemonium

53 Cornell L. Rev. 45, 92–94 (1967)

When a lawyer examines title to a piece of land, his title opinion is usually meant to reflect fully and accurately the present state of the complete record title. If he is both competent and careful, it will. And if all his requirements are satisfied, there seems to be little reason for any other expert handling a subsequent transaction involving the same land to cover the same ground again. He should simply pick up at the point in time when the first examiner left off. But since the bar has steadfastly refused to set up standards of competence for specialties within the law, and both examiners operate separately, with independent liabilities, the one dares not trust the other. Of course, within the same firm, whether it be a firm of lawyers or a title insurance company, no examiner ever retraces the steps of another, except perhaps unwittingly. The writer understands that in Florida, where a high percentage of the conveyancing bar participates in the same bar-related title insuring organization, it is becoming the practice for participating lawyers to rely on the prior opinions of other participants. But until the liabilities of *all* examining experts are backed by the financial resources of the same organization, the waste resulting from repeated re-examinations of the same title will never be eliminated completely.

It may seem old hat to say so, but the writer does not see how the problem can be solved completely without resort to some type of official registration of the present state of the title — a sort of official title opinion that is constantly kept up to date. In other words, the need is for some type of Torrens system. Such a system is not really such a radical departure from the recording system, except that the initial title examination results in an opinion that has official sanction, and each subsequent transaction is ineffective until officially noted on that "opinion." Thus, there is no need to retain for future examiners the records of all those past transactions on which the opinion is based. Under a Torrens system, of course, the initial title examination must be accompanied by an action in rem. But there are many land titles on which a quiet title action must be brought at some time or other, and, unlike the registration suit under a Torrens system, such an action does not have the advantage of being a "once-for-all" affair; an action of the same type may again become necessary to cleanse the records of accumulated "debris." Moreoever, since many laymen are already familiar with a Torrens-type system in the motor vehicle registration laws, it should be much less likely to defeat their natural expectations than a marketable title act.

From the lawyers' point of view, there are two possible objections to a soundly-conceived, efficient title registration system. First, there will be an official check of their work product each time they handle a title transaction under a registered title. But a similar check exists under the recording system, namely, that provided by a subsequent title examiner. To have such a check provided immediately, rather than at the time of some subsequent title transaction, may, of course, be more embarrassing for the lawyer, but it is certainly better for the system. And the standards used in making the check are likely to be more uniform under a Torrens system. Second, a Torrens system may deprive lawyers of fees. But this fear is surely groundless. Lawyers would have to bring the initial registration suits under a Torrens system; many members of the conveyancing bar could be employed as special masters to examine titles for initial registration and, more permanently, as registrars, and lawyers will still have to handle all subsequent title transactions up to the point at which the executed instrument is sent to be registered. Lawyers should not find it difficult to justify charging the same fees for handling transactions under a Torrens system that they charge under the recording system.

The writer is not necessarily suggesting that any particular Torrens act now on the books of any state or country is completely satisfactory; but surely it is possible to devise one that will operate just as quickly in effecting transfers as the recording system. While keeping titles far more reliable, a Torrens system can eliminate the tremendous waste and inefficiency of the recording acts. It is a baffling fact that the United States is rapidly becoming virtually the only country in the world whose land title system is not founded upon Torrens-type principles. The writer finds it incredible that a system which seems to work quite well almost everywhere else cannot be satisfactorily adapted to the United States. If all the brainpower expended by law professors and by the property-law sections of local, state, and national bar associations on marketable title acts were expended instead on devising a model Torrens act, surely a satisfactory adaptation could be found.[130]

With the opposition of the legal profession out of the way, only the abstractors and title insurance companies would be left. Their opposition is inveterate, because, as a Torrens system increases, they must decrease. Yet as long as these parasites that make their living off the inadequacies of the recording system succeed in enlisting the conveyancing bar in support of the proposition that "a little title examination is a good thing" (though all agree that too much is pure hell), legislatures are likely to continue to pass and courts to uphold, halfway measures like the marketable title acts, hoping to keep the whole present absurd system from collapsing under its own weight.

b. Protection Provided

One of the most obvious advantages of a land registration system is the greater ease it provides for ascertaining the state of a title, as so much can be told just by examining the registration certificate. But in no jurisdiction is this advantage carried to its logical extreme and the certificate made the exclusive indicium of title. Wherever land registration is permitted, there are exceptions to what appears on the certificate necessarily being the sole or conclusive indication of legally protected rights in the registered land parcel. Valid off-certificate interests may exist and registered interests may even be invalid, the number and character of these possible exceptions to the binding effect of the certificate varying somewhat among jurisdictions with registration systems. This problem of off-certificate risks is analogous to that of off-record risks under the recording acts, and similar reasons apply in each of the two systems for making exceptions to a centralized public record of the state of the title. To some extent, off-certificate risks can be protected

---

130. Professor Simes acknowledges that, in undertaking the research project initiated by the ABA Section on Real Property, Probate and Trust Law, which culminated in the publication of Simes & Taylor, he "disregarded as useless any investigation of the so-called Torrens Title Registration System." The reason given seems to be that in most American states where such legislation has existed, it hasn't been very successful — which is hardly the sort of reasoning to be anticipated in a project the very object of which is a general reform of inadequate statutory frameworks. He also says, addressing lawyers, that "whether we like it or not," the recording system will continue to be the heart of conveyancing. Simes, supra note 6, at 2358. Why this must be so, *whether the bar likes it or not*, the writer cannot fathom. Has the influence of lawyers and the organized bar in state legislatures atrophied to such an extent that they can do nothing without the support of the abstractors and title insurance companies? The writer feels that, unless lawyers resort to some co-operative plan such as the Florida Lawyers' Title Guaranty Fund, their role in land transactions will, sooner or later, be completely eliminated by the competition of title companies: "If you can't lick 'em, join 'em." A Torrens system, on the other hand, might well serve to rescue the conveyancing bar from such a fate, by eliminating every service title companies presently provide that cannot be considered the practice of law. Of course, there are those who fail to see any reason why the title companies should not be allowed to supplant lawyers completely in land transactions, but the writer is definitely not one of them.

against by examining the premises, questioning knowledgeable parties or searching other public records, as is true of off-record risks under the recording acts. This ancillary checking is often done by lawyers in private practice representing land owners, claimants, prospective buyers or lenders. Such lawyers also bring initial registration proceedings and make registration submissions to the public examiners. Land title registration tends to reduce but not eliminate the title work of lawyers in private practice. Built into land registration systems are state administered insurance schemes applicable to all registered land parcels. These schemes provide compensation to some categories of persons who suffer losses in dealing with registered titles. The scope of coverage varies in different places but in some jurisdictions is more restrictive than the usual title insurance coverage offered by private insurers in the United States to those with recorded interests in land. Private title companies also will insure Torrens titles, and in the Chicago area, for example, such coverage is rather common.

NOTES AND QUESTIONS

1. Express off-certificate exceptions are characteristic of Torrens statutes in the United States, although the statutes differ in the number and kind of exceptions. Typical of the exception statutes is Minn. Stat. Ann. § 508.25(6) (West Supp. 1992):

> Every person receiving a certificate of title pursuant to a decree of registration and every subsequent purchaser of registered land who receives a certificate of title in good faith and for a valuable consideration shall hold it free from all encumbrances and adverse claims, excepting only the estates, mortgages, liens, charges, and interests as may be noted in the last certificate of title in the office of the registrar, and also excepting any of the following rights or encumbrances subsisting against it, if any:
>
> (1) liens, claims, or rights arising or existing under the laws or the constitution of the United States, which this state cannot require to appear of record;
>
> (2) the lien of any real property tax or special assessment;
>
> (3) any lease for a period not exceeding three years when there is actual occupation of the premises thereunder;
>
> (4) all rights in public highways upon the land;
>
> (5) the right of appeal, or right to appear and contest the application, as is allowed by this chapter;
>
> (6) the rights of any person in possession under deed or contract for deed from the owner of the certificate of title;
>
> (7) any outstanding mechanics lien rights which may exist under sections 514.01 to 514.17, and
>
> (8) any lien for state taxes.
>
> No existing or future lien for state taxes arising under the laws of this state for the nonpayment of any amounts due under chapter 268 or any tax administered by the commissioner of revenue may encumber title to lands registered under this chapter unless filed under the terms of this chapter.

Why do you think the legislature included the exceptions listed in this section of the Minnesota statutes? Would any of them be valid encumbrances on Torrens titles even though not registered and not made exceptions by statute? How can a title examiner ascertain if a particular Minnesota land title is burdened with encumbrances of the kind listed in § 508.25?

Some of the other American Torrens Act exception sections are Hawaii Rev. Stat. § 501.82 (Michie. 2006); and Mass. Gen. Laws Ann. c. 185, § 46 (West 2003).

2. American Torrens statutes generally provide that owners of registered land titles may not lose their titles by adverse possession. See, for example, Minn. Stat. Ann. § 508.02 (West 2002). What rationale is there for such a position?

3. Mass. Gen. Laws Ann. c. 185, § 46 (West 2003), provides in part:

"Every plaintiff receiving a certificate of title in pursuance of a judgment of registration, and every subsequent purchaser of registered land taking a certificate of title for value and in good faith, shall hold the same free from all encumbrances except those noted on the certificate, and any of the following encumbrances which may be existing. . . ."

The Massachusetts Supreme Judicial Court has held that purchasers of registered land take subject to unregistered interests of which they had actual knowledge when they took. "Any other construction would ignore the wording of section 46 which provides that one acquires registered land free from unregistered encumbrances if he is a purchaser for value and in 'good faith.'" Killam v. March, 316 Mass. 646, at 651, 55 N.E.2d 945, at 948 (1944). The *Killam* case was followed in Butler v. Haley Greystone Corp., 347 Mass. 478, 198 N.E.2d 635 (1964).

4. In Petn. of Willmus, 568 N.W.2d 722 (Minn. App. 1997), the court held that a person acquiring a Torrens registered land interest takes subject to nonregistered interests of which the acquirer had actual notice but is not on constructive notice of any nonregistered interests mentioned in documents referred to in the certificate of title.

5. Basic to each Torrens system is a government-administered assurance fund available to compensate those suffering losses from operation of the system. In American Torrens states the fund is financed by payments from persons initially registering land and generally also from certain classes of transferors or transferees of registered titles. The amount of the payment, under most statutes, is one-tenth of 1 percent of the value of the property, valuation determined either by the registrar, a court, or from the last general property tax assessment. If the land subsequently increases in value, additional payments need not be made.

Each Torrens state has restrictions on when and under what circumstances those suffering losses may recover from the fund. Typical of such restrictions are those provided for in Mass. Gen. Laws Ann. c. 185, § 101 (West 2003):

A person who, without negligence on his part, sustains loss or damage by reason of any error, omission, mistake or misdescription in any certificate of title or in any entry or memorandum in a registration book, or a person who, without negligence on his part, is deprived of land or of any estate or interest therein, by the registration of another person as owner of such land or of any estate or interest therein, through fraud or in consequence of any error, omission, mistake or misdescription in any certificate of title or in any entry or memorandum in a registration book may institute an action in contract in the superior court for compensation from the assurance fund for such loss, damage or deprivation; but a person so deprived of land or of any estate or interest therein, having a right of action or other remedy for the recovery of such land, estate or interest, shall exhaust such remedy before resorting to the action of contract herein provided. This section shall not deprive the plaintiff of any action of tort which he may have against any person for such loss or damage or deprivation of land or of any estate or interest therein. If the plaintiff elects to pursue his remedy in tort, and also brings an action of contract under this chapter, the action of contract shall be continued to await the result of the action of tort.

6. The English registration system differs in important respects from the usual American Torrens system as set forth in American Torrens statutes. If interest in Torrens revives substantially in the United States, some features of the English system are likely to be enacted in American Torrens statutes to reduce the cost of initial registration and enhance general efficiency of operation. Among aspects of the English system that American states conceivably may borrow are these:

(1) initial registration by an administrative official, the registrar, rather than a court, with the registrar having considerable discretion in determining whether or not titles are adequate to merit registration;

(2) compulsory registration in certain counties and boroughs, eventually to include all sections of the country, whenever a freehold is conveyed or a long-term lease is executed or transferred;

(3) parties in possession may have their titles registered "as is" at the time of registration, with subsequent transactions subject to the act and a possibility of the "as is" title becoming absolute with the passage of time;

(4) land may be, and often is, registered with the exact boundaries left undetermined, the so-called general boundaries rule that reduces expenses and the prospect of dispute associated with registration; and

(5) registration is centralized in district land registries, each serving a sizable geographic area, and most public contact with the registrar's office is by mail.

On recent changes in the English registration law, including creating a framework in which interests in registered land may be created or transferred by electronic conveyancing, see Bogusz, Bringing Land Registration Into the Twenty-First Century — The Land Registration Act 2002, 65 Modern L. Rev. 556 (2002).

Lane and Edson, Improving Land Title Registration Systems[29]

III-16 and 17 (1978)

Despite the serious problems revealed by the history of land title registration laws in the United States, the concept of state guaranteed land titles has logical appeal and practical advantages and deserves consideration in any review of ways to achieve land title reform. However, the historical record demonstrates that there will be no future for the title registration system in this country unless the cost of initial registration can be cut substantially and unless the security provided by a certificate of title can be made equivalent to the protection now provided by title insurance. Cost reductions can be achieved by streamlining the initial registration procedure to remove those procedural requirements that can be eliminated without denying due process or sacrificing substantial accuracy of the registration decree. Acceptable security will inevitably follow if the coverage of a certificate of title is broad, if the registration procedure is well administered, if a readily accessible and ample assurance fund is maintained to compensate for errors, and if the system is designed to assure that registrations occur with sufficient frequency to familiarize the real estate industry and the public with the system.

---

29. A report prepared for the U.S. Department of Housing and Urban Development, by Lane and Edson, pursuant to a contract with Booz, Allen and Hamilton.

Several factors have appeared that could contribute substantially to the revival and strengthening of a title registration approach.

First, the courts are likely to be more receptive to expedited — and hence faster and less costly — procedures for initial registration of land titles than might have been acceptable when the first Torrens statutes were enacted in the United States over 75 years ago. Although the courts have adhered to and frequently strengthened the fundamental protections of individuals guaranteed by federal and state constitutions, they have also become more flexible in sanctioning the procedures by which government actions are taken as long as fundamental rights are preserved. Thus, for example, the courts would now most likely approve a properly drafted title registration procedure conducted entirely by an administrative agency, subject only to judicial review for errors of law.

Second, the federal government has demonstrated an increased interest in urban development and a willingness to work with municipal and county governments for the improvement of American urban life. Through the contracts issued under the Real Estate Settlement Procedures Act and still broader federal planning programs, the federal government can stimulate much needed reform in land title records. Moreover, the federal government may be willing to contribute to the success of any land title registration system through its varied roles as purchaser, lienholder, lender and insurer of loans, although no willingness to do so has yet been demonstrated by the Department of Justice, the Internal Revenue Service, or the Federal National Mortgage Association. . . .

Third, dissatisfaction with present land transfer mechanisms and costs has increased to the point where lawyers and landowners may be receptive once again to experimenting with an effective title registration system.

A fourth factor referred to by recent writers as facilitating the implementation of a title registration system is the recent enormous advances in the processing, storage and retrieval of large amounts of data. However, while these technological advances permit a more rapid, economical consolidation of and access to records, and so must be taken into account, they do not address the principal problems faced by a title registration system.

3. *Automation of Land Title Record Keeping Systems*

Greatly improved data storage and retrieval, using computer technology, is one of the most important developments in modern times. As the technology has improved and its costs reduced, the acquisition and use of information has become far more efficient. The operations of many organizations, including many businesses and some government agencies, have been revolutionized by data system automation relying heavily on computers. However, local government offices that maintain records pertinent to land titles are an exception to this modern trend: Few are automated, and almost none are state-of-the-art. The technology is available; the effective demand is not. Why is this? One reason is the cost of changeover. To fully convert the accumulated documentation in a recorder's office to complete computer automation would be extremely expensive, even in small counties. Converting relevant tax and court records would add greatly to this cost. A much less expensive approach would be to automate only new records as they come in, relying on the old system for searching back records — a this-day-forward approach. But even such an approach would be costly and the inefficiency benefits much less.

Another explanation for the lack of local government land record automation is that there is no influential constituency pushing for it; and powerful interest groups — including title insurers, the conveyancing bar, and abstracters — are prone to oppose major modernization efforts, for these groups profit from the existing archaic system. The present cost burden is borne principally by land owners, mostly home buyers, many of whom do not understand that a more efficient system would have reduced their acquisition costs, and anyway they may never incur these costs again, a deterrent to seeking change.

It also should be recognized that in counties with comprehensive private title plants, substantial realization of automation benefits commonly is being realized, for many of these private plants are extensively automated. Searches in private plants generally are fast and accurate. This is a further explanation as to why public land title records continue to be maintained in such an antiquated manner. The big disadvantage of private title plants, however well-structured, is, of course, the cost of maintaining a double set of land records, public records in addition to private ones, a cost passed on to home owners and other ultimate consumers of land title data.

It should be noted, too, that in many small population counties, with relatively small accumulations of land records and a low volume of new transactions, the present largely manual system works rather well. Upkeep costs are cheap and searches usually neither difficult nor very time consuming. It is in the middle-sized and larger counties, or those growing rapidly, that current land title inefficiencies become most burdensome.

Eventually, government land title records are likely to be fully automated in most communities. But this reform is seen by taxpayers and county executives as such a low-priority need that it probably will be slow in coming and a gradual transition when it does come. Compared to such needs as crime prevention, education, public health, and better streets and highways, improved land records do not generate much enthusiasm.

NOTE

For a detailed discussion of the emergence of electronic conveyancing, see Patton and Palomar on Land Titles, ch. 15 (2003 & Supp. 2006).

Lane and Edson, Land Title Recordation Systems: Legal Constraints and Reforms[30]

V-10 to 13 (1978)

The automation of land title records utilizing advanced computerized techniques for recording, storing and retrieving large volumes of data holds considerable

30. A report prepared for the U.S. Department of Housing and Urban Development, pursuant to a contract with Booz, Allen and Hamilton. Footnotes omitted.

promise for increasing the efficiency of recording offices, both internally and for its users. . . .

The legal constraints on automating land title records will vary depending upon the coverage of the automated system. Policy makers considering the desirability of automating the land title records will have to make an initial set of decisions among the following:

1. *Automate only selected functions in the recording office.* For example, it might be found most economical for a moderately busy recording office with extensive micro-filming equipment already in place to automate only their grantor-grantee indexes, but retain the microfilm system for copying and storing documents. A number of private title plants combine automated functions with manual functions.

2. *Automate all title records in the recording office.* This option would establish a single automated system for all indexes and records maintained in the recording office.

3. *Automate all title records in the county or state.* This would be a far more ambitious undertaking and can be achieved in one of two ways. One way would be to enact legislation to force all land title information presently existing outside of the recording office to be recorded in the recording office where it would be placed in the recording office's automated system. The principal changes here would involve judgment liens, real estate tax liens and assessments, transfers by will or intestate succession, and federal and state income tax liens. . . .

The other way to achieve a fully automated state-wide title information system would be to automate the data existing in these other government offices — the tax assessor's and collector's office, the courts, the bureaus of vital statistics, and so forth — and then interconnect the data information systems so they may all be accessed from the terminals serving the recording office. This program would be a very expensive undertaking and probably politically infeasible because of the extent of interjurisdictional coordination required.

Any policy decision to automate the land title records must also address whether the automation should be prospective only or retroactive as well. While it would be clearly desirable to achieve a completely automated system as rapidly as possible, budgetary limitations might limit the extent to which back records can be read into the automated system. . . .

Assuming for present purposes that it is practical to consider automating only the recording office, as it presently functions, the minimum legal requirements are not many. They are:

1. *Eliminate all restrictive statutory specifications governing how land title records should be maintained.* Laws in those states that require that indexes and copies of recorded documents be maintained in bound volumes must be repealed. So too must those laws requiring the use of micro-filming techniques. The authorizing legislation should impose the duty to maintain records on the recording office, but should leave it to that office to determine how best to accomplish it. . . .

2. *Eliminate the requirement that grantor-grantee indexes be maintained and substitute some form of parcel or geographic index.* Although a grantor-grantee index can be computerized, an entire automated record-keeping system must be organized around the individual parcel, and the parcel or geographic index is the key access point to the system. This should be the legal index on which purchasers are legally entitled to rely.

3. *Establish a system of parcel identifiers and require that every conveyancing document include its unique parcel identifier.* The problem is that the metes and bounds method

of parcel description is too lengthy for practical use by a computer. . . . [T]he parcel identifier should be a number, but the number does not have to be related to the geographic location of the parcel. The parcel identifier number can be arbitrary and random as long as only one number is assigned to each parcel and that number is never reassigned to any other parcel in the jurisdiction.

In addition to these three requirements, there are a number of other statutory provisions that would be desirable to have to establish and operate an efficient automated title records system. Some of these are listed without regard to their relative importance. Other desirable provisions could probably be added to this list.

1. *Establish a system of personal identifiers and require that every conveyancing document identify the parties with their personal identifiers.* An automated system can function without personal identifiers, and automated private title plants do not now have personal identifiers. But the efficiency of the system is reduced. Because of the duplication of names, and because of the possibility of variant and sound-alike names, the automated system will have to retrieve a considerable amount of unnecessary information that the title searcher must then sort through manually. Complex systems have been developed by which computers will search through judgment information to identify all identical, variant and like-sounding names, but individual judgments are ultimately necessary to determine whether any of these names relate to the owner of the parcel in issue. These complexities can be eliminated with a universal system of unique personal identifiers. Then the computer would be able to limit its search to a single unique identifier, whether a number or a combination of words and numbers.

As discussed earlier in Part II-A, given the problems with using social security numbers, the best approach to a unique personal identifier might be to use the person's full name followed by numerals representing his birth date. . . .

2. *Place the risk of indexing errors on the recording party.* In a manual system . . . it seemed to be the better, but minority view to place the burden of loss from indexing errors on the party submitting the document for recordation since he can later check to be sure that the document has been indexed correctly. In an automated system, the recording office is able to return a copy of the indexing entry to the recording party much faster than in a manual system. Such a legal requirement would provide a helpful verification of the correctness of the entries made into the computerized data system.

3. *Reduce the length of title histories through marketable title acts.* By reducing the necessary length of title histories, the transitional period to a completely automated recording office system can be shortened without having to transcribe existing recorded information to the data processing system.

4. *Establish a state review and coordination function.* The operation of computers are not widely understood by non-specialists, and experience with computerized operations is probably lacking in most county recording offices. Effective computer hardware and software salesmen could have an undue influence in the local decision-making process. Further, it would be desirable to have the computerized system throughout the state as nearly uniform and compatible as possible, both for the convenience of the conveyancing professionals who will be dealing with recording offices and their requirements in more than one county, and to permit an eventual linkage of the county title records with the pertinent state-maintained records and with information in other counties. A state office, staffed with experienced persons, would seem vitally important to provide technical assistance to the

county offices seeking to establish automated offices and to assure state-wide compatibility. North Carolina has established such an office as part of its state land records management program. . . .

5. *Establish standard form legal instruments.* The efficiency of a computerized operation would be enhanced if standard legal forms were prepared for those real estate transactions that are capable of standardization. This should include most single family residential transactions. . . .

There are other measures that would help an efficient automated operation that may not require legislation if there is authority to adopt them by regulation or administrative implementation. These would include:

1. *Machine readable documents.* Optical scanners are now available to read and record written documents using special type faces which nevertheless are also readable by persons. This type can be easily inserted into most ball-type standard typewriters. Thus, it would seem to be feasible to require that all conveyancing documents being recorded be typed with machine readable type.

2. *Require summary information to accompany conveyancing documents being recorded.* As a condition for recording, certain summary information should be provided on a special form which includes the names of the parties, their personal identifiers, a description of the property and its parcel identifier, the type of conveyancing document being recorded, and the date. This information will facilitate the entry of the data into the computerized system, whether done manually or by machine-readable type. . . .

3. *Establishment of multiple computer terminals.* Once the recording office information has been fully automated, there is no reason why arrangements cannot be made for title attorneys and abstractors and title insurance companies to have computer terminals in their own offices, to be used 24 hours a day at their convenience.

NOTES AND QUESTIONS

1. Strong arguments are being made for adoption of integrated data information systems to be used by all local government offices that assemble or use data on land within their jurisdictions. These include not only recorders' offices but offices of court clerks, tax assessors, planning and zoning departments, public works departments, and those offices responsible for imposing and enforcing environmental protection. Important to a comprehensive integrated land data system is a more detailed and precise form of land mapping, one that includes not only boundaries but topography, types of soils, land usage — including exact structure locations, and permitted zoning. Mapping systems of this type are called multipurpose cadastres and the comprehensive systems are referred to as geographic information systems. Efficient implementation of these comprehensive systems requires extensive use of computers. It also requires new surveys of land parcels with descriptions in accord with a standard coordinate system. A fully automated land title record system, using currently available technology, is briefly described in Dansby, Automating Title Records, 6 Prob. & Prop. no. 1 at 24 (Jan./Feb. 1992). Needed statutory changes to authorize such a system are also considered in the article.

Full automation of the recording process is a desirable feature of a geographic information system and would enable remote access to all title data by lawyers and title companies. A geographic information system can be implemented gradually as new conveyancing transactions are recorded. Prospects for achieving substantially improved land records, including those pertaining to titles, may be increased by the appeal of an integrated system that will benefit so many different local government operations. On geographic information systems, see J. Antenucci et al., Geographic Information Systems: A Guide to Technology (1991); P. Burrough, Principles of Geographical Information Systems for Land Resources Assessment (1986); P. Dale and J. McLaughlin, Land Information Management (1988); W. Huxhold, An Introduction to Urban Geographic Information Systems (1991); and Dansby and Onsrud, The Geographic Info System — A Map for the Future, 3 Prob. & Prop. 20 (Jan./Feb. 1989).

2. What would be the effect on the private title insurance industry of an integrated public land record system with data stored in government-maintained direct-access storage devices? Would this make private title plants obsolete? Would it encourage replacement of private title insurance by Torrens registration? Is there any likelihood that such an integrated and fully automated system will be developed and operated by title insurers or other private businesses?

3. Is there a risk that an integrated public land record system will collect and distribute some kinds of data that should remain confidential and not be accessible through public records? If so, what kinds of data might be subject to such abuse? And could the system be controlled so that if confidential information were stored, it would be released only to authorized personnel?

4. A highly efficient reform, once in place, is one that would make administration of the recording acts a state obligation and then automate all recorded document records at a central location. Local officials, lawyers, and title insurers would have access to all recorded data in the state through computer hookups. Economies of scale from such a centralized system would, however, quite likely result in far fewer public employees, probably generating opposition from public employees and their unions to instituting the system.

5. Still another reform proposal is to privatize official public land record keeping. The title companies, and in some places abstracters, have shown that they can create and maintain private title plants that are complete, accurate, and easy to use. Why not turn over to these private enterprises the responsibility of recorders' offices and the centralized consolidation of court and tax records pertaining to local land? Where comprehensive private title plants exist, make them the public records. This would eliminate the need for dual sets of recorded instruments and in many counties result in more competent and probably cheaper public record keeping.

6. A thorough and careful analysis of the relative merits of the recording and Torrens systems concludes that the potential of computerization has changed the debate over which system is preferable, and that for "most of the United States, the appropriate choice would be a computerized recording system, with privately or publicly supplied title insurance." McCormack, Torrens and Recording: Land Title Assurance in the Computer Age, 18 Wm. Mitchell L. Rev. 61 (1992). However, Professor McCormack sees advantages to each system if fully computerized, including for recording, less costly and difficult government administration of the system, more rapid processing of new data, no expensive and dilatory initial registration procedures, and widespread understanding by American lawyers and judges as to how a recording system works. Torrens registration, by comparison, includes

advantages of quality control on data input and a format that cuts off the relevance of much old title data, something difficult to replicate effectively in a recording act system, even a computerized one. But McCormack recognizes that gaining political support for his computerization and related land title assurance reforms will take time, patience, and sustained effort. Change will not come quickly or easily.

CHAPTER SIX

Common Interest Communities: Co-ops, Condos, and Homeowners Associations

A quiet revolution has overtaken the housing scene. Not so long ago, in a legal if not social sense, most homeowners had little entanglement with their neighbors. The single-family detached structure resting securely upon its own lot dominated the market. Home-ownership for most Americans meant a fee simple title to that lot, and one should not underestimate the symbolism that this evoked. There were, of course, occasional exceptions. Row-housing, with its party wall arrangements, was quite abundant in a few older urban neighborhoods; and in parts of New York City and Chicago, high-rise cooperatives offered almost the only option for those seeking shelter equity. And residential subdivisions, bound together by a declaration of covenants and restrictions regulating land use, have been around for more than a century.

What has changed dramatically, however, both in volume and complexity has been the spread of common interest communities. These are developments in which the housing unit itself is only part of the physical package that the owner acquires. Coupled thereto is an interest, variously defined, in common areas that the unit owner must share with other residents. These common facilities may include only the land, hallways, and structural elements of the building itself, as in high-rise apartments, but today's homebuyers may also be getting much in the way of recreational and social amenities: swimming pools, tennis courts, community centers, nature trails, open space, etc. The Community Associations Institute estimates that there are more than 286,000 common interest communities as of 2006, housing more than 57 million residents—nearly 20 percent of the population. More than half of these are homeowners associations, roughly 40 percent are condominiums, and 5 to 7 percent are cooperatives.

This chapter looks closely at several law-related problems that have emerged as American homebuyers relinquish some of their sturdy independence in favor of "membership" in a common interest community ("CIC"), whether stock-cooperative, condominium, or homeowners association—the latter two by far the more usual.

PROBLEM

You are the attorney for a residential developer. She owns a tract of land that she wishes to develop into a 200-unit housing subdivision. The proposed venture will include extensive common recreational facilities, such as tennis courts, an artificial lake, and a community center; these will be available to all families within the subdivision. To help preserve first-growth woodland, the developer intends to rely upon the "cluster" provisions of the local zoning ordinance. In addition, all of the units will share party walls, so that the proposed layout will consist of 50 structures, each having four "town-house" units.

Your task is to create the legal structure that will implement your client's physical design in a form most likely to appeal to a melange of potential "home buyers," lenders, local officials and, of course, your client. The materials in this chapter should help you consider the legal design, which, as you should assume, can take one of three forms:

1. The development would be divided into 200 parcels, one per unit, to be sold individually in fee simple absolute. An association of homeowners would also be formed, in which membership would be compulsory. The developer then would either retain title to the recreational areas, which she would lease to the association, or transfer title to the association.

2. The developer would create a cooperative corporation, to which she would transfer title to the entire subdivision. Homebuyers would acquire stock in the corporation and a long-term proprietary lease in their individual units. The lease would also entitle stockholders to use the recreational facilities.

3. The developer would create a condominium association, which would manage all common areas. The developer would transfer to each home buyer a fee simple interest in the interior living space of his or her unit and a co-tenancy interest in all the remaining real estate, including the recreational facilities.

As you consider the materials in this chapter, what do you see as the principal attractions and disadvantages of each legal arrangement?

A.   CHOOSING A SHARED FACILITIES ARRANGEMENT

1. Introduction to the Stock-Cooperative

Berger, Land Ownership and Use[*]

226-227 (3d ed. 1982)

The cooperative apartment (co-op) occupies a small, localized corner in the housing market. Found chiefly in a few urban areas, New York City the principal situs, the co-op remains an option to the condominium for those persons who wish to combine apartment occupancy and the advantages of homeownership.

We cannot date or place the origin of the co-op, but New York City's first cooperative apartment building, and perhaps the first in the United States, was built in 1876.[1] In the years preceding the Great Depression, the luxury co-op began

---

[*] Adapted by author for this casebook, with new text and footnotes.

1. Hansmann, Condominium and Cooperative Housing: Transactional Efficiency, Tax Subsidies, and Tenure Choice, 20 J. Leg. Studies 25, 27 (1991). As early as 1886, a Manhattan co-op was involved in a lawsuit; Barrington Apartment Assn. v. Watson, 45 S. Ct. (38 Hun.) 545.

to abound in Chicago and New York[2] — two cities where the well-to-do practiced the apartment habit, and, in 1927, the first middle-income co-op, Amalgamated Houses, rose in the Bronx. The Depression struck hard at all forms of real estate; because of their financial interdependence, co-ops were especially vulnerable. Nine of every ten co-ops went broke. When World War II began, the co-op movement was in near collapse.

In the postwar era, the co-op staged a comeback.[3] Several factors helped. Congress, in 1942, passed the forerunner of Internal Revenue Code § 216, creating near-parity (regarding deductions for interest and property taxes) between homeowner and cooperator. The war-occasioned rise in tax rates gave the upper-income apartment dweller further incentive to reduce his tax burden by switching from a rental to a cooperative unit. The tenant's desire, in this rare instance, paralleled his landlord's, for the latter, faced with the wearying prospect of rent control, often wanted to sell out; his easiest (and most profitable) chance of doing so lay in conversion to cooperative and the giving of first option, usually at a reduced "insider price," to his present tenants. A series of federal and state subsidy programs geared to the co-op format, most notably New York's Mitchell-Lama Law (Private Housing Finance Law §§ 10–37), enacted in 1956, stimulated new co-op construction. And, finally, banks became more willing to help finance the purchase of co-op apartments, easing a credit barrier to the marketing of more expensive units. Cf. Joselow, Making Cooperative Unit Mortgages More Liquid, Real Est. Rev. 103 (Fall 1983).

Legal Arrangement. Title to the land and building is held by a single entity — usually a corporation, although a trust is sometimes used. Only those who are to become apartment "owners," the cooperators, may obtain a corporate (trust) interest; each cooperator acquires shares based on the value of his apartment. The right to occupy the apartment is embodied in a "proprietary" lease between the corporation (trust), as landlord, and the cooperator, as tenant. Under the lease provisions, the cooperator pays a periodic rental or assessment; this charge covers the cooperator's *pro rata* share of the project's expenses, including debt service, maintenance, taxes, insurance, capital improvements, and reserves. Ordinarily the lease is for an initial three-to-five year term, but is automatically renewable for like terms at the tenant's election.

Management of the cooperative is performed by a board of directors, elected by the project members in accordance with the governing bylaws. The directors fix the amount of the periodic assessment and enforce the lease against delinquent stockholder-tenants. Default may result in a member's eviction and in the forced sale of his stock and lease.

---

2. New York City had at least 125 cooperative apartment buildings by 1929, and Chicago had over 100 by 1930; Hansmann, note 1 supra, at 27.

3. The cooperative reached its post-war zenith of popularity in 1976, when it comprised 2.2 percent of the multifamily housing stock; U.S. Dept. of Housing and Urban Development, Annual Housing Survey: 1983, Part A, General Housing Characteristics (Current Housing Reports set. H-150-83 (1984)).

2. Introduction to the Condominium

Berger, Condominium: Shelter on a Statutory Foundation[4]

63 Colum. L. Rev. 987 (1963)

Mrs. Sullivan: "I am glad to hear about this [condominium] type of ownership. It is the first time I heard of it."

Mr. Addonizio: "This is a new concept, as far as I am concerned, but it is very
interesting."

Senator Sparkman: "I must say I am intrigued by it. . . ."

Seldom have hard-nosed lawmakers greeted innovation more cordially than
they have greeted the condominium. For whatever reason — whether the persua-
siveness of its Puerto Rican proponents, the allure of a concept whose origins
are said to predate Caesar, the inattention of its natural enemies, or simply its
inherent merit — Congress was quick to bring condominium apartments within
the Federal Housing Administration's (FHA) mortgage insurance powers by adding
Section 234 to the National Housing Act.[5] There has followed an astonishing burst
of activity among legal writers, bar committees, state assemblies, and members of
the real estate profession. Today, familiarity with condominium is widespread; yet
only three years ago Congress's housing experts were hearing of it for the first time.

What is this condominium that has aroused such sudden interest? According to
its Latin meaning, condominium is co-ownership; however, co-ownership is not
today its primary feature. The most common modern instance of condominium is a
multi-unit dwelling each of whose residents enjoys exclusive ownership of his
individual apartment. With "title" to an apartment goes a cotenant's undivided
interest in the common facilities — the land, the hallways, the heating plant, etc.
Remarkably flexible, condominium is susceptible of an endless variety of legal
formulations and can be adapted to a multiplicity of land uses or project designs.
But in all of its forms its principal goal remains constant: to enable occupants of a
multi-unit project to achieve more concomitants of ownership than are now available either to renters or to cooperators. . . .

A still greater disadvantage (of the cooperative) is that, for purposes of
mortgage financing and property taxation, the cooperator's stock-lease "estate"
lacks sufficient personality to support an individual obligation.[6] As a result the
entire cooperative structure is burdened by a blanket mortgage and a single tax
assessment. By saddling the venture with overall liens, the stock-cooperative
imposes upon the tenants the duty of meeting collectively the tax and debt
service obligations as they fall due; frequently the two items exceed two-thirds of

---

4. Adapted by the author for use in this casebook. New footnotes supplied.

5. Curiously, § 234, which started it all, delivered fewer than 2,000 units of condominium dwellings in
the first five years after its enactment. U.S. Department of Housing and Urban Development, 1966
Statistical Report.

6. Changes in state and federal law have facilitated financing of the equity portion of the cooperative
stock-lease interest. New York State now allows lenders to make loans "secured" by the stock-lease equity.
For example, savings banks may now loan on such security up to its full appraised value. N.Y. Banking
Law § 103(5) (McKinney 2006). And Congress, in 1974, gave the FHA authority to insure a mortgage on
the equity in a cooperative dwelling unit. National Housing Act § 203(n). Note, however, that the equity
mortgage is necessarily a subordinate lien wherever a blanket mortgage encumbers the project.

the monthly assessment. Stipulate a vigorous economy, modest inflation, housing undersupply, healthy reserves, a competitive location, and no problems of disrepair or obsolescence, and the concern over this financial interdependence is academic. If a tenant defaults, the cooperative may quickly terminate his status and find a replacement able to discharge the delinquent's *pro rata* obligation. There is no assurance, however, of the permanence of satisfactory conditions. Unsatisfactory conditions, moreover, breed further delinquency by stepping up the need for new cooperators at a time when their supply is shrinking. Since the blanket tax and financing burden remains fairly constant, any additional charges upon the surviving cooperators may affect adversely both their ability to pay and their desire to remain current. The calamitous experience of stock-cooperatives during the early 1930s reveals the risks inherent in the snowballing of individual defaults. Higher standards for the selection of tenants, larger down payment requirements, and the immediate funding of reserves would be forms of prophylaxis, but they would also discourage the wider use of cooperatives among lower- and middle-income families.

The massive conversion of New York City rental apartments into co-ops and condominiums during the 1980s led to massive defaults at the end of the decade with the downturn in the City's economy. Most conversions had taken place under the so-called "non-eviction" procedure, which allowed non-purchasing tenants to remain in possession after the conversion plan became effective. Since a non-eviction plan required that only fifteen percent of the units be sold, sponsors typically held a substantial number of unsold units after the building became a co-op or condominium. Financially hard-pressed sponsors began to default on their common-area assessments, and by 1989, according to the New York State Attorney General's office, sponsors of more than 400 converted buildings were in arrears. In many cases, however, successful workouts averted failure. . . .

Even if the risk of financial interdependence has been overdrawn, the blanket mortgage scheme imposes serious disadvantages upon the cooperator. He lacks the flexibility with regard to debt reduction, refinancing, or resale that the home owner enjoys. He cannot shift his assets or take advantage of earnings peaks or asset increments to reduce or eliminate the mortgage affecting his unit. Refinancing, which is often needed to effect modernization, modify debt service charges, "borrow against one's equity," or facilitate resale, is not possible unless the cooperator can persuade his fellow stockholders to refinance the blanket debt. This disadvantage is especially significant at the time of resale if the unit has an enhanced equity value and if the venture permits the cooperator to realize the gain, for the seller is more likely to deal with a buyer who must borrow in order to arrange the purchase. If the seller himself takes back the financing, he must defer the conversion into cash of his equity value. The new stockholder-tenant, who carries the heavier costs of a secondary loan whatever its source, may pose an added hazard for his fellow interdependent cooperators.

By enabling the unit owner to undertake an individual financing program, the condominium offers a major and perhaps critical advantage over the present-day cooperative. Yet the condominium relinquishes none of the ownership benefits afforded by stock-cooperatives — voice in its management, permanence of tenure, avoidance of profit to the landlord, and tax savings. . . .

III.   CREATION OF THE CONDOMINIUM

To inform interested parties of the nature of the enterprise and its internal organization two important documents must be executed and recorded — the declaration
and the operating by-laws.

The declaration serves roughly the same function for the condominium as the
subdivision map and restrictive covenants serve in a tract development. It includes a
legal description of the underlying land, a description in lay terms of the building,
apartment units, and common facilities, and a statement in fractions of each owner's share of rights and duties with respect to the common premises. This fraction
fixes permanently the unit owner's *pro rata* burden of the common expenses and
his share in any profit or distribution of capital. It is also the measure of his voice in
the management. Because taxing officials will need a formula for apportioning a
project's total value among the separate units, the fraction may be used to compute
each apartment's assessment. And finally, the fraction may provide a basis for
limiting the unit owner's individual liability for liens and for the claims of the
project's creditors.[7]

Beyond these essential features, the content of the declarations may vary in
accordance with the requirements of individual statutes. Nevertheless, most
declarations will contain provisions regarding the establishment of an entity to
manage the condominium's day-to-day affairs, measures to be taken against delinquent owners — such as the power to lien an individual unit, designation of persons
upon whom process may be served, arrangements for blanket casualty and liability
insurance, and procedures to be followed in the event of project destruction or
obsolescence. The statutes may mandate some of these provisions, for example, the
designation of persons to receive process; they will legitimize others, such as the
power to impose assessment liens. For the internal administration of a condominium, by-laws are needed to regulate matters such as building maintenance, budget-
ing, assessment and collection, capital improvements, and occupant control. . . .

Either the declaration or the by-laws will also include various restraints upon the
unit owner's freedom to alienate. Two involve the physical and legal integrity of the
project: a restraint against partition of the common areas while the structure
remains intact and subject to the condominium regime, and a bar against transfers
that would divide ownership of a unit from ownership of the corresponding share of
the common areas. Generally the unit owner's freedom to choose a vendee or
tenant will also be restricted. . . .

Finally, the declaration will normally include the condominium plans and either
a subdivision map or a statement of metes and bounds describing each of the units.
These descriptions . . . are later incorporated in the deed of conveyance that the
condominium member receives when he acquires his interest.

Heretofore the most common form of condominium management has been the
unincorporated "Association of Owners." Unit ownership automatically bestows
the status of association membership, which carries the privileges of voting for a
board of directors and taking part in the association's business meetings. In turn,

---

7. Management of the condominium by an unincorporated association makes each unit owner liable
for any unpaid contract claim against the association. The liability is joint and several, which means that
the creditor may recover against any unit owner, who, in turn, must then seek contribution from his
fellow owners. Berger, Condominium: Shelter on a Statutory Foundation, 63 Colum. L. Rev. at 1007.
What steps might the condominium take to insulate the unit owner against this risk?

the board elects the association officers and, together with these and perhaps a manager, it directs the condominium's daily operations. . . .

3. Introduction to the Homeowners Association

Hyatt, Condominium and Home Owner Associations: Formation and Development[*]

24 Emory L.J. 977, 980-983 (1975)

A housing development utilizing a homes association[8] may take many forms. The project might be a conventional subdivision, attached housing, cluster housing, or a variety of other construction forms, including combinations of the possible forms. The first essential difference between the homes association and the condominium is that the individual purchaser acquires title to a dwelling unit. The owner's title includes the exterior of the unit and may also include a portion of the land adjacent to the unit. The second major difference is that the property not owned individually as dwelling units is owned by an association composed of the unit owners, rather than by the unit owners in common.

The condominium and homes association developments have a common feature which is crucial to an appreciation of the many legal complexities involved: membership in the association is mandatory. Each purchaser, by accepting a deed, becomes an association member and submits to the authority of the association and the restrictions upon the use of the property contained in the Declaration of Condominium or in the Declaration of Covenants, Conditions, and Restrictions.

The role and function of the condominium association and the homeowners association in the homes association context are essentially identical. Therefore, having established the definitional framework, this article will refer to the "association" as including both except where the context necessitates separate treatment.

Basic to the development of an association is an appreciation of its role and function. First, the association provides a vehicle for the individual unit owners to work together. An "important aspect of the [community association] lies in its basic nature as a privately owned and operated vehicle of service to a specific community." However, because all owners automatically become members of the association upon taking title and because the association is empowered to levy and collect assessments, to make and enforce rules, and to permit or deny certain uses of the property, it can exert tremendous influence upon the individual's property rights which are normally enjoyed as a concomitant part of fee simple ownership. It is this degree of control that raises the association to a level approaching that of a municipal government.

---

[*] Footnotes renumbered.

8. The terms "landed homes association," "automatic homes association," and "homeowners association" refer to the same concept. For simplicity's sake, the term "homes association" will be used as inclusive of all; it should be noted that the landed association holds title to common areas, while in other possible forms of homes associations, this might not be the case.

This dual role as a service oriented business and regulatory authority is a direct result of the powers conferred upon the association by the declaration which created it. Filed before the sale of the first unit, the declaration immediately brings the association into existence; the complacent assumption by some developers that the association does not exist until control is surrendered to the homeowners not only is incorrect but also is a miscalculation of the developer's own responsibility and hence his potential liability for failure to discharge the duties of and to protect the interests of the association.

Whether developer- or homeowner-controlled, the association must be operated in accordance with the declaration, by-laws, and governing statute, if any, in full recognition of the rights and responsibilities of the owners individually and of the association. The officers and directors must concern themselves, as would the officers and directors of any corporation, with business details such as finances, asset and property management, taxation, insurance, employee relations, and many other considerations inherent in operating a substantial business. The need to observe scrupulously the declaration and by-laws and to consider carefully the long-range effects of these provisions when originally drafting them is best illustrated by the association's regulatory role as a "minigovernment."

In the condominium context, state law ordains the creation of the association; in both forms of development, moreover, the creating documents are filed with and enforced through the state courts. In most cases, the association provides for its members' utility services, road maintenance, street and common area lighting, and refuse removal; in many cases, it also provides security services and various forms of communication within the community. There exists, therefore, a clear analogy to the municipality's police and public safety functions; moreover, these functions are financed through assessments, or taxes, levied upon the members of the community association. The governmental role which creates a special concern for strict observance of the dictates of due process of law is made more acute by the power of the association through its rule-making authority and through its assessment authority to regulate the use and enjoyment of property. This "power of levy" is a distinctive characteristic of the association and removes it from a mere voluntary neighborhood civic group. The declaration, which must be strictly construed and obeyed,[9] establishes a variety of use restrictions including, for example, restrictions upon sale and leasing,[10] exterior alterations, use of the common area, parking, and even limitations upon the nature of uses to which the interior of the unit may be placed. In addition, a typical declaration will empower the board of directors to make rules and to establish penalties for violations thereof. The imposition of penalties, whether fines collected as a lien upon the property or a denial of the use of facilities enforced by injunction, certainly represents a quasi judicial power to affect an individual's property rights.

9. Hoover Morris Development Co., Inc. v. Mayfield, 233 Ga. 593, 212 S.E.2d 778 (1975).

10. The author finds so-called "right of first refusal" clauses a vestige of an era he would like to believe has, and should have, passed. Developers say that they must include such provisions in order to satisfy the buyers who generally do not know or care whether or not the provision exists. The new Georgia Condominium Act, however, specifically continues the practice and modifies existing law only by imposing a time-notice limitation.

NOTES AND QUESTIONS

1. In addition to the unit owner's exposure in contract for any claims against the governing board, the condominium member may face several other forms of individual liability that the co-op member does not usually have. The various liabilities are grounded in tort, mortgage debt, and real estate tax debt (rarely). Explain. Cf. Berger, Condominium: Shelter on a Statutory Foundation, 63 Colum. L. Rev. 987, 1019 (1963). Which of these liabilities would follow the unit owner in a homes association?

2. Most buildings as they age require major capital improvements. Would it be easier in a co-op or a condominium to finance a substantial renovation? Similarly, for expansion of the recreational facilities? Also compare a condominium and a homeowners association.

3. Every state, the District of Columbia, and Puerto Rico now have condominium enabling statutes. In an effort that began in the early 1970s, the National Conference of Commissioners on Uniform State Laws has sought to offer comprehensive legislation that would apply, insofar as possible, not only to condominiums, but also to the other forms of common ownership. This effort has led to a series of Uniform Acts, to wit:

Uniform Condominium Act, adopted 1977;

Uniform Planned Community Act, adopted 1980;

Uniform Condominium Act (amended), adopted 1980;

Model Real Estate Cooperative Act, adopted 1981;

Uniform Common Interest Ownership Act (UCIOA), adopted 1982;

Uniform Common Interest Ownership Act (amended), adopted 1994.

As of late 2006, only Virginia has adopted the Model Real Estate Cooperative Act, and only Oregon and Pennsylvania have adopted the Uniform Planned Community Act. Thirteen states (Alabama, Arizona, Maine, Minnesota, Missouri, Nebraska, New Mexico, North Carolina, Pennsylvania, Rhode Island, Texas, Virginia, and Washington) have enacted the 1980 version of the Uniform Condominium Act; three states (Louisiana, Michigan, and Wisconsin) have borrowed parts of the 1980 Act, and New Hampshire has taken the 1977 version. Alaska, Colorado, Connecticut, Minnesota, Nevada, West Virginia, and Vermont have enacted UCIOA, which has been described as an "amalgam of the three acts designed for condominiums, cooperatives and planned communities."

4. Although the terminology and details vary, other legal systems often provide for arrangements similar to condominiums, cooperatives, and homeowners associations. Indeed, the condominium originated in the civil law. Common law countries have adapted in different ways to the need for equity ownership in individual units within common developments. For example, the law in England and Wales does not provide for condominiums, but a system has evolved for selling long-term leaseholds to units within a development. The terms of this "ownership" are defined by the lease, which can be freely transferred or mortgaged. See C.G. Van Der Merwe, A Comparative Study of the Distribution of Ownership Rights in Property in an

Apartment or Condominium Scheme in Common Law, Civil Law and Mixed Law Systems, 31 Ga J. Int'l & Comp. L. 101 (2002); Daniel G.M. Marre and Alexandre R. Cole, Comparative View of Laws Governing Condominium-Type Projects, 19-JUL Constr. Law. 15 (1999).

5. There is concern that CICs are leading to the "secession of the successful," as upper-income families choose to live in CICs that provide a higher level of services — parks and recreational facilities, security guards, snow clearance, and so on — than are available to those who live outside the CIC. This concern is heightened by the growth in gated communities, where there is a stark physical separation of the CIC from the surrounding neighborhoods. As people move into CICs, they may be less willing to pay taxes and support bond issuances to pay for public services for the broader community. Does this mean that the rise of CICs will further erode our ability to adequately support many types of public investment?

On the flip side, the unit owners are typically liable for property, sales, and income taxes that support public investments and services such as sewer and road construction and repair, garbage collection, and police protection. However, these same "public goods" may be provided by the community association, so the unit owners can end up paying twice — once through taxes for public services they do not use, and a second time through their assessments. Does this mean that the rise of CICs will enhance our ability to support many types of public investment? And should members of CICs be entitled to a tax credit, deduction, or exemption to correct for this double burden, as some argue?

B. SELECTED PROBLEMS

1. The Cooperative Apartment: Realty, Personalty, or Hybrid?

State Tax Commission v. Shor

43 N.Y.2d 151, 371 N.E.2d 523, 400 N.Y.S.2d 805 (1977)

BREITEL, Chief Judge. This is a proceeding to enforce a money judgment, under CPLR article 52 on behalf of three creditors and lienors of the debtor Shor. They sought an order for the distribution of proceeds from the sale of Shor's interest in his co-operative apartment. Fidelity National Bank, a judgment creditor of Shor interpleaded as a respondent, opposed the motion, asserting a prior lien on the proceeds. Special Term granted the motion, and a unanimous Appellate Division affirmed. Fidelity appeals.

The issue is whether the debtor's interest in his co-operative apartment, that is, a stock certificate in the co-operative corporation and a "proprietary" leasehold granted by the corporation, is a "chattel real," and hence, real property under CPLR 5203, thereby entitling a judgment creditor to a lien on the property merely upon docketing his judgment.

The order of the Appellate Division should be affirmed.

The ownership interest of a tenant-shareholder in a co-operative apartment is *sui generis*. It reflects only an ownership of a proprietary lease, and therefore arguably an interest in a chattel real, conditional however upon his shareholder interest in the co-operative corporation, an interest always treated as personal property. The leasehold and the shareholding are inseparable. For some special purposes, the real property aspect may predominate (see Grenader v. Spitz, 2 Cir., 537 F.2d 612, 617-620, *cert. den.* 429 U.S. 1009, 97 S. Ct. 541, 50 L. Ed. 2d 619; cf. United Housing Foundation v. Forman, 421 U.S. 837, esp. 854-860, 95 S. Ct. 2051, 44 L. Ed. 2d 621, *reh. den.* 423 U.S. 884, 96 S. Ct. 157, 46 L. Ed. 2d 115). But, where priorities of judgment creditors are involved, the stock certificate and lease involved in the typical co-operative apartment transaction fit better, legally and pragmatically, although with imperfect linguistic formulation, into the statutory framework governing personal property. Since a co-operative apartment leasehold, inseparable from co-operative shares, is not a chattel real for purposes of CPLR 5203, Fidelity did not obtain a lien merely upon docketing its judgment.

In 1951, Shor purchased 1,400 shares in 480 Park Avenue Corp., a co-operative apartment corporation. He received a stock certificate and a proprietary lease on a duplex apartment. The lease provided the lessor with a "first lien" on Shor's shares of stock for all monetary obligations arising under the lease. Eventually, on February 23, 1973, Shor was evicted for nonpayment of maintenance charges, dating from 1971, and 480 Park Avenue Corp. claims a first lien of $63,908.22 for back maintenance, with interest, expenses, and attorneys' fees.

Well before Shor's eviction, in July, 1967, Shor, as guarantor of a loan made by Chase to a corporate borrower, had granted Chase "a security interest in [and] a general lien upon . . . all money, instruments, securities, documents, chattel paper . . . and any other property, rights and interests of the undersigned, which at any time shall come into the possession or custody or under the control of the Bank." Chase had previously obtained possession of Shor's stock certificate and proprietary lease as collateral. Following various defaults, Chase, on April 28, 1972, obtained a judgment against Shor for $44,222.67. Based on the judgment with added interest and expenses, Chase asserts a first lien of $67,800.17 plus attorneys' fees in this proceeding.

On April 9, 1971, the State Tax Commission filed its first tax warrant against Shor. The commission levied execution on Chase on December 22, 1971, restraining Chase from making any transfer of the collateral. A similar levy was made on 480 Park Avenue Corp. on December 15, 1972. The Tax Commission's lien is for an amount greater than the total of the proceeds from the eventual sale of the apartment.

On August 9, 1973, on motion of Chase, and upon stipulation among Chase, the Tax Commission, and 480 Park Avenue Corp., Special Term authorized the sale of the collateral. All other creditors of Shor consented to the sale reserving any liens and priorities they might have in the proceeds. Appellant Fidelity insisted on payment of $5,000 in return for its consent. On April 24, 1974, the sale realized $141,000. Chase now holds that sum in escrow at interest pending the outcome of this proceeding.

Not in dispute are the priorities among Chase, the Tax Commission, and 480 Park Avenue Corp. Those three subject to court approval, stipulated, on July 24, 1974, to divide the sale proceeds thus: $56,000 to 480 Park Avenue Corp., $64,000 to Chase, and the balance, plus accrued interest, to the Tax Commission. Then, on January 9, 1975, Chase interpleaded other creditors of Shor, seeking to distribute the fund according to the July 24 stipulation, and to be discharged from liability to the interpleaded respondents. All of the interpleaded respondents, save Fidelity, defaulted.

Fidelity had obtained and docketed a judgment against Shor, for $152,589, on February 6, 1970, before Chase obtained any judgment against Shor, before Shor fell behind in his payments to 480 Park Avenue Corp. and before the State Tax Commission filed its warrants. Fidelity, however, never executed on the property. Although $40,000 of Fidelity's judgment was paid, the remainder, plus interest, exceeds the fund in escrow. Fidelity's contention is simple: Shor's interest in his co-operative is a chattel real, and hence treatable as real property (CPLR 105, subd. [r]). Therefore, docketing of the 1970 judgment gave Fidelity a lien on the property (CPLR 5203, subd. [a]), and hence priority over all other creditors, none of whom, Fidelity asserts, obtained liens until after 1970.

The growth of co-operative ownership of apartment buildings, throughout the Nation, but especially in New York City, has created legal problems not resolved by uncritical resort either to the rubrics governing real property or those governing personal property (see Silverman v. Alcoa Plaza Assoc., 37 A.D.2d 166, 173, 323 N.Y. S.2d 39, 45 [Steuer, J., dissenting]). The co-operative corporation owns the land and the building. Shares in the corporation are sold to each apartment "owner," who receives a stock certificate, not a deed to real property. The shares entitle the shareholder to a long-term apartment "proprietary" lease. (See 4B Powell, Real Property [Rohan-rev. ed.], par. 633.4.) One has, therefore, a mixed concept and terminology, superficially resembling the traditional rental apartment lease, except, for example, that the lessee pays monthly maintenance charges and is subject to assessments instead of rent. For some purposes it is a lease; for others it is a compact between co-operative corporation and co-operative tenant. In any case the rights of the tenant are initiated by the capital investment made in the shares of the co-operative corporation. (On the paradoxes with respect to co-operative apartment buildings and the desirability of legislative clarification see 4B Powell, Real Property, pars. 633.51-633.52.)

By viewing the shares of stock as the dominant aspect of the co-operative transaction, as respondents do, one could easily conclude linguistically that the co-operative "owners" hold only personal property, little different from the shareholders in a commercial real estate corporation. By focusing instead on the proprietary lease, as does appellant Fidelity, one could equally well conclude linguistically that the interest of the co-operative "owner" is real property, or at least a chattel real, which is treated as real property under the applicable CPLR provisions. Both approaches are overly facile. Neither the stock certificate nor the lease, inseparably joined, can appropriately be viewed or valued in isolation from the other. Nor may a dynamic jurisprudence ignore the manner in which economic affairs are conducted or the perception that the members of society have in conducting their affairs (see Cardozo, Nature of the Judicial Process, pp. 60–64).

CPLR 5203, governing priorities and liens upon real property, provides, in part: "No transfer of an interest of the judgment debtor in real property, against which property a money judgment may be enforced, is effective against the judgment creditor . . . from the time of the docketing of the judgment with the clerk of the county in which the property is located." CPLR 105 (subd.[r]) provides that, for purposes of the CPLR, real property includes chattels real. Thus, if Shor's interest in his co-operative apartment were a chattel real, Fidelity would have priority over all creditors with liens created after February 6, 1970, the date its judgment was docketed in New York County.

By contrast, CPLR 5202 and 5234, governing rights and priorities of judgment creditors in personal property, require delivery of execution to the Sheriff before a creditor may obtain priority in the property. Since Fidelity has never delivered an execution, if the lease and stock certificate are treated as personal property, Fidelity's interest must be subordinated to those of the other creditors.

Persuasive in this case are the 1971 amendments to the Banking Law which indicate strongly that priorities in the stock certificate and proprietary lease of a co-operative apartment corporation are to be treated under principles governing personal property (Banking Law, § 235, subd. 8-a; § 380, subd. 2-a). Both sections, dealing with permissible investments for various financial institutions, permit loans to finance purchase of ownership interests in co-operative apartments, provided the investment "is secured within ninety days from the making of the loan by an assignment or transfer of the stock or other evidence of an ownership interest of the borrower and a proprietary lease." (See, also, Banking Law § 103, subd. 5.) No recording is required, as it would be in the case of a mortgage on real property (see, e.g., Banking Law, § 235, subd. 8, par. [1]; see, also, 4B Powell, Real Property [Rohan-rev. ed.], par. 633.51[3]).

These provisions indicate a legislative intention that lenders in possession of the relevant documents of title be secure from claims of subsequent creditors without any filing or recording of the security interest. Thus, a possessory security interest in co-operative apartment stock and lease would be much like a possessory security interest in ordinary chattel paper, which requires no filing for perfection (see Uniform Commercial Code, § 9-305). By contrast, if the "ownership" interest in a co-operative apartment were to be treated as real property, mere possession without recording would subordinate the lender's security interest to claims of other classes of creditors (see Real Property Law, § 291; Lien Law, § 13). Such a result could not have been intended by the Legislature seeking to protect the interests of banking depositors. . . .

Lastly, but cogent to the point of controlling, short of violation of public policy or positive law, co-operative tenants, co-operative corporations, and third parties dealing with them do not now, if they ever did, treat co-operative tenancies as chattels real. Indeed, the legislative response in the 1971 amendments to the Banking Law confirm this perception of the nature of the relationship in co-operative apartments and the quality of the property interest involved. The common-law process does not drag unwillingly the people it serves into a rigidly fenced corral, kicking, but reflects the fair conduct and expectations of fair, reasonable persons (see Gray, Nature and Sources of the Law, p. 282). . . .

Accordingly, the order of the Appellate Division should be affirmed, without costs. Jasen, Gabrielli, Jones, Wachtler, Fuchsberg and Cooke, JJ., concur.

Order affirmed.

NOTES AND QUESTIONS

1. New York now requires that a security interest in a co-op be perfected by filing a financing statement, not by possession of the cooperative stock certificate and proprietary lease as was previously required. N.Y.U.C.C. § 9-301(d) (McKinney's 2006).

(These provisions also establish a statutory lien for the cooperative corporation securing the owner's obligations to the corporation, and provide that this "Cooperative Organization Security Interest" is perfected as of the date of the creation of the cooperative interest, without any need for filing. N.Y.U.C.C. § 9-308(h) (McKinney's 2006).) Whether the holding in *Shor* survives these enactments is unclear. See In re Pandeff, 201 B.R. 865, 867 n.8 (Bankr. S.D.N.Y. 1996) (questioning, without deciding, the continuing validity of *Shor*).

2. Silverman v. Alcoa Plaza Assn., 37 A.D.2d 166, 323 N.Y.S.2d 39 (1971), which the *Shor* opinion cites, illustrates the personalty versus realty issue in yet another context. There plaintiff had defaulted on his contract to purchase a co-op apartment and later sued to recover his $15,400 deposit after learning that the owner had sold the unit to another for the same price. At issue was whether the Uniform Commercial Code covered this transaction. If the stock-lease could be characterized as "goods," the defendant would be limited to its actual damages from plaintiff's breach. If the stock-lease was deemed "realty," the defendant could retain the deposit by way of forfeiture, without proof of damages. In holding for the plaintiff, the divided court wrote:

> A proprietary lease is no different from any other type of lease. It is personal property. Co-operative apartment stock is nevertheless stock, like any other stock in a corporation owning real estate. It does not appear that the pairing of the two together does anything to create a new classification of real estate. Important too, to the consideration herein, is the fact that the law frowns upon forfeiture or penalty. True as stated there are specific instances where the law mandates forfeiture as well as penalty. These situations are however limited in kind and scope and should not be unduly expanded except when clearly mandated. [323 N.Y.S.2d at 45.]

At pages 46-47 of his dissenting opinion, Justice Steuer reasoned:

> Concepts of what is realty and what personalty are not static and are no exception to the proposition that the law accommodates to new developments as they occur. Co-operative apartments made their appearance long after classic distinctions between realty and personalty were formulated, and the guidelines to classification should be established by the inherent nature of the property right rather than mere superficial resemblances to other forms. This is no new idea. For instance, while a lease for 99 years is still a lease, it is nevertheless realty, because, despite the form, in actuality the leaseholder has all the attributes of ownership.
>
> Applying the principle to the co-operative shares, it is at once apparent that the dominant characteristic of such shares is the right to a proprietary lease, which is the essential and particularizing aspect of such shares (Penthouse Props. v. 1158 Fifth Ave., 256 App. Div. 685, 692) distinguishing them from the ordinary evidences of corporate stock ownership. While the owner does not acquire a fee in the apartment, he does possess so many of the rights and obligations peculiar to fee ownership that the status is for practical purposes indistinguishable. To name a few of these which have received statutory or decisional recognition: The shareholder has been authorized to bring summary eviction proceedings to obtain possession (Curtis v. Le May, 186 Misc. 853). The Statute of Frauds applicable to real estate transactions applies to sales of cooperative stock (Frank v. Rubin, 59 Misc. 2d 796). . . . Federal and New York State income tax laws give the same privileges to co-operative share owners as they do to fee owners in many respects (see U.S. Code, tit. 26, § 121, subd. [d], par. [3]; §§ 216, 1034, and

New York Tax Law § 360, subd. 12). In addition, alienability, liability for maintenance and repairs, as well as the privileges of making interior alterations, give a popular recognition to the status of realty quite in accord with the decisional law which treats this type of property as realty.

Accord: Shulkin v. Dealy, 132 Misc. 2d 371, 504 N.Y.S.2d 342 (Sup. Ct. 1986).

3. Ordinarily, the public sale of shares of stock is subject to federal securities regulation, yet there is widespread agreement that the denomination of the purchaser's interest in a cooperative corporation as "stock" does not, by itself, create a security under the federal acts. Cf. United Housing Foundation, Inc. v. Forman, page 734 infra. When the New York legislature revised U.C.C. Article 8 in 1997 and 2001, it provided expressly that co-ops were securities within the meaning of that article. See N.Y.U.C.C. §§ 8-201(e), 8-110(c), 8-204(3) (McKinney's 2006).

4. Note, Legal Characterization of the Individual's Interest in a Cooperative Apartment: Realty or Personalty?, 73 Colum. L. Rev. 250-288 (1973), mentions still other problem areas where the real versus personal classification may make a difference. These include:

a. The taxability of the transfer; for example, the New York sales tax applies to the retail sale of "tangible personal property";

b. The spousal co-ownership of the cooperative interest; for example, New York common law permitted the creation of a tenancy by the entirety in real property only; Cf. Stewart v. Stewart, 118 A.D.2d 455, 499 N.Y.S.2d 945 (1986). It was only in 1996 that a statute enabled the creation of tenancy by the entirety interests in a cooperative apartment. N.Y. Est. Powers & Trusts Law § 6-2.1 and § 6-2.2 (McKinney's 2006).

c. Estate administration; for example, should a cooperative interest be classified as real estate or stock when interpreting the provisions of a will? Cf. Matter of Turner, 36 Misc. 2d 684, 233 N.Y.S.2d 108 (Sup. Ct. 1962) (bequest of real property does not include shares in cooperative apartment); Matter of Carmer, 71 N.Y.2d 781, 525 N.E.2d 734 (1988) (residuary legatee awarded proceeds from the sale of shares in cooperative apartment despite clause leaving all shares of common or preferred stock to specific legatee).

5. Reversing the trial court, which had concluded that shares to a cooperative apartment, being personal property, could not be partitioned, the Appellate Division ordered partition, and wrote as follows:

> Moreover, in reflecting on the expectations that co-owners of a cooperative apartment have with respect to their property interest and the personal conflicts which trigger an action for partition, common sense tells us that the differences arising between co-owners that would compel one owner to seek to alienate his property interest could have little, if anything, to do with their ownership of stock. Those differences will, in all likelihood, involve conflicts concerning such issues as use and occupancy of the apartment, disagreements as to each owner's respective financial obligations regarding the apartment, or disagreements as to entitlement to income tax deductions for payment of real property taxes or mortgage interest. Simply put, judicial intervention is sought because there has been a breakdown in the relationship between the co-owners impinging on their ability to enjoy peacefully their occupancy rights to the apartment, making the focus of the action for partition, quite naturally, the apartment, not the stock. [Chiang v. Chang, 137 A.D.2d 371, 372, 529 N.Y.S.2d 294, 295 (1988).]

6. As the purchaser of the shares in a cooperative apartment, what assurances would you seek that the seller has "good title"? See Matthew J. Leeds, Condominium and Cooperative Apartment Title Insurance Policies *in* Title Insurance 2006: Mastering Critical Issues Facing Buyers, Sellers & Lenders, Practising Law Institute Order No. 8646 (2006).

7. The Model Real Estate Cooperative Act contains the following provision:

> Unless the declaration provides that the cooperative interests are real estate for all purposes, the cooperative interests are personal property. [The cooperative interests are subject to the provisions of (insert reference to State Homestead Exemptions), even if they are personal property.]

In explaining this choice, the commissioners comment:

> 1. The classification of the cooperative interests as real property or as personal property is significant for purposes of such matters as tenure, sales, recordation, transfer taxes, property taxes, estate and inheritance taxes, testate and intestate succession, mortgage lending, perfection, priority and enforcement of liens, and rights of redemption.
>
> 2. The section deals with an important theoretical and practical issue which pervades the cooperative field: whether a tenant-stockholder holds an interest in real or in personal property. The section resolves that question by permitting the declarant [sponsor] to decide that issue for each cooperative on a project-by-project basis. By so doing, the section seeks to avoid changing traditional practice in the various states.

The editors of this casebook have seen little evidence that courts decide the classification question on a "project-by-project" basis, rather than as a general rule, as in the *Shor* decision. Nor have courts adopted a single rule — i.e., realty or personalty, instead of a rule tailored to the issue at hand.

Would it not be preferable for a legislature to indicate, as to each of the matters listed in the above comment, whether the cooperative interest is to be treated as personalty or realty, as New York has sometimes done?

2. *Liability in Tort*

White v. Cox

17 Cal. App. 3d 826, 95 Cal. Rptr. 259 (1971)

FLEMING, Associate Justice. Plaintiff White owns a condominium in the Merrywood condominium project and is a member of Merrywood Apartments, a non-profit unincorporated association which maintains the common areas of Merrywood. In his complaint against Merrywood Apartments for damages for personal injuries White avers he tripped and fell over a water sprinkler negligently maintained by Merrywood Apartments in the common area of Merrywood. The trial court sustained Merrywood's demurrer without leave to amend and entered judgment of dismissal. White appeals.

The question here is whether a member of an unincorporated association of condominium owners may bring an action against the association for damages caused by negligent maintenance of the common areas in the condominium project. In contesting the propriety of such an action defendant association argues that because it is a joint enterprise each member is both principal and agent for every other member, and consequently the negligence of each member must be imputed to every other member. Hence, its argument goes, a member may not maintain an action for negligence against the association because the member himself shares responsibility as a principal for the negligence of which he complains. (6 Am. Jur. 2d, Associations and Clubs, § 31.) Since 1962 the trend of case law has flowed toward full recognition of the unincorporated association as a separate legal entity. A member of an unincorporated association does not incur liability for acts of the association or acts of its members which he did not authorize or perform. (Orser v. George, 252 Cal. App. 2d 660, 670–671, 60 Cal. Rptr. 708.) A partner in a business partnership has been allowed to maintain an action against the partnership for the loss of his truck as a result of partnership negligence. (Smith v. Hensley (Ky.), 354 S.W.2d 744, 98 A.L.R.2d 340.) In the latter case the court declared that the doctrine of imputed negligence, which would normally bar a partner's recovery against the partnership, was an artificial rule of law which should yield to reason and practical considerations; since the partnership would have been liable for damages to the property of a stranger, no just reason existed for denying recovery for damages to the property of a partner. In affirming a judgment for plaintiff the court said: ". . . under a realistic approach, seeking to achieve substantial justice, the plaintiff should be held entitled to maintain the action."

In view of these developments over the past decade we conclude that unincorporated associations are now entitled to general recognition as separate legal entities and that as a consequence a member of an unincorporated association may maintain a tort action against his association.

Does this general rule of tort liability of an unincorporated association to its members apply in the specific instance of a condominium? A brief review of the statutory provisions which sanction and regulate the condominium form of ownership will clarify the nature of what we are dealing with. A condominium is an estate in real property consisting of an undivided interest in common in a portion of a parcel of real property together with a separate interest in another portion of the same parcel. (Civ. Code, § 783.) A project is the entire parcel of property, a unit is the separate interest, and the common areas are the entire project except for the units. (Civ. Code, § 1350.) Transfer of a unit, unless otherwise provided, is presumed to transfer the entire condominium. (Civ. Code, § 1352.) Ownership is usually limited to the interior surfaces of the unit, a cotenancy in the common areas, and nonexclusive easements for ingress, egress, and support. (Civ. Code, § 1353.) Typically, a condominium consists of an apartment house in which the units consist of individual apartments and the common areas consist of the remainder of the building and the grounds. Individual owners maintain their own apartments, and an association of apartment owners maintains the common areas. The association obtains funds for the care of the common areas by charging dues and levying assessments on each apartment owner.

The original project owner must record a condominium plan (Civ. Code, § 1351), and restrictions in the plan become enforceable as equitable servitudes (Civ. Code, § 1355). The plan may provide for management of the project by the condominium owners, by a board of governors elected by the owners, or by an elected or appointed agent. Management may acquire property, enforce restrictions, maintain the common areas, insure the owners, and make reasonable assessments. (Civ. Code, §§ 1355, 1358.) Only under exceptional circumstances may the condominium project be partitioned. (Civ. Code, § 1354; Code Civ. Proc., § 752b.) Zoning ordinances must be construed to treat condominiums in like manner as similar structures, lots, or parcels. (Civ. Code, § 1370.) Condominium projects with five or more condominiums are subject to rules regulating subdivided lands and subdivisions. (Bus. & Prof. Code, §§ 11004.5, 11535.1.) Individual condominiums are separately assessed and taxed. (Rev. & Tax. Code, § 2188.3.) Savings and loan associations may lend money on the security of condominium real property. (Fin. Code, § 7153.1.)

California's condominium legislation parallels that of other jurisdictions (see Law of Condominium, Ferrer & Stecher (1957)), and a review of this legislation brings out the two different aspects of the typical condominium scheme. (1) Operations. These are normally conducted by a management association created to run the common affairs of the condominium owners. The association functions in a manner comparable to other unincorporated associations in that it is controlled by a governing body, acts through designated agents, and functions under the authority of bylaws, etc. (the plan). In this aspect of the condominium scheme the management association of condominium owners functions as a distinct and separate personality from the owners themselves. (2) Ownership. In its system of tenure for real property the condominium draws elements both from tenancy in common and from separate ownership. Tenancy in common has also been brought into the structure of the management association, for under Civil Code section 1358 the management association holds personal property in common for the benefit of the condominium owners. In a formal sense, therefore, the condominium owners are tenants in common of the common areas and the personal property held by the management association, and they are owners in fee of separate units, which are not separate in fact. It is apparent that in its legal structure the condominium first combines elements from several concepts — unincorporated association, separate property, and tenancy in common — and then seeks to delineate separate privileges and responsibilities on the one hand from common privileges and responsibilities on the other. At this juncture we . . . pose two questions. Does the condominium association possess a separate existence from its members? Do the members retain direct control over the operations of the association?

Our answer to the first question derives from the nature of the condominium and its employment of the concept of separateness. Were separateness not clearly embodied within the condominium project the unit owners would become tenants in common of an estate in real property and remain exposed to all the consequences which flow from such a status. We think the concept of separateness in the condominium project carries over to any management body or association formed to handle the common affairs of the project, and that both the condominium project and the condominium association must be considered separate legal entities from its unit owners and association members.

For answer to our second question we turn to the statutory scheme, whence it clearly appears that in ordinary course a unit owner does not directly control the activities of the management body set up to handle the common affairs of the condominium project. To illustrate from the facts at bench: White owns his individual unit and a one-sixtieth interest in the common areas of Merrywood. An administrator controls the common affairs of Merrywood and maintains the common area where White tripped over the sprinkler. The administrator is appointed by and responsible to a board of governors. The board of governors is elected by the unit owners in an election in which each owner has one vote, owners vote by proxy, and cumulative voting is allowed. White is not a member of the board of governors. The Merrywood condominium plan succinctly warns, "In case management is not to your satisfaction, you may have no recourse." . . . [We] would be sacrificing reality to theoretical formalism to rule that White had any effective control over the operation of the common areas of Merrywood, for in fact he had no more control over operations than he would have had as a stockholder in a corporation which owned and operated the project.

. . . We concluded, therefore, that a condominium possesses sufficient aspects of an unincorporated association to make it liable in tort to its members. The condominium and the condominium association may be sued in the condominium name under authority of section 388 of the Code of Civil Procedure. The condominium and the condominium association may be served in the statutory manner provided for service on an unincorporated association (Corp. Code, § 24003–24007), and individual unit owners need not be named or served as parties in a negligence action against the condominium and the condominium association.[3]

We conclude (1) the condominium association may be sued for negligence in its common name, (2) by a member of the association, (3) who may obtain a judgment against the condominium and the condominium association.

The judgment of dismissal is reversed.

Compton, J., concurs.

ROTH, Presiding justice (concurring).

I concur.

I agree that a member of an unincorporated association of condominium owners may sue the association in tort. (Code Civ. Proc., § 388.) However, the majority opinion fails to define or distinguish the extent to which individual unit owners in a condominium project may become liable to another unit owner or to a third person for tortious conduct arising in the common areas of the condominium project.

---

3. We express no opinion on what property execution may be levied to satisfy a judgment against the condominium and the condominium association. With reference to liens for labor, services, or materials, the last sentence of Civil Code section 1357 reads:

> The owner of any condominium may remove his condominium from a lien against two or more condominiums or any part thereof by payment to the holder of the lien of the fraction of the total sum secured by such lien which is attributable to his condominium.

It could be implied from the sense of the section that a condominium owner may satisfy his portion of any liability arising out of the operation of the condominium project by the payment of his proportionate share of the liability. Such a conclusion would conform to what has been written on the subject by text writers (Rohan and Reskin, Condominium Law and Practice (1970), Chapter 10A, and 4 Powell on Real Property, section 633.25), and parallels what has been achieved by statute in other states. Alaska, Massachusetts, and Washington provide that a cause of action in tort relating to the common areas may be maintained only against the association of apartment owners. A judgment lien becomes a common expense and is removed from an individual condominium upon payment by the individual owner of his proportionate share. (Alaska Stat., Title 34, § 34.07.260; Annot. Laws of Massachusetts, Chap. 183A, § 13; Rev. Code of Washington Annot., § 64.32.240.) District of Columbia, Idaho, and Maryland provide more generally that any judgment lien against two or more condominium owners may be removed from an individual condominium upon payment by the condominium owner of his proportionate share. (Dist. of Columbia Code Encyclopedia, § 5-924(c); Idaho Code, § 55-1515; Annot. Code of Maryland, Art. 21, § 138.) In contrast is Mississippi, whose code declares that individual owners have no personal liability for damages caused by the governing body or connected with use of the common area. (Miss. Code Annot., § 896-15.)

In footnote 3, the majority declines to hold on "what property execution may be levied to satisfy a judgment against the condominium and the condominium association."

When as at bench a judgment of dismissal entered after a demurrer without leave to amend has been sustained the question of a levy of execution may not be properly before this court. However, the question of the identities of the parties liable is not settled in this case nor is the basis of the liability of parties other than the association, to wit, Merrywood Apartments.

The ownership of the common areas in a condominium project is vested in the individual unit owners as tenants in common. (Civ. Code, § 1353(b).) Thus, even though, as the majority holds, the association may be sued in its separate name, it is apparent that the legal owners of the common areas are not immunized from liability by virtue of the mere existence of the association.

A comparative study of California condominium legislation with that in other states shows that the question of the individual unit owner's tort liability in cases arising in the common areas has not been regulated by statute. The majority's suggestion that section 1357 of the Civil Code, in providing for the aliquot satisfaction of liens for labor, services, or materials, also provides for the distribution of tort liability among the owners is too great a strain on the expressly limited wording of that code section. This suggestion has been questioned by at least one commentator (Comment, 77 Harv. L. Rev. 777, 780, fn. 24) and it does not square with the fact that California has followed the lead of most states and has failed to provide adequate regulation or protection of the individual owner's interests in the case of torts arising from the common areas. (See Rohan, Perfecting the Condominium as a Housing Tool: Innovations in Tort Liability and Insurance (1967), 32 Law and Contemporary Problems 305, 308; Kerr, Condominium — Statutory Implementation (1963), 28 St. John's L. Rev. 1, 42-43; Comment, supra, 77 Harv. L. Rev. 777, 780.) The absence of an express statutory scheme for the re-distribution of tort liability, such as those found in the Alaska, Massachusetts and Washington legislation, is ample warning that the problem of protecting the individual unit owner from tort liability which, it should be noted, may exceed the value of his unit[2] (whether it be to another unit owner or to a third person) is yet an open question in California.

One practical answer is, of course, insurance taken out by the association to cover liability in respect of the common areas. (See Kerr, supra, at 43.)[3] It might then be argued depending on the terms of the written declaration between unit owners that, at least as between suing and defendant unit owners, the maximum amount of liability of defendant unit owners has been contractually limited to the maximum of the insurance taken out by the association.

At bench we have the declaration upon which the project at bench is grounded before us only insofar as its terms are reflected by the permit of the Commissioner of Corporations.

2. Thus, in California, the co-owners may have to respond for injuries arising out of the common areas in terms of the personal tort liability of tenants in common, which according to the common law and our statutory law results in joint and several liability. (Code Civ. Proc., § 384; 86 C.J.S. Tenancy in Common § 143.)

3. In California, the governing body of a condominium project may obtain insurance on behalf of, and for the benefit of condominium owners. (Civ. Code, § 1355(b)(2).)

The permit, after setting forth the plan of management and powers of the Board of Governors, sets forth in pertinent part that the Board of Governors shall have the power to:

Contract and/or pay for fire, casualty, liability and other insurance and bonding of its members, maintenance, gardening, utilities, materials, supplies, services and personnel necessary for the operation of the project, taxes and assessments which may become a lien on the entire project or the common area, and reconstruction of portions of the project which are to be rebuilt after damage or destruction.

The above excerpt or summary (in the Permit) from the declaration is substantially similar to the powers set forth in section 1355, subdivision (b)(2) of the Civil Code, which empowers the Board of Governors to obtain ". . . fire, casualty, liability, workmen's compensation and other insurance insuring condominium owners, and for bonding of the members of any management body."

It occurs to me, therefore, on the limited record before this court that each unit holder of the project has by contract delegated to the Board of Governors which operates the project the power and responsibility to obtain adequate liability insurance for the project to cover claims of third persons and also adequate insurance to cover negligence actions of unit owners against the association and actions which any unit owner might bring against other unit owners because of the negligence of the association.

It seems to me therefore that any failure by management to obtain adequate insurance or any insurance leaves a unit holder injured by negligence of management (as distinguished from independent negligence of a fellow unit owner) with the right to proceed against the association to the extent of its insurance if any and with no right to proceed against other unit owners. A suit by one other than a unit owner is a question not raised by the litigation at bench, and cannot be similarly circumscribed. Generally, tenants in common may be joined as defendants and their liability is joint and several (Code Civ. Proc., § 384), and the apportionment of liability as between unit owners is, of course, a difficult and vexing question. (See generally, 86 C.J.S. Tenancy in Common § 143.)

NOTES AND QUESTIONS

1. Most, but not all, courts have agreed with White v. Cox. See, e.g., Strayer v. Covington Creek Condominium Assn., 678 N.E.2d 1286 (Ind. App. 1997) (unit owner cannot sue unincorporated condominium association of which he is a member).

2. What standard of care should the law impose on the governing association vis-à-vis the unit owners, nonmember residents (e.g., short-term lessees), and nonresident invitees? Are there any reasons to regard the association's standard of care any differently from that of a residential landlord?

3. The principal case deals with association liability for common law negligence, but notice that the concurrence raises the potential liability of the association's *management* for negligence. How, if at all, does the liability of the association members (unit owners) differ from that of the assocation boardmembers? See Note, The Proper Extent of Liability a Condominium Unit Owner Should Have for Injuries Caused by a Limited Common Element, 19 St. John's J. Legal Comment. 637 (2005).

3. Enforcement Procedures

a. Suit for Possession Against Non-Performing Owner

1915 16th St. Co-Operative Assn. v. Pinkett

84 A.2d 58 (D.C. 1951)

CAYTON, Chief Judge. A co-operatively owned apartment house sued one of its member-tenants for possession of an apartment, charging that he owed three months rent under his lease. He denied the charge and the trial court ruled in his favor. Plaintiff brings this appeal. No brief has been filed by counsel for appellee, hence we do not know what position he takes on this appeal. But the issues are revealed in the pleadings, evidence, and documentary exhibits, and in a memorandum of the trial judge on which the decision was based. Defendant John R. Pinkett, Jr., on July 17, 1950, entered into a "contract to purchase co-operative apartment" from plaintiff at an agreed price of $7950. Under the terms of the contract he made an initial deposit of $90 and agreed to pay $410 more to make up a $500 settlement figure. The agreement provided for payments of $90 per month, made up as follows: $54.50 on account of the deferred purchase money, $25 for maintenance, and $10.50 on a note of $386.50 which Pinkett gave to complete the settlement. The purchase agreement recited that at settlement Pinkett was to receive a certificate of ownership and a "proprietary lease" under which he was to have the right to "own and use" the apartment "as long as he remains a member of the association and abides by all the terms of this contract." On the same day a "proprietary lease" was signed by the parties running in favor of Pinkett for 99 years. Among the provisions of the lease was one authorizing the termination thereof "in case the Lessee shall default in the payment of any obligation required hereunder, or of any installment thereof." The same article of the lease also provided that upon termination the lessor would have the right "to reenter the demised premises and to remove all persons and personal property therefrom, either by summary dispossess proceedings or by any suitable action or proceeding at law . . . and to repossess the demised premises in its former state as if this lease had not been made."

Mr. Pinkett took possession and made two monthly payments of $90 each for July and August 1950. He has paid no more but has continued in default and in possession of the apartment.

In December 1950, plaintiff-owner brought this suit for possession in the Municipal Court alleging that Pinkett was in possession under a leasehold and was in default of payment of rent for the three months from September 17 to December 16. In his answer defendant denied that he was a tenant of plaintiff and denied being in default. The trial court in a written memorandum found that there was no intent on the part of plaintiff and defendant to create the relationship of landlord and tenant, that the contract was one for the purchase of an apartment and that the monthly sums payable by defendant were not rent but were payments on account of the purchase. The judge also ruled that there was in form a landlord-tenant relationship but that in substance defendant was the owner of the apartment with the "exclusive right to personal, perpetual use thereof as a dwelling," and that as between defendant and the other occupants in the building the relationship was in effect a partnership for their mutual benefit.

In testing the correctness of these rulings we must look to the transaction as a whole, to the writings between the parties, to the circumstances under which they were made, and to the matters with which they deal, and thereby determine the intent of the parties and the status they created.

The evidence discloses that defendant's right to possession was based initially on his purchase agreement, but more directly on his "proprietary lease." Undoubtedly the purchase agreement vested in him some of the attributes of an owner or landlord. This has been recognized in this jurisdiction, the courts holding that a member of a co-operative apartment house corporation may, when he desires possession for his own use, sue as a "landlord" under the local Rent Act and maintain a possessory action against a tenant who refused to yield an apartment to him. Abbot v. Bralove, D.D.C., 81 F. Supp. 532, affirmed 85 U.S. App. D.C. 189, 176 F.2d 64; Glennon v. Butler, D.C. Mun. App., 66 A.2d 519; Hicks v. Bigelow, D.C. Mun. App., 55 A.2d 924. But none of these cases held that the "landlord" status of such a co-operative member was his only legal status. On the contrary, they all were confined to a situation where a co-operative member was suing a tenant in possession.

What then is the status of a purchaser-lessee like this one who has defaulted in his payments to his co-operative corporation? We think the answer is clearly to be found in the lease between them. There it is provided, as we have already seen, that the lessee's right to possession is lost if he defaults in the payment of any installments due and that the lessor is expressly given the right of reentry. As applied to the facts of this case, we can think of no practical difference between this and conventional lease agreements. What it amounts to is that the lessee is given the right of occupancy so long as he does not default in his monthly payments, but that when default occurs the co-operative corporation has the right to terminate the lease. This right of termination has been recognized even in New York where some courts have treated such a relationship as in effect a partnership. Tompkins v. Hale, 172 Misc. 1071, 15 N.Y.S.2d 854, affirmed 259 App. Div. 860, 20 N.Y.S.2d 398.

We have concluded that the plaintiff had a right to maintain the suit, that defendant's right to possession derived from the lease, and that by his default under the lease such right has been lost. Accordingly, the Municipal Court is instructed to enter judgment for plaintiff for possession. . . .

Defendant may still wish to redeem his lost rights by bringing his payments up-to-date. If so we assume that the trial court would entertain an appropriate motion filed by him, accompanied by a tender of all payments in arrears together with interest and costs. See Trans-Lux Radio City Corp. v. Service Parking Corp., D.C. Mun. App., 54 A.2d 144.

Reversed.

ON MOTION FOR REHEARING

Before Cayton, Chief Judge, and Hood and Quinn, Associate Judges.

CAYTON, Chief Judge. Appellee filed a motion for rehearing and pursuant to our order oral argument has been had thereon. . . .

We must adhere to our previous ruling that there was a default under the lease and that by reason of such default the co-operative had a right to sue for and recover possession. . . .

HOOD, Associate Judge (dissenting). I joined in the original opinion in this case, but on further study I have concluded that such opinion was erroneous. I am now convinced that the Landlord and Tenant Branch of the Municipal Court had no jurisdiction to render a judgment for possession of the apartment.

The statute, Code 1940, 11-735, provides summary remedy for possession of real estate in a definitely limited class of cases. Aside from cases arising after sale under deed of trust or foreclosure of mortgage and cases of forcible entry and detainer (and obviously the present case falls in neither of those classes), the trial court may entertain suits for possession of real estate only in those cases where the conventional relation of landlord and tenant exists.

Whatever may be the exact relation between a corporation holding title to a cooperative apartment house and one to whom it has sold one of the apartment units, the relationship is far more than the conventional relationship of landlord and tenant. One who holds stock or other certificate entitling him to use of a cooperative apartment is generally said to have "purchased" the apartment, Wardman Const. Co. v. Flynn, 60 App. D.C. 357, 54 F.2d 831, and in effect is regarded as the owner of it. 542 Morris Park Ave. Corporation v. Wilkins, 120 Misc. 48, 197 N.Y.S. 625. It has been said that although the corporation holds legal title the entire equitable estate is distributed proportionately among the owners of the apartments and that ownership of an apartment constitutes an interest in real property. In re Pitts' Estate, 218 Cal. 184, 22 P.2d 694. This court has said that the purchaser of a cooperative apartment "is more than a mere tenant or lessee" and "has most of the attributes of an owner." Hicks v. Bigelow, D.C. Mun. App., 55 A.2d 924.

The parties recognized this in their dealings. Appellee contracted to purchase a "Certificate of Ownership" which would "entitle him to the perpetual use and occupancy" of the apartment. Appellant agreed "to cause to be conveyed to the purchaser a right of perpetual use as evidenced by a Proprietary Lease." The contract, the certificate of ownership and the proprietary lease are not severable. They must be considered together. Appellant would have the court disregard everything but the lease and consider the case as nothing more than an ordinary landlord and tenant proceeding. The complaint alleges appellee has defaulted in payment of rent, but in fact appellee agreed to pay no rent.

The transaction is not one of leasing property in exchange for payment of rent but in essence is a purchase or capital investment.

In my opinion the corporation may not bring an action in the landlord and tenant court to oust the owner from possession, treating him as a mere tenant and ignoring his rights under his contract of purchase and certificate of ownership. His right to possession was what he purchased and if such right is to be terminated then all the rights and obligations between the parties ought to be adjusted. This proceeding would leave the rights and obligations under the contract of purchase unsettled and unadjusted. . . .

In short, I think that before the corporation can take back that which it sold, all rights and obligations between the parties under the contract of purchase and the proprietary lease must be settled and that this cannot be done in a summary landlord and tenant proceeding.

NOTES AND QUESTIONS

1. Accord: Jordan v. Placer Holding Co., 213 Ga. App. 218, 444 S.E.2d 112 (Ga. App.,1994); Earl W. Jimerson Housing Co., Inc. v. Butler, 102 Misc. 2d 423, 425 N.Y. S.2d 924 (App. Term 1979); Model Real Estate Cooperative Act 3-115(a)(1981).

Contra: Plaza Road Co-op., Inc. v. Finn, 201 N.J. Super. 174, 492 A.2d 1072 (App. Div. 1985) (relationship between association and a cooperator-shareholder not that of landlord-tenant for the purpose of a summary dispossession action). The New York court in 333-335 East 209th St. HDFC v. McDonnell, 134 Misc. 2d 1022, 513 N.Y.S.2d 935 (Civ. Ct. 1987), refused to permit the eviction of the owner of a cooperative apartment for violating the house rule that barred dogs absent a clear statement in the proprietary lease that this was a substantial obligation of the tenancy.

2. *Compare a condominium or homes association.* A unit owner fails to pay her assessment on the common areas or breaks the project's rules. What is "management's" remedy?

3. The condominium statutes in Alaska and Washington authorize the association, upon obtaining the approval of a majority of unit owners and upon serving a 10-day's notice, to sever all utility service to a delinquent owner. Alaska Stat. 34.07.220 (2005); Wash. Rev. Code Ann. 64.32.200 (2006). Discuss the pros and cons of this approach to nonpayment of assessments.

4. The cooperative tenant loses his lease for nonpayment of rent. Does he also lose his "equity" in the apartment? Suppose that the corporation can resell the apartment for $100,000. To whom does the $100,000 belong? What analogies apply: default by installment land vendee; by mortgagor on power of sale mortgage; by lessee who has installed costly improvements?

5. A related issue, which informs whether there has been a default, is whether statutes protective of "tenants" extend to the owners of cooperative apartments. Examples are

a. Warranty of habitability: McMunn v. Steppingstone Mgmt. Corp., 131 Misc. 2d 340, 500 N.Y.S.2d 219 (Civ. Ct. 1986) (warranty applies to proprietary lessees, although it may be interpreted differently than in rental building); see also Christopher S. Brennan, Note, The Next Step in the Evolution of the Implied Warranty of Habitability: Applying the Warranty to Condominiums, 67 Fordham L. Rev. 3041 (1999);

b. Rights regarding household pets: Linden Hill No. 1 Cooperative Corp. v. Kleiner, 124 Misc. 2d 1001, 478 N.Y.S.2d 519 (Civ. Ct. 1984) (proprietary lessees enjoy similar rights);

c. Occupancy restrictions: Southridge Cooperative Section No. 3, Inc. v. Menendez, 141 Misc. 2d 823, 535 N.Y.S.2d 299 (Civ. Ct. 1988) (state law barring landlord from restricting occupancy of residential premises to tenant and his immediate family applies to proprietary lessees).

b. Enforcement of the Association Lien for Unpaid Charges

American Holidays, Inc. v. Foxtail Owners Association

821 P.2d 577 (Wyo. 1991)

CARDINE, Justice.

Appellant, mortgagee of a shared interest in a time-share condominium, challenges the trial court's decree of foreclosure which subordinated its mortgage to appellee's lien for unpaid condominium assessments. We affirm the decision of the trial court.

Appellant states the issue to be resolved as follows: "Did the court err in holding as a matter of law that the homeowner's assessment lien had priority over a previously filed mortgage?"

Condoshare Jackson Limited Partnership recorded a Declaration of Condominium for the Foxtail Condominium Project on January 6, 1981. This Declaration created appellee, the Foxtail Owners Association (Association). The Association was given numerous responsibilities for maintenance and upkeep of the Foxtail condominium units and common areas. It was empowered to levy assessments against the shared interest of each of the Foxtail condominium owners in order to pay its expenses. These assessments were to be secured by a lien on each shared interest and would bear interest and court costs if not paid.

On September 16, 1984, Edward L. Meier and Clara Zo Meier (Meiers) executed a note and mortgage deed secured by a shared interest in one of the Foxtail units in favor of The Time Store, Inc., a Colorado corporation (Time Store). This mortgage deed was recorded on March 8, 1985. The mortgage deed contained a legal description which made the shared interest "subject to the terms, covenants, conditions, and restrictions contained in the Declaration." The Time Store's mortgage interest passed by assignment and is now held by appellant American Holidays, Inc. (American Holidays).

The Meiers defaulted on the mortgage with American Holidays on December 1, 1985. They also failed to pay Association dues as required by the Declaration. On October 10, 1989, the Association filed two Notices of Lien for unpaid dues with the Teton County Clerk. Then, on January 30, 1990, the Association filed this complaint for foreclosure, which named the Meiers and American Holidays as defendants.

The trial court entered a Summary Judgment and Decree of Foreclosure on January 3, 1991. Both the Association and American Holidays were given judgment against the Meiers. The court further found that American Holidays' interest was subordinate to the Association's lien for unpaid assessments, interests, costs and attorney fees, "even if the mortgage [had been] filed [for record] prior to the time the lien mature[d]." The decree of foreclosure provided that upon foreclosure sale the proceeds would be applied: First, to the costs of the sale; second, toward satisfaction of the Association's assessment lien; and third, toward satisfaction of the mortgage held by American Holidays. Any surplus would be paid to the Meiers. American Holidays filed a timely notice of appeal from this decision. . . .

Wyoming Statute 34-1-121 (a) (July 1990 Repl.) provides in part that

> [e]ach and every deed, mortgage, instrument or conveyance touching any interest in lands, made and recorded, according to the provisions of this chapter, shall be notice to and take precedence of any subsequent purchaser or purchasers from the time of delivery of any instrument at the office of the register of deeds (county clerk), for record.

Appellant's mortgage was recorded prior to the recordation of appellee's lien statement, but subsequent to the recordation of the Declaration of Condominium for the Foxtail Condominium Project. The question to be resolved is that of appellant's priority status relative to that of appellee, considering the recording dates and the subordination clauses contained in the Declaration and in the Meiers' mortgage.

It is undisputed that American Holidays' interest is subject to the provisions of the Declaration, which by its terms are made covenants running with the land binding on "any person acquiring, leasing, or owning an interest in the real property and improvements comprising the Project, and to their respective administrators, personal representatives, heirs, successors, and assigns." The mortgage, whose mortgagee interest was assigned to American Holidays, also describes the property as being subject to the terms of the Declaration.

Our review of authority connected with this issue shows no previous Wyoming cases on point. Cases from other jurisdictions show that the issue of priority has been resolved, generally, in either one of two ways. First, many jurisdictions have applied a statutory scheme governing condominium assessment priority. See e.g., Towne Realty, Inc. v. Edwards, 156 Wis. 2d 344, 456 N.W.2d 651 (1990); First Federal Savings Bank v. Eaglewood Court Condominium Ass'n, Inc., 186 Ga. App. 605, 367 S.E.2d 876 (1988); Brask v. Bank of St. Louis, 533 S.W.2d 223 (Mo. Ct. App. 1975). Wyoming has no such statute, and so we do not find these cases to be helpful.

Second, some jurisdictions have held, in the context of homestead exemption priority, that an association's lien for assessments is a contractual lien which relates back to the time of filing the declaration. See Bessemer v. Gersten, 381 So. 2d 1344 (Fla. 1980); Accord, Inwood North Homeowners' Ass'n, Inc. v. Harris, 736 S.W.2d 632, 636 n. I (Tx. 1987); In re Lincoln, 30 B.R. 905 (Bankr. D. Colo. 1983). For reasons stated below, we think that the *Bessemer* rule properly applies to this case, and that the lien for assessments which attached when the mortgagee's interest was created relates back to the time of filing of the Declaration.

The *Bessemer* case gives no rationale for its holding that an association's lien relates back to the time of recording. We follow it in this case because we believe it reflects the intent of the original covenantor as revealed in the terms of the Declaration.

We consider first the language of the Declaration itself to determine its effect on the interests of the parties. In interpreting the covenants contained in a condominium declaration, we will follow our general rule that we seek to discern the intent of the parties, and especially that of the grantor.

. . . The Declaration contained a provision, quoted in part above, subjecting the property to its terms and creating a covenant running with the land:

2.01 Submission to Condominium Ownership. . . .

All of said property and all Common Facilities and Unit Furnishings are and shall be subject to the covenants, conditions, restrictions, uses, limitations, and obligations set forth herein, each and all of which are declared and agreed to be for the benefit of said Project and each Condominium therein and in furtherance of a plan for improvement of said property and division thereof into Condominiums. Each and all of the provisions hereof shall be deemed to run with the land and shall be a burden and a benefit to the Declarant, and to any person acquiring, leasing, or owning an interest in the real property and improvements comprising the Project, and to their respective administrators, personal representatives, heirs, successors, and assigns.

Any subsequent mortgage or encumbrance was made subject to the terms of the Declaration:

4.05 Separate Mortgages. . . .

Any mortgage or other encumbrance of any Shared Interest shall be subject [to] and subordinate to each and all of the provisions of this Declaration and, in the event of foreclosure, the provisions of this Declaration shall be binding upon any Shared Owner whose title is derived through foreclosure by private power of sale, judicial foreclosure, or otherwise.

The Declaration provided for assessments to be made by and paid to the Association:

9.01 Agreement to Pay Assessments. . . .

[E]ach Shared Owner by the acceptance of instruments of conveyance and transfer of his Shared Interest, whether or not it be so expressed in said instruments, shall be deemed to covenant and agree with each other and with the Association to pay to the Association all assessments made by the Association for the purposes provided in this Declaration.

These assessments would bear interest at the rate of one percent per month. Finally, the Declaration provided that such assessments would constitute a lien on the property:

9.04 Lien for Assessments

All sums assessed to the Shared Owner of any Shared Interest in a Condominium within the Project pursuant to the provisions of this Article IX, together with interest thereon as provided herein, shall be secured by a lien on such Shared Interest in favor of the Association. To evidence a lien for sums assessed pursuant to this Article IX, the Association may prepare a written notice of lien setting forth the amount of the assessment, the date due, the amount remaining unpaid, the name of the Shared Owner of the Shared Interest, and a description of the Shared Interest. Such a notice shall be signed and acknowledged by a duly authorized officer of the Association and may be recorded in the office of the County Clerk of Teton County, State of Wyoming. No notice of lien shall be recorded until there is a delinquency in payment of the assessment. Such lien may be enforced by judicial foreclosure by the Association in the same manner in which mortgages or trust deeds on real property may be foreclosed in the State of Wyoming. In any such foreclosure, the Shared Owner shall be required to pay the costs and expenses of such proceeding (including reasonable attorneys' fees) and such costs and expenses shall be secured by the lien being foreclosed.

The trial court found that this language was plain and unambiguous and that it subjected any interest of a mortgagee to the Association's lien for assessments, interest, costs and attorneys fees, even if the mortgage was recorded prior to the time that the lien matured. We agree that the Association's lien has priority because the Declaration subordinated all subsequent encumbrances to its provisions.

Section 4.05 of the Declaration has the effect of a subordination agreement, to which appellant became a party when it took assignment of the mortgage interest. A subordination agreement controls even over real property priorities established by law. Arundel Federal Savings & Loan Ass'n v. Lawrence, 65 Md. App. 158, 499 A.2d 1298, 1302 (1985). Thus, sellers of unimproved land routinely subordinate their prior purchase money mortgage to a mortgage lien for construction purposes in order that land may be improved. Cf. 2 G. Glenn, Glenn on Mortgages 352 (1943); G. Osborne, Handbook on the Law of Mortgages 212 at 387 (2nd ed. 1970). And prior condominium subscription agreements creating a vendee's lien are frequently made subject to a lien for a building loan mortgage. G. Nelson & D. Whitman, Real Estate Finance Law 13.3 at 947–49 (2nd ed. 1985).

The scope of the subordination is described in Section 4.05 of the Declaration. This section provides that any mortgage or other encumbrance is subject to and subordinate to "each and all" of the provisions of the Declaration. No exception is made for the Association assessment provisions of Article 9. Since these assessment provisions are to be enforced by the existence of a lien, the lien provision itself should also take priority.

Appellant notes that Section 9.04 provides for recordation of a written notice of lien once default occurs. It argues that the lien has the priority date of this recordation. However, this provision for recording written notice of lien is designed only to provide recorded notice once the payments are in default. It differs from the underlying lien created by the terms of the Declaration itself, which comes into being as soon as the owner of the shared interest takes his interest subject to the Declaration. See *Bessemer*, 381 So. 2d at 1348.

Furthermore, the only way to give effect to the subordination clause, which should control over the result achieved under a pure application of the recording statute, is to hold that the Association's lien relates back to the time the Declaration was recorded. That way, any subsequent encumbrance of the shared interest would have a later priority than the Association's lien for assessments, as implicitly provided for in the Declaration. Therefore, we hold that the priority date of the Association's lien relates back to the time that the Declaration was recorded and, as a covenant running with the land, binds the holders and assignees of a subsequent mortgagee interest.

Appellant cites a case which achieved a contrary result based on facts similar to those of this case. St. Paul Federal Bank for Savings v. Wesby, 149 Ill. App. 3d 1059, 103 Ill. Dec 390, 501 N.E.2d 707 (1986), *cert. denied* 114 Ill. 2d 557, 108 Ill. Dec. 425, 508 N.E.2d 736 (1987). We distinguish *Wesby* in that the declaration in that case expressly provided that the assessment did not become a lien until the unit owner failed to make payment. Also, the Declaration specifically provided that the lien for unpaid assessments was subordinate to the lien of a prior recorded first mortgage. Thus, we are not persuaded by the *Wesby* case.

Our decision affirming the trial court is correct as a matter of law. We note also that it is fair and reasonable and benefits both parties. The assessments are used by the Association for insurance, repairs, maintenance, and upkeep of the condominium unit. The benefit to the mortgage holder is that the condominium unit is maintained in good repair and condition and its value maintained. The Association benefits in that all units are kept in good repair and condition and total property values are enhanced.

Because American Holidays' mortgage interest was subordinate to the Declaration, including the provision for the Association's lien, the lien took priority over the mortgage when the Association foreclosed. Therefore, the trial court properly ordered that the proceeds of the foreclosure sale be apportioned to pay off the lien and expenses connected thereto prior to payment of the mortgage.

The order of the trial court is affirmed.

NOTES AND QUESTIONS

1. Section 3-116(b) of the Uniform Condominium Act provides that a first mortgage recorded before the date on which a condominium assessment becomes

delinquent has priority over the claim of the assessment, except with respect to those "common expenses assessments based on the periodic budget adopted by the association . . . which would have become due in the absence of acceleration during the six months immediately preceding institution of an action to enforce the [mortgage] lien."

Because a well-drafted mortgage on a condominium unit provides that the borrower's failure to pay condominium assessments becomes a mortgage default, mortgage holders (including junior mortgagees) can take steps to limit their vulnerability to the lien for assessments arrears; R. Silverman, Foreclosing on a Condominium Project, Real Estate Rev. (Summer 1991) 22, 25. What steps should the mortgagee take to be certain that the borrower's common charge payments are current?

2. In some states, such as New York, a condominium statute may give a first mortgage on the residential condominium unit priority over association liens, where the mortgage was recorded before the association filed its lien; cf. Crossland Savings Bank FSB v. Saffer, 153 Misc. 2d 287, 580 N.Y.S.2d 813 (Sup. Ct. 1992).

3. What are the arguments for and against giving the association lien retroactivity vis-à-vis the following kinds of liens against the unit? first mortgage? second mortgage? mechanics' lien? income tax lien? property tax lien?

4. Where the association lien gains retroactive priority, should the priority extend not only to unpaid common expenses but also to fines and individual charges? Cf. e.g., Elbadramany v. Oceans Seven Condominium Assn., 461 So. 2d 1001 (Fla. App. 1984) (fine for improperly parking a boat in the condo parking lot not a "common expense" and under Florida statute not subject to the association lien); Rothenberg v. Plymouth #5 Condominium Assn., 511 So. 2d 651 (Fla. App. 1987) (similarly, charge for bus service to areas outside the condominium property). What enforcement mechanism would the association have as to charges not covered by the common expense lien?

5. In a stock-cooperative, the common area charges determine the rental under the proprietary lease. Suppose that the owner of a cooperative apartment pledges his stock and lease as security for a co-op loan, and that the lender perfects its lien on March 1st; two months later, the owner fails to pay his May rental. What is the priority of the unpaid May "common charges" vis-à-vis the lien of the co-op loan?

6. Some unit owners have tried without avail to claim that the homestead exemption immunized their properties against foreclosure of the association lien for unpaid common charges; Whispering Pines West Condominium Assn., Inc. v. Treantos, 780 P.2d 26 (Colo. App. 1989); Johnson v. First Southern Properties, 687 S.W.2d 399 (Tex. App. 1985). Both courts held that the condominium lien took precedence over the homestead exemption, which did not accrue until after the unit owner acquired the homestead subject to the terms of the condominium declaration. This view is criticized in Comment, 38 Baylor L. Rev. 987 (1986).

7. Should an association be able to foreclose a lien for the relatively modest charges that often are due, or is this too drastic a remedy? If not, how else can the association enforce the owners' obligations to stay current on their charges? See Gemma Giantomasi, Note, A Balancing Act: The Foreclosure Power of Homeowners' Associations, 72 Fordham L. Rev. 2503 (2004).

4. Restraints on Alienation

Jones v. O'Connell

189 Conn. 648, 458 A.2d 355 (1983)

PETERS, Associate Justice.

This case concerns the right of owners of a cooperative apartment building to impose restraints on the right to alienate one of the cooperative apartments. The plaintiffs, Conrad Jones and Florence McNulty, who had entered into a contract of sale for a cooperative apartment, brought suit against the defendants, Walter F. O'Connell, Pauline F. O'Connell, Margaret Cavanaugh, Christopher H. Smith and Harbor House, Inc., to enjoin the defendants' disapproval of the contemplated sale. The plaintiffs also sought monetary damages from the individual defendants for their tortious interference with the plaintiffs' contract. After a trial to the court, judgment was rendered for the defendants and the plaintiffs have appealed.

The underlying facts are undisputed. In 1975, the defendant Walter F. O'Connell transferred property at 252-58 Main Street, Southport, to a newly formed Connecticut corporation, the defendant Harbor House, Inc., so that Harbor House might hold the property as a cooperative residential apartment house. The defendant Christopher H. Smith, an attorney, prepared the appropriate documentation, consisting of a memorandum of offering for the stock, proprietary leases for the individual apartments, and by-laws for the corporation. From the time of the first meeting of the corporation, the Harbor House directors have been the individually named defendants, Walter and Pauline O'Connell, Christopher Smith, and Margaret Cavanaugh.

In 1979, just before the present controversy arose, the leasehold interests in Harbor House, manifested by ownership of stock and assignments of proprietary leases, were distributed among the defendants and the plaintiffs as follows: The plaintiff Florence McNulty owned 11.2 percent of the stock and was the lessee of apartment 1A. The plaintiff Conrad Jones owned 25.5 percent of the stock and was the lessee of apartment 2. The defendant Margaret Cavanaugh owned 25.5 percent of the stock and was the lessee of apartment 3. The defendant Walter O'Connell owned 37.8 percent of the stock and was the lessee of apartments 1B, 1C and 4.

On November 5, 1979, the plaintiffs entered into a written contract for Florence McNulty to sell her stock in Harbor House and to assign her proprietary lease in apartment 1A to Conrad Jones. This contract of sale was expressly made "subject to the approval of the directors or shareholders of the Corporation as provided in the Lease or the corporate by-laws." Had the transfer to Jones been approved, he would have become the owner of 36.7 percent of the Harbor House stock and the lessee of two apartments, one underneath the other. Jones was interested in acquiring additional living space for his family because in 1979, one year after his acquisition of apartment 2, he had remarried and become the stepfather of two daughters, aged 9 and 13.

Any lessee's right to sell shares and to assign a proprietary lease in Harbor House is expressly made conditional upon the consent of the Harbor House board of directors, or of at least 65 percent of the corporation's outstanding shares, by virtue of separate and somewhat inconsistent provisions in the Harbor House documentation. Under the memorandum of offering, assignments are to be approved only for persons of suitable "character and financial responsibility." Under the proprietary lease, however, consent to assignments can be granted or withheld "for any reason or for no reason." The corporate by-laws are silent as to what may constitute an adequate basis for withholding consent to an assignment.

The plaintiffs were unable to procure the requisite consent for their contemplated transfer. First the board of directors and later the stockholders of Harbor House refused to approve their contract of sale. Subsequent to this disapproval, Walter O'Connell and Margaret Cavanaugh offered to purchase the stock and the lease of apartment 1A from Florence McNulty, an offer she refused because of her commitment to Conrad Jones. The present litigation then ensued.

In the trial court, after an exhaustive examination of the plaintiffs' claim, judgment was rendered for the defendants. The court found that the defendants had acted reasonably and in good faith, and that the plaintiffs had failed to prove their various claims of wrongful interference with their contract. Each of these conclusions is challenged on this appeal. We find no error.

The plaintiffs' principal claim of error asserts that the evidence presented at trial fails to support the trial court's conclusion and finding that the defendants acted reasonably in disapproving the transfer of the stock and the leasehold interest appurtenant to apartment 1A. Before we reach that issue, however, we must first determine the standard by which the propriety of the defendants' withholding of their consent is to be measured.

Although this court has not previously confronted the question of restraints on alienation of property interests in cooperative residential apartments, we have addressed the legality of such restraints on alienation in related contexts. On the one hand, in cases involving the construction of wills involving the devise of both real and personal property, we have noted that "[t]he law does not favor restraints on alienation and will not recognize them unless they are stated 'in unequivocal terms'; Williams v. Robinson, 16 Conn. 517, 523 [1844]"; Romme v. Ostheimer, 128 Conn. 31, 34, 20 A.2d 406 (1941); and that "[i]t is the policy of the law not to uphold restrictions upon the free and unrestricted alienation of property unless they serve a legal and useful purpose." Peiter v. Degenring, 136 Conn. 331, 336, 71 A.2d 87 (1949); Colonial Trust Co. v. Brown, 105 Conn. 261, 278–81, 135 A. 555 (1926). See generally Manning, The Development of Restraints on Alienation Since Gray, 48 Harv. L. Rev. 373, 401–406 (1935), and Schnebly, Restraints Upon the Alienation of Legal Interests, 44 Yale L.J. 961, 1186, 1380 (1935). On the other hand, in a case involving a lease provision requiring that a lessor consent in writing to the assignment of a commercial lease, we have cited with approval the majority rule that "the lessor may refuse consent and his reason is immaterial." Robinson v. Weitz, 171 Conn. 545, 549, 370 A.2d 1066 (1976), relying on Segre v. Ring, 103 N.H. 278, 279, 170 A.2d 265 (1961).

An assessment of how to apply these competing principles to restraints on the alienation of cooperative apartments must take account of the reality that cooperative ownership is in many ways *sui generis*, a legal hybrid. For some purposes, the "owner" of such an apartment has legal title and an interest in real property, while for other purposes his rights as a tenant of the corporation and a holder of its stock more closely resemble an interest in personal property. [Citations omitted.]

As did the trial court, we deem it appropriate to take a middle road in enforcing provisions that impose conditions upon the transfer of the hybrid cooperative apartment. Provisions conditioning transfers upon the consent of the cooperative corporation are neither automatically void nor automatically valid. If the provisions are stated unequivocally, and serve a legal and useful function, i.e., the reasonable protection of the financial and social integrity of the cooperative as a whole, they are not barred by our policy disfavoring restraints on alienation. Such provisions are permissible, however, only insofar as they are limited to the purpose for which they are designed. Unlimited consent clauses, permitting disapproval of transfers for any reason whatsoever, or for no reason, constitute illegal restraints because they fail sufficiently to recognize the legitimate interest of the holder of a leasehold to enjoy reasonable access to a resale market. These distinctions are consistent with the holdings of the majority of courts in other jurisdictions that have addressed this issue. See, e.g., Mowatt v. 1540 Lake Shore Drive Corporation, 385 F.2d 135, 136–37 (7th Cir. 1967); Alexy v. Kennedy House, Inc., 507 F. Supp. 690, 699 (E.D. Pa. 1981); Logan v. 3750 North Lake Shore Drive, Inc., 17 Ill. App. 3d 584, 589–91, 308 N.E.2d 278 (1974); 68 Beacon Street, Inc. v. Sohier, 289 Mass. 354, 360–62, 194 N.E. 303 (1935); Sanders v. The Tropicana, 31 N.C. App. 276, 282, 229 S.E.2d 304 (1976). Contra, in part, Weisner v. 791 Park Avenue Corporation, 6 N.Y.2d 426, 434, 190 N.Y.S.2d 70, 160 N.E.2d 720 (1959); see also Bratt, supra, 783–85; Note, Co-operative Apartment Housing, 61 Harv. L. Rev. 1407, 1416–20 (1948); Tiffany, supra, 483.79.

Applying these principles to the provisions of the Harbor House documentation, we agree, for two reasons, with the trial court's conclusion invalidating the clause in the proprietary lease purporting to permit consent to an assignment of the lease to be granted or withheld "for any reason or for no reason." As a matter of interpretation, that clause is not unequivocal, because it must be read conjointly with the memorandum of offering which limits the authority to disapprove assignments to cases in which the transferee is a person of unsuitable "character and financial responsibility." Given our reluctance to enforce restraints on alienation, the limited clause in the memorandum of offering must prevail over the unqualified consent clause in the proprietary lease. As a matter of public policy, furthermore, we hold, as do the authorities cited above, that only consent clauses reasonably tailored to the protection of the legitimate interests of the cooperative serve the kind of "legal and useful purpose" which protects them from avoidance as illegal restraints on alienation.

We must turn then to the plaintiffs' assertion that the trial court, on the evidence before it, erred in determining that the defendants acted reasonably, in light of the interests of the cooperative as a whole, in refusing consent to the transfer of apartment 1A. Although the defendants, at the time of their vote as directors and as stockholders, had specified no reasons for their withholding of consent, they did provide the court at trial with the propositions upon which they had relied. No special issue has been raised on this appeal that the delay in notifying the plaintiffs of the reasons for the denial of consent materially prejudiced the plaintiffs.

The trial court's memorandum of decision sets forth the reasons given by the defendants for withholding consent to the contemplated transfer. These reasons have nothing to do with the financial responsibility of Jones, which is conceded. Instead, they focus on Jones' tenancy of apartment 2 and upon functional consequences of a combined tenancy for apartments 2 and 1A. The defendants claimed that Jones was responsible for a recurrently unlocked front hall entrance door, that Jones had misled the defendants about his intended use of apartment 2, that Jones had behaved abrasively at a corporation meeting considering the Harbor House budget, that Jones and his guests had misused the cooperative parking lot, and that

Jones' stepdaughters were noisy. The trial court found some of these reasons unproven, and the others of minor significance. The defendants also maintained that the character of the building would be destroyed by having one family occupy apartments on the first and second floors connected for purposes of access only by the common stairway for the building as a whole. This ordinary everyday use of the two apartments would make the stairway a part of the two affected apartments in such a way as to interfere with its common use by the other tenants, who had an interest in the preservation of the building as a cooperative with six separate apartments. Relying principally on this structural reason, the trial court concluded that the defendants "had reasons to deny consent which were based on character, and the purposes and interests of their co-operative."

The plaintiffs argue that this structural reason is insufficient in light of the Harbor House by-laws that specifically authorize the board of directors to permit an owner of one or more apartments "to combine all or any portions of any such apartments into one or any desired number of apartments; and . . . to incorporate other space in the building not covered by any proprietary lease, into one or more apartments covered by a proprietary lease. . . ." The by-laws do not, however, require combinations of apartments to be approved, particularly where impairment of common access would be likely to result from the combination. The trial court did not err in finding that the structural problem, arguably aggravated by the irritations associated with Jones' occupation of apartment 2, furnished a basis for denying consent that was reasonably rooted in the purposes and interests of the cooperative apartment living and that reasonably served to protect the financial and social integrity of the cooperative as a whole. . . .

There is no error.

Chianese v. Culley

397 F. Supp. 1344 (S.D. Fla. 1975)

FULTON, Chief Judge. The plaintiffs in this lawsuit allege in a two count complaint that Article XII F of the Declaration of Condominium of the defendant San Remo, Inc. constitutes an illegal restraint on alienation of property, and that the defendants have discriminated against them on the basis of their religion or national origin. The parties to this cause have stipulated that the issue raised in count one, being a purely legal issue, may be resolved by the Court based on memoranda of law submitted by each side. These memoranda have now been received, and the issue to be resolved by the Court in this Order is whether Article XII F of the Declaration of Condominium of San Remo, Inc. (hereinafter, Article XII F) constitutes an illegal restraint on alienation of property. Neither count two of the complaint, which alleges that the defendants have discriminated against the plaintiffs on the basis of their religion or national origin, nor the counterclaim or crossclaim, is before the Court at this time.

The facts of this case are not complicated. The defendants Culley are husband and wife and were the owners of apartment number 548, Villa Raphael in the San Remo Condominium. The plaintiffs contracted to purchase this condominium unit from the defendants Culley, but said defendants refused to close the transaction because San Remo, Inc. and its directors asserted its rights under Article XII F of the

Declaration of Condominium, and provided an alternate purchaser for the unit in question. At that point, the plaintiffs filed this lawsuit, alleging that Article XII F constituted an illegal restraint against alienation of property and that the defendants were discriminating against the plaintiffs on the basis of their religion or national origin. After this lawsuit was filed, the defendants Culley issued a warranty deed to the plaintiffs Chianese, but the defendants San Remo continue to refuse to recognize the consummation of the transaction between the Culleys and the Chianeses. The issue before the Court at this point is thus whether Article XII F of the San Remo Declaration of Condominium constitutes an illegal restraint on alienation of property.

Article XII F provides in pertinent part as follows:

> F. Conveyances — In order to secure a community of congenial residents and thus protect the value of the apartments, the sale, leasing and mortgaging of apartments by any owner other than the Developer shall be subject to the following provisions so long as the apartment building in useful condition exists upon the land:
>
> > (1) Sale or lease-No apartment owner may dispose of an apartment or any interest therein by sale or by lease without approval of the Association, except to another apartment owner. If the purchaser or lessee is a corporation that approval may be conditioned upon the approval of those individuals who will be occupants of the apartment. The approval of the Association shall be obtained as follows:
> >
> > > (a) Notice to Association. An apartment owner intending to make a bona fide sale or a bona fide lease of his apartment or any interest therein shall give notice to the Association of such intention, together with the name and address of the proposed purchaser or lessee, together with such other information as the Association may require.
> > >
> > > (b) Election of Association. Within sixty (60) days after receipt of such notice, the Association must approve the transaction or furnish a purchaser or lessee approved by the Association who will accept terms as favorable to the seller as the terms stated in the notice. Such purchaser or lessee furnished by the Association may have not less than sixty (60) days subsequent to the date of approval within which to close the transaction. The approval of the Association shall be in recordable form and delivered to the purchaser or lessee. . . .

The general rule is that the right to convey property is one of the incidents of ownership, and the law will not permit the rights of ownership to be fettered by the imposition of restraints by grantors who both seek to convey their properties and at the same time maintain control over them. 61 Am. Jur. 2d Perpetuities and Restraints on Alienation § 93. This right to convey hearkens back to the Statute of Quia Emptores in the year 1290, and the right to alienate one's property has been accepted as an incident of an estate in fee simple ever since. Thus, if Article XII F is found to constitute an absolute restraint against alienation of property, that article is void. Davis v. Geyer, 151 Fla. 362, 9 So. 2d 727 (1942); Holiday Out in America at St. Lucie, Inc. v. Bowes, 285 So. 2d 63 (Fla. App. 4th Dist. 1973).

Florida Statutes Chapter 711.04(1) provides that "A condominium parcel is a separate parcel of real property, the ownership of which may be in fee simple, or any other estate in real property recognized by law." The complaint alleges, and the defendants have not contested, that the condominium parcel in question was owned by the Culleys in fee simple.

The plaintiffs cite Davis v. Geyer, 151 Fla. 362, 9 So. 2d 727 (1942) as being dispositive of the issue at bar. That case held that a provision in an agreement to convey property reading "No sale of the said property is to be made by the party of the first part until the same is approved by the party of the second part" was invalid since it constituted an unlimited restraint on alienation of property.

Article XII F provides that the condominium association upon notice must, within sixty days, either approve the proposed purchaser or furnish another purchaser who will accept terms equally favorable to the seller. This provision is distinguishable from that in Davis v. Geyer. That case involved an absolute restriction against sale without the permission of the second party: should that party withhold permission, for whatever reason, the property could never be sold. Article XII F does not contain such an absolute restriction. By its terms, within sixty days, the association must either provide another purchaser or approve the proposed purchaser. Thus, at the close of the sixty day period, the property can be sold, whether to the seller's purchaser or to the one provided by the association. Article XII F is thus not an absolute restraint, such as was found in the Davis v. Geyer case, but rather grants instead a "pre-emptive option" or "right of first refusal" to the condominium association.

The Restatement of Property, Vol. 4 § 413(1) takes the position that a provision that the owner shall not sell his property without giving a designated person the opportunity to meet any offer received does not constitute an invalid restraint on alienation, provided that such provision does not violate the rule against perpetuities. Plaintiffs in their memo stipulate that the rule against perpetuities is not applicable to condominiums under Florida Statute 711.08(2). The Florida courts have followed the Restatement position, and have upheld provisions similar to that contained in Article XII F. . . .

While covenants which restrict the use of land are not favored, they will be enforced if they are confined to lawful purposes, are within reasonable bounds, and are expressed in clear language. Zoda v. Zoda, 292 So. 2d 412 (Fla. App. 2d Dist. 1974). Article XII F complies with these requirements. The stated purpose of Section XII F is to insure "a community of congenial residents." "The very nature of the condominium concept of ownership requires a degree of control in the management" thereof. Holiday Out in America at St. Lucie, Inc. v. Bowes, 285 So. 2d 63 (Fla. App. 4th Dist. 1973). Chapter 711.08(1)(l) of the Florida Statutes states that the declaration of condominium shall provide for "such other provisions not inconsistent with this law as may be desired, including but not limited to those relating to . . . use restrictions, limitation upon conveyance, sale, leasing, purchase, ownership and occupancy of units. . . ." Chapter 711.08(1)(l) thus clearly provides for and anticipates limitations on the sale of condominium units, providing that such restrictions are valid under the law. This Court has previously held herein that Article XII F does not constitute an illegal restraint against alienation, but is instead a valid and enforceable pre-emptive right granted to the condominium association. Likewise, the provision under Article XII F that the association must, upon notice, either approve the seller's purchaser or provide another purchaser for the same price is reasonable. . . .

Pursuant to the foregoing discussion, the Court finds that Article XII F of the San Remo Declaration of Condominium does not constitute an illegal restraint on the alienation of property, but that Article XII F grants instead a valid and enforceable right of first refusal to the condominium association. Accordingly, the Court finds in favor of the defendants as to the issue raised in Count One of the complaint.

NOTES AND QUESTIONS

1. Contrast the restraint in *Jones* with that in *Chianese*. These typify the arrangements one tends to find, respectively, in a cooperative and condominium. Would *Chianese*'s first count have succeeded if the San Remo condominium had barred him under a *Jones*-type restriction? In weighing a restraint on sale, should courts treat co-ops and condos differently because one gets stock and lease in the cooperative and the other a fee interest (usually) in the condominium? What factors should the courts consider? What is the status of title if a co-op or condo unit were transferred without complying with the "approval" procedures?

Some fairly dated authority survives which would allow a co-op board to grant or withhold consent to an assignment (sale) of a proprietary lease "for any reason or for no reason," as an extension of the state's landlord and tenant law; see, e.g., 68 Beacon Street v. Sohier, 289 Mass. 354, 194 N.E. 303 (1935); Weisner v. 791 Park Avenue Corp., 6 N.Y.2d 426, 160 N.E.2d 720 (1959); but see Bentley v. 75 East End Owners, Inc. 26 B.R. 69 (S.D.N.Y. 1982), where a federal bankruptcy judge described such a provision as "unconscionable" to the extent that it would prevent a Chapter 11 debtor from selling his apartment at a fair price. One author has argued that courts or legislatures should validate such "subjective consent powers," in both co-ops and condominiums; Vincent DiLorenzo, Restraints on Alienation in a Condominium Context: An Evaluation and Theory for Decision Making, 24 Real Prop., Prob. and Trust J. 403 (1989).

2. Note that *Chianese*'s second count claimed religious and ethnic discrimination. Fair housing laws, including the federal Civil Rights Act of 1968, would generally cover a shared facilities development. However, the federal statute allows the owner of a single-family house to avoid compliance if he does not engage a broker. 42 U.S.C.A. § 3603(b)(1)(1977). Should that grace apply (the statute is unclear) to a unit owner in a condo or homes association if his unit is a one-family detached structure?

3. If a co-op were required, as in *Jones*, to treat assignment requests reasonably, which of the objections below would seem reasonable?

(a) The proposed assignee is a prominent official of a right-wing anti-Semitic organization. The cooperative fears that his presence in the building might invite angry protests from activist Jewish groups;

(b) The proposed assignees are an unmarried couple;

(c) The proposed assignee is giving his seller a purchase money mortgage for 90 percent of the contract price.

4. The unit owner wants to rent her unit out. As to whether a restraint is reasonable, are the considerations different in a rental and a sales situation? In a short-term rental (less than three months) and a long-term rental (more than one year)? Consider Seagate Condominium Assn. v. Duffy, 330 So. 2d 484 (Fla. App. 1976), where the declaration barred leasing "as a regular practice for business, speculative, [or] investment . . . purposes"; the Board could grant, however, a short-term exception "to meet special situations or avoid undue hardship." The court upheld the restraint. See also Kroop v. Caravelle Condominium, 323 So. 2d 307 (Fla. App. 1975) (owner could not lease unit more than once).

5. One use of common interest communities has been to establish communities focused on the needs and preferences of older residents, including many communities that bar children as residents. This raises a difficult balancing act between the preferences of those who prefer an adult community and the need to prevent undue discrimination. The Fair Housing Amendments Act of 1988, 42 U.S.C.A. §§ 3601-3617 (Supp. 1992), extended fair housing protection to include "familial status," defined as individuals under the age of 18 domiciled with a parent or legal custodian. The result was to make the creation of "adult communities" significantly more difficult.

Adult communities may qualify for an exemption where the housing is intended for, and solely occupied by, persons 62 years of age or older, or intended and operated for occupancy by at least one person 55 years of age or older per unit. The Secretary was empowered to issue regulations that would permit an exemption for communities with an 80 percent occupancy factor (of persons 55 years of age or older) where significant facilities and services designed to meet the physical or social needs of older persons are present. The 1988 amendments were seen as overly restrictive by supporters of adult-only communities, and in 1995 Congress passed the Housing for Older Persons Act, Pub. L. No. 104-76, 109 Stat. 787 (1995) (codified as amended in 42 U.S.C. § 3607), which eliminated the requirement that the community provide significant facilities or services for the elderly. See Nicole Napolitano, Note, The Fair Housing Act Amendments and Age Restrictive Covenants in Condominiums and Cooperatives, 73 St. John's L. Rev. 273 (1999); Jonathan I. Edelstein, Family Values: Prevention of Discrimination and the Housing for Older Persons Act of 1995, 52 U. Miami L. Rev. 947 (1998).

6. The *Chianese* plaintiffs stipulated that the condominium's preemptive right was beyond the scope of the Rule Against Perpetuities. The Florida statute supports that view. Fla. Stat. Ann. 718.104(5)(1988). So, too, does the Uniform Condominium Act, 2-103(b), where states have adopted it. But the Rule may be a source of concern unless care is taken by the drafters of the condominium documents. See, e.g., The Cambridge Co. v. East Slope Inv. Corp., 700 P.2d 537 (Colo. 1985), and the discussion in R. Natelson, Law of Property Owners Associations 600-608 (1989).

5. Protecting the Consumer

The age of consumerism has arrived. This has led, quite predictably, to growing governmental oversight of the housing developer who undertakes a multi-unit, shared facilities project. Where everything the home buyer acquires lies within the four corners of his lot and where title passes via a one-page deed, the consumer, aided by his lawyer, can reasonably fend for himself. Where, however, the buyer is paying also for the right to enjoy amenities that he must share with others (and that still others may own) and where the title papers cover dozens of pages, the consumer and even his lawyer might welcome a wary, tough-minded regulator. As the project becomes ever more ambitious, so, too, does the prospect of overreaching, under-financing, and plain, downright crookedness.

In the section following we will look at two different aspects of consumer protection; (a) regulating the offering statement; and (b) efforts to redress the uneven bargain.

a. **Regulating the Offering Statement**

Securities Act of 1933 — Release No. 5347[*]

January 4, 1973

GUIDELINES AS TO THE APPLICABILITY OF THE FEDERAL
SECURITIES LAWS TO OFFERS AND SALES OF CONDOMINIUMS OR UNITS IN A
REAL ESTATE DEVELOPMENT

The Securities and Exchange Commission today called attention to the applicability of the federal securities laws to the offer and sale of condominium units, or other units in a real estate development, coupled with an offer or agreement to perform or arrange certain rental or other services for the purchaser. The Commission noted that such offerings may involve the offering of a security in the form of an investment contract or a participation in a profit sharing arrangement within the meaning of the Securities Act of 1933 and the Securities Exchange Act of 1934.[11]

Where this is the case any offering of any such securities must comply with the registration and prospectus delivery requirements of the Securities Act, unless an exemption therefrom is available, and must comply with the anti-fraud provisions of the Securities Act and the Securities Exchange Act and the regulations thereunder. In addition, persons engaged in the business of buying or selling investment contracts or participations in profit sharing agreements of this type as agents for others, or as principal for their own account, may be brokers or dealers within the meaning of the Securities Exchange Act, and therefore may be required to be registered as such with the Commission under the provisions of Section 15 of that Act.

The Commission is aware that there is uncertainty about when offerings of condominiums and other types of similar units may be considered to be offerings of securities that should be registered pursuant to the Securities Act. The purpose of this release is to alert persons engaged in the business of building and selling condominiums and similar types of real estate developments to their responsibilities under the Securities Act and to provide guidelines for a determination of when an offering of condominiums or other units may be viewed as an offering of securities. Resort condominiums are one of the more common interests in real estate the offer of which may involve an offering of securities. However, other types of units that are part of a development or project present analogous questions under the federal securities laws. Although this release speaks in terms of condominiums, it applies to offerings of all types of units in real estate developments which have characteristics similar to those described herein.

The offer of real estate as such, without any collateral arrangements with the seller or others, does not involve the offer of a security. When the real estate is offered in conjunction with certain services, a security, in the form of an investment contract, may be present. The Supreme Court in Securities and Exchange Commission v. W. J. Howey Co., 328 U.S. 293 (1946) set forth what has become a generally accepted definition of an investment contract: "a contract, transaction or scheme

---

* Footnotes renumbered.
    11. It should be noted that where an investment contract is present, it consists of the agreement offered and the condominium itself.

whereby a person invests his money in a common enterprise and is led to expect profits solely from the efforts of the promoter or a third party, it being immaterial whether the shares in the enterprise are evidenced by formal certificates or by nominal interests in the physical assets employed in the enterprise." (298) The *Howey* case involved the sale and operation of orange groves. The reasoning, however, is applicable to condominiums.

As the Court noted in *Howey*, substance should not be disregarded for form, and the fundamental statutory policy of affording broad protection to investors should be heeded. Recent interpretations have indicated that the expected return need not be solely from the efforts of others, as the holding in *Howey* appears to indicate.[12] For this reason, an investment contract may be present in situations where an investor is not wholly inactive, but even participates to a limited degree in the operation of the business. The "profits" that the purchaser is led to expect may consist of revenues received from rental of the unit; these revenues and any tax benefits resulting from rental of the unit are the economic inducements held out to the purchaser.

The existence of various kinds of collateral arrangements may cause an offering of condominium units to involve an offering of investment contracts or interests in a profit sharing agreement. The presence of such arrangements indicates that the offeror is offering an opportunity through which the purchaser may earn a return on his investment through the managerial efforts of the promoters or a third party in their operation of the enterprise.

For example, some public offerings of condominium units involve rental pool arrangements. Typically, the rental pool is a device whereby the promoter or a third party undertakes to rent the unit on behalf of the actual owner during that period of time when the unit is not in use by the owner. The rents received and the expenses attributable to rental of all units in the project are combined and the individual owner receives a ratable share of the rental proceeds regardless of whether his individual unit was actually rented. The offer of the unit together with the offer of an opportunity to participate in such a rental pool involves the offer of investment contracts which must be registered unless an exemption is available.

Also, the condominium units may be offered with a contract or agreement that places restrictions, such as required use of an exclusive rental agent or limitations on the period of time the owner may occupy the unit, on the purchaser's occupancy or rental of the property purchased. Such restrictions suggest that the purchaser is in fact investing in a business enterprise, the return from which will be substantially dependent on the success of the managerial efforts of other persons. In such cases, registration of the resulting investment contract would be required.

In any situation where collateral arrangements are coupled with the offering of condominiums, whether or not specifically of the types discussed above, the manner of offering and economic inducements held out to the prospective purchaser play an important role in determining whether the offerings involve securities. In this connection, see Securities and Exchange Commission v. C. M. Joiner Leasing Corp., 320 U.S. 344 (1943). In *Joiner*, the Supreme Court also noted that:

---

12. SEC v. Glenn W. Turner Enterprises, Inc., CCH Fed. Sec. L. Rep. 893, 605 (D.C. Ore. No. 72-390, May 25, 1972). See also State v. Hawaii Market Center, Inc., 485 P.2d 105 (1971) (cited in Securities Act Release No. 5211 (1971)); and Securities Act Release No. 5018 (1969) regarding the applicability of the federal securities laws to the sale and distribution of whiskey warehouse receipts.

"In enforcement of [the Securities Act], it is not inappropriate that promoters' offerings be judged as being what they were represented to be." (353) In other words, condominiums, coupled with a rental arrangement, will be deemed to be securities if they are offered and sold through advertising, sales literature, promotional schemes or oral representations which emphasize the economic benefits to the purchaser to be derived from the managerial efforts of the promoter, or a third party designated or arranged for by the promoter, in renting the units.

In summary, the offering of condominium units in conjunction with any one of the following will cause the offering to be viewed as an offering of securities in the form of investment contracts:

1. The condominiums, with any rental arrangement or other similar service, are offered and sold with emphasis on the economic benefits to the purchaser to be derived from the managerial efforts of the promoter, or a third party designated or arranged for by the promoter, from rental of the units;

2. The offering of participation in a rental pool arrangement; and

3. The offering of a rental or similar arrangements whereby the purchaser must hold his unit available for rental for any part of the year, must use an exclusive rental agent or is otherwise materially restricted in his occupancy or rental of his unit.

In all of the above situations, investor protection requires the application of the federal securities laws.

If the condominiums are not offered and sold with emphasis on the economic benefits to the purchaser to be derived from the managerial efforts of others, and assuming that no plan to avoid the registration requirements of the Securities Act is involved, an owner of a condominium unit may, after purchasing his unit, enter into a non-pooled rental arrangement with an agent not designated or required to be used as a condition to the purchase, whether or not such agent is affiliated with the offeror, without causing a sale of a security to be involved in the sale of the unit. Further a continuing affiliation between the developers or promoters of a project and the project by reason of maintenance arrangements does not make the unit a security.

In situations where commercial facilities are a part of the common elements of a residential project, no registration would be required under the investment contract theory where (a) the income from such facilities is used only to offset common area expenses and (b) the operation of such facilities is incidental to the project as a whole and are not established as a primary income source for the individual owners of a condominium or cooperative unit.

The Commission recognizes the need for a degree of certainty in the real estate offering area and believes that the above guidelines will be helpful in assisting persons to comply with the securities laws. It is difficult, however, to anticipate the variety of arrangements that may accompany the offering of condominium projects. The Commission, therefore, would like to remind those engaged in the offering of condominiums or other interests in real estate with similar features that there may be situations, not referred to in this release, in which the offering of the interests constitutes an offering of securities. Whether an offering of securities is involved necessarily depends on the facts and circumstances of each particular case. The staff of the Commission will be available to respond to written inquiries on such matters.

By the Commission.

Ronald F. Hunt
Secretary

NOTES AND QUESTIONS

1. Securities Act of 1933 — Release No. 5347 has been the key SEC statement to date regarding condominiums and "all types of units within real estate developments." Suppose your client wishes to develop a resort condominium whose units may be rented out to transients when the owner is not present. Can your client avoid registration without meeting one of the Act's exemptions? As a practical matter, what do you see as the advantage and disadvantage to the developer of an SEC registration?

2. In their comment on Release No. 5347, two SEC specialists lent the following advice to rental pool developers seeking to avoid SEC registration. At a minimum, the offering statement should provide that the unit owner may use his own rental agent; the unit owner may choose not to rent out his unit; and net rental proceeds are to be sent directly to the owner. In addition, the authors warned the developer's salespeople against recommending only one rental agent, or discussing income or tax benefits deriving from rental activity, or estimating rental income. A fortiori, the offering statement must also be silent as to these matters. Dickey and Cutler, Apartment Construction News, Sept. 1973; cf. SEC, No Action Letter, Re: Big Sky of Montana, Inc., March 14, 1973.

Whether these efforts would be enough became questionable after Hocking v. Dubois, 885 F.2d 1449 (9th Cir. 1989) (en banc), *cert. denied,* 110 S. Ct. 1805 (1990). The court held that the sale of a condominium, if presented as part of the same transaction with an optional rental pool offered by an independent third party, can be classified as the sale of a security.

In 2004, however, the SEC issued a no-action letter granting greater leeway to the developer of a condominium hotel to provide information to potential purchasers about rental programs available in connection with the sale of condominium units, fractionals, and club membership plans. Intrawest Corporation, 2002 SEC No-Act.[*]753 LEXIS 787 (Nov. 8, 2002).

Intrawest develops condominium hotels, in which the vast majority of its buyers enter into rental management agreements with Intrawest serving as the rental manager. In its request, Intrawest agreed to the following limitations on its sale activities:

- The sole reference to rental management in either written or oral sales presentations will be "ownership may include the opportunity to place your home in a rental arrangement."
- Upon a request for further information, the sales representative may suggest speaking to a rental management company representative, whether or not affiliated with the developer.
- Some physical separation will exist between the retail sales and the rental management operations.
- Real estate salespersons will not discuss economic or tax benefits of rental arrangements.
- No projections of rental rates or expected occupancies will be made by any person.
- Information about rentals will not be volunteered by a sales representative but can only be provided in response to a specific inquiry.

- The rental agreement will permit owners to have unlimited use of their units subject only to prior reservations by the rental management company.

In response, the SEC agreed that Intrawest can mention the existence of a rental program in written and oral sales and promotional materials by using a statement such as "ownership may include the opportunity to place your unit in a rental management arrangement"; and can enter into a rental management agreement at the time the purchase agreement is signed but prior to closing, provided the agreement is contingent upon the closing of the sale.

3. Rohan and Reskin, Condominium Law and Practice (1985), contains two illustrative SEC prospectuses for rental pool condominiums. The prospectus for Gentle Winds, a 250-unit condominium in the Virgin Islands, contains 100 pages of close print, financial schedules, legal documents, and room layouts. Id. at 18.07(l). The "short form" prospectus for Inn of the Seventh Mountain, an 84-unit resort hotel condominium in Oregon, runs only 23 pages but contains no legal documents. Id. at 18.07[2]. Each contains in boldface the legend appearing on all SEC prospectuses:

These Securities Have Not Been Approved or Disapproved by the Securities and Exchange Commission, Nor Has the Commissioner Passed Upon the Accuracy or Adequacy of the Prospectus. Any Representation to the Contrary Is a Criminal Offense.

This legend exemplifies the controlling spirit of the Securities Act of 1933, which relies upon full disclosure to protect the offeree and not upon a prior regulatory decision as to whether the offering is sound or not. Some states, by contrast, give their securities' officials the power to approve or disapprove a proposed offering. In the present context, which attitude better serves the prospective purchaser of a resort condominium?

Section 5(a) of the Securities Act of 1933 makes it unlawful, absent an exemption, to sell a security using the means or instruments of interstate commerce or the mails unless a registration statement is in effect as to that security. However, the SEC does allow a developer to feel the market pulse before filing his registration statement provided he does not accept down payments, purchase commitments, or "indications of interest." Securities Act of 1933, Release No. 5382, April 9, 1973. How might the developer premarket without crossing the divide?

4. Section 3(a)(11) of the Securities Act of 1933 grants an exemption for so-called intrastate offerings. For real estate offerings, this requires that the property, the offerees, and the issuer all be located within the same state. For the issuer, this means his principal place of business; for the offerees, this means their permanent home. Securities Act of 1933, Rule 147, Release No. 5450, January 7, 1974.

Section 4(2) of the Act exempts transactions that do not involve a public offering. Congress has not defined "public offering," but the SEC, in Securities Act of 1933, Regulation D, Fed. Sec. L. Rep. (CCH) §5875F (April 14, 1989), gives some guidance to issuers. Rule 506 is the operative statement; it contains a safe harbor provision that limits the offering to 35 nonaccredited purchasers and an unlimited number of accredited investors. Accredited investors include banks, investment firms, businesses with assets totaling at least $5 million and individuals whose net worth exceeds $1 million. In addition, for a project to qualify under a Rule 506 exemption, it must be presented in a manner that enables the nonaccredited buyer to evaluate the merits and risks of the proposed investment.

5. Even if the sponsor qualifies for a registration exemption, the Securities Act of 1933 provides civil remedies *whenever* the transaction involves a security. Section 12 (2) enables the buyer to recover damages for material misstatements or omissions in the registration statement (if one exists) and in all written and oral sales materials. Two other provisions deal only with offerings that require registration. Section 12(1) allows the buyer to rescind and recover his down payment whenever the sponsor sells unregistered securities in violation of the Act. Where registration has occurred, Section 11 allows the buyer to recover damages for material misstatements or omissions of material fact in either the registration statement or prospectus.

6. The United States Supreme Court has held that the marketing of cooperative interests is not *per se* the offering of "securities" within the purview of the Securities Act of 1933 and the Securities Exchange Act of 1934. United Housing Foundation Inc. v. Forman, 421 U.S. 837 (1975). Writing for the Court, Justice Powell declared:

> We reject at the outset any suggestion that the present transaction, evidenced by the sale of shares called "stock" must be considered a security transaction simply because the statutory definition of a security includes the words "any . . . stock." Rather we adhere to the basic principle that has guided all the Court's decisions in this area: "[I]n searching for the meaning and scope of the word 'security' in the Act[s], form should be disregarded for substance and the emphasis should be on economic reality" . . . Common sense suggests that people who intend to acquire only a residential apartment in a state-subsidized cooperative, for their personal use, are not likely to believe that in reality they are purchasing investment securities simply because the transaction is evidenced by something called a share of stock.
>
> . . . The Court of Appeals, as an alternative ground for its decision, concluded that a share in Riverbay was also an "investment contract" as defined by the Securities Acts. . . . We perceive no distinction, for present purposes, between an "investment contract" and an "instrument commonly known as a security." In either case, the basic test for distinguishing the transaction from other commercial dealings is "whether the scheme involves an investment of money in a common enterprise with profits to come solely from the efforts of others." Howey, 328 U.S., at 301 . . .
>
> There is no doubt that purchasers in this housing cooperative sought to obtain a decent home at an attractive price. But that type of economic interest characterizes every form of commercial dealing. What distinguishes a security transaction — and what is absent here — is an investment where one parts with his money in the hope of receiving profits from the efforts of others, and not where he purchases a commodity for personal consumption or living quarters for personal use. [421 U.S. at 858.]

7. The tenant-stockholders of Co-op City (Riverbay), the development involved in the *Forman* case, enjoyed a state subsidy; they could not, under the New York law, resell their shares at a profit. Nonsubsidized (or so-called luxury) cooperatives place no limit on their members' profit opportunity. As a result, persons buying such co-op apartments usually consider the investment aspects of their purchase.

The Court's opinion in *Forman* kept alive the possibility that the sponsors of nonsubsidized projects would be required to register their offering as an investment contract.

Faced directly with that issue, the Second Circuit held that the securities acts did not apply. Grenader v. Spitz, 537 F.2d 612 (2d Cir. 1976), *cert. denied,* 429 U.S. 1009 (1976). The lawsuit involved the conversion of a 60-unit rental building into a wholly residential cooperative. The sponsors had filed an offering plan with state officials but had not registered with the SEC. Tenant-stockholders sued for damages alleging that the offering plan contained misleading statements or omissions of material facts.

The court's opinion stressed that the building had no commercial tenants and insignificant income from coin-operated laundry and cable TV, and that the shareholder-tenants were not to receive any distribution from the earnings and profits of the Corporation. There still remained the distinguishing feature of possible resale profit, but this did not convince the court:

> We note initially that the *Howey* test first requires that the investor be led to expect profits! There is nothing in the record before us to support the contention that the investor here was attracted by the prospect of realizing a profit on his investment. . . . The offering plan . . . is barren of any representation or intimation of anticipated profits. Unlike the hawking siren song of the promoter, the plan here is a prosaic recitation of the financial facts underlying their transaction with an *exhaustive* [sic] recitation of the physical properties and condition of the Building and the apartments offered as well as the terms of the tenancy and the obligations of the lessee. There is no reference to the possibility or probability of profits. . . . There is a further flaw in [tenants'] argument. *Howey* requires that the profits arise "solely from the efforts of the promoter or a third party." . . . Realistically [appreciation in value] will depend upon the general housing market, the status of the neighborhood and the availability of credit. See Berman and Stone, Federal Securities Law and the Sale of Condominiums, Homes and Homesites, 30 Bus. Law. 411, 422-24 (1975). [537 F.2d at 618-619.]

8. After *Forman* and *Grenader,* do any situations remain where *residential* co-ops (or condominiums) might still be subject to federal regulation? Suppose that the sponsor has retained a long-term management contract? Or that the sponsor has retained title to the recreational facilities which he leases to the project? Or that the tenant-stockholders can prove that they relied upon commercial rentals to decrease carrying charges and increase share values?

9. The cooperative offering in Grenader v. Spitz was first submitted to the state Attorney General, who has the power to regulate "any public offering or sale in or from the State of New York of participation interests in real estate ventures including cooperative interests in realty." N.Y. Gen. Bus. Law 352-e (McKinney 1984). This power extends to planned unit developments and condominiums. SEC registration would not have obviated the need to follow state procedure.

The New York procedures are quite elaborate. Documentation worthy of a full-dressed SEC registration must accompany the request for state approval. Levine, Registering a Condominium Offering in New York, 19 N.Y.L.F. 493 (1974).

New York is one of several states (the number grows) that systematically regulate co-op and condominium ventures. In many other states, offerings may sometimes be subject to blue-sky control; for example, the Uniform Securities Act (now adopted in 43 states) defines securities to include "investment contracts."

What are the arguments for entrusting states with primary authority over the marketing of shared facilities developments? What are the arguments against?

10. Although most states use the *Howey* criteria, some determine the status of an offering through the "risk capital" test. This test broadens the reach of *Howey* to cover offerings primarily designed to attract risk capital, regardless of the managerial involvement of the investor. See Comment, The Economic Realities of Condominium Registration Under the Securities Act of 1933, 19 Ga. L. Rev. 747, 753-755 (1985). For an example of a state statute embodying the risk capital test, see Ga. Code Ann. § 10-5-2(16)(2006).

11. The Interstate Land Sales Full Disclosure Act, 15 U.S.C. §§ 1701 et seq. (1982), applies to the purchase of unbuilt condominium units, and requires comprehensive disclosures subject to remedies including recission, damages, injunctive relief, and even criminal penalties. Winter v. Hollingsworth Properties, Inc., 777 F.2d 1444 (11th Cir. 1985). The court held that if the sale is nonexempt, the developer must register the condominium and comply with HUD regulations. See Markus, Application of Interstate Land Sales Full Disclosure Act to Condominiums, 22 Real Prop., Prob. and Trust J. 41 (1987).

The Act does exempt projects of less than 50 units and projects where the unit is either completed before it is sold or must contractually be finished within two years of sale. To gain this latter exemption, the sponsor must complete not only the housing unit but also all recreational and other common facilities that are included in the purchase.

The Office of Interstate Land Sales Registration, a division of the Department of Housing and Urban Development, administers the program. Before offering lots in a non-exempt subdivision, the promoter must obtain a HUD-approved Property Report. The Report is a full disclosure of detail such as the promoters' financial and criminal background, topography, climate, nuisances, deed restrictions, road access, utilities, municipal services, and taxes. For a sample subdivision filing, see [1977] Hous. and Dev. Rep. (BNA) § 150:0351.

b.   Developer Control and Self-Dealing

181 East 73rd Street Co. v. 181 East 73rd Tenants Corp.

954 F.2d 45 (2d Cir. 1992)

OAKES, Chief Judge:

We must decide in this appeal to whom Congress accorded the right to terminate a self-dealing lease pursuant to section 3607 of the Condominium and Cooperative Abuse Relief Act of 1980, 15 U.S.C. §§ 3601-3616 (1988) ("Abuse Relief Act") and who may waive that right. The case arises from a conversion of a twenty-story building, located at 181 East 73rd Street in Manhattan, from rental property to cooperative ownership. The building contains 116 apartments and street-level commercial property, including three stores, a restaurant, and a parking garage. Plaintiff 181 East 73rd Street Co. ("Sponsor"), the former owner of the building, sponsored the conversion,[1] and defendant 181 East 73rd Tenants Corporation

---

1. A sponsor is "any person, partnership, joint venture, corporation, company, trust, association or other entity who makes or takes part in a public offering or sale . . . of securities consisting primarily of shares or participation interests or investment in real estate, including cooperative interests in realty." 13 N.Y.C.C.R.R. § 18.1(c)(1) (1984).

("Tenants Corporation") acquired title to the building. As part of the conversion plan, Tenants Corporation — still controlled by officers and directors appointed by Sponsor — executed a ninety-nine year Master Lease that demised the commercial property back to the Sponsor.

The shareholders of Tenants Corporation subsequently voted to terminate, pursuant to section 3607 of the Abuse Relief Act, the portion of the Master Lease that covered the fifty-two car parking garage. Sponsor brought a declaratory judgment action challenging the validity of the termination on the grounds that Tenants Corporation had waived its termination right. In addition, Sponsor sought damages and rent reduction. Tenants Corporation counterclaimed, seeking attorneys' fees and a declaratory judgment as to both the validity of the termination of the garage portion of the Master Lease and the unconscionability of the entire Master Lease under New York law. Both parties moved for summary judgment. Judge Richard Owen of the United States District Court for the Southern District of New York granted Tenants Corporation's motion finding that the termination was valid, denied both the unconscionability and attorneys' fees claims, and, following a hearing and a report by a magistrate, granted Sponsor's claim for rent apportionment. Sponsor appeals the district court's ruling that the lease termination was valid and Tenants Corporation cross-appeals the denial of attorneys' fees.

I.

In New York, a typical cooperative or condominium conversion commences with the distribution of an offering plan to tenants who reside in the building.[3] Through the offering plan a sponsor seeks to solicit the statutorily required percentage of subscription agreements from current residents of the target building. N.Y.Gen. Bus.Law § 352-eeee(2)(c)-(d) (McKinney 1984) (governing conversions in New York City). The Sponsor, in compliance with this procedure, submitted a preliminary offering statement to the New York State Attorney General in 1984. The Attorney General rejected the plan on the grounds that the rent specified in the Master Lease would not keep pace with the costs of maintaining the space.

After the Attorney General approved an amended plan the building tenants formed an association to negotiate additional amendments to the plan. The association gathered "no-buy" pledges from over 85% of the current tenants, thus, blocking conversion under an eviction plan.[4] The pledges forced Sponsor to negotiate with the

---

3. The term "offering plan" connotes a two-step process. First, the sponsor submits a preliminary offering statement or "red herring" to the New York State Attorney General's Office for approval. The sponsor also must notify all current tenants of the conversion proposal and provide them with a copy of the statement. Second, once the Attorney General's office approves the preliminary offer, the sponsor may issue the final offer — known as the "black book" — and solicit acceptance agreements. N.Y.Gen. Bus.Law §§ 352-e(2), 352-eeee(2)(f) (governing conversions in New York City) (McKinney 1984). See generally New York State Attorney General, Cooperative and Condominium Conversion Handbook 8-15 (1989) (hereinafter Conversion Handbook); Comment, Cooperative and Condominium Conversions in New York: The Tenant in Occupancy, 31 N.Y.L.Sch.L.Rev. 763, 764-65 (1986).

4. New York law permits two forms of conversion plans, eviction and non-eviction plans. An eviction plan, which requires that 51% of the tenants in occupancy on the date the Attorney General approves the offering plan for filing sign purchase agreements, provides for the eviction of non-purchasing tenants. A non-eviction plan permits non-purchasing tenants to remain in the building, but to proceed under such a plan at least 15% of the residential units must be purchased by either current tenants or purchasers who plan to live in the unit. N.Y.Gen.Bus.Law § 352-eeee(2)(c)-(d) (McKinney 1984); *see also Conversion Handbook, supra,* at 10, 16-17.

tenants' association before the conversion could proceed. Following negotiation, the parties agreed upon, among other terms, a ninety-nine year Master Lease of the commercial properties at a fixed annual rent plus 19.5% of the rent increases Sponsor received through subletting the property.

On May 15, 1985, the closing occurred and the Master Lease was executed. At the time of the closing, Tenants Corporation was still controlled by Sponsor; however, on June 10, 1985, the tenants elected a new board of directors, replacing Sponsor's nominees.

By 1987, the Master Lease had become a drain on the resources of Tenants Corporation. The Master Lease did not require Sponsor to assume a share of taxes, operating expenses, or services required to maintain the commercial property; as a result of a disproportionate escalation of these costs, Tenants Corporation found itself bound to a long-term lease under which there was an ever-increasing disparity between the rent received and the market value of the properties. In early May 1987, more than two-thirds of the unit holders who held residential units in the building voted to terminate the garage portion of the Master Lease pursuant to section 3607. Notice of Termination was sent to Sponsor on May 8, 1987.

For our purposes, the story might have ended here if not for the discovery of asbestos on the premises of the building. On June 28, 1985, an inspection of the building by the New York City Department of Health revealed asbestos in the garage, boiler room, basement, laundry room, and penthouse patios. The inspector issued a Notice of Violation. On July 22, 1985, the Department of Health ordered the abatement of the asbestos conditions. This order sparked debate as to whether Sponsor or Tenants Corporation was financially liable for the abatement.

On October 25, 1985, the President of Tenants Corporation and a representative of Sponsor signed a letter agreement ("asbestos agreement") that Sponsor would pay roughly two-thirds of the cost of asbestos removal, and Tenants Corporation would pay the remaining one-third. The asbestos agreement, in pertinent part, stated that:

> The Tenants Corp. specifically retains and reserves its right to claim any non-asbestos related defaults of the Lease or Cooperative Plan by the Sponsor. *Except as set forth herein, the Lease remains unmodified and is hereby ratified and confirmed, and remains in full force and effect.* The Tenants Corp. and the Sponsor represent that to the best of their knowledge no defaults presently exist under the Lease and there are no defenses, offsets, or counterclaims against the enforcement by Tenants Corp. of any of the agreements, terms, covenants or conditions of the Lease.

Joint Appendix 131, 132 (emphasis added). The central issue before us is whether the above language resulted in ratification of the Master Lease and, thus, in effect, constituted a waiver of the unit holders' section 3607 right to terminate a self-dealing lease.

II.

The Abuse Relief Act seeks to eliminate the potential for abuse to which the conversion process lends itself. Congress undertook the delicate task of deterring these abuses without preventing conversions from taking place. *See* 15 U.S.C. § 3601(a)(3), (b) (1988); H.R.Conf.Rep. No. 1420, 96th Cong., 2d Sess. 162-63 (1980), *reprinted in* 1980

U.S.Code Cong. & Admin. News pp. 3506, 3617, 3707-08. Section 3607 of the Abuse
Relief Act targeted a particular form of abuse to which tenants were vulnerable, namely,
self-dealing leases arranged by sponsors. Sponsors have an economic incentive to take
advantage of the temporary control they exert over tenants' corporations to bind
tenants to long-term, self-dealing leases — leases that potentially deprive the tenants
of valuable assets. Congress chose to counteract this powerful potential for abuse by
arming the new unit holders of a conversion project with an equally potent weapon, the
federal right to terminate self-dealing leases without having to resort to judicial action.
See H.R.Conf.Rep. No. 1420, 96th Cong., 2d Sess. 168 (1980), *reprinted in* 1980 U.S.Code
Cong. & Admin. News pp. 3617, 3713.

Section 3607 creates a two-year window during which unit holders of a tenants'
corporation can bring hindsight to bear on the question whether certain leases and
contracts with the sponsor constitute the best use of their collective assets. No proof
of one-sidedness or unconscionability is required for the exercise of the termination right. *See West 14th Street Commercial Corp. v. 5 West 14th Street Owners Corp.,* 815
F.2d 188, 200-01 (2d Cir.), *cert. denied,* 484 U.S. 850 & 871, 108 S.Ct. 151 & 200, 98
L.Ed.2d 107 & 151 (1987). Nor does negotiation between prospective unit holders
and the developer, as occurred in the present case, render the termination right
inapplicable. *Id.* The Abuse Relief Act extends the right to any contract that: (1)
provides for the operation of the condominium or cooperative association or
concerns property serving the unit holders; (2) is between the unit holders or the
tenants corporation and the developer or an affiliate of the developer; (3) was
entered into while the tenants corporation was controlled by the developer; and (4)
extends for a period of more than three years.[6] To invoke the termination right,
two-thirds of the unit holders must approve the termination[7] within two years of the
earlier of two events: the date on which developer control ceases or the date on
which the developer owns 25% or less of the units.[8]

---

6. Section 3607(a) provides in pertinent part:

(a) Any contract or portion thereof which is entered into after October 8, 1980, and which —
   (1) provides for operation, maintenance, or management of a condominium or cooperative
       association in a conversion project, or of property serving the condominium or coopera-
       tive unit owners in such project;
   (2) is between such unit owners or such association and the developer or an affiliate of the
       developer;
   (3) was entered into while such association was controlled by the developer through special
       developer control or because the developer held a majority of the votes in such associa-
       tion; and
   (4) is for a period of more than three years. . . . ,
       may be terminated without penalty by such unit owners or such association.

15 U.S.C. § 3607(a) (1988).

7. Section 3607(c) provides:

   A termination under this section shall be by a vote of owners of not less than two-thirds of the
units other than the units owned by the developer or an affiliate of the developer.

15 U.S.C. § 3607(c) (1988).

8. Section 3607(b) provides:

(b) Any termination under this section may occur only during the two-year period beginning on
    the date on which —
   (1) special developer control over the association is terminated; or
   (2) the developer owns 25 per centum or less of the units in the conversion project, whichever
       occurs first.

15 U.S.C. § 3607(b) (1988).

A. APPLICATION OF THE STATUTORY ELEMENTS

If we set aside for the moment the alleged ratification of the Master Lease by Tenants Corporation, the undisputed record reveals that the parking garage portion of the Master Lease falls within the reach of the section 3607 termination right. The on-site parking garage constitutes "property serving the . . . cooperative unit owners," which satisfies the first element of section 3607(a). *See West 14th Street*, 815 F.2d at 198-99. The Master Lease was entered into between Sponsor — a developer as defined by section 3603(14) — and Tenants Corporation — a cooperative association as defined by section 3603(9) — which satisfies the second requirement of section 3607(a). Because directors appointed by Sponsor controlled Tenants Corporation when the contracts were signed, Tenants Corporation was under "special developer control," as defined by section 3603(22), at the time the contracts were entered into; thus, the third element of section 3607(a) is satisfied. *See 2 Tudor City Place Assoc. v. 2 Tudor City Tenants Corp.*, 924 F.2d 1247, 1253 (2d Cir.), *cert. denied*, 502 U.S. 822, 112 S.Ct. 83, 116 L.Ed.2d 56 (1991). The ninety-nine year Master Lease satisfies the fourth requirement of section 3607(a), that the lease be of more than three years' duration.

The parties similarly agree that the manner in which Tenants Corporation invoked the termination right satisfied section 3607(b)-(d): the lease was terminated by a two-thirds vote of the unit holders within two years of the termination of special developer control, and the requisite notice was delivered to Sponsor. The case before us arises over the effect of the ratification language in the asbestos agreement.

B. RATIFICATION AND WAIVER

Underlying this dispute are divergent interpretations of who holds the section 3607 termination right; the parties, consequently, arrive at different answers to the question of who may waive that right by ratifying a self-dealing lease. Sponsor contends, in effect, that the termination right is held by the Tenants Corporation; thus, ratification by the Board of Directors in the asbestos agreement removed the lease from the realm of self-dealing leases, constituting a waiver of the termination right. Sponsor, in essence, characterizes the situation as analogous to a corporation adopting promoters' pre-incorporation contracts. In contrast, Tenants Corporation argues that the termination right belongs solely to the unit holders, and, accordingly, only they may waive that right.

According to Sponsor, once a tenants' corporation is controlled by an independent board of directors, the board may ratify self-dealing leases. Such a ratification constitutes a waiver of the termination right. In support of this argument, Sponsor relies on *West 14th Street*, in which we stated in dicta that, in certain circumstances, ratification might bind a corporation to a contract. *West 14th Street*, 815 F.2d at 199-200.

Sponsor's argument is problematic, even if we were to accept its account of ratification. Although the Board of Directors of Tenants Corporation authorized its President to sign an asbestos agreement, as the district court noted, no vote was taken by the Board on whether to ratify the Master Lease. Even the *West 14th Street* account of ratification does not permit inadvertent waiver of the termination right, but instead requires a vote by the Board on the matter of the adoption of a contract. *West 14th Street*, 815 F.2d at 200.

Furthermore, we offered the discussion of ratification in *West 14th Street* in the context of determining the parties to a contract, within the meaning of the Abuse Relief Act. In this appeal, Sponsor seeks to apply this teaching to the distinct issue of who may waive the termination right. To equate these issues masks the complexities of the newly-fashioned federal termination right by applying the traditional jurisprudence of pre-incorporation contracts to a novel situation.

By means of a convoluted argument, the sponsor in *West 14th Street* contended that contracts that had been signed by the sponsor and the tenants' *corporation* were in fact between the developer and a tenants' *group* that had negotiated amendments to the offering plan, and thus the contracts did not satisfy the second requirement of section 3607(a). This argument, if followed to its logical conclusion, would have proved more than the sponsor wanted — the tenants' corporation would not have been legally bound by the contracts. The sponsor sought to avoid this pitfall by arguing that the tenants corporation had ratified the contract when 80% of the tenants of the building purchased shares in the cooperative. We rejected the ratification portion of this argument on the grounds that:

> Although ratification could serve to bind Owners Corp. to the contracts, *see* 1A W. Fletcher, *Cyclopedia of the Law of Private Corporations* § 210 (C.V. Swearingen rev. ed. 1983), no ratification took place. That event only occurs upon a vote of the board of directors to adopt the contracts, *id.*; it does not occur through the purchase of stock in the corporation. *West 14th Street*, 815 F.2d at 200.

West 14th Street's account of ratification — designed to resolve the issue whether ratification could occur through the purchase of shares in a cooperative — casts little light on the question at hand. We must decide whether ratification by the board of directors may remove a lease from the realm of self-dealing leases, an action which constitutes, in effect, a waiver of the termination right. A board of directors does not have the authority to waive a right held by the stockholders or unit holders. *See* 1A W. Fletcher, *Cyclopedia of the Law of Private Corporations* § 210 (C.V. Swearingen rev. ed. 1983) ("The directors are the central authority of the corporation to do all acts which need not be done by the whole body of stockholders . . ."). Congress crafted the termination right as a right held jointly by the unit holders. To ensure that the right would be used in accordance of the will of the unit holders, Congress required a formal vote by at least two-thirds of the unit holders before the right could be exercised. This procedure reveals that Congress envisioned the right as fundamental to possession of a unit in the cooperative or condominium and intended to temper the exercise of the right through collective debate. Although Congress did not specify a procedure by which the unit holders could waive the termination right, given the assignment of the right to unit holders and the commitment to quasi-consensual exercise of that right, we can safely assume Congress did not intend to exclude the unit holders from the waiver decision. In holding that the waiver decision lies with the unit holders, however, we do not reach the related question of the procedure by which the unit holders may waive that right. The unit holders, in the matter before us, never considered whether to ratify the lease and thereby waive the termination right; therefore, no waiver occurred. . . .

Affirmed.

Cantonbury Heights Condominium Assn., Inc. v. Local Land Development, LLC

273 Conn. 724, 873 A.2d 898 (2005)

BORDEN, J.

This appeal involves the proper interpretation of a particular clause of the declaration[9] for Cantonbury Heights, a common interest community created pursuant to the Common Interest Ownership Act (act), General Statutes § 47-200 et seq.[10] The plaintiff, Cantonbury Heights Condominium Association, Inc., appeals from the trial court's grant of summary judgment in favor of the defendants, Local Land Development, LLC, and Supreme Industries, Inc. The plaintiff contends that the trial court improperly interpreted the declaration. We reverse the judgment in part.

The plaintiff brought this eight count complaint: (1) seeking to quiet and settle title to undeveloped real property in the common interest community; (2) alleging trespass on the real property; (3) alleging negligence with respect to the defendants' title search and work on the real property; (4) seeking indemnification from the defendants for any costs arising from environmental law violations caused by the defendants' actions on that real property; (5) alleging that the defendants' actions constituted conversion; (6) alleging that the defendants' actions constituted unjust enrichment; (7) alleging that the defendants' actions constituted statutory theft; and (8) alleging that the defendants' actions constituted unfair trade practices. The plaintiff sought temporary and permanent injunctions to prevent the defendant from exercising any rights with respect to the property, as well as damages for the defendants' actions to that point. After the trial court denied the plaintiff's motion for a temporary injunction, the plaintiff moved to reargue. Following several hearings, the trial court reaffirmed its prior decision and denied the permanent injunction as well. The defendants then moved for summary judgment, which the trial court granted as to all counts of the complaint. This appeal followed.

The following facts and procedural history are undisputed for the purposes of this appeal. Cantonbury Development Limited Partnership, the original developer of the condominium complex known as Cantonbury Heights, filed an initial declaration establishing nine condominium units with associated common elements and reserving to itself certain special declarant rights, including the authority to exercise development rights. Those development rights included the right to create up to 132 additional condominium units. Cantonbury Development Limited Partnership subsequently transferred the special declarant rights to Cantonbury Heights Associates, which exercised certain of those rights to bring the total number of units built to sixty-seven before financial difficulties forced it to assign the rights, along with

9. A declaration is an instrument recorded and executed in the same manner as a deed for the purpose of creating a common interest community. General Statutes § 47-220.

10. General Statutes § 47-202(7) provides in relevant part: " 'Common interest community' means real property described in a declaration with respect to which a person, by virtue of his ownership of a unit, is obligated to pay for (A) real property taxes on, (B) insurance premiums on, (C) maintenance of, or (D) improvement of, any other real property other than that unit described in the declaration. . . ."

ownership of two unsold units, to Mechanics Savings Bank. Mechanics Savings Bank sold the two units it owned before executing a quit claim deed to transfer the special declarant rights to General Financial Services, Inc.

After acquiring the special declarant rights from General Financial Services, Inc., by quit claim deed, the defendant received approval from the Canton zoning commission to construct sixty-three additional condominium units in those areas designated as Phase III and Phase IV on the Cantonbury Heights site plan. In preparation for construction, Moosehead Land Clearing removed trees and other material from the area to be developed pursuant to a contract with the defendant. The defendant also contracted with West Central Enterprises, Inc., to perform excavation work in the area and with Supreme to perform site preparation work.

Before the defendant could proceed further, town authorities halted the site preparation efforts, and state authorities cited the defendant for violation of environmental laws. First, the town of Canton issued an order to cease and desist excavation and grading operations because those operations may have been caus-ing soil erosion into wetlands and watercourses both on and off the construction site at Cantonbury Heights. The town also claimed that the defendant had failed to comply with the terms and conditions of a permit issued by the Canton inland wetlands and watercourses agency and to construct improvements in accordance with approved drawings. Shortly thereafter, the Connecticut department of environmental protection issued a notice of violation, in which it claimed that the defendant had violated certain provisions of the general permit for the dis-charge of stormwater and dewatering wastewaters associated with construction activities. Then, the Canton inland wetlands and watercourses agency issued a revised cease and desist order requiring the defendant to obtain approval for a modification of the general permit and to develop a management plan for the long-term operation and maintenance of sediment and erosion control measures installed as a result of the initial cease and desist order. Finally, the department of environmental protection issued a notice of violation to the plaintiff, in which it claimed that, if the plaintiff owned the property on which the defendant had begun development work, the plaintiff may be in violation of the law and subject to its ongoing enforcement action.

Even before receiving the notice of violation from the department of environ-mental protection, the plaintiff had initiated the present action, seeking a tempo-rary injunction against the defendant to prevent it from exercising any special declarant rights in Cantonbury Heights. After receiving the notice of violation, the plaintiff amended its complaint to include a count sounding in indemnity for any costs incurred by the plaintiff as a result of the violations alleged by the department of environmental protection. . . .

The [trial] court's finding that the defendant's special declarant rights had not expired was dispositive of seven of the eight counts in the plaintiff's amended complaint. On the fourth count of the amended complaint, which sounded in indemnity for any costs incurred by the plaintiff as a result of violations alleged by the department of environmental protection, the trial court ruled for the defen-dants on the basis of its earlier ruling that the defendant had corrected all violations and had brought the project into compliance with the orders of the department of environmental protection and the Canton inland wetlands and watercourses agency. . . .

I

On seven of the eight counts in the complaint, the court granted summary judgment in favor of the defendants because it concluded, based on its interpretation of the declaration, that the defendant had authority to exercise the development rights contained in the declaration.[5] Our review of that conclusion begins with a review of the declaration's operative terms.

Article VIII of the declaration, entitled "Development Rights and Other Special Declarant Rights," contains those terms relevant to our resolution of the present case. Section 8.1 of article VIII reserves certain development rights to the declarant including "[t]he right to add Units and Limited Common Elements in the location shown as 'Development Rights Reserved in this Area' on the Survey and Plans." Section 8.2 of article VIII then places certain limitations on the development rights, providing in relevant part: "(a) The Development Rights may be exercised at any time, but not more than 21 years after the recording of the initial Declaration; (b) Not more than a total of 132 additional Units may be created under the Development Rights . . . (e) No Development Rights may be exercised unless approved pursuant to Section 18.5."

Section 8.2 of article VIII of the declaration does not contain all of the limitations on the development rights, however, because, although § 8.1 reserves the development rights, § 8.4 makes the authority to *exercise* those rights a special declarant right. Thus, any limitation placed on the special declarant rights also effectively operates as a limitation on the development rights. Section 8.9 contains the relevant limitations on the special declarant rights. Therefore, the determination of whether the defendant's development rights have expired pursuant to the declaration requires an interpretation of § 8.9.

Because the declaration operates in the nature of a contract, in that it establishes the parties' rights and obligations, we apply the rules of contract construction to the interpretation of § 8.9 of article VIII. In ascertaining the contractual rights and obligations of the parties, we seek to effectuate their intent, which is derived from the language employed in the contract, taking into consideration the circumstances of the parties and the transaction. *Alstom Power, Inc. v. Balcke-Durr, Inc.,* 269 Conn. 599, 610, 849 A.2d 804 (2004); *Levine v. Advest, Inc.,* 244 Conn. 732, 745, 714 A.2d 649 (1998). We accord the language employed in the contract a rational construction based on its common, natural and ordinary meaning and usage as applied to the subject matter of the contract. *Alstom Power, Inc. v. Balcke-Durr, Inc.,* supra, at 610, 849 A.2d 804. Where the language is unambiguous, we must give the contract effect according to its terms. Id. Where the language is ambiguous, however, we must construe those ambiguities against the drafter. *Hartford Electric Applicators of Thermalux, Inc. v. Alden,* 169 Conn. 177, 182, 363 A.2d 135 (1975). This approach corresponds with the general rule that "[a]ny ambiguity in a declaration of condominium must be construed against the developer who authored the declaration." 15A Am Jur.2d, Condominiums and Cooperative Apartments § 8 (2000). . . .

Section 8.9 of article VIII of the declaration provides: "Unless sooner terminated by a recorded instrument executed by the Declarant, any Special Declarant Right

---

5. The following counts of the complaint were resolved based on the trial court's interpretation of the declaration: count one to quiet title to the property; count two for trespass; count three for negligence; count five for conversion; count six for unjust enrichment; count seven for statutory theft; and count eight for unfair trade practices.

may be exercised by the Declarant so long as the Declarant is obligated under any warranty or obligation, owns any units or any Security Interest on any Units, or for 21 years after recording the Declaration, whichever is sooner. Earlier termination of certain rights may occur by statute. Additional limitations occur in Article XVIII." Neither termination by a recorded instrument nor by statute applies in the present case, and we need not address the limitations in article XVIII. Thus, the disputed portion of § 8.9 of article VIII is the following language: "so long as the Declarant is obligated under any warranty or obligation, owns any units or any Security Interest on any Units, or for 21 years after recording the Declaration, whichever is sooner."

The parties disagree about two aspects of this language of § 8.9 of article VIII of the declaration: (1) whether each of the listed conditions operates as an independent trigger to terminate special declarant rights; and (2) what types of obligations satisfy the requirement that the declarant be "obligated under any . . . obligation . . ." With respect to the first aspect, the plaintiff argues that in order to give effect to the phrase "whichever is sooner," each condition must be read as an independent trigger that terminates special declarant rights. In other words, according to the plaintiff's interpretation, the declarant must be obligated under a warranty or obligation *and* own a unit *and* maintain a security interest on a unit, *and* less than twenty-one years must have elapsed since the recording of the declaration in order for the declarant to exercise special declarant rights. The defendant counters that the phrase "whichever is sooner," coupled with the twenty-one year time limit constitutes a termination provision, and that as long as less than twenty-one years have elapsed, the declarant need only be obligated under a warranty or obligation *or* own a unit or a security interest on a unit. We agree with the defendant.

We discern no ambiguity in the language of § 8.9 of article VIII of the declaration allowing special declarant rights to be exercised for twenty-one years or until the declarant no longer satisfied any of the other conditions, whichever occurred sooner. In essence, the plaintiff suggests that we insert the word "and" between the first two conditions and replace the word "or" with "and" between the ownership and security conditions to create the phrase "under any warranty or obligation, *and* owns any units *and* any Security Interest on any Units, or for 21 years. . . ." (Emphasis added.) When a list is joined by the disjunctive "or," as this one is, common usage strongly suggests that each item in the list be read to be separated by "or," not "and." Contrary to the plaintiff's assertions, this interpretation still gives effect to the phrase, "whichever is sooner," because that phrase is intended to compare the declarant's ability to satisfy any one of the other conditions to the twenty-one year time limit. The plaintiff seeks to create ambiguity where it does not exist and to resolve the ambiguity by inserting words in the language of the declaration with no justification for doing so.

With respect to the second aspect, namely, what types of obligations satisfy the condition that the declarant be under an obligation,[6] the plaintiff argues that only obligations *to the unit owners* qualify. The defendant counters that the term includes

---

6. No dispute exists between the parties with regard to the defendant's ability to satisfy any of the conditions other than whether it still has obligations pursuant to the declaration. Twenty-one years have not passed since the declaration was recorded. The defendant neither has any warranty obligations, nor does it own or maintain a security interest in any of the units. Therefore, the special declarant rights remain viable if, and only if, the defendant remains obligated under any obligation contemplated by § 8.9 of article VIII of the declaration.

tax, expense and liability obligations associated with its position as the declarant. Because each of the parties offers a reasonable interpretation of the term in light of the origin and the purpose of the declaration, we conclude that the contract is ambiguous as to what type of obligation the declarant must be under to satisfy the § 8.9 limitation on the special declarant rights. "If the language of the contract is susceptible to more than one reasonable interpretation, the contract is ambiguous." *United Illuminating Co. v. Wisvest-Connecticut, LLC,* supra, 259 Conn. at 671, 791 A.2d 546.

Normally, where the contract language is not definitive, the determination of the parties' intent is a question of fact, and the trial court's interpretation is subject to reversal on appeal only if it is clearly erroneous. *HLO Land Ownership Associates Ltd. Partnership v. Hartford,* 248 Conn. 350, 357, 727 A.2d 1260 (1999). In the present case, however, the trial court did not indicate whether it considered the term "obligation" to be ambiguous. Regardless, we conclude that the term is ambiguous, and that the trial court failed to apply properly the rule of contract construction that requires ambiguities to be construed against the drafter.

The plaintiff bases its contention that the term "obligation" must refer to obligations to unit owners on three premises: (1) including obligations to third parties in the meaning of the term would eliminate all limitations on the exercise of special declarant rights except the twenty-one year time limit; (2) relevant portions of the act support this interpretation; and (3) the use of the term "warranty" in conjunction with "obligation" supports this interpretation. In addition, the plaintiff proffers a plausible reason why its interpretation has a natural practical effect. We conclude that the plaintiff's proffered interpretation of "obligation" is sufficiently plausible to invoke the rule of construction against the drafter of the declaration.

First, the tax liabilities and other obligations that the declarant owes to third parties remain in place until the declarant fully exercises all development rights, or those rights lapse for other reasons. For instance, General Statutes § 47-204(c) continues the declarant's tax liability so long as he has reserved development rights: "Any portion of the common elements for which the declarant has reserved any development right shall be separately taxed and assessed against the declarant, and the declarant alone is liable for the payment of those taxes." Thus, including the tax liabilities as an "obligation" pursuant to § 8.9 of article VIII of the declaration results in circular support between the tax liabilities and the development rights: the declarant maintains special declarant rights, which include development rights, because he has tax liabilities, and has tax liabilities because he maintains the development rights. Such a result would render the other limitations in § 8.9, other than the twenty-one year time limit, mere surplusage. If tax liabilities satisfy the "obligation" condition, the declarant would always be under an "obligation" until all of the development rights were exercised, making the warranty, ownership and security interest conditions meaningless.

Second, the language and structure of General Statutes § 47-246 mirrors § 3-104 of the Uniform Common Interest Ownership Act (uniform act). See Uniform Common Interest Ownership Act § 3-104, 7 U.L.A. 99 (2002). That section governs which obligations and liabilities are imposed upon a third party who assumes declarant status through a transfer of the existing declarant's interest in a common interest community, as occurred in the present case. The comment to § 3-104 of the uniform act identifies two issues associated with imposing obligations and liabilities on the successor declarant along with the section's objective in resolving those issues. Id., comment, 101. "First, what obligations and liabilities *to unit owners* (both existing and future) should a declarant retain, notwithstanding his transfer of interests. Second, what obligations and liabilities may fairly be imposed upon the declarant's successor in interest. . . . This section strikes a balance between the obvious need to protect the interests of unit owners and the equally important need to protect innocent successors to a declarant's rights. . . . The general scheme of the section is to impose upon a declarant continuing obligations and liabilities for promises, acts, or omissions undertaken during the period that he was in control of the community, while relieving a declarant who transfers all or part of his special declarant rights in a project of such responsibilities with respect to the promises, acts, or omissions of a successor over whom he has no control." (Emphasis added.) Id. Although § 8.9 of article VIII of the declaration deals with limitations on special declarant rights, rather than the transfer of those rights, the plaintiff argues that this comment indicates that the obligations contemplated by the uniform act, and, by reference, the act, are those obligations to unit owners, not to third parties. Thus, the use of the term "obligation" in the declaration, which must adhere to the requirements of the act, creates a plausible inference that the parties intended that obligation to be to the unit owners.

Third, the use of the phrase "obligated under any warranty or obligation" in § 8.9 of article VIII of the declaration suggests that the terms "warranty" and "obligation" implicate duties to the same party. Where a provision contains two or more words grouped together, we often examine a particular word's relationship to the associated words and phrases to determine its meaning pursuant to the canon of construction *noscitur a sociis*. *Connecticut National Bank v. Giacomi*, 242 Conn. 17, 33, 699 A.2d 101 (1997). . . .

Finally, the plaintiff proffers a plausible practical effect of its interpretation of the clause. The plaintiff's interpretation of the clause prevents the declarant from extending development of the common interest community out over such a long period of time that it harms the investments of the existing unit owners in their properties. The plaintiff contends that a development pattern that results in the addition of new units in the same development as considerably older existing units adversely affects the interests of all unit owners because the value of the existing units decreases while, at the same time, purchasers of the new units must pay higher maintenance fees than a new unit normally would require in order to perform the necessary upkeep, such as roofing and siding replacement, on the existing units. Requiring the declarant to initiate the next phase of development in the community while he still has obligations to the existing unit owners in order to protect the development rights, on the other hand, facilitates the creation of a comprehensive, cohesive condominium development by forcing the declarant either to proceed with development of follow-on phases in a timely manner or to maintain an ownership or security interest in the existing units and risk the adverse effects of extending the development period.

The defendant maintains, however, that limiting the term "obligation" to obligations to unit owners requires this court to do three things: (1) add the phrase "to existing unit owners" after the term "obligation" in the existing declaration; (2) ignore the word "any" that precedes "warranty or obligation"; and (3) ignore the provisions of the act that impose obligations, such as taxes and other duties, on the declarant. Furthermore, the defendant argues, the term "obligation" in the declaration is not ambiguous, and the trial court did not find it to be so. In essence, the defendant claims that the declaration language "obligated under any . . .

obligation" means just that; any obligation suffices to preserve the special declarant rights. Although the defendant's interpretation is certainly plausible, it does not suffice to render the plaintiff's interpretation implausible. At most, it simply shows that the language at issue is ambiguous.

In sum, we are not completely persuaded by either party's interpretation of the declaration. Thus, we must rely upon the applicable rule of contract construction, namely, where the language is ambiguous we must construe those ambiguities against the drafter. *Hartford Electric Applicators of Thermalux, Inc. v. Alden,* supra, 169 Conn. at 182, 363 A.2d 135. As the successor in interest to the rights of the original declarant, the defendant stands in its shoes. Accordingly, we conclude that the term "obligation" in § 8.9 of article VIII of the declaration refers to obligations to the unit owners. Because the defendant neither has any obligations to the unit owners nor satisfies any of the other conditions necessary to preserve the special declarant rights, the defendant possesses no special declarant rights, including the authority to exercise development rights. . . .

NOTES AND QUESTIONS

1. What was the purpose of the "special declarant's rights" in *Cantonbury?* Can you imagine other rights the developer might legitimately want to retain beyond those accorded to purchasers?

2. When a developer retains title to the ground under the development or amenities that are part of the community, entering into a long-term lease with the association, one critical element is the "escalation clause" — since the lease is likely to extend for decades, the rents must increase at some rate to keep from being eaten away by inflation. In 1988, Florida passed a statute prohibiting the inclusion or enforcement of escalation clauses in condominium leases. Fla. Stat. § 718.4015 (2006). The statute defines an escalation clause as any clause providing for a rental increase "at the same percentage rate as any nationally recognized and conveniently available commodity or consumer price index." Would this language also invalidate an escalation at one-half the percentage increase in the consumer price index? What is the impact of such an escalation clause on the real cost of a condominium unit? Of a statute prohibiting such a clause?

3. Although the garage lease in *181 East 73rd* is one example, the predominant form of self-dealing condominium contracts involves long-term leases of recreational facilities. Cf. Point East Management Corp. v. Point East One Condominium Corp., Inc., 282 So. 2d 628 (Fla. 1973); Beeman v. Island Breakers, A Condominium, Inc., 577 So. 2d 1341 (Fla. App. 1990). Generally, the developer retains title to the facilities and then leases them to the condominium association at inflated prices. In *Beeman,* had the escalation clause in the swimming pool lease not been invalidated, the developer would have received $200 million in rental over the 99 years of the lease on an initial $45,000 investment. How would you calculate a "fair" rental return? For general discussion, see Comment, Developer Leases Under the Condominium and Cooperative Abuse Relief Act of 1980, 15 Hofstra L. Rev. 631 (1986).

In addition to the *per se* rule barring escalation clauses, Florida courts also refuse to enforce developer leases if the lease produces "unconscionable" results, Fla. Stat. § 718.122 (2006), or is not "fair and reasonable," Fla. Stat. § 718.302(1) (2006). A lease that is unconscionable can hardly be fair and reasonable, but a lease that is not fair and reasonable need not also be unconscionable. Explain.

4. The Uniform Condominium Act § 3-105 (1977) provides:

If entered into before the executive board elected by the unit owners [after the developer relinquishes control] takes office, (1) any management contract, employment contract, or lease of recreational or parking areas or facilities, (2) any other contract or lease to which [the developer is a party], or (3) any contract or lease which is not bona fide or which was unconscionable to the unit owners at the time entered into under the circumstances then prevailing, may be terminated without penalty by the association at any time . . . upon not less than [90] days notice to the other party.

The Uniform Common Interest Ownership Act § 3-105 (1982) contains identical language.

5. A related problem is how and when the developer should turn control over the governing board to the purchasers, particularly when the developer still holds unsold units. Suppose that 51 units in a 100-unit project remain unsold; is it reasonable for the sponsor to retain control of the governing board? Suppose that 25 units remain unsold; is it reasonable for the sponsor to retain two (three) seats on a five-person governing board? Cf. Barclay v. DeVeau, 384 Mass. 676, 429 N.E. 323 (1981) (developer allowed to appoint two of the three members of the governing board until he owned fewer than 12 units in a 130-unit project). If the developer retains control over the board, what are the board members' duties to other unit owners? See Gary A. Poliakoff, Transition of Control of the Community Association from the Unit Owners' Perspective, 16-APR Prob. & Prop. 49 (2002).

C. THE GOVERNING BODY'S RULE-MAKING POWER

1. The Sources and Limits of Power

The governing body's rule-making and other decisional powers usually derive from either the declaration or the by-laws of the common interest community. Unit owners, increasingly, have sued their governing board for project mismanagement or arbitrary conduct, to protest special assessments, or for improper refusal to consent to a unit sale, and are asking courts to set aside association actions as unreasonable or arbitrary, and on procedural or public policy grounds. The disputes reported below provide some indication of the range of tensions between the governing body and aggrieved unit owners and the way courts are grappling with these issues.

Mulligan v. Panther Valley Property Owners Association

337 N.J. Super. 293, 766 A.2d 1186 (2001)

The opinion of the court was delivered by WEFING, J.A.D.

Plaintiff owns a home in Panther Valley, a private common-interest residential community in Warren County. Defendant Panther Valley Property Owners Association (Association) is a non-profit corporation that was organized in 1968 for the purpose of governing the community. The Association acts through an elected Board of Trustees; the individual defendants are members of the Association's Board. Plaintiff, as a result of her home ownership, is a member of the Association.

In October 1998, the Association, through a vote of its membership, adopted six amendments to the community's Declaration of Covenants and Restrictions (Declarations) and the Association's bylaws. Plaintiff filed suit challenging five of those amendments. The trial court upheld three of the amendments and struck down two. The parties appeal and cross-appeal from the trial court's judgment. After a careful review of the entire record in light of the arguments advanced on appeal, we affirm in part and reverse in part.

The first of these amendments declared, in substance and effect, that no individual registered as a Tier 3 offender under *N.J.S.A.* 2C:7-8(c)(3) ("Megan's Law") could reside in Panther Valley. Tier 3 is the highest classification within Megan's Law. In order for an individual to be classified as a Tier 3 registrant, that individual must be a sex-offender who has been deemed to pose a high risk of re-offending. . . . The trial court upheld the amendment precluding such Tier 3 registrants from residing within Panther Valley.

The second amendment authorized the Association to file with the Warren County Clerk a "Notice of Continuing Violation" if a member persisted in violating Panther Valley's Declaration or the Association's bylaws or rules. The trial court concluded that amendment was invalid because it did not require the Association to give notice to a member before filing such a Notice.

The third amendment provided that an owner could be liable for the Association's counsel fees and costs if the Association were required to file suit to enforce the Declaration, its bylaws or rules. The trial court struck down that amendment.

The fourth amendment set forth a procedure governing a member's inspection of the Association's books and records. The trial court concluded the amendment was facially valid.

The fifth amendment established minimum qualifications for members who wished to be elected to the Association's Board of Trustees. The trial court again concluded the amendment was facially valid.

I

The threshold issue to be determined is the proper standard governing judicial review of these amendments. It is important to note that plaintiff's challenge to the validity of these amendments does not revolve around the manner in which they were adopted, e.g., compliance with procedural requirements. Rather, her challenge is directed to the substance of the amendments themselves.

Plaintiff contends in essence that the amendments should be measured under a test of reasonableness. She asserts that each of these amendments fail that test. She maintains that each of these amendments represents a diminution of her ownership rights and, in consequence, is invalid. Defendants, on the other hand, assert that the amendments should be analyzed under what is termed the business judgment rule to determine if they are authorized by statute and the applicable documents governing the parties' relationship and to see if they violate any constitutional or statutory provision or conflict with public policy; defendants assert the amendments are entitled to a presumption of validity. According to defendants, each of these amendments represents an authorized action by the membership.

There is no reported case in New Jersey which clearly resolves the question of what standard a reviewing court should employ in such a context, where the membership has voted to amend the community's Declaration and the Association bylaws. Other reported cases in New Jersey which have considered such amendments have, generally, arisen following action by the community's board of trustees. *See, e.g., Thanasoulis v. Winston Towers 200 Ass'n,* 110 *N.J.* 650, 542 *A.*2d 900 (1988), in which the Court struck down two amendments to the association's rules and regulations adopted by the board. In *Siller v. Hartz Mountain Assocs.,* 93 *N.J.* 370, 382, 461 *A.*2d 568 (1983), in the context of a suit by individual unit owners to prevent settlement between the condominium developer and the condominium association of claims related to alleged defects in construction, the Court spoke of the association's board occupying a position analogous to a corporation's board of directors. Perhaps the clearest explication of the business judgment rule is contained in *Papalexiou v. Tower West Condominium,* in which individual unit owners challenged the authority of the board to levy a special emergency assessment upon the membership. In upholding the assessment, the court said:

> The refusal to enforce arbitrary and capricious rules promulgated by governing boards of condominiums is simply an application of the "business judgment" rule. This rule requires the presence of fraud or lack of good faith in the conduct of a corporation's internal affairs before the decisions of a board of directors can be questioned. If the corporate directors' conduct is authorized, a showing must be made of fraud, self-dealing or unconscionable conduct to justify judicial review. . . . Although directors of a corporation have a fiduciary relationship to the shareholders, they are not expected to be incapable of error. All that is required is that persons in such positions act reasonably and in good faith in carrying out their duties. Courts will not second-guess the actions of directors unless it appears that they are the result of fraud, dishonesty or incompetence.
> [*Papalexiou v. Tower West Condo.,* 167 N.J.Super. 516, 527, 401 A.2d 280 (Ch. Div.1979) (citations omitted).]

In *Chin v. Coventry Square Condominium Ass'n,* 270 *N.J.Super.* 323, 637 A.2d 197 (App. Div.1994), we considered amendments to the association's bylaws. It is not possible to tell from the opinion whether the challenged amendments were passed by the association's board or the membership as a whole. In our decision, however, we noted the existence of these two tests and concluded that the challenged amendments could not withstand scrutiny even under the business judgment rule. 270 *N.J.Super.* at 329, 637 A.2d 197.

We pause first to note the unique nature of Panther Valley. It is a gated residential community located within the Township of Allamuchy; it is comprised of more than 2,000 homes, including single-family homes, townhouses and condominium units. *State v. Panther Valley Prop. Owners Ass'n,* 307 *N.J.Super.* 319, 322, 704 A.2d 1010 (App.Div.1998) (holding that the Association, having asked the Warren County Prosecutor to assume jurisdiction to enforce the provisions of Title 39 over its private roads, lacked the authority to impose independent fines upon its members who committed traffic violations within its borders). The development itself, in light of the mix of ownership types, is not a condominium development but is more properly referred to as a "common interest development." *Id.* at 327, 704 A.2d 1010. The Association as a whole is thus not subject to the terms and provisions of the Condominium Act, *N.J.S.A.* 46:8B-1 to -38, *Id.* at 328, 704 A.2d 1010, for only "[a] small minority of the units are governed by the Condominium Act." *Id.* at 327, 704 A.2d 1010. In certain contexts, however, the condominium statute may be considered "instructive" and looked to for guidance. *Id.* at 332, 704 A.2d 1010.

Although Justice Schreiber noted in *Siller* that there is some authority for the proposition that condominium ownership existed as long ago as ancient Rome, *Siller, supra,* 93 *N.J.* at 375, n. 4, 461 *A.*2d 568, such common interest developments are generally considered a relatively recent phenomenon. Carl B. Kress, *Beyond Nahrstedt: Reviewing Restrictions Governing Life in a Property Owner Association,* 42 *UCLA L.Rev.* 837, 842 (1995), (hereinafter Kress). Common interest developments are the fastest growing form of housing in the United States. Armand Arabian, *Condos, Cats, and CC & RS: Invasion of the Castle Common,* 23 *Pepp. L.Rev.* 1 (1995), (hereinafter Arabian). New Jersey is among the states in which residential community associations are most common. David J. Kennedy, *Residential Associations as State Actors: Regulating the Impact of Gated Communities on Nonmembers,* 105 *Yale L.J.* 761, 793, n. 24 (1995), (hereinafter Kennedy). The law governing the relationships among an association, its board and its members has been described as being "in its infancy, or at best early adolescence. . . ." Stewart E. Sterk, *Minority Protection in Residential Private Governments,* 77 *B.U. L.Rev.* 273, 307 (1997). One indication that the courts are, indeed, grappling with new concepts is the split that exists in the different approaches of different jurisdictions.

California, for instance, has adopted the "reasonableness" test, *Nahrstedt v. Lakeside Village Condominium Ass'n,* 8 *Cal.* 4th 361, 33 *Cal.Rptr.* 2d 63, 878 *P.*2d 1275 (1994), while New York has adopted the "business judgment" rule. *Levandusky v. One Fifth Avenue Apartment Corp.,* 75 *N.Y.*2d 530, 554 *N.Y.S.*2d 807, 553 *N.E.*2d 1317 (1990). Some courts and commentators recognize a distinction between considering original recorded restrictions, i.e., those extant at the time of purchase, and later-adopted ones. *Ridgely Condo. Ass'n v. Smyrnioudis,* 105 *Md.App.* 404, 660 *A.*2d 942, 948 (1995), *aff'd* 343 *Md.* 357, 681 *A.*2d 494 (1996); *Sterk, supra,* 77 *B.U. L.Rev.* at 338-39. Other cases turn upon whether the restriction at issue was improperly incorporated in the association's bylaws, rather than the community's underlying declaration. *Shorewood West Condo. Ass'n v. Sadri,* 140 *Wash.*2d 47, 992 *P.*2d 1008 (2000) (leasing restriction contained in amendment to bylaws rather than the condominium declaration unenforceable).

The majority of jurisdictions appear to employ the reasonableness standard. *Arabian, supra,* 23 *Pepp. L.Rev.* at 11. We are satisfied that, in the context of this case, the appropriate test to measure the validity of these amendments is that of reasonableness. We reach that conclusion for several reasons. First, we recognize that we are dealing with amendments to the documents governing life at Panther Valley, as opposed to original provisions. None of the terms to which plaintiff objects were contained within the Declaration and bylaws to which she gave her assent by her decision in 1976 to purchase a home at Panther Valley. As amendments, we do not consider them entitled to the "very strong presumption of validity" that some courts have attached to restrictions imposed by a common interest community from the outset of its development. *Ridgely, supra,* 660 *A.*2d at 947, quoting *Hidden Harbour Estates, Inc. v. Basso,* 393 *So.*2d 637, 639 (Fla.App. 4 Dist. Ct.1981).

Additionally, we note that under Section 4 of Article XI of the Declaration, the Declaration can be amended at any time by a simple majority vote of the Association's members. By contrast, many common interest communities permit amendments to the declaration only by a substantial majority of the owners, thus affording greater protection to the affected parties. *Kress, supra,* 42 *UCLA L.Rev.* at 841. This, for example, is the approach of the Uniform Common Interest Ownership Act, a statute that has been passed in a number of states, although not yet in New Jersey.

Finally, these amendments were passed by the membership as a whole, rather than the Association's board of trustees. Thus, the analytical framework which provides the justification for the business judgment rule, see *Papalexiou, supra,* is absent.

Because these amendments all reflect changes adopted substantially after plaintiff took up residence at Panther Valley, and because the governing documents require no more than a simple majority vote, we are unwilling to afford them the presumption of validity for which defendants contend. We are satisfied that plaintiff is entitled in the context of this case to have these amendments judged on their reasonableness.

II

We turn then to the amendments at issue. We have concluded that the second amendment, which authorizes the filing of a Notice of Continuing Violation, does not pass the test of reasonableness but that the third, fourth and fifth amendments do pass that test. As to the first amendment, however, which precludes residency at Panther Valley by a Tier 3 offender, we decline to pass upon the issue for we are satisfied that the parties did not create a sufficient record in this matter, which was handled as a summary proceeding, to permit a reviewing court to reach a decision that can take into account and reflect the various competing policy considerations.

Plaintiff asserts three reasons why this first amendment is invalid. She contends that it is an unlawful infringement on her right to alienate her property, that it compels her to violate the law by obligating her to seek out and identify such Tier 3 registrants and that it is contrary to public policy. The first two are wholly insubstantial in our view and if plaintiff's argument were confined to them, we would reject her position out of hand.

Defendants have supplied as part of the record in this case statistics that were compiled by the Office of the Attorney General in connection with its overall responsibility for monitoring Megan's Law matters. According to those figures, there were, as of July 30, 1999, only 80 Tier 3 registrants within the entire State of New Jersey. New Jersey has, as of the 2000 census, a population in excess of 8,400,000; that there may be 80 individuals out of a total of 8.4 million to whom plaintiff may not sell her home cannot, in our judgment, seriously be considered an unlawful restriction upon her right to sell or lease her home.

In addition, the restriction, if indeed it can be considered one, does not fall unfairly upon plaintiff; it affects all members of the Association equally. Thus, plaintiff, if she sought to sell or lease her home, would not be relegated to a smaller potential market than another Panther Valley resident. ("Courts appear[ ] far more likely to reject changes that involved potential special privileges for individuals than they [are] to reject changes applicable to the entire population of unit owners." Patrick A. Randolph, Jr., *Changing the Rules: Should Courts Limit the Power of Common Interest Communities to Alter Unit Owners' Privileges in the Face of Vested Expectations?,* 38 *Santa Clara L.Rev.* 1081, 1082 (1998).) . . .

Her second asserted reason flies in the face of the plain language of the amendment. It imposes no such obligation upon her.

The third, however, gives us pause, at least in one regard. Although not contained within the record before us, we are aware that other similar common interest communities within the State have passed similar restrictions upon residency by Tier 3 registrants. 156 *N.J.L.J.* 361 (May 3, 1999). We do not know from the record how many common interest communities exist within the State and we do not know from the record how many of those communities have seen fit to adopt comparable restrictions and whether they have determined to include a broader group than Tier 3 registrants. We are thus unable to determine whether the result of such provisions is to make a large segment of the housing market unavailable to one category of individual and indeed perhaps to approach "the ogre of vigilantism and harassment," the potential dangers of which the Supreme Court recognized even while upholding the constitutionality of Megan's Law. *Doe v. Poritz,* 142 *N.J.* 1, 110, 662 A.2d 367 (1995).

The record is deficient in another regard as well for it is entirely unclear if the Association performs quasi-municipal functions, such that its actions perhaps should be viewed as analogous to governmental actions in some regards. As to this issue, see, e.g., *Kennedy, supra,* 105 *Yale L.J.* 761; John B. Owens, *Westec Story: Gated Communities and the Fourth Amendment,* 34 *Am.Crim. L.Rev.* 1127 (1997). We do know, from *State v. Panther Valley, supra,* that the Association has turned over to the township the responsibility for traffic enforcement, for instance, and is precluded from acting independently in that sphere. The record does not disclose whether certain services are provided by the township and others by the Association. It may be somewhat instructive in this regard that we have concluded in another matter involving Panther Valley that the Association's newsletter, "The Panther," could not be compelled to publish an ad submitted by the plaintiff that was apparently critical of the local first-aid squad. *William G. Mulligan Found. for the Control of First Aid Squadders & Roving Paramedics v. Brooks,* 312 *N.J.Super.* 353, 711 A.2d 961 (App. Div.1998).

We recognize, of course, that Tier 3 registrants (and indeed convicted criminals) are not a protected group within the terms of New Jersey's Law Against Discrimination. *N.J.S.A.* 10:5-3. Nor have we been pointed to any authority deeming them handicapped. In this regard, however see *Arnold Murray Constr., L.L.C. v. Hicks,* 621 N.W.2d 171 (S.D.2001), in which the court upheld the eviction of a handicapped tenant who posed a direct threat to the health and safety of other tenants without the necessity of attempting to provide reasonable accommodations under the federal Fair Housing Act. It does not necessarily follow, however, that large segments of the State could entirely close their doors to such individuals, confining them to a narrow corridor and thus perhaps exposing those within that remaining corridor to a greater risk of harm than they might otherwise have had to confront.

Common interest communities fill a particular need in the housing market but they also pose unique problems for those who remain outside their gates, whether voluntarily or by economic necessity. The understandable desire of individuals to protect themselves and their families from some of the ravages of modern society and thus reside within such communities should not become a vehicle to ensure that those problems remain the burden of those least able to afford a viable solution.

We hasten to add that we recognize that not all gated communities are refuges for the wealthy. They are a spreading phenomenon that can be found among all economic strata. Owens, *supra,* 34 *Am.Crim. L.Rev.* at 1136-37. Their growth has been fueled by the public's fear of crime and need for safety. *Ibid.*; Kennedy, *supra,* 105 *Yale L.J.* at 766.

The Supreme Court has long cautioned against the dangers inherent in courts, presented with a meager record, ruling upon questions having a broad social and legal impact. *Jackson v. Muhlenberg Hosp.*, 53 *N.J.* 138, 249 *A.2d* 65 (1969). . . .

Because we have concluded, for the reasons we have set forth, that the record was insufficient to permit determination of the issue, we reverse that portion of the trial court's judgment upholding the validity of the first amendment to the Association's Declaration.

We have considered whether the paucity of the record is a matter that could be cured upon remand. We have, however, determined that a remand is not appropriate. We see no reason to depart from the general practice that a plaintiff who failed initially to present sufficient evidence to the trial court is, ordinarily, not entitled to a remand to cure that deficiency.

III

A

We turn now to plaintiff's remaining challenges to the trial court's judgment. The membership voted to amend the Association's bylaws on the subject of a member's inspection of the Association's books and records. Prior to amendment, Article XIV of the bylaws provided that "all books, records, papers and files of the Association shall be open, upon request" for inspection by a member. . . . It also authorized inspection by an attorney or certified public accountant representing a member and, in appropriate instances, the township. Its only limitation was a reference to "reasonable business hours."

The amended article restricted such inspection to a review of the books for the current fiscal year and the two preceding fiscal years. It required a request for inspection to be in writing and to be served not less than ten business days before the requested date for inspection. It limited any one inspection to no more than two hours in length and provided that if all the records could not be reviewed in that time, an additional date would be provided within five business days. It authorized the Board to draft reasonable rules and regulations governing such inspections and further authorized the Board to withhold from inspection any documents that in "its reasonable business judgment" would

1. Constitute an unwarranted invasion of privacy.
2. Constitute privileged information under the attorney-client privilege.
3. Involve pending or anticipated litigation or contract negotiations.
4. Involve the employment, promotion, discipline, or dismissal of a specific committee member or employee.

Plaintiff argues that the ten-day notice requirement is illegal and that the amendment as a whole is too broad. She asserts that it restricts rights she previously possessed and will hamper members' attempts to assure themselves that the Association is being properly governed. . . .

As to her final argument of overbreadth, we agree with the trial court that it is better dealt with on a case-by-case basis. The members of the Association's board occupy a fiduciary position vis-à-vis the Association and the membership. Any response to a request for inspection of books and records must be made in good faith and cannot be structured with an eye to self-protection. Plaintiff has not hesitated in the past to seek judicial relief from Association actions she has considered improper. *See, e.g., Mulligan Found. v. Brooks, supra; State v. Panther Valley Prop. Owners Ass'n, supra.* We have no doubt that she will remain vigilant against the possibility of improper self-dealing or negligent governance. We thus affirm that portion of the trial court's judgment that upheld the fourth amendment. . . .

IV

A

The Association has cross-appealed from the portions of the trial court's judgment that struck down two amendments. The members voted to supplement Article X of the Declaration by adding the following language:

> In the event the Association files a lawsuit, counterclaim or third-party claim . . . against any owner to enforce any term or provision of . . . [the Association's Declaration, bylaws or rules] and [it] prevails in its claims, [it] shall be entitled to collect reasonable costs and attorneys' fees from the Owner. . . . Should [it] seek to collect its reasonable costs and fees, it will cause the costs and fees to be set forth in the judgment or order . . . adjudicating the claim. Collection . . . may be enforced . . . as if the attorneys' fees and costs were an Assessment owed by the particular Owner, except as otherwise determined by a court having jurisdiction over the claim.

An earlier amendment had also sought to afford the Association a right to seek counsel fees but had been struck down by the same trial court in an earlier lawsuit between the same parties. The trial court concluded the instant amendment was also invalid; the trial court struck down the amendment because it was not authorized by statute and plaintiff had not assented to it.

The statutory prong of the trial court's reasoning is based upon the fact that Panther Valley is not a condominium community and thus does not fall within the fee-shifting provision of the Condominium Act, *N.J.S.A.* 46:8B-15(e). We do not consider that dispositive, however. As we noted earlier, while the condominium statute is not conclusive, it may provide guidance. *State v. Panther Valley Prop. Owners Ass'n, supra,* 307 *N.J.Super.* at 332, 704 A.2d 1010.

One of the core foundations of a common interest community is a sharing of expenses for maintenance among the residents. If the community, however, is compelled to shoulder higher legal expenses because of the intransigence of a small number, we cannot consider it unfair or unreasonable for the Association to seek to lessen the burden upon its other members by seeking to have the uncooperative member contribute to the attorneys' fees required to vindicate the Association's rights.

Nor is it dispositive that plaintiff did not agree with the amendment and thus there was no contract between the parties. The Declaration provided from the outset that it could be amended; the Association could not be deprived of the ability to add provisions to the Declaration that its experience proved warranted. Plaintiff has maintained throughout this litigation that the amendments at issue should be measured under the reasonableness standard; we are unable to consider this amendment unreasonable. We thus reverse that portion of the trial court's judgment that struck down the third amendment.

B

The membership also voted to amend Section 8 of Article XV of the bylaws. Article XV deals generally with enforcement of the community's covenants, bylaws, rules and regulations. Section 8 authorizes the Association to file with the Warren County Clerk a Notice of Violation if the Covenant's Committee has determined "that a continuing violation exists with respect to any Owner. . . ." The trial court concluded this amendment was invalid because a Notice of Violation could be filed without notice to the affected owner.

Defendants argue that the trial court improperly read Section 8 in isolation. They urge that when it is viewed in the overall context of Article XV, there is ample provision for notice to an affected owner.

We do not agree. We conclude that there is a qualitative difference between the private enforcement techniques encompassed within the balance of Article XV and the attempt to create a publicly-recorded lien upon an owner's property. We concur with the trial court that an affected owner is entitled to receive notice before any Notice of Violation is submitted for recording with the County Clerk.

We have noted at several points that the governance of Panther Valley is not subject to the Condominium Act. We are unable, however, to perceive any reason in logic or policy that would obviate the necessity for notice before establishing a lien upon an owner's property. We concur in the analysis expressed in *Loigman v. Kings Landing Condominium Ass'n*, 324 *N.J.Super.* 97, 734 A.2d 367 (Ch. 1999), that requiring notice can only further the presumed purpose of the association, to be paid. We thus affirm that portion of the trial court's judgment that struck down the second amendment. . . .

Pertzsch v. Upper Oconomowoc Lake Association

248 Wis. 2d 219, 635 N.W.2d 829 (Ct. App. 2001)

BROWN, J.

The Upper Oconomowoc Lake Association appeals from an order reversing the decision of the Association's Architectural Control Committee to deny the request of Steven and Doris Pertzsch to build a lakeside boathouse. The court reasoned that the Committee's reliance on the fact that no other lakeside boathouse existed rendered its decision arbitrary and capricious in light of the express terms of the restrictive covenant allowing boathouses. We affirm.

On June 1, 1999, the Pertzsches purchased property on Upper Oconomowoc Lake. As required in the controlling covenants, the Pertzsches provided the Committee with the plans and specifications for the construction of a home and a detached, lakeside boathouse and requested the necessary consent for the construction of both buildings. The Committee approved the Pertzsches' house plan but denied their request for a lakeside boathouse.

The covenants controlling the Committee's decision are contained in an agreement executed in 1961. The agreement provided for the creation of the Committee and granted it certain powers, duties and responsibilities relating to the construction of buildings and other structures. These powers and duties stem from the specific requirement that all construction plans and specifications be approved by the Committee. The paragraphs relevant to this dispute state in part:

(1) LAND USE AND BUILDING TYPE: No lot shall be used, except for residential purposes. No building shall be erected, altered, placed, or permitted to remain on any lot other than one detached single family dwelling not to exceed two stories in height and a private garage for not more than three cars, except that a boat house may be permitted with consent of the Architectural Control Committee.

(2) ARCHITECTURAL CONTROL: No building shall be erected, placed, or altered on any lot until the construction plans and specifications and a plan showing the location of the structure have been approved by the Architectural Control Committee as to quality of workmanship and materials, harmony of external design with existing structures, and as to location with respect to topograph and finish grade elevation and setback, front, back and side. No fence or wall shall be erected, placed or altered on any lot nearer to any street than the minimum building setback line unless similarly approved. . . .

(5) DWELLING LOCATION: No dwelling shall be located on any lot nearer to the front lot line or nearer to the side street line or nearer to the lakeshore, than the minimum building setback lines shown on the recorded plat and in any event, no dwelling shall be located on any lot nearer than fifty (50) feet to the lakeshore or nearer than fifty (50) feet to the front lot line, or nearer than thirty-five (35) feet to any side street line. No building shall be located nearer than ten (10) feet to an interior lot line. No dwelling shall be located on any interior lot nearer than thirty-five (35) feet to the rear lot line. For the purpose of this covenant, eaves, steps, and open porches shall not be considered as part of a building, provided, however, that this shall not be construed to permit any portion of a building on a lot to encroach upon another lot. That prior to commencement of structures of any kind, the Architectural Control Committee must approve all setback lines and all construction in writing. Said Committee is further granted control over construction of piers and any other structures extending into or on the water and written consent must be approved prior to commencement of construction as to length, width, and location.

While the record shows that the Committee has previously approved many boat storage structures attached to a garage or home, it has never before been presented with a plan to construct a detached, lakeside boathouse. . . .

We now address the Association's argument that paragraph one is a "stand alone" provision that contains a standardless consent-to-construction covenant. We also find this argument to be completely without merit. If the Association were correct, then paragraph two would be superfluous. [U]nder the explicit terms of the covenants, the Committee is authorized to approve or deny a request for a boathouse exclusively on the basis of those standards set forth in paragraph two.[3]

---

3. Because we reject the argument that the covenants contain no specific standard of approval for boathouses, we also reject the Association's reliance on Dodge v. Carauna, 127 Wis.2d 62, 377 N.W.2d 208 (Ct. App.1985). In that case, we held that where a common grantor reserves the right to approve construction of a building by arbitrary standards, the exercise of that right must be reasonable. Id. at 66-67, 377 N.W.2d 208. We stated that a finding of reasonableness would depend on the developer's intent and objectives and the relation of the structure to its surroundings and to other buildings in the subdivision. Id. at 67, 377 N.W.2d 208. The Association asks us to remand this case for a finding on these evidentiary issues. However, because the standards of approval in this case are not arbitrary, but are clear and specific, we are precluded from inquiring into the developer's intent or into any other evidentiary matters outside the four corners of the agreement. See Zinda v. Krause, 191 Wis.2d 154, 171, 528 N.W.2d 55 (Ct. App.1995) (where the language of the covenant expresses a purpose contrary to the developer's subjective state of mind, the language of the covenant controls); Hall v. Church of the Open Bible, 4 Wis.2d 246, 248, 89 N.W.2d 798 (1958) (parol evidence is not admissible to establish any intent other than that clearly expressed in the instrument itself).

We now turn to the central issue in this case, which is whether the Committee properly applied the standards in paragraph two of the agreement when it denied the Pertzsches' request for a boathouse as stated in this excerpt of the letter:

> The grounds for said refusal include but are not limited to: its failure to conform to existing structures then and there existing; for not being in harmony of external design with existing structures with respect to topograph elevation and setback.
>
> Whereas the covenants and restrictions obligate us to evaluate the impact on the entire subdivision, and whereas all of the other lots have been developed without permanent raised structures within fifty to seventy feet of the water, we find the boathouse to be nonconforming to the intent of harmony in setback, topography, and structure, therefore, we do not find that this exception would be in the interest of the riparian owners.

Under paragraph two of the agreement, the first criterion the Committee must consider is quality of workmanship and materials. The denial letter does not state that the quality of workmanship and materials is unacceptable. Therefore, we assume that the Committee had no objection to the boathouse based on this criterion.

The second criterion is harmony of external design with existing structures. The Committee construed this standard to mean that it can deny a detached boathouse because it is out of character with the existing structures in the community. Under this interpretation of the standard, the plans for the boathouse fail because there are no other lakeside boathouses. This, we believe, is what the Committee intended to communicate by its letter when it stated, "whereas all of the other lots have been developed without permanent raised structures within fifty to seventy feet of the water."

However, the Committee misconstrues its mandate under this criterion. We believe the key word is "design." In order for the Committee to deny the boathouse within the terms of this criterion, it would have to make a decision based on the specific external design of the boathouse compared to the design of other existing structures. Again, the letter is silent with respect to this matter and therefore we assume the Committee had no objection to the architectural style of the boathouse.

The third criterion which the Committee must consider is location. The agreement is very specific as to what this criterion entails: "location with respect to topograph and finish grade elevation and setback, front, back and side." This means that the Committee can reject a building design or plan if the Committee does not approve of the configuration of its surface features with respect to its surroundings. For example, the Committee would be authorized to deny a boathouse if it was too high or improperly positioned on the lot relative to its surroundings. The letter makes clear, however, that the Committee mistakenly believed it was authorized under this standard to reject the boathouse because it was within fifty to seventy feet of the lake. The explicit language of paragraph five states that this restriction applies only to dwellings: "No dwelling shall be located on any lot nearer than fifty (50) feet to the lakeshore." To assume that the term "dwelling" includes a boathouse strains the language beyond its logical meaning. Later in this paragraph it states: "No building shall be located nearer than ten (10) feet to an interior lot line." Clearly, this latter sentence would include the boathouse while the former sentence would not.

To summarize, we find that the grounds for refusal expressed in the denial letter show that the Committee misconstrued its mandate. The Committee has no authorization to use the standards in the covenant to effectuate an express prohibition of detached, lakeside boathouses when the agreement expressly allows such structures to be built. While the Committee can control construction of boathouses using the criteria in paragraph two, it cannot ban them entirely.

Nevertheless, we are sympathetic with the thrust of the Association's objection, which is that the Pertzsches' boathouse is not in harmony with the general plan or scheme that has evolved in the Upper Oconomowoc Lake community. We are also cognizant of the holding in Zinda v. Krause, 191 Wis.2d 154, 167, 528 N.W.2d 55 (Ct. App.1995), that "where the purpose of a restrictive covenant may be clearly discerned from the terms of the covenant, the covenant is enforceable against any activity that contravenes that purpose." We cannot apply *Zinda* in this case, however, because we, like the Association, are constrained by the language of the agreement which allows boathouses to be constructed. Therefore, we must apply the rule that has long been the law in Wisconsin[5] that deed restrictions must be strictly construed to favor unencumbered and free use of property and any derogation of such use must be expressed in clear, unambiguous and peremptory terms. Crowley v. Knapp, 94 Wis.2d 421, 434-35, 288 N.W.2d 815 (1980). Because we conclude that the Committee was not authorized to refuse the Pertzsches' request for a boathouse for the reasons stated in the denial letter, we affirm the order of the trial court.

Order affirmed.

ANDERSON, J. (concurring).

I join in the result because we are bound by precedent. Cook v. Cook, 208 Wis.2d 166, 189, 560 N.W.2d 246 (1997). . . .

While zoning has been considered a legitimate restriction on the private use of real property, restrictive covenants imposed upon real property by owners and developers have not enjoyed the same status. As the lead opinion makes abundantly clear, Wisconsin disfavors privately imposed restrictions on the use of land. I believe that the time has come to abandon an out-of-date public policy in favor of a public policy that recognizes:

> [H]ousing today is ordinarily developed by subdividers, who, through the use of restrictive covenants, guarantee to the homeowner that his house will be protected against adjacent construction which will impair its value, and that a general plan of construction will be followed. Restrictions enhance the value of the subdivision property and form an inducement for purchasers to buy lots within the subdivision. A covenant requiring submission of plans and prior approval before construction is one method by which guarantees of value and of adherence to a general scheme of development can be accomplished and maintained.

---

5. We acknowledge that some jurisdictions now question whether rules of strict construction should apply where the meaning of a subdivision's protective covenants are at issue and the dispute is among homeowners. See Riss v. Angel, 131 Wash.2d 612, 934 P.2d 669, 675-76 (1997). These jurisdictions view restrictive covenants as valuable land use planning devices, Joslin v. Pine River Dev. Corp., 116 N.H. 814, 367 A.2d 599, 601 (1976), and liberally construe restrictive covenants to give effect to the intent or purpose of the covenants rather than free use of the land. *Riss,* 934 P.2d at 676. However, in this case, the agreement unambiguously manifests an intent to allow boathouses, and we do not believe even a liberal construction of the covenants can overcome this clear expression.

Davis v. Huey, 620 S.W.2d 561, 565 (Tex.1981) (citations omitted).

The public policy favoring the free use of land has been abandoned in Restatement (Third) of Prop.: Servitudes § 4 (Introductory Note) (1998):

> The general principles governing servitude interpretation . . . adopt the model of
> interpretation used in contract law and displace the older interpretive model used in
> servitudes law that emphasized the free use of land, sometimes at the expense of
> frustrating intent. In adopting this model, this Restatement follows the lead of courts
> that have recognized the important and useful role servitudes play in modern real-
> estate development. To the extent that the old canon favoring free use of land remains
> useful, its function is served in cautioning against finding that a servitude has been
> created where the parties' intent is unclear . . . and in construing servitudes to avoid
> violating public policy. . . . It also may play a role in limiting the creation of servitudes
> that burden fundamental rights . . . and limiting the rulemaking powers of communi-
> ty associations. . . . Aside from those situations, *construing in favor of free use of land*
> *should play no role in interpreting modern servitudes.* (Emphasis added.)

"[T]o ascertain and give effect to the likely intentions and legitimate expectations" of property owners, id., the RESTATEMENT adopts a new principle governing the interpretation of restrictive covenants:

Interpretation of Servitudes
(1) A servitude should be interpreted to give effect to the intention of the parties
ascertained from the language used in the instrument, or the circumstances surrounding creation of the servitude, and to carry out the purpose for which it was created.

   (2) Unless the purpose for which the servitude is created violates public policy, and
unless contrary to the intent of the parties, a servitude should be interpreted to avoid
violating public policy. Among reasonable interpretations, that which is more consonant with public policy should be preferred.

Id.

The justification for a new principle to guide the interpretation of restrictive
covenants is provided in the commentary:

> The rule that servitudes should be interpreted to carry out the intent of the parties and
> the purpose of the intended servitude departs from the often expressed view that
> servitudes should be narrowly construed to favor the free use of land. It is based in the
> recognition that servitudes are widely used in modern land development and ordi-
> narily play a valuable role in utilization of land resources. The rule is supported by
> modern case law.

Id. § 4.1 cmt. a.

When this modern approach is employed by courts to review decisions of an
architectural control committee, the question is no longer whether the committee's
decision inhibits the free use of land but whether its decision is reasonable. See
Allen Oshinski, Restrictive Covenants and Architectural Review: Some Suggested
Standards, 27 J. Marshall L. Rev. 939, 941 (1994). The RESTATEMENT imposes a
duty upon a committee "to act reasonably in the exercise of its discretionary powers

including . . . design-control powers." Restatement (Third) of Prop.: Servitudes § 6.13(1)(c). See also Marvin J. Nodiff, Decision Making in the Community Association: Do the Old Rules Still Apply?, 52 J. Mo. B. 141, 147 (1996). In applying the rule of reasonableness, one court places "special emphasis on arriving at an interpretation that protects the homeowners' collective interests." Riss v. Angel, 131 Wash.2d 612, 934 P.2d 669, 676 (1997).

If I were to apply the modern approach to the decision of the Committee in this case, I would start with the discretion given to the Committee to grant permission to build a detached boathouse. Majority at ¶3. In exercising this discretion, the Committee's mandate is to enforce the restrictive covenants in such a manner as to give effect to the intent of the covenants and to protect the interest of all the homeowners in the subdivision. That there have been no other requests to construct detached boathouses in the subdivision, Majority at ¶4, demonstrates the collective interest of the members of the Upper Oconomowoc Lake Association that all boat storage structures be attached to a garage or home. Because the Committee must take into consideration the collective interest of the homeowners, the proposed boathouse's "harmony of external design with existing structures" and "location with respect to topograph," Majority at ¶3, it is reasonable for the Committee to decide that the intent of the restrictive covenants is not given effect by permitting the construction of a detached boathouse. Normandy Square Ass'n v. Ells, 213 Neb. 60, 327 N.W.2d 101, 104 (1982) (it was reasonable for an architectural review committee to deny permission to build a fence because it violated the harmony of external design and location in relation to the surrounding structures and topography).

If I could use the modern approach to interpreting restrictive covenants, I would approve the action of the Committee because the proposed detached boathouse changed the neighborhood ambiance, backdrop and setting. The proposed boathouse would be the subdivision's only detached boat storage. These factors furnish an objective, reasonable and nonarbitrary basis for denying permission under the modern approach embodied in the RESTATEMENT.

NOTES AND QUESTIONS

1. The condominium, a form that did not exist at common law, depends on a statutory foundation pursuant to which a declaration may be filed that establishes the powers of the condominium board. The homeowners association and the cooperative emerged from common law bases — to simplify, the homeowners association from the law of servitudes and the cooperative from corporate and landlord/tenant law. As noted above, many states have now adopted legislation governing the creation and powers of all common interest communities, which provides the framework for the CC&Rs or declaration establishing the association.

2. The Restatement (Third) of Property: Servitudes provides the following enunciation of the duties of the community association:

§ 6.13 Duties Of A Common-Interest Community To Its Members

(1) In addition to duties imposed by statute and the governing documents, the association has the following duties to the members of the common-interest community:

(a) to use ordinary care and prudence in managing the property and financial affairs of the community that are subject to its control;

(b) to treat members fairly;

(c) to act reasonably in the exercise of its discretionary powers including rulemaking, enforcement, and design-control powers;

(d) to provide members reasonable access to information about the association, the common property, and the financial affairs of the association.

(2) A member challenging an action of the association under this section has the burden of proving a breach of duty by the association. Except when the breach alleged is ultra vires action by the association, the member has the additional burden of proving that the breach has caused, or threatens to cause, injury to the member individually or to the interests of the common-interest community.

3. *Standard of review.* The *Mulligan* court applied a "reasonableness" standard in its review of actions of the association membership or board. As noted in *Mulligan*, however, some courts have applied a more lenient test borrowed from corporate law, the business judgment rule. The leading case is Levandusky v. One Fifth Ave. Apartment Corp., 75 N.Y.2d 530, 554 N.Y.S.2d 807, 553 N.E.2d 1317 (1990), in which a member of a co-op did renovations to his kitchen in the process of which he moved a steam riser and installed certain air conditioners without permission of the board, which then ordered that they be removed.

As cooperative and condominium home ownership has grown increasingly popular, courts confronting disputes between tenant-owners and governing boards have fashioned a variety of rules for adjudicating such claims. In the process, several salient characteristics of the governing board homeowner relationship have been identified as relevant to the judicial inquiry.

As courts and commentators have noted, the cooperative or condominium association is a quasi-government — "a little democratic sub society of necessity" (Hidden Harbour Estates v. Norman, 309 So.2d 180, 182 [Fla.Dist.Ct.App.]). The proprietary lessees or condominium owners consent to be governed, in certain respects, by the decisions of a board. Like a municipal government, such governing boards are responsible for running the day-to-day affairs of the cooperative and to that end, often have broad powers in areas that range from financial decisionmaking to promulgating regulations regarding pets and parking spaces. Authority to approve or disapprove structural alterations, as in this case, is commonly given to the governing board.

Through the exercise of this authority, to which would-be apartment owners must generally acquiesce, a governing board may significantly restrict the bundle of rights a property owner normally enjoys. Moreover, as with any authority to govern, the broad powers of a cooperative board hold potential for abuse through arbitrary and malicious decisionmaking, favoritism, discrimination and the like.

On the other hand, agreement to submit to the decisionmaking authority of a cooperative board is voluntary in a sense that submission to government authority is not; there is always the freedom not to purchase the apartment. The stability offered by community control, through a board, has its own economic and social benefits, and purchase of a cooperative apartment represents a voluntary choice to cede certain of the privileges of single ownership to a governing body, often made up of fellow tenants who volunteer their time, without compensation. The board, in return, takes on the burden of managing the property for the benefit of the proprietary lessees. . . .

It is apparent, then, that a standard for judicial review of the actions of a cooperative or condominium governing board must be sensitive to a variety of concerns — sometimes competing concerns. Even when the governing board acts within the scope of its authority, some check on its potential powers to regulate residents' conduct, life-style and property rights is necessary to protect individual residents from abusive exercise, notwithstanding that the residents have, to an extent, consented to be regulated and even selected their representatives (*see*, Note, *The Rule of Law in Residential Associations*, 99 Harv.L.Rev. 472 [1985]). At the same time, the chosen standard of review should not undermine the purposes for which the residential community and its governing structure were formed: protection of the interest of the entire community of residents in an environment managed by the board for the common benefit.

We conclude that these goals are best served by a standard of review that is analogous to the business judgment rule applied by courts to determine challenges to decisions made by corporate directors. A number of courts in this and other states have applied such a standard in reviewing the decisions of cooperative and condominium boards (see, e.g., *Kirsch v. Holiday Summer Homes*, 143 A.D.2d 811, 533 N.Y.S.2d 144; *Schoninger v. Yardarm Beach Homeowners' Assn.*, 134 A.D.2d 1, 523 N.Y.S.2d 523; *Van Camp v. Sherman*, 132 A.D.2d 453, 517 N.Y.S.2d 152; *Papalexiou v. Tower W. Condominium*, 167 N.J.Super. 516, 401 A.2d 280; *Schwarzmann v. Association of Apt. Owners*, 33 Wash.App. 397, 655 P.2d 1177; *Rywalt v. Writer Corp.*, 34 Colo.App. 334, 526 P.2d 316). We agree with those courts that such a test best balances the individual and collective interests at stake. Developed in the context of commercial enterprises, the business judgment rule prohibits judicial inquiry into actions of corporate directors "taken in good faith and in the exercise of honest judgment in the lawful and legitimate furtherance of corporate purposes." (*Auerbach v. Bennett*, 47 N.Y.2d 619, 629, 419 N.Y.S.2d 920, 393 N.E.2d 994, *supra*.) So long as the corporation's directors have not breached their fiduciary obligation to the corporation, "the exercise of [their powers] for the common and general interests of the corporation may not be questioned, although the results show that what they did was unwise or inexpedient." (*Pollitz v. Wabash R.R. Co.*, 207 N.Y. 113, 124, 100 N.E. 721.)

Application of a similar doctrine is appropriate because a cooperative corporation is — in fact and function — a corporation, acting through the management of its board of directors, and subject to the Business Corporation Law. There is no cause to create a special new category in law for corporate actions by coop boards.

We emphasize that reference to the business judgment rule is for the purpose of analogy only. Clearly, in light of the doctrine's origins in the quite different world of commerce, the fiduciary principles identified in the existing case law — primarily emphasizing avoidance of self-dealing and financial self-aggrandizement — will of necessity be adapted over time in order to apply to directors of not-for-profit homeowners' cooperative corporations. For present purposes, we need not, nor should we determine the entire range of the fiduciary obligations of a cooperative board, other than to note that the board owes its duty of loyalty to the cooperative — that is, it must act for the benefit of the residents collectively. So long as the board acts for the purposes of the cooperative, within the scope of its authority and in good faith, courts will not substitute their judgment for the board's. Stated somewhat differently, unless a resident challenging the board's action is able to demonstrate a breach of this duty, judicial review is not available.

In reaching this conclusion, we reject the test seemingly applied by the Appellate Division majority and explicitly applied by Supreme Court in its initial decision. That inquiry was directed at the *reasonableness* of the board's decision; having itself found that relocation of the riser posed no "dangerous aspect" to the building, the Appellate Division concluded that the renovation should remain. Like the business judgment rule, this reasonableness standard — originating in the quite different world of governmental agency decisionmaking found favor with courts reviewing board decisions (*see, e.g., Amoruso v. Board of Managers*, 38 A.D.2d 845, 330 N.Y.S.2d 107; *Lenox Manor v. Gianni*, 120 Misc.2d 202, 465 N.Y.S.2d 809; *see*, Note, *Judicial Review of Condominium Rulemaking*, op. cit., at 659-661 [discussing cases from other jurisdictions]).

As applied in condominium and cooperative cases, review of a board's decision under a reasonableness standard has much in common with the rule we adopt today. A primary focus of the inquiry is whether board action is in furtherance of a legitimate purpose of the cooperative or condominium, in which case it will generally be upheld. The difference between the reasonableness test and the rule we adopt is twofold. First — unlike the business judgment rule, which places on the owner seeking review the burden to demonstrate a breach of the board's fiduciary duty — reasonableness review requires the board to demonstrate that its decision was reasonable. Second, although in practice a certain amount of deference appears to be accorded to board decisions, reasonableness review permits — indeed, in theory requires — the court itself to evaluate the merits or wisdom of the board's decision (see, e.g., *Hidden Harbour Estates v. Basso*, 393 So.2d 637, 640 [Fla.Dist.Ct.App.]), just as the Appellate Division did in the present case. The more limited judicial review embodied in the business judgment rule is preferable. In the context of the decisions of a for-profit corporation, "courts are ill equipped and infrequently called on to evaluate what are and must be essentially business judgments * * * by definition the responsibility for business judgments must rest with the corporate directors; their individual capabilities and experience peculiarly qualify them for the discharge of that responsibility." (*Auerbach v. Bennett*, 47 N.Y.2d, *supra*, at 630-631, 419 N.Y.S.2d 920, 393 N.E.2d 994). Even if decisions of a cooperative board do not generally involve expertise beyond the usual ken of the judiciary, at the least board members will possess experience of the peculiar needs of their building and its residents not shared by the court.

Several related concerns persuade us that such a rule should apply here. As this case exemplifies, board decisions concerning what residents may or may not do with their living space may be highly charged and emotional. A cooperative or condominium is by nature a myriad of often competing views regarding personal living space, and decisions taken to benefit the collective interest may be unpalatable to one resident or another, creating the prospect that board decisions will be subjected to undue court involvement and judicial second-guessing. Allowing an owner who is simply dissatisfied with particular board action a second opportunity to reopen the matter completely before a court, which — generally without knowing the property — may or may not agree with the reasonableness of the board's determination, threatens the stability of the common living arrangement.

Moreover, the prospect that each board decision may be subjected to full judicial review hampers the effectiveness of the board's managing authority. The business judgment rule protects the board's business decisions and managerial authority from indiscriminate attack. At the same time, it permits review of improper decisions, as when the challenger demonstrates that the board's action has no legitimate relationship to the welfare of the cooperative, deliberately singles out individuals for harmful treatment, is taken without notice or consideration of the relevant facts, or is beyond the scope of the board's authority.

75 N.Y.2d 530, 536-39, 554 N.Y.S.2d 807, 810-13, 553 N.E.2d 1317, 1320-23 (some citations omitted).

4. Should provisions contained in the recorded CC&Rs or Declaration be entitled to greater deference than rules or regulations adopted by the board after a unit owner has purchased her unit? Some courts have held so, while others find that any provision properly adopted should be tested by the same standard whether it was passed before or after the complainant's purchase.

5. *Alternative dispute resolution and access to the courts.* Suppose the CC&Rs contain a provision requiring that any dispute between owner(s) and the association be resolved by binding arbitration. Would this effectively preclude judicial review of all association actions and decisions? Suppose the CC&Rs provided that unit owners will resolve any disputes *with any other unit owners* through binding arbitration?

Given the nature of many CIC disputes and the fact that the parties will likely be together for many years after the "resolution" of the particular issue, would it make sense for the parties to be obligated to attempt mediation before filing a suit? See Scott E. Mollen, Alternate Dispute Resolution of Condominium and Cooperative Conflicts, 73 St. John's L. Rev. 75 (1999). Fla. Stat. Ann. § 718.1255 (2006) requires owners to submit certain categories of disputes with the governing board to nonbinding arbitration by an arbitrator with the Division of Florida Land Sales, Condominiums, and Mobile Homes of the Department of Business and Professional Regulation. The parties are entitled to seek *de novo* judicial review, although the statute oddly provides that "the final decision of the arbitrator shall be admissible in evidence in the trial *de novo*."

2. The Association as Mini-Government

The powers and responsibilities of a community association are comparable in many ways to those of a local government. As provided in the governing documents, the association may have the power to maintain and improve the common elements (including potentially, recreational facilities, utilities, roads, lobbies, and so forth), make and enforce rules regarding the use of the individual units and common elements, to have a say in the leasing or sale of units, to approve or disapprove of unit owners' improvement plans, and to levy assessments against the individual units to support all of these functions.

The decisions of a local government are subject, however, to judicial review, including determinations of any possible violations of an individual's constitutional rights, such as the rights to free speech and assembly, equal protection of the laws, and the right to be free from governmental takings except for public use and with just compensation. But what protections do owners have against the arbitrary, unfair, or unwise decisions of the association board? Should community associations be subject to the same checks and balances as government entities, or should a person who chooses to join a common interest community be held strictly to the contractual rights and obligations they accepted in joining?

Stewart E. Sterk, Minority Protection in Residential Private Governments[*]

77 B.U. L. Rev. 273, 288-307, 320-329 (1997)

II. MAJORITY RULE AND ITS LIMITS

A. WHY MAJORITY RULE?

Much of our legal system — both public and private — is based on the assumption that collective decisions should be made by majority vote. . . .

[*] Some footnotes omitted. — EDS.

The majority rule principle is not limited to government institutions. Corporate decisions, too, are generally decided by majority vote, whether that of shareholders or directors. And majority rule is the organizing principle for decision making in many other private organizations.

The natural question is why we should look to majority rule as a basis for making important social decisions. Few of us believe that important scientific questions should be resolved by majority rule. If 51% of the members of a calculus class concluded that the derivative of $3x^2$ was 5x, should they be entitled to have that answer marked correct on an examination? Fewer still believe that religious truth can or should be determined by majority vote. Yet, we continue to rely on majority rule to make determinations of political and financial significance. Why?

One answer stems from the premise that every member of a collective body should share equally in political power. If less than a majority could bind the whole to act, proponents of action each would wield more political power than a larger body of opponents. Conversely, if action required a supermajority, opponents of an action each would enjoy more power than any individual proponent. Only majority rule preserves equality among all members of the group.

The premise that political power should be equally distributed is central to prominent, if controversial, justifications for judicial review of legislative action. In particular, John Hart Ely has argued that courts should, as a matter of constitutional law, protect those most likely to be excluded from political power in a majoritarian regime.[55] Indeed, even those who question process-based theories of judicial review often start from the premise that political power should be distributed equally.[56]

Equal distribution of political power cannot, however, serve as an absolute principle. The principle is incoherent without some delineation of the political realm. Not all decisions can be treated as political decisions over which all members of the collective body have an equal say. Voting rights provide the most extreme example. If we treat voting rights as a political issue to be decided by majority rule, a majority would be empowered to disenfranchise members of the collective body. Such disenfranchisement would clearly violate the principle that political power be distributed equally.

To make the equal distribution principle coherent, the principle itself must be subject to limits. To identify those limits, one must start by identifying reasons for distributing power equally (and, derivatively, for allowing majorities to rule). One reason is that sharing political power increases the power of individuals to shape their own lives in a society marked by state regulation. Another is that giving each citizen an equal say in governmental decision making processes may also promote self-respect among the citizenry . . .

These reasons for distributing power equally are peculiar to notions of citizenship in a coercive state, but less persuasive in the context of a voluntary association. Concerns about self-determination are less critical in voluntary organizations,

55. See John Hart Ely, Democracy and Distrust 75-100 (1980) (advancing a process-based representation-reinforcement theory of minority protection); see also Jesse Choper, Judicial Review and the National Political Process 71-72 (1980); Louis Lusky, By What Right? 131, 138-39 (1975).

56. See, e.g., Frank I. Michelman, Welfare Rights in a Constitutional Democracy, 1979 Wash. U. L.Q. 659, 675-78 (arguing that inequality of resources creates a substantial bias in the functioning of majoritarian institutions, and suggesting that constitutionalization of a form of welfare rights would better equalize political power).

because the choice to join — or to leave — gives an individual a measure of control, even if the individual has no "voice" in the organization's decision making process.[60] Concerns about promoting self-respect, too, appear less significant in voluntary organizations, because the individual can choose not to participate in an organization whose governing rules are offensive.

Other reasons for equal distribution of power, and hence for majority rule, translate more easily from the public to the private sphere. In particular, majority rule in any sphere can be viewed as a form of applied utilitarianism, likely to produce better outcomes than other decision making processes. Since each individual typically is the best respecter of his own interests, a decision making system will produce better outcomes if participation is open to all individuals with a stake than if power is divorced from interest. . . .

When members of the collective have an unequal stake in the collective's decisions, the costs of gathering information suggest that weighing votes by stake will generate better outcomes. Members with the greatest stake have the greatest incentive to invest resources in acquiring information about the wisdom of alternative courses of action. Assuming information contributes positively to the quality of decisions, those members with a greater stake are, therefore, likely to make better decisions. On this theory, rules like "one share, one vote" are more likely to generate optimal outcomes than rules like "one shareholder, one vote."

Finally, equal distribution of power among members of a collective body may create a tighter sense of community among members of the collective, causing each member to take better account of the interests of the others. To the extent that this sort of community increases individual happiness and improves the quality of decision making, these benefits should be capable of realization in a privately created collective body.

Thus, the case for majority rule is a substantial one. At the same time, as we have already seen, majority rule can never be an absolute principle. What remains for the next subpart is an exploration of the reasons for limiting majority rule.

B. LIMITS ON MAJORITY RULE

1. PROTECTING FUNDAMENTAL RIGHTS

The argument that majorities ought not be permitted to abridge fundamental rights has become a staple in American constitutional theory.[68] The argument

---

60. For the classic work comparing "exit" and "voice" as mechanisms for influencing organizational outcomes, see Albert O. Hirschman, Exit, Voice, and Loyalty 40-41 (1970). Professor Gregory Alexander has suggested that lumping all "voluntary" organizations together and treating them under the same legal rubric is a mistake. Alexander distinguishes between voluntary associations formed for instrumental ends and "communities . . . drawn together by shared visions that constitute for each of them their personal identity." Gregory S. Alexander, Group Autonomy: Residential Associations and Community, 75 Cornell L. Rev. 1, 26 (1989). Alexander uses the monastery as an example of an organization in which membership is essential to the realization of self-identity. See id. at 27. Alexander also suggests that homeowner associations have community elements and should not be treated simply as groups created by contract. See id. at 42. And, indeed, once a homeowner becomes a member of an association, she does, in many ways, become bound up with the group. "Exit" becomes difficult. See infra Part III. Nevertheless, with a community association, unlike a monastery, it is difficult to see how the initial decision to join could be a decision largely outside of the homeowner's control.

68. See, e.g., David A.J. Richards, A Theory of Free Speech, 34 UCLA L. Rev. 1837, 1877 (1987) (arguing that the inalienable right of conscience cannot be surrendered to the state); Mark V. Tushnet,

rests on the simple premise that majority rule is not an end in itself, but a means of assuring that government respects personal liberties and promotes social welfare. If one views liberty of conscience, a measure of personal autonomy, or even security from economic predation as more essential to a liberal society than political liberty, one would support constraining the power of political majorities when these critical interests are at stake.[69] Moreover, if majority rule is designed to foster equal input into the political process, it is self-evident that majorities should not be permitted to entrench their own powers by limiting the franchise.

Rights theorists, however, face a critical hurdle: if not by majority rule, how does the society determine which rights merit protection against majoritarian depredation? Our legal system entrusts judges with the power to decide which rights to protect; how they should exercise that power remains a matter of considerable controversy. . . . Ultimately, however, our legal system finds it critical to locate limits on majority rule in the Constitution itself, however that document is interpreted.[70] The Constitution commands respect in part because of its status as a contract ratified by each of the sovereign states and in part out of recognition that the Founders themselves, removed from the heat of battle over particular issues that have since arisen, were well positioned to set ground rules for the majority's exercise of power.

However powerful rights theory is as a basis for judicial review of legislative decisions, it furnishes little justification for overturning decisions of the majority of a homeowners' association or condominium board. Most of the issues that arise in these contexts are not the sort that one would consider fundamental to the existence of a liberal society.[77] Consider, however, those issues that some might deem fundamental: restrictions on signs or other expressive activity, for example.[78]

Foreword, Symposium on Democracy and Distrust: Ten Years Later, 77 Va. L. Rev. 631, 634 (1991) (identifying the rights-based approach with Justice Blackmun's opinion in Roe v. Wade, and treating it as one of the major currents in contemporary constitutional theory).

69. For the position that liberty of conscience merits protection against majority rule, see Kent Greenawalt, Speech, Crime, and the Uses of Language 177-79 (1989) (enunciating a broad view of the protection of political expression), and David A.J. Richards, A New Paradigm for Free Speech Scholarship, 139 U. Pa. L. Rev. 271, 275 (1990) ("Constitutionally legitimate political power must respect substantive spheres of moral independence—like liberty of conscience."). For the argument that economic interests merit protection against majority rule, see Richard Epstein, Takings: Private Property and the Power of Eminent Domain 308 (1985).

70. See, e.g., Griswold v. Connecticut, 381 U.S. 479, 483-86 (1965) (finding a constitutional right of privacy in penumbras emanating from explicit constitutional protections).

77. Parking restrictions, satellite dish prohibitions, and assessment levels, for instance, would appear to abridge "fundamental" rights only to property absolutists—the very people most likely to advocate enforcement of contractual arrangements. Compare, e.g., Epstein, supra note 70, at 306-31 (advocating protection of economic interests against majority rule), with Epstein, supra note 5, at 924-25 (advocating routine enforcement of privately created servitudes when majority-rule procedures are in effect).

78. A few states have held, as a matter of state constitutional law, that certain private property owners (shopping center owners) may not prohibit expressive activity on their property. See Pruneyard Shopping Ctr. v. Robins, 447 U.S. 74, 76, 79 (1980) (affirming, against Takings and Due Process challenges, a California court's holding that the state constitution required a shopping center owner to permit speech and petitioning); Batchelder v. Allied Stores Int'l, Inc., 445 N.E.2d 590, 590 (Mass. 1983) (holding that, under the Massachusetts Constitution, a person may solicit public office nomination signatures in the mall area of a privately owned shopping center); Alderwood Assoc. v. Washington Envtl. Council, 635 P.2d 108, 117 (Wash. 1981) (holding that Washington law permitted the solicitation of signatures at privately owned shopping centers). The United States Supreme Court has held, as a matter of federal constitutional law, that a shopping center owner is free to restrict expressive activity. See Hudgens v. NLRB, 424 U.S. 507, 520-21 (1976) (denying right to picket); Lloyd Corp. v. Tanner, 407 U.S. 551, 552, 570 (1972) (denying right to distribute handbills).

Existing constitutional jurisprudence permits individuals to execute limited waivers even of First Amendment rights. Thus, although government may not unduly limit the speech rights of employees, no comparable limitation applies in the absence of state action; private employers, and presumably other private entities, are free to restrict the speech of employees.[79] If a private entity can condition one's livelihood on suppression of speech, there seems to be little reason to prevent a home-owners' association from demanding that its residents obey duly enacted speech restrictions.[80]

2. PROMOTING DELIBERATION

Civic republican scholars — particularly Frank Michelman and Cass Sunstein — have justified judicial review on the ground that legislative actions are too often the product of dealmaking and too rarely the product of deliberation. Civic republicans reject the pluralist notion that political processes are designed to aggregate the preferences of individual citizens, contending instead that legislation should be the product of a process that emphasizes deliberation about the wisdom of alternative policies. . . .

Civic republicans value deliberation for its transformative promise. In their view, political discussion can generate in citizens a set of preferences both different, and apparently more accurate, than the preferences those same citizens had before engaging in collective dialogue.[85] On this theory, then, mere aggregation of pre-political preferences leads to sub-optimal social results. . . .

Deliberative decision making is not an unqualified "good." Deliberation requires time and energy that could be devoted to other pursuits, including deliberation about other matters. . . . [W]hen people make decisions about their own self-interest, our legal system is generally content to permit them to deliberate as much — or as little — as they like. . . .

79. See Rendell-Baker v. Kohn, 457 U.S. 830, 834, 836-37 (1982) (holding that a private school could fire employees without concern for constitutional claims that such firings inhibited free speech).

80. The same arguments apply to restrictions on religion, for instance, or to restrictions on economic harm. In each case, a potential homeowner might choose to purchase in a community that protects her against unwanted restrictions. If, however, she chooses to purchase in a community that restricts religious practice or threatens particular economic harms, she might be treated as waiving any constitutional protections she might otherwise have had.

85. See id. at 27 ("Any view in which the true, primary interests of individuals are 'exogenous' or prior to politics is unrepublican. Republicanism rejects the idea that political activity is, at best, a mere means to the advancement of those prior interests. . . ."). Sunstein echoes the same theme: "The republican position is . . . that existing desires should be revisable in light of collective discussion and debate, bringing to bear alternative perspectives and additional information." Sunstein, supra note 81, at 1549. Sunstein continues:

A central point here is that individual preferences should not be taken as exogenous to politics. . . . [P]rivate preferences may be a product of adaptation by the disadvantaged and interest-induced beliefs on the part of the relatively well-off. Republicans are thus unlikely to take existing preferences and entitlements as fixed. Both are permissible objects of political deliberation.

Id.; see also Frank I. Michelman, Law's Republic, 97 Yale L.J. 1493, 1528 (1988) (noting that republican politics "contemplates . . . a self whose identity and freedom consist, in part, in its capacity for reflexively critical reconsideration of the ends and commitments that it already has and that make it who it is").

3. REDUCING AGENCY COSTS

Majority rule, like any other collective decision making process short of unanimous agreement, binds some people to the decisions of others. This raises two significant issues. First, how, and how well, do majorities determine individual preferences? Second, how well do majorities aggregate those preferences? These sorts of problems are often categorized as agency costs.

Majority determination of preferences is a problem because we generally assume that each person is the best judge of his own interests. In a market, each participant can only bind herself — the person whose preferences she knows best. By contrast, in a collective regime marked by majority rule, all participants are bound by decisions that some of them believe are not in their interests. Even if we assume that all participants in a collective enterprise try to act in the interests of the body as a whole, they will be judging the interests of people they understand less well than themselves. And, of course, the assumption that participants do, or should, try to act in the common interest rather than in their individual interests is a hotly contested one.

Even if we assume that participants in a collective process could accurately assess the interests of other participants, the problem of aggregating those interests remains. If we assume that individuals best know their own interests, aggregating interests reduces to aggregating preferences. In a system of majority rule, then, how do the minority's preferences get counted in the aggregation process? One answer is that the voting process itself gives minority preferences adequate attention, and that in a democracy, as Bruce Ackerman has observed, minorities are supposed to lose.[102]

Unless majority rule is itself the ultimate end, that answer is inadequate. The question instead must be whether majority rule is suited to achieve the ends for which the collective enterprise is designed. To the extent, for instance, that one views redistribution of resources as an appropriate collective goal, one might conclude that majorities are likely to give inadequate weight to the preferences of those without resources to contribute in the pluralist process.

Whatever its merit in the public law context, the notion that redistribution of resources constitutes an appropriate collective goal is less plausible within privately created associations. If potential members knew that an association was likely to redistribute resources, potential targets of redistribution would be highly unlikely to join. Hence, in the context of private associations, criticisms of majority rule as insufficiently redistributive are largely irrelevant.

A more plausible model for a privately created collective enterprise is the Buchanan and Tullock model of the state as an enterprise created by individuals hoping to increase their utility by eliminating external costs and securing external benefits. According to this model, a system in which majorities always rule would be ill-suited to serve the ends of the enterprise's members. Because majority rule does not account for intensity of preferences, many individuals would be unwilling to join a collective enterprise in which a mere majority of members could trample on important individual interests.

---

102. See Bruce Ackerman, Beyond Carolene Products, 98 Harv. L. Rev. 713, 719 (1985) ("[M]inorities are supposed to lose in a democratic system — even when they want very much to win and even when they think (as they often will) that the majority is deeply wrong. . . .").

As the number of issues and interest groups confronting the collective grows, the risk to minority interests shrinks. Each group seeking to garner support for action promoting its own strongly held preferences on an issue will trade votes with members of other groups, increasing the chance for each group to implement its strongly held preferences. Indeed, vote trading increases the likelihood that minorities with strongly held preferences will wield too much power as they overwhelm the interests of larger but more diffuse groups who face greater difficulty organizing into a successful pressure group.[110] Nevertheless, much constitutional scholarship rests on the premise that interest-group politics will inadequately protect the interests of "discrete and insular" minorities.

Hence, to the extent that the range of decisions facing community associations is relatively small, majority rule may risk undervaluing the interests of minority members. This problem is not, as we shall see, unique to community association law.

III.   CONTRACT AS A CONSTRAINT ON PROTECTION OF MINORITY INTERESTS

A.   THE CONTRACT ARGUMENT

The public law debate over protection of minority interests has, in essence, been a debate about the terms of the social contract. Since the social contract represents a theoretical construct rather than a historical event, scholars in a variety of disciplines and with a variety of perspectives have devoted much energy to identifying its appropriate terms. In their classic work on public choice, Buchanan and Tullock developed models of collective decision making "[b]y approaching the problem of the calculus of the single individual as he confronts constitutional choices, not knowing with accuracy his own particular role in the chain of collective decisions that may be anticipated to be carried out in the future."[113] Similarly, Rawls expounds his principles of justice by constructing a hypothetical bargain among persons so situated that "no one is able to design principles to favor his particular condition."[114] Because the hypothetical choices are made by hypothetical people with hypothetical characteristics, the shape of the resulting social contract — and particularly the scope of minority protections — might vary enormously.

No comparable problems afflict the constitutions that govern private residential communities. By purchasing a home in a community governed by a declaration that contemplates an association with rulemaking power, a flesh-and-blood person agrees to abide by the association's rules. If purchasers want protection against interference with important rights, declarations can be drafted to secure those protections. If purchasers want to ensure deliberation in the association's processes, declarations can provide appropriate procedures for association action. If purchasers are concerned about agency costs, covenants can be drafted to reduce those costs.

It would be absurd to argue that a prospective home purchaser will find it worthwhile to negotiate for declaration provisions that maximize her own welfare. If, however, protections against association action are important, developers should

---

110. See Mancur Olson, The Logic of Collective Action 127-28 (2d ed. 1971) (arguing that the groups most likely to be successful in a pluralist process are small interest groups in which each member has a large stake).

113. Buchanan & Tullock, supra note 76, at 92.

114. Rawls, supra note 65, at 12.

find it worth their while to design attractive provisions that will induce homeowners to choose their developments, in the same way that homeowners choose units with attractive kitchens and bathrooms.[116] Choosing among governance provisions is much less onerous for potential homeowners than designing those provisions. And, of course, the potential homeowner concerned about community association governance retains the option to buy a home not subject to association governance.

Moreover, few people casually decide to purchase a home. Because purchasing a home is the largest single investment most people will make, they generally take time to assess the quality of that investment. In many jurisdictions, though certainly not all, purchasers are routinely represented by counsel who provide advice about any dangers associated with community association governance. As a result, home purchasers have both the incentive and the opportunity to become informed about their decision to purchase in a development governed by a community association.

That, in sum, is the contract argument against extending more protection to community association minorities than is provided in the governing documents themselves.

B. OBJECTIONS TO THE CONTRACT ARGUMENT

The contract argument, for all of its credibility, faces at least three challenges. First, because provisions creating association powers are bundled with other items more significant to housing consumers, a consumer's purchase should not necessarily be treated as a decision to be bound by association governance. Second, the contract argument for providing less protection to minorities in private settings assumes a distinction between the private and public spheres, a distinction that is in fact illusory. Third, the contract argument ignores the "good faith" requirement and other doctrines of contract law that routinely operate to constrain power apparently bestowed by one party to a contract on the other. This subpart considers these three challenges.

1. THE BUNDLING PROBLEM

In arguing that all servitudes should be subject to discretionary judicial review, Gregory Alexander has invoked the "bundling" problem.[117] Alexander notes that a land purchaser might buy subject to a servitude, even if the purchaser did not want the servitude. He rejects the notion that such a purchaser would obtain a discounted price to compensate for the unwanted servitude, arguing that because of the complexity of the transaction, the purchaser might not have focused on the servitude provision. If Alexander's argument has force for servitudes made explicit in the deed, the argument carries even more force with respect to association power

---

116. Moreover, the increasing sophistication of community association lawyers makes it more feasible to tailor declarations to reflect particular market concerns. Thus, community association lawyers have their own professional group, the Community Associations Institute, which sponsors the usual range of seminars and publications for interested practitioners. See, e.g., Community Ass'ns Inst., supra note 2.

117. See Alexander, supra note 91, at 894. Alexander attributes the term "bundling" to Mark Kelman. See generally Mark Kelman, A Guide to Critical Legal Studies 107-09 (1987) (applying bundling theory to explain courts' treatment of coercive covenants running with the land).

to impose new obligations on the purchaser; the purchaser might well have failed to focus on those unknown obligations.

Alexander expressly relies on the premise that purchasers engage in irrational behavior.[118] Taken broadly, as Alexander recognizes, this premise challenges not merely enforcement of bundled agreements, but enforcement of all contracts. Taken more narrowly to apply only when contracts involve bundling, the premise is peculiar. Every decision to enter into a contract involves bundled choices. A golf club member can hardly complain about a club dress code or a monthly charge for uneaten meals on the grounds that he agreed to those burdens only unwillingly as the price for using the club's golf course. An academic could not likely avoid teaching responsibilities by contending that he was forced to accept them as the price of joining a faculty. Every commitment requires some sacrifice of personal autonomy, but if we preclude people from making commitments, we exact from them an even greater sacrifice of autonomy. . . .

2. THE ASSERTED EMPTINESS OF THE PUBLIC-PRIVATE DISTINCTION

The contract argument against minority protections assumes that an agreement to purchase a unit subject to association governance is fundamentally different from the purchase of a home subject to state and municipal governance. That supposed distinction, however, has been hotly contested. Gerald Frug, for one, has argued that some cities, like many homeowner associations, were initially formed by the unanimous consent of all residents.[125] Frug has suggested, moreover, that the circumstances of original formation lose significance with the passage of time, as "children take over their parents' homes, and the like."[126]

One might also argue that the decision to reside in a particular municipality, like the decision to purchase in a particular common interest community, is a "voluntary" act that signifies consent to be governed in accordance with the municipality's charter. Indeed, Charles Tiebout theorizes that competition among municipalities regulates municipal provision of public goods, because potential residents shop among municipalities to find one that provides the mix of public goods best suited to their desires.[127] . . .

The argument that minorities choose to submit to local government power just as they choose to submit to community association power, however, should not be dispositive. . . . In general, the constraints imposed on a potential purchaser deciding whether to buy a home in an area governed by a community association are far less significant than the constraints facing a resident trying to decide whether to move into (or to leave) a particular municipality.[128] A lifelong resident

---

118. See id. at 895.

125. See Gerald E. Frug, Cities and Homeowner Associations: A Reply, 130 U. Pa. L. Rev. 1589, 1590 n.5 (1982) (citing the Mayflower Compact as an example of a voluntary agreement forming a city).

126. Id. at 1590-91.

127. See Charles M. Tiebout, A Pure Theory of Local Expenditures, 64 J. Pol. Econ. 416, 418 (1956).

128. For an empirical study suggesting that few citizens leave municipalities out of dissatisfaction with political processes, see David Lowery & William E. Lyons, The Impact of Judicial Boundaries: An Individual-Level Test of the Tiebout Model, 51 J. Pol. 73, 92-93 (1989). See also Wallace E. Oates, On Local Finance and the Tiebout Model, Am. Econ. Rev., May 1981, at 93, 93 (questioning the assumptions underlying the Tiebout model).

of New York City might find the costs of leaving to be daunting, even if the resident was fed up with City policies. Without leaving the city, however, the same person would be free to choose among many apartments and homes, governed by a variety of community associations or subject to no associations at all. . . . [A]lthough the difference is largely a matter of degree, contract does provide somewhat greater justification for binding minority members to the decisions of a community association than for binding minority residents to the decisions of a local government.

3. CONSTRAINTS ON POWER INTERNAL TO CONTRACT LAW

A unit owner's agreement to abide by the decisions of a community association does not immediately obligate the owner to perform a specified act or pay a particular sum of money. Rather, the agreement binds the unit owner to determinations the association might make in the future. As a result of the agreement, the association has power to impose new duties not specified in the agreement itself. This situation resembles the classic relational contract, "characterized by uncertainty about factual conditions during performance and an extraordinary degree of difficulty in describing specifically the desired adaptations to contingencies."[129] The agreement, here embodied in the Declaration, deals with the uncertainty by creating a mechanism for coping with future problems: association governance.

When relational contracts appear to put one party at the mercy of another, contract doctrine constrains the broad discretion conferred on one party, either by holding the agreement unenforceable altogether or by reading the agreement's terms to limit discretion. The extreme example of an agreement unenforceable because it would give one party complete discretion over the other is a contract to enslave oneself.[130] By contrast, the obligation to deal in good faith, implied in all contracts, construes the contract's terms to limit a party's discretion, even when the letter of the agreement appears to confer that discretion. . . .

The point is not to define limits on a community association's exercise of discretion; that enterprise is the focus of the next Part. Instead, the point is that contract law constrains the exercise of discretion even when the parties have not included explicit limits on its exercise. . . . Moreover, even if courts should defer to community association decisions, the basic point remains: the existence of a contract among unit owners does not end discussion about the scope of association power or the desirability of affording protection to minority members. Because contract law generally constrains the exercise of discretion by contracting parties, one would also expect to see limits on the exercise of community association discretion. In examining those limits, an appropriate next step would be to explore the other area in which contractually created decision making bodies exercise discretion in ways that displease minority members: corporate law. . . .

---

129. Charles J. Goetz & Robert E. Scott, Principles of Relational Contracts, 67 Va. L. Rev. 1089, 1127 (1981); see also Gillette, supra note 122, at 1413-17 (exploring the relational nature of community associations).

130. Cf. U.S. Const. amend. XIII (prohibiting slavery and involuntary servitude).

V. MINORITIES IN THE COMMUNITY ASSOCIATION CONTEXT:
ADDRESSING CONCRETE PROBLEMS

As we have seen, despite its apparent advantages, majority rule risks undervaluing minority interests. By outvoting the minority, the majority avoids confronting and evaluating minority concerns. This results in two sorts of inefficiency. First, the organization itself may take actions that generate costs without commensurate benefits. Second, the prospect of such actions may discourage others from entering into collective enterprises, even when collective action could eliminate inefficient holdout and freerider problems.

In the corporate setting, institutional constraints on the behavior of managers and majority shareholders mitigate some of the most serious difficulties of majority rule. When institutional constraints are inadequate, an express contract among the members may reduce the risk of harm to the minority. One of the lessons from close corporation law, however, is that the range of opportunities for collective action is so great that express contracts cannot contemplate all of the circumstances that might lead a majority to act opportunistically. Legal rules may therefore be helpful in defining the appropriate scope of majority power. . . .

A. COMMUNITY ASSOCIATION DECISIONS THAT REDISTRIBUTE MARKET VALUE

Start with two relatively uncontroversial assumptions. First, unit owners in common interest communities generally expect net benefit, not net harm, from community association activity. Second, because their units represent a large portion of their total assets, unit owners tend to be risk averse with respect to their units. Given these assumptions, it is not difficult to see that unit owners generally would oppose giving community associations the power to take actions that redistribute market value from some units to others.[187] The risk of redistribution is a net harm to risk averse owners, a harm not counterbalanced by any benefit, since purely redistributive actions create no net benefit for the community.[188]

Moreover, to the extent that associations deal with too few issues to permit effective formation of shifting coalitions, the risk that the majority will not account for minority preferences is significant. Members of the majority on one issue will be unlikely to worry that they might need minority support on some other issue. At the time the association is formed, potential members would find it difficult to anticipate, and prohibit, all potential forms of redistribution, so that failure to bar a particular action in the Declaration or in the association's bylaws would hardly establish that association members were willing to confer uncontrolled power on the majority. The case for judicial invalidation of purely redistributive actions, then, is particularly strong.

---

187. Indeed, even if we assume that unit owners are risk neutral, they might oppose redistributive actions to the extent those actions encourage members of the association to engage in unproductive rent-seeking, rather than more productive activity. On similar grounds, Easterbrook and Fischel justify prohibitions on redistribution in publicly held corporations, where they assume shareholders are risk neutral. See Easterbrook & Fischel, supra note 9, at 124-26 (likening prohibitions on redistribution to prohibitions on theft).

188. Moreover, as Robert Ellickson has pointed out, even if residents are not risk averse, the administrative costs of redistributive programs make redistribution a negative sum game. See Ellickson, supra note 1, at 1525 (noting that administrative expenses will result in a dead-weight loss to unit owners).

Few association actions are purely redistributive, however. Most redistributive actions serve some community purpose. As we have seen, a number of scholars have championed deliberation-promoting rules as a means of persuading victims of redistribution that their losses are necessary to promote the common good. But to the extent that the burden of the action falls on a small number of unit owners, redistribution should not be necessary to promote the common good. The association would not face a heavy administrative burden if forced to compensate affected unit owners for the harm they suffer. Risk averse unit owners would certainly support a compensation requirement. Hence, one would expect courts to invalidate any measure that significantly reduces the market value of a particular unit or set of units, even if the association's action creates some community-wide benefit.[191]

Ridgely Condominium Ass'n v. Smyrnioudis[192] furnishes perhaps the best illustration. In *Ridgely*, a mixed-unit condominium had 232 units, seven of which were commercial units with access both from the outside and from the interior lobby of the building. After the commercial units were sold, the association, for security reasons, enacted a bylaw prohibiting customers of the commercial units from using the interior lobby. This made access to those units less attractive and consequently made them less valuable. The court invalidated the bylaw as unreasonable. Of course, if security had been a significant concern for the residential users, they could easily have compensated the seven commercial users for loss of lobby access. Their failure to do so made the case an easy one for the court. The governing principle is analogous to that which the *Wilkes* court invoked in the close corporation context: an action that serves a permissible purpose — here, improving security — is nevertheless invalid if the same purpose could have been accomplished without harm to minority members (here, by compensating the commercial unit owners).

Similarly, in Boyles v. Hausman,[195] the Nebraska Supreme Court invalidated a covenant, affecting only a minority of landowners, that prohibited building within 120 feet of a county road. The association imposed the covenant after the complaining unit owner had purchased his parcel. The covenant significantly diminished his parcel's value. Had the association compensated the unit owner for the value of an easement over his parcel, the association's position would have been more defensible. As it was, however, the association's action constituted unnecessary redistribution, and the court responded accordingly.[196] . . .

---

191. If the association offered just compensation to those whose land would decline in value as a result of the association's proposed regulation, there would be little reason to invalidate the regulation. Cf. Ellickson, supra note 1, at 1536-37 (suggesting that courts imply taking clauses into declarations). However, whether courts should order compensation, rather than simply invalidate the regulation and give the association the opportunity to draft a new regulation with compensation, is a different question. In any event, associations appear rarely to have offered harmed landowners compensation for losses resulting from regulation.

192. 660 A.2d 942 (Md. Ct. Spec. App. 1995).

195. 517 N.W.2d 610, 618 (Neb. 1994).

196. The court wrote: "The law will not subject a minority of landowners to unlimited and unexpected restrictions on the use of their land merely because the covenant agreement permitted a majority to make changes to existing covenants." Id. at 617. See also Blood v. Edgar's, Inc., 632 N.E.2d 419, 420 (Mass. App. Ct. 1994), in which a mixed-use condominium association decided to subsidize a rental program that benefited only residential unit owners. When the sole commercial owner attacked the subsidy, the court held that the association had no power to alter the previous practice, which had been to assure that the rental program was self-sustaining. See id. at 422-23.

C. DECISIONS THAT DEPRIVE UNIT OWNERS OF
IDIOSYNCRATIC VALUE

1. THE FRAMEWORK

Community association decisions can have an impact—positive or negative—on particular homeowners, even if those decisions have no impact on the market value of the units. Suppose, for instance, that an association is about to decide whether to improve existing swimming pool facilities and expand the hours during which the pool is open. Suppose further that these enhancements will cost $100 per year per unit owner. For Sally Swimmer, who would have paid $200 per year for upgraded pool facilities, the proposal is attractive. Lucy Landlubber, by contrast, would not willingly pay even a dollar for the upgrade, because she never uses the facilities. Each of the other association members values the enhancements somewhere between zero and $200 per year. If a majority of association members approves the upgrade, and approves an assessment of $100 per year to pay for the enhancement, should a court step in to protect Lucy, who has been made $100 per year worse off as a result of the association's action?

At first glance, one might dismiss Lucy's complaint by noting that Lucy could simply sell her unit and avoid the $100 annual expense. The very fact that a majority of unit owners supported the improvements and was willing to pay the annual assessment is good evidence that potential buyers would find the benefit worth the cost. If the majority preferences of existing owners reflect the preferences of potential buyers, Lucy will not suffer any loss in market value as a result of the pool improvements.

The problem with this approach is that it denies Lucy the idiosyncratic value she almost certainly attaches to her unit. Economic theory teaches that all current owners of housing (and, for that matter, other assets) value their units more than the market does; if they did not, they would be indifferent to selling their units and moving or remaining. With housing, there is a particularly good reason for assuming that owners attach idiosyncratic value to their units: moving is costly, both in terms of finances as well as changed affiliations (new schools, new neighbors) and personal attachments. In other words, the cost of "exit" for Lucy is high, often higher than the loss she might suffer at the association's hands.

Lucy's predicament is not the "bundling" problem she would face when deciding whether to purchase a unit with a swimming pool she does not want. In that situation, Lucy would not yet have formed the attachments that make leaving difficult in the case where the association approves pool renovations after she has lived in the community for a time. Moreover, because Lucy's attachments in the latter situation lock her into her current unit, she has less incentive to make an informed decision about pool improvements than if she was deciding whether to buy in the first place.

Focusing on Lucy's predicament, however, obscures the advantages of sustaining the association's action. First, there is good reason to believe that the majority's gains will exceed the minority's losses. Sheer numbers do not capture intensity of preferences, but in the case of community association decisions, those with intense preferences have two alternatives: they can seek to influence the association's decision, or they can move. The first option is likely to be more effective in the community association context than in the close corporation, because majority members of the association must confront members of the minority on a regular basis — in the neighborhood or when using common facilities. Regular contacts like these would be quite uncomfortable if it was clear that the majority was ignoring strongly held preferences of the minority. Thus, the majority will be more inclined to compromise . . .

In addition, because units in a common interest community are readily marketable — unlike minority interests in close corporations — the exit option furnishes the ultimate safety valve for dissident residents of a common interest community. So long as the association's actions do not redistribute market value from some units to others, those who are particularly unhappy with the association's decision know that, at worst, they can sell their unit at the market price. Moving would result in a loss of idiosyncratic value, but there is no way to protect both the minority's intense preferences and its idiosyncratic value without imposing parallel — and presumptively larger — costs on the majority. That is, if we assume that some members of the majority are at least as likely to have intense preferences as members of the minority, annulling the association's action would put the former to the same choice. Either they could stay, their intense preferences ignored, or they could leave, losing whatever idiosyncratic value they attach to their units. Collective action problems make it virtually impossible to solve the dilemma by compensating minority members. As long as the losses the minority suffers are not reflected in market value, no readily available mechanism exists for determining what compensation should be paid, or who should pay it.

Two analogies to close corporation law suggest that the majority ought to prevail in cases like Lucy's. First, we have seen that even in a close corporation case like *Wilkes*, in which the court protected a minority shareholder against a freeze-out, the court indicated that the majority shareholders would be entitled to disadvantage the minority shareholder if they could not accomplish their legitimate business purpose without harming the minority shareholder.[213] If a community association cannot accomplish a purpose of importance to a majority of unit owners without diminishing the idiosyncratic value of minority unit owners, the *Wilkes* principle suggests that the majority should prevail.

Second, a number of states have enacted statutes authorizing dissolution of close corporations when those in control have oppressed minority shareholders. These statutes permit controlling shareholders to avoid dissolution by purchasing the shares of the minority shareholders at a fair price.[215] In effect, then, a dissenting shareholder who establishes that her expectations of corporate office or employment have been unjustifiably frustrated by the majority's action is entitled to recover only the market value of her shares, not whatever idiosyncratic value she attached to her job or affiliation with the company. There is good reason for denying dissenting shareholders (and dissenting unit owners) compensation for lost idiosyncratic value: that value is notoriously difficult to measure.

To the extent these analogies to close corporation law are appropriate, they suggest that those who join an association generally expect that the association could pursue policies that most members would find beneficial, so long as those policies do not redistribute market value among units. On the other hand, this presumption of association power should serve merely as a default rule. When

213. See supra text accompanying notes 175-83.
215. See Cal. Corp. Code § 2000(a); N.Y. Bus Corp. Law § 1118(a).

parties have revealed expectations that association power is limited, those expectations should be honored.

The most obvious way for parties to reveal their expectations about the scope of association power is to make them explicit in the documents creating the association. Thus, if the Declaration limits association power to alter appurtenances without unanimous approval of record owners, an association majority should not be able to convert a tennis court into a parking area.[219] Similarly, the Declaration can limit the power of the association board by requiring supermajorities for particular actions. Moreover, if the Declaration explicitly permits particular land-owner activities, one would not expect that an association could prohibit those activities without amendment to the Declaration. Simply enacting a rule should be insufficient.[221]

Even when the Declaration is silent about association behavior, if a unit owner makes a substantial and obvious investment, either financial or emotional, with the expectation, created by existing association structure, that certain behavior would be permitted, the association should be estopped from regulating that behavior if it took no steps to stop the unit owner from making the investment. Property law often protects expectations, whether or not reduced to a writing, when a party has made investments that all parties understand he would not have made but for the expectation.[222] Zoning law's non-conforming use doctrines provide similar protection for expectations: if a party develops land for a particular use, subsequent zoning regulation changes do not generally require immediate cessation of the pre-existing use. The same principles should serve to limit community association action. For instance, if a unit owner erected a satellite dish or installed a washer and dryer without any notice that these devices were prohibited, courts could appropriately enjoin the association from enforcing any subsequently enacted prohibition against that unit owner. Similarly, a prohibition on pets even if enforceable prospectively, ought not to require a particular unit owner to part with a pet acquired without notice of any restriction. . . .

Neuman v. Grandview at Emerald Hills, Inc.

861 So. 2d 494 (Fla. App. 4th Dist. 2003)

Warner, J.

We deny the motion for rehearing, withdraw our previously issued opinion, and substitute the following in its place.

219. See Gilmore v. Ciega Verde Condo. Ass'n, 601 So. 2d 1325, 1325 (Fla. Dist. Ct. App. 1992) (rejecting an association's attempt to convert a tennis court into a parking lot without the unanimous consent of its residents, as required by its CC&Rs); Young v. Ciega Verde Condo. Ass'n, 600 So. 2d 528, 528 (Fla. Dist. Ct. App. 1992) (same).

221. See, e.g., Parkway Gardens Condo. Ass'n v. Kinser, 536 So. 2d 1076 (Fla. Dist. Ct. App. 1988) (holding unenforceable a rule prohibiting pets when the Declaration permitted them).

222. American property law generally imposes on neighbors the obligation to cooperate with each other. See generally Sterk, supra note 212, at 95-103 (discussing the scope of the obligation). In particular, a neighbor generally may not stand silent while his neighbor makes substantial investments, and then require the neighbor to forfeit those investments. See id. at 59-63 (discussing various easement and boundary dispute doctrines that protect neighbors who have made substantial investments in reliance on an understanding, sometimes mistaken, about their right to use their land). Presumably, the obligation to cooperate should be even stronger in the community association context, in which the parties have a continuing formal legal relation, as well as a social relation as neighbors.

The issue presented in this case is whether a condominium association rule banning the holding of religious services in the auditorium of the condominium constitutes a violation of section 718.123, Florida Statutes (2002), which precludes condominium rules from unreasonably restricting a unit owner's right to peaceably assemble. We hold that the rule does not violate the statute and affirm.

Appellee Grandview is a condominium association with 442 members, appellants being two of the members. Appellants reside at Grandview condominium during the winter months. The common elements of the condominium include an auditorium that members can reserve for social gatherings and meetings. Grandview enacted a rule governing the use of the auditorium in 1982, which provided that the auditorium could be used for meetings or functions of groups, including religious groups, when at least eighty percent of the members were residents of Grandview condominium. Generally, the only reservations made for the auditorium on Saturdays were by individual members for birthday or anniversary celebrations.

In January 2001, several unit owners reserved the auditorium between 8:30 and noon on Saturday mornings. While they indicated they were reserving it for a party, they actually conducted religious services. Approximately forty condominium members gathered for the services.

Upon discovering that religious services were being conducted on Saturdays in the auditorium, several other members complained to the Board of Directors ("Board"). The Board met in February to discuss restrictions on the use of the auditorium and common elements for religious services and activities. The meeting became very confrontational between those members supporting the use of the auditorium for religious services and those opposing such use. Based upon the controversial nature of the issue, the Board's desire not to have a common element tied up for the exclusive use of a minority of the members on a regular basis, and to avoid conflicts between different religious groups competing for the space, the Board first submitted the issue to a vote of the owners. Seventy percent of the owners voted in favor of prohibiting the holding of religious services in the auditorium. The Board then voted unanimously to amend the rule governing the use of the auditorium. The new rule provided that "[n]o religious services or activities of any kind are allowed in the auditorium or any other common elements."

Appellants filed suit against Grandview seeking injunctive and declaratory relief to determine whether the rule violated their constitutional rights or was in violation of section 718.123, and whether the rule was arbitrarily and capriciously enacted by the Board. Grandview answered, denying that the rule was arbitrary or violated appellants' statutory or constitutional rights. Appellants moved for a temporary injunction alleging that Grandview was not only preventing the owners from holding religious services, it was also prohibiting the use of the auditorium for holiday parties, including Christmas and Chanukah, based upon its prohibition against using the common elements "for religious activities of any kind." The court granted the motion as to the use of the auditorium for religious activities of any kind but denied it as it applied to the holding of religious services. Based upon the temporary injunction as to religious activities, Grandview amended its rule to limit the prohibition to the holding of religious services in the auditorium.

At a hearing on appellants' motion for a permanent injunction against the rule, the appellants relied primarily on section 718.123, which prohibits condominium associations from unreasonably restricting the unit owners' rights to peaceable assembly. They argued that religious services fell into the category of a "peaceable assembly," and a categorical ban on the holding of religious services was *per se* unreasonable. Grandview maintained that it had the right to restrict the use of its common elements. Because the right of peaceable assembly did not mandate a right to conduct religious services, it had the right to poll its members and restrict the use based upon the majority's desires. As such, Grandview maintained the exercise of this right was reasonable.

In its final order denying the injunction, the court determined that because no state action was involved, the unit owners' constitutional rights of freedom of speech and religion were not implicated by Grandview's rule. The court determined that the rule did not violate section 718.123, as the condominium association had the authority to enact this reasonable restriction on the use of the auditorium. Appellants challenge that ruling.

Chapter 718, Florida's "Condominium Act," recognizes the condominium form of property ownership and "establishes a detailed scheme for the creation, sale, and operation of condominiums." Woodside Vill. Condo. Ass'n v. Jahren, 806 So.2d 452, 455 (Fla.2002). Thus, condominiums are strictly creatures of statute. See id. The declaration of condominium, which is the condominium's "constitution," creates the condominium and "strictly governs the relationships among the condominium units owners and the condominium association." Id. at 456. Under the declaration, the Board of the condominium association has broad authority to enact rules for the benefit of the community. See id.

In Hidden Harbour Estates, Inc. v. Norman, 309 So.2d 180, 181-82 (Fla. 4th DCA 1975), this court explained the unique character of condominium living which, for the good of the majority, restricts rights residents would otherwise have were they living in a private separate residence:

> It appears to us that inherent in the condominium concept is the principle that to promote the health, happiness, and peace of mind of the majority of the unit owners since they are living in such close proximity and using facilities in common, each unit owner must give up a certain degree of freedom of choice which he might otherwise enjoy in separate, privately owned property. Condominium unit owners comprise a little democratic sub society of necessity more restrictive as it pertains to use of condominium property than may be existent outside the condominium organization.

Section 718.123(1) recognizes the right of the condominium association to regulate the use of the common elements of the condominium:

> All common elements, common areas, and recreational facilities serving any condominium shall be available to unit owners in the condominium or condominiums served thereby and their invited guests for the use intended for such common elements, common areas, and recreational facilities, subject to the provisions of s. 718.106(4). *The entity or entities responsible for the operation of the common elements, common areas, and recreational facilities may adopt reasonable rules and regulations pertaining to the use of such common elements, common areas, and recreational facilities. No entity or entities shall unreasonably restrict any unit owner's right to peaceably assemble* or right to invite public officers or candidates for public office to appear and speak in common elements, common areas, and recreational facilities.

(Emphasis added).

The statutory test for rules regarding the operation of the common elements of the condominium is reasonableness. The trial court found the rule preventing use of the auditorium for religious services was reasonable in light of the Board's concern for a serious potential for conflict of use which could arise among competing religious groups. Having polled the members and determined that a majority of the members approved the ban, the Board's rule assured that the auditorium was "available to unit owners in the condominium or condominiums served thereby and their invited guests for the use intended" in accordance with the statute. § 718.123(1).

The appellants' main argument both at trial and on appeal suggests that because the statute mandates that the Board may not "unreasonably restrict any unit owner's right to peaceably assemble," § 718.123(1), a categorical prohibition of all religious services exceeds the Board's powers, as the right to meet in religious worship would constitute the right to peaceably assemble. However, the right to peaceably assemble has traditionally been interpreted to apply to the right of the citizens to meet to discuss public or governmental affairs. See United States v. Cruikshank, 92 U.S. 542, 551-52, 23 L.Ed. 588 (1875). Assuming for purposes of this argument that the right to gather for religious worship is a form of peaceable assembly, the rule in question bans this particular form of assembly, but not all right to assemble. Certainly, a categorical ban on the right of members to use the auditorium for any gathering would be contrary to statute. However, the statute itself permits the reasonable regulation of that right. Prohibiting those types of assembly which will have a particularly divisive effect on the condominium community is a reasonable restriction. See Hidden Harbour, 309 So.2d at 181-82. The Board found that permitting the holding of regular worship services and the competition among various religious groups for use of the auditorium would pose such conflict. Where the condominium association's regulations regarding common elements are reasonable and not violative of specific statutory limitations, the regulations should be upheld. See Juno By the Sea N. Condo. Ass'n v. Manfredonia, 397 So.2d 297, 302 (Fla. 4th DCA 1980). The trial court found the restriction reasonable under the facts. No abuse of discretion has been shown.

The judgment of the trial court is affirmed.

STONE and STEVENSON, JJ., concur.

NOTES AND QUESTIONS

1. *"Functional equivalence" and the application of constitutional limitations.* Could a local government pass an ordinance permitting the use of public space for peaceable assemblies of any kind except for religious services? If not, should a homeowners association be able to adopt such a measure? In Marsh v. Alabama, 326 U.S. 501, 506 (1946), the Supreme Court addressed the rights of individuals in a privately owned company town:

> Ownership does not always mean absolute dominion. The more an owner, for his advantage, opens up his property for use by the public in general, the more do his rights become circumscribed by the statutory and constitutional rights of those who use it.

A series of subsequent cases have defined and circumscribed this broad language. Consider Hudgens v. N. L. R. B., 424 U.S. 507 (1976), Justice Stewart writing for the Court:

> "The question is, Under what circumstances can private property be treated as though it were public? The answer that *Marsh* gives is when that property has taken on All the attributes of a town, i.e., 'residential buildings, streets, a system of sewers, a sewage disposal plant and a "business block" on which business places are situated.' 326 U.S., at 502, 66 S.Ct., at 277. I can find nothing in *Marsh* which indicates that if one of these features is present, e. g., a business district, this is sufficient for the Court to confiscate a part of an owner's private property and give its use to people who want to picket on it." Id., at 332, 88 S.Ct., at 1615.

Another series of cases has held that first amendment rights of access and free speech sometimes apply to privately owned shopping centers. See Amalgamated Food Employee Union Local 590 v. Logan Valley, 391 U.S. 308 (1968) (First Amendment protects picketing at privately owned shopping center, where picketing was directly related to the activities of the shopping center); Lloyd Corp. v. Tanner, 407 U.S. 551 (1972) (First Amendment does not protect right of antiwar protesters to pass out handbills in private shopping center); Pruneyard Shopping Center v. Robbins, 447 U.S. 74 (1980) (interpretation of California State Constitution that shopping center owner must permit petitioning by private parties does not violate the First Amendment free speech rights of the owner nor constitute a taking of private property); New Jersey Coalition Against War in the Middle East v. J.M.B. Realty Corp., 650 A.2d 757 (N.J. 1994) (New Jersey constitution protects the right of individuals to distribute leaflets about public issues inside private shopping centers).

So, to what extent are the powers of a homeowners association to control its property akin to "absolute dominion," and to what extent are those powers "circumscribed by the statutory and constitutional rights of those who use it"? In *Mulligan,* the court declined to rule on the validity of the restriction against Tier 3 sex offenders, and in its discussion noted that "it is entirely unclear if the Association performs quasi-municipal functions, such that its actions perhaps should be viewed as analogous to governmental actions in some regards." What difference would this make?

These issues have generated a considerable literature. See, e.g., Adrienne Iwamoto Suarez, Covenants, Conditions, and Restrictions . . . on Free Speech? First Amendment Rights in Common-Interest Communities, 40 Real Prop. Prob. & Tr. J. 739 (2006); Josh Mulligan, Finding a Forum in the Simulated City: Mega Malls, Gated Towns, and the Promise of PruneYard, 13 Cornell J. L. & Pub. Pol'y (2004); David L. Callies et al., Ramapo Looking Forward: Gated Communities, Covenants, and Concerns, 35 Urb. Law. 177, 182 (2003); Steven Siegel, The Constitution and Private Government: Toward the Recognition of Constitutional Rights in Private Residential Communities Fifty Years After Marsh v. Alabama, 6 Wm. & Mary Bill Rts. J. 461, 464 (1997); John B. Owens, Westec Story: Gated Communities and the Fourth Amendment, 34 Am. Crim. L. Rev. 1127, 1136 (1997); Harvey Rishikof & Alexander Wohl, Private Communities or Public Governments: The State Will Make the Call, 30 Val. U. L. Rev. 509, 512 (1996); David J. Kennedy, Residential Associations as State Actors: Regulating the Impact of Gated Communities on Nonmembers, 105 Yale L.J. 761, 766-767 (1995).

2. *State action.* In *Neuman,* the trial court held that there was no state action that would bring the board's decision to ban religious services from the common areas under constitutional limitations, a ruling the appellate court did not address. Consider Gerber v. Longboat Harbour North Condo, Inc., 724 F. Supp. 884, 886-887 (M.D. Fla. 1989), in which a condominium owner challenged a rule barring the display of the American flag except on specified occasions.

> In 1947, the United States Supreme Court sounded the death knell for those among our number who would deny minorities the housing of their choice simply because of the color of their skin through racially restrictive covenants. In *Shelley v. Kraemer,* 334 U.S. 1, 68 S.Ct. 836, 92 L.Ed. 1161 (1948), the six participating justices held that, while the Fourteenth Amendment does not reach purely private conduct, judicial enforcement of restrictive covenants constitutes state action, triggering the protections of the Fourteenth Amendment's Due Process and Equal Protection Clauses.
>
> Applying the principles of *Shelley* to the situation sub judice, this Court finds that judicial enforcement of private agreements contained in a declaration of condominium constitutes state action and brings the heretofore private conduct within the ken of the Fourteenth Amendment, through which the First Amendment guarantee of free speech is made applicable to the states.
>
> It cannot be gainsaid that judicial enforcement of a racially restrictive covenant constitutes state action. It offends logic to suppose that equal protection of the law could be guaranteed by the very government whose judicial arm seeks to deny it. To suggest that judicial enforcement of private covenants abridging protected speech is not state action is, *mutatis mutandis,* equally repugnant to reason.
>
> Defendant's actions in denying Plaintiff his Constitutionally guaranteed right to display the American Flag were illegal *ab initio,* and this Court so holds. . . .
>
> This Court has read and weighed the opinion of the Florida Second District Court of Appeal in *Quail Creek Property Owners Association, Inc. v. Hunter,* 538 So.2d 1288 (Fla.App.1989) (on rehearing). This Court cannot agree with its conclusion that judicial enforcement of racially restrictive covenants is state action and judicial enforcement of covenants which restrict one's right to patriotic speech is not state action. Enforcement of private agreements by the judicial branch of government is state action for purposes of the Fourteenth Amendment, as the Highest Court in the land declared it to be in *Shelley*; it cannot be said that the terms of the agreement either increase or decrease the extent to which government is involved. It is an exercise in sophistry to posit that courts act as the state when enforcing racially restrictive covenants but not when giving effect to other provisions of the same covenant.

But see Midlake on Big Boulder Lake Condominium Assoc. v. Capuccio, 673 A.2d 340 (Pa. 1996) (no state action in enforcement of prohibition on signs; *Shelley* is limited to cases of racial discrimination); cf. Goldberg v. 400 East Ohio Condominium Assn., 12 F. Supp. 2d 820 (N.D. Ill. 1998) (condominium association rule barring distribution of fliers is not state action absent action for judicial enforcement).

3. If an association rule cannot be challenged on constitutional grounds, could a court void it under the doctrine that servitudes are not enforceable if they violate public policy?

CHAPTER SEVEN

Advanced Topics in Land Finance

A. LOAN COMMITMENTS

The borrower-lender relationship starts before a loan is made, when the borrower applies and the parties enter into negotiations. It is not uncommon for the parties to enter into a loan commitment—an agreement to make a loan in the future, upon the satisfaction of certain conditions. Loan commitments were once relatively brief, a page or two setting out the terms of the proposed loan. However, as mortgage finance has grown more varied and complex, it has become common for loan commitments to be detailed agreements setting forth the terms of the loan and conditions precedent in great detail.

Loan commitments are the source of a tremendous amount of litigation, in large part because either the lender or the borrower may find that, in the period between the execution of the commitment and the issuance of the loan, circumstances have changed and it is no longer so interested in completing the transaction. In the simplest cases, movements in interest rates create incentives to back out of the deal. As the following cases show, litigation arises on a host of factors.

Chemical Realty Corp. v. Home Fed. S&L Assn. of Hollywood

310 S.E.2d 33 (N.C. App. 1983)

Plaintiff sued defendant to recover damages for an alleged breach of contract. In its complaint, plaintiff claimed that defendant had agreed to a "takeout" or purchase of the plaintiff's construction loan to Landmark Hotel, Inc. (hereinafter, Landmark). Plaintiff alleged that it had made a construction loan to Landmark in reliance on defendant's promise to provide the long-term financing of the Landmark hotel. Defendant refused to make the long-term loan to Landmark after plaintiff had advanced funds under the construction loan.

Plaintiff alleged that defendant had a contractual duty to fund the long-term loan for two reasons. First, defendant had issued a permanent loan commitment to Landmark in which defendant promised, under certain terms, to provide long-term financing for Landmark's hotel. Plaintiff alleged that it was a third party beneficiary of defendant's permanent loan commitment to Landmark. Second, defendant sent a letter to plaintiff agreeing to purchase the construction loan note and accept an assignment of the deed of trust held by plaintiff as long as there had been no default of the terms of the permanent loan commitment. Plaintiff alleged that this letter created a direct contractual duty running from defendant to plaintiff. Plaintiff's amended complaint asked for $5,694,951.56 in damages.

In its answer, defendant denied that plaintiff was a third party beneficiary of the permanent loan commitment and denied that its letter to plaintiff formed a contract. Defendant also alleged that it had no obligation under the permanent loan commitment since the terms of the commitment had not been fulfilled.

The stipulations and evidence at trial tended to show the following. Landmark's predecessor-in-interest had acquired some land in Asheville on which it planned to build a hotel. It entered into negotiations with defendant for a long-term mortgage loan to finance the hotel. On 14 April 1972 defendant issued a permanent loan commitment letter which Landmark's predecessor-in-interest executed and returned along with a $60,000.00 commitment fee. The commitment letter was later modified to substitute Landmark as the borrower, and in other minor aspects.

The commitment letter included the following pertinent terms. Defendant committed itself to loan $6,000,000.00 for the proposed hotel, as described in a feasibility report, to be disbursed upon completion of the hotel. The loan was conditioned on receipt of an appraisal of not less than $8,000,000.00 for the real estate to be encumbered. The loan was "subject to an acceptable management contract to be executed by the borrower and the Hyatt House Hotel Corp." It was also subject to defendant being placed in the position of a mortgagee holding a valid first lien, with title insurance to be provided by a company acceptable to defendant. Payment of the $60,000.00 commitment fee by 15 May 1972 kept the commitment in effect for one year from the date of the 14 April 1972 commitment letter. Six-month extensions of the commitment could be obtained by payment of an additional $30,000.00 fee for each extension; however, any extension fee had to be paid fifteen days prior to the expiration of the outstanding commitment. The commitment was to automatically terminate upon, among other things, the failure of defendant "to receive written certification from all applicable Government Authorities indicating that the completed project has been approved by them. . . ."

Landmark's proposed contract with Hyatt House Hotel Corp. was rejected by defendant because Hyatt wanted defendant to subordinate its interests as first mortgagee to Hyatt. Landmark then proposed Motor Inn Management, Inc. (hereinafter, MIM) and on 13 November 1972 defendant agreed to accept MIM as the management company instead of Hyatt.

Also in November, 1972, a broker approached plaintiff about becoming the construction lender for the Landmark project. Plaintiff reviewed the permanent loan commitment of defendant and issued a construction loan commitment to Landmark on the condition that Landmark, plaintiff, and defendant would enter into a tripartite buy-sell agreement whereby plaintiff's construction loan would be repaid from defendant's permanent loan. Not until after the construction loan commitment had been issued in December of 1972 did plaintiff enter into negotiations with defendant for this proposed takeout agreement. Defendant refused to enter the tripartite agreement proposed by plaintiff. Defendant felt that the proposed agreement would have forced it to take out the construction loan "come hell or high water." Plaintiff modified its construction loan commitment on 7 February 1973 to eliminate the requirement of a tripartite agreement.

Plaintiff and defendant continued to discuss the arrangements by which defendant would become Landmark's permanent lender. Plaintiff and an intermediary broker worked out terms that were acceptable to defendant. These terms were set forth in an undated letter executed by defendant and delivered to the intermediary in early April, 1973. The intermediary passed the undated letter on to plaintiff. The letter stated in part that,

> This is to confirm that the Commitment and amendments, copies of which are attached hereto, is in full force and effect as of the date hereof, that there have been no modifications thereof and that no modifications shall be made without your consent and pursuant to such commitment. This is to confirm that:
>
> 1. We have received, in full satisfaction of the terms of paragraph numbered 1 of the Commitment, an MAI appraisal indicating a value in the Premises, upon completion of the improvements of at least $8,000,000;
>
> 2. We have reviewed the Chicago Title Insurance Company commitment for Title Insurance No. 73-U-00006 attached hereto as marked up with deletions crossed through and additions noted thereon; Chicago Title Insurance Company is acceptable to us as the title insurer and policy to be issued to us pursuant to paragraph 5 of our commitment . . . will be satisfactory and acceptable by us.
>
> . . . .
>
> 4. We have found acceptable and approved the Management Contract dated December 26, 1972 between Asheville Development Associates and Motor Inn Management, Inc. as assigned to the Borrower satisfying the terms of paragraph numbered 4 of the Commitment;
>
> 5. We have received the $60,000 commitment fee referred to in paragraph numbered 8 on the Commitment and agree that we will accept from you the additional $90,000 commitment fee at the closing of the construction loan whereupon the Commitment will be automatically extended to October 14, 1974;
>
> . . . .
>
> 6. The issuance of (a) the Certificate of Completion referred to in Section 307 of the Contract for Sale of Land For Private Redevelopment by and between Overland Investments, Ltd. and Housing Authority of The City of Asheville and (b) a Certificate of Occupancy, will satisfy the conditions of paragraph numbered 9(a) of the Commitment;
>
> . . . .
>
> 10. We have approved, in all respects the First Mortgage Real Estate Note and Deed of Trust, copies of which are attached hereto, and agree that at the appropriate time, as provided in the Commitment, we will purchase said First Real Estate Note from you, without recourse, and accept the assignment of said Deed of Trust provided however that the loan is not in default under the terms of our Commitment or our loan documents. We have also approved the form of the assignment of the Deed of Trust to be made by you to us, a copy of which is attached hereto.
>
> 11. We have reviewed the Construction Note and Construction Deed of Trust attached hereto including the language incorporating therein the First Mortgage Real Estate Note and Deed of Trust referred to in 10 above. We understand that the Guaranty and Endorsement on the Construction Note will be executed at the closing of your construction loan with Landmark Hotel, Inc. and will survive an assignment of your note to us. We understand that the terms and provisions of the First Mortgage Real Estate Note and Deed of Trust referred to in 10 above will automatically become operative upon an assignment of the Deed of Trust and Note to us from you.

Defendant extended its original commitment to 15 April 1973 "for purposes of facilitating the closing of the construction loan." Plaintiff closed the construction loan to Landmark on 13 April 1973. No representative of defendant was present at the construction loan closing. Plaintiff disbursed $30,000.00 directly to defendant the same day to obtain a six-month extension of the permanent loan commitment. It disbursed another $60,000.00 a few days later to extend the permanent loan commitment through 14 October 1974.

At the closing, Landmark executed a building loan mortgage note in the principal amount of $6,000,000.00 and delivered it to plaintiff. Attached to the building loan mortgage note as Exhibit A was a first mortgage real estate note in the principal amount of $6,000,000.00, also executed by Landmark and delivered to plaintiff. The building loan mortgage note provided that if it was purchased by defendants, its terms would be superseded by those of the first mortgage real estate note.

The building loan mortgage note was secured by a construction loan deed of trust executed by Landmark on the same day. Plaintiff was the beneficiary and Sydnor Thompson served as trustee. Attached to the construction loan deed of trust as Exhibit B was a permanent loan deed of trust executed by Landmark. The Trustee was Thomas Wharton, who represented the broker acting as an intermediary between plaintiff and defendant. The construction loan deed of trust provided that upon the purchase of the building loan mortgage note and the assignment of the construction loan deed of trust to defendant, the terms of the permanent loan deed of trust would supersede those of the construction loan deed of trust. The construction loan deed of trust, with the permanent loan deed of trust attached as Exhibit B, was recorded in the Buncombe County Office of the Register of Deeds.

Plaintiff advanced $4,867, 249.43 to Landmark from 13 April 1973 to 10 October 1974 under the construction loan. Landmark used the funds to build the hotel and prepare it for doing business. The construction was certified as substantially complete on 10 October 1974.

During construction of the hotel, several events occurred pertinent to the permanent loan commitment. The management contract with MIM appeared to be at an impasse, and MIM and Landmark sued each other for breach of that contract. Landmark ordered MIM to cease performance of its pre-opening duties in March, 1974. MIM notified all concerned parties in July of 1974 that it deemed its obligations to plaintiff and defendant terminated due to Landmark's breach of the management contract. Defendant informed plaintiff that it was worried about the collapse of the management contract and about a lease agreement between Landmark and Orbital Industries, Inc. Neither Landmark nor plaintiff proposed a substitute management company acceptable to defendant. The Housing Authority of Asheville refused to issue a certificate of completion, which had been requested, for the hotel in October, 1974.

Landmark was unable to pay all the bills for the hotel on 9 October 1974, and on that day, a representative of Landmark tendered the hotel keys to a representative of plaintiff, who refused to accept them. On 10 October 1974 Landmark closed the hotel due to a lack of operating funds. . . .

On 14 October 1974 representatives of plaintiff arrived at defendant's hometown office prepared to close the permanent loan to Landmark. Defendant refused plaintiff's tender of the construction loan note and deed of trust. Defendant indicated that the terms of the permanent loan commitment had not been met and that the economy was too uncertain for it to finance as risky a venture as the hotel. Plaintiff then asked for an extension of the permanent loan commitment. Defendant refused this request.

Landmark filed a voluntary petition in bankruptcy on 18 November 1974. On 11 February 1976 plaintiff received permission to foreclose its deed of trust. Plaintiff held a public foreclosure sale three months later and was the successful bidder at $3,000,000.00. Plaintiff subsequently sold the property to its wholly-owned subsidiary, which in turn sold the hotel to Vector Hospitality Associates. . . .

The case was then tried before the trial court sitting without a jury. After making findings of fact and conclusions of law, the trial court entered judgment for the defendant. Plaintiff appealed. . . .

WELLS, Judge.

Plaintiff first contends that the trial court erred in failing to find and conclude that a contract existed between plaintiff and defendant. Plaintiff also contends that the trial court should have found and concluded that it was a third party beneficiary of defendant's permanent loan commitment. We hold that the trial court did not adequately address these issues.[1]

G.S. § 1A-1, Rule 52(a)(1) of the Rules of Civil Procedure requires a trial judge hearing a case without a jury to make findings of fact and conclusions of law. To comport with Rule 52(a)(1), the trial court must make "a specific statement of the facts on which the rights of the parties are to be determined, and those findings must be sufficiently specific to enable an appellate court to review the decision and test the correctness of the judgment." *Quick v. Quick*, 305 N.C. 446, 290 S.E.2d 653 (1982) (citation omitted). Rule 52(a)(1) does not require recitation of evidentiary facts, but it does require specific findings on the ultimate facts established by the evidence, admissions and stipulations which are determinative of the questions involved in the action and essential to support the conclusions of law reached. *Id.* See also *Farmers Bank v. Michael T. Brown Distributors, Inc.*, 307 N.C. 342, 298 S.E.2d 357 (1983).

Although the letter written by Home Federal to Chemical appears from an agreement supported by consideration by Home Federal to purchase Chemical's construction loan upon compliance with certain conditions precedent, the trial court's only finding of fact with respect to the letter was that "Home Federal, by Wohl, executed an undated letter being Defendant's Exhibit 154 for identification purposes." This finding is an evidentiary fact, not an ultimate fact. The trial court failed to make any finding of fact regarding whether defendant owed any contractual duty to plaintiff. Such findings are necessary to a valid judgment in this action. As the North Carolina Supreme Court has stated,

> Effective appellate review of an order entered by a trial court sitting without a jury is largely dependent upon the specificity by which the order's rationale is articulated. Evidence must support findings; findings must support conclusions; conclusions must support the judgment. Each step of the progression must be taken by the trial judge, in logical sequence; each link in the chain of reasoning must appear in the order itself. Where there is a gap, it cannot be determined on appeal whether the trial court correctly exercised its function to find the facts and apply the law thereto.

---

1. In *Chemical Realty Corp. v. Home Federal Savings & Loan Association of Hollywood*, 40 N.C.App. 675, 253 S.E.2d 621, *disc. rev. denied and app. dismissed*, 297 N.C. 612, 257 S.E.2d 435 (1979), *app. dismissed*, 444 U.S. 1061, 100 S.Ct. 1000, 62 L.Ed.2d 744 (1980), we upheld the trial court findings that a contract existed between Home Federal and Landmark. These findings were made solely to establish jurisdiction over the defendant, do not go to the merits of this case or determine the contractual rights of plaintiff and defendant, and therefore do not constitute the law of the case on the respective contractual rights or obligations of plaintiff and defendant.

Coble v. Coble, 300 N.C. 708, 268 S.E.2d 185 (1980).

Although the trial court's order contains more than forty-one separate findings of fact, the evidence, stipulations, and pleadings in the instant case present questions of fact which were ignored in those findings, but which must be resolved before judgment can be entered. On remand, the following issues should be resolved by proper findings and conclusions.

(1) Was there a promise by defendant, supported by consideration, to plaintiff to purchase plaintiff's construction loan?

(2) If defendant made no promise, did defendant's actions provide the basis for plaintiff to become a creditor beneficiary of defendant's permanent loan commitment?

(3) If plaintiff contracted with defendant, or had third party beneficiary status, what were the conditions precedent and material terms that had to be complied with before defendant's duty to plaintiff to perform arose?

(4) Were those terms and conditions substantially complied with?

(5) If Landmark and/or plaintiff had not fulfilled the conditions precedent and material terms on 14 October 1974, did plaintiff timely request defendant to extend the permanent loan commitment beyond 14 October 1974?

(6) If plaintiff did make a timely request to extend the permanent loan commitment, to what extent did plaintiff incur foreseeable and ascertainable damages by defendant's refusal to extend?

Defendant contends that even if the trial court failed to make all the necessary findings arising under the evidence, the findings it made adverse to plaintiff and supported by the evidence are sufficient to sustain the trial court's conclusions and judgment. We cannot agree. The trial court's findings having failed to address crucial aspects of the rights and obligations of the parties arising upon the evidence, we can make no assumptions as to what the result will be when the evidence in the case is properly sifted, addressed, and treated at the trial level.

The parties to this appeal have submitted extensive briefs; plaintiff has brought forward a number of exceptions we have not addressed; but we perceive that it would be untimely and unproductive for us to deal with plaintiff's other exceptions because of the obvious need for the heart of this case to be reconsidered at the trial level.

Because we perceive there are no questions raised in the appeal as to admission of evidence or credibility of witnesses, we conclude that it is unnecessary to order a new trial, and that the case may be properly considered on remand on the existing record.

For the reasons stated, the judgment of the trial court must be reversed and the case remanded for further proceedings consistent with this opinion.

Reversed and remanded.

VAUGHN, C.J., and JOHNSON, J., concur.

Ralls v. First Fed. Savings and Loan Assoc. of Andalusia

422 So.2d 764 (Ala. 1982)

ALMON, Justice.

This case involves a dispute over a loan commitment issued by First Federal Savings and Loan Association of Andalusia (First Federal) to John G. Ralls. The defense to Ralls's action is accord and satisfaction.

Ralls acquired a franchise permitting him to operate a Days Inn Motel. In 1978, he began investigating the feasibility of constructing and operating a motel in Evergreen, Alabama. He discussed construction loans with several lending institutions and on August 28, 1978, Ralls submitted a loan application for $600,000 to First Federal. He discussed the proposed loan with Miss Maggie Rodgers, the Executive Vice-President and Managing Officer of First Federal. Miss Rodgers testified that at the time the loan application was made, she told Ralls there would be an eight-month completion date on any construction loan. On October 27, 1978, First Federal sent Ralls a commitment letter stating in part:

"The loan was approved for 20 years at 10% interest rate. The 10% interest rate is *guaranteed* subject to your paying 1% of our 2% initial service charge." (Emphasis added.)

The letter made no mention of a completion date.

On December 21, 1978, Ralls met with Miss Rodgers to accept the commitment. At that time he paid $6,000 representing 1% of the initial 2% service charge. Miss Rodgers testified she made a notation on her copy of the commitment letter that the completion date would be eight months from December 21, 1978, and also brought this to Ralls's attention. Miss Rodgers made another notation on the letter stating that $6,000 had been paid "guaranteeing [the] 10% rate."

Ralls testified that he had not been told of the completion date at the time of the loan application and that it was only mentioned by Miss Rodgers after he had paid the $6,000 on December 21, 1978. His testimony as to the completion date was as follows:

"Well, I went over to pay six thousand dollars and after she wrote the check out, she said, 'we're going to have to put a date on it,' and she came up with the August 21st and I told her that I had never built a motel and what if I didn't get it finished by then and she said, 'we've never failed to give anybody an extension yet,' — that's what she told me — so I didn't worry about the date. . . ."

Ralls also testified that he did not know the completion date had been put on First Federal's copy of the commitment letter until shortly before the trial and that the first time a completion date was mentioned was after he had paid the $6,000. He further testified that he told First Federal that he did not want the loan unless it would be at the 10% interest rate.

Miss Rodgers filled out the check and check stub for Ralls when he paid the 1% fee. On the check stub she wrote: "1% guaranteeing 10% interest for 600,000." On the check itself she wrote "1% — 10% interest."

On January 9, 1979, Miss Rodgers sent a letter to the Conecuh County Bank stating First Federal had received $6,000 from Ralls that guaranteed him a 20-year loan at 10% interest. The letter authorized interim financing through the Conecuh County Bank. This letter made no mention of a completion date.

On April 12, 1979, Miss Rodgers notified Ralls that the First Federal board of directors did not approve extension of his 10% loan past August 21, 1979, but would be happy to extend the loan for a few months at the prevailing interest rate at the time of closing.

When it became apparent that the project would not be completed by August 21, 1979, Ralls wrote Miss Rodgers on August 5, 1979, asking for an extension. Miss Rodgers wrote Ralls on August 9, 1979, stating the board of directors could not extend the loan at 10% but could extend the loan commitment until the motel was completed, subject to the prevailing interest rate at the time of closing.

The motel was not completed until a few days before the loan was closed at 12% on December 5, 1979. Interest rates at that time had increased considerably.

Ralls subsequently filed suit against First Federal, claiming breach of contract, fraud, and misrepresentation and deceit. At the close of all the evidence, the trial judge granted First Federal's motion for a directed verdict.

Ralls contends the trial court misinterpreted the law when it held that the loan closing on December 5, 1979, at 12% rather than 10%, constituted an accord and satisfaction as a matter of law.

Ralls contends his acceptance of the loan at 12% interest could not operate as an accord and satisfaction because he entered into the loan agreement under duress. The gist of Ralls's argument is that at the time he accepted the loan, he was in such dire need of funds, as a result of the actions of First Federal, that he had no choice but to accept the loan no matter what the interest rate. Specifically, the question presented is whether economic duress can be successfully asserted to defeat the defense of accord and satisfaction.

The economic duress is asserted not to vitiate a contract, but as a defense to the assertion by First Federal that the signing of the 12% loan effected an accord and satisfaction. Economic duress is, under proper circumstances, a viable legal principle.

> "Many authorities recognize the doctrine that economic duress or business compulsion vitiates a contract induced thereby. . . .
>
> " . . .
>
> "While the doctrine of economic duress or business compulsion is constantly being expanded by the courts, it may be invoked only to prevent an injustice and not to accomplish an injustice. The doctrine applies only to special, unusual, or extraordinary situations in which unjustified coercion is used to induce a contract, as where extortive measures are employed, or improper or unjustified demands are made, under such circumstances that the victim has little choice but to accede thereto."

17 C.J.S. *Contracts* § 177 (1963) (citations omitted). We see no reason why courts should recognize economic duress to entirely invalidate a contract but not to avoid a defense of accord and satisfaction.

Since duress is ordinarily a matter for the jury, *see, Day v. Ray E. Friedman & Company*, 395 So.2d 54 (Ala.1981), Ralls claims the trial court erred in directing a verdict for First Federal. We are inclined to agree.

In order to survive a motion for a directed verdict, the contestant must present a scintilla of evidence. *Bardin v. Jones*, 371 So.2d 23 (Ala.1979); Rule 50(e), A.R.C.P. The reviewing court must examine the record to see if there exists a scintilla of evidence in support of the complaint. *Perdue v. Mitchell*, 373 So.2d 650 (Ala.1979).

The evidence presented by Ralls, viewed in a light most favorable to him, tended to show that First Federal guaranteed him a 10% interest rate. The only limitation on that guarantee was the completion date. However, the evidence concerning the completion date was in conflict. Ralls testified that Miss Rodgers told him they would have to put a limitation date on the loan but not to worry about it because they had never refused an extension to a loan commitment. Miss Rodgers's testimony was otherwise, but this is the type of factual dispute that should be submitted to the jury.

If the jury found Miss Rodgers had in fact represented to Ralls that there would be no problem getting an extension, then it would follow that Ralls was justified in committing himself financially to the point where he had no choice but to later accept the loan regardless of the higher interest rate.

After reading the record and reviewing the evidence, we are of the opinion that Ralls presented a jury question in support of his theory of recovery. Therefore, it was error to direct a verdict in favor of First Federal. Accordingly, the judgment appealed from is reversed and the cause is remanded for retrial.

Reversed and remanded.

TORBERT, C.J., and FAULKNER, EMBRY and ADAMS, JJ., concur.

NOTES AND QUESTIONS

1. *Types of commitments.* A *bilateral* commitment obligates both the borrower and lender, so that the lender must make the loan and the borrower must accept it. In contrast, under a *unilateral* or *standby* commitment, the lender commits to making the loan, but the borrower is not obligated to take the loan. This leaves the borrower freedom to seek other financing if interest rates drop in the interim. When a borrower believes that rates are likely to decline, a standby commitment gives a construction lender assurance that funds will be there to pay off the construction loan without locking in the current, presumably high, interest rate for the permanent financing. In *Chemical Realty* the construction lender tried to argue that it was a third party beneficiary of the borrower's takeout commitment. This issue is sometimes avoided by use of a *trilateral* commitment, in which the takeout lender contracts with both the borrower and the construction lender to provide the permanent financing.

2. *Negotiating the final loan terms.* What has to be contained in a commitment for it to be binding on the parties? Even if the parties intend to be bound, if they did not agree to the fundamental terms of the loan, the agreement is nothing more than an unenforceable "agreement to agree." Of course, the commitment will typically not contain all of the loan terms (although it is sometimes possible to negotiate the loan in advance and include the loan documents as an attachment to the commitment), and the gaps will have to be filled in by negotiations between the parties before the loan can close.

In Teachers Ins. & Annuity Assoc. v. Butler, 626 F. Supp. 1229 (S.D.N.Y. 1986), TIAA had entered into a commitment with the borrower for a $20 million takeout loan at 14.25% with an equity kicker and a 17-year lock-in period before prepayment would be permitted. Interest rates dropped during the construction period, and as it came close to the time for the loan to be funded, the parties deadlocked over a term not mentioned in the commitment—whether TIAA was entitled to a default prepayment fee if borrower defaulted during the lock-in period. The court found that the borrower had created the negotiation deadlock to escape its obligation to borrow:

Under New York law, a duty of fair dealing and good faith is implied in every contract . . . . Obviously, the Commitment Letter did not contain, and the parties understood that it did not contain all the final and definitive terms that were to be incorporated in the closing documents. Both parties were required to negotiate in good faith with respect to the closing documents needed to consummate the transaction. Defendants breached that duty to negotiate in good faith and therefore breached the contract with Teachers.

626 F. Supp. at 1232.

3. In many jurisdictions the Statute of Frauds requires that agreements to lend money be in writing. Would the *Ralls* case come out differently if the Statute of Frauds applied?

Woodbridge Place Apartments v. Washington Square Capital, Inc.

965 F.2d 1429 (7th Cir. 1992)

Before WOOD, Jr., MANION, and KANNE, Circuit Judges.

HARLINGTON WOOD, Jr., Circuit Judge.

This controversy highlights the distinction between an option contract and a conditional bilateral contract, as well as breach and the failure of a condition precedent.

The lenders and borrower entered into an agreement where the lenders agreed to loan over 4.6 million dollars if certain conditions were satisfied on the date of closing. The loan never funded because some of these conditions were not satisfied. The borrower now asks this court to uphold the district court judgment requiring lenders to return the standby deposit that the borrower laid down when entering into this agreement. The borrower does not seem to argue that the contract's language contemplates such a return. Rather, the borrower argues that the law requires the return because the deposit is an unenforceable penalty. The lenders, on the other hand, argue that the deposit is enforceable under one of three theories: the deposit serves as consideration for an option contract; the deposit serves as consideration for the expense of the lender's loan commitment; or the deposit constitutes an enforceable liquidated damage provision.

The resolution of this case turns on the nature of the agreement between the borrower and lenders: whether the lenders provided the borrower with an option for a loan with the standby deposit serving as consideration for this option, so that only the lenders were bound to carry through with the loan; whether the parties entered into a conditional bilateral contract so that both sides were committed to perform assuming the satisfaction of the conditions precedent; or whether the parties entered into essentially two agreements, one agreement in which the lenders agreed to commit to loan a specified sum of money at a specified interest rate in exchange for the standby deposit, and one where both the lenders and the borrower agreed to carry through with the loan assuming the satisfaction of the conditions precedent.

I

In 1984 Woodbridge Place Apartments Limited Partnership ("Woodbridge Partnership") developed Woodbridge Place Apartments ("Woodbridge Apartments"), a 192-unit apartment complex in Evansville, Indiana. Woodbridge Partnership's sole general partner is Robert Jarrett. Late in 1986, Woodbridge Partnership decided to replace the financing on Woodbridge Apartments. For this purpose, Jarrett was introduced to Jerry Karem, a mortgage broker associated with Citizens Fidelity Bank of Louisville, Kentucky. Karem put Jarrett in contact with Washington Square Capital ("Washington Square"). In the negotiations with Jarrett, Washington Square acted on behalf of two lenders, Northern Life Insurance Company ("Northern Life") and Ministers Life Insurance Company ("Ministers Life"). All of Jarrett's dealings were with Karem; he had no direct contact with Northern Life, Ministers Life or Washington Square.

With Karem's assistance, Jarrett executed a mortgage application on behalf of Woodbridge Partnership. . . . Washington Square conceded at oral argument that this application constituted a form application which it or the lenders drafted. This loan application set forth the basic format for the mortgage loan and it set forth the conditions necessary for the funding of the loan. Jarrett, acting on behalf of Woodbridge Partnership, simply filled in that information necessary to tailor this form to its needs. As such, with Karem's assistance, Jarrett filled in the requested loan amount of $4,665,000 for a term of 10 years at an interest rate of 9¼% based on a 30-year amortization schedule with Woodbridge Apartments serving as the mortgage security for this loan.

Paragraph 11(i) of this form application provides for a 3% standby deposit. A dispute over the nature of the standby deposit provided for in this paragraph is what brings the parties to this court. This paragraph reads as follows:

> Refundable Standby Deposit and Inspection Fee: A Refundable Standby Deposit ("Standby Deposit") of 1% of the Loan amount is submitted with this Application, and an additional 2% of the Loan shall be paid within 5 days of our receipt of the Commitment to increase the Standby Deposit to $139,950. It will be transferred to the Lender and be refunded at a reasonable time after funding and receipt by Lender of the original Note and title policy. In the event we do not consummate the Loan in accordance with the Commitment, we [borrower] shall pay the fees and expenses of your Special Counsel, and further, we shall have no right to any refund of the Standby Deposit, and the same shall become the sole property of the Lender. In addition, an inspection fee of $500 has been enclosed to defray the cost of inspection of the Premises and Improvements, this Commitment being subject to Lender's inspection and approval of the Premises. If the Premises are not as described in the accepted submission, appraisal report or plans and specifications, this Commitment shall become null and void and the standby fee shall not be returned. However, should the Lender wrongfully refuse to fund the Loan, the Standby Deposit and inspection fee shall be refunded.

In filling out the loan application, Jarrett, acting on behalf of Woodbridge Partnership, typed in a modification to paragraph 11(i) which stated that, "In lieu of the 2% additional points, the Borrower will furnish the Lender with an irrevocable Letter of Credit in a form acceptable to the Lender." The lenders accepted this modification. Woodbridge Partnership deposited $46,650.00 with Washington Square on January 22, 1987. . . .

After agreement was reached, Jarrett deposited a Letter of Credit secured by a certificate of deposit in the amount of $93,000.00. On June 12, 1987, Washington Square, acting on behalf of the lenders, sent a letter acknowledging both the existence of an agreement and the receipt of the remainder of the standby deposit.

According to the loan commitment, the loan was to fund by the close of July 1987. The loan agreement provided for numerous conditions which had to be satisfied in order for the loan to fund. The loan never funded because a few of these conditions were not satisfied, including an apparently significant condition — the minimum occupancy requirement. That is, Woodbridge Apartments did not meet the 93% minimum occupancy requirement at the time in which the loan was to close. The district court concluded that the lenders benefitted from the loan's failure to fund because interest rates increased between the time in which the agreement was entered and the closing date.

II

* * *

C. Ambiguous Nature of the Relevant Provision

What is at issue is the enforceability of the 3% standby deposit provision in a mortgage loan commitment. The parties seem to agree that the language of the loan commitment contemplates a refund in one situation: if the lenders wrongfully refuse to fund the loan. The plaintiffs-appellees, Woodbridge Partnership and Jarrett, (hereinafter collectively referred to as "Woodbridge Partnership") do not assert that the lenders wrongfully refused to fund this loan. Rather, Woodbridge Partnership argues it is entitled to a refund because this provision is a penalty provision — an unenforceable attempt to provide for damages. Washington Square, however, argues that this is not a penalty provision. Indeed, Washington Square argues that this provision is not a damage provision at all. Instead, Washington Square argues that the standby deposit constitutes consideration.

Washington Square sets forth two theories in support of its argument that the deposit fee constitutes consideration. One theory is that the deposit constitutes consideration for Washington Square's irrevocable offer to carry through with the loan if the conditions are satisfied. The second theory is that the deposit constitutes a "commitment fee" which serves as consideration for the risk that lenders incur in committing to fund a loan in the future at a specified interest rate. Alternatively, Washington Square argues that even if this is a damage provision, it is a reasonable and valid liquidated damage provision, not an unenforceable penalty provision.

Washington Square has presented us with some rather persuasive precedent to support its argument that this court should reverse the district court and enforce this standby deposit provision. In light of this precedent, we cannot deny that standby deposits are standard in the industry and the great majority of courts enforce such provisions under one of several theories. [Citations omitted.] Although numerous courts have indeed upheld somewhat similar provisions in other loan agreements, the enforceability of deposits in the loan commitment context will depend on the wording of the particular agreement at issue. This means that we must look to the contract before us in deciding the enforceability of the standby deposit rather than relying on the general notion that courts enforce such provisions.

Respecting the freedom to contract, courts are generally reluctant to interfere with bargained-for agreements between parties. John D. Calamari & Joseph M. Perillo, the law of contracts § 14-31 (1987). This is particularly true in the consideration context where courts generally do not test the adequacy of a party's consideration. *See, for example, id.* at § 4-14; *Harrison-Floyd Farm Bureau Co-op Assoc. Inc., v. Reed,* 546 N.E.2d 855, 857 (Ind.Ct.App. 1989). The damage context, however, is one area of contract law where courts are more willing to interfere with the terms of bargained-for agreements. CALAMARI, *supra* at § 14-31. Indeed, courts closely scrutinize damage provisions in order to determine if a contract's so-called damage provisions are in reality an attempt to assess penalties. *Id.* For this reason, the argument that $139,500.00 constitutes invalid consideration is less likely to prevail than the argument that $139,500.00 constitutes an unenforceable penalty. And, accordingly, the characterization of the standby deposit provision and the nature of this contract as a whole is essential to the resolution of this case.

We must first look to a contract's language in deciding any contract dispute. The problem is that the disputed provision fails to characterize the standby deposit as either consideration for an option, consideration for a commitment ("commitment fee"), or as a damage provision. Indeed, the standby deposit provision fails to use any one of numerous operative terms which might help to resolve this ambiguity. For example, this provision does not even mention such terms as consideration, commitment, fee, damage, or option.

Washington Square's failure to use any operative language indicating the nature of the standby deposit distinguishes this case from some of the other cases in which similar provisions were enforced as option contracts or commitment fees. That is, many of the cases which have upheld similar deposits under an option or commitment fee theory involved contracts which either labeled the deposit as a fee, or at least stated that the deposit constituted consideration. *See, for example, Goldman,* 248 A.2d at 158-59 (contract indicated that deposit constituted a fee); *D & M Dev. Co. v. Sherwood and Roberts, Inc.,* 93 Idaho 200, 202, 457 P.2d 439, 441 (1969) (document labeled deposit as "consideration for your [the mortgage broker] obtaining written commitments for all three loans. . . ."). We have no such language in this contract.

D. NATURE OF THE AGREEMENT AS A WHOLE

The fact that the relevant provision is ambiguous, however, is not determinative if the language of the agreement as a whole gives us some guidance as to the nature of this provision. First, we address whether the nature of this contract indicates that the standby deposit constitutes a commitment fee. If this deposit constitutes a commitment fee, then this means there are essentially two contracts between the parties: one contract in which the lender agrees to commit funds for the future supported by the deposit as consideration, and one contract to loan money if certain conditions are met in exchange for the agreed interest of 9¼%.

Nothing in the nature of this bilateral contract indicates that the standby fee constitutes consideration for the lender's risk in committing funds in the future. Indeed, Washington Square has pointed to no contractual language indicating that the loan commitment constitutes essentially two contracts. For this reason, the structure of the agreement seems to dictate against such a conclusion.

Next, we must address whether the unilateral nature of this agreement indicates that the standby deposit constitutes consideration for an option contract. Washington Square argues it does.

Assuming *arguendo* that this is an option contract in which only Washington Square is obligated to carry through with the loan, Washington Square's argument that the standby deposit constitutes consideration for such an option is persuasive. This is especially true when we consider that under traditional contract theory some consideration is necessary to make an option contract enforceable. CALAMARI, *supra* § 2-25(b). Moreover, a damage provision has no place in this loan commitment if it truly constitutes an option contract because, as Washington Square has pointed out, damages are appropriate only when there is a breach of contract. [Citations omitted.]

The problem, however, is that it is far from clear whether or not this loan commitment constitutes an option contract or a conditional bilateral contract. The agreement's language fails to resolve this issue because the drafters of this agreement not only failed to specify the nature of the standby deposit, but the drafters also failed to specify whether or not the agreement between the parties constitutes an option contract or a bilateral conditional contract.

In order for the loan commitment to constitute an option agreement, the loan commitment must be one in which binds the lenders and not the borrowers. In other words, if both the borrower and lenders are bound to carry through with the loan upon satisfaction of the specified conditions, then the loan commitment could only be a bilateral conditional agreement. Under such a reading the option theory fails. *See B.F. Saul Real Estate*, 683 S.W.2d at 534 (relied on the fact that only the lender was obligated to carry through with the loan commitment in concluding that the standby deposit constituted consideration). Recognizing this fact, Washington Square asserts that the agreement between the parties did not obligate the borrower to carry through with the loan. However, the agreement's language offers no definitive support for this proposition because the loan application and the accompanying letters fail to indicate whether the borrower is bound to accept the loan if the conditions are met. Indeed, one reasonable reading of this loan commitment leads to the conclusion that the borrower has covenanted to make a good faith effort to satisfy the conditions and that the borrower is obligated to carry through with the loan if the conditions are satisfied.

It appears that confusion over the unilateral versus bilateral nature of mortgage loan commitments is not new to the courts. In fact, in *Lincoln National Life Insurance Co. v. NCR Corp.*, 772 F.2d 315, 319 (7th Cir.1985), this court noted the variety of holdings on this issue. Of course, the determination of the unilateral versus bilateral nature of the agreement will differ depending on the wording of the agreement before the court. Nonetheless, when a loan commitment's language fails to resolve the ambiguity some jurisdictions tend to presume that loan commitments are bilateral conditional contracts and some tend to presume that loan commitments constitute irrevocable offers. For example, New York courts apparently presume that loan commitments constitute bilateral agreements. *See, for example, Murphy v. Empire of America, FSA*, 746 F.2d 931, 934 (2d Cir.1984). Other jurisdictions seem to presume that ambiguously worded mortgage loan commitments constitute option contracts in which only the borrower is obligated. *See, for example, B.F. Saul Real Estate*, 683 S.W.2d at 534; *Lowe*, 127 Cal.Rptr. at 28-29; 54 Cal.App.3d at 729-30. Moreover, a third interpretation of ambiguously worded loan commitments is that neither side is bound. This was the interpretation that this court adopted in *Runnemede Owners, Inc. v. Crest Mortgage Corp.*, 861 F.2d 1053, 1056-57 (7th Cir.1988), when construing a loan commitment under Illinois law.

We have found no cases, nor has either party cited any cases, where the Indiana courts have considered the unilateral versus bilateral nature of mortgage loan commitments. However, the district court in *Lincoln National Life Insurance Co. v. NCR Corp.*, 603 F.Supp. 1393 (D.C.Ind.1984), *affirmed on other grounds*, 772 F.2d 315 (7th Cir.1985), interpreted a loan commitment under Indiana law. In that case the district court construed the document against the drafter in order to find that the contract was binding on both parties. . . .

E. Standby Deposit Provision Constitutes a Damage Provision

. . . Extrinsic evidence and rules of construction are two vehicles for deciphering contractual intent from ambiguous documents. *Tastee-Freez Leasing Corp. v. Milwid*, 173 Ind.App. 675, 365 N.E.2d 1388, 1390 (1977). Resolving the nature of an ambiguous contract through extrinsic evidence is a factual determination which is evaluated under the clearly erroneous standard. *See, for example, English Coal Co., Inc. v. Durcholz*, 422 N.E.2d 302, 308-09 (Ind.Ct.App.1981) (citing *Brumfield, Tr. v. State ex rel. Wallace*, 206 Ind. 647, 190 N.E. 863 (1934)). The district court conducted a two-day trial in this case. However, the district court opinion does not indicate that it relied on evidence submitted during this trial in determining that the standby deposit provision constitutes a damage provision. Rather, it appears that without explicitly stating so the district court followed the rule of construction which requires courts to construe agreements against the drafter. *See* District Court Memorandum at 5 ("The applicable clause here does not indicate that the deposit is a fee for either the issuance of the commitment to make the loan or as a fee for an option for the loan. If a mortgage lender wishes the deposit to be treated as such, it should state so in the refundable standby deposit clause."). Therefore, there is no factual finding to which we can give deference. And, in any event, it appears that the extrinsic evidence fails to resolve the issue either way because Indiana courts look to objective outward manifestations of contractual intent, not to some private intent of one of the parties. *Crabtree v. Lee*, 469 N.E.2d 476 (Ind.Ct.App.1984); *Robinson v. Fickle*, 167 Ind.App. 651, 340 N.E.2d 824 (1976). *See also Western & Southern Life Ins. Co. v. Vale*, 213 Ind. 601, 12 N.E.2d 350 (1938). The record contains no evidence indicating that the parties communicated their understanding of this provision to one another while negotiating the loan agreement.

Considering that the district court did not base its contractual interpretation on extrinsic evidence, we will turn to rules of construction. While the evaluation of extrinsic evidence to decipher the intent of an ambiguous contract is a question of fact, the application of rules of construction in order to interpret an ambiguous contract is a question of law for the courts reviewed *de novo*. *See, for example, McGann & Marsh Co. v. K & F Mfg. Co.*, 179 Ind.App. 411, 385 N.E.2d 1183, 1187 (1979). Indiana courts invoke the cardinal rule of construction that, "[a]mbiguities in a contract are to be strictly construed against the party who prepared the contract." *See, for example, Durcholz*, 422 N.E.2d at 309 (citation omitted). The parties conceded at oral argument that either Washington Square or the lenders, not Woodbridge Partnership, drafted the form application which contained the bulk of the contractual terms between the parties. Construing the standby provision against the drafter leads to the conclusion that this ambiguously worded provision is a damage provision rather than a provision for consideration.

If this standby deposit was intended as consideration, it would have been easy for the lenders to state this in the loan application. And, if such an intent had been stated, or even hinted at, this would be an entirely different case. But, as it stands, the lenders never indicated in the contractual language or in the negotiations what purpose the standby deposit was intended to serve. Nor did the lenders indicate whether the agreement constituted an option contract or a conditional bilateral agreement.

The district court concluded that the lenders were not harmed by this loan's failure to fund. To the contrary, the district court indicated that the lenders benefitted from this failure because the interest rates went up, meaning that the lenders were able to lend money at a higher interest rate than that agreed to in the loan commitment with Woodbridge Partnership. These factual findings are supported by the record and we take these findings as true. . . .

F. UNAVAILABILITY OF LIQUIDATED DAMAGES

Now that we have determined that this is a damage provision, the next question is whether this can be enforced against Woodbridge Partnership as a liquidated damage provision in the context of this case. The district court held that this provision constitutes an unenforceable penalty provision. The district court reached this decision after concluding that this "provision does not attempt to secure an amount for the non-breaching party which is reasonably proportionate to the amount of actual damages likely to occur by failure of the loan to fund." District Court Memorandum at 7. We, however, need not address whether this provision is a valid liquidated damage provision because liquidated damages are not available on the facts before this court.

Washington Square, in support of its earlier argument that the standby deposit served as consideration, emphasized that damages are only appropriate upon breach. We agree. *See, for example, Ryan,* 813 S.W.2d at 596; *Madonna,* 546 N.E.2d at 1150; and *B.F. Saul Real Estate,* 683 S.W.2d at 534.

In its decision the district court stated that, "For reasons not pertinent to this action, the plaintiff failed to satisfy the *conditions* of funding the loan." (Emphasis added.) The fact that the district court used the label "conditions" indicates that the district court viewed the failure to fund as a failure of a condition precedent, not as a breach of some covenant. The defendants-appellants have not challenged this characterization on appeal. . . .

Not only does it appear that Washington Square has effectively conceded that the contract failed because of a failure of a condition rather than breach, the language of the contract also supports this conclusion. Both parties agree that at least one primary reason for the loan's failure to fund was that Woodbridge Apartments, the proposed security for the mortgage loan, dipped below the required 93% minimum occupancy rate. The provisions which outline this minimum occupancy requirement are contained in Schedule I of the loan commitment. Paragraph 2 of this schedule refers to these occupancy requirements as "conditions." We see no reason not to hold the drafters to this chosen label. . . .

The Indiana courts pointed out in *Billman* and *Keliher* that breach sometimes results from the failure of a condition precedent under the theory of implied covenants. *See, for example, Keliher,* 534 N.E.2d at 1138; *Billman,* 391 N.E.2d at 673. *But see Baker,* 519 N.E.2d at 195 (condition did not impose a covenant of good faith). For example, Indiana courts often imply a covenant of good faith when the satisfaction of a condition is within the control of one of the parties. *See, for example, Keliher,* 534 N.E.2d at 1138; *Billman,* 391 N.E.2d at 673. *But see Baker,* 519 N.E.2d at 195. In such situations, if the party in control fails to make a good faith effort to satisfy the condition, this party has breached the implied covenant. Nonetheless, the district court made no finding of bad faith, nor did the district court otherwise indicate that Woodbridge Partnership breached either an implied or express covenant. And, the defendants-appellants do not allege that the district court erred in failing to make such a finding. We must assume, therefore, that the contract failed because of a failure of a condition precedent, and not because of a breach of contract. Liquidated damages are therefore inappropriate. As such, the district court correctly ordered Washington Square to return the standby deposit.

* * *

III

For the foregoing reasons, we affirm the district court so far as the district court ordered Washington Square to refund $139,500.00 of the deposit. However, considering Washington Square's concession on the issue of prejudgment interest, we reverse and remand that portion of the district court decision which pertains to the award of prejudgment interest. On remand, the district court should determine the appropriate amount of prejudgment interest owed to the plaintiffs-appellants.

Parties shall bear their own costs.

Affirmed in part, and reversed and remanded in part.

B.   THE GROUND LEASE

1.   Introduction

Whalen, Commercial Ground Leases, 2d ed.

1-2, 8-10, 17-19 [Prac. L. Inst. 2002]

COMMERCIAL GROUND LEASES

Commercial ground leases are instruments by which a fee owner leases real property for an extended term to a tenant who intends to develop the property by constructing improvements or renovating existing improvements. After completion, the improvements will be leased to one or more rent-paying occupancy tenants (technically, subtenants) to produce income. Ground leases are frequently used for shopping centers, office buildings, hotels, and other commercial projects. They are significantly unlike other commercial leases, primarily in two respects: they are typically for much longer terms; and the tenant usually needs mortgage loan financing secured by the property.

The modern commercial ground lease is a phenomenon of the post-World War II "building booms," which have affected every major city in North America. Renewed interest in ground leases in the 1950s led to the adoption in the leading commercial states, such as New York and Massachusetts, of statutes authorizing leasehold mortgage loans for institutional lenders. In a more recent development of significance for attorneys, in 1980 the American Bar Association published Model Leasehold

Encumbrance Provisions. Leasehold financing and the commercial ground lease have come of age.

Typically, the ground lease involves land leased by a developer/tenant from the landowner with the undertaking to either build new improvements or substantially renovate existing improvements on the property. Comparable relationships between the landlord and tenant are sometimes created when an owner sells existing improvements only, retaining ownership of the land, and leases the land to the purchaser, who becomes the tenant under a ground lease; and when the owner sells and leases back the land only from an investor, who becomes the landlord under the ground lease, while the "tenant" retains ownership of the improvements.

In each of these cases, the distinguishing characteristic is a lease of the land with the tenant owning all or a substantial portion of the equity in the improvements. Normally this means that the rental paid to the landowner is not based upon the value of all of the real property, but only upon the value of the land and any portion of the improvements the landlord may own. The substantial income-producing equity in the improvements owned by the tenant can be financed, sold, and otherwise dealt with independently of the fee ownership of the land.

The landlord's continuing interest in the property is essentially an annuity, represented by the ground rent payable by the tenant, together with a right of reversion that will inure to the landlord upon expiration of the lease. The annuity is in effect secured by the tenant's equity position in the property: if the ground rent is not paid, the landlord may terminate the ground lease for default and obtain present possession and ownership of the improvements. As long as the ground lease is in effect, possession and control of the land and improvements is in the tenant. . . .

WHY GROUND LEASES?

Before discussing specific lease issues, it is worthwhile considering first some of the reasons why groundowners and developers sometimes become landlord and tenant with respect to commercial property rather than partners or seller and buyer.

THE LANDOWNER

In most circumstances, a ground lease is used for a commercial real estate project because the landowner refuses to sell her land. Occasionally a situation will arise where the owner of real property *cannot* sell ground that the developer is interested in developing, due to a lack of legal authority to sell. This will sometimes happen with governmental agencies (e.g., a port district) and less frequently with private entities (e.g., a trust).

Much more often the groundowner is simply unwilling to sell for one or more reasons.

Long-term Investment Policies. Institutions, and sometimes private individuals who are protecting the long-range interests of their families, as a matter of policy may want to maximize fee ownership of real property.

Their investment horizons can extend for fifty or one hundred years or more. Owners with these objectives may be willing to consider only lease proposals.

Tax Incentives. Frequently, an owner of property is unwilling to sell because her tax basis in the property is nominal, so that a sale would generate a substantial taxable gain. The structure of the Internal Revenue Code, including the estate tax provisions, may encourage holding commercial real estate until death in order to obtain a basis step-up.

Sometimes a tax-free exchange under Internal Revenue Code Section 1031 can be used to solve this problem, frequently involving the exchange of income-producing (and depreciable) improved real property for the property that the developer wishes to obtain (which may be raw land or have obsolete improvements). The landowner will still have a relatively low carryover tax basis with respect to the property received in the exchange.

From the groundowner's standpoint, the long-term ground lease has the advantage of not being a taxable sale. It was once relatively common to see ground leases that contained an option to purchase granted to the tenant, which option was exercisable on the death of the groundowner. That sort of option may still serve some purposes, but does not provide answers to fundamental issues of the ground lease relationship that must be resolved in order for the tenant to obtain project financing.

Investment Considerations. Often the owner of real estate simply wishes to maintain ownership of particular property because she believes it is the best available investment. The alternative in the event of a sale is to take the proceeds after paying applicable taxes and purchase some other investment: stocks, municipal bonds, bank deposits, oil and gas leases, or other real estate, for example. Many investors have been convinced that real property is the safest long-term investment available, and many are also concerned that alternative investments may involve unacceptable levels of risk.

Valuation. Many landowners find it difficult to establish a "reasonable" price for their property due in part to market uncertainties (e.g., inflation and interest rates) and in part to uncertainties created by changes in government policies, including local land use codes and federal income tax legislation.

Theoretically, the market should establish a price for land or any other asset based on current and projected levels of return for alternative investments, levels of risk, economic growth, inflation, and other factors; however, all markets are at best imperfect, and land is an illiquid and unique commodity. Landowners sometimes conclude that they cannot determine with confidence what the "fair market" price should be except at levels so high that the developer, on the other side of the same uncertain equation, cannot justify the expense.

The ground lease as an alternative to selling presents advantages that will frequently appeal to the groundowner who is disinclined or uncertain about selling. For the right project with the right developer, a well structured ground lease can provide (1) a minimum reasonable return reflecting the current value of the property; (2) through any of several available means, a participation in the project that should keep the return reasonable in relationship to market value over time; and (3) further value in the long-term ownership of land, which will revert to the landowner on expiration of the lease, together with the improvements built on the property.

THE DEVELOPER

From the developer's viewpoint, a ground lease might be attractive in a purely economic sense as a relatively inexpensive means of financing acquisition of the land, especially when the market (or the landowner) values the land in excess of what the developer's project can comfortably afford to pay. The ground lease is a form of project financing: particularly when the landowner agrees to "subordinate" her land to the tenant's financing, a ground lease will increase the developer's leverage in the project and reduce any equity requirement. Nevertheless, most developers may conclude that the problems of dealing with a ground lease outweigh the advantages in a complex commercial development. . . .

RELATIONSHIPS

A ground lease puts the parties into specific sorts of legal relationships, creating particular legal categories for the parties that may affect their rights against one another and even against third parties.

THE GROUNDOWNER

The groundowner is the landlord under the lease. For the most part, her rights and remedies will be determined by the terms of the lease, although there is a vast law of landlord and tenant accumulated over hundreds of years that will have some influence, particularly with respect to matters not specifically addressed by the lease documents. In most jurisdictions a complete landlord-tenant relationship can be created by nothing more than an oral agreement, a nod or a wink, although the agreement may not be fully enforceable (e.g., having intended a long-term lease, orally they may create only a month-to-month tenancy terminable on thirty days' notice).

As landlord, the groundowner has a significant interest in the form of the "reversion," i.e., upon expiration or earlier termination of the lease, the landlord will obtain full ownership and possession of the land and the real property improvements installed on the land by the developer/tenant (although this too may be varied by the terms of the lease). Meanwhile, the fee interest may be transferred, mortgaged, or sold by the landlord separately from the "ownership" of the improvements and the leasehold estate.

THE DEVELOPER

The developer is a tenant and not an owner of land. The developer will generally be "owner" of the improvements and the personal property installed or maintained on the land. The tenant in effect owns a "leasehold estate" in the land and the real property improvements, which is a terminable estate at law (as opposed to the "indefeasible" estate of a fee owner). In plain English, that means that the right of the tenant to possession of the property may be terminated in a variety of circumstances with the result that the developer/tenant's entire interest in the project is lost. That is expected to occur upon expiration of the lease term and may occur before the latest expiration date in a number of circumstances: failure to exercise an option to renew, "default" without completion of a cure, damage or destruction without rebuilding, and condemnation, to name the most common.

Equity investors in the project will usually become members in an entity that is the "tenant"; the developer (or an affiliate) will usually be another member in the same partnership.

LENDERS

The biggest issue for the developer's lender is the nature of the lender's collateral: is the collateral a fee interest in the land (which would require some action by the landowner to submit her fee title to the lender's mortgage or deed of trust) or is the collateral limited to the tenant's leasehold interest in the property? If the collateral is only the leasehold estate, then it may be lost entirely if the ground lease is terminated; if the leasehold mortgage is foreclosed, the lender will be required to pay the ground rent and comply with other provisions of the lease.

OCCUPANCY TENANTS

The persons and firms who will actually occupy the project when it is completed and pay the rentals that are necessary to repay the lender, pay the ground rent, and provide a return to the equity participants are not technically tenants, but rather subtenants of the developer/tenant. In the event of a termination of the ground lease, the sublease-hold estates of the occupancy subtenants are automatically terminated.

CONTRACTORS

Contractors, materialmen, and persons performing labor or services with respect to the property may also be affected in that their lien rights (in the event of nonpayment for materials or services) may attach to the fee interest in the land or may be limited only to the developer/tenant's leasehold estate. Similarly, local taxing authorities may be affected in terms of upon whom or upon what property taxes can be levied. . . .

PROBLEM

X owns a commercially zoned midtown parcel that she acquired years ago for $1 million. The parcel's present market value is $5 million. If X sells the parcel, she will pay $1.4 million in taxes (35 percent federal and state combined capital gains rate), which would leave X with $3.6 million for reinvestment. If X enters into a long-term ground lease, D will pay X an annual net ground rental of $450,000 (based on 9 percent of the parcel's market value) for an initial ten-year term and will pay upward adjustments thereafter to reflect any increased market value. Armed with D's lease-hold obligations (which include a duty to improve the property), X may now borrow $3.6 million (X receives the proceeds tax free), pledging the rental stream or mortgaging the fee as security. X's debt service on her $3.6 million loan comes only to $432,000 yearly (10 percent interest, level payment debt service, 18-year maturity).

Do you see any fallacy in this analysis? Or by leasing rather than selling, can X have her cake while also eating it?

2. Taxation of the Leasehold Interest

The ground-tenant, as the owner of investment property, is entitled to deduct all ordinary and necessary expenses, which will include, of course, ground rental, real estate taxes, operating costs, repairs, and mortgage interest. Two other categories of expenditure will concern the tax-wise ground-tenant: any leasehold acquisition costs and, more importantly, the investment in building improvements.

Acquisition costs may involve brokerage fees, closing expenses, and any premium paid to the prior tenant for a leasehold assignment. The cost of building improvements may involve not only the expenditure on a new structure but also tenant removal and demolition costs on the previous structure.

The ground-tenant must capitalize and then write off the acquisition and improvement costs. What must be determined is the appropriate write-off period. Most ground leases contain one or more renewal clauses, which give the tenant the privilege of extending the term for many years.

Except during TEFRA's brief life (1981-1986), when the 15-year[2] recovery period for real estate improvements was shorter than the initial term of most ground leases, the existence of options complicates the calculation of amortization and depreciation allowances. To illustrate the problem, assume tenant builds an office building having a 31.5-year recovery period. The tenant holds a 25-year ground lease with two 20-year renewal options. How should tenant write off the construction costs: Amortize on a 25-year schedule? Amortize on a 45-year or 65-year schedule? Depreciate on a 31.5-year schedule?

Congress, seeking to provide tenants with easily followed guidelines, has enacted the following Code provision:

Internal Revenue Code of 1986

§ 178 *Amortization of Cost of Acquiring a Lease*

(a) General Rule. — In determining the amount of the deduction allowable to a lessee for exhaustion, wear and tear, obsolescence, or amortization in respect of any cost of acquiring the lease, the term of the lease shall be treated as including all renewal options (and any other period for which the parties reasonably expect the lease to be renewed) if less than 75 percent of such cost is attributable to the period of the term of the lease remaining on the date of its acquisition.

(b) Certain Periods Excludable. — For purposes of subsection (a), in determining the period of the term of the lease remaining on the date of acquisition, there shall not be taken into account any period for which the lease may subsequently be renewed, extended or continued pursuant to an option exercisable by the lessee.

NOTES AND QUESTIONS

1. You will note that the current statutory test applies only to leasehold amortization. The Senate explanation indicates that the cost of tenant-built improvements is to be recovered under the rules applicable to other taxpayers, without regard to the lease term. On termination of the lease, the lessee who does not retain the improvements is to compute gain or loss by reference to the adjusted basis of the improvements at that time.

2. Self-evidently, tenant may only depreciate improvements for which he has paid. Conversely, landlord may not write off lessee-built improvements during the

---

2. The recovery period (except for low-income housing) rose to 18 years in 1984 and to 19 years in 1985.

leasehold term. When the lease terminates, possession and ownership of the improvements then pass to the fee owner. The lease may require landlord to pay tenant a sum based on the improvement's current value, or some fraction thereof, on the termination date. What tax consequences would flow, for example, if landlord paid the terminating tenant $10 million for the tenant-built improvements?

Suppose, instead, that the fee owner pays nothing at leasehold termination for improvements having a current $10 million value: What tax consequences would flow from that event? See I.R.C. §§ 109, 1017.

3. The Leasehold Mortgage

a. Structure and Terms

York, The Ground Lease and the Leasehold Mortgage

99 Banking L. Journal 709-721 (1982)

Most long-term ground leases contain provisions allowing the tenant to encumber its leasehold estate pursuant to a mortgage or deed of trust in order to obtain financing for construction of a project being developed by the tenant. Unless the landlord is also agreeable to encumbering its fee interest in the land, the leasehold estate will be the only security for the lender. It is obvious that any termination of the lease for any reason would cause a complete loss of the lender's security; therefore, protection against such loss of security is just one of the reasons counsel for a lender contemplating a leasehold mortgage loan will want to review carefully the provisions of the lease.

This article discusses the principal factors lender's counsel should consider. Even where the landlord executes a deed of trust encumbering its fee interest in the land as additional security for the loan, the provisions of the lease will be important to the tenant and to the lender in order to ensure that the tenant will be able to obtain any necessary refinancing in the future.

GENERAL CONSIDERATIONS

The attorney for the leasehold mortgagee should be involved in the negotiation and drafting of the lease from the outset. Too often the attorney for the leasehold mortgagee is presented with a lease which has already been negotiated between the landlord and the tenant (or one which has been executed). It is then difficult to obtain the modifications which are required to make it acceptable to the lender.

However, often the identity of the lender is not known at the time the lease is originally executed. In such situations, and because the particular requirements of each lender are somewhat different, it is advisable to include a provision in the lease to the effect that the landlord will agree to make such further reasonable modifications as a leasehold mortgagee may request, provided that the amendment does not significantly adversely affect landlord's rights under the lease or reduce the rental thereunder. While typically the landlord's initial reaction is to reject any such provision, it often can be included when the landlord is made to realize that obtaining financing for the project is the landlord's concern as much as it is the tenant's.

When the attorney for the lender participates in the negotiation of the lease, he should review the entire lease from the viewpoint of the tenant. The factors which are mentioned in this article are only some of the factors with which the lender should be concerned. In the event of a foreclosure, the lender usually seeks to obtain a new tenant to take over the project; it would be difficult to obtain a new tenant if there are provisions in the lease which are objectionable to a prospective tenant, even if they do not directly relate to the leasehold financing aspects. Consequently, the lease must be satisfactory in all respects from the viewpoint of the tenant.

In most cases, fee title to the improvements will remain with the tenant until the expiration of the lease; therefore, any leasehold mortgage will actually be both a leasehold mortgage (as to the land) and a fee mortgage (as to the buildings and improvements). This is often overlooked in preparing the loan documents and in dealing with related matters such as title insurance.

TERM OF THE LEASE

Obviously, the term of the lease must be at least as long as the term of the loan. Otherwise, the security for the loan would be extinguished prior to the loan being paid. However, most lenders require that the lease term be at least as long as the amortization schedule of the loan, and usually somewhat longer. Many times, the state laws regulating loans made by institutional lenders will set minimum standards regarding the term of the lease to be mortgaged, such as setting a minimum "cushion" between the expiration date of the lease and the maturity date of the loan (the most common being that the loan term cannot exceed 75 percent of the unexpired lease term).

One should not rely on unexercised renewal options for satisfying the requirement of the length of the term. Occasionally a lender will permit an option to renew a lease to be included in the minimum term calculation if it is expressly enforceable by the leasehold mortgagee. In such a case, the renewal option should be self-executing so that no affirmative action is required from the landlord following exercise of the option by the tenant. While this minimizes the risk that the landlord's trustee-in-bankruptcy will avoid a renewal option, it appears to this author that the possible adverse consequences are so significant that the ability to renew the lease should not be relied upon.

The lease should also provide for a specific commencement date of the term. Where the term of a lease is to commence only on the happening of some specified condition and the condition may never occur, the lease may be held void as violating the rule against perpetuities.[3] Some leases provide that the term of the lease commences only upon completion of construction of the improvements. In California it has been held that a lease does not violate the rule against perpetuities if the term is to commence upon completion of construction of a building and if it is contemplated that the building will be completed in a reasonable time amounting to less than twenty-one years.[4] There should be no unsatisfied conditions to the

3. See First & C Corp. v. Wencke, 253 Cal. App. 2d 719, 61 Cal. Rptr. 531 (1967).
4. Wong v. DiGrazia, 60 Cal. 2d 525, 35 Cal. Rptr. 241 (1963). See also Cal. Civ. Code § 715.6.

commencement of the term when the loan is made, unless the lender is certain that it can ensure that such conditions will be fulfilled.

Rent

Virtually all long-term leases today have rent escalation clauses. It is impossible to set specific guidelines because of the numerous variations on the types of escalation provisions which exist. Some provisions require periodic appraisals of the rental value of the property, others are tied to an objective indicator such as the Consumer Price Index, and others contain a combination of methods. The attorney reviewing the lease must be certain that, at a minimum, the provision is clear and unambiguous.

Use of a formula based upon the Consumer Price Index should be discouraged. While such a formula is easy to apply, it may have no relationship to the rental value of real property in the area concerned. If used, the leasehold mortgagee should require a ceiling on the amount of increase which may occur each year. Generally, formulas based upon income generated from the property (such as percentage rent clauses) are satisfactory.

If the landlord and the tenant have already agreed on a formula which the lender believes to be unsatisfactory, sometimes it is possible to provide that the escalation clause is "subordinate" to the leasehold mortgage so that it would not be binding on the mortgagee in the event of a foreclosure. Even in such a case, at the time of a foreclosure the rents could have escalated to such a level that the project is no longer viable. Therefore, it should be made clear that increases in rent even if occurring prior to foreclosure are not binding on the lender.

Use of the Leased Premises

In the event of a foreclosure by the leasehold mortgagee, the mortgagee will seek to locate a new tenant and will want the premises to be usable for as broad a number of uses as possible. Usually, a foreclosure occurs only because the original project was not successful. Accordingly, great latitude must be allowed the lender. In the event the landlord is reluctant to allow the tenant to use the property except for limited uses, the use clause should be modified so that the restrictions will not apply following a foreclosure.

Of course, the attorney should carefully review "radius" restrictions, exclusive use provisions, and other provisions which may violate laws regulating restraints on trade.

Improvements

In most cases, improvements on the property will belong to the tenant. If construction of the improvements commenced prior to the execution of the lease or if there are existing improvements, it may be necessary for all parties who have an interest in the property to execute quitclaim deeds of the improvements to the tenant. The lease should provide that the improvements belong to the tenant until the expiration or other termination of the lease, unless a "new lease" is entered into pursuant to the default provisions discussed below under "Defaults by the Tenant."

INSURANCE

The lease should require that all insurance policies include a standard mortgagee endorsement and be noncancellable without at least thirty days' prior written notice to the landlord and to the leasehold mortgagee. The leasehold mortgagee should be allowed to hold the originals of all insurance policies if it desires. In the event of a casualty, the lease should provide that all proceeds will be paid to the leasehold mortgagee or to an independent trustee to be applied in accordance with the provisions on casualty.

CASUALTY

In the event of a casualty, the leasehold mortgagee often would prefer to be able to use the insurance proceeds to reduce the loan (or to pay it off entirely). However, in view of the landlord's typically strong bargaining position on this point, as well as judicial authority which limits the ability of the lender in this regard,[5] this usually is not possible. If the lease is strictly a "ground" lease, with a flat rental based solely on the value of the land, the lender may believe that the landlord has no interest in requiring the improvements to be rebuilt. However, often the landlord has negotiated a ground rent which includes a percentage rent or other amounts based upon income from the property, and the landlord has a strong interest in having the improvements reconstructed. If nothing else, the landlord has some residual interest in the improvements following the expiration of the lease. Therefore, usually there will be some provisions requiring the tenant to reconstruct the improvements.

However, the tenant's obligations should be limited to the extent of the insurance proceeds. If the landlord insists that the tenant have an unconditional obligation to rebuild the improvements, the lender should require that such provision not be binding on the leasehold mortgagee except as to a limited monetary amount or to the extent insurance proceeds are available. As stated above under "Insurance," proceeds should be paid to a trustee controlled by the mortgagee who then disburses the proceeds as reconstruction progresses. In the event of any excess proceeds, they should belong to the tenant; the leasehold mortgage itself will provide for the disposition of such proceeds, presumably to the reduction of the loan.

There should also be limitations on the requirement that the tenant restore the improvements when the cause of the loss is not insurable. In the event a loss occurs during the last five years of the term, the tenant's only obligation should be to clear the property of debris, utilizing insurance proceeds to the extent available; any excess proceeds should belong to the landlord. There should also be no obligation to reconstruct in the event of a loss involving a substantial portion of the premises. When a loss is substantial, the parties may wish to review entirely the use and financing of the property and should not be locked into rebuilding the improvements which previously existed.

---

5. See, e.g., Milstein v. Security Pac. Bank, 27 Cal. App. 3d 482, 103 Cal. Rptr. 16 (1972).

CONDEMNATION

Even though in most cases the parties agree that condemnation is an unlikely event, condemnation provisions are extremely important to the lender. If the property is taken either in whole or in part through eminent domain proceedings, the lender wants its loan to be paid off to the fullest extent possible and, in the event of a partial condemnation, wants its remaining security to be adequate.

The lease should provide that in the event of a total taking, the lease automatically terminates. In the event of a partial taking, the tenant should have the option to terminate the lease if a substantial portion of the premises is taken (as with casualty, the definition of "substantial" should be defined as precisely as possible, such as by a percentage of the net leasable floor area of the project). If there is a partial taking which is not a substantial taking, there should be no termination of the lease, and the rent should be reduced pursuant to a formula, such as one which takes into account the value of the premises taken to the value of the premises prior to the taking. A formula based upon the area taken should not be utilized unless all portions of the premises are of equal value.

Provisions relating to the allocation of the award frequently are heavily negotiated among landlord, tenant, and the leasehold mortgagee. From the mortgagee's point of view, the preferred allocation is for any award to be applied first to the unpaid balance of the loan. If such a provision can be negotiated, the mortgagee is not generally concerned with how the landlord and tenant divide the remainder of the award. Frequently, however, the landlord will not agree to such a provision. In such an event, it is generally acceptable for the landlord and the tenant to divide the award based upon the values of their respective estates in the property. The landlord should be entitled to receive the value of the fee interest subject to the lease, and the tenant should be entitled to receive the value of the leasehold (including renewal options), which may include a "bonus value." In the event of a partial taking which is not a substantial taking which would allow the tenant to terminate the lease, then the condemnation proceeds should be held by the mortgagee as trustee to be used for restoration of the premises remaining after the taking, and any excess proceeds should be divided between landlord and tenant. The tenant should not be required to expend more than the net amount received from a partial taking in order to restore the improvements. In the event of a temporary taking, all proceeds should belong solely to the tenant unless the taking extends beyond the term of the lease including any renewals.

To avoid any doubt on the question, the lender should be specifically permitted to participate in any condemnation proceeding.

SUBLEASES

Frequently, it is the subleases which generate the income from which the tenant makes its payments under the leasehold mortgage loan. As a result, the ability of the tenant to freely sublease the property is of vital concern. The lease should specifically allow the tenant to sublet all or any part of the premises without the landlord's consent. Also, the landlord should agree not to disturb the possession of any subtenant which has been approved by the leasehold mortgagee even if the original ground lease is terminated. The ground lease should contain a covenant that all subleases will provide that they cannot be modified so as to reduce the rent, change renewal rights, shorten the term, or provide for prepayment of rent without the consent of the leasehold mortgagee. The purpose of this covenant is to insure that should the lender take over the property following a default, it will find in effect the same subleases on which it relied in making the loan in the first place. The lease should also provide that subleases must be expressly subordinate to the ground lease (as well as to any "new lease" as discussed under "Defaults by the Tenant" below).

In the event of a termination of the ground lease for a noncurable default and the issuance to a lender of a "new lease," the subleases might be inadvertently cut off. Therefore, the lease should require that all subleases contain an attornment provision whereby the subtenant agrees to recognize the leasehold mortgagee as its new landlord if the leasehold mortgagee assumes that position under a "new lease." In that manner, the lender will be assured of rental income after it has executed the new lease.

ASSIGNMENT

The tenant must have the right at any time to mortgage its leasehold interest without any restrictions. Therefore, the lease should be expressly made mortgage-able by the tenant. It should also be freely assignable by the tenant. In the event of foreclosure, the lender must have absolute freedom to dispose of the lease. It is important that the lease be freely assignable so that an assignment in lieu of foreclosure or an assignment pursuant to a foreclosure sale are not improper assignments. It is not acceptable for the right of assignment to be conditioned upon the consent of the landlord, even if such consent is "not to be unreasonably withheld," for there are too many possibilities for a landlord to assert that it has reasonable grounds for withholding consent.

DEFAULTS BY THE TENANT

The most important provisions in any ground lease which is to be mortgageable relate to defaults by the tenant. It is vital that the lease not be terminated because of a default by a tenant without notice to the lender and an opportunity to cure. There are many variations on the actual provisions which are utilized to satisfy this requirement, and some institutional lenders require certain specialized language. There are also some model provisions prepared by a subcommittee of the American Bar Association.[6]

The important points to be covered are as follows: the mortgagee must be entitled to receive notice of any default by the tenant; and the leasehold mortgagee must be provided a reasonable opportunity to cure beyond the time permitted the tenant to cure. For example, it should be provided that if the tenant defaults and does not cure the default within the notice and grace period provided in the lease, then the landlord will give the leasehold mortgagee a notice that the tenant has failed to cure the default and that the mortgagee shall have sixty days after such additional notice to cure or commence to cure the default. If a default is of a nature

6. See Subcommittee on Leasehold Encumbrances. Committee on Leasing, ABA Real Property, Probate & Trust Law Section, "Model Leasehold Encumbrance Provisions," 15 Real Prop. Prob. & Tr. J. 395 (1980).

which is not curable within such time, the leasehold mortgagee should have such additional time as necessary provided it is proceeding diligently to cure the default or is commencing foreclosure proceedings.

Some defaults cannot be cured by the leasehold mortgagee. These defaults are generally personal to the tenant and include such matters as the insolvency or bankruptcy of the tenant. Therefore, the lease should not allow the landlord to automatically terminate the lease upon such a default (even though such a clause may be wholly or partially unenforceable under the Bankruptcy Act), but it should provide that the landlord may not terminate the lease or exercise its remedies so long as the leasehold mortgagee continues to pay all rent and diligently proceeds to cure all defaults which are curable by the leasehold mortgagee.

The lease should also provide that any default not curable by the mortgagee will be waived by the landlord when the mortgagee assumes the position of the tenant following foreclosure or assignment in lieu of foreclosure.

It should be provided that any action taken by the leasehold mortgagee to cure the default must be accepted by the landlord as though performed by the tenant itself. The mortgagee should be permitted to enter the property if necessary to cure any default.

If the leasehold mortgagee takes possession of the lease through foreclosure or assignment in lieu of foreclosure, the lease should provide that the mortgagee is liable for the tenant's obligations only for the time it is in possession of the lease. In addition, many lenders require that the landlord's recourse against any leasehold mortgagee be solely against the mortgagee's interest in the lease.

There should also be provisions requiring the landlord to enter into a "new lease" with the leasehold mortgagee for the unexpired term of the lease. This new lease should be on the same terms and conditions as the original lease. It should also be provided that the new lease will be subject to no new encumbrances or other matters adversely affecting title other than those which may have been created by the tenant. Virtually all institutional lenders require such "new lease" provisions as an ultimate fallback in the event the lease is terminated inadvertently or because of a default not susceptible to cure by the lender. However, the enforceability of such provisions is unclear.[7]

MODIFICATION, CANCELLATION, AND MERGER

There should be a clause which specifically prohibits any modification, amendment, cancellation, or termination of the lease without the leasehold mortgagee's written consent and which prohibits any surrender of the lease without the mortgagee's consent. Lenders for many years have been concerned with the potential ability of a trustee in bankruptcy of a landlord to disaffirm a ground lease. Section 365(h) of the Bankruptcy Code now provides that if the trustee of a bankrupt landlord rejects a lease, the lessee may treat it as terminated by such rejection, or at the lessee's election may remain in possession for the balance of the term and any renewal or extension that is enforceable under applicable nonbankruptcy law. The ground lease as well as the leasehold mortgage should contain a provision (1) expressly barring the tenant from exercising the right of termination afforded

---

7. See Levitan, Leasehold Mortgage Financing: Reliance on the "New Lease" Provision, 15 Real Prop. Prob. & Tr. J. 413 (1980).

by this section without the prior written consent of the leasehold mortgagee; or (2) which expressly vests such rights solely in the leasehold mortgagee.

In order to prevent extinguishment of the lease through a merger of the leasehold estate and the fee estate, the lease should provide that there will be no such merger even if both estates are held directly or indirectly by the same person or entity.

ESTOPPEL CERTIFICATES

The landlord should be required to provide, when requested and without cost, an estoppel certificate to insure a prospective or current leasehold mortgagee that the lease is in full force and effect without any present defaults (or any event having occurred which, with the passage of time and/or the giving of notice, would constitute a default). Preferably, the estoppel certificate should attach a copy of the lease and any amendments and should set forth the commencement and termination dates of the lease. The landlord should also be required to represent whether there are any offsets or counterclaims against the tenant and provide any other information which a leasehold mortgagee may reasonably request.

TITLE

At the time the loan is made and the leasehold deed of trust recorded, title to the property should be carefully reviewed by counsel for the lender. A short form or memorandum of the ground lease must be recorded and must be prior to any encumbrance which is not satisfactory to the lender. There can be no deeds of trust or other liens which are prior to the lease and which could extinguish the lease if foreclosed. In this regard, it is not satisfactory for the beneficiary under a prior deed of trust to execute a "nondisturbance agreement" with respect to the lease, because, among other things, virtually all lenders and the laws which regulate their investments require that the lease be prior to any other encumbrance. In addition, the enforceability of such an agreement may be in doubt in the event of the landlord's bankruptcy. The lease should also contain a specific provision to the effect that any encumbrance later placed on the premises will be subordinate to the lease and to any leasehold mortgage.

The loan policy of title insurance issued to the mortgagee should insure that the estate encumbered by the deed of trust is a leasehold estate as to the land and a fee estate in all improvements.

GROUND SUBLEASES

Mortgages on ground subleases present a difficult problem primarily because the lender's security is extinguished if either the master lease or the sublease is terminated for any reason. Because of the special risks involved in a sublease situation, many lenders are reluctant to loan on the basis of a sublease and there are often special laws applicable to institutional lenders regulating such loans. Great care must be taken to make sure that the sublessor's estate survives the termination of the master lease. The master lessor must agree, for example, that in the event of the termination of the master lease for any reason, the sublease will automatically become a direct lease between the master lessor and subtenant. The master lessor and its tenant (the sublessor) must agree not to allow any deed of trust or other lien to be placed either on the fee estate or on the leasehold estate under the master lease if the foreclosure of such lien would extinguish the master lease or the sublease.

The master lease must be reviewed carefully to ensure that all of its provisions are consistent with the sublease. For example, if the master lease provides that in the event of a condemnation the tenant receives only the portion of any award representing the value of the improvements, and the landlord receives all of the award for the land, the sublease, being subject to the master lease, could not possibly grant the subtenant the right to receive the value of its sublease estate in the land.

CONCLUSION

When a lender secures a loan by acquiring a mortgage on a ground leasehold estate, it becomes, in effect, a tenant once removed. As a result, the provisions of the ground lease are of vital importance to such secured lender. The attorney representing the lender must review all of the lease provisions with care, and the attorneys representing the landlord and the tenant should be aware of the lender's concerns and how to satisfy them while still protecting their own clients' interests.

Thomas, The Mortgaging of Long-Term Leases[8]

39 Dicta 363, 379-382 (1962)

III. THE MORTGAGE

Once the provisions of the lease have been satisfactorily resolved, the drafting of the mortgage will be comparatively easy, almost anticlimactic. Speaking generally, most of the standard provisions of a fee mortgage should be found in a leasehold mortgage with little or no change. There are, however, a number of provisions which must be added to a leasehold mortgage. Most of them will be fairly obvious. Few should cause much argument by borrower's counsel. The landlord, of course, has no direct concern with the terms of the mortgage — unless he has agreed to join it. It is considered prudent practice, however, to require the landlord to agree to recognize any authorization granted by the tenant mortgagor to the mortgagee to exercise tenant's rights under the lease. The more common of the distinctive leasehold mortgage provisions in addition to the difference in description, are summarized in the following paragraphs.

A. Conformity with Lease Requirements. — The mortgage itself may not contain provisions inconsistent with those of the lease. Of frequent consideration in this area are the use of proceeds of fire insurance or of an award for a taking in condemnation. However, the mortgage may impose additional obligations on the borrower-tenant if the lease seems inadequate. An example would be a requirement that the tenant furnish additional insurance policies with a standard mortgagee clause, if the lease did not permit one on policies to be furnished the landlord. If the age of the building is such that ordinary insurance might be substantially inadequate to effect the restoration required by the lease, the mortgage should

8. Footnotes have been omitted — Eds.

require the tenant to carry insurance on a replacement basis to cover physical depreciation. If the lease does not provide for a rental abatement while damage is being restored, the ability of the tenant to continue to pay the rent and other lease changes should be assured by the mortgage requiring the tenant to maintain rent insurance or business interruption insurance.

B. Tenant to Comply with Lease. — The mortgage will require the tenant to agree expressly to perform or comply with all of the covenants of the tenant to be performed under the lease. The lease will have provided for a notice by the landlord to the mortgagee of any default under the lease which could form a basis for termination. If there are other possible notices from the landlord of which the mortgagee wishes to learn, the mortgage may provide that copies be sent by the tenant to the mortgagee. In addition, if the lease clauses are considered inadequate, the mortgage may require the tenant to furnish evidence of payment of ground rent, taxes, etc., before any grace period given in the lease has expired. The mortgage should expressly provide that the failure of the tenant to perform and subsequent performance by the mortgagee will not remove the default as between tenant and mortgagee but that until the tenant shall have reimbursed the mortgagee for the cost of performance, the mortgagee will have the right to accelerate and add the cost to the mortgage debt.

C. Shortening of Tenant's Grace Period under the Lease. — Depending upon the provisions in the lease which require the landlord to give the mortgagee notice of the tenant's defaults and the opportunity to cure them, the mortgage may require the tenant to cure any such defaults within a shorter period than that permitted the mortgagee, so that the mortgagee will have time within which to cure if the tenant does not.

D. Prohibition of Lease Modification or Termination. — The mortgage will, of course, prohibit the tenant from agreeing to any modification or termination or surrender of the lease without the mortgagee's consent. Notifying the landlord of the existence of the mortgage may be sufficient to prevent the landlord from agreeing to any such modification, termination or surrender, but an express agreement by the landlord is more satisfactory. Incidentally, the lease will probably require the tenant to notify the landlord of any leasehold mortgage and the mortgage will require the tenant to give such notice. The mortgagee should nevertheless be satisfied beyond question that the notice has been given.

E. Control of Arbitration. — If the lease provides for arbitration in any particular aspect, the mortgagee may require the tenant to authorize the mortgagee to represent the tenant in certain areas of arbitration or in certain circumstances. Again, it would be well to have the landlord agree to recognize such authorization.

F. Control of Renewal of Term. — If the tenant has the right to renew the lease, the mortgagee should be authorized to renew on behalf of, and in the name of, the tenant if the tenant fails to renew at any time when the security of the mortgage would be jeopardized by such failure. Again, the landlord should recognize such authorization or it should be clear, as a matter of law, that the landlord cannot refuse to recognize the authorization.

G. Fee Interest Acquired by Tenant to Be Subject to Mortgage. — Any purchase option in the tenant should be covered by the mortgage expressly and although it would be an unusual situation in which the mortgagee would be justified in insisting that the tenant exercise such an option, it should continue with the lease in the event of foreclosure. In any event, the mortgage should provide that if the tenant should acquire the fee of all or any portion of the leased property whether by exercise of a purchase option or otherwise, the fee would immediately become subject to the mortgage and the mortgagor would execute whatever confirmatory instrument might be required. However, provision should be made to prevent a merger of the lease in the fee if, under state law, the consequent disappearance of the lease would permit valued subtenants to effectively claim that the sublease falls with the disappearance of the primary lease.

H. Subleases. — In a majority of large real estate financings the terms of occupancy and the financial responsibility of the occupying tenants are of primary importance, whether the property be an office building, a shopping center, a department store or a post office. We are here concerned, however, only with the aspects of such leasing as may peculiarly relate to leasehold financing. In this context, the occupancy leases are subleases.

First, it should be apparent that the subleases must be integrated with the primary lease and that no rights can be granted the subtenants more extensive than those granted under the primary lease. Indeed, it is not uncommon for the sublease to contain an express stipulation to that effect.

In the second place, if the primary lease provides for a new lease to the mortgagee in the event of termination of the primary lease . . . any sublease considered valuable by the mortgagee must contain a covenant by the subtenant to attorn to the lessee under any such new lease. Otherwise the subtenant may effectively claim that the sublease and his obligations thereunder fall with the termination of the primary lease. As a matter of fact, a subtenant of a large amount of space may well require the overlandlord to agree that if the lease is terminated and the mortgagee does not obtain a new lease, either the subtenant may obtain a new lease on the same terms as the primary lease or the overlandlord will recognize the continuance of the sublease as a direct lease from the overlandlord. Careful drafting will provide for such recognition by the overlandlord during the period in which the mortgagee is making up his mind whether or not to take a new lease.

An ABA group, the Subcommittee on Leasehold Encumbrances, of the Committee on Leasing, Real Property Division, has issued a Report that contains "model" leasehold encumbrance protective provisions for use in long-term leases. The Report at page 399 speaks of these provisions as reflecting an attempt "to fine tune the balancing of the interests of the landlord and of the leasehold lender."

The Subcommittee devoted special attention to the matter of the tenant's non-curable default:

> In addition to the many areas considered, special consideration was given to the desirability of "New Lease" provisions which require a fee owner to enter into a New Lease with the leasehold mortgagee at such mortgagee's request in the event of a termination of the leasehold. The use of the New Lease provisions which have been added as subsection (h) to these model provisions is elective. The use of such provisions is sufficiently well established in practice to warrant their use although dependence by the mortgagee upon the availability of a New Lease may be dangerous. One must consider the possibility of intervening third party rights and of whether the obligation to enter into the New Lease would be effected by proceedings under the Bankruptcy Code involving the lessor . . . The tenant should seek to modify the renewal provision of the lease to permit the leasehold mortgagee to exercise renewal options if the lessee fails to do so. . . .

(h) New Lease, (Optional Provision)

In the event of the termination of this Lease as a result of Tenant's default Landlord shall, in addition to providing the notices of default and termination as required by subsections (e) and (f) above of this section [Insert section number of lease], provide each Leasehold Mortgagee with written notice that the Lease has been terminated, together with a statement of all sums which would at that time be due under this Lease but for such termination, and of all other defaults, if any, then known to Landlord. Landlord agrees to enter into a new lease ("New Lease") of the Demised Premises with such Leasehold Mortgagee or its designee for the remainder of the term of this Lease, effective as of the date of termination, at the rent and additional rent, and upon the terms, covenants and conditions (including all options to renew but excluding requirements which are not applicable or which have already been fulfilled) of this Lease, provided:

(i) Such Leasehold Mortgagee shall make written request upon Landlord for such New Lease within 60 days after the date such Leasehold Mortgagee receives Landlord's Notice of Termination of this Lease given pursuant to this subsection-(h).

(ii) Such Leasehold Mortgagee or its designee shall pay or cause to be paid to Landlord at the time of the execution and delivery of such New Lease, any and all sums which would be at the time of execution and delivery thereof be due pursuant to this Lease but for such termination and, in addition thereto, all reasonable expenses, including reasonable attorney's fees, which Landlord shall have incurred by reason of such termination and the execution and delivery of the New Lease and which have not otherwise been received by Landlord from Tenant or other party in interest under Tenant. Upon the execution of such New Lease, Landlord shall allow to the Tenant named therein as an offset against the sums otherwise due under this subsection (h)(ii) or under the New Lease, an amount equal to the net income derived by Landlord from the Demised Premises during the period from the date of termination of this Lease to the date of the beginning of the Lease term of such New Lease. In the event of a controversy as to the amount to be paid to Landlord pursuant to this subsection (h)(ii), the payment obligation shall be satisfied if Landlord shall be paid the amount not in controversy, and the Leasehold Mortgagee or its designee shall agree to pay any additional sum ultimately determined to be due plus interest [at the rate of 8 percent per annum] and such obligation shall be adequately secured.

(iii) Such Leasehold Mortgagee or its designee shall agree to remedy any of Tenant's defaults of which said Leasehold Mortgagee was notified by Landlord's Notice of Termination and which are reasonably susceptible of being so cured by Leasehold Mortgagee or its designee.

(iv) Any New Lease made pursuant to this subsection (h) and any renewal Lease entered into with a Leasehold Mortgagee pursuant to section [Insert section number of lease], hereof shall be prior to any mortgage or other lien, charge or encumbrance on the fee of the Demised Premises and the Tenant under such New Lease shall have the same right, title and interest in and to the Demised Premises and the buildings and improvements thereon as Tenant had under this Lease.

(v) The Tenant under any such New Lease shall be liable to perform the obligations imposed on the Tenant by such New Lease only during the period such person has ownership of such Leasehold Estate.

15 Real Prop. Prob. and Tr. J. 395, 399, 406-408 (1980).

NOTE

1. For a thoughtful examination of potential problems in enforcing a "new lease" provision, see Levitan, Leasehold Mortgage Financing: Reliance on the

"New Lease" Provision, 15 Real Prop. Prob. and Tr. J. 413 (1980). Among the issues Levitan raises are the possibility that a bankruptcy trustee could reject the lease, thereby terminating the new lease provision, and the risk that the provision could be held to violate the rule against perpetuities.

Thus far, our examination of groundlease financing has focused largely on the needs and concerns of the construction (and then takeout) lender, and we have noted that subjecting the owner's fee to the mortgage can be a valuable way to reduce the risk involved in leasehold financing. However, the owner has concerns as well. This next reading sheds light on the risks faced by the owner, and steps that may mitigate those risks.

Emanuel B. Halper, Planning and Construction Clauses in a Subordinated Ground Lease

17 Real Est. L. J. 48 (1988)

. . . One reason why ground leases are interesting is that they differ so much from each other. A ground lease clause that is perfectly reasonable in one context is absolutely preposterous in another. In particular, the presence or absence of a subordination clause influences many other ground lease clauses profoundly.

WHAT IS A GROUND LEASE SUBORDINATION CLAUSE?

Ground lease subordination clauses usually have nothing to do with the classical concept of subordination. Real estate developers and their lawyers (who have never been the most articulate people in our society) have confused the two ideas. I figure that the confusion began when developers, who were accustomed to buying land for a large purchase price and a small down payment, shifted to ground leasing. Before they shifted to ground leasing, their negotiations to purchase land focused on the amount of the purchase price and how and when the purchase price would be paid. To the extent they could, many would attempt to defer as much of the purchase price as possible and for as long as possible. The deferred portion of the purchase price was usually secured by a purchase money mortgage. Naturally, many of these developers became adept at negotiating the provisions of their deferred payment purchase money mortgages.

Some of these provisions necessarily dealt with the developer's subsequent efforts to develop the project and finance the cost of development.

As you know, almost all developers need to finance the cost of constructing improvements to the land (and sometimes the cost of the land as well) by borrowing as much money as they can pursuant to a construction loan. Customarily, lenders insist that construction loans be secured by a first mortgage lien against the land and the buildings to be constructed. Because of his need to grant a first mortgage to secure a construction loan, a developer who purchased land, deferred the payment of a part of the purchase price, and secured the deferred payment with a purchase money mortgage was faced with two alternatives: He could convince the construction lender to lend him additional funds to pay off the deferred payments due with respect to the purchase money land mortgage, or he could convince the landowner to subordinate the lien of the purchase money land mortgage to the lien of the construction loan mortgage.

Clearly, purchaser-developers usually preferred to convince landowners to subordinate the lien of a deferred payment purchase money land mortgage rather than to borrow more money from their construction lenders and pay off the landowners with the additional funds. Interest payable on purchase money mortgages is often much lower than interest payable on construction loans. In addition, construction lenders prefer to lend less than the entire project development cost and want to know that someone other than the lender has money in the deal. That someone can be the landowner.

Accordingly, the developers learned that they usually end up needing much less of their own cash by not paying off the debt secured by a purchase money land mortgage and getting the landowner to subordinate the lien of the land mortgage to the lien of the construction loan mortgage and permanent loan mortgage.

As some developers learned that you need even less cash when you lease land rather than buy it, I figure that they jumped into the new way of dealing with much exhilaration but without much preparation or understanding. It seems to me that the developers' negotiators just superimposed the way they drafted purchase money mortgages on the ground leases they confronted without bothering to learn much about the new subject matter. They knew how to talk to a landowner from whom they were purchasing land for a little cash and a lot of deferred payments secured by a purchase money mortgage; they'd try to convince him that the lien of his purchase money mortgage should be subordinated to the lien of a mortgage securing a construction loan or a construction loan and permanent loan. Unfortunately, when they were negotiating ground leases instead of purchase money mortgages, they approached the document in exactly the same way. They (absurdly) asked the landowner to subordinate his land (or the ground lease) to one, two, or all mortgages the tenant might want executed.

Of course, you can't subordinate land, and the idea of a landlord subordinating a ground lease is nonsense.

THE NEEDS OF TENANT-DEVELOPERS

Actually, a properly drafted subordinated ground lease should not require the landowner to subordinate anything. It should require the landowner to execute a mortgage (or mortgages) of his land to accommodate a loan (or loans) made to the tenant for the purpose of developing the land. Subordination is meaningless in this context.

Ground lease tenant-developers have needs that are similar to the needs of purchaser-developers. However, the needs of tenant-developers are more difficult to satisfy than the needs of purchaser-developers. For example, the need to borrow most or all of the funds needed to discharge the cost of development from an institutional lender is common to purchaser-developers and tenant-developers. Purchaser-developers can provide security for their mortgage loans by mortgaging the fee simple (ownership estate); they can forget about landowners after they buy and pay for the land. Tenant-developers usually attempt to solve their need to provide adequate security for their mortgage loans by taking one of two paths. Sometimes they try to organize the ground lease in a salutary way so that an institutional lender would be willing to lend the funds he needs to develop the project against the security of the leasehold estate alone. More often, they try to convince the landowner that the deal won't work unless he executes a mortgage to secure a loan to be made to the tenant-developer for the purpose of financing the development.

A landowner's decision whether he will or will not execute a mortgage of his land to accommodate a loan to be made to a tenant-developer has profound consequences on the risks to be taken by the landowner, the institutional lender, and the tenant-developer. If a landowner executes a mortgage to secure a loan made to the tenant-developer, the landowner faces the possibility that he will lose his land entirely in case the tenant fails to pay the mortgage debt or in case the tenant is in default under the mortgage documents in other respects. On the other hand, if the ground lease doesn't require the landowner to execute a mortgage of the land (in real estate slang, the lease is unsubordinated), the mortgagee faces the loss of the security (the leasehold mortgage) for its investment in case the tenant defaults under the ground lease. In a financial climate in which lenders of a large percentage of commercial permanent mortgage loans customarily agree to limit the borrower's liability to the proceeds of the security and not to seek repayment from other assets of the borrower, the loss of the security can mean the loss of all hope for repayment.

Given this state of affairs, the most significant issue that must be faced by the parties to a ground lease is whether the landlord will subordinate (execute a mortgage of his land to secure a loan made to the tenant). If the landlord refuses to subordinate, the tenant's reaction to the other clauses of the ground lease must be influenced by the need to convince a mortgagee to lend against the security of the leasehold estate alone. However, if the landlord agrees to subordinate, his reaction to many other clauses of the ground lease must be influenced by this decision and the risks he undertakes as a result of this decision.

Although the aroma of subordination permeates all of a subordinated ground lease, this article will focus on the effect of subordination on the planning and construction clauses.

Before we go any further, I'd like to stop using the word "subordinate" when I refer to the landlord's execution of a mortgage of his land to secure a loan made to his tenant. What's really happening is that a landowner is encumbering his property to accommodate his tenant's need to borrow money. So I call this kind of mortgage an "accommodation mortgage."

PLANNING AND SITE PREPARATION

A landowner's agreement to execute his tenant's mortgage should cause plenty of anxiety at the beginning of a ground lease relationship. The clauses that deal with the beginning of a ground lease relationship focus on the process of planning and preparing for the construction of buildings and other improvements on the land.

IN THE EVENT CONSTRUCTION IS ABANDONED

Construction is fraught with danger for a landowner who executes an accommodation mortgage. The most obvious danger is the possibility that the tenant will be unable to manage the construction properly or that construction will be abandoned for one reason or another.

Such an event might be a blessing in disguise for the landowner if the lease were an unsubordinated ground lease. If that were the case and the tenant abandoned the project after building only part of the improvements he planned, the landowner might have a good shot at a windfall. He might acquire something of value for no investment or effort as a result of a default by the tenant.

However, when a landowner has executed an accommodation mortgage, the most likely prospect in store for the landowner as a result of a tenant's failure to comply with his construction obligations is disaster. Mismanaged or abandoned construction would probably be a default under the accommodation mortgage; the mortgage lender would be able to accelerate the debt and foreclose against the security. Since, in the case of a subordinated ground lease, the security also includes a mortgage of the landowner's fee simple (ownership) estate in the land, the landowner might lose his land for no fault of his own.

Naturally, a landowner who agrees to execute an accommodation mortgage should exhibit uncommon concern about the project the tenant intends to construct on the land. The construction process should be unraveled and examined from tip to toe to provide a relatively safe path for the landowner. . . .

No landowner should execute a mortgage securing a construction loan unless he gets practical assurances that the debt will be repaid from a source other than a foreclosure of the land. Moreover, a tenant-developer should not be permitted to demolish an existing building or evict its occupants unless he agrees to build a much better building and provide tangible financial assurances that the much better building will be completed within a reasonable time. Similarly, a landowner who executes a subordinated ground lease needs a clause to govern eviction and demolition procedures. The clause should provide for safety valves to make sure that the landowner won't lose his income stream, his land, or any buildings on the land. The most obvious safety valve for a landowner in this regard is to make sure that the developer he deals with knows what he is doing and has the financial clout to make the development work. Assuming that the developer is an okay person, a landowner can find a measure of protection against the very real dangers of the planning and construction process by getting personal guarantees of the developer, a security deposit, a letter of credit, or a combination of them.

Although tenant-developers often do agree to provide personal guarantees or other financial assurances to keep a landowner happy during the construction process, the personal guarantees or other assurances they give are temporary. Developers want them to end when the value added to the land by the tenant-developer's construction activities is large enough to make a reasonable landowner feel that he won't lose his land. Sometimes, a landowner might be sufficiently comfortable to release the personal guarantees or third-party assurances when construction will have progressed to a point at which the new is significantly better than the old. In other circumstances, landowners won't agree to release the personal guarantees or third-party assurances until construction is complete and a new income stream replaces the old.

DETERMINING WHAT WILL BE BUILT

If a landowner is expected to execute a mortgage to finance the construction of a building that hasn't been built yet, the lease needs machinery to determine what's to be built. To get there, the lease should describe the proposed project — at least in general terms. It would be even better to adopt a set of plans and specifications in the lease, but developers aren't usually ready to commit themselves to many of the detailed features of a project when they execute a ground lease. The next best thing is for the ground lease to provide for a procedure to adopt plans and specifications that are acceptable to the landowner.

In unsubordinated ground leases, tenant-developers seldom agree to extensive limitations on the kinds of buildings that may be constructed on leased land. Landowners are usually willing to play a completely passive role when an unsubordinated ground lease is on the table. They can afford to be passive. In the case of an unsubordinated ground lease, nothing very bad can happen to the landowner if the tenant-developer's project can't make it.

But a landowner who agrees to execute an accommodation mortgage can't afford to be completely passive as to the kind of building the tenant-developer expects to build. When he executes an accommodation mortgage, he risks losing his land to the mortgagee if the development proves to be unsuccessful. If the landowner is willing to take the risk that he will lose all he owns as a result of the tenant-developer's mistake, the tenant-developer should make a reasonable effort to assure the landowner that there won't be a mistake.

Of course, landowners can't expect complete control. A landowner who is smart enough to control every aspect of development and has sufficient resources to effectuate the development doesn't need a developer. He shouldn't enter into a ground lease in the first place.

The negotiation about the description of the kind of building that may be built on the land must balance the fear of the landowner that the building will be a flop and that his birthright will be squandered against the (hopefully) superior personal and financial resources of the developer. The results should be a rather general description of the permissible improvements that will allow considerable flexibility to the developer on the one hand but protect the landowner against the construction of a white elephant on the other hand.

Ground leases are usually executed long before a tenant-developer can make a detailed commitment to construct a particular type of building. However, tenant-developers can commit themselves, even at the outset, to criteria that will be sufficient to calm even a very nervous landowner. The criteria should include at least a general description of the expected use of the building, the appropriate number of stories, and the approximate floor area. Of course, the developer should be able to choose from several different alternative types of buildings. Likewise, the criteria dealing with the height and floor area of the building should give the developer enough latitude to make prudent business decisions.

When the landowner and tenant-developer agree on criteria for the buildings to be constructed, the landowner can relax for awhile. The tenant-developer has a great deal of work to do before his next significant move. Before developers build on a site, they usually investigate site conditions, search title, prepare environmental studies, and gather other relevant information about the land. They also (usually) plan their project, organize a construction program, prepare conceptual drawings, and make arrangements to borrow the funds they need to finance construction. In the case of commercial and industrial developments, they try to lease large blocks of space to important tenants before they start building.

Ultimately, a tenant-developer will employ an architect to prepare plans and specifications for construction of the proposed improvements. Plans and specifications are developed in stages pursuant to a procedure that involves consultation, criticism, and negotiation between the developer and architect.

A landowner who executes a subordinated ground lease should want to play a role in this process. Naturally, he should not be in a position to dictate to the tenant-developer or to pass on the decorative aspects of the building. However, he should be able to review the plans and specifications at various stages and be able to squawk if the plans vary materially from the criteria established in the ground lease or fail to comply with applicable legal requirements.

The culmination of the process of developing plans and specifications is a set of detailed specifications and working drawings. The detailed specifications and working drawings later become a part of a general construction contract between the tenant-developer and a construction contractor. And when the construction contract is executed, the most anxiety-provoking part of the biography of a subordinated ground lease is about to begin.

CONSTRUCTION

The fact that a landowner has executed or is required to execute a mortgage of his land to secure a loan made to the tenant of his land should cast a shadow on the construction clause of a ground lease. The knowledge that he is obligated to execute accommodation mortgages should motivate a landowner to concentrate on the possibility that he risks losing his land or a part of it as a result of a mishap in the construction process. He should negotiate the construction clause with this idea in mind and insist on inserting clauses that will provide him with safeguards against the kind of turbulence you see when construction is botched.

As I mentioned before, developers don't usually build buildings with their own money. Long before they start building, developers busy themselves with making arrangements for loans to finance the cost of development. Most developers won't even break ground for construction until construction loan commitments for the project have been executed. Moreover, the mortgage securing the construction loan is also usually executed and recorded before construction begins.

In the case of a subordinated ground lease, the landowner is asked to execute the mortgage at the same time the developer does so. Accordingly, a subordinated ground lease landlord does not have the luxury of inspecting completed buildings before he executes an accommodation mortgage. He can't ask that the construction mortgage closing be postponed until the end of construction so that he can determine whether the construction conforms to the ground lease, to the plans and specifications, and to legal requirements. He must execute the mortgage document at the beginning of the construction process.

Unless a subordinated ground lease provides for appropriate prerequisites to the obligation of the landowner to execute an accommodation mortgage and provides for additional safeguards after the mortgage is executed, the only thing the landlord will be able to do to protect himself will be to pray that he will be shielded from harm by divine providence or by the integrity of the tenant-developer.

If I were a landowner negotiating a subordinated ground lease, I'd insist on a lot of prerequisites to the obligation to execute an accommodation mortgage. However, there is not sufficient space to present a careful analysis of the kinds of prerequisites a landowner should demand.

The focus of this sermon is narrower. For now, I'll concentrate on how a subordinated ground lease should regulate the construction process to provide an additional safety net for the landowner after the accommodation mortgage is executed.

Problems Directly Related to Construction Loan Agreements

One crucial principle for a landowner's negotiator is to make sure that the tenant complies with all of its obligations as the mortgagor under the accommodation mortgage and all of its covenants as borrower under the additional documents executed in connection with an accommodation mortgage. In the case of a construction loan mortgage, one of the additional documents borrowers (mortgagors) are required to execute is a construction loan agreement. Among other things, construction loan agreements usually set forth procedures pursuant to which the loan proceeds are to be disbursed and provide for many covenants and warranties on the part of the borrower-mortgagor-developer (who, in the context of a ground lease, is also the tenant).

Mortgage documents often contain cross-default provisions under which the mortgage debt will be accelerated in case of a default under a construction loan agreement. Needless to say, the acceleration of a mortgage debt caused by a default under a construction loan agreement is just as destructive to the interests of a landowner as the acceleration of a mortgage debt caused by a default under the mortgage.

To lay a foundation for a series of clauses that cumulatively provide a safeguard for the landowner, the construction clause of the ground lease should include a covenant by the tenant to comply with all of the tenant's obligations as borrower under a construction loan agreement executed in connection with an accommodation mortgage (as well as the accommodation mortgage itself and all other agreements executed in connection with the accommodation mortgage).

However, a landowner can't rely on the expectation that the construction loan agreement of any lender that might commit to the project will include all of the clauses necessary to minimize potential construction problems. So, it's still better to provide for additional covenants in the ground lease to govern individual construction issues that parallel many of the covenants customarily found in construction loan agreements.

With this principle in mind, let's review some of the basic questions that should be considered.

What Will Be Constructed?

Naturally, a landowner who encumbers his property with a mortgage that secures his tenant's construction loan wants to know that the loan proceeds will be applied to the construction of an economically and structurally sound building. This goal can be achieved in part by a careful description of the buildings the tenant is permitted to construct on the land. As of the date on which a ground lease of the so-called subordinated variety is executed, a tenant-developer isn't ready to commit himself fully as to the details of the buildings he intends to build. Consequently, I recommended that the buildings and other improvements be described in the ground lease in a general way and that guidelines be adopted for the preparation and negotiation of, and agreement on, detailed plans and specifications after the execution of the ground lease itself. In the course of these post-lease execution negotiations, the landowner should see to it that the detailed plans and specifications describe a legal, structurally sound, and economically viable building that fits harmoniously with its environment.

To complete this thought, the landowner should propose that the lease require that the buildings be constructed in accordance with the detailed plans and specifications.

How Good Will the Quality of the Work Be?

The tenant-developer should be required to construct the buildings and other improvements in a good and workmanlike manner and in accordance with good construction practices. Construction should conform to all applicable requirements of governmental bodies and the insurance companies with which the tenant is required to insure the building.

When Will Construction Begin?

Until a landowner actually executes an accommodation mortgage, the landowner needn't lose too much sleep worrying about when construction will start. As long as the tenant pays rent every month and doesn't ask the landowner to execute an accommodation mortgage, the absence of construction shouldn't be excessively troublesome.

A landowner's concern about the beginning of construction should increase significantly when an accommodation mortgage securing a construction loan is executed. . . . [A] construction loan agreement customarily requires that construction begin by an agreed-on date. The landowner needs parallel protection in the ground lease. To this end, the construction clause of a subordinated ground lease should require the tenant to begin construction within a fixed number of days after a construction loan accommodation mortgage is executed by the landowner (perhaps instead of a fixed number of days after the execution of the lease).

Who Will Come Up with the Money to Pay for the Work?

Construction lenders don't like to be the sole source of funds for a project. They often demand to know that the developer has sufficient resources to bridge the gap between the project development cost and the proceeds of the construction loan.

Similarly, a landowner should negotiate for a ground lease provision that requires his tenant-developer to provide information on the developer's ability to pay for the construction he is about to begin. To this end, the developer should agree to submit a budget to the landowner before construction begins. The budget should break down the project development cost in reasonable detail and list the sources of funding. . . .

When Will Construction Be Finished?

Construction loan agreements also customarily require the borrower to prosecute construction diligently and to complete construction before a fixed outside date designated in the agreement. Subordinated ground leases should contain parallel clauses.

HOW SHOULD THE PROCEEDS OF CONSTRUCTION LOANS BE HANDLED?

If you're a landowner who is about to execute a subordinated ground lease, you'd better do some serious thinking about what will happen to the proceeds of the loan to be secured by the mortgage you will be bound to execute. It's one thing to agree to burden your land with the lien of a debt to repay funds used by your tenant to build a building on your land. It's quite another to encumber your property to secure a loan when the proceeds of the loan will be used by the tenant-developer to finance his latest venture into professional sports.

Lenders are usually very careful about disbursing construction loan proceeds. Most of the time, a construction loan agreement will provide that the loan proceeds are to be disbursed in stages as construction progresses. Typically, they provide for monthly disbursement of loan proceeds to the borrower. The developer (who, in the case of a ground lease, is also the tenant) is able to get the money only in bits and pieces as his contractors perform the construction work, and he must use the funds to pay off the contractors.

The amount of the disbursements is usually determined by reference to certificates of architects or engineers. The architects or engineers, in turn, base their certificates on their observations, on tests they make, and on requisitions submitted by contractors and subcontractors.

[However,] a landowner who executes a subordinated ground lease can't assume that the proceeds of the tenant's construction loan will be disbursed prudently or in accordance with the customary procedure.

The ground lease itself should provide that the loan proceeds will be disbursed as construction progresses and pursuant to an orderly procedure. The procedure should include a requirement for disbursement pursuant to requisitions of contractors and certification by a dependable architect or engineer on the basis of his observations and testing. The tenant should be obliged to invest a significant amount of his own funds in the construction before any of the proceeds of the construction loan are disbursed. The percentage of the work that has been completed should always exceed the percentage of the construction loan proceeds that have been disbursed. The lender should be required to withhold a part (usually 10 percent) of the loan proceeds to which the tenant-developer would have been entitled otherwise to make sure that sufficient funds remain on hand to permit the project to be completed. If the cost of completing the work at any given time exceeds the part of the loan proceeds that haven't yet been disbursed, the tenant should be required to advance more of his own funds to bridge the gap.

Unlike a mortgagee, a ground lease landlord is not lending funds and doesn't have the opportunity to take charge of the disbursement proceeds. However, he is taking a special risk as the construction loan is being disbursed and deserves to know what's going on. A subordinated ground lease should require the tenant-developer to report monthly to the landowner on the progress of construction and the disbursement of the construction loan proceeds. Copies of the contractors' requisitions and the architect's or engineer's certificates should be forwarded to the landowner.

PROBLEMS NOT DIRECTLY RELATED TO CONSTRUCTION LOAN AGREEMENTS

. . . Subcontractors who construct improvements to property on behalf of developers and don't get paid by the developers are often in a position to seek payment from the value of the property itself. They can do this pursuant to the lien laws of various states. . . . A mechanic's lienor and a materialman's lienor have the right to foreclose against the liened property to recover the amount he should have been paid.

This is another way for the landowner to lose his land. Of course, a landowner really doesn't care whether he loses his land to an accommodation mortgagee or a mechanic's lienor.

There's no absolutely certain antidote for this poison. Even the most beautifully drafted ground lease construction clause is likely to be ineffective in the event of the tenant-developer's inability to cope with the process of constructing improvements to the land and paying the contractors who supply the materials and perform the work.

What can be done? A landowner who agrees to execute an accommodation mortgage can find a measure of protection in a covenant that requires that the improvements be constructed pursuant to a fixed price (or guaranteed maximum) price contract between the developer and a reputable and financially responsible general contractor. This kind of arrangement is not the only way to compensate a general contractor for constructing improvements, and many developers prefer not to deal with general contractors at all. But a landowner who executes a subordinated ground lease is usually better off when the tenant-developer enters into a construction contract with a general contractor, and he's usually still better off when the construction contract provides for a fixed or guaranteed maximum price.

Frequently, developers are happy to employ general contractors to perform the necessary construction work because developers are usually required by their construction lenders to execute personal guarantees that the improvements will be constructed in accordance with the construction loan agreement. At least to the extent they can, they like to pass on this obligation to a general contractor who, in turn, agrees to complete the job for a fixed price or a guaranteed maximum price.

To button up the fixed or guaranteed price general contract a bit, a landowner might bargain further for a requirement that the tenant-developer obtain a performance bond and payment bond from an impeccable, financially secure surety company with respect to the contract.

Because a developer's own personal guarantee of construction depends in part on the ability of the general construction contractor to fulfill his obligations, developers themselves are naturally concerned about the financial resources of the general contractor. Those who aren't keen on their ability to evaluate the financial position of general contractors willingly turn to surety companies for aid. Surety companies are often willing to issue performance bonds with respect to contractors' obligations under construction contracts, and their willingness usually turns on their evaluation of the reliability and creditworthiness of the contractor.

Performance bonds are essentially limited guarantees by deep-pocketed surety companies that the principal obligor (the contractor) will live up to his obligations under a construction contract. A performance bond enables a developer to look to the surety company in case the general contractor fails to live up to his obligations. However, a performance bond is not an insurance policy. The obligation of the surety depends partly on the performance by the developer of his obligations (principally, the obligation to pay the contractor) under the construction contract. Sureties also limit their liability by a fixed amount or "penal sum," which customarily has been the same amount as the contract price under the construction contract.

What a landowner can expect to get out of a performance bond is the comfort that the tenant-developer will have additional muscle to deal with the kind of trouble that you find daily in the course of construction. . . .

A payment bond (which usually accompanies a performance bond) assures subcontractors that the general contractor will pay them. A payment bond helps a tenant-developer and a landowner in that it encourages subcontractors to bid. In that respect, you might see a payment bond as a way to keep the bidding for subcontracts competitive. That, in turn, may help keep the construction contract price low. It also helps the landowner and developer in that a subcontractor who is actually paid by a surety is not a potential source of trouble to a developer or landowner.

If you're about to represent a landowner ready to execute a subordinated ground lease, this stuff has probably been frightening to you. But don't cry. You're not alone with your fears; the construction process is probably almost as frightening to developers and the people who represent them. To make the construction process work, they customarily risk their own cash and provide personal guarantees to construction lenders. . . .

CONCLUSION

I would have liked to have ended this article on a note of optimism, but I can't. As I searched for some harmonious chord, I conjured visions of plans and specifications that contain no provision for heating or air conditioning, construction contractors who refuse to pay subcontractors for no good reason, jurisdictional strikes, incompetent supervision, football pools among the skilled tradesmen, fraudulent certification, and organized theft of materials.

If you're looking for euphoria, maybe you should become a negligence lawyer.

b.   Real or Chattel Mortgage

Harbel Oil Co. v. Steele

83 Ariz. 181, 318 P.2d 359 (1957) (page 210 supra)

c.   Some Concerns of the Leasehold Mortgagee

(1)   Alienation Restraints

City of Gainesville v. Charter Leasing Corp.

483 So. 2d 465 (Fla. D. Ct. App. 1986)

ERVIN, Judge.

The City of Gainesville (City) appeals from a final judgment foreclosing a mortgage secured by a lease on certain premises owned by the City at its airport. The City urges on appeal that the lower court erroneously entered final judgment in favor of appellee on the ground that certain conditions stated in the lease were not complied with by appellee or its predecessors; that a default had occurred under the terms of the lease, and therefore the lower court had no right to enter foreclosure of the mortgage on the leasehold. We affirm.

On June 28, 1979, the City, as lessor, entered into an agreement with Sopwith Camel, Inc., leasing to the latter certain premises located at the Gainesville Regional Airport, in order for Sopwith to conduct a "fixed based" operation, providing aircraft fueling services. Sopwith, in turn, subleased its rights under the lease, with the City's approval, to Dewkat II, Inc. (Dewkat). Dewkat thereafter obtained a loan from the Wauchula State Bank, mortgaging its leasehold as security for the loan. Wauchula State Bank assigned the mortgage and the underlying note to Charter Air Center, which in turn transferred the same to appellee, Charter Leasing Corporation. None of the assignments following the assignment of the note and mortgage to Wauchula State Bank were approved by the City, as, the City contends, the terms of the lease required.

Dewkat eventually defaulted on the note and mortgage and appellee Charter Leasing Corporation brought suit against Dewkat, seeking both foreclosure of the mortgage and declaratory relief as to its interests in the lease. Later joined as a defendant, the City affirmatively defended below, and argues now on appeal that because Dewkat violated certain provisions of its lease with the City before the assignment of the note and mortgage to appellee, and of which appellee was aware, a default under the terms of the lease occurred; that the lease was thereafter terminated, and appellee was therefore not entitled to possession of the premises. The specific breaches of the lease which the City contends occurred, insofar as they are material to this appeal, include: . . . the failure of Dewkat or appellee to seek approval from the City for the transfer of the note and mortgage to anyone other than a bank or lending institution for financing purposes, as required by paragraph 15.a. of the lease. . . .

The City next argues that the lower court ignored the provisions of paragraph 15.a., requiring the City's approval of a transfer of any interest in the lease for financing purposes unless such transfer is to a bank or lending institution. Paragraph 15.a. states in pertinent part: "Except for sale or assignment of this lease to a bank or lending institution for financing purposes, no sublease, transfer or assignment by the lessee of this lease or of any part hereof or interest herein, directly or indirectly, voluntarily or involuntarily, shall be made unless such sublease, transfer or assignment is first approved by the CITY in writing, which approval shall not be unreasonably withheld." (Emphasis supplied).

In finding for Charter Leasing Corporation, the lower court determined that the assignments from Wauchula State Bank to Charter Air Center, and from it to Charter Leasing Corporation were not assignments pursuant to paragraph 15.a. of the lease, because the assignments were of a promissory note and a mortgage — not a lease. As such they were not covered by the terms of paragraph 15.a., and therefore no prior approval was required by the City in writing. We agree.

The mortgage upon the leased property given as security for the note to Wauchula State Bank by Dewkat, and subsequently assigned, was not, under the terms of the lease, a "sublease, transfer or assignment by the lessee of this lease or of any . . . interest herein." (e.s.) Section 697.02, Florida Statutes, in effect at all applicable times involved, provides: "A mortgage shall be held to be a specific lien on the property therein described, and not a conveyance of the legal title or of the right of possession." A mortgage is a species of intangible property, creating a lien on the land, but is not an interest in the land. Waldock v. Iba, 114 Fla. 786, 153 So. 915 (1934). Because Florida is a lien theory state, the "assignment of a mortgage lien is not 'a conveyance' or a 'transfer' of 'any interest' in land covered by the mortgage, but is only an assignment or transfer of the lien created by the mortgage." United of Florida, Inc. v. Illini Federal Savings and Loan Association, 341 So. 2d 793, 794 (Fla. 2d DCA 1977) (quoting Garrett v. Fernauld, 63 Fla. 434, 57 So. 671, 672 (1912)).

As an assignee of a mortgage on real property cannot acquire an interest in real property, neither can an assignee of a mortgage on a leasehold of real property acquire an interest in the leasehold. Such a transfer therefore cannot be deemed to violate a non-assignable clause of the lease. "Since a mortgage in Florida is not a transfer of title to the leasehold, but merely a lien upon it . . . the voluntary action of a lessee in mortgaging the leasehold is not such a transfer as would violate a non-assignable provision." Great Southern Aircraft Corp. v. Kraus, 132 So. 2d 608, 609-10 (Fla. 3d DCA 1961); accord Gould, Inc. v. Hydro-Ski International Corporation, 287 So. 2d 115, 116 (Fla. 4th DCA 1974); see also 36 Fla. Jur. 2d Mortgages § 22 (1982).

The judgment below is in its entirety
Affirmed.

JOANOS and BARFIELD, JJ., concur.

NOTES AND QUESTIONS

1. Great Southern Aircraft Corp. v. Kraus, 132 So. 2d 608 (Fla. D. Ct. App. 1962), cited in the court's opinion, involved the validity of a leasehold mortgage given without the lessor's consent where the ground lease required consent for any sale or assignment. Besides holding that under the lien theory of mortgages, the mortgaging of the leasehold was not a leasehold assignment, the court issued *dictum* that any transfer resulting from a mortgage default would not require the landlord's consent either, as this would be an involuntary transfer by operation of law. Would this *dictum* include the transfer of the lease in lieu of foreclosure? But see Whalen, Commercial Ground Leases 12-2 (2002) ("In 'lien theory', the original mortgage may not be an assignment, but the sale at foreclosure is").

2. The *Great Southern Aircraft Corp.* opinion also cited several other "operation of law" situations that a generalized "non-assignment without consent" clause would not reach: Hockman v. Sunhew Petroleum, 92 Mont. 174, 11 P.2d 778 (1932) (judgment execution); Miller v. Fredeking, 101 W. Va. 643, 133 S.E. 375 (1926) (bankruptcy); Crouse v. Mitchell, 130 Mich. 347, 90 N.W. 32 (1902) (assignment for benefit of creditors).

3. As you know, a few states still regard themselves as "title" states. In such places, the mortgaging of a leasehold may be subject to a non-assignment proviso. Even in lien states, although the original mortgage would not be deemed an assignment, and, arguably, the transfer of the lease at a mortgage foreclosure sale would be an "exempt" transaction, if the purchaser at the foreclosure sale suffers the restraint, this may restrict the lender's ability to realize upon its collateral.

4. Wholly apart from wishing an unimpaired ability to obtain mortgage financing, the ground-tenant must also consider that it may someday become a mortgagee itself should it sell the lease and take back a junior purchase money mortgage.

(2)   Liability for the Performance of Leasehold Covenants

Bloor v. Chase Manhattan Mortgage and Realty Trust

511 F. Supp. 12 (S.D.N.Y. 1979)

WHITMAN KNAPP, District Judge.

This is an action by James Bloor, Trustee in Bankruptcy of Invesco Holding Corporation, brought for breach of a lease agreement against defendant Chase Manhattan Mortgage and Realty Trust ("Chase REIT"). Defendant Chase REIT has moved for summary judgment. As set forth in the complaint, the pertinent facts are:

On November 1, 1974, plaintiff was appointed Trustee of Invesco Holding Corporation in proceedings for reorganization of certain corporations under Chapter X of the Bankruptcy Act. At that time, he took title in fee simple from the 315 West Fifty Seventh Street Corporation of certain real property located at 315 West 57th Street and 330 West 58th Street, New York, N.Y. (the "premises"). Since 1961, the premises had been subject to a ground lease between 315 West Fifty Seventh Street Corporation as landlord, and Hyman and Irving Shapiro, as tenants (hereinafter referred to in the singular as "tenant"). In 1971 the Shapiros mortgaged their interest under the ground lease to Chase REIT.

Plaintiff upon his appointment as trustee, became the successor to the landlord's interest under the ground lease. The ground lease, as amended in 1975, provided for the payment by the tenant to the landlord as "rent" and "additional rent" all real estate taxes, water and sewage charges, interest and principal payments on a certain first mortgage to the New York City Employees Retirement System, a monthly deposit of $17,000 to a certain escrow fund to be held by the landlord, and a net rental of $200,000 per year.

The lease also contained a provision (in Article EIGHTEENTH) that upon its termination by default or summary proceedings, the tenant should continue to be liable to the landlord for rent and additional rent as it came due (less any net rent collected by the landlord for use of the premises), and gave the landlord at any time after default the option of serving a notice on the tenant requiring him to pay "liquidated damages" measured by the total rent and additional rent then remaining due, less the fair rental value of the premises for the remaining term of the lease.

In April of 1976, following the Shapiros' failure to meet their obligations under the ground lease, Chase REIT began making payments due the landlord. On July 15, 1976 Chase REIT accepted from the Shapiros an assignment of their interest as tenant under the ground lease; it did not, however, contract to assume the tenant's obligations.

On October 29, 1976, Chase REIT assigned all of its interest in the premises to Stevens & Edwards, Inc. and ceased making rental payments. Prior to such assignment, Chase REIT had neglected to make water and tax payments totalling approximately $127,489.

On November 15, 1976, the ground lease being in default, the trustee gave written notice to Stevens & Edwards and to Chase REIT that it was electing to terminate the ground lease as of November 26, 1976.

On January 10, 1977 the trustee commenced a summary proceeding against Stevens & Edwards in the Civil Court of the City of New York. In its petition the trustee alleged, as its first cause of action, that Stevens & Edwards was improperly holding over after the expiration of the ground lease on November 26, 1976, and as a second cause of action, that Stevens & Edwards was in default in the payment of rent.

On February 11, 1977 a stipulation was entered into in open court terminating the summary proceeding. The stipulation provided that a judgment giving possession of the premises to the trustee would be entered pursuant to the holdover cause of action, but that the claim for nonpayment of rent would be withdrawn. The parties also agreed that in the event that Stevens & Edwards made the appropriate payments under the lease within sixty days, the trustee would reinstate it as tenant.

On April 29, 1977, pursuant to a warrant issued in the summary proceeding, possession of the premises was delivered to the trustee. On August 10, 1977 the trustee served on Chase REIT notice of election to claim liquidated damages under Article EIGHTEENTH.

The trustee seeks to collect from Chase REIT all rent and additional rent unpaid under the lease. Because Chase REIT never contracted to assume any of the tenant's liabilities, there is no privity of contract between it and the trustee. Therefore, the trustee can prevail only to the extent it can establish liability under the doctrine of privity of estate. See Tate v. McCormick (Gen. Term 2d Dept. 1880) 23 Hun. 218; Mann v. Munch Brewery (1919) 225 N.Y. 189, 121 N.E. 746.

There is no doubt as to Chase REIT's liability accruing prior to October 29, 1976, when Chase REIT assigned to Stevens & Edwards its interest under the lease. The critical questions pertain to obligations accruing during the period between that day and April 29, 1977 while Stevens & Edwards was purportedly in possession of the premises, and subsequent thereto, when the trustee had concededly accepted possession of the premises from the marshal in the dispossess proceedings.

It is the trustee's position: first, that the assignment to Stevens & Edwards was a sham as Chase REIT was in fact in possession at all times until April 29, 1977 when the marshal delivered the premises, and second, that on November 15, 1976 when the trustee served its notice to terminate, Chase REIT, as tenant actually in possession, became liable under Article EIGHTEENTH for all rent and additional rent until the end of the term, such liability to be measured until August 10, 1977 (when the trustee exercised its Article EIGHTEENTH option for liquidated damages) by the total amount of rent and additional rents as they accrued less any monies the trustee may have received by leasing the premises, and thereafter by the liquidated damage formula.

Chase REIT, on the other hand, claims that it terminated its privity of estate by the October 29th assignment to Stevens & Edwards and thereby relieved itself of all subsequent liability to the trustee; and that, in any event, it cannot be held liable for any payments falling due after April 29, 1977 when the trustee accepted possession from the marshal.

These questions are presented to us by Chase REIT's motion for summary judgment. For reasons that follow, we find the existence of a question of fact with respect to the period prior to the day on which the trustee accepted possession from the marshal, but grant summary judgment with respect to any liability falling due thereafter.

I. The Period Prior to the Trustee's Acceptance of Possession from the Marshal

Ordinarily a person is liable only for the obligations he agrees to assume. Accordingly, a mortgagee of a lease will not be held to have assumed the liabilities of his mortgagor to the latter's landlord. However, the ancient common law doctrine of privity of estate is an exception to this rule. Although the mortgagee is not a party to the landlord-tenant agreement, and is therefore not in privity of contract with the landlord, if the mortgagee accepts assignment of the mortgagor's lease and enters into possession of the premises, he comes into privity of estate with the landlord, thereby becoming liable for any of the tenant's obligations which accrue during such privity of estate, provided that the obligation "touches and concerns" the land. Mann v. Munch Brewery, supra (at 195, 121 N.E. 746).

Apparently the common law judges who created this doctrine recognized it to be a harsh one when applied to a non-assuming mortgagee, and therefore fashioned a relatively easy escape hatch which allowed the mortgagee to relieve himself of all obligations to the landlord by any valid assignment of the lease to a third party. It is Chase REIT's position that it did so assign the lease to Stevens & Edwards on October 26, 1976, and that summary judgment should be granted with respect to any liability said to have accrued thereafter. The trustee, on the other hand, contends that this assignment was "colorable" and fraudulent and should be wholly disregarded. It is our conclusion that while under applicable New York decisions it may well be difficult for the trustee to establish his position, a question of fact exists with respect to any obligations accruing prior to April 29, 1977, when the trustee took possession of the property.

The most elaborate discussion of the privity of estate doctrine as applicable to the situation before us is to be found in the various opinions in Century Holding Co. v. Ebling Brewing Co. (App. Term, 1st Dept. 1917), 98 Misc. 226, 162 N.Y.S. 1061 (App. Term, 1st Dept. 1917), 167 N.Y.S. 52 (1st Dept. 1918), 185 App. Div. 292, 173 N.Y.S. 49. In that case, a mortgagee who had accepted a lease assignment, thereafter attempted to relieve itself of liability by assigning the lease to one of its employees. The first opinion (written by Hon. Irving Lehman, subsequently Chief Judge of the New York Court of Appeals, with the concurrence of Hon. Edward R. Finch also a subsequent Court of Appeals judge) reversed a judgment for the plaintiff landlord which had been entered on a jury verdict finding the assignment to have been "colorable" and fraudulent. In his opinion, Judge Lehman set forth the two necessary elements for the establishment of privity of estate: the mortgagee must have accepted assignment of the lease, and thereafter must have entered upon and assumed possession of the premises.[9] Once such possession has been assumed the mortgagee becomes liable for rent accruing during his possession, and for all "covenants in the original lease which run with the land." (162 N.Y.S. at 1064, quoting Stewart v. Long Island R.R. Co. (1886) 102 N.Y 601, 8 N.E. 200.) This liability could be terminated, however, by reassignment of the lease to any third party, "together with the note for which the lease was security." (162 N.Y.S. at 1065). Judge Lehman ruled that so long as such assignment was legally effective, it could not be found "colorable" and fraudulent simply because it was made to an assetless

---

9. In Lynch v. Joseph (4th Dept. 1930) 228 App. Div. 367, 240 N.Y.S. 176, it was held that possession need not be actual, but could be symbolized by delivery and acceptance of the assignment.

employee of the assignor solely for the purpose of relieving the assignor of liability. Furthermore, the fact that the subtenant of the assignor remained in possession of the premises would not defeat the assignment. Concluding that the combination of all of these factors was insufficient to sustain a jury's finding either that the assignment was colorable and fraudulent, or that the assignee had been acting as "agent" for the assignor, the Appellate Term reversed and ordered a new trial.

The second Appellate Term decision in *Century Holding* was upon appeal from a directed verdict against the landlord. Observing that "collateral security cannot be effectively assigned without an assignment of the debt which it secures," the court found a question of fact to exist as to whether the assignor had actually assigned to its employee its interest in the note which had been secured by the lease, and ordered yet another trial on that issue (167 N.Y.S. at 54).

The third opinion, upon direct appeal to the Appellate Division, resulted in sustaining a jury verdict in the landlord's favor. That jury had specifically found that the note had not been assigned to the employee, and also that the assignment of the lease had been made in bad faith since the defendant-assignor had actually intended to "continue in possession, dominion, and control of the premises." (173 N.Y.S. at 51.) Although the Appellate Division ruled that the evidence fully supported the jury's finding that the note had never been assigned to the employee, it did not rest its decision upholding the verdict on that finding. Rather, it went on to determine (largely upon the considerations Judge Lehman had previously found inadequate) that the employee had been acting as "mere agent or dummy" of the defendant assignee, and that there had therefore been no "bona fide transfer of the lease . . . which would relieve the defendant of its liability to pay rent." (167 N.Y.S. at 54.)

So far as we can determine, these are the most recent New York opinions dealing extensively with an assignee's attempt to end privity of estate liability by assignment to a third party. (See also Lynch v. Joseph (4th Dept. 1930) 228 App. Div. 367, 240 N.Y.S. 176, for a brief reference to assignment as relief from liability under privity of estate.) Although it requires little discussion to demonstrate that these opinions require us to hold that the question is one of fact which cannot be disposed of on summary judgment (even Judge Lehman sent the matter back for a new trial), we have attempted a detailed analysis in the hope that it will encourage the parties to do further research which will shed more light on how the question should be resolved at trial.

II. THE PERIOD AFTER THE TRUSTEE OBTAINED POSSESSION FROM THE MARSHAL

The trustee's argument that he is entitled to recover damages for the loss of rent until the end of the lease's original term is based on the following language in Article EIGHTEENTH:

> In the event that this lease be terminated by summary proceedings, or otherwise, as above provided, and whether or not the premises be re-let, the Landlord shall be entitled to recover from the Tenant and the Tenant shall pay to the Landlord as follows: . . . (b) An amount equal to the amount of all rent and additional rent reserved under this lease, less the net rent, if any collected by the Landlord on re-letting the demised premises which shall be due and payable by the Tenant to the

Landlord on the several days on which the rent and the additional rent reserved under this Lease would have become due and payable . . . Provided however, that if this lease shall be terminated after a default specified in subdivision (2) of Article SEVENTEENTH, the Landlord may at any time thereafter, at its option, which shall be exercised by the service of a notice on the Tenant, collect from the Tenant and the Tenant shall pay . . . (liquidated damages measured by the difference between the rent due for the remainder of the term less the fair rental value of the premises).

It will be recalled that the trustee did not send the notice called for in the last quoted proviso until some time after it had acquired possession from the marshal and any privity of estate existing between it and Chase REIT had been terminated. The trustee contends, however, that the words "shall pay" in the third line of subdivision (1) fix the entire liability at the time of default, and that the trustee's exercise of its option merely governs the measure of damages.

In view of the fact that provisions like the one quoted are commonplace in New York, we find it altogether remarkable that there does not seem to be a single case deciding whether a landlord can, in circumstances such as these, invoke such a provision against one whose obligations to the landlord arose solely through privity of estate. The parties have cited no such case and our independent research has uncovered none.

However, it is our conclusion that the New York Court of Appeals, if ever presented with the question, would decide it against the landlord. In the first place, the New York courts seem to recognize privity of estate as a harsh doctrine when applied against one who has never contracted to assume any obligation.[10] Moreover, the basic purpose of the doctrine as we read the cases is to provide the landlord with some assurance that the day-to-day obligations of its lease will be attended to by a person actually in possession, and it is unnecessary to such purpose to impose upon the temporary possessor future penalties that the original tenant had contracted to assume.

Moreover, the New York Court of Appeals by dictum has given clear support to the position. In Mann v. Munch Brewery, supra, it was found that the assignee unlike Chase REIT in the case at bar had contracted to assume the obligations of the lease. The assignee was accordingly held liable under a clause providing that after the tenant had been dispossessed he shall nonetheless "continue to remain liable for the payment of the rent . . . until the expiration of the entire term thereof." (at 194, 121 N.E. 746.) There was clear dictum, however, that he would not have been so liable had he not contracted to assume the lease's obligations. (at 194, 121 N.E. 746.)

We accordingly conclude that Chase REIT is not liable for any rents or additional rent falling due after the day in which the marshal delivered possession to the trustee and grant partial summary judgment to that extent, but otherwise deny the motion for summary judgment.

---

10. Its harshness is aptly illustrated by the facts at bar. So far as we can determine, Chase REIT gained absolutely nothing by accepting the assignment from the Shapiros. It could have effectively managed the property through their agency. Or, if it were desirable to get them out of the picture, it could have caused them to assign the lease directly to Stevens & Edwards, thus avoiding the whole question.

NOTES AND QUESTIONS

1. Judge Knapp states that the mortgagee, upon taking possession of the premises after an assignment of the mortgagor's lease, becomes liable for any of the "tenant's obligations which accrue during such privity of estate, provided that the obligation 'touches and concerns' the land." When does a leasehold covenant "touch" and not "touch and concern" the land?

2. Maryland is a so-called "intermediate title" state, whereby the mortgagee is entitled to the right of immediate possession upon a mortgage default. In Williams v. Safe Deposit & Trust Co., 167 Md. 499, 175 A. 331 (1934), Williams held a leasehold mortgage on which a default occurred. Although the mortgagee never actually took possession, the court held that Williams qua assignee would be liable to perform the leasehold covenants following the mortgage default.

3. In South Lakeview Plaza v. Citizens National Bank of Greater St. Louis, 703 S.W.2d 84 (Mo. Ct. App. 1985), tenant assigned its lease to bank as a condition to receiving a $95,000 loan, and the bank (surprisingly) assumed the lease. Despite the bank's assertion that the parties intended to create only a collateral security mortgage, the court treated the assignment as absolutely effective, regardless of the purpose of the assignment, and would not apply Missouri law that the mortgage of a leasehold estate in itself does not effect an assignment.

(3)   The Durability of the Underlying Security Interest

Old Stone Capital Corp. v. John Hoene Implement Corp.

647 F. Supp. 916 (D. Idaho 1986)

RYAN, District Judge.

This is a diversity action seeking foreclosure of certain real property. On December 10, 1979, various documents were executed with the ultimate effect being that Old Stone Capital Corporation made a $250,000.00 operating capital loan to John Hoene Implement Corporation (JHI) (now defunct). JHI was the lessee of the subject commercial property owned by Philomena Davis, formerly known as Philomena Hoene. In order to secure the loan from Old Stone, JHI granted Old Stone a leasehold deed of trust on its leasehold estate in the Davis property. Accompanying the deed of trust was an assignment of rents and a security agreement on personal property. On the same date, JHI and Davis entered into an amended lease for a new term of ten years, coextensive with the term of the loan. Davis agreed to enter into a subordination agreement and to sign an estoppel certificate. Copies of all of these documents are appended to the memorandum of Davis in support of her Motion for Summary Judgment. JHI defaulted on the loan and Old Stone took possession of the personal property which secured the loan and now seeks to foreclose on the subject commercial property.

Davis contends that she agreed to subordinate only her leasehold interest in the property in question, as that was the only interest which was the subject of the leasehold mortgage executed by JHI. Old Stone contends that Davis agreed to subordinate not only her interest in the leasehold, but her entire fee interest in the property to Old Stone's deed of trust. It is for this court, on the cross-motions for summary judgment, to determine whether the documents are unambiguous and the question may be answered as a matter of law, or whether ambiguities are present necessitating a trial.

Davis argues that she only granted subordination on her interest in the leasehold estate. In doing so, she states that she subjected her interest in the leasehold to foreclosure, which would mean that the sale of the leasehold would not be subject to the obligation to pay rent for the remaining term of the lease and she would lose that lease money. In the converse situation, if the leasehold estate were simply sold without the existence of a subordination, then the obligation to pay rent would remain in the buyer of the lease. She notes that the total lease payment after January 1, 1980, to the expiration of the lease would be $144,000.00.

Davis argues that the subordination agreement could only prioritize the interest which Old Stone had, and the only interest which it had was in the leasehold. Since subordination merely changes priorities, a leasehold mortgage could not be transformed into a fee mortgage through subordination. Finally, she points out that if Old Stone had intended for her to subordinate her fee interest and not her interest in the lease, she could have executed her own mortgage of her fee interest. Old Stone contends that there is nothing conceptually disjointed in subordinating a fee interest to provide incentive for a mortgage on a leasehold interest.

While Old Stone vehemently argues that the subordination is not a mortgage, it appears that the subordination should be characterized as a mortgage. In *Rush v. Anestos*, 104 Idaho 630, 661 P.2d 1229 (1983), the court stated: I.C. § 45-901 defines a mortgage as a "contract excepting a trust deed or transfer in trust by which specific property is hypothecated for the performance of an act without the necessity of a change of possession." I.C. § 45-904 provides that "[e]very transfer of an interest in property other than in trust to secure the performance of any obligation of the trustor or other person named in the trust instrument, made only as a security for the performance of another act, is to be deemed a mortgage." A security instrument, however it is called, is a mortgage whenever real property is encumbered as security for a debt or liability. *Kendrick v. Davis*, 75 Wash. 2d 456, 452 P.2d 222 (1969). Id. 104 Idaho at 634, 661 P.2d 1229 (citation omitted) (footnote omitted). The court further cited *Kendrick* for the proposition that an instrument may in form be a deed or an assignment, but if the intent is to use the property as security, it will be a mortgage.

Old Stone argues that the subordination agreement was an inducement and not security for the loan. In its supplemental memorandum, the plaintiff states:

> The issue is whether the ultimate effect of these transactions was one in which Davis had mortgaged her property to secure the debts of another. The answer is decidedly "no." Davis mortgaged nothing. She pledged nothing. She executed no personal guaranty. She did nothing to otherwise secure, i.e., become liable for, JHIC's debt. Rather, Davis became junior in priority, i.e., subordinated her interest in the property to Old Stone's deed of trust lien.

Supplemental Memorandum Re: Summary judgment, filed August 14, 1986, at 12. Davis could subordinate her interest in the leasehold and become "junior in priority, *i.e., subordinated* her interest in the property to Old Stone's deed of trust lien." *Id.* However, the subordination of an interest cannot be accomplished if the beneficiary of the subordination does not have a like interest which prior to the subordination is junior. Davis could not subordinate her fee interest as Old Stone did not have an interest in the fee and, therefore, no interest which would become senior to her interest in the fee. If, in fact, the intent was for Davis to face the risk she now encounters, in reality she has mortgaged her fee. While Old Stone argues that Davis did nothing to secure, i.e., become liable for JHI's debt, it seems that the obligation of JHI was to repay the loan and the purpose of having the fee interest at risk would be to enable Old Stone to foreclose on the fee interest and satisfy the loan. Therefore, she would be pledging her fee interest as security for and as a source of repayment for the debt of JHI. The contract would be a mortgage.

Idaho Code § 45-1001 (1977) provides that any interest in real property which is capable of being transferred may be mortgaged. Idaho Code § 45-901 (1977) provides that a mortgage is a contract excepting a trust deed or transfer in trust by which specific property is hypothecated for the performance of an act without the necessity of a change of possession. Idaho Code § 45-902 (1977) provides that a mortgage, deed of trust, or transfer in trust can be created, renewed or extended only by writing executed with the formalities required in the case of a grant or conveyance of real property. It goes without any argument or challenge that the subordination agreement was not *executed with the formalities required in the case of a grant or conveyance of real property.* Idaho Code § 45-1502(3) (Supp.1986) provides that a trust deed means a deed executed in conformity with the act and conveying real property to a trustee in trust to secure the performance of an obligation of the grantor or other person named in the deed to a beneficiary. It appears from the documents that the subordination agreement was transferred to the trustee who kept all of the documents relative to this transaction. However, Idaho Code § 45-902 (1977) again incorporates the deed of trust and requires that it be executed with the formalities required in the case of a grant or conveyance of real property. It is not arguable that the subordination agreement complies with the formalities of the conveyance of real property pursuant to Idaho Code § 55-601 (1977).

In summary, the nature of a subordination is such that the beneficiary of the subordination must have a competing interest which, after the subordination, becomes senior to that which, before the subordination, was the senior interest. In this case, Old Stone never had an interest in the fee of Davis's property, but only pursuant to the leasehold mortgage a junior interest in the leasehold. After the subordination, Old Stone's interest in the leasehold became superior to Davis's interest in the leasehold. By its very nature, the vehicle of subordination could not be used to grant Old Stone an interest in the fee. In order to have an interest in Davis's fee estate, a mortgage or deed of trust must have been executed. No such instrument was executed. Further, the subordination agreement cannot be elevated to the position of a mortgage or deed of trust since it lacks the formalities of such required under Idaho law. The subordination agreement could not, as a matter of law, grant any interest in the fee, upon which foreclosure could be had, to Old Stone. Foreclosure is only possible on the deed of trust affecting the leasehold.

By her reply brief, Davis has set up certain defenses to the foreclosure on the leasehold. She, therefore, moves for summary judgment on her defenses to the Complaint in foreclosure.

Davis states that the subordination document makes her a surety on the loan from Old Stone. A subordination of an interest to a like interest does not automatically make one a surety, but simply changes the priority in the event of foreclosure.

Davis sets up this surety argument in order to show that when an extension of time for payment was granted by Old Stone to JHI, it materially altered her position, thereby discharging her from her suretyship. As noted by Old Stone, whether she is a surety involves questions of fact. Whether the modification was material, whether Davis was a compensated surety, and whether she demonstrated prejudice or injury if in fact she was a compensated surety, are questions of fact.

Next, Davis argues that the subordination agreement effects an interest in real property and involves a contract to answer for the debt of another implicating the statute of frauds pursuant to Idaho Code § 9-503 (1977) and § 9-505 (1977). A simple answer to this argument is that Davis has never raised the statue of frauds defense in responsive pleading and cannot now assert that claim.

Finally, Davis points out that the lease was terminated subsequent to JHI filing bankruptcy. The estoppel certificate expressly authorized Davis to terminate the lease if Old Stone elected not to cure JHI's default. Davis argues that the consequence of the termination of the lessee's rights upon the lease is that all interest of third persons acquired and held by them under the lease are also terminated since they can acquire no rights in the premises other than those of the original lessee. Once the interest of Old Stone evaporated upon the termination of the lease, her interest in the leasehold was again senior and secure. Old Stone, in reply, states that this assertion engenders numerous questions of fact. Old Stone does not raise any substantive argument to counter this evaporation theory, but merely states that it is in contradiction to her earlier argument that she is a surety. Old Stone contends that if Davis is a surety, then suretyship does not evaporate upon the termination of the lease and she is obligated to the extent of her suretyship. Davis can argue these defenses in the alternative.

Plaintiff has not suggested that Davis's termination of the lease is somehow violative of the estoppel certificate. Therefore, once the leasehold was terminated, the subject matter of the leasehold mortgage evaporated and Old Stone had nothing. The estoppel certificate gives Old Stone the right, but not the obligation, to maintain the leasehold in existence. It appears that Old Stone elected not to keep the leasehold in existence and allowed its termination, thereby losing its security. Summary judgment is appropriate on this ground.

Based upon the foregoing and the court being fully advised in the premises,

IT IS HEREBY ORDERED that Old Stone's Motion for Partial Summary judgment should be, and is hereby, DENIED.

IT IS FURTHER ORDERED that Davis's Motion for Summary Judgment should be, and is hereby, GRANTED.

NOTES AND QUESTIONS

1. From the leasehold mortgagee's vantage, Murphy's law governs this case: Everything that could possibly go wrong did so. The subordination agreement failed to subject the fee to the leasehold mortgage. The lessee's bankruptcy terminated the ground lease. The fee owner's surety status may well have been discharged. Can the Old Stone Capital Corp., which made a $250,000 loan, retrieve anything from this disaster?

2. Whalen, Commercial Ground Leases 5-18 (2002), in its discussion of subordination, recommends, at a minimum, that the subordination agreement contain

language unequivocally subjecting the fee to the mortgage: "including any technical granting clause or other language required to create a mortgage or deed of trust under local law." The author also recommends that the landlord join in the mortgage instrument, but not the promissory note. In return, the landlord will want a mortgage provision exonerating the landlord for payment of the loan or for performance of any of the other mortgage covenants. Finally, the author suggests that the landlord should execute an assignment of sublease rentals.

3. In Jacob Hoffman Brewing Co. v. Wuttge, 234 N.Y. 469, 138 N.E. 411 (1923), tenant, behind on his rent, voluntarily surrendered possession of the premises to the landlord. The leasehold mortgagee sought unsuccessfully to reinstate the lease, claiming that the tenant, having granted the mortgagee an interest in the leasehold, had no right or power to destroy the interest by surrendering the lease. The court wrote:

> Surely the mortgage given by the tenant to this plaintiff could not reduce the lessor's rights under the lease or prevent him from pursuing any and all of his remedies for the nonperformance of the covenants. When Wuttge failed to pay his rent, the owner was not called upon to consult the tenant's assignees, mortgagees, or subtenants before taking action. . . . He could accept the voluntary surrender of the premises and enter into possession and re-let them according to the terms and conditions of the lease.

Although a leasehold mortgage would almost certainly bar the mortgagor from voluntarily surrendering the ground lease, what practical steps can the mortgagee take to prevent that occurrence? If the lessor accepts a surrender, especially where no leasehold default has taken place, might this not be a tortious interference with the mortgagee's business advantage?

(4) Bankruptcy

Precision Industries, Inc. v. Qualitech Steel SBQ, LLC

327 F.3d 537 (7th Cir. 2003)

ILANA DIAMOND ROVNER, Circuit Judge.

In this case of first impression at the circuit level, we are asked to reconcile two distinct provisions of the Bankruptcy Code: 11 U.S.C. § 363(f), which authorizes the sale of a debtor's property free of any "interest" other than the estate's, and 11 U.S.C. § 365(h), which protects the rights of the lessee when the debtor rejects a lease of estate property. The bankruptcy court in this case construed a sale order issued pursuant to section 363(f) to extinguish the possessory rights bestowed by a lease of the estate's land. The district court disagreed, reasoning that sections 363(f) and 365(h) conflict and that the more specific terms of the latter provision concerning leaseholds trump those of the former, in this way preserving the lessee's possessory interest even after a section 363(f) sale. Precision Indus., Inc. v. Qualitech Steel SBQ, LLC, 2001 WL 699881 (S.D.Ind. April 24, 2001). We reverse, concluding that under the plain terms of section 363(f), the sale order extinguished the lessee's possessory interest.

I

The debtors in the underlying bankruptcy proceedings — Qualitech Steel Corporation and Qualitech Steel Holdings Corporation (collectively, "Qualitech") — owned and operated a steel mill on a 138-acre tract of land in Pittsboro, Indiana. Before it entered bankruptcy, Qualitech had entered into two related agreements with appellees Precision Industries, Inc. and Circo Leasing Co., LLC (collectively, "Precision"). A detailed supply agreement executed on June 29, 1998, provided that Precision would construct a supply warehouse at Qualitech's Pittsboro facility and operate it for a period of ten years so as to provide on-site, integrated supply services for Qualitech. The second agreement, a land lease executed on February 25, 1999, specified that Qualitech would lease to Precision the property underlying the warehouse for a period of ten years. In exchange for nominal rent of $1 per year, the lease granted Precision exclusive possession of the warehouse and any other improvements or fixtures it installed on the land for the term of the lease; and in the event of an early termination or default under either the lease or the supply agreement, Precision had the right to remove all improvements and fixtures from the property. Assuming no default, Qualitech had the right at the end of the lease term to purchase the warehouse, its fixtures, and other improvements for $1. In accordance with the two agreements, Precision built and stocked a warehouse on the leased property and Qualitech began purchasing goods from Precision. The lease was never recorded.

Heavily in debt, Qualitech filed a Chapter 11 bankruptcy petition on March 22, 1999. On June 30, 1999, substantially all of Qualitech's assets were sold at auction for a credit bid of $180 million to a group of senior pre-petition lenders that held the primary mortgage on the Pittsboro property. On August 13, 1999, at the conclusion of a noticed hearing, the bankruptcy court entered an order approving the sale (hereinafter, the "Sale Order"). Precision, which had notice of the hearing, did not object to the Sale Order. That order directed Qualitech to convey its assets to the pre-petition lenders — referred to in the Sale Order collectively as the "purchaser" — "free and clear of all liens, claims, encumbrances, and interests," except for specifically enumerated liens, pursuant to section 363(f), among other provisions of the Code. R. 492 at 6-7 ¶2 (emphasis supplied). All persons and entities holding interests other than those expressly preserved in the Sale Order were barred from asserting those interests against the purchaser. Id. at 8 ¶6. The pre-petition senior lenders subsequently transferred their interest in the purchased assets to newly-formed Qualitech Steel SBQ, LLC ("New Qualitech"), which assumed the rights of the purchaser under the Sale Order and took title to the Pittsboro property. The Sale Order also reserved for the purchaser the debtor's right to assume and assign executory contracts pursuant to 11 U.S.C. § 365. R. 492 at 9 ¶9. Although the sale closed on or about August 26, 1999 without assumption of either the lease or the supply agreement with Precision, negotiations toward that end continued and the parties extended the deadline for assumption on four occasions. Those negotiations did not prove successful, however, with the result that Precision's lease and supply agreement were *de facto* rejected. See 2001 WL 699881, at *9 & n. 8.

By December 3, 1999, Precision had completely vacated and padlocked the warehouse. Shortly thereafter, New Qualitech, without Precision's knowledge or consent, hired a locksmith and changed the locks on the building. New Qualitech's takeover of the warehouse led to a dispute over whether Precision's possessory interest in the leased property, pursuant to section 365(h), survived the bankruptcy sale. Finding itself locked out of the warehouse, Precision filed a diversity suit in the district court contending that New Qualitech was guilty of trespass, conversion, wrongful eviction, breach of an implied contract, and estoppel. New Qualitech in turn asked the district court to refer Precision's complaint — which was premised on the notion that Precision retained a possessory interest in the warehouse under the lease — to the bankruptcy court, and New Qualitech also filed a request with the bankruptcy court asking it to clarify that the Sale Order had extinguished Precision's possessory interest. The district court obliged New Qualitech by referring Precision's complaint to the bankruptcy court, and that court in turn resolved the matter of Precision's possessory interest in New Qualitech's favor.

Based on the terms of both section 363(f) and the Sale Order itself, the bankruptcy court determined that New Qualitech had obtained title to Qualitech's property free and clear of any possessory rights that Precision otherwise might have enjoyed under its lease. In relevant part, the court held that Precision's possessory interest was among those interests extinguished by the Sale Order:

> The interest[ ] of Precision as a lessee under the Lease is an "interest" within the meaning of the Sale Order. The sale of the Indiana Facilities pursuant to 11 U.S.C. § 363(b), (f), and (k) was free and clear of all liens, claims, encumbrances and interests [and therefore] acted to convey the Indiana Facilities free and clear of the interests of Precision as lessee under an unrecorded lease.

R. 601 at 5 ¶6. The court emphasized that "[t]he Sale Order was unequivocal and not left open to interpretation." Id. at 7 ¶11. Implicitly, the bankruptcy court rejected the notion that the provisions of section 365(h) acted to preserve Precision's rights as a lessee in the face of the Sale Order.

> [T]he Court is forced to conclude that under the circumstances and the plain language of the Sale Order [New Qualitech] holds the assets acquired from [Qualitech] free and clear of the Lease and all interest of Precision in the . . . real estate acquired by the Purchaser from the Debtor. The Lease has been extinguished by the Sale Order and the Sale Order is no longer subject to attack by Precision.
>
> Precision is barred from asserting any interest in the real estate acquired by the Purchaser from [Qualitech]. . . . Precision may take no further action to enforce the Lease against [New Qualitech] or the Indiana Facilities.

Id. at 9-10 ¶¶16, 17.

Precision appealed the bankruptcy court's decision, and the district court reversed. . . . New Qualitech filed a timely notice of appeal from the district court's decision. We have jurisdiction pursuant to 28 U.S.C. § 158(d). *See, e.g.,* In re Golant, 239 F.3d 931, 934 (7th Cir. 2001).

II

Our task in this appeal is straightforward. We must decide whether a sale order issued under section 363(f), which purports to authorize the transfer of a debtor's property "free and clear of all liens, claims, encumbrances, and interests," operates to extinguish a lessee's possessory interest in the property, or whether the terms of section 365(h) operate to preserve that interest. This is, of course, a question of law, making our review of the district court's decision de novo. *See, e.g., APS Sports Collectibles, Inc. v. Sports Time, Inc.*, 299 F.3d 624, 628 (7th Cir. 2002). . . .

As in all statutory interpretation cases, we begin with the statutory language. E.g., Hughes Aircraft Co. v. Jacobson, 525 U.S. 432, 438, 119 S.Ct. 755, 760, 142 L.Ed.2d 881 (1999). Statutory terms or words will be construed according to their ordinary, common meaning unless they are specifically defined by the statute or the statutory context requires a different definition. E.g., Walters v. Metropolitan Educ. Enters., Inc., 519 U.S. 202, 207, 117 S.Ct. 660, 664, 136 L.Ed.2d 644 (1997). The Supreme Court has repeatedly instructed "that courts must presume that a legislature says in a statute what it means and means in a statute what it says there. [Citations omitted.] When the words of a statute are unambiguous, then, this first canon is also the last: 'judicial inquiry is complete.'" Connecticut Nat'l Bank v. Germain, 503 U.S. 249, 253-54, 112 S.Ct. 1146, 1149, 117 L.Ed.2d 391 (1992) (*quoting Rubin v. United States*, 449 U.S. 424, 430, 101 S.Ct. 698, 701, 66 L.Ed.2d 633 (1981)).

We must also have in mind our obligation to construe the two statutory provisions at issue in this case in such a way as to avoid conflicts between them, if such a construction is possible and reasonable. As the Supreme Court has observed:

> [W]e "are not at liberty to pick and choose among congressional enactments, and when two statutes are capable of co-existence, it is the duty of the courts, absent a clearly expressed congressional intention to the contrary, to regard each as effective." *Morton v. Mancari*, 417 U.S. 535, 551, 94 S.Ct. 2474, 2483, 41 L.Ed.2d 290 (1974). We should read federal statutes "to give effect to each if we can do so while preserving their sense and purpose." *Watt v. Alaska*, 451 U.S. 259, 267, 101 S.Ct. 1673, 1678, 68 L.Ed.2d 80 (1981); see also *United States v. Fausto*, 484 U.S. 439, 453, 108 S.Ct. 668, 676-77, 98 L. Ed.2d 830 (1988).

Pittsburgh & Lake Erie R.R. Co. v. Railway Labor Executives' Ass'n, 491 U.S. 490, 510, 109 S.Ct. 2584, 2596, 105 L.Ed.2d 415 (1989) . . . With these principles in mind, we turn to the language of the statutory provisions at issue here.

Section 363 generally provides for the use, sale, or lease of property belonging to the bankruptcy estate. As relevant here, subsections (b) and (c) permit the trustee of a bankruptcy estate to sell estate property either within the normal course of a debtor's business (in which case the sale may take place without prior notice and a hearing) or outside the normal course of business (in which case, as here, notice and hearing are mandatory). Subsection (f) makes clear that the property, under specified conditions, may be sold unencumbered of interests held by others:

> The trustee may sell property under subsection (b) or (c) of this section free and clear of *any interest* in such property of an entity other than the estate, only if—
>
> (1) applicable nonbankruptcy law permits sale of such property free and clear of such interest;
> (2) such entity consents;
> (3) such interest is a lien and the price at which such property is to be sold is greater than the aggregate value of all liens on such property;
> (4) such interest is in bona fide dispute; or

    (5) such entity could be compelled, in a legal or equitable proceeding, to accept
        a money satisfaction of such interest.

(Emphasis ours.) Finally, subsection (e) provides that "on request of an entity that
has an interest in property . . . proposed to be . . . sold . . . by the trustee, the
court, with or without a hearing, shall prohibit or condition such . . . sale . . . as
is necessary to provide adequate protection of such interest." We note that although
section 363(f) refers to the powers and obligations of the "trustee," these are
powers and obligations which, in a Chapter 11 case, inure to the debtor-in-
possession. See 11 U.S.C. § 1107(a).

    The Bankruptcy Code does not define "any interest," and in the course of
applying section 363(f) to a wide variety of rights and obligations related to estate
property, courts have been unable to formulate a precise definition. *Folger Adam
Security, Inc. v. DeMatteis/MacGregor, JV*, 209 F.3d 252, 258 (3d Cir.2000). But the
Code itself does not suggest that "interest" should be understood in a special or
narrow sense; on the contrary, the use of the term "any" counsels in favor of a broad
interpretation. *See United States v. Gonzales*, 520 U.S. 1, 5, 117 S.Ct. 1032, 1035, 137 L.
Ed.2d 132 (1997). As commentators have pointed out, the Supreme Court else-
where has observed that the term "interest" is a broad term no doubt selected by
Congress to avoid "rigid and technical definitions drawn from other areas of the
law. . . ." *Russello v. United States*, 464 U.S. 16, 21, 104 S.Ct. 296, 299, 78 L.Ed.2d 17
(1983); *see* Steven R. Haydon & Nancy J. March, *Sale of Estate Property Free and Clear of
Real Property Leasehold Interests Pursuant to § 363(f): An Unwritten Limitation?*, 19
AMERICAN BANKR. INST. J. 20, 20 (2000) (hereinafter, "*Unwritten Limitation?*").
The *Russello* Court thus concluded that "interest," as used in the Racketeer Influenced and Corrupt Organizations statute, 18 U.S.C. § 1963(a)(1), "comprehends
all forms of real and personal property, including profits and proceeds." 464 U.S. at
21, 104 S.Ct. at 299, 104 S.Ct. 296. . . .

    Here, we likewise conclude that the term "any interest" as used in section 363(f)
is sufficiently broad to include Precision's possessory interest as a lessee. BLACK'S
defines "interest" to mean "[a] legal share in something; all or part of a legal or
equitable claim to or right in property." BLACK'S LAW DICTIONARY, 816 (7th
ed.1999). The right that a leasehold confers upon the lessee is one to possess
property for the term of the lease. It is, therefore, not simply a right that is
connected to or arising from the property, *see In re Trans World Airlines, Inc.*, 322
F.3d 283, 289-90 (3d Cir.2003), but a (limited) right to the property itself. That right
readily may be understood as an "interest" in the property. *FutureSource LLC v.
Reuters Ltd.*, *supra*, 312 F.3d at 285; *see also In re Downtown Athletic Club of New York
City, Inc.*, 44 Collier Bankr.Cas.2d 342, 2000 WL 744126, at *4 (S.D.N.Y. June 9,
2000) ("under the expansive interpretation of 'any interest' under § 363(f)(4),
Defendants' asserted possessory rights as lessees fall within the scope of this section");
In re Taylor, 198 B.R. 142, 162 (Bankr.D.S.C.1996) ("it appears that a leasehold is a
type of 'interest' that fits within the plain text of the . . . statute"); *see also C.H.E.G.,
Inc. v. Millenium Bank*, 99 Cal.App.4th 505, 121 Cal.Rptr. 2d 443, 448 (2002)
(holding that contractual right to commission in event of sale of property leased
from debtor is an "interest" in estate property that may be extinguished pursuant to
section 363(f)). This inclusive interpretation of the phrase "any interest" is consistent with the expansive use of that same phrase in other provisions of the Code. See,

e.g., 11. U.S.C. § 541(a)(3), (4), (5), and (7) (identifying various interests comprising property of the estate).

Because Precision's right to possess the property as a lessee qualifies as an interest for purposes of section 363(f), the statute on its face authorized the sale of Qualitech's property free and clear of that interest. Although the statute conditions such a sale on the satisfaction of one of five conditions, the parties before us do not dispute that at least one of those conditions was satisfied. On the contrary, both parties to the appeal proceed from the premise that section 363(f) standing alone permits the sale of estate property free and clear of a lessee's possessory interest.

Where the parties lock horns is on whether the terms of section 365(h) conflict with and override those of section 363(f). Section 365 generally provides the trustee (and here, the debtor-in-possession, see § 1107(a)) with the right to reject executory contracts, a power that serves to relieve the debtor of contractual obligations that are unduly burdensome. *See N.L.R.B. v. Bildisco & Bildisco*, 465 U.S. 513, 528, 104 S.Ct. 1188, 1197, 79 L.Ed.2d 482 (1984). However, insofar as lessees of the estate's property are concerned, the power of rejection is limited so as to preclude eviction of the lessee. In relevant part, section 365(h)(1)(A)(ii) provides:

> If the trustee rejects an unexpired lease of real property under which the debtor is the lessor and—
>
> . . .
>
> (ii) if the term of such lease has commenced, the lessee may retain its rights under such lease . . . that are in or appurtenant to the real property for the balance of the term of such lease and for any renewal or extension of such rights to the extent that such rights are enforceable under applicable non-bankruptcy law.

The terms of section 365(h) thus allow a lessee to remain in possession of estate property notwithstanding the debtor-in-possession's decision to reject the lease. In this way, the statute strikes a balance between the respective rights of the debtor-lessor and its tenant: the lessee retains the right to possess the property for the remainder of the term it bargained for, while the rejection frees the debtor-lessor of other burdensome obligations that it assumed under the lease (as, for example, the duty to provide services to the lessee). *See Taylor*, 198 B.R. at 165-67 (summarizing legislative history and case law); *In re LHD Realty Corp.*, 20 B.R. 717, 719 (Bankr.S. D.Ind.1982); *Unwritten Limitation?*, 19 AM. BANKR. INST. J. at 22.

The district court, following the lead of other lower courts, concluded that the limitations imposed by section 365(h) vis à vis rejection of leases necessarily conflict with and override the debtor-in-possession's ability to sell estate property free and clear of a lessee's possessory interest. But for the reasons that follow, we conclude that the terms of section 365(h) do not supersede those of section 363(f).

First, the statutory provisions themselves do not suggest that one supersedes or limits the other. Notably, sections 363 and 365 both contain cross-references indicating that certain of their provisions are subject to other statutory mandates. *See* §§ 363(d), 365(a). But nowhere in either section 363(f) or section 356(h) is there a similar cross-reference indicating that the broad right to sell estate property free of "any interest" is subordinate to the protections that section 365(h) accords to lessees. The omission suggests that Congress did not intend for the latter section to limit the former. . . .

Second, the plain language of section 365(h)(1)(A) suggests that it has a limited scope. By its own terms, that subsection applies "[i]f the trustee [or debtor-in-possession] *rejects* an unexpired lease of real property. . . ." (Emphasis supplied.) Here what occurred in the first instance was a sale of the property that Precision was leasing rather than a rejection of its lease. Granted, if the Sale Order operated to extinguish Precision's right to possess the property — as we conclude it did — then the effect of the sale might be understood as the equivalent of a repudiation of Precision's lease. *See Taylor*, 198 B.R. at 166 ("[t]o allow a sale free and clear of a leasehold interest pursuant to §363 . . . would effectively provide a debtor with means of dispossessing the lessee"). But nothing in the express terms of section 365(h) suggests that it applies to any and all events that threaten the lessee's possessory rights. Section 365(h) instead focuses on a specific type of event — the rejection of an executory contract by the trustee or debtor-in-possession — and spells out the rights of parties affected by that event. It says nothing at all about sales of estate property, which are the province of section 363. The two statutory provisions thus apply to distinct sets of circumstances. [Citations omitted.]

Third, section 363 itself provides for a mechanism to protect the rights of parties whose interests may be adversely affected by the sale of estate property. As noted above, section 363(e) directs the bankruptcy court, on the request of any entity with an interest in the property to be sold, to "prohibit or condition such . . . sale . . . as is necessary to provide adequate protection of such interest." Because a leasehold qualifies as an "interest" in property for purposes of section 363(f), a lessee of property being sold pursuant to subsection (f) would have the right to insist that its interest be protected. "Adequate protection" does not necessarily guarantee a lessee's continued possession of the property, but it does demand, in the alternative, that the lessee be compensated for the value of its leasehold — typically from the proceeds of the sale. *See Unwritten Limitation?*, 19 AM. BANKR. INST. J. at 22 & n. 5, citing, *inter alia, In re Murel Holding Corp.*, 75 F.2d 941, 942 (2d Cir.1935) (L.Hand, J.), and *La Jolla Mortgage Fund v. Rancho El Cajon Assocs.*, 18 B.R. 283, 286 (Bankr.S.D.Cal.1982). Lessees like Precision are therefore not without recourse in the event of a sale free and clear of their interests. They have the right to seek protection under section 363(e), and upon request, the bankruptcy court is obligated to ensure that their interests are adequately protected.

With these points in mind, it is apparent that the two statutory provisions can be construed in a way that does not disable section 363(f) vis à vis leasehold interests. Where estate property under lease is to be sold, section 363 permits the sale to occur free and clear of a lessee's possessory interest — provided that the lessee (upon request) is granted adequate protection for its interest. Where the property is not sold, and the debtor remains in possession thereof but chooses to reject the lease, section 365(h) comes into play and the lessee retains the right to possess the property. So understood, both provisions may be given full effect without coming into conflict with one another and without disregarding the rights of lessees.

We are persuaded that it is both reasonable and correct to interpret and reconcile sections 363(f) and 365(h) in this way. It is consistent with the express terms of each provision, and it avoids the unwelcome result of reading a limitation into section 363(f) that the legislature itself did not inscribe onto the statute. Congress authorized the sale of estate property free and clear of "any interest," not "any interest except a lessee's possessory interest." The interpretation is also consistent with the process of marshaling the estate's assets for the twin purposes of maximizing creditor recovery and rehabilitating the debtor, which are central to the Bankruptcy Code. *Unwritten Limitation?*, 19 AM. BANKR. INST. J. at 22-23, *citing* Basil H. Mattingly, *Sale of Property of the Estate Free and Clear of Restrictions and Covenants in Bankruptcy*, 4 AM. BANKR. INST. L. REV. 431, 451-52 (1996).

Thus, section 363(f), as we interpret that provision, permitted the bankruptcy court to allow the sale of Qualitech's Pittsboro property unencumbered by Precision's possessory interest as a lessee. Precision neither objected to the sale nor sought the protection that was available under section 363(e). Its possessory interest was extinguished by the sale.

III

As the sale of Qualitech's property terminated Precision's possessory interest in the property as a lessee, we REVERSE the district court's judgment to the contrary.

NOTES AND QUESTIONS

1. *Bankruptcy Code section 365(h).* In general, a bankrupt party can choose to accept or to reject its executory contracts and leases, and if a lease is rejected, the other party has a claim for compensation for the breach within the bankrupty proceeding—a claim that rarely makes the party whole. As an alternative, Congress has given any tenant of the debtor the power, under section 365(h), to "retain its rights under such lease (including rights such as those relating to the amount and timing of payment of rent and other amounts payable by the lessee and any right of use, possession, quiet enjoyment, subletting, assignment, or hypothecation) that are in or appurtenant to the real property for the balance of the term of such lease and for any renewal or extension of such rights to the extent that such rights are enforceable under applicable nonbankruptcy law." 11 U.S.C. § 363(h). Thus, if the bankrupt landlord rejects the lease, the tenant may retain its possession as long as it lives up to its obligations under the lease. This right is not only of vital interest to tenants but it is critical to any leasehold financing, because a leasehold mortgagee's greatest fear is that the leasehold could somehow be terminated, eliminating its security.

2. *Qualitech*, the first circuit court case to consider the relation between the "sale free and clear" provision of section 363(f) and the leasehold protections of section 365(h), created quite a stir in the financing community and has been severely criticized by commentators. See Christopher C. Genovese, Precision Industries v. Qualitech Steel: Easing the Tension Between Sections 363 and 365 of the Bankruptcy Code? 39 Real Prop. Prob. & Tr. J. 627 (2004); Michael St. Patrick Baxter, Section 363 Sales Free and Clear of Interests: Why the Seventh Circuit Erred in Precision Industries v. Qualitech Steel, 59 Bus. Law 475(2004); Robert M. Zinman, Precision in Statutory Drafting: The Qualitech Quagmire and the Sad History of § 365(h) of the Bankruptcy Code, 38 J. Marshall L. Rev. 97 (2004). Most previous cases had held that the general provision of section 363(f) had to yield to the more specific protections that section 363(h) created for tenants. See, e.g., Churchill Props. III, L.P., 197 B.R. 283 (Bankr. N.D. Ill. 1996). However, *Qualitech* seems to

have created a new avenue for a bankruptcy lessor to eliminate a lease, one that does away with the tenant's right under section 365(h) to retain possession of the premises so long as the tenant honors its own obligations under the leasehold.

3. While *Qualitech* is of great concern to tenants and leasehold mortgagees, it is important to note that Precision failed to take a number of important steps within the bankruptcy proceeding to protect its leasehold interest. First, it did not object to the sale of the assets free and clear of its interest, nor did it insist that the Sale Order entered by the Bankruptcy Court preserve its leasehold rights. Once the time to appeal the Sale Order had expired, Precision lost its right to challenge the court's order selling the property free of Prescision's rights even if that order was errone-ous. Second, section 363(e) provides that upon sale of the property free and clear of Precision's leasehold, Precision was entitled to "adequate protection" of its interest in the property if it so requested. Precision Industries did not make this request. Finally, as the Seventh Circuit notes, section 363(f) only permits sale of property free and clear of the rights of others if one of five circumstances exists:

(1) applicable nonbankruptcy law permits sale of such property free and clear of such interest;
(2) such entity consents;
(3) such interest is a lien and the price at which such property is to be sold is greater than the aggregate value of all liens on such property;
(4) such interest is in bona fide dispute; or
(5) such entity could be compelled, in a legal or equitable proceeding, to accept a money satisfaction of such interest.

Precision failed to argue that these conditions were not satisfied, an argument it would likely have won. See In re Haskell, 321 B.R. 1 (Bankr. D. Mass. 2005) (sale free and clear of leasehold not permitted where the elements of 363(f) are not met); In re Taylor, 198 B.R. 142 (Bankr. D.S.C. 1996) (same).

C. THE SALE-LEASEBACK

1. *Background*

The sale-leaseback has become a fixture on the American commercial scene. Endlessly versatile, this financing device is well known both to real estate and corporate specialists, and has become routine in our capital centers and smaller cities. To complete this course without a thorough understanding of the sale-leaseback is to bathe without water.

The sale-leaseback transaction, as this term denotes, comprises two simultaneous events: the sale of property to an investor or institutional lender and the long-term lease of the property back to the seller, generally a developer, operator, or user. The sale-leaseback of tangible property occurs widely: airplanes, tankers, and construc-tion equipment are typical subject matter. But real estate transactions remain the concern of this course, so we will examine the sale-leaseback as it involves land, or land and buildings, or, sometimes, even a building alone.

Homburger, Real Estate Sale-Leasebacks

1-2 — 1-4 (1992)

HISTORY OF SALE-LEASEBACK TRANSACTIONS

The sale-leaseback technique was first used in England in the late 19th Century.[11] It first became popular in the United States sometime during the 1940s. Early sale-leaseback transactions were fairly simple. The buyers generally were institutions with special tax advantages, such as educational institutions, pension funds, and other tax-free institutions. The sellers were usually large corporations with substantial amounts of assets tied up in real estate. Since the 1950s, developers and financiers have expanded the basic sale-leaseback concept to dizzying heights of complication. In large part, this was due to William Zeckendorff, Sr., who developed the "pineapple" theory of sale-leaseback financing as part of a development concept called the "Hawaiian technique." The basis of this theory is simple: If a piece of real estate is broken into separate parts (e.g., fee interest in the land and reversionary interest in the building, fee interest in the building, sublease of the building, management agreement to operate the building, subleases of parts of the building, etc.), and each of those parts is marketed to different entities who are willing to pay top price for the particular part of the estate, then the total value of all of the parts is worth more than the value of the undivided property.[12] This technique has been embraced and expanded by syndicators and financial institutions as a means of maximizing their economic returns and their tax benefits.[13]

Over the years, sale-leaseback financing transactions have proven to be good investments for buyer-lessors such as charitable and educational institutions, pension funds, institutional investors, and real estate investment trusts looking for "bond-like" passive investments. Individual investors and syndicated partnerships seeking tax shelters have also profited. In recent years, buyer-lessors have utilized sale-leaseback transactions as a means of participating in both the cash flow and the proceeds of financing the leasehold estate.

Seller-lessees have found such transactions an effective way of obtaining funds in unfavorable mortgage markets. Sale-leasebacks are an effective means of raising funds in excess of amounts available from first mortgage loans. Avoiding second mortgage financing or refinancing of an advantageous first mortgage can have great financial rewards. Seller-lessees may also realize certain tax advantages from such transactions.

---

11. The first case documenting the use of a sale-leaseback transaction was Yorkshire Ry. Wagon Co. v. Maclure, 21 Ch. D. 309 (1881). In that case, the Cornwall Minerals Railway Company (Railway Company) solicited the Yorkshire Railway Wagon Company (Wagon Company) for a loan offering locomotives and wagons for security. Since the Railway Company could not legally borrow any more money, the parties agreed that it would sell 15 locomotive engines and 200 wagons to the Wagon Company. The Wagon Company would then lease the equipment back to the Railway Company for a term of five years. The Railway Company had an option to repurchase the assets at the end of the term for a nominal sum. A dispute arose when the Railway Company failed to make its rental payments. A lower court judge viewed the transaction as a loan and thus declared it void. The appellate court, however, upheld the loan on the ground that the parties intentionally designed the transaction to circumvent the illegality of an outright loan.

12. Weil, Land Leasebacks Move Up Fast as Financing Technique, 1 Real Est. Rev. 65, 65 (Winter 1972).

13. Cary, Corporate Financing Through Sale and Leaseback of Property: Business, Tax and Policy Considerations, 62 Harv. L. Rev. 1, 2 (1948).

THREE BASIC TYPES OF SALE-LEASEBACK TRANSACTIONS

Despite an infinite number of innovative modifications and combinations, the framework of a sale-leaseback can be categorized into three basic types. Each entails different real estate and tax ramifications.

The first type of transaction involves the sale-leaseback of land and improvements that are owned by the buyer-lessor. Thus, the buyer-lessor enjoys the tax benefits that come with ownership of the improvements. This holds true even if the transaction involves the sale of (1) land and improvements owned and used by the seller-lessee prior to the sale or (2) unimproved land upon which the buyer-lessor is to construct improvements for the seller-lessee. The seller-lessee's sole interest is as a tenant.

The second kind of transaction involves the sale-leaseback of land or improvements only. If only the land is sold, the seller-lessee retains ownership of existing and to-be-constructed improvements during the term of the lease. The seller-lessee enjoys the tax benefits that come with ownership of the improvements. The buyer-lessor acquires ownership of the land and a reversionary or future interest in the existing or future improvements.[14] If only the improvements are sold, the buyer-lessor obtains ownership of the improvements and the corresponding tax benefits while the seller-lessee retains ownership of the underlying land. The ownership of land and improvements must be consolidated in one of the parties to the transaction at the end of the lease term.

The last variation of sale-leasebacks involves personal property. . . .

Lifton, Practical Real Estate in the '80s

497-499 (2d ed. 1982)

SALE VS. MORTGAGE

Patently, the sale and leaseback transaction has many of the elements of mortgage financing: the property is used as collateral to raise money, and the party receiving the money enters into an obligation, in the case of a user-lessee supported by its credit, to make regular payments sufficient to return the funds advanced plus pay an interest factor for the use of the money. The form of transaction is flexible enough to accommodate a real sale or a financing transaction, depending on the parties' aims. At one end of the spectrum is the true sale and leaseback. The property is sold at an arm's length price, based on its fair market value, and leased back to the seller at a fair rental that would be arrived at in an arm's length negotiation between a landlord and a tenant. At the end of the initial term of the lease, there may be renewal options that are based on the then market value of the

---

14. See, e.g., In re PCH Associates, 60 Bankr. 70 (S.D.N.Y. 1986) (corporation purportedly purchased and leased back the land upon which a hotel was situated); Papago Tribal Utility Authority v. F.E. R.C., 773 F.2d 1056, 1058 (9th Cir. 1985), cert. denied, 475 U.S. 1108 (1986) (public service company sold its steam electric generating station to General Electric Company and immediately leased it back, and "[t]he net result was that General Electric paid $50.6 million for the tax benefits of owning [the station] . . . while [the public service company] retained use and control of the facility"); Harris v. Metropolitan Mall, 112 Wis. 2d 487, 334 N.W.2d 519 (1983) (a partnership sold a shopping center mall building, but not the underlying land, and leased it back from an individual investor who was looking for a tax shelter).

property or tied to the realistic rentals for the earlier term. When the last renewal option expires, the tenant has no further interest in the property. If the tenant has an option to purchase, it is at the fair market value at the time of exercise or at a presently determined price which stands up as a reasonable estimate of the future fair market value.

At the other end of the spectrum is a transaction that has the characteristics of a secured loan. The property is sold at a price lower or higher than the true value of the property, related solely to the capitalized value of the rent to be paid under the lease. The rent will be lower or higher than a realistic rent for that property because the rent represents a return of the funds advanced for the purchase and a charge for the use of the money. After some specified period, the purchaser-lessor may have the right to "put" the property to the lessee, which is obligated to buy it, at a price which pays the seller back for the property and, taken together with the lease rents, provides a return on its funds outstanding to that date. Alternatively, the lessee may have an option at the end of the lease to extend the term at an unrealistically low rent or to buy the property back for an unrealistically low price.

As we shall see, substantially different tax and legal consequences flow from the characterization of the transaction as a mortgage loan rather than as a sale and leaseback. In the tax realm, whether the transaction is a "true" sale and leaseback, rather than a secured loan, has perplexed even (or especially) the Supreme Court. See Frank Lyon Co. v. United States, page 857 infra.

Del Cotto, Sale and Leaseback: A Hollow Sound When Tapped?

37 Tax L. Rev. 1, 3-9 (1981)

COMMERCIAL AND TAX ATTRIBUTES OF THE SALE AND LEASEBACK

Although the sale and leaseback can serve what many view as legitimate commercial and business needs, parties to the transaction understand that this form may also provide mutual tax advantages. For the seller, the primary tax advantage is full deductibility of rental payments as ordinary and necessary business expenses, despite the fact that under a loan theory these payments include an interest portion and the amortized sale price of the property. Thus, over the lease term the seller-lessee will deduct rental payments equal to the full fair market value of the property, whereas with conventional mortgage financing only the interest portion of the payment would be deductible and no deduction would be allowed for amortized principal payments.

Of course, with conventional financing, as owner the seller-lessee would be able to take depreciation deductions, but only with respect to depreciable items, thus excluding land from the depreciation base. Hence, the rental deduction under the sale and leaseback is usually preferable to a depreciation deduction in that in effect it allows for depreciation of land. This feature is particularly attractive if the ratio of land cost to improvement cost is high. Or, if the property has appreciated in value, through rental deductions a sale and leaseback in effect allows depreciation of full market value, rather than of only the cost of the property. Similarly, if the property has been fully depreciated, sale and leaseback generates deductions otherwise unavailable. Furthermore, a sale and leaseback obviates determination of the property's salvage value and exclusion of it from the depreciable amount.

Even on property that has not been depreciated to any great extent, sale and leaseback provides the advantage of what is essentially accelerated depreciation. The rental deductions not only represent the full value of the property, they are deducted over the term of the lease, the length of which may be for a shorter period than the useful life of the property. . . .

With respect to deductions, then, by financing with a sale and leaseback rather than conventional borrowing, the seller hopes to acquire rental deductions and is willing to forego deductions for depreciation and interest. The advantage gained by a rental deduction is offset somewhat by loss of a remainder interest in the property at the end of the lease term, unless the seller is also given a repurchase option, which in turn would invite recharacterization of the transaction as a financing rather than as a sale.

Assuming the transaction is respected as a sale, an additional tax consequence of a sale and leaseback is current recognition of the seller's gain or loss. By timing the transaction under section 1231, the seller may recognize ordinary losses, and capital gains, while retaining use and possession of property which is needed for business operations. If the adjusted basis of the asset is higher than its fair market value, a loss may be recognized, reducing tax liability or perhaps permitting a refund of a prior year's taxes. If, however, the adjusted basis of the asset is less than its fair market value, the taxpayer can utilize a sale and leaseback to recognize gain in order to take advantage of offsetting losses which could otherwise be wasted. Gain on the sale of a section 1231 asset, however, may be subject to depreciation recapture and taxed as ordinary income rather than as long-term capital gain.

Turning to the buyer-lessor, the sale and leaseback offers an investment on which at least part of the rentals received will not be taxed due to an offsetting depreciation deduction. Although the buyer must include the full rental payments in gross income, deductions for depreciation and interest on any mortgage debt are allowed. As owner, the investor can claim a depreciation deduction based on cost, including any mortgage debt, which, in an arm's length transaction, would be the full market value of the property.

On the other hand, if the buyer were treated as a conventional lender rather than a buyer-lessor, only the interest portion of the payments received would be includable in gross income. The remainder would be a return of capital. For tax-exempt organizations, this difference between the two transactions is irrelevant if the organization can pay cash. If, however, the sale and leaseback is debt-financed by the organization, all or some portion of the rental payments would be subject to taxation under sections 511 and 514 as "unrelated business income." Though the nonexempt buyer is in a less advantageous position, there are advantages it can, and will, pursue. The buyer can leverage its investment, borrowing at a lower rate than the rate at which the interest portion of the rental payment is calculated. With newly constructed, highly leveraged real estate, the sale and leaseback can be structured so that interest and accelerated depreciation deductions exceed rental payments, thus sheltering nonrental income from taxation. In addition, if the property is newly constructed, the buyer may be eligible for an investment tax credit.

A variety of nontax considerations recommend utilizing the sale and leaseback device. "[E]ven were there no tax inducements whatsoever some corporations today would enter into these transactions for the business and legal advantages they may afford."[15] A primary advantage of the sale and leaseback from the seller's perspective is that the seller receives the proceeds from the sale of a nonliquid asset yet retains for a term the use and possession of the asset. This retained use may be important in a variety of situations in which the seller plans eventually to terminate its relationship with the property. . . .

. . . Even sellers who do not wish ultimately to dispose of property may use a sale and leaseback where the combination of the retained possessory term and other advantages override loss of the remainder. This situation often arises in the use of a sale and leaseback as a financing device in order to provide the seller with working capital. Given the earning potential of working capital, taxpayers may prefer not to tie it up in nonliquid assets. Indeed, some contend that from the seller's perspective the principal purpose of a sale and leaseback is to increase or conserve working capital. In this respect, the sale and leaseback form of financing is particularly advantageous in that it often provides the seller with 100 percent of the fair market value of the property sold. In contrast, other financing arrangements — mortgage loans or corporate bonds — may yield only 75 to 80 percent of the value of the property. Hence, the sale and leaseback enables a company to obtain greater aggregate capital than through other forms of financing, while retaining for a term the use and possession of the asset sold.

These advantages of the sale and leaseback recommend its use in a variety of business situations. Builders and developers can effectively use the sale and lease-back device as a financing tool for construction purposes. By selling undeveloped or partially improved land for cash and leasing it back, the builder acquires capital for construction. The sale and leaseback serves a similar function in providing expansion opportunities for businesses needing to enlarge existing facilities or build new ones. A company can build or enlarge its plant or store to meet its specifications, sell it to an investor to recoup its cash investment, and then lease it back. If the company is unable to obtain the initial construction financing, a buyer can be found and the sale proceeds used to finance the costs of construction. Hence, the company can have the use and possession of a physical facility tailored to its needs without sacrificing working capital for fixed assets. This consideration is especially important for businesses like retail stores which require large amounts of working capital for inventory and operating expenses. For these businesses, the sale and leaseback also affords the advantage of piecemeal financing. The sale and leaseback of one or more units can be timed to coincide with the need for funds to finance new units. Thus, funds are acquired as needed, in contrast to debt financing through the sale of a company's securities, where funds may be received over a short period. . . .

There are other commercial and business reasons why a sale and leaseback may or must be used in lieu of conventional financing.[16] Suffice it to say here that although the desire to avoid taxes does not contaminate a commercially sound sale and leaseback, such desires have led to substantial litigation in a continuing struggle to determine whether tax consequences should literally follow form.

15. Cary, Tax Aspects of the Sale and Leaseback of Corporate Property, 7 N.Y.U. Inst. Taxn. 599, 601 (1949).

16. Accounting considerations are summarized in Cook, Sales and Leasebacks, BNA Tax Mgmt. Portfolio 36-3d, at A-5 through A-35 (1981).

2. *Taxation of Sale-Leaseback Transactions*

a. **Recharacterization**

Frank Lyon Company v. United States

435 U.S. 561, 98 S. Ct. 1291, 55 L. Ed. 2d 550 (1978)

Mr. Justice BLACKMUN delivered the opinion of the Court.

This case concerns the federal income tax consequences of a sale-and-leaseback in which petitioner Frank Lyon Company (Lyon) took title to a building under construction by Worthen Bank & Trust Company (Worthen) of Little Rock, Ark., and simultaneously leased the building back to Worthen for long-term use as its headquarters and principal banking facility.

I

The underlying pertinent facts are undisputed. They are established by stipulations, App. 9, 14, the trial testimony, and the documentary evidence, and are reflected in the District Court's findings.

Lyon is a closely held Arkansas corporation engaged in the distribution of home furnishings, primarily Whirlpool and RCA electrical products. Worthen in 1965 was an Arkansas-chartered bank and a member of the Federal Reserve System. Frank Lyon was Lyon's majority shareholder and board chairman; he also served on Worthen's board. Worthen at that time began to plan the construction of a multi-story bank and office building to replace its existing facility in Little Rock. About the same time Worthen's competitor, Union National Bank of Little Rock, also began to plan a new bank and office building. Adjacent sites on Capitol Avenue, separated only by Spring Street, were acquired by the two banks. It became a matter of competition, for both banking business and tenants, and prestige as to which bank would start and complete its building first.

Worthen initially hoped to finance, to build, and to own the proposed facility at a total cost of $9 million for the site, building, and adjoining parking deck. This was to be accomplished by selling $4 million debentures and using the proceeds in the acquisition of the capital stock of a wholly owned real estate subsidiary. This subsidiary would have formal title and would raise the remaining $5 million by a conventional mortgage loan on the new premises. Worthen's plan, however, had to be abandoned for two significant reasons:

1. As a bank chartered under Arkansas law, Worthen legally could not pay more interest on any debentures it might issue than that then specified by Arkansas law. But the proposed obligations would not be marketable at that rate.

2. Applicable statutes or regulations of the Arkansas State Bank Department and the Federal Reserve System required Worthen, as a state bank subject to their supervision, to obtain prior permission for the investment in banking premises of any amount (including that placed in a real estate subsidiary) in excess of the bank's capital stock or of 40% of its capital stock and surplus. See Ark. Stat. Ann. § 67-547.1 (Supp. 1977); 12 U.S.C. § 371d (1976 ed.) [12 U.S.C.S. § 371d]; 12 C.F.R. § 265.2(f)(7) (1977). Worthen, accordingly, was advised by staff employees of the Federal Reserve System

that they would not recommend approval of the plan by the System's Board of Governors.

Worthen therefore was forced to seek an alternative solution that would provide it with the use of the building, satisfy the state and federal regulators, and attract the necessary capital. In September 1967 it proposed a sale-and-leaseback arrangement. The State Bank Department and the Federal Reserve System approved this approach, but the Department required that Worthen possess an option to purchase the leased property at the end of the 15th year of the lease at a set price, and the federal regulator required that the building be owned by an independent third party.

Detailed negotiations ensued with investors that had indicated interest, namely, Goldman, Sachs & Company; White, Weld & Co.; Eastman Dillon, Union Securities & Company; and Stephens, Inc. Certain of these firms made specific proposals.

Worthen then obtained a commitment from New York Life Insurance Company to provide $7,140,000 in permanent mortgage financing on the building, conditioned upon its approval of the titleholder. At this point Lyon entered the negotiations and it, too, made a proposal.

. . . Lyon in November 1967 was approved as an acceptable borrower by First National City Bank for the construction financing, and by New York Life, as the permanent lender. In April 1968 the approvals of the state and federal regulators were received.

In the meantime, . . . Worthen itself began construction.

In May 1968 Worthen, Lyon, City Bank, and New York Life executed complementary and interlocking agreements under which the building was sold by Worthen to Lyon as it was constructed, and Worthen leased the completed building back from Lyon:

1. Agreements between Worthen and Lyon. Worthen and Lyon executed a ground lease, a sales agreement, and a building lease.

Under the ground lease dated May 1, 1968. . . . Worthen leased the site to Lyon for 76 years and 7 months through November 30, 2044. The first 19 months were the estimated construction period. The ground rents payable by Lyon to Worthen were $50 for the first 26 years and 7 months and thereafter in quarterly payments:

12/1/94 through 11/30/99 (5 years)	—	$100,000 annually
12/1/99 through 11/30/04 (5 years)	—	$150,000 annually
12/1/04 through 11/30/09 (5 years)	—	$200,000 annually
12/1/09 through 11/30/34 (25 years)	—	$250,000 annually
12/1/34 through 11/30/44 (10 years)	—	$10,000 annually.

Under the sales agreement dated May 19, 1968. . . . Worthen agreed to sell the building to Lyon, and Lyon agreed to buy it, piece by piece as it was constructed, for a total price not to exceed $7,640,000, in reimbursements to Worthen for its expenditures for the construction of the building.

Under the building lease dated May 1, 1968. . . . Lyon leased the building back to Worthen for a primary term of 25 years from December 1, 1969, with options in Worthen to extend the lease for eight additional 5-year terms, a total of 65 years. During the period between the expiration of the building lease (at the latest,

November 30, 2034, if fully extended) and the end of the ground lease on November 30, 2044, full ownership, use, and control of the building were Lyon's, unless, of course, the building had been repurchased by Worthen. . . . Worthen was not obligated to pay rent under the building lease until completion of the building. For the first 11 years of the lease, that is, until November 30, 1980, the stated quarterly rent was $145,581.03 ($582,324.12 for the year). For the next 14 years, the quarterly rent was $153,289.32 ($613,157.28 for the year), and for the option periods the rent was $300,000 a year, payable quarterly. . . . The total rent for the building over the 25-year primary term of the lease was $14,989,767.24. That rent equaled the principal and interest payments that would amortize the $7,140,000 New York Life mortgage loan over the same period. When the mortgage was paid off at the end of the primary term, the annual building rent, if Worthen extended the lease, came down to the stated $300,000. Lyon's net rentals from the building would be further reduced by the increase in ground rent Worthen would receive from Lyon during the extension.

The building lease was a "net lease," under which Worthen was responsible for all expenses usually associated with the maintenance of an office building, including repairs, taxes, utility charges, and insurance, and was to keep the premises in good condition, excluding, however, reasonable wear and tear.

Finally, under the lease, Worthen had the option to repurchase the building at the following times and prices:

11/30/80 (after 11 years)	—	$6,325,169.85
11/30/84 (after 15 years)	—	$5,432,607.32
11/30/89 (after 20 years)	—	$4,187,328.04
11/30/94 (after 25 years)	—	$2,145,935.00.

These repurchase option prices were the sum of the unpaid balance of the New York Life mortgage, Lyon's $500,000 investment, and 6% interest compounded on that investment.

2. Construction financing agreement. By agreement dated May 14, 1968. . . . City Bank agreed to lend Lyon $7,000,000 for the construction of the building. This loan was secured by a mortgage on the building and the parking deck, executed by Worthen as well as by Lyon, and as assignment by Lyon of its interests in the building lease and in the ground lease.

3. Permanent financing agreement. By Note Purchase Agreement dated May 1, 1968. . . . New York Life agreed to purchase Lyon's $7,140,000 6 3/4% 25-year secured note to be issued upon completion of the building. Under this agreement Lyon warranted that it would lease the building to Worthen for a noncancelable term of at least 25 years under a net lease at a rent equal to the mortgage payments on the note. Lyon agreed to make quarterly payments of principal and interest equal to the rentals payable by Worthen during the corresponding primary term of the lease. . . . The security for the note were a first deed of trust and Lyon's assignment of its interests in the building lease and in the ground lease. . . . Worthen joined in the deed of trust as the owner of the fee and the parking deck.

In December 1969 the building was completed and Worthen took possession. At that time Lyon received the permanent loan from New York Life, and it discharged the interim loan from City Bank. The actual cost of constructing the office building and parking complex (excluding the cost of the land) exceeded $10,000,000.

Lyon filed its federal income tax returns on the accrual and calendar year basis. On its 1969 return, Lyon accrued rent from Worthen for December. It asserted as deductions one month's interest to New York Life; one month's depreciation on the building; interest on the construction loan from City Bank; and sums for legal and other expenses incurred in connection with the transaction.

On audit of Lyon's 1969 return, the Commissioner of Internal Revenue determined that Lyon was "not the owner for tax purposes of any portion of the Worthen Building," and ruled that "the income and expenses related to this building are not allowable . . . for Federal income tax purposes." . . . He also added $2,298.15 to Lyon's 1969 income as "accrued interest income." This was the computed 1969 portion of a gain, considered the equivalent of interest income, the realization of which was based on the assumption that Worthen would exercise its option to buy the building after 11 years, on November 30, 1980, at the price stated in the lease, and on the additional determination that Lyon had "loaned" $500,000 to Worthen. In other words, the Commissioner determined that the sale-and-leaseback arrangement was a financing transaction in which Lyon loaned Worthen $500,000 and acted as a conduit for the transmission of principal and interest from Worthen to New York Life.

All this resulted in a total increase of $497,219.18 over Lyon's reported income for 1969, and a deficiency in Lyon's federal income tax for that year in the amount of $236,596.36. The Commissioner assessed that amount, together with interest of $43,790.84, for a total of $280,387.20.

Lyon paid the assessment and filed a timely claim for its refund. The claim was denied, and this suit, to recover the amount so paid, was instituted in the United States District Court for the Eastern District of Arkansas within the time allowed by 26 U.S.C. § 6532(a)(1) (26 U.S.C.S. § 6532(a)(1)).

After trial without a jury, the District Court, in a memorandum letter-opinion setting forth findings and conclusions, ruled in Lyon's favor and held that its claimed deductions were allowable. 75-2 U.S.T.C. 9545 (1975); 36 A.F.T.R. 2d 75-5059 (1975). It concluded that the legal intent of the parties had been to create a bona fide sale-and-leaseback in accordance with the form and language of the documents evidencing the transactions. It rejected the argument that Worthen was acquiring an equity in the building through its rental payments. It found that the rents were unchallenged and were reasonable throughout the period of the lease, and that the option prices, negotiated at arm's length between the parties, represented fair estimates of market value on the applicable dates. It rejected any negative inference from the fact that the rentals, combined with the options, were sufficient to amortize the New York Life loan and to pay Lyon a 6% return on its equity investment. It found that Worthen would acquire an equity in the building only if it exercised one of its options to purchase, and that it was highly unlikely, as a practical matter, that any purchase option would ever be exercised. It rejected any inference to be drawn from the fact that the lease was a "net lease." It found that Lyon had mixed motivations for entering into the transaction, including the need to diversify as well as the desire to have the benefits of a "tax shelter." . . .

The United States Court of Appeals for the Eighth Circuit reversed. 536 F.2d 746 (1976). It held that the Commissioner correctly determined that Lyon was not the true owner of the building and therefore was not entitled to the claimed deductions. It likened ownership for tax purposes to a "bundle of sticks" and undertook its own evaluation of the facts. It concluded, in agreement with the Government's contention, that Lyon "totes an empty bundle" of ownership sticks. Id., at 751. It stressed the following: (a) The lease agreements circumscribed Lyon's right to profit from its investment in the building by giving Worthen the option to purchase for an amount equal to Lyon's $500,000 equity plus 6% compound interest and the assumption of the unpaid balance of the New York Life mortgage. (b) The option prices did not take into account possible appreciation of the value of the building or inflation. (c) Any award realized as a result of destruction or condemnation of the building in excess of the mortgage balance and the $500,000 would be paid to Worthen and not Lyon. (d) The building rental payments during the primary term were exactly equal to the mortgage payments. (e) Worthen retained control over the ultimate disposition of the building through its various options to repurchase and to renew the lease plus its ownership of the site. (f) Worthen enjoyed all benefits and bore all burdens incident to the operation and ownership of the building so that, in the Court of Appeals' view, the only economic advantages accruing to Lyon, in the event it were considered to be the true owner of the property, were income tax savings of approximately $1.5 million during the first 11 years of the arrangement. Id., at 752-753. The court concluded, id., at 753, that the transaction was "closely akin" to that in Helvering v. Lazarus & Co., 308 U.S. 252, 84 L. Ed. 226, 60 S. Ct. 209 (1939). "In sum, the benefits, risks, and burdens which (Lyon) has incurred with respect to the Worthen building are simply too insubstantial to establish a claim to the status of owner for tax purposes. . . . The vice of the present lease is that all of (its) features have been employed in the same transaction with the cumulative effect of depriving (Lyon) of any significant ownership interest." 536 F.2d, at 754.

We granted certiorari, 429 U.S. 1089, 51 L. Ed. 2d 534, 97 S. Ct. 1097 (1977), because of an indicated conflict with American Realty Trust v. United States, 498 F.2d 1194 (CA4 1974).

II

This Court, almost 50 years ago, observed that "taxation is not so much concerned with the refinements of title as it is with actual command over the property taxed — the actual benefit for which the tax is paid." Corliss v. Bowers, 281 U.S. 376, 378, 74 L. Ed. 916, 50 S. Ct. 336 (1930). In a number of cases, the Court has refused to permit the transfer of formal legal title to shift the incidence of taxation attributable to ownership of property where the transferor continues to retain significant control over the property transferred. E.g., Commissioner v. Sunnen, 333 U.S. 591, 92 L. Ed. 898, 68 S. Ct. 715 (1948); Helvering v. Clifford, 309 U.S. 331, 84 L. Ed. 788, 60 S. Ct. 554 (1940). In applying this doctrine of substance over form, the Court has looked to the objective economic realities of a transaction rather than to the particular form the parties employed. The Court has never regarded "the simple expedient of drawing up papers," Commissioner v. Tower, 327 U.S. 280, 291, 90 L. Ed. 670, 66 S. Ct. 532, 164 A.L.R. 1135 (1946), as controlling for tax purposes when the objective economic realities are to the contrary. "In the field of taxation, administrators of the laws, and the courts, are concerned with substance and realities, and formal written documents are not rigidly binding." Helvering v. Lazarus & Co., 308 U.S., at 255, 84 L. Ed. 226, 60 S. Ct. 209. See also Commissioner v.

P.G. Lake, Inc., 356 U.S. 260, 266-267, 2 L. Ed. 2d 743, 78 S. Ct. 691 (1958); Commissioner v. Court Holding Co., 324 U.S. 331, 334, 89 L. Ed. 981, 65 S. Ct. 707 (1945). Nor is the parties' desire to achieve a particular tax result necessarily relevant. Commissioner v. Duberstein, 363 U.S. 278, 286, 4 L. Ed. 2d 1218, 80 S. Ct. 1190 (1960).

In the light of these general and established principles, the Government takes the position that the Worthen-Lyon transaction in its entirety should be regarded as a sham. The agreement as a whole, it is said, was only an elaborate financing scheme designed to provide economic benefits to Worthen and a guaranteed return to Lyon. The latter was but a conduit used to forward the mortgage payments, made under the guise of rent paid by Worthen to Lyon, on to New York Life as mortgagee. This, the Government claims, is the true substance of the transaction as viewed under the microscope of the tax laws. Although the arrangement was cast in sale-and-leaseback form, in substance it was only a financing transaction, and the terms of the repurchase options and lease renewals so indicate. It is said that Worthen could reacquire the building simply by satisfying the mortgage debt and paying Lyon its $500,000 advance plus interest, regardless of the fair market value of the building at the time; similarly, when the mortgage was paid off, Worthen could extend the lease at drastically reduced bargain rentals that likewise bore no relation to fair rental value but were simply calculated to pay Lyon its $500,000 plus interest over the extended term. Lyon's return on the arrangement in no event could exceed 6% compound interest (although the Government conceded it might well be less. . . . Furthermore, the favorable option and lease renewal terms made it highly unlikely that Worthen would abandon the building after it in effect had "paid off" the mortgage. The Government implies that the arrangement was one of convenience which, if accepted on its face, would enable Worthen to deduct its payments to Lyon as rent and would allow Lyon to claim a deduction for depreciation, based on the cost of construction ultimately borne by Worthen, which Lyon could offset against other income, and to deduct mortgage interest that roughly would offset the inclusion of Worthen's rental payments in Lyon's income. If, however, the Government argues, the arrangement was only a financing transaction under which Worthen was the owner of the building, Worthen's payments would be deductible only to the extent that they represented mortgage interest, and Worthen would be entitled to claim depreciation; Lyon would not be entitled to deductions for either mortgage interest or depreciation and it would not have to include Worthen's "rent" payments in its income because its function with respect to those payments was that of a conduit between Worthen and New York Life. . . .

III

There is no simple device available to peel away the form of this transaction and to reveal its substance. The effects of the transaction on all the parties were obviously different from those that would have resulted had Worthen been able simply to make a mortgage agreement with New York Life and to receive a $500,000 loan from Lyon. Then *Lazarus* would apply. Here, however, and most significantly, it was Lyon alone, and not Worthen, who was liable on the notes, first to City Bank, and then to New York Life. Despite the facts that Worthen had agreed to pay rent and that this rent equaled the amounts due from Lyon to New York Life, should anything go awry in the later years of the lease, Lyon was primarily liable. No matter how the transaction could have been devised otherwise, it remains a fact that as the agreements were placed in final form, the obligation on the notes fell squarely on Lyon. Lyon, an ongoing enterprise, exposed its very business well-being to this real and substantial risk.

The effect of this liability on Lyon is not just the abstract possibility that something will go wrong and that Worthen will not be able to make its payments. Lyon has disclosed this liability on its balance sheet for all the world to see. Its financial position was affected substantially by the presence of this long term debt, despite the offsetting presence of the building as an asset. To the extent that Lyon has used its capital in this transaction, it is less able to obtain financing for other business needs. . . .

The Court of Appeals acknowledged that the rents alone, due after the primary term of the lease and after the mortgage has been paid, do not provide the simple 6% return which, the Government urges, Lyon is guaranteed, 536 F.2d, at 752. Thus, if Worthen chooses not to exercise its options, Lyon is gambling that the rental value of the building during the last 10 years of the ground lease, during which the ground rent is minimal, will be sufficient to recoup its investment before it must negotiate again with Worthen regarding the ground lease. There are simply too many contingencies, including variations in the value of real estate, in the cost of money, and in the capital structure of Worthen, to permit the conclusion that the parties intended to enter into the transaction as structured in the audit and according to which the Government now urges they be taxed. It is not inappropriate to note that the Government is likely to lose little revenue, if any, as a result of the shape given the transaction by the parties. No deduction was created that is not either matched by an item of income or that would not have been available to one of the parties if the transaction had been arranged differently. While it is true that Worthen paid Lyon less to induce it to enter into the transaction because Lyon anticipated the benefit of the depreciation deduction it would have as the owner of the building, those deductions would have been equally available to Worthen had it retained title to the building. The Government so concedes. Tr. of Oral. Arg. 22-23. The fact that favorable tax consequences were taken into account by Lyon on entering into the transaction is no reason for disallowing those consequences. We cannot ignore the reality that the tax laws affect the shape of nearly every business transaction. See Commissioner v. Brown, 380 U.S. 563, 579-580, 14 L. Ed. 2d 75, 85 S. Ct. 1162 (1965) (Harlan, J., concurring). Lyon is not a corporation with no purpose other than to hold title to the bank building. It was not created by Worthen or even financed to any degree by Worthen.

The conclusion that the transaction is not a simple sham to be ignored does not, of course, automatically compel the further conclusion that Lyon is entitled to the items claimed as deductions. Nevertheless, on the facts, this readily follows. As has been noted, the obligations on which Lyon paid interest were its obligations alone, and it is entitled to claim deductions therefor under § 163(a) of the 1954 Code, 26 U.S.C. § 163(a) (26 U.S.C.S. § 163(a)).

As is clear from the facts, none of the parties to this sale-and-leaseback was the owner of the building in any simple sense. But it is equally clear that the facts focus upon Lyon as the one whose capital was committed to the building and as the party, therefore, that was entitled to claim depreciation for the consumption of that capital. The Government has based its contention that Worthen should be treated as the owner on the assumption that throughout the term of the lease Worthen was acquiring an equity in the property. In order to establish the presence of that growing equity, however, the Government is forced to speculate that one of the options will be exercised and that, if it is not, this is only because the rentals for the extended term are a bargain. We cannot indulge in such speculation in view of the District Court's clear finding to the contrary. We therefore conclude that it is Lyon's capital that is invested in the building according to the agreement of the parties, and it is Lyon that is entitled to depreciation deductions, under § 167 of the 1954 Code, 26 U.S.C. § 167 (26 U.S.C.S. § 167); Cf. United States v. Chicago B. & Q. R. Co., 412 U.S. 401, 37 L. Ed. 2d 30, 93 S. Ct. 2169 (1973).

IV

We recognize that the Government's position, and that taken by the Court of Appeals, is not without superficial appeal. One, indeed, may theorize that Frank Lyon's presence on the Worthen board of directors; Lyon's departure from its principal corporate activity into this unusual venture; the parallel between the payments under the building lease and the amounts due from Lyon on the New York Life mortgage; the provisions relating to condemnation or destruction of the property; the nature and presence of the several options available to Worthen; and the tax benefits, such as the use of double declining balance depreciation, that accrue to Lyon during the initial years of the arrangement, form the basis of an argument that Worthen should be regarded as the owner of the building and as the recipient of nothing more from Lyon than a $500,000 loan.

We, however, as did the District Court, find this theorizing incompatible with the substance and economic realities of the transaction: the competitive situation as it existed between Worthen and Union National Bank in 1965 and the years immediately following; Worthen's undercapitalization; Worthen's consequent inability, as a matter of legal restraint, to carry its building plans into effect by a conventional mortgage and other borrowing; the additional barriers imposed by the state and federal regulators; the suggestion, forthcoming from the state regulator, that Worthen possess an option to purchase; the requirement, from the federal regulator that the building be owned by an independent third party; the presence of several finance organizations seriously interested in participating in the transaction and in the resolution of Worthen's problem; the submission of formal proposals by several of those organizations; the bargaining process and period that ensued; the competitiveness of the bidding; the bona fide character of the negotiations; the three-party aspect of the transaction; Lyon's substantiality and its independence from Worthen; the fact that diversification was Lyon's principal motivation; Lyon's being liable alone on the successive notes to City Bank and New York Life; the reasonableness, as the District Court found, of the rentals and of the option prices; the substantiality of the purchase prices; Lyon's not being engaged generally in the business of financing; the presence of all building depreciation risks on Lyon; the risk, borne by Lyon, that Worthen might default or fail, as other banks have failed; the facts that Worthen could "walk away" from the relationship at the end of the 25-year primary term, and probably would do so if the option price were more than the then-current worth of the building to Worthen; the inescapable fact that if the building lease were not extended, Lyon would be the full owner of the building, free to do with it as it chose; Lyon's liability for the substantial ground rent if Worthen decides not to exercise any of its options to extend; the absence of any understanding between Lyon and Worthen that Worthen would exercise any of the purchase options; the nonfamily and nonprivate nature of the entire transaction; and the absence of any differential in tax rates and of special tax circumstances for one of the parties — all convince us that Lyon has far the better of the case.

In so concluding, we emphasize that we are not condoning manipulation by a taxpayer through arbitrary labels and dealings that have no economic significance. Such, however, has not happened in this case.

In short, we hold that where, as here, there is a genuine multiple-party transaction with economic substance which is compelled or encouraged by business or regulatory realities, is imbued with tax-independent considerations, and is not shaped solely by tax-avoidance features that have meaningless labels attached, the Government should honor the allocation of rights and duties effectuated by the parties. Expressed another way, so long as the lessor retains significant and genuine attributes of the traditional lessor status, the form of the transaction adopted by the parties governs for tax purposes. What those attributes are in any particular case will necessarily depend upon its facts. It suffices to say that, as here, a sale-and-leaseback, in and of itself, does not necessarily operate to deny a taxpayer's claim for deductions.

The judgment of the Court of Appeals, accordingly, is reversed. It is so ordered.

Mr. Justice White dissents and would affirm the judgment substantially for the reasons stated in the opinion in the Court of Appeals for the Eighth Circuit. 536 F.2d 746 (1976).

NOTES AND QUESTIONS

1. "We cannot ignore the reality that the tax laws affect the shape of nearly every business transaction." Frank Lyon Co. v. United States, at page 863 supra.

The departure point in your understanding of the sale and leaseback is to consider why it matters to the taxpayers that the transaction not be recast as a mortgage, and, also, why justice Blackmun almost certainly is mistaken when he asserts that "the Government is likely to lose little revenue, if any, as a result of the shape given the transaction by the parties." Id.

To help understand the tax stakes, consider first with the mindset of a buyer-lessor the treatment of both a sale and leaseback and an equivalent mortgage. To use a simple illustration: B acquires property from A for $1,000,000, which he leases back to A at a $100,000 yearly rental. Cost recovery in the first year is $31,746. If B were to lend A $1,000,000 on an equivalent basis, debt service would be $31,746 yearly; the first year's interest component would be $90,000.

Income of Buyer-Lessor/Lender

	Sale-Leaseback	Secured Loan
Income	Rent: $100,000	Interest: $90,000
Less Cost Recovery	$31,746	—
Taxable Income	$68,254	$90,000

Although B's cash flow is the same in either case, B's taxable income in year one, reduced by the cost recovery deduction, is lower under a sale and leaseback than it would be had B made an equivalent $1,000,000 loan. On the other hand, A would suffer a reciprocal disadvantage.

Deduction of Seller-Lessee/Borrower

	Sale-Leaseback	Secured Loan
Expense	Rent: $100,000	Interest: $90,000
Less Cost Recovery	—	$31,746
Tax Deduction	$100,000	$121,746

Although A would incur a $100,000 outlay, whether in rent or debt service, his relevant deductions in year one would be $21,746 less in the event of a sale and leaseback. A would be reluctant to structure this transaction as a sale and leaseback unless (a) the extra deductions were worth more to B than to A, and (b) B was prepared, in some fashion, to share with A these tax benefits — for example, by paying a somewhat inflated price for the property.

This analysis suggests that a common scenario for a sale and leaseback is one which involves an investor "suffering" higher marginal rates than those applicable to the user-lessee. Despite Justice Blackmun's belief that the outcome of the *Frank Lyon* case would be tax neutral, it seems that as a commercial bank Worthen was able to shelter income even without the cost recovery deduction, and that cost recovery in this case was, indeed, more useful to Lyon than to the bank. Wolfman, The Supreme Court in the *Lyon's* Den: A Failure of Judicial Process, 66 Cornell L. Rev. 1075, 1094-1098 (1981).

2. As you are aware, the relative advantage which the buyer-lessor enjoys over the mortgagee in the early years stems from the excess of cost recovery over that part of the rental payment which is a surrogate for "mortgage amortization." Alluding again to our illustration, B's $21,746 "decrease" in taxable income is simply the difference between the $31,746 in cost recovery and the $10,000 of amortization which A would pay (and B would not report) had the transaction been cast as a mortgage. But some years later the relative advantage shifts away from the buyer-lessor as his cost recovery deductions drop, and — on a level payment mortgage — the amortization component rises. To illustrate the fifteenth year, once again from B's vantage:

Income of Buyer-Lessor/Lender

	Sale-Leaseback	Secured Loan
Income	Rent: $100,000	Interest: $30,000
Less Cost Recovery	$31,746	—
Taxable Income	$68,254	$30,000

The shoe is now on the other foot, and B — as the buyer-lessor — will suffer more taxable income from this transaction than he would incur as a straight mortgagee. Reciprocally, A — as the seller-lessee — will now be better off:

Deduction of Seller-Lessee/Borrower

	Sale-Leaseback	Secured Loan
Expense	Rent: $100,000	Interest: $30,000
Less Cost Recovery	—	$31,746
Tax Deduction	$100,000	$61,746

These shifting tax fortunes reflect a fundamental difference in the treatment of "cost recovery" by an owner of depreciable property and by a mortgage holder. The lender recovers its capital tax-free only as the principal of its investment, the loan, is repaid. Lenders, in effect, amortize their loan for tax purposes on a sinking fund theory of capital recovery. The amortization curve, you will recall, is up-sloping parabolic. By contrast, where the tax code allows the owner to recover his cost on an accelerated basis, as present law does for equipment, and as the Code allowed for real estate prior to 1986, the cost-recovery curve is down-sloping parabolic. Even straight-line depreciation on today's 31.5-year schedule for commercial real estate will outstrip the amortization of a 20-year, 8.50 percent, mortgage during the mortgage's first six years. Wolfman, note 1 supra, at 1089.

3. Turning your attention to the Court's rationale, how persuaded are you that Justice Blackmun has given lawyers and judges useful guidelines for distinguishing between a "good" and "bad" sale and leaseback. Among the factors that to the Court seemed to "reveal the substance" of this transaction were that:

a. Lyon was primarily liable on the permanent loan to New York Life;

b. Lyon had committed $500,000 of its own capital to this transaction;

c. If Worthen chose not to exercise its repurchase option, Lyon would be gambling that the rental value of the building during the last ten years of the ground lease, at a time when the ground rental was minimal, would be sufficient to recoup its investment;

d. Here there was a "genuine multiple-party transaction with economic substance compelled or encouraged by business or regulatory realities";

e. One felt the cumulative impact of the 26 factors set forth under Part IV of the opinion.

As its title implies, Wolfman, The Supreme Court in the *Lyon's* Den: A Failure of Judicial Process, 66 Cornell L. Rev. 1075 (1981), takes strong exception to the Court's decision. The author also reports that early in 1981 Worthen repurchased the bank building from Lyon — in accordance with the lease repurchase option terms. For each of the 11 years during which the lease remained in effect (1969-1980), Lyon's depreciation and interest deductions exceeded its rental income. Had Lyon remained the owner after 1981, its rental income would have exceeded the relevant deductions. Id. at 1101.

4. The Court in *Lyon* refused to apply Helvering v. Lazarus & Co., 308 U.S. 252 (1939). There the department store taxpayer sold its property to a bank and immediately leased it back for 99 years, obtaining in the same transaction successive

purchase options. Although the Supreme Court opinion in *Lazarus* does not disclose the option prices, these were based on the unamortized balance of the moneys which the bank had provided the taxpayer. 32 B.T.A. 633 (1935). The *Lazarus* Court disregarded the sale and leaseback form and, over the Commissioner's(!) objection, recast the transaction as a mortgage.

In *Lyon*, how convincing is Justice Blackmun when he writes:

> The effects of the transaction on all the parties were obviously different from those that would have resulted had Worthen been able simply to make a mortgage agreement with New York Life and to receive a $500,000 loan from Lyon. Then Lazarus would apply. Here, however, and most significantly, it was Lyon alone, and not Worthen, who was liable on the notes, first to City Bank, and then to New York Life. [435 U.S. at 576.]

What if the New York Life loan had been nonrecourse?

Alternatively, what if New York Life had purchased the property directly and then had leased it back to Worthen?

Michael A. Yuhas and James A. Fellows, Sale-Leasebacks Revisited: The Old and the New of Federal Tax Law

31 Real. Est. L. J. 9 (2002)

. . . Since the advent of *Lyon*, the courts have attempted to fashion a workable standard for assessing the economic substance of sale-leaseback transactions. Their decisions have reflected two key elements that are most often discussed in considering the transaction. Specifically, in order for a sale-leaseback to be respected for Federal income tax purposes, the seller must prove either that (a) the underlying transaction was supported by economic substance, or (b) the transaction was motivated by a sound business purpose sufficient to justify the form of the transaction.[17]

THE ECONOMIC SUBSTANCE TEST

The purpose of the economic substance test is to ensure that the transaction generates an economic profit to the buyer-lessor independent of tax considerations. If the transaction does not possess economic substance, it will be characterized as a financing device, and the seller-lessee will be considered the "tax owner" of the property. But just what does this esoteric term "economic substance" mean in the context of Federal tax law?

In *Estate of Franklin*, the Ninth Circuit Court of Appeals stated that the presence of economic substance was predicated on whether the buyer's investment in the underlying property would be expected, at the outset, to yield equity in the property that the buyer could not prudently abandon.[18] According to the *Franklin* decision and its progeny, the test for economic substance, i.e., the "prudent abandonment"

17. See, for example, Rice's Toyota World, Inc. v. Commissioner of Internal Revenue, 81 T.C. 184, 1983 WL 14860 (1983), decision *aff'd in part, rev'd in part on other grounds*, 752 F.2d 89 (4th Cir. 1985).

18. Franklin's Estate v. C. I. R., 544 F.2d 1045 (9th Cir. 1976), *aff'g* Estate of Franklin v. Commissioner of Internal Revenue, 64 T.C. 752, 1975 WL 3035 (1975).

test, should be an analysis of the objective factors indicating whether the transaction has a reasonable opportunity of producing a profit, exclusive of tax benefits.

The key factor relied upon by the courts in determining whether or not economic substance prevails is whether or not the seller has transferred an equity interest to the buyer. If not, the IRS (and the courts) will contend that a true sale has not taken place, and that the seller remains the "tax owner" of the property. Whether or not an equity interest has been transferred or not depends on whether the buyer has acquired not only legal title, but most of the benefits and burdens of ownership as well.

One factor that is supportive of a transfer of equity interest is a purchase price approximating the fair market value of the property. Generally, the buyer will not be considered to have an equity interest if the purchase price appreciably exceeds the property's fair market value. In *Narver*, the Tax Court refused to find a valid sale where the sale price exceeded the property's fair market value.[19] Citing the *Franklin* court's "prudent abandonment" test, the Tax Court noted that even after 15 years of principal payments by the buyer-lessor, the outstanding mortgage on the property would still substantially exceed the property's fair market value. The buyer-lessor in this case would most certainly be acting prudently if it abandoned the property, especially since the mortgage was nonrecourse. The court correctly noted that the primary reason for the buyer-lessor remaining "in the deal" was that it was a related party to the seller-lessee, so the entire transaction had a predominant tax-avoidance motive.

Another determining factor if an equity interest exists is the ability of the buyer to resell the property for a profit.[20] Two elements necessary for profit potential are (a) appreciation potential in the property, and (b) the ability of the buyer-lessor to benefit from such appreciation. The second factor is crucial. If an equity interest really exists, there must be no meaningful restriction in the lease agreement on the buyer-lessor to realize a profit on a later sale. The opportunity for profit may be hollow if the lease agreement grants the seller-lessee the right to lease the property at a fixed rental rate for the entire useful life of the property. Moreover, if a lease agreement contains a clause allowing the seller-lessee the right to renew the lease at less than a fair rental rate, it will be presumed that a perpetual lease exists, allowing the seller to retain all of the benefits of property ownership. Thus, the buyer-lessor is deprived of the opportunity to sell the property at a profit and arguably would not be considered to have acquired a true equity interest in the property. On the other hand, a true equity interest exists if, at the inception of the lease, any renewal rental option is reasonable. This is consistent with a bona fide lessor-lessee relationship. In such cases, the lessor runs the risk that the lessee will not exercise the renewal option, and therefore a significant risk of ownership resides with the buyer-lessor.

Another evidence of an equity interest residing with the buyer-lessor is the absence of any bargain purchase option allowing the seller-lessee to repurchase the property at an amount significantly less than its expected fair market value at that time. If a bargain purchase option exists in the lease contract, then it is presumed that the seller-lessee will exercise this option. The IRS and the courts will generally view the existence of a bargain purchase option as evidence of a financing arrangement, rather than a true sale, because the buyer-lessor has no ability to share in the property's

19. Narver v. Commissioner of Internal Revenue, 75 T.C. 53, 1980 WL 4626 (1980), *opinion aff'd*, 670 F.2d 855 (9th Cir. 1982).
20. Sanderson v. C.I.R., T.C. Memo. 1985-477, 1985 WL 15104 (1985).

appreciation in value. In this instance, the seller-lessee will usually, absent any other controlling factors, be considered the "tax owner" of the property, and will be allotted the depreciation deductions on the property.

Likewise, the seller-lessee will be deemed the "tax owner" of the property if the repurchase option is set to approximate the unamortized principal on the loan obtained by the buyer-lessor to construct the improvements on the property. This is nothing more than a disguised bargain purchase option, if the seller-lessee waits to exercise the option toward the end of the amortization period, when the amount it has to pay to repurchase the property is relatively small. In *Sun Oil* the Third Circuit Court of Appeals concluded that the existence of such a repurchase option was indicative that the buyer-lessor had no true equity in the property, and the seller-lessee was the "tax owner" of the property.[21]

The courts have also focused on the rental payments themselves to determine if the buyer-lessor has a true equity interest in the property. For example, the courts have analyzed the amount of the annual rental payments to determine if there is enough cash flow available for distribution to the buyer after the annual mortgage payments have been made.[22] Another factor indicative of a financing device rather than a true sale is when rental payments are less than fair market value. The courts have usually found that the buyer-lessor does not have an equity interest in the property if the rental payments can be applied to the option price allowed the seller-lessee for reacquisition of the property.[23] Such a provision is much too indicative of the seller-lessee retaining the benefits as "tax owner" of the property. In this situation, an implied financing arrangement is the result, and the depreciation deduction is granted the seller-lessee.

EQUITY INTERESTS AND RIGHTS AND RESPONSIBILITIES

The courts will also review the lease agreement to determine whether the purported sales transaction truly shifts the "risks and responsibilities" to the buyer-lessor. If the seller-lessee retains most of the "risks and responsibilities" of ownership, the transaction will be considered an implied financing arrangement, rather than a true sale. One such factor the courts will review is whether or not the seller agrees to indemnify and hold the buyer harmless from any and all claims and liability for damage that occurs on the property. Such a "hold harmless" agreement indicates the absence of any risk and responsibilities being passed to the buyer-lessor. Also suggestive of the absence of risk to the buyer is the lack of any obligation to make repairs or any expenditures for improvement to the property, which is of course typical in a triple net lease situation.

Another indication that a true sale has not occurred is when the lease agreement contains a "hell or high water" clause. Pursuant to a "hell or high water" provision, there is no diminution of the seller's rental payments even in the event of a casualty or total destruction of the property. Thus, even if the property is totally destroyed, the seller-lessee is liable for the full monthly rentals for the remainder of the lease term. In this instance, then, the seller-lessee has retained most of the risks and

21. Sun Oil Co. v. C. I. R., 562 F.2d 258 (3d Cir. 1977), rev'g Sun Oil Co. v. C.I.R., T.C. Memo. 1976-40, 1976 WL 3238 (1976).

22. See, for example, Hilton v. Commissioner of Internal Revenue, 74 T.C. 305, 1980 WL 4523 (1980), *judgment aff'd*, 671 F.2d 316 (9th Cir. 1982).

23. Frenzel v. C.I.R., T.C. Memo. 1963-276, 1963 WL 701 (T.C. 1963).

responsibilities of ownership, similar to any other debtor who has borrowed money to acquire and use property.

A review of the rights of the parties upon a condemnation of the leased premises may also suggest that the seller continues to enjoy certain benefits that traditionally are reserved to the owner of the property. If the seller is entitled to the condemnation proceeds upon a formal taking by a public authority, the seller-lessee will continue to be the "tax owner" of the property. In some cases, the seller, upon learning of the threat of condemnation, possesses the legal right to make a "rejectable offer" to purchase the property for an amount equal to the present value of future rental payments, plus a contractual premium. If the property is reacquired, the seller-lessee could then sell the repurchased property to the public authority at its current fair market value, ensuring a substantial profit. Should the buyer-lessor reject the offer, then the seller-lessee is given the contractual right to the condemnation proceeds, or at least is given the contractual right to have the buyer-lessor provide replacement real estate equal in value to the condemned property. Such a repurchase option, coupled with the right to the condemnation proceeds and/or the right of substitution, are significant benefits that reside with the seller-lessee, who would be considered the "tax owner" of the property in such a situation.

THE BUSINESS PURPOSE TEST

A transaction may still qualify as a true sale, even if the economic substance test is failed, if it can be shown that the transaction possessed a bona fide "business purpose." The inquiry into the business purpose test tends to be an investigation of the parties' subjective motivation for entering into the sale-leaseback agreement. As such, it does not have the tests of objective measurement usually found in the economic substance test.

The business purpose test focuses on the business reasons for entering into the transaction, exclusive of any tax consequences of the transaction. A transaction entered into solely for favorable tax consequences would fail the business purpose test (although it could still be considered a true sale under the economic substance test). In the *Lyon* decision, the Supreme Court found the fact that conventional financing was precluded by federal and state regulations established a bona fide business purpose to the sale-leaseback. Limitations on the amount of conventional debt the seller-lessee could incur would also satisfy the business purpose test for consummating a sale-leaseback arrangement. In *Hilton*, the court found that a business purpose existed where conventional financing would only grant the taxpayer 75 percent financing of the acquisition costs, whereas a sale-leaseback arrangement provided the taxpayer with 100 percent financing.[24] Entering into a sale-leaseback transaction in order to obtain a more favorable balance sheet (no liability shown for future rentals) should also satisfy the business purpose test, as such a motive operates independently of tax consequences. Eliminating debt from the balance sheet can allow the seller-lessee to meet other loan covenants established by other creditors, as well as increase the potential to obtain future financing.

---

24. See Hilton v. Commissioner of Internal Revenue, 74 T.C. 305, 1980 WL 4523 (1980), *judgment aff'd*, 671 F.2d 316 (9th Cir. 1982).

b. Sale versus Exchange

Another tax aspect of the sale and leaseback involves the treatment of losses, should any result from the first step of the transaction. Ideally, the seller would like to obtain ordinary loss recognition. Several pitfalls lie in the way. The first hazard, already mentioned, is that the sale will be treated as a loan. The second hazard, since the purchase price is not always related to market values, is that the commissioner, relying upon § 482, will rewrite the transaction to rectify artificial distortions of income; to date, the commissioner has not seized this power. The final hazard, the nonrecognition feature of § 1031, is considered in the following case.

Leslie Co. v. Commissioner

64 T.C. 247 (1975), aff'd, 539 F.2d 943 (3d Cir. 1976)

IRWIN, Judge. Respondent determined deficiencies in petitioner's income tax as follows:

Year	Deficiency
1965	$176,551.77
1966	50,700.90
1968	155,770.75

The issues presented for our determination are (1) whether the sale and leaseback of property by petitioner in 1968 constituted an exchange of property of a like kind within the meaning of section 1031(a) and, if so, (2) whether petitioner should be entitled to depreciate the property under any of the methods specified in section 167(b) and to avail itself of investment credits pursuant to section 38.

The deficiencies in 1965 and 1966 result from the disallowance of net operating loss carrybacks and investment credit carrybacks based on a claimed net operating loss in 1968 and are completely dependent upon our determination of whether the sale and leaseback comes within the purview of section 1031.

FINDINGS OF FACT

Some of the facts have been stipulated and the stipulation of facts, together with the exhibits attached thereto, are found accordingly.

Petitioner Leslie Co. (hereinafter referred to as Leslie or petitioner) is a New Jersey corporation primarily engaged in the design, manufacture, and industrial distribution of pressure and temperature regulators and automatic instantaneous water heaters. . . .

For many years prior to 1966 Leslie operated its entire business, plant, and office in Lyndhurst, N.J. In 1966 Leslie determined that the Lyndhurst plant would be inadequate for future use and decided to construct a new facility in Parsippany. Upon completion of the new plant the Lyndhurst property was to be sold. Pursuant to the decision to move, Leslie acquired land in Parsippany in March 1967.

On October 30, 1967, after having explored other financing possibilities without success, Leslie agreed to a sale and leaseback of the land with improvements to the Prudential Insurance Co. of America (hereinafter referred to as Prudential). The agreement provided that Prudential would enter into a contract for the purchase and leaseback of the Parsippany property, subject, inter alia, to the following requirements and conditions:

1. The sale price shall not exceed $2,400,000 or the actual cost of land, building and other improvements erected thereon, whichever is the lower. . . .

2. Leslie Co. shall have erected and completed on the above premises a one story, 100% sprinklered, masonry and steel industrial building containing approximately 185,000 square feet. . . . The building is to be constructed and improvements made according to detailed plans and specifications which have been approved by The Prudential. Any changes to the plans . . . must be approved by Prudential prior to commencement of construction. . . .

4. Prudential will be furnished with the following prior to closing:

(a) A lease with Leslie Co. satisfactory in form and substance to Prudential and Leslie Co. for a term of 30 years at an absolute net rental of $190,560, or 7.94% of purchase price if less than $2,400,000 to be paid monthly, in advance, in equal monthly installments. The lease shall include two (2) renewal options of 10 years each with an absolute net annual rental of $72,000, or 3% of purchase price if less than $2,400,000. The lease shall further include a rejectable offer to purchase at the end of the fifteenth, twentieth, twenty-fifth or thirtieth year based on the following schedule:

at the end of the 15th year	$1,798,000
at the end of the 20th year	$1,592,000
at the end of the 25th year	$1,386,000
at the end of the 30th year	$1,180,000

On December 16, 1968, after completion of the plant as approved by Prudential, Leslie delivered the deed to the Parsippany property to Prudential for $2.4 million. The fair market value of the property at the time of sale was in the neighborhood of $2.4 million. Contemporaneously with the transfer of title to Prudential, Leslie and Prudential entered into the lease as specified in the above agreement. The annual net rental of $190,560 was comparable to the fair rental value of similar types of property in the northern New Jersey area. The lease also provided that all condemnation proceeds, net of any damages suffered by Leslie with respect to its trade fixtures and certain structural improvements, would become the property of Prudential without deduction for the leasehold interest of petitioner.

Leslie's total cost in purchasing the land and constructing the plant was $3.187 million, consisting of the following:

Land	$ 255,000
Building	2,410,000
Paving and landscaping	72,000
Boiler (including special features)	140,000
Special electrical wiring	138,000

Miscellaneous personal property	140,000
(including certain special items)	
Interim finance costs	20,000
Selling costs	12,000
Total cost	3,187,000

Leslie would not have entered into the sales part of the transaction without the guarantee of the leaseback.

The Parsippany plant was not in operation on December 16, 1968, the date of closing, and did not become fully operational until mid-January 1969. The useful life of the new plant was stipulated to be 30 years.

Leslie sold the Lyndhurst plant for $600,000 when it moved into the Parsippany facilities.

Leslie is not a dealer in real estate.

On its 1968 corporate income tax return Leslie reported the disposition of the Parsippany property as a sale with a gross sale price of $2.4 million and a cost of $3,187,414 with a loss thereon of $787,414. The claimed loss resulted in a net operating loss of $366,907, which was carried back to 1965. In addition, an investment credit of $436.41, not utilizable in 1968 on account of the claimed net operating loss was carried back to 1965. An investment credit of $50,700, likewise not utilizable in 1968 on account of the claimed net operating loss, was carried back to 1966. Respondent, in disallowing the claimed loss, thereby disallowed all of the claimed carrybacks. Respondent would allow the loss as a cost of obtaining the 30-year lease and permit it to be amortized over the period of the lease.

Leslie treated the claimed loss as an unrecovered cost of plant construction on its books to be amortized over 30 years.

Prudential treated the rental receipts as rental income and depreciated the property on its corporate income tax returns.

OPINION

Respondent, relying upon section 1.1031(a)-1(c), Income Tax Regs.,[25] and Century Electric Co., 15 T.C. 581 (1950), *aff'd.*, 192 F.2d 155 (8th Cir. 1951), *cert. denied*, 342 U.S. 954 (1952), submits that the sale and leaseback between petitioner and Prudential falls within the nonrecognition provisions of section 1031, and that, therefore, petitioner's claimed loss is not allowable. In the same breath, respondent would allow the claimed loss as a "cost" of acquiring the leasehold and amortize it over the 30-year term. Petitioner, on the other hand, submits that there was no "exchange" within the meaning of section 1031, and that, therefore, the claimed

---

25. "(c) No gain or loss is recognized if (1) a taxpayer exchanges property held for productive use in his trade or business, together with cash, for other property of like kind for the same use, such as a truck for a new truck or a passenger automobile for a new passenger automobile to be used for a like purpose; or (2) a taxpayer who is not a dealer in real estate exchanges city real estate for a ranch or farm, or exchanges a leasehold of a fee with 30 years or more to run for real estate, or exchanges improved real estate for unimproved real estate; or (3) a taxpayer exchanges investment property and cash for investment property of a like kind."

loss must be recognized. We agree with petitioner that section 1031 is inapplicable and that the loss must be recognized. The amount is not in dispute.

As an exception to the general rule requiring the recognition of all gains and losses, section 1031 must be strictly construed. See sec. 1002 and the regulations thereunder, particularly sec. 1.1002-1(b), Income Tax Regs. In order for this nonrecognition provision to come into play it must first be established that an exchange occurred. An exchange is defined in the regulations as a transaction involving the reciprocal transfer of property, as distinguished from a transfer of property for a money consideration. Sec. 1.1002-1(d), Income Tax Regs. See also Vernon Molbreak, 61 T.C. 382, 390-392 (1973), aff'd. per curiam, 509 F.2d 616 (7th Cir. 1975).

In the instant situation petitioner executed a sale and leaseback agreement with respect to the Parsippany property. It is clear that the sale and leaseback were merely successive steps of a single integrated transaction. It is also equally clear that petitioner, unable to obtain financing to construct a new plant, employed the sale and leaseback mechanism to obtain the needed new facilities. These factors, however, do not dispose of the issue.

While the leaseback arrangement was a necessary condition to the sale, we are of the opinion that, based on the record before us, the leasehold herein did not have any separate capital value which could be properly viewed as a portion of the consideration paid or exchanged. Petitioner received $2.4 million on the sale of the property. The sale and leaseback agreement, executed prior to construction of the new facility, provided that the sale price was to be actual cost to petitioner or $2.4 million, whichever was less. This was based on Prudential's appraisal of the worth of the property after improvements. As it turned out, the actual cost to construct the new facilities (including purchase of the land) totaled $3.187 million. Although we are troubled by the disparity between $2.4 million and $3.187 million, the only evidence in the record (and this presented by respondent) indicated that the fair market value of the property as improved at the date of sale was in the neighborhood of $2.4 million, not $3.187 million. Respondent has also not objected to petitioner's proposed finding of fact that the property as improved had a fair market value of $2.4 million at the date of sale.[26] We also note that the evidence presented indicated that this valuation was comparable to the fair market value of similar types of property in the area. The annual net rental was also comparable to the fair rental value of similar types of property in the area. Based on the record before us, we have no choice but to find that the fair market value of the property was within the $2.4 million range. In our judgment, therefore, the sole consideration paid for the property was the $2.4 million in cash. The leasehold, while integral to the transaction, had no separate capital value and was not a part of the consideration. See City Investing Co., 38 T.C. 1, 9 (1962). In support of our finding that the leasehold had no capital value in and of itself at the time of the sale, we also note that in addition to the fact of the sale price and net rentals being for fair value, the condemnation clause in the lease agreement provided (with certain

26. We hypothesize that respondent's willingness to accept petitioner's proposed finding of fair market value was due to his desire to ensure that the transaction would not be characterized as merely financial with title in substance remaining with petitioner. At the same time, relying upon Century Electric Co., 15 T.C. 581 (1950), he must have assumed that this Court would disregard the fair market values in finding sec. 1031 applicable. What he has failed to take into account is that it must first be determined that an "exchange" occurred for sec. 1031 to apply.

exceptions not material herein) that in the event of condemnation all proceeds would be paid to Prudential without deduction for the leasehold interest. This clause, while clearly not conclusive on the issue, is further evidence of a lack of capital value.

Respondent, however, in the body of his reply brief, argues that since petitioner's cost exceeded the contract price, the difference must be equal to the capital value of the lease. We find this unsupported by the evidence presented. In essence, it would appear that respondent is arguing that although the leasehold had no capital value, it had a premium value to petitioner. The excess expenditures over $2.4 million would not be a loss as such to petitioner since it would be able to utilize the improvements as lessee and thus would be willing to spend more than $2.4 million. Although this argument seems to comport to economic realities, it does not give the leasehold value. The difference between $2.4 million and $3.187 million is clearly attributable to the cost of building the plant (including the purchase of land); it is not attributable to the leasehold. While it may be true that it was only because of the leasehold that petitioner was willing to spend $3.187 million, it does not follow that the leasehold had a value equal to the difference between $2.4 million and $3.187 million. To reach such a result, it must be shown that the fair market value of the improved property was $3.187 million, not $2.4 million. This was not done.

From an accounting standpoint it is true that the loss, being an extraordinary item, may cause a distortion of income. That is probably why petitioner amortized the unrecovered costs over the 30-year term in its financial statements. Petitioner's treatment of the item on the books, however, is not dispositive of the issue for tax purposes. It is not at all uncommon to find that the book and tax treatment of a given transaction differ. Although losses may be amortized for book purposes, nothing in the Code permits such amortization for tax purposes.

When all the cards are on the table, the fact remains that petitioner had a cost basis of $3.187 million in the improved property and realized $2.4 million on the sale. The bonafideness of the sale was not questioned by respondent. As stated previously, since the evidence indicates that petitioner would be paying a net rent comparable to the fair rental value, the leasehold could have no value at the time of sale, and thus could not be a part of the consideration paid. It was merely a condition precedent to the sale; no more and no less. The fact that petitioner was willing to sell the property "only with some kind of leaseback arrangement included does not of itself detract from the reality of the sale." Cf. City Investing Co., supra.

We, therefore, conclude that there was a bona fide sale of the property and not an "exchange" within the meaning of section 1031. See Jordan Marsh Co. v. Commissioner, 269 F.2d 453 (2d Cir. 1959), nonacq. Rev. Rul. 60-43, 1960-1 C.B. 687, rev'g. a Memorandum Opinion of this Court. We need not consider *Century Electric Co.*, supra, and its possible conflict with *Jordan Marsh Co.* since we have found that there was no "exchange" within the meaning of section 1031. We do note, though, that if an "exchange" had been found, then, assuming "like kind" property, the fair market value of such property would appear not to be relevant.

Since the nonrecognition provisions of section 1031 are not applicable, the general rule of recognition under 1002 applies.

Because of our holding in the above issue we need not consider the other issue presented.

Reviewed by the Court.

Decision will be entered for the petitioner.

TANNENWALD, J., dissenting. If I understand the majority opinion correctly, its rationale is (1) the sale and leaseback constituted "integral parts of a single transaction" but this factor is not dispositive of the issue of whether there was an exchange under section 1031, and (2) since the sales price and the lease rental were "for fair value," the lease lacked "capital value" and "the transaction must be classified as a bona fide sale and not as an exchange." I think this rationale is erroneous.

I start from the premise that the record supports a finding that the price Prudential paid for the property was equal to its fair market value and that the lease rental was "fair" (as to which the record, to put it mildly, is sparse). But the fact of the matter is that although the lease in the instant case may not have had "capital value" in the normal sense of that term, it did have a value beyond the fair rental value to the petitioner herein.

Whatever the respective values of the lease and the fee, it is clear from the record herein that petitioner entered into the transaction with its eyes wide open. It knew at the outset that Prudential would acquire the full benefit (in the form of title to the fee) of all of its expenditures with regard to the property. It committed itself to expend whatever sums it took to construct the building with those improvements required by its own special needs and to pay the legal fees and other costs required to consummate the transaction with Prudential. The record herein contains insufficient evidence to support a finding that the petitioner did not contemplate or should not have reasonably contemplated the possibility of a cost overrun; indeed, the record tends to indicate that the opposite was the case. The reason for petitioner's willingness to run the risk of this financial exposure is obvious; in order to operate its business, it needed and was entitled to obtain the lease from Prudential. Thus, the lease had a value to this petitioner beyond the rental value, namely, any excess cost that it might incur. In this respect, the situations of the taxpayers in both Jordan Marsh Co. v. Commissioner, 269 F.2d 453 (2d Cir. 1959), rev'g. T.C. Memo, 1957-237, and Century Electric Co. v. Commissioner, 192 F.2d 155 (8th Cir. 1951), aff'g. 15 T.C. 581 (1950), are clearly distinguishable. In both those cases, the costs in excess of the fair market value of the fee and/or the fair value of the lease were incurred long before the transaction under scrutiny (in one case, 12 years, and in the other, 13 years). It could not possibly be said that those costs were undertaken in order to consummate the transaction. Here, by way of contrast, petitioner incurred the excess costs for the express purpose of engaging in the transaction with Prudential. Under these circumstances, petitioner, unlike the taxpayer in *Jordan Marsh*, was not "clos[ing] out a losing venture" (see 269 F.2d at 456), i.e., a venture that did not start out on a predetermined course.

Under my reasoning, it is unnecessary for me to decide the extent to which the decision or rationale of the Second Circuit Court of Appeals in *Jordan Marsh* is in conflict with *Century Electric*. See City Investing Co., 38 T.C. 1, 7 (1962). I have no hesitancy, however, in holding that, even though there was a sale and not an exchange under section 1031, the excess expended by petitioner over the cash received from Prudential, as far as the petitioner is concerned, should be considered as akin to a bonus paid for the lease and amortized over its term. University Properties, Inc., 45 T.C. 416 (1966), aff'd, 378 F.2d 83 (9th Cir. 1967), and cases cited therein.

Raum, Drennen, Quealy, and Hall, JJ., agree with this dissent.

[Dissenting opinions of Quealy and Wilbur, JJ., omitted.]

NOTES AND QUESTIONS

1. Accord Crowley Milner and Co. v. Commissioner, 76 T.C. 1030 (1981), *aff'd*, 689 F.2d 635 (6th Cir. 1982).

2. Before trial, Leslie Co. amended its petition to argue, in the alternative, that the transaction, if not a sale, should be viewed as a mortgage financing arrangement, entitling Leslie Co. to the depreciation deductions and the investment tax credit. 539 F.2d at 945 n.6. In view of the court's holding, this issue was not reached. Had this been necessary, what outcome would you have foreseen?

3. The *Leslie Co.* opinion mentions two circuit court decisions. Century Electric Co. v. Commissioner, 192 F.2d 155 (8th Cir. 1951), *cert. denied*, 342 U.S. 954 (1952), which the government had cited, and Jordan Marsh Co. v. Commissioner, 269 F.2d 453 (2d Cir. 1959), on which taxpayer had relied. Refusing to find any kind of exchange, the Tax Court concluded (incorrectly!) that neither decision controlled the outcome; but the two cases stand as the leading—and somewhat contradictory—authority as to when a leaseback might result in a nontaxable exchange.

The facts in *Century Electric* first: Taxpayer owned business property carried on its books at $531,000. A small college purchased the property for $150,000 and immediately leased it back for 95 years at an aggregate rental of $367,000 for the first 25 years and $11,400 per year thereafter. In refusing to allow taxpayer the benefit of a $381,000 loss deduction, the court simply cited the Treasury Regulation that equates a lease of at least 30 years and "real estate" as property of like kind. Treas. Reg. § 1.1031(a)-(c)(2).

Now the facts in *Jordan Marsh*: A department store owned business property with a book value of $4,770,000. It sold the property for $2,300,000 on a leaseback for 30 years and 3 days, with renewal options for another 30 years. The annual lease rental during the initial term was $138,000, concededly the full rental value, and full rental value was also to be paid during any renewal. The seller was given no repurchase option. The commissioner disallowed the tax loss on the basis of *Century Electric* and the Treasury Regulations. The Tax Court upheld him. 29 T.C. 1281 (1957). Despite the apparent similarity between this and the *Century Electric* case, the Second Circuit reversed the commissioner, holding—as did the court in *Leslie Co.*—that the *Jordan Marsh* transaction was a sale and not an exchange; by taking this position, the Second Circuit did not reach the issue of "likeness" between a 30-year lease and a fee simple:

. . . By the transaction its capital invested in the real estate involved had been completely liquidated for cash to an amount fully equal to the value of the fee. This, we hold, was a sale—not an exchange within the purview of § 112(b).

The Tax Court apparently thought it of controlling importance that the transaction in question involved no change in the petitioner's possession of the premises; it felt that the decision in Century Electric Co. v. Commissioner of Internal Rev., supra, controlled the situation here. We think, however, that the case was distinguishable on the facts. For notwithstanding the lengthy findings made with meticulous care by the Tax Court in that case, 15 T.C. 581, there was no finding that the cash received by the taxpayer was the full equivalent of the value of the fee which the taxpayer had conveyed to the vendee-lessor, and no finding that the leaseback called for a rent which was fully equal to the rental value of the premises. . . .

269 F.2d 453, 456-457 (2d Cir. 1959).

Although the Second Circuit's reasons are sound for treating the *Jordan Marsh* transaction as a sale, its effort to distinguish *Century Electric* is, at best, unconvincing. The Eighth Circuit certainly seemed satisfied (or, at least, kept any doubts to itself) that the sales price measured the market value. With such equivalence, the lease-back has no independent monetary value, the transfer of a fee for cash is a sale, and the Eighth Circuit erred in believing that it had to decide whether the "exchange" was of like kind.

By distinguishing, rather than repudiating, the *Century Electric* precedent, the Second Circuit stresses an imaginary conflict between itself and the Eighth Circuit over nontaxable exchanges, whereas a real conflict was brewing over the distinction between sale and exchange. The commissioner has refused to follow *Jordan Marsh*. Rev. Rul. 60-43, 1960-1 Cum. Bull. 687.

A loss that is disallowed, as in *Century Electric*, will be treated as an acquisition cost of the leaseback and amortized over the leasehold term. 192 F.2d 155, 160; cf. Int. Rev. Code of 1954, § 162. The leaseback term in *Century Electric* was 95 years, far longer than the estimated useful life of the undepreciated improvements that were the subject of the transaction. The court, in rejecting taxpayer's contention that the loss should be apportioned between the land and improvements in proportion to their respective bases, argued that the taxpayer had "invested" in a leasehold and not in its constituent properties.

4. If a sale and leaseback transaction should result in gain instead of loss, which side of the sale versus exchange argument would taxpayer and the commissioner each be most likely to advance?

5. *Transactions between related parties.* Taxpayers who might be tempted to push a close family or business relationship into an advantageous sale and leaseback will find the Code a minefield. For example, the Code does not recognize any loss incurred on a sale between members of a family (brothers and sisters, spouses, ancestors, and lineal descendants), between an individual and a "controlled" corporation, between the grantor and fiduciary of a trust, and between the fiduciary and beneficiary of a trust. Int. Rev. Code of 1954, § 267. For a detailed treatment of sale and leasebacks between related parties, see Anderson, Tax Factors in Real Estate Operations 303-310 (2d ed. 1965); Burke, Why Some Sale and Leaseback Arrangements Succeed While Others Fail, 26 J. Taxn. 130, 132-133 (1967).

c. The Issue of Genuineness

Estate of Franklin v. Commissioner

544 F.2d 1045 (9th Cir. 1976)

SNEED, Circuit Judge. This case involves another effort on the part of the Commissioner to curb the use of real estate tax shelters.[27] In this instance he seeks to

---

27. An early skirmish in this particular effort appears in *Manuel D. Mayerson*, 47 T.C. 340 (1966), which the Commissioner lost. The Commissioner attacked the substance of a nonrecourse sale, but based his attack on the nonrecourse and long-term nature of the purchase money note, without focusing on whether the sale was made at an unrealistically high price. In his acquiescence to *Mayerson*, 1969-2 Cum. Bull. xxiv, the Commissioner recognized that the fundamental issue in these cases generally will be whether the property has been "acquired" at any artificially high price, having little relation to its fair market value. "The Service emphasizes that its acquiescence in Mayerson is based on the particular facts

disallow deductions for the taxpayers' distributive share of losses reported by a limited partnership with respect to its acquisition of a motel and related property. These "losses" have their origin in deductions for depreciation and interest claimed with respect to the motel and related property. These deductions were disallowed by the Commissioner on the ground either that the acquisition was a sham or that the entire acquisition transaction was in substance the purchase by the partnership of an option to acquire the motel and related property on January 15, 1979. The Tax Court held that the transaction constituted an option exercisable in 1979 and disallowed the taxpayers' deductions. *Estate of Charles T. Franklin*, 64 T.C. 752 (1975). We affirm this disallowance although our approach differs somewhat from that of the Tax Court.

The interest and depreciation deductions were taken by TwentyFourth Property Associates (hereinafter referred to as Associates), a California limited partnership of which Charles T. Franklin and seven other doctors were the limited partners. The deductions flowed from the purported "purchase" by Associates of the Thunderbird Inn, an Arizona motel, from Wayne L. Romney and John E. Romney (hereinafter referred to as the Romneys) on November 15, 1968.

Under a document entitled "Sales Agreement," the Romneys agreed to "sell" the Thunderbird Inn to Associates for $1,224,000. The property would be paid for over a period of ten years, with interest on any unpaid balance of seven and one-half percent per annum. "Prepaid interest" in the amount of $75,000 was payable immediately; monthly principal and interest installments of $9,045.36 would be paid for approximately the first ten years, with Associates required to make a balloon payment at the end of the ten years of the difference between the remaining purchase price, forecast as $975,000, and any mortgages then outstanding against the property.

The purchase obligation of Associates to the Romneys was nonrecourse; the Romneys' only remedy in the event of default would be forfeiture of the partnership's interest. The sales agreement was recorded in the local county. A warranty deed was placed in an escrow account, along with a quitclaim deed from Associates to the Romneys, both documents to be delivered either to Associates upon full payment of the purchase price, or to the Romneys upon default.

The sale was combined with a leaseback of the property by Associates to the Romneys; Associates therefore never took physical possession. The lease payments were designed to approximate closely the principal and interest payments with the consequence that with the exception of the $75,000 prepaid interest payment no cash would cross between Associates and Romneys until the balloon payment. The lease was on a net basis; thus, the Romneys were responsible for all of the typical expenses of owning the motel property including all utility costs, taxes, assessments, rents, charges, and levies of "every name, nature and kind whatsoever." The Romneys also were to continue to be responsible for the first and second mortgage until the final purchase installment was made; the Romneys could, and indeed did, place additional mortgages on the property without the permission of Associates. Finally, the Romneys were allowed to propose new capital improvements which

in the case and will not be relied upon in the disposition of other cases except where it is clear that the property has been acquired at its fair market value in an arm's length transaction creating a bona fide purchase and a bona fide debt obligation." Rev. Rul. 69-77, 1969-1 Cum. Bull. 59.

Associates would be required to either build themselves or allow the Romneys to construct with compensating modifications in rent or purchase price.

In holding that the transaction between Associates and the Romneys more nearly resembled an option than a sale, the Tax Court emphasized that Associates had the power at the end of ten years to walk away from the transaction and merely lose its $75,000 "prepaid interest payment." It also pointed out that a *deed* was never recorded and that the "benefits and burdens of ownership" appeared to remain with the Romneys. Thus, the sale was combined with a leaseback in which no cash would pass; the Romneys remained responsible under the mortgages, which they could increase; and the Romneys could make capital improvements.[28] The Tax Court further justified its "option" characterization by reference to the nonrecourse nature of the purchase money debt and the nice balance between the rental and purchase money payments.

Our emphasis is different from that of the Tax Court. We believe the characteristics set out above can exist in a situation in which the sale imposes upon the purchaser a genuine indebtedness within the meaning of section 167(a), Internal Revenue Code of 1954, which will support both interest and depreciation deductions. They substantially so existed in *Hudspeth v. Commissioner*, 509 F.2d 1224 (9th Cir. 1975), in which parents entered into sale-leaseback transactions with their children. The children paid for the property by executing nonnegotiable notes and mortgages equal to the fair market value of the property; state law proscribed deficiency judgments in case of default, limiting the parents' remedy to foreclosure of the property. The children had no funds with which to make mortgage payments; instead, the payments were offset in part by the rental payments, with the difference met by gifts from the parents to their children. Despite these characteristics this court held that there was a bona fide indebtedness on which the children, to the extent of the rental payments, could base interest deductions. *See also American Realty Trust v. United States*, 498 F.2d 1194 (4th Cir. 1974); *Manuel D. Mayerson*, 47 T.C. 340 (1966).

In none of these cases, however, did the taxpayer fail to demonstrate that the purchase price was at least approximately equivalent to the fair market value of the property. Just such a failure occurred here. The Tax Court explicitly found that on the basis of the facts before it the value of the property could not be estimated. 64 T.C. at 767-768.[29] In our view this defect in the taxpayers' proof is fatal.

Reason supports our perception. An acquisition such as that of Associates if at a price approximately equal to the fair market value of the property under ordinary circumstances would rather quickly yield an equity in the property which the

28. There was evidence that not all of the benefits and burdens of ownership remained with the Romneys. Thus, for example, the leaseback agreement appears to provide that any condemnation award will go to Associates. Exhibit 6-F, at p. 5.

29. The Tax Court found that appellants had "not shown that the purported sales price of $1,224,000 (or any other price) had any relationship to the actual market value of the motel property. . . ." 64 T.C. at 767.

Petitioners spent a substantial amount of time at trial attempting to establish that, whatever the actual market value of the property, Associates acted in the good faith *belief* that the market value of the property approximated the selling price. However, this evidence only goes to the issue of sham and does not supply substance to this transaction. "Save in those instances where the statute itself turns on intent, a matter so real as taxation must depend on objective realities, not on the varying subjective beliefs of individual taxpayers." *Lynch v. Commissioner*, 274 F.2d 867, 872 (2d Cir. 1959). *See also Bornstein v. Commissioner*, 334 F.2d 779 (1st Cir. 1964); *MacRae v. Commissioner*, 294 F.2d 56 (9th Cir. 1961). . . .

purchaser could not prudently abandon. This is the stuff of substance. It meshes with the form of the transaction and constitutes a sale.

No such meshing occurs when the purchase price exceeds a demonstrably reasonable estimate of the fair market value. Payments on the principal of the purchase price yield no equity so long as the unpaid balance of the purchase price exceeds the then existing fair market value. Under these circumstances the purchaser by abandoning the transaction can lose no more than a mere chance to acquire an equity in the future should the value of the acquired property increase. While this chance undoubtedly influenced the Tax Court's determination that the transaction before us constitutes an option, we need only point out that its existence fails to supply the substance necessary to justify treating the transaction as a sale *ab initio*. It is not necessary to the disposition of this case to decide the tax consequences of a transaction such as that before us if in a subsequent year the fair market value of the property increases to an extent that permits the purchaser to acquire an equity.[30]

Authority also supports our perception. It is fundamental that "depreciation is not predicated upon ownership of property *but rather upon an investment in property. Gladding Dry Goods Co.*, 2 B.T.A. 336 (1925)." *Mayerson, supra* at 350 (italics added). No such investment exists when payments of the purchase price in accordance with the design of the parties yield no equity to the purchaser. *Cf. Decon Corp.*, 65 T.C. 829 (1976); *David F. Bolger*, 59 T.C. 760 (1973); *Edna Morris*, 59 T.C. 21 (1972). In the transaction before us and during the taxable years in question the purchase price payments by Associates have not been shown to constitute an *investment in the property*. Depreciation was properly disallowed. Only the Romneys had an investment in the property.

Authority also supports disallowance of the interest deductions. This is said even though it has long been recognized that the absence of personal liability for the purchase money debt secured by a mortgage on the acquired property does not deprive the debt of its character as a bona fide debt obligation able to support an interest deduction. *Mayerson, supra* at 352. However, this is no longer true when it appears that the debt has economic significance only if the property substantially appreciates in value prior to the date at which a very large portion of the purchase price is to be discharged. Under these circumstances the purchaser has not secured "the use or forbearance of money." *See Norton v. Commissioner*, 474 F.2d 608, 610 (9th Cir. 1973). Nor has the seller advanced money or forborne its use. *See Bornstein v. Commissioner*, 334 F.2d 779, 780 (1st Cir. 1964); *Lynch v. Commissioner*, 273 F.2d 867, 871-872 (2d Cir. 1959). Prior to the date at which the balloon payment on the purchase price is required, and assuming no substantial increase in the fair market value of the property, the absence of personal liability on the debt reduces the transaction in economic terms to a mere chance that a genuine debt obligation may arise. This is not enough to justify an interest deduction. To justify the deduction the debt must exist; potential existence will not do. For debt to exist, the purchaser, in the absence of personal liability, must confront a situation in which it is presently reasonable from an economic point of view for him to make a capital investment in the amount of the unpaid purchase price. *See Mayerson, supra*

---

30. These consequences would include a determination of the proper basis of the acquired property at the date the increments to the purchaser's equity commenced.

at 352.[31] Associates, during the taxable years in question, confronted no such situation. Compare Crane v. Commissioner, 331 U.S. 1, 11-12, 67 S. Ct. 1047, 91 L. Ed. 1301 (1947).

Our focus on the relationship of the fair market value of the property to the unpaid purchase price should not be read as premised upon the belief that a sale is not a sale if the purchaser pays too much. Bad bargains from the buyer's point of view—as well as sensible bargains from buyer's, but exceptionally good from the seller's point of view—do not thereby cease to be sales. See Commissioner v. Brown, 380 U.S. 563, 67 S. Ct. 1047, 91 L. Ed. 1301 (1965); Union Bank v. United States, 285 F.2d 126, 128, 152 Ct. Cl. 126 (1961). We intend our holding and explanation thereof to be understood as limited to transactions substantially similar to that now before us.

Affirmed.

3. Bankruptcy

The recharacterization issue also arises in bankruptcy court. In these proceedings, it is usually the debtor (seller-lessee) urging that the arrangement created a disguised security agreement or even a joint venture rather than a true sale-leaseback. Contrast the two cases that follow:

In re Opelika Manufacturing Corp.

67 B.R. 169 (N.D. Ill. 1986)

MEMORANDUM AND ORDER

ROBERT L. EISEN, Chief Judge.

This matter came to be heard on the motion of the debtor in possession, Opelika Manufacturing Corporation ("Opelika" or "debtor"), to extend the time within which it must assume or reject various nonresidential real property leases. In connection therewith, Opelika presently seeks a determination as a matter of law that its Lease Agreement (the "Agreement") with the Pulaski County-Hawkinsville Development Authority (the "Authority"), is in fact no more than a security agreement. For the reasons set forth below, the court, having reviewed the memoranda and documents submitted by the parties, holds that the Agreement in question, although denominated a lease, is, in actuality, a security agreement.

BACKGROUND

On May 1, 1971, Opelika entered into an agreement with the Authority whereby the Authority would purchase and construct a plant in Hawkinsville, Georgia, as well as acquire and install machinery and equipment for use by Opelika, using proceeds from the sale of tax exempt revenue bonds issued by the Authority. Under a Trust Indenture executed on that same date, the Authority assigned its interest in the Agreement to the First National Bank of Chicago, as Trustee (hereinafter the "Trustee").

---

31. Emphasis on the fair market value of the property in relation to the apparent purchase price animates the spirit, if not the letter, of Rev. Rul. 69-77, 1969-1 Cum. Bull. 59.

The debtor now argues that the terms of the Agreement bear no resemblance to a true lessor-lessee relationship but rather demonstrate that Opelika borrowed money which it was obligated to repay with interest, securing its obligation with a deed to the plant and certain equipment. The Trustee, on the other hand, appearing in these proceedings, seeks a determination that the Agreement is a lease to be assumed or rejected by the debtor. The Trustee, in addition to contending that there is no evidence that the parties intended to create a security agreement, posits that there are sufficient indications in the Agreement of a leasehold estate under Georgia law.

DISCUSSION

Section 101(42) of the Bankruptcy Code defines a security agreement for purposes of bankruptcy law as an "agreement that creates or provides for a security interest." 11 U.S.C. § 101(42). Whether a lease constitutes a security interest under the Code depends on whether it constitutes a security interest under applicable state law, H. Rep. No. 95-595, 95th Cong., 1st Sess. 314 (1977) *reprinted in* U.S. Code Cong. & Admin. News, 5787, 5878, 6271 (1978). The Agreement in question, which encompasses both real and personal property, provides that it is to be governed by Georgia law. Section 1-201(37) of the Georgia Commercial Code, like its Uniform Commercial Code counterpart, provides in relevant part as follows:

> Whether a lease is intended as security is to be determined by the facts of each case; however, (a) the inclusion of an option to purchase does not itself make the lease one intended for security, and (b) an agreement that upon compliance with the terms of the lease the lessee shall become or has the option to become the owner of the property for no additional consideration or for a nominal consideration *does* make the lease one intended for security.

Ga. Code § 109A1-201(37) (emphasis added).

In determining whether or not a transaction is intended to be a true lease, courts look beyond the form of the transaction to its economic reality. *In re Nite Lite Inns*, 13 B.R. 900, 908 (Bankr. S.D. Ca. 1981). *See also Matter of Kassuba*, 562 F.2d 511, 513 (7th Cir. 1977); *Fox v. Peck Iron and Metal Co., Inc.*, 25 B.R. 674, 688 (Bankr. S.D. Ca. 1982). The court in *In re Central Foundry Company*, 48 B.R. 895 (Bankr. N.D. Ala. 1985), a case factually similar to the present situation, was required to determine whether a "lease" was a true lease or a disguised security agreement. The "lease" term in *Central Foundry* was tied to the maturity and retirement of the bond issue. In addition, the "rent" was payable when the interest payments on the bond came due; the "rent" payment also included a payment on outstanding principal of the bond issue; the "lessee" had an unconditional obligation to pay "rent"; and the "lessee" was obligated to purchase a certain pollution control system at the end of the "lease" term for a nominal consideration of $10.00. The court there held that the terms of the "lease" clearly showed the land and equipment were being used to secure the indebtedness on the bond issue through which the construction was financed.

With respect to the Agreement in issue, Opelika is obligated under section 12.1 to purchase the Project for $10.00 at the expiration or sooner termination of the "lease term" following full payment of the bonds. Clearly such a provision does make the present "lease" one intended as security under section 1-201(37) of the Georgia Commercial Code. *See also In re Seatrain Lines*, 20 B.R. 577 (Bankr. S.D.N.Y. 1982) (fact that amount of purchase option was unrelated to market value of property was strong evidence that transaction was one intended for security). Moreover, the Agreement contains additional indicia of a financing agreement as enunciated in *Central Foundry* and other relevant authority, e.g., Opelika may terminate its "lease" by redeeming the bonds (section 11.1); the payment of "rent" is unconditional as long as any bonds remain due (section 5.5); and the "rent" bears no relationship to the value of the right to use the property but is directly tied to repayment of the bonds (section 5.3).

Other provisions of the Agreement demonstrate that the Authority did not retain the normal risks and responsibilities of lessor status. For example, if the project could not be constructed and equipped with funds from the bond sale, Opelika was *required* to complete construction and equip the plant at its own expense (section 4.6); Opelika, at its sole discretion can make modifications or improvements to the plant (section 6.1(b)); the Authority has no obligation to renew, repair or replace any obsolete or unnecessary "leased" equipment in the plant and Opelika at its sole discretion may sell, trade in, exchange or scrap any such equipment (section 6.2); Opelika may grant or release easements, licenses or rights of way over the property (section 8.4); and Opelika may assign the Agreement without the Authority's consent but the Authority may not sell, assign, transfer or convey the project (sections 9.1 and 9.3).

Despite the foregoing, the Trustee nonetheless contends the Agreement is a true lease, relying primarily on the decision of the Supreme Court of Georgia in *DeKalb County Board of Tax Assessors v. W. C. Harris & Co.*, 248 Ga. 277, 282 S.E.2d 880 (1981), wherein long-term leases with the city development authority were held to be taxable as leasehold estates rather than fee simple estates. Since *DeKalb County* is also a factually similar case, the Trustee focuses on provisions of the subject Agreement similar to those on which the court in *DeKalb* relied in finding sufficient indications of a leasehold under Georgia law, e.g., the Agreement limits expenditures which Opelika can make on the property (section 8.7); the Agreement requires Opelika to remain primarily liable if the property is sublet (section 9.1(a)); the Authority agrees not to convey or sell the property during the lease term (section 9.3); and, in the event of default by Opelika, the Authority may terminate the lease and exclude the lessee from possession (section 10.2(c)).

It is important to note that the decision in *DeKalb* focused on those aspects of a lease inconsistent with fee ownership in the context of a tax case, a significant difference. Nevertheless, even were this court to find those terms of the Agreement on which the Trustee relies similar to the dispositive terms of the leasehold in *DeKalb*, the terms taken as a whole in the context of the weight of authority point persuasively to the conclusion that the parties herein intended to create a security interest rather than a true lease. *See In re Pacific Express, Inc.*, 780 F.2d 1482 (9th Cir. 1986). Therefore, insofar as this "lease" is really a disguised security agreement, assumption or rejection under section 365 is inapplicable. Id.

SO ORDERED.

In re Omne Partners II

67 B.R. 793 (D.N.H. 1986)

MEMORANDUM OPINION

JAMES E. YACOS, Bankruptcy Judge.

This adversary proceeding brings before the court the question of the characterization and present status of a real estate transaction involving the "OMNE Mall" located in Portsmouth, New Hampshire. The debtor-defendant operates and manages this "Factory Outlet" discount mall facility.

On March 20, 1986, the debtor filed a Chapter 11 petition seeking reorganization relief in this court. On April 7, 1986, the plaintiffs, hereinafter referred to as the "Pension Fund" or "Fund," filed a complaint seeking a determination as to their rights to possession of the property and its rents, and for other relief.

The Fund takes the position that it effectively terminated the debtor's rights as lessee under the underlying ground lease of the mall property prior to the bankruptcy filing, and that the debtor has wrongfully refused to vacate the property and to return control and possession of the same to the Pension Fund as the owner under a terminated lease.

The debtor answered and denied that its rights had been effectively terminated prior to the bankruptcy. The debtor also counterclaimed for a declaratory judgment that the transaction in question was not a true lease at all, but rather was a disguised financing transaction under a "sale-and-leaseback" in which the Pension Fund should be viewed as merely a mortgagee-lender regarding the property.

The City of Portsmouth, which provided some of the funds required to put the mall in operation, took as part of its collateral a security interest in the lease in question, and has been permitted to intervene as a party defendant and joins with the debtor in challenging the assertion by the Pension Fund that the lease had been terminated prior to bankruptcy. The City also apparently joins in the debtor's contention that the transaction in question was a financing arrangement rather than a lease, but couples this contention with the further request that this court "validate the interest of the intervenor as a mortgagee on the premises referred to in the agreement."

By agreement of the parties this adversary proceeding has been split into "First Trial" and "Second Trial" phases. The "First Trial" phase, involving an evidentiary hearing on October 24, 1986, and a further oral argument hearing on November 21, 1986, deals solely with the question of the characterization, or recharacterization, of the real property transaction in question. Left for the "Second Trial" phase is the separate question as to whether the lease, if that is what it is determined to be, was terminated prior to bankruptcy.

The evidence submitted indicates a multi-party transaction for development and operation of the Portsmouth mall property. In round numbers, the debtor was required to obtain a total of $12,600,000 in funding for the project. This included $3,000,000 from the limited partners of the debtor and $2,100,000 from the City of Portsmouth as its part of a HUD grant for industrial development. The debtor also obtained $4,800,000 from a construction lender for the mall improvements and $2,700,000 from the Pension Fund under the transaction here in issue.

The transaction with the Pension Fund was closed on May 1, 1984, under a sale-leaseback in which the debtor transferred the land to the Fund and the trustees of the Fund executed a 30-year ground lease to the property back to the debtor. Under the agreement, the debtor deeded the property to the Fund for a sale price of $1,000,000, and the Fund agreed to make additional site improvement advances up to 1.5 million dollars concerning the mall. This amount was later increased to 1.7 million dollars. The ground lease is what is commonly referred to as a "triple net lease" transaction in which the lessee obligates itself to pay certain taxes, charges, costs and expenses attributable to the property which otherwise would be born directly by the owner-lessor.

The debtor's chief contention is that it bore all the normal obligations of ownership and that the "rental payments" provided under the lease transaction were admittedly defined in terms of the recovery by the Pension Fund of its investment into the transaction. This, the debtor says, establishes that the economic substance of the transaction was simply secured financing. The debtor argues therefore that it should be declared to be the "owner" of the property, notwithstanding the recorded deed showing the Pension Fund as owner, and the recorded lease showing the debtor as lessee. The debtor also raises a number of additional facets of the lease transaction which it contends adds to this "economic substance" argument. The Fund contends that a number of other facets of the overall transaction negate the debtor's argument. However, for reasons which appear below in my discussion of the "intent factor," it is unnecessary to go into all of these contentions in detail for present purposes.

It is well established that a bankruptcy court, as a court of equity, may "look through form to substance" in determining the true nature of a transaction relating to rights of parties against a bankruptcy estate. . . .

In the context of sale-leaseback realty transactions, however, this power should be exercised only upon a showing by "clear and convincing evidence" by the debtor that the transaction should be deemed a disguised financing transaction. *Fox v. Peck Iron & Metal Co., supra*, at p. 688. *See also Seaboard Terminal Corp. v. Western Maryland R.R. Co.*, 108 F.2d 911 (4th Cir. 1940). Moreover, the intent of the parties in the transaction is factually the key issue in such cases. *Matters of Kassuba*, 562 F.2d 511 (7th Cir.1977): *Fox v. Peck Iron & Metal Co.*, [25 B.R. 674, 688 (S.D. Cal. 1982)].

It is also important to identify the purpose relevant to the Bankruptcy Code for which the characterization is being made. In the present case the characterization is relevant because it will determine whether the debtor can seek to realize an "equity of redemption" in the property, as it would be able to do as a mortgagor-borrower, by virtue of the confirmation of a reorganization plan, with or without a "cram-down" provision, as provided in § 1129 of the Bankruptcy Code.

On the evidence presented I conclude that the debtor has failed to meet its burden of clear and convincing evidence that the transaction in question was understood by the parties, and had the economic substance, as being a disguised financing transaction rather than the lease transaction it purported to be. There is no question that these parties, both being sophisticated in such complex financing transactions, negotiated and intended the transaction to be a lease rather than a loan transaction.

The debtor in fact first approached the Pension Fund on the basis of a loan transaction with regard to its mall project. In November of 1982 the debtor asked the Fund to consider a construction loan for the project. The Fund rejected that request the same month and indicated that it did not wish to get involved in any construction lending. At that time the Fund had a dispute with the Department of Labor regarding its involvement in construction loans involving union labor.

In December of 1982 the debtor replied to this rejection by suggesting that perhaps a sale-leaseback transaction could be structured for the project. The debtor's representatives met with the Fund trustees in January of 1983 with regard to this proposal. The trustees of the Fund at that meeting indicated their reluctance to consider this alternative proposal but agreed to further negotiations. These negotiations went on throughout 1983 and it was not until November of 1983 that the Pension Fund finally agreed to the transaction in question. As part of that transaction the debtor was required to give its opinion of counsel that the Fund would receive good title as owner of the property from the debtor, and that the Fund would be provided appropriate title insurance written by the debtor's attorney as agent to protect the Fund's interest as owner of the property.

On this showing I find that the debtor understood that it was important to the Pension Fund that the transaction in question be accomplished through a sale-leaseback rather than a construction loan, and that the debtor agreed to that structuring of the transaction. It also appears clear that if the debtor had broached the concept that it should have some "protection for its equity from foreclosure" in the transaction, the Pension Fund would not have agreed to go forward. The debtor actually did not bring up the matter in the negotiations.

There is likewise no evidence to support a finding that a disguised financing transaction was involved. Obviously, the deed of ownership to the Pension Fund was on record, for all interested parties to see, as was the lease with all its terms and conditions. No misleading of creditors dealing with the debtor, which was a concern of this court involving an equipment lease transaction, in *In re North American Rental*, 54 B.R. 574 (Bankr. D.N.H. 1985), or an ownership claim to the "technology" of a computer company, in *In re Bedford Computer Corporation*, 61 B.R. 594 (Bankr. D.N.H. 1986), is involved in the present case.

A case with very similar facts to the present case appears in *Matters of Kassuba*, 562 F.2d 511 (7th Cir. 1977). The Court of Appeals for the Seventh Circuit there held that a recharacterization of a sale-leaseback transaction was properly denied. The Court emphasized that many of the "economic substance" factors are relevant only when the intent of the parties is disputed. Id., at p. 514.

The court of appeals in the *Kassuba* decision also made the following comment pertinent to the "equity of redemption" argument being made by the debtor in the present case:

> Thus, the parties by contract, may create a set of mutual economic benefits that is similar to a mortgage without conferring on each other the rights and liabilities of judicial foreclosure, if that is what they actually intend. The substance of the transaction that a court of equity will examine is not its economic effect, which the parties determine by their agreement, but instead it is what their agreement is. What would be a contract case at law remains in equity a contract case.

The same emphasis on the intent of the parties appears in the decision of the Court of Appeals for the Fourth Circuit in *Seaboard Terminals Corp. v. Western Maryland R.R. Co.*, supra, at pp. 915-916.

I am aware that some courts have downplayed the importance of the "intent factor" in these recharacterization situations. To some extent, it can be argued that it is logically inconsistent to say that the characterization of a commercial transaction depends upon the intent of the parties and yet also say a court of equity can look through form to the economic substance of the transaction. I do not believe however that bankruptcy judges have a warrant from Congress to run roughshod over the economic landscape recharacterizing commercial transactions entered into by sophisticated parties—restating them in terms of their "economic substance" contrary to their negotiated and agreed form—in the absence of some *triggering factor* permitting such recharacterization, i.e., an actual ambiguity in the documentation, a substantial factual dispute as to the intent of the parties, or some "disguise" or "misleading" aspect to the transaction.

I also find some comfort for this approach in the Supreme Court's decision in the analogous tax avoidance/recharacterization situation in *Frank Lyon Co. v. United States*, 435 U.S. 561, 98 S. Ct. 1291, 55 L. Ed. 2d 550 (1978). In that case a state bank which could not finance a new building by conventional mortgage or other financing, due to various state and federal regulatory requirements, entered into a sale-leaseback agreement with the Frank Lyon Company. The Court of Appeals for the 8th Circuit held that the tax commissioner had correctly determined that Lyon was not the true owner of the building and was not entitled to claimed tax deductions as an owner. It likened ownership to "a bundle of sticks" and concluded after reviewing the net lease transaction involved that Lyon "totes an empty bundle of ownership sticks." 536 F.2d 746, 751 (1976).

The Supreme Court in *Frank Lyon* reversed, concluding that the transaction was not a sham transaction, notwithstanding the fact that the lease rental payments were defined in terms of recovering the investment made into the property by the Frank Lyon Company. The Court commented:

> It is true, of course, that the transaction took shape according to Worthen's [the lessee bank's] needs. As the Government points out, Worthen throughout the negotiations regarded the respective proposals of the independent investors in terms of its own cost of funds. E.g., App. 355. It is also true that both Worthen and the prospective investors compared the various proposals in terms of the return anticipated on the investor's equity. But all this is natural for parties contemplating entering into a transaction of this kind. Worthen needed a building for its banking operations and other purposes and necessarily had to know what its cost would be. The investors were in business to employ their funds in the most remunerative way possible. And, as the Court has said in the past, a transaction must be given its effect in accord with what actually occurred and not in accord with what might have occurred.

[435 U.S. at 576, 98 S. Ct. at 1299].

The Supreme Court in *Frank Lyon* also made the following pertinent commentary as to sale-leasebacks as essentially new, hybrid real estate transactions: "As is clear from the facts, none of the parties to this sale and lease-back was the owner of the building in any simple sense."

For all of the foregoing reasons I conclude that the debtor must be denied its attempt to recharacterize the transaction herein question [sic]. A separate judgment to that effect will be entered. This leaves for determination at the "Second Trial" the question of whether the leasehold interest of the debtor was effectively terminated pre-bankruptcy by the lessor Pension Fund.

NOTES AND QUESTIONS

1. How was the debtor-"lessee" in *Opelika* advantaged by the court's determination that the transaction was a security agreement? For a thoughtful examination of the issues, see Thomas C. Homburger and Karl L. Marschel, Recharacterization Revisited: A View of Recharacterization of Sale and Leaseback Transactions in Bankruptcy after Fifteen Years, 41 Real Prop. Prob. & Tr. J. 123 (2006).

2. The court in *Omne Partners II* relied largely on its reading of the parties' intention to create a sale-leaseback, rather than the "loan" that the debtor

originally sought. Yet one treatise states that a key factor that might lead a bankruptcy court to recharacterize a sale-leaseback transaction is the lessee's original loan request. Thomas C. Homburger et al., Structuring Real Estate Sale-Leasebacks 5-3 (1992).

3. In re Nite Lite Inns, 13 B.R. 900 (S.D. Cal. 1981), involved the bankruptcy of a motel developer, whose troubles mounted because of delays and cost overruns during the motel's construction. At the core of a complex transaction, the debtor had agreed to sell the completed motel to a buyer-lessor and to lease back the property for 29 years with a renewal option for another 25 years. Because of the debtor's difficulties, the "sale" collapsed, but only after the buyer had deposited $800,000 into escrow toward the purchase price.

In the Chapter 11 proceeding, the buyer claimed that § 365(j) of the Bankruptcy Code entitled it to a "lien" in the amount of the escrow deposit. The debtor answered that the sale-leaseback was "really nothing more than a disguised financing," and that the buyer should be treated as an unsecured "lender." The court, in agreeing with the debtor, gave in part this explanation:

> The evidence of the parties' intent in this transaction is somewhat equivocal. On the one hand, throughout their negotiations, Nite Lite [debtor] and Burke Investors [buyer] referred to their agreement as a sale-leaseback. Furthermore, all the documentation created by their lawyers reinforced this preference. On the other hand, individuals bent on disguising the true nature of their business dealings can hardly be expected to disclose their unstated intentions, especially in the writings they create. . . . Also, Burke characterized the intent of Burke Investors in this transaction as that of a "passive investor," looking only for a secure and profitable return on their invested capital. These remarks indicate that Burke Investors was not interested in obtaining any of the attributes of ownership which traditionally attend to landlord status.
>
> When the underlying economic substance of the leaseback is examined it becomes clear that this transaction was merely a disguised financing arrangement. . . . For all practical purposes, Nite Lite was the "owner" of the motel property despite the transaction. First, the parties expressly referred to the Lease Agreement as a "net-net-net" lease. This meant that the "lessee-seller," Nite Lite, was responsible for payment of all real estate taxes, the procurement of fire and liability insurance and the undertaking of repairs and maintenance of the motel property, at no cost to Burke Investors. . . . Third, Nite Lite was to pay all utility costs associated with the motel property. Fourth, Nite Lite was granted a broad right to alter or modify the motel property after notice had been given to Burke Investors. . . .
>
> With respect to the question of "rentals" it is clear that the "rent" charged under the Lease Agreement did not simply reflect fair compensation for the use of the motel property. It was designed to amortize Burke Investors' costs in purchasing the motel property and also provide a rate of return on that investment. . . .

Do you agree with the court that the enumerated factors, singly or together, contradict the buyer's claim of a "true" sale-leaseback?

4. Recharacterization may result in the purported "sale" being treated as a usurious loan. See, e.g., Rochester Capital Leasing Corp. v. K & L Litho Corp., 13 Cal. App. 3d 697, 91 Cal. Rptr. 827 (1970).

5. In re PCH Associates, 60 B.R. 870 (S.D.N.Y. 1986), resulted in a sale-leaseback agreement being recast as a joint venture. Because of the court's holding, the

debtor was excused from making the lease rental payments to its co-venturer "lessor."

6. In *Opelika*, the court largely disregarded *DeKalb* because that case had "focused on those aspects of a lease inconsistent with fee ownership in the context of a tax case, a significant difference." Does this mean that the criteria for determining for whether a transaction is a sale-leaseback rather than a disguised financing is different in a tax case than it is in a bankruptcy case?

4. Other Uses for the Sale-Leaseback

1. *In lieu of a second mortgage.* X built a 408-unit garden apartment project costing $5.25 million. He obtained a $4.65 million mortgage at 10.7 percent constant. This left X with a $600,000 equity and a net cash flow after debt service of $102,000 yearly (17 percent).

X then sold the land (only) to a pension fund for $652,000. Simultaneously, X leased back the land for 99 years at an annual ground rental of $75,000. Net result: X had an annual cash flow of $27,000 on zero cash investment, retained all depreciation deductions, and would be able to refinance the first mortgage since the pension fund agreed to subordinate the fee for the entire 99-year term of the lease. Cf. Mortgage & Real Estate Executive's Report, pp. 2-3 (May 21, 1971).

2. *As the key to a real estate exchange.* X owned a 165-acre farm valued at $1.5 million, subject to a $1.275 million mortgage. X wanted to realize a return on his equity investment without paying a capital gains tax on the sale of the farm, which he had owned for 30 years.

Y owned an apartment house valued at $1.6 million, subject to a $1.185 million mortgage. Y had no incentive to sell the property, which was in top condition. But Y would happily convert some or all of its equity into cash.

An exchange was worked out that imaginatively met both X's and Y's objectives. Y obtained the farm at the $1.5 million figure (which it then sold). X obtained the apartment house at the "reduced" price of $1.41 million. Simultaneously, X leased back the apartment house to Y; the ground rental gave X a satisfactory return on his equity. The key provision was a repurchase option (at $1.41 million), permitting Y to recover the fee interest in the apartment house should it ever wish to. Cf. Mortgage & Real Estate Executive's Report, pp. 4-5 (May 21, 1971).

3. *Lease-layering.* Once the seller becomes the tenant under a net lease in a sale-leaseback transaction, he can take the further step of selling the lease and *sub*leasing back. The practice is described below:

> William Zeckendorf, the dynamic president of Webb & Knapp, may have been the originator of this type of transaction. He conceived of various layers of leases analogous to the varying types of securities (common stock, preferred stock, first-mortgage bonds, second-mortgage bonds, and debenture bonds) issued by a corporation, each carrying a return related to the risk involved. Applying this graduated-risk system to real estate, the sale-leaseback of property by an insurance company would be the first step, entailing the company assuming a modest risk as fee owner, analogous to the risk in a high-credit, low-interest bond.
>
> The lease could then be sold by the lessee to an investor, with a sublease back to the seller who would operate the property. The main lease (often called a "sandwich

lease") would produce a fixed return to its holder represented by the difference between the rent payable by the sublessee to the main lessee and the rent payable by the main lessee to the fee owner. This main lease would involve somewhat more risk than ownership of the fee since the holder of the main lease has a fixed rental obligation to the fee owner that would continue even if the sublessee defaulted. It is possible to add another layer to the "sandwich" by creating an intermediate sublease, which would make the operating lease a sub-sublease.

The value of the main and intermediate leaseholds would be determined by capitalizing the returns received by the respective lessees in their landlord capacities. The sub-sublease (the operating position) has a real estate value, since the tenant operates the property and therefore receives space rents, provides management and building services, and has all the other incidents of ownership. In addition, leasehold mortgages can be placed on each lease. And, of course, the fee may be mortgaged if the purchaser is capable of mortgaging it and desires to do so.

If the holder of a "sandwich lease" insists on participating in the fruits of the operation of the property, the lease can provide that the holder (lessor) will receive a percentage of the income that the operating subtenant derives from the property over and above the fixed sublease rental.[32] This adds to the value of the "sandwich" lessee's position. A provision of this type can also be used in a straight sale-leaseback, where the seller-lessee retains the operating portion.

Lease-layering can also be used in a sale-leaseback deal that separates the land from the building. In one actual transaction, a corporation with nationwide operations proposed to construct a new building for its home office through sale-leaseback financing. Initially, the corporation sold the land to an investor and leased it back, with the investor agreeing in the lease to construct the building for the corporation. The investor sold the land, subject to the corporation's leasehold, to a REIT which, in this particular instance, had no need for depreciation deductions. The investor-seller then leased the land back from the REIT, retaining in the lease its obligation to construct the building as provided in the initial lease to the corporate seller. This second ground lease also provided that the investor, as the intermediate tenant, would retain ownership of the building to be constructed. The rent on this second "sandwich lease" was, of course, less than the rent to be paid by the original corporate seller under its leaseback. The intermediate lease also provided for the joinder by the REIT landlord in a mortgage to be obtained by the investor, the proceeds of which were used to construct the building. The REIT then provided a leasehold mortgage loan on such lease. As a result of this multilayered transaction, 100 percent financing was provided to construct the new building.

Sillcocks, Financial Sense in Sale and Real Estate Leasebacks, 5 Real Est. Rev. 89, 94-95 (Spring 1975).

---

32. If the landlord is a REIT or a pension or profit-sharing trust, the additional rent must be based on gross income only and the tenant must be restricted from making subleases providing for rent in any way based on net income. The Internal Revenue Code specifically bars these tax-favored trusts from directly or indirectly participating in a tenant's net income.

D. SECURITIZATION

1. *Securitization of Commercial Real Estate Markets*

Michael H. Schill, The Impact of the Capital Markets on Real Estate Law and Practice

32 J. Marshall L. Rev. 269 (1999)

Over the past twenty years, the real estate markets of the United States have been swept by enormous change. A sector of the economy that had long been resistant to change, real estate has been and is continuing to be transformed by the process of securitization on both the debt and equity side. Just twenty years ago, the vast majority of single family residential mortgage loans were provided by local banks or savings and loan associations that held the debt in their portfolios until maturity or prepayment. Today, most single family mortgage debt is sold into the secondary mortgage market and converted into securities. Ten years ago, mortgage loans for commercial properties were largely originated and held by commercial banks, pension funds or insurance companies. In recent years, with the exception of the meltdown of the commercial mortgage-backed securities market in the summer of 1998, the proportion of commercial loans that were securitized rapidly grew. Just six or seven years ago, real estate investment trusts (REITs) were commonly thought of as the investment entity that crashed and burned in the 1970s. In the last two or three years, however, REITs have increasingly come to be seen as a dominant, if not preeminent ownership vehicle in many real estate markets throughout the nation. . . .

As the securitization of home mortgage loans exploded in the 1980s, the commercial mortgage debt market was much slower to join the securitization bandwagon. A number of factors accounted for the relatively slow growth of commercial mortgage-backed securities during this period. Perhaps most importantly, no secondary mortgage market for commercial mortgage loans was created by the federal government. Thus, the secondary mortgage market for commercial mortgages had to be created in a piecemeal fashion by a variety of institutional investors and Wall Street. In addition, certain characteristics of commercial mortgages made them a bit more difficult to securitize. Commercial mortgage loans tend to be much larger than residential loans. Therefore, the number of loans in a pool tends to be smaller, creating greater risk due to less opportunity for diversification.

Commercial mortgage loans are also more idiosyncratic than residential loans. Commercial properties are typically quite different from each other, requiring much more due diligence than pools based upon relatively similar single family loans. Moreover, the loan documentation for commercial properties tends to be much more voluminous and non-uniform as compared to residential properties. Finally, without a secondary mortgage market backed by federal or quasi-federal guarantees, the commercial mortgage-backed securities market required experimentation with different methods of credit enhancement such as letters of credit and overcollateralization.

Nevertheless, throughout the late 1980s and 1990s, the commercial mortgage-backed securities market grew significantly. . . . [I]n 1991, $4.3 billion in commercial mortgage-backed securities were issued. This volume of issuance increased by

850% to $41.0 billion in 1997. As a proportion of outstanding commercial mortgage debt, the growth in number of commercial mortgage-backed securities has also been strong. . . . [I]n 1990, $758 billion of mortgages secured by commercial properties were outstanding of which less than $5 billion had been securitized. By the first quarter of 1998, $855 billion of commercial mortgages were outstanding and over $102 billion had been securitized (a 20-fold increase).

THE SECURITIZATION OF EQUITY IN REAL ESTATE

Just as the capital markets have dramatically affected the debt structure of real estate, they have also had a tremendous impact on equity. In recent years, REITs have taken the real estate market by storm. A REIT is typically formed as a corporation or trust under state law. To qualify as a REIT under the Internal Revenue Code, the REIT must meet a long list of requirements concerning its investments and beneficial owners. Most important, a REIT must distribute 95% of its net earnings each year to its owners in the form of dividends. Failure to do this will result in financial penalties or loss of its status under the tax law. As long as a REIT adheres to these requirements, it will be subject to only one layer of taxation, a distinct advantage over organizing as a corporation. Like a corporation, however, the beneficial owners of the REIT are insulated from liability. In addition the REIT is an extremely liquid investment vehicle with shares of many REITs trading freely in the stock market.

REITs are not a new invention. In the late 1960s and early 1970s, REITs grew rapidly. Unlike today, the majority of REIT assets were in land and construction loans rather than in equity interests in real estate.[42] Mortgage REITs typically borrowed short-term to finance these loans and were caught as market interest rates rapidly increased in the early 1970s. As a result, many REITs failed during this period and it has taken over a decade for the industry to rebound.

The current resurgence of REITs began in the 1980s with the growth of equity REITs and took off during the early 1990s. This corresponds to the period following the slump in real estate that occurred during the recession of 1989–1991. During this period, traditional sources of real estate capital dried up as banks, pension funds and life insurance companies overreacted to the lax credit standards and losses of the 1980s and early 1990s. The REIT became a way for real estate to amass capital as the nation emerged from the recession. . . . [T]he number of equity REITs rose from 25 in 1984 to 176 in 1997, a 600% increase. In addition, the capitalization of REITs (defined as the price of shares multiplied by the number of shares outstanding) shot up by an astounding factor of 55, increasing from $2.3 billion in 1984 to $127.8 billion in 1997.

According to the estimates of one real estate analyst . . . as of June 30, 1997, REITs accounted for over one-third (35.2%) of all institutional real estate in the United States.[43] Only pension funds had a greater share (39.4%) of equity interests in the sector.

* * *

42. Barry Ziering et al., The Evolution of Public and Private Market Investing in the New Real Estate Capital Markets, 14 Real Est. Fin. 22 (1997).

43. ERE Yarmouth and Real Estate Research Corporation, Emerging Trends in Real Estate 1998 (1998), available in (last modified July 10, 1998) <http://www.208.240.92.174/rsch/trends1998/index.htm>.

THE IMPACT OF CAPITAL MARKETS ON THE PRACTICE OF REAL ESTATE LAW

Regardless of its ultimate impact on the structure of the real estate industry, the growing securitization of real estate equity and debt has already had a tremendous impact on the practice of real estate law. As Wall Street makes itself felt in real estate, real estate lawyers increasingly must master and apply legal principles that used to be the province of lawyers from other departments. Among the many new areas real estate lawyers must understand are the disclosure requirements mandated by federal securities laws, the practices and requirements of ratings agencies, how to structure deals in entities that are bankruptcy-remote, and how to advise REIT clients to structure transactions so as to preserve their favorable tax treatment.

In addition to mastering and applying the principles that used to be the province of lawyers from different departments, the practice of real estate law itself has changed. For example, in real estate financing transactions, the days when every firm had its own idiosyncratic forms for mortgage transactions are rapidly coming to an end. The use of relatively standard documents and deal structures first became commonplace in single family home mortgage transactions. Indeed, with respect to mortgages on single family homes, most lawyers have typically given up trying to get originators to accept provisions that vary from the Fannie Mae or Freddie Mac forms because such provisions would make the loans unsaleable in the secondary mortgage market.

This rigidity over terms is also beginning to find its way into commercial mortgages. More often the requirements of the rating agencies are dictating the form and content of commercial mortgages. To veer away from these requirements could potentially cost the issuer of mortgage-backed securities an investment grade and thereby have an adverse impact on returns.

Indeed, in 1996, the Capital Consortium, a joint effort of the National Realty Committee, the Mortgage Bankers Association and the National Realtors Association, did the heretofore unthinkable by issuing model mortgage forms to be used in commercial mortgage transactions.[44] The forms contain a number of provisions that are designed to make the mortgage loan acceptable to rating agencies. Among the provisions that vary most from those used in many mortgages are: 1) absolute prohibitions on secondary financing; 2) single-purpose entity/bankruptcy remote covenants; 3) extensive covenants to provide information about the property; and 4) requirements to use proceeds from casualty or condemnation awards for restoration. The forms have not caused lawyers to entirely abandon their idiosyncratic forms or favorite representations or warranties. However, they have formed the basis for greater uniformity of terms in commercial lending transactions.

THE IMPACT OF THE CAPITAL MARKETS ON THE SUBSTANTIVE LAW OF REAL ESTATE

Although there can be no doubt that the securitization of real estate debt and equity has changed the form of real estate transactions as well as the way real estate lawyers practice their profession, the same cannot be said for the underlying substantive law of real estate. For years, commentators have argued that the linkage of real estate markets to national securities markets would mark the end of the divergent legal

---

44. See The Capital Consortium, Capital Markets Initiatives, June 25, 1996, at 15-57. For a description of the Capital Consortium's proposed mortgage forms see Joseph Philip Forte, A Capital Markets Mortgage: A Ratable Model For Main Street and Wall Street, 31 Real Prop. Prob. & Tr. J. 489 (1996).

rules that apply from state to state, governing much including conveyancing practices, title and the law of mortgage foreclosure.[45] According to these arguments, idiosyncratic state real estate laws would add transaction costs to increasingly interstate transactions concerning real estate. The successful linkage of real estate credit and equity markets to national capital markets would therefore create incentives for eliminating differences among the states.

The growth of the national capital markets for real estate has been used to justify the adoption of uniform laws. However, the track record among states in voluntarily adopting the uniform laws promulgated by the National Commissioners on Uniform Laws has been dismal.[46] The Uniform Land Transaction Act (ULTA) was not adopted by a single state.[47] Efforts to carve out the Uniform Land Security Interest Act (ULSIA) similarly failed to succeed. In light of the overwhelming success of the Uniform Commercial Code, the resistance of states to uniform real estate laws has puzzled both the advocates of uniform laws as well as many academic commentators.[48]

Uniformity was forced on states, however, in certain instances by the federal government. Among the notable legislation was Congress's passage of the Depository Institutions Deregulation and Monetary Control Act of 1980, which preempted state anti-usury laws on loans secured by first mortgages on residential properties; the Garn-St. Germain Depository Institutions Act of 1982, which preempted state laws limiting the right of lenders to enforce due-on-sale clauses in mortgages; and two statutes in 1981 and 1994 substituting a federal law of mortgage foreclosure for mortgages held by the federal government. . . .

. . . The exponential growth of REITs and mortgage-backed securities despite the persistence of these non-uniform laws suggests to me that they are not major impediments to the capital markets. Nevertheless, the growth of the market for commercial mortgage-backed securities probably increases the likelihood that these laws will gradually be forced out by competitive forces. With respect to home mortgage loans, to the extent that non-uniform laws generate costs, it is likely that these costs are not entirely borne by citizens of the states that enacted them, but instead a portion of the costs are likely to be externalized. Externalities result because Fannie Mae and Freddie Mac do not price loans differentially to account for the risk of state laws. It is unclear why they do not do this since information and technology exists that would permit the practice. One possibility is that the costs of the non-uniform laws are so low that the cost to the agencies of pricing the risk would exceed the benefits. Alternatively Fannie Mae and Freddie Mac, as quasi-federal agencies subject to political forces and Congressional oversight may be wary of angering members of Congress from particular states. No similar political impediment would exist to state-by-state pricing in the commercial mortgage-backed securities market if such pricing were efficient and would generate higher profits.

There is also some reason to believe that the costs of these types of laws would be higher for commercial as compared to residential mortgage-backed securities and

45. Robin P. Malloy, The Secondary Mortgage Market—A Catalyst for Change in Real Estate Transactions, 39 Sw. L.J. 991, 991-92 (1986).

46. Patrick A. Randolph, Jr., The Future of American Real Estate Law: Uniform Foreclosure Laws and Uniform Land Security Interest Act, 20 Nova L. Rev. 1109, 1128 (1996).

47. See Ronald Benton Brown, Whatever Happened to ULTA?, 20 Nova L. Rev. 1017, 1018 (1996).

48. See 20 Nova L. Rev. 1017 (1996) (a recent volume of the Nova Law Review devoted to a symposium entitled, "Whatever Happened to the Uniform Land Transactions Act?").

that the corresponding benefits of the laws to borrowers might be lower. The size of an individual residential loan or set of loans from a state with costly borrower protection laws is likely to be insignificant when considered in the context of the entire pool of mortgages backing a particular issue of securities. As Professor Randolph correctly noted in a recent article, however, the number of loans in a commercial mortgage-backed security pool is much smaller and any one loan is likely to have a far greater impact.[49] Therefore, if non-uniform mortgage foreclosure laws were to raise costs significantly, they would likely have a much bigger impact now than they would have had before the recent growth of commercial mortgage-backed securities. In addition, rates of foreclosure for commercial mortgages are typically higher than those for single family loans.[50] Since non-uniform mortgage foreclosure and borrower protection laws generate costs only when foreclosure takes place, the costs are therefore likely to be greater in the context of commercial mortgage-backed securities.

Finally, the benefits of non-uniform mortgagor protection laws are likely to be less for commercial as compared to residential borrowers. Commercial borrowers are much more likely to be sophisticated and risk neutral than are homebuyers. In addition, they typically are more diversified and better able to absorb the risk of foreclosure. Although I am not making an argument that these laws should be changed, I do believe that the forces that will likely challenge their continued existence are probably stronger today than at any time in our past.

Conclusion

In the future, real estate professionals are likely to experience a world quite different from the one we have become accustomed to. For investors, securitization of both debt and equity is likely to make real estate more like other types of commodities and subject to the same market pressures. For lawyers, the practice will never be the same. Although significant changes in the substantive law of real estate will likely be slow in coming, the practice of law has already changed forever and will continue to evolve. The real estate lawyer will have to add securities law, corporate law and bankruptcy law to his or her repertoire. Now more than ever, the term "dirt law" is a misnomer for the profession.

49. Randolph, supra note 73, at 1129.

50. See Inside Mortgage Finance Publications, The Mortgage Market Statistical Annual For 1998 422-23 (1998). In December 1996, the proportion of commercial mortgage loans that were in the process of foreclosure (1.10%) was higher than the proportion of all one to four family home loans in foreclosure (0.91%). Id. The disparity between the two types of loans was substantially greater in 1995 and 1994 when foreclosure rates for commercial were almost twice those of residential mortgage loans.

2. *Real Estate Investment Trusts*

Alvin L. Arnold, Real Estate Transactions — Structure and Analysis with Forms

---

§ 16:109. Generally

A REIT is a vehicle for group investment in real estate, just as a mutual fund is a vehicle for group investment in stocks or bonds. REITs are a creation of the Internal Revenue Code because the necessary condition for their success, again like a mutual fund, is an exemption from double taxation — tax at the corporate or trust level as well as at the shareholder or beneficiary level. Provided tax rules are met, REITs themselves pay no income tax; only shareholders (beneficiaries) pay tax on dividend distributions.

REITs were created by Congress in 1960 to give small investors the opportunity to share in the ownership of real estate (either a single property or a diversified portfolio) or to share in the profits of mortgage lending. Prior to 1960, group investment in real estate by private investors took the form either of

(1) share ownership in a business corporation that developed or operated real estate or

(2) partnership shares in a real estate limited partnership (syndicate).

The relatively small number of real estate corporations that were publicly owned (some of which were listed on the New York Stock Exchange and American Stock Exchange) preceded by some years the development of the real estate limited partnership as an investment vehicle. While, in theory, a real estate corporation could produce satisfactory results for shareholders even after paying the corporate income tax, just as do regular business corporations, they never commanded a large public following.

In the late 1950s, another vehicle for group real estate investment became popular — the real estate limited partnership (commonly known as a "real estate syndicate"). While syndicates had been popular in the 1920s, they had been abandoned as an investment vehicle following the Great Depression of the 1930s. However, they became popular once again in the late 1950s when real estate professionals recognized the unique feature of the partnership form — partnerships are not recognized as an independent tax entity so that income taxes do not have to be paid at the partnership level. Instead, profits (and tax losses) could be passed through directly to individual partners, with the result that after tax profits were higher and tax losses could be used to shelter profits from other sources. Real estate partnerships, however, had some significant disadvantages. The most important was the lack of liquidity; partnership interests could not be sold easily (if at all) because of the absence of a secondary market. In addition, real estate partnerships were treated as securities subject to federal and state regulation, with the result that a lengthy and expensive process was involved each time a syndicate was organized. Also, the tax laws affecting partnerships were complex and in some cases it was not clear as to whether a particular partnership would be treated as such under the tax laws. Consequently, as public interest in real estate increased (partly due to the sharp rise in the values of private homes, which stimulated an interest in the investing public in commercial real estate), the real estate industry sought legislation that would permit public investment in real estate to be as relatively uncomplicated as in stocks and bonds. The result was the creation of the REIT.

Whereas stock and bond mutual funds are set up in corporate form, the original form for real estate funds was the *trust*, as the name indicates. (Now, REITs may take either a trust or corporate form.) . . .

§ 16:110. Impressive Long-Term Record

A study in 2005 by the research firm of Torto Wheaton Research (TWR), titled "Thus Far REITs Are Winning," says that over the past four decades, REITs have had a superior risk-adjusted performance compared to the overall stock and bond markets, as well as direct real estate investments. The report compares average returns and risk-adjusted returns for the equity REIT index as recorded by the National Association of Real Estate Investment Trusts (NAREIT) with returns for the major stock market indices and the Lehman Brothers government bond index. For each of four periods ending in 2004 — ten, fifteen, twenty and twenty-seven years — REITs consistently beat all alternative investment vehicles. Over the longest period of twenty-seven years, the average annual return for REITs was 15.8% (as determined by NAREIT) compared to 10.3% for both the Dow Jones Industrial Average and the S&P 500. The annual bond return was 9.2%. The average annual return for direct investment in real estate (as determined by the National Council of Real Estate Investment Fiduciaries — NCREIF) was 9.7%. For the ten years ending in 2004, the average annual REIT return was 16.2%, again beating all other alternatives.

An interesting question is why REIT prices have been considerably higher (by 400–600 basis points) than returns from direct real estate investments over the longer term. According to the report, since the dividend provided by REIT stocks is about the same as the income return provided by direct real estate investments, the consistently better performance of REITs must be due to higher growth rates in stock prices compared to property prices. The reason for this may be that REIT managers can quickly move capital to real estate in recovering markets, so creating strong positive demand that has an instant impact on REIT prices. And the greater liquidity of REIT stocks gives managers the ability to readjust positions quickly when property markets enter a downturn.

Finally, two other possible explanations may account for the better performance of REIT stocks. The first is that REITs are better managed because of more investment discipline (the public REITs must disclose significant information about their holdings). The other is that REITs tend to specialize in a particular property type, possibly enabling them to be more innovative in developing new investment products and also enabling them to more quickly adapt to changing market conditions and to changes in the financial and regulatory environment.

§ 6:112. Investing in REITs

REITs can be classified in two ways: according to the type of investments they make and according to whether they have an infinite or a finite life. With regard to the type of investment, REITs fall into three groups:

(1) *Equity REITs.* Equity REITs invest in income-producing properties or in raw land, either on an all-cash basis or utilizing debt financing. Most early REITs took the equity form, and it seems clear that Congress, in passing tax legislation creating

REITs, considered the equity REIT as the typical format. An equity REIT may distribute to shareholders only its after-tax income (while retaining the nontaxable cash flow attributable to depreciation write-offs) or distribute the nontaxable cash flow as well, in which case it is treated as a return of equity to shareholders. To the extent that any cash flow was retained by the trust, it permits the trust to grow by purchasing additional properties.

(2) *Mortgage REITs.* This type of REIT is a financial intermediary, comparable to a bank or thrift that loans money on the security of real estate. REITs became important financial intermediaries in the 1970s when funds for construction and permanent loans became scarce. The scarcity was due to an inflationary trend that pushed interest rates above those permitted to be paid by thrifts and banks, with the result that these traditional sources of financing for real estate saw a substantial decline in their deposit growth. Builders and developers, forced to look elsewhere for funds, turned to mortgage REITs. The REITs, not subject to regulation with respect to interest rates that could be charged, responded with enthusiasm and made large numbers of highly risky loans in exchange for high fees and interest rates. Often staffed with relatively inexperienced personnel, the REITs ignored warning signals of a forthcoming recession, which came in the mid-1970s. The results were severe losses for many mortgage REITs and the virtual collapse of this form of REIT ownership. However, there remain a number of sound mortgage REITs that specialize in the various forms of financing, such as land sale-leasebacks, and second mortgages on private houses.

(3) *Combination (hybrid) REITs.* A hybrid REIT can be defined as one that has at least 30% of its assets in both the mortgage and equity categories. . . .

§ 16:113. Investing in REITs — Advantages of REITs
As an investment form, a REIT has some significant advantages over alternative real estate investments. These include the following:

- *Liquidity.* Possibly the single greatest disadvantage of real estate as an investment is its illiquidity — the inability to sell within a reasonable time at a price close to true market value. The reason is that every parcel of real estate is unique and requires the owner to find a buyer who needs property having the same characteristics as that offered for sale. In addition, since real estate is permanent and indestructible, every parcel of real estate has a history that must be checked by the buyer to be sure that the present owner can convey the title contracted for. While a real estate partnership moves one step away from the direct ownership of real estate, the purchase and sale of partnership interests in the secondary market is almost as difficult (if not more so) than the direct sale of real estate. The REIT, however, is the first major effort to "securitize" real estate that has been successful. By having the real estate owned by an REIT, which in turn issues shares of stock (technically, shares of beneficial ownership in the case of a trust), the real estate is made liquid because the shares can easily be traded . . .

- *Existing and stable yield.* Since the reason for the existence of the REIT form is to distribute income to its shareholders without the burden of a tax at the corporate level, REITs almost always invest assets in existing income properties or interest-bearing mortgages. REITs normally do not own unproductive raw land nor are they engaged in the development process (which in any case would be barred by the requirement that REITs be passive investors). Consequently, investors can expect an immediate income return and since it comes from established properties, a return that should be reasonably stable. By comparison, real estate limited partnerships often invest in raw land or new developments so that income is nonexistent or volatile.

- *Daily pricing.* Unlike real estate partnerships and other non-public real estate investing formats, REITs are valued daily by the marketplace, with prices available to the general public. This is important for certain types of investors, such as pension funds, that require periodic valuation. [Non-REIT forms of real estate investment, by comparison, require individual appraisals which are time consuming and expensive. . . .]

- *Assurance of tax status.* The conditions that must be met by an REIT to be assured of tax-favored status are set forth clearly in Sections 856 to 860 of the Internal Revenue Code. By comparison, real estate limited partnerships, in order to avoid being taxed as associations (corporations), must meet requirements that are much less clear and which often require litigation in order for a final determination to be made.

- *Full disclosure.* Although both REITs and real estate limited partnerships must make written disclosures to investors as to the details of their structure and investments, REIT disclosures are much less complex than those of a partnership because the applicable law is far less complicated. In addition, REITs are unable to engage in some of the more esoteric forms of real estate investment and financing and so need not make complicated disclosures to investors. Finally, the relationship between the trustees of an REIT and its shareholders is much more clearly defined than that between a general partner and the limited partners of a real estate partnership.

§ 16:114. Investing in REITs — Disadvantages of REITs

The major disadvantages of the REIT investment format are the obverse signs of two of the major advantages: liquidity and daily pricing. Since REIT shares can be easily traded because there is an active market of buyers and sellers and prices are set daily, periods of over-enthusiasm and excessive pessimism can drive REIT prices far above or below the "market value" of the underlying real estate assets. In addition, since REIT shares trade primarily on yield, they often are compared to fixed income securities, such as bonds, and thus are susceptible to "interest rate risks," i.e., price changes due to changes in overall levels of interest rates. . . .

* * *

§ 16:118. Tax Aspects of REITs — General Tax Rules

A corporation, trust or association specializing in real estate and mortgage investments, which meets certain status requirements as to ownership and purpose and which satisfies certain gross income and asset diversification requirements, may elect to be taxed as an REIT.

If an organization meets the REIT requirements, it will be taxed only on its undistributed income and capital gains. However, the alternative minimum tax may apply to the organization with respect to its tax preference for depreciation taken in excess of straight line depreciation and also on the portion of other tax preference items not distributed to its shareholders. Distributed income, on the other hand, is taxed directly to the shareowners. . . .

An organization must meet the following ownership and purpose requirements to qualify as an REIT:

- *Number of persons.* Beneficial ownership in the organization must be held by at least 100 persons for at least 335 days during a tax year of 12 months or for a proportionate part of a tax year of less than 12 months. The days need not be consecutive.
- *Transferable shares.* The beneficial ownership must be evidenced by transferable shares or transferable certificates of beneficial interest. The term "shares" includes shares of stock.
- *Management.* The organization's management must be in the hands of one or more trustees or directors, with the trustees generally holding legal title to the organization's property and having exclusive authority over management.
- *Corporate attributes.* The organization, in addition to central management, also must possess all other necessary attributes that would (except for the REIT tax provisions) cause it to be taxed as a corporation.
- *No concentrated ownership.* Five or fewer individuals may not own (directly or indirectly) more than half of the value of the organization's stock during the last six months of its tax year.

The income requirements of an REIT are divided into three categories:

(1) *95 percent rule.* 95% or more of an REIT's gross income must be dividends, interest, rents from real property, gains from the sale of securities and real property, and abatements and refunds of real property taxes.
(2) *75 percent rule.* At least 75% of the REIT's income must, in one manner or another, be derived from real property. Included within the 75% category are rents from real property, interests on obligations secured by mortgages on real property, qualified temporary investment income, gain from the sale of real property, dividends and other distributions from other REITs, and abatements and refunds of taxes on real property.
(3) *30 percent rule.* Short-term gains on security sales and gains on the sale of real property held for less than four years (apart from involuntary conversions) must represent less than 30% of the REIT's gross income.

The interaction of the 95% and 75% tests requires at least 75% of the REIT's income to be derived from real property, while the remaining 20% must be derived either from real property or from sources from which a regulated investment company is required to derive most of its income. . . .

Two tests as to the nature of their investments must be met by REITs:

(1) *75 percent test.* At least 75% of the value of the REIT's assets must be in real estate assets, cash and cash items, and government securities.
(2) *25 percent test.* Not more than 25% of the value of the REIT's assets may be represented by securities (other than those described in the preceding paragraph) of any one issuer in an amount greater in value than 5% of the

REIT's total assets and not more than 10% of the voting securities of the issuer.

* * *

§ 16:120. REITs as Financing Sources

REITs have been utilized by some developers as a source of financing that is less expensive (or more available) than from traditional institutional sources. The REIT either may hold as its sole asset a permanent mortgage secured by a single real estate project (a "single purpose" REIT) or may hold a number of mortgages secured by a portfolio of properties. In most cases, such an REIT is of the finite type (with a specified life equal to the mortgage term). The developer organizes the REIT at the time a development project is conceived. The REIT offers shares to investors, with the specified purpose of utilizing the capital raised to finance the proposed development. The REIT then gives to the developer a permanent loan takeout commitment, upon the strength of which the developer is able to obtain construction financing. When the project is completed and the permanent loan funded, the REIT earns interest income that is distributed to its shareholders. In exchange for an interest rate that may be somewhat below current market rates, the REIT may be given a participation in increased cash flow generated by the property, which participation will be distributed to the shareholders as additional interest. Alternatively, the REIT may be structured as an equity trust, in which case the REIT would give the developer a commitment to purchase the property upon completion, which commitment would act as a takeout for the construction lender. The developer in this situation would receive its compensation in the form of a development fee and/or the difference between the sales price to the REIT (reflecting market value of the completed project) and the costs to the developer of land and construction.

An REIT also may be utilized by a development or investment company owning a portfolio of existing properties. The company can divide into two separate entities. One entity is a newly created REIT that would own the real estate, passing through to its shareholders taxable income without a tax at the corporate level. The other entity is the existing development or operating company, which acts as the management firm for the REIT or engages in new development with financing provided by the REIT. The advantage of the split up is that taxable income is subject only to a single tax at the shareholder level; as a result, distributions to shareholders are substantially increased and the combined value of the REIT shares and the original company shares rises substantially. . . .

NOTES AND QUESTIONS

1. *Distribution of net income.* To avoid paying tax on their earnings, REITs are required to distribute at least 90 per cent of their taxable income as dividends each year. As a result, REITs cannot expand by retaining their profits, but must instead raise new capital or borrow in order to acquire new investments. The distribution requirement makes REITs attractive to many institutional investors, which are looking for steady income. A second effect, however, is that REIT management

must justify its performance regularly to seek new capital from investors or lenders, which may be partly responsible for the extraordinary record of returns that REITs have developed.

2. *Tax treatment of REIT distributions.* While the passive activity loss rules treat income from real estate limited partnerships as passive, REIT distributions are portfolio income. REITs may also distribute their long-term capital gains by issuing a designated capital gain dividend, in which case taxpayers may report the income as long-term capital gains. REIT losses, of course, are not passed through to individual investors because the REIT is treated as a separate corporation. For an excellent comparison of REITs versus public limited partnerships as investment vehicles, including their respective tax treatment, see Thomas A. Jesch, The Taxation of "Opportunistic" Real Estate Private Equity Funds and U.S. Real Estate Investment Trusts (REITs) — An Investor's Comparative Analysis, 34 Real Est. L.J. 275 (2005).

3. *REITs and mezzanine financing.* The requirement that most REIT assets be invested in real estate and loans secured by real estate raised a difficult issue as mezzanine financing increasingly displaces subordinated mortgage financing (see pages 928-934, infra). A subordinated mortgage loan clearly would be a permitted investment, but is a mezzanine loan, which is secured by ownership interests in the borrower (typically a special purpose entity created to own and operate the real property) rather that a direct interest in the underlying real property? In Rev. Proc. 2003-65, the I.R.S. answered affirmatively, setting forth requirements which, if met, permit a mezzanine loan to be treated as a loan secured by real estate.

4. *International REITs.* Many investors are interested in diversifying their holdings globally, but purchasing real estate in a foreign country presents many issues — the need to understand the local marketplace, to manage real estate in a distant location, and so forth. REITs have become an important vehicle for the internationalization of real estate portfolios, as non-US investors purchase shares in U.S. REITs, and as U.S. investors purchase shares in overseas REITS. While REITs started in the U.S., over the past decade they have expanded to nearly 20 nations, including markets as diverse as Hong Kong, Japan, the Netherlands, France, and Belgium. REITs have been permitted in the United Kingdom and in Germany only since January 1, 2007, and other countries are sure to follow. The tax treatment and requirements of REITs in most countries follow the U.S. model closely.

5. *UPREITs.* An Umbrella Partnership REIT (UPREIT) is sometimes used to allow members of a limited partnership to diversify their holdings and increase their liquidity. An UPREIT does not own property directly, but rather owns interests in a limited partnership (called the operating partnership or OP), as general partner or as owner of a wholly-owned subsidiary that serves as the general partner. In a typical UPREIT transaction, the partners in a real estate limited partnership contribute their partnership shares to the OP and in return receive partnership interests in the OP ("OP Units"). OP Units generally receive the same income distribution as holders of the UPREIT shares and are convertible into shares in the UPREIT. This exchange of partnership interests can be done on a tax-free basis, with taxes only owed when the partner sells her OP interest, converts it into shares of the UPREIT, or the OP sells the property. The OP acquires interests in multiple properties in this way, so that each OP unit represents an interest in a pool of properties rather than just the property owned by the prior partnership. See generally Chadwick M. Cornell, REITS and UPREITS: Pushing the Corporate Law

Envelope, 145 U. Pa. L. Rev. 1565 (1997); Russell J. Singer, Understanding REITS, UPREITS, and DOWN-REITS, and the Tax and Business Decisions Surrounding Them, 16 Va. Tax Rev. 329 (1996).

3. Commercial Mortgage Backed Securities

American Bar Association Section of Taxation Committee on Financial Transactions Subcommittee on Asset Securitization,[51] Legislative Proposal to Expand the REMIC Provisions of the Code to Include Nonmortgage Assets

46 Tax L.R. 299 (1991)[52]

I. INTRODUCTION

The securitization of mortgage loans and other debt obligations has evolved dramatically during the last decade. Residential mortgage loans were the first type of obligation to be securitized, and they continue to represent the majority of securitized assets today.[53] As mortgage securitization evolved and became more sophisticated, it became apparent that existing federal income tax law inadequately addressed many of the issues relating to securitization and was hindering the development of the market. In 1986, Congress responded to the needs of the secondary mortgage market by enacting the real estate mortgage investment conduit (REMIC) provisions of the Code.[54] Today, REMIC securities dominate the secondary mortgage market. Although the securitization of nonmortgage debt obligations began later than and, therefore, lags mortgage securitization in its development, it is evolving in a manner that is similar in most respects to mortgage securitization. The securitization of nonmortgage obligations is faced with the same inadequacies and lack of safe harbors in existing federal income tax law that have been addressed for the secondary mortgage market by the REMIC provisions of the Code. . . .

---

51. This legislative proposal represents the individual views of the members of the Section of Taxation who prepared it and does not represent the position of the American Bar Association or the Section of Taxation. The Council of the Section of Taxation, without adopting the proposal as Section policy, has approved its transmittal to officials of the Treasury Department and the Joint Committee on Taxation.

The proposal was drafted by the following individual members of the Committee on Financial Transactions: Barbara A. Byrd, Steven D. Conlon, Robert C. MacDonald, Thomas R. Popplewell, and Kenneth Whyburn. It was compiled and edited by George C. Howell, III, who at the time was the chair of the Subcommittee on Asset Securitization. Helpful comments were provided by Peter C. Aberg, Bruce W. Bantz, David M. Gruppo, Danny P. Jackson, Michael L. Schler, and Nelson Soares. The proposal was reviewed by Joel D. Zychick of the Committee on Government Submissions and by Frederic L. Ballard, Jr., a member of the Section's Council.

52. Copyright © (1992) by the New York University School of Law; American Bar Association Section of Taxation Committee on Financial Transactions Subcommittee on Asset Securitization.

53. There are many aspects of residential mortgage loans that make them easy to securitize and to market to investors: (1) creditworthiness; (2) standardized nature; (3) relatively small loan principal amount; (4) large volume of loan originations; (5) qualifying asset treatment for thrift institutions; and (6) participation and encouragement by the U.S. government in the development of the secondary mortgage market.

54. Tax Reform Act of 1986, Pub.L. No. 99-514, § 671, 100 Stat. 2085, 2309 (codified at IRC §§ 860A-860G) [hereinafter 1986 Act].

A. THE DEVELOPMENT OF MORTGAGE SECURITIZATION

1. MORTGAGE-BACKED BONDS

The precursor of securitization was the mortgage-backed bond, which made its appearance many years ago as a way for banks and thrift institutions to finance their mortgage lending operations. Mortgage-backed bonds are general obligations of an issuer secured by a pool of mortgage loans held by the issuer. The mortgage loans securing the bonds typically have a market value that is substantially higher than the principal amount of the bond offering at the time the bonds are issued. The issuer periodically must compare the market value of the mortgage pool to the outstanding principal amount of the bonds. If the market value of the mortgage loans falls below a specified multiple of the outstanding principal amount of the bonds, the issuer must restore the required level of collateralization by either collateralizing the bonds with additional mortgage loans, paying down the principal amount of the bonds, or defeasing the bonds. Unlike in the case of a true securitization, the payment terms of the bonds generally do not match or depend upon the cash flows to the issuer from the mortgage pool. For example, prepayments on mortgage loans collateralizing the bonds may not necessarily result in prepayments on the bonds.

Mortgage-backed bonds still are issued today. However, because they do not involve the matching of cash flows between the mortgage loans and the bonds (this is commonly referred to as "duration matching"), they are perceived as a less efficient form of securitization than other methods of mortgage securitization discussed below.

2. AGENCY AND NONAGENCY PASS-THROUGH CERTIFICATES

In 1970, the Government National Mortgage Association (GNMA) created the first publicly traded mortgage pass-through certificates representing an undivided percentage interest in a trust containing specified mortgage loans.[55] Payment of principal and interest on the certificates was guaranteed by GNMA. Because the pass-through certificates represented an undivided pro rata interest in all of the mortgage loans in the pool, there was a precise matching of cash flows from the underlying mortgage loans to the payments on the certificates, net of certain fees paid to the mortgage loan servicer, GNMA, and the custodian.

The Internal Revenue Service has determined that trusts issuing such mortgage pass-through certificates are classified as grantor trusts for federal income tax purposes.[56] As grantor trusts, the mortgage pass-through trusts escape tax at the entity level on income received on the mortgage loans, and the holders of the

---

55. H. Lore, Mortgage-Backed Securities 2-5 (1986-87 ed.).

56. Rev.Ruls. 70-544 and 70-545, 1970-2 C.B. 6, 8, modified, Rev.Rul. 74-169, 1974-1 C.B. 147; see also Rev.Rul. 75-192, 1975-1 C.B. 384 (same treatment for mortgage pass-through certificates guaranteed by the Federal Housing Administration (FHA) and the Veterans Administration (VA)). Under the entity classification regulations, a mortgage pass-through trust technically is classified as an "investment trust." Reg. § 301.7701-4(c). As the foregoing rulings indicate, however, an investment trust is considered a grantor trust for purposes of determining the federal income tax consequences applicable to both the trust and the beneficiaries. See IRC §§ 671-679.

mortgage pass-through certificates generally are treated as owning directly their share of the mortgage loans for federal income tax purposes.[57]

Following GNMA's lead, the Federal National Mortgage Association (FNMA) and the Federal Home Loan Mortgage Corporation (FHLMC) began issuing mortgage pass-through certificates with similar types of payment guarantees. Although, unlike GNMA, FNMA and FHLMC are not federal agencies, FNMA and FHLMC mortgage pass-through certificates are accorded agency status by the credit markets because of their close relationships with the United States government. Accordingly, GNMA, FNMA, and FHLMC guaranteed mortgage pass-through certificates are commonly referred to as "agency pass-through certificates." The Service has held that the trusts issuing FNMA and FHLMC mortgage pass-through certificates are classified as grantor trusts for federal income tax purposes.

In 1977, Bank of America issued the first major nonagency guaranteed mortgage pass-through certificates. Subsequently, numerous nonagency guaranteed pass-through certificates have been issued. At first, the issuance of nonagency guaranteed mortgage pass-through certificates was subject to various securities laws limitations that were not applicable to agency pass-through certificates.[58] Those limitations were substantially lifted by the Secondary Mortgage Market Enhancement Act of 1984.[59] The Service has not distinguished nonagency certificates from agency certificates in its grantor trust analysis.

3. MULTIPLE CLASS TRUSTS AND THE "SEARS REGULATIONS"

A major drawback of the mortgage pass-through certificate as an investment is the prepayment risk to the certificate holder. The requirements of grantor trust status dictate that prepayments on the mortgage loans held by the trust be passed through to the holders of the pass-through certificates almost immediately after receipt.[60]

---

57. Rev.Rul. 70-544, 1970-2 C.B. 6; Rev.Rul. 70-545, 1970-2 C.B. 8. Such treatment is particularly advantageous for certain special classes of investors (e.g., real estate investment trusts (REITs), savings and loan associations (S&Ls), and other types of thrift institutions) because the underlying mortgage loans typically constitute qualifying assets for such investors.

58. An issuer of nonagency mortgage-backed securities had to consider whether such securities were subject to registration as publicly offered securities under the Securities Act of 1933, Pub.L. No. 73-22, ch. 33, title I, § 6, 48 Stat. 78, codified at 15 U.S.C. § 77(f) (hereinafter the 1933 Act). Registration of publicly offered securities under the 1933 Act entails significant effort and expense. An issuer also had to consider the impact of various state laws regarding the sales of securities (typically referred to as state "blue sky" laws). State blue sky laws are not uniform among the states and are often perceived as outdated or unduly restrictive. The lack of uniformity among state blue sky laws imposes additional complexity and expense in offering securities in several states.

59. Pub.L. No. 98-440, 98 Stat. 1689. Congress enacted the Secondary Mortgage Market Enhancement Act of 1984 (SMMEA) to facilitate the issuance of mortgage-backed securities by private participants in the secondary mortgage market. S.Rep. No. 293, 98th Cong., 2d Sess. 3 (1984). SMMEA relaxed margin requirements for nonagency guaranteed mortgage pass-through certificates and improved the treatment of such certificates for purposes of the net capital requirements for securities dealers. Pub.L. No. 98-440, § 102, 98 Stat. 1689, 1690; S.Rep. No. 293, supra at 3, 6-9. SMMEA also preempted state legal investment restrictions and blue sky laws. Pub.L. No. 98-440, § 106, 98 Stat. 1689, 1691-92. The preemption of state law by SMMEA is considered one of its most significant provisions. Section 106(b) of SMMEA does contain a so-called "opt out" provision permitting any state to enact legislation within seven years of the date of the enactment of SMMEA that specifically overrides the general preemption of SMMEA over state legal investment and blue sky laws. 98 Stat. at 1692. . . .

60. In order for a trust to qualify as a grantor trust under the Code and to avoid the imposition of corporate tax, the trustee must have no power under the trust agreement to vary the investments of the trust. See Reg. § 301.7701-4(c). Accordingly, there are substantial limitations on the trustee's power to reinvest cash received by the trusts. See, e.g., Rev.Rul. 75-192, 1975-1 C.B. 384 (limiting reinvestment of

Accordingly, the maturity of an investment in a mortgage pass-through certificate is uncertain. That uncertainty increases the yield that the secondary market demands for investments in mortgage pass-through certificates.

In February 1984, Sears Mortgage Securities Corporation formed a trust that issued innovative mortgage pass-through certificates. Unlike prior mortgage pass-through trusts, in which the rights of all certificate holders were identical with respect to the pool of mortgage loans held by the trust, the Sears trust issued multiple classes of certificates in a "fast pay/slow pay" structure. Although the prepayment risk was not entirely eliminated, "compartmentalization" of that risk permitted the cash flows from the mortgage loans to be repackaged into short-term, medium-term, and long-term certificate classes.[61] Because the repackaged cash flows were better tailored to the needs of various investor groups than were the unrefined cash flows from the mortgage loans and because of the upward sloping yield curve then prevailing in the marketplace, underwriters could sell the multiple class certificates at an aggregate blended yield that was lower than the yield demanded by investors under a comparable single class mortgage pass-through structure.

On April 27, 1984, the Service issued News Release 84-58, which announced that the trust classification regulations would be revised generally to treat multiple class investment trusts as associations taxable as corporations, rather than as grantor trusts, for federal income tax purposes. Proposed regulations to that effect were issued simultaneously with the news release, and substantially similar final regulations were adopted on March 21, 1986. Because the entity level taxation threatened by the news release and the proposed regulations halted Sears' proposed second offering of multiple class certificates, the regulations are commonly referred to as the "Sears Regulations."

4. DEVELOPMENT OF CMOS AND THE OWNER TRUST

Despite the issuance of the Sears Regulations, market participants have continued to use an alternative structure for compartmentalizing prepayment risk under which the fast pay/slow pay securities are designed to qualify as debt for federal income tax purposes. Payments on the various classes of debt are in the aggregate closely matched to the cash flows received by the issuer on the underlying mortgage loans or pass-through certificates. The debt securities generally take the form of bonds and are commonly referred to as "collateralized mortgage obligations" (CMOs). The CMO format largely avoids two levels of taxation through the

---

amounts received by an investment trust prior to distribution to its certificate holders). The limitations relating to the trustee's power to vary investments have prevented trusts that issue mortgage pass-through certificates from fully satisfying the structuring needs of secondary mortgage market participants because, for example, prepayments received on mortgage loans held by such trusts must be distributed to holders of the mortgage pass-through certificates on the next regular distribution date. Id.

61. Each class had a different priority with respect to the principal payments received on the trust's mortgage loans. The differing priorities of the various classes of certificates allowed the compartmentalization of the prepayment risk on the mortgage loans held by the trust. For example, the holder of a Class D Certificate knew that principal paid on the mortgage loans held by the trust would be distributed to retire all of the Class A, Class B and Class C Certificates before any principal would be distributed with respect to his Class D Certificate. Using assumptions about future prepayment patterns, investors could determine an expected maturity range for each class with some assurance.

deduction by the issuer of interest paid on the CMOs, which offsets a corresponding amount of interest income from the collateral.

The first CMO offerings generally were issued by limited-purpose finance subsidiaries. Financial accounting guidelines, promulgated in 1985, typically required CMOs issued by a limited purpose finance subsidiary to be included as liabilities on the consolidated balance sheet of the parent corporation.[62] In order to avoid carrying large amounts of debt on their financial accounting balance sheets,[63] many CMO sponsors soon began using so-called "owner trusts" as the issuing vehicle. Under an owner trust structure, the sponsor transfers mortgage loans or pass-through certificates to a trust, which issues CMOs to the public. The sponsor sells to investors the certificates of beneficial interest, which represent equity ownership of the mortgage collateral subject to the CMO debt issued by the trust. Provided that no single investor owns more than 50% of the beneficial interest in the trust, neither the sponsor nor any of the investors are required to include the CMO liability on their financial accounting balance sheet.[64]

Although CMOs provide a method for creating fast pay/slow pay securities without incurring two levels of taxation, structuring CMOs as debt for federal income tax purposes causes transactional inefficiencies. For example, the issuer generally is unable to match precisely the cash flows on the mortgage collateral with the issuer's payment obligation on the CMOs. The issuer also is required to retain a meaningful residual interest in the cash flows from the mortgage collateral in excess of amounts that could be attributed to compensation received by a mere administrator of the CMOs or servicer of the collateral.[65] In connection with the retention of a meaningful residual interest, the issuer normally is required to have certain rights to call the CMOs and to substitute collateral. The various tax-related restrictions placed on CMO offerings are perceived by the market as a severe handicap because they adversely affect the price that sponsors receive for their mortgage loans in the secondary market. . . .

---

62. FASB Technical Bulletin No. 85-2, Accounting for Collateralized Mortgage Obligations (CMOs) (Mar. 18, 1985). Technical Bulletin No. 85-2 provides special rules for determining when CMOs must be included on the issuer's balance sheet as liabilities for financial accounting purposes. In addition, an issuer's financial accounting balance sheet generally is consolidated with that of its parent.

63. Treating CMOs as liabilities for financial accounting purposes was perceived as disadvantageous for sponsors of CMO transactions because it artificially inflated the amount of debt on their consolidated balance sheets. Nonetheless, in situations where sale treatment would cause the sponsor to recognize a loss for financial accounting purposes, treating CMOs as liabilities rather than as a sale could be beneficial to the sponsor.

64. FASB Accounting Research Bull. No. 51, Consolidated Financial Statements ¶2 (Aug. 1959), as amended, FASB Statement of Financial Accounting Standards no. 94, Consolidation of All Majority-Owned Subsidiaries ¶13 (Oct. 1987).

65. A residual interest generally represents the economic right to (1) the difference between (a) the cash flow received on the mortgage loans and (b) the cash payments required to be made on the CMOs and any administrative expenses, and (2) the earnings received from the temporary investment of cash flow received on the collateral prior to making payments of principal and interest on the CMOs (the float).

II. CURRENT ACTIVITY IN THE MARKETPLACE

A. ASSET SECURITIZATION STRUCTURES

1. GENERAL CONCEPT

Asset securitization is the process of raising funds through the issuance of marketable securities the payments on which are derived from the cash flows received on a specified pool of debt obligations or receivables. The basic steps in any asset securitization transaction usually are the same: (1) the pooling of the obligations or receivables; (2) the allocation of the cash flows from the asset pool into securities with different risk, duration, and payment frequency profiles; and (3) the sale of the securities. The sponsor may make an "arbitrage" profit if the sum of the price of the securities sold and the value of any retained securities and servicing fees is greater than the value or price of the unsecuritized assets.

There are a number of potential benefits to securitization. One such benefit is increased liquidity for both investors and the sponsor. To transfer unsecuritized assets, it is often necessary to execute individual assignments or endorse individual promissory notes and prepare and file individual evidences of security interests for each asset. However, once the assets are securitized, liquidity is improved because a transfer of an interest in the asset pool can be made simply by registering a transfer of a security. If the security is issued in a public offering and is widely held, an investor also will have liquidity because of the active secondary market that generally arises in such circumstances. Securitization creates liquidity for investors because it produces a ready market for the sponsor's assets and typically reduces the overall cost to the sponsor of financing those assets.

Securitization also may benefit the sponsor's financial statements. For example, if the offering of the assets-backed securities properly is treated under generally accepted accounting principles (GAAP) as a sale of the underlying assets (which occurs when there has been a shifting of the financial risks associated with ownership and is referred to as an "off-balance sheet financing" because both the assets and the liabilities are removed from the sponsor's GAAP balance sheet), there will be a reduction in the sponsor's liabilities and often an improved return on the sponsor's total assets for GAAP purposes. In addition, the sponsor may use securitization as a tool for better matching the average maturity of its liabilities with the average life of its assets in order to reduce its interest rate exposure.[66]

Finally, securitization increases the efficiency of the secondary capital markets. It is a more efficient form of financial intermediation than that provided by banks and other financial institutions because both the transaction costs and the spread between borrower yields and lender yields are lower. Moreover, securitization provides efficient functional segmentation in that it allocates the risks and tasks associated with financial intermediation to the parties who can most cheaply and effectively bear those risks and perform those tasks.

---

66. Because principal payments received on the securitized assets generally are used to pay down the related securities, asset securitization generally achieves a closer durational match between assets and liabilities than usually can be obtained through more conventional forms of financing.

2. PRINCIPAL LEGAL AND TAX STRUCTURES

Asset-backed securities are issued with a variety of legal structures. Most offerings use one of the following structures:

(1) A pass-through certificate of beneficial interest in a trust that is classified as a fixed investment trust taxable as a grantor trust for federal income tax purposes.

(2) A collateralized debt obligation (CDO) issued by a limited purpose corporation, owner trust, or limited partnership. The most common type of CDO is a CMO, which was discussed in Section I.

(3) A hybrid instrument that takes the legal form of a beneficial interest in a trust but that is characterized as indebtedness for federal income tax purposes.

(4) Preferred stock that is issued by a limited-purpose corporation and classified as stock for both federal income tax and applicable state corporate law purposes, including adjustable rate and money market preferred stock.

(5) A REMIC, which is a federal income tax classification in which the qualifying entity's legal form is irrelevant.

With the exception of REMICs, all of the above structures are employed in securitizing both mortgages and other types of assets. Furthermore, each of the first four structures imposes tax related inefficiencies on the issuer that are more severe than those imposed by a REMIC structure. . . .

e. REMICs

. . . The election of REMIC status for an entity or an asset pool affects only the taxation of the issuer and the holders of the securities, while the securities law, state law, and GAAP consequences of the transaction remain unchanged. The REMIC rules remove many of the tax-based inefficiencies in mortgage-backed security structures, including the necessity for the issuer of multiple class CDOs to maintain equity or an ownership interest in the residual cash flow from the collateral, the need to provide at least some mismatching between the payments on CDOs and the cash flows on the related collateral, limitations on multiple classes of ownership and the transferability of interests in grantor and owner trusts, and other complexities resulting from the need to obtain pass-through tax treatment for the issuer. Because REMIC treatment is not governed by the form of a particular transaction, sponsors can design mortgage-backed securities transactions to qualify for either debt or sale treatment for GAAP purposes, depending on the sponsor's particular financial accounting objectives. Under the so-called "exclusivity rule," REMICs generally will be the exclusive means for issuing multiple maturity mortgage-backed securities after 1991 without subjecting residual income to double taxation. Therefore, except for limited situations, current techniques for issuing multiple maturity non-REMIC CMOs will be unavailable beginning in 1992.

There are a number of structuring benefits that derive from the REMIC legislation. The issuer of the REMIC interests may be a trust, corporation, partnership, or even a segregated pool of assets that is not an entity for state law purposes. The securities may be in the form of pass-through securities, debt, stock, or partnership interests. REMIC securities backed by the proper type of mortgage loans are qualifying assets for REITs and thrift institutions, which are required to invest in certain classes of real estate related assets to obtain their desired tax treatment.

A REMIC can issue two types of securities: regular interests and residual interests. For federal income tax purposes, a regular interest is treated as debt of the REMIC. A residual interest is treated much like a partnership interest in a partnership that has issued bonds. Multiple classes of regular interests are allowed, but only a single class of residual interest may be issued by each REMIC. . . .

NOTES AND QUESTIONS

1. *Understanding the players.* An understanding of the CMBS market starts with an appreciation of the different parties involved in the course of a transaction. The loan is first made by an *originator*, perhaps a commercial bank or a mortgage bank. The originator will often sell the loan to a *warehouser*, which gathers loans until enough have been collected for a securities issuance. The warehouser transfers the loans to a special purpose entity (SPE), also called a special purpose vehicle, often a subsidiary of the investment bank managing the issuance (the SPE is often a REMIC). The SPE sells securities to the public, generating the cash to pay the warehouser (or originator) for the loans. A trustee is responsible to the investors, overseeing the operations of the SPE, ensuring that payments are made to the securities holders as required, and so forth. The trustee is also responsible for contracting with a *servicer*, who services the loans (that is, managing the relationship with the borrowers, collecting mortgage payments, administering the escrows required under the loan documents, and so forth). When a loan becomes distressed (missing payments or going into default), the servicer will generally transfer the loan to a separate entity called a *special servicer* which handles workout negotiations or enforcement proceedings against the borrower.

2. *Rating agencies.* The prices and yields on bonds have long been determined by the riskiness of those bonds as indicated by ratings provided by Standard & Poors, Duff & Phelps, Moody, or Fitch's. These rating agencies study the financial health of the issuer, the strength of the borrowers under the mortgages, the diversification of the mortgage pool, the legal and economic terms of the securities, and a host of other factors in deciding what rating to grant. The higher the rating, the more investors will pay (or, put another way, the higher the rating, the lower the return the investors will demand). Agencies will raise or lower their ratings on a security over time, as the health of the issuer or other factors change.

For the CMBS market to flourish, it was important that the rating agencies provide this same type of information to potential investors in CMOs, and the price issuers receive on the sale of their CMOs depends heavily on the ratings the issuance receives. The rating agencies, in turn, have developed guidelines for the structuring of deals, specifying the types of legal structures, credit enhancement, and other factors required to earn a high rating. As discussed in the next section, the requirements of the ratings agencies drive the structuring of loans that are intended to end up in a CMBS pool.

3. *Classes of securities.* The great advantage of the CMO over traditional pass-through certificates is the ability to structure different classes of securities (called tranches, French for "slices") with different durations, risk profiles, and expected returns, so as to satisfy the needs of investors with different preferences. The actual

structure can involve scores of distinct securities, but a few simple examples convey a sense of the structures.

> Example 1: Consider a REMIC that issues two classes of securities. The first entitles the holders to all of the interest paid on the mortgages in the pool (an "interest only" or "IO" strip), while the second entitles the holders to all of the principal repaid on those mortgages ("principal only" or "PO" strips).

> Example 2: Securities in a $100 million pool of mortgages, where Tranche A is entitled to the first $80 million of principal repaid, plus the interest on the unpaid amount until they have received the full $80 million. Tranche B is entitled to the next $15 million of principal repaid plus interest on it; Tranche Z is entitled to the remaining interest and principal.

Consider each of these tranches from the point of view of a potential investor. How risky is the investment? Over what period of time will the investment be recovered? How would the value of each respond to a recession? To a drop in interest rates?

4. The Effects of Securitization on Mortgage Loan Terms

Securitization has been a blessing for borrowers, but not an unmixed one. By allowing investors to purchase liquid interests in mortgage loans, with varying risk/ reward profiles, it has increased the flow of captial into real estate and lowered interest rates. At the same time, however, securitization has required that the interests of investors drive the structuring of the mortgage deal, increasing the up-front costs and reducing flexibility. As shown below, the needs of investors have become paramount in the negotiations between mortgage borrowers and lenders.

Carl J. Seneker, II, How to Document Securitized Commercial Real Estate Mortgage Loans

Modern Real Estate Transactions, 1129-1148 (ALI-ABA 2006[67])

A SECURITIZED MORTGAGE LOAN is a commercial real estate mortgage loan that is underwritten and documented to ensure that it will be marketable to investors in the commercial mortgage backed securities ("CMBS") market. Real estate securitization is an increasingly important aspect of real estate financing and investment, and thus, of real estate practice. To document a mortgage loan successfully for securitization, counsel must be thoroughly familiar with the requirements of the public markets and rating agencies and must be able to negotiate, draft, and assemble the necessary documentation effectively and efficiently. At the outset, note that the loan documentation standards for traditional mortgage loans and loans destined for securitization differ. In addition, there may be differences in documentation attributable to the nature of the assets that the mortgages will encumber and the identity of the borrower.

For example, for a securitization that is limited to a group of mortgage loans in which a single borrower and its affiliates own all of the underlying mortgaged assets, cross-collateralization of the loans is common. The size and diversity of assets in the loan pool will affect the marketability of the offering and its rating. At the same time, there may be some flexibility in the negotiation of loan documents. These types of single borrower offerings, however, have become relatively rare given the larger pool size and diversity requirements that have emerged as the CMBS market has matured.

For loan pools involving multiple borrowers — which represent by far the bulk of the CMBS offerings — the sponsor is typically either a portfolio lender (commonly linked with an investment bank) or a conduit lender. There will usually be less flexibility in the documentation package — the CMBS market demands consistency to ensure reliable cash flows and for purposes of supporting issuer representations and warranties and loan servicing. Because of the lack of true cross-collateralization among the loans in the pool, securitization will typically require an unrated subordinate tranche that will assume the ultimate risk of nonpayment. Other so-called credit enhancement devices may also be employed, as discussed later in this article.

Most CMBS vehicles are structured as trusts that meet real estate mortgage investment conduit ("REMIC") requirements for favorable tax treatment. The financial asset securitization investment trust ("FASIT") legislation that became effective in late 1997 offers additional structuring flexibility not available to REMICs in areas such as prepayments and ability to modify or substitute mortgages in the pool. However, FASITs are subject to different tax consequences upon creation of the mortgage pool.

Both REMICs and FASITs permit an array of tranches of investment interests having differing cash flows and timing of payments in order to appeal to investors with varying cash flow profiles and risk tolerances. Typically, the structure will contemplate the creation of a number of regular interests that will be rated according to cash flows and risk profiles, together with a subordinated residual interest which will not be rated.

The rating agency for the CMBS offering will do extensive due diligence and analysis addressing both credit and property conditions for at least the more sizable or significant loans to be included in the loan pool. Provisions included in the mortgage loan documents can have an important relationship to the due diligence conclusions reached by the rating agency. Accordingly, significant changes in certain key provisions which the rating agency assumes will be included in the mortgage documents can be detrimental to the offering and can affect the viability of the securitization.

In a number of instances, the rating agency will require one or more forms of credit enhancement to issue the desired investment rating. Credit enhancement may include, for example, cross-collateralization features, one or more guaranties, the creation of reserves for certain types of property exposure, letters of credit, the use of a larger unrated subordinated residual interest, and the like.

From the real estate perspective, the size of the mortgage pool, and the diversity of the borrowers, property types, and geographic location of the underlying mortgaged assets, will be important factors that can mitigate property-related risk and support a higher investment rating for particular interests.

Securitized offerings require the creation of loan servicing arrangements to provide for the collection of payments on the underlying mortgage loans, monitoring of the cash flow from the loans, and periodic reports to investors. A master servicer will have responsibility for collecting loan payments and forwarding them to investors, along with periodic reports. The master servicer also may assume certain limited obligations to make servicing advances or monthly loan payment advances in the event of cash flow shortfalls. A special servicer will have responsibility for addressing loan defaults and carrying out any necessary loan workouts, foreclosures, receiverships, and sales of property acquired through foreclosure. It is not uncommon for the special servicer to hold some or all of the subordinated residual interest and to enjoy special incentive compensation tied to successful completion of its responsibilities.

Loan Documentation in Securitized Mortgage Transactions

In the origination of loans intended for securitization, a central purpose of the documentation will be to ensure that the mortgage loan terms are sufficient to eliminate or mitigate interruptions in cash flow to the investors. Cash flow risk derives primarily from:

- Potential borrower payment defaults (whether on account of factors within the borrower's control or unfavorable market conditions, such as nonrenewal of a lease by a major tenant);
- Inability to refinance the loan at maturity (commonly, securitized loans are not fully amortized and have balloon payments due at maturity); and
- The occurrence of a voluntary or involuntary prepayment of the loan.

Assurance of Steady Cash Flow

Three critical requirements for securitization relate to this assurance of a steady cash flow stream:

- Different forms of credit enhancement, as noted above, may be required to cover potential interruptions in cash flows.
- Prepayment of the mortgage loans will be prohibited unless adequate market prepayment premiums are paid or a defeasance structure is used (i.e., U.S. Government securities are substituted for the mortgaged properties with payment schedules that match the required cash flow profile for the various tranches of the CMBS offering). In a defeasance arrangement, the loans are technically not prepaid; rather, the collateral for the loans is changed to allow release of the mortgages encumbering the original real property interests.
- Extensive information regarding the borrower, the performance of the encumbered property, and the loan itself is required to be provided on an ongoing basis. This information and disclosure trail is needed for the initial CMBS offering under applicable securities laws, for the full and free flow of current information to support the secondary market for the sale of investor interests, and for ease of servicing of the loans.

Single Purpose Entity

The borrower under a mortgage loan to be included in a securitized pool will be required to be organized as a single purpose entity ("SPE") to ensure that the property owner will not become financially overextended by business operations that are unrelated to the mortgaged property and to eliminate or minimize bankruptcy risk. In appropriate cases, particularly those involving the more substantial loans in a CMBS offering (e.g., loans in a principal amount exceeding $20 million), the borrower will also be required to be organized as a bankruptcy remote entity. For a comprehensive discussion of the use of bankruptcy remote entities in securitizations and structured finance transactions, see William L. Myers, The Use of Bankruptcy-Remote Entities in Real Property Securitizations and Structured Financings, 15 Cal. Real Prop. J. 24 (1997).

The basic requirements for the creation of an SPE that is bankruptcy remote include the following:

- The business purpose of the SPE must be limited to owning and operating the mortgaged property. No assets may be acquired other than those related to the mortgaged property.
- The borrower must be prohibited from incurring additional indebtedness. In the relatively recent past, borrowers were sometimes given very limited flexibility to place fully subordinated junior nonrecourse debt on the property that was payable solely from excess cash flow, with the junior lender having no ability to enforce the junior debt until after the senior securitized debt has been paid in full. In more recent years, however, most types of junior secured debt have been prohibited and additional "financing," if needed, has been placed in the form of mezzanine debt or preferred equity where the mezzanine lender or preferred equity holder will have the right to proceed only against the borrower's partnership or LLC interests at the entity level . . .
- The borrower must maintain a separate legal existence in all respects from any affiliated or related entities . . .
- No pledges of assets or guaranties of the debts of any other entity will be permitted, except for any liabilities expressly permitted to be guaranteed by the loan documents.
- Adequate capitalization must be maintained.
- At the corporate level, the bankruptcy remote structure will typically require at least one independent director with veto power over major decisions, including in particular a bankruptcy filing. There are, however, issues of fiduciary duty responsibilities created by this structure. Under corporate law principles, an independent director must act in the best interests of the company, which under certain circumstances could conceivably require a bankruptcy filing. A fiduciary duty could also extend to company creditors under certain circumstances. See In re Kingston Square Associates, 214 B.R. 713 (Bankr. S.D.N.Y., 1997).

If the borrower is a partnership or an LLC, the above tests will be applied at the general partner/managing member level as well.

In some cases, the lender making the mortgage loan may require the issuance of a substantive nonconsolidation opinion from the borrower's counsel (to the effect that the borrower will not be consolidated into a bankruptcy proceeding involving its affiliated companies) if the SPE is a member of a group of related companies or has a general partner or managing member which is a member of such a group. As discussed below, these opinions can be very difficult and expensive to render.

KEY TERMS OF MORTGAGE DOCUMENTS

The following portion of this article will focus on the key terms and provisions that are typically required in securitized mortgage loan documents. These requirements will constrain counsel's ability to negotiate the documentation package. In general, the provisions in the loan documents that directly affect the cash flow stream from the underlying mortgaged properties are highly sensitive to the rating agencies and investors, and there will be only very limited or no ability to modify these provisions.

This limitation is now generally understood by most borrowers as conduit loans have proliferated. In rare instances where the lender is an institution that has important institutional relationships with a particular borrower, some limited flexibility may exist. However, most securitized loans are nonrecourse, with only limited recourse carveouts, and the reliability of an unbroken cash flow stream from the property or from some credit enhancement vehicle is critical.

TOP TEN LIST

Although not an exhaustive list, consider this "Top Ten" list of issues when documenting securitized mortgage loans:

PREPAYMENTS

There will typically be a lock-in period during which no prepayment will be permitted, and then a further period during which prepayment may be permitted only upon payment of a make whole premium. Alternatively, it is becoming more common that a defeasance structure will be used once the lock-in period expires. In very limited instances, the borrower may be able to negotiate for a prepayment premium that is based on a declining fixed percentage of the loan principal in return for agreeing to pay a higher base interest rate, or the borrower may be able to buy down the standard lock-in period by agreeing to pay a higher base rate.

A prepayment premium will typically also be required upon the occurrence of an involuntary prepayment, such as following damage or destruction or condemnation, or upon an attempt to redeem from foreclosure following a borrower default, including where the event triggering the prepayment occurs during the lock-in period. See Calif. Civ. Code § 2954.10 (West 1993) for special California documentation requirements relating to the enforcement of prepayment premiums following a borrower default.

RESERVES

Rating agencies may require the creation of reserve funds to support and ensure the adequacy of cash flow. There is a wide array of possible reserves, including capital replacements, environmental mitigation, tenant improvements, leasing commissions, deferred maintenance items, debt service coverage, and the like. . . .

LOCKBOX CONTROLS

Lockbox controls are designed to eliminate the risk that the property management company or the borrower will misapply the income from the property. However, they can impede the efficient operation of the property if the controls are too cumbersome.

Lockbox provisions are not always required, or may be required only upon the occurrence of a default or other event giving rise to concern about ability to pay or misapplication of property revenues. (Query how, as a practical matter, a lender would be able to enforce an agreement to create a lockbox at a time when the borrower is in default or the property is otherwise troubled. Presumably, a receiver may have to be sought for the property if the borrower is not cooperative.) When a lockbox is required, it is typical to include provisions that will give the property manager or borrower access on an agreed basis to any excess funds after payment of operating expenses, debt service, property taxes, insurance premiums, and reserves. In some cases, waiver of a lockbox requirement may be given in return for the execution of a guaranty from a borrower affiliate covering misapplication of property income. Also, some lenders will seek to impose recourse liability on the principals of the borrower in the case of intentionally misapplied revenues.

PERIODIC OPERATING REPORTS AND STATEMENTS

Compliance by the borrower with reporting requirements is important to the loan servicing functions, as well as the ability to sell investor certificates in the secondary market. Typical requirements for periodic operating reports and statements include:

- Quarterly and annual rent rolls and operating statements;
- Annual balance sheets and income statements (certified or audited);
- Annual operating budgets (including capital replacements and improvements); and
- Property management and marketing reports, security deposit reconciliation, and bank statements (usually on request).

These reports are early warning signals for possible impairment or interruption of cash flow. They may also be used, in combination with financial covenants, to trigger restrictions on distributions or dividends to the borrower's equity owners. . . .

LEASING RESTRICTIONS

It is common to include leasing guidelines in the loan documents that require active ongoing marketing efforts by the borrower and impose limitations on the economic terms of any significant leases. When the consent of the lender is required for a particular lease, it is common to include a reasonableness standard for such consent and also to permit the execution of a market form of SNDA (subordination and nondisturbance agreement). Because of the nature of the loan servicing relationships, however, it is difficult to construct hard and fast time limits for lender responses to requests for consent.

RESTRICTIONS ON ASSIGNMENT AND TRANSFER

These restrictions are important to ensure that the SPE/bankruptcy remote ownership structure is kept intact, and that management and control of the property is retained by an entity acceptable to the lender.

Note the importance of applying any transfer restrictions to cover the transfer of ownership interests in the borrowing entity (and perhaps lower entity tiers) as well as the transfer of interests in the property itself. Some lenders will allow certain limited transfers among affiliates and for estate planning purposes, as long as the SPE status is maintained. Some permitted transfers may also require rating agency signoff.

It is also not unusual to find provisions that will allow a single one-time transfer by the borrower to a new SPE, subject to meeting a debt service coverage test, rating agency signoff, title policy endorsement, payment of a transfer fee to the lender, payment of all lender and rating agency costs by the borrower, written assumption of the loan by the new SPE, and similar requirements.

As noted above, junior financing secured by a lien on the mortgaged property is not usually allowed and the rating agencies have become quite rigid in maintaining this restriction. The reason is that junior financing may substantially increase the risk of bankruptcy, as well as possibly create divided loyalties. As also noted above, in certain cases junior financing may be permitted at a level above the title holding borrowing entity (e.g., loans from borrower affiliates that are deeply subordinated and enforceable only against the affiliated parent entity to the extent necessary to gain control of the borrower).

INSURANCE AND REBUILDING

The mortgage loan documents will contain explicit requirements for insurance coverage for the property, including casualty, business interruption, and general liability insurance.

The documents will typically permit rebuilding after damage or destruction (given the desire to ensure a steady cash flow stream, rebuilding would usually be preferred by the lender to premature repayment of the loan). . . .

COMPLIANCE WITH LAWS

Compliance of the mortgaged property with applicable laws will be important because the CMBS issuer will typically represent and warrant as to the compliance of the properties in the mortgage pool with applicable laws.

Essentially, this requirement raises an underwriting issue regarding how deep and detailed will the pre-funding due diligence investigations extend to determine the property's compliance with laws. Commonly, a zoning endorsement to the lender's title policy will be required along with (where available) a favorable zoning and building code compliance letter from local officials and/or an opinion or zoning memorandum from counsel. Keep in mind, however, that other non-zoning laws will also be involved that may be more difficult to address, including the requirements of the Americans with Disabilities Act and some environmental and health and safety measures.

NONRECOURSE CLAUSE

Securitized commercial mortgage loans are commonly nonrecourse with only limited recourse carveouts. Because of the SPE structure used in such loans, recourse against the personal assets of the borrower (other than the mortgaged property) is effectively limited in any event (although the free cash balances of the borrowing entity could be significant in particular cases). Thus, the issue often becomes whether any guarantees will be obtained from the principals or affiliates of the borrower. Also, in states such as California, one action or antideficiency rules may come into play to restrict the institution of personal actions against a borrower or the recovery of deficiency judgments.

Note also that if a recourse carveout is breached, the issue arises whether the borrower or its principals should be liable to the lender for the entire amount of the loan or only to the extent of the damage or loss actually suffered by the lender (essentially the amount of any deficiency after a foreclosure sale).

Nonrecourse clauses appear in a variety of formats, and with a seemingly never ending expansion of the number of recourse carveouts. Many lenders employ full recourse liability for such egregious matters as fraud, bankruptcy, violation of SPE requirements, and perhaps environmental liabilities. On the other hand, events such as the creation of junior liens, unpermitted transfers, misapplication of funds, and commission of waste, will commonly produce liability limited to the amount of the lender's resulting loss or damage. A lender might also require so-called "exploding" or "springing" guarantees by one or more borrower principals which would be activated by a bankruptcy filing or a challenge (at least if unsuccessful or done for the purpose of delay) to the exercise by the lender of its default remedies.

RIGHT OF LENDER TO ASSIGN

Securitized loans will include express language giving the lender the right to assign the loan and the servicing of the loan. . . .

Some borrowers remain concerned about not knowing who will end up holding the loan servicing responsibilities, particularly for those loans where it is likely that the borrower will need to deal with the lender or loan servicer on a relatively frequent basis for consents and approvals (e.g., major leases). Needless to say, one of the costs to the borrower of accepting a securitized loan is the lack of control over the identity of the lender, as well as potential difficulties (and the related costs) associated with obtaining consents for even relatively routine matters involving the real estate collateral, such as granting partial releases of small portions of the property to be conveyed to a local government for maintenance purposes, particularly if a REMIC compliance opinion will be required as a condition of the consent. . . .

NOTES

1. *Special purpose entities and "bankruptcy remoteness."* Where the lender intends to include a commercial loan in a securitization, the borrower will normally be an SPE — a legal entity established specifically to hold the real estate and serve as the

borrower for the loan. This SPE will be subject to a number of restraints to try to ensure that it cannot become a debtor in a bankruptcy proceeding, nor be caught up in a bankruptcy proceeding of the owner of the SPE, because bankruptcy can inhibit the lender's ability to collect on the loan or result in a "cramdown" that limits the amount the lender will ultimately recover on the loan. The SPE is made "bankruptcy remote" by a number of measures, such as providing that it will engage in no other business except for owning this parcel of property; prohibiting it from entering into any debt except for this mortgage loan; and providing for an independent director controlled by the lender whose consent is required for any bankruptcy filing by the SPE. The lender will also normally require an opinion letter from the borrower's counsel that the SPE is not likely to be "substantively consolidated" in any bankruptcy of the borrower's parent company or owner.

The borrower is not the only bankruptcy remote SPE involved in a securitized loan, however. The issuer, which owns the pool of mortgage loans and issues the securities, will also be required to be an SPE, so that the securities holders can be as protected as possible against the risk that the issuer, or its parent company, may become a bankruptcy debtor.

For discussions of the various techniques intended to make these entities "bankruptcy remote" and examinations of their efficacy, see, e.g., Adam B. Weissburg, Special Purpose Bankruptcy Remote Entities, *in* Commercial Real Estate Financing 2005: What Borrowers & Lenders Need to Know Now, 512 PLI/Real 237 (2005); Report by the Committee on Bankruptcy and Corporate Reorganization of the Association of the Bar of the City of New York, New Developments in Structured Finance, 56 Bus. Law. 95 (2000); William L. Myers, The Use of Bankruptcy-Remote Entities in Real Property Securitizations and Structured Financings, 15 Cal. Real Prop. J. 24 (1997); Marshall E. Tracht, Contractual Bankruptcy Waivers: Reconciling Theory, Practice, and Law, 82 Cornell L. Rev. 301 (1997).

2. *Fairness, efficiency, and securitization.* Securitization has grown to be a massive force in the economy. It is not limited to (the trillions of dollars of) residential and commercial mortgages, but practically any asset that generates a stream of income can be sold to an SPE that issues securities to the public — credit card receivables, auto loans, equipment leases, structured litigation settlements, and even music royalties. There is an extensive literature debating the costs and benefits of asset securitization. Advocates point to the reduction in financing costs and greater availability of capital to borrowers who might otherwise be closed out of the financial markets. Critics contend that securitization, by removing assets from the parent corporation, threaten to externalize the costs of business failure onto noncontractual creditors (like tort victims) and employees, to the unfair and inefficient benefit of securities holders. See, e.g., Steven L. Schwarcz, Securitization Post-Enron, 25 Cardozo L. Rev. 1539 (2004); Thomas E. Plank, The Security of Securitization and the Future of Security, 25 Cardozo L. Rev. 1655 (2004); Lois R. Lupica, Circumvention of the Bankruptcy Process: The Statutory Institutionalization of Securitization, 33 Conn. L. Rev. 199 (2000); David Gray Carlson, The Rotten Foundations of Securitization, 39 Wm. & Mary L. Rev. 1055, 1064 (1998); Lois R. Lupica, Asset Securitization: The Unsecured Creditor's Perspective, 76 Tex. L. Rev. 595 (1998); Christopher W. Frost, Asset Securitization and Corporate Risk Allocation, 72 Tul. L. Rev. 101 (1997).

George Lefcoe, Yield Maintenance and Defeasance: Two Distinct Paths to Commercial Mortgage Prepayment

28 Real Est. L.J. 202 (2000)

This article compares two arrangements for commercial mortgage prepayment—yield maintenance and defeasance—and explains why CMBS issuers prefer defeasance, and why some portfolio commercial mortgage lenders might not.

Highly leveraged real estate owners who don't sell or refinance in good times risk losing their properties if their mortgages fall due when real estate values are too low to support refinancing. With the typical commercial fixed-rate loan maturing in 7 to 10 years, owners are lucky to catch one good cycle. Portfolio lenders know this and allow prepayment, usually through yield maintenance clauses.[68] Yield maintenance formulas are calculated to cover the lender's reinvestment loss when prepaid loans bear above-market rates.

Issuers of commercial mortgage-backed securities (CMBS) prefer mortgage prepayment by defeasance.[69] Because approximately half of all commercial mortgages are originated for inclusion in CMBS packages, borrowers, lenders, and, in some situations, judges will need to know the difference between yield maintenance and defeasance. This article compares the two arrangements and explains why CMBS issuers prefer defeasance and why many commercial mortgagors might not.

A Nutshell Comparison

Under a yield maintenance formula, the borrower discharges the debt with a onetime fee sufficient to enable the lender, reinvesting at current rates, to earn no less than it would have earned had the borrower not prepaid. By contrast, defeasance effects no early termination of the debt. Instead, the borrower is allowed to substitute for the mortgage a carefully assembled package of noncallable and non-prepayable U.S. government obligations.

Quite often, the costs of yield maintenance and defeasance will be nearly the same, except for the considerable expense of arranging defeasance. Most yield maintenance clauses peg the prepayment premium to the difference between the original mortgage interest rate and the market rate of a Treasury obligation of comparable maturity to the unexpired term of the prepaid debt.

If the purpose of the premium is to offset any loss the lender might otherwise suffer upon reinvesting prepaid sums, the mortgage/Treasury differential over-compensates the lender. Treasury obligations, being safer than mortgages, command lower rates. One lawyer offers the example of a $10 million loan, with 10-year maturity and an 8 percent interest rate, being prepaid one minute after origination, at a time when Treasuries of comparable maturity were yielding 6.5 percent. Along with repayment of the $10 million, the borrower's prepayment fee would be

---

68. For a onetime fee or higher interest rate, some portfolio lenders will agree to allow prepayment without penalty or according to a fixed or sliding-scale premium.

69. Anticipating the possibility that borrowers may not be able to sell or refinance when the loan principal falls due, many CMBS mortgage loans do not treat as a default failure to repay at maturity. Instead, the interest rate is increased, and all net operating income is allocated to principal repayment, called hyperamortization.

$1.1 million even though rates hadn't changed at all during the intervening minute.[70] In similar circumstances, the defeasing borrower would have to purchase more than $11 million worth of Treasuries to fund an account yielding 8 percent interest, in precisely the amounts and at the same times the mortgage payments would have been due.[71]

Comparing the costs of yield maintenance to defeasance requires a close look at the particular yield maintenance provision. Some yield maintenance clauses are less expensive than defeasance because the borrower's obligation is calculated as the difference between the current Treasury rate and the Treasury rate at the date of loan origination, or between a current mortgage rate and the original mortgage loan rate. Other yield maintenance clauses are more expensive than defeasance because they set a minimum payment of 1 percent of the prepaid loan balance regardless of interest rates. When rates have risen enough so that the borrower can purchase Treasuries for less than the prepaid mortgage balance, the borrower's defeasance cost could be lower than a 1 percent yield maintenance premium. But under many yield maintenance clauses, the borrower pays absolutely nothing when the current rate exceeds the original yield. Regardless of interest rate trends, the defeasing borrower always incurs the expense of purchasing Treasury obligations.

Besides reinvestment losses, yield maintenance prepayment could result in two additional types of losses to lenders: the costs of processing the new loan and temporary reductions in interest income while the lender "parks" the funds in low-yielding, short-term government securities, pending mortgage reinvestment. Most yield maintenance provisions disregard these items, realistically assuming that lenders recoup fully their loan origination costs from borrower fees, and reinvest funds almost instantaneously. But some lenders levy fixed fees or reserve the right to recoup these costs, if incurred, from the prepaying borrower.

THE DEFEASANCE PROCESS

Defeasance costs consist of processing fees and the actual cost of acquiring the Treasuries. The borrower's request to defease must be supported by the opinion of a recognized rating agency, prepared at the borrower's expense, that the defeasance will not cause a downgrade, qualification or withdrawal of the then-current ratings on the mortgage certificate. Once the servicer designated in the CMBS offering accedes to the request, the borrower will pay processing fees, and for the preparation of a defeasance security agreement, a comfort letter from the borrower's Certified Public Accountant that the cash flow from the substituted collateral exactly matches all scheduled mortgage payments, and a legal opinion that the borrower has fully complied with all defeasance requirements, including Treasury Regulations regarding REMICs (Real Estate Mortgage Investment Conduits) (more about this later). The borrower will also have to form a special-purpose entity to act as the successor borrower.

---

70. Sam W. Galowitz, "The Myth of the Yield Maintenance Formula," 15 Real Est. Fin. J. 27, 29 (Fall 1999). Further, some yield maintenance formulas neglect to credit the borrower by discounting to present value the lump-sum payment the lender is receiving well ahead of schedule.

71. Michael Schonberger, "Defeasance: A Prepayment Substitute," 15 Real Est. Fin. J. 37 (Fall 1999). The more efficiently the defeasance account is structured, the closer its costs will approximate a comparable yield maintenance formula.

Actually accumulating the matching Treasury collateral is complicated because of the many differences between mortgages and Treasuries. Principal is repaid on a Treasury at maturity, while most loans call for periodic amortization. Treasury interest is payable semiannually and not compounded, while mortgage interest is payable monthly and compounded. Most prepaying borrowers will require the services of a bond trader.

A poorly arranged defeasance can be quite costly, particularly when the Treasuries purchased produce payments in advance of actual need on which the borrower earns nothing. In one case, a borrower, arranging a securitized loan, sued its financial advisors for breach of contract and its legal advisors for malpractice partly because of a defeasance clause giving the lender the first right to purchase the U.S. obligations. The borrower's expert testified that the total cost of defeasing the borrower's $174 million note could range between $223,776,000 and $292,612,920, depending on the efficiency of the execution.[72]

WHY YIELD MAINTENANCE PROVISIONS FAIL PREPAID MORTGAGE BONDHOLDERS

Yield maintenance formulas calculated at the loan level don't guarantee that all bondholders will be made whole when loans are prepaid.

To offer an example, consider a $50 million loan, all principal due in 10 years, secured by two twin office towers, each appraised by the lender at $37.5 million. The interest rate is fixed at 8 percent. One day after the loan closes, the borrower receives and accepts an offer of $45 million for one of the towers. Providentially, the borrower had contracted for the right to prepay $30 million of the debt in exchange for a release of the mortgage on one tower.

Under a yield maintenance provision, the borrower's prepayment fee would depend significantly on the precise language of the clause. Suppose the provision defined original yield as 8 percent and current yield as a Treasury of like maturity, then trading at 5.5 percent. The borrower would be liable for 2.5 percent, the difference between 8 percent and 5.5 percent, multiplied by the prepaid sum, discounted to present value. Had the yield maintenance clause measured original and current yield from the same yardstick — utilizing mortgage or Treasury rates in both instances — the borrower would incur no prepayment fee obligation.

Now consider the position of bondholders if the mortgage loan had been securitized before the partial prepayment. For simplicity, assume that the securitization contained only the one underlying mortgage of $50 million.

The issuer created an A and a B tranche ("tranche" is French for "slice"). The A tranche investor purchased the right to receive the first principal and interest payments, at 7 percent, on $30 million. The B tranche investor bought the right to receive the next $20 million at 7.7 percent. Finally, the issuer sold to C an interest-only (IO) strip for the 1 percent premium on the A tranche — the difference between the mortgagor's 8 percent interest rate and the A tranche investor's 7 percent coupon rate.

C's purchase was especially important to the issuer because, besides fee income, the issuer's profit depends on the spread between the mortgage interest rate and what bond investors receive. The issuer could patiently pocket the difference each month but preferred cash now, as do most issuers.

---

72. "Sage Realty Corp. v. Proskauer Rose, LLP," NYLJ, Apr. 6, 1999, at 27, col. 2.

Again, assume that the mortgagor partially prepaid one day after A, B, and C purchased their respective interests. A will be fully repaid. Because securitized debt is traded at a spread above Treasuries, whether A can reinvest in a comparable 7 percent deal depends on whether Treasury rates, and the spread between Treasuries and mortgage rates, have remained constant. Assuming no change in these numbers, the A tranche holder will be able to reinvest without loss — except for transactions costs. Those costs could be more than covered by the borrower's yield maintenance fee. But there would be no source of recovery from a yield maintenance clause precisely calculated to measure the mortgagee's reinvestment loss.

B's situation is enviable. Far from costing B anything, the borrower's prepayment delivers a windfall to B. Before prepayment, B's loan-to-value (LTV) ratio was 66 percent. After prepayment, it would improve to 53 percent. Given that A had accepted 7 percent on an LTV of 40 percent, what would B have rationally accepted? The difference between that rate and 7.7 percent is the measure of B's windfall. Anything B recovers from the mortgagor's yield maintenance fee adds to B's windfall.

C stands to suffer a substantial loss. The mortgagor's obligation to pay interest ceases with prepayment. C will get nothing, unless the borrower is obligated for a prepayment fee and C has been given the right to receive it. Of course, knowledgeable purchasers of IO strips consider prepayment fee allocation formulas in deciding what they will pay. "There is seemingly no end to the number of ways underwriters can distribute the penalties."[73]

Defeasance saves the CMBS issuer struggling to devise an acceptable formula for allocating yield maintenance payments fairly among competing classes of bondholders by assuring that all the investors in the securitized pool continue to receive their payments on schedule. The cash keeps flowing, but from U.S. Treasury obligations, not a mortgage, increasing the value of the investment by the amount investors prefer government bonds to mortgages.

REMIC RULES

The Real Estate Mortgage Investment Conduit is a Tax Code-authorized vehicle that enables mortgage investors to purchase shares of pooled mortgages while avoiding the double taxation of interest income, first at the conduit level when interest payments that mortgagors make to loan services are forwarded to the bond trustee and, again, when bondholders receive their payments from the trustee.[74]

Tax at the entity level is only avoided if the REMIC remains an entirely passive recipient of interest payments, not actively engaged in trading, originating, or servicing mortgages. Otherwise, REMICs could compete unfairly with businesses that are subject to entity-level tax, or be exploited by such firms to defer or avoid tax on "active" earnings.[75] REMICs are taxed on 100 percent of the income derived

73. Manus J. Clancy & Michael Constantino III, "The Effects of Prepayment on the Bond Structures of CMBS," in The Handbook of Commercial Mortgage-Backed Securities 139, 146 (Fabozzi & Jacob eds., 1997).

74. Joseph L. Ferst & Milton K. Miyashiro, "Federal Income Taxation of REMICs and CMBS," in The Handbook of Commercial Mortgage-Backed Securities (Fabozzi & Jacob eds., 2d ed. 1999).

75. Diane M. Sullivan, "Why Does Tax Law Restrict Short-term Trading Activity for Asset Securitization?," 17 Va. Tax. Rev. 609, 623 (1998).

from prohibited sources. The REMIC must consist of a fixed pool of "qualified" mortgages, basically, loans acquired at the REMIC startup date or acquired within three months pursuant to a contract entered on that date. Loans cannot be prepaid within the first two years of startup, which explains the two-year "lock out" in all REMIC-securitized mortgages.

Except for precisely defined "defective obligations" (mainly, loans in or near default), no mortgage may be substituted for another originally included in a REMIC pool. This rules out substituting one mortgaged property for another, an option that would save the borrower the cost of the spread between Treasury and mortgage rates. Only Treasury obligations can be substituted for prepaid mortgages, and only two years after the REMIC startup date.

An alternate tax pass-through entity, available since 1996, known as a FASIT (Financial Asset Securitization Investment Trust) accommodates the debtor substituting one asset for another with no adverse tax consequences. FASITs were designed to allow the securitization of revolving consumer debt — car and credit card loans — and are allowed to substitute debt instruments. Thus, while a REMIC could not invest in construction loans, to be "taken out" with long-term financing, a FASIT could. But FASITs have rarely been used for securitized mortgages. They raise numerous, as yet unanswered tax questions and would result in significant front-end tax liabilities for some securitized mortgage issuers. . . .

LEGAL ENFORCEABILITY OF PREPAYMENT PROHIBITIONS, YIELD MAINTENANCE, AND DEFEASANCE

Except in bankruptcy, courts have universally enforced absolute prohibitions against prepayment (variously called "lock outs" or "lock ins"). They also uphold yield maintenance provisions, even those that significantly overcompensated the lender because they carry a premium based on the difference between the contract mortgage rate and the Treasury rate at the time of prepayment.[76] Some lawyers are dismayed by this, recalling Corbin's admonition that "justice requires nothing more than compensation measured by the amount of the harm suffered."[77]

Analyzed as liquidated damage clauses, prepayment provisions that predictably overcompensate lenders could be faulted as unreasonably high, unnecessary because the lender's damages can readily be calculated at date of breach and in excess of actual loss, calculated ex post. To avoid applying these familiar limits on liquidated damages clauses, some courts characterize prepayment fees not as damages for breach at all, but as contracts for alternate performance, like options. Other courts emphasize that such provisions should be upheld in commercial mortgage loans because they are, presumably, "fairly bargained."

Conventionally, the "fairly bargained" standard was an attempt to identify "process" unconscionability, so that courts could reserve their intervention in the private contract arena to alleviating the plight of helpless or desperate borrowers. Commercial mortgagors don't easily fit within that class of protected consumers, despite their occasional claims to the contrary.

---

76. Dale Whitman, "Mortgage Prepayment: A Legal and Economic Analysis," 40 UCLA L. Rev. 851 (1993); Restatement of the Law (Third) of Property (Mortgages) 410-413 (1997).

77. Corbin, Contracts § 1057, at 334.

Another rationale for denying commercial mortgagors relief from harsh prepayment clauses is that prepayment arrangements figure prominently, if often subtly, in loan pricing. When courts limit lenders to actual loss, instead of enforcing agreed prepayment penalties, borrowers reap a windfall by obtaining free what would have cost them a higher interest rate or front-end fee. To avoid unjust enrichment, borrowers should be made to reimburse lenders for lost earnings. Courts recognizing the legitimacy of the lender's claim might well decide not to interfere with the contract in the first place, anticipating that in many cases what the borrower saves in prepayment relief will be offset by the lender's foregone interest on the underlying loan.

To protect undersecured and unsecured creditors, many bankruptcy courts limit prepaid lenders to actual damages, rigorously calculated to return no more than reinvestment loss,[78] unless the lender had agreed to a prepayment formula yielding a lesser sum. The leading bankruptcy case striking down an overcompensatory yield maintenance clause as contrary to state liquidated damage law was simply mistaken in its analysis of the applicable state law.[79] Several bankruptcy courts have predicated their opinions on Section 506(b) of the Bankruptcy Code. That section empowers bankruptcy judges to allow secured creditors "reasonable fees, costs or charges." Although some bankruptcy courts allow as a "reasonable" fee overcompensatory yield maintenance fees,[80] most limit the lender to actual reinvestment loss.

A legal threat to REMICs would arise from a black letter prescription in the Restatement of the Law (Third) Property (Mortgages), if courts took it seriously. Probably thinking only of portfolio lenders, the Restatement authors would allow borrowers to contravene an absolute prohibition against prepayment by providing "substitute security equal in value to the mortgage obligation . . . that is substantially the equivalent of cash."[81]

This provision would impair REMIC tax status if mortgagors prepaid during the two-year lock-out period; interest received on the collateral would be subject to entity-level tax. Also, the Restatement would not limit substitute collateral to U.S. government obligations. It would allow borrowers to replace mortgages with "short-term certificates of deposit issued by financial institutions and fully covered by federal deposit insurance" and "short-term commercial paper issued by large firms and highly rated by national rating agencies." REMIC tax status only extends to Treasuries.

The Restatement authors appear to have overlooked the difference between portfolio and CMBS lenders in another respect. The Restatement defends prepayment provisions that overcompensate lenders as not necessarily inefficient by contending that mortgagors can simply renegotiate with lenders to "split" the savings achievable by refinancing at lower rates. Portfolio lenders might well renegotiate, especially if they were also providing the refinancing.

---

78. W. Barry Blum, "The Oversecured Creditor's Right to Enforce a Prepayment Charge As Part of Its Secured Claim Under 11 USC Section 506(b)," 98 Com. LJ 78 (1993).

79. In re Skyler Ridge, 80 BR 500 (Bankr. CD Cal. 1987) (purporting to apply Kansas law). The court's analysis of Kansas's liquidated damage law was repudiated in TMG Life Ins. Co. v. Barney Ashner, 898 P2d 1145, 1160 (Kan. 1995).

80. Financial Ctr. Assocs. of E. Meadow, LP v. TNE Funding Corp., 140 BR 829 (EDNY 1992).

81. Restatement of the Law (Third) of Property (Mortgages) § 6.2(b) (1997).

REMIC trustees and servicers are severely limited in their authority to modify the provisions of loans not in default. Renegotiating the prepayment provision could constitute an impermissible loan modification, and result in a 100 percent tax on interest following the modification.

Tax considerations aside, renegotiation would be more difficult than in a portfolio loan because CMBS bondholders are not all affected in the same way by prepayment. The class of bondholders who would forfeit the "excess" prepayment fee implicit in an overcompensatory yield maintenance provision would seldom be the same class of bondholders who would benefit from the credit-enhancing effect of a prepayment on the loan portfolio. Prepayment is often a blessing to the holders of the "first loss piece" and, usually the holders of the mezzanine or "B" interests, described in the above example. But it can leave the holders of interest-only strips in the cold. To defend overcompensatory prepayment fees as efficient, in the CMBS context, some rationale is required other than the borrower's ability to renegotiate.

CONCLUSION

Each commercial real estate borrower's challenge lies in pricing the difference between yield maintenance and defeasance provisions, mindful of its own anticipated prepayment needs. In shopping for loans, borrowers will not necessarily have to choose between portfolio and CMBS lenders. Some CMBS lenders offer yield maintenance and other prepayment options to lure borrowers who resist defeasance. Conversely, even portfolio lenders, until now content with yield maintenance clauses, may desire the option of securitizing their loans, leading them toward defeasance.

Courts are more likely than ever to regard prepayment provisions as contracts for alternate performance, not penalties for breach, precisely because commercial mortgagors have choices, and loan rates, increasingly, take account of prepayment arrangements because CMBS issuers and investors are pricing them.

5. *Mezzanine Loan and Preferred Equity Investments*

Andrew R. Berman, "Once a Mortgage, Always a Mortgage" — The Use (and Misuse) of Mezzanine Loans and Preferred Equity Investments[*]

11 Stan. J.L. Bus. & Fin. 76, 105-110 (2005)

III. THE EMERGENCE OF NON-TRADITIONAL FINANCING TECHNIQUES: MEZZANINE LOANS AND PREFERRED EQUITY INVESTMENTS

A major NYC real estate developer recently completed a real estate refinancing of The Daily News Building — one of the many properties held in his vast real estate portfolio. The Daily News Building, located on East 42nd Street in midtown Manhattan, is what real estate brokers like to refer to as a "trophy" office building. It contains over one million square feet of office space, and was recently estimated to be worth approximately $250 million dollars. Unable to sell The Daily News Building at the price he desired, the owner instead chose to refinance the property for

*. Footnotes omitted - Eds.

about $240 million dollars. After paying off the existing first mortgage from the loan proceeds of this refinancing, the owner was able to pocket almost $80 million dollars.

How did the owner of The Daily News Building achieve this alchemy? He was able to structure a transaction that actually consisted of several separate real estate financings: (i) a first mortgage loan for $155 million made by Deutsche Bank, (ii) a mezzanine loan for $83 million made by Capital Trust, a New York investment fund; and (iii) a preferred equity investment in the amount of $53 million made by SL Green, a New York real estate investment trust. While no longer unusual, this real estate owner combined conventional mortgage debt with two new non-traditional financing techniques: mezzanine financing and preferred equity investments.

A. MEZZANINE LOANS

The term "mezzanine financing" in the financial markets describes an array of financings such as junk bonds, unrated debt, unsecured notes, zero-coupon bonds, deferred interest debentures, and convertible loans. The legal structure of these financing methods varies not just by industry, but also reflects responses to unique regulatory and market concerns. Typically, however, all mezzanine financing refers to debt that is subordinate to another type or class of debt but senior to equity. Many have analogized it to a theater where mezzanine debt is the mezzanine section sitting between the orchestra (senior debt) and the balcony (equity).

In the real estate capital markets, the term "mezzanine financing" also refers to debt that sits between senior debt and the borrower's equity. In this case, mezzanine debt is junior to the mortgage loan but senior to the borrower's equity. A mezzanine loan in the real estate industry typically refers to debt that is secured solely by the mezzanine borrower's indirect ownership of the mortgage borrower — the entity that actually owns the income producing real property. This same underlying real property also serves as collateral for the senior mortgage lender.

In a mezzanine loan, neither the mezzanine borrower nor lender actually holds any direct real property interest in the underlying land serving as collateral. Rather, their respective interests are derived solely from the mezzanine borrower's (direct or indirect) ownership of the equity in the underlying mortgage borrower. The mezzanine borrower grants to the mezzanine lender a lien on its equity in the mortgage borrower pursuant to a written instrument (typically a security agreement), and thereafter the mezzanine lender holds an effective lien on the collateral at least vis-à-vis the mezzanine borrower.

Similar to junior mortgage financing, the national rating agencies also dictate to a large extent the form and structure of mezzanine financing. For instance, in a typical mezzanine financing, the rating agencies require that the underlying organizational documents of the mezzanine borrower only permit certain specified activities. As a corporate law matter, the mezzanine borrower may only own the direct or indirect equity in the mortgage borrower and it is typically prohibited from undertaking any other corporate or business activity. Because of these organizational limitations, this type of entity is referred to as a "special purpose" entity (SPE).

The rating agencies often also require the underlying organizational documents of the mezzanine borrower to prohibit or significantly curtail its ability to file any type of petition for bankruptcy, insolvency, or reorganization. These types of

provisions and limitations are optimistically considered to make an entity "bankruptcy remote," and the industry refers to such an entity as a bankruptcy remote
entity (BRE). In order to qualify as a SPE/BRE, the rating agencies also require
strict limits on the type and amount of permitted additional indebtedness and
require their approval of the identity of, and the review of the management,
finances, and experience of, the mezzanine lender. These limitations represent,
in part, the agencies' attempt to avoid the substantive consolidation of the mezzanine borrower's assets with another bankrupt but related entity.

Since the mezzanine lender's collateral is equity in another entity, the collateral
is technically personal property; therefore Article 9 of the Uniform Commercial
Code (UCC) applies rather than local mortgage law. By recording a UCC-1
Financing Statement in the appropriate recording office, the mezzanine lender
can also generally ensure that its lien is effective and superior to most other third-
parties'. Similar to mortgage law, once the Financing Statement describing the
collateral is properly recorded, the mezzanine lender's security interest becomes
perfected and is thereafter generally superior to that of subsequent lien holders,
judgment lien creditors and bona fide purchasers.

Mezzanine loans differ significantly with traditional loans secured by real estate
where the mortgage borrower directly owns income producing real property. With a
mortgage loan, the mortgage borrower grants a lien on its real property pursuant to
a written instrument (typically a mortgage or in some states, a deed of trust), and
thereafter the lender holds an effective mortgage lien on the collateral. In addition,
since the rights and remedies of a mortgagee are inextricably linked to the mortgaged real property, the law of the state where the real property is located typically
governs the enforceability of the lender's principal remedies (i.e., lender's right to
obtain a receiver or foreclose the mortgage lien). By recording the mortgage in the
land records where the property is located, a mortgage lender can also generally
ensure that its lien is effective and superior to most other third-parties'.

In addition, because of the interplay between federal bankruptcy law and mortgage law, a mortgagee may typically assert a powerful arsenal of rights and remedies
against both the mortgage borrower and any third party claiming any of the
bankrupt debtor's assets, including any junior secured lender, unsecured creditor,
or equity investor. The mortgage law of most states, for example, permits a mortgagee to appoint a receiver for the property, foreclose the mortgage and sell the real
property, and eliminate many subordinate junior liens and encumbrances adversely
affecting the value of the collateral. By granting the mortgagee the power to
eliminate certain junior liens and encumbrances, the mortgage foreclosure process
typically enables a mortgagee to sell the property at the foreclosure sale for a higher
price, thereby increasing the cash available to repay the outstanding debt.

Compared to the senior mortgage lender's right to foreclose its senior mortgage,
the mezzanine lender's right to foreclose on the equity interests of the mezzanine
borrower is both riskier and of somewhat limited value. Whereas a mortgagee's
foreclosure rights derive from its mortgage on the borrower's real property, a
mezzanine lender's remedies derive solely from its lien on personal property (i.e.,
the equity in the mezzanine borrower). And unlike a mortgagee's right to foreclose
all junior liens and encumbrances on the underlying real property, a mezzanine
lender has no rights to foreclose any other liens on the underlying real property—a
mezzanine lender's rights are limited solely to foreclosing junior liens on the equity
in the mezzanine borrower and not the real property. Even after a successful

foreclosure of a mezzanine loan, therefore, the underlying mortgage property remains subject to the lien of the senior mortgage as well as any other liens, leases and other encumbrances previously recorded against the mortgage property. Furthermore, the existence of a default under the mezzanine loan suggests that there is probably inadequate cash flow or some other problem with the fundamentals of the real estate venture; therefore, it is likely that there will also be new tax liens, mechanics liens, and perhaps even judgment liens recorded against the underlying mortgaged property. These other liens only further deteriorate the value of the mezzanine lender's collateral.

Unfortunately for many mezzanine lenders, even their right to foreclose junior liens on their own collateral — the equity in the mezzanine borrower — is often of little value. Since the mezzanine loan documents typically prohibit any other liens on the lender's collateral and because of its limited marketability, it is unlikely (except in the case of fraud or willful violation of the mezzanine loan documents) that there are any other junior liens on the equity anyway. Oftentimes, the mezzanine lender's sole remedy is to foreclose its lien on the equity and then attempt to sell the equity at a UCC foreclosure sale. But the rating agencies also restrict the mezzanine lender's ability to foreclose on its collateral without compliance with many conditions. For example, the agencies all require that the mezzanine lender obtain a "No Downgrade Letter" — written confirmation from the rating agencies that the mezzanine lender's enforcement actions will not cause a downgrade of the rating of the related CMBS issuance which is secured or contains the related senior mortgage on the underlying real property. In addition, mezzanine lenders typically must also deliver to the rating agencies a new non-consolidation bankruptcy opinion. This opinion is typically prepared by a nationally recognized law firm and concludes that it is unlikely that the assets of the mortgage borrower will be substantively consolidated with the mezzanine borrower (or any other affiliated entities) in case of a bankruptcy.

In addition, since there is typically no active market for the purchase and sale of the equity in the mezzanine borrower and no other bidders, the mezzanine lender often has no choice other than to bid-in and "buy" the equity at the foreclosure sale. In such a case, the mezzanine lender still has not received any cash proceeds, although after the foreclosure sale, the mezzanine lender at least has direct day-to-day control of the mezzanine borrower (and, therefore, also indirect control of the mortgage borrower and the underlying real property). Only then may the mezzanine lender (in its new capacity as the indirect owner of the mortgage borrower) attempt to force a sale of the mortgaged property. But as discussed above, this right is of limited value since the underlying real property remains subject to the senior mortgage, which generally prohibits the sale of the real property and contains an extensive set of restrictive covenants and other prohibitions. The fact remains that even after a successful foreclosure on its collateral — the equity of the mezzanine borrower — the mezzanine lender is still just an owner in the underlying mortgage borrower. As equity, the mezzanine lender's claims are structurally subordinated and junior to every other secured or unsecured creditor of the mortgage borrower.

B. PREFERRED EQUITY FINANCING

In a preferred equity transaction, the financing source (the Preferred Member) typically makes an investment (generally in the form of a capital contribution) in the underlying mortgage borrower. In exchange for its investment, the financing source receives equity in the mortgage borrower, and if the senior mortgage prohibits such an investment directly in the mortgage borrower, the financing source makes an investment in a newly formed entity that indirectly owns the underlying mortgage borrower.

The Preferred Member has special rights including a preferred rate of return on its investment and accelerated repayment of its capital. The organizational documents of the investment entity (i.e., the Preferred Equity Borrower) typically provide that the Preferred Member receives its preferred return (representing the interest component) before any other member receives any cash distributions. In addition, if the real estate venture is successful, the Preferred Member typically also has the right to receive certain cash distributions of excess cash flow. Since these distributions are usually applied to reduce the recipient's capital account, the Preferred Member typically also receives the repayment of its initial investment prior to the other equity investors. Because of these special rights, preferred equity transactions are analytically similar to traditional loans since the preferred rate of return basically reflects interest and the accelerated repayment of the capital reflects repayment of principal.

Although these preferential payments make the Preferred Member senior to the other equity investors, the Preferred Member is still just an equity owner in the Preferred Equity Borrower. As a result, it usually remains junior to all secured or unsecured creditors. Because of this unique structure, a Preferred Member in a preferred equity financing "occupies an identical position in the capital structure and in relation to the property cash flow as a mezzanine financing. . . ." However, a Preferred Member "differs significantly because it already has an equity ownership interest and does not need to foreclose any pledge to gain an equity ownership interest . . . in the borrower."

The national rating agencies usually require that the underlying senior mortgage and/or mezzanine loan prohibit or otherwise severely restrict any distributions to equity unless there is sufficient excess cash flow from the underlying income producing property. And typically there is excess cash flow only after the payment of a wide variety of expenses and obligations of the mortgage borrower (e.g., (i) interest and principal under the mortgage or mezzanine loan; (ii) required cash reserves for debt service, principal prepayment, capital improvements, tenant leasing expenses, and taxes and insurance operating expenses of the mortgage property; and (iii) trade creditors, taxing authorities, judgment lien and other creditors). Consequently, the Preferred Member doesn't ordinarily receive any cash distribution unless the enterprise is successful, there is excess cash flow and all other expenses and debt obligations have been satisfied in full. No matter that a preferred equity transaction is substantively similar to a loan — since preferred equity is not legally structured as debt, a Preferred Member does not have the same rights as a creditor of the mortgage borrower. Given these structural realities, a Preferred Member is likely to receive its preferred rate of return and the repayment of its initial investment only if the mortgage borrower realizes its lofty economic projections, generates sufficient cash flow, and repays in full all its outstanding debt obligations.

On the other hand, if the venture fails to earn sufficient cash flow to repay the senior mortgage, it is likely that the Preferred Equity Borrower will default since there will also be insufficient funds to pay the Preferred Member its preferred return or capital. In order to maintain the fiction that preferred equity is not debt, however, the transaction documents typically refer to these "defaults" as "Change of Control Events." And, if a Change of Control Event occurs, most preferred equity arrangements provide that day-to-day control and management of the Preferred Equity Borrower automatically and immediately shifts to the Preferred Member. This "change of control" mechanism effectively makes the Preferred Member's remedies similar to a mezzanine lender. As discussed above, a mezzanine lender in order to enforce its rights typically would foreclosure its lien on the equity interests, thereby seizing day-to-day control of the mezzanine borrower. In this way, the mezzanine lender gains indirect but effective control of the mortgage borrower and the underlying mortgaged property. Unlike the mezzanine loan, however, the Preferred Member's financing arrangement is structured as an equity investment rather than secured debt. Therefore, there is no collateral and the Preferred Member has no foreclosure rights. However, after a Change of Control Event occurs, the Preferred Member effectively controls the mortgage borrower by virtue of the contractual provisions contained in the organizational documents of the borrower.

Although the Preferred Member will effectively control the mortgage borrower after a Change of Control Event occurs, the shift in control does nothing to eliminate any of the liens, contractual obligations, mortgages, and other obligations binding upon the mortgage borrower. Similar to a mezzanine lender, therefore, the Preferred Member also takes the "collateral" (i.e., control of the mortgage borrower) subject to the senior mortgage and any other existing liens and obligations. And unlike a mortgage lender, neither the mezzanine lender nor Preferred Member may foreclose upon and thereby eliminate any of these liens or encumbrances. In addition, preferred equity investments are also subject to certain bankruptcy risks such as the possibility that a bankruptcy court would recharacterize its equity investment as debt.

Furthermore, many senior mortgages prohibit any change in the composition of the direct equity investors in the mortgage borrower or a material change in the parties exercising effective control over the mortgage borrower. If the Preferred Member begins to exercise control of the mortgage borrower as a result of the occurrence of a Change in Control Event, therefore, it is likely that there would also be a default under the senior mortgage. Any default under the senior mortgage or the commencement of a mortgage foreclosure action substantially reduces the value of the Preferred Member's investment in the mortgage borrower. As a result, these mortgage prohibitions often leave the mezzanine lender and Preferred Member without any effective remedy.

NOTES AND QUESTIONS

1. In what ways is mezzanine financing like a junior mortgage loan, and in what ways does it differ? If you were a lender, which would you prefer? How do these compare with a preferred equity investment?

2. Mezzanine financing and preferred equity financing take established legal rules and apply them in a novel way in real estate finance. These structures have been widely adopted in recent years, so that billions of dollars in financing now depend on the legal treatment of these structures even though there is not much of a basis for predicting how courts will treat them. Mortgage law, developed over the past five

centuries, does not have a clear answer to many of the questions that such structures raise. For example, could the preferred financing structure be held an impermissible clog on the equity of redemption? What would be the implications of such a ruling?

3. Mezzanine and preferred equity financing normally include provisions that, upon default, grant the lender control, or a say in management, of the ownership entity. This carries obvious advantages for the lender, but consider the risks that it may raise. Could a mezzanine lender be considered a partner or joint venturer, losing its rights as a creditor? Could a lender be held liable for breach of fiduciary duties to its "partners" when it exercises its control rights in its own best interest? For a discussion of these issues, among others, see John C. Murray, Mezzanine Financing: Legal and Title Issues (2003), available on the Web site for the First American Title Insurance Company.

E. VALUING REAL ESTATE AND INVESTMENTS

1. *Present Value and Return on Investment*

a. Present Value Analysis

The concept of present value (also known as the "time value of money") is central to all financial analysis, business, and tax planning. Some basic examples:

- Present value is needed in all sorts of business calculations. Consider which is better: an investment that will return $800 in three years, or one that will return $1,200 in four years. Answering a question like this requires present value analysis.
- Tax lawyers use present value analysis constantly: Suppose as part of her tax planning, a woman places assets in trust, retaining an interest for herself for life then to go to her grandchildren. What is the value of the gift today, on which gift tax must be paid? The answer is found using present value analysis.
- In many divorce settlements, one of the most valuable assets is pension rights; but what is the value today of the right to receive $40,000 per year for the remainder of your life, starting 22 years from now? This is a present value problem.
- In a wrongful death suit, how much should the jury award to compensate for the earnings that the decedent would have earned in the future? The answer is determined by present value analysis, and millions of dollars can depend on the lawyer's ability to convince the jury that her expert has offered a better analysis than the other side's expert.

(1) *The Basics of Present Value*
The present value of a payment or object to be received in the future is the value today of the right to receive that payment or object in the future. Obviously, it is worth more to you to receive $100 today than to get that same $100 a year from now.

How much more? Well, assume an interest rate of 10 percent. If you had $100 today, how much would you have a year from now?

$100 + 10% of $100 = $110, which is the same as

$$\$100 \times [1 + 10\%] = \$110.$$

So, the formula is that $X today is worth $\$X \times (1 + r)$ next year, where "r" is the annual interest rate.

How much is $100 today worth *two* years from now? Well, take the amount it is worth in one year and add in another year's interest:

$$\$100 \times (1 + 10\%) \times (1 + 10\%) = \$100 \ (1 + 10\%)^2 = \$121.00; \text{ or, in other words:}$$

$X today is worth $\$X \times (1 + r)^2$ two years from now.

In general: if PV is the amount today, FV_1 is the value one year from today, and FV_n is the value n years from today, then:

$PV \times (1 + r)^n = FV_n$, which we can rearrange to be:

$$PV = \frac{FV_n}{(1 + r)^n}.$$

(2)   Choosing an Interest Rate

The interest rate that is used to "discount" future dollars into present dollars should reflect the risk of the investment. That is, if the future income is certain to be paid, then a lower discount is appropriate (called the "risk-free rate"). If the future income is not certain to be paid, a higher discount rate must be used — the riskier, the higher the interest rate.

This should make some intuitive sense: Discounting by a higher interest rate results in a lower present value, and obviously the possibility of receiving $1,000 one year from today is worth less than the *certainty* of receiving $1,000 one year from today!

In general, the discount rate is the rate that an investor today would demand as the return on an investment with a risk that is the same as the risk of the future cash flow you are valuing.

Some examples follow:

1. Your aunt has promised to give you a Volkswagon convertible upon graduation from law school. The car is worth $22,000, and you have one year until graduation. Assuming a 9 percent discount rate, what is the value today of your aunt's promised graduation gift?

Answer: You are looking for the present value of $22,000 to be received one year from today, at a 9 percent discount rate.

$$PV = FV/(1 + r)^n = \$22,000/(1 + .09)^1 = \$20,183.49$$

Suppose instead that you had two years until graduation. What would the present value be?

Answer: You are now looking for the present value of $22,000 to be received *two* years from today, at a 9 percent discount rate.

$$PV = FV/(1 + r)^n$$
$$= \$22,000/(1 + .09)^2$$
$$= \$22,000/1.1881 = \$18,516.96$$

Another way to see this: If you had $18,516.96 today, and invested it for one year at 9 percent, at the end of the year you would have $18,516.96 × 1.09 = $20,183.49. Investing that for another year at 9 percent, you have $20,183.49 × 1.09 = $22,000. So, if you had $18,516.96 today, you could invest it to have exactly $22,000 in two years. In other words, $18,516.96 today is worth the same as $22,000 in two years, given a 9 percent interest rate.

2. A friend of yours who is planning to go to law school tells you that her fairy godmother has agreed to pay her tuition, $30,000, each year for the next three years. The first payment is due today. What is the value of the payments her fairy godmother has promised to make, assuming a 6 percent discount rate (a low rate, since fairy godmothers are very reliable!)?

Answer:

$$PV = \frac{FV_0}{(1 + r)^0} + \frac{FV_1}{(1 + r)^1} + \frac{FV_2}{(1 + r)^2}$$

$$= \frac{\$30,000}{1} + \frac{\$30,000}{1.06} + \frac{\$30,000}{1.1236}$$

$$= \$30,000 + \$28,301.89 + \$26,699.89$$

$$= \$85,001.78$$

To put it another way, if the fairy godmother were to set aside $85,001.78, and can invest it in CDs yielding 6 percent, it will be enough to cover the tuition for all three years.

HOW TO DETERMINE REAL ESTATE RETURN
ON INVESTMENT

The Mortgage and Real Estate Executive's Report 5-7 (June 16, 1985)

Return on investment (ROI) analysis has come a long way since buy and sell decisions were made strictly on the basis of the first year cash-on-cash return. (Some would argue that the original method remains the best.)

All of the more recent ROI techniques seek to estimate annual returns over a fairly long period—five or 10 years in most cases. The trend to long-range projections reflects the fundamental change in the source of equity capital for real estate. Formerly, equity came mostly from sophisticated real estate professionals who put up their own money and relied on their judgment in making investments. For them, the current profit and loss statement was all they needed. (It was also true that returns were often much higher than today, affording a cushion against mistakes.)

Now, however, equity capital comes primarily from large institutional investors (pension funds and equity-sharing lenders) and from the public (via syndicates and real estate investment trusts). For these investors, detailed projections substitute for the "intuitive" sense of the professional.

A projected ROI will be worth looking at only if two conditions are met: (1) the projected figures (rentals, expenses, resale prices, etc.) have been carefully and conservatively arrived at; and (2) the method of estimating the return on investment is clearly understood by the investor. This second condition is the subject of this article. (The examples used in the article were prepared by Robert A. Stanger & Co., and appear in the current issue of The Stanger Report.)

COMPOUNDED GROWTH RATE IS KEY MEASURE

The most popular technique for measuring ROI is the internal rate of return (IRR). The workings (and limitations) of IRR are detailed below, and it is then compared with the adjusted rate of return (ARR) method. Before doing this, however, some comments should be made about compound interest and the concept of compounded growth rate.

Compound interest, as everyone knows, is interest on interest. If $100 is deposited in a five-year certificate of deposit with a guaranteed annual rate of 10 percent, the sum will grow to $161.05 at the end of the term. The original $100 grows to $150 ($10 interest per year for five years).

The additional $11.05 represents compound interest — the interest earned each year on the prior accumulated interest.

The special feature of a certificate of deposit with a guaranteed yield, as with a zero coupon bond, is that no reinvestment risk exists. That is, the accumulated interest will earn the same return as the original deposit. Thus, we can say with certainty that the above investment will have a compounded growth rate of 10 percent over its five-year term. In virtually all other types of investments, however, there is a reinvestment risk and it is this factor that leads to confusion about the meaning of the internal rate of return.

CALCULATING INTERNAL RATE OF RETURN

We have just seen that when (1) the annual rate of return on an initial investment is known and (2) each year's gain will itself earn the same rate of return (compounded return), it is a simple matter to calculate the future value of the initial investment.

Now suppose the future value (total of future economic benefits) is known and the investor wants to determine the annual rate of compounded return. He must reverse the process just described. This in essence is the internal rate of return technique.

TABLE [7-1]
12% IRR

(1) Annual Beginning of Year	Investment	(2) Economic Benefits	(3) Present Value Factor	(4) Present Value
1	$10,000			—
2	—	5,000	.893	$4,465
3	—	3,000	.797	2,391
4	—	1,800	.712	1,282
5	—	1,500	.636	954
6	—	900	.567	510
7	—	500	.506	233
8	—	330	.453	149
Totals	$10,000	$13,030		$10,004
Reinvestment Earnings		$ 4,008		
Net Worth in Year 8*		$17,038		

*Assumes reinvested benefits earn 6% after tax per annum.

Table [7-1] illustrates how IRR works. An initial investment of $10,000 will produce a value of $13,030 as a result of seven annual repayments or tax benefits. By using a present value table, we can determine the compounded interest rate that will permit an initial $10,000 sum to grow to $13,030 as indicated in column 2. That compounded interest rate is 12 percent.

This may be more clearly understood if the initial investment of $10,000 is viewed as a number of separate investments, each equal to the present value of each future payment (i.e., the present values listed in column 4). For example, $4,465 of the initial investment is treated as repaid to the investor at the beginning of Year 2 together with $535 of interest (or a total of $5,000). This represents an annual return of 12 percent. The second segment of the initial investment, $2,391, is repaid at the beginning of the third year together with $609 of interest. This also represents a compounded return of 12 percent, and so on for the remaining five payments.

REINVESTMENT EARNINGS ARE IGNORED

The important point to note about the process just described is that IRR does not show the compound annual growth on the entire initial investment, but only for the period of time each segment is invested. Thus, when comparing IRRs for different investments, it is necessary to make an assumption about the reinvestment rate on payments by the investor prior to the end of the overall holding period.

COMPARING INVESTMENTS

To show the importance of including a reinvestment factor when comparing the total return from different investments, compare Tables [7-1] and [7-2] infra. Table [7-2] shows the annual returns (including return of principal in the final year) from an investment of $10,000 in a tax-free bond yielding 8.5 percent. The total value of the annual payments is $15,950, $2,920 more than the total payments in Table [7-1]. However, the IRR of the tax-free bond investment is only 8.5 percent, 3.5 percent less than the IRR in Table [7-1]. The reason is obvious. Most of the annual returns in Table [7-1] come in the earlier years, while the opposite is true in Table [7-2]. (That is, the average holding period is shorter in Table [7-1].) Thus, when the reinvestment of annual returns is ignored, Table [7-1] shows the higher return.

However, the conclusion may change depending on the assumption one makes about reinvestments. The lower portions of Tables [7-1] and [7-2] compare the two investments when it is assumed that annual benefits are reinvested at a 6 percent after-tax rate of return until the end of the overall holding period of seven years. It then turns out that the tax-free bond shows the higher return. The reason is that the real estate investment, which returns most of the initial investment in the early years, subjects more of the initial investment to a lower reinvestment rate of only 6 percent. In the case of the tax-free bond, although the initial rate is only 8.5 percent, a larger proportion of the initial investment earns that range for a longer period of time; consequently, less of the initial investment must be reinvested at the 6 percent rate.

TABLE [7-2]
8.5% IRR

Beginning of Year	(1) Investment	(2) Annual Economic Benefits	(3) Present Value Factor	(4) Present Value
1	$10,000	—	—	—
2	—	850	.921	$783
3	—	850	.849	722
4	—	850	.783	666
5	—	850	.722	614
6	—	850	.665	565
7	—	850	.612	520
8	—	10,850	.565	6,130
Totals	$10,000	$15,950		$10,000

Reinvestment Earnings $ 1,184
New Worth in Year 8* $17,134

*Assumes reinvested benefits earn 6% after tax per annum.

WHAT IRR REALLY TELLS THE INVESTOR

As can be seen from the tables, the internal rate of return tells an investor what the compounded interest rate is on equity remaining in the particular investment at any given point. It does not represent the compounded return on the total initial investment over the entire holding period. Therefore, it is essential for the investor to make some assumption about a reinvestment rate.

In the example shown in Table [7-1], if annual returns could be reinvested at the same 12 percent rate the initial investment earns, then it could be said that the $10,000 put up in year 1 earns 12 percent compounded annually through the end of year 8. If the reinvestment rate is more or less than 12 percent, then the total return on the investment over the holding period will be different from 12 percent.

<h2 style="text-align:center">USING THE ADJUSTED RATE OF RETURN</h2>

The adjusted rate of return (ARR) is a better way of comparing investments because it specifically identifies a reinvestment rate to be applied to amounts repaid to the investor during the holding period. Table [7-3] infra combines the information contained in Tables [7-1] and [7-2] to show how an ARR is calculated. When reinvestment of benefits is assumed at 6 percent after tax, the tax-free bond shows an ARR of 8 percent, versus 7.9 percent for the real estate investment.

TABLE [7-3]
Adjusted Rate of Return

Year	"12% IRR Partners"			Bond Yielding 8.5% After Tax		
	Investment	Annual Economic Benefits	Earnings from Reinvestment of Benefits*	Investment	Annual Economic Benefits	Earnings from Reinvestment of Benefits*
1	$10,000	—	—	$10,000	—	—
2	—	$ 5,000	—	—	850	—
3	—	3,000	$ 300	—	850	$ 51
4	—	1,800	498	—	850	105
5	—	1,500	636	—	850	162
6	—	900	764	—	850	223
7	—	500	864	—	850	287
8	—	330	946	—	850	365
Totals	$10,000	$13,030	$4,008	$10,000	$15,950	$1,184
Total Returns**		$17,038			$17,134	
Adjusted Rate of Return		7.9%			8.0%	

*Assumes reinvested benefits earn 6% after tax per annum.
**Total annual economic benefits plus total earnings reinvestment.
Source: The Stanger Report.

Observation: Of course, even the ARR cannot determine precisely the future return, since the reinvestment rate can only be assumed. Nevertheless, it provides a much sounder comparison between alternative investments than does the IRR. Note that in the case of a zero coupon bond or certificate of deposit, the ARR and the IRR are identical, since in these investments the reinvestment rate is guaranteed to be the same as the rate on the original investment.

NOTES AND QUESTIONS

1. Discounted cash flow analysis is the foundation for most real estate and business valuation, and many books and articles have been written on the subject. DCF involves forecasting the income that will be earned, and discounting back those earnings at an appropriate interest rate to find the present value of the investment. In predicting the income that is likely to be earned, an investor will normally consider various scenarios, and estimate the effect that different

developments would have on valuation. For example, in purchasing an apartment building, the prospective buyer might examine scenarios where the rental market is strong (low vacancy rates and high rents), medium, and weak (higher vacancy rates and lower rents), and see how the value changes.

2. The discount rate to use in finding the present value of the expected future income is critical, because different assumptions on the discount rate can dramatically affect the present value calculation. A building expected to generate $1 million per year forever would be worth $10 million at a 10 percent discount rate, but $14.3 million at a 7 percent discount rate.

So how does a potential investor determine the rate to use? The rate should reflect the return the investor requires to make an investment with the amount of risk presented by this project. If the property is new and fully leased to strong tenants, the risks are relatively low and the discount rate would be low. For an older building in a marginal part of town where future demand and rents are uncertain, the risks (and therefore the discount rate) would be higher. For a fuller discussion, see Alvin L. Arnold, The Real Estate Investor's Deskbook, § 2:74 (3d ed. 2007).

3. *Direct Capitalization.* A rougher calculation related to DCF analysis is the direct capitalization of income. In direct capitalization, an estimate is made of the expected annual net operating income from the property, and the investor determines how much she can pay for the property given that expected income, and earn the return she needs to justify the investment. Mathematically, this is straightforward: Simply divide the expected annual income by a capitalization rate (the investor's required rate of return) to generate an estimate of the property's value. Thus, if a property is expected to generate $50,000 per year and is capitalized at an 8 percent cap rate, the value would be $50,000/.08 = $625,000 (again, to put it into words: An investor who is considering buying a building that generates net income of $50,000 per year would earn an 8 percent annual return on her investment if she paid $625,000). See Alvin L. Arnold, The Real Estate Investor's Deskbook, §§ 2:30-2:35 (3d ed. 2007).

Real estate professionals routinely talk about "cap rates" for different types of property, which they use to generate quick estimates of property values. These cap rates are the average returns that investors are demanding in purchasing these types of properties, and the cap rates change constantly as interest rates, the real estate market, the broader economy, and other investment markets change. As with the discount rate in DCF analysis, cap rates are higher for riskier properties. Professionals keep up on cap rates by watching sales and appraisals, and through surveys that report on the current cap rates in different markets (both geographically and by property type).

2. Real Estate Appraisals

Paula K. Konikoff, CFO's Guide to Real Estate Appraisals

534 PLI/Real 843, 850-859 (2006)

Reprinted and adapted from the PLI Course Handbook, Negotiating Commercial Leases:
How Owners & Corporate Occupants Can Avoid Costly Errors Spring 2006 (Order #8608)

* * *

What Is an Appraisal?

An appraisal is an opinion of value at a specific date and under certain conditions and assumptions specified in the appraisal. The appraiser's methodology and conclusions should mirror the thinking of buyers and sellers active in the relevant marketplace. This means that an appraised value is not necessarily the appraiser's personal opinion and not the client's opinion, and the appraisal might not be in conformity with academic research. The appraisal is the appraiser's emulation of the thinking of players in the market. If the marketplace assumes, as it sometimes does, that all multitenant office properties would reach 95 percent occupancy, then the appraiser should use that assumption in the valuation. If the marketplace indicates that 6 percent is an acceptable cash-on-cash return for a regional mall, then the appraiser should use that first-year return, even if he or she would personally seek an 8.5 percent cash-on-cash return from an investment of equivalent perceived risk.

An appraisal is not a guarantee of achievable price or a prognostication of future achievable rent rates. The information presented in cash flow projections is generally based on well-researched and -supported historical and current (first year of projection) amounts with appreciation rates applied to those amounts in a formulaic manner. Again, the appraiser should be attempting to reproduce the projections that potential buyers and sellers of the property would use in formulating their offers.

The Uniform Standards of Professional Appraisal Practice ("USPAP"), 2006, defines "appraisal" as "[t]he act or process of developing value; an opinion of value." These concepts of developing an opinion underlie appraisal theory and practice and must be remembered when appraisal analyses and conclusions are relied on.

The Appraisal of Real Estate, pages 602-603 states:

> Because an appraised value is an opinion, it implies a range in which property value may fall. That range usually reflects the range of conclusion from two or more approaches [within the appraisal report] but the final value opinion need not fall within this range. For example, an appraiser may report a value estimate of $9,400,000 to represent a result drawn from two approaches with preliminary conclusions of $9,390,000 and $9,380,000. In this case, the value conclusion is not statistically derived. It is outside the range indicated by the two approaches but it reflects the market value of the property based on the two approaches. . . .
>
> An appraisal is an opinion of value. Although it is an impartial, expert, and reasoned conclusion formed by a trained professional based on an analysis of all relevant evidence, it is still an opinion. . . . Subtle differences in the appraisal objectives or the real property interests being appraised may account for differences in value indications.

These aspects of judgment and opinion almost always create differences in value conclusions among appraisers. And, the fact that an appraisal is an opinion based on judgment requires the user of an appraisal to critically assess the validity and reasonableness of the assumptions and data used to arrive at the final conclusion of value.

It is important to remember that this professional opinion is as of a specified date and subject to specified conditions. An unexpected change in the leasing status or physical condition of the property would have an effect on value, as would changes in the local or national real estate market, or changes in capital markets. Even though you may not agree with the assumptions stated in the appraisal, you must be aware that the value estimated is based entirely on those assumptions; should the assumptions change, so would the value. . . .

WHAT IS AN APPRAISAL REPORT?

USPAP provides the minimum requirements for the presentation of an appraisal report. It is possible to request an oral response, or a short version of a narrative report (a restricted use appraisal report). Regardless of the form of presentation, USPAP's SCOPE OF WORK RULE requires that the amount of research performed in every appraisal permits the appraiser to produce credible assignment results.

WHICH ARE THE VALUE DETERMINATIVE ASSUMPTIONS?

Almost every choice an appraiser makes in the analysis of the subject property and its economic environment has an effect on value. But there are some broad areas that control value more than others, and the client can have some input regarding some of these crucial issues.

DEFINITION OF VALUE

The USPAP requires that each appraisal set forth the definition of value being considered. This is one of the most basic and value-determinative selections made by the appraiser.

RECONCILIATION OF VALUE INDICATIONS AND FINAL VALUE ESTIMATE
REPORT OF DEFINED VALUE

The importance of the selection and expression of the definition of value is stressed in The Appraisal of Real Estate, which states:

> The purpose of the valuation process is to estimate the value of a real property interest, so the specific type of value and the interests involved must be clearly identified [page 74].
>
> When the word value is applied to real estate, it must be qualified. The statement 'The value of your property is $150,000' is not specific enough to be meaningful to real estate professionals. If, however, an appraiser says, 'Your property is estimated to have a market value of $150,000' an explicit meaning is conveyed. Of necessity, appraisers refer to market value, insurable value, liquidation value, and other precisely identified and defined types of value [page 586].

The choice of definition of value carries with it assumptions that will have an effect on the final value conclusion. Market value determines the price to be paid by a typical buyer to a willing seller who is not under any duress or time pressure to dispose of the property. Liquidation value is still the price paid by a typical buyer, but it is assumed that the seller must dispose of the property within a time period that is shorter than the "normal" marketing time. Liquidation value is generally lower than market value, as it carries a discount for the short marketing period.

Investment value is the price to be paid by a specific class of buyer that will use income, expense, and/or yield assumptions that are different from those being used by typical buyers in the marketplace. Investment value is most often higher than market value, as the assumptions may be based on a buyer who has a particular tenant to immediately occupy a large block of currently vacant space, or one who can provide management or insurance or maintenance at a lower cost than the typical buyer, or one who seeks a yield lower than that being sought in the market due to tax status, portfolio considerations, etc. Value in use, which is the value of a specific property for a specific purpose, may be most useful for companies needing to value operating plants.

Although FIRREA requires that market value be estimated, it is appropriate to request that other values be estimated as well, provided the appraisal fee is negotiated to include this additional work. USPAP allows appraisers to estimate values other than market value, provided these definitions are clearly set forth in the appraisal.

HIGHEST AND BEST USE

Another underlying (and value-determinative) decision is the appraiser's determination of highest and best use. Highest and best use is defined in The Appraisal of Real Estate:

> [T]he reasonably probable and legal use of vacant land or an improved property, which is physically possible, appropriately supported, financially feasible, and that results in the highest value [page 275].

If an appraiser believes that the highest and best use of a particular property is its current or existing use, for example, as a warehouse, he or she will appraise it as such. If another appraiser values the property and believes that its highest and best use is for residential development, he or she will appraise it as such. In such a situation, it is probable that the value estimates will differ significantly.

USPAP only requires the highest and best use of a property to be developed if necessary for credible assignment results in a market value appraisal (Standards Rule 1-3(b)). The highest and best use of the subject land as if vacant at the appraisal date is considered apart from the highest and best use of the property as it is improved. Therefore, when neighborhoods or demographic forces are changing, it is possible that the highest and best use of the subject land may be for high-rise office development, but the current improvement (such as, a parking garage) is worth more than the value of the land as if vacant less the costs of razing the garage. Therefore, the highest and best use as improved would be as a parking garage, even though this is different from the highest and best use of the land as if vacant.

If relevant, an appraisal determines the highest and best use of the land underlying the subject property as if it were vacant, as well as the highest and best use of the property as it is currently improved. The highest and best use of vacant land or an improved property is that use which meets the following tests:

1. Physically possible. The highest and best use is restricted to those uses which are physically capable of being placed on the site.

2. Legally permissible. The highest and best use must conform to all zoning regulations and deed restrictions affecting the subject site. Probable amendments and variances to such restrictions also should be considered.
3. Financially feasible. The highest and best use must be among those uses that are physically possible and legally permissible and which will produce a net return to the owner.
4. Maximally productive. Once all other tests are met, the appraiser selects that use which results in the highest net return to the owner as the highest and best use.

These academic tests are difficult for the user of an appraisal to understand, difficult for the appraiser to apply, and often too costly to analyze thoroughly. Appraisal practitioners have responded to these problems by simplifying the highest and best use analysis while continuing to address the purpose of the analysis. This pragmatic result is well described in The Appraisal Journal, April 1993, page 272:

> [T]hese theories do not simulate the thinking of an actual buyer, who is usually predisposed to a particular use for the property and seldom relies on these criteria for help in estimating the highest and best use. Finally, financial feasibility and maximal productivity tests fail to account for the fact that not all commercial real estate is income property.
>
> Appraisers do, however, consider the land use patterns in the area, what comparable sales were used for after the sale, and the supply and demand for various uses. For improved property, appraisers know that if the land value exceeds the value as improved, the improvements may be of no value. When estimating the highest and best use, appraisers appear to rely on much less complicated and more practical methods. . . .

Suffice it to say that regulations require appraisers to consider the issue of highest and best use, and so it will be part of the appraisal report you receive. . . .

WHAT VALUATION METHODOLOGIES ARE USED?

There are three traditional appraisal approaches that are considered, although not necessarily developed, in each valuation. All three are based on the principal of substitution, which affirms that a prudent purchaser has alternate courses of action available:

- Construct a similar improvement on presently vacant land (cost approach).
- Acquire an equally desirable existing property offering comparable utility (comparable sales approach).
- Acquire a substitute income stream of comparable quality, quantity, and durability (income approach).

THE COST APPROACH

The cost approach assumes that a potential purchaser of the subject property would not pay more for the subject than the value of the subject land, as if vacant, plus the depreciated reconstruction cost of the subject improvements.

The appraiser estimates the land value by using the sales comparison technique of comparing the subject land, as if vacant, to parcels of land with similar size, zoning, and utility that were recently sold. The prices of those "comparable" land transactions are adjusted to account for differences between the subject and comparable properties. Construction costs are usually estimated by reference to published sources or actual costs of similar buildings. The costs must then be reduced by the amount of depreciation existing at the subject property. Depreciation may be attributable to physical, functional, or external factors. Physical depreciation may be curable (the roof leaks) or incurable (normal wear and tear over the life of the building). Functional obsolescence is associated with poor design or construction features (thirty-foot ceiling heights in a property type where twenty-eight feet is most efficient). External (or economic) obsolescence is attributable to conditions lying outside the property itself, such as changing neighborhood or poor market conditions (a factory adjacent to a farm that has become a residential subdivision; a suburban office building in a market that is 35 percent vacant).

This approach is most relevant for special-purpose properties such as manufacturing or research facilities, refineries, grain storage facilities, milling buildings, saw mills, airport buildings, and so on. It is also more reliable for newer properties than older ones; an integral part of the cost approach is the determination of accrued depreciation. Since that estimate is fairly subjective, the less depreciation, the more reliable the result.

THE COMPARABLE SALES APPROACH

This approach develops a value conclusion through an analysis of physically similar properties that have been sold ("comparable properties" or "comparable sales"), adjusting the sale prices for differences between the properties sold and the property being appraised. The key to this approach is the availability of sales of sufficiently similar properties that occurred close to the valuation date between parties that are not related or under duress.

The sales comparison approach develops an estimate of value on a "price per unit" basis. The unit selected is the one most commonly used with regard to the subject property type. The units most often used are price per square foot or acre for vacant land, price per gross (inside of exterior wall to inside of exterior wall) square foot of building area for warehouses and factories, price per gross or usable (rentable) square foot for office properties. There are exceptions and additions to this list, and the appropriate unit should be stated and explained in the appraisal report.

If there are sufficient transactions of comparable properties, the sales comparison approach is a valid tool for appraising properties that are owner-occupied. However, when there are few transactions in the marketplace or the property is relatively unique, this approach becomes less reliable. . . .

THE INCOME APPROACH

This approach is only relevant if the subject property is of a type (office, warehouse, etc.) that is commonly rented to third parties. If the subject property is physically suited to either owner occupancy, single tenancy, or multitenancy, the property should be appraised in a way that is consistent with market behavior. If a corporate headquarters facility being valued is physically suitable for multitenant occupancy, but similar headquarters buildings in the subject area are only used by owners, the income approach will probably not be used by the appraiser.

The income approach is, however, the most meaningful way to appraise income-producing properties. In this approach, a value conclusion is developed by converting a property's anticipated income stream into value through the capitalization process, which can take the form of "direct" capitalization (dividing the selected capitalization or yield rate into one pro forma year of net income) or a discounted cash flow analysis, which involves developing cash flow projections over an assumed holding period (generally ten years), estimating the sale price at the end of that holding period using direct capitalization, and converting the resulting net income amounts and proceeds of the future sale to present value with the application of a discount rate.

Accuracy in valuing property using the income approach also suffers for reasons based on the same market problems as the other two approaches. Yield rates acceptable to investors cannot be supportably developed because of the lack of income-driven sales transactions. Markets have been overbuilt and so are experiencing previously unheard-of vacancy rates, causing more creative leasing structures to be offered. Since landlords do not want the tenant market to know how much they might be willing to give away in the form of concessions to secure a lease, appraisers have little "real" information about recent leases. Thus, the revenue projections in the income approach are based on limited and often incomplete or inaccurate data. . . .

In many cases, the income approach will not be developed in the appraisal of corporate property. But when it is a viable approach, the reader must be comfortable with all the income, expense, and yield assumptions made by the appraiser. If the owner of the property cannot understand, or does not agree with, what the appraiser has done, it is appropriate to have an in-depth conversation with that appraiser.

How Is the Final Value Estimate Selected?

After presenting the relevant approaches to value, the appraisal report concludes with a reconciliation of the values estimated by each approach. The appraiser should not calculate the average of the values presented by the approaches used; rather, the appraiser should select the value he or she believes is most reasonable and best supported. The final value estimate is generally within the range presented by the estimates derived from each of the approaches used. . . .

Ballance v. Rinehart

105 N.C. App. 203, 412 S.E.2d (1992)

Greene, Judge.

. . . Plaintiff instituted this action on 11 February 1991 seeking damages for economic loss allegedly caused by defendant's negligent performance of a real estate appraisal. In her complaint, plaintiff alleges that she purchased a house owned by Jack and Annie Horton after relying on a real estate appraisal prepared by defendant in which defendant stated that the house was in good condition. Plaintiff further alleges that soon after the purchase, she discovered that the house had serious structural defects and that defendant breached his duty of ordinary care by failing to discover the defects. Plaintiff alleges that defendant knew or should have known at the time that he rendered the appraisal report that, although the appraisal report was prepared for Peoples Bank and Trust Company (Peoples Bank), other persons, particularly potential home buyers, would rely on the report as verification of the condition and value of the property. . . . Plaintiff filed an amended complaint on 16 May 1991, which added to plaintiff's original complaint the allegations that the appraisal report was also prepared for Jack Horton and that "defendant knew or should have known that [owner] Jack Horton could potentially show the appraisal to potential buyers of the home." On 11 June 1991, the trial court entered an order in open court granting defendant's motion and dismissing plaintiff's complaint.

* * *

The dispositive issue is whether a licensed real estate appraiser who performs an appraisal of real property at the request of a client owes a prospective purchaser of such property who relies on the appraisal a duty to use reasonable care in the preparation of the appraisal.

. . . Plaintiff argues that the trial court's dismissal of her claim is improper since this Court has previously recognized the right of a home buyer, in the absence of contractual privity with the appraiser, to recover damages for economic loss proximately caused by negligence in the performance of a real estate appraisal. Plaintiff cites in support thereof *Alva v. Cloninger,* 51 N.C.App. 602, 277 S.E.2d 535 (1981), where this Court reversed a directed verdict for defendant real estate appraiser on plaintiff home buyer's claim for negligent misrepresentation. Like plaintiff in the instant case, the plaintiff in *Alva* alleged that he had suffered economic loss by relying on defendant's appraisal which indicated that the home purchased by plaintiff was in good condition when in fact the house contained serious defects. In reversing the directed verdict for the defendant, we held that "there was evidence from which a jury could have concluded that defendant [appraiser] should have reasonably foreseen and expected that plaintiffs would rely on the appraisal report" performed by defendant. *Alva,* 51 N.C.App. at 610-11, 277 S.E.2d at 540.

The facts in *Alva,* however, are quite different from those in the instant case. Specifically, although the defendant in *Alva* prepared the appraisal report at the request of NCNB Mortgage Corporation (NCNB), the following additional facts formed the basis of our holding: NCNB was the lending institution from whom plaintiff was in the process of obtaining the purchase money for the house; plaintiff was listed by name as the borrower on defendant's work order; plaintiff himself paid the appraisal fee; and defendant had transacted enough similar business with the lending institution that he should have been aware of the importance of his appraisals to borrowers for whom the appraisals were indirectly performed. Plaintiff in the instant case alleges simply, without specifying the original purpose for which the appraisal at issue was performed, that defendant provided the appraisal, as requested, to his clients, and that plaintiff ultimately saw it and relied on it.

Defendant contends that the present case is controlled not by *Alva* but by *Raritan River Steel Co. v. Cherry, Bekaert & Holland,* 322 N.C. 200, 367 S.E.2d 609 (1988). In *Raritan,* Intercontinental Metals Corporation (IMC) retained the defendants, a firm of certified public accountants and individual partners working for the firm, to provide an audit report on IMC's financial status. The plaintiffs, Raritan River Steel Company (Raritan) and Sidbec-Dosco, extended credit to IMC on the basis of what they contended was an incorrect overstatement of IMC's net worth contained in the audit report prepared by the defendants. The plaintiffs sought to hold the defendants liable for losses resulting from the extension of credit to IMC.

In assessing the scope of an accountant's liability for negligent misrepresentation to persons other than the client for whom the financial audit was prepared, our Supreme Court adopted the approach set forth in the Restatement (Second) of Torts § 552 (1977), which provides:

Information Negligently Supplied for the Guidance of Others.

(1) One who, in the course of his business, profession or employment, or in any other transaction in which he has a pecuniary interest, supplies false information for the guidance of others in their business transactions, is subject to liability for pecuniary loss caused to them by their justifiable reliance upon the information, if he fails to exercise reasonable care or competence in obtaining or communicating the information.

(2) . . . [T]he liability stated in Subsection (1) is limited to loss suffered

(a) by the person or one of a limited group of persons for whose benefit and guidance he intends to supply the information or knows that the recipient intends to supply it; and

(b) through reliance upon it in a transaction that he intends the information to influence or knows that the recipient so intends or in a substantially similar transaction.

Restatement (Second) of Torts § 552 (1977). The *Raritan* Court rejected as too expansive the position adopted by some courts which extends liability to all persons whom the accountant should reasonably foresee might obtain and rely on the financial information. In doing so, the Court emphasized the policy reasons which justify establishing a narrower class of plaintiffs to whom an accountant owes a duty of care, such as the lack of control by accountants over the distribution of their reports and the fact that accountants do not benefit if their clients decide to use the report for purposes other than those communicated to the accountant. *See Raritan,* 322 N.C. at 212-13, 367 S.E.2d at 616. After applying § 552, the Court held that Sidbec-Dosco had stated a legally sufficient claim against the defendants for negligent misrepresentation by alleging that at the time that the defendants prepared the audited financial statements for IMC, they knew: (1) the statements would be used by IMC to represent its financial condition to creditors who would extend credit on the basis of them; and (2) Sidbec-Dosco and other creditors would rely on those statements. *Id.* at 216, 367 S.E.2d at 618.

For the following reasons, we find *Raritan* instructive in assessing the liability of a real estate appraiser for negligent misrepresentation to prospective purchasers of the appraised property with whom the appraiser is not in contractual privity. Like an accountant, real estate appraisers have no control over the distribution of their reports once rendered and therefore cannot limit their potential liability. Moreover, like an accountant, a real estate appraiser performs an appraisal pursuant to a contract with an individual client, often a lending institution or a homeowner. For example, in the case of a homeowner who requests an appraisal in connection with a refinancing transaction, the real estate appraiser does not benefit if the homeowner later decides to distribute the appraisal to a prospective purchaser of his home. As the *Raritan* Court noted with regard to accountants:

> [A client's distribution of the audit opinion to others] merely exposes [the accountant's] work to many whom he may have no idea would scrutinize his efforts. We believe that in fairness accountants should not be liable in circumstances where they are unaware of the use to which their opinions will be put. Instead, their liability should be commensurate with those persons or classes of persons whom they *know* will rely on their work.

Raritan, 322 N.C. at 213, 367 S.E.2d at 616 (emphasis added). For these reasons, we conclude that §552, which limits the class of persons to whom certain suppliers of information may be held liable for negligent misrepresentation, is the appropriate standard under which to assess a real estate appraiser's liability.

Applying this standard to the instant case, we conclude that plaintiff has failed to sufficiently allege that she is a person for whose benefit and guidance defendant *intended* to supply the appraisal report, or that defendant *knew* that the recipients of the report, Peoples Bank and Jack Horton, intended to supply it to plaintiff. In fact, plaintiff's complaint is devoid of any alleged purpose for which Peoples Bank and Jack Horton requested the appraisal in question. Defendant could have supplied the appraisal in question as part of a refinancing transaction between Peoples Bank and Jack Horton, with no intention that a third party would later see and rely on the report. In addition, as previously discussed, the instant case is distinguishable from *Alva* in light of the fact that the plaintiff in *Alva,* although not in actual contractual privity with defendant appraiser, was so closely connected to the rendering of the appraisal report that the defendant appraiser could be deemed to have known that NCNB intended to supply it to plaintiff. In such a case, the §552 standard is satisfied. Here, nothing in her complaint indicates that plaintiff played any part, directly or indirectly, in procuring the appraisal at issue. Comment h to §552 makes it clear that liability does not extend to situations where the maker "merely knows of the ever-present possibility of repetition to anyone, and the possibility of action in reliance upon it, on the part of anyone to whom it may be repeated." Restatement (Second) of Torts §552, comment h. Accordingly, plaintiff's complaint fails to state a claim under §552 of the Restatement (Second) of Torts, and therefore was properly dismissed by the trial court.

Affirmed.

WELLS and PARKER, JJ., concur.

NOTES AND QUESTIONS

1. As the excerpt above indicates, appraisal is an art rather than a science and two different appraisers may arrive at substantially different conclusions as to value — hence the common joke that MAI (for Master Appraisal Institute) stands for "Made As Instructed." But this is not a laughing matter: appraisals serve critical roles in the real estate marketplace and in legal disputes involving real property. They provide the basis for loan underwriting, providing the measure of "value" in loan-to-value ratio. They are used in establishing property taxes, which are a major cost in real estate, they form the basis for many ground-rent adjustment clauses, for the

payments owed under shared appreciation mortgages, for condemnation awards, and for insurance payments.

Subjective judgments by the appraiser are an unavoidable issue, but fraud is another matter. Deliberately false appraisals play an important role in mortgage fraud, predatory lending, and other forms of misconduct. In the wake of the savings and loan crisis of the late 1980s, in which unwise and fraudulent mortgage lending played an important role, the federal government tightened the regulation of appraisers. The Real Estate Appraisal Reform Amendments, Title XI of the Financial Institutions Reform, Recovery and Enforcement Act of 1989 (FIRREA),[105] imposed two important, if imperfect, protections. First, it required that appraisals used for mortgage lending be prepared by appraisers licensed by the states in accordance with specific licensing standards. Second, it required that these appraisals be in writing and that they conform to certain specific methods and standards. See, e.g., Comment, Cherokee W. Wooley, Regulation of Real Estate Appraisers and Appraisals: The Effects of FIRREA, 43 Emory L.J. 357 (1994); Joanne Robbins Hicken, Real Estate Appraisers and Appraisals: Changes Mandated by FIRREA, 20 Real. Est. L.J. 157 (1991).

2. *Appraiser liability.* Courts have split on the liability of appraisers to third parties, some adhering to the traditional need for "privity" and others following the guidelines of Restatement § 552. For more on the case law and its merits, see Albert L. Wheeler, III, Real Estate Appraisal Malpractice Liability to Nonprivy Third Parties: Questioning the Applicability of Accountant Liability to Third Party Cases, 25 Real Prop. Prob. & Tr. J. 723 (1991).

3. Assume you are drafting a ground lease that will reset the rents periodically based on the value of the land. How would you provide for the selection of the appraiser? How would you define the instructions to be given to the appraiser? And how would the parties resolve any disputes as to these matters, or as to the validity of the ultimate appraisal?

4. Valuation is a central issue in a great deal of real estate–related litigation, from condemnation and tax proceedings to bankruptcy cases. The challenge for the lawyer is to understand the appraisal process in such detail that each assumption made by the opponent's expert can be challenged, while bolstering the testimony of your own expert—all in terms that a lay jury can understand. See Michael Rikon, Overview of a Valuation Trial, *in* Condemnation 101: Fundamentals of Condemnation Law and Land Valuation SL050 ALI-ABA 133 (2006); Stephanie Hutchins Autry, Techniques That Work: Selecting and Trying Your Condemnation Case to a Jury, *in* Eminent Domain and Land Valuation Litigation, L049 ALI-ABA 291 (2006); Robert F. Reilly, How to Build a Strong Real Estate Appraisal Report, 23-SEP Am. Bankr. Inst. J. 44 (2004).

---

105. Pub. L. No. 101-73, 103 Stat. 183 (1989).

APPENDIX A

Glossary of
Real Estate Terms

Madway, A Mortgage Foreclosure Primer

8 Clearinghouse Rev. 146, 178-181 (July 1974)

Abstract of Title—A summary of conveyances, transfers, *mortgages* and any other factual evidence which may confirm or impair the validity of title to real property.

Acceleration Clause—A clause in a *note,* a *deed of trust* or *mortgage* providing that if the *mortgagor* fails to pay any of his payments when due or breaches any of the other covenants in the *mortgage* instrument, the balance of the obligation becomes immediately due and owing.

Accrued Interest—*Interest* that has been earned but not collected.

Amortization—The process of repaying a loan by equal periodic installments calculated to retire the principal at the end of a fixed period and to pay *accrued interest* on the outstanding balance.

Appraisal—The act of placing an estimate of the real or *market value* on real estate.

Assessed Valuation—The valuation placed by a local governmental unit upon real property for purposes of real estate taxation. Usually, it is less than the *market value* of the property. The relationship between *assessed* and *market value* varies widely from place to place.

Assessment—Usually a charge made against property by a state, county, city or other authorized taxing jurisdiction.

Assignee—The party to whom a *note* and the *mortgage* or *deed of trust* it secures have been transferred, usually for consideration.

Assignor—The party who assigns or transfers the *note* and the *mortgage.*

Assumption of Mortgage—The act of taking title to real estate and assuming payment of the outstanding indebtedness on it.

Balloon Mortgage—A type of *mortgage* loan which involves regular monthly payments for *interest* plus either no or partial *amortization* of the loan principal, so that at the end of the *term* of the *mortgage* there is a lump sum payment, commonly called a balloon payment, of the remaining principal due.

Beneficiary—The person designated to receive the payment from the borrower (*trustor*) under a *deed of trust,* usually the lender or its *assignee.*

Closing—Meeting of parties to adjust final sale figures, taxes, etc., and to sign and deliver *mortgage* and property title transfer documents.

Cloud on Title—An instrument, such as deed, *deed of trust, mortgage,* tax or *assessment,* judgment, or decree, that, if valid, would impair the title to land.

Collateral—The specific real property the borrower pledges as security for a loan.

Collateralized Mortgage Obligation (CMO)* — A form of mortgage-backed security in which mortgages are pledged as security for obligations owed to investors. The investors' interests can be separated into different classes (called tranches) with different payment terms and risks.

Commercial Mortgage-Backed Securities (CMBS)* — Mortgaged-backed securities that are based on commercial, rather than residential, mortgage loans.

Commitment — A promise by a lender to make a specific loan to a prospective borrower.

Compound Interest — Interest computed on both the original principal and its *accrued interest.*

Conduit Loan* — A loan held or intended to be held by a pass through entity such as a REMIC that issues securities backed by the loan.

Conventional Mortgage — In modern mortgage parlance, a *mortgage* that is not insured, guaranteed and/or subsidized by any governmental or quasi-governmental agency. It should be noted that conventional mortgages are often insured by private mortgage insurers.

Conveyance — The transfer of the title to land from one person, or class of persons, to another.

Correspondent — A mortgage loan correspondent; a mortgage banker who *services* mortgage loans as agent for the owner of the mortgage. Also applied to the mortgage banker in his role as originator of mortgage loans for the investor.

Credit Enhancement* — An arrangement established by the issuer of securities to increase the credit rating of the securities by reducing the risk of nonpayment, such as overcollateralizing the securities, maintaining reserves, arranging a letter of credit to cover shortfalls, or securing a third-party guarantee.

Deed of Trust — Essentially a three-party *mortgage;* the owner, as *trustor,* conveys the property to a *trustee* to hold for the benefit of a *beneficiary,* the lender, to secure payment of a debt or obligation owed to the *beneficiary.* The deed of trust invariably gives the *trustee* the power to sell the property upon demand of the beneficiary in the event of a default.

Debt Service — The regular payments that are made to pay off the principal of a mortgage loan, plus *interest* on the unpaid balance of the principal.

Debt Service Constant — A factor that, multiplied by the total loan amount, or total principal, yields the annual *debt-service* payment (principal plus interest) required to amortize a loan.

Decree of Foreclosure and Sale — In judicial foreclosure jurisdiction, the court decree or judgment that establishes the amount of the *mortgage* debt and orders the property sold to satisfy the debt.

Deed in Lieu of Foreclosure* — A transfer of the equity of redemption from the borrower to the mortgage lender, ending the borrower's rights in the mortgaged property.

Default — The nonperformance of a duty arising under a *note, mortgage or deed of trust or installment land sale contract.*

Defeasance* — (1) A provision or instrument that nullifies or terminates an interest or estate in land; (2) replacing the original collateral for a debt with Treasury securities that generate income sufficient to repay the debt. This ensures the mortgage holder will receive the full return it contracted for, while allowing the borrower to free the property from the lien of the mortgage.

Deficiency—The difference between the amount of the mortgage indebtedness and any lesser amount recovered by the mortgagee from the foreclosure sale.

Deficiency Judgment—A personal judgment created by a court decree for the amount of the deficiency against any person liable for the mortgage debt.

Down Payment—The amount of cash that a buyer is required to put up in order to purchase a piece of property; it is equal to the purchase price minus the amount of any mortgage loans used to finance the purchase.

Direct-Reduction Mortgage—A *mortgage* directing that all payments must be used for reduction of the outstanding balance of the principal.

Discount Points—Amount paid by the borrower to the lender to secure a mortgage loan. One point is equal to one percent of the loan.

Due-on-Sale or Encumbrance—A clause in a *mortgage* or *deed of trust* providing that if the mortgagor or trustor sells, transfers or in any way encumbers the property (e.g., gives a *second mortgage* or *deed of trust,* permits a lien to attach), the *acceleration clause* is triggered and the balance of the obligation becomes due.

Encumbrance—A claim or *lien* attached to a piece of property, limiting in some way the owner's rights to the property.

Escrow Account—An account in which the borrower's monthly payments for taxes and insurance are placed and held in trust by the lender.

Executory Deed in Lieu of Foreclosure* —An agreement by the mortgagor that upon a future default, the mortgagor will grant the mortgagee a deed in lieu of foreclosure; if it is enforced, the executory deed in lieu of foreclosure works essentially as a waiver of the equity of redemption upon a future default.

Equity of Redemption—The right of a *mortgagor* to redeem his property after he has breached some covenant of the *mortgage,* usually by failing to make a payment when due, and the *mortgagee* has elected to accelerate the balance of the obligation. Redemption is accomplished by payment of the entire debt, plus accrued interest and costs. The equity of redemption must be distinguished from the *statutory right of redemption.* The former is a creature of equity, while the latter, of statute. The equity of redemption is cut off when the foreclosure sale takes place. In jurisdictions which provide a statutory right of redemption, that right usually accrues upon the foreclosure sale and remains available to the mortgagor for a specified period of time, in some places, up to two years. In effect, it permits him to oust the party who purchased the property at the foreclosure sale and regain possession by paying the foreclosure sale price or the amount of the outstanding obligation, plus accrued interest and costs, depending on the statute.

Execution—A writ issued by a judicial officer and directed to a sheriff, constable, marshal or commissioner appointed by the court to enforce a judgment against the property or person of a judgment debtor.

Federal Home Loan Banks—A national system of eleven regional banks established by the Home Loan Bank Act of 1932 to provide facilities for savings and loan associations and similar institutions, mutual savings banks, and life insurance companies, in connection with their home-mortgage lending activities, on condition that they become members of the system.

Federal National Mortgage Association ("FNMA" or "Fannie Mae")—An association organized February 10, 1938 under the provisions of the National Housing Act. During its earlier years, it was grouped under a series of federal departments and agencies and was authorized to purchase, or commit for purchase, FHA insured and Veterans' Administration guaranteed mortgage loans. Funds for those mortgage purchases were obtained by FNMA by borrowing from the Treasury. In 1954, Congress rechartered FNMA into a mixed private-public ownership corporation. Under the Housing and Urban Development Act of 1968, FNMA was spun off from the federal government as a government sponsored but privately owned corporation. By purchasing mortgages, the FNMA provides a "secondary market" for mortgages, thus permitting home mortgage lenders to increase their liquidity and make more money available for new loans.

First Mortgage—A type of *mortgage* where the property which secures it has no other mortgages with prior or greater rights to the property; a *mortgage* that is a first lien on the property pledged as security.

Forbearance—The act of refraining from taking legal action despite the fact that a *mortgage* is in *default*—usually granted only when the *mortgagor* makes a satisfactory arrangement by which the *default* will be cured at a future date.

Foreclosure—The legal process by which a *mortgagor* is deprived of his interest in the property. Usually, property is sold, either pursuant to a court *decree of foreclosure* or pursuant to a *power of sale* provision. The proceeds of the sale are customarily applied to pay off the amount still owed on the *note* which the *mortgage* secured, plus the expenses of the foreclosure proceeding and/or the sale.

Fully Amortized Mortgage—A method of repaying a mortgage loan which involves regular payments for *interest* plus *amortization* of the loan principal so that at the end of the term the principal has been entirely repaid.

Garnishment—An attachment of assets in the possession of a third person.

General National Mortgage Association ("GNMA" or "Ginnie Mae") —Created by the Housing and Urban Development Act of 1968, GNMA is part of the U.S. Department of Housing and Urban Development. GNMA operates a number of "special assistance" programs under which it buys certain categories of FHA and VA mortgages at prices above the *market price,* thus encouraging lenders to make loans falling in these categories. Many of these "special assistance" programs are conducted pursuant to the "tandem plan," under which GNMA buys mortgages at prices more favorable than the *market price* and then sells them to *FNMA* or other investors at prevailing market prices, absorbing the difference between the GNMA price and the higher *market price* as a subsidy.

Grant—A generic term applicable to all transfers of an interest in real property.

Grantee—A person to whom a *grant* is made.

Grantor—The person by whom the *grant* is made.

Ground Lease* —A lease, typically for an extended term, of undeveloped land or a lease of land but not the improvements on the land.

Ground Lease Financing* —Financing secured by a mortgage on the borrower's interest in a long-term ground lease.

Holder—The current owner of an indebtedness secured by a *mortgage* or *deed of trust.*

Homestead Estate—The rights of record, belonging to a family or head of a household in real estate owned and occupied as a home, that are exempt from seizure by creditors.

Hypothecate—To pledge a thing without delivering the title or possession of it to the pledgee.

Installment Land Sales Contract—An agreement whereby a seller agrees to convey title to real property to a buyer when the buyer has paid the seller the purchase price of the property, with *interest* at a specified rate, and with the payment schedule spread over a number of years. Depending upon the jurisdiction, this type of financing arrangement places the buyer in the position of the tenant except that, after the pay-out period, the seller conveys his interest in the land to the buyer. The buyer receives no deed until he pays the seller the entire purchase price, and the seller may have all of the remedies of a landlord against the defaulting buyer.

Income Limits—Family income limits established for admission to FHA, and FmHA homeownership programs. Limits are based on family size, type of dwelling and cost of living in the area.

Interest Rate—The rate at which the amount charged for use of money is computed.

Interest Reduction Programs—Programs operated by FHA and FmHA which subsidize the market *interest rate* on mortgage loans for low and moderate-income housing, thus lowering the cost to the buyer.

Interim Financing—Loans covering land and construction costs, current real estate taxes, and other incidental expenses during the construction period.

Institutional Lender—A mortgage lender that invests its own funds in *mortgages* and carries a majority of such loans in its own portfolio, e.g., mutual savings banks, life insurance companies, commercial banks, savings and loan associations. Although individuals or mortgage companies may hold and service mortgage loans, they are not generally classified as institutional lenders.

Junior Mortgage—A type of *mortgage* where the property which it secures already has one or more *mortgages* on it with prior or greater rights.

Late Charge—A penalty permitted by FHA covering any monthly payment not made by the 15th of the month in which the payment is due. The FHA usually permits 2% of the monthly payment as a late charge. Many lenders exact a late charge for delinquency on *conventional mortgage* loan installments.

Lender—Any mortgage lender, e.g., mutual savings bank, commercial bank, savings and loan association, etc., that invests its own funds in *mortgages*. Also, the *holder* of the *mortgage*, the permanent lender for which the mortgage banker services the loan.

Level-Payment Mortgage—A *mortgage* that provides for the payment of like sums at periodic intervals during its term. Part of the payment is credited to the *interest* for the time involved, and the balance is used to amortize the principal.

Lien—A hold or claim one person has upon the property of another as security for a debt. In many states, a *mortgage* is regarded as a lien.

Loan Trust Funds—In FHA loans, the funds accumulated to take care of taxes, fire insurance, mortgage insurance and premiums as they become due and payable.

Loan-Value Ratio—The relationship between the amount of the loan and the appraised value of the property, usually expressed as a percentage.

Market Value—The price at which a property could be sold on the open market, free of the pressures created by a forced sale.

Maturity—Termination of the period a note or obligation has to run.

Mechanic's Lien—A claim created by statute in most states, in favor of mechanics or other persons who have performed work or furnished materials in and for the erection or repair of a building.

Moratorium—A period during which a borrower has a legal right to delay payment obligations. Especially, a period granted in an emergency or generally by a moratorium law.

Mortgage—A contract by which specific property is *hypothecated* as security for the performance of an act or the payment of a debt.

Mortgage-Backed Securities (MBS)*—Securities that represent interests in, or are secured by, a pool of mortgage loans; MBS include mortgage-backed bonds, collateralized mortgage obligations, pass-through securities, and participation certificates.

Mortgage Insurance Premium—The price paid by the borrower for insurance under FHA and VA loans. The insurance is furnished by the federal government in favor of the lender, and insures payment of the loan in event that the proceeds of a foreclosure sale fail to cover the outstanding balance of the obligation.

Mortgage Note—A promissory note secured by a mortgage on specific real property.

Mortgage Portfolio—The aggregate of mortgage loans held by a mortgage lender.

Mortgage Risk—A hazard of loss of principal and/or interest in the lending of funds secured by a mortgage.

Mortgagee—The lending party under the terms of a *mortgage.*

Mortgagor—The borrowing party who pledges property to secure the loan.

Note—See *mortgage note,* supra.

Open-End Mortgage—A *mortgage* or *deed of trust* so written as to secure and permit additional advances on the original loan.

Package Mortgage—See *open-end mortgage,* supra.

Plat—A map showing the dimensions of a piece of real estate based upon the legal descriptions.

Power of Sale—A provision in a *mortgage* or *deed of trust* which empowers a *mortgagee* or *trustee,* without resort to any judicial procedures, to sell the property in the event of *default* by the *mortgagor* and apply the proceeds of the sale to satisfy the obligation, the costs of invoking the procedure (e.g., attorneys' fees, recordation fees, etc.), and the expenses of sale.

Points—The percentage deduction from the nominal amount of a discounted loan. On a $1000 loan discounted two points, the borrower receives $980.

Prepayment Penalty—A penalty exacted from the borrower for the right to repay a debt before it actually becomes due.

Prepayment Risk*—The risk to the holder of a debt or bond that the obligation will be paid off before maturity, depriving the holder of the full stream of cash flow that was expected.

Private Mortgage Insurance (PMI)*—Insurance offered by a commercial insurer that protects a lender against loss in case of default by the mortgage borrower. PMI is often required on high-LTV loans.

Purchase Money Mortgage—A *mortgage* given to the seller by the buyer to secure in whole or in part the purchase price of real property.

Quiet Title—An action to judicially determine the rights and interests to specific real property.

Real Estate Investment Trust (REIT)*—A publicly traded corporation or trust that invests in real estate and/or mortgage loans and that, by meeting certain requirements, including investing in permitted real estate investments and distributing at least 90% of its net income as dividends, can avoid entity-level tax. REITs can actively manage their investment portfolios, which REMICs are not permitted to do.

Real Estate Mortgage Investment Conduit (REMIC)*—A business entity (corporation, partnership, trust, etc.) that invests in qualified mortgages and other permitted investments as required by the tax code to avoid taxation at the entity level. Most collateralized mortgage obligations are issued by REMICs.

Reinstatement—The curing of all defaults by a borrower; the restoration of a loan to current status through payment of arrearages.

Refinancing—The process of obtaining a new *mortgage* loan when the old note has been partially repaid. The proceeds of the new loan are customarily used to repay the outstanding balance of the old.

Refunding—The process of refinancing a debt that cannot be paid conveniently when due.

REIT*—see *Real Estate Investment Trust*, supra.

REMIC*—see *Real Estate Mortgage Investment Conduit*, supra.

Right of Redemption—See *equity of redemption*, supra.

Risk Rating—A process by which risks are divided and evaluated, as to neighborhood, property, the *mortgagor*, and the *mortgage* pattern.

Satisfaction—A written instrument evidencing the full payment of a *mortgage* debt and extinguishing the *mortgage lien*.

Second Mortgage—A type of *junior mortgage* where the property is encumbered by only one other *mortgage*, the first *mortgage*, that has prior or greater right to the property.

Secondary Financing—A loan secured by a second *mortgage* or *deed of trust*.

Servicing—The collection of payments of *interest* and principal and *trust-fund* items such as fire insurance, taxes, and others on a note. Servicing by the lender also consists of operational procedures covering accounting, bookkeeping, insurance, tax records, loan-payment-follow-up, delinquent loan-follow-up, and loan analysis. Servicing may be performed either by the *holder* of a *mortgage note* or by its agent appointed for that purpose.

Standing Mortgage—A method of repaying a mortgage loan which involves a regular payment for interest but no *amortization* of the loan principal.

Straw—A person or firm named as the owner of a piece of property, when in fact it is in reality a front for the real owner.

Strict Foreclosure—A type of foreclosure proceeding used in a few states in which title is vested directly in the mortgagee by court degree without holding a foreclosure sale.

Subordinated Ground Lease Financing*—Financing secured not only by a ground lessee's leasehold estate, but also by the fee ownership of the ground lessor.

Subordination—The written acknowledgment of the creditor that the debt due to him by the debtor is inferior to a debt due another creditor by the same debtor.

Tandem Plan—See *General National Mortgage Association*, supra.

Term—The time period in which a loan must be repaid.

Term Mortgage—A *mortgage* having a specific *term*, usually not over five years, during which interest is paid but the principal is not reduced.

Title Insurance—Insurance to protect a property owner from loss if a title proves imperfect.

Trust Deed—See *Deed of Trust* supra.

Trustee—A person in whom property is vested for the purpose of securing performance of an obligation.

Trustor—The borrower under a *deed of trust*.

Usury—Taking, or contracting for, a rate of interest in excess of that permitted by law.

Waiver of Lien—A written evidence in many states from a contractor or material-man surrendering his right of lien to enforce collection of a debt against property.

Waste—Damage to property by willful neglect, abuse, misuse, etc.

Yield—Effective return on a *mortgage* based upon the face rate of interest and the price paid for the *mortgage.*

Yield Maintenance Premium*—A prepayment premium calculated to compensate the lender for any loss caused by the borrower's prepayment. The amount of a yield maintenance premium will increase if the borrower prepays when mortgage rates are low, and will decrease if prepayment occurs when mortgage rates are high.

Yield Spread Premium*—Points or a fee paid by a lender to a mortgage broker for securing a loan that carries a higher rate of interest.

* Definition added by the editors of this casebook.

APPENDIX B

Exclusive Authorization and Right to Sell (Multiple Listing)

Reprinted with permission, CALIFORNIA ASSOCIATION OF REALTORS®. Endorsement not implied.

CALIFORNIA ASSOCIATION OF REALTORS®

RESIDENTIAL LISTING AGREEMENT
(Exclusive Authorization and Right to Sell)
(C.A.R. Form RLA, Revised 4/06)

1. **EXCLUSIVE RIGHT TO SELL:** _____ ("Seller")
   hereby employs and grants _____ ("Broker")
   beginning (date) _____ and ending at 11:59 P.M. on (date) _____ ("Listing Period")
   the exclusive and irrevocable right to sell or exchange the real property in the City of _____,
   County of_____, Assessor's Parcel No. _____,
   California, described as:_____ ("Property").

2. **ITEMS EXCLUDED AND INCLUDED:** Unless otherwise specified in a real estate purchase agreement, all fixtures and fittings that are attached to the Property are included, and personal property items are excluded, from the purchase price.
   ADDITIONAL ITEMS EXCLUDED: _____.
   ADDITIONAL ITEMS INCLUDED: _____
   Seller intends that the above items be excluded or included in offering the Property for sale, but understands that: **(i)** the purchase agreement supersedes any intention expressed above and will ultimately determine which items are excluded and included in the sale; and **(ii)** Broker is not responsible for and does not guarantee that the above exclusions and/or inclusions will be in the purchase agreement.

3. **LISTING PRICE AND TERMS:**
   A. The listing price shall be: _____
      _____ Dollars ($ _____).
   B. Additional Terms:_____

4. COMPENSATION TO BROKER:
   Notice: The amount or rate of real estate commissions is not fixed by law. They are set by each Broker individually and may be negotiable between Seller and Broker (real estate commissions include all compensation and fees to Broker).
   A. Seller agrees to pay to Broker as compensation for services irrespective of agency relationship(s), either ☐ _____ percent of the listing price (or if a purchase agreement is entered into, of the purchase price), or ☐ $ _____,
      AND _____, as follows:
      (1) If during the Listing Period, or any extension, Broker, Seller, cooperating broker, or any other person procures a buyer(s) who offers to purchase the Property on the above price and terms, or on any price and terms acceptable to Seller. (Broker is entitled to compensation whether any escrow resulting from such offer closes during or after the expiration of the Listing Period.)
   OR (2) If within _____ calendar days **(a)** after the end of the Listing Period or any extension, or **(b)** after any cancellation of this Agreement, unless otherwise agreed, Seller enters into a contract to sell, convey, lease or otherwise transfer the Property to anyone ("Prospective Buyer") or that person's related entity: **(i)** who physically entered and was shown the Property during the Listing Period or any extension by Broker or a cooperating broker; or **(ii)** for whom Broker or any cooperating broker submitted to Seller a signed, written offer to acquire, lease, exchange or obtain an option on the Property. Seller, however, shall have no obligation to Broker under paragraph 4A(2) unless, not later than **3 calendar days** after the end of the Listing Period or any extension or cancellation, Broker has given Seller a written notice of the names of such Prospective Buyers.
   OR (3) If, during the Listing Period or any extension, without Broker's prior written consent, Seller cancels this Agreement, withdraws the Property from sale or makes it unmarketable, or the Property is conveyed, leased, rented or otherwise transferred.
   B. If completion of the sale is prevented by a party to the transaction other than Seller, then compensation due under paragraph 4A shall be payable only if and when Seller collects damages by suit, arbitration, settlement or otherwise, and then in an amount equal to the lesser of one-half of the damages recovered or the above compensation, after first deducting title and escrow expenses and the expenses of collection, if any.
   C. In addition, Seller agrees to pay Broker: _____
   D. Seller has been advised of Broker's policy regarding cooperation with, and the amount of compensation offered to, other brokers.
      (1) Broker is authorized to cooperate with and compensate brokers participating through the multiple listing service(s) ("MLS"): **(i)** by offering MLS brokers: either ☐ _____ percent of the purchase price, or ☐ $ _____
      OR (ii) (if checked) ☐ as per Broker's policy.
      (2) Broker is authorized to cooperate with and compensate brokers operating outside the MLS as per Broker's policy.
   E. Seller hereby irrevocably assigns to Broker the above compensation from Seller's funds and proceeds in escrow. Broker may submit this Agreement, as instructions to compensate Broker pursuant to paragraph 4A, to any escrow regarding the Property involving Seller and a buyer, Prospective Buyer or other transferee.
   F. **(1)** Seller represents that Seller has not previously entered into a listing agreement with another broker regarding the Property, unless specified as follows: _____
      (2) Seller warrants that Seller has no obligation to pay compensation to any other broker regarding the Property unless the Property is transferred to any of the following individuals or entities: _____

      (3) If the Property is sold to anyone listed above during the time Seller is obligated to compensate another broker: **(i)** Broker is not entitled to compensation under this Agreement; and **(ii)** Broker is not obligated to represent Seller in such transaction.

Seller acknowledges receipt of a copy of this page.
Seller's Initials (_____)(_____)

RLA REVISED 4/06 (PAGE 1 OF 3) Print Date

Reviewed by _____ Date _____

EQUAL HOUSING OPPORTUNITY

RESIDENTIAL LISTING AGREEMENT - EXCLUSIVE (RLA PAGE 1 OF 3)

Property Address: _____ Date: _____

5. **OWNERSHIP, TITLE AND AUTHORITY:** Seller warrants that: **(i)** Seller is the owner of the Property; **(ii)** no other persons or entities have title to the Property; and **(iii)** Seller has the authority to both execute this Agreement and sell the Property. Exceptions to ownership, title and authority are as follows: _____ .

6. **MULTIPLE LISTING SERVICE:** All terms of the transaction, including financing, if applicable, will be provided to the selected MLS for publication, dissemination and use by persons and entities on terms approved by the MLS. Seller authorizes Broker to comply with all applicable MLS rules. MLS rules allow MLS data to be made available by the MLS to additional Internet sites unless Broker gives the MLS instructions to the contrary. MLS rules generally provide that residential real property and vacant lot listings be submitted to the MLS within 48 hours or some other period of time after all necessary signatures have been obtained on the listing agreement. However, Broker will not have to submit this listing to the MLS if, within that time, Broker submits to the MLS a form signed by Seller (C.A.R. Form SEL or the locally required form) instructing Broker to withhold the listing from the MLS. Information about this listing will be provided to the MLS of Broker's selection unless a form instructing Broker to withhold the listing from the MLS is attached to this listing Agreement.

7. **SELLER REPRESENTATIONS:** Seller represents that, unless otherwise specified in writing, Seller is unaware of: **(i)** any Notice of Default recorded against the Property; **(ii)** any delinquent amounts due under any loan secured by, or other obligation affecting, the Property; **(iii)** any bankruptcy, insolvency or similar proceeding affecting the Property; **(iv)** any litigation, arbitration, administrative action, government investigation or other pending or threatened action that affects or may affect the Property or Seller's ability to transfer it; and **(v)** any current, pending or proposed special assessments affecting the Property. Seller shall promptly notify Broker in writing if Seller becomes aware of any of these items during the Listing Period or any extension thereof.

8. **BROKER'S AND SELLER'S DUTIES:** Broker agrees to exercise reasonable effort and due diligence to achieve the purposes of this Agreement. Unless Seller gives Broker written instructions to the contrary, Broker is authorized to order reports and disclosures as appropriate or necessary and advertise and market the Property by any method and in any medium selected by Broker, including MLS and the Internet, and, to the extent permitted by these media, control the dissemination of the information submitted to any medium. Seller agrees to consider offers presented by Broker, and to act in good faith to accomplish the sale of the Property by, among other things, making the Property available for showing at reasonable times and referring to Broker all inquiries of any party interested in the Property. Seller is responsible for determining at what price to list and sell the Property. **Seller further agrees to indemnify, defend and hold Broker harmless from all claims, disputes, litigation, judgments and attorney fees arising from any incorrect information supplied by Seller, or from any material facts that Seller knows but fails to disclose.**

9. **DEPOSIT:** Broker is authorized to accept and hold on Seller's behalf any deposits to be applied toward the purchase price.

10. **AGENCY RELATIONSHIPS:**
    A. **Disclosure:** If the Property includes residential property with one-to-four dwelling units, Seller shall receive a "Disclosure Regarding Agency Relationships" form prior to entering into this Agreement.
    B. **Seller Representation:** Broker shall represent Seller in any resulting transaction, except as specified in paragraph 4F.
    C. **Possible Dual Agency With Buyer:** Depending upon the circumstances, it may be necessary or appropriate for Broker to act as an agent for both Seller and buyer, exchange party, or one or more additional parties ("Buyer"). Broker shall, as soon as practicable, disclose to Seller any election to act as a dual agent representing both Seller and Buyer. If a Buyer is procured directly by Broker or an associate-licensee in Broker's firm, Seller hereby consents to Broker acting as a dual agent for Seller and such Buyer. In the event of an exchange, Seller hereby consents to Broker collecting compensation from additional parties for services rendered, provided there is disclosure to all parties of such agency and compensation. Seller understands and agrees that: **(i)** Broker, without the prior written consent of Seller, will not disclose to Buyer that Seller is willing to sell the Property at a price less than the listing price; **(ii)** Broker, without the prior written consent of Buyer, will not disclose to Seller that Buyer is willing to pay a price greater than the offered price; and **(iii)** except for (i) and (ii) above, a dual agent is obligated to disclose known facts materially affecting the value or desirability of the Property to both parties.
    D. **Other Sellers:** Seller understands that Broker may have or obtain listings on other properties, and that potential buyers may consider, make offers on, or purchase through Broker, property the same as or similar to Seller's Property. Seller consents to Broker's representation of sellers and buyers of other properties before, during and after the end of this Agreement.
    E. **Confirmation:** If the Property includes residential property with one-to-four dwelling units, Broker shall confirm the agency relationship described above, or as modified, in writing, prior to or concurrent with Seller's execution of a purchase agreement.

11. **SECURITY AND INSURANCE:** Broker is not responsible for loss of or damage to personal or real property, or person, whether attributable to use of a keysafe/lockbox, a showing of the Property, or otherwise. Third parties, including, but not limited to, appraisers, inspectors, brokers and prospective buyers, may have access to, and take videos and photographs of, the interior of the Property. Seller agrees: **(i)** to take reasonable precautions to safeguard and protect valuables that might be accessible during showings of the Property; and **(ii)** to obtain insurance to protect against these risks. Broker does not maintain insurance to protect Seller.

12. **KEYSAFE/LOCKBOX:** A keysafe/lockbox is designed to hold a key to the Property to permit access to the Property by Broker, cooperating brokers, MLS participants, their authorized licensees and representatives, authorized inspectors, and accompanied prospective buyers. Broker, cooperating brokers, MLS and Associations/Boards of REALTORS® are **not** insurers against injury, theft, loss, vandalism or damage attributed to the use of a keysafe/lockbox. Seller does (or if checked ☐ does not) authorize Broker to install a keysafe/lockbox. If Seller does not occupy the Property, Seller shall be responsible for obtaining occupant(s)' written permission for use of a keysafe/lockbox.

13. **SIGN:** Seller does (or if checked ☐ does not) authorize Broker to install a FOR SALE/SOLD sign on the Property.

14. **EQUAL HOUSING OPPORTUNITY:** The Property is offered in compliance with federal, state and local anti-discrimination laws.

15. **ATTORNEY FEES:** In any action, proceeding or arbitration between Seller and Broker regarding the obligation to pay compensation under this Agreement, the prevailing Seller or Broker shall be entitled to reasonable attorney fees and costs from the non-prevailing Seller or Broker, except as provided in paragraph 19A.

16. **ADDITIONAL TERMS:** _____
_____
_____

Seller acknowledges receipt of a copy of this page.
Seller's Initials (_____)(_____)

RLA REVISED 4/06 (PAGE 2 OF 3)

Reviewed by _____ Date _____

RESIDENTIAL LISTING AGREEMENT - EXCLUSIVE (RLA PAGE 2 OF 3)

Property Address: _____ Date: _____

17. **MANAGEMENT APPROVAL:** If an associate-licensee in Broker's office (salesperson or broker-associate) enters into this Agreement on Broker's behalf, and Broker or Manager does not approve of its terms, Broker or Manager has the right to cancel this Agreement, in writing, within **5 Days** After its execution.

18. **SUCCESSORS AND ASSIGNS:** This Agreement shall be binding upon Seller and Seller's successors and assigns.

19. **DISPUTE RESOLUTION:**

A. **MEDIATION:** Seller and Broker agree to mediate any dispute or claim arising between them out of this Agreement, or any resulting transaction, before resorting to arbitration or court action, subject to paragraph 19B(2) below. Paragraph 19B(2) below applies whether or not the arbitration provision is initialed. Mediation fees, if any, shall be divided equally among the parties involved. If, for any dispute or claim to which this paragraph applies, any party commences an action without first attempting to resolve the matter through mediation, or refuses to mediate after a request has been made, then that party shall not be entitled to recover attorney fees, even if they would otherwise be available to that party in any such action. THIS MEDIATION PROVISION APPLIES WHETHER OR NOT THE ARBITRATION PROVISION IS INITIALED.

B. **ARBITRATION OF DISPUTES: (1)** Seller and Broker agree that any dispute or claim in law or equity arising between them regarding the obligation to pay compensation under this Agreement, which is not settled through mediation, shall be decided by neutral, binding arbitration, including and subject to paragraph 19B(2) below. The arbitrator shall be a retired judge or justice, or an attorney with at least 5 years of residential real estate law experience, unless the parties mutually agree to a different arbitrator, who shall render an award in accordance with substantive California law. The parties shall have the right to discovery in accordance with Code of Civil Procedure §1283.05. In all other respects, the arbitration shall be conducted in accordance with Title 9 of Part III of the California Code of Civil Procedure. Judgment upon the award of the arbitrator(s) may be entered in any court having jurisdiction. Interpretation of this agreement to arbitrate shall be governed by the Federal Arbitration Act.

(2) EXCLUSIONS FROM MEDIATION AND ARBITRATION: The following matters are excluded from mediation and arbitration: (i) a judicial or non-judicial foreclosure or other action or proceeding to enforce a deed of trust, mortgage, or installment land sale contract as defined in Civil Code §2985; (ii) an unlawful detainer action; (iii) the filing or enforcement of a mechanic's lien; and (iv) any matter that is within the jurisdiction of a probate, small claims, or bankruptcy court. The filing of a court action to enable the recording of a notice of pending action, for order of attachment, receivership, injunction, or other provisional remedies, shall not constitute a waiver of the mediation and arbitration provisions.

"**NOTICE: BY INITIALING IN THE SPACE BELOW YOU ARE AGREEING TO HAVE ANY DISPUTE ARISING OUT OF THE MATTERS INCLUDED IN THE 'ARBITRATION OF DISPUTES' PROVISION DECIDED BY NEUTRAL ARBITRATION AS PROVIDED BY CALIFORNIA LAW AND YOU ARE GIVING UP ANY RIGHTS YOU MIGHT POSSESS TO HAVE THE DISPUTE LITIGATED IN A COURT OR JURY TRIAL. BY INITIALING IN THE SPACE BELOW YOU ARE GIVING UP YOUR JUDICIAL RIGHTS TO DISCOVERY AND APPEAL, UNLESS THOSE RIGHTS ARE SPECIFICALLY INCLUDED IN THE 'ARBITRATION OF DISPUTES' PROVISION. IF YOU REFUSE TO SUBMIT TO ARBITRATION AFTER AGREEING TO THIS PROVISION, YOU MAY BE COMPELLED TO ARBITRATE UNDER THE AUTHORITY OF THE CALIFORNIA CODE OF CIVIL PROCEDURE. YOUR AGREEMENT TO THIS ARBITRATION PROVISION IS VOLUNTARY.**"

"**WE HAVE READ AND UNDERSTAND THE FOREGOING AND AGREE TO SUBMIT DISPUTES ARISING OUT OF THE MATTERS INCLUDED IN THE 'ARBITRATION OF DISPUTES' PROVISION TO NEUTRAL ARBITRATION.**"

| Seller's Initials _____ / _____ | Broker's Initials _____ / _____ |

20. **ENTIRE AGREEMENT:** All prior discussions, negotiations and agreements between the parties concerning the subject matter of this Agreement are superseded by this Agreement, which constitutes the entire contract and a complete and exclusive expression of their agreement, and may not be contradicted by evidence of any prior agreement or contemporaneous oral agreement. If any provision of this Agreement is held to be ineffective or invalid, the remaining provisions will nevertheless be given full force and effect. This Agreement and any supplement, addendum or modification, including any photocopy or facsimile, may be executed in counterparts.

By signing below, Seller acknowledges that Seller has read, understands, received a copy of and agrees to the terms of this Agreement.

Seller _____ Date _____
Address _____ City _____ State _____ Zip _____
Telephone _____ Fax _____ E-mail _____

Seller _____ Date _____
Address _____ City _____ State _____ Zip _____
Telephone _____ Fax _____ E-mail _____

Real Estate Broker (Firm) _____ DRE Lic. # _____
By (Agent) _____ DRE Lic. # _____ Date _____
Address _____ City _____ State _____ Zip _____
Telephone _____ Fax _____ E-mail _____

THIS FORM HAS BEEN APPROVED BY THE CALIFORNIA ASSOCIATION OF REALTORS® (C.A.R.). NO REPRESENTATION IS MADE AS TO THE LEGAL VALIDITY OR ADEQUACY OF ANY PROVISION IN ANY SPECIFIC TRANSACTION. A REAL ESTATE BROKER IS THE PERSON QUALIFIED TO ADVISE ON REAL ESTATE TRANSACTIONS. IF YOU DESIRE LEGAL OR TAX ADVICE, CONSULT AN APPROPRIATE PROFESSIONAL.

This form is available for use by the entire real estate industry. It is not intended to identify the user as a REALTOR®. REALTOR® is a registered collective membership mark which may be used only by members of the NATIONAL ASSOCIATION OF REALTORS® who subscribe to its Code of Ethics.

Published and Distributed by:
REAL ESTATE BUSINESS SERVICES, INC.
a subsidiary of the California Association of REALTORS®
525 South Virgil Avenue, Los Angeles, California 90020

SURE TRAC
The System for Success®

RLA REVISED 4/06 (PAGE 3 OF 3)

| Reviewed by _____ Date _____ |

EQUAL HOUSING OPPORTUNITY

RESIDENTIAL LISTING AGREEMENT - EXCLUSIVE (RLA PAGE 3 OF 3)

APPENDIX C

California Residential Purchase Agreement and Joint Escrow Instructions

Reprinted with permission, CALIFORNIA ASSOCIATION OF REALTORS®. Endorsement not implied.

**CALIFORNIA
RESIDENTIAL PURCHASE AGREEMENT
AND JOINT ESCROW INSTRUCTIONS**
For Use With Single Family Residential Property — Attached or Detached
(C.A.R. Form RPA-CA, Revised 1/06)

Date _____, at _____, California.

1. OFFER:
  A. **THIS IS AN OFFER FROM** _____ ("Buyer").
  B. **THE REAL PROPERTY TO BE ACQUIRED** is described as _____
    _____, Assessor's Parcel No. _____, situated in
    _____, County of _____, California, ("Property").
  C. **THE PURCHASE PRICE** offered is _____
    _____ Dollars $ _____
  D. **CLOSE OF ESCROW** shall occur on _____ (date)(or ☐ _____ **Days** After Acceptance).

2. FINANCE TERMS: Obtaining the loans below **is a contingency** of this Agreement unless: **(i)** either 2K or 2L is checked below; or **(ii)** otherwise agreed in writing. Buyer shall act diligently and in good faith to obtain the designated loans. Obtaining deposit, down payment and closing costs **is not a contingency**. Buyer represents that funds will be good when deposited with Escrow Holder.
  A. **INITIAL DEPOSIT:** Buyer has given a deposit in the amount of . . . .$ _____
    to the agent submitting the offer (or to ☐ _____), by personal check
    (or ☐ _____), made payable to _____
    which shall be held uncashed until Acceptance and then deposited within **3 business days** after
    Acceptance (or ☐ _____), with
    Escrow Holder, (or ☐ into Broker's trust account).
  B. **INCREASED DEPOSIT:** Buyer shall deposit with Escrow Holder an increased deposit in the amount of . . . .$ _____
    within _____ **Days** After Acceptance, or _____
  C. **FIRST LOAN IN THE AMOUNT OF** . . . .$ _____
    (1) NEW First Deed of Trust in favor of lender, encumbering the Property, securing a note payable at
      maximum interest of _____% fixed rate, or _____% initial adjustable rate with a maximum
      interest rate of _____%, balance due in _____ years, amortized over _____ years. Buyer
      shall pay loan fees/points not to exceed _____ (These terms apply whether the designated loan
      is conventional, FHA or VA.)
    (2) ☐ FHA ☐ VA: (The following terms only apply to the FHA or VA loan that is checked.)
      Seller shall pay _____% discount points. Seller shall pay other fees not allowed to be paid by
      Buyer, ☐ not to exceed $ _____. Seller shall pay the cost of lender required Repairs
      (including those for wood destroying pest) not otherwise provided for in this Agreement, ☐ not to
      exceed $ _____. (Actual loan amount may increase if mortgage insurance premiums,
      funding fees or closing costs are financed.)
  D. **ADDITIONAL FINANCING TERMS:** ☐ Seller financing, (C.A.R. Form SFA); ☐ secondary financing, ...$ _____
    (C.A.R. Form PAA, paragraph 4A); ☐ assumed financing (C.A.R. Form PAA, paragraph 4B)
    _____
    _____
  E. **BALANCE OF PURCHASE PRICE** (not including costs of obtaining loans and other closing costs) in the amount of . . .$ _____
    to be deposited with Escrow Holder within sufficient time to close escrow.
  F. **PURCHASE PRICE (TOTAL):** . . . .$ _____
  G. **LOAN APPLICATIONS:** Within **7 (or** ☐ _____ **) Days** After Acceptance, Buyer shall provide Seller a letter from lender or mortgage loan broker stating that, based on a review of Buyer's written application and credit report, Buyer is prequalified or preapproved for the NEW loan specified in 2C above.
  H. **VERIFICATION OF DOWN PAYMENT AND CLOSING COSTS:** Buyer (or Buyer's lender or loan broker pursuant to 2G) shall, within **7 (or** ☐ _____ **) Days** After Acceptance, provide Seller written verification of Buyer's down payment and closing costs.
  I. **LOAN CONTINGENCY REMOVAL: (i)** Within **17 (or** ☐ _____ **) Days** After Acceptance, Buyer shall, as specified in paragraph 14, remove the loan contingency or cancel this Agreement; **OR (ii)** (if checked) ☐ the loan contingency shall remain in effect until the designated loans are funded.
  J. **APPRAISAL CONTINGENCY AND REMOVAL:** This Agreement is (OR, if checked, ☐ is NOT) contingent upon the Property appraising at no less than the specified purchase price. If there is a loan contingency, at the time the loan contingency is removed (or, if checked, ☐ within **17 (or** ☐ _____ **) Days** After Acceptance), Buyer shall, as specified in paragraph 14B(3), remove the appraisal contingency or cancel this Agreement. If there is no loan contingency, Buyer shall, as specified in paragraph 14B(3), remove the appraisal contingency within **17 (or** ☐ _____ **) Days** After Acceptance.
  K. ☐ **NO LOAN CONTINGENCY** (If checked): Obtaining any loan in paragraphs 2C, 2D or elsewhere in this Agreement is NOT a contingency of this Agreement. If Buyer does not obtain the loan and as a result Buyer does not purchase the Property, Seller may be entitled to Buyer's deposit or other legal remedies.
  L. ☐ **ALL CASH OFFER** (If checked): No loan is needed to purchase the Property. Buyer shall, within **7 (or** ☐ _____ **) Days** After Acceptance, provide Seller written verification of sufficient funds to close this transaction.

3. CLOSING AND OCCUPANCY:
  A. Buyer intends (or ☐ does not intend) to occupy the Property as Buyer's primary residence.
  B. **Seller-occupied or vacant property:** Occupancy shall be delivered to Buyer at _____ AM/PM, ☐ on the date of Close Of Escrow; ☐ on _____; or ☐ no later than _____ **Days** After Close Of Escrow. (C.A.R. Form PAA, paragraph 2.) If transfer of title and occupancy do not occur at the same time, Buyer and Seller are advised to: **(i)** enter into a written occupancy agreement; and **(ii)** consult with their insurance and legal advisors.

RPA-CA REVISED 1/06 (PAGE 1 OF 8) Print Date

Buyer's Initials (_____)(_____)
Seller's Initials (_____)(_____)

EQUAL HOUSING OPPORTUNITY

Reviewed by _____ Date _____

CALIFORNIA RESIDENTIAL PURCHASE AGREEMENT (RPA-CA PAGE 1 OF 8)

Property Address: _____   Date: _____

C. **Tenant-occupied property: (i) Property shall be vacant** at least **5 (or ☐ _____) Days** Prior to Close Of Escrow, unless otherwise agreed in writing. **Note to Seller: If you are unable to deliver Property vacant in accordance with rent control and other applicable Law, you may be in breach of this Agreement.**

OR **(ii)** (if checked) ☐ **Tenant to remain in possession.** The attached addendum is incorporated into this Agreement (C.A.R. Form PAA, paragraph 3.);

OR **(iii)** (if checked) ☐ **This Agreement is contingent** upon Buyer and Seller entering into a written agreement regarding occupancy of the Property within the time specified in paragraph 14B(1). If no written agreement is reached within this time, either Buyer or Seller may cancel this Agreement in writing.

D. At Close Of Escrow, Seller assigns to Buyer any assignable warranty rights for items included in the sale and shall provide any available Copies of such warranties. Brokers cannot and will not determine the assignability of any warranties.

E. At Close Of Escrow, unless otherwise agreed in writing, Seller shall provide keys and/or means to operate all locks, mailboxes, security systems, alarms and garage door openers. If Property is a condominium or located in a common interest subdivision, Buyer may be required to pay a deposit to the Homeowners' Association ("HOA") to obtain keys to accessible HOA facilities.

4. **ALLOCATION OF COSTS** (If checked): Unless otherwise specified here, this paragraph only determines who is to pay for the report, inspection, test or service mentioned. If not specified here or elsewhere in this Agreement, the determination of who is to pay for any work recommended or identified by any such report, inspection, test or service shall be by the method specified in paragraph 14B(2).

   A. **WOOD DESTROYING PEST INSPECTION:**

     (1) ☐ Buyer ☐ Seller shall pay for an inspection and report for wood destroying pests and organisms ("Report") which shall be prepared by _____, a registered structural pest control company. The Report shall cover the accessible areas of the main building and attached structures and, if checked: ☐ detached garages and carports, ☐ detached decks, ☐ the following other structures or areas _____. The Report shall not include roof coverings. If Property is a condominium or located in a common interest subdivision, the Report shall include only the separate interest and any exclusive-use areas being transferred and shall not include common areas, unless otherwise agreed. Water tests of shower pans on upper level units may not be performed without consent of the owners of property below the shower.

   OR **(2)** ☐ **(If checked)** The attached addendum (C.A.R. Form WPA) regarding wood destroying pest inspection and allocation of cost is incorporated into this Agreement.

   B. **OTHER INSPECTIONS AND REPORTS:**

     (1) ☐ Buyer ☐ Seller shall pay to have septic or private sewage disposal systems inspected _____.

     (2) ☐ Buyer ☐ Seller shall pay to have domestic wells tested for water potability and productivity _____.

     (3) ☐ Buyer ☐ Seller shall pay for a natural hazard zone disclosure report prepared by _____.

     (4) ☐ Buyer ☐ Seller shall pay for the following inspection or report _____.

     (5) ☐ Buyer ☐ Seller shall pay for the following inspection or report _____.

   C. **GOVERNMENT REQUIREMENTS AND RETROFIT:**

     (1) ☐ Buyer ☐ Seller shall pay for smoke detector installation and/or water heater bracing, if required by Law. Prior to Close Of Escrow, Seller shall provide Buyer a written statement of compliance in accordance with state and local Law, unless exempt.

     (2) ☐ Buyer ☐ Seller shall pay the cost of compliance with any other minimum mandatory government retrofit standards, inspections and reports if required as a condition of closing escrow under any Law. _____.

   D. **ESCROW AND TITLE:**

     (1) ☐ Buyer ☐ Seller shall pay escrow fee _____.
     Escrow Holder shall be _____.

     (2) ☐ Buyer ☐ Seller shall pay for **owner's** title insurance policy specified in paragraph 12E _____.
     Owner's title policy to be issued by _____.
     (Buyer shall pay for any title insurance policy insuring Buyer's **lender**, unless otherwise agreed in writing.)

   E. **OTHER COSTS:**

     (1) ☐ Buyer ☐ Seller shall pay County transfer tax or transfer fee _____.

     (2) ☐ Buyer ☐ Seller shall pay City transfer tax or transfer fee _____.

     (3) ☐ Buyer ☐ Seller shall pay HOA transfer fee _____.

     (4) ☐ Buyer ☐ Seller shall pay HOA document preparation fees _____.

     (5) ☐ Buyer ☐ Seller shall pay the cost, not to exceed $ _____, of a one-year home warranty plan, issued by _____
     with the following optional coverage: _____.

     (6) ☐ Buyer ☐ Seller shall pay for _____.

     (7) ☐ Buyer ☐ Seller shall pay for _____.

5. **STATUTORY DISCLOSURES (INCLUDING LEAD-BASED PAINT HAZARD DISCLOSURES) AND CANCELLATION RIGHTS:**

   A. (1) Seller shall, within the time specified in paragraph 14A, deliver to Buyer, if required by Law: (i) Federal Lead-Based Paint Disclosures and pamphlet ("Lead Disclosures"); and (ii) disclosures or notices required by sections 1102 et. seq. and 1103 et. seq. of the California Civil Code ("Statutory Disclosures"). Statutory Disclosures include, but are not limited to, a Real Estate Transfer Disclosure Statement ("TDS"), Natural Hazard Disclosure Statement ("NHD"), notice or actual knowledge of release of illegal controlled substance, notice of special tax and/or assessments (or, if allowed, substantially equivalent notice regarding the Mello-Roos Community Facilities Act and Improvement Bond Act of 1915) and, if Seller has actual knowledge, an industrial use and military ordnance location disclosure (C.A.R. Form SSD).

     (2) Buyer shall, within the time specified in paragraph 14B(1), return Signed Copies of the Statutory and Lead Disclosures to Seller.

     (3) In the event Seller, prior to Close Of Escrow, becomes aware of adverse conditions materially affecting the Property, or any material inaccuracy in disclosures, information or representations previously provided to Buyer of which Buyer is otherwise unaware, Seller shall promptly provide a subsequent or amended disclosure or notice, in writing, covering those items. **However, a subsequent or amended disclosure shall not be required for conditions and material inaccuracies disclosed in reports ordered and paid for by Buyer.**

Buyer's Initials (_____)(_____)
Seller's Initials (_____)(_____)

RPA-CA REVISED 1/06 (PAGE 2 OF 8)

Reviewed by _____ Date _____

EQUAL HOUSING OPPORTUNITY

CALIFORNIA RESIDENTIAL PURCHASE AGREEMENT (RPA-CA PAGE 2 OF 8)

Property Address: _____ Date: _____

(4) If any disclosure or notice specified in 5A(1), or subsequent or amended disclosure or notice is delivered to Buyer after the offer is Signed, Buyer shall have the right to cancel this Agreement within **3 Days** After delivery in person, or **5 Days** After delivery by deposit in the mail, by giving written notice of cancellation to Seller or Seller's agent. (Lead Disclosures sent by mail must be sent certified mail or better.)

(5) Note to Buyer and Seller: Waiver of Statutory and Lead Disclosures is prohibited by Law.

B. NATURAL AND ENVIRONMENTAL HAZARDS: Within the time specified in paragraph 14A, Seller shall, if required by Law: **(i)** deliver to Buyer earthquake guides (and questionnaire) and environmental hazards booklet; **(ii)** even if exempt from the obligation to provide a NHD, disclose if the Property is located in a Special Flood Hazard Area; Potential Flooding (Inundation) Area; Very High Fire Hazard Zone; State Fire Responsibility Area; Earthquake Fault Zone; Seismic Hazard Zone; and **(iii)** disclose any other zone as required by Law and provide any other information required for those zones.

C. DATA BASE DISCLOSURE: Notice: Pursuant to Section 290.46 of the Penal Code, information about specified registered sex offenders is made available to the public via an Internet Web site maintained by the Department of Justice at www.meganslaw.ca.gov. Depending on an offender's criminal history, this information will include either the address at which the offender resides or the community of residence and ZIP Code in which he or she resides. (Neither Seller nor Brokers are required to check this website. If Buyer wants further information, Broker recommends that Buyer obtain information from this website during Buyer's inspection contingency period. Brokers do not have expertise in this area.)

6. CONDOMINIUM/PLANNED UNIT DEVELOPMENT DISCLOSURES:

A. SELLER HAS: 7 (or ☐ _____) Days After Acceptance to disclose to Buyer whether the Property is a condominium, or is located in a planned unit development or other common interest subdivision (C.A.R. Form SSD).

B. If the Property is a condominium or is located in a planned unit development or other common interest subdivision, Seller has **3 (or ☐ _____) Days** After Acceptance to request from the HOA (C.A.R. Form HOA): **(i)** Copies of any documents required by Law; **(ii)** disclosure of any pending or anticipated claim or litigation by or against the HOA; **(iii)** a statement containing the location and number of designated parking and storage spaces; **(iv)** Copies of the most recent 12 months of HOA minutes for regular and special meetings; and **(v)** the names and contact information of all HOAs governing the Property (collectively, "CI Disclosures"). Seller shall itemize and deliver to Buyer all CI Disclosures received from the HOA and any CI Disclosures in Seller's possession. Buyer's approval of CI Disclosures is a contingency of this Agreement as specified in paragraph 14B(3).

7. CONDITIONS AFFECTING PROPERTY:

A. Unless otherwise agreed: **(i) the Property is sold (a) in its PRESENT physical condition as of the date of Acceptance and (b) subject to Buyer's Investigation rights; (ii)** the Property, including pool, spa, landscaping and grounds, is to be maintained in substantially the same condition as on the date of Acceptance; and **(iii)** all debris and personal property not included in the sale shall be removed by Close Of Escrow.

B. SELLER SHALL, within the time specified in paragraph 14A, DISCLOSE KNOWN MATERIAL FACTS AND DEFECTS affecting the Property, including known insurance claims within the past five years, AND MAKE OTHER DISCLOSURES REQUIRED BY LAW (C.A.R. Form SSD).

C. NOTE TO BUYER: You are strongly advised to conduct investigations of the entire Property in order to determine its present condition since Seller may not be aware of all defects affecting the Property or other factors that you consider important. Property improvements may not be built according to code, in compliance with current Law, or have had permits issued.

D. NOTE TO SELLER: Buyer has the right to inspect the Property and, as specified in paragraph 14B, based upon information discovered in those inspections: **(i)** cancel this Agreement; or **(ii)** request that you make Repairs or take other action.

8. ITEMS INCLUDED AND EXCLUDED:

A. NOTE TO BUYER AND SELLER: Items listed as included or excluded in the MLS, flyers or marketing materials are **not** included in the purchase price or excluded from the sale unless specified in 8B or C.

B. ITEMS INCLUDED IN SALE:

(1) All EXISTING fixtures and fittings that are attached to the Property;

(2) Existing electrical, mechanical, lighting, plumbing and heating fixtures, ceiling fans, fireplace inserts, gas logs and grates, solar systems, built-in appliances, window and door screens, awnings, shutters, window coverings, attached floor coverings, television antennas, satellite dishes, private integrated telephone systems, air coolers/conditioners, pool/spa equipment, garage door openers/remote controls, mailbox, in-ground landscaping, trees/shrubs, water softeners, water purifiers, security systems/alarms; and

(3) The following items: _____
_____

(4) Seller represents that all items included in the purchase price, unless otherwise specified, are owned by Seller.

(5) All items included shall be transferred free of liens and without Seller warranty.

C. ITEMS EXCLUDED FROM SALE: _____
_____

9. BUYER'S INVESTIGATION OF PROPERTY AND MATTERS AFFECTING PROPERTY:

A. Buyer's acceptance of the condition of, and any other matter affecting the Property, is a contingency of this Agreement as specified in this paragraph and paragraph 14B. Within the time specified in paragraph 14B(1), Buyer shall have the right, at Buyer's expense unless otherwise agreed, to conduct inspections, investigations, tests, surveys and other studies ("Buyer Investigations"), including, but not limited to, the right to: **(i)** inspect for lead-based paint and other lead-based paint hazards; **(ii)** inspect for wood destroying pests and organisms; **(iii)** review the registered sex offender database; **(iv)** confirm the insurability of Buyer and the Property; and **(v)** satisfy Buyer as to any matter specified in the attached Buyer's Inspection Advisory (C.A.R. Form BIA). Without Seller's prior written consent, Buyer shall neither make nor cause to be made: **(i)** invasive or destructive Buyer Investigations; or **(ii)** inspections by any governmental building or zoning inspector or government employee, unless required by Law.

B. Buyer shall complete Buyer Investigations and, as specified in paragraph 14B, remove the contingency or cancel this Agreement. Buyer shall give Seller, at no cost, complete Copies of all Buyer Investigation reports obtained by Buyer. Seller shall make the Property available for all Buyer Investigations. Seller shall have water, gas, electricity and all operable pilot lights on for Buyer's Investigations and through the date possession is made available to Buyer.

Buyer's Initials (_____)(_____)
Seller's Initials (_____)(_____)

Reviewed by _____ Date _____

EQUAL HOUSING OPPORTUNITY

Property Address: _____ Date: _____

10. **REPAIRS:** Repairs shall be completed prior to final verification of condition unless otherwise agreed in writing. Repairs to be performed at Seller's expense may be performed by Seller or through others, provided that the work complies with applicable Law, including governmental permit, inspection and approval requirements. Repairs shall be performed in a good, skillful manner with materials of quality and appearance comparable to existing materials. It is understood that exact restoration of appearance or cosmetic items following all Repairs may not be possible. Seller shall: **(i)** obtain receipts for Repairs performed by others; **(ii)** prepare a written statement indicating the Repairs performed by Seller and the date of such Repairs; and **(iii)** provide Copies of receipts and statements to Buyer prior to final verification of condition.

11. **BUYER INDEMNITY AND SELLER PROTECTION FOR ENTRY UPON PROPERTY:** Buyer shall: **(i)** keep the Property free and clear of liens; **(ii)** Repair all damage arising from Buyer Investigations; and **(iii)** indemnify and hold Seller harmless from all resulting liability, claims, demands, damages and costs. Buyer shall carry, or Buyer shall require anyone acting on Buyer's behalf to carry, policies of liability, workers' compensation and other applicable insurance, defending and protecting Seller from liability for any injuries to persons or property occurring during any Buyer Investigations or work done on the Property at Buyer's direction prior to Close Of Escrow. Seller is advised that certain protections may be afforded Seller by recording a "Notice of Non-responsibility" (C.A.R. Form NNR) for Buyer Investigations and work done on the Property at Buyer's direction. Buyer's obligations under this paragraph shall survive the termination of this Agreement.

12. **TITLE AND VESTING:**
    A. Within the time specified in paragraph 14, Buyer shall be provided a current preliminary (title) report, which is only an offer by the title insurer to issue a policy of title insurance and may not contain every item affecting title. Buyer's review of the preliminary report and any other matters which may affect title are a contingency of this Agreement as specified in paragraph 14B.
    B. Title is taken in its present condition subject to all encumbrances, easements, covenants, conditions, restrictions, rights and other matters, whether of record or not, as of the date of Acceptance except: **(i)** monetary liens of record unless Buyer is assuming those obligations or taking the Property subject to those obligations; and **(ii)** those matters which Seller has agreed to remove in writing.
    C. Within the time specified in paragraph 14A, Seller has a duty to disclose to Buyer all matters known to Seller affecting title, whether of record or not.
    D. At Close Of Escrow, Buyer shall receive a grant deed conveying title (or, for stock cooperative or long-term lease, an assignment of stock certificate or of Seller's leasehold interest), including oil, mineral and water rights if currently owned by Seller. Title shall vest as designated in Buyer's supplemental escrow instructions. THE MANNER OF TAKING TITLE MAY HAVE SIGNIFICANT LEGAL AND TAX CONSEQUENCES. CONSULT AN APPROPRIATE PROFESSIONAL.
    E. Buyer shall receive a CLTA/ALTA Homeowner's Policy of Title Insurance. A title company, at Buyer's request, can provide information about the availability, desirability, coverage, and cost of various title insurance coverages and endorsements. If Buyer desires title coverage other than that required by this paragraph, Buyer shall instruct Escrow Holder in writing and pay any increase in cost.

13. **SALE OF BUYER'S PROPERTY:**
    A. This Agreement is NOT contingent upon the sale of any property owned by Buyer.
    OR B. ☐ (If checked): The attached addendum (C.A.R. Form COP) regarding the contingency for the sale of property owned by Buyer is incorporated into this Agreement.

14. **TIME PERIODS; REMOVAL OF CONTINGENCIES; CANCELLATION RIGHTS: The following time periods may only be extended, altered, modified or changed by mutual written agreement. Any removal of contingencies or cancellation under this paragraph must be in writing (C.A.R. Form CR).**
    A. **SELLER HAS: 7 (or ☐ _____) Days** After Acceptance to deliver to Buyer all reports, disclosures and information for which Seller is responsible under paragraphs 4, 5A and B, 6A, 7B and 12.
    B. **(1) BUYER HAS: 17 (or ☐ _____) Days** After Acceptance, unless otherwise agreed in writing, to:
        (i) complete all Buyer Investigations; approve all disclosures, reports and other applicable information, which Buyer receives from Seller; and approve all matters affecting the Property (including lead-based paint and lead-based paint hazards as well as other information specified in paragraph 5 and insurability of Buyer and the Property); and
        (ii) return to Seller Signed Copies of Statutory and Lead Disclosures delivered by Seller in accordance with paragraph 5A.
    (2) Within the time specified in 14B(1), Buyer may request that Seller make repairs or take any other action regarding the Property (C.A.R. Form RR). Seller has no obligation to agree to or respond to Buyer's requests.
    (3) By the end of the time specified in 14B(1) (or 2I for loan contingency or 2J for appraisal contingency), Buyer shall, in writing, remove the applicable contingency (C.A.R. Form CR) or cancel this Agreement. However, if **(i)** government-mandated inspections/ reports required as a condition of closing; or **(ii)** Common Interest Disclosures pursuant to paragraph 6B are not made within the time specified in 14A, then Buyer has **5 (or ☐ _____) Days** After receipt of any such items, or the time specified in 14B(1), whichever is later, to remove the applicable contingency or cancel this Agreement in writing.
    C. **CONTINUATION OF CONTINGENCY OR CONTRACTUAL OBLIGATION; SELLER RIGHT TO CANCEL:**
        (1) Seller right to Cancel; Buyer Contingencies: Seller, after first giving Buyer a Notice to Buyer to Perform (as specified below), may cancel this Agreement in writing and authorize return of Buyer's deposit if, by the time specified in this Agreement, Buyer does not remove in writing the applicable contingency or cancel this Agreement. Once all contingencies have been removed, failure of either Buyer or Seller to close escrow on time may be a breach of this Agreement.
        (2) Continuation of Contingency: Even after the expiration of the time specified in 14B, Buyer retains the right to make requests to Seller, remove in writing the applicable contingency or cancel this Agreement until Seller cancels pursuant to 14C(1). Once Seller receives Buyer's written removal of all contingencies, Seller may not cancel this Agreement pursuant to 14C(1).
        (3) Seller right to Cancel; Buyer Contract Obligations: Seller, after first giving Buyer a Notice to Buyer to Perform (as specified below), may cancel this Agreement in writing and authorize return of Buyer's deposit for any of the following reasons: **(i)** if Buyer fails to deposit funds as required by 2A or 2B; **(ii)** if the funds deposited pursuant to 2A or 2B are not good when deposited; **(iii)** if Buyer fails to provide a letter as required by 2G; **(iv)** if Buyer fails to provide verification as required by 2H or 2L; **(v)** if Seller reasonably disapproves of the verification provided by 2H or 2L; **(vi)** if Buyer fails to return Statutory and Lead Disclosures as required by paragraph 5A(2); or **(vii)** if Buyer fails to sign or initial a separate liquidated damage form for an increased deposit as required by paragraph 16. **Seller is not required to give Buyer a Notice to Perform regarding Close of Escrow.**
        (4) Notice To Buyer To Perform: The Notice to Buyer to Perform (C.A.R. Form NBP) shall: **(i)** be in writing; **(ii)** be signed by Seller; and **(iii)** give Buyer at least 24 (or ☐ _____) hours (or until the time specified in the applicable paragraph, whichever occurs last) to take the applicable action. A Notice to Buyer to Perform may not be given any earlier than **2 Days** Prior to the expiration of the applicable time for Buyer to remove a contingency or cancel this Agreement or meet a 14C(3) obligation.

Buyer's Initials (_____)(_____)
Seller's Initials (_____)(_____)

Reviewed by _____ Date _____

Property Address: _____   Date: _____

D. EFFECT OF BUYER'S REMOVAL OF CONTINGENCIES : If Buyer removes, in writing, any contingency or cancellation rights, unless otherwise specified in a separate written agreement between Buyer and Seller, Buyer shall conclusively be deemed to have: **(i)** completed all Buyer Investigations, and review of reports and other applicable information and disclosures pertaining to that contingency or cancellation right; **(ii)** elected to proceed with the transaction; and **(iii)** assumed all liability, responsibility and expense for Repairs or corrections pertaining to that contingency or cancellation right, or for inability to obtain financing.

E. EFFECT OF CANCELLATION ON DEPOSITS: If Buyer or Seller gives written notice of cancellation pursuant to rights duly exercised under the terms of this Agreement, Buyer and Seller agree to Sign mutual instructions to cancel the sale and escrow and release deposits to the party entitled to the funds, less fees and costs incurred by that party. Fees and costs may be payable to service providers and vendors for services and products provided during escrow. **Release of funds will require mutual Signed release instructions from Buyer and Seller, judicial decision or arbitration award. A party may be subject to a civil penalty of up to $1,000 for refusal to sign such instructions if no good faith dispute exists as to who is entitled to the deposited funds (Civil Code §1057.3).**

15. **FINAL VERIFICATION OF CONDITION:** Buyer shall have the right to make a final inspection of the Property within **5 (or _____) Days** Prior to Close Of Escrow, NOT AS A CONTINGENCY OF THE SALE, but solely to confirm: **(i)** the Property is maintained pursuant to paragraph 7A; **(ii)** Repairs have been completed as agreed; and **(iii)** Seller has complied with Seller's other obligations under this Agreement.

16. **LIQUIDATED DAMAGES: If Buyer fails to complete this purchase because of Buyer's default, Seller shall retain, as liquidated damages, the deposit actually paid. If the Property is a dwelling with no more than four units, one of which Buyer intends to occupy, then the amount retained shall be no more than 3% of the purchase price. Any excess shall be returned to Buyer. Release of funds will require mutual, Signed release instructions from both Buyer and Seller, judicial decision or arbitration award. BUYER AND SELLER SHALL SIGN A SEPARATE LIQUIDATED DAMAGES PROVISION FOR ANY INCREASED DEPOSIT. (C.A.R. FORM RID)**

Buyer's Initials _____/_____	Seller's Initials _____/_____

17. **DISPUTE RESOLUTION:**

A. MEDIATION: Buyer and Seller agree to mediate any dispute or claim arising between them out of this Agreement, or any resulting transaction, before resorting to arbitration or court action. Paragraphs 17B(2) and (3) below apply to mediation whether or not the Arbitration provision is initialed. Mediation fees, if any, shall be divided equally among the parties involved. If, for any dispute or claim to which this paragraph applies, any party commences an action without first attempting to resolve the matter through mediation, or refuses to mediate after a request has been made, then that party shall not be entitled to recover attorney fees, even if they would otherwise be available to that party in any such action. THIS MEDIATION PROVISION APPLIES WHETHER OR NOT THE ARBITRATION PROVISION IS INITIALED.

B. ARBITRATION OF DISPUTES: (1) Buyer and Seller agree that any dispute or claim in Law or equity arising between them out of this Agreement or any resulting transaction, which is not settled through mediation, shall be decided by neutral, binding arbitration, including and subject to paragraphs 17B(2) and (3) below. The arbitrator shall be a retired judge or justice, or an attorney with at least 5 years of residential real estate Law experience, unless the parties mutually agree to a different arbitrator, who shall render an award in accordance with substantive California Law. The parties shall have the right to discovery in accordance with California Code of Civil Procedure §1283.05. In all other respects, the arbitration shall be conducted in accordance with Title 9 of Part III of the California Code of Civil Procedure. Judgment upon the award of the arbitrator(s) may be entered into any court having jurisdiction. Interpretation of this agreement to arbitrate shall be governed by the Federal Arbitration Act.
(2) EXCLUSIONS FROM MEDIATION AND ARBITRATION: The following matters are excluded from mediation and arbitration: (i) a judicial or non-judicial foreclosure or other action or proceeding to enforce a deed of trust, mortgage or installment land sale contract as defined in California Civil Code §2985; (ii) an unlawful detainer action; (iii) the filing or enforcement of a mechanic's lien; and (iv) any matter that is within the jurisdiction of a probate, small claims or bankruptcy court. The filing of a court action to enable the recording of a notice of pending action, for order of attachment, receivership, injunction, or other provisional remedies, shall not constitute a waiver of the mediation and arbitration provisions.
(3) BROKERS: Buyer and Seller agree to mediate and arbitrate disputes or claims involving either or both Brokers, consistent with 17A and B, provided either or both Brokers shall have agreed to such mediation or arbitration prior to, or within a reasonable time after, the dispute or claim is presented to Brokers. Any election by either or both Brokers to participate in mediation or arbitration shall not result in Brokers being deemed parties to the Agreement.

"NOTICE: BY INITIALING IN THE SPACE BELOW YOU ARE AGREEING TO HAVE ANY DISPUTE ARISING OUT OF THE MATTERS INCLUDED IN THE 'ARBITRATION OF DISPUTES' PROVISION DECIDED BY NEUTRAL ARBITRATION AS PROVIDED BY CALIFORNIA LAW AND YOU ARE GIVING UP ANY RIGHTS YOU MIGHT POSSESS TO HAVE THE DISPUTE LITIGATED IN A COURT OR JURY TRIAL. BY INITIALING IN THE SPACE BELOW YOU ARE GIVING UP YOUR JUDICIAL RIGHTS TO DISCOVERY AND APPEAL, UNLESS THOSE RIGHTS ARE SPECIFICALLY INCLUDED IN THE 'ARBITRATION OF DISPUTES' PROVISION. IF YOU REFUSE TO SUBMIT TO ARBITRATION AFTER AGREEING TO THIS PROVISION, YOU MAY BE COMPELLED TO ARBITRATE UNDER THE AUTHORITY OF THE CALIFORNIA CODE OF CIVIL PROCEDURE. YOUR AGREEMENT TO THIS ARBITRATION PROVISION IS VOLUNTARY."

"WE HAVE READ AND UNDERSTAND THE FOREGOING AND AGREE TO SUBMIT DISPUTES ARISING OUT OF THE MATTERS INCLUDED IN THE 'ARBITRATION OF DISPUTES' PROVISION TO NEUTRAL ARBITRATION."

Buyer's Initials _____/_____	Seller's Initials _____/_____

Buyer's Initials (_____)(_____)
Seller's Initials (_____)(_____)

RPA-CA REVISED 1/06 (PAGE 5 OF 8)

Reviewed by _____ Date _____

EQUAL HOUSING
OPPORTUNITY

CALIFORNIA RESIDENTIAL PURCHASE AGREEMENT (RPA-CA PAGE 5 OF 8)

Property Address: _____   Date: _____

18. **PRORATIONS OF PROPERTY TAXES AND OTHER ITEMS:** Unless otherwise agreed in writing, the following items shall be PAID CURRENT and prorated between Buyer and Seller as of Close Of Escrow: real property taxes and assessments, interest, rents, HOA regular, special, and emergency dues and assessments imposed prior to Close Of Escrow, premiums on insurance assumed by Buyer, payments on bonds and assessments assumed by Buyer, and payments on Mello-Roos and other Special Assessment District bonds and assessments that are now a lien. The following items shall be assumed by Buyer WITHOUT CREDIT toward the purchase price: prorated payments on Mello-Roos and other Special Assessment District bonds and assessments and HOA special assessments that are now a lien but not yet due. Property will be reassessed upon change of ownership. Any supplemental tax bills shall be paid as follows: **(i)** for periods after Close Of Escrow, by Buyer; and **(ii)** for periods prior to Close Of Escrow, by Seller. TAX BILLS ISSUED AFTER CLOSE OF ESCROW SHALL BE HANDLED DIRECTLY BETWEEN BUYER AND SELLER. Prorations shall be made based on a 30-day month.

19. **WITHHOLDING TAXES:** Seller and Buyer agree to execute any instrument, affidavit, statement or instruction reasonably necessary to comply with federal (FIRPTA) and California withholding Law, if required (C.A.R. Forms AS and AB).

20. **MULTIPLE LISTING SERVICE ("MLS"):** Brokers are authorized to report to the MLS a pending sale and, upon Close Of Escrow, the terms of this transaction to be published and disseminated to persons and entities authorized to use the information on terms approved by the MLS.

21. **EQUAL HOUSING OPPORTUNITY:** The Property is sold in compliance with federal, state and local anti-discrimination Laws.

22. **ATTORNEY FEES:** In any action, proceeding, or arbitration between Buyer and Seller arising out of this Agreement, the prevailing Buyer or Seller shall be entitled to reasonable attorney fees and costs from the non-prevailing Buyer or Seller, except as provided in paragraph 17A.

23. **SELECTION OF SERVICE PROVIDERS:** If Brokers refer Buyer or Seller to persons, vendors, or service or product providers ("Providers"), Brokers do not guarantee the performance of any Providers. Buyer and Seller may select ANY Providers of their own choosing.

24. **TIME OF ESSENCE; ENTIRE CONTRACT; CHANGES:** Time is of the essence. All understandings between the parties are incorporated in this Agreement. Its terms are intended by the parties as a final, complete and exclusive expression of their Agreement with respect to its subject matter, and may not be contradicted by evidence of any prior agreement or contemporaneous oral agreement. If any provision of this Agreement is held to be ineffective or invalid, the remaining provisions will nevertheless be given full force and effect. **Neither this Agreement nor any provision in it may be extended, amended, modified, altered or changed, except in writing Signed by Buyer and Seller.**

25. **OTHER TERMS AND CONDITIONS,** including attached supplements:
    A. ☑ Buyer's Inspection Advisory (C.A.R. Form BIA) _____
    B. ☐ Purchase Agreement Addendum (C.A.R. Form PAA paragraph numbers: _____) _____
    C. ☐ Statewide Buyer and Seller Advisory (C.A.R. Form SBSA) _____
    D. _____

26. **DEFINITIONS:** As used in this Agreement:
    A. **"Acceptance"** means the time the offer or final counter offer is accepted in writing by a party and is delivered to and personally received by the other party or that party's authorized agent in accordance with the terms of this offer or a final counter offer.
    B. **"Agreement"** means the terms and conditions of this accepted California Residential Purchase Agreement and any accepted counter offers and addenda.
    C. **"C.A.R. Form"** means the specific form referenced or another comparable form agreed to by the parties.
    D. **"Close Of Escrow"** means the date the grant deed, or other evidence of transfer of title, is recorded. If the scheduled close of escrow falls on a Saturday, Sunday or legal holiday, then close of escrow shall be the next business day after the scheduled close of escrow date.
    E. **"Copy"** means copy by any means including photocopy, NCR, facsimile and electronic.
    F. **"Days"** means calendar days, unless otherwise required by Law.
    G. **"Days After"** means the specified number of calendar days after the occurrence of the event specified, not counting the calendar date on which the specified event occurs, and ending at 11:59PM on the final day.
    H. **"Days Prior"** means the specified number of calendar days before the occurrence of the event specified, not counting the calendar date on which the specified event is scheduled to occur.
    I. **"Electronic Copy" or "Electronic Signature"** means, as applicable, an electronic copy or signature complying with California Law. Buyer and Seller agree that electronic means will not be used by either party to modify or alter the content or integrity of this Agreement without the knowledge and consent of the other.
    J. **"Law"** means any law, code, statute, ordinance, regulation, rule or order, which is adopted by a controlling city, county, state or federal legislative, judicial or executive body or agency.
    K. **"Notice to Buyer to Perform"** means a document (C.A.R. Form NBP), which shall be in writing and Signed by Seller and shall give Buyer at least 24 hours **(or as otherwise specified in paragraph 14C(4))** to remove a contingency or perform as applicable.
    L. **"Repairs"** means any repairs (including pest control), alterations, replacements, modifications or retrofitting of the Property provided for under this Agreement.
    M. **"Signed"** means either a handwritten or electronic signature on an original document, Copy or any counterpart.
    N. **Singular and Plural** terms each include the other, when appropriate.

Buyer's Initials (_____)(_____)
Seller's Initials (_____)(_____)

Reviewed by _____ Date _____

EQUAL HOUSING OPPORTUNITY

CALIFORNIA RESIDENTIAL PURCHASE AGREEMENT (RPA-CA PAGE 6 OF 8)

Property Address: _____   Date: _____

27. AGENCY:

    A. DISCLOSURE: Buyer and Seller each acknowledge prior receipt of C.A.R. Form AD "Disclosure Regarding Real Estate Agency Relationships."

    B. POTENTIALLY COMPETING BUYERS AND SELLERS: Buyer and Seller each acknowledge receipt of a disclosure of the possibility of multiple representation by the Broker representing that principal. This disclosure may be part of a listing agreement, buyer-broker agreement or separate document (C.A.R. Form DA). Buyer understands that Broker representing Buyer may also represent other potential buyers, who may consider, make offers on or ultimately acquire the Property. Seller understands that Broker representing Seller may also represent other sellers with competing properties of interest to this Buyer.

    C. CONFIRMATION: The following agency relationships are hereby confirmed for this transaction:
Listing Agent _____ (Print Firm Name) is the agent of (check one): ☐ the Seller exclusively; or ☐ both the Buyer and Seller.
Selling Agent _____ (Print Firm Name) (if not same as Listing Agent) is the agent of (check one): ☐ the Buyer exclusively; or ☐ the Seller exclusively; or ☐ both the Buyer and Seller. Real Estate Brokers are not parties to the Agreement between Buyer and Seller.

28. JOINT ESCROW INSTRUCTIONS TO ESCROW HOLDER:

    A. The following paragraphs, or applicable portions thereof, of this Agreement constitute the joint escrow instructions of Buyer and Seller to Escrow Holder, which Escrow Holder is to use along with any related counter offers and addenda, and any additional mutual instructions to close the escrow: 1, 2, 4, 12, 13B, 14E, 18, 19, 24, 25B and 25D, 26, 28, 29, 32A, 33 and paragraph D of the section titled Real Estate Brokers on page 8. If a Copy of the separate compensation agreement(s) provided for in paragraph 29 or 32A, or paragraph D of the section titled Real Estate Brokers on page 8 is deposited with Escrow Holder by Broker, Escrow Holder shall accept such agreement(s) and pay out from Buyer's or Seller's funds, or both, as applicable, the Broker's compensation provided for in such agreement(s). The terms and conditions of this Agreement not set forth in the specified paragraphs are additional matters for the information of Escrow Holder, but about which Escrow Holder need not be concerned. Buyer and Seller will receive Escrow Holder's general provisions directly from Escrow Holder and will execute such provisions upon Escrow Holder's request. To the extent the general provisions are inconsistent or conflict with this Agreement, the general provisions will control as to the duties and obligations of Escrow Holder only. Buyer and Seller will execute additional instructions, documents and forms provided by Escrow Holder that are reasonably necessary to close the escrow.

    B. A Copy of this Agreement shall be delivered to Escrow Holder within **3** business days after Acceptance (or ☐ _____). Buyer and Seller authorize Escrow Holder to accept and rely on Copies and Signatures as defined in this Agreement as originals, to open escrow and for other purposes of escrow. The validity of this Agreement as between Buyer and Seller is not affected by whether or when Escrow Holder Signs this Agreement.

    C. Brokers are a party to the escrow for the sole purpose of compensation pursuant to paragraphs 29, 32A and paragraph D of the section titled Real Estate Brokers on page 8. Buyer and Seller irrevocably assign to Brokers compensation specified in paragraphs 29 and 32A, respectively, and irrevocably instruct Escrow Holder to disburse those funds to Brokers at Close Of Escrow or pursuant to any other mutually executed cancellation agreement. Compensation instructions can be amended or revoked only with the written consent of Brokers. Escrow Holder shall immediately notify Brokers: **(i)** if Buyer's initial or any additional deposit is not made pursuant to this Agreement, or is not good at time of deposit with Escrow Holder; or **(ii)** if Buyer and Seller instruct Escrow Holder to cancel escrow.

    D. A Copy of any amendment that affects any paragraph of this Agreement for which Escrow Holder is responsible shall be delivered to Escrow Holder within **2** business days after mutual execution of the amendment.

29. BROKER COMPENSATION FROM BUYER: If applicable, upon Close Of Escrow, **Buyer** agrees to pay compensation to Broker as specified in a separate written agreement between Buyer and Broker.

30. TERMS AND CONDITIONS OF OFFER:

This is an offer to purchase the Property on the above terms and conditions. All paragraphs with spaces for initials by Buyer and Seller are incorporated in this Agreement only if initialed by all parties. If at least one but not all parties initial, a counter offer is required until agreement is reached. Seller has the right to continue to offer the Property for sale and to accept any other offer at any time prior to notification of Acceptance. Buyer has read and acknowledges receipt of a Copy of the offer and agrees to the above confirmation of agency relationships. If this offer is accepted and Buyer subsequently defaults, Buyer may be responsible for payment of Brokers' compensation. This Agreement and any supplement, addendum or modification, including any Copy, may be Signed in two or more counterparts, all of which shall constitute one and the same writing.

RPA-CA REVISED 1/06 (PAGE 7 OF 8)

Buyer's Initials (_____)(_____)
Seller's Initials (_____)(_____)

Reviewed by _____ Date _____

EQUAL HOUSING
OPPORTUNITY

CALIFORNIA RESIDENTIAL PURCHASE AGREEMENT (RPA-CA PAGE 7 OF 8)

Property Address: _____   Date: _____

31. EXPIRATION OF OFFER: This offer shall be deemed revoked and the deposit shall be returned unless the offer is Signed by Seller and a Copy of the Signed offer is personally received by Buyer, or by _____, who is authorized to receive it by 5:00 PM on the third Day after this offer is signed by Buyer (or, if checked, ☐ by _____ (date), at _____ AM/PM).

Date _____   Date _____

BUYER _____   BUYER _____

_____   _____

(Print name)   **(Print name)**

_____

(Address)

32. BROKER COMPENSATION FROM SELLER:
   A. Upon Close Of Escrow, **Seller** agrees to pay compensation to Broker as specified in a separate written agreement between Seller and Broker.
   B. If escrow does not close, compensation is payable as specified in that separate written agreement.

33. ACCEPTANCE OF OFFER: Seller warrants that Seller is the owner of the Property, or has the authority to execute this Agreement. Seller accepts the above offer, agrees to sell the Property on the above terms and conditions, and agrees to the above confirmation of agency relationships. Seller has read and acknowledges receipt of a Copy of this Agreement, and authorizes Broker to deliver a Signed Copy to Buyer.
   ☐ (If checked) **SUBJECT TO ATTACHED COUNTER OFFER, DATED** _____.

Date _____   Date _____

SELLER _____   SELLER _____

_____   _____

(Print name)   **(Print name)**

_____

(Address)

(__/__)   **CONFIRMATION OF ACCEPTANCE:** A Copy of Signed Acceptance was personally received by Buyer or Buyer's authorized
(Initials)   agent on (date) _____ at _____ AM/PM. **A binding Agreement is created when a Copy or Buyer's authorized agent whether or not confirmed in this document. Completion of this confirmation is not legally required in order to create a binding Agreement; it is solely intended to evidence the date that Confirmation of Acceptance has occurred.**

REAL ESTATE BROKERS:
A. Real Estate Brokers are not parties to the Agreement between Buyer and Seller.
B. Agency relationships are confirmed as stated in paragraph 27.
C. If specified in paragraph 2A, Agent who submitted the offer for Buyer acknowledges receipt of deposit.
D. COOPERATING BROKER COMPENSATION: Listing Broker agrees to pay Cooperating Broker **(Selling Firm)** and Cooperating Broker agrees to accept, out of Listing Broker's proceeds in escrow: **(i)** the amount specified in the MLS, provided Cooperating Broker is a Participant of the MLS in which the Property is offered for sale or a reciprocal MLS; or **(ii)** ☐ (if checked) the amount specified in a separate written agreement (C.A.R. Form CBC) between Listing Broker and Cooperating Broker.

Real Estate Broker (Selling Firm) _____   License # _____
By _____ License # _____ City _____ Date _____
Address _____ City _____ State _____ Zip _____
Telephone _____ Fax _____ E-mail _____

Real Estate Broker (Listing Firm) _____   License # _____
By _____ License # _____ Date _____
Address _____ City _____ State _____ Zip _____
Telephone _____ Fax _____ E-mail _____

ESCROW HOLDER ACKNOWLEDGMENT:
Escrow Holder acknowledges receipt of a Copy of this Agreement, (if checked, ☐ a deposit in the amount of $ _____), counter offer numbers _____ and _____, and agrees to act as Escrow Holder subject to paragraph 28 of this Agreement, any supplemental escrow instructions and the terms of Escrow Holder's general provisions.

Escrow Holder is advised that the date of Confirmation of Acceptance of the Agreement as between Buyer and Seller is _____

Escrow Holder _____ Escrow # _____
By _____ Date _____
Address _____
Phone/Fax/E-mail _____
Escrow Holder is licensed by the California Department of ☐ Corporations, ☐ Insurance, ☐ Real Estate. License # _____

(__/__)   **REJECTION OF OFFER:** No counter offer is being made. This offer was reviewed and rejected by Seller on
(Seller's Initials) _____ (Date)

Published and Distributed by:
REAL ESTATE BUSINESS SERVICES, INC.
a subsidiary of the California Association of REALTORS®
525 South Virgil Avenue, Los Angeles, California 90020

Reviewed by _____ Date _____

RPA-CA REVISED 1/06 (PAGE 8 OF 8)

Multistate Adjustable Rate Note

ADJUSTABLE RATE NOTE
(LIBOR One-Year Index (As Published In *The Wall Street Journal*)
Rate Caps–Fixed Rate Conversion Option)

THIS NOTE CONTAINS PROVISIONS ALLOWING FOR CHANGES IN MY INTEREST RATE AND MY MONTHLY PAYMENT. THIS NOTE LIMITS THE AMOUNT MY ADJUSTABLE INTEREST RATE CAN CHANGE AT ANY ONE TIME AND THE MAXIMUM RATE I MUST PAY. THIS NOTE ALSO CONTAINS THE OPTION TO CONVERT MY ADJUSTABLE RATE TO A FIXED RATE.

_____, _____   _____   _____
                          [City]   [State]

_____
                    [Property Address]

1. BORROWER'S PROMISE TO PAY

In return for a loan that I have received, I promise to pay U.S. $_____ (this amount is called "Principal"), plus interest, to the order of Lender. Lender is _____. I will make all payments under this Note in the form of cash, check or money order.

I understand that Lender may transfer this Note. Lender or anyone who takes this Note by transfer and who is entitled to receive payments under this Note is called the "Note Holder."

2. INTEREST

Interest will be charged on unpaid principal until the full amount of Principal has been paid. I will pay interest at a yearly rate of _____%. The interest rate I will pay may change in accordance with Section 4 of this Note.

The interest rate required by this Section 2 and Section 4 or 5 of this Note is the rate I will pay both before and after any default described in Section 8(B) of this Note.

3. PAYMENTS

(A) Time and Place of Payments

I will pay principal and interest by making a payment every month.

I will make my monthly payments on the first day of each month beginning on _____, _____. I will make these payments every month until I have paid all of the principal and interest and any other charges described below that I may owe under this Note. Each monthly payment will be applied as of its scheduled due date and will be applied to interest before Principal. If, on _____, _____, I still owe amounts under this Note, I will pay those amounts in full on that date, which is called the "Maturity Date."

I will make my monthly payments at _____ or at a different place if required by the Note Holder.

(B) Amount of My Initial Monthly Payments

Each of my initial monthly payments will be in the amount of U.S. $_____. This amount may change.

(C) Monthly Payment Changes

Changes in my monthly payment will reflect changes in the unpaid principal of my loan and in the interest rate that I must pay. The Note Holder will determine my new interest rate and the changed amount of my monthly payment in accordance with Section 4 or 5 of this Note.

4. ADJUSTABLE INTEREST RATE AND MONTHLY PAYMENT CHANGES

(A) Change Dates

The adjustable interest rate I will pay may change on the first day of _____, _____, and on that day every 12th month thereafter. Each date on which my adjustable interest rate could change is called a "Change Date."

(B) The Index

Beginning with the first Change Date, my adjustable interest rate will be based on an Index. The "Index" is the average of interbank offered rates for one-year U.S. dollar-denominated deposits in the London market ("LIBOR"), as published in *The Wall Street Journal.* The most recent Index figure available as of the date 45 days before each Change Date is called the "Current Index."

If the Index is no longer available, the Note Holder will choose a new index that is based upon comparable information. The Note Holder will give me notice of this choice.

(C) Calculation of Changes

Before each Change Date, the Note Holder will calculate my new interest rate by adding _____ percentage points (_____%) to the Current Index. The Note Holder will then round the result of this addition to the nearest one-eighth of one percentage point (0.125%). Subject to the limits stated in Section 4(D) below, this rounded amount will be my new interest rate until the next Change Date.

The Note Holder will then determine the amount of the monthly payment that would be sufficient to repay the unpaid principal that I am expected to owe at the Change Date in full on the Maturity Date at my new interest rate in substantially equal payments. The result of this calculation will be the new amount of my monthly payment.

(D) Limits on Interest Rate Changes

The interest rate I am required to pay at the first Change Date will not be greater than _____% or less than _____%. Thereafter, my adjustable interest rate will never be increased or decreased on any single Change Date by more than two percentage points from the rate of interest I have been paying for the preceding 12 months. My interest rate will never be greater than _____%, which is called the "Maximum Rate."

(E) Effective Date of Changes

My new interest rate will become effective on each Change Date. I will pay the amount of my new monthly payment beginning on the first monthly payment date after the Change Date until the amount of my monthly payment changes again.

(F) Notice of Changes

The Note Holder will deliver or mail to me a notice of any changes in my adjustable interest rate and the amount of my monthly payment before the effective date of any change. The notice will include information required by law to be given to me and also the title and telephone number of a person who will answer any question I may have regarding the notice.

5. FIXED INTEREST RATE CONVERSION OPTION

(A) Option to Convert to Fixed Rate

I have a Conversion Option that I can exercise unless I am in default or this Section 5(A) will not permit me to do so. The "Conversion Option" is my option to convert the interest rate I am required to pay by this Note from an adjustable rate with interest rate limits to the fixed rate calculated under Section 5(B) below.

The conversion can only take place on (1) if the first Change Date is 21 months or less from the date of this Note, the third, fourth or fifth Change Date, or (2) if the first Change Date is more than 21 months from the date of this Note, the first, second or third Change Date. Each Change Date on which my interest rate can convert from an adjustable rate to a fixed rate also is called the "Conversion Date." **I can convert my interest rate only on one of these Conversion Dates.**

If I want to exercise the Conversion Option, I must first meet certain conditions. Those conditions are that: (i) I must give the Note Holder notice that I want to do so at least 15 days before the next Conversion Date; (ii) on the Conversion Date, I must not be in default under the Note or the Security Instrument; (iii) by a date specified by the Note Holder, I must pay the Note Holder a conversion fee of U.S. $_____; and (iv) I must sign and give the Note Holder any documents the Note Holder requires to effect the conversion.

(B)   Calculation of Fixed Rate

My new, fixed interest rate will be equal to Fannie Mae's required net yield as of a date and time of day specified by the Note Holder for: (i) if the original term of this Note is greater than 15 years, 30-year fixed rate mortgages covered by applicable 60-day mandatory delivery commitments, plus five-eighths of one percentage point (0.625%), rounded to the nearest one-eighth of one percentage point (0.125%); or (ii) if the original term of this Note is 15 years or less, 15-year fixed rate mortgages covered by applicable 60-day mandatory delivery commitments, plus five-eighths of one percentage point (0.625%), rounded to the nearest one-eighth of one percentage point (0.125%). If this required net yield cannot be determined because the applicable commitments are not available, the Note Holder will determine my interest rate by using comparable information. My new rate calculated under this Section 5(B) will not be greater than the Maximum Rate stated in Section 4(D) above.

(C)   New Payment Amount and Effective Date

If I choose to exercise the Conversion Option, the Note Holder will determine the amount of the monthly payment that would be sufficient to repay the unpaid principal I am expected to owe on the Conversion Date in full on the Maturity Date at my new fixed interest rate in substantially equal payments. The result of this calculation will be the new amount of my monthly payment. Beginning with my first monthly payment after the Conversion Date, I will pay the new amount as my monthly payment until the Maturity Date.

BORROWER'S RIGHT TO PREPAY

I have the right to make payments of Principal at any time before they are due. A payment of Principal only is known as a "Prepayment." When I make a Prepayment, I will tell the Note Holder in writing that I am doing so. I may not designate a payment as a Prepayment if I have not made all the monthly payments due under this Note.

I may make a full Prepayment or partial Prepayments without paying any Prepayment charge. The Note Holder will use my Prepayments to reduce the amount of Principal that I owe under this Note. However, the Note Holder may apply my Prepayment to the accrued and unpaid interest on the Prepayment amount before applying my Prepayment to reduce the Principal amount of this Note. If I make a partial Prepayment, there will be no changes in the due dates of my monthly payments unless the Note Holder agrees in writing to those changes. My partial Prepayment may reduce the amount of my monthly payments after the first Change Date following my partial Prepayment. However, any reduction due to my partial Prepayment may be offset by an interest rate increase.

(7) LOAN CHARGES

If a law, which applies to this loan and which sets maximum loan charges, is finally interpreted so that the interest or other loan charges collected or to be collected in connection with this loan exceed the permitted limits, then: (a) any such loan charge shall be reduced by the amount necessary to reduce the charge to the permitted limit; and (b) any sums already collected from me that exceeded permitted limits will be refunded to me. The Note Holder may choose to make this refund by reducing the Principal I owe under this Note or by making a direct payment to me. If a refund reduces Principal, the reduction will be treated as a partial Prepayment.

(8) BORROWER'S FAILURE TO PAY AS REQUIRED

(A) Late Charges for Overdue Payments

If the Note Holder has not received the full amount of any monthly payment by the end of _____ calendar days after the date it is due, I will pay a late charge to the Note Holder. The amount of the charge will be _____% of my overdue payment of principal and interest. I will pay this late charge promptly but only once on each late payment.

(B) Default

If I do not pay the full amount of each monthly payment on the date it is due, I will be in default.

(C) Notice of Default

If I am in default, the Note Holder may send me a written notice telling me that if I do not pay the overdue amount by a certain date, the Note Holder may require me to pay <u>immediately the full amount of Principal</u> that has not been paid and all the interest that I owe on that amount. That date must be at least 30 days after the date on which the notice is mailed to me or delivered by other means.

(D) No Waiver By Note Holder

Even if, at a time when I am in default, the Note Holder does not require me to pay immediately in full as described above, the Note Holder will still have the right to do so if I am in default at a later time.

(E)   Payment of Note Holder's Costs and Expenses

If the Note Holder has required me to pay immediately in full as described above, the Note Holder will have the right to be paid back by me for all of its costs and expenses in enforcing this Note to the extent not prohibited by applicable law. Those expenses include, for example, reasonable attorneys' fees.

9.   GIVING OF NOTICES

Unless applicable law requires a different method, any notice that must be given to me under this Note will be given by delivering it or by mailing it by first class mail to me at the Property Address above or at a different address if I give the Note Holder a notice of my different address.

Any notice that must be given to the Note Holder under this Note will be given by mailing it by first class mail to the Note Holder at the address stated in Section 3(A) above or at a different address if I am given a notice of that different address.

10.   OBLIGATIONS OF PERSONS UNDER THIS NOTE

If more than one person signs this Note, each person is fully and personally obligated to keep all of the promises made in this Note, including the promise to pay the full amount owed. Any person who is a guarantor, surety or endorser of this Note is also obligated to do these things. Any person who takes over these obligations, including the obligations of a guarantor, surety or endorser of this Note, is also obligated to keep all of the promises made in this Note. The Note Holder may enforce its rights under this Note against each person individually or against all of us together. This means that any one of us may be required to pay all of the amounts owed under this Note.

11.   WAIVERS

I and any other person who has obligations under this Note waive the rights of Presentment and Notice of Dishonor. "Presentment" means the right to require the Note Holder to demand payment of amounts due. "Notice of Dishonor" means the right to require the Note Holder to give notice to other persons that amounts due have not been paid.

12.   UNIFORM SECURED NOTE

This Note is a uniform instrument with limited variations in some jurisdictions. In addition to the protections given to the Note Holder under this Note, a Mortgage, Deed of Trust, or Security Deed (the "Security Instrument"), dated the same date as this Note, protects the Note Holder from possible losses that might result if I do not keep the promises that I make in this Note. That Security Instrument describes how and under what conditions I may be required to make immediate payment in full of all amounts I owe under this Note. Some of those conditions read as follows:

(A) Until I exercise my Conversion Option under the conditions stated in Section 5 of this Adjustable Rate Note, Uniform Covenant 18 of the Security Instrument shall read as follows:

Transfer of the Property or a Beneficial Interest in Borrower. As used in this Section 18, "Interest in the Property" means any legal or beneficial interest in the Property, including, but not limited to, those beneficial interests transferred in a bond for deed, contract for deed, installment sales contract or escrow agreement, the intent of which is the transfer of title by Borrower at a future date to a purchaser.

If all or any part of the Property or any Interest in the Property is sold or transferred (or if Borrower is not a natural person and a beneficial interest in Borrower is sold or transferred) without Lender's prior written consent, Lender may require immediate payment in full of all sums secured by this Security Instrument. However, this option shall not be exercised by Lender if such exercise is prohibited by Applicable Law. Lender also shall not exercise this option if: (a) Borrower causes to be submitted to Lender information required by Lender to evaluate the intended transferee as if a new loan were being made to the transferee; and (b) Lender reasonably determines that Lender's security will not be impaired by the loan assumption and that the risk of a breach of any covenant or agreement in this Security Instrument is acceptable to Lender.

To the extent permitted by Applicable Law, Lender may charge a reasonable fee as a condition to Lender's consent to the loan assumption. Lender also may require the transferee to sign an assumption agreement that is acceptable to Lender and that obligates the transferee to keep all the promises and agreements made in the Note and in this Security Instrument. Borrower will continue to be obligated under the Note and this Security Instrument unless Lender releases Borrower in writing.

If Lender exercises the option to require immediate payment in full, Lender shall give Borrower notice of acceleration. The notice shall provide a period of not less than 30 days from the date the notice is given in accordance with Section 15 within which Borrower must pay all sums secured by this Security Instrument. If Borrower fails to pay these sums prior to the expiration of this period, Lender may invoke any remedies permitted by this Security Instrument without further notice or demand on Borrower.

(B) If I exercise my Conversion Option under the conditions stated in Section 5 of this Adjustable Rate Note, Uniform Covenant 18 of the Security Instrument described in Section 12(A) above shall then cease to be in effect, and Uniform Covenant 18 of the Security Instrument shall instead read as follows:

Transfer of the Property or a Beneficial Interest in Borrower. As used in this Section 18, "Interest in the Property" means any legal or beneficial interest in the Property, including, but not limited to, those beneficial interests transferred in a bond for deed, contract for deed, installment sales contract or escrow agreement, the intent of which is the transfer of title by Borrower at a future date to a purchaser.

If all or any part of the Property or any Interest in the Property is sold or transferred (or if Borrower is not a natural person and a beneficial interest in Borrower is sold or transferred) without Lender's prior written consent, Lender may require immediate payment in full of all sums secured by this Security Instrument. However, this option shall not be exercised by Lender if such exercise is prohibited by Applicable Law.

If Lender exercises this option, Lender shall give Borrower notice of acceleration. The notice shall provide a period of not less than 30 days from the date the notice is given in accordance with Section 15 within which Borrower must pay all sums secured by this Security Instrument. If Borrower fails to pay these sums prior to the expiration of this period, Lender may invoke any remedies permitted by this Security Instrument without further notice or demand on Borrower.

WITNESS THE HAND(S) AND SEAL(S) OF THE UNDERSIGNED.

.... (Seal)
                                                          -Borrower

.... (Seal)
                                                          -Borrower

.... (Seal)
                                                          -Borrower

[Sign Original Only]

APPENDIX E

Mortgage
New York–Single Family

_____[Space Above This Line For Recording Data] _____

MORTGAGE

WORDS USED OFTEN IN THIS DOCUMENT

(A) "Security Instrument." This document, which is dated _____,
_____, together with all Riders to this document, will be called the "Security
Instrument."

(B) "Borrower."_____
_____, whose address
is _____ sometimes will be called
"Borrower" and sometimes simply "I" or "me."

(C) "Lender."_____ will be
called "Lender." Lender is a corporation or association which exists under the laws
of _____. Lender's address is _____.

(D) "Note." The note signed by Borrower and dated _____, _____,
will be called the "Note." The Note shows that I owe Lender _____
Dollars (U.S. $_____) plus interest and other amounts that
may be payable. I have promised to pay this debt in Periodic Payments and to
pay the debt in full by _____, _____.

(E) "Property." The property that is described below in the section titled "Description of the Property," will be called the "Property."

(F) "Loan." The "Loan" means the debt evidenced by the Note, plus interest, any
prepayment charges and late charges due under the Note, and all sums due under
this Security Instrument, plus interest.

(G) "Sums Secured." The amounts described below in the section titled "Borrower's Transfer to Lender of Rights in the Property" sometimes will be called the
"Sums Secured."

(H) "Riders." All Riders attached to this Security Instrument that are signed by
Borrower will be called "Riders." The following Riders are to be signed by Borrower
[check box as applicable]:

☐ Adjustable Rate Rider	☐ Condominium Rider	☐ Second Home Rider
☐ Balloon Rider	☐ Planned Unit Development Rider	☐ Other(s) [specify]_____
☐ 1-4 Family Rider	☐ Biweekly Payment Rider	

(I) "Applicable Law." All controlling applicable federal, state and local statutes, regulations, ordinances and administrative rules and orders (that have the effect of law) as well as all applicable final, non-appealable, judicial opinions will be called "Applicable Law."

(J) "Community Association Dues, Fees, and Assessments." All dues, fees, assessments, and other charges that are imposed on Borrower or the Property by a condominium association, homeowners association or similar organization will be called "Community Association Dues, Fees, and Assessments."

(K) "Electronic Funds Transfer." "Electronic Funds Transfer" means any transfer of money, other than by check, draft, or similar paper instrument, which is initiated through an electronic terminal, telephonic instrument, computer, or magnetic tape so as to order, instruct, or authorize a financial institution to debit or credit an account. Some common examples of an Electronic Funds Transfer are point-of-sale transfers (where a card such as an asset or debit card is used at a merchant), automated teller machine (or ATM) transactions, transfers initiated by telephone, wire transfers, and automated clearinghouse transfers.

(L) "Escrow Items." Those items that are described in Section 3 will be called "Escrow Items."

(M) "Miscellaneous Proceeds." "Miscellaneous Proceeds" means any compensation, settlement, award of damages, or proceeds paid by any third party (other than Insurance Proceeds, as defined in, and paid under the coverage described in, Section 5) for: (i) damage to, or destruction of, the Property; (ii) Condemnation or other taking of all or any part of the Property; (iii) conveyance in lieu of Condemnation or sale to avoid Condemnation; or (iv) misrepresentations of, or omissions as to, the value and/or condition of the Property. A taking of the Property by any governmental authority by eminent domain is known as "Condemnation."

(N) "Mortgage Insurance." "Mortgage Insurance" means insurance protecting Lender against the nonpayment of, or default on, the Loan.

(O) "Periodic Payment." The regularly scheduled amount due for (i) principal and interest under the Note, and (ii) any amounts under Section 3 will be called "Periodic Payment."

(P) "RESPA." "RESPA" means the Real Estate Settlement Procedures Act (12 U.S.C. §2601 et seq.) and its implementing regulation, Regulation X (24 C.F.R. Part 3500), as they might be amended from time to time, or any additional or successor legislation or regulation that governs the same subject matter. As used in this Security Instrument, "RESPA" refers to all requirements and restrictions that are imposed in regard to a "federally related mortgage loan" even if the Loan does not qualify as a "federally related mortgage loan" under RESPA.

BORROWER'S TRANSFER TO LENDER OF RIGHTS IN THE PROPERTY

I mortgage, grant and convey the Property to Lender subject to the terms of this Security Instrument. This means that, by signing this Security Instrument, I am giving Lender those rights that are stated in this Security Instrument and also those rights that Applicable Law gives to lenders who hold mortgages on real property. I am giving Lender these rights to protect Lender from possible losses that might result if I fail to:

(A) Pay all the amounts that I owe Lender as stated in the Note including, but not limited to, all renewals, extensions and modifications of the Note;

(B) Pay, with interest, any amounts that Lender spends under this Security Instrument to protect the value of the Property and Lender's rights in the Property; and

(C) Keep all of my other promises and agreements under this Security Instrument and the Note.

DESCRIPTION OF THE PROPERTY

I give Lender rights in the Property described in (A) through (G) below:

(A) The _____,

[Street]

_____, New York _____.

[City, Town or Village]   [Zip Code]

This Property is in _____County. It has the following legal description:

(B) All buildings and other improvements that are located on the Property described in subsection (A) of this section;

(C) All rights in other property that I have as owner of the Property described in subsection (A) of this section. These rights are known as "easements and appurtenances attached to the Property;"

(D) All rights that I have in the land which lies in the streets or roads in front of, or next to, the Property described in subsection (A) of this section;

(E) All fixtures that are now or in the future will be on the Property described in subsections (A) and (B) of this section;

(F) All of the rights and property described in subsections (B) through (E) of this section that I acquire in the future; and

(G) All replacements of or additions to the Property described in subsections (B) through (F) of this section and all Insurance Proceeds for loss or damage to, and all Miscellaneous Proceeds of the Property described in subsections (A) through (F) of this section.

BORROWER'S RIGHT TO MORTGAGE THE PROPERTY AND BORROWER'S OBLIGATION TO DEFEND OWNERSHIP OF THE PROPERTY

I promise that: (A) I lawfully own the Property; (B) I have the right to mortgage, grant and convey the Property to Lender; and (C) there are no outstanding claims or charges against the Property, except for those which are of public record.

I give a general warranty of title to Lender. This means that I will be fully responsible for any losses which Lender suffers because someone other than myself has some of the rights in the Property which I promise that I have. I promise that I will defend my ownership of the Property against any claims of such rights.

PLAIN LANGUAGE SECURITY INSTRUMENT

This Security Instrument contains promises and agreements that are used in real property security instruments all over the country. It also contains other promises and agreements that vary in different parts of the country. My promises and agreements are stated in "plain language."

COVENANTS

I promise and I agree with Lender as follows:

1. Borrower's Promise to Pay. I will pay to Lender on time principal and interest due under the Note and any prepayment, late charges and other amounts due under the Note. I will also pay all amounts for Escrow Items under Section 3 of this Security Instrument.

Payments due under the Note and this Security Instrument shall be made in U.S. currency. If any of my payments by check or other payment instrument is returned to Lender unpaid, Lender may require my payment be made by: (a) cash; (b) money order; (c) certified check, bank check, treasurer's check or cashier's check, drawn upon an institution whose deposits are insured by a federal agency, instrumentality, or entity; or (d) Electronic Funds Transfer.

Payments are deemed received by Lender when received at the location required in the Note, or at another location designated by Lender under Section 15 of this Security Instrument. Lender may return or accept any payment or partial payment if it is for an amount that is less than the amount that is then due. If Lender accepts a lesser payment, Lender may refuse to accept a lesser payment that I may make in the future and does not waive any of its rights. Lender is not obligated to apply such lesser payments when it accepts such payments. If interest on principal accrues as if all Periodic Payments had been paid when due, then Lender need not pay interest on unapplied funds. Lender may hold such unapplied funds until I make payments to bring the Loan current. If I do not do so within a reasonable period of time, Lender will either apply such funds or return them to me. In the event of foreclosure, any unapplied funds will be applied to the outstanding principal balance immediately prior to foreclosure. No offset or claim which I might have now or in the future against Lender will relieve me from making payments due under the Note and this Security Instrument or keeping all of my other promises and agreements secured by this Security Instrument.

2. Application of Borrower's Payments and Insurance Proceeds. Unless Applicable Law or this Section 2 requires otherwise, Lender will apply each of my payments that Lender accepts in the following order:
First, to pay interest due under the Note;

Next, to pay principal due under the Note; and

Next, to pay the amounts due Lender under Section 3 of this Security Instrument. Such payments will be applied to each Periodic Payment in the order in which it became due.

Any remaining amounts will be applied as follows:

First, to pay any late charges;

Next, to pay any other amounts due under this Security Instrument; and

Next, to reduce the principal balance of the Note.

If Lender receives a payment from me for a late Periodic Payment which includes a sufficient amount to pay any late charge due, the payment may be applied to the late Periodic Payment and the late charge. If more than one Periodic Payment is due, Lender may apply any payment received from me: First, to the repayment of the Periodic Payments that are due if, and to the extent that, each payment can be paid in full; Next, to the extent that any excess exists after the payment is applied to the full payment of one or more Periodic Payments, such excess may be applied to any late charges due.

Voluntary prepayments will be applied as follows: First, to any prepayment charges; and Next, as described in the Note.

Any application of payments, Insurance Proceeds, or Miscellaneous Proceeds to principal due under the Note will not extend or postpone the due date of the Periodic Payments or change the amount of those payments.

3. Monthly Payments For Taxes And Insurance.

(a) Borrower's Obligations. I will pay to Lender all amounts necessary to pay for taxes, assessments, water charges, sewer rents and other similar charges, ground leasehold payments or rents (if any), hazard or property insurance covering the Property, flood insurance (if any), and any required Mortgage Insurance, or a Loss Reserve as described in Section 10 in the place of Mortgage Insurance. Each Periodic Payment will include an amount to be applied toward payment of the following items which are called "Escrow Items:"

(1) The taxes, assessments, water charges, sewer rents and other similar charges, on the Property which under Applicable Law may be superior to this Security Instrument as a Lien on the Property. Any claim, demand or charge that is made against property because an obligation has not been fulfilled is known as a "Lien;"

(2) The leasehold payments or ground rents on the Property (if any);

(3) The premium for any and all insurance required by Lender under Section 5 of this Security Instrument;

(4) The premium for Mortgage Insurance (if any);

(5) The amount I may be required to pay Lender under Section 10 of this Security Instrument instead of the payment of the premium for Mortgage Insurance (if any); and

(6) If required by Lender, the amount for any Community Association Dues, Fees, and Assessments.

After signing the Note, or at any time during its term, Lender may include these amounts as Escrow Items. The monthly payment I will make for Escrow Items will be based on Lender's estimate of the annual amount required.

I will pay all of these amounts to Lender unless Lender tells me, in writing, that I do not have to do so, or unless Applicable Law requires otherwise. I will make these payments on the same day that my Periodic Payments of principal and interest are due under the Note.

The amounts that I pay to Lender for Escrow Items under this Section 3 will be called "Escrow Funds." I will pay Lender the Escrow Funds for Escrow Items unless Lender waives my obligation to pay the Escrow Funds for any or all Escrow Items. Lender may waive my obligation to pay to Lender Escrow Funds for any or all Escrow Items at any time. Any such waiver must be in writing. In the event of such waiver, I will pay directly, when and where payable, the amounts due for any Escrow Items for which payment of Escrow Funds has been waived by Lender and, if Lender requires, will promptly send to Lender receipts showing such payment within such time period as Lender may require. My obligation to make such payments and to provide receipts will be considered to be a promise and agreement contained in this Security Instrument, as the phrase "promises and agreements" is used in Section 9 of this Security Instrument. If I am obligated to pay Escrow Items directly, pursuant to a waiver, and I fail to pay the amount due for an Escrow Item, Lender may pay that amount and I will then be obligated under Section 9 of this Security Instrument to repay to Lender. Lender may revoke the waiver as to any or all Escrow Items at any time by a notice given in accordance with Section 15 of this Security Instrument and, upon the revocation, I will pay to Lender all Escrow Funds, and in amounts, that are then required under this Section 3.

I promise to promptly send to Lender any notices that I receive of Escrow Item amounts to be paid. Lender will estimate from time to time the amount of Escrow Funds I will have to pay by using existing assessments and bills and reasonable estimates of the amount I will have to pay for Escrow Items in the future, unless Applicable Law requires Lender to use another method for determining the amount I am to pay.

Lender may, at any time, collect and hold Escrow Funds in an amount sufficient to permit Lender to apply the Escrow Funds at the time specified under RESPA. Applicable Law puts limits on the total amount of Escrow Funds Lender can at any time collect and hold. This total amount cannot be more than the maximum amount a lender could require under RESPA. If there is another Applicable Law that imposes a lower limit on the total amount of Escrow Funds Lender can collect and hold, Lender will be limited to the lower amount.

(b) Lender's Obligations. Lender will keep the Escrow Funds in a savings or banking institution which has its deposits insured by a federal agency, instrumentality, or entity, or in any Federal Home Loan Bank. If Lender is such a savings or banking institution, Lender may hold the Escrow Funds. Lender will use the Escrow Funds to pay the Escrow Items no later than the time allowed under RESPA or other Applicable Law. Lender will give to me, without charge, an annual accounting of the Escrow Funds. That accounting will show all additions to and deductions from the Escrow Funds and the reason for each deduction.

Lender may not charge me for holding or keeping the Escrow Funds, for using the Escrow Funds to pay Escrow Items, for making a yearly analysis of my payment of Escrow Funds or for receiving, or for verifying and totaling assessments and bills. However, Lender may charge me for these services if Lender pays me interest on the Escrow Funds and if Applicable Law permits Lender to make such a charge. Lender will not be required to pay me any interest or earnings on the Escrow Funds unless either (1) Lender and I agree in writing that Lender will pay interest on the Escrow Funds, or (2) Applicable Law requires Lender to pay interest on the Escrow Funds.

(c) Adjustments to the Escrow Funds.

Under Applicable Law, there is a limit on the amount of Escrow Funds Lender may hold. If the amount of Escrow Funds held by Lender exceeds this limit, then there will be an excess amount and RESPA requires Lender to account to me in a special manner for the excess amount of Escrow Funds.

If, at any time, Lender has not received enough Escrow Funds to make the payments of Escrow Items when the payments are due, Lender may tell me in writing that an additional amount is necessary. I will pay to Lender whatever additional amount is necessary to pay the Escrow Items when the payments are due, but the number of payments will not be more than 12.

When I have paid all of the Sums Secured, Lender will promptly refund to me any Escrow Funds that are then being held by Lender.

4. Borrower's Obligation to Pay Charges, Assessments And Claims. I will pay all taxes, assessments, water charges, sewer rents and other similar charges, and any other charges and fines that may be imposed on the Property and that may be superior to this Security Instrument. I will also make ground rents or payments due under my lease if I am a tenant on the Property and Community Association Dues, Fees, and Assessments (if any) due on the Property. If these items are Escrow Items, I will do this by making the payments as described in Section 3 of this Security Instrument. In this Security Instrument, the word "Person" means any individual, organization, governmental authority or other party.

I will promptly pay or satisfy all Liens against the Property that may be superior to this Security Instrument. However, this Security Instrument does not require me to satisfy a superior Lien if: (a) I agree, in writing, to pay the obligation which gave rise to the superior Lien and Lender approves the way in which I agree to pay that obligation, but only so long as I am performing such agreement; (b) in good faith, I argue or defend against the superior Lien in a lawsuit so that in Lender's opinion, during the lawsuit, the superior Lien may not be enforced, but only until the lawsuit ends; or (c) I secure from the holder of that other Lien an agreement, approved in writing by Lender, that the Lien of this Security Instrument is superior to the Lien held by that Person. If Lender determines that any part of the Property is subject to a superior Lien, Lender may give Borrower a notice identifying the superior Lien. Within 10 days of the date on which the notice is given, Borrower shall pay or satisfy the superior Lien or take one or more of the actions mentioned in this Section 4.

Lender also may require me to pay a one-time charge for an independent real estate tax reporting service used by Lender in connection with the Loan, unless Applicable Law does not permit Lender to make such a charge.

5. Borrower's Obligation to Maintain Hazard Insurance or Property Insurance. I will obtain hazard or property insurance to cover all buildings and other improvements that now are, or in the future will be, located on the Property. The insurance will cover loss or damage caused by fire, hazards normally covered by "Extended Coverage" hazard insurance policies, and any other hazards for which Lender requires coverage, including, but not limited to earthquakes and floods. The insurance will be in the amounts (including, but not limited to, deductible levels) and for the periods of time required by Lender. What Lender requires under the last sentence can change during the term of the Loan. I may choose the insurance company, but my choice is subject to Lender's right to disapprove. Lender may not disapprove my choice unless the disapproval is reasonable. Lender may require me to pay either (a) a one-time charge for flood zone determination, certification and tracking services, or (b) a one-time charge for flood zone determination and certification services and subsequent charges each time remappings or similar changes occur which reasonably might affect the flood zone determination or certification. If I disagree with the flood zone determination, I may request the Federal Emergency Management Agency to review the flood zone determination and I promise to pay any fees charged by the Federal Emergency Management Agency for its review.

If I fail to maintain any of the insurance coverages described above, Lender may obtain insurance coverage, at Lender's option and my expense. Lender is under no obligation to purchase any particular type or amount of coverage. Therefore, such coverage will cover Lender, but might or might not protect me, my equity in the Property, or the contents of the Property, against any risk, hazard or liability and might provide greater or lesser coverage than was previously in effect. I acknowledge that the cost of the insurance coverage so obtained might significantly exceed the cost of insurance that I could have obtained. Any amounts disbursed by Lender under this Section 5 will become my additional debt secured by this Security Instrument. These amounts will bear interest at the interest rate set forth in the Note from the date of disbursement and will be payable with such interest, upon notice from Lender to me requesting payment.

All of the insurance policies and renewals of those policies will include what is known as a "Standard Mortgage Clause" to protect Lender and will name Lender as mortgagee and/or as an additional loss payee. The form of all policies and renewals will be acceptable to Lender. Lender will have the right to hold the policies and renewal certificates. If Lender requires, I will promptly give Lender all receipts of paid premiums and renewal notices that I receive.

If I obtain any form of insurance coverage, not otherwise required by Lender, for damage to, or destruction of, the Property, such policy will include a Standard Mortgage Clause and will name Lender as mortgagee and/or as an additional loss payee.

If there is a loss or damage to the Property, I will promptly notify the insurance company and Lender. If I do not promptly prove to the insurance company that the loss or damage occurred, then Lender may do so.

The amount paid by the insurance company for loss or damage to the Property is called "Insurance Proceeds." Unless Lender and I otherwise agree in writing, any Insurance Proceeds, whether or not the underlying insurance was required by Lender, will be used to repair or to restore the damaged Property unless: (a) it is not economically feasible to make the repairs or restoration; (b) the use of the Insurance Proceeds for that purpose would lessen the protection given to Lender by this Security Instrument; or (c) Lender and I have agreed in writing not to use the Insurance Proceeds for that purpose. During the period that any repairs or restorations are being made, Lender may hold any Insurance Proceeds until it has had an opportunity to inspect the Property to verify that the repair work has been completed to Lender's satisfaction. However, this inspection will be done promptly. Lender may make payments for the repairs and restorations in a single payment or in a series of progress payments as the work is completed. Unless Lender and I agree otherwise in writing or unless Applicable Law requires otherwise, Lender is not required to pay me any interest or earnings on the Insurance Proceeds. I will pay for any public adjusters or other third parties that I hire, and their fees will not be paid out of the Insurance Proceeds. If the repair or restoration is not economically feasible or if it would lessen Lender's protection under this Security Instrument, then the Insurance Proceeds will be used to reduce the amount that I owe to Lender under this Security Instrument. Such Insurance Proceeds will be applied in the order provided for in Section 2. If any of the Insurance Proceeds remain after the amount that I owe to Lender has been paid in full, the remaining Insurance Proceeds will be paid to me.

If I abandon the Property, Lender may file, negotiate and settle any available insurance claim and related matters. If I do not answer, within 30 days, a notice from Lender stating that the insurance company has offered to settle a claim, Lender may negotiate and settle the claim. The 30-day period will begin when the notice is given. In either event, or if Lender acquires the Property under Section 22 of this Security Instrument or otherwise, I give Lender my rights to any Insurance Proceeds in an amount not greater than the amounts unpaid under the Note and this Security Instrument. I also give Lender any other of my rights (other than the right to any refund of unearned premiums that I paid) under all insurance policies covering the Property, if the rights are applicable to the coverage of the Property. Lender may use the Insurance Proceeds either to repair or restore the Property or to pay amounts unpaid under the Note or this Security Instrument, whether or not then due.

6. Borrower's Obligations to Occupy The Property. I will occupy the Property and use the Property as my principal residence within 60 days after I sign this Security Instrument. I will continue to occupy the Property and to use the Property as my principal residence for at least one year. The one-year period will begin when I first occupy the Property. However, I will not have to occupy the Property and use the Property as my principal residence within the time frames set forth above if Lender agrees in writing that I do not have to do so. Lender may not refuse to agree unless the refusal is reasonable. I also will not have to occupy the Property and use the Property as my principal residence within the time frames set forth above if extenuating circumstances exist which are beyond my control.

7. Borrower's Obligations to Maintain And Protect The Property And to Fulfill Any Lease Obligations.

(a) Maintenance and Protection of the Property. I will not destroy, damage or harm the Property, and I will not allow the Property to deteriorate. Whether or not I am residing in the Property, I will keep the Property in good repair so that it will not deteriorate or decrease in value due to its condition. Unless it is determined under Section 5 of this Security Instrument that repair is not economically feasible, I will promptly repair the Property if damaged to avoid further deterioration or damage. If insurance or Condemnation (as defined in the definition of Miscellaneous Proceeds) proceeds are paid because of loss or damage to, or Condemnation of, the Property, I will repair or restore the Property only if Lender has released those proceeds for such purposes. Lender may pay for the repairs and restoration out of proceeds in a single payment or in a series of progress payments as the work is completed. If the insurance or Condemnation proceeds are not sufficient to repair or restore the Property, I promise to pay for the completion of such repair or restoration.

(b) Lender's Inspection of Property. Lender, and others authorized by Lender, may enter on and inspect the Property. They will do so in a reasonable manner and at reasonable times. If it has a reasonable purpose, Lender may inspect the inside of the home or other improvements on the Property. Before or at the time an inspection is made, Lender will give me notice stating a reasonable purpose for such interior inspection.

   8. Borrower's Loan Application. If, during the application process for the Loan, I, or any Person or entity acting at my direction or with my knowledge or consent, made false, misleading, or inaccurate statements to Lender about information important to Lender in determining my eligibility for the Loan (or did not provide Lender with such information), Lender will treat my actions as a default under this Security Instrument. False, misleading, or inaccurate statements about information important to Lender would include a misrepresentation of my intention to occupy the Property as a principal residence. This is just one example of a false, misleading, or inaccurate statement of important information.

   9. Lender's Right to Protect Its Rights in The Property. If: (a) I do not keep my promises and agreements made in this Security Instrument; (b) someone, including me, begins a legal proceeding that may significantly affect Lender's interest in the Property or rights under this Security Instrument (such as a legal proceeding in bankruptcy, in probate, for Condemnation or Forfeiture (as defined in Section 11), proceedings which could give a Person rights which could equal or exceed Lender's interest in the Property or under this Security Instrument, proceedings for enforcement of a Lien which may become superior to this Security Instrument, or to enforce laws or regulations); or (c) I have abandoned the Property, then Lender may do and pay for whatever is reasonable or appropriate to protect Lender's interest in the Property and Lender's rights under this Security Instrument.

   Lender's actions may include, but are not limited to: (a) protecting and/or assessing the value of the Property; (b) securing and/or repairing the Property; (c) paying sums to eliminate any Lien against the Property that may be equal or superior to this Security Instrument; (d) appearing in court; and (e) paying reasonable attorneys' fees to protect its interest in the Property and/or rights under this Security Instrument, including its secured position in a bankruptcy proceeding. Lender can also enter the Property to make repairs, change locks, replace or board up doors and windows, drain water from pipes, eliminate building or other code violations or dangerous conditions, have utilities turned on or off, and take any other action to secure the Property. Although Lender may take action under this Section 9, Lender does not have to do so and is under no duty to do so. I agree that Lender will not be liable for not taking any or all actions under this Section 9.

   I will pay to Lender any amounts, with interest, which Lender spends under this Section 9. I will pay those amounts to Lender when Lender sends me a notice requesting that I do so. I will pay interest on those amounts at the interest rate set forth in the Note. Interest on each amount will begin on the date that the amount is spent by Lender. This Security Instrument will protect Lender in case I do not keep this promise to pay those amounts with interest.

   If I do not own, but am a tenant on the Property, I will fulfill all my obligations under my lease. I also agree that, if I acquire the full title (sometimes called "Fee Title") to the Property, my lease interest and the Fee Title will not merge unless Lender agrees to the merger in writing.

   10. Mortgage Insurance. If Lender required Mortgage Insurance as a condition of making the Loan, I will pay the premiums for the Mortgage Insurance. If, for any reason, the Mortgage Insurance coverage ceases to be available from the mortgage insurer that previously provided such insurance and Lender required me to make separate payments toward the premiums for Mortgage Insurance, I will pay the premiums for substantially equivalent Mortgage Insurance coverage from an alternate mortgage insurer. However, the cost of this Mortgage Insurance coverage will be substantially equivalent to the cost to me of the previous Mortgage Insurance coverage, and the alternate mortgage insurer will be selected by Lender.

If substantially equivalent Mortgage Insurance coverage is not available, Lender will establish a non-refundable "Loss Reserve" as a substitute for the Mortgage Insurance coverage. I will continue to pay to Lender each month an amount equal to one-twelfth of the yearly Mortgage Insurance premium (as of the time the coverage lapsed or ceased to be in effect). Lender will retain these payments, and will use these payments to pay for losses that the Mortgage Insurance would have covered. The Loss Reserve is non-refundable even if the Loan is ultimately paid in full and Lender is not required to pay me any interest on the Loss Reserve. Lender can no longer require Loss Reserve payments if: (a) Mortgage Insurance coverage again becomes available through an insurer selected by Lender; (b) such Mortgage Insurance is obtained; (c) Lender requires separately designated payments toward the premiums for Mortgage Insurance; and (d) the Mortgage Insurance coverage is in the amount and for the period of time required by Lender.

If Lender required Mortgage Insurance as a condition of making the Loan and Borrower was required to make separate payments toward the premiums for Mortgage Insurance, I will pay the Mortgage Insurance premiums, or the Loss Reserve payments, until the requirement for Mortgage Insurance ends according to any written agreement between Lender and me providing for such termination or until termination of Mortgage Insurance is required by Applicable Law. Lender may require me to pay the premiums, or the Loss Reserve payments, in the manner described in Section 3 of this Security Instrument. Nothing in this Section 10 will affect my obligation to pay interest at the rate provided in the Note.

A Mortgage Insurance policy pays Lender (or any entity that purchases the Note) for certain losses it may incur if Borrower does not repay the Loan as agreed. Borrower is not a party to the Mortgage Insurance policy.

Mortgage insurers assess their total risk on all Mortgage Insurance from time to time. Mortgage insurers may enter into agreements with other parties to share or change their risk, or to reduce losses. These agreements are based on terms and conditions that are satisfactory to the mortgage insurer and the other party (or parties) to these agreements. These agreements may require the mortgage insurer to make payments using any source of funds that the mortgage insurer may have available (which may include Mortgage Insurance premiums).

As a result of these agreements, Lender, any owner of the Note, another insurer, any reinsurer, any other entity may receive (directly or indirectly) amounts that come from a portion of Borrower's payments for Mortgage Insurance, in exchange for sharing or changing the mortgage insurer's risk, or reducing losses. If these agreements provide that an affiliate of Lender takes a share of the insurer's risk in exchange for a share of the premiums paid to the insurer, the arrangement is often termed "captive reinsurance."

It also should be understood that: (a) any of these agreements will not affect the amounts that Borrower has agreed to pay for Mortgage Insurance, or any other terms of the Loan. These agreements will not increase the amount Borrower will owe for Mortgage Insurance, and they will not entitle Borrower to any refund;

and (b) any of these agreements will not affect the rights Borrower has—if any—regarding the Mortgage Insurance under the Homeowners Protection Act of 1998 or any other law. These rights may include the right (a) to receive certain disclosures, (b) to request and obtain cancellation of the Mortgage Insurance, (c) to have the Mortgage Insurance terminated automatically, and/or (d) to receive a refund of any Mortgage Insurance premiums that were not earned at the time of such cancellation or termination.

11. Agreements About Miscellaneous Proceeds; Forfeiture. All Miscellaneous Proceeds are assigned to and will be paid to Lender.

If the Property is damaged, such Miscellaneous Proceeds will be applied to restoration or repair of the Property, if (a) the restoration or repair is economically feasible, and (b) Lender's security given in this Security Instrument is not lessened. During such repair and restoration period, Lender will have the right to hold such Miscellaneous Proceeds until Lender has had an opportunity to inspect the Property to verify that the work has been completed to Lender's satisfaction. However, the inspection will be undertaken promptly. Lender may pay for the repairs and restoration in a single disbursement or in a series of progress payments as the work is completed. Unless Lender and I agree otherwise in writing or unless Applicable Law requires interest to be paid on such Miscellaneous Proceeds, Lender will not be required to pay Borrower any interest or earnings on the Miscellaneous Proceeds. If the restoration or repair is not economically feasible or Lender's security given in this Security Instrument would be lessened, the Miscellaneous Proceeds will be applied to the Sums Secured, whether or not then due. The excess, if any, will be paid to me. Such Miscellaneous Proceeds will be applied in the order provided for in Section 2.

In the event of a total taking, destruction, or loss in value of the Property, the Miscellaneous Proceeds will be applied to the Sums Secured, whether or not then due. The excess, if any, will be paid to me.

In the event of a partial taking, destruction, or loss in value of the Property in which the fair market value of the Property immediately before the partial taking, destruction, or loss in value is equal to or greater than the amount of the Sums Secured immediately before the partial taking, destruction, or loss in value, the Sums Secured will be reduced by the amount of the Miscellaneous Proceeds multiplied by the following fraction: (a) the total amount of the Sums Secured immediately before the partial taking, destruction, or loss in value divided by (b) the fair market value of the Property immediately before the partial taking, destruction, or loss in value. Any balance shall be paid to me.

In the event of a partial taking, destruction, or loss in value of the Property in which the fair market value of the Property immediately before the partial taking, destruction, or loss in value is less than the amount of the Sums Secured immediately before the partial taking, destruction, or loss in value, the Miscellaneous Proceeds will be applied to the Sums Secured whether or not the sums are then due.

If I abandon the Property, or if, after Lender sends me notice that the Opposing Party (as defined in the next sentence) offered to make an award to settle a claim for damages, I fail to respond to Lender within 30 days after the date Lender gives notice, Lender is authorized to collect and apply the Miscellaneous Proceeds either to restoration or repair of the Property or to the Sums Secured, whether or not then due. "Opposing Party" means the third party that owes me Miscellaneous Proceeds or the party against whom I have a right of action in regard to Miscellaneous Proceeds.

I will be in default under this Security Instrument if any civil or criminal action or proceeding that Lender determines could result in a court ruling (a) that would require Forfeiture of the Property, or (b) that could damage Lender's interest in the Property or rights under this Security Instrument. "Forfeiture" is a court action to require the Property, or any part of the Property, to be given up. I may correct the default by obtaining a court ruling that dismisses the court action, if Lender determines that this court ruling prevents Forfeiture of the Property and also prevents any damage to Lender's interest in the Property or rights under this Security Instrument. If I correct the default, I will have the right to have enforcement of this Security Instrument discontinued, as provided in Section 19 of this Security Instrument, even if Lender has required Immediate Payment in Full (as defined in Section 22). The proceeds of any award or claim for damages that are attributable to the damage or reduction of Lender's interest in the Property are assigned, and will be paid, to Lender.

All Miscellaneous Proceeds that are not applied to restoration or repair of the Property will be applied in the order provided for in Section 2.

12. Continuation of Borrower's Obligations And of Lender's Rights.

(a) Borrower's Obligations. Lender may allow me, or a Person who takes over my rights and obligations, to delay or to change the amount of the Periodic Payments. Even if Lender does this, however, I will still be fully obligated under the Note and under this Security Instrument unless Lender agrees to release me, in writing, from my obligations.

Lender may allow those delays or changes for me or a Person who takes over my rights and obligations, even if Lender is requested not to do so. Even if Lender is requested to do so, Lender will not be required to (1) bring a lawsuit against me or such a Person for not fulfilling obligations under the Note or under this Security Instrument, or (2) refuse to extend time for payment or otherwise modify amortization of the Sums Secured.

(b) Lender's Rights. Even if Lender does not exercise or enforce any right of Lender under this Security Instrument or under Applicable Law, Lender will still have all of those rights and may exercise and enforce them in the future. Even if: (1) Lender obtains insurance, pays taxes, or pays other claims, charges or Liens against the Property; (2) Lender accepts payments from third Persons; or (3) Lender accepts payments in amounts less than the amount then due, Lender will have the right under Section 22 below to demand that I make Immediate Payment in Full of any amounts remaining due and payable to Lender under the Note and under this Security Instrument.

13. Obligations of Borrower And of Persons Taking Over Borrower's Rights or Obligations. If more than one Person signs this Security Instrument as Borrower, each of us is fully obligated to keep all of Borrower's promises and obligations contained in this Security Instrument. Lender may enforce Lender's rights under this Security Instrument against each of us individually or against all of us together. This means that any one of us may be required to pay all of the Sums Secured. However, if one of us does not sign the Note: (a) that Person is signing this Security Instrument only to give that Person's rights in the Property to Lender under the terms of this Security Instrument; (b) that Person is not personally obligated to pay the Sums Secured; and (c) that Person agrees that Lender may agree with the other Borrowers to delay enforcing any of Lender's rights, to modify, or make any accommodations with regard to the terms of this Security Instrument or the Note without that Person's consent.

Subject to the provisions of Section 18 of this Security Instrument, any Person who takes over my rights or obligations under this Security Instrument in writing, and is approved by Lender in writing, will have all of my rights and will be obligated to keep all of my promises and agreements made in this Security Instrument. Borrower will not be released from Borrower's obligations and liabilities under this Security Instrument unless Lender agrees to such release in writing. Any Person who takes over Lender's rights or obligations under this Security Instrument will have all of Lender's rights and will be obligated to keep all of Lender's promises and agreements made in this Security Instrument except as provided under Section 20.

14. Loan Charges. Lender may charge me fees for services performed in connection with my default, for the purpose of protecting Lender's interest in the Property and rights under this Security Instrument, including, but not limited to, attorneys' fees, property inspection and valuation fees. With regard to other fees, the fact that this Security Instrument does not expressly indicate that Lender may charge a certain fee does not mean that Lender cannot charge that fee. Lender may not charge fees that are prohibited by this Security Instrument or by Applicable Law.

If the Loan is subject to Applicable Law which sets maximum loan charges, and that Applicable Law is finally interpreted so that the interest or other loan charges collected or to be collected in connection with the Loan exceed permitted limits: (a) any such loan charge will be reduced by the amount necessary to reduce the charge to the permitted limit; and (b) any sums already collected from me which exceeded permitted limits will be refunded to me. Lender may choose to make this refund by reducing the principal owed under the Note or by making a direct payment to Borrower. If a refund reduces principal, the reduction will be treated as a partial prepayment without any prepayment charge (even if a prepayment charge is provided for under the Note). If I accept such a refund that is paid directly to me, I will waive any right to bring a lawsuit against Lender because of the overcharge.

15. Notices Required under this Security Instrument. All notices given by me or Lender in connection with this Security Instrument will be in writing. Any notice to me in connection with this Security Instrument is considered given to me when mailed by first class mail or when actually delivered to my notice address if sent by other means. Notice to any one Borrower will be notice to all Borrowers unless Applicable Law expressly requires otherwise. The notice address is the address of the Property unless I give notice to Lender of a different address. I will promptly notify Lender of my change of address. If Lender specifies a procedure for reporting my change of address, then I will only report a change of address through that specified procedure. There may be only one designated notice address under this Security Instrument at any one time. Any notice to Lender will be given by delivering it or by mailing it by first class mail to Lender's address stated on the first page of this Security Instrument unless Lender has given me notice of another address. Any notice in connection with this Security Instrument is given to Lender when it is actually received by Lender. If any notice required by this Security Instrument is also required under Applicable Law, the Applicable Law requirement will satisfy the corresponding requirement under this Security Instrument.

16. Law That Governs this Security Instrument; Word Usage. This Security Instrument is governed by federal law and the law of New York State. All rights and obligations contained in this Security Instrument are subject to any requirements and limitations of Applicable Law. Applicable Law might allow the parties to agree by contract or it might be silent, but such silence does not mean that Lender and I cannot agree by contract. If any term of this Security Instrument or of the Note conflicts with Applicable Law, the conflict will not affect other provisions of this Security Instrument or the Note which can operate, or be given effect, without the conflicting provision. This means that the Security Instrument or the Note will remain as if the conflicting provision did not exist.

As used in this Security Instrument: (a) words of the masculine gender mean and include corresponding words of the feminine and neuter genders; (b) words in the singular mean and include the plural, and words in the plural mean and include the singular; and (c) the word "may" gives sole discretion without any obligation to take any action.

17. Borrower's Copy. I will be given one copy of the Note and of this Security Instrument.

18. Agreements about Lender's Rights If the Property Is Sold or Transferred. Lender may require Immediate Payment in Full of all Sums Secured by this Security Instrument if all or any part of the Property, or if any right in the Property, is sold or transferred without Lender's prior written permission. If Borrower is not a natural Person and a beneficial interest in Borrower is sold or transferred without Lender's prior written permission, Lender also may require Immediate Payment in Full. However, this option shall not be exercised by Lender if such exercise is prohibited by Applicable Law.

If Lender requires Immediate Payment in Full under this Section 18, Lender will give me a notice which states this requirement. The notice will give me at least 30 days to make the required payment. The 30-day period will begin on the date the notice is given to me in the manner required by Section 15 of this Security Instrument. If I do not make the required payment during that period, Lender may act to enforce its rights under this Security Instrument without giving me any further notice or demand for payment.

19. Borrower's Right to Have Lender's Enforcement of this Security Instrument Discontinued. Even if Lender has required Immediate Payment in Full, I may have the right to have enforcement of this Security Instrument stopped. I will have this right at any time before the earliest of: (a) five days before sale of the Property under any power of sale granted by this Security Instrument; (b) another period as Applicable Law might specify for the termination of my right to have enforcement of the Loan stopped; or (c) a judgment has been entered enforcing this Security Instrument. In order to have this right, I will meet the following conditions:

(a) I pay to Lender the full amount that then would be due under this Security Instrument and the Note as if Immediate Payment in Full had never been required;

(b) I correct my failure to keep any of my other promises or agreements made in this Security Instrument;

(c) I pay all of Lender's reasonable expenses in enforcing this Security Instrument including, for example, reasonable attorneys' fees, property inspection and valuation fees, and other fees incurred for the purpose of protecting Lender's interest in the Property and rights under this Security Instrument; and

(d) I do whatever Lender reasonably requires to assure that Lender's interest in the Property and rights under this Security Instrument and my obligations under the Note and under this Security Instrument continue unchanged.

Lender may require that I pay the sums and expenses mentioned in (a) through (d) in one or more of the following forms, as selected by Lender: (a) cash; (b) money order; (c) certified check, bank check, treasurer's check or cashier's check drawn upon an institution whose deposits are insured by a federal agency, instrumentality or entity; or (d) Electronic Funds Transfer.

If I fulfill all of the conditions in this Section 19, then this Security Instrument will remain in full effect as if Immediate Payment in Full had never been required. However, I will not have the right to have Lender's enforcement of this Security Instrument discontinued if Lender has required Immediate Payment in Full under Section 18 of this Security Instrument.

20. Note Holder's Right to Sell the Note or an Interest in the Note; Borrower's Right to Notice of Change of Loan Servicer; Lender's and Borrower's Right to Notice of Grievance. The Note, or an interest in the Note, together with this Security Instrument, may be sold one or more times. I might not receive any prior notice of these sales.

The entity that collects the Periodic Payments and performs other mortgage loan servicing obligations under the Note, this Security Instrument, and Applicable Law is called the "Loan Servicer." There may be a change of the Loan Servicer as a result of the sale of the Note. There also may be one or more changes of the Loan Servicer unrelated to a sale of the Note. Applicable Law requires that I be given written notice of any change of the Loan Servicer. The notice will state the name and address of the new Loan Servicer, and also tell me the address to which I should make my payments. The notice also will contain any other information required by RESPA or Applicable Law. If the Note is sold and thereafter the Loan is serviced by a Loan Servicer other than the purchaser of the Note, the mortgage loan servicing obligations to me will remain with the Loan Servicer or be transferred to a successor Loan Servicer and are not assumed by the Note purchaser unless otherwise provided by the Note purchaser.

Neither I nor Lender may commence, join or be joined to any court action (as either an individual party or the member of a class) that arises from the other party's actions pursuant to this Security Instrument or that alleges that the other has not fulfilled any of its obligations under this Security Instrument, unless the other is notified (in the manner required under Section 15 of this Security Instrument) of the unfulfilled obligation and given a reasonable time period to take corrective action. If Applicable Law provides a time period which will elapse before certain action can be taken, that time period will be deemed to be reasonable for purposes of this paragraph. The notice of acceleration and opportunity to cure given to me under Section 22 and the notice of the demand for payment in full given to me under Section 22 will be deemed to satisfy the notice and opportunity to take corrective action provisions of this Section 20. All rights under this paragraph are subject to Applicable Law.

21. Continuation of Borrower's Obligations to Maintain and Protect the Property. The federal laws and the laws of New York State that relate to health, safety or environmental protection are called "Environmental Law." Environmental Law classifies certain substances as toxic or hazardous. There are other substances that are considered hazardous for purposes of this Section 21. These substances are gasoline, kerosene, other flammable or toxic petroleum products, toxic pesticides and herbicides, volatile solvents, materials containing asbestos or formaldehyde, and radioactive materials. The substances defined as toxic or hazardous by Environmental Law and the substances considered hazardous for purposes of this Section 21 are called "Hazardous Substances." "Environmental Cleanup" includes any response action, remedial action, or removal action, as defined in Environmental Law. An "Environmental Condition" means a condition that can cause, contribute to, or otherwise trigger an Environmental Cleanup.

I will not do anything affecting the Property that violates Environmental Law, and I will not allow anyone else to do so. I will not cause or permit Hazardous Substances to be present on the Property. I will not use or store Hazardous Substances on the Property. I also will not dispose of Hazardous Substances on the Property, or release any Hazardous Substance on the Property, and I will not allow anyone else to do so. I also will not do, nor allow anyone else to do, anything affecting the Property that: (a) is in violation of any Environmental Law; (b) creates an Environmental Condition; or (c) which, due to the presence, use, or release of a Hazardous Substance, creates a condition that adversely affects the value of the Property. The promises in this paragraph do not apply to the presence, use, or storage on the Property of small quantities of Hazardous Substances that are generally recognized as appropriate for normal residential use and maintenance of the Property (including, but not limited to, Hazardous Substances in consumer products). I may use or store these small quantities on the Property. In addition, unless Environmental Law requires removal or other action, the buildings, the improvements and the fixtures on the Property are permitted to contain asbestos and asbestos-containing materials if the asbestos and asbestos-containing materials are undisturbed and "non-friable" (that is, not easily crumbled by hand pressure).

I will promptly give Lender written notice of: (a) any investigation, claim, demand, lawsuit or other action by any governmental or regulatory agency or private party involving the Property and any Hazardous Substance or Environmental Law of which I have actual knowledge; (b) any Environmental Condition, including but not limited to, any spilling, leaking, discharge, release or threat of release of any Hazardous Substance; and (c) any condition caused by the presence, use or release of a Hazardous Substance which adversely affects the value of the Property. If I learn, or any governmental or regulatory authority, or any private party, notifies me that any removal or other remediation of any Hazardous Substance affecting the Property is necessary, I will promptly take all necessary remedial actions in accordance with Environmental Law.

Nothing in this Security Instrument creates an obligation on Lender for an Environmental Cleanup.

NON-UNIFORM COVENANTS

I also promise and agree with Lender as follows:

(22) **Lender's Rights If Borrower Fails to Keep Promises and Agreements. Except as provided in Section 18 of this Security Instrument, if all of the conditions stated**

in subsections (a), (b) and (c) of this Section 22 are met, Lender may require that I pay immediately the entire amount then remaining unpaid under the Note and under this Security Instrument. Lender may do this without making any further demand for payment. This requirement is called "Immediate Payment in Full."

If Lender requires Immediate Payment in Full, Lender may bring a lawsuit to take away all of my remaining rights in the Property and have the Property sold. At this sale Lender or another Person may acquire the Property. This is known as "Foreclosure and Sale." In any lawsuit for Foreclosure and Sale, Lender will have the right to collect all costs and disbursements and additional allowances allowed by Applicable Law and will have the right to add all reasonable attorneys' fees to the amount I owe Lender, which fees shall become part of the Sums Secured.

Lender may require Immediate Payment in Full under this Section 22 only if all of the following conditions are met:

(a) I fail to keep any promise or agreement made in this Security Instrument or the Note, including, but not limited to, the promises to pay the Sums Secured when due, or if another default occurs under this Security Instrument;

(b) Lender sends to me, in the manner described in Section 15 of this Security Instrument, a notice that states:

(1) The promise or agreement that I failed to keep or the default that has occurred;

(2) The action that I must take to correct that default;

(3) A date by which I must correct the default. That date will be at least 30 days from the date on which the notice is given;

(4) That if I do not correct the default by the date stated in the notice, Lender may require Immediate Payment in Full, and Lender or another Person may acquire the Property by means of Foreclosure and Sale;

(5) That if I meet the conditions stated in Section 19 of this Security Instrument, I will have the right to have Lender's enforcement of this Security Instrument stopped and to have the Note and this Security Instrument remain fully effective as if Immediate Payment in Full had never been required; and

(6) That I have the right in any lawsuit for Foreclosure and Sale to argue that I did keep my promises and agreements under the Note and under this Security Instrument, and to present any other defenses that I may have; and

(c) I do not correct the default stated in the notice from Lender by the date stated in that notice.

23. **Lender's Obligation to Discharge this Security Instrument.** When Lender has been paid all amounts due under the Note and under this Security Instrument, Lender will discharge this Security Instrument by delivering a certificate stating that this Security Instrument has been satisfied. I will pay all costs of recording the discharge in the proper official records. I agree to pay a fee for the discharge of this Security Instrument, if Lender so requires. Lender may require that I pay such a fee, but only if the fee is paid to a third party for services rendered and the charging of the fee is permitted by Applicable Law.

24. **Agreements about New York Lien Law.** I will receive all amounts lent to me by Lender subject to the trust fund provisions of Section 13 of the New York Lien Law. This means that I will: (a) hold all amounts which I receive and which I have a right to receive from Lender under the Note as a trust fund; and (b) use those

amounts to pay for "Cost of Improvement" (as defined in Section 13 of the New York Lien Law) before I use them for any other purpose. The fact that I am holding those amounts as a trust fund means that for any building or other improvement located on the Property I have a special responsibility under the law to use the amount in the manner described in this Section 24.

25. Borrower's Statement Regarding the Property [check box as applicable].

☐ This Security Instrument covers real property improved, or to be improved, by a one or two family dwelling only.

☐ This Security Instrument covers real property principally improved, or to be improved, by one or more structures containing, in the aggregate, not more than six residential dwelling units with each dwelling unit having its own separate cooking facilities.

☐ This Security Instrument does not cover real property improved as described above.

BY SIGNING BELOW, I accept and agree to the promises and agreements contained in pages 1 through 19 of this Security Instrument and in any Rider signed by me and recorded with it.

Witnesses:

_____   _____ (Seal)
                                                                -Borrower

_____   _____ (Seal)
                                                                -Borrower

_____ **[Space Below This Line for Acknowledgment]** _____

APPENDIX F

Deed of Trust

_____[Space Above This Line For Recording Data] _____

DEED OF TRUST

DEFINITIONS

Words used in multiple sections of this document are defined below and other words are defined in Sections 3, 11, 13, 18, 20 and 21. Certain rules regarding the usage of words used in this document are also provided in Section 16.

(A) "Security Instrument" means this document, which is dated _____, _____, together with all Riders to this document.

(B) "Borrower" is _____. Borrower is the trustor under this Security Instrument.

(C) "Lender" is _____. Lender is a _____ organized and existing under the laws of _____. Lender's address is _____. Lender is the beneficiary under this Security Instrument.

(D) "Trustee" is _____.

(E) "Note" means the promissory note signed by Borrower and dated _____, _____. The Note states that Borrower owes Lender _____ Dollars (U.S. $ _____) plus interest. Borrower has promised to pay this debt in regular Periodic Payments and to pay the debt in full not later than _____.

(F) "Property" means the property that is described below under the heading "Transfer of Rights in the Property."

(G) "Loan" means the debt evidenced by the Note, plus interest, any prepayment charges and late charges due under the Note, and all sums due under this Security Instrument, plus interest.

(H) "Riders" means all Riders to this Security Instrument that are executed by Borrower. The following Riders are to be executed by Borrower [check box as applicable]:

☐ Adjustable Rate Rider   ☐ Condominium Rider   ☐ Second Home Rider

☐ Balloon Rider   ☐ Planned Unit Development Rider   ☐ Other(s) [specify] _____

☐ 1-4 Family Rider   ☐ Biweekly Payment Rider

(I) "Applicable Law" means all controlling applicable federal, state and local statutes, regulations, ordinances and administrative rules and orders (that have the effect of law) as well as all applicable final, non-appealable judicial opinions.

(J) "Community Association Dues, Fees, and Assessments" means all dues, fees, assessments and other charges that are imposed on Borrower or the Property by a condominium association, homeowners association or similar organization.

(K) "Electronic Funds Transfer" means any transfer of funds, other than a transaction originated by check, draft, or similar paper instrument, which is initiated through an electronic terminal, telephonic instrument, computer, or magnetic tape so as to order, instruct, or authorize a financial institution to debit or credit an account. Such term includes, but is not limited to, point-of-sale transfers, automated teller machine transactions, transfers initiated by telephone, wire transfers, and automated clearinghouse transfers.

(L) "Escrow Items" means those items that are described in Section 3.

(M) "Miscellaneous Proceeds" means any compensation, settlement, award of damages, or proceeds paid by any third party (other than insurance proceeds paid under the coverages described in Section 5) for: (i) damage to, or destruction of, the Property; (ii) condemnation or other taking of all or any part of the Property; (iii) conveyance in lieu of condemnation; or (iv) misrepresentations of, or omissions as to, the value and/or condition of the Property.

(N) "Mortgage Insurance" means insurance protecting Lender against the nonpayment of, or default on, the Loan.

(O) "Periodic Payment" means the regularly scheduled amount due for (i) principal and interest under the Note, plus (ii) any amounts under Section 3 of this Security Instrument.

(P) "RESPA" means the Real Estate Settlement Procedures Act (12 U.S.C. §2601 et seq.) and its implementing regulation, Regulation X (24 C.F.R. Part 3500), as they might be amended from time to time, or any additional or successor legislation or regulation that governs the same subject matter. As used in this Security Instrument, "RESPA" refers to all requirements and restrictions that are imposed in regard to a "federally related mortgage loan" even if the Loan does not qualify as a "federally related mortgage loan" under RESPA.

(Q) "Successor in Interest of Borrower" means any party that has taken title to the Property, whether or not that party has assumed Borrower's obligations under the Note and/or this Security Instrument.

TRANSFER OF RIGHTS IN THE PROPERTY

This Security Instrument secures to Lender: (i) the repayment of the Loan, and all renewals, extensions and modifications of the Note; and (ii) the performance of Borrower's covenants and agreements under this Security Instrument and the Note. For this purpose, Borrower irrevocably grants and conveys to Trustee, in trust, with power of sale, the following described property located in the _____ of _____:
[Type of Recording Juridiction]   [Type of Recording Juridiction]

which currently has the address of _____

[Street]

_____, California _____ ("Property Address"):

[City]   [Zip Code]

TOGETHER WITH all the improvements now or hereafter erected on the property, and all easements, appurtenances, and fixtures now or hereafter a part of the property. All replacements and additions shall also be covered by this Security Instrument. All of the foregoing is referred to in this Security Instrument as the "Property."

BORROWER COVENANTS that Borrower is lawfully seised of the estate hereby conveyed and has the right to grant and convey the Property and that the Property is unencumbered, except for encumbrances of record. Borrower warrants and will defend generally the title to the Property against all claims and demands, subject to any encumbrances of record.

THIS SECURITY INSTRUMENT combines uniform covenants for national use and nonuniform covenants with limited variations by jurisdiction to constitute a uniform security instrument covering real property.

UNIFORM COVENANTS. Borrower and Lender covenant and agree as follows:
1. Payment of Principal, Interest, Escrow Items, Prepayment Charges, and Late Charges. Borrower shall pay when due the principal of, and interest on, the debt evidenced by the Note and any prepayment charges and late charges due under the Note. Borrower shall also pay funds for Escrow Items pursuant to Section 3. Payments due under the Note and this Security Instrument shall be made in U.S. currency. However, if any check or other instrument received by Lender as payment under the Note or this Security Instrument is returned to Lender unpaid, Lender may require that any or all subsequent payments due under the Note and this Security Instrument be made in one or more of the following forms, as selected by Lender: (a) cash; (b) money order; (c) certified check, bank check, treasurer's check or cashier's check, provided any such check is drawn upon an institution whose deposits are insured by a federal agency, instrumentality, or entity; or (d) Electronic Funds Transfer.

Payments are deemed received by Lender when received at the location designated in the Note or at such other location as may be designated by Lender in accordance with the notice provisions in Section 15. Lender may return any payment or partial payment if the payment or partial payments are insufficient to bring the Loan current. Lender may accept any payment or partial payment insufficient to bring the Loan current, without waiver of any rights hereunder or prejudice to its rights to refuse such payment or partial payments in the future, but Lender is not obligated to apply such payments at the time such payments are accepted. If each Periodic Payment is applied as of its scheduled due date, then Lender need not pay interest on unapplied funds. Lender may hold such unapplied funds until Borrower makes payment to bring the Loan current. If Borrower does not do so within a reasonable period of time, Lender shall either apply such funds or return them to Borrower. If not applied earlier, such funds will be applied to the outstanding principal balance under the Note immediately prior to foreclosure. No offset or claim which Borrower might have now or in the future against Lender shall relieve Borrower from making payments due under the Note and this Security Instrument or performing the covenants and agreements secured by this Security Instrument.

2. Application of Payments or Proceeds. Except as otherwise described in this Section 2, all payments accepted and applied by Lender shall be applied in the following order of priority: (a) interest due under the Note; (b) principal due under the Note; (c) amounts due under Section 3. Such payments shall be applied to each Periodic Payment in the order in which it became due. Any remaining amounts shall be applied first to late charges, second to any other amounts due under this Security Instrument, and then to reduce the principal balance of the Note.

If Lender receives a payment from Borrower for a delinquent Periodic Payment which includes a sufficient amount to pay any late charge due, the payment may be applied to the delinquent payment and the late charge. If more than one Periodic Payment is outstanding, Lender may apply any payment received from Borrower to the repayment of the Periodic Payments if, and to the extent that, each payment can be paid in full. To the extent that any excess exists after the payment is applied to the full payment of one or more Periodic Payments, such excess may be applied to any late charges due. Voluntary prepayments shall be applied first to any prepayment charges and then as described in the Note.

Any application of payments, insurance proceeds, or Miscellaneous Proceeds to principal due under the Note shall not extend or postpone the due date, or change the amount, of the Periodic Payments.

3. Funds for Escrow Items. Borrower shall pay to Lender on the day Periodic Payments are due under the Note, until the Note is paid in full, a sum (the "Funds") to provide for payment of amounts due for: (a) taxes and assessments and other items which can attain priority over this Security Instrument as a lien or encumbrance on the Property; (b) leasehold payments or ground rents on the Property, if any; (c) premiums for any and all insurance required by Lender under Section 5; and (d) Mortgage Insurance premiums, if any, or any sums payable by Borrower to Lender in lieu of the payment of Mortgage Insurance premiums in accordance with the provisions of Section 10. These items are called "Escrow Items." At origination or at any time during the term of the Loan, Lender may require that Community Association Dues, Fees, and Assessments, if any, be escrowed by Borrower, and such dues, fees and assessments shall be an Escrow Item. Borrower shall promptly furnish to Lender all notices of amounts to be paid under this Section. Borrower shall pay Lender the Funds for Escrow Items unless Lender waives Borrower's obligation to pay the Funds for any or all Escrow Items. Lender may waive Borrower's obligation to pay to Lender Funds for any or all Escrow Items at any time. Any such waiver may only be in writing. In the event of such waiver, Borrower shall pay directly, when and where payable, the amounts due for any Escrow Items for which payment of Funds has been waived by Lender and, if Lender requires, shall furnish to Lender receipts evidencing such payment within such time period as Lender may require. Borrower's obligation to make such payments and to provide receipts shall for all purposes be deemed to be a covenant and agreement contained in this Security Instrument, as the phrase "covenant and agreement" is used in Section 9. If Borrower is obligated to pay Escrow Items directly, pursuant to a waiver, and Borrower fails to pay the amount due for an Escrow Item, Lender may exercise its rights under Section 9 and pay such amount and Borrower shall then be obligated under Section 9 to repay to Lender any such amount. Lender may revoke the waiver as to any or all Escrow Items at any time by a notice given in accordance with Section 15 and, upon such revocation, Borrower shall pay to Lender all Funds, and in such amounts, that are then required under this Section 3.

Lender may, at any time, collect and hold Funds in an amount (a) sufficient to permit Lender to apply the Funds at the time specified under RESPA, and (b) not to exceed the maximum amount a lender can require under RESPA. Lender shall estimate the amount of Funds due on the basis of current data and reasonable estimates of expenditures of future Escrow Items or otherwise in accordance with Applicable Law.

The Funds shall be held in an institution whose deposits are insured by a federal agency, instrumentality, or entity (including Lender, if Lender is an institution whose deposits are so insured) or in any Federal Home Loan Bank. Lender shall apply the Funds to pay the Escrow Items no later than the time specified under RESPA. Lender shall not charge Borrower for holding and applying the Funds, annually analyzing the escrow account, or verifying the Escrow Items, unless Lender pays Borrower interest on the Funds and Applicable Law permits Lender to make such a charge. Unless an agreement is made in writing or Applicable Law requires interest to be paid on the Funds, Lender shall not be required to pay Borrower any interest or earnings on the Funds. Borrower and Lender can agree in writing, however, that interest shall be paid on the Funds. Lender shall give to Borrower, without charge, an annual accounting of the Funds as required by RESPA.

If there is a surplus of Funds held in escrow, as defined under RESPA, Lender shall account to Borrower for the excess funds in accordance with RESPA. If there is a shortage of Funds held in escrow, as defined under RESPA, Lender shall notify Borrower as required by RESPA, and Borrower shall pay to Lender the amount necessary to make up the shortage in accordance with RESPA, but in no more than 12 monthly payments. If there is a deficiency of Funds held in escrow, as defined under RESPA, Lender shall notify Borrower as required by RESPA, and Borrower shall pay to Lender the amount necessary to make up the deficiency in accordance with RESPA, but in no more than 12 monthly payments.

Upon payment in full of all sums secured by this Security Instrument, Lender shall promptly refund to Borrower any Funds held by Lender.

4. Charges; Liens. Borrower shall pay all taxes, assessments, charges, fines, and impositions attributable to the Property which can attain priority over this Security Instrument, leasehold payments or ground rents on the Property, if any, and Community Association Dues, Fees, and Assessments, if any. To the extent that these items are Escrow Items, Borrower shall pay them in the manner provided in Section 3.

Borrower shall promptly discharge any lien which has priority over this Security Instrument unless Borrower: (a) agrees in writing to the payment of the obligation secured by the lien in a manner acceptable to Lender, but only so long as Borrower is performing such agreement; (b) contests the lien in good faith by, or defends against enforcement of the lien in, legal proceedings which in Lender's opinion operate to prevent the enforcement of the lien while those proceedings are pending, but only until such proceedings are concluded; or (c) secures from the holder of the lien an agreement satisfactory to Lender subordinating the lien to this Security Instrument. If Lender determines that any part of the Property is subject to a lien which can attain priority over this Security Instrument, Lender may give

Borrower a notice identifying the lien. Within 10 days of the date on which that notice is given, Borrower shall satisfy the lien or take one or more of the actions set forth above in this Section 4.

Lender may require Borrower to pay a one-time charge for a real estate tax verification and/or reporting service used by Lender in connection with this Loan.

5. Property Insurance. Borrower shall keep the improvements now existing or hereafter erected on the Property insured against loss by fire, hazards included within the term "extended coverage," and any other hazards including, but not limited to, earthquakes and floods, for which Lender requires insurance. This insurance shall be maintained in the amounts (including deductible levels) and for the periods that Lender requires. What Lender requires pursuant to the preceding sentences can change during the term of the Loan. The insurance carrier providing the insurance shall be chosen by Borrower subject to Lender's right to disapprove Borrower's choice, which right shall not be exercised unreasonably. Lender may require Borrower to pay, in connection with this Loan, either: (a) a one-time charge for flood zone determination, certification and tracking services; or (b) a one-time charge for flood zone determination and certification services and subsequent charges each time remappings or similar changes occur which reasonably might affect such determination or certification. Borrower shall also be responsible for the payment of any fees imposed by the Federal Emergency Management Agency in connection with the review of any flood zone determination resulting from an objection by Borrower.

If Borrower fails to maintain any of the coverages described above, Lender may obtain insurance coverage, at Lender's option and Borrower's expense. Lender is under no obligation to purchase any particular type or amount of coverage. Therefore, such coverage shall cover Lender, but might or might not protect Borrower, Borrower's equity in the Property, or the contents of the Property, against any risk, hazard or liability and might provide greater or lesser coverage than was previously in effect. Borrower acknowledges that the cost of the insurance coverage so obtained might significantly exceed the cost of insurance that Borrower could have obtained. Any amounts disbursed by Lender under this Section 5 shall become additional debt of Borrower secured by this Security Instrument. These amounts shall bear interest at the Note rate from the date of disbursement and shall be payable, with such interest, upon notice from Lender to Borrower requesting payment.

All insurance policies required by Lender and renewals of such policies shall be subject to Lender's right to disapprove such policies, shall include a standard mortgage clause, and shall name Lender as mortgagee and/or as an additional loss payee and Borrower further agrees to generally assign rights to insurance proceeds to the holder of the Note up to the amount of the outstanding loan balance. Lender shall have the right to hold the policies and renewal certificates. If Lender requires, Borrower shall promptly give to Lender all receipts of paid premiums and renewal notices. If Borrower obtains any form of insurance coverage, not otherwise required by Lender, for damage to, or destruction of, the Property, such policy shall include a standard mortgage clause and shall name Lender as mortgagee and/or as an additional loss payee and Borrower further agrees to generally assign rights to insurance proceeds to the holder of the Note up to the amount of the outstanding loan balance.

In the event of loss, Borrower shall give prompt notice to the insurance carrier and Lender. Lender may make proof of loss if not made promptly by Borrower.

Unless Lender and Borrower otherwise agree in writing, any insurance proceeds, whether or not the underlying insurance was required by Lender, shall be applied to restoration or repair of the Property, if the restoration or repair is economically feasible and Lender's security is not lessened. During such repair and restoration period, Lender shall have the right to hold such insurance proceeds until Lender has had an opportunity to inspect such Property to ensure the work has been completed to Lender's satisfaction, provided that such inspection shall be undertaken promptly. Lender may disburse proceeds for the repairs and restoration in a single payment or in a series of progress payments as the work is completed. Unless an agreement is made in writing or Applicable Law requires interest to be paid on such insurance proceeds, Lender shall not be required to pay Borrower any interest or earnings on such proceeds. Fees for public adjusters, or other third parties, retained by Borrower shall not be paid out of the insurance proceeds and shall be the sole obligation of Borrower. If the restoration or repair is not economically feasible or Lender's security would be lessened, the insurance proceeds shall be applied to the sums secured by this Security Instrument, whether or not then due, with the excess, if any, paid to Borrower. Such insurance proceeds shall be applied in the order provided for in Section 2.

If Borrower abandons the Property, Lender may file, negotiate and settle any available insurance claim and related matters. If Borrower does not respond within 30 days to a notice from Lender that the insurance carrier has offered to settle a claim, then Lender may negotiate and settle the claim. The 30-day period will begin when the notice is given. In either event, or if Lender acquires the Property under Section 22 or otherwise, Borrower hereby assigns to Lender (a) Borrower's rights to any insurance proceeds in an amount not to exceed the amounts unpaid under the Note or this Security Instrument, and (b) any other of Borrower's rights (other than the right to any refund of unearned premiums paid by Borrower) under all insurance policies covering the Property, insofar as such rights are applicable to the coverage of the Property. Lender may use the insurance proceeds either to repair or restore the Property or to pay amounts unpaid under the Note or this Security Instrument, whether or not then due.

6. Occupancy. Borrower shall occupy, establish, and use the Property as Borrower's principal residence within 60 days after the execution of this Security Instrument and shall continue to occupy the Property as Borrower's principal residence for at least one year after the date of occupancy, unless Lender otherwise agrees in writing, which consent shall not be unreasonably withheld, or unless extenuating circumstances exist which are beyond Borrower's control.

7. Preservation, Maintenance and Protection of the Property; Inspections. Borrower shall not destroy, damage or impair the Property, allow the Property to deteriorate or commit waste on the Property. Whether or not Borrower is residing in the Property, Borrower shall maintain the Property in order to prevent the Property from deteriorating or decreasing in value due to its condition. Unless it is determined pursuant to Section 5 that repair or restoration is not economically feasible, Borrower shall promptly repair the Property if damaged to avoid further deterioration or damage. If insurance or condemnation proceeds are paid in connection with damage to, or the taking of, the Property, Borrower shall be responsible for repairing or restoring the Property only if Lender has released proceeds for such purposes. Lender may disburse proceeds for the repairs and restoration in a single payment or in a series of progress payments as the work is completed. If the insurance or condemnation proceeds are not sufficient to repair or restore the Property, Borrower is not relieved of Borrower's obligation for the completion of such repair or restoration.

Lender or its agent may make reasonable entries upon and inspections of the Property. If it has reasonable cause, Lender may inspect the interior of the improvements on the Property. Lender shall give Borrower notice at the time of or prior to such an interior inspection specifying such reasonable cause.

8. Borrower's Loan Application. Borrower shall be in default if, during the Loan application process, Borrower or any persons or entities acting at the direction of Borrower or with Borrower's knowledge or consent gave materially false, misleading, or inaccurate information or statements to Lender (or failed to provide Lender with material information) in connection with the Loan. Material representations include, but are not limited to, representations concerning Borrower's occupancy of the Property as Borrower's principal residence.

9. Protection of Lender's Interest in the Property and Rights Under this Security Instrument. If (a) Borrower fails to perform the covenants and agreements contained in this Security Instrument, (b) there is a legal proceeding that might significantly affect Lender's interest in the Property and/or rights under this Security Instrument (such as a proceeding in bankruptcy, probate, for condemnation or forfeiture, for enforcement of a lien which may attain priority over this Security Instrument or to enforce laws or regulations), or (c) Borrower has abandoned the Property, then Lender may do and pay for whatever is reasonable or appropriate to protect Lender's interest in the Property and rights under this Security Instrument, including protecting and/or assessing the value of the Property, and securing and/or repairing the Property. Lender's actions can include, but are not limited to: (a) paying any sums secured by a lien which has priority over this Security Instrument; (b) appearing in court; and (c) paying reasonable attorneys' fees to protect its interest in the Property and/or rights under this Security Instrument, including its secured position in a bankruptcy proceeding. Securing the Property includes, but is not limited to, entering the Property to make repairs, change locks, replace or board up doors and windows, drain water from pipes, eliminate building or other code violations or dangerous conditions, and have utilities turned on or off. Although Lender may take action under this Section 9, Lender does not have to do so and is not under any duty or obligation to do so. It is agreed that Lender incurs no liability for not taking any or all actions authorized under this Section 9.

Any amounts disbursed by Lender under this Section 9 shall become additional debt of Borrower secured by this Security Instrument. These amounts shall bear interest at the Note rate from the date of disbursement and shall be payable, with such interest, upon notice from Lender to Borrower requesting payment.

If this Security Instrument is on a leasehold, Borrower shall comply with all the provisions of the lease. If Borrower acquires fee title to the Property, the leasehold and the fee title shall not merge unless Lender agrees to the merger in writing.

10. Mortage Insurance. If Lender required Mortgage Insurance as a condition of making the Loan, Borrower shall pay the premiums required to maintain the Mortgage Insurance in effect. If, for any reason, the Mortgage Insurance coverage required by Lender ceases to be available from the mortgage insurer that previously provided such insurance and Borrower was required to make separately designated payments toward the premiums for Mortgage Insurance, Borrower shall pay the premiums required to obtain coverage substantially equivalent to the Mortgage Insurance previously in effect, at a cost substantially equivalent to the cost to Borrower of the Mortgage Insurance previously in effect, from an alternate mortgage insurer selected by Lender. If substantially equivalent Mortgage Insurance coverage is not available, Borrower shall continue to pay to Lender the amount of the separately designated payments that were due when the insurance coverage ceased to be in effect. Lender will accept, use and retain these payments as a non-refundable loss reserve in lieu of Mortgage Insurance. Such loss reserve shall be non-refundable, notwithstanding the fact that the Loan is ultimately paid in full, and Lender shall not be required to pay Borrower any interest or earnings on such loss reserve. Lender can no longer require loss reserve payments if Mortgage Insurance coverage (in the amount and for the period that Lender requires) provided by an insurer selected by Lender again becomes available, is obtained, and Lender requires separately designated payments toward the premiums for Mortgage Insurance. If Lender required Mortgage Insurance as a condition of making the Loan and Borrower was required to make separately designated payments toward the premiums for Mortgage Insurance, Borrower shall pay the premiums required to maintain Mortgage Insurance in effect, or to provide a nonrefundable loss reserve, until Lender's requirement for Mortgage Insurance ends in accordance with any written agreement between Borrower and Lender providing for such termination or until termination is required by Applicable Law. Nothing in this Section 10 affects Borrower's obligation to pay interest at the rate provided in the Note.

Mortgage Insurance reimburses Lender (or any entity that purchases the Note) for certain losses it may incur if Borrower does not repay the Loan as agreed. Borrower is not a party to the Mortgage Insurance.

Mortgage insurers evaluate their total risk on all such insurance in force from time to time, and may enter into agreements with other parties that share or modify their risk, or reduce losses. These agreements are on terms and conditions that are satisfactory to the mortgage insurer and the other party (or parties) to these agreements. These agreements may require the mortgage insurer to make payments using any source of funds that the mortgage insurer may have available (which may include funds obtained from Mortgage Insurance premiums).

As a result of these agreements, Lender, any purchaser of the Note, another insurer, any reinsurer, any other entity, or any affiliate of any of the foregoing, may receive (directly or indirectly) amounts that derive from (or might be characterized as) a portion of Borrower's payments for Mortgage Insurance, in exchange for sharing or modifying the mortgage insurer's risk, or reducing losses. If such agreement provides that an affiliate of Lender takes a share of the insurer's risk in exchange for a share of the premiums paid to the insurer, the arrangement is often termed "captive reinsurance." Further:

(a) Any such agreements will not affect the amounts that Borrower has agreed to pay for Mortgage Insurance, or any other terms of the Loan. Such agreements will not increase the amount Borrower will owe for Mortgage Insurance, and they will not entitle Borrower to any refund.

(b) Any such agreements will not affect the rights Borrower has — if any — with respect to the Mortgage Insurance under the Homeowners Protection Act of 1998 or any other law. These rights may include the right to receive certain disclosures, to request and obtain cancellation of the Mortgage Insurance, to have the Mortgage Insurance

terminated automatically, and/or to receive a refund of any Mortgage Insurance premiums that were unearned at the time of such cancellation or termination.

11. Assignment of Miscellaneous Proceeds; Forfeiture. All Miscellaneous Proceeds are hereby assigned to and shall be paid to Lender.

If the Property is damaged, such Miscellaneous Proceeds shall be applied to restoration or repair of the Property, if the restoration or repair is economically feasible and Lender's security is not lessened. During such repair and restoration period, Lender shall have the right to hold such Miscellaneous Proceeds until Lender has had an opportunity to inspect such Property to ensure the work has been completed to Lender's satisfaction, provided that such inspection shall be undertaken promptly. Lender may pay for the repairs and restoration in a single disbursement or in a series of progress payments as the work is completed. Unless an agreement is made in writing or Applicable Law requires interest to be paid on such Miscellaneous Proceeds, Lender shall not be required to pay Borrower any interest or earnings on such Miscellaneous Proceeds. If the restoration or repair is not economically feasible or Lender's security would be lessened, the Miscellaneous Proceeds shall be applied to the sums secured by this Security Instrument, whether or not then due, with the excess, if any, paid to Borrower. Such Miscellaneous Proceeds shall be applied in the order provided for in Section 2.

In the event of a total taking, destruction, or loss in value of the Property, the Miscellaneous Proceeds shall be applied to the sums secured by this Security Instrument, whether or not then due, with the excess, if any, paid to Borrower.

In the event of a partial taking, destruction, or loss in value of the Property in which the fair market value of the Property immediately before the partial taking, destruction, or loss in value is equal to or greater than the amount of the sums secured by this Security Instrument immediately before the partial taking, destruction, or loss in value, unless Borrower and Lender otherwise agree in writing, the sums secured by this Security Instrument shall be reduced by the amount of the Miscellaneous Proceeds multiplied by the following fraction: (a) the total amount of the sums secured immediately before the partial taking, destruction, or loss in value divided by (b) the fair market value of the Property immediately before the partial taking, destruction, or loss in value. Any balance shall be paid to Borrower.

In the event of a partial taking, destruction, or loss in value of the Property in which the fair market value of the Property immediately before the partial taking, destruction, or loss in value is less than the amount of the sums secured immediately before the partial taking, destruction, or loss in value, unless Borrower and Lender otherwise agree in writing, the Miscellaneous Proceeds shall be applied to the sums secured by this Security Instrument whether or not the sums are then due.

If the Property is abandoned by Borrower, or if, after notice by Lender to Borrower that the Opposing Party (as defined in the next sentence) offers to make an award to settle a claim for damages, Borrower fails to respond to Lender within 30 days after the date the notice is given, Lender is authorized to collect and apply the Miscellaneous Proceeds either to restoration or repair of the Property or to the sums secured by this Security Instrument, whether or not then due. "Opposing Party" means the third party that owes Borrower Miscellaneous Proceeds or the party against whom Borrower has a right of action in regard to Miscellaneous Proceeds.

Borrower shall be in default if any action or proceeding, whether civil or criminal, is begun that, in Lender's judgment, could result in forfeiture of the Property or other material impairment of Lender's interest in the Property or rights under this Security Instrument. Borrower can cure such a default and, if acceleration has occurred, reinstate as provided in Section 19, by causing the action or proceeding to be dismissed with a ruling that, in Lender's judgment, precludes forfeiture of the Property or other material impairment of Lender's interest in the Property or rights under this Security Instrument. The proceeds of any award or claim for damages that are attributable to the impairment of Lender's interest in the Property are hereby assigned and shall be paid to Lender.

All Miscellaneous Proceeds that are not applied to restoration or repair of the Property shall be applied in the order provided for in Section 2.

12. Borrower Not Released; Forbearance By Lender Not a Waiver. Extension of the time for payment or modification of amortization of the sums secured by this Security Instrument granted by Lender to Borrower or any Successor in Interest of Borrower shall not operate to release the liability of Borrower or any Successors in Interest of Borrower. Lender shall not be required to commence proceedings against any Successor in Interest of Borrower or to refuse to extend time for payment or otherwise modify amortization of the sums secured by this Security Instrument by reason of any demand made by the original Borrower or any Successors in Interest of Borrower. Any forbearance by Lender in exercising any right or remedy including, without limitation, Lender's acceptance of payments from third persons, entities or Successors in Interest of Borrower or in amounts less than the amount then due, shall not be a waiver of or preclude the exercise of any right or remedy.

13. Joint and Several Liability; Co-signers; Successors and Assigns Bound. Borrower covenants and agrees that Borrower's obligations and liability shall be joint and several. However, any Borrower who co-signs this Security Instrument but does not execute the Note (a "co-signer"): (a) is co-signing this Security Instrument only to mortgage, grant and convey the co-signer's interest in the Property under the terms of this Security Instrument; (b) is not personally obligated to pay the sums secured by this Security Instrument; and (c) agrees that Lender and any other Borrower can agree to extend, modify, forbear or make any accommodations with regard to the terms of this Security Instrument or the Note without the co-signer's consent.

Subject to the provisions of Section 18, any Successor in Interest of Borrower who assumes Borrower's obligations under this Security Instrument in writing, and is approved by Lender, shall obtain all of Borrower's rights and benefits under this Security Instrument. Borrower shall not be released from Borrower's obligations and liability under this Security Instrument unless Lender agrees to such release in writing. The covenants and agreements of this Security Instrument shall bind (except as provided in Section 20) and benefit the successors and assigns of Lender.

14. Loan Charges. Lender may charge Borrower fees for services performed in connection with Borrower's default, for the purpose of protecting Lender's interest in the Property and rights under this Security Instrument, including, but not limited to, attorneys' fees, property inspection and valuation fees. In regard to any other fees, the absence of express authority in this Security Instrument to charge a specific fee to Borrower shall not be construed as a prohibition on the charging of such fee. Lender may not charge fees that are expressly prohibited by this Security Instrument or by Applicable Law.

If the Loan is subject to a law which sets maximum loan charges, and that law is finally interpreted so that the interest or other loan charges collected or to be collected in connection with the Loan exceed the permitted limits, then: (a) any such loan charge shall be reduced by the amount necessary to reduce the charge to the permitted limit; and (b) any sums already collected from Borrower which exceeded permitted limits will be refunded to Borrower. Lender may choose to make this refund by reducing the principal owed under the Note or by making a direct payment to Borrower. If a refund reduces principal, the reduction will be treated as a partial prepayment without any prepayment charge (whether or not a prepayment charge is provided for under the Note). Borrower's acceptance of any such refund made by direct payment to Borrower will constitute a waiver of any right of action Borrower might have arising out of such overcharge.

15. Notices. All notices given by Borrower or Lender in connection with this Security Instrument must be in writing. Any notice to Borrower in connection with this Security Instrument shall be deemed to have been given to Borrower when mailed by first class mail or when actually delivered to Borrower's notice address if sent by other means. Notice to any one Borrower shall constitute notice to all Borrowers unless Applicable Law expressly requires otherwise. The notice address shall be the Property Address unless Borrower has designated a substitute notice address by notice to Lender. Borrower shall promptly notify Lender of Borrower's change of address. If Lender specifies a procedure for reporting Borrower's change of address, then Borrower shall only report a change of address through that specified procedure. There may be only one designated notice address under this Security Instrument at any one time. Any notice to Lender shall be given by delivering it or by mailing it by first class mail to Lender's address stated herein unless Lender has designated another address by notice to Borrower. Any notice in connection with this Security Instrument shall not be deemed to have been given to Lender until actually received by Lender. If any notice required by this Security Instrument is also required under Applicable Law, the Applicable Law requirement will satisfy the corresponding requirement under this Security Instrument.

16. Governing Law; Severability; Rules of Construction. This Security Instrument shall be governed by federal law and the law of the jurisdiction in which the Property is located. All rights and obligations contained in this Security Instrument are subject to any requirements and limitations of Applicable Law. Applicable Law might explicitly or implicitly allow the parties to agree by contract or it might be silent, but such silence shall not be construed as a prohibition against agreement by contract. In the event that any provision or clause of this Security Instrument or the Note conflicts with Applicable Law, such conflict shall not affect other provisions of this Security Instrument or the Note which can be given effect without the conflicting provision.

As used in this Security Instrument: (a) words of the masculine gender shall mean and include corresponding neuter words or words of the feminine gender; (b) words in the singular shall mean and include the plural and vice versa; and (c) the word "may" gives sole discretion without any obligation to take any action.

17. Borrower's Copy. Borrower shall be given one copy of the Note and of this Security Instrument.

18. Transfer of the Property or a Beneficial Interest in Borrower. As used in this Section 18, "Interest in the Property" means any legal or beneficial interest in the Property, including, but not limited to, those beneficial interests transferred in a bond for deed, contract for deed, installment sales contract or escrow agreement, the intent of which is the transfer of title by Borrower at a future date to a purchaser.

If all or any part of the Property or any Interest in the Property is sold or transferred (or if Borrower is not a natural person and a beneficial interest in Borrower is sold or transferred) without Lender's prior written consent, Lender may require immediate payment in full of all sums secured by this Security Instrument. However, this option shall not be exercised by Lender if such exercise is prohibited by Applicable Law.

If Lender exercises this option, Lender shall give Borrower notice of acceleration. The notice shall provide a period of not less than 30 days from the date the notice is given in accordance with Section 15 within which Borrower must pay all sums secured by this Security Instrument. If Borrower fails to pay these sums prior to the expiration of this period, Lender may invoke any remedies permitted by this Security Instrument without further notice or demand on Borrower.

19. Borrower's Right to Reinstate After Acceleration. If Borrower meets certain conditions, Borrower shall have the right to have enforcement of this Security Instrument discontinued at any time prior to the earliest of: (a) five days before sale of the Property pursuant to any power of sale contained in this Security Instrument; (b) such other period as Applicable Law might specify for the termination of Borrower's right to reinstate; or (c) entry of a judgment enforcing this Security Instrument. Those conditions are that Borrower: (a) pays Lender all sums which then would be due under this Security Instrument and the Note as if no acceleration had occurred; (b) cures any default of any other covenants or agreements; (c) pays all expenses incurred in enforcing this Security Instrument, including, but not limited to, reasonable attorneys' fees, property inspection and valuation fees, and other fees incurred for the purpose of protecting Lender's interest in the Property and rights under this Security Instrument; and (d) takes such action as Lender may reasonably require to assure that Lender's interest in the Property and rights under this Security Instrument, and Borrower's obligation to pay the sums secured by this Security Instrument, shall continue unchanged. Lender may require that Borrower pay such reinstatement sums and expenses in one or more of the following forms, as selected by Lender: (a) cash; (b) money order; (c) certified check, bank check, treasurer's check or cashier's check, provided any such check is drawn upon an institution whose deposits are insured by a federal agency, instrumentality or entity; or (d) Electronic Funds Transfer. Upon reinstatement by Borrower, this Security Instrument and obligations secured hereby shall remain fully effective as if no acceleration had occurred. However, this right to reinstate shall not apply in the case of acceleration under Section 18.

20. Sale of Note; Change of Loan Servicer; Notice of Grievance. The Note or a partial interest in the Note (together with this Security Instrument) can be sold one or more times without prior notice to Borrower. A sale might result in a change in the entity (known as the "Loan Servicer") that collects Periodic Payments due under the Note and this Security Instrument and performs other mortgage loan servicing obligations under the Note, this Security Instrument, and Applicable Law. There also might be one or more changes of the Loan Servicer unrelated to a sale of the Note. If there is a change of the Loan Servicer, Borrower will be given written notice of the change which will state the name and address of the new Loan Servicer, the address to which payments should be made and any other information RESPA requires in connection with a notice of transfer of servicing. If the Note is sold and thereafter the Loan is serviced by a Loan Servicer other than the purchaser of the Note, the mortgage loan servicing obligations to Borrower will remain with the Loan Servicer or be transferred to a successor Loan Servicer and are not assumed by the Note purchaser unless otherwise provided by the Note purchaser.

Neither Borrower nor Lender may commence, join, or be joined to any judicial action (as either an individual litigant or the member of a class) that arises from the other party's actions pursuant to this Security Instrument or that alleges that the other party has breached any provision of, or any duty owed by reason of, this Security Instrument, until such Borrower or Lender has notified the other party (with such notice given in compliance with the requirements of Section 15) of such alleged breach and afforded the other party hereto a reasonable period after the giving of such notice to take corrective action. If Applicable Law provides a time period which must elapse before certain action can be taken, that time period will be deemed to be reasonable for purposes of this paragraph. The notice of acceleration and opportunity to cure given to Borrower pursuant to Section 22 and the notice of acceleration given to Borrower pursuant to Section 18 shall be deemed to satisfy the notice and opportunity to take corrective action provisions of this Section 20.

21. Hazardous Substances. As used in this Section 21: (a) "Hazardous Substances" are those substances defined as toxic or hazardous substances, pollutants, or wastes by Environmental Law and the following substances: gasoline, kerosene, other flammable or toxic petroleum products, toxic pesticides and herbicides, volatile solvents, materials containing asbestos or formaldehyde, and radioactive materials; (b) "Environmental Law" means federal laws and laws of the jurisdiction where the Property is located that relate to health, safety or environmental protection; (c) "Environmental Cleanup" includes any response action, remedial action, or removal action, as defined in Environmental Law; and (d) an "Environmental Condition" means a condition that can cause, contribute to, or otherwise trigger an Environmental Cleanup.

Borrower shall not cause or permit the presence, use, disposal, storage, or release of any Hazardous Substances, or threaten to release any Hazardous Substances, on or in the Property. Borrower shall not do, nor allow anyone else to do, anything affecting the Property (a) that is in violation of any Environmental Law, (b) which creates an Environmental Condition, or (c) which, due to the presence, use, or release of a Hazardous Substance, creates a condition that adversely affects the value of the Property. The preceding two sentences shall not apply to the presence, use, or storage on the Property of small quantities of Hazardous Substances that are generally recognized to be appropriate to normal residential uses and to maintenance of the Property (including, but not limited to, hazardous substances in consumer products).

Borrower shall promptly give Lender written notice of (a) any investigation, claim, demand, lawsuit or other action by any governmental or regulatory agency or private party involving the Property and any Hazardous Substance or Environmental Law of which Borrower has actual knowledge, (b) any Environmental Condition, including but not limited to, any spilling, leaking, discharge, release or threat of release of any Hazardous Substance, and (c) any condition caused by the presence, use or release of a Hazardous Substance which adversely affects the value of the Property. If Borrower learns, or is notified by any governmental or regulatory authority, or any private party, that any removal or other remediation of any Hazardous Substance affecting the Property is necessary, Borrower shall promptly take all necessary remedial actions in accordance with Environmental

Law. Nothing herein shall create any obligation on Lender for an Environmental Cleanup.

NON-UNIFORM COVENANTS. Borrower and Lender further covenant and agree as follows:

22. Acceleration; Remedies. Lender shall give notice to Borrower prior to acceleration following Borrower's breach of any covenant or agreement in this Security Instrument (but not prior to acceleration under Section 18 unless Applicable Law provides otherwise). The notice shall specify: (a) the default; (b) the action required to cure the default; (c) a date, not less than 30 days from the date the notice is given to Borrower, by which the default must be cured; and (d) that failure to cure the default on or before the date specified in the notice may result in acceleration of the sums secured by this Security Instrument and sale of the Property. The notice shall further inform Borrower of the right to reinstate after acceleration and the right to bring a court action to assert the non-existence of a default or any other defense of Borrower to acceleration and sale. If the default is not cured on or before the date specified in the notice, Lender at its option may require immediate payment in full of all sums secured by this Security Instrument without further demand and may invoke the power of sale and any other remedies permitted by Applicable Law. Lender shall be entitled to collect all expenses incurred in pursuing the remedies provided in this Section 22, including, but not limited to, reasonable attorneys' fees and costs of title evidence.

If Lender invokes the power of sale, Lender shall execute or cause Trustee to execute a written notice of the occurrence of an event of default and of Lender's election to cause the Property to be sold. Trustee shall cause this notice to be recorded in each county in which any part of the Property is located. Lender or Trustee shall mail copies of the notice as prescribed by Applicable Law to Borrower and to the other persons prescribed by Applicable Law. Trustee shall give public notice of sale to the persons and in the manner prescribed by Applicable Law. After the time required by Applicable Law, Trustee, without demand on Borrower, shall sell the Property at public auction to the highest bidder at the time and place and under the terms designated in the notice of sale in one or more parcels and in any order Trustee determines. Trustee may postpone sale of all or any parcel of the Property by public announcement at the time and place of any previously scheduled sale. Lender or its designee may purchase the Property at any sale.

Trustee shall deliver to the purchaser Trustee's deed conveying the Property without any covenant or warranty, expressed or implied. The recitals in the Trustee's deed shall be prima facie evidence of the truth of the statements made therein. Trustee shall apply the proceeds of the sale in the following order: (a) to all expenses of the sale, including, but not limited to, reasonable Trustee's and attorneys' fees; (b) to all sums secured by this Security Instrument; and (c) any excess to the person or persons legally entitled to it.

23. Reconveyance. Upon payment of all sums secured by this Security Instrument, Lender shall request Trustee to reconvey the Property and shall surrender this Security Instrument and all notes evidencing debt secured by this Security Instrument to Trustee. Trustee shall reconvey the Property without warranty to the person or persons legally entitled to it. Lender may charge such person or persons a reasonable fee for reconveying the Property, but only if the fee is paid to a third party (such as the Trustee) for services rendered and the charging of the fee is permitted under Applicable Law. If the fee charged does not exceed the fee set by Applicable Law, the fee is conclusively presumed to be reasonable.

24. Substitute Trustee. Lender, at its option, may from time to time appoint a successor trustee to any Trustee appointed hereunder by an instrument executed and acknowledged by Lender and recorded in the office of the Recorder of the county in which the Property is located. The instrument shall contain the name of the original Lender, Trustee and Borrower, the book and page where this Security Instrument is recorded and the name and address of the successor trustee. Without conveyance of the Property, the successor trustee shall succeed to all the title, powers and duties conferred upon the Trustee herein and by Applicable Law. This procedure for substitution of trustee shall govern to the exclusion of all other provisions for substitution.

25. Statement of Obligation Fee. Lender may collect a fee not to exceed the maximum amount permitted by Applicable Law for furnishing the statement of obligation as provided by Section 2943 of the Civil Code of California.

BY SIGNING BELOW, Borrower accepts and agrees to the terms and covenants contained in this Security Instrument and in any Rider executed by Borrower and recorded with it.

Witnesses:

_____   _____ (Seal)
                                                                     -Borrower

_____   _____ (Seal)
                                                                     -Borrower

_____ **[Space Below This Line for Acknowledgment]** _____

APPENDIX G

Warranty Deed

This indenture, made the _____ day of _____, two thousand and _____, between _____, party of the first part, and _____, party of the second part,

Witnesseth, that the party of the first part, in consideration of Ten Dollars and other valuable consideration paid by the party of the second part, does hereby grant and release unto the party of the second part, the heirs or successors and assigns of the party of the second part forever.

All that certain plot, piece or parcel of land, with the buildings and improvements thereon erected, situate, lying and being in the _____.

Together with all right, title and interest, if any, of the party of the first part of, in and to any streets and roads abutting the above-described premises to the center lines thereof; Together with the appurtenances and all the estate and rights of the party of the first part in and to said premises; To Have and To Hold the premises herein granted unto the party of the second part, the heirs or successors and assigns of the party of the second part forever.

And the party of the first part, in compliance with Section 13 of the Lien Law, covenants that the party of the first part will receive the consideration for this conveyance and will hold the right to receive such consideration as a trust fund to be applied first for the purpose of paying the costs of the improvement and will apply the same first to the payment of the cost of the improvement before using any part of the total of the same for any other purpose.

And the party of the first covenants as follows: that said party of the first part is seized of the said premises in fee simple, and has good right to convey the same; that the party of the second part shall quietly enjoy the said premises; that the said premises are free from incumbrances, except as aforesaid; that the party of the first part will execute or procure any further necessary assurance of the title to said premises; and that said party of the first part will forever warrant the title to said premises.

The word "party" shall be construed as if it read "parties" whenever the sense of this indenture so requires.

In witness whereof, the party of the first part has duly executed this deed the day and year first above written.

In presence of: _____

State of New York
County of _____ } ss.

On the _____ day of _____, 20__, before me personally came _____, to be known to be the individual _____ described in and

1017

who executed the foregoing instrument, and acknowledged that _____ executed the same.

State of New York ⎫
County of _____ ⎬ ss.
                                ⎭

On the _____ day of _____, 20___, before me personally came _____, to me known, who, being by me duly sworn, did depose and say that ___, he resides at No. _____ ; that__he is the _____ of _____, the corporation described in and which executed the foregoing instrument; that__he knows the seal of said corporation; that the seal affixed to said instrument is such corporate seal; that it was so affixed by order of the board of directors of said corporation, and that__he signed h__name thereto by like order.

State of New York ⎫
County of _____ ⎬ ss.
                                ⎭

On the _____ day of _____, 20___, before me personally came _____, the subscribing witness to the foregoing instrument, with whom I am personally acquainted, who, being by me duly sworn, did depose and say that — he resides at No. _____ ; that — he knows _____ to be the individual described in and who executed the foregoing instrument; that — he, said subscribing witness, was present and saw _____ execute the same; and that — he, said witness, at the same time subscribed h — name as witness thereto.

APPENDIX H

Settlement Statement

A. **Settlement Statement**	U.S. Department of Housing and Urban Development	OMB Approval No. 2502-0265 (expires 11/30/2009)

B. Type of Loan

1. ☐ FHA 2. ☐ FmHA 3. ☐ Conv. Unins.	6. File Number:	7. Loan Number:	8. Mortgage Insurance Case Number:
4. ☐ VA 5. ☐ Conv. Ins.			

C. Note: This form is furnished to give you a statement of actual settlement costs. Amounts paid to and by the settlement agent are shown. Items marked "(p.o.c.)" were paid outside the closing; they are shown here for informational purposes and are not included in the totals.

D. Name & Address of Borrower:	E. Name & Address of Seller:	F. Name & Address of Lender:

G. Property Location:	H. Settlement Agent:	
	Place of Settlement:	I. Settlement Date:

J. Summary of Borrower's Transaction		K. Summary of Seller's Transaction	
100. Gross Amount Due From Borrower		**400. Gross Amount Due To Seller**	
101. Contract sales price		401. Contract sales price	
102. Personal property		402. Personal property	
103. Settlement charges to borrower (line 1400)		403.	
104.		404.	
105.		405.	
Adjustments for items paid by seller in advance		**Adjustments for items paid by seller in advance**	
106. City/town taxes to		406. City/town taxes to	
107. County taxes to		407. County taxes to	
108. Assessments to		408. Assessments to	
109.		409.	
110.		410.	
111.		411.	
112.		412.	
120. Gross Amount Due From Borrower		**420. Gross Amount Due To Seller**	
200. Amounts Paid By Or In Behalf Of Borrower		**500. Reductions In Amount Due To Seller**	
201. Deposit or earnest money		501. Excess deposit (see instructions)	
202. Principal amount of new loan(s)		502. Settlement charges to seller (line 1400)	
203. Existing loan(s) taken subject to		503. Existing loan(s) taken subject to	
204.		504. Payoff of first mortgage loan	
205.		505. Payoff of second mortgage loan	
206.		506.	
207.		507.	
208.		508.	
209.		509.	
Adjustments for items unpaid by seller		**Adjustments for items unpaid by seller**	
210. City/town taxes to		510. City/town taxes to	
211. County taxes to		511. County taxes to	
212. Assessments to		512. Assessments to	
213.		513.	
214.		514.	
215.		515.	
216.		516.	
217.		517.	
218.		518.	
219.		519.	
220. Total Paid By/For Borrower		**520. Total Reduction Amount Due Seller**	
300. Cash At Settlement From/To Borrower		**600. Cash At Settlement To/From Seller**	
301. Gross Amount due from borrower (line 120)		601. Gross amount due to seller (line 420)	
302. Less amounts paid by/for borrower (line 220)	( )	602. Less reductions in amt. due seller (line 520)	( )
303. Cash ☐ From ☐ To Borrower		603. Cash ☐ To ☐ From Seller	

Section 5 of the Real Estate Settlement Procedures Act (RESPA) requires the following: • HUD must develop a Special Information Booklet to help persons borrowing money to finance the purchase of residential real estate to better understand the nature and costs of real estate settlement services; • Each lender must provide the booklet to all applicants from whom it receives or for whom it prepares a written application to borrow money to finance the purchase of residential real estate; • Lenders must prepare and distribute with the Booklet a Good Faith Estimate of the settlement costs that the borrower is likely to incur in connection with the settlement. These disclosures are mandatory.

Section 4(a) of RESPA mandates that HUD develop and prescribe this standard form to be used at the time of loan settlement to provide full disclosure of all charges imposed upon the borrower and seller. These are third party disclosures that are designed to provide the borrower with pertinent information during the settlement process in order to be a better shopper.

The Public Reporting Burden for this collection of information is estimated to average one hour per response, including the time for reviewing instructions, searching existing data sources, gathering and maintaining the data needed, and completing and reviewing the collection of information.

This agency may not collect this information, and you are not required to complete this form, unless it displays a currently valid OMB control number.

The information requested does not lend itself to confidentiality.

Settlement Statement

L. Settlement Charges

700. Total Sales/Broker's Commission based on price $		@	% =		Paid From Borrowers Funds at Settlement	Paid From Seller's Funds at Settlement
Division of Commission (line 700) as follows:						
701. $		to				
702. $		to				
703. Commission paid at Settlement						
704.						

800. Items Payable In Connection With Loan

				Paid From Borrowers	Paid From Seller's
801. Loan Origination Fee	%				
802. Loan Discount	%				
803. Appraisal Fee	to				
804. Credit Report	to				
805. Lender's Inspection Fee					
806. Mortgage Insurance Application Fee to					
807. Assumption Fee					
808.					
809.					
810.					
811.					

900. Items Required By Lender To Be Paid In Advance

901. Interest from	to	@$	/day			
902. Mortgage Insurance Premium for			months to			
903. Hazard Insurance Premium for			years to			
904.			years to			
905.						

1000. Reserves Deposited With Lender

1001. Hazard insurance	months@$	per month		
1002. Mortgage insurance	months@$	per month		
1003. City property taxes	months@$	per month		
1004. County property taxes	months@$	per month		
1005. Annual assessments	months@$	per month		
1006.	months@$	per month		
1007.	months@$	per month		
1008.	months@$	per month		

1100. Title Charges

1101. Settlement or closing fee	to		
1102. Abstract or title search	to		
1103. Title examination	to		
1104. Title insurance binder	to		
1105. Document preparation	to		
1106. Notary fees	to		
1107. Attorney's fees	to		
(includes above items numbers:	)		
1108. Title insurance	to		
(includes above items numbers:	)		
1109. Lender's coverage	$		
1110. Owner's coverage	$		
1111.			
1112.			
1113.			

1200. Government Recording and Transfer Charges

1201. Recording fees: Deed $	; Mortgage $	; Releases $		
1202. City/county tax/stamps: Deed $	; Mortgage $			
1203. State tax/stamps: Deed $	; Mortgage $			
1204.				
1205.				

1300. Additional Settlement Charges

1301. Survey	to		
1302. Pest inspection to			
1303.			
1304.			
1305.			

1400. Total Settlement Charges (enter on lines 103, Section J and 502, Section K)		

Table of Cases

Principal cases appear in italics.

INDEX